MW01029469

The Canonical Hebrew Bible
A Theology of the Old Testament

The
CANONICAL
HEBREW BIBLE

A Theology of the Old Testament

Rolf Rendtorff

Translated by

David E. Orton

BLANDFORD FORUM

Tools for Biblical Study series, 7

The publication of this work was supported by funding from the Goethe Institute.

Translated by David E. Orton from the German:
Theologie des Alten Testaments. Ein kanonischer Entwurf,
copyright © Neukirchener Verlag, Neukirchen-Vluyn 2001

Published by Deo Publishing
PO Box 6284, Blandford Forum, DT11 1AQ, UK

Copyright © 2005, 2011 Deo Publishing

Printed in the United Kingdom by Henry Ling Limited, at the Dorset Press, Dorchester, DT1 1HD

All rights reserved. No part of this publication may be reproduced, translated, stored in a retrieval system, or transmitted in any form or by any means, electronic, mechanical, photocopying, recording or otherwise, without prior written permission from the publisher.

The Odyssea Greek font used to publish this work is available from Linguist's Software, Inc., www.linguistsoftware.com, PO Box 580, Edmonds, WA 98020-0580 USA, tel. (425) 775-1130.

British Library Cataloguing-in-Publication data
A catalogue record for this book is available from the British Library

ISSN   1566-2101
ISBN   90-5854-020-0
       978-905854-020-1

Contents

Part I

Introduction
The Old Testament as Canon

1. The Canonical approach

The Old Testament is a theological book. An account of the "Theology of the Old Testament" therefore scarcely requires special justification. A justification of the theological approach that provides the basis for such a Theology, however, is indeed called for. In the recent history of theology various models have been set up. The account may have a *systematic* structure. Here, key terms which the structure follows may be oriented towards a particular dogmatic tradition or be chosen by the individual author in each case. Other accounts have underlying historical concepts, taking their orientation either from the chronological course of Israel's history or more from the development of theological ideas and terms within the Old Testament. Here the boundaries between "Theology of the Old Testament" and "History of the Religion of Israel" are fluid.

Gerhard von Rad (1962/1965) presented a new approach which takes another route. He follows the canonical basis of the biblical scriptures and devotes a separate part of his overall account to each of the two first parts of the Hebrew canon, the Torah (Pentateuch) and the Prophets. The present book follows this approach, but develops it a step further, not only assuming the canonical basis of the Hebrew Bible but also making the texts themselves, in their present "canonical" shape, the point of departure for the account. This interpretation of the texts occurs within the context of historical-critical biblical research. It goes a step beyond the methodological approaches in widespread current use by following to its end the path of transmission that has emanated in the present shape of the text and by focusing its primary attention on this final form. Diachronic aspects are certainly not ignored; however, essentially they are considered in relation to the contribution they may make to the understanding of the texts in their present, final, form.

The predominant interest in the final shape of the texts is grounded largely in the fact that the texts in this form became the foundation of the faith, doctrine and life of the two biblical faith communities, the Jewish and the Christian, remaining so right through to the beginning of the modern period. The emergence of modern historical-critical biblical research means a break in tradition at this point. But this does not have to be the last word. Rather, biblical criticism, notwithstanding the other tasks it has set itself over time, must once again find a way to take the present biblical text seriously and understand it. With this task, the Theology presented here is broadly "canonical," since it takes the Bible seriously as the founding document of the Jewish and Christian faith communities.

In accordance with the task we are undertaking, Part I is devoted to the biblical texts themselves. The account thus consistently follows the canonical order of the biblical books, in the sequence of the Hebrew canon. It attempts to bring the theological intentions of the texts into discussion by going step by step into the texts themselves. "It would be fatal for our understanding if we tried to order the world of Israel's testimony from the outset according to theological contexts, which, though familiar to us, have nothing at all to do with the circumstances in which Israel ordered its own theological thinking. The most legitimate form of theological discourse in relation to the Old Testament is thus still 'retelling' (*Nacherzählung*)" (von Rad 1962, 134).

Such a "retelling" is attempted in Part I. The interpreter schooled in historical-critical biblical studies is confronted by some not inconsiderable difficulties in this attempt. It was, after all, an essential point of departure for modern historical-critical exegesis that the texts often appear to lack cohesion or are recognizably disparate, so that they seem to issue a veritable challenge to diachronic analysis and the discerning of earlier stages in their history of development. By devoting itself to this task, however, modern biblical criticism largely lost the present form of the text from view. In particular the authors of the text before us found themselves cast in the role of "editors," revisers, supplementers etc., who were considered of lesser value, and worthy of less attention, than the "original" authors—despite the fact that in many cases the "authors" are unknown or not traceable, or that, as in the case of the prophetic books, the composers of the "original" words cannot generally be equated with the authors of the written texts.

The present attempt at retelling is fully aware of these difficulties. It sees its primary task, however, in allowing the intentions of those who gave the texts their present shape to come into their own. It is a matter of "recovering" texts which have largely got lost in their present form as a result of critical analysis. It will be necessary at many points to refer to diachronic problems or to examine them in more detail in order to clarify the complex shape of the present text. A "reconstruction" of earlier stages of the present text, however, lies in principle outside the remit of this account.

It would be a complete misunderstanding of this approach to see in it an attempt to smooth over contradictions or to harmonize the biblical texts. The guiding interest is not the uncovering of tensions or contradictions in the texts, however, but rather the question how the authors of the extant texts understood them in their present form and how they wanted their readers to understand them. As a rule we can assume that tensions in the text that are discernible to the present-day exegete were not hidden from the authors of the final text either. We should therefore not attempt to put the tensions to one side by means of critical atomization of the texts into contradiction-free "original" text elements; rather, we should endeavor to interpret the tensions within the texts. Only thus can historical-critical exegesis reach its true goal, the understanding of the texts.

The methodological questions touched upon very briefly here are dealt within in more detail in Part III (§§ 23, 24), in the context of recent scholarly discussion (cf. also 1991a). At that point we also deal in more detail with the relationship between the Jewish and Christian understanding of the Old Testament and with the question of a "Biblical Theology" of the Old and New Testament.

Part II builds upon the basis of Part I. It deals with "themes" found in the various books of the Old Testament which seem to exceed the boundaries of the individual books in their contexts. The selection of topics emerges directly from the Old Testament texts dealt with in Part I. Their order follows as far as possible their order of appearance in the "retelling" of the biblical books, beginning with the topic of "Creation" (Gen 1) [→§5], followed by the topic of "Covenant" (Gen 9) [→§6], etc. This then produces the need for a degree of systematization of the account, in particular to bring more complex thematic associations to bear on the account. Such systematizations are naturally determined by our own access to the topics and do not in all cases find their justification in the Old Testament material itself. To this extent,

in the second part the account comes close in some ways to systematically oriented outlines of the theology of the Old Testament. At the
same time historical questions also arise, so that at some stages there
will also be points of agreement with historically oriented discussions.
In Part II once again the tension-filled variety of the Old Testament
texts will be visible.

2. The structure of the Old Testament canon

When we speak of the canon of the Old Testament we immediately
encounter a terminological problem. The term "Old Testament"
comes from Christian parlance and presupposes a relationship to the
"New Testament." Understood in this way, the Old Testament is one
of the two parts of the Christian "Bible." The Hebrew Bible was already the Jewish Holy Scripture before this. In Jewish tradition it is
often referred to as "the books" (*hass'farîm*) or "the holy books" (*sifrê
haqqodeš*), and also as "the Holy Scriptures" (*kitbê haqqodeš*) or as "reading" (*miqra'*) or by the acronym תנ״ך (TaNaKh), which is formed by
the initial letters of the three parts of the Hebrew canon, *tôrah*, *n'bî'îm*
(prophets) and *k'tûbîm* (writings).

It is not only the terms of these collections that differ, however, but
also their scope and the arrangement of the writings contained in
them. The canon of the Hebrew Bible is divided up into three parts:
the Torah, namely the first five books, often referred to by the Greek
term "Pentateuch" [→In 139] and, following Luther, as the five "books
of Moses"; the Prophets, which contain the books of Joshua to Kings,
as the "Former Prophets" (*n'bî'îm ri'šônîm*) [→In 174] and the prophetic
books proper as "Latter Prophets" (*n'bî'îm 'aharônîm*) [→In 199]; the Writings [→In 258], in which all those books are collected which do not
belong to one of the first two groups.

Christian tradition adopted a collection of Greek translations of the
canonical books that came into being in hellenistic Judaism, as well as
a number of other writings transmitted only in Greek, which however
never attained canonical status in the Jewish world. Together with the
New Testament they form the Christian Greek Bible, the "Septuagint."
The order of the books in this collection differs quite considerably from
those in the Hebrew Bible. Thus the Writings with "historical" content from the third part of the canon are placed among the "historical
books": Ruth (on account of the chronological information in Ruth

1.1) following Judges, the books of Chronicles, followed by Ezra–Nehemiah, following the books of Kings, then after the two non-canonical books of Tobit and Judith, the book of Esther, and finally the two non-canonical books of Maccabees. There then follow first most of the books of the third part of the canon as "Wisdom books," complemented by the non-canonical books of the Wisdom of Solomon and Jesus Sirach (Ecclesiasticus). The prophetic books form the last part of the canon, complemented by Lamentations, which follows the book of Jeremiah along with the non-canonical book of Baruch with the Letter of Jeremiah, and the book of Daniel, which is placed after Ezekiel. Thus in general as well as in particular it is evident that there is a different concept of the canon than in the Hebrew Bible (cf. Zenger 1995a).

In their overall structure the German translations follow the Greek tradition, which also underlay the Latin translation, the Vulgate, which for a long period was considered binding. Luther, however, took out the writings not found in the Hebrew canon and added them to the Old Testament as "Apocrypha." His translation of the Old Testament was based on the Hebrew text.

The account given in this book follows the canon of the Hebrew Bible. Its division into the three main parts, of Torah, the Prophets and the Writings, has been undisputed since the canon gained fixed form. This is already evident in the second century BCE, when in the prologue to the book of Sirach the source of the account is given as the "Law" (νόμος), the Prophets and the other Writings. The arrangement of the individual books in the Torah and the "Former Prophets" is not subject to fluctuations. In the "Latter Prophets," in some manuscripts Jeremiah is in first position, which is also justified in a passage of the Talmud (*Baba bathra* 14b); the present sequence with Isaiah in front has, however, asserted itself and is found in all editions of the Hebrew Bible since book printing came in. The sequence of the books in the third part of the canon was in dispute for some time. In many manuscripts the book of Ruth is in first place (thus also *Baba bathra* 14b), in others the books of Chronicles; here too the position of Chronicles at the end of the canon asserted itself up to the advent of book printing. There are however still fluctuations in the order of the books of Job and Proverbs.

The sequence of the three parts of the canon corresponds to their theological significance. The Torah, the Pentateuch, forms the basis for the life and thought of Israel: for its understanding of God and the world, for its self-understanding and for the rules of the cult and human life in community. The other parts of the canon are related to the Torah. At the conclusion of the Torah we read: "And there has not arisen a prophet since in Israel like Moses, whom the Lord knew face to face" (Deut 34.10) [→**87**]. The Torah concludes with a look towards prophecy, but all the prophets who follow are subordinate to the one Prophet through whom God gave his Torah. The conclusion of the canon of the prophets reflects the same relationship the other way round: "Remember the law of my servant Moses" (Mal 3.22 [4.4]) [→**312**]. The whole prophecy is to be understood with reference to the Torah, including when attention is turned to the end-times, the return of the prophet Elijah (Mal 3.23f. [4.5f.]).

The third part of the canon, finally, also refers back to the Torah. Psalm 1.1f. reads: "Blessed is the man … his delight is in the law of the Lord" [→**319**]. The Psalms too, "Israel's response" to God's acting and speaking, cannot be understood without the Torah, and the study of the varied message of the Psalms is placed alongside the study of the Torah. The Torah also enters into a relationship with Wisdom (e.g. Ps. 37.30f.), which finally opens up into the wisdom-influenced song of praise to Torah (Ps 119) [→**320**], which seems never to want to come to an end.

Apart from such explicit references under the rubric of Torah, in all parts of the canon multiple references to the first part are in evidence: references to what is reported and commanded there, to the Creation and the story of human beginnings, to the story of God's dealings with the patriarchs of Israel, to the revelation of God on Sinai and the gift of the commandments. One can even say that most of the books of the canon of the Hebrew Bible could not be fully understood without knowledge of the Pentateuch to which they frequently directly or indirectly refer.

3. Three ways of speaking of and with God

A closer look at the three parts of the canon shows up further specific differences and relationships between them. Particularly conspicuous is the way in which God is spoken of or spoken with. One might venture to say: in the first part of the canon *God acts*, in the second *God speaks*, and in the third part of the canon *people speak* to God and of God.

This needs further development and clarification. The first part of the canon is marked by God's activity. God is always present as the direct actor. Even when God speaks, in the first instance this is an act: in the Creation, in the establishment of the covenant with humanity and everything that is created, in the election of Abraham, in the giving of the Torah on Sinai and finally in the leading of Israel as far as the borders of the promised land. In the later parts of the canon God acts and speaks with such directness only in very special exceptional situations. God's action also provides the bases for everything that follows. After the conclusion of the first part of the canon nothing more occurs that is fundamentally new. Everything that now happens must be seen in the light of it and be justified in relation to what has been established in the first part of the canon, the Torah.

In the second part of the canon, the spoken word of God dominates the center. This applies in particular to the books of the "Latter Prophets." The texts collected in them contain almost exclusively divine discourse, often with the expression "Thus says the Lord," which is characteristic of the proclamation and introduction of prophetic speech. The prophetic divine speech is an address to Israel. It confronts Israel with the will of God, i.e. ultimately with what has been set down in the first part of the canon. Here, prophetic speech reacts to the behavior and actions of Israel in its history and its present.

This shows the function of the division of the prophetic canon into two. The history into which the "Latter Prophets" speak has been passed before the reader in the books of the "Former Prophets." In these books two prophets are already to be found who introduce their words with the expression "Thus says the Lord" (1 Sam 10.18; 15.2; 2 Sam 7.5, 8 etc.) [→**105, 113**]. But there they only accompany the extended narratives about the history in which people themselves now act, and label them by clearly marked critical accents. The prophets of the second part of the prophetic canon pick up on this and lead the reader back again to particular phases and particular points in this history [→**157**]. Thus the prophetic word becomes a commentary on the history of Israel in the time of the kings.

Gerhard von Rad's heading for the third part of the canon was "Israel before Yahweh (Israel's Response)" (1962, 366). This characterizes two essential elements that come to the fore in this collection of writings. In the first place, in many of the psalms and songs of lament Israel itself is the speaking subject, whether in the form of the common "We" or in the "I" of the individual praying and lamenting Israelite. Secondly, much more frequently than in other parts of the canon the address to God is found in liturgical or individual prayer, in worship, praise and thanksgiving or in lament. And this address is always a response to what has been proclaimed and experienced; at the same time it contains the expectation, hope and petition for God's saving attention. But also in the other writings of the third part of the canon, especially in those influenced by wisdom, convictions, experiences and insights from Israel's "everyday life" are represented or, as in the case of Qohelet, reflected upon critically and queried. The book of Job also belongs in this context, for here the wisdom traditions are discussed in a controversial way, and in a particularly extreme sense "before God."

The three parts of the canon stand in a constant mutual relationship. There is scarcely a theme that does not appear in some way in several or all parts of the canon. The themes are often viewed from quite different perspectives and with different sorts of presuppositions, and their various aspects illuminate and complement one another. Thus the variety of voices within the Hebrew Bible gains its quite specific structure through the arrangement of the canon.

4. Preliminary remarks

4.1 Terminology

The term "Old Testament" is today disputed and also open to misunderstanding. To date, however, there is no generally accepted alternative. In "Old Testament" research, the term continues to be used by representatives of all participating religions and denominations. It can therefore continue to be used, as long as one is aware of the problems associated with it. Since the Hebrew canon is made the basis for this book, in what follows I shall in general use the term "Hebrew Bible," which is in common usage in inter-religious and interdenominational scholarly interpretation. For adjectival use, we shall have to stay with "Old Testament."

A more difficult issue is the use of the divine name. In Old Testament usage the divine name is transmitted only with its consonants, *yhwh*, the "Tetragrammaton." The name was not pronounced in Jewish tradition, nor is it pronounced by Jews today. Since the end of the Middle Ages the pronunciation *Jehovah* was in use, based on an erroneous reading of the Hebrew text, until in the nineteenth century the presumed pronunciation *Yahweh* was reconstructed on the basis of ancient Greek transcriptions. Since then many Christian scholars write and pronounce it like this. In the international arena however, the spelling without vowels has been maintained, often with capital letters: YHWH or JHWH. Since ancient times, the Tetragrammaton has been rendered in translations by κύριος or *dominus*, and in European languages by "LORD," "Herr'" etc.

In what follows as a rule I refer to the God of the Hebrew Bible as "God." In particular contexts, e.g. in relation to disputes with other deities, I use the form "Yhwh." In word-for-word quotations from the Hebrew text I use the form "LORD" except in such combinations as "Yhwh Zebaot." Occasionally the spelling "Yahweh" appears in quotations from secondary literature.

4.2. Bibliography
Bibliographic references in this book give those authors to whose work I refer directly or indirectly and whom I therefore wish to name. They also mention secondary literature in which a position mentioned in the text is spelt out in detail or further elaborated. The two often go hand in hand. The bibliographic references are cited only with the author's name and year of publication, as listed in the Bibliography. My own works are cited only by year of publication.

4.3. Cross-references
In my *Introduction* (*Das Alte Testament. Eine Einführung*, 1983), I provided a series of cross-references in the margin. In the present work such references are given within the text, in square brackets, in bold type and prefaced by an arrow, thus: [→**145**]. The majority of these are references to related discussions of the texts and topics elsewhere within this book; some are approximate. References prefaced by "*In*" are to my *Introduction* (German edition).

4.4. Biblical references
Versification in the German Bible (after Luther) generally follows the Hebrew Bible, while English Bibles follow the versification of the Vulgate (itself based on the Septuagint). For comparison of the divergences readers are referred to the chart in *The SBL Handbook of Style* (Peabody, Mass., 1999), Appendix E (pp. 172-175). *The Canonical Hebrew Bible* retains the Hebrew versification given in the original German, but endeavors to add the equivalent English Bible reference where appropriate. Occasionally an asterisk ★ is used as a reminder that versification varies.

§ 1

The Pentateuch

Preliminary remarks

Jewish tradition refers to the first five books of the Hebrew Bible as the "Torah." This reflects the fact that they form the basis and the heart of the Jewish faith tradition [→89], since Torah is at the same time the all-embracing term for this whole tradition. In Christian tradition these five books are generally referred to as the "Pentateuch." Luther gave them the name "The Five Books of Moses," in line with the post-biblical tradition that Moses was the author of this entire body of material.

The Pentateuch [→*In* 166] comprises a variety of traditions, many of which differ starkly from one another in age and provenance. In modern Old Testament scholarship, the dominant interest has been in the individual traditions, their provenance and their age, and this has largely determined accounts of the theology of the Old Testament. The attempt will now be made to make the Pentateuch in its present, final form the basis for a theological exposition. This certainly does not mean that the results of Pentateuchal research to date will be ignored. Rather, they will be advanced, as attention is devoted to the final result of the long process of tradition to which the present form of the Pentateuch owes its origin, and as this is made the real subject of consideration. Thus the text is not taken apart into hypothetically deduced earlier components which are then separately expounded and theologically interpreted. Rather, the text is read in its present context, and the tensions, and in some cases even contradictions, which have arisen as a result of the bringing together of different elements of tradition are in each case viewed and interpreted as such.

Different layers of tradition are clearly discernible in the Pentateuch, distinguishable from each other in particular through their language and their theological emphases. Most clearly in evidence is a layer that can be called "priestly" and is found especially in the first four books of the Pentateuch. It is quite clearly discernible in the characteristic linguistic phraseology it uses, so that there are few differences of opinion as to its contours. It is, however, questionable whether this layer ever existed on its own, as many scholars continue to assume. According to this view the Pentateuch was pieced together from various "sources" that originally existed independently of each other; in this context the priestly "source" is referred to as the "Priestly Document" or "P." But it seems to me more likely that the extensive priestly materials first found form in their connection with other, "non-priestly" materials and are therefore best understood together as a "composition layer" (cf. 1977, 130ff; Blum 1990a, 219ff). However the view, widely accepted since Julius Wellhausen's day, that the priestly layer as a whole contains the most recent elements of the pentateuchal tradition and is to be dated to the time of the Babylonian Exile (597-538) or shortly afterwards, remains unaffected.

The contours of the other, "non-Priestly" materials are considerably less clear. Up until a few decades ago the dominant, almost unchallenged view was that there must have been one or more older "sources," which were given the names "Yahwist" and "Elohist." Their existence as independent, coherent literary entities has, however, since been queried, and opinion is greatly divided as to their date of origin (cf. Blenkinsopp 1992) [→**14f**]. In view of more recent discussion, in what follows I shall adopt the view that the many "pre-priestly" materials in the Pentateuch did not have the form of independent "sources" or such like, but that they too were first collated and shaped in a "composition." This "pre-priestly" composition shows evidence of close linguistic and theological connections with Deuteronomy and may therefore be referred to as "deuteronomistic" (cf. Blum 1990a, 7ff). The "priestly" composition builds upon it.

Finally, Deuteronomy constitutes an entity in its own right [→**74**]. In its present form it does not come from a single cast, but shows evidence of various stages of tradition. Doubtless it was included in the final composition of the Pentateuch and left its mark on it. The character of the Pentateuch as Torah in particular has been fundamentally determined in large part by Deuteronomy (cf. Crüsemann 1992). For justification of the following discussion I refer in particular to the discussion in Blenkinsopp (1992) and the work of Blum (1990a) and Crüsemann (1992).

1. The Book of Genesis

1.1 Primordial history

1.1.1 In the beginning God created

"In the beginning God created the heaven and the earth." With this sentence the first chapter of the book of Genesis begins [→*In* **140**]. The first word in the Hebrew sentence, *bʿrēʾšît*, "in the beginning," gave the book its name in Jewish tradition. This sentence also forms the beginning of the Pentateuch, the beginning of the Old Testament as a whole and thereby the beginning of the Bible, both the Jewish and the Christian. This sentence therefore also stands at the beginning of a "Theology of the Old Testament," which understands the Old Testament (the Hebrew Bible) as a theological book and reads it in its given context [→**§23**].

This sentence speaks of the beginning of God's dealings with the world, with humanity and with Israel. It is an absolute beginning; there is no previous history. The word *bʿrēʾšît*, "in the beginning," only occurs with this meaning at this point in the Hebrew Bible [→**§5**]. The subject of the sentence is God. His action sets history in motion. The verb *bārāʾ*, "create," is also special from a linguistic point of view: it is one of the very few verbs in biblical Hebrew that are only used with God as subject [→**191**]. It thus expresses the sovereignty of God's action. The pairing of "heaven and earth" has a dual function. First, it points forward to the immediately following unfolding of the divine act of creation, which comprises heaven and earth; it is repeated with this meaning in the summary at the conclusion of the sixth and last day of creation (Gen 2.1). Second, the word pair is frequently used in the Hebrew Bible as a comprehensive expression of the "world" as a whole and at the same time as the realm of God's operation (Deut 3.23; 4.39; 1 Kgs 8.23; Isa 1.2; 49.13; 66.1; Jer 23.24; Ps 96.11; 113.6; 1 Chron 29.11) [→**76, 169**]. God created absolutely *everything*. This will be elaborated in what follows.

Verse 2 seems to cast doubt on the absoluteness of the beginning. The earth was already in existence. But it was still *tohû wābohû*, in chaos, "without form and void," "desolate and waste," not yet suited for "habitation" (Isa 45.18). There is a mythological tradition behind this, according to which the creator God had to win the world in a struggle with Chaos. But here, in the first chapter of the Bible, God does not have to fight. He speaks (v. 3) [→**332**]. He speaks, and it is done: light comes into being. This creates the precondition for distinction, which at the same time is a separation (*hibdîl*). God separates the newly created light from the chaotic darkness and makes it an object of creation, adding it into the newly created order: the light is now called "day" and the darkness "night" (v. 5). The firmament too (*rāqî*ʿ), which God now calls "heaven," serves as a separation, separating the chaotic water in the heavenly ocean above from the other water below (vv. 6-8); the latter has to make space for the "dry" land, which is now given the name "earth, while the water is called "sea" (vv. 9f). Thus heaven and earth are created, and at the same time the chaotic elements of darkness and water are included in the creation.

Step by step the world is built up further in works of creation each day (cf. Steck 1975). Finally God creates man, or more precisely: people, man and woman, "in his image" (vv. 26f) [→**18f**]. He blesses them with fertility and delegates to them responsibility for administering the world on his orders (v. 28). God sees that everything is "very good" (v. 31). On the seventh day he rests from his work of creation and blesses and "hallows" this day (2.1-3).

This first chapter of the Bible constitutes an impressive, self-contained account of the coming into being of the world and of human beings. At the same time it forms the beginning of the biblical "primordial history" (Gen 1–11) and interrelates with the other texts in this section in a variety of ways. Directly after the first creation account there follows a second, which reaches beyond the creation and tells of the fate of the first human couple (2.4–3.24). It views the creation from another perspective. While in Gen 1 a broadly spanned, systematic sketch of the creation of the world is unfolded, in 2.4ff the concern is with people and their immediate living area. Thus this second text as it were gives an account of the first human couple in more concrete detail.

From the earliest days of historical-critical work on the Old Testament it has been generally assumed that these two creation accounts were not composed by the same author. The second account is rightly considered to be the older of the two. While emphasis used to be placed on the independence of the two texts (and of corresponding texts in the rest of the Pentateuch), in more recent work interest has been directed more to their interconnections. Their integration is not ascribed to a mere "redaction" [→**12**] but is understood, rather, in the context of a "composition," which in very deliberate and nuanced work linked together texts of varying ages and provenances and related them to each other. The connection between the two creation accounts is made by means of the introductory formula in 2.4a, which is to be understood as the heading for the second account (Cross 1973, 302; Blum 1990a, 291; similarly Blenkinsopp 1992, 60).

The creation of man is presented in the second chapter as a direct act of God: first the creation of the man, whom God forms from clay and into whom God breathes the "breath of life" (2.7f), then that of the woman, whom he forms (*bānāh*: literally, "builds") from the "rib" taken from the man (? the word *ṣēlāʿ* does not have this meaning anywhere else; cf. *ThWAT* 6, 1059ff). Unlike 1.27b, where the word is treated as a plural and is differentiated by the adjectives "male" and "female" [→§5.4], in 2.22-24 the equivalent opposition between *ʾiššāh* "woman" and *ʾîš* "man" is expressly and emphatically introduced (cf. Trible 1993, 120ff). A further differentiation and sharpening over against Gen 1 is found in the formulation of the commission given to the man to "cultivate and preserve" the garden allocated to him to live in (v. 15). Unlike the charge to have dominion in 1.28, however, in view here is the narrower inhabited area of ch. 2.

This second (older) creation account is not, however, at an end at this point. Its continuation is found in a narrative (ch. 3) in which it is no longer God who is the active party, but where it is his creations who begin to act in their own right. Thus begins, as it were, the story of humanity, and it begins with the "fall from grace." This narrative, whose reception history is one of the longest among the Old Testament texts, is quite isolated within the Hebrew Bible itself. "No prophet, psalm, or narrator makes any recognizable reference to the story of the fall" (von Rad 1972, 74). But its significance within the framework of primordial history is perfectly clear: it marks the end of the first chapter of the story of humanity, in which humans lived in immediate, and unmediated, proximity to God. Its end comes because humans wanted to be "like God," which (notwithstanding the many layers of meaning in this statement) here means: to be responsible for their own decisions. And they may, and must, do this outside the Garden of Eden, which post-biblical tradition has called "Paradise."

The use that humans make of their freedom to be responsible for themselves is catastrophic: the first deed recounted is a murder, fratricide in fact (ch. 4). We see here what humans are capable of. But we also see, with inescapable clarity, that God will not allow this: Cain is banished from the human community. God gives humans the freedom do decide their own actions. But already here he sets the first basic limits within which these actions must be performed, and later he will elaborate and on this and develop it (cf. Gen 9.6; Ex 20.13) [→18].

This first misuse of freedom continues the line begun in the "fall" and it leads on (by way of the uninhibited vengefulness of Lamech [Gen 4.23f] and the myth-reflecting "marriages with angels" [6.1-4]) ultimately to God's "regretting" having created humans (6.6). Here we see a profound tension in the first chapters of the Bible. The world God created was "very good." But humans, who are a central component of his creation, are not "good." So it is certainly no coincidence that in the first creation account the work of creating humans (1.26-28) does not conclude with the verdict "good," as in the case of the preceding objects of creation, but is merely included in the general verdict (1.31). Humans were faced with the possibility of recognizing good and evil; and through their actions they finally took things so far that God had to acknowledge that "every imagination of the thoughts of [their] heart was only evil continually" (6.5). The author of the first creation account could already see this and perhaps intended deliberately to avoid a counterpart to this statement (Cassuto 1961, 59f, 302).

The texts do not attempt to explain this tension between God's "good" creation and the "evil" imagination of the human heart. Their authors, however, write in the full awareness that they can only view the world from the viewpoint of those who live "after the flood," i.e. outside the area of the undisturbed symbiosis of the creatures with their creator, which they describe as the original, primordial situation. From their own experience they know that humans are not "good," but capable of, and frequently prone to, sins of all kinds. And from tradition they know that the elemental tension between the original "good" design of divine creation and what humans have made of it, almost meant the end of this creation.

At this point the two text layers that have been brought together in the composition of the primordial history are closely interwoven. Twice we read "Yhwh/God saw." He saw the condition of humans, the "evil imagination" of their hearts (6.5); and he saw the condition of the entire earth, which finds its expression in a word-for-word echo of the "seeing" of God at the conclusion of the creation story (1991b, 124): "And God saw everything that he had made, and behold, it was very good" (1.31) [→14]; and now: "And God saw the earth, and behold, it was corrupt" (6.12). It was full of "violence" (*ḥāmās*, v. 11), for "all flesh" (i.e. humans and animals) had "corrupted their way" (v. 12).

Then God "regretted" (6.6) [→**§15**]. The basic contradiction between God's good creation and its perversion by humans (and also by animals) finds expression in an extreme theological "border statement" (*Grenzaussage*, Jeremias 1975/97, 25). God reacts like a human being (cf. 1 Sam 15.29b): it "grieved him to his heart" (Gen 6.6b); in torment of soul, he decides to annihilate his work.

1.1.2 Noah found grace

But the narrative, which is heading towards the annihilation of creation, abruptly stalls: "But Noah found grace in the eyes of the LORD" (6.8). A single human being is spared the general verdict on the evil of humans. Back in 5.29 his name was interpreted as "comforter," and in 6.9 we read that he was "righteous" and "blameless" (*ṣaddîq tāmîm*). Later tradition too calls Noah the exemplary righteous man, together with Daniel and Job (Ezek 14.14, 20) [→**243**]; but nowhere do we read what his righteousness consisted in. But he is chosen to begin a new chapter of human history: "This is the history of the generations of Noah" (6.9). God shares with him his decision to annihilate the world (v. 13) and announces to him at the same time that he wants to conclude with him and all humans and animals that are to go into the Ark with him, a "covenant" that they will stay alive (v. 18). Noah himself and the readers of this story know this, when the great annihilating flood, the "waters of Noah" (Isa 54.9) [→**193**] come upon the earth. They know that the story of God's creation is not quite over yet.

When Noah has survived the flood in the Ark, and presents the first sacrifice (8.20), God talks to himself once again "in his heart." He repeats the statement about the "evil imagination" of the human heart, but he now draws the opposite conclusion from this: "I will never again curse the ground because of man ... neither will I ever again destroy every living creature as I have done." Humans have not changed, but God has, as it were, overcome his regret, once and for all: "While the earth remains, seedtime and harvest, cold and heat, summer and winter, day and night, shall not cease" (vv. 21f). The future existence of the world will no longer be dependent on human behavior. God lets the world continue and puts up with humans as they are.

This promise that God makes is once again solemnly confirmed. (Here again the priestly text layer [Gen 9] is closely linked with the older one [8.21f], forming the overarching framework of the composition [1991b].) God sets up a "covenant" (*b'rît*) with humans and with all living creatures which have left the Ark, and therefore with all future inhabitants of the earth (9.8-17). The content of this covenant is that there will be no further annihilation by means of a flood, but that this world and all its inhabitants will have a continuing existence from now on. This means, however, that people now living on the earth are descendants of Noah. Humans remain *b'nê 'ādam*, children of Adam (cf. e.g. Ps 115.16). But the line traced back to Adam is broken, and the promises made to humans at the time of creation now apply to Noachic humanity in a mediated and partially altered manner (cf. Greenberg 1970).

Central statements from the first creation account are therefore picked up again (9.1-7). But unlike Gen 1, Gen 9 now speaks of the reality of the post-diluvian world in which readers of the text themselves live. First God repeats the blessing of fertility from the sixth day of creation (9.1, cf. 1.28) [→14]. But there then follows a sharp contrast: instead of the peaceful co-existence of all living creatures to date, "fear and dread" will now hold sway, because God has given all animals into the hands of humans (9.2). The direct connection between this sentence and the fertility blessing of v. 1 makes this new description of the relationship between humans and animals look very much like the exercise of the human domination over creation ordered by the creator. In v. 3 this is elaborated, when (with a verbal link to 1.29) animals are assigned to humans for food (with the express exclusion of the consumption of blood, v. 4). But it remains clear that this alteration to the original order of creation means at the same time the end of "paradisal" peace. The human being is now both the "image of God and the dread of animals" (Ebach 1986). Here too the text does not offer an interpretation; but it states that this change in the post-diluvian world is in accordance with the will of God.

Humanity too is endangered, and the mutual relationship between humans in this altered world must be regulated. Since the first human act when responsibility was given was one of fratricide (Gen 4) [→15], the first commandment that God gives humans is the prohibition of killing another human being, the "shedding of blood" (9.6). The justification for this is simple and basic: because the creator has created human beings "in the image of God" [→14]. The killing of a human means damage to, indeed the destruction of, the image of God.

Hence, "If someone destroys a human being, the Scripture regards it as if he has destroyed a whole world" (*Sanhedrin* IV.5). The existence of this altered post-diluvian world is confirmed by the covenant which God sets up with humans and all creatures (9.8ff). God sets up a "sign" [→§6] of this: his rainbow in the clouds (9.12ff; cf. Zengler 1983). God binds himself by means of this sign: he will see (*rā'āh*) the rainbow and "remember" the "eternal" covenant (*b'rît 'ôlām*) he has set up (vv. 15f; cf. also 8.1). But humans too can see the rainbow when it "appears," i.e. when it is visible (*nir'āh*, v. 14). They know then that they can rely on the promise of God given in the covenant and that the world in which they live will continue to exist.

Thus begins a new stage in the history of God's dealings with the world and humanity. It is continued in a dual manner. The nations of the world spread out and become differentiated. The beginnings of this occur already with the sons of Noah, who represent the three main groups of nations (9.18f), and then it continues in the "genealogy" (ch. 10). Here humanity as a whole is taken as a unity as it was created (von Rad 1962, 175). At the same time, however, a counter-movement is discernible. In the primordial history we read the very general remark: "At that time men began to call upon the name of the LORD" (Gen 4.26b). The circle of Yhwh-worshipers within humanity at the time is not more precisely indicated or restricted. But in the blessings and curses on the sons of Noah (Gen 9.25-27) we then read: "Blessed be Yhwh, the God of Shem" (v. 26). The special relationship to Yhwh now applies only to a particular section of humanity. As yet there is no talk of Israel. But it is already included in the name Shem, for Shem is "the father of all the children of Eber," i.e. of the "Hebrews" (10.21; cf. Crüsemann 1981). From here, the narrowing line of the genealogies (11.10ff) runs on towards Abraham.

But the course of the narrative is interrupted once again, turned upside down, in fact, by the narrative of the building of the tower of Babel (11.1-9). Humanity does not want to acknowledge its variety and its dispersal over the entire earth (10.32). In the present narrative context we read also: humans do not want to obey God's commandment to "fill the earth" (Gen 1.28) [→15]. They want to maintain a unity that no longer exists. They want to demonstrate the power of this unity by means of a tower, the top of which reaches "to heaven." This indicates a rivalry with the celestial world of the gods, as in an inscription on the famous ziggurat of Babylon, which may have served as a model for the biblical account: "to let its top compete with heaven" (*TUAT* II, 491ff, l. I, 36f). This is not explained in Gen 11, however, but the emphasis is placed elsewhere: humans want to "make a name" for themselves (12.2). So he "disperses" the nations once again (*pûṣ*, 11.8), as had already begun with the structuring of humanity by the descendants of Noah (9.19, same verb). The "one speech" (*śāpāh* 11.1) that they hold in common must give way once again (11.9) to the variety of languages (*l'šonôt* 10.5, 20, 31). Many interpreters take this as a punishment of ambitious humanity, and the narrative is indeed ambivalent. But in the end the notion of the re-establishment of the variety of humanity intended at creation dominates (cf. Jacob 1934, 301ff; Uehlinger 1990). The common history of Noachic humanity thus comes to an end. The nations of the world in their vast variety do not again come into view as a totality, and with the history of Abraham a new stage begins in the story of God's dealings with humans. The future of the "families of the earth," however, is already included in God's plans (12.3).

The biblical primordial history shows its readers both things: the greatness and beauty of creation and its derailment and endangering by humans. But it also reassures them that God wants to retain and maintain his creation despite human sinfulness. This is where readers stand, then as today. There is no longer any undistorted view of creation (cf. Jeremias 1990).

Even the magnificent first chapter of the Bible cannot and must not be read without its sequel, that of sin, flood and finally of God's covenant with all living creatures. This gracious promise of God alone makes it possible for present-day readers too to direct their view again and again to the creation and, despite everything, to admire it in its greatness and beauty.

In the broader context of the Pentateuch other perspectives from the primordial history emerge too. Thus, at the conclusion of creation, the seventh day is blessed and hallowed by God (Gen 2.3) [→**14**], and in the talk of God's "resting" (*šābat*) the name of the Sabbath (*šabbāt*) rings through; but it is not yet specifically mentioned. After the Israelites have learned of the sabbath for the first time as a divine regulation, in the wilderness, without knowing it already (Ex 16) [→**50**], the celebration of the sabbath is finally inserted as a cultic rule in the context of the restoration of the Sinai sanctuary (Ex 31.12-17). The Israelites are to acknowledge that "I am the LORD, who sanctifies you" (v. 13) [→**66, 77**].

At the conclusion of the sixth day of creation, we read: "And God saw everything that he had made, and behold, it was very good" (Gen 1.31) [→**14**]; in sharp contrast to this, before the flood begins we read: "And God saw the earth, and behold, it was corrupt" (6.12) [→**17**]. This resounds once again at the end of the account of the construction of the sanctuary at Sinai: "And Moses saw all the work, and behold, they had done it; as the LORD had commanded, so had they done it" (Ex 39.43a; cf. also Gen 2.1f with Ex 39.32a; 40.33b [→**66**]; cf. Zenger 1983, 170ff; Blum 1990, 306f).

The parallelism between Gen 1.31 and Ex 39.43 is as clear as the difference between them. In both cases the concluding "see" is followed by the blessing (Gen 2.3a; Ex 39.43b); but the verdict "very good" is the property of the creator—Moses can only confirm the full accordance of the constructed sanctuary with the divine plan. But between them stands the flood as the divine reaction to human sin. The great significance of the Sinai sanctuary in its relation to creation cannot be understood without this.

1.2 The Patriarchal history [→§7]

1.2.1 The Lord spoke to Abraham

"The LORD spoke to Abram" (Gen 12.1). With this address to the "patriarch" Abraham (on the name change, see 17.5 [→**27**]), after all the general part, the particular part of the biblical story begins: the history of Israel. Abraham is chosen by God, from the totality of the nations, for a new beginning. Old Testament texts express this in different ways: God "takes" Abraham "out" (Gen 24.7; Josh 24.3), he "calls" him (Isa 51.2), he "recognizes" him (Gen 18.19) and to use a thoroughly theological term, he "chooses" him (*bāḥar* Neh 9.7) [→**§6.4**]. In the latter instance, the prayer in Neh 9, the election of Abraham is regarded as the second fundamental act of God after creation (v. 6) [→**399**].

The call of Abraham signifies a radical new beginning. He alone is chosen out of the whole of the rest of the nations of the world. This is emphasized all the more by the fact that God commands him to release himself from all aspects of his life thus far: land, relations and paternal household. He faces a new beginning with the threefold divine promise: land, vast number of descendants and blessing (vv. 1b, 2). This provides the decisive key terms for the first phase of the history of Israel, which now begins in the narrative form of the family history.

At the same time this first divine address to Abraham makes clear that his election from among the nations certainly does not mean that the history of his people that now begins will be unrelated to that of other nations [→§20]. The land which God wants to "show" Abraham (12.1), is identified as the "land of Canaan" (v. 5), and an added note states: "at that time the Canaanites were in the land" (v. 6b).

Thus begins the story of Israel in a land in which the members of another nation live, who bear the name of the land. This name is also maintained in what follows (e.g. Gen 13.12; 50.5; Ex 6.4; Josh 14.1). In God's speech we read, further, that Abraham and his descendants can expect "blessing" and "cursing" action from other nations. In a metrically worded divine saying, which probably derives from older tradition (cf. Gen 27.29; Num 24.9) [→72], this expectation is contrasted with the promise that God will react protectively and caringly in response (v. 3a). And those nations that will "bless" Israel will in turn have a share in Abraham's blessing (v. 3b).

In the story that now begins, readers of these texts stand as members of the nation that regards Abraham as its forefather. This story is marked essentially by the problem of the existence of Israel in its land. Israel does not see itself as indigenous, but regards the land into which Abraham has migrated and in which Israel now lives, as given by God.

This implies two basic aspects in particular: on the one hand the possession of the land and life in it means particular relationships with other nations, both peaceful and inimical. The history of Israel is thus always the history of "Israel among the nations," near and far, for better and for worse. Second, at any time God can take back the gift of the land on account of Israel's behavior. Israel's dwelling in this land is thus never without jeopardy. In the course of the story that will now be told, this second aspect gains increasingly in significance.

1.2.2 I will give you the land

The first thing Abraham does is to traverse the land, in order to take it symbolically into his possession (Gen 12.6-9), in particular through the building of altars in Shechem and Beth-El. The relation to God is thus the first thing that constitutes Abraham's relationship to the land. God appears to him and gives him the promise: "To your descendants I will give this land" (v. 7) [→§8]. This promise runs like a scarlet thread through the whole of the story of the patriarchs. It applies to all three patriarchs, with variations in the formulation leaving traces of the step-by-step development of the composition as a whole (13.15, 17; 15.7, 18; 26.3f; 28.13; 35.12; cf. 24.7; 48.4; cf. 1977, 42ff).

The land has been promised to the fathers, and they live in it; but it is not their property. In a divine speech in Gen 15.13-16 it is predicted that the Israelites will return to the land promised to them only after a period of sojourn as *gēr*, non-domiciled protected citizen, and of oppression "in a land that is not theirs," which points to the stay in Egypt and the exodus [→§9]. In another (priestly) tradition the land is repeatedly described as *'ereṣ m'ġûrîm* (e.g. 17.8; 28.4), usually translated as "land of sojournings," i.e. the land in which Abraham and his descendants live in the status of the *gēr*.

Nonetheless the land has central significance for the patriarchal stories as a whole. Abraham receives the divine commandment to move from Mesopotamia into the land of Canaan (12.1). Later, Jacob, after a lengthy absence on account of his flight from his brother Esau (which is approved of by his father Isaac in the priestly version in 27.46–28.5), receives an order to return in the same direction (31.13). Isaac is impeded from moving to Egypt during a famine (26.2f), while later on, in God's speech to Jacob, we read: "Do not be afraid to go down to Egypt" (46.3f) [→32]. These texts are expressly related to each other in the literary composition and show that God has allocated the land to the patriarchs to live in and that they should therefore not leave it against his will (cf. Blum 1984, 300). Abraham's direction to his servant, who is supposed to collect a bride for Isaac from Mesopotamia, on no account to take Isaac there himself (24.6) is to be seen in this context.

Only Abraham's trek to Egypt during a famine (12.10-20) does not fit this pattern. In the overall context it is clear that this is a "digression" of Abraham's own, which in addition leads to the endangerment of Israel's matriarch and which is reversed by the intervention of God himself. In the narrative this is made clear by the fact that Abraham is brought back step for step to where he last had his tent and the altar at which once again he can worship God (13.1-4).

Later, in connection with the famine Isaac experiences, at which point express reference is made back to the time of Abraham (26.1), the alert reader will see that Abraham should not have wandered off to Egypt but that God would have kept him alive if he had stayed in the land, as he did with Isaac (26.12).

It is difficult to see how Genesis 14 fits in with our understanding of the patriarchal history. With its warlike scenes the narrative presents quite a different picture from the other patriarchal stories; moreover it is difficult to follow the historical course of the events related. Abraham's generous refraining from plunder (vv. 22-24), however, fits well with his behavior towards Lot, related immediately before this, to whom he left the choice of his share in the land (13.8ff). Lot's place of residence (Sodom) and Abraham's (the oaks of Mamre) correspond to those of ch. 13. Finally, the beginning of ch. 15 with its divine promise of a rich "reward" connects well with Abraham's restraint at the end of ch. 14 (cf. Blum 1984, 462ff n.). Thus despite its difference the narrative seems to be deliberately related to the present context.

The scene of Abraham's meeting with Melchizedek, the king of šālēm, priest of 'ēl 'elyôn (14.18-20) also is in isolation within the Abraham stories, but has various connections with other texts in the Hebrew Bible, via the name Melchizedek (cf. Ps 110.4), the designation of Jerusalem as šālēm (Ps 76.3) and the divine epithet 'elyôn (Deut 32.8; Ps 46.5; 47.3 etc.) [→§15]. This section thus constitutes an interesting and important element of tradition.

The story of the forefathers, then, is the beginning of the story of Israel in the land God has promised it. Many texts allude to matters known or familiar to later readers, for instance particular places like the "oaks of Mamre" (Gen 18) or the "pillar of salt" at the Dead Sea (19.26), cultic sites like that at Beth-El (28.10ff) or Shechem (33.20) [→29], customs such as a particular food taboo (32.32), and so on. In the consciousness of later generations, the patriarchs are inextricably linked with the land, and conversely the land and life in it are associated with remembrance of the patriarchs. But still it did not belong to them. Abraham is only able fully to acquire a burial site, the cave of Machpelah (ch. 23), so that his wife Sarah (23.19) and he himself (25.9f) will no longer be "sojourners" in death. (According to 49.31 Isaac and Rebekkah too were buried there, along with Jacob's wife Leah.)

But then the patriarchal narratives end with Jacob and his sons, i.e. the whole family of "Israel" (cf. 32.29; 35.10), leaving the land (46.1ff) [→32]. They do this with express divine permission, which is linked with the promise that God will make them a great nation in Egypt and finally lead them back into the promised land (vv. 3f). Jacob himself again builds a bridge back from Egypt, where the Israelites became such oppressed and enslaved foreigners (cf. Ex 22.20; 23.9 etc.), to the promised land, in which they already have a stake, by arranging for his own burial in the cave of Machpelah (29.29f; 50.12f). Finally, at the conclusion of the story of the patriarchs, Joseph recalls the divine promises to Abraham, Isaac and Jacob, of return to, and ultimate possession of the land (50.24). Thus the story of Abraham's posterity stays open for the future promised by God, even in the following time of servitude in Egypt.

1.2.3 You will be a great nation

The second main theme in the patriarchal story was announced in Gen 12.2 as: "I will make you a great nation." The problem inherent in this announcement is known to the reader from the comment in 11.30 that Sarah (at this point still Sarai, cf. 17.15) was infertile. This problem is dramatically accentuated in the first episode following their arrival in the land, when during his digression to Egypt Abraham pretends Sarah is his sister and thus accepts the fact that she might disappear into Pharaoh's harem (12.10-20); it is only through God's direct intervention (v. 17) that she is rescued from this. The narrative remains oddly without comment, even though readers know that the existence of the whole nation of Israel is in peril at this point.

In what follows, the problem of Abraham's posterity is then shown from the most varied angles. In the first place, it is repeatedly promised to him and his sons by God, often in images which seem to exceed all bounds: it will be as numerous as the stars (15.5; 26.4) or as the dust of the earth (13.16; 28.14, cf. 32.13; 22.17), or rather a great nation (12.2; 18.18; 46.3) or even a multitude of nations (17.4-6; 35.11). On the other hand the realization of the promise is constantly impeded, which provides the narratives with part of their dramatic force. When Sarah is in danger of being taken into Pharaoh's harem (12.10-20) it is not expressly mentioned that the promise just given was imperiled, but this is clear to readers. After that, Sarah's childlessness is one of the dominant narrative elements in the Abraham story. Not only does it provide the grounds for conflict between the two women, Sarah and Hagar (16; 21.8-21), but it also forms the leitmotiv of the divine visit to the oaks of Mamre (18), when once again, as several times beforehand (15.4; 17.19), the birth of a son to Sarah herself is expressly promised (18.10, 14). This son will be Isaac, whose name *yiṣḥāq* constantly reminds us of Sarah's laughter (*ṣāḥaq*, vv. 12, 13, 15a,b; cf. 21.6). With Isaac the series of "patriarchs" [→§7] as bearers of the promise continues.

Isaac's late arrival brings a second aspect into view: the relationship between Isaac and Ishmael, the son of Abraham and Hagar (16.15). Connections between them are reflected here which give graphic detail to what is expressed already in 12.3, 5f: that Israel does not live in isolation but stands in relation to other peoples [→§20], some of which are regarded as close relatives. Tradition has preserved only very little about the Ishmaelites (cf. 25.12-18). What is clearer is the relationship in the next generation, in which the problem of childlessness is first repeated (25.21), but then twins are born (vv. 24-26): Jacob and Esau, i.e. Israel (32.29; 35.10) and Edom (25.30; 36). The tense relationship between the two brothers, as recounted in the "Jacob–Esau cycle" (Gunkel 1910, 291f) in Gen 25.21ff; 27; 32f, reflects at the same time relations between Israel and its south-eastern neighbor, with which it was connected by a varied, and occasionally hostile history. Many texts testify to the profundity of the split between the two peoples caused by this enmity at different times (cf. Num 20.14-21; 2 Sam 8.13f; 1 Kgs 11.14-22; 2 Kgs 8.20-22; 14.7; Isa 34; Jer 49.7-22; Ezek 25.12-14; Amos 1.11f; Obad; Lam 4.21f). Finally, relations with the eastern neighbors Moab and Ammon through the line of Lot, the nephew and companion of Abraham, are narratively recorded (Gen 19.30-38).

1.2.4 Interpretations

If the Genesis stories are read in context, it is evident that in many of them human activity is in the foreground, without God himself appearing in speech or action. Theological points are often kept implicit and are often visible only in the light of the broader context. Other texts on the other hand are determined entirely by the speech and actions of God, and the theological messages are central to them. These texts belong to various stages in the history of the emergence of the present whole and place different emphases; but they all have their significance within and for the present context.

(a) Abraham
Genesis 15 opens with a divine speech, and Abraham is the conversation partner who responds. After his hesitant question, "LORD, what can you give me?" (v. 2) we read, following God's renewed promise, "And he believed" (*he' 'min*, v. 6). This sentence contrasts oddly with its immediate and its wider context. Within the chapter, in v. 8 we have another hesitant question of Abraham's and in ch. 16 his desperate attempt to force the fulfillment of the promise of a son in his own

way. But this verse already points beyond itself: to the promise of the
son to Sarah (21.1ff) that will ultimately be fulfilled, to the severe test
Abraham had to—and did—withstand (22), and finally to the installment he makes towards possession of the land as he acquires a small
plot (23). The reader is told here already that ultimately Abraham's
faith, his confidence in the reliability of the promises and the guidance
of God, will determine his image as a whole. Later tradition also
knows that God found Abraham's heart "faithful" (*ne' 'mân*, Neh 9.8,
from the same root as *he' 'min* in Gen 15.6).

Gen 15.6 continues further: "and he reckoned it to him as righteousness." The linguistic structure of the verse leaves the subject of
this second half of the verse open. According to the traditional interpretation, God counted Abraham's faith as righteousness. But in medieval Jewish interpretation we already find the view that it is Abraham who recognizes and acknowledges God's promise as an expression
of God's righteousness (cf. Gaston 1980; Mosis 1989; cf. Oeming
1983). This finds support in Neh 9, where, like a liturgical response to
the sentence that God found Abraham's heart "faithful," we read "for
you (God) are righteous" (*ṣaddîq*, v. 8). God's righteousness here is his
faithfulness to his promise. Abraham believed in God's faithfulness and
confirmed it, as it were, by "acknowledging" it.

Finally, in ch. 15 we meet once again the word *b'rît*, "covenant,"
which the reader has already met as a central theological term in ch. 9.
There God had committed himself to the existence of the world in his
covenant with humanity and the whole of creation [→**19**]; now in the
covenant he promises Abraham and his posterity (15.7) the possession
of the land: "To your descendants I give this land" (v. 18). As in ch. 9,
this covenant agreement is purely a promise of God's, which is not
linked to any condition on the human side (cf. Kutsch 6f). But as if by
an oath (Lohfink 1967) God binds himself to Abraham and his descendants.

Chapter 17 too contains almost exclusively divine speech. The
chapter opens with a solemn address to Abraham, who for the main
part remains a silent partner. To begin with, God introduces himself
with the formula, "I am *'ēl šadday*," which is characteristic of "priestly"
language [→**11**]. The word *b'rît* is taken up again and here too comprises the promise of a great posterity (17.2, 4-6). This is expanded by
Yhwh's comprehensive promise, "to be your and your descendants'
God" (v. 7). In one essential respect, however, Gen 17 goes beyond

covenant statements up to this point. God's promises, which are marked by a two-fold "I," placed in an emphatic forward position (v. 1bβ, 4), are followed by a second part, introduced with an emphatic "you" (v. 9aβ): "Keep the covenant!" Here there are two sides to the "covenant": the divine promise and the human response. As the "sign of the covenant" (v. 11), circumcision [→53] is an integral part of the covenant, and its observance is made a mandatory duty. But the existence of the covenant, i.e. the validity of the God-given promises, is not jeopardized if it is not kept; the consequences affect only the individual transgressor (v. 14; cf. Crüsemann 1992, 342f).

The passage Gen 18.16-33 is quite a different sort of text. Nowhere else in the Hebrew Bible, after the banishment of the first human couple from the Garden of Eden, do we find a human being so directly face to face with God. Yhwh has previously eaten as Abraham's guest (18.1ff), if partially incognito as one of three men. After they leave, Abraham accompanies the trio; two of them continue in the direction of Sodom, "but Yhwh still stood before Abraham" (v. 22). This was the original wording: but the "scribes" (according to tradition, the "men of the great synagogue"; cf. Abot I.1) took offense at the šᵉkînāh (the "indwelling" of God on earth) standing before Abraham, because "stand before" can also mean "serve" (e.g. 1 Kgs 17.1). So they changed the text to "but Abraham still stood before Yhwh;" the change has been preserved as a *tiqqûn sofᵉrîm*, an "alteration of the scribes" (cf. Biblia Hebraica).

God first talks to himself, saying that he wants to make Abraham a great and strong people and that he cannot therefore keep from him what he plans to do. So Abraham becomes "God's Co-Knower" (Jacob 1934, 447). And then Abraham begins a conversation with God on the question whether in the imminent annihilation of Sodom God intends to "destroy the righteous with the wicked" (v. 23). The decision itself is not open to discussion; so it is not a matter of Abraham's petitioning for Sodom. Nor is the possibility of distinguishing between the "righteous" (*ṣaddîq*) and the "wicked" (*rāšāʿ*) seen as a problem. Rather, at issue is a double question: whether God, "the judge of the whole earth," lets justice reign (v. 25) and whether the presence of a minority of righteous persons can turn the fate of a predominantly ungodly community. The conversation proceeds in a dramatic movement from fifty righteous down to ten, ending there. The (unexpressed) message is: ten righteous would have been enough to save the city, but they were not to be found. So God has dealt justly. Behind this lies the question whether the fate of Jerusalem in the year 586 could have been averted if there had been more righteous persons in the city (cf. Isa 1.9; Blenkinsopp 1983b, 51f).

In Gen 22 we encounter defamiliarization-like theological statements within a narrative that is anything but clear. God "tests" Abraham (v. 1). Here God seems to veil himself, for only here in the patriarchal history is he designated with the impersonal *hā'ᵉlohîm*, "the God" (or "the Deity") (vv. 1, 9). And in the rest of the narrative God appears only in the form of his messenger (or "angel," *mal'ak yhwh*, vv. 11, 15). In what does the "testing" of Abraham consist? Certainly not simply in a hard test of obedience. In the present context the narrative contains the paradox that God himself is threatening to destroy everything he has promised to Abraham, which Abraham has believed, despite all his doubts, and which God has ultimately also fulfilled. If Abraham must now sacrifice his only legitimate son, then everything will have been in vain. Is this not precisely what the test is: to obey when God seems to contradict himself so fundamentally? Abraham does what God has told him to do. He obeys, because he believes (but the word does not appear here). He believes, we could say with Gen 15.6 (and Neh 9.8), that God is just. And when the test has been passed and God has given Abraham his son back, he repeats through his messenger the promises which have accompanied and determined the patriarchal narrative from the beginning (vv. 15-18).

These interpretive texts illuminate the figure of Abraham from quite different perspectives. He is the believer, who takes God's "righteousness," his faithfulness to his promises [→**27**], at face value (Gen 15.6). He is the first to experience the special attention of the divine "covenant" with Israel which finds expression in the promise of the land (15.18-20), in the promise of great posterity and blessing and in the constant attention of God (17.2-8), and to which he is supposed to respond with the circumcision of all the male members of his family (vv. 9-14). He comes through a severe temptation and test of faith and passes it (ch. 22). And finally in a theological disputation with God he gives an answer to the question whether God acted justly when he had Jerusalem destroyed (18.16-33). The "judge of the whole earth" acted justly both times, toward both Sodom and Jerusalem.

(b) Jacob

Jacob's encounters with God are rather more veiled throughout. There is never a direct confrontation between God and Jacob as with Abraham. But the placement of the encounters with God in the present context is very striking:

The Jacob story ... is supported like a bridge between two pillars, by the Bethel story (Gen 28) at one end and the Penuel story (Gen 32.22ff) at the other. In each of the two cases the paradox of the divine action is very acute: when Jacob has experienced the most devastating bankruptcy, when all seems lost, and blessing seems to have turned to curse, God adds his blessing to him. And when the narrative shows him in a state of wellbeing, when he thinks all he has to do is get through the dispute with Esau, that is when God attacks him like a ghost in the night. And here too it is all about blessing! (v. 26) (von Rad, 1972, 22).

In Beth-El he meets God in a dream (Gen 28.10-22). From an open heaven God reveals himself to Jacob as he once did to Abraham: "I am the LORD" (v. 13; cf. 15.7). When he flees, God gives him the promises (vv. 13f) he previously gave to Abraham (13.15f etc.) and Isaac (26.3f): that he will give them the land and make them a great nation. With the emphatic promise "I am with you" (v. 15) the divine speech includes preservation and return and thereby links the promises with Jacob's personal story. Jacob's return too is initiated by a direct speech by God, which says once again, "I will be with you" (31.3).

But then there is a divine encounter of quite a different sort. Before he meets Esau again Jacob must survive a fight at the Jabbok at night (32.23ff)—not with Esau, as he had expected, but with a "man" who does not reveal his identity (v. 30). But after he is fortunate enough to survive the contest, Jacob recognizes who it is that has fought with him in disguise: "I have seen God face to face" (v. 31; cf. Terrien 1978, 85ff). This God now blesses him before he meets Esau again, thereby "legitimizing" (Elliger 1951) Isaac's deceitfully acquired blessing. From the beginning of the story of the two brothers, the reader knows that God has planned the preeminence of the younger (25.23). But now, after Jacob has come through this last peril, despite his deceitful action (ch. 27) it is expressly put into effect.

Something else occurs in this encounter too: God gives Jacob a new name, Israel [→§7]. This is the first time that the name occurs in the Bible, interpreted in a mysterious way: "for you have striven with God and with men, and have prevailed" (32.28). Did Jacob win? He has survived, and he now has a limp (v. 32). But God has blessed him (v. 30), and the future lies before him, not just his own future, but "Israel's" future. So shortly after this Jacob dedicates an altar to the "God of Israel" (33.20) [→**§15**]; this term for God too occurs for the first time here.

Soon the narrator also begins to refer to Jacob by the name of "Israel," for instance at the beginning of the Joseph story (37.3). And when Israel/Jacob departs for Egypt, God speaks to him once again in a night vision and repeats his promise, "I will go down with you ..." (46.1-4).

(c) Joseph

The Joseph story (Gen 37–50) can be read quite differently. In the present context it forms an indispensable bridge between the patriarchal narratives which take place in the land of Canaan, and the continuation of the story of the people of Israel in Egypt. But it can also be seen very clearly as an independent literary unit, which exceeds everything else in Genesis in extent. Viewed thus, it exhibits very marked features of a didactic wisdom narrative. Joseph is absolutely the embodiment of the wisdom ideal of a "young man ... with the best education and discipline, of piety and worldly wisdom" (von Rad 1953, 122 = 274f).

Joseph's actions are determined entirely by his religious convictions (cf. Meinold 1975/76, 320). To Potiphar's wife, who attempts to seduce him, he responds: "How can I do this great wickedness, and sin against God?" (39.9). His ability to interpret dreams he emphatically attributes to God in each case (40.8; 41.16). But even the narrator remembers to say again and again, "The Lord was with Joseph" and blessed his actions (39.2, 3, 21, 23); so the whole thing is a story of guidance.

Finally the Joseph story is given its theological interpretation by means of a few brief remarks of Joseph's. When he reveals himself to his brothers, he explains to them, "God sent me before you" (45.5). And then finally, "You meant evil against me; but God meant it for good" (50.20). Thus in retrospect not only does Joseph's life-story seem to have been directed by God, but also the story of his whole family, which was kept alive in time of famine through the God-given opportunity to move to Egypt.

1.2.5 Israel moves to Egypt

"Israel in Egypt"—in this first place this means Jacob in Egypt. From his renaming (see above on Gen 32.29) Jacob is frequently called "Israel" in the Genesis narratives, and in the last chapters of Genesis the name dominates. So at the beginning of the last stage of his life-story, we read that Israel departs (Gen 46.1) and finally settles in Egypt (47.27).

In the concluding chapters of Genesis [→§7], almost imperceptibly a change takes place in the plane of observation. In 46.8ff, on the way to Egypt, the "sons of Israel" are still represented as individuals, and the emigrating family is called "Jacob and his sons" (v. 8); in total there are seventy persons who belong to this family (v. 27). It is then reported that Israel blesses his two grandsons Manasseh and Ephraim, Joseph's sons (Gen 48), thereby preferring the younger one, Ephraim, over the older—the same experience as he himself (Jacob) had had from his birth. But this also resonates with the dominance of the tribe of Ephraim over the tribe of Manasseh. Later Jacob collects his sons (Gen 49) and speaks to them in the "blessing of Jacob" as their father Jacob/Israel (both names are given in v. 2 in a *parallellismus membrorum*). In so doing he no longer speaks to them as merely individuals but at the same time as tribes also. The concluding verse 28 contains both aspects: "All these are the twelve tribes of Israel." Here the sons of Jacob are called "tribes" for the first time (cf. also v. 16); but the continuation turns back to the aspect of the family: "Your father gave this command before he died." Jacob has now become the father of the tribes of the *b'nê yiśrā'el*, the "sons of Israel." The content of his last speech to his sons is of blessing: "He blessed them, blessing each with the blessing suitable to him" (v. 28b) [→21]. This brings the first stage of the history of Israel, which began with the promise of blessing to one, Abraham (12.2), to a conclusion with the blessing of all twelve tribes.

The sons of Jacob/Israel now live in Egypt. But in the last chapters of Genesis the connection to the land of the promise, in which the forefathers lived for generations, is very firmly emphasized and maintained. Jacob/Israel makes arrangements before his death for his burial in a tomb of the fathers (47.29f) in the cave of Machpelah (49.29f) which Abraham had acquired for Sarah's burial (Gen 23); he picks up on the fact that God had said, "… and I will also bring you up again" (46.4). Joseph and his brothers fulfill this last wish with much ado, even with the participation of official Egyptian delegates (50.7-13; in vv. 10f another tradition as to the location of Jacob's grave seems to play a role). Joseph too asks his "brothers," the "sons of Israel," to return his bones to the land of his fathers after his death. He connects this with the memory of the divine promise: "God will visit you and bring you up out of this land to the land which he swore to Abraham, to Isaac, and to Jacob" (50.24f). The stay in Egypt will thus not be permanent, and especially it cannot render ineffective the promise of the land given to the forefathers. This recalls the statement in Gen 15, which once before speaks in the divine speech in vv. 13-16 of a sojourn in a foreign land and a later return from it. There, the negative aspect of life "in a land that is not theirs" and of oppression by the inhabitants is moved to the foreground and the stay in Egypt is thus presented as a forced situation of exile. This aspect is faintly discernible in Gen 50.24f [→**37**] in the promise that God will visit the Israelites and will "accept" them.

Thus the story of the three "patriarchs" and their families ends with the prospect of a return from Egypt into the land promised to the forefathers. This also produces the transition to the book of Exodus.

2. The Books of Exodus to Numbers

2.1 The Exodus

2.1.1 They filled the land

"These are the names of the sons of Israel who came to Egypt." Thus begins the book of Exodus [→*In* 140, 148], which has derived its Hebrew designation as *šᵉmôt*, "names," from the opening sentence. Ex 1.1-5a represents a radically shortened reprise of the list given in Gen 46.8-27 [→32] (with slight changes also to the sequence), which names the relatives of Jacob/Israel who moved to Egypt with him. The concluding number of 70 persons (v. 27) is also repeated (Ex 1.5a), the "sons of Israel" once again being expressly given as "descendants of Jacob."

But then the step from family to "people" occurs. After the death of the first generation (Ex 1.6) the "sons of Israel" multiply so much that the whole land is filled with them (v. 7). The multiplication had also been mentioned briefly in Gen 47.27, directly following the note about Jacob/Israel's settling in Egypt. This is now said in more detail, with reference already to the coming conflicts with the Egyptians. The formulation, "they were fruitful … and multiplied" (v. 7) contains clear resonances not only with the promise of numerous descendants to the patriarchs (Gen 17.6; 28.3; 35.11) [→27, 31], but also with the command to the first human couple (Gen 1.28) [→14] to be fruitful and multiply, and then to Noachic humanity after the flood [→18] (9.1; here in v. 7 we also have the word "teeming" as in Ex 1.7). For the story of the people of Israel it is like a new beginning of creation (Fishbane 1979, 65). The emphasis has shifted strangely: in Gen 1.28; 9.1, 7 people are to fill "the earth" (*hā'āreṣ*); in Ex 1.7 the same word means that "the land" in which they now live is being filled by them. Thus what has been promised to mankind is fulfilled "as an example, prototypically or even vicariously" by Israel (Schmidt 1980, 30).

But here it bears the seeds of conflict. For in the land filled by them, the Israelites are only "sojourners" (so with reference to e.g. Ex 22.20, cf. 2.22 and also Gen 15.13 already) [→20]. And they are not only numerous but also "strong" (v. 7)—a word added to the early words about multiplication here. And precisely this key term provokes the conflict (v. 9). The conflict begins after a generation change which here takes the form of a change of epochs: the first generation dies (v.

6) and then comes "a new king, who knew nothing of Joseph" (v. 8). This means that he did not know, or did not want to know, the whole prehistory: how Joseph came to the court of Pharaoh, how Pharaoh recognized that "the spirit of God was in him" (Gen 41.38) [→**31**], what services Joseph had given to Egypt and that on account of this his family was able to come to Egypt. Quite by contrast to the friendly behavior of the earlier Pharaoh (Gen 47.1-12), the new one sees the Israelites as a threat. They are too strong, and in the case of conflict they could align themselves with the enemy (vv. 9f). And he no longer sees in them the family of Joseph or Jacob but "the people of the Israelites" (Ex 1.9).

This is the first time that the "sons of Israel," the Israelites, are called a "people" (*'am*). A fundamental change in the perspective of the account is visible here. Thus far the talk was of the "sons of Israel" [→**§7**] as if of a wider family, and the acting individuals were always clearly recognizable; Israel now appears as a people, a collective entity which acts and is led as a unit. One gains the impression that it was not just Pharaoh, but also the narrator, and even the Israelites themselves, who no longer knew anything about Joseph. His name does not occur again until Ex 13.19, where it is reported that Moses takes Joseph's bones with him when leaving Egypt. But now, at the beginning of the book of Exodus, Moses is not yet in view either. The people of the Israelites does not have a representative to speak for it. It is dumbly exposed to oppression. Even God is silent.

In this change a difference in the traditional material comes to expression. The patriarchal story is conceived as a story of individuals, as a family history, while the Egypt and exodus tradition is conceived as a national history. Each of these two narrative traditions has its own prior history, and both have been the subject of much scholarly research and analysis (cf. Westermann 1975; W.H. Schmidt 1983; H. Schmid 1986). In the present context the narratives of (Joseph and) Jacob/Israel in Egypt link these two traditions together into the one great history of Israel under the guidance of God.

Three times Pharaoh raises his voice to hinder the further multiplication of the Israelites. First he orders them to be set to work as slaves (vv. 9-14). The same terms crop up here as in Gen 15.13 [→**23**]: "oppress" (*'innāh*) and "enslave" (*he'ĕbîd*). But the Israelites continue to multiply, so that the Egyptians are "terrified." They have to acknowledge that stronger powers are at work here. Pharaoh's next command to the midwives, to kill all new-born boys at birth, is disobeyed (vv.

15-21). Their justification for this is simple: they fear God (vv. 17, 21). But their behavior is clever, so that they are able to outwit the king of the land of wisdom. And the people of Israel increases further in number and becomes even stronger (v. 20b). Thereupon Pharaoh commands pure murder: all new-born Hebrew boys are to be thrown into the Nile (v. 22)—a brutal act of desperation which shows that Pharaoh has already lost the fight. But it remains for the reader to understand that the hidden activity of the God of Israel lies behind this [→**44f**].

2.1.2 She called him Moses

No more is related about the result of the royal edict. In the present context it appears only as an introduction to what now follows (2.1-10). An Israelite boy is born [→**§12**] and removed from the persecution in an innovative way, released in a reed basket on the Nile. The child is not thrown into the Nile to be killed, but is consigned to the Nile to be saved. The reader is immediately aware that this is not just any child. The motif of the endangered birth of the hero and his rescue is known also from other ancient religions (cf. the birth legend of King Sargon of Akkad, *AOT* 234f; *RTAT* 123f). But to begin with, the narrative gives no hint of the future fate of this child (unlike, for instance, the narratives of the birth of Samuel in 1 Sam 1f or of Samson in Judg 13) [→**103**]. In addition, to start with, it runs in quite another direction: the child comes to the Egyptian court, whereby his connection with the people he comes from appears to be cut. In the wider context once again there is a special accent here, in that the birth of the future leader and savior of Israel is brought into a close relationship with the Egyptian court, the head of which had tried precisely to hinder this birth. Again, as in the narrative of the midwives (1.15-21), it is women—the mother and sister of the new-born child and the Egyptian princess—who perform the life-saving actions (cf. Exum 1983). And as Joseph was able to bring the Israelites to Egypt as a result of his rise in the court of Pharaoh, so can Moses survive through the action of a member of the court, the daughter of Pharaoh, and thus grow into the role ordained for him. This strange rescue story provides him with an Egyptian name, more precisely a short name lacking the theophoric element found in such names as "Thutmoses," meaning "God X has fathered him." "So he was quite simply a 'son'. The only question is, whose son?" (Thomas Mann, *Das Gesetz*). The narrative turns this motif of the foreign name as it were into its opposite when the Egyptian princess is made to give a Hebrew etymology: "I have pulled him out of the water" (playing on the Hebrew *māšāh*, "pull out," v. 10b).

The narrative skips a number of years and has Moses immediately "go out to his brothers" (2.11-14). We are not told how Moses knows who he really is. The readers know it, but the narrative leaves it in the air. Moses does not act like an Israelite forced laborer but like a privileged Egyptian. By means of his intervention against the Egyptians and his attempt to smooth a quarrel between two "Hebrews," he seems to the Israelites to be someone who aspires to high office: "Who made you a prince and a judge over us?" (v. 14). The questioner does not know that later there will be a concrete answer to this rhetorical question: God did it (cf. Ex 18.13ff). But this remains hidden for the time being, and Moses has to flee because Pharaoh wants to have him killed (v. 15a).

2.1.3 Lead my people out of Egypt

This flight seems to signify the end of the brief episode of Moses' return to his "brothers" (vv. 15b-22). He flees into the wilderness, into the "land of Midian," where he is taken for an Egyptian—or even pretends that he is one (v. 19). The encounter scene takes place beside a well; it is told very succinctly but with the elements familiar to us from Gen 24.11ff and 29.1ff, leading to a marriage. He himself takes some of the water drawn from the well (v. 19b), and the future savior of Israel "saves" (*hôšîaʿ*, v. 17; cf. Alter 1981, 51-58)—but these resonances remain inexplicit. Moses now decides to stay with the "man" (v. 21), also described as the "priest of Midian." The naming of his first son Gershom (v. 22) seals as it were his existence as a "stranger" (*gēr*) in a foreign land (recalling Gen 15.13 once again).

But then a change begins. The short passage 2.23-25 contains two important statements. First: the "new king" (1.8), the same Pharaoh who sought Moses' life (2.15), has died. This would free the way for Moses' return to Egypt (cf. 4.19). But much more important is the second statement: God "hears" how the Israelites groan and "cry" (*zāʿaq*) under their forced labor and "sees" and "recognizes" Israel's need, and therefore "remembers" the covenant [→§6] he concluded with Abraham, Isaac and Jacob. Now, in Israel's time of need, God's covenant promise must and will be honored. The assurance that God will "accept" his people, which Joseph had recalled before his death (Gen 50.24) [→33], will also be fulfilled.

The tool God has chosen for the salvation of Israel is Moses. But as yet Moses himself knows nothing of this. He seems as far removed

from the history of his people and thus from the history of God's dealings with his people as it was possible to be: half Israelite, half Egyptian, and now a refugee who has joined up with a Midianite as his
stockman. He now journeys a little farther "behind the wilderness"
(Ex 3.1ff), coming—unintentionally, and obliviously—to the "mountain of God." This is his first encounter with this spot, to which he
will later return with all Israel for the most significant meeting with
God in the Hebrew Bible and in the history of this people as a whole
(Ex 19ff) [→**52**].

The mountain is here referred to by the name of "Horeb," whereas in Ex 19ff
it is called "Sinai." Both names are common in the Hebrew Bible (Sinai
roughly twice as frequently as Horeb), though Deuteronomy (with the exception of 33.2 in a poetic context) uses only Horeb (1.2, 6, 19 etc.). Scholarly
opinion is divided as to whether the two names originally referred to different
mountains, and also whether the term "mountain of God" in Ex 3f and 1 Kgs
19.8ff [→**139**] originally referred to a third mountain. Possibly Deuteronomy
avoided the name Sinai for theological reasons and introduced instead the
name Horeb as a code for "wilderness" (Perlitt 1977). But there is no dispute
that in the present context of the biblical texts both names mean the same
mountain (cf. *ABD* 6.47-49).

Here Moses is suddenly pushed by the narrator into the ranks of the
great individual figures of Israel's prehistory: God "appears" to him (v.
2), as he had done with the patriarchs (Gen 12.7; 17.1; 18.1; 26.2, 24;
35.9). First he appears in disguise, represented by his messenger (or
"angel," *mal'āk*), as happened before with Abraham (Gen 22.11, 15)
[→**§15**]. The messenger is hidden in the mysterious flame which makes
the thorn-bush burn but does not consume it. But when Moses approaches, God calls him by his name, as he called Abraham (Gen 22.1,
11) [→**28**] and Jacob (46.2), and Moses answers as they did: "Here am
I!" And now God draws him completely into the patriarchal story by
introducing himself: "I am the God of your father, the God of Abraham, the God of Isaac and the God of Jacob" (v. 6); and Moses covers
his head, afraid of catching sight of the deity (*hā*ʾ*lohîm*, cf. 1994, 16)
(which could be fatal; cf. e.g. Ex 33.20; Judg 6.22f).

   Then, however, the scene expands into a large divine speech and a
dialogue between Moses and God. This puts Moses as it were on a par
with Abraham, since no one else before him had conversed with God
with such intensity (Gen 15; 17; 18.16-33) [→**26**], and no one else will

do so after him. But the beginning of the conversation already makes the basic difference clear. What God says to Moses does not concern Moses himself but the people, "my people," as God calls them at the beginning of his speech (3.7). The divine speech picks up what has already been said at the turning point in 2.23-25: God has "seen" and "heard the crying" and "recognizes" what the Israelites are suffering, and has decided to lead them out (cf. Ska 1989, 119f). And Moses is to do this: "Go ... and lead my people, the sons of Israel, out of Egypt" (v. 10).

The double problem in this commission is immediately evident, however. First: "I will send you to Pharaoh" (v. 10) and Moses' prompt answer: "Who am I that I should go to Pharaoh?" (v. 11). And then: "... and bring the sons of Israel out of Egypt—they will not believe me" (4.1).The commission goes in two directions: to Pharaoh and to the Israelites, and in both directions it is fraught with problems. But God's first and basic answer is: "I will be with you" (3.12). The stories of the patriarchs resonate here again, in which we read again and again: "I will be with you." This is particularly marked in the Jacob story [→**29**], where this divine assurance is found at all the important stages on his path: at the flight from Esau (Gen 28.15), at the instruction to return (31.3) and on the way to Egypt (46.4). Conversely, Isaac experiences this assurance because God instructs him *not* to go to Egypt (26.3) [→**23**]. The fellow inhabitants of the land, too, see and say to Abraham and Isaac: "God is with you" (21.22; 26.28).

There is a second part to God's answer. "This will be the sign for you that I have sent you: When you lead the people out of Egypt, you will serve God (*hā'' lôhîm*) on this mountain." Moses had been shifted into the company of the patriarchs by the "appearance" of God; now he is placed in the context of the prophetic tradition. "Send" (*šālaḥ*) is a very characteristic word for this [→**172**]. For instance, Isa 6.8: "Whom shall I send, and who will go for us?" And Isaiah's answer: "Here am I, send me!" (Cf. also Jer 1.7 etc.) The sign will serve to legitimate Moses, but it will not be recognizable until after the event. This too corresponds to the tradition regarding the legitimation of a prophet [→**82, 143, 217**], that it is only recognizable in retrospect (Deut 18.21f; 1 Kgs 22.28; Jer 28.8f). And for the reader, the sign promised to Moses will manifest itself when Moses arrives at Sinai and ascends "to God" (*'el-hā'' lôhîm*, Ex 19.3) [→**52**].

2.1.4 Yhwh is my name

(a) Exodus 3.13-15

Moses is faced with the question of his legitimation and authority on
two sides, toward Pharaoh and toward the Israelites. The second question is the first to loom large. The Israelites are going to ask: "Who is
this "God of the fathers" who has sent you? But what does this question mean at this point? Is it just a way of dressing up Moses' own
question? Does he really know with whom he is speaking? To judge
from the course of the narrative he is hardly in a position to know. His
Israelite mother took care of him only as a wet-nurse, and after that he
grew up at the Egyptian court. He knows only that a deity (see on v. 6
above) is speaking with him, and the narrator continues to have him
address "the deity" (*hā'lōhîm*, vv. 11, 13). This deity has introduced
himself to him as the "God of your father" or as the God of the fathers
[→§7], with the list of names. But Moses must now know the name if
he is to appear and act in the service of this God.

God's answer is given in three steps, and it is only in the third of
these that a real answer comes: "YHWH, the God of your fathers ...
that is my name" (v. 15). This is preceded by another answer (v. 14):
'ehyeh 'ăšer 'ehyeh, "I will be who I will be," or "I will exist as the one I
will exist as" (Buber). This is not a name; but neither is it a statement
about who or how God is, as the Septuagint took it: ἐγώ εἰμι ὁ ὤν,
"I am the being one." Rather, here is picked up again what God had
said to Moses previously: "I will be with you" (*'ehyeh 'immāk*, v. 12)
[→40]. And that is also how he will pass it on to the Israelites: the one
who promises you, "I will be," i.e. I will be with you, he is the one
who has sent me. Here the *'ehyeh* sounds almost like a name, and that
is how it resonates with Hosea too: "You are not my people and I am
not your *'ehyeh*" (1.9).

But then the name Yhwh is named, and he is equated with the
"God of the fathers" (v. 15). Do the Israelites to whom Moses is sent
know this name? If they no longer knew anything about Joseph, then
perhaps they had also forgotten their religious traditions. Before this
point too the explicit naming of this name is only rarely mentioned.
The divine "I" in the addresses to the patriarchs is generally followed
by God's self-designation as "God of the fathers" (Gen 26.24; 28.13;
46.3) or as *'ēl šadday* (17.1; 35.11, see below on Ex 6). Only twice does
God call himself Yhwh when speaking to the patriarchs (15.7; 28.13).

This leaves in the air the question whether in the narrator's opinion Moses could connect with something familiar to the Israelites when naming the name.

So it is all the more significant that the name Yhwh is introduced at this point with great emphasis and some degree of solemnity: "This is my name for all time (Luther: all eternity)." For here begins not only the history proper of Israel as a nation, but from now on its allegiance to this God [→**§6**] is a fundamental element of Israel's identity. So it is quite appropriate that on his first audience with Pharaoh Moses begins with the words, "Thus says YHWH, the God of Israel" (Ex 5.2).

The name Yhwh has meaning not only for the delimitation of Israel over against the outside world but in particular for the internal "memorial," "from generation to generation." The language of the Psalms is echoed here (Ps 30.5; 97.12; 102.13; 135.13 etc.). Remember the name and the deeds of God, that is what Israel will do in its services and its prayers when it has been freed from Egyptian slavery. So by the equation of the solemnly proclaimed name of Yhwh with the God of the fathers, Israel is as it were placed back into the patriarchs' relationship with God, but now in quite a new way as a nation. And when Moses, equipped with the ability to perform legitimating miracles (4.1-9) and accompanied by Aaron, who is to be his "mouth" (4.15f), comes to the Israelites and reports everything to them, we read: "The people believed" (4.31).

(b) Exodus 6.2-8

Surprisingly, we encounter another introduction of the name Yhwh in Ex 6.2-8. After Moses' first, unsuccessful appearance before Pharaoh (ch. 5) God speaks to him again. This divine speech picks up and extends what resounded when the turning-point was announced in 2.23-25 [→**37**]: God "remembers" the covenant which he made with the fathers, and promises the Israelites that they will be led out of oppression in Egypt. The divine speech that begins in v. 2b is constructed according to a strict pattern dominated by the formula "I am YHWH" (*'ᵃnî yhwh*, vv. 2bβ, 6aα, 8bβ, also 7b). This sentence is the key to the whole divine speech: thus far God has appeared to the fathers by the name of *'ēl šadday* (Gen 17.1; 35.11; cf. 28.3; 48.3) [→**27**], but now he announces to them his name Yhwh. This announcement occurs in the frequently recurring, almost liturgical phrase, "I am YHWH" [→**§15**].

We meet it here for the first time and it is found time and again in other books of the Hebrew Bible.

At the same time another line of tradition is picked up, which moves God's covenant (*b'rît*) with the forefathers into the center (v. 4). In a clear reference to Gen 17 there is a reminder of the content of the covenant in the promise of the "land of sojournings" (*'ereṣ m'gûrîm*, 17.8). But this promise is given quite a new meaning, since it is spoken in another, distant land, to people who are living in slavery. So to the covenant promise is added the assurance that God has heard the groaning of the Israelites under the yoke of forced labor and that he will lead them out of slavery in Egypt (vv. 5f). God "remembers his covenant." This reminds us of God's covenant agreement with Noah (Gen 9.15f) [→19]; already in the flood story, when God "remembers" (Gen 8.1) we have a turning-point.

Yet another element is taken up from Gen 17. There the covenant agreement [→§6] is introduced by Yhwh's promise to be "God to you and your descendants after you" (v. 7). We now read: "I will take you for my people, and I will be your God" (Ex 6.7). Here full expression is given to the mutual belonging between Yhwh and Israel (cf. 1995, 20ff). Here it is linked first with the solemn proclamation of the Yhwh-name on the one hand, and second with the imminent leading out of Egypt. The latter is repeated once again (cf. v. 6) and emphatically introduced with the "knowledge statement" (Zimmerli 1954): "You will know that I am Yhwh, your God ..." (v. 7b). The leading out from Egyptian slavery and the leading into the land promised to the fathers will effectuate and reinforce this knowledge.

Exodus 6.2-8 [→11] belongs to the priestly layer of the text, which is clearly evident from the linguistic structure and especially the divine name *'ēl šadday* (cf. Gen 17.1; 35.11). The passage stands in a certain tension with Ex 3.14f [→40], where the name Yhwh has already been introduced. The position of this text after the failure of Moses' first deliberations with Pharaoh is, however, thoroughly plausible. In addition, through the explicit mention of the patriarchs (v. 2) a connection is made to the first revelation of the name in Ex 3, in which Yhwh presents himself as the "God of the fathers." As in other passages, priestly parts of the text have not been inserted "seamlessly" into the text but clearly deliberately inserted at this point, having a particular compositional function for the broader context (cf. Ska 1982; 1989; with a different emphasis, Blum 1990a, 232ff).

Chapters 3 and 6 of Exodus thus have a fundamental function in a variety of respects. They introduce Moses, who will be the dominant figure from this point on to the end of the Pentateuch [→**93**]. They associate with the person of Moses the explicit annunciation of the Yhwh name to Israel. And they announce the imminent liberation of Israel from servitude, also in direct connection with Moses. With Moses, the history of Israel as a nation enters its first decisive stage.

2.1.5 The people believed

At the beginning, however, Moses certainly does not prove to be a willing partner for God. He raises objections. First of all: "If they do not believe me …" (4.1). So God equips him with powers which the Egyptian magicians also possess (vv. 2-9; cf. 7.11f). But Moses is not satisfied: "I cannot speak" (v. 10). This places him once again in the prophetic tradition, associating him with Jeremiah in particular (Jer 1.6 [→**204**]); ability to speak plays a significant part with Isaiah and Ezekiel, too (Isa 6.5-7; Ezek 2f [→**172, 235**]). God's (somewhat ill-tempered, v. 11) answer sounds like his answer to Jeremiah: "Now therefore go, and I will be (once again the *'ehyeh* of 3.12, 14!) with your mouth and teach you what you shall speak" (v. 12). But Moses says no. He does this in a linguistic form similar to the divine *'ehyeh 'ašer 'ehyeh* (3.14): "Send, I pray, some other person" (more accurately: "Send [your message] through the person who want to send"; cf. Vriezen 1950, 502). But the answer is very clear, and is not found like this with any prophet.

God's reaction is surprising. He is angry, but nonetheless he responds to Moses' refusal and sends another—not in place of Moses, though, but as his "mouth": his brother Aaron. God repeats that he will be with Moses' mouth, and indeed now also with Aaron's mouth (vv. 14-16). When Moses and Aaron have got together (vv. 27f) the most important preconditions are met for everything that will follow. For up to Aaron's death (Num 20.22-29) [→**73**] the two brothers work in partnership—in very different ways, with different functions and certainly not always harmoniously, but in such a way that together they effectuate God's plans with Israel.

The brief episode Ex 4.24-26 is one of the most difficult texts in the Old Testament. The context would suggest the real problem was Moses' marriage with a non-Israelite woman, since this would mean the son was not circumcised, and the family as a whole would not fully belong to Israel. Yhwh therefore attempts to kill Moses at the moment he returns from the area of Midian.

Thereupon Zipporah performs "a complex symbolic act," in which she as it were consummates her marriage with Moses over again with the blood of her son's foreskin, underlining this with the declaratory formula, "Surely you are a bridegroom of blood to me!" The missing family connection is thus constructed and the danger eliminated. (Cf. Blum 1990c).

Moses and Aaron eventually come back to the Israelites, report everything to them and show their credentials through their miracles (4.29-31). "And the people believed." This sentence concludes the section that began with the proclamation of the turning-point in 2.23-25 [→**37**]. In a long, complex story, the preconditions for Israel's liberation from slavery in Egypt have now been met. Moses' doubting question, "If they do not believe me?" (4.1; cf. vv. 5, 8, 9) has also been answered—though certainly not once and for all (cf. 6.9) [→**46**].

2.1.6 I do not know Yhwh

Moses' and Aaron's first appearance before Pharaoh (5.2-5) contrasts sharply with what has gone before. Moses appears before Pharaoh with the (prophetic) messenger's formula [→*In* **123**], "Thus says YHWH, the God of Israel" and conveys to him Yhwh's demand: "Let my people go, that they may hold a feast to me in the wilderness." Pharaoh's answer is abrupt. He not only rejects Moses' demand but adds the provocative sentence: "Who is YHWH? ... I do not know YHWH." The contrast with the preceding self-revelation of Yhwh, his annunciation of the release of Israel from Egypt and the people's belief could not be greater. At the same time Pharaoh shows himself to be a resolute opponent to Yhwh—in a sharpness of confrontation unequalled in the Hebrew Bible.

This formulates the real topic of the dramatic chapters that follow. It is not just a matter of the liberation of Israel; rather, the ever-worsening "plagues" that overcome the Egyptians in what follows are a response to Pharaoh's arrogant challenge of Yhwh. As a sort of prelude to the plague narratives we learn from 7.1-7 that the "plagues" are to be understood primarily as "signs and wonders" (v. 3b) [→**46**]. The aim of Yhwh's action, we read, is: "The Egyptians shall know that I am YHWH, when I stretch forth my hand upon Egypt and bring out the people of Israel from among them" (v. 5). Moses and Aaron first try to convince Pharaoh with their miraculous credentials (7.8-13) and immediately before the first "plague" Moses declares to Pharaoh, once again introducing his words with the messenger formula, "By this you shall know that I am YHWH" (7.17). The call to recognize and acknowledge Yhwh's power [→**§15**] runs like a scarlet thread through the plague narratives (8.6, 18; 9.14, 29). This shows that this recognition is the main goal of the "plagues." Israel too is itself to acknowledge "that I am YHWH, your God, who brings you out from under the burdens of the Egyptians ..." (6.6); and later they are to pass on this acknowledgement to the next generations (10.1f). (Cf. Kegler 1990.)

But Pharaoh's heart remains "hardened." This statement, which constantly recurs in the plague narratives (from the prelude in 7.3 to the last plague in 11.10), is the counterpart to the "signs and wonders" which Yhwh performs by the hands of Moses and Aaron and through which Yhwh is to be "known." It is not just a matter of counterparts but of competition, since Pharaoh is presented as the exemplary opponent of Yhwh. After his abrupt "I do not know Yhwh" (5.2) he continues to refuse to "acknowledge" him. The subject of the hardening of heart changes: sometimes it is Pharaoh who hardens his own heart (8.11, 28; 9.34), sometimes his heart "hardens" (7.13, 14, 22; 8.15; 9.7, 35), but then also Yhwh hardens Pharaoh's heart (in anticipation 4.21; 7.3, and then from the sixth "plague" onwards: 9.12; 10.1, 20, 27; 11.10; 14.4, 8, 17).

Pharaoh is the opponent in various regards. He oppresses Israel, the people to whom Yhwh has promised his presence. He refuses in a very fundamental way to "acknowledge" Yhwh: he does not want to know him at all, he takes no note of him. And so he does not want to acknowledge Yhwh's power either, considering himself to be stronger. He makes himself an Anti-God. This idea is not developed in the plague narratives themselves, but in the concluding interpretation of the events we read: "On all the gods of Egypt I will execute judgments: I am YHWH" (Ex 12.12; cf. Num 33.4). Pharaoh represents the anti-divine power. It appears in the form of the powerful king, but in him at the same time the "gods of Egypt" stand against the one God. They stand as representatives of the "gods of the nations," who are "nothings" to Yhwh (Ps 96.5) [→**48**]. The hymn Ex 15.1-17 describes this fight as a primordial struggle in which Yhwh demonstrates his superiority over all the gods (v. 11).

2.1.7 This day shall be a memorial to you
Immediately before the last, decisive stage in this argument has been reached, the narrative gets stuck. After the dramatic accounts of the disputes with Pharaoh and the events of the first nine "plagues," the

stipulations for the Passover and the closely associated Mazzot, the feast
of "unleavened bread," are now given in great detail (Ex 12f). The
traditions collected here about these two festivals obviously originally
had no direct connection with the dramatic narratives of the present
context. Now, however, they are closely linked with the events of the
last "plague," the killing of the Egyptian firstborn, and the exodus of
the Israelites that follows.

In 5.1, 3; 7.16; 8.23f (cf. already 3.18) we read that the Israelites want to celebrate a sacrifice to Yhwh "in the wilderness." It is disputed whether there is an
underlying independent tradition to this or whether this claim only serves as a
pretext to be able to leave the land. Many interpreters relate this statement to
the Passover, even though no explicit connection is made anywhere. Others
think of the festival on Sinai or of the sacrificial meal with Jethro, the priest of
Midian. The question must remain open (cf. W.H. Schmidt 1988, 251ff) [→52].

The context that emerges is complex. This day is to be a "memorial"
for Israel; on this day all future generations are to celebrate a festival
for Yhwh (12.14) [→393]; for "on that very day the LORD brought the
people of Israel out of the land of Egypt" (v. 51). It is the day of liberation from oppression. But it is also the night in which Yhwh went
through Egypt and killed all the firstborn while the Israelites were
saved by the blood of the Passover lamb painted on the entrances to
their houses (vv. 12f; cf. v. 27; 13.14f). This last terrible intensification
of the Egyptian plagues is viewed by the Israelites as a visible expression of the "strong hand" with which God led them out of Egypt
(13.9, 16). The great significance of this event and the constant reminder of it in all subsequent generations of Israel is marked right at
the beginning by the fact that the Israelite year [→§11] is to begin with
this double festival (12.2; cf. also Lev 23.5ff; Num 28.16ff; Deut 16.1ff).
   The same night the Israelites leave (Ex 12.29ff) and at first the departure seems to run smoothly (13.7-22). But then a phase of high
drama begins again. Pharaoh is not beaten yet. He reverses his decision
once again (12.31f; cf. already 8.4, 21ff; 9.27f; 10.16f, 24) and pursues
the Israelites, who have already left (Ex 14). And then comes the decisive demonstration of Yhwh's power: he divides the sea, lets Israel pass
through, letting Pharaoh and his forces sink in it afterwards. When the
Israelites see this "great hand" of God, they believe (14.31) [→44]—as
they did before, when Moses told them of God's liberation plans
(4.31). And so what God began when he commissioned Moses has
reached its goal.

This account of the exodus of Israel out of Egypt has thus two climaxes: the last "plague" and the killing of the Egyptian firstborn, linked with the Passover, and the passing of the Israelites through the Reed Sea, linked with the destruction of the Egyptian forces. Both events can be recalled individually, or together (e.g. Ps 136.10-15) as the "signs and wonders" (Deut 6.22 etc.) that God performed in order to free his people from servitude. This act of God, the leading of Israel out of Egypt—from Israel's point of view, the march out of Egypt, the Exodus [→**§9**]—is the determinative event in Israel's history, for all time to come. God introduces himself at the beginning of the Decalogue with the words, "I am the LORD your God, who brought you out of the land of Egypt, out of the house of bondage" (Ex 20.2; Deut 5.6) [→**53**]; more briefly in Hosea: "I am the LORD your God from the land of Egypt" (Hos 12.10[9]; 13.4) [→**273**]. For its part, Israel can address God as the one who led his people out of Egypt, and can derive from this the hope of helping, saving and forgiving action in the future (Ex 32.11; Lev 26.45 etc.) [→**61, 69, 78**].

At the same time the exodus marks the end of the first stage in the history of Israel, after the family of Jacob had become the nation. The texts that deal directly with the exodus events do not mention the preceding stage, the story of the families of Abraham, Isaac and Jacob. These texts clearly have their own literary prehistory, which was not at first narratively connected with the patriarchal history. But for the reader of the Pentateuch in its present form there is no doubt that with the exodus the divine promises to the patriarchs start to be fulfilled. After all, God had told Abraham already that his descendants would not return to the land promised him until the end of a lengthy period of oppression in the foreign land (Gen 15.13-16). Later, Jacob moved to Egypt with express divine permission and there received the assurance that God would make him a great nation there and bring him back again (46.3f). At last Joseph recalled this assurance and had his brothers swear to take his body with them on their return to the land of the forefathers (50.24f) [→**33**]. Moses now honors this oath (Ex 13.19), and the next generation will complete it by burying Joseph (Josh 24.32).

In the immediate context of the exodus narrative the "hymnic confession" (Strauß 1985) of Ex 15.1-19 [→**45**] takes up the "belief" of the Israelites from 14.31 and leads it on through Israel's wanderings (vv. 14-16) through to Zion (v. 17). Other creed-like or hymnic texts lead from the deliverance from Egypt in a direct line to the land that was promised to the forefathers and in which Israel was living at the time the texts were composed (or from which it was driven during the exile) (Deut 6.21-23; 26.5-9; Ps 136.10-22 etc.). So the exodus is not only a departure, but also the beginning of a new stage in the story of Israel.

2.2 Israel on the way: the first stage

2.2.1 By a prophet the Lord brought Israel up from Egypt

Where will Israel's path lead after the departure from Egypt? The reader can see the broad context of the Pentateuch narrative: the people of Israel has proceeded from the family of the patriarchs and stands under the promise that God will give them the land in which the fathers, Abraham, Isaac and Jacob lived. For Moses the answer to this question does not at first seem so obvious. In the first divine speech addressed to him when he is called, God said that he would lead the Israelites out of Egypt [→38] into "a good and broad land, a land flowing with milk and honey, to the place of the Canaanites, the Hittites, the Amorites, the Perizzites, the Hivites, and the Jebusites" (3.8). The land is introduced here as an unknown land, populated by foreign nations. (This does, though, recall the promised of the land in the covenant assurance in Gen 15.19ff.) In the second divine speech in Ex 6.2-8, however, the reference back to the fathers and the promise made to them is unmistakable (vv. 4, 8) [→41]. And in the context of the stipulations concerning the Mazzot festival, the two statements are linked: "And when the Lord brings you into the land of the Canaanites ..., which he swore to your fathers to give you, a land flowing with milk and honey ..." (13.5; cf. v. 11) [→45]. So Moses knows that the promised land lies before them as the ultimate goal of the wanderings. The reader is given a further indication when in 13.17f there is talk of a "diversion" by comparison with the "nearer" route (into the "land of the Philistines" and thus into the coastal plain of the land of the fathers). Whether the Israelites themselves know where they are headed, however, is not said.

There is another indication of the goal of this journey. In Ex 3.12 God announced a "sign" to Moses at the foot of the "mountain of God": "When you lead the people out of Egypt, you will serve God on this mountain." "This mountain" [→40], on which God first announced the salvation of Israel from Egyptian oppression (cf. Crüsemann 1992, 50ff), is thus the first goal for Moses after the liberation of Israel. The narrative moves resolutely in this direction, even if this is not explicit (Ex 19.1) [→**52**]. The further course of the narrative then shows that the stay on the "mountain of God," i.e. on Sinai, was to be only a temporary one (Num 10.11f) [→**69**]. After this a new stage in the stay in the wilderness begins, which ultimately extends to forty years, until at last the final goal of the path, the land promised to the fathers, is reached.

The stage in Israel's history that now follows has quite different features. The wanderings have a double goal: Sinai and the promised land. The stay on Sinai has on one hand the character of an interim stop, but on the other hand the basic structures of Israelite law and the cult are established and developed there in great detail, so that this stage has central significance [→**52**]. The reports of the time before and after the stay on Sinai are themselves highly complex. On the one hand, it is a time of divine guidance in the most varied shapes and forms. On the other, however, there are constant reports of the dissatisfaction of the Israelites, even of rebellion, directed against Moses but in the final analysis also against God. Both aspects are interwoven and are maintained throughout the whole sequence of narratives from the departure from Egypt through to the borders of the promised land.

God leads Israel from the moment of departure onwards. In Ex 13.21f we read that God moves ahead of the people in the form of a pillar of cloud by day and a pillar of fire by night. The pillar of cloud and fire means not only guidance but also protection. In the threat from the Egyptian pursuers at the Reed Sea the column appears at the end of the procession and thus between the Israelites and the Egyptians; it prevents the latter from attacking and finally plunges them into a state of panic and confusion, so that Israel is saved (14.19-25). On Sinai the cloud then connects with the newly erected sanctuary. When it lies above the sanctuary, the Israelites stay where they are; if it rises, they move on (Ex 40.26-38; Num 9.15-23) [→**70**]. Later, after the first unsuccessful attempt to invade Canaan, in his petition for the people Moses holds up this form of God's guidance as particularly significant, using it to persuade him to intervene (Num 14.13f).

Another form of divine guidance is the "messenger" or "angel" (*mal'āk*) of God. At the Reed Sea he appears with the pillar of cloud to save Israel from the Egyptians (Ex 14.19). After the proclamation of the commandments on Sinai God promises that the *mal'āk* will go with them on the way to the promised land, in particular to keep Israel from worshiping the foreign gods (23.20-24) [→**56**]. After the dramatic dispute about the "Golden Calf," too, God promises Moses that his *mal'āk* will still accompany Israel on its continuing way (32.34; 33.2) [→**54**]. In 33.14f, finally, the accompanying presence of God is described as his "countenance" (*pānîm*). All these forms in which God's presence and guidance appear, behind which there are certainly various traditions, express the fact that God wants to lead his people to the goal he has himself planned, despite all resistance from outside and on the part of Israel itself.

The narratives give abundant reports of the long journey in the wilderness. The problems in the foreground are those determined by the situation in the wilderness, in the first place by lack of water and hunger. The interest of the narratives is not, however, directed to these problems themselves, but to the reactions to them. In particular, the Israelites see the difference between their present situation in the wilderness and their earlier situation in Egypt, and comparison of the two seems to result in a clear decision in favor of the "fleshpots" of Egypt (Ex 16.3). The freedom from slavery under which they had suffered so much seems to them to be less of an advantage compared with the hunger and thirst they are now having to suffer. They thus begin to "murmur" (Ex 15.24 etc.)

This topic generally dominates the accounts of Israel's journey through the wilderness. There will be various reasons for the breadth of the elaboration here. For one thing, many of the "murmuring stories" contain etiological elements. Some of them provide explanations of place names and were probably first transmitted as local legends: Marah ("bitter water," Ex 15.22-26), Massah and Meribah ("proof" and "contention," 17.1-7 and Num 20.1-13), Taberah ("firebrand," Num 11.1-3), Kibroth-Hataavah ("greedy-graves," Num 11.4-35); others explain wilderness phenomena such as manna (Ex 16) and locust swarms (Ex 16.13; Num 11.31ff); others again tell of threats from enemies (Ex 18.8-16) or snakes (Num 21.4-9). But more important than the derivation and presumed original meaning of the individual accounts is the question of what significance these texts have in their present context. They all deal with conflicts, primarily those between the "people" and Moses. But Moses is of course God's envoy, and the narratives often state that the people's laments and complaints are ultimately directed against God (Ex 16.8; Num 11.1 etc.).

So Moses stands between the people and God. Towards the people he represents the voice of God, explaining, warning, often strictly and even angrily. But then again and again he finds himself in the situation of having to plead with God on the people's behalf. This gives the image of Moses [→**§12**] a new dimension. While at first he was God's ambassador, standing up in the name of God and for his people against the hostile king, now he also stands up against his own people in the name of God—and more than once also against God in the name of his people and on their behalf. The image of Moses we find in these texts is a very complex one. Right at the beginning there are features which place Moses in the same line as the patriarchs of Genesis, especially in the directness of his conversations with God [→**38**]. But already here it is clear that, unlike the patriarchs, Moses does not speak only for himself, but right from the start he is sent in as a mediator between God and the "people"—an entity not yet found in the patriarchal narratives. This feature gains a new aspect in that God "sends" Moses with a particular task (Ex 3.12-15) [→**40**], just as later he will send prophets (Isa 6.8; Jer 1.7, etc.) |→**173, 204**|. The element of refusal also belongs in this context, especially the use of the messenger formula, "Thus says the LORD" (Ex 5.1 etc.), with which the prophets frequently convey God's message (1 Sam 2.27; 10.18; Amos 1.3 etc.).

Moses is, however, more than a prophet [→**§17**], and different too. There are in particular two moments that make him a unique figure in relation to the other prophets we meet in the Hebrew Bible. For one thing, the directness of Moses' contacts with God is reported, unlike anything we find with other prophets. This finds expression at a number of points in the account in the text, and in the conflict with Aaron and Miriam, who want to query this exalted position of Moses' (Num 12.1ff), the solemn divine speech (vv. 6-8) expressly emphasizes that God wants to speak "mouth to mouth" with Moses only (v. 8; cf. Ex 33.11: "face to face, as a man speaks to his friend"). The spirit (*rûaḥ*) of God that rests on Moses is so powerful that even a portion of it, spread among seventy elders, transports them into prophetic ecstasy (*hitnabbē'*, Num 11.25). On the other hand Moses is a representative and leader of the people, without compare among other figures in the biblical history of Israel. He is the precursor of all coming leaders of Israel: Joshua, the "judges," Samuel and the kings. But he is also more than all of them. His task is much bigger than theirs, completely incomparable in fact. Moses is the first to have to lead and guide this people, and he has to bring them to the place where the history of this people begins in a way comparable with other peoples. This aspect also comes to expression in the words of Num 12.6-8: "Not so with my servant (*'abdî*) Moses. He is entrusted with all my house" (v. 7). Here, Moses' position in relation to God is compared with the "place of the top slave, who at the same time is his master's trusted one, to whom his master's whole 'household' is entrusted" (Noth 1966, 85). This understanding of the figure of Moses also finds expression in the prophet Hosea: "By a prophet the LORD brought Israel up from Egypt, and by a prophet he was preserved" (Hos 12.14[13]) [→**273**].

2.3 Israel on Sinai

2.3.1 I have brought you to me

"On the third new moon after the people of Israel had gone forth out of the land of Egypt, on that day they came into the wilderness of Sinai" (Ex 19.1). Here the chronology of the book of Exodus marks the beginning of the second great stage after the departure from Egypt (12.2f, 40f, 51; cf. 16.1) [→**45**]. This stage contains one of the lengthiest coherent bodies of text in the Hebrew Bible (Ex 19.1–Num 10.10) [→**69**]; the next date in Num 10.11 then relates to the departure from Sinai and therewith the beginning of the third and last stage before the arrival in the promised land.

Israel has now reached one of the two goals mentioned to Moses by God when he announced the exodus: the mountain of God, on which God first appeared to Moses and told him of the liberation of Israel (cf. Ex 3.12) [→**40**]. Even if this is not yet the last, final stop on the way that began with the departure from Egypt, still it is much more than a mere staging-post. Here Israel receives the instructions by which it is to shape its life: life before and with God and life with each other.

Once again the key figure is Moses. While the people camp in the desert, facing Mount Sinai (19.2), Moses alone climbs the mountain to God (*hā'elohîm*, v. 3, as in Ex 3.6, 12; cf. 1991d). From there God calls him (*wayyiqrā'*, as in 3.4) and in the first divine speech which Moses is to pass on to Israel (19.4-6), God gives him as it were a commentary on the decisive turning-point at which Israel now stands. He points back to the deliverance from Egypt and God's powerful and protective guidance on the way, like "on eagles' wings." Then we read: "I brought you to myself." Here it is especially clear that Israel's stay in Sinai is not only an interim stop, but that for the first time Israel is "with God" here. Here too, notwithstanding the complex prehistory, Israel's demand to Pharaoh, that Israel wants to serve its God in the wilderness (4.23; 7.16, 26; 8.16 etc.; cf. 3.12), reaches its fulfillment [→**44**].

With its introductory "and now" (*w⁽attāh*), v. 5 marks the new situation. Israel is to listen to the voice of God, i.e. to the instructions he is about to announce, and is to keep its part of the covenant (*b⁽rît*) formulated in them. This will bring about a quite special, unique relationship between Israel and God, in which Israel becomes God's "property" "before all nations." Here the choice of Abraham, which stands right at the beginning of Israel's prehistory (Gen 12.1-3) [→**21**], is extended to the people of Israel which has grown out of Abraham's posterity. The "keeping" of the covenant (*šāmar*), which was made compulsory to Abraham already in the form of circumcision (Gen 17.9) [→**28**], is now applied to the instructions which are about to be announced. In this way the people of Israel which had seemed almost to be alienated from its history with God during the slavery in Egypt, is now placed squarely into the succession of its forefather [→**§7**], Abraham.

The statement about Israel's special position in the future is followed by a postscript in which God as it were lays out his credentials for choosing Israel from among the nations: "for all the earth is mine" (v. 5b). God is the creator of the world and thus at the same time the creator of all the nations. He can decide freely which people he wants to call into a special relationship with him. The history of Israel thereby finds its place in the history of God's dealings with the world, which begins with the creation. This special position [→**§6**] was already set out in the call of Abraham and is now extended in all respects to the people of Israel. The consequence of this special position for Israel will be that it will become a "nation of priests" and a "holy nation" (see below on Ex 24 [→**57**]).

This first divine speech on Sinai introduces a very extensive and extraordinarily complex collection of texts. Collected in it are legal and cultic traditions of various provenances and different ages. What all these instructions basically have in common is that they are given by God at the point when Israel has emerged from servitude into freedom but has not yet settled in the land God has granted it. Liberated Israel is alone with God, here at Sinai, and receives from him the instructions for the whole of its future life.

Thus God begins to speak again, this time from a powerful theophany on Mount Sinai (19.16ff), directly to the gathered people of Israel. He shares with them a first, brief and resonant collection of divine commandments and prohibitions: the Decalogue (Ex 20.2-17). The introductory words are reminiscent of the earlier "self-introduction" of God towards Moses. At that point the message was: "You shall know that I am the LORD your God, who has brought you out from under the burdens of the Egyptians" (6.7b) [→**44**]. Now, after this has happened, the divine speech begins: "I am the LORD your God, who brought you out of the land of Egypt, out of the house of bondage" (20.2). The whole further history of God with Israel stands under the sign of the liberation that has taken place. The God who has led Israel into freedom now begins to establish in more detail relations between himself and his people.

The first and most important instruction grows directly out of the memory of the divine act of liberation: "You shall have no other gods before me" (v. 3). The liberation of Israel entails the exclusive relationship to the liberating God. Any relation with other gods would be directly aimed against the one to whom Israel owes its freedom and thus its whole existence [→**§20**]. It would be done to him "in his face" (*'al pānay*), as Buber literally and aptly translates. The fashioning of images that could be used for worship also belongs to this, whether images of the deity himself, or of other creatures (vv. 4, 5a). The prohibition of images distinguishes Israel fundamentally from all the other religions of its ancient eastern environment. It corresponds with the basic intention of this prohibition that it directly follows the requirement of the exclusive worship of the one God, who has liberated Israel by his actions in history.

The unconditionality of these basic requirements of the Yhwh-faith is further underlined in that Yhwh says of himself that he is a "jealous God" (*'ēl qannā'*, vv. 5b, 6) [→**76**]. Here this means that he himself will watch out that the exclusivity of Israel's relations with him is not harmed. This self-declaration of God therefore has a dual orientation: punitively against his "haters," i.e. against those who show themselves to be his enemies by not following his commandments—but benevolently towards those who keep the commandments.

2.3.2 The Lord said to Moses: Say to the Israelites

After the proclamation of God's first ten commandments, there is a sudden dramatic caesura. The people are seized by fear at the violent phenomena accompanying the divine speech and ask Moses to speak to God alone. "Let not God speak to us, lest we die" (Ex 20.19). So from now on the Israelites receive all the instructions given on Sinai through the mediation of Moses. This has double consequences. First, the Decalogue is very clearly set apart from all the other commandments and laws. It was only this that God spoke in Israel's immediate hearing. Second, it means that Moses grows into another role, greater than those thus far. His task as mediator between God and people is vastly extended in that he alone is party to the full import of the instructions that now follow and which he passes on to the people (or the priests). Later, we hear not only of the "Torah of Yhwh" [→§10] or the "Torah of God" but also of the "Torah of Moses" (Josh 23.6 etc.) [→100]. Moses himself [→§12] has become the lawgiver.

The commandments and laws which Moses is to pass on to the Israelites are of a wide variety of kinds and from a wide diversity of backgrounds. Various individual collections of texts are clearly distinguishable, which were presumably originally independent of each other before they became connected in the present context as components of the divine Torah mediated through Moses. Among them we find narrative sections, sometimes surrounding the legal passages, sometimes interrupting them. Thus Ex 24 and ch. 19 [→57] together form a narrative unit dealing with the solemn covenant on Sinai, comprising besides the Decalogue (20.2-17) another collection of commandments, generally known as the "Book of the Covenant" (20.22–23.33). Chapters 32–34 on the other hand, with their report on the construction of the "Golden Calf," which marks a dramatic querying of the covenant just concluded, interrupt the block of priestly-cultic regulations that begins in ch. 25. At the same time, however, they stand in a tense mutual relationship with chs. 19–24. The complex literary data thus show that Moses had to grow into the role of the summarizing mediator of the law.

The "Book of the Covenant" (Ex 20.22–23.33), the name of which has been predicated on 24.7 in recent exegesis, is generally viewed as the oldest partial collection of the Sinai legislation. It has clearly been very carefully composed from various text groups (cf. Crüsemann 1992, 132-234). The most extensive texts are then the priestly-cultic texts that begin with Ex 25, dealing primarily with the building of the sanctuary at Sinai and the establishment of the cult; they extend as far as the departure from Sinai in Num 10.10. Within this body of material, Lev 17–26 [→68] is frequently viewed as a separate collection labeled the "holiness code"; these chapters are however so interwoven with the other priestly texts that they are better understood in association with them.

The first substantial commandment that Moses is to pass on to the people (Ex 20.22–23.33) begins with the same expression as the first divine speech on Sinai: "You have seen" (20.22; cf. 19.4). There it referred to God's great deed in Egypt (with an allusion to the "seeing" in 14.13, 30f); here it now links up with the preceding proclamation of the Decalogue: "You have seen that I spoke with you from heaven" (cf. Deut 4.36). The Israelites "saw" (20.18) the voice of God with its powerful accompanying phenomena and were terrified as a result. What follows is therefore given to them through the mediation of Moses. It is the continuation of what God had himself proclaimed in direct speech to Israel. And in first position once again we have the commandment not to make images of any gods (20.23), as was already expressed in the Decalogue as the elaboration of the commandment to venerate and worship Yhwh alone (20.4f) [→**54**]. This collection of commandments looks forward to a time when Israel will live in the land that God has promised to give them. Directly connected with the prohibition of divine images is an instruction about the building of an altar (20.24ff): "In every place where I cause my name to be remembered ('*azkîr*) I will come to you and bless you." (This recalls the "remembering" [*zēker*] of the Name from Ex 3.15 [→**40**].) The sanctuaries which God himself has marked and legitimated by his presence are contrasted in the concluding section of this collection of commandments with the sanctuaries of the present inhabitants of the promised land. By means of his "messenger" (*mal'āk*) God will lead Israel into the land (23.20ff), the entirety of which is here called "place" (*māqôm*), and the Israelites will hear his voice (as they did the voice of God on Sinai, 19.5) [→**52**] and not worship the gods of the other nations, but rather destroy their monuments (23.24). Above all, they will not conclude any covenant (*b'rît*) with these nations and their gods (v. 32).

These fundamental commandments relating to the exclusive worship of Yhwh are framed by quite different sorts of legal rulings. Two groups of texts stand out in particular. The first of these are regulations intended to serve for appropriate legal rulings and are addressed to those who have to make judgments (esp. 21.1–22.16). These regulations are together described in Ex 21.1 as "judgments" (*mišpātîm*) [→**§10**]. They deal with numerous legal cases introduced in each case with "if," and are concerned in particular with infringements of physical integrity and misdemeanors relating to property. "Punishments" are not set for these cases, but rules are set up for compensation between culprit and victim, setting on the one hand the limits of imprisonment and on the other ground rules for restitution or compensation. In 23.1-8 rules are added for the court case. Those who have to make legal judgments on behalf of the public are here warned not to be diverted by rumors (v. 1), majority opinion (v. 2) or even bribery (v. 8) from the task of clearly separating justice from injustice. In particular the rights of the poor should not be infringed (v. 6); but the opposite (v. 3) would also be against God's requirement, who says of himself: "For the LORD will not hold him guiltless" (v. 7b).

Another group of texts has to do especially with those in need of special attention and consideration: aliens, i.e. those who are not full citizens and thus not in possession of full rights (22.20; 23.9), the poor (22.24-26), widows and orphans (22.21). Indeed, even the enemy's or opponent's animal suffering under its burden, or lost (23.4f), needs attention and help. Here the boundary of "law" is crossed and sympathy and mercy are made compulsory.

All this is transmitted as a divine speech to Moses and passed on by him to the Israelites. The Decalogue and the "Book of the Covenant" are the first central parts of what may be called in summary the "Torah" (see on Deut 4 below [→**75**]).

2.3.3 The covenant which the LORD makes with you

The message of this first section of the Torah is given a narrative framework with the introduction to the whole Sinai narrative in Ex 19 and the report of the concluding of the covenant as the first climax in Israel's encounter with God on Sinai in ch. 24. Already in the divine speech in 19.4-6 [→**52**] there is advance reference to the covenant: Israel is to keep the covenant (v. 5). Now that this covenant has been given content and concrete shape through the giving of the commandments in the Decalogue and the "Book of the Covenant," there follows a confirmation in a solemn covenant-concluding ceremony (24.3-8).

The covenant agreement is made with Israel as the totality of the twelve tribes [→**32**], which finds expression in the erection of twelve pillars (24.4). Then what was announced in 19.6 is taken up in a surprising way: Israel as a whole is to be a "nation of priests" and a "holy nation." "Priests," according to this, are thus not individuals or a particular group distinguished and separated from the rest of the people by their special "holiness," but the nation as a whole. This is finds appropriate expression in the fact that it is "the young men of the Israelites" who present the sacrifices which form the central component of the covenant-making ceremony (24.5; cf. Blum 1990a, 51f). Since the whole nation is a nation of priests, even the young can perform priestly functions and thus represent the nation as a whole.

The word *b'rît* "covenant" [→§6] has a central role here. Moses has previously announced "all the words of the Lord" to the people (v. 3) and then written them down. Now he reads them out again from the "Book of the Covenant" (*sôfer habb'rît*, v. 7). The people answer both times with the same words as at the arrival at Sinai: "All the words that the LORD speaks/has spoken, we will do" (19.8; 24.3, 7; in 24.7 the words "and we will hear" are added in reinforcement). The resumption of this clearly marks the fact that Israel's encounter with God that began in Ex 19 has reached its goal. The covenant has been confirmed in all respects. The covenant ceremony comes to its conclusion when Moses sprinkles half the blood of the sacrificial animals on the people as the "blood of the covenant" (*dam-habb'rît*, v. 7). (Nowhere else in the OT is such a ritual found; it can perhaps be understood by analogy to priestly purification [Ex 29.20f; Lev 8.22f] [→67], as there too the blood of sacrificial animals is applied to people [cf. Ruprecht 1980, 165ff].)

After the "young men" have been awarded the commissioning with a cultic task, the "elders" are honored with a quite special meeting with God (24.9-11). Upon God's instruction (v. 1) Moses ascends the mountain with 70 elders, "and they saw the God of Israel." The "elders," who represented the whole nation just as the "young men" did, are granted a very unusual favor. To "see" God is forbidden to humans, as God himself later says to Moses: "No man can see me and remain alive" (33.20) [→62]. So this scene on the mountain is something quite special and unique (see below on v. 11). The "seeing" of God is however further specified and at the same time qualified. They see "under his feet as it were a pavement of sapphire stone, like the very heaven for clearness" (v. 10). What they see, then, is not God "himself" but only the footstool of the enthroned God, the king (which reminds one of the "kingdom of priests" in 19.6). In a similar way, Isaiah also "sees" God, the "king YHWH of Hosts" (Isa 6.5) [→172], but only the hem of the divine robe is described in any detail (v. 1); and in Ezekiel's great vision above the sapphire stones everything is lost in the dazzling splendor, the appearance of which the prophet can also compare with the multiple colors of the rainbow (Ezek 1.26ff) [→234]. The elders thus see God "from below" and their seeing (*rā'āh*) is further qualified as "beholding" (*ḥāzāh*)—a quite specific expression for the prophetic "beholding" of God [→§17]. Perhaps it is also a restriction or veiling, that we do not read they saw "Yhwh" but "the God of Israel" (v. 10) and "the deity" (*ha"lohîm*) [→§15]. In Isaiah's case too, it is not said that he saw "Yhwh" but the "LORD" (*'adonay*) (Isa 6.1; cf. Cassuto 1967, 314).

At the end the special and unusual aspects of this encounter on the mountain are once again emphasized: "Against the 'plans' (the word is only found here) of the Israelites he (i.e. God) did not raise his hand" (v. 11). They were allowed to live on although they had "beheld" God; indeed, "they ate and drank." This is supposed to express, first, that they had survived this dangerous encounter in one piece. One might also think of a festive common meal, comparable with the communal meal after a sacrificial slaughter (cf. Gen 31.54; Ex 18.12; Deut 12.7, 18 etc.) [→§11]. But the frequently used term "covenant meal" is certainly inappropriate; it would assume that the two covenant "partners," God and Israel, eat and drink together—a notion quite foreign to the Hebrew Bible.

With this scene on the mountain the narrative arch that began with Moses' first encounter with God on the mountain of God, has come to its goal: Israel has worshiped God "on this mountain," as Moses had promised as a testifying sign of his call by God (Ex 3.12) [→40]. The first great stage in Israel's path to liberation from Egyptian slavery has thereby come to its conclusion. Israel has met God as a nation chosen by God in a special way, as a "priestly" and "holy" nation. Through Moses God has formed a covenant with the nation, and finally the nation itself has "beheld" God through its representatives. A higher and more intensive stage in the encounter with God is not conceivable.

Here an ideal relationship between Israel and God is presented. An essential element in this is that Israel "keeps" its part of the covenant— as was expressed as a condition for this ideal relationship between Israel and God in 19.5. Israel itself has confirmed many times that it wants to honor all the words of God that are given in this covenant and written down in the "Book of the Covenant" (19.8; 24.3, 7). So this is, as it were, the snapshot of an ideal situation in which Israel, the "holy" nation, stands unrestrictedly in covenant with God and thus shares his direct nearness. The further course of the narrative, however, shows that this situation is not a lasting one.

2.3.4 Once again: Herewith I make a covenant

The narrative now runs on two different levels, also with regard to geography. Moses is called by God to the mountain once again and ascends together with his servant Joshua (Ex 24.12ff). He stays there for forty days and forty nights and receives from God the instructions for the building of a sanctuary and its cultic facilities (chs. 25-31). Meanwhile, in the camp of the Israelites below a rejection of the way in which Moses is leading the people develops, which puts all the resistance and conflict experienced hitherto in the shade [→§16]. The people destroy the covenant that has just been concluded with dramatic radicalism, by making themselves a God of their own (32.1-6). The fundamental crisis that arises from this and its resolution are the focus of chs. 32-34. After this the other narrative thread continues with the account of the execution of the instructions that Moses received on the mountain (chs. 35-40 and their continuation in the book of Leviticus) [→64].

At first sight these two narrative planes seem to have very little connection. They also have different backgrounds. (Chapters 25-31 and 35-40 [→11], texts relating to the establishment of the cult, belong to the priestly level of composition.) In the overall narrative plot and also in a number of details, however, they are clearly connected and refer to each other (cf. Utzschneider 1988). The establishment of the sanctuary means the creation of a place in which God wants to "dwell" with his people and thus be present with them (25.8), even after Israel's unique and unrepeatable encounter with God in his representatives (24.9-11) [→58]. But rebellion against Moses subverts the preparations for this. The people do not want to wait for Moses. In their words all the ill-feeling towards "this man Moses," just as previously expressed in the "murmuring stories" [→50], comes to a head once again: "We do not know what has become of him" (32.1). But more clearly than ever before they now even say that their protest is directed not only against Moses but also against the God in whose name and mission he acts. They want their own gods, which are to "go before them." So they cause the astonishingly malleable Aaron (but see below) to make a divine image for them, and he makes them a "calf," a young bull and thus an image of an animal, precisely what was expressly forbidden at the beginning of the Decalogue (20.3-5) [→54].

It seems that everything that Israel has learned so far on Sinai has been destroyed. Israel had been placed in a unique place of nearness to God, in that its "holiness" and the keeping of the covenant were indissolubly linked together (Ex 19.5f) [→53] and the covenant had been solemnly sealed and confirmed by Israel (24.3-8) [→57]. Israel has now canceled its participation and made itself a god of its own: "These are your gods, O Israel, which led you out of Egypt" (v. 4b). The peculiar plural form (the word generally used for God, *'elohîm*, is grammatically speaking a plural, but here, as already in v. 1, the verb is also given in the plural!) recalls the account of Jeroboam's two bull images (1 Kgs 12.28) [→**129**]. In particular the infringement of the basic first commandment "You shall have no other gods beside me" (Ex 20.3) comes emphatically to expression. The opposing position against the *one* God Yhwh could not be sharper. In addition, the sacrificing and eating and drinking (v. 6) mimic the grand scenes of the covenant ceremony and the meal on Mount Sinai (24.5, 11) in a blasphemous orgy. (In the divine speech [v. 8] we hear that they have even bowed down and worshiped the bull image.)

But the narrative contains a moment of ambivalence: Aaron's behavior. He had replaced Moses as substitute during his absence (Ex 24.14). Now the people gather against him (v. 1; cf. Num 16.3) and he accedes to their wishes. But he evidently understands what is happening with the manufacture of the "Golden Calf" in a different way than the people, for he announces a feast "for YHWH" (v. 5). So he does not see an antithesis to Yhwh in the bull image. Nor is there any indication that he equates the bull image with Yhwh. Rather, the narrative leaves him in an oddly indefinite, compromising attitude, which is, if anything, reinforced by his later defense before Moses (cf. Childs 1974, 364ff).

So, though Aaron is involved in the affair with the "Golden Calf," he is not compromised to such an extent that he cannot assume the role earmarked for him in the cult. For on the other narrative level, Moses has meanwhile received the instruction to appoint Aaron and his sons to the priestly office at the sanctuary that is to be set up (Ex 28f). And it emerges later how much depends on this office for Israel (cf. esp. Lev 16) [→**67**]. In the continuation of the narrative Aaron is now for the time being relegated to the background.

In the foreground and the center stands once again Moses [→**§12**], this time in the extremely dramatic sharpening of his position as mediator between God and the people. For God wants to destroy Israel (Ex 32.10). For the second time in the history of humanity God breathes such a radical plan of destruction: the first time against the whole of creation, which was his own great work (Gen 6.5ff) [→**15?**], now against the people of Israel, which he himself had called his "possession before all nations" (Ex 19.5) [→**53**] and for whose liberation and guidance he had engaged all his efforts. Moses gets into a situation similar to Noah in his day, who was the only one to "find grace" (Gen 6.8); for as the opposite pole to his decision to destroy Israel, God says to Moses: "I will make you a great nation" (Ex 32.10b). He wants to begin again with Moses where he started with Abraham (Gen 12.2) [→21]. But unlike Noah, Moses can oppose this divine plan by insisting on this point and taking God at his own word, given to Abraham, Isaac and Jacob/Israel as a solemn oath: that he would make their descendants as numerous as the stars in the heavens and that he would give these descendants the land promised them for all time (Ex 32.13). Once again Moses thus proves himself as petitioner for his people (cf. Aurelius 1988), this time in a situation that threatens Israel's very existence. It is only thanks to his pleading that Israel can live on.

At the same time, however, Moses demonstrates in a highly dramatic way the situation that Israel has brought about through its idolatry. He smashes the two tables of the law that God gave him on the mountain (v. 19). The covenant [→§6] is broken. Everything has changed. Even if the following chapters show that God's history with Israel continues, nonetheless it is always the story *after* the sin with the "Golden Calf," through which Israel destroyed the first, "original" covenant of Sinai. This too recalls the primordial history, which shows clearly that everything can be viewed only from the perspective of after the flood. So too here: from this moment onwards, Israel lives *after* the breaking of the covenant (cf. 1991b).

But can Israel live on? And how will God behave towards Israel in future? The complex texts of Ex 32-34 center on these questions. After Moses' first petition we read: "Then the Lord regretted the evil that he had said he would bring on the people" (32.14). This sentence as it were anticipates the result of the disputes that follow. For Moses will first have to fight a dramatic wrestling match with God over his way with Israel in the future. He declares that he will share Israel's fate if God turns down his petition (this is how v. 32b is to be understood; cf. Janowski 1982, 144f). But God hears Moses' plea and once again commissions him to lead Israel further along the path indicated by God.

But a new problem now arises: God will not himself travel with them (33.3) but will merely send his "angel" (*mal'āk*) (32.34; 33.2). Elsewhere the *mal'āk* always appears as Yhwh's representative (e.g. Ex 23.20f) [→56]; but here this announcement of God's involves a degree of reserve: the *mal'āk* is not Yhwh himself. But finally Moses wrestles the concession out of God that he will himself go with them (33.16f). God's justification is: "You have found grace in my eyes and I know you by name." So everything depends on the person of Moses—as on the person of Noah in his day; for it is said only of these two people in the Hebrew Bible that they "found grace (favor) in the eyes of God" (Gen 6.8; Ex 33.17).

This special position enjoyed by Moses finds its last climax in a theophany. Moses desires—all too boldly, in the opinion of some interpreters—to see God's *kābôd*, his "glory" (33.18) [→§15]. But God grants only that he see him from behind, and he protects him with his own hand against the danger of seeing what he should not see (vv. 22f) —another parallel to Noah, behind whom God sealed the ark with his own hand (Gen 7.16)! And then God moves on and calls out his name: "YHWH, YHWH, a God merciful and gracious, slow to anger, and abounding in steadfast love and faithfulness ... to the third and the fourth generation" (Ex 34.6f). The words of the Decalogue resonate here (Ex 20.5f); but the abundance of God's attributes is developed much further here, and at the forefront stand his grace, mercy, long-suffering and faithfulness. It is this that Moses hears, though he does not see it, and that will accompany him on the way ahead.

But the covenant is still broken. Now, however, begins the decisive step towards its restoration. Moses asks God to extend the grace he himself has been vouchsafed to the people of Israel (34.9). He knows that this is a stubborn people; God has said it himself and has thereby justified his earlier decision to destroy this people (32.9f; cf. 33.3, 5). Nothing has changed in this regard. But Moses asks God to forgive the people this guilt and sin and to accept it again as his property, and he includes himself in this ("our guilt and sin"). And God answers: "Behold I make a covenant" (34.10). He grants this covenant to the stubborn, sinful people. The basis for this is exclusively divine forgiveness. Here once again the parallel with the Noachic covenant is quite clear: The "imagination of man's heart" remains evil (Gen 8.21) [→18], and Israel still remains a "stubborn" people. But God's forgiving grace overcomes this hurdle and again concludes the covenant with his people. And just as the keeping of the first covenant is not dependent on the behavior of people, so too that of the Sinai covenant; for God has restored it, even though he knows Israel's sinfulness.

This text has a quite central significance. Throughout the whole of the Hebrew Bible the decisive question again and again is how God behaves in relation to Israel when it infringes his commandments, departs from his ways, or "breaks" the covenant (or whatever the wording may be). God punishes Israel in many different ways, often seeming to abandon it—but in the end he does not give up: he does not break his covenant. The justification for this stands at this place, at which God's covenant with Israel was first made, then broken by Israel and finally restored by God in full awareness that Israel itself will never be in a position to keep the covenant in its own strength. But God keeps it; it is *šomēr habb'rît*, the faithful God who keeps his covenant (Deut 7.9; 1 Kgs 8.23 etc.) [→**78**].

God concludes the covenant with Moses and with Israel (v. 27) "in accordance with these words" which God had previously spoken (vv. 11-26) and which Moses is now to write down. The words take up again much of what has already been said in earlier legal communications. The main concern is with the exclusive worship of Yhwh and the festivals and cultic procedures connected with it. As on the first occasion (24.8f) [→**57**] the words on the basis of which God concludes the covenant are written down. Distinguished from these in the present narrative context are the "ten words" that God himself (according to v. 1) writes on the tables, which Moses has made in place of the first one, smashed by him because of the "Golden Calf" (34.1, 4, 28). Once again Moses has spent forty days and forty nights on Sinai (cf. 24.18) [→**59**] and when he comes down, his face is shining, so that he has to hide the radiance from the eyes of the Israelites, who are disconcerted by it (34.29-35). This feature again underlines the special position enjoyed by Moses, which separates and marks him off from all other people.

The whole section Ex 32-34 has clearly been put together from a variety of elements; though they can be read and understood coherently in their present context, they still comprise a number of tensions of various kinds. A great deal of exegetical wisdom has been applied to the interpretation of the prehistory of these chapters, but this has not produced accepted solutions in all respects. This applies in particular to the collection of laws in 34.11-26 (often called the "cultic decalogue" or "Yhwh's right of privilege"). The question of its relation to the Decalogue and the "Book of the Covenant" is as vexed as that of its relationship to the narrative context. Recent studies have paid increasing attention to the present framework and cross-connections.

A special problem is presented by the section Ex 33.7-11. In the previous chs. 25-31 God has informed Moses in great detail of the nature of the tent sanctuary that he is to erect and in which God will dwell in the midst of Israel; in chs. 35-40 the account of the execution of this follows. But the tent spoken of in 33.7-11 is quite a different one—it stands outside the camp, indeed "far off" from it (v. 7). Moses calls it the "tent of meeting" (*'ohel mô'ed*), because one can "seek" God there. In particular Moses himself goes there, however, and God meets with him by descending in the pillar of cloud.

This section (behind which there presumably stands a separate tradition) has to be explained with reference to its immediate context: after the sinning that occurred in connection with the "Golden Calf," God is far away from Israel. Only Moses is in conversation with him, and God meets Moses only outside the camp. So this is an important element of Moses' mediator function, which eventually leads to God's turning once again to Israel. (On this understanding of the tent of meeting cf. also Num 11.4-12.8; Deut 31.14f; 34.10 and the discussion by Childs 1974, 591ff; Gunneweg 1990.)

2.3.5 I will dwell in the midst of them

Before all these dramatic arguments God had already shown Moses on the mountain, on another narrative plane one might say, the "model" (*tabnît*) of the "sanctuary" [→**§11**] (*miqdāš*), Yhwh's "dwelling-place" (*miškān*) (Ex 25.8f) and its cultic facilities and given him the task of constructing it (Ex 25–31). Moses now sets to without delay, putting the commission into practice and thereby preparing the place for the presence of God with his people (Ex 35–40).

A second, fundamental aspect of the significance of Israel's stay in Sinai comes in here: Israel is "with God" here (cf. Ex 19.4) [→**52**], it has received the Torah, and this has been confirmed in the covenant agreement; now with the portable sanctuary the precondition is created for God's constant presence with his people Israel: "I will dwell among the people of Israel, and will be their God. And they shall know that I am the LORD their God, who brought them forth out of the land of Egypt that I might well among them; I am the LORD their God" (Ex 29.45f).

This is an astonishing statement. According to this it is practically the goal of Israel's being led out of Egypt that God should dwell in the midst of them (cf. 1997b, 508). At the same time this means that he will travel with them and that the divine "residence" will accompany them. The cloud above the sanctuary, in which the presence of God is manifest, now takes on the function of signaling Israel's breaking and setting up camp on the way (Ex 40.36f; Num 10.11). This also makes apparent the broad context in which the construction of the sanctuary on Sinai stands. On the seventh day God calls Moses to him in the cloud which veils his *kābôd*, to show him the model of the sanctuary (Ex 24.16). This continues, as it were, the creation story, as God's "blessing" and "hallowing" of the seventh day of creation (Gen 2.3)

[→**14**] now gains concrete shape in the construction of the sanctuary, God's "residence." And when the construction is concluded, Moses contemplates the finished work and blesses it (Ex 39.43), just as God did with his work of creation on the seventh day.

The basic statement, "I will be their God," which was expressed to Abraham (Gen 17.8) [→**27**] and to Moses in Egypt (Ex 6.7) [→**41**] is repeated (Ex 29.45b). Here, as in Ex 6.7f, it is reinforced by the "knowing" saying that follows: "They will know that I am the LORD, their God..." (v. 46). In both cases the basic criterion of the "knowing" is that God has led Israel out of Egypt. But then a crucial shift of emphasis emerges: according to Ex 6.7f the leading out occurred in order to bring Israel into the land promised to the fathers, but according to 29.46 "that I might dwell among them." Everything is oriented towards God's dwelling in the midst of his people.

The "dwelling" is not, however, something static. God "meets" with the Israelites in the sanctuary (Ex 29.43), which is therefore also called *'ohel mô'ēd*, "tent of meeting" (v. 42, but cf. above on Ex 33.7 [→**64**]). This meeting is made possible by God himself having his *kābôd*, which represents his presence, transferred from Sinai (24.16f) into the newly erected sanctuary (40.34f). The *kābôd* fills the whole sanctuary, so that Moses cannot enter until God himself calls him in (Lev 1.1), as previously on Sinai (Ex 24.16b, 18). And after the presentation of the first sacrifices in the newly erected sanctuary, the *kābôd* appears to the whole people (Lev 9.23).

So Israel is with God—and God dwells in the midst of Israel. Israel is at its goal—and God is at the goal too. The Midrash says: "From the beginning of the creation of the world onwards, the Holy One, blessed be He, had a desire to create communion with those below (i.e. people)" (*Genesis Rabbah* 3.9). This desire has now found its fulfillment. (On this cf. Janowski 1987; Köckert 1989; Blum 1990a, 293ff.)

2.3.6 You will be holy, for I am holy

God's dwelling in the midst of Israel means at the same time the constant presence of his "holiness." His "residence" (*miškān*) is the "sanctuary" (*miqdāš*), which he himself consecrates (Ex 29.43f). Israel must now take great care to maintain this holiness and to keep on restoring it after the many occasions when it inevitably gets harmed. God himself puts into Israel's hands the rules according to which this is to be done.

At this point a new book begins in the Hebrew Bible [→*In* **153**]. In the Jewish tradition it is again known by its opening word, *wayyiqra'* "And he called," while its Latinized Greek name "Leviticus" refers to its content, cultic law.

This new departure marks the transition from the instructions for the construction of the sanctuary to the rules for the cultic life that is to be carried out in it. The two books are closely connected with each other, however, as God calls Moses to him from the cloud covering the just-erected "tent of meeting" (Lev 1.1).

At the center of cultic life [→**§11**] stands the burnt offering altar, which is to be "sanctified" after its construction (Ex 29.36f), so that the daily sacrifices can be presented on it (vv. 38-42). The sacrificial cult performed on this altar partly serves for "communication" with the deity and also between the sacrificers: so we have the "burnt offering" (*'olāh*, Lev 1; 6.1-6), the "cereal offering" (*minḥāh*, Lev 2; 6.7-11) and the "peace offering" (*zebāḥ šelāmîm*, Lev 3; 7.11-21). But of special importance are the sacrifices that serve to restore the holiness, "atonement," especially the "sin offering" (*ḥaṭṭā'ṭ* Lev 4.1–5.13; 6.17-23), as well as the "guilt offering" (*'āšām*, Lev 5.14-26; 7.1-7). (For detail, cf. 1967 and 1985ff.)

The sacrificial cult is carried out by "Aaron and his sons," who are "consecrated" in elaborate ceremonies and are thereby commissioned as priests (Ex 28f; Lev 8) and then perform the first sacrifices (Lev 9). They, and the later priests after them, are responsible in a quite special way for guaranteeing the holiness of the divine residence. How threatening and perilous this office can be is evident right away in a short scene in which two of Aaron's sons, Nadab and Abihu, are struck by the divine punishment on account of an illegitimate smoke offering (Lev 10.1-5).

A central position is taken by the annual "day of atonement," the *yôm hakkippurîm* (Lev 16; 23.26-32). What happens here is a concentrated form of what the individual sin offering already achieves to a lesser degree: the removal of "impurities" (Lev 16.16), through which the purity and thus the holiness of the sanctuary has been affected in the course of a year. In order to make God's residence in the midst of Israel possible, it is necessary again and again to restore the holiness of the divine dwelling-place.

But the Israelites must also contribute to the maintenance of the holiness. The law concerning the day of atonement in Lev 11–15 and
17–26 is thus framed by texts that can be summarized under the heading of "Sanctification of the People of God" (Blum 1990a, 318). Almost like a refrain they repeat the formula: "You shall be holy, for I
am holy" (Lev 11.44, 45; 19.2; 20.26; 21.8; cf. 20.7f; 22.31f etc.). At
issue here is keeping away from "impure" animals (ch. 11), the removal of bodily impurities (chs. 11–15), sexual and family laws (chs.
18; 20), cultic regulations of various kinds (chs. 17; 22; 23), and special
regulations for the priests (ch. 21), besides other things. Everything is
viewed in particular from the aspect formulated especially explicitly in
22.32: "You shall not profane my holy name, but I will be hallowed
among the people of Israel; I am the LORD who sanctify you." This
also shows, however, that many regulations presuppose Israel's life in
the land, for instance rules about the harvest (19.9f, 23ff) and the festivals that go with it (23.10ff, 39ff), about the sale of plots of land and
the sabbath year (ch. 25), on hospitality for strangers (19.33f), the designation of Israelite citizens as "people of the land" (20.2, 4) and so on.

A variety of traditions have been collected in these chapters. Lev 17–26 is
often viewed as a law collection in its own right and is termed the Holiness
Code. Doubtless these chapters show particular characteristics, such as the
paraenetic style, which is not generally found in "priestly" texts [→**11**]. It has,
however, become clear in recent scholarly discussion that its separation from
the context is not watertight, partly because the expression "You shall be holy,
for I am holy" is already found in ch. 11, which emphasizes the central place
of ch. 16 within this collection (cf. Blum 1990a, 318ff; Crüsemann 1992,
323ff).

The broadly spread chapters on God's dwelling with Israel and on
Israel's holiness lead into the concluding chapter, Lev 26. It refers back
to God's self-revelation to Moses: "I am the LORD, your God" (v. 1;
cf. Ex 6.7) [→**42**], and once again it sharpens the fundamental
commandments of the Decalogue: not to have any foreign gods and to
keep the sabbath (vv. 1f) [→**54**]. This is connected with an "if" ('*im*) (v.
3), which makes two things clear: God wants to distribute the abundance of his gifts to Israel; but the two-sidedness of the covenant, as
was already expressed to Abraham (Gen 17.9ff) [→**28**] and then on the
arrival at Sinai [→**53**], has to be guaranteed by Israel's keeping, for its
part, the divine commandments and instructions. So this "if" has a
double sequel: in the description of the gifts that God wants to "give"

(vv. 4ff)—and in the subsequent "but if not" (vv. 14ff). These are in principle almost utopian promises about the fertility of the land and the peace of life in it (vv. 4-6), and phrases from the creation story resound: "be fruitful and multiply," which are linked with the memory of God's covenant with Noah (v. 9; cf. Gen 9.1) [→**18**]. God repeats the promise of his dwelling with Israel (v. 11) and continues it in the words about God's "walking" (*hithallēk*) in the midst of Israel (v. 12), as it were as the counterpart to Abraham's walking before God (Gen 17.1; cf. also Enoch in 5.22, 24 and Noah in 6.9). The full, double-sided statement of Israel's belonging to God surfaces again: "I will be your God and you shall be my people," which so far was only to be heard in Ex 6.7. And finally the whole thing is given its express conclusion through the reminder of the leading of Israel out of Egypt (v. 13), as God had announced it to Moses.

So the divine speeches in Ex 6 and Lev 26 bracket together Exodus and Sinai as the two great deeds of God at the beginning of his history with his people, Israel (cf. Blum 1990a, 325ff).

But then the other side follows, a series of laws that starts up time and again with "but if not" (vv. 14, 18, 21, 23, 27) and proclaiming as the consequence of not observing the divine commandments a series of increasingly terrible catastrophes that will come upon the land and its inhabitants. Finally the Israelites will be led away into captivity and the land will lie waste (v. 33). Then it will at last receive the sabbath rest that the Israelites have denied it for so long (vv. 34f), thereby offending against the commandment of God that was given them immediately beforehand (25.2-7). Much of this is reminiscent of prophetic words of judgment, and much of it reveals the experiences of disaster, persecution, destruction and exile that lie behind the formulations.

But that is not the end of it. The Israelites will acknowledge their sins (vv. 40f) and God will remember his covenant [→**§6**] (vv. 42, 45). This throws a bridge back again, this time as far as the patriarchs (v. 42), and the "memory" of the covenant, once again to Ex 6.5 and thus to the exodus (v. 45). God will not therefore break his covenant, nor will he leave Israel in the lurch in exile either (v. 44). So the giving of the law on Sinai ends with a powerful confirmation of God's faithfulness to the covenant.

2.4 Israel on the way: The second stage

2.4.1 The Israelites set out

Before the preparations for Israel's departure from Sinai begin, a new book opens up once again in the Hebrew Bible [→*In* **156**]. Its Hebrew designation derives from the first sentence: *b'midbar*, "In the desert." The Latin term "Numeri," "Numbers," taken from the Greek, refers to the gathering of the Israelites reported in the first chapter.

"In the second year, in the second month, on the twentieth day of the month ... the people of Israel set out" (Num 10.11f), almost exactly one year after their arrival in Sinai (Ex 19.1) [→**52**]. But the situation is completely different now: in the midst of Israel is the divine "residence," which is here called the "tabernacle of the testimony," i.e. of the tables of the law which Moses had laid in the ark (Ex 40.20f). And when the Israelites set out now, they are given the signal for this by the cloud which sits upon the sanctuary and then rises (Ex 40.34ff; Num 9.15ff; 10.11f) [→**49**]. Once again it is clear that the stay in Sinai has not been permanent, but that it was not just an episode either; for now Israel lives with the sanctuary at its center, which at the same time directs the requirement of holiness to the people and to each individual.

Num 10.13-28 describes how the breaking of camp is to proceed, the detailed camp arrangement as set out in Num 2 being presupposed. This constructs the connection between the details on Israel's cultic life around the sanctuary at its center and the narratives on the second part of the wilderness wanderings. For now quite different problems arise, some of which resemble those of the first period of wanderings, especially the "murmuring" [→**50**] of the people (Num 11; 20.1-13) and the consequences of this for Moses and Aaron. (In what their transgression consisted at the waters of Meribah is unclear [→**87**].) Other conflicts presuppose the special meeting between God and Moses at Sinai (Num 12), and in addition the rules about holiness and priesthood, which lead to the rebellion incited by the "Korah gang" (Num 16–18). Particular features of the image of Moses only now emerge in full clarity, especially Moses' spiritual gifts (Num 11.16-30) and his clear preeminence and superiority with respect to Aaron and Miriam and all the prophets (ch. 12).

The hazards and conflicts on this path come together once more in a dramatic way when the Israelites come into the vicinity of the land that is their real goal. Moses sends out envoys to reconnoiter the lie of the land (Num 13). They return and report on the one hand great fertility and on the other the strength of the inhabitants of the land, to which the Israelites would not be equal. The people then refuse to move on and even want to set up another leader to take them back to Egypt (14.1-4) [→**§16**]. The conflict between the Israelites and Moses (and Aaron) that arises from this as well as that between the Israelites and Yhwh seems like a repetition of the Sinai conflict (Ex 32–34) [→**59**] and once again brings Moses into the role of the advocate. Again God wants to destroy the whole people and make a new start with Moses alone (Num 14.12; cf. Ex 32.10). And again Moses succeeds in moving God to make concessions by reminding him constantly of his repeatedly mentioned readiness to forgive and confronting him with his own words from Sinai (Num 14.17-19; cf. Ex 34.6f) [→**63**]. God's punishment for the Israelite's stubbornness ultimately consists in the fact that Israel has to stay in the wilderness for forty years, until all the currently responsible men have died.

It is evident from its conclusion that this narrative has a key function, in various regards. For one thing, it makes clear how irksome Israel's path to the promised land is. In some summary formulations this way seems smooth and unproblematic, for instance Deut 26.8f: "The LORD led us out of Egypt with a mighty hand and an outstretched arm ... and he brought us into this place and gave us this land, a land flowing with milk and honey." Here exodus and the conquest of the land come quite close together, while in the book of Numbers, according to the account in chs. 13f forty difficult years lie between them as the divine punishment for unbelieving and stubborn Israel. Here, even clearer than at Sinai is the fact that God's forgiveness and his adherence to the promises given to the patriarchs does not mean that Israel will remain unpunished. But it also conveys the message that the next generation [→**§22**] will not have to bear the sins of the fathers, but that they will come into the land promised by God. The central significance of this statement for the book of Numbers and thereby for the whole stage of Israel's wandering from Sinai up to the borders of the promised land is visible in the fact that two reports are given of a great census of the people. Before the departure from Sinai, on God's orders the total number of all the Israelite men of twenty years of age and older (Num 1.3ff) is established. The same formula is found again first in Num 14.29, where God's judgment that those responsible for the "murmuring" against him in the wilderness should die, is related expressly to those who are twenty years of age and over.

In Num 26, finally, a new general assembly of the Israelites of twenty years and over is executed and thereafter established that none of those assembled the first time was still alive (vv. 64f). So the forty-year period means a complete change of generations and thus a new beginning, which for the next generation stands again under the divine promise (cf. Olson 1985).

On the continuing pathway into the promised land Israel now has a series of encounters with other nations and their representatives. Here memories and experiences in relations with the immediate neighbors have been set down, mainly in short accounts. The Edomites refuse passage to the Israelites, who make a detour (Num 20.14-21). There are no problems in traversing the area of the Moabites (21.13-20). But then there are reports of a series of military engagements in which Israel is successful: with the "Canaanite," the king of Arad (21.1-3), with Sihon, the king of the "Amorites" (21.21-32) and with Og, the king of Bashan (21.33-35). The tradition concerning Israel's way to the promised land has attached special significance to the two last-mentioned encounters. Their land is first divided among Israelite tribes: to Reuben and Gad as well as the half-tribe Manasseh (32.33). Then in Deuteronomy's retrospect they are not only mentioned in detail (Deut 2.26–3.11) [→74], but also named in other historical summaries as the beginning of the divine handover of the land to Israel (Ps 135.10-12; 136.17-22; Neh 9.22) [→§21]. Israel's "conquest" thus begins here already in Transjordan before the crossing of the Jordan (cf. 1995b).

Finally a report is given of a last attempt to hold Israel up on its route (Num 22–24). The Moabite king Balak engages Balaam, the "soothsayer" (as he is titled in Josh 13.22), to curse Israel. But Yhwh prevents him from doing this and changes his words into a blessing. This complex narrative fits in with the overall scheme, in which Israel is led closer and closer to the promised goal under the guidance and protection of God. In the words of blessing that God puts on Balaam's lips (23.7-10, 18-24; 24.3-9, 15-19 [20-24]), a great future is predicted for Israel. So the contrast could hardly be greater when immediately afterwards the Israelites allow themselves to be seduced by Moabite women into participation in the cult of the Ba'al of Pe'or (25.1ff), thereby offending against the express prohibition given on Sinai (Ex 23.32f; 34.15f) [→56]. This scene looks like a repetition of the scout story of Num 13f [→70]. Once again the people rebels at a moment when fulfillment of the divine promises is almost within their grasp.

Again God punishes the people with a plague (25.8f); and like Caleb and Joshua then (14.6-10, 24, 30), now only one individual is exempted because he has stood up to the great majority: Phinehas (25.7-13; cf. Olson 1985, 160).

This apostasy of the Israelites to foreign gods and the subsequent plague, to which many succumbed, means at the same time a decisive caesura. Immediately afterwards the second assembly takes place, at which it is established that none of those who had assembled the first time was around any longer (Num 26.64f). This second deviation from the divine commandments was thus the last act of the old generation. It will only be the next generation that completes the entry into the land. Aaron has already died (Num 20.22-29) and now Moses' succession is arranged, since he himself is not permitted to cross the Jordan himself to lead the people into the promised land (cf. 20.12). This task falls to Joshua (27.12-23) [→**86**].

The multi-layered narrative sequence of the book of Numbers is repeatedly interrupted by paragraphs dealing with cultic law. The connection with the narrative context is often not immediately evident. (Douglas 1993 sees in the alternation between narrative and legal passages a structural element of the book of Numbers.) In some cases, however, it is clear that we have here supplements and more precise explanations of rules given earlier [→*In* **156**], e.g. 15.1-16 cf. Lev 1–3; 15.22-31 cf. Lev 4f; 28f cf. Lev 23.

The book of Numbers, then, seems to have been given its final shape only later than the book of Leviticus, so that it was able to pick up such supplements.

The epoch of which the book of Numbers tells has an exemplary character for the whole of the subsequent history of the people of Israel. It is dominated by the tension between the divine commandments which Israel received on Sinai and Israel's constantly re-emerging inability to live up to these commandments. The wilderness generation was granted participation in the great appearance of God and the giving of the commandments on Sinai, but it failed even to live in accordance with these commandments. Its fate makes both aspects clear in an exemplary way: the punishment of God, which finds expression in a forty-year period of suffering—and the longsuffering of God, with which in the end he keeps to his covenant and does not reject Israel. Both are repeated in a variety of ways in the subsequent epochs in the history of the people of Israel.

3. Deuteronomy

The flow of the narrative is broken once again. Before the account of the previously announced death of Moses and thus of the transfer of the leadership of the people to Joshua, Moses once again applies himself to a very long speech. In its center stands a collection of laws (Deut 12–26), framed by detailed introductory (chs. 1–11) and concluding speeches (27–34, supplemented by some further texts). Unlike the preceding books of the Pentateuch this book, Deuteronomy, contains hardly any narrative elements [→*In* 159]. On the other hand both the speeches and the laws are given many justifications, explanations and polemical reflections which could be termed "theological" in the narrower sense of the word (cf. Smend 1982). To that extent Deuteronomy is perhaps the most theological book in the Hebrew Bible. In addition, through its central position it has decisively marked the overall understanding of the Pentateuch and thus also the overall understanding of the Hebrew Bible (cf. Herrmann 1971).

This book gets its Hebrew name, *d'barîm*, "Words," once again from the opening words, "These are the words." Its Greek/Latin name "Deuteronomy" means "second law" and comes from the Greek Septuagint translation of Deut 17.18 (and Josh 8.32), where the Hebrew text runs "record of the law." There can be no doubt that Deuteronomy has a history of its own and was not initially linked with the preceding or following books. But it is just as clear that in the present context Deuteronomy has close connections with the preceding books. This applies to the laws as well as the narrative parts of the introductory chapters (cf. Crüsemann 1992, 235ff and Blum 1990, 176ff).

So Deuteronomy in its present form, which as far as its origins are concerned is certainly not "unified," is an integral part of the Pentateuch.

3.1 What nation has such a righteous Torah?

Deuteronomy is formulated almost entirely as a speech of Moses. This gives expression to the distinction that already marked the giving of the law on Sinai: only the Decalogue was spoken to Israel by God himself, and all the other commandments and laws are given to Moses and passed on by him to the people (Ex 20.18-21) [→**54**]. We are reminded of this in detail once again in the repetition of the Decalogue in Deut 5 (vv. 23-31).

But beforehand the significance of the divine commandments for Israel unfolds with great emphasis and breadth. The first speech of Moses begins with a historical introduction in which Moses recapitulates again the events of Sinai up to the border of the promised land, "beyond the Jordan" (chs. 1–3). Then in ch. 4 there follows a grandly conceived sermon, the first section of which climaxes in the sentence, "What great nation is there, that has statutes and ordinances so righteous as all this law?" (Deut 4.8). Here (as in the introduction 1.5) the word "Torah" appears in its meaningful, untranslatable sense [→57]. It means more, and other things, than just "law." It is an expression for the whole of the "revelation of the divine will" (von Rad 1962, 235) and comprises "law" and "gospel" (Crüsemann 1992, 8f) [→§10].

At the same time, Israel is defined here by the Torah. Israel is the nation that has the Torah, and this distinguishes it from all the nations (4.6). And through the gift of the Torah, Israel is also the nation that is close to its God, closer than even "great nations" can claim to be (v. 7). This does not make Israel itself a "great nation" within a world marked by the changing domination of superpowers. But little Israel, still without political shape on the banks of the Jordan, the Israel addressed by Moses, and the concrete political Israel to which Deuteronomy is oriented, is forcefully made conscious of the fact that through the closeness of this God, wherever Israel calls upon him, and through his Torah, it possesses gifts that far exceed anything the "great nations" have.

The admonition to keep the Torah is now concentrated on the Decalogue: the Ten Words which Israel itself heard, when God spoke them out of the fire like thunder (vv. 12f) [→63]. In this very dense theological speech the Ten Words are equated with the "covenant" which God concluded with Israel on Horeb/Sinai. More precisely: they are described as the content of the covenant which God has commanded should be kept. Then as the explanation of the first commandment the prohibition of images is justified with a surprising turn of argument: on Horeb Israel has only heard, it has not seen anything (vv. 12, 15); so it is not to make any image to worship either. This relates not only to the images of human beings, male or female, and of all conceivable kinds of animals (vv. 16-18), but also includes the heavenly bodies (v. 19).

This is again surprising, and doubly so. For one thing, the Moses sermon is extending the statements of the Decalogue about the prohibition of images into a new dimension. New experiences with other religions are certainly reflected in this. The formulations of the prohibition of images in the Decalogue had primarily Canaanite cultic traditions in view, while the cult of the stars was an important element of Babylonian religion, which Israel encountered already before the exile in Babylon and then especially during that exile. Secondly, however, it is extremely surprising that the astrological cult was not simply rejected, but that it says that Yhwh allocated the stars to other nations for veneration. This statement is singular. It not content to leave the nations with their veneration of their gods (cf. e.g. Mic 4.5) [→295] but it even allocates them to them. On the one hand this gives expression to the infinite superiority of Yhwh, who also has the sun, moon and stars at his disposal. On the other hand this once again separates Israel off clearly from the other nations. Its relationship to God is justified in a quite different way: through the leading out of Egypt, which is described here with an especially memorable expression for the trials and suffering as "iron furnace" (v. 20). The contrast between these two aspects sets the consistent history-relatedness of the Israelite concept of God on the agenda in an impressive way.

The covenant [→§2] now moves into the center of attention, and the prohibition of images appears as its essential content. Israel is not to forget the covenant, since God is a "jealous" God (vv. 23f) [→54]. If Israel should offend against it, it will be driven into exile and dispersion (vv. 25-28)—until it finally seeks and finds God again and returns to him (vv. 29-31). Then it will be clear that God is not only a jealous God, but ultimately a merciful God and that he himself will never forget the covenant that Israel has forgotten (v. 31). This passage is reminiscent of the great chapter of Lev 26 [→68], which also ends with the banishment of Israel, with the assurance that God will remember his covenant. Repeatedly, and in quite different contexts, the Hebrew Bible emphasizes that despite everything Israel does, and despite all the punishments that he will visit upon Israel, God will keep to his covenant, remember it and not forget it.

The last section of this great introductory speech (vv. 32-40) also contains extremely weighty theological statements. Once again it picks up the theme of Israel's special position from vv. 5-8 and leads on to the sentence that Israel will "know that the LORD is [*the*] God; there is no other besides him" (v. 35). This "monotheistic" statement [→§15] is reinforced further: "The LORD is [*the*] God in heaven above and on the earth beneath; there is no other" (v. 39) [→14]. That this world-ruling God has turned to the little nation of Israel, that he has "chosen" it (*bāhar*) [→**§6**], has its ground in God's love for the patriarchs of Israel (v. 37; cf. 1981). Israel's leading out of Egypt (v. 37) has its ground in this as well as the requirement to keep God's commandments (v. 40).

The passage Deut 4.1-40 thus offers a very detailed and also concentrated development of important foundations for deuteronomistic theology (cf. Lohfink 1965). Even already in its approach it displays the central function of Deuteronomy and its theology not only for the Pentateuch but in a particular way for the whole of the Hebrew Bible.

3.2 Hear, O Israel!

The second great speech of Moses begins in Deut 4.44 with the words: "This is the Torah." The central significance of the word "Torah," which had already come to the fore in 4.8, comes forcibly to expression again. The word covers the whole block of material from the Decalogue (ch. 5) through the following paraenetic speeches (chs. 6–11) through to the great collection of laws (chs. 12–26 with the added chs. 27f). Torah in the narrower sense means in the first place the commandments and laws themselves as listed in the "book of the Torah" (20.10; cf. Josh 1.8) [→**§10**]; but then also everything that is said in justification and explanation of it, and finally also the proclamations of the consequences of the keeping or neglect of the commandments (Deut 29.20, 61).

The Decalogue is placed in a broadly sweeping narrative context in ch. 5, which describes the fearful reaction of the Israelites to the divine voice of thunder and their request to Moses that he accept the commandments of God on his own. Here the special place of the Decalogue is spelt out even more explicitly than in Ex 20 [→**54**]. The Decalogue itself is largely identical in wording to that in Ex 20. The most important difference lies in the justification for the sabbath commandments: in Ex 20.11 it is justified with God's resting on the seventh day of creation; in Deut 5.15, on the other hand, the social aspect of the resting is emphasized and there is a reminder of the forced labor in Egypt. A characteristic element of deuteronomic theology is already apparent in this.

At the beginning of the far-ranging paraenetic speech that follows the Decalogue there is a short sentence of great theological and historical significance: "Hear, O Israel! The Lord is our God. The Lord is *one*" (6.4). This Shema' Yisra'el is probably the most important sentence in the history of the Jewish religion. It is said twice in the course of the Jewish day, together with the sentence that follows: "and you shall love the LORD your God with all your heart, and with all your soul and with all your might" (v. 5). (The justification for its liturgical use is derived from vv. 6-9.) In New Testament times this sentence was already considered to be the "greatest commandment" (Mk 12.28-34 and parr.). Here it is placed at the head of a long paraenetic speech which can be understood as an exposition of the Decalogue, in particular of its introductory sentences on the exclusivity of the worship of Yhwh and the prohibition of images.

In the process, at first the leading out of Egypt is given pride of place, as the decisive saving act of God [→47]. In the answer to the son's question, why the Israelites keep these commandments, the history of Israel's slavery in Egypt, the powerful divine rescue from there and the (still at this point in the future) gift of the promised land, is all recapitulated in a creed-like summary. This provides the essential justification for Israel's need to keep the commandments given to it by God. This will be Israel's "righteousness" (6.20-25).

The cultic delimitation in respect of other nations, which is made Israel's duty (7.1-5), is justified in Israel's election (cf. already 4.37). In 7.6 this is elaborated in a central sentence: "For you are a people holy to the Lord your God; the Lord your God has chosen you to be a people for his own possession, out of all the peoples that are on the face of the earth" (7.6). Election means selection, separation from the totality of the nations. What has already been said under the aspect of the gift of the Torah and of God's nearness to Israel (see above on 4.7f) is now further elaborated. The nations [→§20] are also in view, but Israel is given a special task among them. It is a "holy nation," which again means a separated one, withdrawn from the general profane round. And a nation that in a special way is God's property.

But now the question arises, how Israel will deal with this privilege. In the following chapters Israel is warned against various possibilities of overestimating itself. The grounds for the election of Israel do not lie in it being the biggest of the nations. On the contrary, it is the smallest (7.7). God's election is grounded in his unmerited love for Israel and in the "oath" that he has already given to the forefathers. That is why he led Israel out of the Egyptian house of slavery—that too is one of his deeds of election (v. 8). And in this he proves himself also to be the "defender of the covenant" [→121, 399], which however only applies to those who keep his commandments (vv. 9ff). This tight connection between leading out of Egypt, election and covenant shows once again how closely and concentratedly the various theological aspects are connected together in deuteronomic parlance. Another self-overestimation could lie in the fact that Israel might think, as it enjoys the gifts of the land: I gained this wealth in my own strength. No, once again it is God's faithfulness to his covenant, which he swore to the forefathers and is now realizing in this way (8.17f). Finally, Israel might even think that it is to its own righteousness that it owes the occupation of the land. But on the contrary: Israel is a stiff-necked people, and once again it is because of the oath to the forefathers that God has given Israel the land (9.4-6). The words about Israel's being "stiff-necked" then revive detailed memories of the events on Sinai/Horeb, where this was a decisive key term (9.7-10, 11; cf. Ex 32.9; 33.3, 5; 34.9) [→62]. Finally the admonition to fear God and to keep the commandments flows into the demand that this stubbornness should be abandoned, and that people's hearts be circumcised instead (10.16).

3.3 These are the laws and prescriptions

In Deut 12.1 the great collection of laws then begins, which the paraenetic texts have been leading up to since the introduction in 4.44. It does not end until ch. 26.

The prescriptions and laws in this collection [→*In* 163] display many connections to the preceding collections of laws. There are good reasons why the "Book of the Covenant" (Ex 20.22-23, 33) is generally considered to be older than Deuteronomy, and the "priestly" texts including Lev 17–26 (often called the Holiness Code) to be younger. The question therefore arises whether Deuteronomy was intended to supplement or to replace the "Book of the Covenant." It is entirely conceivable that the first intention was a replacement. In the merging of the two bodies of law within the present Pentateuch, however, they gain a new function, in that together with the other legal traditions of the Pentateuch they form the *one* "Torah of Sinai" given by Moses, which has to be taken in its variety and interpreted further in a "halakhic" way (cf. Blum 1990a, 200f). On the structure of the law corpus of Deut 12–26 [→*In* 162] cf. Crüsemann 1992, 241f.

The law collection begins, like the Book of the Covenant before it, with a law pertaining to the altar, or the place of worship (Deut 12; cf. Ex 20.24-26) [→56]. But now a new aspect appears: after Israel has taken possession of the land, the legitimate sacrificial cult is possible only at *one* location. God himself will choose the place for this, or to be more precise, "elect" it (vv. 5, 11, 14 etc., using the same word as for the election of Israel, see above on Deut 4.37 [→**77**]), and he will "let his name dwell there" (v. 11; cf. v. 5). This is one of the decisive foundations of the book of Deuteronomy: the centralization of the sacrificial cult in *one* place. The Book of the Covenant already talked about God "proclaiming" his name at particular places (Ex 20.24) [→**56**]; but the wording can refer to several places where God will come to Israel and bless it. Here in Deuteronomy it is only *one* place to which Israel may bring its sacrifices; all other places are expressly excluded (vv. 13f). Oddly enough the name of this place is never given in Deuteronomy. There can be no doubt that Jerusalem is meant; but the narrative situation is maintained, according to which Israel cannot yet know at this point what place God will finally elect, when it has crossed the Jordan.

This demand for the centralization of the cult in a single place is a concretization of the first commandment, as has already been laid out in the *Sh'ma' Yiśrā'ēl* (see above on Deut 6.4 [→**77**]): *one* God—*one* sanctuary. The cult centralization in Jerusalem is one of the most doggedly effective commandments of Deuteronomy. It has all kinds of consequences, above all the permission for "profane" slaughter. Since it is impossible (even in an Israel that has shrunk as a result of the political developments) to carry out all slaughtering at the temple in Jerusalem, the Israelites are allowed to slaughter and eat meat "to their heart's desire" and "in all places" (vv. 15, 20ff). This could be forbidden in the ideal circumstances in which Israel's life was centered around the tent sanctuary in the camp (Lev 17.3f). But the reality of life in the land does not allow this. The requirement of unity and uniqueness of the place where sacrifices are presented involves permission for profane slaughter. Consumption of the blood of a slaughtered animal, however, is repeatedly forbidden in explicit terms (vv. 16, 23-25). This shows that non-cultic slaughter remains within the Israelite religious tradition, as set down for humanity after the flood, according to Gen 9.4 [→**19**] (cf. also Lev 17.10-14).

Further cultic requirements are added. The concern with them, in part in sermonic form, is for the preservation of the exclusive worship of Yhwh and the rejection of foreign cultic practices (12.29–14.2), and the maintenance of the purity and "holiness" of Israel through abstinence from eating particular animals held to be culticly impure (14.3-21; cf. Lev 11).

This again shows that the permission for profane slaughter in Deuteronomy certainly does not lead generally in a profane direction.

In 14.22-29 there follow requirements concerning the giving of a tenth of the annual harvest. They clearly have very special significance, since they are taken up once again in 26.12-15 [→**84**], where they form the last of the commandments for the festive concluding ceremony in vv. 16-19. Two main features emerge here. In the first place, the tithing commandment links up with the requirement of the unity of the cultic place in ch. 12: the tenth, or its equivalent in money, may only be consumed at the sanctuary (14.22-26). But the second regulation seems more important: every third year the whole tithe is to be delivered to the individual localities and placed at the disposal of the Levites, as well as strangers, orphans and widows, i.e. those groups that do not own land (vv. 27-29). It is also this last regulation that is taken up once again when the tithing commandment is repeated at the end of the whole giving of the law (26.12f). It can be described as the "beginning of a real social legislature." It is closely connected with the hope and prayer that God will bless Israel for this social behavior (14.29; 26.15). Solidarity and blessing belong closely together here (Crüsemann 1992, 254, 262ff).

The regulations concerning the sabbath year, Passover and other festivals in 15.1–16.17 continue the theme of tithing, in that they deal with the social consequences of the sacred seasons [→**§10**], especially in the form of the canceling of debts (15.1-11), and the releasing of slaves (15.12-18) and the participation of all groups in the sacrificial meals (16.11, 14; cf. also 12.12, 18). Once again in this theme one can see a framework function within the deuteronomic law collection, in that in the last part of it too, in 23.16-25, 19, laws for the protection of the socially disadvantaged are to be found.

A further block of laws deals with public offices and institutions (16.18–18.22). At the beginning of this stands the law concerning the appointment of "judges and scribes" (16.18-20). The people is to create its own justice organization, which forms the basis of all other institutions: "Justice, and only justice (*sedeq sedeq*, you shall follow" (v. 20). This also involves, alongside the speaking of righteous judgment, in particular that there is no "respecting of persons" and no bribery (v.

19); a death sentence can only be given on the basis of the testimony of two or three witnesses (17.6f). These requirements of the judiciary are also once again connected with the commandment regarding the purity and unity of the cult: through the prohibition of Massebahs and Asherahs, i.e. wooden and stone cultic symbols (16.21f) [→144], the requirement of the umblemished condition of the sacrificial animals (17.1) and the ordering of prosecution in court of the cultic worship of foreign deities (17.2-5).

Finally there is talk in 17.8-13 of a supreme central authority, to which such cases as are too difficult for the local courts are to be presented. It consists of priests and a supreme judge. Their decisions are binding and count as *tôrāh* (v. 11). Israel is to "turn neither to the right nor to the left of them." This phrase is used elsewhere of the divine *tôrāh* mediated by Moses (5.32; 28.14). The central authority as such also reminds us of what is said in Ex 18.13-26 on Moses' position in relation to the judges he himself appointed (vv. 22, 26). So the talk here is of a supreme court in Israel which can make decisions with the same authority as Moses (Crüsemann 1992, 120).

It is only now that there is mention of a king [→§13] (Deut 17.14-20). The position of the law of kings in the context already makes it clear that the king is in no way above the law. On the contrary: he is expressly duty-bound to keep the law constantly "before his eyes," by having a copy of "this *tôrāh*" made, and to follow it precisely (vv. 18f). In other respects too the rules about the king contain, in particular, limitations. He is not to possess a surfeit of the typical elements and means of the exercise of power: horses for the implementation of military power, wives in order to foster foreign-policy relationships, silver and gold (vv. 16f). And his heart is not to be exalted above his brothers (v. 20). An odd tension marks the choice of king. The people appoint him, and he has to come from the ranks of the people; but he has to have been chosen by God (v. 15). The events of the late monarchic period seem to ring through here, in which "the people" (the *'am-hā'āreṣ*) appointed the king but kept to the divinely chosen Davidic dynasty (2 Kgs 21.24; 23.30).

Finally there follow legal rulings for two further groups: priests and prophets. In the case of the first the concern is mainly with rules for their share in the sacrifices, from which they have to live (Deut 18.1-8). The provisions that follow are extremely complex (vv. 9-22). First of all they speak in detail of the prohibition of all conceivable cult practices, but especially of conjurations and consultations of extra-human powers. None of this is for Israel. God has provided something else for it: "A prophet like me" [→**§17**], says Moses, "from among you, from your brethren" (v. 15). God will "raise him up," and indeed (this is evidently what we are to understand) time and again. "Him you shall heed," for he will speak in the Mosaic succession what God puts in his mouth (v. 18). So here the prophet first opposes the interpreters of signs and consulters of oracles, which Israel does not need. Israel experiences the will of God through the prophets in the succession of Moses. Then, however, the question arises how Israel is to know whether a prophet is really speaking in the name of God or whether he is only speaking in presumption, or even in the name of other gods. The answer seems extremely pragmatic: a prophetic word that is not fulfilled does not come from God, even if it is spoken in the name of God (v. 22). This answer hinders a premature condemnation of a prophet whose words do not meet with general approval. It is only the fulfillment that can show whether it was a true or a false prophecy. This paragraph continues what has already been said about Moses earlier: that he is the only true prophet (Num 12.6-9). But now sights are set on the future. There will always be a successor to Moses, appointed by God, who will speak with Moses' authority; for Israel will be reliant on this prophetic voice time and again.

In the following body of laws, which stands at the center of the whole collection of laws, the concern is with the preservation of life (19.1–21.9). Very varied topics are linked together here: the creation of towns of refuge (19.1-13), further rules about the testimony of witnesses (vv. 15-20), procedures to follow in the case of an unknown murderer (21.1-9). Oddly enough, the "war laws" are found in this context (ch. 20). The sense in their being located here lies in the fact that they do not really deal with war but with the possibilities and necessities of "humane" behavior in the case of war. They begin with an extensive list of possible hindrances to participation in military service. Anyone who has started something and not yet concluded it should see to this first: "house-warm" his newly built house (v. 5), reap the first harvest from his newly planted vineyard (v. 6), marry his fiancée (v. 7). That life should go on is more important than war. Indeed, even someone who is afraid should stay at home (v. 8), as protection for him and for the others he might infect with his fear. When the fight begins, an attempt is to be made to come to an amicable agreement before the battle, in order to spare human life (vv. 10f). And finally in the case of a lengthy siege even the fruit-trees are to be spared (vv. 19f).

What we find in chs. 21–25 is a rather variegated mixture of laws and rules. The dominant ones are the laws in 21.10–23.15, which have to do with questions of family and sexuality, while in 23.16–25.19 laws on the protection of the socially disadvantaged form an important proportion. Here too care for the protection of the life of the individual as well as the community of the family and tribe is continually in evidence.

The law collection comes to an end. It becomes clear here that the giving of the land is the decisive matter for Israel's life. The community of Israel, addressed in the informal second-person singular, is as it were individualized as the individual Israelite who is to appear before the priest with the first-fruits of the land and confess: "I declare this day to the LORD your God that I have come into the land which the LORD swore to our forefathers to give us" (26.3) [→§8]. And then follows a detailed confession which recapitulates the path from servitude in Egypt through to the entry into the land "flowing with milk and honey" (vv. 5-9). The first-fruits of the field are the visible expression of the blessing, for which the worshiper gives thanks by presenting them (v. 10). After the regulation for the delivery of the tithe in the third year (see above on 14.27-29), the whole thing ends with a solemn prayer: "Look down from your holy dwelling place, from heaven, and bless your people Israel and the land you have given us, as you promised to our forefathers, a land flowing with milk and honey" (v. 15).

3.4 This day you are a people for his own possession

Again and again in Deuteronomy we read "this day." The Israel that is being addressed has it impressed upon it time and again that everything that happened back on Horeb between God and Israel and everything that has been said to Israel, does not belong to the past, but that the addressees themselves are directly meant. So in the introduction to the Decalogue we can read something that sounds almost over the top:

"The LORD our God made a covenant with us at Horeb. It was not with our fathers that the LORD made this covenant, but with us, with all of us who are alive here today" (Deut 5.2f). However decisively important the fathers [→§7] constantly are, it is all up to those that are alive today. It is with them that God has concluded the covenant, it is to them that the Torah applies.

The threefold "this day" then marks the ceremony of commitment at the end of the proclamation of the law as a whole, in which the two parts of the "covenant formula" (see above on Ex 6.7 [→41]) are ceremonially proclaimed (Deut 26.16-19): on Yhwh's part "to be your God" (v. 17) and on Israel's part "to be the people for his own possession" (v. 18). The basis for this mutual commitment is formed by the "statutes and ordinances" which Moses has presented to the people thus far (v. 16). Israel now commits itself anew to keep these statutes and ordinances, the "Torah," and thereby accepts in all respects the repeatedly made promise that they are to be God's "people of possession."

There are a number of indications that there is a connection between Deut 26.1-19 and the report of the ceremonial covenant conclusion of King Josiah after the discovery of the book of the law in the temple, reported in 2 Kgs 23.1-3, even if many individual questions remain open (cf. Crüsemann 1992, 321).

This commitment ceremony forms the transition to the broadly structured concluding part which provides the framework for the law collection in correspondence with the introductory chapters Deut 1–11. In these chapters too, the "this day" resonates again and again, so too in the quotation chosen as a superscription to this section in 27.9. The style once again is paraenetic and often sermonic. The intensity with which these laws are emphasized and the keeping of them exhorted is again evident. One of the dominant themes is blessing and cursing as consequences of the observation or neglect of the Torah. With its sweeping description of the consequences of non-observation of the Torah, ch. 28 recalls Lev 26 [→68], though it does end without mention of the conversion of Israel and of God's turning to it anew. That is not found until the subsequent chapter 30.

In this chapter we now also meet a number of remarkable statements about the Torah. After all the announced punishments for not keeping the law have overcome Israel, it will repent, and God will graciously turn to it again and things will go better for it than before (30.1-10). There then follows a surprising statement about the possibility of fulfilling the Torah [→§10]: it is not too hard and not too far away, not in heaven and not on the other side of the sea. "But the word is very near you; it is in your mouth and in your heart, so that you can do it" (v. 14). This recalls the eschatological expectation of Jeremiah, that God will write the Torah in the hearts of the Israelites (Jer 31.31-34) [→227]; but here it already seems almost to be reality. It is as if the author of this text, after all the detailed descriptions of the consequences of the curse, not only wants to describe blessing as the consequence of repentance but also to encourage people to recognize the Torah as fulfillable and livable, and to act accordingly. "Choose life," we read a few verses later (Deut 30.19), "for he, God, is your life" (v. 20).

3.5 No prophet like Moses

At the end, Moses once again speaks, to talk about the time after his death (Deut 31.1ff). There are two things above all else that he must see to. One is his own succession. Joshua is already prepared for this (vv. 3, 7f, 14f, 23; cf. Num 27.12-23) [→73]. But there can be no true successor, and there does not have to be one, for Moses' all-important life's task is now completed: he has presented Israel with the divine Torah in its full abundance and in all its details. And so the other thing that remains to be done is to record the Torah in writing. Moses himself takes up this task (v. 9) and thereby creates the "Book of the Torah" (v. 26), which can later be called the "Book of the Torah of Moses" (Josh 8.31 etc.). It is to be regularly read in public (Deut 31.10-13) and it is to be constantly to hand and before their eyes (cf. Josh 1.8; Ps 1.2) [→98, 319].

In his last words, however, Moses very emphatically warns against not keeping the Torah, indeed he says in advance that Israel will break the covenant that God has concluded with it, and that God will punish it for this (Deut 31.16-18). This is developed in great detail in a song that Moses is to write down, like the Torah, and which the Israelites are to learn (31.19-22; 32.1-44). The song first describes Israel's guilt (32.15-21) and the consequences of the divine punishment (vv. 22ff), until in a sudden turnabout, we read: "For the LORD will vindicate his people, and have compassion on his servants" (v. 36). Now God's wrath is turned against the foreign gods, which are not gods: "I, even I am he, and there is no god beside me." And so "I wound and I heal" (v. 39). So even in this depiction of the forthcoming history of Israel's distress, the mercy of God and his faithfulness to his covenant has the last word.

The song is followed by a second poetic text, a "blessing" over the tribes of Israel (33.1-29), comparable with the words of Jacob over his sons in Gen 49 [→31]. Unlike the song in ch. 32, the blessing of the tribes is not introduced as a word of God but as Moses' own words. So they form a sort of testament, which closes with the words: "Blessed are you, O Israel! Who is like you, a people saved by the LORD?" (v. 29). So at the end the song of praise about Israel's special position as the people of God dominates, as was already revealed in the introduction to Deuteronomy, especially in ch. 4 [→74], though this time in different terminology.

Moses was not permitted to enter the land of promise to which he had led Israel. In Deut 3.23-27 it is recorded that he besought God to let him go over and see the land, but God rejected this abruptly and categorically. The reason for this strange prohibition remains unclear to the reader. In Num 20.12 [→70] the prohibition is pronounced in a short sentence with the justification, "because you (Moses and Aaron) did not believe in me, to sanctify me in the eyes of the people of Israel." In what the unbelief consisted is not expressly said. Perhaps in that Moses struck the rock with his stick, twice in fact (v. 11), instead of "speaking" with him, as God had told him to do (v. 8)? In any case, this scene is brought to mind once again at the "waters of discord" (Deut 32.51). Then God shows Moses the whole land from Mount Nebo, from the north to the south, which he now wants to give to Israel as the fulfillment of his promise: "This is the land of which I swore to Abraham, to Isaac and to Jacob, 'I will give it to your descendants'" (34.4; Gen 12.7 etc.) [→22]. This closes the circle from God's first speech to Abraham to the last words to Moses, from the beginning of the story of Israel's election to its fulfillment in the giving of the land.

Moses dies and God buries him. His grave remains unknown to people (Deut 34.5f). The last word about him reads: "And there has not arisen a prophet since in Israel like Moses, whom the LORD knew face to face" (v. 10). This emphasizes once again, in conclusion and summary, Moses' unique position. At the moment of his call he had already been placed in a quite unique relationship with God (Ex 3.7–

4.17) [→**39**]. God had "appeared" to him and had promised him, "I will be with you" (Ex 3.12) as with the patriarchs; here already he had spoken to him "face to face" (cf. Ex 33.11; cf. Num 12.8: "from mouth to mouth") [→**51**], God had "sent" him like a prophet (3.10) [→**40**], and Moses introduced his speeches like a prophet: "Thus says the LORD" (4.22; 5.1 etc.). God had announced his name, Yhwh, to him (3.14f; 6.2f), which was to be and remain his name through all generations. It was Moses to whom God first said: "I will take you for my people, and I will be your God" (Ex 6.7), thereby creating the two-way covenant relationship with Israel. Moses is in many regards the "mediator" who stands in between, who represents and mediates in two directions: between God and Israel and between Israel and God; between Israel and Pharaoh and between God and Pharaoh. Above all Moses lets his mediator position between Israel and God become a figure without analogy in the history of biblical Israel. He as it were tips out the divine anger over Israel when he smashes the tablets of the law and destroys the "Golden Calf" (Ex 32.19f) [→**62**]. But at the same time he acts as the petitioner for his people before God and literally wrestles with God for the existence of Israel (Ex 32.11-14, 30-34; Num 14.10-20) [→**70**]. And so he is called by the title of honor, "Servant of Yhwh" (*'ebed yhwh*) (Deut 34.5), to whom the whole household of his Lord is entrusted (Num 12.7). And besides all this he gave Israel the Torah.

But why is Moses once again emphatically called "prophet"? And why is he so unambiguously raised above all the other prophets? This sentence at the end of Deuteronomy was formulated at a time when Israel had already had centuries of experience with prophets. Moses is now brought into comparison with them, or more precisely: they are brought into comparison with him. "No prophet like Moses" [→**§17**]; this leaves the prophets their prophetic dignity, but it formulates a standard against which they are to be measured. As to what this standard is there can be no doubt at the end of Deuteronomy: the Torah. The reception and passing-on of the Torah by Moses remain unique and unrepeatable. And they remain prior and superior to all prophecy.

This heavy emphasis on the special place of the "prophet" Moses at the end of the first part of the canon, the Torah, is given its decisive accent by the fact that immediately after it follows the second part of the canon, the "prophets." They are now placed after it in the sequence and at the same time ordered with it and under it. The prophets themselves do not have a Torah to proclaim like Moses. But God will "put my words in his mouth, and he shall speak to them all that I command him" (Deut 18.18; cf. Jer 1.9, 7) [→**82, 204**]. The prophets speak in the name of God when they are ordered to do so by God and pass on what he has commissioned them to pass on (Deut 18.20). But what they say will always be classed as, and subordinated to, the Torah that Moses alone proclaimed. The last sentences of the canon of the prophets reflect these statements about the classification of "law and prophets": "Remember the law of my servant Moses, the statutes and ordinances that I commanded him at Horeb for all Israel" (Mal 3.22 [4.4] [→**313**]; cf. Blenkinsopp 1977, 120ff). This remains the first task of the prophets. It is, however, linked to the other one, which is expressed in the eschatological hope [→**§22**] and finds its personification in the figure of Elijah: "Behold I will send you Elijah the prophet before the great and terrible day of the LORD comes" (3.23 [4.5]).

4. The Pentateuch as the Founding Document of Israel

The Pentateuch, "the Torah," forms the basis and the core of the canon of the Hebrew Bible. No other part of the biblical canon contains central statements of Israel's religious self-understanding in such abundance and in such concentration. No other part, furthermore, has been edited and shaped in such an intensive and varied way. On account of this background history the Pentateuch shows, in a constantly surprising way, two things: inner tensions and even opposing viewpoints, and at the same time a great unity and self-containedness (cf. Patrick 1995).

The Pentateuch is the part of the Hebrew Bible that reached its final canonical form earliest. This shows the great significance that is attached to the collection and compositional shaping of the traditions contained in it. At the same time the Pentateuch also has fundamental significance for the other parts of the canon of the Hebrew Bible. Most of the other books would not be fully understandable without knowledge of the Pentateuch, to which they frequently refer, directly or indirectly.

But above all the Pentateuch contains the account of the decisive foundations of Israel's existence: the election of Israel by the one God, the promise of the land, the liberation from Egyptian servitude, the establishment of the cult, and the giving of the Torah. The Pentateuch describes the path taken by Israel until, step by step, it reaches the point at which life in the promised land can begin, on the basis of these foundations laid in the Pentateuch. This path taken by Israel, however, is placed in a greater, comprehensive framework: the Pentateuch begins with the creation of the world and of the whole of humanity. The elect Israel stands firmly in the center of the texts that follow; but it is not alone in the world, indeed it is only "the fewest of all peoples" (Deut 7.7) [→**78**]. This is impressively brought to expression in the primordial history through the great framework in which Israel does not in the first instance even appear. At the same time another decisive point is unmistakably brought out: God is *one*. Whatever kinds of questions and doubts and claims to the contrary may emerge in the course of the history of Israel, the fact that God is *one* and that besides him there are no other gods and that this one created the whole world and humanity, is pronounced incontrovertibly in the first sentence of the Hebrew Bible as the basis and precondition for everything that will follow [→**13**]: "In the beginning God created the heavens and the earth." For God there is no beginning, and besides God there is no creator.

The dramatic events of the primordial history make us aware of another decisive precondition of the life of Israel and the whole of humanity: humans do not live in a disruption-free creation. The first human couple already infringed God's rules, and then sin grew and became prevalent, so that God decided to destroy creation again. Only his own "regret" stopped him destroying them altogether, so that finally he concluded a covenant with the only one who found grace in his eyes, Noah, promising him that despite the continuing sinfulness of humanity he would never again threaten creation with annihilation (Gen 9) [→**18**]. What will be repeated later in the history of God's dealings with Israel (cf. Ex 32–34) [→**61**] is presented here already in advance: sinful humanity lives, as Israel also does, only on the basis of the mercy of God, which he has promised in a covenant agreement.

Against this background, Abraham is called. With him the first period of Israel's history begins. The term "election" is not expressly applied to Abraham here (as in Neh 9.7) [→**399**]; but in Deuteronomy the reason for the election of Israel is given as God's love for the fathers (Deut 4.37; 7.6-8) [→**77**]. So this first epoch is marked by the calling and election of Israel's ancestor out of the world of nations as a whole. To some degree, what happened with Noah after the flood is repeated here again: God begins a new chapter in his history with humanity with an individual. From now on this small episode in the history of humanity is the central topic of the texts of the Hebrew Bible. But the nations always remain in view, and they will have a share in the blessing that Abraham receives from God (Gen 12.3) [→**20**].

For the reader of this story of Israel's origins, it is never in doubt for a moment that the God who calls and leads Abraham is none other than the *one* the text has been talking about from the creation of the world onwards. Later in Deuteronomy this connection is spelt out explicitly: "To the LORD your God belong the heavens, even the highest heavens, the earth and everything in it. Yet the LORD set his affection on your forefathers and loved them, and he chose you, their descendants, above all the nations, as it is today" (Deut 10.14f). So this first constitutive element of the existence of Israel is already set out in God's first address to Abraham: the *one* God has chosen Israel.

The second element too becomes into view right at the beginning: the promise of the land. This one does, however, appear in a very much less unambiguous form than the first. Already in the first words God addresses to Abraham, he speaks of the "land that I will show you" (Gen 12.1) [→**21**]. But just a little later, when Abraham crosses this land for the first time, the promise says: "To your descendants I will give this land" (v. 7). Occasionally the wording is also more direct: "I will give it to you" (13.17), but in the whole of the story of the patriarchs it remains clear that the land does not yet belong to the fathers. With the Cave of Machpelah near Hebron, Abraham acquires, as it were on installment, a small piece of the land as his own property and as a symbolic tomb for his wife Sarah (ch. 23) [→**24**] and later also for himself (25.9f), and afterwards also for other members of the family (49.31). But the fathers remain strangers in this land, and finally they leave it for an uncertain future.

But the theme of the promised land remains present and immediately comes back into the foreground when God once again calls an individual to continue his history with Israel: Moses. At first the talk is only of a "good and broad land, a land flowing with milk and honey," to which God intends to lead the Israelites, out of forced labor in Egypt (Ex 3.8). But then in a solemn divine speech the connection with the fathers is restored, with whom God has "established a covenant," "to give them the land of Canaan, the land in which they dwelt as sojourners" (6.4) [→**41**]. From the moment of the departure from Egypt on, the land is then constantly present as the goal of the simply endless wanderings through the wilderness. But it remains an unattained goal, and at the conclusion of the narrative of the Pentateuch Moses is allowed to see it only from the other side of the Jordan before he dies (Deut 34.1-5) [→**87**]. The story from Abraham to Moses narrated in the Pentateuch is thus a story of the unfulfilled promise of the land. But no other theme dominates and characterizes this epoch in the story as this one does.

The path to the promised land is interrupted by the stay on Sinai. It is here that the essential equipment for its religious and social life is placed in Israel's hands. Here Israel is "with God" (cf. Ex 19.4) [→**52**], and God takes up residence in the midst of Israel; for—we read here— he has led Israel out of Egypt specifically "that I might dwell among them" (Ex 29.46). God now lives in a tent in the middle of the camp of the wandering people. Here the structures of the later communal life in the land are as it were pre-formed and practiced in the smallest of spaces and in the most extreme concentration: the sacrifices with their center in the annual "great day of atonement" [→**67**] and multiple forms of "sanctification" and the rejection and removal of impurity, which might disturb the sanctity of the nation massed around the dwelling-place of God. It will be an ideal time that will never return, when Israel is in the promised land. In this ideal shape the forms of cultic life can be set out pure and untroubled by the realities of everyday life.

The instructions about the establishment of the cult and the preservation of purity are part of the Torah that Israel receives from God on Sinai through the mouth of Moses. But the Torah contains much more than this, namely an abundance of regulations for human coexistence under the real circumstances of life in the land. On Sinai Israel receives the foundational Ten Commandments [→**53, 77**], which it hears direct from the mouth of God, and then the further commandments and laws which Moses receives from God and passes on to Israel. After the difficult path through the wilderness and after the forty-year stay in the wilderness, for which Israel itself is to blame, Moses gives the Israelites further commandments to complete, supplement, and also reformulate the Torah [→**79**]. It is to this last great proclamation of the Torah that the Pentateuch ultimately is leading. Through this proclamation the Pentateuch itself as a whole becomes Torah.

With Deuteronomy, the figure of Moses too stands dominant and influential at the end of the Pentateuch. In retrospect it is clear that he is altogether the dominant figure of the Pentateuch. Four of the five books of the Pentateuch are concerned with him. Two other figures stand out before him: Noah and Abraham [→**17, 21**]. But what distinguishes Moses from these two is above all that not only is he the only one who has dealings with God, but that he stands between God and Israel. He leads the people, he teaches them, he represents them as petitioner before God and he gives them the Torah [→**86**]. From Israel's point of view he is the first leader figure—a ruler figure, but of a rule without an institutionalized force. This is one of the decisive messages of the Moses tradition to Israelite posterity: that Israel can only really be led by a person who stands in direct contact with God and who receives from this relationship the instructions for the leading of this people, of whose special position among the nations Deuteronomy has spoken in such elevated terms. Moses is more than a prophet, but he is also more than all those who will lead the people after him: more than Joshua, the judges, Samuel and the kings. He sets standards by which those who come after him must be measured, but which are in fact matched by none of them.

§ 2

The "Former Prophets"

Preliminary considerations

In Jewish tradition the books that follow the Torah are given the general term "Prophets." The first reason for this is that the authors of the books of Joshua to Kings were viewed as prophets: Joshua, Samuel, also considered to be the author of the book of Judges, and Jeremiah as author of the books of Kings.

The title "Former Prophets" (*nᵉbî'îm ri'šonîm*) [→In 174] distinguishes these books from the "Latter Prophets" (*nᵉbî'îm 'aḥᵃrônîm*), Isaiah to Malachi. The books of the "Former Prophets" do indeed contain many kinds of reports of the work of prophets; unlike the "Latter Prophets," however, these are given in the context of more detailed reports, while in the "Latter Prophets" the prophetic words themselves are the main focus of interest.

In the Christian tradition, following the Septuagint, the books of the "Former Prophets" are counted among the "Historical Books." The book of Ruth, however, is inserted after the book of Judges, while in the Hebrew canon it is found in the last section under the "Writings." The books of the "Former Prophets" are largely marked by "deuteronomistic" language and theology, which comes to the fore especially in structuring elements of the account. In this regard they have a clear connection with the Pentateuch.

Noth (1943) proposed the thesis of a "Deuteronomistic History" [→In 194] which included the book of Deuteronomy and extended as far as the end of 2 Kings. He did not regard Deuteronomy as part of the Pentateuch, so that the latter shrank to a "Tetrateuch." By contrast, the older view, generally dominant since Wellhausen, took Joshua, the first book of the "Former Prophets," as belonging with the preceding five books and spoke of a "Hexateuch" (so also von Rad 1938).

The two views reflect different conclusions from the fact that in many regards the Pentateuch is connected with the subsequent books, which describe the progress of the history that begins in the Pentateuch (cf. Zenger *et al.* 1995, 34ff). In both cases, however, the clearly recognizable canonical shape of the Pentateuch as a unity was not sufficiently taken into account; more recent studies have shown this clearly once again (cf. Blum 1990, Blenkinsopp 1992, Crüsemann 1992).

1. Israel without Moses

1.1 From Moses to Samuel (an overview)

With the death of Moses the first, fundamental epoch in Israel's history comes to an end. The last sentences of Deuteronomy have left us with the question who or what will come after Moses. If one views the books of the "Former Prophets" from this angle, three phases stand out; they differ in length and vary greatly in character.

First, Joshua appears as the direct successor of Moses (Josh 1.1-9; cf. Deut 34.9). He had been prepared for this long before (Num 27.15-23). It is emphasized very clearly, however, that as Moses' successor he does not have the same standing as him. In Josh 1.1 Moses is given the title of honor "Servant of YHWH," while Joshua is called the "servant of Moses." (On Josh 24.29 see below [→**98**].) God says to Joshua that he will be with him as he was with Moses (Josh 1.5). But the important thing is that Joshua is to act entirely in accordance with the Torah that Moses has laid upon him (v. 7) and that he is to keep "this book of the Torah" [→**§10**] before his eyes and on his lips (v. 8). So Joshua is the executor of the Torah given by Moses.

He is still to a much greater degree a successor to Moses than any of the leader and ruler figures that would come after him. He is, albeit to a lesser degree, a charismatic leader, one directly appointed by God. The special thing about him is that the leadership charisma has been transferred to him from Moses by the laying-on of hands (Num 27.18-23; Deut 34.9) [→**95**]. He is often also the recipient of a direct word from God (Josh 1.1; 3,7; 4.1 etc.). But his difference from Moses is always clear in these instances: there is never a conversation between Joshua and God. Nor does Joshua act as a petitioner but prays together with the Elders in a crisis situation (7.6-9) [→**99**]. The most striking thing is the difference with regard to the Torah: God gave it by the mouth of Moses and Moses wrote it down personally. Joshua has this book in front of him, and it is entirely beyond his area of competency to change anything or add anything.

So this first phase is marked by a leadership figure who stands expressly in the Mosaic succession. It is Joshua's job to bring to a conclusion the outstanding parts of the divine promises given through Moses: the accession of the land of Canaan. Joshua is to take the land in line with the divine instructions and distribute it among the Israelite tribes. With the fulfillment of this task his mission is ended. It only remains for him to admonish the Israelites to keep the Torah (chs. 23f). We hear nothing of a succession. In particular we are not told that Joshua (or the author of the book of Joshua) raised this question. Joshua dies (24.29), and this brings the first stage after Moses to an end. Looking back, it is rooted firmly in the Mosaic tradition. It has no perspective on the future.

In the second phase, then, there is nothing for it to connect to. Israel is without a leader, "acephalous," one might say (see below). But to begin with, this does not seem to be a problem, for Joshua has admonished the Israelites as a whole to "serve the LORD," and they have ceremonially agreed to do so (Josh 24.16-24). Thus the history of the time of Joshua ends on a positive note: the generation of Joshua kept its promise (24.31). But then the decisive break occurs: the generation after Joshua "did not know the LORD, or the work which he had done for Israel" (Judg 2.10) [→100]. The consequence was that the Israelites "served the Baals; and they forsook the LORD, the God of their fathers, who had brought them out of the land of Egypt" (vv. 11f). A story begins that is determined by a turning away from YHWH [→§20], oppression of the Israelites by enemy peoples as a result of YHWH's anger, help from the saving figures ("judges") called by God, and recurrent apostasy.

In the account in the book of Judges, this chapter in the story is viewed entirely from the point of view of Israel's relationship with YHWH and is marked by great instability. In particular, Israel has no steady leadership, since the "judges" (Judg 3.9, 15) raised up by God are only "saviors" sent on an *ad hoc* basis. After their death the situation reverts to that which pertained after the death of Joshua: the Israelites do "what was evil in the sight of the LORD" (3.7, 12; 4.1 etc.), i.e. they "serve other gods."

The Judges account, however, is oriented less in a backward direction and rather more in a forward direction, with regard to the next phase. So at the end we read: "In those days there was no king in Israel;

every man did what was right in his own eyes" (21.25; cf. 17.6) [→**103**]. In retrospect the lack of order in this period looks little short of anarchic. There is no authority to say what is right and just, and to ensure that this is maintained. From a later point of view, this would only be possible for a king.

From a historical point of view the "Judges period" reflects the earliest recognizable epoch in the history of Israel. At this time the individual tribes largely led their own lives and joined forces under a common leadership, appointed *ad hoc* in times of threat. This can be called a "segmentary society" without a constant leadership, and so "acephalous" (cf. Crüsemann 1978, 203; Donner 1984/86, 153f, 2176f; whether the list of the "minor judges" in Judg 10.1-5; 23.7-15 permits us to conclude that there was a continuous office of law-enforcement or magistracy is disputed). So for later generations it was appropriate to look back from the point of view of the monarchic period. The time of Moses and Joshua however belongs to the realm of a far earlier, ideal era.

The conclusion of the book of Judges already looks forward to the following phase: the period of the monarchy. But the transition that leads to it is extremely problematic. First of all a figure appears who links up with earlier traditions much more than announcing something new: Samuel. He grows up in Shiloh, where he "serves YHWH" (1 Sam 2.11, 18) [→**103**]; he is never described as a priest, however. Instead we find the title "prophet" (3.20) [→**§17**], and an account is given of a direct divine commission (3.1-14, cf. v. 21); further, we read that Samuel "judged" Israel (7.6, 15-17). So in the picture we are given of Samuel various features of a quite unusual function of religious leadership in Israel are united. The "elders of Israel" lay on him their wish to appoint a king "like all the nations" (8.5). In the divine answer the problems associated with this demand are brought into sharp focus: the desire for a king means that God is no longer to be king over Israel. Earlier Gideon, one of the "judges" of Israel, had used similar words to express the problem when a corresponding demand was made of him: "I will not rule over you, and my son will not rule over you; the LORD will rule over you" (Judg 8.23).

Nonetheless God, and Samuel as his representative, gives his permission for the appointment of a king. Thus begins the third phase [→**§13**] "after Moses." Once again it shows a connection with the preceding phase, in that Saul appears like one of the "judges" and gains a military victory for Israel (1 Sam 11.1-11). But then, after Saul's anointing by Samuel and his appointment as the first king of Israel,

deep-seated conflicts arise between the two of them [→**105**] (esp. 1 Sam
13.7b-14; 15.10-30).

Fundamentally differing concepts of rulership in Israel are reflected
in this, which have left traces in these texts (cf. Crüsemann 1978). Here
the prophet Samuel retains control as the representative of the culticly
established view of the exclusive rule of YHWH. In the next stage under
the kingship of David the balance shifts. The prophets become "court
prophets," who, though they criticize the king in the name of God, are
no longer able to question his power (cf. e.g. 2 Sam 12) [→**112**].

Thus it is only after an interim period lasting many generations that
Israel once again has a continuous leadership. But this leadership is
quite different from that of Moses. The direct connection between the
king and God is missing, and the authority of the proclamation of the
Torah is missing. So it seems almost inescapable that right from the
beginning of the monarchy a religious opposition should arise—an
inspecting authority, as it were: the prophets. Thus with the beginning
of the monarchy a time of prophecy also arises, which will accompany
the monarchy more or less continuously to its end.

1.2 I will be with you as I was with Moses

"Moses my servant is dead." With these words a new epoch in the
history of Israel begins (Josh 1.2) [→*In* **175**]. Everything that now follows is history "after Moses." No replacement of Moses can be his
equal (Deut 34.10) [→**87**]. In the first words of the book of Joshua this
comes very pointedly to expression: Moses is the "servant" (*'ebed*) of
God—a title of honor that is accorded only to very few outstanding
people (cf. previously Num 12.7) [→**51**]. Joshua is his "helper"
(*mᵉšārēt*)—also a title of honor, but with reference to Moses, whose
"helper" Joshua was [→**59**], long before (Ex 24.13; 33.11; Num 11.28).
It is not until Josh 24.29 (=Judg 2.8) that Joshua is, as it were, post-
humously awarded the title of "servant of YHWH." But he merely
continued Moses' work and did not add anything of his own.

His most important duty is to lead Israel into the land that God has
promised it. Accompanying him is the divine promise: "as I was with
Moses, so I will be with you" (Josh 1.5). Here the promise to Moses,
"I will be with you" (Ex 3.12) [→**40**] is repeated verbatim. Moses is in
fact almost "omnipresent" in the book of Joshua. Joshua is to "do
according to all the law which Moses my servant commanded you"

(Josh 1.7), as we read right at the beginning. And after the successful occupation of the land, we are told: "As the LORD had commanded Moses his servant, so Moses commanded Joshua, and so Joshua did; he left nothing undone of all that the LORD had commanded Moses" (11.15). Here the whole thing is anchored further back in God's commission to Moses. The Israelites too see and accept this line from Moses to Joshua: "Just as we obeyed Moses in all things, so we will obey you; only may the LORD your God be with you, as he was with Moses!" (1.17). Through the successful execution of Moses' tasks Joshua is "exalted" by God (14.4a); but even this is immediately an occasion for comparison with Moses: "and they stood in awe of him, as they had stood in awe of Moses, all the days of his life" (v. 14b). We hear echoes of the reaction of the people after their rescue at the Reed Sea: "and the people feared the LORD; and they believed in the LORD and in his servant Moses" (Ex 14.31) [→46].

This echo is no coincidence. Just as it was through God's deed that Israel was saved at the Reed Sea, so too in the final analysis it is always God himself, time and again, who gives Israel the victory, giving it the land that he has promised it. As a result many events almost have the character of cultic processions: such as the first great event, the procession through the Jordan headed by the priests bearing the "Ark of the Covenant" (Josh 3f); and then the taking of the city of Jericho, in which, in a seven-fold ceremonial procession, once again with the ark in front, the rams' horns are blown and finally the walls are made to collapse (ch. 6).

An example of divine aid hurrying ahead is presented in the prehistory of the conquest of Jericho [→§20]. The Canaanite prostitute Rahab declares to the Israelite scouts whom she has hidden in her house her knowledge that "the LORD has given you the land," mentioning also the miraculous exodus of the Israelites from Egypt and the victory over kings Sihon and Og, and assuring them that the inhabitants of the land are in a state of great fear (Josh 2.9-11). The latter is also the decisive message which the scouts pass on when they return (v. 24).

But there is also a setback. The disloyalty with regard to parts of the booty from the sacking of Jericho that should have been dedicated to God (cf. Josh 6.19, 24) leads to a heavy defeat for Israel when they attempt to take the city of Ai (7.1-5). This "theft of Achan" is seen as a transgression of the covenant (vv. 11, 15), so that God withdraws his promise to be with Israel (v. 12), until this sin has been atoned for by the death of the person responsible. Visible underneath this are notions and rules with cultic-magical dimensions, which we only partially understand. The emphasis here, however, lies on the demand of obedience, of keeping the rules that are constitutive for the "covenant" between YHWH and Israel. The fulfillment of the promise given by God relating to the land can be endangered by a breach of the covenant on the part of Israel.

So the report of this episode in the context of the otherwise so successful completion of the occupation of the land also contains an admonition and warning not to break the covenant. After Israel has removed this "scandal" (v. 15) from its midst (vv. 24-26) it can take the next steps in the occupation of the land promised by God (8.1-29).

After Joshua has taken the whole land, "just as the LORD said to Moses," he divides it as inheritance (*naḥ°lāh*) among the tribes (Josh 11.23). When this is completed, the circle is closed once again: "Thus the LORD gave to Israel all the land which he swore to give to their fathers; and having taken possession of it, they settled there" (21.43). So here the line is drawn from the beginnings of the story of God's dealings with Israel through to the fulfillment of the promise that was already made at that time (cf. Gen 12.7) [→**22**]. In his farewell speech Joshua once again binds the Israelites to "the book of the Torah of Moses" (23.6) and thus reverts to the role of the successor. But he himself has no successor. Israel as a whole is now charged with observance of the Law (cf. Schäfer-Lichtenberger 1995, 217f). Looking to the future, the danger of deviation from the Torah and the consequences of this loom large (23.12f, 15f).

1.3 Everyone did what was right in his eyes

The texts of the book of Judges can be read from very divergent points of view [→**In 177**]. Its title, *šofṭîm*, "Judges," comes from the individual figures that dominate its account. These are the savior figures, sent time and again by God when Israel is in dire straits, and who in the introductory passage Judg 2.11-19 are referred to summarily as "judges" (vv. 16-19). At other points they are referred to as "saviors" (*môšî°* 3.9, 15), or it is said that they "saved Israel" (3.31; 6.14f etc.). So the book of Judges is a book of the repeatedly experienced rescue of Israel by men and women sent by God.

But the introduction also reports why Israel so frequently finds itself in times of oppression. It is the time after the death of Joshua, i.e. after the definitive end of the time of Moses, which has been extended by one generation by his successor Joshua. The Israelites are now without political and spiritual leadership, and the next generation no longer knows about all that God had done for Israel; in fact, they "did not know the LORD" (2.10).

A new problem arises: the Israelites now live in the direct vicinity of other nations who worship other gods. There is an obvious temptation to join in with the cult of these nations (Judg 2.12). Already when the law was given on Sinai this danger was mentioned and a warning given of it (Ex 23.23f) [→56]. In particular the close connection with other nations in the form of treaties and intermarriage is regarded as dangerous and is therefore forbidden (Ex 23.32; 34.12f). Instead, the cultic sites of the peoples that are conquered or driven away must be destroyed and removed. In Moses' farewell speech too, the book of Deuteronomy, this warning appears repeatedly (Deut 7.1-5 etc.) [→78] and finally at the beginning of the book of Judges it is proclaimed by a "messenger (or: angel) of YHWH" (Judg 2.1-5).

Immediately after this we read: "the people of Israel did what was evil in the sight of the LORD" (Judg 2.11). So it had come to that, the Israelites were worshiping the gods of the surrounding nations [→§20], especially Baal, the chief god of the Canaanite pantheon. These gods are often referred to together as "Baals" (*bᵉ'ālîm*, 2.11), or female deities are mentioned alongside Baal, such as Astarte (2.13) and Asherah (3.7), both also in the plural. So here it is less a matter of the worship of particular individual deities and more the fundamental problem of participation in Canaanite cults. From this point of view the period of the judges is a time of perpetual apostasy from Yhwh.

These two aspects are linked together in a rather stereotypical sequence: the Israelites worship strange gods—Yhwh gives them into the hands of an enemy—the Israelites "cry" to Yhwh—Yhwh raises up a savior for them, who rescues them—the land has forty years of rest (e.g. 2.11-19, also 3.7-11 as "exemplary tale" etc.). This scheme shows that the book of Judges is concerned to present these two aspects precisely in their connection to each other: the disobedience and apostasy of Israel and the help of God. The "crying" of Israel for help recalls its earlier crying under the oppression in Egypt (cf. Ex 2.23) [→37]. But now Israel's woes are its own fault. Nonetheless the cry for help leads again and again to Yhwh's intervention. This reminds us of texts in the Pentateuch, which speak of Israel's falling away from Yhwh, of subsequent trouble, which is often cleverly represented as being sent by God himself, and finally of gracious rescue (Lev 26; Deut 4; 28ff etc.) [→68, 76, 86]. In the book of Judges, however, time and again there is a new apostasy, so that Israel's behavior is shown in a negative light through this whole era.

It is essentially their military successes that are reported of the judges. In some cases we read that the "spirit (*rû'ḥ*) of YHWH" came over the persons concerned and made them capable of his deeds (3.10; 6.34; 11.29). On one occasion it is a woman, Deborah, who is called a "prophetess" and a "female judge," who in the name of Yhwh gives Barak the task of leading the fight against the Canaanites (Judg 4). She announces that Yhwh will give the enemy into Barak's hand (vv. 7, 14) and thus into her own hand (v. 9), just as he previously gave the Israelites into the hand of the Canaanite king Jabin (v. 2).

Gideon, finally, has a special position. To begin with he is told of his calling by a "messenger (or: angel) of YHWH" (Judg 6.11-24), the accompanying promise "I will be with you" recalling the call of Moses (Ex 3.12) [→40]. Then in a nocturnal action he destroys his father's altar of Baal and the Asherah belonging to it and with the wood from them presents a sacrifice for Yhwh on a makeshift altar (Judg 6.25-32). This is the only time in the book of Judges that there is a report of Israelite resistance to the cult of Baal. Finally, Gideon is asked by the Israelites to accept a hereditary rule over Israel for himself and his descendants (8.22f). Gideon turns this down with the words: "I will not rule over you, and my son will not rule over you; the LORD will rule over you" (Judg 8.23). Though this speaks of "ruling" (*māšal*) and not of "reigning" (*mālak*), a critical attitude toward the monarchy comes to expression, which is regarded as incompatible with the rule of Yhwh (cf. Crüsemann 1978, 42-54). This attitude is visible once again at the beginning of the book of 1 Samuel.

In all, the book of Judges presents the picture of a somewhat chaotic, even anarchic period. This is reinforced by the turbulent narratives of Samson (Judg 13–16) and the reports of internal Israelite fighting (chs. 19–21). The note at the end of the book marks the situation at the threshold of the establishment of the monarchy: "In those days there was no king in Israel; every man did what was right in his own eyes" (21.25; cf. 17.6).

1.4 Called to be a prophet

The birth narrative in 1 Sam 1 signals a new beginning [→*In* **180**]. For the reader this a direct answer to the concluding sentence of the book of Judges (cf. 1991c). The birth of the boy on the basis of an answer to prayer and his dedication to the sanctuary are considerably reinforced in the literary composition by the Psalm-like prayer of Hannah (2.1-10), which goes far beyond the framework of her personal fate. The psalm praises God's power over his enemies and his help for the weak and ends with the request that God will give his king strength and will "exalt the power of his anointed" (v. 10). So we have been given the decisive key terms which the text will be concerned with in what follows. The king, who according to the last words of the book of Judges, is imminently expected, will be anointed by Samuel. (Because of this prediction, in Jewish tradition Hannah is regarded as one of the seven female prophets in the Hebrew Bible; cf. *Megilla* 14a.)

At the same time the psalm shows itself to be an important element of the composition of the story of the monarchy, in particular the story of David. For at the end of this historical section (and also at the end of 2 Sam), the notes that ring out in the two psalm-like texts in 2 Sam 22 and 23.1-7 are picked up once again [→**114**]. Here, as there, God is described as a "rock" (1 Sam 2.2; 2 Sam 22.3 etc.; 23.3), his epiphany is depicted in a similar way (1 Sam 2.10; 2 Sam 22.8ff), the motif of exalting and humiliating, of killing and bringing to life is found here as it is there (1 Sam 2.6-8; 2 Sam 22.17-20, 28), and at the end we read in each case of God's blessing and help for the king, the "anointed" (*māšîᵃḥ*, 1 Sam 2.10b; 2 Sam 22.51) [→**§13**], David's name being mentioned in 2 Sam 22. So in retrospect for the reader the significance of this beginning becomes quite clear again.

But first, interest is focused on Samuel himself. The figure of Samuel is not automatically comparable with any of the others that came before or after him. Already the story of his birth and youth sets out the special nature of his beginnings in unusual detail: the detailed account of his mother Hannah's answer to prayer (1.1-20), his dedication to temple service (2.19-28), Hannah's psalm of praise (2.1-10) and the nocturnal receipt of a word from God, which at once makes him the counterpart to the priestly house of Eli (3.1-18). In a summarizing note we then read that all his words carried weight (3.19) and that "all Israel from Dan to Beer-sheba knew that Samuel was established as a prophet of the LORD" (v. 20). This formula recalls Num 12.7 [→**51**], where it is said that Moses is "known" to the whole house of Yhwh. The difference is very clear, because Moses is expressly distinguished from all other prophets in this saying. Nonetheless, here Samuel is deliberately brought into the vicinity of the "prophet" Moses (cf. Ps 99.6). This is underlined once again by the statement that God continued to reveal himself to Samuel through his word in Shiloh (v. 21). So Samuel is not far removed from the picture of the prophet as given in Deut 18.8 [→82]and—in contrast—in 18.22.

But Samuel is "more than a prophet" [→§17]. He is described as having a leadership function with different aspects to it. In the narrative of the loss of the ark in the battle with the Philistines (1 Sam 4–6) Samuel is not mentioned. This silence is clearly in deliberate contrast to the following chapter, in which we read of an impressive victory of the Israelites over the Philistines under Samuel's leadership (7.2-14; cf. ABC V, 956). Here Samuel appears in a role comparable with those of the "great judges," when he gains a victory with God's help [→104]. But before this Samuel has called on the Israelites to remove the foreign gods from their midst, and the Israelites have complied with this. And then Samuel does not fight, but prays (vv. 5, 9). He is thus also comparable with Moses in the role of the petitioner [→§12] (cf. Aurelius 1988, 145). The concluding note (7.15-17) then shows him as a "judge" who gives legal judgments at different places—perhaps comparable with the "minor judges" [→97]. According to 8.1, when he was old, Samuel also appointed his sons as "judges," and v. 3 says that this meant the function of magistracy. So his position comprises more than one of the "offices" mentioned in this period.

In 1 Sam 8, finally, Samuel is finally shown in an undisputed role of leadership. The "elders of Israel" turn to him in a question of Israel's existence and present him with a very fundamental decision: he is to appoint a king "like all the nations" have (8.5). Here Samuel's special standing is again particularly impressive, when he enters into conversation with God, as no one had done since Moses (8.6-9). God's answer seems highly contradictory. On the one hand the wish for a king is sharply criticized, since it is directed not only against the leadership position of Samuel but against that of God himself: "for they have not rejected you, but they have rejected me from being king over them" (v. 7). Indeed, the wish for a king is even presented as an expression of the Israelites having served other gods time and again since they were led out of Egypt (v. 8). On the other hand, God gives Samuel the instruction to comply with the wish in spite of everything, but at the same time to make the negative sides of the monarchy clear to them (v. 9; cf. vv. 11-18).

The same ambivalence is evident in the following chapters. A positive report of the emergence of the monarchy is given in two different narrative versions: in the story of the secret anointing of Saul by Samuel (1 Sam 9.1-10, 16) and in the report of Saul's appointment as king after his victory over the Ammonites (ch. 11). In 10.17-27 and ch. 12 on the other hand the critique of the monarchy is once again dominant, even though it ends once again with the granting of the wish for a king. Samuel, as a positive figure, is again contrasted with the expected negative appearance of the king (12.1-5 in contrast to 8.11-17). He warns the people not to abandon Yhwh and follow the *tōhû*, the "nothing," i.e. other gods (12.21). He will continue to fulfill his role as petitioner for the people in the future too (12.19, 23). So Israel now has its king, "like all the nations," and it has to live with him, for better or for worse: "if you still do wickedly, you shall be swept away, both you and your king" (12.25, cf. v. 15).

1.5 I repent that I have made Saul king

The critical view of the kingship finds confirmation in its first phase. Right at the beginning a conflict arises between Samuel and Saul, which already signals the end of Saul's reign. This conflict also shows very clearly the tensions between political and military interests and necessities of the kingship on the one hand and the cuticly grounded notion of the sole rule of Yhwh on the other. The concrete point of conflict is formed by the presentation of a sacrifice, the time and performance of which Samuel had reserved for himself (1 Sam 13.7b-14; cf. 10.8), which Saul however presents himself, so as to keep his military team together. According to Samuel's words this means disobedience to the command of Yhwh, which has far-reaching consequences. God will not now realize his original intention to "establish" Saul's kingship "forever," but has already selected another man "after his own heart" to reign over Israel (vv. 13f). Who this man is, however, is not yet said.

The conflict is further exacerbated when Saul offends against the instruction given by Samuel that all the booty from the campaign against the Amalekites should be "banished," i.e. destroyed (1 Sam 15). This time there is talk of a veritable reproach of Saul. A word of God comes to Samuel: "I repent that I have made Saul king" (v. 11, cf. v.

35), and later Samuel himself says to Saul: "Because you have rejected the word of the LORD, he has also rejected you from being king" (v. 23b, cf. v. 26). Once again there is mention of the "neighbor" "who is better than you" and to whom God will "give the kingdom of Israel" (v. 28). Saul himself also confesses, finally, that he "obeyed the voice of the people" and thus "transgressed the commandment of the LORD" (15.24). Here a very clear alternative is expressed. The king chosen and appointed by God must not listen to the voice of the people more than the divine word.

In Samuel's speech another alternative is set out. Saul has said—whether honestly or in order to justify himself—that the animals that were not killed in carrying out the ban have been set aside for sacrifice for Yhwh. Samuel answers this with a saying in prophetic-poetic language, the core of which is formed by the sentence: "to obey is better than sacrifice, and to hearken than the fat of rams" (vv. 22f). This is reminiscent of sayings of the "Latter Prophets," e.g. Hos 6.6 [→**269**]. Here it has its function in the conflict between Samuel and Saul: obedience to the divine word is the most important thing; even sacrifices must take second place to this.

Saul's kingship has failed. At the beginning of his rule it was said that the "spirit of God" came upon him and made him capable of his first military successes (1 Sam 11.6). Now we read that the "spirit of YHWH" has left him and that he is afflicted by an "evil spirit from YHWH" (16.14). God has taken his hand off Saul and even turned it against him; he has become his enemy (28.16). So Saul becomes a "tragic" figure in an almost classical sense (cf. Exum 1992). Everything that follows is nothing but Saul's long drawn-out struggle to put off the end of his kingship. The narrator almost puts on his lips the insight that David will become king (24.21). Jonathan too, Saul's potential successor, has to confirm this (23.16-18).

The latter shows that the failure of Saul's kingship does not mean the failure of the divinely condoned establishment of a monarchy [→**§13**] in Israel. God does not "repent" of the establishment of the monarchy, but of appointing Saul as its first representative. At the same time, though his name is not mentioned, attention is directed towards the successor (13.14; 15.28). So this word of the "repenting" or "regret" of God stands in exact parallel to that of the primordial narrative: just as there God regrets having made humanity (Gen 6.6f) [→**17**] but then after the end of the flood guarantees the continuing existence of creation (8.21f; 9.8-17), so he now regrets having appointed Saul as king, but soon afterwards guarantees to the already earmarked successor David the establishment of his dynasty (2 Sam 3.9f; 7.12, 16 etc.; cf. Jeremias 1975/97) [→**113**]. Like humanity after the flood, so now Israel lives in the tense knowledge of the failure and rejection of Saul and at the same time of the divine guarantee for the establishment of David's dynasty.

Finally this conflict also shows that as yet there is no independent kingship. Samuel remains the dominant figure. He appoints Saul, and the latter is accountable to him. The decision about selection and rejection remains with God, and he has his delegated representative, the "prophet" Samuel, pass it on and execute it. Again this shows the unique position of Samuel. Before him there was no one who could decide over the political leadership of Israel with such consummate power. According to 1 Sam 8.4f [→**104**] it was also the opinion of the leading representatives of the tribes of Israel that only Samuel was able to make this decision. However the historical circumstances may be reconstructed in detail (cf. Donner 1984/86, 169-85, [2]193-210; Edelman 1991), it is in any case clear that Samuel has a very special place in the presentation of the biblical account (cf. 1997e). As we have shown, in more than one respect he stands in the succession of Moses. He is described as a prophet (1 Sam 3.20), the echo of Num 12.7 being clear; he approaches God as petitioner for Israel (1 Sam 7.5, 9); he stands in direct conversation with God (8.6-9), and also he does not simply accept God's decisions without contradiction (15.11, 35). Finally, he follows God's command to anoint Saul's successor (16.1ff); but he does not do this without objections (v. 2), as was the case with Moses (Ex 4) and will later be the case with other prophets (Isa 6.5; Jer 1.6 etc.). However, with the last step Samuel now introduces a new era in Israel's history.

2. Israel among kings and prophets
The first period

2.1 Anoint him! He's the one!

The report of the anointing of David (1 Sam 16.1-13) forms the contrasting parallel to the report of the anointing of Saul (9.15–10.8). It starts off with the express remark that God has rejected Saul and chosen a new king (16.1) [→**§13**]. What follows takes place as with Saul: God tells Samuel to anoint the one he has chosen, and indicates this person to him at the decisive moment: "This is he" (9.17; 16.12). As in Saul's case (10.10; 11.6) the Spirit of Yhwh comes upon David (16.13). But this time this comes as the direct consequence of the anointing and also as a permanent gift of the spirit: "from that day forward." In contrast to this we read in the next verse: "the Spirit of the LORD departed from Saul, and an evil spirit from the LORD tormented him" (v. 14).

The first meeting between the two of them occurs under very similar circumstances. David, the gifted young harpist, is called to Saul's court to drive away the evil spirit from Saul when it afflicts him (vv. 15-23). No one other than David himself, however, knows that he has already been secretly designated as Saul's successor. But there is a strong hint in the commendation of David, though the speaker himself does not realize it: "and the LORD is with him" (v. 18).

But David is not yet Saul's successor but his counterpart. Yet the dispute between them is an unfair contest. The reader knows that Saul's time is over and that the future belongs to David. Saul's son Jonathan too, the potential "crown prince," knows it and says so explicitly (23.16-18). Finally, Saul has to confirm it himself (24.21). In so doing he also expresses the essential difference between his own kingship and that of David: David's kingdom will last.

First, however, a very varied story is played out between Saul and David. The reports of this in 1 Sam 17–2 Sam 1 have clearly been put together from disparate traditional material, and they are only interpreted now and again by means of suggestive indications (cf. 1971). After Saul's first failed attempt to "pin David to the wall" with his spear (1 Sam 18.11; cf. 19.9f), a number of comments follow which interpret the conflict from the perspective of God's preference for David, showing at the same time the tragic moment in Saul's fate: "Saul was afraid of David, because the LORD was with him but had departed from Saul" (18.12). In vv. 14-16 this is further reinforced: David was successful in everything he did, because God was with him; Saul was more and more fearful but the whole nation loved David as the successful commander of the army. This is at the same time the cue for a long story of persecution and flight. It is given another special aspect in that Saul's children are on David's side and are helpful to him in his flight: Michal, whom Saul had given David as his wife (18.17-29; 19.11-17), and Jonathan (19.1-7; 20; 23.16-18), whose love for David was "wonderful, passing the love of women" (2 Sam 1.26).

Samuel appears two more times: first in a last meeting with David, who had fled to him (1 Sam 19.18-24). Saul, pursuing David, also turns up, and like his messengers before him flies into a "prophetic" rage. The whole thing leads up to the interpretation of the saying, "Is Saul among the prophets?" and thus proves to be a parallel tradition to 10.10-12. This short anecdotal narrative however also makes it plain that Samuel has disappeared from the story as an active figure following the anointing of David. This becomes even clearer on his second appearance, when in a nocturnal act Saul has the dead spirit of Samuel called up (23.3-25). Here the latter once again repeats the divine judgment of rejection against Saul (vv. 16-19), which Samuel had already pronounced a number of times during his life (esp. 15.11, 23b, 26) [→**106**].

The story of David's flight contains quite varied elements. For one thing, it reports how out of his precarious situation David builds up his own power position as guerrilla leader (1 Sam 21.1-10; 22.1-4; 25) and occasional vassal of the Philistine king Achish of Gath (21.11-16; 27.1-28; 29), sometimes leading campaigns on his own initiative (23.1-5; 27.8-12; 30). His careful planning for the future is evident in the fact that he sends parts of his booty to the inhabitants of the towns in the area of the southern tribe of Judah, thus indebting them to him (cf. 2 Sam 2.1-4). Furthermore, the conflict with Saul leads to ever more dramatic situations. Saul does not even flinch from having the whole priesthood of the Nob sanctuary killed for having supported David (23.6-28). A number of times David escapes only by the skin of his teeth (23.6-28). Twice, though, it is reported that David spares Saul, though he could have killed him (24; 26). Here David is shown in a particularly positive light, because it is not just out of noble sentiments that he spares Saul but above all because he sees in him as king the "anointed (*māšîªḥ*) of YHWH" (24.7, 11; 26.9, 11, 16, 23) [→**§13**]. A quite special element, in addition, is that David constantly inquires of the divine oracle (22.10, 15; 23.2, 4, 9-12; 30.7f; 2 Sam 2.1; 5.18f, 23f).

Saul finally dies in battle against the Philistines and along with him his son Jonathan (1 Sam 31). This seems to clear David's pathway to power. The provisions he has made make it easy for him to establish himself first in Judah. Once again led by the divine oracle (and by his "grand political instincts" [Donner 1984/86, 191, ²217]), in Hebron he has himself anointed king over the "house of Judah" by the "people of Judah" (2 Sam 2.1-4).

Almost incidentally an extremely significant development gets underway: the political separation of North and South. Whether Judah had belonged to Saul's empire is disputed [→**127**]. But certainly for

David there was no separate political entity of "Judah." At this point a new power center comes into being through David's initiative which will later become the religious center for the whole of Israel.

After a brief interlude with the ill-fated kingship of Saul's son Ishbaal (2 Sam 2.8-4, 12), the northern tribes also turn to David.

In the complex passage 5.1-3 we read first that "all the tribes of Israel" come to David in Hebron and emphasize their allegiance to him: "we are your flesh and bone." They recall David's time as Saul's military commander and remind him of a divine message: "the LORD said to you, You shall be shepherd of my people Israel, and you shall be *nāgîd* over Israel." The title *nāgîd* had already been applied to Saul on his anointing by Samuel (1 Sam 9.16; 10.1). On the first conflict between Samuel and Saul Samuel announced that God had appointed a man "after his own heart" as *nāgîd* over his people (13.14), and Abigail too (who is therefore regarded in Jewish tradition [*Megilla* 14a] alongside Hannah as a prophetess) expresses the expectation that God will appoint David as *nāgîd* over Israel (25.30). This tradition is picked up and carried further here by the tribes of Israel. Finally, we then read that the "elders of Israel" come to David in Hebron. There he concludes a treaty with them, and they anoint him king over "Israel" (2 Sam 5.3).

The terminology is not entirely uniform here. In the tradition about Saul Samuel uses the title *nāgîd* at the secret anointing of Saul (1 Sam 9.16; 10.1); after this, in public the talk is regularly of the "king" (10.24; 11.14f). So here *nāgîd* seems to have a more strongly religious tone. In David's case the anointing story is under the rubric of "king" (16.1), though no title is used at the anointing itself (vv. 12f). But in David's case too the title *nāgîd* appears in the above-mentioned texts (13.14; 25.30) in the sense of the designation already applied by God, though David is not yet king. This is also how it is used by the representatives of the tribes of Israel (2 Sam 5.2), while following this at the anointing there is again talk of the "king" (v. 3). In 6.21 and 7.8 too the title *nāgîd* is found in a religious context; on the other hand it is never used as a label for the king in the political sense. (On this cf. Mettinger 1976; Campbell 1986, 47-61; *ThWAT* V, 212ff.)

The term "Israel" now has a double meaning [→**§21**]. It remains the overall term for the nation which understands itself as a whole as the community of the descendants of Jacob/Israel, finding in this both its common identity and its distinction from other peoples. In particular in the area of religious language this aspect of the name is dominant.

But at the same time "Israel" has now become the designation of a kingdom that is clearly distinguished from the kingdom of "Judah" [→**127**]. There is an awareness of this distinction as long as David and following him Solomon reign over both kingdoms in a personal union (cf. e.g. 2 Sam 5.5; 1 Kgs 1.35). After the death of Solomon and the break-up of the personal union (1 Kgs 12) it reappears once again, and in a sharper form.

2.2 Your house and kingdom will be established

David has arrived at the goal of his plans and wishes [→**§13**]. He is king of Judah and king of Israel and thus combines in his person a plenitude of power that has never previously been seen in Israel. In comparison with the beginnings of the kingship under Saul, David's political independence is very clearly in evidence. There is no Samuel-like figure to have an influence on his political decisions. His anointing as king of Judah (2 Sam 2.4) is reported without any religious emphasis, and even the anointing as king of Israel, despite the preceding reminder of the earlier designation as *nāgîd*, is the occasion for a contract in which nothing is said about the religious function of the king (5.3). Nor is there any note about associated sacrifices such as in 1 Sam 11.15, when one might imagine that they would be relevant.

The first thing we are told about David after he has become king of Israel is the occupation of the city of Jerusalem (2 Sam 5.6-9). In retrospect this seems an especially cleverly planned act. David thereby created a capital city independent of the tribes of Judah and Israel, lying furthermore in a central position between the areas of his two kingdoms. Up to that point the small Jebusite town had remained largely untouched by political developments, evidently because of its relative insignificance and unfavorable location for trade, but also because of its strong fortifications (cf. Alt 1925). It now became the center of the empire established by David and soon also the center of Israelite religion [→**§14**]. David gave the conquered "mountain fortress Zion" the name "City of David" (v. 9, cf. v. 7). This gives expression to the fact that this city belonged only to the king and was thus independent of the Israelite tribes.

In the style of the narrative the significance of this step is clearly marked by the short passage 2 Sam 5.10-12, in which religious notes are sounded again: "David became more and more powerful, because the LORD God Almighty was with him" (v. 10). Here earlier statements are recalled, that "the LORD was with him" (1 Sam 16.18; 18.12, 14) [→**108**]. The name Yhwh, linked with the ark, already resounds at this point (see below). After the note about the first important international relations with the king of Tyre and the construction of a palace (v. 11) we then read again: "And David knew that the LORD had established him as king over Israel and had exalted his kingdom for the sake of his people Israel" (v. 12). This again corresponds with an earlier remark, according to which Saul acknowledged that God was with David (1 Sam 18.28). Now David himself recognizes this and he relates it above all to his kingdom, which had just experienced confirmation through the international recognition. At the same time, however, this concluding sentence emphasizes that God has exalted the kingdom "for the sake of his people Israel." The future of David's kingdom, which this sentence already has in mind, is thus closely linked with the future of "Israel."

The next, again well-considered step of David is to bring the "Ark of God" to Jerusalem (2 Sam 6.1-19) [→**§11**]. In the battle with the Philistines it had been brought from its earlier situation in Shiloh and had then been lost to the Philistines. After this it had been sent back by the Philistines and had finally found a temporary resting place in Kiryath-Jearim (1 Sam 4.1–7.1). It seems then to have been more or less forgotten; according to 7.2 it had been standing there for twenty years before Saul was anointed by Samuel. The reader remembers the divine threats against the house of Eli the priest at the ark sanctuary in Shiloh (2.27-36; 3.11-14) and the fate of Eli and his family [→**104**] after the loss of the ark (4.12-18, 19-22). David now collects the ark, associated with so many important traditions, and brings it to Jerusalem. Here the solemn divine name associated with it is mentioned: "Yhwh Zebaot, who is enthroned above the Cherubim" (2 Sam 6.2; cf. 1 Sam 4.4) [→**§15**]. Again a new chapter in the history of Jerusalem begins, which will turn out to have greater consequences than the previous episodes. Jerusalem now becomes the center of the religion of Israel and later indeed the only place where the cultic worship of the God of Israel could be carried out. All this lies still a long way ahead, but the introduction of the ark into Jerusalem was the first step, laying the foundations for further developments.

The narrative marks the situation now reached as a decisive point: "The king was settled in his palace and the LORD had given him rest from all his enemies around him" (2 Sam 7.1). At this point the prophet Nathan appears (vv. 2ff). The presence of a prophet is not specially emphasized here. In 1 Sam 22.5 the prophet Gad had already been briefly mentioned, who gave David the instruction to stay in the land of Judah—certainly a reference to the later significance of Judah for the beginning of David's reign. Now with Nathan another prophet appears and in what follows both repeatedly intervene in events (2 Sam 12; 24 etc.). So here there is a continuity with the story of Samuel and Saul as well as with David's beginnings. The present prophets cannot be simply compared with Samuel [→**103**]; but they are on the spot and they appear with a clear divine authority with regard to the king.

The conversation between David and Nathan (2 Sam 7.1-17) has two interlinked themes. The connecting keyword is "house." David indicates the plan to build a house for the ark of God, which is currently residing in a tent, as he himself has a house made of cedar wood (v. 2). Nathan first gives a courteous answer, which ends with the emphatic "for the LORD is with you" (v. 3). But then he comes back with a detailed divine saying. This appears in the first place to reject David's plan to build a house for the ark and thus for God himself. God has so far never demanded of the Israelites that they should build him a house (vv. 5-7). But then the theme changes and thereby also the meaning of the word "house." With an express address to David (v. 8) Nathan gives a backward look at David's call and leadership hitherto, ending with the sentence: "The LORD declares to you that the LORD himself will establish a house for you" (v. 11b). The "house" is now David's dynasty, which God plans to establish from this point on [→**§13**]. The following section then connects both aspects of the word "house": David's descendant, whose kingdom God will establish, "*he* is the one who will build a house for my name" (v. 13). Only after God has set up the house of David will the next occupant of this house also build a house for God (more precisely: for his name, see below on 1 Kgs 8 [→**129**]). After the establishment of the kingdom and God's presence has been promised (vv. 13b-15), Nathan's speech once again returns to a heavily emphasized promise for the "house" and throne of David, both of which will remain established "forever" ('*ad 'ôlām*) (v. 16).

This "saying of Nathan the wise," as it is commonly termed, is a key text for the account of the time of David in the present context and also for the "royal ideology" which is evident in other texts of the Hebrew Bible. The history of the emergence of this passage and its interrelationship with such texts as Pss 89 and 132 are the subject of lively discussion (cf. Mettinger 1976, 43-63; Waschke 1987). With its concentrated theological statements in this case this text retains its quite special meaning. It recapitulates the story of David, whom God has taken away from "behind the flock" and made a "*nāgîd* over my people, over Israel" [→110]; with whom God has been (cf. 1 Sam 16.18; 2 Sam 5.10 etc.), wherever he went; whose enemies he destroyed; whose name he intends to make great among the great names of the world (vv. 8f). All this, however, occurs not just for David's sake, but for the sake of Israel (v. 10, cf. also previously 5.12). So he has also created peace for David before all his enemies (cf. v. 1) and so he wants to build him a "house" (v. 11). The following story harks back to this founding episode in the Davidic dynasty and of the resulting promise for its continuing existence.

What is striking here is that the initial question regarding the house for God is only once taken up again with reference to the expected son of David (v. 13). On the other hand after the promise to David (v. 11) the word "house" occurs a further seven times in this chapter, in reference to the "house of David." This applies especially to David's great prayer in vv. 18-29, in which he humbly thanks God for the promise of the dynasty and extends this thanks in two respects: in a confession of the unique deity of Yhwh (v. 22) and in praise to God for having liberated Israel, having given it a great name, made it his people and having become its God (vv. 23f; cf. 1995, 34). Here God's promise to David is tied in very closely with God's promises to Israel (cf. also already 5.12; 7.10). In 2 Sam 23.5 and Ps 89.4 [→103, 321], among other places, God's relationship to David is also referred to by the word *b'rît*, "covenant," which makes it an aspect of the divine covenant with Israel (cf. Waschke 1987, 167f).

2.3 From your own household I will bring calamity upon you

The "prophecy of Nathan" in 2 Sam 7 marks the climax of the story of the kingdom of David. At the same time it forms the transition to the period of his life that now follows and his reign, which stands increasingly under a shadow. One can in fact distinguish two fundamentally different periods: "David under the blessing" (2 Sam 2–7) and "David under the curse" (2 Sam 9–24) (Carlson 1964). Both of these are sharply emphasized by the appearance of the prophet Nathan (chs. 7 and 12).

The second period begins with David's double sin: his adultery with Bathsheba and his treacherous removal of her husband Uriah (2 Sam 11). The turning point is hinted at already in the remark: "But the thing David had done displeased the LORD" (v. 27).

Then the prophet Nathan comes on the scene. He had first shown himself—like Samuel—as the bearer of God's confirmation of David's kingship (ch. 7), but now he appears as a sharp critic of the king and as a proclaimer of the divine punishment [→§17]: "You are the man!" (12.7). David confesses: "I have sinned against the LORD" (v. 13). But now everything has changed. The child that has been produced through the adulterous relationship must die (v. 14) and God will bring calamity upon him out of his own household (v. 11). Nonetheless, the promises for David's dynasty which Nathan has previously announced are not revoked. And of David's son Solomon, to whom Bathsheba gives birth after the death of the first child, it is said: "The LORD loved him" (v. 24).

But there now follows a long sequence of narratives about scandals and intrigues in David's family, which are quickly focused on the question of the succession: the firstborn son Amnon rapes his sister (2 Sam 13.1-22); his brother Absalom, evidently the next in line to the throne (nothing more is said of David's second son Kileab [3.3]), has him killed (13.23-37); Absalom has to flee, is pardoned and organizes a rebellion, which forces David to flee from Jerusalem, but ends with Absalom's death (13.38–19.44). Finally the next oldest, Adonijah, attempts to have himself crowned king; but by a well-contrived court intrigue Nathan succeeds in getting David to set up Bathsheba's son Solomon as his successor (1 Kgs 1.1-40). Unlike in Saul's case, despite all this turmoil it is never in doubt that the fights are all contained within the family of David, so that the Davidic dynasty promised by Nathan is never in danger.

All this is, however, related in extremely secular terms. It is only in one single brief note that the author lets it be known that God still has his hand in all of this: he has the good counsel of Ahithophel for the immediate persecution of David thwarted, "in order to bring disaster on Absalom" (17.14) and thereby save David.

So one can say that the "tradition of the Davidic succession" (Rost 1926) is also "in a very marked sense theological historiography," in that it shows "the first functioning of the prophecy of Nathan" (von Rad 1962, 329, cf. von Rad 1944, 37f = 183f). But it leaves visible only the "profane" side of this kingship and it shows it in an extremely realistic way in its endangerment and humiliation. In the picture of David in the subsequent story of the reign and in other sections of the Hebrew Bible the features of the first part of the story of David become clearer again and connect with other elements to effectively produce a "royal ideology" which occasionally contains truly "messianic" aspects [→§13].

A strangely isolated piece is the narrative of David's erection of an altar on the threshing-floor of the Jebusite Araunah in Jerusalem (2 Sam 24). This is embedded in the narrative of a census ordered by David, which is regarded as a sin and punished with a plague, in which the prophet Gad has a decisive role to play. The occasion of the account is the erection of an altar on the precise spot where the angel of pestilence sent by Yhwh stood when Yhwh stopped him (vv. 16, 18ff). Here it is not said how this cultic site relates to the later temple. In 1 Chron 22.1, however, we read the explicit statement that this is to be the place for the temple and the burnt-offering altar. There is evidently an underlying tradition according to which the Israelite temple was erected in Jerusalem on the site of an older Jebusite temple that was converted by Solomon (Rupprecht 1977). In the report of the construction of the temple in 1 Kings 6, however, there is no mention of this background.

2.4 God gave Solomon wisdom and insight

[→*In* 185] In the appointment of the successor we see once again, and to a greater degree, the independent position that the kingdom has achieved during David's reign. The idea of the dynasty has also established itself to such an extent that it is now just a question of which of David's sons will be the one to succeed him. This question is decided, however, among the leading and rival political groups; unlike when David was appointed king, when the representatives of the tribes played a decisive role (2 Sam 2.4; 5.1-3) [→109], the people now have no part in the process. A divine designation does, however, take place as with Saul and David. The reader knows the brief note about the newborn Solomon in 2 Sam 12.24, "The LORD loved him" [→114]; but there is no reference to that at this point. Nathan the prophet appears here only as a skillful champion of Solomon.

Instead, surprisingly another element comes into play. In his farewell speech David warns his son Solomon to observe the "Torah of Moses" (1 Kgs 2.1-4) [→§10]. The texts had not mentioned this since the days of Joshua. The (deuteronomistic) author now makes a connection with the beginnings of Israel "without Moses." He reminds us that since then the Torah of Moses was given to Israel as a guideline and that every instance of rulership in Israel stands in the Mosaic succession. David announces his death with the same words as Joshua did in his day: "I am about to go the way of all the earth" (1 Kgs 2.2; cf. Josh 23.14). Then he continues with words that recall the first divine speech to Joshua: "So be strong, show yourself a man" with the added charge to observe all the statutes and commandments in the Torah of Moses, "so that you may prosper in all you do" (cf. Josh 1.7) [→**98**]. In the charge to follow the Torah, there is an echo of the deuteronomic rules for the king (Deut 17.18-20) [→**82**].

Finally, David recalls the divine promises for his sons given in the "prophecy of Nathan" (1 Kgs 2.4; cf. 2 Sam 7.12-16) [→**104**]. But a conditional point is added which is not found in this form in 2 Sam 7: "*If* your descendants watch how they live ..., you will never fail to have a man on the throne of Israel." Solomon reiterates the same expression in slightly adapted wording later in his "temple dedication prayer" (1 Kgs 8.25, see below [→**121**]) and it reappears, once again with variations and this time in a much more intense form, in Solomon's second dream vision (9.5-9; see below [→**122**]). So right at the beginning of Solomon's reign the warning is displayed that his rule will only be established on the condition that the Torah of Moses is followed exactly. At the same time, retrospectively David is viewed in a different light. During his own reign there was no explicit talk of the Torah. We read only once in a brief comment: "David ensured (literally: did) justice and right for all his people" (2 Sam 8.15). Now David talks to Solomon as if he is someone who has himself fully kept the Torah. This also comes to expression soon afterwards in the dream vision Solomon has, where Solomon says that his father (1 Kgs 3.6) "was faithful to you and righteous and upright in heart" and where God himself then declares that David obeyed God's statutes and commands (v. 14). This picture of David then also underlies the regular assessments of the succeeding kings, all of whom are measured against David; only once do we read the qualification that David did not depart from any of the commandments throughout the whole of his life "except in the case of Uriah the Hittite" (1 Kgs 15.5) [→**128**].

The picture that now follows of the beginning of Solomon's reign is highly ambivalent. First, David continues his speech (1 Kgs 2.5-9) by demanding of Solomon, in an abrupt transition, that in his "wisdom" (vv. 6, 9) he ensure that the gray heads of two men with whom David still has an account open will not be able to go to the grave in peace:

Joab and Shimei. Solomon understands the matter only too well and removes two of his own enemies at the same time: his brother Adonijah and Adonijah's supporter, Abiathar the priest (vv. 13-46). So Solomon's reign begins with some concentrated killing, for which David remains partially responsible.

Then the scene changes, and God appears to Solomon in a dream at night (1 Kgs 3.4-15). This lays the foundation for quite a different picture of Solomon. God grants Solomon a wish, and as a modest, still young and inexperienced ruler Solomon asks for a "listening heart" so as to be able to govern the people, whom he describes when talking to God as "your people" (vv. 8f). God grants him this request and wealth and honor besides, which Solomon had not asked for. He will receive both in such measure as to exalt him above the kings before and after him and also above his contemporaries (vv. 12f).

This provides us with the key terms for what follows. Solomon first demonstrates his wisdom [→§19] as an unconventional judge (1 Kgs 3.16-28), so that all Israel recognizes "that he had wisdom from God" (v. 28). Then another aspect of the "wisdom and understanding" that God has given Solomon is related (5.9-14): Solomon composed a large number of songs and sayings, dealing in particular with topics from various realms of nature. This sort of wisdom is compared with the wisdom of the "sons of the east" and Egypt [→*In* 114], i.e. with the two great cultural centers of the world of the time, and described as greater than all of these. There is an allusion here to the "list science" of the great ancient near eastern cultures which was concerned with the collection and systematic ordering of all known natural phenomena. Emphasized as the special feature of Solomon's wisdom is the fact that he reproduced this knowledge about nature in the form of sayings and songs (cf. Alt 1951). These two texts, which deal with exemplary aspects of Solomon's wisdom, are laid like a framework around further texts in which details of Solomon's administrative system are given and the extent of his area of rule is described (4.1–5.8). Particular emphasis is also placed on how peacefully and contentedly Judah and Israel lived under the rule of Solomon (4.20; 5.4b, 5). The proverbial phrase that everyone is able to sit in safety "under his own vine and fig tree," which is found as an eschatological promise in prophetic texts (Mic 4.4; Zech 3.10) [→**295**], is used here as an expression of the situation current under the rule of Solomon.

2.5 I have built the house for the name of the LORD

Now that Solomon's rule has been established and God has given him "rest on every side" (1 Kgs 5.18[4]), he returns to the point at which his father once was, in the same situation (2 Sam 7.1): he wants to build "a temple for the name of the LORD, his God" (1 Kgs 5.17, 19[3, 5]) [→§11]. He refers to the express declaration in the "prophecy of Nathan" that David's son would build this temple (2 Sam 7.12f; 1 Kgs 5.19[5] [→113]. A wide-ranging report then begins about the construction of the temple and the royal palace as well as the dedication of the temple (1 Kgs 5.15[3]-8.66). The author makes his first theological point when the external building of the temple is completed (6.11-13). God announces his willingness to fulfill the promise given to David: "And I will live among the Israelites and will not abandon my people Israel." But he prefixes this again with a conditional clause, which ties this promise to Solomon's following God's statutes and commands (see above on 2.4 [→116]). A grandly structured chapter on the dedication of the temple follows. At the beginning and the end there is a narrative section: on the bringing of the ark (1 Kgs 8.1-13) and on the concluding sacrificial ceremony and the festival of booths (vv. 62-66). A second, inner framework is formed by two sections in which Solomon turns to the assembled celebrants and "blesses" them, which with the words "blessed be (*bārûk*) the LORD" is followed first by a sort of theological commentary (vv. 14-21) and secondly by a paraenesis (vv. 54-61). At the center of it is an extensive prayer of Solomon (vv. 22-53) [→121]. All parts of this chapter are filled with weighty theological statements, which show clear signs of being related to the theology of Deuteronomy, but which also contain individual elements and are not without mutual tensions. This chapter obviously has great significance not only for the story of Solomon, but also beyond (cf. Long 1984; Nelson 1987).

First we read that Solomon has the "ark of the covenant" brought from the City of David, where it has been standing since its transportation to Jerusalem by David (2 Sam 6) [→112], into the temple and has it set up in the place prepared for it in the Holy of Holies (the *d'bîr*) (1 Kgs 8.1-9). This brings out the continuity with the beginnings of the story of the ark. It is emphasized that in the ark were the two stone tablets put there by Moses on Horeb/Sinai (cf. Deut 10.1-5; cf. Ex 25.21; 40.20) [→70]. (The "only" / "nothing except" in v. 9 may relate to differing traditions such as that given in Heb 9.4, that the ark also contained a gold jar of manna and Aaron's budding staff; however, both of these were to be kept "in front of" the ark of the covenant according to Ex 16.13-34 or Num 17.23-26[7-10].) When the ark has been set up in the Holy of Holies, something happens that occurred previously on Sinai: the "cloud" and in it the "glory (*kābôd*) of YHWH" fills the temple, so that the priests, like Moses cannot enter (1 Kgs 8.10f; cf. Ex 40.34f) [→**66**]. So God demonstratively takes up residence in the temple. So now not only the ark but the temple as a whole stands in continuity with Israel's fundamental encounter with God on Sinai. This was already echoed in the divine word on the completion of the temple building, where we read that God intends to "live among the Israelites" (1 Kgs 6.13)—a verbatim resumption of the divine promise on Sinai (Ex 29.45) [→**64**].

There is also talk of God's residence in 1 Kgs 8.12f. This short passage, often described as the "temple dedication saying," presents special problems.

It appears to be quite isolated in relation to its context. In particular, the Septuagint, however, presents a reading that differs in a number of respects. There the passage is found at another place, namely following 8.53. The introductory formula, which in the MT reads "Then Solomon said," is longer, and there is also a concluding formula: "this is recorded in the Book of Songs." The content of this "song" itself begins in the LXX with a sentence not found in the MT. Literally it says: "The LORD has recognized the sun in the heavens." Wellhausen (1899, 269) suggested that the Greek ἐγνώρισεν should be taken as rendering a Hebrew הבין, but which was a misread הכין, so that the sentence reads: "The sun in the heavens, he, YHWH, created." This reading has been generally accepted, though it is usually translated: "Yhwh has put the sun in the heavens," or similar. This gives an antithetical opposition to the sentence transmitted also in the MT: "YHWH has said that he would dwell in a dark cloud." But the Masoretic text does not contain this opposition.

God wants to live in the "darkness of the cloud" (*ʿărāpel*). Does this mean: in the separated darkness of the Holy of Holies in the temple? This would make sense in the context; but the term is also used of the dark cloud on Sinai "in which God was" (Ex 20.21; Deut 4.11; 5.22) [→**54, 75**] and as an accompanying phenomenon at his heavenly theophany (Ps 18.10 = 2 Sam 22.10; Ps 97.2; cf. *ThWAT* 6.397ff). Solomon's statement in the next verse sets another tone: "I have indeed built a magnificent temple for you, a place for you to dwell for ever" [→**48**]. The temple is the place where God is enthroned as king (cf. Ex 15.17f; Mettinger 1982, 26f, 33ff). So quite different notions of God's residence are juxtaposed here (see also on v. 27).

Solomon now commences a speech to the whole "assembly of Israel" (vv. 14-21), in which he once again reminds them in detail of God's promise to David through Nathan, which has now been fulfilled. Hence Solomon has been able to build the house for the name of God and to give the ark the central place in it. This was also the point of departure in 2 Sam 7 [→**112**]: that David toyed with the idea of creating a home for the ark (v. 2). At that time God's answer was first: "Are you the one to build *me* a house to dwell in?" (v. 5); of David's son and successor it is then said: "he will build a house for my name" (v. 13). The house for the ark is thus a house "for Yhwh"; but already there it is understood as a house "for the name of YHWH." Solomon quotes the divine speech of 2 Sam 7 in a form that is expanded along these lines: "I have not chosen a city in any tribe of Israel to have a temple built for my Name to be there" (1 Kgs 8.16). The language of Deuteronomy is evident here (12.5, 11, 21 etc.; cf. Mettinger 1982, 49f) [→**77**].

An extensive prayer of Solomon follows, which is often referred to as Solomon's "prayer of dedication." In the introduction to this, weighty theological tones are found with statements made also at key points in Deuteronomy (v. 23): there is no God like Yhwh "in heaven above and on the earth below" (cf. Deut 4.39); he is the "keeper of the covenant and favor towards those who continue wholeheartedly in his way" (cf. Deut 7.9) [→**79**]. And then the question: "But will God really dwell on earth?" (v. 27). Here the differences in the conception of God's residence that became visible already in vv. 12f are made explicit. The statement of the "Name of God" gains a quite precise function: all the heavens are unable to contain God—how much less the temple; but God has his "Name" live there, and when people pray at this site God will hear it in his residence in heaven (vv. 28-30).

This also sets out the main concern of Solomon's prayer. The temple is the place where humans pray to God, as individuals (vv. 31f), as the people of Israel (vv. 33-40, 44-51), or even as strangers (vv. 41-43). The occasion for the prayers can be of all kinds: personal guilt (vv. 31f), the distresses and dangers of war (vv. 33f, 40f), natural catastrophes (vv. 35f, 37-40) and finally captivity and exile (vv. 46-51). In exile the Israelites will then pray "towards the land you gave their fathers, towards the city you have chosen and the temple I have built for your Name" (v. 48, cf. v. 44). At the heart of this section (vv. 46-48) we find an impressive interaction between the two verbs *šābāh* "lead away captive" (four times) and *šûb* "turn back" (three times), the

forms of which are partly identical (with the exception of the emphasis): they are carried away and they will turn back in the land to which
they have been transported (Levenson 1982, cf. Long 1984, 103)
[→§9]. The return is not yet in view here, however, for the prayer is
that the exiles will be shown mercy by their conquerors (v. 50). In the
whole prayer the petition to be heard is introduced with the frequently repeated expression "hear from heaven" (vv. 30, 32, 35, 36,
39, 43, 45, 49). Once again it is said that God lives in heaven. So he
can also hear the prayers of those who pray from exile in a distant land
in the direction of the temple.

2.6 He did not act like his father David

After the completion of the construction of the temple and the palace
and the achievement of "all he had desired to do" (1 Kgs 9.1, cf. v.
19), God appears to Solomon "a second time, as he had appeared to
him at Gibeon" (v. 2). The reference back to the first theophany (3.4-
15) [→117] is the decisive point here, for nothing is said about how the
second theophany took place; the reader is again expected to think of
this as a night dream. These two dream visions have a structuring function for the whole story of Solomon (Noth 1968, 195f). The first opens
up the quite positively drawn stage of Solomon's reign, in which his
wisdom and the construction of the temple form the decisive themes.
The divine promises are given a conditional element here, though this
is not specially emphasized: "if you walk in my ways ..." (3.14). But
now something new is being introduced. The second dream vision
(9.3-9) begins with a promise that the preceding prayer of Solomon's
will be heard (vv. 3-5), which is again introduced with an "if." Then a
renewed "if" follows, however, which contains a detailed proclamation of woe (vv. 6-9). The address changes from the singular "you,"
directed to Solomon, to "you" plural, which turns to Israel as a whole.
If Israel turns away from God, then it will be driven out of the land
that God has given it, and the temple will be destroyed, so that everyone will see it and be horrified by it. This introduces or prepares the
second stage in Solomon's reign. At the same time, however, this
proclamation of woe reaches far beyond the time of Solomon and resonates with the sound of the destruction of the temple and exile [→§21].

First, however, all sorts of unconnected things, in various literary
forms, are told us which pick up on the positively drawn picture of the
first part of Solomon's reign: about activities in foreign relations, con-

nected with shipping and trade (9.10-14, 26-28; 10.11f, 22, 28f) and about Solomon's immense wealth (10.14-21, 23-25, 26f), with the climactic account of the visit of the Queen of Sheba in between (1 Kgs 10.1-10, 13). This queen is, as it were, the representative of all the distant lands to which Solomon's fame has spread, and she wants to convince herself of it with her own eyes and ears. But she not only admires everything she sees and hears, as the expression of the wisdom of Solomon, but she also praises God for having set Solomon on the throne "out of eternal love for Israel" so that he will "maintain justice and righteousness," as she adds (v. 9).

Some of these items of information must impress the reader, who knows the preceding texts in the Hebrew Bible or the concepts contained in them, as at least ambivalent. The spectacular accumulation of gold and other riches (10.14ff) stands in striking contrast to what is said in Deut 17.17b [→82]; moreover the acquisition of huge numbers of horses (10.26) is in contradiction with Deut 17.16. The splendor of the throne that Solomon has made, according to 10.18-20, would scarcely have met with the approval of the authors of Deut 17. So the author already reveals an aspect critical of Solomonic rule. This applies also to the information about forced labor (9.15-23). In this section, in contrast to 5.27-37 it is emphasized that no Israelites are pressed into forced labor. Nonetheless the detailed remarks on the use of Israelites for all possible services show clear parallels to the critical "king-law" that Samuel conveyed before the beginning of the kingdom (1 Sam 8.11-17; cf. Crüsemann 1978a, 70ff) [→105].

The note about the move of Pharaoh's daughter whom Solomon had married into the house built for her (9.24; cf. 7.8b) points clearly already to the negative consequences of Solomon's relations with foreign women, which will later be presented as the main reason for his apostasy from the true faith (11.1ff). Here, though, this is balanced by the report of Solomon's frequent sacrifices (9.25).

But with the beginning of ch. 11 the negative aspects of Solomon's behavior move into the foreground. The multiplicity of foreign women is given as the prime reason for Solomon's departure from the path his father David had previously exhorted him to follow (2.3) [→116] and which had been at the center of the two dream visions (3.4; 9.4) [→117, 122]. In the report of Solomon's behavior (11.1-8) there is an explicit reminder of the time when Israel came into the land given it by God and God forbade close relationships and in particular marriage with members of the nations living in the land (Ex

34.15f; Deut 7.1-5) [→**78**]. This is precisely what Solomon had done
by taking into his harem not only Pharaoh's daughter but women
from the neighboring peoples. Women from the immediate neighbors
are mentioned: Moabite, Ammonite and Edomite women, and from
the northern neighbors Sidonite (i.e. Phoenician) and finally "Hittite"
women (evidently as representatives of the pre-Israelite population of
Canaan; cf. e.g. Gen 15.20; Josh 3.10; see also 1 Kgs 9.20) [→**§20**].

Solomon is accused of having "followed" these gods (11.5) as he
should have followed Yhwh. Furthermore he had built "high-places"
for the gods of his wives outside the city, thus legitimating the cults of
these non-Israelite gods (vv. 7f) [→**131**]. He was thus the first to institute a kind of negative cultic reform, to be contrasted in the subsequent story with a very small number of positive cultic reforms (cf.
Hoffmann 1980).

This shows that Solomon was not as completely devoted to God as
his father David had been (11.4, 6). This is a further key statement for
the assessment of the subsequent monarchic period. All subsequent
kings are measured against David. The latter himself is presented above
all as the ideal king according to the will of God, whose heart was
"fully devoted to the Lord his God" (11.4) and he "followed the LORD
completely" (v. 6). It is noteworthy here that this positive assessment
of David does not appear in the David story itself in this form but only
in the Solomon story (cf. already 2.3, then 3.3, 6; 9.4 etc.) [→**116**].
Here David is depicted as the ideal figure for reference, against whom
all subsequent kings are measured. At the same time Solomon appears
as the first of them who does not completely correspond to the ideal.

The consequence of Solomon's misbehavior will be that God will
take the kingdom away from him (11.11). But now David [→**§13**] once
again comes into play, this time in Solomon's favor. "For the sake of
his father David" God will not carry out his judgment as long as
Solomon is alive, but only on his son (v. 12); and "for the sake of my
servant David" he will not even take the kingdom completely away
from his son but leave him one of the twelve tribes to rule over (v. 13;
here "for the sake of Jerusalem" is added). So David stands at the beginning of the story of the dynasty founded by him in a dual role: as a
seldom matched ideal but at the same time as guarantor for an albeit
limited continuation of the existence of the dynasty.

But for Solomon the pathway is set out. God raises a contender
against him (*śāṭān*) in the Edomite Hadad (11.14-22) and then another
in the person of Rezon (vv. 23-25). But the decisive threat to his rul-

ership comes from within: as a protest against his forced labor system. One of the specially gifted workers in this system, Jeroboam, rebels against the king (11.26-40). At this crucial point a prophet now comes on the scene. In the designation of Solomon as David's successor the prophet Nathan had been an active participant; since then, however, no prophets have appeared in the story of Solomon [→§17]. Now the prophet Ahijah of Shiloh appears, this time as an opponent of the king. This marks a rather dramatic turn of events. The time of the "court prophets" is over. From now on prophets arise in opposition to the monarchy [→156] or against individual kings. Ahijah is the first in this long series of prophets.

Ahijah announces to Jeroboam in a symbolic act and its interpretation that God will tear the kingship away from Solomon and give Jeroboam ten of the tribes of Israel. In the long divine speech (11.31-39) he repeats the statements in the divine word to Solomon (cf. vv. 11-13) [→124] and adds further promises for a future dynasty of Jeroboam's, which will be comparable with those of David (vv. 37f, see below). Solomon tries to kill Jeroboam, but he is able to escape to Egypt. But the reader now knows that David's rule over the twelve tribes of Israel is now coming to an end. And the story of Solomon goes out, as it were, on a whimper. It remains only to report the extent of his reign over "all Israel": a round forty years (v. 42), as had David before him (2.11).

2.7 David and Solomon (summary)

David [→§13] is not just the most frequently mentioned king in the Hebrew Bible. His name is the most commonly mentioned name of all, more frequent even than that of Moses. The extent of the texts that mention him is again comparable only with those about Moses. (If one adds the books of Chronicles, the texts about David actually exceed those about Moses.) The mentions of David however reach far beyond the texts that deal with him as a person and his story. Much of what is said about him in other texts or is linked with his name has no direct connection with the narratives and reports of his life and work. Obviously the traditions linked with David's name were more varied and multi-layered than those handed down to us in the books of Samuel and the beginning of Kings.

But in the narrative traditions too, the picture of David has various layers, and is in fact ambivalent. There are in particular two aspects

that mark out his significance. In the first place David is the king chosen by God and anointed by the prophet Samuel and thereby also the
founder of the dynasty whose establishment is confirmed by the
prophet Nathan and which ruled in Jerusalem for four hundred years.
In the second place he made Israel a great power in the Near East
through his great successes in military campaigns and foreign policy,
unparalleled after him. Besides this, however, the texts give little cause
to view his personal lifestyle as particularly exemplary or to testify to
any special commitment of his to religious matters.

This picture changes with the transfer of rule to Solomon. In his
farewell speech David warns his son Solomon to keep the "Torah of
Moses" (1 Kgs 2.1-4) [→**116**], while otherwise in David's own reign
there was never any explicit discussion of the Torah. From now on,
the picture that David followed God's statutes and commandments in
an exemplary way predominates (e.g. 3.14). This statement however in
each case has the function of measuring Solomon's behavior against it,
whether in admonition to follow David's example or in the judgment
that he has not done this. So in the books of Kings David is first stylized as the counterpart of Solomon, as the exemplary, Yhwh-faithful
king.

Conversely, through the contrast with the ideal picture of David, a
negative general judgment arises for the reign of Solomon. Solomon
seems, from the perspective of the end, like the "failed successor"
(Schäfer-Lichtenberger 1995, 356ff). But this does not correspond at
all with the account of his reign in matters of detail. Solomon built the
temple that David had already planned [→**119**] and thus made Jerusalem
also the cultic center of Israel. His quite unwarlike foreign-political
relationship brought him great international respect, alongside his cultivation of "wisdom" [→**117f**]. It is true of Solomon too that, albeit to a
lesser degree than for David, outside the books of Kings there are
other traditions in circulation about him, which link up fully with
these positive sides of his rule. In the account of his rule itself, however, a religiously justified negative judgment is made of him, the precondition for which is the contrast with the ideal picture of David.

The reason for this is clear: David's rule over "all Israel," i.e. over
the whole area of "Judah" and "Israel," had already come to an end
with Solomon's reign. The ideal rule of the Davidic dynasty, it
seemed, had collapsed because of the failure of his successor Solomon.
This failure was then interpreted in a summarizing retrospect from the
deuteronomistically influenced view as a failure to keep the Torah of

Moses. In particular the maintenance of the cults of foreign deities by Solomon's wives [→**123**] was bound to seem like a transgression of the law of exclusive worship of Yhwh and thus was understood as the decisive reason for the fall of the reign over "all Israel" that had been set up by David. Thus Solomon appears "on the one hand as the great temple-builder ..., but on the other hand also as the idolater, on whom the abiding promise of 2 Sam 7 nevertheless rested" (Donner 1984/86, 229, ²256). The prophetic word to David, that "the sword shall never depart from your house" and that God will "bring calamity on you out of your own household" (2 Sam 12.10f) seems almost forgotten by comparison. (Cf. however 1 Kgs 15.5 [→**117**].). David has become increasingly an integral ideal figure. Responsibility for the end of his empire has been transferred entirely to his successor.

The summarizing retrospect on the reign of David and Solomon finally shows too that the beginning and end are decisively marked by prophetic words which as it were form a framework around this epoch. David is anointed king by Samuel (1 Sam 16.1-13) [→**107**] and his anointing gains special weight by dint of the fact that David represents the alternative to Saul, whom God rejected. Later Nathan promises David the permanency of his dynasty (2 Sam 7) [→**112**]. The possibility of the end of this first period of the Israelite monarchy is first envisioned in a dream vision given to Solomon (1 Kgs 9.1-9) [→**122**]. But then in Ahijah of Shiloh a new prophet turns up who announces the definitive end of the rule of the Davidic dynasty over Israel and Judah (1 Kgs 11.29-39) [→**125**]. Thus the beginning, divine confirmation and end of this epoch are marked by three prophetic figures.

3. Israel and Judah among kings and prophets
Continuation and conclusion

3.1 Israel fell from the house of David

The end of the dominion of the Davidic dynasty over "all Israel" is represented in the tradition as an extremely complex process. The transition from Solomon to his son Rehoboam seems at first not to be problematic. As in the change from David to Solomon the dynastic inheritance is not brought into doubt and there is nothing to indicate that there were any problems in relation to the person of the successor. Instead, however, social conflict comes to the fore, arising as a result of the hard forced labor which Solomon had laid upon his subjects. The resistance to this had already formed while Solomon was alive (see above on 1 Kgs 11.26-40 [→**124**]); now it comes fully to light. Evident in the account is a striking similarity to the situation of the Israelites during their forced labor in Egypt, from which they were freed by Moses (cf. Kegler 1983; Albertz 1992, 219).

This conflict at the same time makes clear that the connection between the two political entities of "Judah" and "Israel," which David had united under his rule (cf. 2 Sam 2.4 and 5.1-5) [→**111**], was by no means stable. On the contrary, the social conflict draws its political charge precisely from the fact that the northern tribes, i.e. "Israel," do not immediately recognize the new king from the Davidic dynasty but demand new negotiations with him. And when Rehoboam is not prepared to alleviate the labor conditions the negotiations break down. The narrative indicates this as a fulfillment of the word of God given to Jeroboam by the prophet Ahijah (1 Kgs 12.15). So then Jeroboam too, who had previously led the revolt against Solomon, is proclaimed king over Israel (1 Kgs 12.20).

In the role played by the prophet Ahijah of Shiloh [→**§17**] a further important aspect is evident. According to the narrative of 1 Kgs 11.26-40 he moved Jeroboam to rebel against Solomon by means of a symbolic act and an associated divine message [→**125**]. The way in which he appeared shows a clear change in the role of the prophet in relation to his "predecessors." Nathan and Gad stood in a close relationship to the king and the royal court. (Gad is even described as *ḥozēh dāwid*, "David's seer," 2 Sam 24.11 [→**115**].) Ahijah however meets Jeroboam "on the way" outside Jerusalem and presents him with a message directed against the royal house. He repeats the announcement previously given in a divine speech to Solomon that God will "tear" the kingdom away from Solomon (vv. 31-36, cf. vv. 11-13), and now applies this to Jeroboam: God will transfer the rule of ten of the tribes of Israel to him (v. 31; v. 11 says: "to one of your subordinates"). The reason given is again the worship of foreign gods, though once again the contrast with the exemplary behavior of David is emphasized (v. 33b). The dual qualification "for David's sake" is repeated: the kingdom will not be taken from Solomon during his lifetime and his son will be left a tribe (vv. 34-36). This is justified on the grounds that for David a "lamp" should be kept in Jerusalem (v. 36), a statement that will be met several more times later on (cf. 1 Kgs 15.4; 2 Kgs 8.19) [→**145, 147**].

So here three quite different ways of looking at the end of the reign of the Davidic dynasty over "all Israel" are linked together: the social rebellion against forced labor, the political secession of the northern tribes and the worship of foreign gods. The political collapse of the reign of David and Solomon is, however, presented as the consequence of religious waywardness. The situation that now arises is regarded as a fundamental new beginning and Jeroboam is given the same promises that were previously given to David: God will be with him and will build him a firm (*ne'mān*) house, as he did for David (cf. 2 Sam 7.16) [→113]. This promise is, however, introduced by an "if": "If you do whatever I command you ... as David my servant did" (11.38). On this condition Jeroboam is appointed by divine order as David's successor over the ten tribes of Israel. (On the text of 1 Kgs 11.29-40 cf. H. Weippert 1983.)

All this was spoken before the death of Solomon. But it is then realized in dramatic conflicts between the representatives of the northern tribes and Rehoboam, Solomon's son and successor (1 Kgs 12.1-19). "So Israel has been in rebellion against the house of David to this day" (v. 19). With the appointment of Jeroboam as king over "all Israel" (here with the express exception of the tribe of Judah, v. 20), there are now two kings in the succession of David and Solomon. According to 1 Kgs 11.37f Jeroboam appears as the true successor of David [→§13], while the Davidide Rehoboam is merely the administrator of the remainder, left to him "for David's sake." Once again he sets about winning back the rule of all Israel by force of arms; but the word of a "man of God" by the name of Shemaiah holds him back from this (12.20-24). So the split between north and south, between "Israel" and "Judah" is maintained. (In what follows I shall frequently use the term "northern kingdom" for "Israel" so as to avoid confusion with the still customary broader concept of Israel.)

The political secession of the northern tribes is quickly followed by cultic separation. Jeroboam founds two sanctuaries [→§11], one in the south of his kingdom in Beth-El, the other in Dan in the north (1 Kgs 12.26-33). Beth-El had an old cultic tradition which was traced back to the time of the patriarchs (cf. Gen 28.10-22) [→31]; the tradition of Dan was connected with the time of the judges (cf. Judg 18). These sanctuaries were expressly described as alternative foundations to Jerusalem, which could be politically dangerous because of its great attractiveness (vv. 26f). The sanctuary at Beth-El is later called "royal sanctuary" [→286] and "temple of the kingdom" (Amos 7.13), in which

terms the political claim comes to expression. Jeroboam has golden
bull images set up in the two sanctuaries as religious symbols. In a clear
echo of Ex 32 [→60] they are described as "calves"; this word could be
meant pejoratively, but can also be taken in the sense of "young animals." This does not mean we should assume the bulls themselves are
supposed to represent the deity but rather pedestals on which the (invisible) deity was thought of as standing (cf. the illustration BRL 102);
so the bull images formed a correspondence with the ark in the temple
in Jerusalem, on which Yhwh was also imagined to be invisibly enthroned. A decisive departure from the cultic tradition that had become established in Jerusalem is in evidence here. At the same time,
however, this newly formed cultic tradition is anchored in the previous history of Israel through the call to worship, which agrees with Ex
32.8: "Here are your gods, O Israel, who brought you up out of
Egypt!" (v. 28).

The report of these cult establishments by Jeroboam is written from
a Judean or Jerusalemite point of view. Hence the deviations from the
tradition there are in the foreground. Thus the erection of the bull
images is not, as in Ex 32, represented as an offense against the commandment to worship Yhwh alone, but as an individual formation of
new traditions. But this is precisely where the "sin" (v. 30) lies, because "the people" now made their pilgrimage to these sanctuaries and
thus moved away from the only legitimate Israelite cultic tradition
[→80]. Jeroboam also demonstrates the deviation from the Jerusalem
tradition in setting up a festival after the Judean model, but on another
date (v. 32). This may well be the annual harvest festival, the "feast of
tabernacles," which is celebrated, according to the festival calendar in
Lev 23.34, on the 15th day of the seventh month, while Jeroboam has
his festival take place a month later, on the 15th of the eighth.

The cultic measures reported of Jeroboam go further still. We read
that he set up "high places" (1 Kgs 12.31). The term "cultic high-
place" (*bāmāh*) means the local sanctuaries that had been around in
Israel since time immemorial (cf. 1 Sam 9.12ff; 1 Kgs 3.4) [→105, 117].
The negative judgment of them shows that the report of Jeroboam's
cultic reforms has been formulated from the viewpoint of Deuteronomy, which recognizes only Jerusalem as the only legitimate place for
the Yhwh cult (cf. Hoffmann 1980, 59ff). That the priests of these
local sanctuaries did not come from the tribe of Levi, too, can only be
taken as a reproach from this later point of view. That these non-
levitical priests could even serve at the central sanctuary, conceived

after the example of Jerusalem, heightens the illegitimacy of this cult in the eyes of the author.

All this is reported in order to show, right from the beginnings of the northern kingdom, the development that determined the history of this kingdom [→**§21**] and which ultimately led to its end. Already in Jeroboam's lifetime it is announced that his cultic projects became a sin to his "house" and that God would put an end to this house for that reason (13.34; 14.14). For Jeroboam had not met the condition on which God had promised him a "house" (11.38): to be like David, to walk in God's way and to keep God's commandments (14.8). So Jeroboam fails just as Solomon did, whose shoes he was supposed to fill, because he was not "like David." The "sins of Jeroboam" lie from here on like a dark shadow over the story of the northern kingdom (14.16; 15.30; 16.31 etc.).

Ahijah of Shiloh then comes on the scene once again (1 Kgs 14.1-18). When Jeroboam's son becomes sick, he sends his wife incognito to the old, blind Ahijah, to ask him about the fate of the child. But Ahijah has learned by way of a divine communication that it is Jeroboam's wife who is coming to him. So he informs her in a long divine speech, what fate awaits the child, the house of Jeroboam and finally all Israel: the child will die (v. 12), the house of Jeroboam will be decimated (vv. 10f) and finally all Israel will be led into exile "because of the sins Jeroboam has committed and has caused Israel to commit" (vv. 15f). Again cultic sins are in the foreground, which are here specified more closely: Jeroboam has made "other gods, idols made of metal" [→**§20**] (v. 9, the word *massēkāh*, "molten image" is also used for the "Golden Calf" at Sinai, Ex 32.4, 8 etc.) [→**60**]; so here Jeroboam's sin is set explicitly in parallel to that at Sinai. Israel has made itself "Asherahs," i.e. wooden cultic symbols representing the goddess Asherah (v. 15, cf. Judg 3.7; 6.25ff) [→**100f**]; this too is counted among Jeroboam's sins. These are as it were the beginning of all subsequent cultic transgressions by Israel, which are already foreseen in the divine words placed on Ahijah's lips.

An even clearer anticipation of the later development is contained in the narrative of the "man of God" who pronounces a prophecy against the altar at Beth-El (1 Kgs 13.1-10). It refers expressly to the later destruction of the altar by Josiah (v. 2; cf. 2 Kgs 23.14-16) [→**151**]. It is difficult to understand the continuation of this scene in the narrative of a second "prophet" (vv. 11-32; the expressions "man of God" and "prophet" are indirectly equated in v. 18) who causes the man of God to stay, against the divine command he has received, which leads to the man of God later being killed by a lion. Reference is also made to this in 2 Kgs 23.17f.

3.2 Only Judah kept to the house of David

The story of the subsequent centuries shows Judah in the rather modest role of the remainder state, which stands entirely in the shadow of the larger and more powerful northern neighbor Israel. For a long time there is war between the two states (1 Kgs 14.30; 15.7, 16, 32). When there is peace later on (22.45), Judah gets involved in Israel's warlike activities (22.2-4, 29ff) [→146], so that one might almost speak of a "veiled vassal-state relationship of Judah in relation to Israel" (Donner 1984/86, 250, ^{2}279).

But Judah had two essential elements on its side which ensured a continuity that was lacking in Israel. One of these was the never seriously challenged rule of the dynasty of David. There were none of the intrigues and usurpations that were the order of the day in the northern kingdom. Only once was the succession of the kings from the Davidic dynasty interrupted, in which the relationship with Israel was the decisive factor. Joram of Judah had married Athaliah, a daughter of Ahab of Israel (2 Kgs 8.18). When their son Ahaziah died in Jehu's revolt against Joram of Israel (9.27) [→147], she seized power in Jerusalem and exterminated Judah's royal family. Only one, Joash, at the time only an infant, was able to be taken to safety and was anointed king after six years of rule by Athaliah by means of a joint coup by the Jerusalem priests and the aristocracy (11.1-16). The dynastic succession was restored [→§13].

This event reveals the second, even more important element in the tradition of Judah: the temple in Jerusalem. In the decades after its construction by Solomon [→119] it had clearly become the dominant center of Jerusalem and thus also of Judah. And so it was possible for the decisive impetus for the restoration of state continuity to come from the temple and its priests. The institution of the new king also occurs in the temple, the king standing "by the column" "in accordance with the rule" (*kammišpāṭ* 11.14), i.e. evidently at the place where the institution of a new king or other important ceremonies were held. Afterwards a covenant [→§6] (*b'rît*) was concluded by Jehoiada the priest—evidently representing the still under-age king—whose partners are God, the king and the people and the content of which is summarized very succinctly: "that they would be the LORD's people" (v. 17; the whole ceremony displays a close relationship to Josiah's covenant in 2 Kgs 23.1-3 [→**150**]; cf. 1995a, 35 and 68).

So despite its political dependency on the northern kingdom of Israel, Judah still had a very marked level of independence. With regard to the overall course of the history of Israel (in the broader sense) the basic elements of the politico-religious complex created by David and Solomon remained continuously in Jerusalem, and that means in Judah: the Davidic kingship and the temple of Jerusalem. They guaranteed Jerusalem and Judah a continuity that was to survive all turmoil and vicissitudes despite its diminutiveness and insignificance and thus formed the essential precondition for the continued existence of the people of Israel even after the loss of its political independence.

3.3 They did evil in the sight of the LORD (an overview)

The history of the two separated kingdoms is presented in a consistently maintained synchronism, in which the beginning of a king's reign is dated according to the year of the rule of the king reigning in the neighboring kingdom at the time (1 Kgs 15.1, 9, 25, 33 etc.). An evaluation of the religious behavior of the king concerned is generally connected with these notes. Here the consequence of the judgment of Jeroboam's behavior is evident: all kings of Israel are given a fundamentally negative judgment, because they kept to the "sins of Jeroboam" [→**131**]. This remark is often connected with the statement: "they did evil in the sight of the LORD" (1 Kgs 15.26, 34 etc.). This is the same statement as we read at the beginning of the time of the judges (Judg 2.11, cf. also already Deut 31.29) [→**100**], the time that was depicted as the darkest and most godless in the history of Israel to date. Thus the whole period of the northern kingdom is viewed in the light of that period [→**§21**]. (On the individual evaluations cf. H. Weippert 1972.)

This almost stereotypical judgment of the kings of Israel forms the framework for an extremely varied history. At an early stage the prediction made by the prophet Ahijah that the house of Jeroboam will be annihilated, is fulfilled, in Baasha's coup against Nadab [→**131**], Jeroboam's son and successor (1 Kgs 15.25-30). But Baasha does not succeed in founding a new dynasty either. During his reign a divine word comes to him through the prophet Jehu ben Hanani, which tells him of the same fate declared to Jeroboam by Ahijah (16.1-4, 7; cf. 14.10f), because he has continued on the "way of Jeroboam" and led Israel into sin; in the report of the fulfillment of this announcement in Baasha's son Elah, there is an additional mention of "worthlessnesses" (*h'balîm*), i.e. worthless gods, through which they incurred God's wrath (16.13). Omri too, who after much ado acquires the dominion of Israel (16.21-23), is given the same verdict; indeed he is said to have done "evil in the eyes of the LORD" even more than all previous rulers, and the "worthlessnesses" are again mentioned in relation to him too (vv. 25f). This is as it were the prelude to the story of Ahab, son of Omri, who has the longest list of cultic misdemeanors. He did "more evil than all before him," even beyond the "sins of Jeroboam." He married the Phoenician king's daughter Jezebel, served Baal by building a Baal temple with an altar for Baal in Samaria, and set up an Asherah pole. This list in 1 Kgs 16.30-33 concludes with the sentence that Ahab "provoked" Yhwh more than all previous kings. The word about "provoking" Yhwh through the sins of the kings of Israel was already used a number of times previously (15.30; 16.2, 13, 26) and its use has its climax here in relation to Ahab.

At this point the prophet Elijah [→§17] comes on the scene. A new element comes to the fore with his appearance: the conflict between Yhwh and Baal (esp. 1 Kgs 18) [→137]. There has only been one previous explicit mention of the worship of these two gods: on the occasion of Gideon's (Jerubbaal's) destruction of the Baal altar of his father's (Judg 6.25-32) [→102]. Once again it is evident that the period of the northern kings is depicted in parallel with the dark history of the judges period, when the conflict between Yhwh and Baal made its first appearance.

Elijah's dramatic arguments with king Ahab (1 Kgs 17–19; 21) end with the announcement that Ahab's house will be "swept away" (21.21f), exactly as had been prophesied of the house of Jeroboam (14.10) [→130]. The execution of this is then in the hands of Elisha, whom Elijah appoints as his successor on divine instructions (19.16, 19-21). The instrument of this will be Jehu (2 Kgs 9f) who is also seen as the executor of the line begun by Elijah (1 Kgs 19.16f). Ahab's son and successor Ahaziah, whose reign is very short, is said again to have served and worshiped Baal (22.54). "His brother and heir to the throne Joram, who succeeded him shortly afterwards, is said not to have done "evil in the eyes of the LORD" like his father and mother, but to have removed the sacred stones of Baal; nonetheless he is still adjudged to have clung to the "sins of Jeroboam" (2 Kgs 3.2f), and it is on him that the fate of the house of Ahab is played out.

It is then Jehu that can be said to have "destroyed Baal worship in Israel" (2 Kgs 10.28). He thereby brings a period in the history of the northern kingdom to an end, in which the Baal cult had come more and more to the fore. So he is promised a dynasty that will last to the fourth generation (v. 30). Nonetheless the reproach of having clung to the "sins of Jeroboam," here specified as "the golden calves at Bethel and Dan" (v. 29), is applied to him too. The comment given on this clinging is that he "was not careful to keep the law of the LORD, the God of Israel" (v. 31) [→§10]. Surprisingly, the Torah is given as a yardstick, for the first time since David's admonition on Solomon's accession to the throne (1 Kgs 2.3) [→116]. This shows the great expectations that were connected with Jehu's reform. But he was unable to fulfill them, any more than Solomon had been able to in his day. And so the only cultic reform in the northern kingdom was not successful either in breaking through the heavy shadow over this kingdom caused by the "sins of Jeroboam." Hence too the judgment on the three successors of Jehu, for whom a longer reign was cut out, is no different from that on the earlier kings of Israel: they continued in the "sins of Jeroboam": Joash (2 Kgs 13.2), Jehoash (13.11) and Jeroboam II (14.24).

In the story of Jeroboam II there is a prophetic "interlude." According to 2 Kgs 14.25 this king recreated the borders of Israel according to a divine prophecy through the prophet Jonah ben Amittai [→293]. Here a prophet appears in a very unfamiliar role, not as a warner and admonisher but as the proclaimer of positive political events. This is confronted in vv. 26f with the fact that God did not say he wanted to blot Israel's name out under heaven. This sounds like a reference to what the prophet Amos proclaimed in the time of Jeroboam II: "The time is ripe for my people Israel" (Amos 8.2) [→286]. Underlying this may be a conflict between the (deuteronomistic) authors of the Kings account and Amos's prophecy of judgment (Crüsemann 1971). At the end of the story of the northern kingdom, however, there is no longer any evidence of such a distance being maintained from the proclamation of Amos (2 Kgs 17.23).

With Jeroboam II the dynasty of Jehu comes to an end. His son Zechariah reigns for only a few months and then becomes the victim of political intrigue. His death is expressly related to the prophecy to Jehu, according to which Jehu's dynasty would sit on the throne of

Israel to the fourth generation (2 Kgs 10.30; 15.12) [→135]. For the next two decades kings succeed each other, sometimes in quick succession, without there being a visible element of continuity again. The negative verdict remains immutably the same (Zechariah 15.9; Menahem 15.18; Pekahiah 15.24; Pekah 15.28). Only Hoshea, the last of the northern kings, is said not to have done evil in the eyes of the Lord like the kings of Israel who preceded him, and there is no mention of the "sins of Jeroboam" (17.2); but this is not further specified, and it does not alter the fact that with this king the northern kingdom of Israel goes under.

The evaluations of the kings of Israel formulated in retrospect show that there are two charges in particular that are laid against them: the maintenance of the northern Israelite state sanctuaries (the "sins of Jeroboam") and the worship of Baal [→§21]. In the latter case the connection with the period of the judges comes to the fore, in which it was described as one of the Israelites' main sins that they served Baal and other deities (Judg 2.11, 13; 3.7 etc.) [→100]. This worship of foreign gods was then presented as the assumption of the cultic practices of the Canaanites. This applies also to Ahab's Baal cult, which is attributed to the influence of his Canaanite wife, Jezebel. In both cases the Baal cult is viewed as a specifically Canaanite element that comes into conflict with the Israelite worship of Yhwh (cf. also Gideon in Judg 6.25-32) [→102]. The historical preconditions are quite different, but in both cases the conflict between Yhwh and Baal appears as a conflict between Israelite and Canaanite religious tradition. The assumption of the Canaanite tradition by the Israelites, however, is the clearest form of deviation from the path on which Yhwh, the God of Israel, has led his people hitherto.

In the reflection on the fate of the northern kingdom in 2 Kgs 17.7-23 [→144] the circle of reproaches is then drawn even wider. The sins of the Israelites were in essence an offense against the God who had brought them out of Egypt into the land (v. 7). There, they immediately began to imitate the customs of the nations that God had driven before them, by adopting their cult practices and worshiping their gods and "idols" (vv. 8-12). In 2 Kgs 17 a further element is added: God had warned Israel and Judah through "his servants the prophets," had called them to repentance and admonished them to observe the Torah (v. 13), and finally threatened them with expulsion from the land (v. 23). Here in summary the prophets, however much they differed as individuals, are described as "my (his) servants, the prophets" [→§17], whose warnings and admonitions Israel had disregarded time and again, so that finally, as God himself had announced through the prophets, the people were led out of their land to Assyria, "and they are still there" (v. 23). With reference to the end of the northern kingdom we read later once again: "they had not obeyed the Lord their God, but had violated his covenant—all that Moses the servant of the LORD commanded. They neither listened to the commands nor carried them out" (18.12). The last words recall the repeated declaration of the Israelites on Sinai that they would listen to and carry out the words of God mediated to them through Moses (Ex 19.8; 24.3, 7) [→**57**].

3.4 Yhwh or Baal

The concise account of the historical events after the separation of the two kingdoms of Israel and Judah suddenly broadens with the appearance of Elijah (1 Kgs 17.1). It is prompted by the mention of the Baal cult of king Ahab in Samaria (16.31-33). Elijah comes on the scene to oppose this. His appearance recalls that of Ahijah of Shiloh [→**125**]: he has no discernible relationship to the royal court but appears as an outsider and a loner. The latter function, however, according to Elijah's own words, is one imposed upon him, since queen Jezebel had eliminated all prophets of Yhwh (18.4) and only Elijah remained (18.22; 19.10). The narratives show that he commands an astonishing authority, even in respect of the king, whom he criticizes with the utmost acerbity. In this he continues the traditional prophetic critique of the monarchy (Albertz 1992, 235ff). But with the conflict between Yhwh and Baal an entirely new element now comes to the fore.

The story of Elijah is first told in the large narrative corpus of 1 Kgs 17–19. The center of this is formed by a dramatic public argument between Yhwh and Baal in ch. 18 (cf. Thiel 1990) [→**§20**]. It is prepared by the unmediated appearance of Elijah before Ahab with the proclamation of a lengthy period of drought (17.1). The grounds for this lie in the preceding list of Ahab's cultic misdemeanors, by which he has "provoked" Yhwh (16.30-33). Elijah's announcement of the drought is to be understood as Yhwh's answer to this behavior of Ahab's, though this is not expressly stated. The consequence is that Ahab now views Elijah as his enemy. So Elijah, following God's instructions, is obliged to seek refuge from persecution by the king (17.2ff). God provides for him in the uninhabited countryside, where he drinks from a stream and ravens bring him food (vv. 5f). Then he has to move into the heathen territory of the neighbors, where by means of miraculous deeds for the widow of Zarephath he as it were in anticipation of the great argument to come provides proof that Yhwh has the gifts of nature at his disposal, corn and oil in this case (vv. 8-16), and even has the power of life and death (vv. 17-24). The only witness of his deeds, the widow of Zarephath, puts it in confessional terms: "Now I know that you are a man of God and that the word of the LORD from your mouth is the truth" (v. 24).

Then—after a preliminary scene with the Yhwh-faithful minister Obadiah (18.7-15)—we come to the encounter between Elijah and Ahab (vv. 16-19). "Troubler of Israel," Ahab calls the prophet. Elijah rejects the reproach and now sets out precisely what had thus far been the unstated theme of the narrative: Ahab's worship of Baal. Elijah challenges him to a competition between the gods on Mount Carmel, to decide the question of "Yhwh or Baal" in public (vv. 20-24). The god who sends down fire on the sacrifice prepared for him will thereby prove that he is "the God" ($h\bar{a}$'$l\bar{o}h\hat{i}m$), i.e. the only God (cf. 1994, 19). In the dramatic argument that now follows, the four hundred prophets of Baal try to get their god to send down fire on the sacrifice they have prepared—but in vain (vv. 25-29). Then Elijah rebuilds the destroyed altar of Yhwh, prepares a bull for a burnt offering and has water poured over the whole thing (vv. 30-35). In the decisive scene Elijah calls upon Yhwh to show the people that he is "the God." Yhwh answers with fire, the sacrifice is consumed, and the people raise the cry of confession, "Yhwh is (alone) God" (vv. 36-39) [→§15]. Finally the narrative is rounded off with the drought being ended by a sudden heavy rainfall—a new demonstration of who is God (vv. 41-46).

Elijah's appearance occurs at a particularly critical point in the history of the northern kingdom. The state promotion of the Baal cult had apparently begun already under Omri [→134]; but with the construction of the temple of Baal in the capital city, Samaria (16.32) Ahab had given it an important new impulse. With his intervention against this development Elijah places himself in the line of his prophetic predecessors from Samuel, through Nathan and Gad to Ahijah, who criticized the politics and religious policies of the kings time and again and also influenced and altered the direction of the political development.

The special character of Elijah's stand lies, first, in the conflict with the Baal cult, sharpened to an extent not found previously. Second, in Elijah we meet for the first time a prophet who is threatened and persecuted by the king. This was the case right at the beginning of his work and it now increases following the dramatic victory of the Yhwh religion on Mount Carmel.

The persecution is at the behest of Jezebel, Ahab's Phoenician wife (19.1f). She is said to have had the prophets of Yhwh put to death (18.4, 13), so that Elijah alone remained (18.22; 19.10). Now she wants to bring her work to a fitting end. Elijah flees, this time in a southerly direction. He is in despair and begs God to take his life (19.4). Here we see a clear connection to Moses, whose office became too burdensome for him and who therefore asked God to take his life (cf. Num 11.14f, cf. Seybold 1973) [→**51**]. This connection is abundantly clear when Elijah, strengthened with sustenance provided by a messenger from God, finally reaches Mount Horeb (vv. 5-8). Here he is accorded an encounter with God, which is described in striking parallelism with Moses' encounter with God on Sinai/Horeb (Ex 33.18-23; 34.5-8) [→**62**]. Elijah finds himself in a cave (1 Kgs 19.9, 13) like Moses in the cleft of a rock (Ex 33.22). God passes over ('*abar* 1 Kgs 19.11; Ex 33.19, 22; 34.6) but like Moses (Ex 33.22f) Elijah is not allowed to see him (1 Kgs 19.13). Then God speaks, but not in the storm, earthquake and fire that precede him (vv. 11f); God is not even in them himself but only in the calm after the storm, in the "voice of hovering silence" that follows them (Buber).

In Ps 29 [→**330**] the three elements, storm, earthquake and fire represent the forms of the divine theophany, visible throughout the world (vv. 5-9). This psalm probably contains "Canaanite" elements of tradition relating to a theophany of Baal. So in the context of 1 Kgs 17–19 in the reference of these elements in the divine encounter with Elijah there may be evidence of a further contribution to the "Yhwh or Baal" theme (cf. Macholz 1980).

Out of this mysterious silence Elijah receives a commission which is considerable in scope and extent (1 Kgs 19.15-17). He is to bring about three changes of personnel which will decisively influence the future history of Israel: he is to "anoint," i.e. designate, a new king for the neighboring kingdom of the Arameans; he is to designate a new king over Israel; and he is to designate his own successor. This shows that the tradition ascribes a key role to Elijah for the following history of Israel. The three figures mentioned are to continue the work Elijah has begun. Their actions will have serious consequences for Israel.

But before the narrative continues, a sentence follows which is "the climax and at the same time the key to the story" (von Rad 1965, 30). God says: "I reserve seven thousand in Israel—all whose knees have not bowed down to Baal and all whose mouths have not kissed him" (v. 18). This is the answer to Elijah's complaint that he is the only one left. Now he is given the promise that in future too, despite all the divine judgments that are to come, there will be a "remnant" that God leaves and with whom the story will go on [→§22].

In accordance with the divine commission Elijah calls Elisha as his successor (19.19-21). But before Elisha starts to exercise his prophetic function, a number of other prophetic figures appear. At no other place in the Hebrew Bible do so many prophets appear in such a short space. They are all occupied with Ahab and his immediate successors and often the Baal cult of Ahab and Jezebel plays a direct or indirect role. The stories of the appearance of other prophets (1 Kgs 20; 22; 2 Kgs 2ff, see below) are interwoven with further accounts of the work of Elijah (1 Kgs 21; 2 Kgs 1f).

The first of these stories shows Elijah in a remarkable conflict with Ahab (1 Kgs 21). Ahab wants to buy a vineyard bordering the palace garden in his second residence, Jezreel; but the owner of the vineyard, Naboth, refuses to sell the "inheritance (*naḥ^lāh*) of his fathers." He appeals to a tradition by which a family's *naḥ^lāh* may not be sold; underlying this is the view formulated in Lev 25.33 [→68] that the land belongs to God and is only loaned to humans [→§10]. Ahab is prepared to comply with this but his wife Jezebel refuses to recognize this Israelite law, which limits the king's right of access and arranges a juridical assassination of Naboth. When Ahab then goes to take possession of the vineyard, Elijah meets him with a sharp divine word of judgment, proclaiming his death and the end of his dynasty (vv. 19-24). But Ahab carries out ceremonies of repentance, and then a divine word comes to Elijah to say that this verdict will not be effective until the next generation (vv. 27-29). This conflict again shows the problem of the "Canaanite" influence on Ahab, from another point of view, the legal side. The narratives clearly shows that Ahab would have been prepared to bow to the Israelite legal tradition but that Jezebel did not even shrink from juridical assassination to assert her notion of the sovereign rights of the king.

Elijah's last appearance shows him in conflict with Ahab's son Ahaziah (2 Kgs 1). Once again religious opposition comes into view. After an accident Ahaziah sends messengers to Baal-Zebub of Ekron to enquire of him whether he will recover. The unsolicited answer of Yhwh, which Elijah passes to the envoys, is: "Is it because there is no God in Israel?" (v. 3). The consultation of another god, a Baal moreover (who was perhaps regarded as the god to consult for sickness), is a clear transgression of the exclusive veneration of Yhwh, to which Israel is committed. This narrative again makes it clear that for Israel there can be only one God. This is carried out in a dramatic account at the end of which Elijah himself stands by the sickbed of the king and tells him of God's judgment that he will die because he has departed from this elementary premise (vv. 15f). So this last (or penultimate) Elijah story (see below on 2 Kgs 2 [→**143**]) once again shows the fundamental significance of the conflict that has emerged here and which will lead, with Elisha's help, to the end of the Omri/Ahab dynasty (see below on 2 Kgs 9f [→**121**]).

In 1 Kgs 20 we find a collection of narratives on prophets [→**§17**] who show another aspect of the prophecy of that time. The prophets remain anonymous, and it is notable that they belong to one group. They are occasionally described as *bᵉnê hannᵉbî'îm*, i.e. as members of a group of prophets, or "prophet's disciples" (v. 35). They appear in a war situation as aids of the king and announce to him divine support in the battle, in the form of a prophetic speech, so that "you will know that I am the LORD" (vv. 13f, 22, 28). But they also criticize the king because he has infringed the commandment banning the Aramean king (vv. 35–43), very much as Samuel had done to Saul (1 Sam 15) [→**106**]. In 2 Kgs 2–9 such groups of prophets appear in Elisha's circle (see below).

While the prophets appear fully independent and on their own against the king, in 1 Kgs 22 we meet a large crowd of prophets who give the king the desired answer to his question whether he should undertake the planned campaign against the Arameans (v. 6). One single prophet opposes them, who "never prophesies anything good ... but always bad" to the king, namely Micaiah ben Imlah. Here a dramatic conflict develops between the four hundred "court prophets" and the one opposition prophet. Micaiah ben Imlah demonstrates a number of new features of prophecy.

First, we meet here for the first time in the history of Old Testament prophecy [→*In* **121**] the report of a vision, or more precisely of two visions. Micaiah "sees" something which does not (yet) exist in the present earthly reality and is thus not visible to human eyes— unless God opens up the prophet's view (cf. Num 12.6) [→51]. To begin with Micaiah sees Israel "scattered like sheep without a shepherd" (v. 17), i.e. he foresees the failure of the planned campaign and the end of the king. Then the vision ascends into the heavenly sphere: in the assembly of the heavenly court God asks: "Who will lure Ahab into attacking Ramoth Gilead and going to his death there?" The anti-regal intent of the vision is even clearer here. Finally "the spirit" (*hārûah*) is given the task of luring Ahab. He wants to achieve this by being "a lying spirit in the mouths of all his prophets" (vv. 19-22). Micaiah finally turns this vision completely against the other prophets and against the king himself (v. 23). Here the prophetic critique of the monarchy and its political ambitions comes into extremely sharp focus. Micaiah ben Imlah thus stands in the line of Samuel, Ahijah of Shiloh and Elijah [→105, 128, 137]. At the same time the problem of "true" and "false" prophecy is presented in sharp focus.

Another topic is thrown up by Micaiah ben Imlah: the question of how to tell the truth of a prophetic divine word. When Ahab has the prophet thrown into prison "until I return safely," Micaiah answers: "If you ever return safely, the LORD has not spoken through me" (vv. 27f). The proof of the truth of the divine word is linked directly to the occurrence of what has been predicted, just as in Deuteronomy (Deut 18.21f) [→82], though from the opposite point of view, so to speak. So Micaiah ben Imlah is a very important figure in the history of prophecy.

Finally, this extremely dense phase of prophecy has its conclusion in the appearance of Elisha. The reports about him show Elisha on the one hand as a very well-contoured individual figure, but depict on the other hand his close, continuous relationship to a group of "prophets' disciples" (*b'nê hann'bî'îm*). He is described as their president or teacher, and his disciples "sit before him" (2 Kgs 6.1) and turn to him with their problems (4.1-7, 38-41; 6.1-7). In Elisha's first appearance it is evident that Elijah also had connections to this group of prophets' disciples. When the two of them go together from Gilgal to Beth-El and then to Jericho, they each meet a group of prophets' disciples, who quiz Elisha about his "lord" or "master" (*'adôn*), whom they evidently also know. As before in Elijah's case (18.22; 19.10, see above), it is clear that no fundamental difference can be drawn between the prophets that stand on their own and those in groups. (Cf. also Sam-

uel's role as "leader" of a "group of prophets" in 1 Sam 19.18-24)
[→**108**].

Elisha's first appearance is at the same time the last of Elijah's (2 Kgs
2). It forms one of the climaxes of early prophecy. Elijah is taken up to
heaven in a chariot of fire and his "spirit" (*rûaḥ*) is transferred to Elisha
(vv. 9-15). Elijah still has a future [→**§22**] (Mal 3.23; the Mishnah says
several times "until Elijah comes," *Sheq* 2.5; *Baba Mezia* 1.8) [→**313**],
but now Elisha is his legitimated and authorized successor (cf. Carroll
1969; Schäfer-Lichtenberger 1989). Elisha has asked Elijah for the
inheritance of the firstborn, and the request is granted. He can now
call upon "YHWH, the God of Elijah" (v. 14)—a very unusual link of
the divine name with a human person (otherwise found only in
2 Chron 34.3).

The picture of Elisha's prophetic activity is varied. As a miracle-
worker he ranks with Elijah (cf. 2 Kgs 4.1-7, 8-37 with 1 Kgs 17.8-
16, 17-24); alongside miracles in a private context or in the narrower
community of the group of prophets (see above) he even has a reputa-
tion as a miraculous healer beyond the boundaries of Israel (2 Kgs 5).
Precisely because of this ability he is described as "the *nābî'* who is in
Samaria" (v. 3) and even as "the *nābî'* in Israel" (5.8; cf. 6.12). Some
of his miracles also have military and political effects (2 Kgs 3.1ff; 6.8–
7.20) [→**142**]. This brings Elisha close to the prophets of 1 Kgs 20. But
at the same time an extremely critical element is shown towards king
Joram, son of Ahab and Jezebel, whom he reproaches with: "Go to
the prophets of your father and the prophets of your mother" (2 Kgs
3.13). In this rejection of Ahab's religious policy Elisha also stands in
the tradition of Elijah. This finally comes to decisive expression when
Elisha charges one of the prophets' disciples to anoint the officer Jehu
as king over Israel in secret and thus to set the revolution against Joram
in motion, which will also mean the end of the Omri/Ahab dynasty
(9.1ff) [→**139**]. In so doing Elisha carries out the task Elijah had been
given on Mount Horeb (1 Kgs 19.16), just as he had previously also
carried out the task of designating Hazael of Damascus as king of Aram
(2 Kgs 8.7-15; cf. 1 Kgs 19.15).

In the century that follows, in which the dynasty of Jehu reigns in
Israel and in which it once again enjoys a flourishing period under the
rule of Jeroboam II (cf. Donner 1984/86, 282-84, ²312-14), the books
of Kings report nothing more about the activities of prophets (cf.
however Hos 8.4a) [→**269**]. It is only in the concluding evaluation of
the history of the northern kingdom that there is mention in summary

of the activity of the prophets, the servants of God (2 Kgs 17.13, 23) [→**137**]. In the collection of the "Latter Prophets," however, it is Hosea and Amos that raise their prophetic voice in the time of Jeroboam (Hos 1.1; Amos 1.1; 7.7ff).

3.5 Judah to the end of the house of David

The evaluations of the kings of Judah differ fundamentally from those of the kings of Israel. The negative connecting element of backward reference to the "sins of Jeroboam" is missing here. Instead two other elements are frequently found that create continuity: the comparison of each ruler with his father and predecessor and the comparison with David. At first, however, the series begins with a very negative judgment of the reign of Rehoboam, which has no such backward reference. The text speaks remarkably enough not of the behavior of the king himself but of what "Judah" did, namely "evil in the eyes of the LORD" (1 Kgs 14.22). A list follows of the cultic sins of the Judahites, with which they "stirred up his jealous anger" than all their "fathers." The indeterminate mention of "fathers" brings the increase of sin through the generations to expression, thoughts again certainly reaching back into the time of the judges [→**§7**]. Listed next are: high-places (*bāmôt*), Massebahs (sacred stones) and Asherah poles, which they had set up "on every high hill and under every spreading tree" (v. 23) [→**207**]. Finally, "dedicated persons," i.e. cult prostitutes, are mentioned and the whole situation is summarized as "the detestable practices of the nations the LORD had driven out before the Israelites," which expressly makes the connection to the time of the judges. Rehoboam, or the effect of his rule on Judah, is thus depicted no less negatively than Jeroboam. The mention of the "high-places" [→**§20**] is of special significance for the further history of Judah and its kings. The maintenance of these is an object of reproach to most of the kings of Judah in the future, because they represented competition to the temple in Jerusalem and thus a danger to the pure worship of Yhwh.

In Rehoboam's son and successor Abijah we immediately meet both references to the predecessors with whom comparison is made. He committed all the sins of his father Rehoboam, and his heart was not fully devoted (undivided, *šālēm*) to Yhwh like the heart of his "father" David (1 Kgs 15.3). Talk of the "undivided heart" was first made at the end of Solomon's concluding address after the temple dedication as a commission to the gathering of the whole "assembly of Israel"

(8.61). But just a little later Solomon himself is said not to have turned his heart undividedly to Yhwh like the heart of his father David (11.4) [→**124**]. Abijah thus stands in the succession of Solomon. At the same time the promise that God will set up a "lamp" in Jerusalem for David comes into force, in that he will keep one of the descendants of David always on the throne and maintain the city himself (15.4; cf. 11.36) [→**128**]. The reason given for this is that David "had done what was right in the eyes of the Lord" (15.5). This counterpart to the more common mention of "evil in the eyes of the LORD" is found here for the first time in the history of the kings. It is later used more frequently in characterizing the kings of Judah who are measured against the model of David [→**147, 150**].

With Abijah's son Asa a turn for the better takes place. He is the first of whom it is said: "he did what was right in the eyes of the LORD, as his father David had done" (15.11). The reason given for this positive verdict are measures taken by Asa which make him look like the first cult reformer, as it were (Hoffmann 1980, 87ff). He removes the cult prostitutes from the land (cf. 14.24) and removes "all the idols (*gillulîm*) his fathers had made" (v. 12). This last statement is again very indeterminate and does not make it clear which "idols" are meant, especially since here the expression occurs for the first time in the history of the kings. One is reminded of the list given in connection with the reign of Rehoboam (14.22-24) [→**145**], particularly since the mention of the "fathers" links up with 14.22. Very much more precise is the information about the removal of the king's grandmother from her office as "queen mother" (*g'bîrāh*, v. 13), which evidently indicates a special function of the king's mother (in this case his grandmother) at the royal court (cf. Donner 1959). She had also assisted with cultic activities and set up a "repulsive image" (*mipleṣet*), which Asa has hauled down and burnt. The meaning of this word, found only here, is still unclear, but this measure shows clearly that Asa made serious efforts to purge the Yhwh cult.

But a shadow is cast over the positive picture of Asa: the high-places did not disappear (v. 14). The wording does not make Asa directly responsible for this, but his positive assessment is clearly limited by this. The text however immediately balances this with the emphatic statement that Asa's heart was turned "undividedly" towards Yhwh. This confirms in him what was missing in his father (v. 3) and he is expressly placed in the succession of David (cf. 11.4). Thus with Asa a series of Judean kings begins who correspond to the picture of David

[→§13], even though in most cases the qualification remains that the high places were not removed. This applies also to Asa's son Jehoshaphat, who walked entirely in the ways of his father Asa and did "right in the eyes of the Lord" (22.43); only the high-places did not disappear. With the supplementary note that "the people" brought sacrifices at the high-places, again a very clear distinction is made between the behavior of the king and the popular high-place cult (v. 44). Finally it is added that Jehoshaphat removed the remaining cult prostitutes who were left from the days of Asa (v. 47). This is evidently not supposed to express a critique of Asa but rather to indicate the continuity of the cult-reforming activity.

But then the series of the positively judged kings of Judah in the Davidic succession is interrupted by the close relations between the following kings and the kings of the northern kingdom, in particular Ahab. Though Jehoshaphat also had maintained relations with the northern kingdom and had even participated in military actions (1 Kgs 22.1-38) [→132], this did not cause any damage to his overall depiction. His son Joram then marries a daughter (according to v. 26 a sister) of Ahab's and thus goes "the way of the kings of Israel" and does "evil in the eyes of the LORD" (2 Kgs 8.18). Here we see very clearly that the generally more positively judged religious policy of Judah is repeatedly endangered by the influence of the northern kingdom of Israel. But still again the assurance comes into force that God will not destroy Judah "for David's sake," to whom he has promised a lasting "lamp" (v. 19; cf. 1 Kgs 11.36) [→128]. In the case of Joram's son Ahaziah, however, about whom the same verdict is given (v. 27), this continuity suddenly breaks off. He is killed in the course of Jehu's revolt against the house of Ahab (9.27f), which opens up the way for the usurpation of his mother Athaliah (ch. 11, see above [→133]).

Athaliah's rule is the only interruption in the continuous succession in the davidic dynasty. After that with Joash (2 Kgs 12.3f) a new series of Judean kings begins who do "right in the eyes of the LORD." In the case of Amaziah, however, there is the reservation that he did not do "as his father David" but as his father Joash (14.3f). The same applies to Azariah, whose behavior is related to that of his father Amaziah (15.3f), and correspondingly to his son Jotham (15.34f; here the form of the name is Uzziah instead of Azariah). Despite this qualification, however, for about a century there is a more positive picture of the religious behavior of the kings of Judah.

But then it is Ahaz, who once again did not do "right in the eyes of the Lord like his father David," but goes "the way of the kings of Israel" (16.2f). He is said to have himself brought sacrifices on the high places (v. 4). In addition, he is reproached for imitating the "detestable ways of the nations the LORD had driven out before the Israelites," by making his son "pass through the fire" (v. 3). Above all he had an altar erected after an Assyrian model in the Jerusalem temple and made dedicatory sacrifices on it (vv. 10-16) [→§11]. In the context this has to be seen as an act of loyalty towards the Assyrians. But nothing is said of to whom this altar and these sacrifices were made, so that they were apparently seen as compatible with the Yhwh cult. Among the cult reforms of Hezekiah also (see next paragraph), there is no mention of the new altar. The negative judgment of Ahaz remains, however. Again we see that it is foreign influences on the religious policy of Judah that are regarded as particularly dangerous.

But then there is another turn-around and a great cult reform is undertaken under Hezekiah (18.1-6). He is described as the first successor of David to correspond entirely to his example: "He did right in the eyes of the LORD, just as his father David had done" (v. 3). Above all he removes the high-places (v. 4) so that now for the first time in the history of Judah this qualification of the positive assessment of the king's cultic behavior can be dropped [→145]. Furthermore he destroys the sacred stones and Asherah poles, though it is not specified where these had been set up. Finally he removes the "brazen serpent" that was venerated in the Jerusalem temple under the name of *n'huštān* and the origins of which were traced back to Moses (Num 21.4-9). These brief notes about Hezekiah's cult reform are supplemented by detailed theological statements, in which we read that before and after Hezekiah there was no king like him and that he kept the commandments given by God through Moses (vv. 5f).

Here the account opens up into a broad narrative of the threat to Jerusalem by the Assyrians and a sickness of Hezekiah. The activity of the prophet Isaiah [→§17] plays a central role here (18.13–20.19). First Isaiah appears in a similar role to Elisha, in which he informs the king in a divine word that Jerusalem will not be taken by the Assyrian king (19.1-7). Then he answers a pleading prayer of Hezekiah in the temple (vv. 14-19) with a detailed divine word (vv. 20-34) which presents itself as a three-part composition: a word of judgment, beginning as a mocking song against the Assyrian king Sennacherib (vv. 21-28), the announcement of a time of peace and prosperity for the "remnant" that goes out from Zion (vv. 29-31) and finally the concrete proclamation that the king of Assyria will not penetrate the city because God will protect it "for my sake and the sake of my servant David" (vv. 32-34).

In this detailed, poetically written text a picture of the prophet is evident that is not otherwise found in the books of the "Former Prophets," but frequently in those of the "Latter Prophets." So it is remarkable that the passage 2 Kgs 18.13–20.19 is also found, with slight changes, in the book of Isaiah (chs. 36-39 [→**183**], with an added psalm in 38.9-20). This is the only passage in the books of Kings in which one of the "writing prophets" has a chance to speak. (For the note about Jonah see above.)

Finally an account is given of a sickness of Hezekiah. Isaiah first announces, with a word from God, that the king is going to die, but then after a pleading prayer of Hezekiah's he is told to declare a new message that Hezekiah will recover and live for a further fifteen years (20.1-7); this is accompanied by miraculous signs (vv. 7-11). This change of a divine announcement on the basis of a prayer by the person concerned recalls the words of Nathan to David (1 Sam 12.7-14) [→**114**] and of Elijah to Ahab (1 Kgs 21.27-29) [→**140**]. Isaiah thus stands in the tradition of these former prophets. And just like these he then pronounces a divine word of judgment on the king in which he declares that the "days will come" when the treasures of the royal house which Hezekiah has shown to the envoys from Babylon will be carried off to Babylon together with the king's sons (2 Kgs 20.12-19). But Hezekiah thinks only of himself: "Will there not be peace and security in my lifetime?" Thus this phase of the kingdom in Judah, too, which began with the great cult reform, ends with a negative outlook on the impending future.

That Hezekiah's reform was not permanent is immediately shown by his son and successor Manasseh (2 Kgs 21.1-18). Manasseh's religious policy stands in blatant contrast to Hezekiah's reform and as it were represents a counter-reform (cf. Hoffmann 1980, 146, 155ff). Manasseh is said to have done "evil in the eyes of the LORD," and again following "the detestable practices of the nations the LORD had driven out before the Israelites" (v. 2, cf. vv. 6, 15, 16), as had previously been said of Ahaz (16.3) [→**147**] and of Judah in the time of Rehoboam (1 Kgs 14.24) [→**145**]. A long list of cultic measures then follows, beginning with the restoration of the high-places that Hezekiah had destroyed, through the erection of Baal altars, the setting up of an image of Asherah in the temple following Ahab's example [→**134**], the institution of the cult for "the whole army of heaven," having his son pass through the fire, through to sorcery, divination, the setting up of necromancers and sign-interpreters (vv. 3-8). This list shows clear echoes of Deuteronomy, sometimes even in the wording (cf. v. 6 with Deut 18.10f) [→**82**]. Manasseh is stylized here as the opposite of Hezekiah; through his actions in Judah and Jerusalem everything is reintroduced that had at last been removed by Hezekiah, and even worse things are added.

This points to the end of the history of Judah and Jerusalem and thus of the history of Israel as a whole [→**§21**]. God had given Israel the land and placed his name "forever" on the temple in Jerusalem. He had promised Israel it would reside permanently in the land, "if they observe everything I have commanded them in accordance with the whole Torah which my servant Moses gave them (vv. 7f). But Hezekiah was the only one after David who could be said to have kept the Torah of Moses. Now we read the summary judgment: "But they did not listen." This repeats what has already been said in retrospect on the end of the northern kingdom (18.12). But under the reign of Manasseh this was exacerbated one last time in that Israel/Judah not only did the same as the peoples God had driven out from before them but did even worse (v. 9).

As before at the end of the history of the northern kingdom (17.7-23) [→**137**] we again read that God has spoken to Judah through "his servants, the prophets" (21.10-15). He announces a fate for Jerusalem and Judah that will be like that of Samaria and the house of Ahab (v. 13). Again it is made clear that Judah has increasingly gone the way of the northern kingdom under Manasseh. But now God will also give "the rest of my inheritance" into the hands of its enemies, "because they have done evil in my eyes and have provoked me to anger from the day their forefathers came out of Egypt until this day" (vv. 14f). It sounds as if a line is being drawn under the history of Jerusalem and Judah.

But once again the pendulum swings back. Reform and counter-reform are followed by a last great reform. Josiah, the eight-year-old grandson of Manasseh who has come to the throne by way of a putsch against his father (21.32f; 22.1), is once again one of the kings of Judah who did "right in the eyes of the LORD." This statement is further reinforced and raised to exemplary significance by the addition: "he walked in all the ways of his father David, not turning aside to the right or to the left" (22.2; cf. Deut 17.20!) [→**82**]. No king had previously received such an accolade.

The reform is prompted by the discovery of a book during work on the temple. The (high) priest Hilkiah who finds it calls it the "book of the law" (*sēfer hattôrāh*, 22.8, cf. v. 11). It is read to the king (now an adult) and it has an alarming effect on him. He "tears his robes" and orders the priest and some court officials to consult God about this book: "Great is the Lord's anger that burns against us because our fathers have not obeyed the words of this book; they have not acted in accordance with all that is written there concerning us" (vv. 11-13).

From the broader context it is clear that the reference is to words as found in Deuteronomy. So everything points to this book of the law being Deuteronomy (or perhaps an earlier form of it) [→**§10**]. However the cultic reality at the time of its "discovery" stands in stark contrast to its demands for "cult unity and cult purity" (Herrmann 1971).

The king's envoys consult the prophetess Hulda (22.14-20). Her answer is ambivalent. At first she confirms the divine decision, pronounced before against Manasseh, that an end will be made to Judah because of its constant departures from God's commandments (vv. 16f). But then a positive word follows for Josiah: because he has humbled himself before God he himself will not experience this calamity (vv. 18-20). The rest of the narrative is then marked entirely by the second part of this message: Josiah begins with comprehensive reforms. It is not until right at the end that the divine judgment announced for Judah and Jerusalem is again mentioned, this time with express reference to Manasseh (23.26f).

The fundamental significance of Josiah's reforms is already demonstratively emphasized at their beginning: the king calls a great gathering in front of the temple, reads out the "book of the covenant" that has been found and "renews the covenant in the presence of the LORD" [→**§6**]. The content of this covenant is the commitment to "follow the LORD and keep his commands, regulations and decrees with all his heart and all his soul, thus confirming the words of the covenant written in this book." Following this we read: "Then all the people pledged themselves to the covenant" (23.1-3).

This ceremonial covenant agreement has a certain parallel in the covenant agreement that Jehoiada the priest concludes with the seven-year-old king Joash and the people after the ending of the reign of Athaliah (2 Kgs 11.17)

[→**133**]. Associated with this too there is a removal of cult objects set up during the foreign rule. In other respects, however, essential differences remain.

Then begins a reform on a grand scale [→**§11**]. It has two main foci: on the one hand the removal of all foreign cults, on the other the concentration of the cult on the temple in Jerusalem. In the structure of the report of the reform it is clear that the second aspect is central (23.8, cf. Lohfink 1987, 217). Great importance is attached to the removal of the *bamôt*, the local sanctuaries. Their continuing existence had been a constant stumbling-block for the religious assessment of the kings of Judah from the time of Rehoboam (cf. 1 Kgs 14.23; 15.14 etc.) [→**145**]. Hezekiah had got rid of them as his first act of reform (2 Kgs 18.4) [→**147**], but again it was Manasseh's first act to reinstate them (21.3) [→**149**]. Now they are desecrated and thereby made cultically unusable. In addition, the priests of these local sanctuaries are removed from there so as to prevent the continuation of the local cults. Finally the concentration on the temple is complemented by the removal of the "high gates," i.e. evidently cultic facilities in the area of the city gates.

Further, in a comprehensive listing wide-scale reform measures are mentioned by which everything that has been assembled in the way of non-Israelite or otherwise illegitimate cultic facilities and practices is removed. Expressly and repeatedly the instigators of these facilities are given as the "kings of Judah" (23.5, 11, 12), and also Manasseh (v. 12) as well as Solomon (v. 13), and for the north of the land Jeroboam (v. 15) and the "kings of Israel" (v. 19). A central role is played by the cultic objects and facilities for other gods: Baal (vv. 4, 5), Asherah (vv. 4, 6, 7), the "lord of heaven" (vv. 4, 5), the sun (v. 11) as well as sun, moon and the signs of the zodiac (v. 5), Molech (v. 10), Ashtoreth, Chemosh and Milcom (v. 13). Finally the reform is also extended to the area of the earlier northern kingdom of Israel, where the high-place sanctuaries are destroyed (vv. 19f), above all that in Beth-El, with express reference being made to the narratives in 1 Kgs 13 (vv. 15-18) [→**132**].

The crowning conclusion of the whole event is a celebration of the Passover "as it is written in this book of the covenant," as no Passover had been observed "since the days of the judges who led Israel, nor throughout the days of the kings of Israel and the kings of Judah" (vv. 21-23). In the concluding note Josiah is once again elevated above all kings before and after him: "Neither before nor after Josiah was there a king like him who turned to the LORD as he did—with all his heart and with all his soul and with all his strength, in accordance with all the law of Moses" (v. 25).

The reader might again think that a line has been drawn here, like at the end of the prophetic word about Manasseh (2 Kgs 21.14f); but this time it seems to be a positive conclusion. All Israel's and Judah's cultic mistakes have been removed by a king who at last was like David, even more than Hezekiah had been, when he "repented" according to the Torah of Moses. In him was fulfilled what David had charged his son and successor with: to keep the Torah of Moses and to live before God with his whole heart and soul (1 Kgs 2.1-4) [→116]. But this positive concluding word is not the last word. The divine word of judgment spoken over Manasseh cannot be set aside even as a result of Josiah's exemplary deeds. It is repeated and confirmed (vv. 26f): God does not "repent" of his great wrath. The word "he did not repent" (lo'-šāb) stands in stark contrast to the statement in the preceding verse, that Josiah was the king who "repented" ('ašer-šab). Josiah's repentance was not enough to turn the wrath of God concerning Judah and Jerusalem.

After Josiah's ignominious death (2 Kgs 23.29f) Judah is swamped in the fighting between Egypt and Babylonia. The following kings are mere pawns in the battles of the great nations. They are all judged with the concise, stereotypical note that they did "evil in the eyes of the LORD." Of the sons of Josiah, Jehoahaz and Eliakim/Jehoiakim it is said that they did evil "just as their fathers had done" (23.32, 37), without their natural father Josiah being mentioned; of Jehoiachin and Mattaniah/Zedekiah we again read "just as his father had done" (24.9) or "just as (his brother) Jehoiakim had done" (24.19). At the beginning of the threat from the Babylonians the divine words of judgment are recalled and also the "sins of Manasseh" (24.3f). There are then no further religious evaluations or comments. The fall of Judah and Jerusalem, the destruction and sacking of the temple, executions and deportations, all this goes on without comment.

It is only right at the end that a note follows, which does not contain any comment but does call for interpretation: 37 years after Jehoiachin has been taken off into exile, the Babylonian king pardons him, releases him from prison and gives him a place at the royal table, together with other deported kings (2 Kgs 25.27-30). This is clearly not a "conclusion" but it leaves open the question of what will happen afterwards. It is not without reason that Jehoiachin is twice described here as "king of Judah" (v. 27). Will there be a king of Judah again? Or what will the future look like?

3.6 Has Israel failed?

The open ending of the account of the history of Israel and Judah leaves the reader with the question: has this story come to a definitive end? Has Israel failed? This question could not be answered with a simple Yes or No at the time, any more than it can today. In a sense, the history of Israel had come to an end. The political structures that had pertained for more than four hundred years in Israel and Judah no longer existed. There was no longer a king and no national sovereignty. And the religious and intellectual center, the temple in Jerusalem, was in ruins. Important sections of the population had been transported into exile in Babylon. So in many regards there was a vacuum and there was no way of telling what the future would bring.

But everything that had formed the content of the life people in Israel and Judah had led in these centuries could not be destroyed by this. The books at the conclusion of which this question had to be posed had of course not yet been written and were not edited and passed on in order to contemplate and lament the end and failure of everything that had been presented in such detail and with such commitment. This is so much more the case when one considers not only the books of the "Former Prophets," the historical books, but also those underlying books that had preceded them and with which they were frequently connected: the books of the Pentateuch with their account of the beginnings of the history of humanity and Israel and of the religious and to some extent also the political bases of Israel's life as a community as well as of the life of the individual as a member of this community.

Whenever each of these books was composed and edited, the fact that they were available or perhaps were just now formed from available traditions, shows very clearly that the life they describe was not at an end. And at the end of the Pentateuch a future after the exile is explicitly contemplated (Deut 30.1-10). One also has to think of the abundance of other texts and writings transmitted in Israel and which brought particular aspects of its life to expression: above all the Psalms, but also other texts from the realm of "writings," as far as such already existed at the time of the end of the state of Judah; finally the transmission and continued writing of the prophetic traditions presupposes a lively interest in a future for Israel.

We know little of the life of the Israelites (or Judahites) in any detail in the centuries after the fall of Jerusalem. But we have a number of very impressive indications of how problems that now arose were dealt with and overcome. Thus the prophet Jeremiah wrote a letter to the exiles in Babylon in which he admonished them and encouraged them to make their lives in exile worth living, not falling into utopian hopes of an early return but still to remain sure of the divine promise that the return would take place one day: "'For I know the plans I have for you', declares the Lord, plans to prosper you and not to harm you, plans to give you hope and a future'" (Jer 29.11) [→**226**]. The book of the prophet Ezekiel is determined entirely by the question of the failure *and* of the future. The prophet sees the future life of Israel in the vision as the resurrection of the dry bones (Ezek 37) [→**256**], and also the throne of a new David comes into view (34.23f; 37.24f). In the book of Isaiah, in chs. 40–55 [→**185**] in particular a voice of lively and theologically reflective hope for the future is heard. In these and many other texts it is clear that the political end of the states of Israel and Judah and even the destruction of Jerusalem and the temple were understood as a deep wound, but certainly not as a definitive end.

If one looks at the books of the "Former Prophets" from this perspective, it is quite plain that they do not talk only about failure. They contain a number of fundamental traditions that were and remained of great significance for Israel's life in general and thus also for its life after the exile. Already in the Pentateuch there is talk of two basic gifts that Israel has received: the Torah given through Moses and the land promised to the fathers, already received on installment (Gen 23). The promise of the land begins really at the beginning of the "Former Prophets" under Joshua's leadership. After that there is talk of two further and no less fundamental gifts: the kingship, connected above all with the name of David, and the temple built by Solomon in Jerusalem. In the account of this period in the books of Samuel and at the beginning of 1 Kings there is no reference to the basic evil of the following period: the worship of foreign gods. On the contrary: already prominently in the choice of the king Samuel called upon the Israelites to remove the foreign gods from their midst, and they obeyed his call: "So the Israelites put away their Baals and Ashtoreths, and served the LORD only" (1 Sam 7.3f) [→**104**]. This removed the main problem of the time of the judges, which is depicted as a time of perpetual apostasy from Yhwh, and a new start was possible. So looking back, Solomon describes the first phase of the period of the monarchy [→**121**] and the temple as a time of God-given "peacefulness" (*mᵉnûḥāh*, 1 Kgs 8.56). This period is thus expressly placed in parallel with the time of the possession of the land, which was described as the first time of "peacefulness" for Israel (Josh 21.44 [→**99**]; cf. Albertz 1989, 41ff). We read even that everyone was able to sit in safety "under his own vine and his own fig tree" (1 Kgs 5.5) [→**119**], an expression found in prophetic texts as an eschatological promise (Mic 4.4; Zech 3.10) [→**295**].

It is only after the conclusion of the building of the temple that the problem of the worship of foreign gods comes up again. At first it is viewed as a possibility in Solomon's second dream vision, with which the second phase of his reign is introduced: "if you … go off to serve other gods and worship them …," and consequences of this are set out (1 Kgs 9.6ff) [→**122**]. It is then Solomon himself who succumbs to the seduction of his foreign wives and thus begins to worship other gods. Ashtoreth, Milcom and Chemosh are mentioned by name (11.4-8; cf. 2 Kgs 23.13). He then is given an announcement of divine judgment which only for David's sake and for Jerusalem's sake will not affect Solomon himself but only his successors (1 Kgs 11.9-13). This announces the trend for the following period.

But the account of the next centuries is by no means tuned one-sidedly to the negative tone of departure from the right path of Yhwh worship. In the history of the kingdom of Judah in particular there are lengthy stages in which we read nothing of the veneration of foreign gods. For most of the kings of Judah the criticism is focused on their allowing the high-place sanctuaries to continue to exist. In retrospect, from the viewpoint of the central cult in Jerusalem these sanctuaries are deemed illegitimate, but generally speaking it is not said that they served the worship of foreign gods. Towards the end all this comes to a head with the alternating reforms of Hezekiah, Manasseh and Josiah. The cultic sins committed in the lengthy reign of Manasseh are then depicted as so serious that ultimately, despite the extremely positive assessment of the reforms of Hezekiah and especially of Josiah, they are the decisive factor for the unhappy end of Judah.

But precisely the comparison of the last great kings of Judah shows clearly for posterity, those that read these stories, what the right way would have been. At the same time the possibility opens up of following these examples and thus opening up a future for the history of Israel and Judah. It is certainly no coincidence that in the reconstruction of social and religious life in Jerusalem and Judah the concentration and limitation of the cult to the temple in Jerusalem introduced by Josiah was presupposed and practiced, clearly without further discussion. This central demand of Deuteronomy thus comes fully into effect and determines religious development from this point on. The cultic prescriptions set down in the "priestly" sections of the Pentateuch also come into their own in this context.

But above all it is of the prophets [→§17] that one must speak at this point. The monarchy was constantly accompanied by prophets, right from the beginning, though in very different ways. Samuel set out the problematic sides of the new constitutional reform of the monarchy programmatically, but then anointed the first kings; Gad and Nathan accompanied the kingship of David with encouragement and also critique; Ahijah of Shiloh announced the end of the kingdom of Solomon and at the same time introduced the rule of Jeroboam; Jehu ben Hanani announced to king Baasha, who had removed the dynasty of Jeroboam, the impending end of his dynasty; Elijah, Micaiah ben Imlah, Elisha and a series of anonymous prophets intervened in various ways in the "culture war" against the Canaanite tendencies of the dynasty of Omri, particularly under Ahab, and at times supported this dynasty, but finally preparing its end; Elijah co-operated in a decisive way in the emergence of the dynasty of Jehu but also predicted its end after only four generations, which even the support from Jonah ben Amittai was not able to stop. (Cf. Blenkinsopp 1995, 138-40.)

The activity of the prophets in the period of the monarchy in Israel and Judah is described in summary terms a number of times. Thus after the report of the fall of Samaria and the deportation of the population of the northern kingdom, following a long list of Israel's cultic deviations, we read: "The LORD warned Israel and Judah through all his prophets and seers: 'Turn from your evil ways. Observe my commands and decrees, in accordance with the entire Law that I commanded your fathers to obey and that I delivered to you through my servants the prophets'" (2 Kgs 17.13).

Here in a—naturally very concise—overview the activity of the prophets is seen especially in the proclamation of the Torah and the exhortation to keep it [→137]. But this summary no doubt hits the nail on the head. The prophetic message, in all its various forms, was always focused on the basic requirements of Yhwh worship, as they formed the basis and the heart of all Israelite legislation.

The expression, "my (his) servants the prophets" is evidently a deliberate reference to the frequent description of Moses as "servant" (*'ebed*) of God. With this title Moses is frequently described as the mediator of the divine Torah; but at one decisive point precisely this title exalts him above the other prophets (Num 12.7) [→**70**]. In this capacity he also predicted the election of Israel as the people of Yhwh and the gift of "rest" in the land (1 Kgs 8.53, 56). This title is now frequently applied to the prophets as a whole (2 Kgs 9.7; 17.13, 23; 21.10; 24.2), but occasionally also to individual prophets: Ahijah of Shiloh (1 Kgs 14.18; 15.29), Elisha (1 Kgs 18.36 in his self-designation; 2 Kgs 9.36; 10.10), Jonah ben Amittai (14.25).

This important role that the prophets play in the account of the history of the monarchy contains a clear answer to the question whether Israel has been a failure. The monarchy did not do justice to its commission to lead the people in the way the Yhwh religion had required as the "constitution" of Israel. And so the political fate of Israel and Judah could and had to be interpreted as the failure of "Israel" as a political entity. At the same time, however, in the account of this history readers are made very clearly aware that there could have been, and still was, another way which was in tune with the demands of the Torah and allowed Israel to be the "chosen people" and the "people of (God's) possession." The prophets had repeatedly pointed to this path, and the writings of the prophets, which now were available following the account of the history of the monarchy, contained an abundance of sayings that could point to a new way that did not have to lead again into ruin.

Interlude
Continuity and Discontinuity in Old Testament Prophecy

The two parts of the canon of the prophets display quite different characteristics. The books of the "Former Prophets" talk of prophets in the framework of narrative traditions. The prophets are generally not the "principal characters" but appear in the context of the historical and political events that the texts report about. In many cases however they more or less directly influence these events. Above all they often give the decisive theological assessment and interpretation in their words and their effects. Thus this first part of the prophetic canon richly deserves its label, the "Former Prophets."

In the second part of the canon of the prophets the picture undergoes a fundamental change. Here we find a large number of books that each bear the name of a prophet and in which the words of this prophet are reported, usually supplemented only by brief narrative components. Here the prophets themselves are in the center ground, while the historical and political context of their activity often comes to expression only in fits and starts or can only be determined indirectly from the prophetic words or from other texts. The different character of these two parts of the canon raises a whole series of questions. First, the question arises why the word of the prophets is presented in such a varied way. Connected with this is the other question whether the type of prophecy is the same in the two parts of the canon or whether fundamental differences or changes can be discerned. Finally the character of the books in which the prophetic words are transmitted throws up quite different interpretative problems than exist with the narrative books. (On this, cf. 1997a.)

We begin with the second question. If one considers the terms used to describe the prophets within the Hebrew Bible, two things emerge. First: there is no clear and exclusive terminology to describe those figures that one can or should term "prophets" [→§17]. The dominant Hebrew expression *nābî*, with its corresponding Greek term προφήτης, is by no means always and everywhere used for the prophets. In particular for the older "writing prophets" it is only seldom used of the prophet that gives his name to the book concerned. But no other term is used for it either. Rather, its appearance and effect shows the prophets as such, independently of any labeling by a particular term. The other question is related to this: despite all the differences in detail fundamentally different forms of prophecy cannot be determined within the story as presented in the Hebrew Bible. Above all, there is no basic difference between the prophets talked about in the first part of the prophetic canon and those in the second. The great prophetic figures like Elijah, Elisha and not least Micaiah ben Imlah "warn us ... against the assumption that the appearance of Amos or Isaiah meant something entirely new to Israel" (von Rad 1965, 64). This means that no clear answer is feasible for the first question of the reasons for the differences in presentation between the "Former" and the "Latter" prophets. "Why we have a book of Amos but no book of Elijah, we can only guess at" (Blenkinsopp 1995, 140).

An essential element of continuity lies in the fact that in the case of all the "former" prophets and many of the "latter" prophets their appearance is in a relationship of tension towards the monarchy. In the account of the biblical texts the beginning of the kingdom is indissolubly linked with the work of the prophet Samuel [→**104**]. Without him there would be no king, since it was he who anointed and appointed a king in accordance with the wishes of the people, first Saul and then David. In the rejection of Saul and the anointing of his successor it becomes clear that in the view of these texts the kingdom does not have any independence of its own, but is dependent on the divine legitimation confirmed by a prophet. This can be granted but can also be withdrawn.

In the time to follow the picture varies. The appearance of prophets however always contains the two elements of support of the king and criticism of his rule through to rejection. This applies in different ways in each case for the prophets in the time of David, Gad and Nathan, for Ahijah of Shiloh [→**113, 125**], who brought about the end of Solomon's rule and thus also the establishment of a separate kingdom in the north under Jeroboam I, and then (after a short, purely negative message of Jehu ben Hanani to Baasha) for the large number of prophets from Elijah through Micaiah ben Imlah and the anonymous prophets and groups of prophets through to Elisha, who with the designation of Jehu once again brings about the end of a dynasty and the beginning of a new one. Throughout this whole time kings and prophets are engaged in an extremely tense relationship with each other.

Jehu's dynasty [→**135**] is the last to receive a prophetic legitimation, and at the same time the last in the northern kingdom of Israel that is blessed with a relatively long rule. For the following time through to the end of the northern kingdom no more reports are found of the appearance of prophets. But here the continuity between the "former" and the "latter" prophets is evident. In Hosea we read: "I will soon punish the house of Jehu for the massacre at Jezreel, and I will put an end to the kingdom of Israel" (Hos 1.4) [→**266**]. Here a prophetic voice is raised which continues the critical line beyond Elisha. Amos names Jeroboam II, the last of the dynasty of Jehu, who reigned for a lengthy period, and predicts his death by the sword (Amos 7.9; cf. vv. 10f) [→**286**]—an announcement that was not fulfilled, however (cf. 2 Kgs 14.29). Hosea and Amos thus stand in the line of the prophets that form a critical opposition to the kingship. But whatever the causes may be for their lack of mention in the books of Kings, at any rate one

can see no sign there of a fundamental change in the relationships between prophets and kings.

The reasons for the "silence of the prophets" (Koch 1981) in the books of
Kings have been discussed many times. Were these material reasons, perhaps
because the prophet's proclamation of judgment was in contradiction to the
hope of the "deuteronomistic" authors of the books of Kings for a future restoration of Israel? (Blenkinsopp 1995, 122). It would be consonant with the
latter that in many of the prophetic books "deuteronomistic" parties and revisions are found; in particular the superscriptions of the prophetic books show
clear deuteronomistic elements (Tucker 1977, 69). This question will not
however be answered unambiguously.

In Judah too the voices of prophets are raised who are publicly at odds
with the monarchy. In Isaiah his great appearance against Ahaz [→**174**]
stands at the center of the first main part of the book (Isa 7). His advi-
sory and critical relations with Hezekiah (chs. 36–39) are also transmitted in the books of Kings (2 Kgs 18.13–20.19) [→**148**]. This is all very
reminiscent of Elisha. In Jeremiah, finally, the alternating relationship
of the prophet to the kings is a constant theme. On occasion there are
even what could well be termed conspiratorial conversations with
Zedekiah (Jer 37f) [→**223**].
     So the relationship with the kingdom as an institution and with the
individual kings places the prophets in the center of the history of their
people. This applies to the prophets of the various periods in basically
the same way. It is nonetheless clear that after the eighth century, the
words of the prophets whose words we find transmitted in the second
part of the prophetic canon, have new elements to them. So the question arises what "the new thing in 8th-century prophecy" (von Rad
1965, 182ff) might be. Von Rad emphasized with continuity: "one
might almost describe the whole of their proclamation as a single con-
temporizing conversation with the tradition." But he then continues:
"but it is as if they were reading something entirely different in these
traditions" (*ibid.* 185). What is the basis for this impression?
     The clearest indication of what is "new" is doubtless the promi-
nence of the prophets as individuals in a very pronounced sense.
"They could say 'I' in a way that Israel had not previously heard" (*ibid.*
183). This individuality also comes to expression in the fact that individual writings now come into being in which an individual is at the
center, whose name they bear. The large extent of the utterances of
each of the prophets is also something entirely new. Finally, there is

no precedent in the older literature for the sometimes extremely artistic turns of phrase in which the prophets declaim. These more external features already make the appearance of the "writing prophets" stand out from all that has come before. And then there is the extraordinary breadth and extent of the topics that they deal with. They not only show a marked knowledge of the faith traditions of Israel but also an astonishing level of knowledge of historical and world-political connections. But above all with the prophets there begins a nuanced "theological" thinking and speaking in the narrower and broader senses. There is nothing comparable before them to what they say about God, his relationship to Israel and the nations, about law and cult and much else besides.

This applies in particular to the salvation-historical traditions of Israel. An especially marked, frequently cited example of this is Amos's statement: "You only have I chosen of all the families of the earth; therefore I will punish you for all your sins" (Amos 3.2) [→**280**]. Here the "election tradition" is certainly not denied. But it is not simply and linearly interpreted as a basis for a continuing saving history of God with Israel, but out of it a special responsibility is derived towards the God who has selected Israel out of the world of the nations. Out of the election tradition a proclamation of the divine punishment of Israel can be deduced. In this line lie many words of the prophets in which they understand salvation-historical traditions in such a way that they become the basis of a critique of Israel's behavior and of the proclamation of a divine judgment.

The prophets thus develop an entirely new, broadly spread understanding of history and especially of its theological dimension. This demonstrates the effort "to understand Israel's behavior in its entirety and to draw out what, in all its historical conditionedness, may be regarded as typical" (von Rad, 1965, 186). This is directly related to the conviction of "God's full power over history. It is so sovereign that no other activity whatsoever seems to have space in history ... It is the "I" of Yahweh that fills the space of history right to the end" (*ibid.* 189f).

The whole thing is to a large extent an intellectual phenomenon. It can be seen in connection with the emergence of intellectual elites in various parts of the world in the period around the middle of the first millennium BCE, which Karl Jaspers has called the "axis period." "This axis of world history now seems to lie around 500 BCE, in the intellectual process that took place between 800 and 200. There lies the most decisive turning point in history. It was then that the human being emerged that we live with to the present day ... Extraordinary things come together at this time." Alongside the great figures in China, India, Iran and finally in Greece, "in Palestine ... the prophets arise from Elijah through Isaiah and Jeremiah to Deutero-Isaiah" (Jaspers 1949/1955, 14f).

This understanding of the prophets from the eighth century can at least go some way towards explaining the odd tension between continuity and discontinuity in the history of Israelite prophecy. It also helps to understand the special position of the prophets, who in their role as "dissident intellectuals" have also gained a position of intellectual leadership in the history of Israelite religion (Blenkinsopp 1995, 144ff). This certainly came about in a lengthy process. The texts show that in their activities the prophets often met rejection, even if it would certainly be too one-sided to characterize them as in "total opposition" (Albertz 1992, 255ff). Above all, from the beginning there were circles in which their words were collected and transmitted. By the arrival of the calamities predicted by the prophets their words gained credibility and increased weight, so that they were passed on and interpreted (cf. Steck 1993). On the one hand this has the consequence that the "historical" wording of what the prophets proclaimed is no longer clearly discernible and that in the intention of the tradents it should not be so either. On the other hand precisely this manner of continuing exposition has provided some of the decisive grounds for the central significance of the prophetic message for biblical religion.

§3

The "Latter Prophets"

1. Problems of interpretation

The reader of the Hebrew Bible who moves on from the end of the second book of Kings to the beginning of the book of Isaiah meets a completely changed situation. The conclusion of the books of Kings has left the reader with an open question: How will Israel's history continue after the fall of Jerusalem and the destruction of the temple? But now there is no narrative thread to follow, and it is difficult for the reader to gain an overview of the large number of books with which he or she is now confronted. There is an abundance of mainly shorter passages of prophetic speech, the connection between which is often not easy to discern and which is only occasionally interrupted by brief narrative sections or notes.

The reader of a German or English Bible translation will not meet this problem in the same way, because here the prophetic books are placed at the end of the Old Testament [→4].

In other regards, however, basically the same applies for the prophetic books as for the Pentateuch and the "Former Prophets" [→11, 94]: they contain material from various times and by various "authors." A basic stock of sayings of the prophet whose name is given to the book in question has been supplemented and revised in the course of its transmission to coming generations. In the process, the great historical events in particular have left traces. One can assume that the books of the prophets from the time of the fall of Jerusalem and the Babylonian exile did not gain their final shape until after the end of the exile and the beginning of the restoration of the political, economic and religious life in Jerusalem and Judah. The changed situation has its echoes in various parts of the texts.

So in the majority of the prophetic books it is scarcely possible to tease out the original words of the prophet in question. The difficulty starts already with the fact that we do not know how and by whom the words spoken by the prophet were committed to writing. In the case of most of the prophets one might easily assume that they wrote down their words themselves. (Ezekiel might form an exception [→**231**].) But it is also only in exceptional cases that we learn something about a possible school of disciples or an individual who might have been able to do this, such as the "disciples" of Isaiah (Isa 8.16) [→**175**] or Jeremiah's "secretary," Baruch (Jer 36) [→**187, 209?**]. So already here there is a certain distance between the spoken and the written word. But this means that as a rule the prophets are not the "authors" of the books that bear their names.

Nonetheless, it may be assumed that in all the prophetic books many words have been preserved and transmitted that were spoken by the prophet in question. That is what gives each of the prophetic books its own unmistakable profile. For the majority of the prophetic books, however, they will also contain texts that derive only from the transmission of the tradition. Such texts were generally written with the intent and conviction of speaking in the name of the prophet concerned. They aim to interpret his words and at the same time to react to changed circumstances. One might in this connection speak of "prophecy of tradents" (cf. Steck 1991, 270ff). Thus many of the prophetic books offer a multifaceted picture and reflect a whole spectrum of different situations, but at the same time are marked by a clearly recognizable character that bears the profile of the prophet in question.

Prophet research was for a long time (and to some extent still is) determined by the search for the "original" words of each prophet and with the most exact determination possible of his historical vantage point and of the situation he was speaking to. The other words were considered "secondary" by comparison, which however did not stop intensive thought often being devoted to them and the conditions in which they came into being. However, the texts in their present shape and the prophetic books as a whole were increasingly lost from view.

This has not least to do with the fact that the prophetic books were primarily viewed from a historical perspective. To a certain extent, if often unconsciously, the temporal and conceptual proximity of the prophetic books to the preceding historical books carried weight. In the case of the prophetic books too, exegesis wanted to know first of all "what really happened." This concern was fuelled additionally by the fact that the historical circumstances of some of the most important prophetic figures are more or less clearly recognizable. In the case of Isaiah, Jeremiah and Ezekiel, and in the case of Amos and again Haggai and Zechariah, the texts reveal individual phases of their biography and make clear how particular prophetic sayings were spoken to particular historical situations. But this is certainly not the case for all the prophetic books, and even for those just mentioned in most cases it applies only to a portion of the texts.

The problem is exacerbated where juxtaposed texts in a prophetic book obviously derive from different times in the history of Israel. This is most clearly the case in the book of Isaiah. In ch. 7 [→**175**] the so-called Syro-Ephraimite war of 734/732 forms the historical context, while in 44.28 and 45.1 [→**191**] the name of the Persian king Cyrus is mentioned, who conquered Babylon in 539. So here texts have been joined together which are separated by two centuries. Scholarly exposition has largely concentrated on this and been content also to reconstruct the various "original" components of the book of Isaiah and to expound each of them separately.

In recent times, however, there have been more and more attempts to focus on Isaiah as a whole and to place in the foreground the question of how the "authors" of the final edition of the book wished this to be understood. From this point of view an attempt is made to understand the book of Isaiah as a complex unit, full of tensions (cf. 1996). The same applies also to other prophetic books in which there is evidence of a similar plurality or even multiplicity of layers.

This means that exegesis on one hand will be concerned to elucidate the person of the prophet in question, but that it will not stop there but will need to continue to ask about the "canonical" Isaiah, Amos etc. This will be done with great care and with awareness of the demanding task of finding a responsible path between the critical atomization of a prophetic book and an uncritical harmonization of obvious tensions. This task is not fundamentally different from that for the other parts of the canon. But here it has special importance by virtue of the fact that the prophets, unlike the authors of the books of the Pentateuch and the "Former Prophets," stand before us as personalities, so that the question of what the individual prophet "really" said and did is almost automatically raised.

It is now crucial with what attitude the interpreter poses and attempts to answer this question. In the traditional "historical-critical" approach to the texts the prime concern is often to tease out what is "historically" accurate and in so doing to be "critical" towards those who altered and obscured this historical "original." This type of exegetical work is often compared, even by many who use it, with the work of archaeologists. This comparison implies a valuation of the individual "layers," which in effect leads to a devaluation of the later layers by comparison with the earlier ones. It is not uncommon for it to be argued that statements of a later editor infringed the intention of the prophet himself, the exegete as a rule attempting to put himself in the supposed position of the prophet and to defend this position against such distortions. A "canonical" exposition will in principle not apply such judgments and valuations. Rather, it will treat the various stages of the history of the text as components of the canonical process, with the same respect that eventually brought about the canonical text in its final form. This means equally that the individual stages of this process are not played off against each other but are interpreted in their continuing dialogue with each other.

Such a view is thus also of great significance for the understanding of the message of the prophetic books, because this is addressed to a generation living after the catastrophes of the fall of the northern kingdom of Israel and the southern kingdom of Judah and finally of exile. The readers of the prophetic texts know that the prophets' message of judgment has been dramatically fulfilled. But they also know that the history of the people of Israel has not yet come to an end, that there is an "afterwards," in which they themselves are living. So for them not only are the prophets' proclamations of judgment significant, but at least as much their justifications. For their present these become appeals not to behave in the way the prophets had to criticize and judge their contemporaries for, but to obey the message of the prophets and follow their insights. Hence precisely those texts that repeatedly break through the prophetic message of judgment, be it with the call to repentance before it is too late, be it with the quiet hope of a possible rescue, or be it finally with the resounding proclamation of imminent salvation. Many of these sayings may have been added to the message of the individual prophets in the course of the process of transmission and the final shaping of the prophetic books. In the light of these the readers may also feel spoken to by the prophetic message of judgment. But they know that even the hardest message of judgment cannot be announced without the future perspective in which there is a continuation of Israel, which must be marked by the concern not to repeat the mistakes of earlier generations and which is willing to take its lead from the notes of hope and promise in the prophetic message.

A comment on terminology. Up to this point, for the prophetic books that form the second half of the second part of the canon of the Hebrew Bible I have generally used the term "Latter Prophets," which is adopted from the Hebrew. In English, the prophetic figures after whom these books are named are frequently called the "writing prophets." This term might create the impression that the prophets themselves are to be understood as "authors." But that this is not the case, generally speaking, has been shown above. But after this misunderstanding has been set aside, this commonly used term can be used uninhibitedly as a designation of the title figures of the various prophetic books or "prophetic writings," where appropriate.

2. The Book of Isaiah

2.1 Preliminary considerations

On a count of chapters, the book of Isaiah is the most extensive book of the "writing prophets," and it is also the most complex [→*In* **201**]. The person of the prophet Isaiah ben Amoz comes into the clear view of the reader in a series of chapters which also contain narrative elements. In the so-called Syro-Ephraimite war of 734/732 he appears before king Ahaz (ch. 7) [→**175**] and later, during the siege of Jerusalem in 701 before king Hezekiah (chs. 36–39) [→**183**]. Many of the prophetic messages in the first half of the book reflect the political and social situation in these decades, which are also framed in the superscript of the book by the mention of the Judean kings Uzziah, Jotham, Ahaz and Hezekiah. Then the situation changes. From ch. 40 [→**184**] it is presupposed that the addressed Israelites are in Babylonian exile, and many prophetic sayings promise an early return. Here we also find the name of the Persian king Cyrus, who conquered Babylon in 539 [→**191**]. But no other prophetic figure to whom the words of this changed time could be ascribed appears. In the concluding chapters, from ch. 56 onwards [→**194f**] the addressees are evidently back in Jerusalem and Judah. Here many themes from earlier sections of the book are taken up again and developed further. Towards the end eschatological expectations are increasingly in evidence.

The prevailing scholarly opinion since the end of the 19th century divided the book into three separate "books": chs. 1–39 (called "Isaiah," sometimes "Proto-Isaiah"), chs. 40–55 ("Deutero-Isaiah" or "Second Isaiah"), chs. 56–66 ("Trito-Isaiah" or "Third Isaiah"). Most recent discussion however has cast doubt on this threefold division. No one doubts that the book of Isaiah contains texts from at least three different time periods. What is in question, however, is the literary independence of the individual parts. From a linguistic and theological point of view the clearest contours are evident for chs. 40–55. However, they have no literarily discernible beginning, and in addition some of the earlier chapters of the book also have clear elements of the same language and theology. This has to do with the other problem, that chs. 1–39 are by no means a unit but display great literary and theological variety. For this reason the separate existence of a book that contained only chs. 1–39 or essential parts of them has become doubtful (Ackroyd 1979; Seitz 1988). Rather, we see that the shaping of these chapters has at many points been influenced by the later chapters. In the prevailing terminology this means that in the shaping of Isa 1–39 the influence of elements from "Deutero-Isaiah" is clearly discernible. For chs. 56–66 this influence is in any case quite obvious. So the book of Isaiah we now have is a unity to a much stronger degree than is generally assumed [→*In* 210]. The person of the 8th-century prophet Isaiah recedes behind the overall prophetic message of the book. From a canonical point of view however the various voices join up with the message of the one "Isaiah," and they gain their profile from the prophet who gave the book its name and who is the only one to be discernible in it as a person: Isaiah ben Amoz. (In general cf. 1996; Jüngling 1995, esp. 313; further, Williamson 1994.)

2.2 The vision concerning Judah and Jerusalem

"The vision concerning Judah and Jerusalem that Isaiah son of Amoz saw" (Isa 1.1). The first sentence of the book of Isaiah indicates one of the basic themes of this great collection of prophetic sayings: Jerusalem, also called Zion [→§14]. The theme is in the superscription and colors the first rhetorical-literary unit, which concludes with the vision of the pilgrimage of the peoples to Zion in 2.1-5. From here on it moves on under changing aspects through the whole book, through to the inclusion of Jerusalem in the hope of the creation of a new heaven and a new earth (65.17f; cf. 66.22) [→**197f**].

But first of all heaven and earth come into view in a quite different function: "Hear, O heavens! Listen, O earth! For the LORD has spoken: 'I reared children and brought them up, but they have rebelled against me'" (1.2). Heaven and earth are called upon as witnesses in the legal dispute God has against his own wayward "sons," i.e. with Israel (v. 3), his "people" (v. 4) [→14]. Thus begins Isaiah's vision of Judah and Jerusalem: with God's suffering from the fact that his people has left the path it should take in accordance with his will.

Here we see what is new in prophecy, with its first representative Isaiah. Its opponent is not the king—he does not come into view in Isaiah until much later (ch. 7) [→175]—but the people, "Israel," as it is called in the language of religious tradition, even when what is meant is the political entity of "Judah." The themes of the dispute are not so much individual actions or conflicts but much more fundamental: Israel is a "sinful people" (1.4). This marks out the situation of the prophet: he stands alone before the people as the representative and proclaimer of the will of God; the prophet has nothing fundamentally new to proclaim. But they have become apostate, have turned away and turned their back on the "Holy One of Israel" [→§16].

At another point this is filled in with more detail: "They have rejected the law of the LORD Almighty (Yhwh Zebaot) and spurned the word of the Holy One of Israel" (5.24). So it is about the Torah, the instruction given by God, which Israel should have followed. The one who gives it is the "Holy One of Israel," who also bears the name associated with the ark in the temple, "Yhwh Zebaot" [→112]. Finally this is again drawn out when Isaiah is to write down a message for later times. It deals with the rejection of the Torah by the stubborn people, for whom the term "sons" is taken up again here and whose resistance is once again directed against the "Holy One of Israel" (30.8-11) [→182].

The place where the Torah should be implemented above all places, is Jerusalem. It was once the "faithful" city, filled with justice, and righteousness (*sedeq*) lived in it (1.21). All this is over now, because care of the law has been neglected. But God will restore it "as at the beginning" so that Zion will again be called "The City of Righteousness, The Faithful City." We then read the programmatic statement: "Zion will be redeemed with justice (*mišpaṭ*), her penitent ones (or returnees?) with righteousness (*ṣᵉdāqāh*)" (1.21-27) [→179, 183]. When this will be, and how it will occur, is left open at this point.

The sacrificial cult [→§11] in the temple has also fallen into neglect. The hands of those who present the sacrifices are covered in blood. More important than the presentation of sacrifices is to do right, and this means in particular: helping the oppressed and gaining justice for widows and orphans (1.10-17). This is one of the texts that are all too frequently misunderstood in a "Protestant" way. The prophet is far away from any rejection of the sacrificial cult *per se*. But a sacrifice presented by hands "bloody" from acts of violence is senseless. So the concluding call sounds out not to desist from presenting sacrifices in future but to learn to do good and seek justice (v. 17).

This first section ends by picking up again on the superscription of the book. Isaiah "sees" "a word about Judah and Jerusalem" (2.1). The view of the "days of Uzziah" and the kings that succeed him (1.1) is now directed ahead to the "end of days" (2.2). The significance of Jerusalem, not only for Israel, but for the whole world, will then be evident, when the peoples carry out their pilgrimage to Zion, for "the law will go out from Zion, the word of the LORD from Jerusalem" (v. 3). The Torah has been given to Israel, but its significance extends far beyond into the world of the nations. The giver of the Torah will create justice between the nations, so that they will no longer wage war with each other (v. 4). But the view of the future will not deflect attention from the present. Rather, it is to serve as an encouragement to Israel, the "House of Jacob," to walk now already in the "light of the LORD" (v. 5), as it will one day radiate over Jerusalem, when the nations throng to it (60.1-3) [→196].

In this first section of prophecies, in which Jerusalem has central position, the most varied time aspects are linked together. We read how Jerusalem once was (1.21), how it now is (vv. 21-23), how it will become again (vv. 26f) and how it will stand, finally, "at the end of days" [→§22], as the central point for the world of the nations (2.2-4). The first verses, however, show the lamentable reality of the present: the land has been severely hurt and devastated by the war, Zion/Jerusalem has remained alone "like a shelter in a vineyard" (1.5-8). Here mixed in with the exchange of voices between the reporter (v. 1), God himself (vv. 2f), and the prophet (vv. 4-6) is also the voice of those affected: "Unless the LORD Almighty had left us some survivors ('a small remnant'), we would have become like Sodom, we would have been like Gomorrah" (v. 9). The "remnant"—this too is a recurrent motif in the book of Isaiah (cf. Webb 1990).

In the second section (2.6–4.6) the change of aspects is even more dramatic: accusations against the "House of Jacob" (2.6), against Judah and Jerusalem (3.1ff), against officials (3.12, 14) and against women ("daughters of Zion" 3.16-24) alternate with the depiction of the ravages of war and anarchic circumstances when the "day of YHWH Zebaot" comes upon "all the proud and lofty" (2.12ff). But in the end there is talk again of the remnant (4.2-6), of what remains in Zion and Jerusalem; it is "called holy" and God will set up a structure providing shelter and shade over Zion, expressed with the same word for the shelter in the vineyard (*sukkāh*, 1.8), as it were a magnificent eschatological counterpart.

These first chapters, then, contain the basic elements of the prophetic proclamation of the book of Isaiah: lament and accusation on account of abandonment of the Torah and hence announcement of the divine judgment—and proclamation and promise of the restoration and of salvation in the last days. In the course of the book the balance changes. In chs. 40ff in particular [→**185**], in which the situation of the exile is presupposed, the saving and comforting words come more strongly to the fore. But as has already been shown, they are certainly not lacking in the first part of the book, and even in the later chapters the critical and punishing elements appear again and again. Both things, judgment and salvation, belong inseparably connected in the prophetic message of the book of Isaiah.

This is again seen in the chapters that now follow. In 5.1 for the first time the "I" of the prophet is heard. The song of the vineyard expresses God's experiences with Israel with a new metaphor. All care and attention has achieved nothing, so God allows the vineyard to run wild and become a wasteland (vv. 1-6). The key to the metaphor is clear: the vineyard is Israel (v. 7). As already in ch. 1, we hear the reproach that justice (*mišpaṭ*) and righteousness (*ṣᵉdāqāh*) have not been done. A first "woe" is added (5.8), which continues through the whole of ch. 5 and is taken up again later in ch. 10 [→**199**]. In the same way a poem is interrupted with a pivotal verse about the untempered wrath of God (5.25) and resumed later (9.11).

This shows the broad scope of this composition. It begins with the devastation of the vineyard in 5.1-7 and ends with the return of the "remnant" to a road that God will travel as he once did the road through the sea during the exodus from Egypt (11.15f; on the "remnant" see already 10.20-22) [→**178**]. Thus once again we see the basic structure of the way from accusation and proclamation of divine judgment through to the restoration of the remnant, as was already discernible in 1.2–2.5 and 2.6–4.6.

2.3 Here am I, send me

In between there is a connected body of texts with quite a different set of themes (6.1–9.6). In ch. 6 the person of Isaiah himself comes into view: "I saw" [→*In* 121]. The prophet describes a vision that is surprisingly closely reminiscent of the vision of Micaiah ben Imlah in 1 Kgs 22.19ff [→142]: "I saw the LORD seated on a throne, high and exalted." As the vision further unfolds the parallels are clear: God, enthroned as king, is surrounded by heavenly beings; he speaks with them and issues orders. The parallel also makes the difference between them clear, however. In the case of Micaiah ben Imlah the concern was with the critical dispute with the Israelite king who was just ruling; in Isaiah's case the bridge reaches further: it is about the future of Israel. The continuity with earlier prophecy is as much in evidence here as ventures into new thematic areas.

Isaiah sees himself placed in a heavenly scene: God, enthroned, is surrounded by heavenly beings singing his praises: he is the "Holy One" [→§15], whose glory (*kābôd*) fills the whole world. Isaiah is frightened to death that his eyes have seen the "king YHWH Zebaot" (v. 5). He knows that no human being who sees God can remain alive (Ex 33.20) [→58, 62]. Indeed: he knows that he has "unclean lips" like the whole nation among whom he lives. They have injured the holiness of God both in word and deed. And not even he, though he has stood up to the people with his sharp criticism, can except himself.

But it becomes clear here that precisely this is the reason that Isaiah is granted this vision. He is now almost physically pulled into the heavenly scene as he is cleansed of his "unclean" lips and purified by the "Serafim" with a glowing coal from the altar (vv. 6f). This prepares him for the moment he hears the divine question, "Whom shall I send? And who will go for us?," so that he can answer: "Here am I. Send me!" (v. 8). The vision was not self-serving. It was intended to equip Isaiah for a special task.

What now follows, however, shows that this scene was not a "call" to become a prophet but a commission with a very particular message. Isaiah has after all already been working as a prophet and speaking in the name of God, so that there have to be good reasons for this vision not standing at the beginning of the book (as in Jeremiah and Ezekiel).

All the more shocking is the content of what is now said to the prophet. At the end of his solemn preparation he is commissioned to preach: "Be ever hearing, but never understanding; be ever seeing, but never perceiving" (v. 9). And then we read as an explanation for himself that with his preaching he is to harden, stop and seal the hearts, ears and eyes of the Israelites, so that they do not see, hear and understand—and turn and be healed (v. 10).

For the present-day interpreter it is difficult to understand this message of "hardening." A way out has often been sought in psychological explanation: this is the result of the depressing experience of Isaiah, that his preaching remained without fruit. But the text does not allow such an interpretation; the divine commission is clear. In addition, the notion of a "hardening" of hearts is also found in other parts of the Hebrew Bible (e.g. with Pharaoh, Ex 4.21 etc.) [→**45**]. It is important not to see this saying in isolation but to read it in its context, in particular in view of what follows.

The prophet's counter-question is surprising: "How long, O LORD?" (v. 11). The question shows that he does not see the hardening commission as an announcement of the definitive end of Israel. The divine answer speaks of a destruction of the cities and of the land, of the deportation of the inhabitants into exile and finally of the annihilation of the last remnants (vv. 11b-13a)—but not "root and branch," because the stump remains, and the stump is "holy seed" (v. 13b). Thus despite the radicalism of its proclamation of woe the divine answer points towards a promising conclusion, however muted it may be. In the end, when everything seems to be over, new life germinates like a new shoot growing out of a tree-stump (cf. Seitz 1993, 52ff).

As things proceed it is also clear that Isaiah does not understand the message about hardening as the "last word." Just a little later he expresses that he hopes in the God who is now "hiding his face from the house of Jacob" (8.17). And he is writing down his message "for future times," so he expects that there will be such times (30.8; cf. von Rad 1965, 158-62). For the reader of the book of Isaiah the bridge is extending even further. After the destruction of the land and the expulsion of the inhabitants, which the divine answer speaks of, have occurred, there is talk of return and reconstruction. The "waste places" (6.11) will become too tight for the many new inhabitants (49.19) [→**193f**] and Jerusalem will no longer be called "Deserted" (62.4). Then the hardening of Israel will also be lifted and they will again "see and know" (41.20), which now is impossible for them (cf. 1989).

2.4 If you do not stand firm in your faith, you will not stand at all

What is recorded in ch. 6 concerned only Isaiah himself. Now he appears in the public arena (ch. 7). In a situation of crisis he appears before the king [→**144**]. This recalls the appearance of Elisha or the anonymous prophets of 1 Kgs 20 [→**142**]. This time it is about the political fate of king Ahaz. The coalition of the northern neighbor states wants to replace him with a king of their choice who is prepared to join the coalition against Assyria (cf. 2 Kgs 16) [→**147f**]. But at the same time it is about the "house of David" (vv. 2, 13). In two weighty divine sentences Isaiah formulates the alternative: "It will not take place, it will not happen" (v. 7); but "If you do not stand firm in your faith, you will not stand at all" (v. 9b). How are these two sayings related? Is the "faith" the precondition for the looming calamity not to happen? The question remains open.

The scene grows as it were beyond itself through the hesitation of Ahaz to ask for a sign offered by the prophet (vv. 11f). An unsolicited sign is then announced to him: the birth of a child by the name of *'immānû'ēl*, "God with us" (v. 14). We do not know whether the meaning of this sign was completely clear to Ahaz and his contemporaries. For interpreters after them these verses are among the great puzzles of the Bible. Who is the "young woman" who will give birth to this child? The Greek translation of the Hebrew word *'almāh* by παρθένος "virgin" has played an important role in the Christian tradition of the "virgin birth" of the Messiah [→**§13**]. But apart from the problem of this (not quite impossible) translation the question who is meant by this woman remains unanswered and unanswerable. Similarly the question of who this child will be; it is not given an answer in the further course of the book of Isaiah either. And in what does the "sign" consist? In the birth of the child, or in the course of his life? Or perhaps rather in his name, "God with us"? One has to take the name as a "symbolic name" like the names of the sons of Isaiah *š°'ār yāsûb* "a remnant turns back" (or: "a remnant returns"? 7.3) and *mahēr šālāl ḥāš baz* "Quick to the plunder—Swift to the spoil" (8.3).

According to the thrust of the text a sign would now be expected indicating calamity for Ahaz, and there is frequent mention of calamity in the following texts. But the name Immanuel means divine care and help. For whom? If not for Ahaz, for whom? (See below on 8.18.)

It has been suggested that in the interpretation of this child one should assume that for the meeting with Ahaz Isaiah is to take his son Shear-Yashub with him (7.3). After the unbelieving refusal of Ahaz to ask for a sign, the announced son could then represent the believing "remnant" (Rice 1978; Webb 1990, 82).

Isaiah's meeting with king Ahaz, which began in 7.3, is not given a conclusion in narrative form. But the following prophetic words show two things: first the end of the two northern kingdoms which now threaten Jerusalem (7.16; 8.4), but then the threat to Judah and Jerusalem from the Assyrians, who are called by God himself [→§20]. Here we see Isaiah's graphic and dramatic language with particular clarity: God will whistle up Israel's enemies like flies and bees (7.18), he will let the Assyrians come upon Israel like a razor (v. 20), and the flood waters of the Euphrates will come over those who scorn their own "gently flowing waters of Shiloah" (8.5-8). These floods will come up to Judah's neck—and then suddenly we hear: Immanuel (end of v. 8)! It is like a stop-sign. However much the nations may rage, and whatever they are planning: it will not happen (vv. 9f; cf. 7.7). For there is one thing in their way: Immanuel—"God with us"! God remains the lord of what happens, and this means: he is with his own people. In the context this does not rule out the waters coming up to their neck—but then *only* up to the neck.

Once again Isaiah's "I" comes into view. God has physically ("with his strong hand") prevented him from going the way of "this people" (8.11). This has brought him into isolation; but he wants to "seal" this "testimony" in his disciples and hope in the Lord, who now "is hiding his face from the house of Jacob" (vv. 16f). He himself and his children with their symbolic names have become a sign for Israel "from the LORD Almighty, who dwells on Mount Zion" (v. 18). This sounds like a final word. In the context it means the end of Isaiah's attempt to let his message (not to go the way of coalition with Assyria in the current danger of the Syro-Ephraimite war) find a hearing among "this people." Do Isaiah and his disciples already belong to the "remnant"? But first attention turns to the future.

2.5 To us a child is born

The identity of the first child, whose birth is announced by Isaiah, remained hidden—except for his name, "Immanuel." Now the birth of a child is announced that will reign—visibly for miles around—on the throne of David (9.1-6). His identity is thus clear: a ruler from the dynasty of David [→§13].

Talk of his "birth" may also mean his enthronement—as in Ps 2.6f, where the king placed by God on the throne is addressed thus [→319]: "You are my son; today I have become your father." The birth (or enthronement) of this new king will be "a great light" for "the people walking in darkness," i.e. in the first place for the areas of northern Israel occupied by the Assyrians (8.23). An impressive victory over the (not further specified) enemies will precede this, a miraculous victory, like that gained by Gideon over the Midianites (9.3; cf. Judg 7) [→102]. The king is named with great names: "Wonderful Counselor, Mighty God, Everlasting Father, Prince of Peace." This is reminiscent of "throne names" like those given to a king in Egypt on his accession to the throne (cf. Wildberger 1960).

But what the prophet expects here is not simply a successor to the king they have had so far. He is looking ahead to a rule that exceeds everything that has come before. Peace will have no end in the kingdom that this king will rule from the throne of David. And above all: "justice and righteousness" will reign "from that time on and for ever." What is now lacking (cf. 1.21; 5.7) [→169, 172] and what God has promised for the future of Jerusalem (1.27) will constitute the rule of this king, and not just for a short time but as far ahead as it is possible to think. What is Isaiah thinking of? Is he pinning such high expectations on the successor of Ahaz? Or is he speaking in a "court style," which puts reality in an embellishing light? Doubtless an "eschatological" element comes into play here [→§22], an expectation that looks forward into a changed and renewed time beyond current human experience. But also other expectations of Isaiah's, e.g. of a "pilgrimage of the people" to Zion (2.1-5), go far beyond what corresponds to everyday experience. Future expectations of the prophets in a time of oppression always contain an element of expectation of a "coming" time. It will be a time in which human society will correspond entirely to what God's will was and is for humanity; and also the relationship between humans and animals and animals with each other will be freed of all negative and hostile proclivities.

This proclamation of a new ruler according to God's will is concluded like a seal with the sentence: "The zeal of the LORD Almighty will accomplish this" (9.7b). This is an emphatic confirmation that God will keep this promise and at the same time a justification for why he is going to do this. That a king will again sit on the throne of

David, that peace will return again with his rule and that above all justice and righteousness will rule once again, all this will occur not just for Israel's sake but for the sake of God himself. So he will watch jealously to ensure that it happens.

Once again we read of a new ruler from the house of David. After the series of woes that began in 5.8 (and was then interrupted) [→**172**] has concentrated on Assyria in 10.5, finally we read of the complete annihilation of this mighty empire. It is compared with a huge forest that in the end is completely felled (10.33f). In contrast with this the image of the "stump" reappears which was found at the conclusion of Isaiah's great vision (6.13) [→**173**]. Again we read of a tree-stump from which a shoot emerges (11.1; the word here is a different one from that in 6.13, but the concept is the same). This time the image looks back further to the beginning of the story of David, into the house of his father Jesse (1 Sam 16). A new shoot will grow from them, a new David as it were, not just a successor.

At the center of the expectations connected with this future ruler are once again justice and righteousness (11.3-5). But before this we read that the "spirit of the LORD" will rest on him (v. 2), as was said of David immediately after his anointing by Samuel (1 Sam 16.13; cf. also 2 Sam 23.2) [→**108**]. The gifts of the spirit with which the new ruler will be equipped are specified further in three pairs of terms: "spirit of wisdom and understanding, spirit of counsel and power, spirit of knowledge and the fear of the LORD."

It is made quite clear here that the expected future ruler will be more and different than a political and military ruler. He is to combine many qualities in himself that are necessary in order to lead and rule a people in the most varied areas of life. And his legal decisions will not only be incorruptible—"by what he sees with his eyes or what he hears with his ears" (v. 3)—but above all social. He gives justice to those right at the bottom of society, the poor and needy, and defends them against those who are otherwise used to getting their way by means of social power (v. 4).

If the ideal description of the king to this point has gone beyond what has hitherto been experienced, so now in one great stride the present world is exceeded with its often life-threatening contrasts through to the future picture of a world in which peace reigns for all, animals and humans alike (11.6-8). There is again an echo of the animal metaphors from the earlier texts: Assyria was like a lion (5.29), other enemies have devoured Israel "with open mouth" (9.12) and the tribes of Israel ate each other up like wild animals (9.20f). All this will then come to an end. But one is also reminded of accounts of a peaceful life together in creation as a whole, as in ancient Near Eastern traditions about the beginnings of world history and as also expressed in Greece as a future expectation, especially in Virgil's famous *Fourth Eclogue* (cf. Wildberger 1971, 440f). But this eschatological view also remains related to human society which is concentrated as it were in a prism on God's "holy mountain," around which however the whole earth is filled with "the knowledge of the LORD as the waters cover the sea" (11.9). Here too once again one might think of the counter-image of the approaching mighty flood-waters of Assyria (8.7) [→**175**].

That the room of history has not been abandoned with this vision of the future is immediately evident: the shoot from the "root of Jesse" will become a sign for the nations (*nēs 'ammîm*) (11.10) and once again we hear the motif of the pilgrimage of the nations (cf. 2.1-5). Above all, however, God will lead back the "remnant of his people" (11.11-16). For this he will not only remove all obstacles among the nations, but also in nature, just as he once did when he led Israel out of Egypt, by creating a road through sea and river, on which the remnant can return in safety. The history of the people of God, burdened at present with so much waywardness and confusion, will then come to its goal.

2.6 In that day you will say: I will praise you, O LORD

A psalm (Isa 12) concludes this first great chapter of prophetic literature (chs. 1-11) which introduces the prophet Isaiah to the reader. This is the "presentation of a prophet" (Ackroyd 1978); but it is much more than just a biographical "presentation" of this prophet, much of whom is certainly contained in it (cf. Blum 1996/97). It offers a whole spectrum of prophetic visions and messages, which begins in the time of the Assyrian threat to Jerusalem and Judah but which then extends far beyond into a time in which these calamities and sufferings will come to an end.

So then this psalm-like text is not really a conclusion. It looks forward to "that day" when God's anger will be turned and he will comfort his people (12.11). This sounds a note that will later become a key word in a decisive passage in Isaiah, where we read: "Comfort, comfort my people!" (40.1) [→**185f**]. There the divine voice announces that for Jerusalem the time of suffering will come to an end and that the return home through the wilderness is imminent. Later God himself says: "I, even I, am he who comforts you" (51.12) [→193] and again right at the end of the book: "As a mother comforts her child, so will I comfort you" (66.13) [→198]. Here we see that the conclusion of the first major corpus of Isaiah texts is worked into a tapestry that encompasses the whole book. Again and again at significant points "signals" are placed which make the reader aware of these connections (cf. 1984).

One such signal lies in the appearance in this concluding and at the same time forward-looking chapter for the first time of the word *yˀšûʿāh* "rescue" or "salvation" (three times in vv. 2f), in which there is a clear echo of the name Isaiah (*yˀšaʿyāhû*, "Yhwh has given salvation"). This word and the associated verb are then found frequently in the language of the later chapters of the book, in which the blissful future and the saving action of God are in the foreground. That the resonance of the name appears at this point once again recalls Isaiah's word at a decisive moment: "I and the children the LORD has given me. We are signs and symbols in Israel" (8.18) [→175]. Not only the children with their symbolic names but also Isaiah himself is a sign to Israel.

With its last verse the psalm once again intones one of the central themes of the proclamation of Isaiah and of the whole book of Isaiah: "Shout aloud and sing, people of Zion, for great is the Holy One of Israel among you" (12.6). From the first chapter (1.8) to the last (66.8) the name of Zion is almost omnipresent in the book of Isaiah. Here it is given a special emphasis through its connection with the other great word of the proclamation of Isaiah: the "Holy One of Israel." That God himself will be present in Jerusalem as the Holy One of Israel is the hopeful concluding word of this first great chapter of the message of the book of Isaiah.

2.7 Who will turn back the hand of the Lord?

Again Isaiah ben Amoz "sees" (13.1; cf. 1.1; 2.1), this time an "oracle" (*maśśāʾ*), which can also be a "burden" (cf. Jer 23.33ff) [→221]. The message with this superscription concerns Babylon, and many further messages introduced by the word *maśśāʾ* follow, concerning cities (Damascus 17.1, Tyre 23.1), countries (Moab 15.1, Egypt 19.11), nations (Philistines 14.28f) and lands (the wilderness by the sea 21.1, Duma [?] 21.11, "in the wilderness" 21.13, the Valley of Vision 22.1), with in between them a "woe" about Cush (Ethiopia), the "land of whirring wings" (18.1). These "oracles to the nations" form a cohesive group of texts; but they are at the same time very varied in kind and relate to a whole range of different contexts.

The texts recall the proclamation of a divine judgment against Assyria in 10.5ff [→**176f**]. Surprisingly enough, however, the subject is no longer Assyria but Babylon. The temporal perspective has shifted, for Babylon does not play a role until the last phase of the history of Judah and is then in Isa 40ff the place of the Judeans' exile. This shift makes it evident again that Isaiah's message reaches far beyond the Assyrian period and that the divine judgment applies also to other arrogant "superpowers" [→**§20**]. But now we see that it is not just a question of a judgment about Babylon and about its king, who is setting himself up in such a blasphemous way (14.4ff), but that the scope is much broader and the whole earth is involved in the devastating events called the "day of Yhwh" (13.6, 9). As before in 2.12ff [→**171**] this day will come upon "the arrogance of the haughty" (13.11). Assyria is also included in this final judgment (14.25) and this picks upon on what resounded repeatedly before in 5.25 and 9.11f [→**172**]: God's hand is "stretched out" (14.26f). Now we see that all this is the execution of the divine plan (14.24, 26f), which no one can thwart. Who will turn back the outstretched hand of God (v. 27)?

This first extensive passage on Babylon (chs. 13f) shows what the prime concern is in these oracles to the nations: God turns his face against the arrogance and hubris of any nation and any people that sets itself against him, just as he also turns his face against the hubris of Israel (2.12ff; cf. Hamborg 1981). His action towards other nations is certainly not in any direct connection with his actions towards Israel. In particular it is clear that it is a misinterpretation of these texts to assume God's judgment on other peoples means salvation for Israel. In these texts Israel is often completely in the background. (This can be shown statistically: the name Jerusalem, found a dozen times in chs. 1–12, is absent from chs. 13–23—with the exception of ch. 22, which is not addressed to foreign nations.) Only once does Israel briefly appear: when the returnees are allowed to intone the mocking song against the toppled king of Babylon (14.1-4). But at the same time this means that God's position towards the nations of the world is not seen only under the aspect of their relations with Israel but that he is the God of all the nations.

The often extremely dramatic depictions of these oracles to the nations hardly contain clear references to particular events in chronological history. This also applies to the immediately following chs. 24–27, which must be viewed together with them. Here the depictions of the divine action of destruction are at first continued. The whole earth is affected by them; no concrete nations are named, and even the "ruined city" (24.10-12) remains anonymous. But then suddenly we read: "for the LORD Almighty will reign on Mount Zion and in Jerusalem" (24.23b). Again, then, this central word: Zion [→§14]. Out of this rises a psalm praising the destruction of the (enemy) fortified city as an act of God (25.1-3). In contrast, God sets up a festive meal for all the nations "on this mountain," i.e. on Mount Zion (25.6), and the following song sings of the restoration of the walls of Jerusalem (26.1ff).

Finally another song rings out, the theme of which is familiar to the reader (or listener): the Song of the Vineyard (27.2-5, 6). The metaphor is the same as in the first vineyard song (5.1-7) [→171]: Israel is the vineyard and God its owner. But the indicators have fundamentally changed. God is not only the owner waiting for the fruits, but at the same time he is the watchman who tends the vineyard night and day and waters it. Thorns and brambles would not enrage him if he found them, but he would tackle them and burn them. This change of image brings God's care for his people, restored after the catastrophe, to expression in an impressive way. And finally the great ram's horn will be blown, so that everyone returns from the countries of exile and worships the Lord in Jerusalem on the "holy mountain" (27.13). Only once beforehand was there mention of the "holy mountain": at the conclusion of the vision of eschatological peace under the rule of the ideal shoot of David (11.9) [→178]. Nothing is said here of the eschatological king; but this emphasized mention of Zion provides an echo of the whole horizon of expectation that began back with the vision of the pilgrimage of the nations to Zion (2.1-5) [→170].

2.8 Woe!—and then rejoicing on Mount Zion

Once again the "woe" cry rings out (28.1) [→172] as before in 5.8-24 and 10.1-19 [→177]. It extends from the beginning of the text unit starting here through to ch. 33, giving these chapters their structuration. The first and last woes are directed to the outside: against Ephraim, the northern kingdom of Israel (28.1), and against a "destroyer" (33.1) who remains anonymous. These texts are close to the words to the nations in chs. 13ff but now it is Israel's immediate enemies that are in focus. (This also applies to the word against Edom in ch. 34, which does not have the added "woe.") The other woes are directed against Israel itself: against Ariel, i.e. Jerusalem (28.1) and against various groups of people in the city (19.15; 30.1; 31.1). As before in chs. 1–12 we see a constant alternation between the annunciation of calamity and destruction on the one hand and restoration and salvation on the other. This emphasizes that in 32.1 the series of "woe"-cries (*hôy*) is interrupted by a "see" (*hēn*), which introduces a positive expectation: a king who will reign with justice and righteousness (cf. 9.6; 11.3-5) [→**176**].

The manifold complaints against the inhabitants of Jerusalem are addressed in two directions in particular. First, the Jerusalemites are seeking their salvation in futile foreign-political activities, especially in allegiance with Egypt (30.2; 31.1). But these efforts are pointless and useless (30.5, 7), they bring only shame and humiliation (30.5); "for the Egyptians are men and not God" (31.3). Here again we hear the divine negation of all human hubris as before in the oracles to the nations in chs. 13ff [→**178**]. Secondly, people no longer trust the prophetic message but mock it (28.7ff) and reject it (30.9ff). But the "Holy One of Israel" does not put up with this rejection (30.11, 12ff). Already Isaiah's first message had denounced Israel's turning away from the "Holy One of Israel" (1.4), whose Torah the Israelites had spurned (5.24) [→**170**]. And the psalm that concludes the introductory "presentation" of the prophet Isaiah ends with the words: "Shout aloud and sing for joy, people of Zion, for great is the Holy One of Israel among you" (12.6) [→**179**].

Here, however, the "Holy One of Israel" points out the alternative: "In repentance and rest is your salvation, in quietness and trust is your strength" (30.15). The answer at first is an abrupt No. Instead, "We will ride off on swift horses" (v. 16). But at this point the reversal occurs, as before in 29.17-24. God will be gracious towards Israel, indeed he is waiting to answer the "people of Zion" when he hears their cry (30.18f). Then Israel will also throw away its silver and golden images (30.22; cf. 31.7) and God will grant it rain and fertility (30.23-26). Finally after the calamitous deeds of the "destroyer" (33.1) Zion/Jerusalem will be restored (vv. 13ff, esp. v. 20), and its inhabitants will be forgiven their sin (*'āwon*) (v. 24). This is a clear reference back to the introduction of the book of Isaiah, where in 1.4 [→**169**] Israel is described as a sinful people full of sin (*'āwon*).

This extremely variable collection of prophetic sayings ends with the prospect of a blissful future (ch. 35) [→**§22**]. As before in the conclusion of the first group of prophetic messages in ch. 12, here too the language is strikingly close to chs. 40ff. Indeed, there are quite direct connections to the introductory chapter of the second main part of Isaiah, ch. 40 [→**185f**]. The wilderness will blossom, and in it there will be a highway (35.1f, 8; 40.3); the glory of the Lord will make its appearance there (35.2b; 40.5); the call rings out: "Be strong, do not fear, your God will come" (35.4; 40.9). So ch. 35 builds the bridge to the following chapters, which are totally colored by future expectation. And again, as already in ch. 12, the last verse speaks of Zion: "the ransomed of the LORD will return. They will enter Zion with singing" (35.10; this is a verbatim quotation from 51.11) [→**193**].

Here we see that the individual parts of the book of Isaiah are very deliberately linked together. One might almost say they have been woven together. Chapter 35 has clearly been formulated precisely for this purpose (Steck 1985). But we have seen time and again that the first part of the book contains varied and very fundamental elements from the second part, especially so in ch. 12, which concludes the first collection of Isaiah's messages in chs. 1–2. These elements have certainly not been inserted "as an afterthought" or "secondarily" but were constantly present in the formulation of the message of "Isaiah" [→**168f**].

2.9 Jerusalem is still preserved

The following chapters, 36–39, have certainly been deliberately placed in this position too. Here they have a changed function by comparison with their earlier appearance in 2 Kgs 18–20 [→**148**]. There the concern was primarily with king Hezekiah and his role in the history of Judah. His radical cultic reform proved an essential reason for the protection of Jerusalem. Now this is placed in the broad context of all the various statements about Zion. In central position is Isaiah's message: "For out of Jerusalem will come a remnant, and out of Mount Zion a band of survivors. The zeal of the LORD Almighty will accomplish this" (37.32). Again Zion is at the center [→**§14**]. At the same time the second part of this message calls attention to another context. We have already come across the "zeal of Yhwh": in the announcement of the birth of a king who will meet all God's expectations for a king in the dynasty he has appointed for Jerusalem (9.6) [→**176f**]. With the same emphasis a blissful future is promised for Jerusalem and its inhabitants.

This also creates a connection with Isa 6.1–9.6, the only section within Isaiah outside chs. 36–39 where we find the prophet in a larger narrative context. In 6.1 and 7.1 historical data are given as in 36.1. In 7.3ff and 36.2ff events occur at the same place, "the aqueduct of the Upper Pool," which is mentioned nowhere else. In both narratives an important role is played by a "sign" (7.10ff; 38.7f) [→175]; and the resonance of the words "high" and "deep" (7.11; 38.8) is scarcely coincidental. It must remain open how far these resonances extend and what they intend to point the reader to—whether for instance to a connection between Hezekiah and the royal child expected according to 9.5f. (The brief mention in 32.1 of a king who would rule with justice and righteousness might be linked with this too.) (On this whole question cf. Ackroyd 1982, Conrad 1988.)

The function of the concluding ch. 39 is especially clear in this context. Babylon now comes on the scene. But it has a different role here than it did in chs. 31f. First it appears as a partner in the renewed ill-advised alliance of a Judahite king. But then Isaiah predicts that Judah's relations with Babylon will be quite different from what Hezekiah hopes. Before the announcements of the annihilation of Babylon in chs. 13f become reality, Judah itself will fall. Hezekiah reacts evasively to this divine word of judgment—after all, Isaiah has announced that the calamity will only affect his sons (v. 7) and so Hezekiah hopes for peace and security for himself (v. 8). What will come afterwards is in the air. This open conclusion at the same time creates a transition to the words that immediately follow: "Comfort, comfort my people" (40.1). The calamity is upon it, and Israel is in need of comfort. Isaiah's proclamation is taken up and continued by the prophetic voices of later generations.

2.10 After the catastrophe

Chapters 40–55 are referred to in biblical scholarship as "Deutero-Isaiah" or "Second Isaiah" [→167]. As mentioned above, they are the most clearly contoured of the three main sections of the book of Isaiah. They are directed to a situation in which the Israelites or Judeans addressed are in exile in Babylon, where however the hope of an end of the exile is already arising, especially as a result of the accession of the Persian king Cyrus, who is threatening the power of the Babylonian empire (44.28; 45.1) [→191]. The language of these chapters is very characteristic in its both poetic and theologically highly reflective nature. It contains many distinctive elements, but in others it agrees with the first part of Isaiah.

These chapters give the impression that their author was a prominent individual personality. However, such a person is nowhere to be discerned, so that many scholars prefer to think of a group of authors. One might also ask whether this anonymous proclaimer is to be counted as a prophet in the narrower sense, familiar to us in Isaiah and other writing prophets, or whether the cultic-liturgical elements of his language lead one to suppose a closer connection with cultic groups, such as temple singers. Much remains open. In what follows we shall thus simply speak of the "prophet."

In shaping the book of Isaiah the authors clearly did not want to have chs. 40–55 appear as a prophet book in its own right but have added it to create a unity with the proclamation of Isaiah ben Amoz (and apparently also beforehand with chs. 56–66). At many points in chs. 1–39 elements of the language and theology of chs. 40–55 have been taken up, in many cases with great emphasis and detail as in chs. 12 and 35 [→**178, 182**]. As a result the book of Isaiah, in all its variety, gains a moment of unity, one of the important features of which is the language of "Deutero-Isaiah." (On the rhetorical and literary structure of chs. 40–55 see esp. Melugin 1976.)

2.10.1 Comfort my people

"Comfort, comfort my people, says your God" (40.1) [→*In* **204**]. That is the turning-point. The comfort hoped for at the end of the first section of Isaiah (12.1) [→**178**] is now proclaimed. The comforting nearness of God comes to expression in the formulas: "my people" and "your God." The actual recipient of the comfort is Jerusalem. Its hard labor is at an end (40.2). At the same time the divine voice confirms what was already indicated in 33.24: the sin or guilt (*'āwon*) spoken of in the first words of Isaiah (1.4) [→**168**] has now been atoned for. So the keyword Jerusalem/Zion again stands at the beginning of a new section as before in the first chapter of Isaiah. Chapters 12 and 35 also, which stand at key pivotal points, each end with the rejoicing of the inhabitants of Zion (23.6) or of the returnees to Zion (35.10). So the reader is prepared for it, but it now becomes the all-pervading theme: the time of exile is at an end, a new future is beginning for Jerusalem.

The return from exile is described as a divine triumphal procession. A highway will be prepared through the desert (40.3f)—a motif that was previously developed in ch. 35. It is in the first place a road on which God himself will enter, so that his glory (*kābôd*) will be revealed to all the world (40.3-5). The cries in front of him will be "Behold your God!" (v. 9), and he will bring the returnees with him as a shepherd brings his herd (vv. 10f). All this confirms what the mouth of the Lord has spoken (v. 5); for "the word of our God remains forever" (v. 8).

This opening of the new chapter in the history of God's dealings with Jerusalem shows clear parallels to the apotheosis granted to Isaiah. After a vision (6.1-3) [→**172**] or audition (40.1f) there is talk twice in both texts of a "voice" (*qôl*) which cries (6.4; 40.3) or speaks (6.8; 40.6). The voice is directly or indirectly addressed to the prophet: "Whom shall I send?" (6.8) and "Cry!" (40.6). The prophet's counter-question, "What shall I cry?" is responded to with the first weighty pronouncement on the superiority and abiding reliability of the word of "our God" (40.6-8). Here we clearly see the close interaction between the individual main parts of the book of Isaiah (cf. 1989, 168ff). The second great prophetic voice picks up on the experiences of the first and announces something new beyond what it has in common with the first (cf. e.g. 42.9). The section 40.1-8 is often understood as the report of a call for the prophet "Second Isaiah." But once again the person concerned remains entirely in the background.

The statement about the superiority of the word of God sets out a central topic of chs. 40ff [→**§15**]. In a whole range of various forms we find again and again: "I am the LORD—besides me there is no God" (45.5, 6, 18, 21 etc.). In a first, grandly conceived and extremely graphic section this is now developed: this God is comparable with no one (40.12-31). The main argument here is that God is the creator of the world: "Do you not know? Have you not heard? The LORD is the everlasting God, the Creator of the ends of the earth" (40.28). But this also shows that this emphasis on the incomparability and superiority of God is not self-serving. This God, who does not tire or grow weary, will also give strength to those who trust in him (vv. 29ff). It is characteristic and fundamental for the theological argumentation of chs. 40ff that the greatness, superiority and uniqueness of God are proclaimed in direct connection with God's unique relationship with Israel, with Israel's former fate and with the coming change in its fortunes. This proclamation will strengthen Israel, i.e. the Judeans in exile in Babylon, allay their doubts and prepare them for the impending return.

The next basic topic follows immediately. In the style of a court case (41.1-5) God calls upon the "islands" and the "nations," i.e. all the peoples of the world, to ask themselves: "Who has stirred (him) up from the east?" No name is given, but the following sentences show that the person concerned is a conquering warrior to whom all eyes now turn and who is later named: Cyrus (cf. 44.28; 45.1) [→191]. He does not come in his own power, he has been called by none other than the One: "I, the LORD—with the first of them and with the last—I am he" (41.4). Here for the first time we meet the clear and full resonance of *'ᵃnî-yhwh* "I am Yhwh." It runs like a constant refrain through chs. 40ff of Isaiah. Sometimes it seems almost formulaic, but at the same time it appears in a range of variations and adaptations. (One variant is found here at the end of v. 4: *'ᵃnî-hû* "I am he," or: "I am the same.") The phrase shows in a particularly memorable way what the concern is here, time and again: *one* only is God, in fact even more unambiguously: there *is* only one God—this one. This is proclaimed and acknowledged time and again before the whole world. But the public proclamation is never given for its own sake but always appears in an entirely concrete context. Both things are constantly present: that this God rejects all competing claims against the exclusivity of his being God—sometimes with mockery of the makers of idols (vv. 6f)—and that he does this for the sake of a single goal: to turn the fortunes of his people Israel and to prepare his people for this change.

In the words to Israel that now follow, restoration and comfort are the content. The address is quite emphatic: "But you (*wᵉ'attāh*), O Israel, my servant, Jacob, whom I have chosen, you descendants of Abraham my friend" (41.8). God's affection for his people Israel is given quite emotional expression; at the same time with its mention of the names of Jacob and Abraham and with the word about election this address covers the whole of God's early salvation history with Israel. Israel is designated with the honorific title of *'ebed*. The word can mean "servant," but is also a title that expresses a position of special confidence, e.g. in relation to a king. It contains the sense of close belonging and nearness. This comes very much to the fore when God calls Israel "my servant"; and it forms the basis for the message, "Do not fear!" (v. 10). It resounds time and again in the following chapters. The reason why Israel need not fear is quite simple and clear: "I am with you." And again: "I am your God"—in another variant of the "I am" formula (*kî 'ᵃnî 'elohêkā*). God will strengthen and help Israel and "uphold" it with his "saving right hand" (v. 10).

The themes and motifs are repeated in a range of variations. Others are added, including some that have been met earlier in the book of

Isaiah. A renewed "Do not be afraid" (41.14) links up with the resumption of the title "the Holy One of Israel" (cf. 1.4; 5.24 etc.)
[→**169f**]. But this title now has an entirely positive turn: the Holy One
of Israel is the helper and redeemer. A further feature of the theological language of Isa 40ff comes into view. The word *gā'al* "redeem" is
only found in this second part of the book of Isaiah. In addition we
have the special linguistic feature that it is used as a substantival participle: "your redeemer." This applies also to other weighty theological
terms. Thus in 43.1 for instance we read: "But now this is what the
LORD says—he who created you, O Jacob, he who formed you, O
Israel"; the participial word "Creator" [→**§5**] is found almost exclusively in Isa 40ff in the Hebrew Bible. The word *môšî*ᵃᶜ "redeemer"
or "savior" is also one of the characteristic features of this language: "I,
even I, am the LORD, and apart from me there is no savior" (43.11),
and then again "your Redeemer" (v. 14) and "Israel's Creator" (v. 15),
linked with the titles "the Holy One of Israel" and "your King." Everywhere one looks, this dense language, which frequently comes close
to hymnic parlance, is in evidence as a special feature of the second
part of Isaiah.

A new element comes in at this point. In 41.12ff the style of the
court case appears again, as before in 41.1-5. Once again the concern
is with the claim to divinity, which comes to expression in the ability
to announce forthcoming events in advance and then to bring them
about. This time, however, the opposing party is expressly mentioned,
and their representatives are called upon to predict something, "so that
we may know that you are gods" (v. 23). But their silence shows that
the supposed gods are not gods in reality, that they are "nothing" (v.
24), only images that are empty breaths of wind (v. 29). This expressly
formulates one of the great themes of Isa 40ff: the confrontation between Yhwh and the other gods [→**§20**]. It was an essential aspect of
the situation of the Judean exiles in their Babylonian environment that
other gods were worshiped there and that in addition the military
victories of the Babylonians appeared to have proved the superiority of
their gods over the God of Israel. The great significance of Isa 40ff lies
not least in the fact that the prophet has posed himself this problem
and countered the claims of other gods with the conviction of the
unique and exclusive deity of Yhwh, the God of Israel. We would
surely be justified in saying that here for the first time we have a recognizably "monotheistic" notion of God in the strict sense [→**§15**].

So in chs. 40 and 41 almost all the important themes of the proclamation of this prophet are collected. Each of them unfolds, as it were, from the other:

- The time of exile is at an end; Jerusalem's guilt has been atoned for, a new future is at hand.
- The word of God, with which he announces this, is immutable.
- The superiority of God is already evident in a creator power, in which none can compare with him.
- God is also in control of historical events, for it was he alone who called Cyrus.
- This proves that he alone, Yhwh, is God. The other gods are not gods at all; they are "Nothing."
- Since this is so, Israel, the Servant of God, need not be afraid.

2.10.2 Jacob/Israel, the Servant of God

Israel, God's Servant, is also at the center of the following chapters. Again and again God addresses Israel as "my Servant" (42.1, 19; 43.10; 44.1, 2, 21). He gives Israel a task: to bring justice (*mišpāṭ*) to the nations (42.1, 3); for the "islands" (v. 4) are waiting for this and for his instruction (*tôrāh*). This commission to the people in exile, which seems at first surprising, is repeated later: "You are my witnesses" (43.10, 12; 44.8). From the context it is clear that the idea is not in the first instance of Israel's active engagement with the nations but that the function of witness lies in its existence and in what God is now doing with it. Even if to begin with they are still blind and deaf (43.8; cf. 42.18-20), from the fate that God alone predicted it becomes evident: "I, even I, am the LORD, and apart from me there is no savior (*môšîʿ*)" (43.11). So they can also become a "light for the gentiles" (42.6) [→§20].

What God is going to create now is something new. This "new thing" supersedes the "former thing," that has already come into being, as God said it would. Again we can see the unique deity of Yhwh, which he will not share with the "gods" (42.8f). Later he can even say that it is no longer time to think of the former things because the new thing that is now springing up is more important (43.18f). God has broken the bars of the prison in Babylonia and will lead his people out as he once led Israel out of Egypt. Just as then he prepared a path through the sea (vv. 16f), so now he will prepare a way through the wilderness (v. 19). And again the people that God himself has prepared [→§9] will proclaim his praise (v. 21).

The divine "Fear not!" accompanies the declarations about the return under God's guidance (43.1-7). But it also has another side to it. God reminds Israel that it has brought its present fate on itself and that this is God's punishment for its blindness (42.24f). So Israel's sin, which is traced back to its ancestors (43.27) [→§7] and which has not been removed through Israel's failed sacrificial cult either (vv. 23f; cf. 1.10-17), still stands between it and God. But now we hear the quite direct: "I, even I, am he who blots out your transgressions ... and remembers your sins no more" (v. 25). What was announced at the beginning by the divine voice (40.2), God himself now says to Israel with an emphatic double "I": that he "blots out" (or "washes away") its sins and remembers it no more. In the middle of this sentence is a word that explains why this is going to happen: "for my own sake." There is no other reason than that God wants, for his own sake, to direct his behavior towards Israel not in accordance with Israel's sin but out of his forgiving grace. Thus this prophet too, whom some like to call a "prophet of salvation," stands entirely in continuity with the earlier prophets and in particular with the Isaiah of the preceding chapters. God's saving attentiveness towards Israel occurs on the basis of the forgiveness of its earlier sins. And once again Israel, the Servant of God, is addressed and the promise of forgiveness is repeated: Israel's sin will blow away like a cloud (44.21f).

In chs. 41–45 the description of Israel as the Servant of God is particularly frequent. In recent exegetical tradition the "Servant" in 42.1 is classed with a particular group of texts called "Servant Songs" (*Gottesknechtlieder*) since the Isaiah Commentary of Bernhard Duhm (1892) (42.1-4[, 5-9]; 49.1-6[, 7-12]; 50.4-9[, 10-11]; 52.13–53.12). This presupposes that these texts derive not from "Deutero-Isaiah" but from another author. This hypothesis has since been accepted by the majority of interpreters; however there has been no consensus on the question of who is meant by the term "Servant of God." In particular the question remains whether an individual figure is in mind, and who this might be. In 49.3 the Servant is expressly addressed as "Israel." In many other regards too there are clear correspondences with the other texts. Thus some recent interpreters dispute the hypothesis of a "Servant" figure differing from Israel more emphatically than was done in the past. Of particular significance in this is the insight that these texts are firmly anchored in the context of chs. 40–55, their connection with the hymns found at specific points (42.10-13; 44.23; 45.8; 48.20f; 49.13; 51.3; 52.9f; 54.1-3) also playing an important role (Mettinger 1983; Matheus 1990).

So Cyrus now appears, his name being given explicitly. The verses that speak of him (44.24–45.7; cf. 41.2) are specially accentuated by their being framed by two hymnic pieces (44.23; 45.8). God's address to Cyrus itself then stands within a heavily significant context. It is framed by the statement that God is the Creator (44.24; 45.7) and that no one besides him can predict and bring about events (44.25; 45.5f). The impending developments are directed entirely to the restoration of Israel, Jerusalem in particular (44.26), and will occur for the sake of Israel (45.4). Cyrus has a place in this divine plan. God calls him "my shepherd" (44.28), i.e. he as it were entrusts his own flock to him (cf. 40.11), and he addresses him as his "anointed one" (*māšî͏̄aḥ*) (45.1) and thus lends him a royal title otherwise granted only to the kings of Israel [→§13].

All this happens despite the fact that Cyrus did not know God (*yāda͏ʿ*, 45.4, 5). But he himself will acknowledge (*yāda͏ʿ*) "that I am the LORD, the God of Israel, who calls you by name" (v. 3); and through Cyrus's deeds the whole world "from the rising of the sun to the place of its setting" will acknowledge (*yāda͏ʿ*, v. 6) that there is no God besides Yhwh. Four times in close succession the phrase *ʾ͏ănî yhwh* "I am the LORD" occurs (vv. 3, 5, 6, 7). And here it is given its most emphatic formulation: "I am the LORD, and there is no other. I form the light and create darkness, I bring prosperity and create disaster; I, the LORD, do all these things" (vv. 6b, 7). That God appoints the heathen king, who does not even know him, as his "shepherd" and his "anointed one," takes the statements about God's activity to their most extreme limits. If there is no God besides Yhwh [→§15], then neither is there anyone who can be held responsible for darkness and disaster, other than this same God.

The prophet presents himself with this consequence of strict monotheistic thinking. He formulates the insight that emerges from this in a sharpened, one might almost say oversharpened, form. Yhwh, the one unique God, "forms" light and "brings" prosperity—but he also "creates" darkness and disaster. The central word in the creation account at the beginning of the Bible, *bārā'*, "create," is applied here to the negative sides of the activity of the creator God. This goes even beyond what is said in the creation account [→§5]: that God includes darkness in the creation, assigning it a function and a name.

Here we now read that he "creates" darkness, i.e. that he is also responsible for its threatening existence. Similarly he also "creates" disaster. Particularly in mind here, evidently, is the political arena, in which disaster (*rāʿ*) stands in opposition to prosperity, i.e. peace (*šālôm*). At the same time the ambivalence comes to expression: the impending calamity for Babylon will mean *šālôm* for Israel. In its fundamental formulation, however, this formulation goes far beyond that statement. Neither other gods nor any other powers can be made responsible for events in this world.

A climax has been reached. Through the appearance of Cyrus the turning point has become clear. Everything is now pressing towards the fall of Babylon, so that the way will become free for Israel's return. Doubters will not be able to impede God's plan (45.9-13), the "makers of idols" (45.14-17) even less so. Rather, all will see that Yhwh alone is the Creator (v. 18) and announces the truth (v. 19). They will all assemble and be persuaded and bow the knee to him (vv. 20-25). Even Bel, the God of Babylon, will have to "bow down" (46.1-4). This prepares the ground for what is said next, after the doubters and despairing are reminded of what God announced at the beginning, who will now bring prosperity and salvation to Zion (46.3-13): Babylon must grovel in the dust! (47.1-15) [→§20]. This mocking song against the "daughter of Babylon" reminds the reader of earlier texts about Babylon (chs. 13f) [→180]. There was anticipation there of what is now about to occur. And in a quite similar way the arrogance and hubris with which Babylon thought itself greater and more exalted than all others is denounced; the further it must now fall.

Once again the prophetic divine speech turns to Jacob/Israel. The note sounded earlier (42.9; 43.19) is now central: God announces something "new" (48.1-11). Once again the one and unique God, the Creator of heaven and earth, confirms that he himself has called the one who will now execute his will for Babylon (vv. 12-19). And then comes the crucial call: "Leave Babylon, flee from the Babylonians! ... The LORD has redeemed his servant Jacob." What is about to occur is a repetition of the way that Israel went once before through the wilderness [→§9], without suffering thirst because God had water flow from the rock for them (vv. 20f). This is now the last time that the name Babylon is mentioned in Isaiah. Attention now turns forward, to Jerusalem.

2.10.3 Zion/Jerusalem restored

In 49.14-17 the program, as it were, of what will unfold in what follows is formulated. Zion [→§14] complains that it has been abandoned by God—as Jacob/Israel had done before (40.27); the answer is again a counter-question (49.15; cf. 40.28): Can a mother forget her child? And even if she were to do this, God will not forget Zion. Its walls are constantly before his eyes, they are engraved on his hands (49.16) as on a clay tablet serving as a blueprint (cf. Ezek 4.1) [→237]. So now the reconstruction and new settlement of the ruined and depopulated city is announced from various points of view. The saying about "waste places" from Isaiah's vision echoes again, as it were as a continuation of the answer to the prophet's question, "How long?" (6.11) [→173]; they will now become too crowded for the many inhabitants (49.19), those of the hitherto infertile and childless (vv. 20f) brought in by their former oppressors (vv. 22f) or newly born (54.1-6). God himself will construct the walls of the city from precious stones and will make the city unassailable (54.11-17). Looking back, the hard fate of Jerusalem is recapitulated once again (51.17-23; 52.1-6); but now God comforts (51.12) [→178], as the psalm in ch. 12 hoped (v. 1) and the divine voice announced in 40.1 [→185]. In the hymnic sections too the message of comfort resonates (49.13; 51.3; 52.9).

What now happens is inserted in the broader context of the story of God's dealings with Israel. The same will now happen to Jerusalem as happened to Abraham and Sarah, who were at first alone and whom God then blessed with many descendants (51.2). The return of the redeemed to Zion is like the procession through the sea during the exodus from Egypt; indeed God's action in preparing the way is even comparable with his work of creation (51.9-11). And just as in the days of Noah God swore never again to send a flood upon the earth, so he now swears that he will never again be angry with Jerusalem (54.9).

In this context the figure of the "Servant of the LORD" again appears (49.1-6[, 7-12]; 50.4-9[, 10-11]; 52.13–53.12). The individual features are now more sharply in focus: God has called the Servant already when in his mother's womb, as is also said of Jeremiah (Isa 49.1, 5; cf. Jer. 1.5); he prepares his mouth and tongue for public speaking (49.2; 50.4) and his ear for hearing (50.4f). And above all, the Servant leads. He is thoroughly despised (49.7), he is beaten and mistreated (50.6; 53 *passim*) and finally meets his death (53.8f, 12). In 49.3 however, the Servant is expressly referred to as "Israel," and much of what is said in these texts about the Servant of the Lord is comparable to other texts that speak of Israel. So on the level of the present text the equation of the Servant with Israel dominates, which is the view invariably maintained in Jewish tradition. Nonetheless the figure of the "Servant of the Lord" is not in the end accessible to an unambiguous interpretation and has repeatedly been subject to the most varied interpretations in the course of history.

Once again Israel's fate is placed in the broader historical context. God reminds them of the "gracious favor" (*ḥesed*) which he showed to David; in the same way he now wants to conclude an "eternal covenant" (*bᵉrît 'ôlām*) [→§6] with Israel (55.3). Just as he made David a "witness for the peoples and prince and master to the nations," so now too Israel is given the function of witness towards the peoples (vv. 4f), as had been announced previously (43.10, 12; 44.8). The peoples will come to Israel "because of the LORD your God, the Holy One of Israel" (55.5); this recalls the pilgrimage of the nations to the "house of the God of Jacob," from which they wanted to receive instruction (2.2-4) [→169f].

Finally, this part of Isaiah ends as it began. The message the prophet was supposed to proclaim was: "The word of our God stands for ever" (40.8) [→185f]. Now we read that the word that proceeds from the mouth of God will not remain without its due effect but "will accomplish what I desire and achieve the purpose for which I sent it" (55.11). While at the beginning the contrast between quickly wilting plants and the life-giving word was emphasized (40.6-8), so now the life-giving strength of the word is compared with the fertility-bringing rain and snow (55.10). That the word "remains" is not meant in a static sense but expresses its constant, unending effectiveness.

When the exiles now make their departure it will not be like it was when they left Egypt "in fearful haste" (Isa 52.12; cf. Ex 12.11; Deut 16.3) [→45], but they will depart in joy and peace (*šālôm*), accompanied by the rejoicing of nature. This will happen in honor of the name of God as a perpetual sign that will not be destroyed (55.12f).

2.11 After the return

The exiles have returned [→*In* 208]. We do not know how many, and we know nothing of the precise circumstances. But neither is it the concern of the book of Isaiah to inform the reader about this. The texts of the last main section of the book show, rather, that life in the old-new homeland now asserts its demands. At the beginning stands the call: "Maintain justice and do what is right" (56.1). This reasserts the theme of the first chapter of Isaiah. There we read: "Zion will be redeemed with justice, her returnees with righteousness" (1.27) [→**169f**]. The returnees are now there and they are now called upon to work together to see that justice and righteousness are reapplied in Israel.

But this call now stands in a new context. The word *ṣᵉdāqāh* shows itself from two different angles. First, it means "righteousness" and corresponds with "justice" (*mišpaṭ*). It is the task of humans to realize this in society. Secondly it means what God is about to do now: the "salvation" (*yᵉšû'āh*) [→**179**] he brings is close at hand, and his *ṣᵉdāqāh*, his saving action, is about to be revealed. The connection between *yᵉšû'āh* (or the expressions *yeša'* and *tᵉšû'āh* which come from the same root) and *ṣᵉdāqāh* is found many times in the second section of Isaiah, e.g. in 51.6, 8, where this pair of terms appears as an expression of the enduring steadfastness of God (cf. also 45.8; 46.13; 51.5) and where *ṣᵉdāqāh* can also be linked with *šālôm* "peace, prosperity" (48.18; 54.13f).

At the beginning of the third part of the book of Isaiah the doing of justice and righteousness that is expected of humans, as was already demanded right from the beginning of the book, is as it were embedded in the impending saving work of God as promised in the second part and as prepared for in the return from exile. The salvation has not yet been definitively realized, but the experience of those that have returned from exile is that it is starting. They are now to shape their life together on the basis of this experience.

This marks the basic tenor of the concluding chapter of Isaiah. The theme of "righteousness" [→**§10**] in its various aspects also dominates the subsequent chapters. Thus there is criticism of the fact that *ṣᵉdāqāh* and *mišpaṭ* are absent (59.9, 14; 59; cf. v. 4), even though people claim to be practicing them (58.2). Instead, social injustices (58.6f) and unrighteousness (57.1; 59 *passim*) hold sway. But when God intervenes he will clothe himself with *ṣᵉdāqāh* and *yᵉšû'āh* (59.17; cf. v. 16), and Israel's own *ṣᵉdāqāh* will parade before it in triumph, while God's glory (*kābôd*) [→**§15**] will bring up the rear (58.8). Here the saving aspect of the term *ṣᵉdāqāh* will be transferred to Israel. This is even more noticeably the case in the large middle part of this last group of chapters, chs. 60–62. In Zion's splendid future, which ch. 60 depicts, it will turn out that God is Israel's "savior" and "redeemer," who appoints "peace" and "righteousness" as a watchman over Israel (60.16f). Israel itself will be clothed with "salvation" and "righteousness" (61.10); Zion's "righteousness" and "salvation" will break forth radiantly and the nations will see its "righteousness" and its "glory" (62.1f). All this will include the people in Jerusalem: "all your people will be righteous" (60.21).

That these chapters presuppose the situation of the returned community is also evident in the fact that there is now mention of the temple and of problems in the cult and participation in the cult. These statements stand in an elevated position at the beginning (56.2-8) and at the conclusion of the third part of the book (66.18-24); in ch. 58, in addition, there is talk of proper fasting and of the keeping of the sabbath. This shows a remarkable openness to the outside world: "My house will be called a house of prayer for all nations" (56.7). "Foreigners" are expressly included (v. 4) and are called "servants" of God (v. 6); indeed, according to 66.21 even access to priestly and levitical office should be open to them—a quite unique statement in the Hebrew Bible [→§20]. Mentioned as special cultic duties that also apply to foreigners (and eunuchs, who are also admitted) are the keeping of the sabbath (56.2, 4, 6) and the observance of the "covenant," i.e. evidently circumcision (vv. 4, 6). If they do this then their burnt offerings and sacrifices will be accepted by God with "favor" (v. 7). Here we see the beginnings of proselytization.

Reflected in these chapters however we also see various problems and tensions within the community. There is mention of idolatry (57.5-13; 65.3-7, 11; 66.3, 17); but this time it is not the gods of mighty nations that struggle for power with Yhwh as in the Babylonian exile that are the concern, but small local cults practiced in their own land. In particular, however, there is evidence of tensions between various groups (cf. Hanson 1975). In ch. 59 criticism and complaint are directed against others, addressed by "you" (vv. 1-3) or as "they" (vv. 4-8), and of whom it is said that their sins separate them from God and that their hands are full of blood. Then follows a forceful complaint against those that speak of themselves in the first person plural (vv. 9-15a). This second group feels oppressed, especially because "justice and righteousness" are not coming into their own (vv. 9, 11, 14); it hopes for the intervention of God, who will bring about "justice and salvation" (v. 17, cf. v. 16) and come as redeemer for

Zion (vv. 15b-20). This is the group that reflects self-critically on Israel's history [→**§21**] in a substantial song of lament (63.7–64.11). Again and again it emphasizes the close relationship of the supplicants to God: "surely they are my people" (63.8), "we are all your people" (64.8; cf. 63.14), "but you are our Father" (63.16; 64.7), "for the sake of your servants" (63.17). Then in the divine answer in ch. 65 an extremely sharp division and distinction is made between the two groups: announcement of judgment for idolaters (vv. 1-7)—but proclamation of salvation for God's "servants" and "elect," for "my people who seek me" (vv. 8-10); then again: "but you who forsake the LORD" (vv. 11f) and finally in quick succession: "my servants"—"but you" (vv. 13-15). The separation carries on into the last chapter, where we even read: "your brothers who hate you" (66.5; cf. also v. 14).

These internal tensions stand under the aspect of God's action in the future: "behold I will create new heavens and a new earth" (65.17; cf. 66.22) [→**§22**]. Then people will no longer think of the "former things" (cf. 43.18). Pain, suffering and lack will be forgotten, indeed the eschatological expectations of peaceful coexistence between all the animals crop up again (65.35; cf. 11.6-8) [→**178**]. But it is quite clear that this announcement of future bliss will not apply to everyone without distinction. Rather, all this will be for the good of the group of those who are now in the minority but who follow the paths of God. This is the eschatological divine community of those whom God himself has preserved, the "remnant" mentioned repeatedly earlier on in Isaiah. Right at the beginning their voice was to be heard (1.9), as it was time and again after that (4.2-6; 7.3; 10.20-22; 11.15f; 37.32).

The last chapter's connection to the beginning of the book is also evident in other regards. The hands of the majority group are full of blood (59.3), which recalls the accusations in 1.15 and their context in 1.10-15 [→**170**]. The concern there is with sacrifices that are not pleasing to God—as in 66.3f, where the motif of innocently shed blood is picked up. The "gardens" mentioned in connection with illegitimate sacrificial practices (1.29; 65.3; 66.17) show a clear resonance. And the message to the people of "Sodom and Gomorrah" in 1.10 is introduced with the words, "Hear the word of the LORD," found also in 66.5 (otherwise only at 28.14 and 39.5). (On this cf. Conrad 1991, 98f; Steck 1991, 265.)

2.12 The major themes of the book of Isaiah

The book of Isaiah is one of the greatest theological books of the Hebrew Bible. The variety and significance of its themes and the often
dramatic changes of situation are comparable with no other book. In
the canonical context the book opens up the series of prophetic books.
At the same time it opens a theological dispute of hitherto unknown
dynamism.

This dynamism has its basis especially in the fact that the prophetic
figures that leave their mark in the various parts of the book stand in
an extremely intense way both "inside" and "outside." On the one
hand they represent in various respects the faith traditions of Israel and
fight with all their strength for their maintenance, proper interpretation and further development, and on the other hand they oppose the
community whose traditions they represent, sometimes with sharp
criticism, sometimes arguing against unbelief and doubts, sometimes
also with the proclamation of new acts of God that go far beyond what
has been the subject of these faith traditions hitherto. They often appear to be outsiders and opponents; at the same time, however, in the
line of biblical tradition there is no doubt that the prophets represent
the true tradition of Israel [→**159**]. This was certainly already the case at
the moment when they proclaimed their message, when they could be
opposed for all kinds of reasons, but certainly not because they had
departed from Israel's faith traditions. This applies all the more in the
context of the Hebrew Bible, in which the prophets are among the
most important representatives of Israel's faith. In the present overall
picture the deviants are those who resisted the message of the prophets
and the prophets themselves.

All this applies to the writing prophets as a whole. In the book of
Isaiah this tension is particularly marked, because there are quite different emphases in the individual parts of the book, as has been set out in
some detail above. So it is all the more striking that a range of basic
theological themes runs through and characterizes the whole book (cf.
1984). In the first place mention should be made of the theme of
"Zion." In no other book of the Hebrew Bible do we meet this word
as often as in Isaiah, and in all three parts of the book it forms an extremely important key term from a theological point of view. The
great religious traditions that have found their way into the Psalms in
particular resound there [→**175**]: of "YHWH Zebaot, who dwells on
Mount Zion" (8.18) and "reigns as king on Mount Zion" (24.23b)

[→181] and of the Torah that proceeds from Zion (2.3) [→170]. But above all Zion as a city, i.e. Jerusalem, with all its inhabitants is in view. From the beginning it is clear that Zion is threatened, abandoned "like a shelter in the vineyard" (Isa 1.8). This aspect is a constant feature of the book of Isaiah. It would be entirely appropriate to call it the "book of concern for Zion."

The threat to Jerusalem appears under quite varied aspects: sometimes as a threat from the outside by enemies, but sometimes from the inside too, through the behavior of its own inhabitants. Here the theme of "Zion" is linked with that of "justice and righteousness," the other major theme of the book of Isaiah. It is evident that Isaiah's critique and accusation against his fellow citizens [→§16] is determined entirely by concern for Zion. This is already very clear in the first chapter. The vehement accusations have in view the hope that Zion will be saved through justice and righteousness and again be called the "city of righteousness" (1.26f) and that then finally the nations will undertake pilgrimages to Zion in order to learn Torah there (2.2-4). But the problem is that justice and righteousness are now missing. This is brought out, among many other texts, in the key metaphor of the vineyard Israel: what God, the owner of the vineyard, is vainly seeking is justice and righteousness (5.1-7). Conversely, the central expectation among the promises and expectations of a future king is always that under his rule justice and righteousness will come into their own (9.6; 11.3-5; 32.1) [→175f]. The program for the returnees begins with the call to realize justice and righteousness (56.1) [→194f], and the depiction of the splendid eschatological future of Zion climaxes with justice and righteousness radiating over it, for all nations to see (62.1f).

A further great key term in the book of Isaiah is the expression "the Holy One of Israel." It is found almost exclusively in the book of Isaiah, but in all parts of that book. But it is used in two quite different ways. The first is evident already at the beginning of the book. In the first speech of complaint against Israel we read: "they have forsaken the LORD; they have spurned the Holy One of Israel" (1.4) [→169]. In what this rejection consists is explained later: "they have rejected the Torah of Yhwh Zebaot and spurned the word of the Holy One of Israel" (5.24; cf. similar reproaches in 5.19; 30.11; 31.1). The holiness of God is closely linked to his righteousness: "YHWH Zebaot will be exalted by his justice, and the holy God will show himself holy by his righteousness" (5.16). So this reproach is part of the accusation about the neglect of justice and righteousness. Hence the relationship with the Holy One of Israel is reversed when Israel's behavior changes. "On that day" the "remnant of Israel" will rely on the Holy One of Israel (10.20), the eyes of the people will look upon him (17.7), the poor will rejoice over him (29.19), and Jacob/Israel will keep his name holy (29.23).

The texts cited so far from the first part of the book of Isaiah all refer to the relationship of people to the "Holy One of Israel." Things are quite different in the second part. Here the majority of references are in first-person speeches by God. The term "the Holy One of Israel" is often connected with other epithets that express God's special relationship to Israel in the characteristic language of chs. 40ff. The Holy One of Israel is Israel's redeemer (41.14; 43.14; 47.4; 48.17; 49.7; 54.5), creator (43.15; 45.11; 54.5), savior (43.3), king (43.15 and husband (54.5); he creates (41.20), elects (49.7) and glorifies (55.5) Israel; and he is the God of the whole earth (54.5). It is remarkable that this central theological expression, found scarcely anywhere else in the Hebrew Bible, has been preserved within the book of Isaiah in these two fundamentally different perspectives. A bridge between the two is again formed by ch. 12. The last verse reads: "Shout aloud and sing for joy, people of Zion, for great is the Holy One of Israel among you" (12.6). So the speech of the Holy One of Israel stands at the beginning and the end of the first major collection of prophetic sayings in chs. 1–12. Here at the end it also includes the speech about Zion.

Finally, one more theme must be mentioned, which is expressly mentioned time and again without being so broadly developed and deeply anchored as the three previously mentioned themes: talk of the "remnant." The significance of this theme for the book of Isaiah as a whole becomes unmistakably clear through its appearance in the first discourse unit of the book: "Unless YHWH Zebaot had left us some survivors, we would have become like Sodom, we would have been like Gomorrah" (1.9). Here a "small remnant" [→170f] speaks, i.e. a small number of survivors of the catastrophe described in the preceding verses. They are not completely destroyed, as happened to Sodom and Gomorrah and as will happen to Babylon (13.19) [→180]. But these survivors, this "remnant," are quite deliberately distinguished from the others who face the fate of Sodom and Gomorrah (1.10). They are a minority. But they will also be the "holy" remnant when God restores Zion (4.2-6), "the remnant that returns," to which the name of Isaiah's son Shear-Yashub pointed (7.3; cf. 10.20-22), who will return like those liberated from Egypt (11.15f), or in the words of another form of the image: the remnant that will go out from Zion (37.32). (On this cf. Webb 1990.)

Talk of the "remnant" is also found in other texts of the Hebrew Bible. But it is not limited to a particular Hebrew term. See §22.

3. The Book of Jeremiah

3.1 Preliminary considerations

No other prophet confronts us in his human form as Jeremiah does [→*In* 212]. In no other prophet do we find a personal fate so directly interwoven with political events as his. And of no other prophet do we have such moving testimonies to the pain of exercising his calling.

We have better information on the external data of the life of Jeremiah than for other prophets. The introductory verses of the book of Jeremiah (1.1-3) mention his origins in the small town of Anathoth to the north east of Jerusalem, which belongs already to the tribe of Benjamin. He comes from a priestly family, of whom we learn nothing of detail; no priestly features are discernible in Jeremiah's life and work. We read further that "the word of the LORD came to him" in the thirteenth year of king Josiah. This must mean the year of his call as a prophet, which the immediately following verses tell us about (1.4-10). According to this his prophetic activity began in 627/6 and according to the further information given in the introduction continued until the destruction of Jerusalem in the eleventh year of king Zedekiah (587/6). So the book of Jeremiah is the testimony of a prophet's life at the time of the fall and finally the end of the kingdom of Judah. Many elements and aspects of these dramatic decades are reflected in the book, so that it also constitutes an important document for this crucial time in history.

The book as a whole presents a very self-contained and impressive picture of the life, proclamation and troubles of the prophet Jeremiah. At the same time, however, very diverse linguistic forms are displayed in it, which point to a gradual growth and the collaboration of various persons or groups in the composition of the book. However, there are no texts, such as there are for instance in Isaiah, that reflect another period, and no references to other prophetic figures either. In addition the book contains very marked individual features found in no other prophet and which cannot be understood as merely the result of formations of tradition. So the book as a whole offers the testimony of the life and work of the prophet Jeremiah as perceived, experienced and presented by his contemporaries in his more or less direct proximity.

This does not rule out the possibility that this process of tradition extended for a lengthy period. In particular, texts that relate to the period after the end of the exile may have been expanded or added. So the book cannot be read as a biography of Jeremiah in the narrower sense. When we speak of "Jeremiah" in what follows, this is therefore not meant in a strictly historical and biographical sense but designates the prophet Jeremiah as we see him in the book of Jeremiah.

Within the book two forms of account are clearly distinguishable: words of the prophet and reports about the prophet. The first are found mainly in chs. 1–25, the latter primarily in chs. 26–45. Within the words of the prophet there is a further difference: a proportion of the words are formulated in poetic language, which stands in the tradition of the words of earlier prophets, but which at the same time also bears very individual traits; another part presents speech-like pieces given in prose, which reveal clear connections in language and theology with Deuteronomy. What part of these "deuteronomistic" texts goes back to Jeremiah himself and what is to be ascribed to a later "redaction" is disputed, as is the question of what texts Baruch may have written down (ch. 36) [→**225**]. But the multi-layered and multi-vocal nature of the work that comes to expression in these questions does not put the overall self-contained impression of the book in any real doubt.

A roughly chronological sequence is discernible in the book. It begins with the call of Jeremiah (ch. 1) and ends with his last words to the group of Judeans who took him with them to Egypt after the fall of Jerusalem, against his will (ch. 44) [→**224**]—and there we lose his tracks. Within the book some texts are dated but appear not to be in chronological order (e.g. 25.1 in the time of Jehoiachim is earlier than 21.1 in the time of Zedekiah). At many points, though, a sequence based on content and text arrangements is evident, which possibly came about before the present final form of the book of Jeremiah.

The Greek translation of Jeremiah in the Septuagint presents a special problem. This version is roughly one seventh shorter than the Hebrew. In addition, sayings against foreign nations that form chs. 46–51 in the Hebrew version are found in the middle of the book (chs. 26–31), and moreover in a different order. Since Hebrew fragments that approximate to the Greek text have also been found among the Qumran texts, there is a lot to suggest that there were two different Hebrew versions, of which the shorter formed the basis for the Greek translation. Apart from the certainly remarkable different positioning of the oracles to the nations (see below on ch. 25 [→**219**]), however, the LXX version does not present any notable differences in content by comparison with the Hebrew. (See Herrmann 1990, 182ff.)

3.2 I have appointed you as a prophet

Unlike Isaiah, Jeremiah comes into view as a person, right from the first moment. He himself is the subject of the first scene of the book, which begins in the first person: "The word of the LORD came (lit.: happened) to me" (*way'hî d'bar yhwh 'elay*, 1.4) [→*In* **123**]. This is something new, that the word of God "happens," that it "comes" to a person. We meet this expression only once in Isaiah (Isa 38.4), and it is not found at all in the Book of the Twelve Prophets, who came earlier than Jeremiah. Now in Jeremiah (and then in Ezekiel) we read time and again: "The word of the LORD came to me" (Jer 1.4, 11, 13; 2.1 etc.) or "to Jeremiah" (14.1; 28.12; 29.30 etc.).

In the divine word that comes to him at this point (1.5), Jeremiah is told that before his birth, in fact before God "formed" (*yāṣar*, cf. Gen 2.7) him in his mother's womb, God "knew," or "recognized" him—*yāda'* can mean both. The notion of "election" that is contained in *yāda'* in Amos 3.2 (and Gen 18.18f) [→**281, 28**] is connoted here too. Already then God had marked him out as a prophet, "dedicated" him, one might say (literally "sanctified," *hiqdîš*). Here the term *nābî'* appears for the prophet, a word that frequently occurs in the reporting texts of the books of Samuel and Kings but which is scarcely ever found in the older "writing prophets." Jeremiah is thus expressly placed in the tradition of the prophets who accompanied Israel's pathway through its history from the early days.

The phrase "*nābî'* for the nations" is very unusual [→**§17**]. In the time of Jeremiah's ministry, Israel (i.e., to be precise, Judah) was drawn as never before into the disputes and confusions of the world of the nations of that time, in which the hitherto dominant structures became unstable and eventually collapsed. This is the "world hour" which Jeremiah is to interpret "as an action of God in history, judgment and renewal" (Buber 1942/1984, 208). He is appointed by God "over nations and kingdoms to uproot and tear down, to destroy and overthrow, to build and to plant" (1.10). What this means is later shown graphically in the activity of the potter whom Jeremiah watches at his work (18.1-10) [→**216**]. Just as the potter decides whether a vessel corresponds to his requirements or not, so too God decides whether a people can exist before him or not, and whether he will "uproot, tear down and destroy" it (v. 7) or "build and plant" it (v. 9). Jeremiah is appointed to proclaim and announce this (vv. 11f).

Jeremiah reacts in shock: "Ah, Sovereign LORD!" (1.6). The contrast with Isaiah's commission is striking. Isaiah says, of his own accord, "Here am I, send me!" (Isa 6.8) [→**173**]. For Ezekiel, the book of the scroll that he has to eat and which is inscribed on the inside and outside with "lament, mourning and woe," becomes "sweet as honey" to him (Ezek 3.3) [→**235**]. But Jeremiah tries to get out of the commission. This recalls Moses' reaction to his "call" (cf. Zimmerli 1969, 16-21). Jeremiah says: "I cannot speak!" (1.6), Moses: "I have never been eloquent ..., I am slow of speech and tongue" (Ex 4.10) [→**43**]. And when later there is mention of Jeremiah's "woe" about the day he was born (Jer 15.10) [→**214**], this also recalls Moses who prays God in desperate situations to blot him out of his "book" (Ex 32.32) [→**62**], and even to kill him (Num 11.15).

"I am only a *na'ar*, a child" (1.6b). Whether this means "I am too young" (Luther) or whether it expresses a subordinate or not yet socially established position, which would not lend his words sufficient weight (Herrmann 1986, 61f), in any case a feeling of unsuitability for this task comes to expression, and there is a sense of fear for the consequences and the enemies that will grow out of it. But God does not accept this protest (v. 7). He will send him (*šālaḥ*) as he sent Moses (Ex 3.12) [→**40**] and Isaiah (Isa 6.8) [→**173**], and his authority will be vindicated in this. And he will not speak with his own words but say what God has given him to say. So he will enter into the role of the prophet in the succession of Moses, whom God will call upon again and again to speak what God tells him to (Deut 18.18). And God will be with him (v. 8) as he was before with Moses (Ex 3.12).

The commission is confirmed and reinforced when God's hand directly touches Jeremiah: "Now, I have put my words in your mouth" (1.9). Again the parallel with Isaiah is obvious, whose "unclean" lips are purified and atoned by one of the "Seraphim" surrounding God with a glowing coal from the altar (Isa 6.6f). But the difference is clear once again. In Isaiah's case the problem is: how can a person with unclean lips, from a people with unclean lips, proclaim the word of

God? For Jeremiah the question is: how can a person who does not feel competent for the task nonetheless proclaim the word of God? God answers this question by himself putting his words in Jeremiah's mouth.

In no other prophet is the task of passing on the word of God formulated so expressly and reflected upon so intensively as in Jeremiah. This is already evident in the fact that the term *dābār*, "word," is found more frequently in Jeremiah than in any other book of the Hebrew Bible (more than 200 times, mostly in application to the divine word, cf. *THAT* I, 435). And after we read that God puts his words in Jeremiah's mouth, he can later even say: "When your words came, I ate them" (15.16) [→**214**]. In the divine speech we read: "I will make my words in your mouth a fire" (5.14), and finally: "Is not my word like fire, and like a hammer that breaks a rock in pieces?" (23.29). The dramatic nature of these statements also shows that behind them there is no coherent theory of the "word of God"; so too, no fundamental distinction is made between statements about the "word" and "the words" of God.

In two brief vision scenes [→*In* **121**] the two main elements of the call scene are now graphically depicted: the word of God and Jeremiah's involvement in the impending historical events. Twice God asks: "What do you see, Jeremiah?" The first time it is a branch of the almond tree, the name of which, *šāqēd*, evokes the divine assurance that he will be "watching" (*šoqēd*) over his word, so that it will indeed be fulfilled (1.11f). He will not leave Jeremiah alone with the word entrusted to him. The second time it is a "boiling pot," the front of which is "tilting away from the north," so that it will necessarily run over in a southerly direction (v. 13). This announces the coming historical events: "From the north" disaster will be poured out (lit.: "opened up" v. 14) on all inhabitants of the land. Soon the "enemy from the north" [→**208**] will become a dominant theme (esp. in 4.5–6.26).

To start with, however, God will summon kings from the north, who will set up their thrones around Jerusalem and the cities of Judah (v. 15). This appears like a court scene, in which the foreign kings function as "community of justice" (Herrmann 1986, 77) [→*In* **94**]: "Then I will take them to court." This addresses another central theme in Jeremiah, which up to this point has been in the background: Israel's sin. "They have forsaken me, burning incense to other gods and worshiping what their hands have made" (v. 16).

This dramatically shows the changed situation by comparison with the time of Isaiah. The worship of foreign gods plays no role there. But now for Jeremiah it becomes a dominant theme. This is the all-important "wickedness" (*rā'āh*) of Israel (v. 16) that will cause God to unleash the "evil," disaster (*rā'āh*) upon Israel (v. 14) [→§19].

The call account returns to its beginning as God repeats his commission (v. 17, cf. v. 7b). He also repeats the encouragement, and he will now "reinforce" Jeremiah, far beyond what can be said of a person: like a fortified city, an iron pillar and a bronze wall (1.18). For now those people will turn against him that have already been referred to (cf. v. 8) and who are now concretely named: the kings of Judah, the officials, priests and the "people of the land," i.e. the representatives of the population of Judah [→§16]. None of them will be able to touch Jeremiah. God repeats his assurance: "I am with you and will rescue you" (v. 19, cf. v. 8).

At the end of the first chapter Jeremiah is now in the full view of the reader: his person, his call as a prophet, his commission to pass on the word of God, the basic elements of his message, the resistance that is to be expected and the promise of God's protection and help. The element of hesitation, his recoiling in the face of the task, indeed the fear of enmity and persecution, sets the tone of this call report. These features repeatedly reappear later also, with great clarity, in the monologues, laments and prayers, the "confessions of Jeremiah" (see below, 3.5 [→213]).

3.3 Married bliss—apostasy to Baal—the enemy from the North

Again the word of God comes to Jeremiah (2.1). It calls on him to speak publicly in Jerusalem. This time the introductory formula is followed by a second: "Thus says the LORD" (*koh 'āmar yhwh*, v. 2) [→*In* 123]. It too is one of the basic elements of prophetic language in Jeremiah. It is, as it were, the consequence of the fact that God has placed his words in the prophet's mouth, so that they are always recognizable as the words of God when he speaks them. Finally, a further formulaic element appears, which shows that the prophetic speech is a divine word, at the same time possessing a structural function: *ne'um yhwh*, "pronouncement of the LORD"; this too is found with particular frequency in Jeremiah (previously 1.8, 15, 19; then 2.3, 9, 12, 19 etc.; cf. 1954b).

The prophetic discourse that begins here as a first-person divine speech develops in all kinds of new ways the theme that Jeremiah was commissioned to proclaim in the introduction: the reproach that Israel has turned to other gods (1.16). This is now placed in a broader, salvation-historical context. At the beginning in the wilderness Israel's relationship with God was unclouded (2.2f); but when they came into the fertile land that God had given them, they no longer asked, "Where is the LORD, who brought us out of Egypt?," but turned to other gods (vv. 4-8) [→§7]. This reproach applies to the "fathers," i.e. to all the generations before those who are now being addressed (v. 5). In particular, however, it applies to the earlier strata talked about earlier (1.18): above all the priests responsible for the observance of the Torah, then the "shepherds" of the people and finally even the prophets (2.8). For the first time there is mention here of the name of the Canaanite god [→§20], who appears again and again as the significant opponent of Yhwh: Baal. Centuries before already there had been those dramatic disputes about the Baal cult in the northern kingdom of Israel, in which the prophets Elijah and Elisha played a crucial role [→137]. Then this problem had raised its head increasingly in Judah too, and now it becomes a central theme in Jeremiah's dispute with his contemporaries. So God now begins a legal dispute with Israel (v. 9).

In the lively language of the following paragraphs the images change: Israel exchanges gods, which no other people would ever do (2.10f); Israel leaves the living source and makes leaky cisterns for itself (v. 13); Israel was a choice vine which has now become "wild" (v. 21); Israel breaks its yoke and tears off its bonds (v. 20), behaves like a camel mare in heat or a wild donkey (vv. 23f). The sexual metaphor contained in the last image is applied also to the cultic domain: the "high-place sanctuaries" are places where Israel commits prostitution "on every high hill and under every spreading tree" (v. 20) [→145]. In the following chapter this is developed further and extended also to the history of the northern kingdom of Israel, Judah's "sister," which has been punished by God on account of this prostitution; but Judah has not taken this on board as a warning (3.6-10).

In between there are frequent sections that speak of the disaster that has already befallen Israel or will do so (2.14-19, 26-28, 35-37). Israel has only itself to blame for this. It is because of its own "wickedness" (again the word rā'āh as in 1.14, 16!) that it is being punished (v. 19).

But then the question suddenly arises whether this story of calamity is then definitive and irreversible. A woman who is divorced by her husband because of marital infidelity cannot return to him (3.1-5). Does this apply to Israel too? Here the word *šûb* "repent, return" appears; it too is one of the common expressions in Jeremiah and is not found as often as here in any other book of the Hebrew Bible. Here it is used in the most varied shades of its meaning: May the divorced wife go back to her husband (3.1)? Will Israel come back to God (v. 7)? Will Judah convert to God (v. 10)? And then God's cry: "Turn/turn back! Turn around!" (3.12, 14, 22; 4.1) The theme of "turning around" becomes the central theme in Jeremiah (Wolff 1951, 131).

Here, then, we have the statements about Israel's sin with the Baal cult, about the punishments that Israel has to suffer as a result, and about the possible turn-around, apparently roughly juxtaposed. The tension seems even greater when the text speaks not only of God's call to repent (3.12, 14, 22; 4.1) but also of the first signs of Israel's repentance: "Yes, we will come to you" (3.22b). Israel makes a confession of its sin (vv. 23-25) and at the same time a confession to its God, the only source of "the salvation of Israel" (v. 23b). And God promises a new beginning: "Break up your unplowed ground! Circumcise your hearts!" (4.1-4). This direct juxtaposition of judgment and salvation recalls the book of Isaiah, especially chs. 1–12. There too, accusation, proclamation of judgment and assurance of restoration stand next to each other, time and again [→171]. This shows that the connection and association of judgment and salvation forms a basic element of the canonical prophetic books. This now applies to the first section of the proclamation of Jeremiah (2.1–4.4), but equally to the whole of the book that follows. This means that even the sharpest preaching of judgment by Jeremiah can never be read without the broad context of God's salvation history with Israel being called to mind.

But the prospect of a blissful future provides only a brief breathing space. The noise of war then sounds: the "foe from the north" is approaching (4.6; 6.1, 22; cf. 1.14). The approach of this enemy [→§20], its archaic cruelty and the consequences for the land and for Jerusalem are described in dramatic descriptions that start up again and again (4.5-31; 6.1-26). But it seems as if only Jeremiah himself sees and hears this, almost physically suffering under it (4.19 etc.), while others scarcely acknowledge it (4.21f etc.). For the reader too the question remains open who is meant by this enemy and whether the concern is with something real and experienced or something anticipated. Perhaps his contemporaries really did not see and hear anything because they could not, or did not want to, see what was facing them. The conflict becomes clear again in the question why all this is happening (5.1-31). The answer is the same as before: Israel has forsaken its God and is serving foreign gods (vv. 7, 11, 19 etc.). And in addition there is no one who "deals honestly and seeks the truth" (vv. 1, 26-28). In this regard the "great" are no better than the "poor" (vv. 4f). It sounds like a concluding word placed in this first section of Jeremiah (chs. 2–6) when we read that God has made Jeremiah a "tester" of his people, who, as a metal-tester tests the material, is to test the "way," i.e. the comportment of this people. But the result is quite negative: the slag is not purged out of the precious metal (6.27-30).

3.4 Temple speech and covenant preaching

Once again the word of God comes to Jeremiah and calls on him to speak out in public (7.1). The proclamation of the word of God he has received is again presented in a special form. It does not say: "And the word came" (with the verbal introduction *wayʰî*, see above on 1.4 [→203]), but "The word that came to Jeremiah from the LORD" (with *haddābār*, "the word," placed at the beginning for emphasis). This formula introduces public actions by Jeremiah: the temple speech (7.1), the covenant sermon (11.1), the visit to the potter, which opens up a broader context (18.1), the public answer to the oracle-seeking king Zedekiah, which introduces the collection of words to the kings (21.1), the public announcement of the victory of the Babylonian king Nebuchadnezzar, which concludes the first part of the book (25.1), the writing down of the divine words in a "book" (30.1), the purchase of a field (32.1) etc., also the repetition, with a slight variation, of the temple speech (26.1), the commission to carry a yoke (27.1) and the writing down of the words on a scroll (36.1). These texts clearly form a consciously shaped context, which connects the important stages in Jeremiah's public ministry.

Jeremiah now has to proclaim his criticism at a central point in Jerusalem: at the gate of the temple (7.2). A public conflict seems unavoidable. The "temple speech" that now follows contains a sharp critique of the current cultic practice [→§11]. At its center stands the question of how the cult and the life of the community relate to each other.

This speech can be called an "alternative sermon" (cf. Thiel 1973, 290ff): either the community lives according to the will and the instructions of God, in which case "I will let you live in this place (v. 3), in the land I gave to your forefathers" (v. 7); or they will rely on the "lying word" which regards temple service as a guarantee of security, independent of moral and just behavior (vv. 4, 8-10), in which case God will destroy this temple as he destroyed the temple in Shiloh, and will "thrust away" the people like the inhabitants of the northern kingdom (vv. 12-15) [→**169f**]. Like Isaiah (Isa 1.10-17), Jeremiah too sees a cult that does not correspond to a community life in accordance with the will of God as a self-deception and a betrayal of God. The "house which bears my Name" will thereby be made a "den of robbers" (v. 11).

Following the Vulgate, at vv. 3 and 7 some translations read: "So I will live with you in this place." The basis for this translation is the same consonantal Hebrew text as for the above translation, but with a different vocalization: *wešakantî 'itťkem* instead of *w'šikkantî 'etkem* (v. 7, in accordance with v. 3). Some recent commentators have followed this on the grounds that the expression *māqôm* "place" means the temple here. In the masoretic text and the Septuagint, however, the meaning is clearly the land in which God will let Israel live and from which he will not expel it if it fulfills the conditions he requires of it.

The dramatic consequences of this performance are not recorded until later (ch. 26), in correspondence with the composition of the book; but the reader can already sense the tension. Jeremiah's own situation is itself now spotlighted: God forbids him to intercede for "this people" (7.16). Here the comparison with Moses comes in again. Moses was the greater intercessor (Aurelius 1988) who time and again saves Israel from threatened annihilation in critical situations through his personal intervention [→**61, 70f**].

Jeremiah is clearly drawn as a successor of Moses, but he is not allowed at this point to act like Moses (Seitz 1989). He did this earlier, which he reminds God about (18.20). But now he is not allowed to do it [→**214**]. And this is not the only prohibition he receives (cf. 11.14; 14.11). The prophet who suffers under his own message, who would like to deflect the impending disaster from his people and whose heart is breaking over it (4.19), is not permitted to stand up for his people. This is one of the keys to the understanding of Jeremiah's situation.

In the following verses new aspects of illegitimate cults crop up. Whole families set up sacrificial ceremonies for the "queen of heaven" (7.17f) [→**§20**], the Babylonian-Assyrian Ishtar, a cult which was evidently very popular at the time (44.15-19); they also worship the sun, moon and the whole host of heaven (8.2). In the temple they have set up "detestable idols" (7.30), and they arrange child sacrifices in the Valley of Ben-Hinnom (v. 31). In this context the critique of the sacrificial cult is again sharpened: God did not order the forefathers to perform sacrifices on their exodus from Egypt but to obey his word (vv. 21-23).

This first public speech resounds again and again later on. This is especially clear in the context of the text composition, which centers around the picture of the potter [→**216**], where themes from the context of the temple speech are taken up again (chs. 18–20, see below). The second informative main section of the book is introduced in ch. 26 with a new account of the temple speech, which then reports on its consequences and thereby introduces a whole series of public appearances and disputations.

First words are again exchanged which announce Israel's fate, with laments of the prophet, which bring to expression his suffering on account of his message and the impending disaster (8.4–9.25). It ends in a fundamental confrontation between the gods, which are only made with hands, and the *one* God, who is without compare and whose name is "YHWH Zebaot" (10.1-16). Here there is a clear connection with texts in Isaiah (e.g. Isa 44.6ff) [→**189**]. And again it ends with the prophet's lament about the impending transportation of the people into captivity, for which it must now gather its belongings together (10.17ff).

With the same introductory formula as the temple speech, in 11.1 a new sermon opens up. The content of the sermon is formed by the "words of the covenant" (v. 2) [→**§6**]. The hearers and readers of the book of Jeremiah knew which covenant was meant—and the readers of the Hebrew Bible know too, having already read it. In the depiction that Moses gives retrospectively of the revelation of the Torah on Sinai/Horeb, we read: "The LORD spoke to you out of the fire ... and he declared to you his covenant, the ten commandments, which he commanded you to follow and then wrote them on two stone tablets" (Deut 4.12f) [→**75**]. Jeremiah's sermon stands in this tradition. God then spoke the words of the covenant to Israel and connected obedience to these words with the assurance: "you will be my people and I will be your God" (v. 4); in addition he connected this with the fulfillment of his responsibilities towards the forefathers, to give them a fertile land (v. 5).

The words of the covenant have another side to them, however: because Israel has not obeyed the voice of God [→§16], he has "brought on them all the words of this covenant" (v. 8). The words of the covenant also contain the announcement of the consequences for the non-observance of the responsibilities of the covenant. The house of Israel and the house of Judah have broken the covenant by turning again to other gods (v. 10, cf. v. 13). God will therefore cause disaster (*rā'āh*) to come upon them (v. 11); this is, as it were, the other side of the coin of the covenant, which will come into force if it is not observed.

As after the temple speech, so too now God forbids Jeremiah to intercede for "this people" (11.14). The prohibition again occurs in direct connection with the proclamation of impending disaster and stops Jeremiah stepping into the breach himself. The agreement between these two speeches of Jeremiah has already become evident in the same wording of the introductory formula (see above on 7.1 [→209]). Now the prohibition of intercession joins these two public appearances even closer together.

3.5 The lamenting prophet

At this point the spotlight moves. After the great covenant sermon and after the prohibition of intercession Jeremiah now begins to speak to himself (11.18). He reflects on his situation. It has become clear to him that he has enemies who are persecuting him and are out to kill him (vv. 19, 21). So he speaks to himself about it and then also to God (v. 20; 12.1-3), who answers him (vv. 21, 22f; 12.5f). A whole series of texts begins here, which have in common that they are not addressed to the public in general but are in some cases Jeremiah's conversations with himself, in some cases prayers and dialogues with God. These texts are usually referred to as the "confessions" of Jeremiah [→*In* 215]. With their tension between quite personal statements and traditional stylistic forms many of them come very close to the "individual laments" of the book of Psalms, so that they can also be called Jeremiah's "poems of lament" (Baumgartner 1917; ET 1987). Counted among this group are 11.18-23; 12.1-6; 15.10f, 15-21; 17.12-18; 18.18-23; 20.7-18.

The confessions often stand at the conclusion of a clearly marked text unit (Thiel 1973, 161f, 286f). The often surprising alternation between the proclamation of the divine word and Jeremiah's conversations with himself as well as his conversations with God about his situation demonstrates to the reader again and again the inner tension in which Jeremiah lives. One might almost say that his prophetic existence consists in this tension, in this split personality, as was expressed before in the call story. So the confessions belong at the "center of any Jeremiah interpretation" (von Rad 1965, 211). But with these texts too the question of the biography of Jeremiah and the rest of the tradition-formation remains open, especially as many of the texts give the impression of being compositions within which various themes are introduced (cf. Carroll 1981, 107-39).

Friends become enemies—a typical element of the songs of lament in the Psalms (e.g. Pss 31.12-14; 41.10; 88.9) [→**328**]. Now it is the people of Anathoth that are out to kill their fellow-citizen Jeremiah (Jer 11.18-23). God assures Jeremiah that he will hold his enemies to account (vv. 22f); but Jeremiah sees another, more far-reaching problem in the confrontation with them: why do the "wicked," the "ungodly" prosper like this (12.1-6)? This problem too occurs frequently in the psalms of lament. The "ungodly" (*rešāʿîm*) are the opponents and counterparts of the petitioners in the Psalms, the "pious" and righteous (*ṣaddîqîm*), e.g. Ps 73 [→**329**]. In the book of Job too this is one of the central themes (e.g. Job 21 [→**345f**]). Jeremiah enters into a formal dispute with God over this question (12.1). But God's answer does not lend validity to Jeremiah's problem: if he already experiences difficulties with a "pedestrian" problem, how is he going to cope with the tasks of his prophetic calling, which are still to come (v. 5)? So already in this first of Jeremiah's poems of lament the personal problem of the prophet again comes into view, with which the reader of the book is already familiar from the first sentences: Jeremiah's awareness of not being up to his task and still of not being able to get out of it.

The lament increases in intensity: "Alas, my mother, that you gave me birth!" (15.10) This cry of lament follows directly on from a particularly harsh word of judgment over Jerusalem, which Jeremiah had to proclaim, and at the end of which the sad fate of the mothers is prophesied (15.5-9). His own lament now goes far beyond what the petitioners of the Psalms dare to say; only in Job are such statements to be found (Job 3 etc.) [→**341**]. His preaching of judgment has again brought him into conflict with his environment, with "the whole land" as we are now told (v. 10). God knows that the prophet is despised on his account (15.15). Indeed, it is precisely his devotion to his prophetic office that brings him into the situation of the one who is persecuted above all others: he "ate" the words of God whenever they came to him (v. 16). They became his heart's delight—but at the same time they isolated him from others and made him lonely (v. 17). The lament turns into an accusation: God has become a "deceptive brook" which has suddenly stopped providing living and life-giving water (v. 18). But again God's answer turns the lament back to the prophet (v. 19). Again the word of "turning around" (*šûb*) occurs, this time in an artistic word-play: "If you repent (*tāšûb*) I will restore you (*waʾašîbᵉkā*) ...; let them turn to you (*yāšubû*), but you must not turn to them (*tāšûb*)." Now it is the prophet himself who is to turn around, and this means: turn back to his task, by speaking "worthy," not "worthless" words, which is what his laments represent in God's view. Here again the mutual relationship between Jeremiah's poems of lament and his call as a prophet is quite clear: if he turns to the situation at the beginning, then what God promised him at that time will come back into force: that he would make him a "brazen wall" and be with him (vv. 20f, cf. 1.18f) [→**206**].

Again and again in the poems of lament the problem arises of enmity which Jeremiah experiences on account of the words of God that he has to proclaim. His opponents mock him and say to him: "Where is the word of the LORD? Let it now be fulfilled!" (17.15). They want to beat him with his own words (18.18). Jeremiah has to put up with this mockery even though he himself was never in favor of the calamity (17.16). In fact, he reminds God that he has stood up for him and interceded for Israel (18.20). But now, like many of the petitioners in the songs of lament, he can only pray that God will destroy his enemies (17.18; 18.21-23; 20.11f; cf. Ps 69.25f; 143.12 etc.)

The last of the poems of lament brings the prophet's conflict with God to its extreme. Two dramatic scenes have preceded it: in a public symbolic act, through the smashing of an earthenware vessel he has demonstrated how God will treat Israel (ch. 19), and thereupon he is beaten by the superintendent of the temple guard and placed in the stocks overnight (20.1-6). This first public mistreatment of Jeremiah appears in the course of the book of Jeremiah as a provisional deep point in his prophetic activity. From these depths the lament is raised:

"O LORD, you have deceived me, and I was deceived; you overpowered me and prevailed" (20.7). This again exceeds all the laments and complaints of Jeremiah hitherto. God has seduced him as one seduces a girl (cf. Ex 22.15), or as a woman persuades a man (Judg 14.15; 16.5), or as God leads people astray through false prophets (1 Kgs 22.20-22; cf. Ezek 14.9) [→143]. He had to do something he did not want to do, which brought him contempt and scorn, but which he could not escape because it would otherwise have burnt his inner being: he had to pass on the preaching of judgment to his people (20.8-10).

Again he hopes that he will see the end of his enemies (vv. 11f). Standing next to this in an almost painful contrast is the hymnic praise for the rescue of the persecuted out of the hands of his enemies (v. 13), as is familiar to us from the psalms of lament (Ps 6.9f; 22.24f) [→327].

But then the lament abruptly turns to the cursing of his own birth. This note has been struck once before (15.10), but now it occurs in a much harsher tone: the "Alas" has become "Cursed!" and the lament ends without any comforting conclusion (20.14-18). At the same time this ends the group of poems of lament in the conception of the book. It remains unstated what this expression of deepest despair means for the life of Jeremiah. His prophetic ministry continues. A new phase begins which is marked above all by public conflict with the kings (chs. 21ff).

3.6 The prophet as sign

Many of Jeremiah's prophetic utterances are collected and transmitted without any mention of the occasion and context. Alongside them, however, there are a large number of reports of Jeremiah's public appearances, and no other prophet is as involved in acts of prophetic proclamation as he is. We have already discussed the two great sermons, the temple speech (ch. 7) and the covenant sermon (ch. 11). Characteristic alongside these are above all the actions in which Jeremiah demonstrates particular elements of his proclamation in symbolic form. Many of them can in fact be described as "acts" (cf. Carroll 1981, 130-35).

The two visions connected with Jeremiah's call [→201], in which the content of a proclamation is graphically presented, belong here: the branch of an almond tree (*šāqēd*) illustrates the "watching" (*šoqēd*) God (1.11f), and the pot of boiling water leaning "away from the north" illustrates the impending disaster from the north (vv. 13f). Here

The Canonical Hebrew Bible

Jeremiah is only a "spectator," as in the potter's workshop, where he observes how the potter rejects a misshapen vessel and from the clay makes another which meets with his approval (18.2-4). For Jeremiah this becomes the graphic sign for God's dealings with Israel: "Like clay in the hand of the potter, so are you in my hand, O house of Israel" (v. 6); and it is just the same for other nations too (vv. 7-10). This interpretation of what has been seen is followed by an announcement of disaster for Israel and the call to repentance (*šûb*); but it remains in vain (vv. 11f).

The visit to the potter's is emphasized by means of the introductory formula, "The word that came to Jeremiah from the LORD" (18.1) and is placed in a series with the great public appearances in the temple speech (ch. 7) [→**209**] and the covenant sermon (ch. 11). At the same time it introduces a broader context. The following narrative sees the prophet in action. He concretizes the potter parable by going out into the Valley of Ben-Hinnom in the company of earlier representatives of Jerusalem's population and the priesthood and there smashing a clay vase with the words: "This is what the LORD Almighty says: I will smash this people and this city ..." (191f, 10f). In the potter narrative there was still the possibility of repentance and therewith of the avoidance of the announced disaster (18.11). The smashing of the clay jar makes it clear that this possibility no longer exists. The disaster will come, ineluctably. This symbolic act is connected in the present context with a sermon of judgment on the child sacrifice on the Topheth high-places in the Hinnom Valley (vv. 3-9, 11b-13), which were spoken of already in the context of the temple speech in ch. 7 (vv. 31f). Jeremiah announces that this valley will in future be called "Valley of Murder" instead of "Topheth" or "Valley of Ben-Hinnom" (7.32; 19.6). Again there is talk of sacrifices for "other gods" [→**§20**] (19.4, 13; cf. 1.16; 7.6, 9 etc.), especially for Baal (v. 5) and for the "host of heaven" (v. 13, cf. 8.2). So as it unfolds, the potter parable becomes also a visible concretization of the temple speech.

Jeremiah repeats his preaching of judgment in the temple courtyard (19.14f), and this public provocation brings mistreatment and punishment upon him (20.1-6). This context of sign-acts and public preaching finally leads to the most profound of all the laments handed down from Jeremiah (20.7-18). Here we see that the sign-act is more than a mere "symbolic action." It becomes a central element of Jeremiah's proclamation, in which he himself and his personal fate become a sign.

The connection of a sign-act with prophetic proclamation and Jeremiah's personal fate is also evident in the narrative context of chs. 27f. The introduction (27.1) places this text again in a series with the other great public appearances [→**209**]. Jeremiah is commissioned by God to make himself a yoke and place it on his neck (27.1f). Again the sign-act is preparation for a prophetic address, the theme of which grows out of the sign-act: "Bow your neck under the yoke of the king of Babylon" (v. 12). This sermon is addressed not only to Zedekiah, king of Judah (vv. 12-15), to the priests and the whole population (vv. 16-22), but also to the kings of the neighboring peoples, whose envoys happen to be at this moment with Zedekiah (vv. 3-11).

Already in the sermons that interpret the sign-act, Jeremiah warns against prophets who "prophesy" against submission to the king of Babylon (27.14, 16-18). But then out of this sign-act a conflict arises which is at the same time symptomatic of the relationship between Jeremiah and the other prophets (ch. 28). The prophet Hananiah opposes him with the opposite message: that God is shortly going to break the yoke of the king of Babylon and will bring back the king of Judah, who has been taken into exile, and all the other exiles as well as the temple objects (vv. 2-4). It is now a question of prophet against prophet. The narrative is full of drama and leaves scope for various interpretations. At first Jeremiah appears to confirm Hananiah's message: "Amen! May the LORD do so!" (v. 6). But does he really mean it? One may certainly assume that Jeremiah would approve of the return of the temple objects and the exiles (cf. 27.18). But now he is bearing the yoke on his neck, the message of which is unmistakable: subjection to the Babylonians is inescapable [→**§16**]. Jeremiah sees himself within a history of prophecy marked by the proclamation of disaster (v. 8); so a prophet who announces disaster needs no additional legitimation. But if a prophet prophesies peace/salvation (*šālôm*), then the proof that this prophet has really been sent by God is only evident when the prophecy comes to fulfillment (v. 9). This recalls Micaiah ben Imlah, who wanted to apply the criterion of the actual coming into being of what is announced even for his message of disaster (1 Kgs 22.27f) [→**143f**].

At first Hananiah has the upper hand. In an antithetical sign-act he breaks the yoke that Jeremiah is carrying on his neck, and repeats his message of peace. Jeremiah does not resist this and does not protest; he "goes on his way" (vv. 10f). It seems as if he is conceding defeat. It is not until later (the Hebrew text says indeterminately "after" this event) that a new divine word comes to Jeremiah (v. 12). This hiatus makes it clear that it is not a matter of Jeremiah having a quick answer ready. This conflict between prophet and prophet is only going to be decided by a new message from God. The metaphor of the sign-act is taken up again and reinforced: instead of a wooden yoke, an iron yoke will represent the rule of the Babylonians (vv. 13f). In addition, Jeremiah is now empowered to speak out clearly that Hananiah and his message of peace have not been sent by God. He announces to Hananiah that he will soon die; and this is what transpires (vv. 15-17).

Alongside these two consequential sign-acts there are others that have quite a different character. Before only a limited number of witnesses the repurchase of a field in Anathoth takes place, for which Jeremiah possesses the right of redemption (*g'ullāh*) (ch. 32). The process would as such scarcely have been remarkable, since it was a perfectly "normal" legal transaction, though one that has its justification in religious law (cf. Lev 25.25ff) [→68]. But the circumstances in which this item of business is conducted make it an act: Jerusalem is besieged and Jeremiah is in prison. In this situation the purchase of a field must seem almost absurd. But the purchase sets up a sign: "Houses, fields and vineyards will again be bought in this land" (32.15). A quite different tone is set here, compared with previous sign-acts. God assures Jerusalem and the whole land of a future. This certainly does not mean a retraction of the announcement of conquest and destruction by the Babylonians. But it does mean that even after that there will still be "future and hope" for Israel (cf. 29.11, see below [→226]). Jeremiah himself is shown in a strangely halting position. In a long prayer he asks God about the meaning of this action in this hopeless situation (vv. 16-25), and God answers in a detailed divine message, which presents the two phases of God's dealings with Israel: the punishment of its sinful behavior and the restoration (vv. 26-44). So here the real sign character lies in the fact that for those who are directly affected a prospect for the future is held open.

In some of the other sign-acts, too, the public character lies rather in the associated sermon or even only in a later publicization of the event. It is not immediately easy to understand the act in which Jeremiah is to bury a new, linen belt by the Euphrates and to dig it up again "after a long time," when it becomes evident that it has been completely ruined (13.1-7). The attached interpretation in a divine word (vv. 8-11) compares this with the impending fate of Israel. In the act itself there is no mention of witnesses, and the following divine word does not contain a commission to announce it in public. So it remains unclear in what way the whole thing becomes a sign-act. In view of the great distance between Jerusalem and the Euphrates a real execution of this action is scarcely conceivable. So is it a vision? Or a message in the form of a narrated sign-act? Or should one assume that for the performance of the action a particular place in the vicinity of Jerusalem is symbolically declared to be the "Euphrates"? This narrative leaves the question open and inserts the reported event in the series of Jeremiah's sign-acts.

The sign-character of the action reported only at the conclusion of the book is clearer, though it takes place at an early point in time: Jeremiah gives a Judean delegation a scroll to take with them to Babylon, on which the threatening words against Babylon are written. These are to be read aloud there, and then the scroll is to be sunk in the Euphrates (51.59-64). It remains open whether and which audience and spectators will be present. In the context of the book of Jeremiah, however, this report has a clear function: Jeremiah has announced disaster for Babylon before. Egypt too, where Jeremiah was forced to spend his last years, becomes the subject of a sign-act. In front of his Judean compatriots Jeremiah buries stones under the gate of the palace of Pharaoh in Tahpanhes, in order to announce that the Babylonian king Nebuchadnezzar will set up his throne there when he has defeated Egypt (43.8-13).

The last two sign-acts combine to form great political and geographical circles which encompass Jeremiah's prophetic speeches. So the "nations" too become the subject of the strangest of his sign-acts. On God's instructions the prophet has "all nations" drink from the "goblet of wrath," whether they want to or not (25.15-29). The names of the nations are listed in a long sequence and they are told that God's judgment will begin in Jerusalem, but then come upon "all the inhabitants of the earth." Here too it is again evident that this cannot have been a real act that was actually carried out. So the question again arises whether this act is visionary, whether it is only related or presented symbolically. The text leaves this open, since in the first instance it is concerned with the message connected to the sign-act. (The Septuagint inserts this passage only at the conclusion of the words to the nations which begin there after 25.13 [→203].)

When there is talk of the prophet as a "sign," then finally the most personal aspect should also be mentioned. Jeremiah's complaint about his loneliness (15.15-21) is followed, as it were as a counter-image, by God's instruction, in which this is presented as an inescapable component of his prophetic office: he is not to raise a family (16.2-4), he is not to go into a house of mourning, neither to lament nor to comfort (vv. 5-7), but not to a wedding celebration either (v. 8). His isolation is to represent the coming fate of Israel, whom God will punish because of their worship of other gods, which started already with their forefathers (vv. 9-13). Here the prophet himself becomes entirely a sign of the fact that within the lifetime of the present generation "the sounds of joy and gladness, the voices of bride and bridegroom" will cease (v. 9).

The texts that present the prophet as a sign thus cover the whole breadth and depth of his proclamation: from world history which includes all the nations through to the most personal area of the prophet's own life, from the harsh announcement of the inescapable, impending end of Israel through to the demonstrative presentation of hope of a life worth living in the future.

3.7 Whom has the LORD sent?

The poems of lament, the sign-acts and many other texts show Jeremiah in conflict with his environment. In the case of no other prophet are the disputes comparable in intensity. The call story already points to the opposition that Jeremiah will have to deal with: the kings of Judah, the officials, priests and the "people of the land," i.e. the representatives of the population of Judah (1.18f) [→206]; often there is additional mention of "the prophets" (2.8; 4.9 etc.). So it is kings and prophets that appear in a special way as counterparts and opponents of Jeremiah. This makes the basic structure of the dispute clear. The matter at issue is the double question: whether Jeremiah's preaching of disaster is really the word of God, or whether he will be vindicated in his predictions of political catastrophe.

In the dispute with other prophets Jeremiah frequently mentions a crucial criterion: whether God has sent a prophet or not [→§17]. For himself—and for readers of the book of Jeremiah—it has been established right from the moment of his call that God has sent him (1.7). So he can also say with great emphasis: "in truth (*be'emet*) the LORD has sent me" (26.15). In his dispute with Hananiah he emphasizes that he stands in continuity with the prophets sent by God (28.8) [→217] and in Jeremiah there is constant talk of such a continuing series of prophets, who are said, almost formulaically, as "all my servants, the prophets," to have been sent by God to Israel (7.25; 25.4 etc.). Readers of the Hebrew Bible know this expression from the retrospect on the end of the northern kingdom, where the decisive cause of Israel's fate is given as the fact that they have not listened to the voice of these prophets sent by God, who called them to repentance (2 Kgs 17.13, 23) [→**137, 149**]. Elsewhere too in Jeremiah we frequently read that Israel despises the prophets (5.11-13), or persecutes them (2.30); so God will make his word fire in Jeremiah's mouth (5.14). In these texts Jeremiah stands in the line of other prophets.

Often, however, "the prophets" appear among Jeremiah's opponents. They are mentioned as a group alongside other social groups, especially next to the priests (5.31; 6.13 etc.) as well as in lengthy lists (2.8, 26 etc.). But then special reproaches are constantly leveled against them. The prophets of the northern kingdom prophesied "by Baal" (23.13) as the generation of the forefathers had done before (2.7f; 23.26f) [→**207**]. But above all the prophets proclaim "peace" (*šālôm*), when there is no coming peace but calamity (6.14; 8.11; 14.13; 23.17). For Jeremiah this means a confrontation, because this message of other prophets is diametrically opposed to his own.

He therefore comes to the conclusion that these prophets speak a "lie" (*šeqer*). In the divine word we read: "The prophets are prophesying lies in my name. I have not sent them or appointed them or spoken to them" (14.14). It is almost a stereotypical phrase in Jeremiah that "the prophets prophesied lies" (5.31; 23.25, 26; 27.10, 14 etc.) or that they "practice deceit" (6.13; 8.10 etc., here together with the priests). This is often connected with the statement that God has not sent them (14.14; 27.15; 29.9 etc.); but they still proclaim their lies in his name (14.14f; 23.25; 27.15 etc.). But it is only dreams that they are proclaiming (23.25-27, 32; 27.9; 29.8). Here an alternative is formulated: "Let the prophet who has a dream tell his dream, but let the one who has my word speak it faithfully" (23.28). This again moves Jeremiah close to Moses, of whom it is said that God speaks with prophets through dreams, but with Moses "from mouth to mouth" (Num 12.6f) [→**51**].

What is played out as a sign in Jeremiah's conflict with the prophet Hananiah (28.15) is extended again and again to "the prophets" as a whole. But in the process these statements have a share in the uncertainty that comes to expression in the account of the confrontation between Jeremiah and Hananiah. It is only on the fulfillment or non-fulfillment of the prophetic proclamation that it can be decided whether the word of the prophet is true or not; and it is only then that one can finally tell whether God has sent the prophet or not. The problem of "false prophecy" cannot be decided theoretically and not once and for all. So the Hebrew Bible also has no word for "false" prophets; the title *nābí'* applies to Jeremiah in the same way as to Hananiah and others (e.g. 29.21-23, see below).

It is only the Greek translation that is marked by the term ψευδο- προφήτης (6.13; 33.7 [=26.7]; 35.1 [=28.1] etc.). But it is precisely the clarity of the distinction that this word introduces that is missing in the Hebrew text, and it is missing above all in respect of Jeremiah, as the texts present him to us.

3.8 Before the gates of Babylon

Even if the texts of the book of Jeremiah are not ordered according to chronological considerations, still in general a clear process is evident. At first, at the center of the prophet's complaints lies Israel's turning towards other gods (1.16), Baal in particular (2.8), and "whoring" at the high-place sanctuaries (2.20) as well as their failure to do justice and righteousness (5.1, 26-28). In the two great sermons in chs. 7 and 11 [→209] too, the concern is with the relationship between worship and lifestyle and the keeping of the "covenant." Here and in the first sign-acts in chs. 18 and 19 [→216] Jeremiah announces the divine judg- ment on Judah and Jerusalem; but the enemy that will carry out this judgment remains unnamed. It is not until ch. 20 that the name first appears of the power that presents the great threat and which from then on as it were dominates the whole book: Babylon (20.4-6).

The collection of sayings about the kings (21.1-23.8) unites quite varied themes and aspects. Several passages are expressly addressed to the "house of Judah" (21.11; 23.1, 6). They contain ethical instruc- tions: to exercise justice, rescue the oppressed (21.12), assist foreigners, orphans and widows in gaining justice and refrain from spilling inno- cent blood (22.3) [→150], the example being Josiah (vv. 15f). In an "alternative sermon" (vv. 3-5, cf. ch. 7) [→209] the observance of these ethical rules is connected with the future establishment of the royal house; in fact at the end of this collection a promise is even declared that "days will come" in which God will raise a "righteous shoot" for David, whose name will be "Yhwh is our righteousness" *yhwh ṣidqenû,* which has an unmistakable resonance with the name of king Zedekiah (*ṣidqiyyāhû*) (23.5f). The following verses (vv. 7f) show that the thought is of the time after the return from exile.

The whole collection is introduced by the report of the enquiry of king Zedekiah to Jeremiah (21.1f). In the context of the book this report presents a harsh contrast to Jeremiah's last poem of lament [→215] which directly precedes it (20.7-18): there the prophet's desperate lament about the inescapable compulsion to pass on the word of God, even though it will bring him only mockery and enmity—here the courteous, rather submissive petition of the king to Jeremiah, to ask God on his behalf (cf. Rudolph 1968, 123). At the same time this text places the reader right in the center of the oppressive situation that had arisen as a result of the siege of Jerusalem by the Babylonians. The king hopes that God will be able to act "as in all his wonders" so that Nebuchadnezzar withdraws (21.2). The reader is bound to think of the very similar scene when during the siege of Jerusalem king Hezekiah asked the prophet Isaiah to intercede and then Jerusalem was saved (Isa 37) [→183, 148]. But this time Jeremiah's answer is an abrupt No. God himself will fight against the Israelites and will give the king and all survivors in the city into the hands of the Babylonians (21.4-7). Jeremiah adds another word to the inhabitants of Jerusalem: only those who leave the city and surrender to the Babylonians will survive (vv. 8-10).

It is certainly the intention of the writer that this chronologically late word introduces Jeremiah's words to the kings. It marks the tone of what Jeremiah proclaimed in the last historical phase towards the kings and prophets: the king of Babylon will come, God himself is sending him; the only way to survive is to surrender and submit to him. It is already said of Jehoiachim that the decisive point of his critique of Jeremiah's words was that Jeremiah proclaimed the coming of the king of Babylon with its horrific consequences (36.29). In his words to Zedekiah Jeremiah then repeats the same message over and again (34.1-7; 37.1-10, 17-21; 38.14-28). The king himself constantly seeks God's message and the advice of Jeremiah as before in 21.1f; but he does this secretly (37.17; 38.16) and he is too weak towards his immediate subjects and advisors to follow these pieces of advice and submit to the Babylonians (38.24-28). So in the end the fate announced to him by Jeremiah hastens to overtake him (39.1-10).

In Jeremiah's dispute with the prophets too the question of how to behave towards the Babylonians becomes the crucial point of conflict.

The sign-act with the yoke is followed by words of Jeremiah against the prophets, in which he thus describes them as liars precisely because they say one should not submit to the king of Babylon (27.14-18) [→221]. Among the exiles in Babylon too there are "lying prophets" who proclaim an early return (28.8f, 15). But finally Jeremiah can only say to Zedekiah: "Where are your prophets who prophesied to you, 'The king of Babylon will not attack you or this land'?" (27.19). This is the last time that the prophets are mentioned. After this they have nothing more to say.

For Jeremiah himself the conquest of Jerusalem by the Babylonians means liberation from the imprisonment in which he had latterly found himself (37.11-16; 38.1-13; 39.11-14). His prophetic word is sought once again, in order to facilitate, as it were, a political decision: should we stay in Judea or emigrate to Egypt? And again his advice is ignored. The group that asks him moves to Egypt against his advice and takes him there with them (42.1–43.7). So Jeremiah is torn away from the center of his prophetic ministry, out of Jerusalem. But even in the isolation of Egyptian exile he again has to function as a prophet. In a sign-act he announces that Egypt will be conquered by the Babylonians (43.8-13). But above all in a final dispute with the Judeans who took him to Egypt he repeats once again the main elements of his prophetic critique and focuses them especially on the cult of the "queen of heaven" [→§20], which appears here as a central element in the apostasy from the worship of Yhwh. So Jeremiah speaks a final word of judgment about this group of refugees and predicts their complete annihilation (ch. 44). The reliability of this proclamation will be confirmed by a "sign," namely the defeat of Pharaoh at the hands of the Babylonians, announced already in the prophetic act (vv. 29f).

Here Jeremiah's voice is silenced. We learn nothing of his further fate, and nor do we hear any laments from him. Only his companion Baruch is spoken of in a brief divine word (ch. 45) which he had already received at the time Jeremiah's words were written down. He gives this only now as a sort of concluding word, as it were as evidence that the divine promise has been fulfilled, that he was able to get away with his life, like booty, despite all the calamity around him.

3.9 Future and hope

Many of Jeremiah's sayings are marked by insight into the inescapability of the impending judgment. It is always clear that the judgment will and must come, because the Israelites refuse to live and act in conformity with the will of God. The call to "repentance" [→**208**] is thus one of the constitutive elements of Jeremiah's proclamation. He is, however, constantly confronted with the rather stereotypical and thus often almost resigned comment: "But you did not hear." The possibility of repentance and thus of obviation of disaster had been offered to Israel, but it did not take up the offer.

The complex shape of the book of Jeremiah makes it difficult to show in detail whether and when Jeremiah gave up hope of repentance. In the first chapters a self-contained section appears which considers this subject from various angles (3.1–4.4). The tone here is a hopeful one. It becomes clear that "repent" can mean turning back to the original relationship with God: "If you will return, O Israel, return to me" (4.1; cf. 3.22; 31.18). In the potter parable too the thought of repentance plays a central role. Here "return" means to turn away from the "evil" (*rā'āh*, 18.8) of the false path [→**216**]: "So turn from your evil ways, each one of you, and reform your ways and your actions" (18.11; cf. 25.5; 26.3 etc.). Here, however, the resistance is already clear: "They will say, 'It's no use. We will continue with our own plans'" (18.12). Jeremiah reproaches the prophets for actually preventing people from turning from their evil ways (23.14). They thus stand in contrast to "my servants the prophets," whose task was precisely to call Israel to repentance (25.4f; 35.15).

The narrative of the writing down of Jeremiah's words by Baruch (ch. 36) attaches high priority to the hope of repentance. The reason for the writing down is precisely the hope that the house of Judah may "perhaps" repent, "each one, from his evil ways" (vv. 3, 7), when they hear all these proclamations of disaster.

In a series of further texts repentance and future expectation have central position. Attention turns first to the Judeans who had been carried off to Babylon in the first deportation in 597. In a vision scene reminiscent of 1.11–14 [→**205**], Jeremiah sees two baskets of figs (ch. 24). Some are very good, the others very bad. This contrast symbolizes the two groups of Judeans, those in exile and those in the homeland. God wants to look on those in exile as on the good figs. They can expect a peaceful future and a new relationship with God. This is unfolded as it were on two planes: God will bring the exiles back into their land and will "build them up and not tear them down, plant them and not uproot them" (v. 6); phrases from the call story echo

here (1.10) [→**204**]. In addition God will put their relationship with
him on a new footing (v. 7). Memorable theological phrases are linked
together: a renewed knowledge of God: "I will give them a heart so
that they will know me, that I am the LORD"; a renewal of the covenant relationship [→**§6**]: "They will be my people and I will be their
God"; complete repentance: "And they will turn to me with their
whole heart." This is actually a tapestry of theological phrases with
which the future relationship with God is described (cf. 1995, 51). It is
notable that the "covenant formula" is here related to the future for
the first time in the book of Jeremiah (contrast 7.23; 11.4). This speaks
of a strong hope of a new beginning after the exile, a new beginning
not only in a social and economic sense, but with a renewed understanding of God's relationship with Israel.

Chapter 29 reports about a letter that Jeremiah sends from Jerusalem
to the community of exiles, the *gôlāh* (vv. 1, 4). Immediately before
this the concern is with Jeremiah's dispute with the prophet Hananiah
(ch. 28) [→**218**]. The letter leads to a new conflict with other prophets,
this time with those among the exiles (vv. 8, 15, 21ff). Jeremiah's message, which leads to vigorous controversy, reads: prepare for a long
duration of the exile, seventy years (v. 10; cf. 25.1-14); then God will
bring you back to your land. "For I know the plans I have for you,"
declares the LORD, "plans to prosper you (*šālôm*) and not to harm you
(*rā'āh*), plans to give you hope and a future" (v. 11) [→**§22**]. Then the
exiles will turn back to God. Though the term *šûb* "repent" is missing
here, still we read that people will call upon God and pray to him, will
seek him and find him (vv. 12, 13a). "When you seek me with all
your heart I will be found by you" (vv. 13b, 14a). Then he will "turn
their captivity" (*šûb š'bût*)—a further instance of the many possible
forms of the word *šûb*. This letter is a key text for the question of how
the exile was understood and dealt with, whether by Jeremiah himself
or by others who continued to formulate the tradition in accordance
with his thinking.

This promise of future restoration provides a connection to the following collection of messages of peace. In 30.2 Jeremiah is called upon
by God to write what follows in a book; chs. 30 and 31 are thus frequently called the "book of comfort." The following chapters 32, the
sign-act of the purchase of the field, and 33 contain sayings about a
prosperous future, so that the whole section from ch. 29 to 33 is presented as a proclamation of prosperity.

At the beginning as it were stands the motto under which all these sayings are summarized: "'The days are coming,' declares the LORD, 'when I will bring my people Israel and Judah back from captivity (*šûb š'bût*) and restore them to the land I gave to their forefathers to possess,' says the LORD" (30.3). The promise of return from exile and the restoration is then repeated in many variations (vv. 8f, 10f, 17, 18-22). In between are depictions of horror (vv. 5-7, 23f) and of Israel's suffering (vv. 12-15). In ch. 31 it is then the proclamations of prosperity that dominate the field, again with many variations, which give the impression of a collection of rather different texts. Here there is talk of gathering together, leading back and restoration of those taken into exile and scattered, of the reconstruction of the land, of comfort and great joy. At the conclusion there is again a sort of summary: "'Just as I watched over them to uproot and tear down, and to overthrow, destroy and bring disaster, so I will watch over them to build and to plant,' declares the LORD" (31.28; cf. 1.10) [→204].

The sayings about the future reach a climax in the promise of a "new covenant" (31.31-34) [→§6]. It will differ from the covenant God made with the forefathers in one essential respect: the Torah will be "written on the hearts" of Israel [→86], so that they will no longer be able to break the covenant as they did before. This new covenant will mean complete knowledge of God as far as Israel is concerned and forgiveness of all sins as far as God is concerned. This expectation and hope sounds like a reflex of earlier statements about the covenant. In 22.9 we read that the decisive reason for the expected destruction of Jerusalem will be "that they have forsaken the covenant of the LORD, their God"; and in 14.21 we find the plea: "Remember your covenant with us and do not break it." The breaking of the covenant on Israel's part must become impossible, so that the danger of God breaking the covenant is banished once and for all. In 32.36-41 this future hope is once again developed from a new angle. God will give the returnees the fear of God in their hearts (vv. 39, 40b) and make an "eternal covenant" with them. The main feature of this covenant will be that God will not cease to "do good" to them (v. 40a). Here too Israel's "heart" will be changed, but God's gracious deeds are right in the foreground.

Finally the promise that God will not break his covenant is extended into the realm of creation. As unbreakable as God's covenant with day and night and with the ordering of the heavens and the earth

(33.20, 25) [→**17f**] will also be his covenant with the house of David (vv. 15f; cf. 23.5f) and the house of Levi (v. 18), and above all with the house of Israel and the house of Judah (v. 14), the two tribes he has chosen (vv. 23-26).

3.10 And the nations?

At the end of the book of Jeremiah there is a collection of sayings against foreign nations (chs. 46-51) [→*In* **128**]. Similar collections are also found in the two other great prophetic books (Isa 13–23; Ezek 25–32) [→**179, 250**]; though there they are in each case within the prophetic book while here they are right at the end.

In the Greek version of Jeremiah [→**202f**], and thus also in its supposed Hebrew *Vorlage*, the words against foreign nations are inserted after 25.13, and the sign-act with the "goblet of wrath" for the nations (Hebrew 25.15-38) forms the conclusion (Greek 32.15-38). This sequence may have been made in analogy to the books of Isaiah and Ezekiel, in which the sayings against the foreign nations are also not found at the end but in the middle of the book.

At the beginning and conclusion of this collection are sayings against the two great powers: Egypt (ch. 46) and in particular detail Babylon (chs. 50 and 51); in between them sayings against neighboring peoples: the Philistines (ch. 47), Moab (ch. 48), the Ammonites (49.1-6), Edom (49.7-22), Damascus (49.23-27), Arabian tribes (49.28-33) and finally against far-away Elam (49.34-39). In the case of the smaller nations and groups these are often only short sketches showing how they are sucked into the confusion of events. Sometimes particular events appear to lie behind them, but a great deal remains unclear to us.

The message against Egypt (ch. 46) is expressly introduced with the consequential victory of Nebuchadnezzar over the Egyptians in the battle of Carchemish in 605 (v. 2). This was as it were the beginning of the end of the hegemony of Egypt. Jeremiah had announced in his sign-act with the yoke that God had given "all these lands" into the hand of Nebuchadnezzar (27.6) [→**217**], and the last saying of his that has come down to us announces the defeat of the Egyptian Pharaoh (44.29f) [→**224**]. In several stages the approach of Nebuchadnezzar (46.13ff) and the defeat of Pharaoh, the whole of Egypt and its gods is described. It is God himself that will do this (vv. 25f). But this is no reason for Israel to fear; rather, it should expect a peaceful return from captivity (vv. 27f). Sayings from the beginning of the "book of comfort" are repeated (30.10f) [→**227**]. This provides a connection between the words to the foreign nations and the main part of the book.

The detailed chapter about Moab (48), on the other hand, has no connection with Jeremiah's earlier sayings. Moab is only occasionally mentioned together with other neighboring peoples (9.25; 27.3), as when it is mentioned among those who will have to drink the "goblet of wrath" (25.21) [→**219**]. In this chapter a centuries-old enmity is unleashed against the proud and arrogant Moab (48.7, 14, 29), which has always mocked and despised Israel (v. 27, cf. 2 Kgs 3.4-27). Its god, Chemosh (vv. 7, 13, 46), was also a religious threat to Israel (1 Kgs 11.7; 2 Kgs 23.13) [→**151**]. And the sayings against Ammon, Edom, Damascus, the Arabian tribes and Elam in ch. 49 have no recognizable connection with earlier messages of Jeremiah's.

While in ch. 49 Babylon implemented the judgment on Egypt that God had sent, now at the conclusion of the oracles to the nations the annihilation of Babylon is announced in a great view of the future (chs. 50f). Events are described which lie beyond Jeremiah's lifetime. Babylon has been destroyed (50.2f and *passim*) and the Israelites make their way home (vv. 4f). These chapters contain various echoes of the oracles concerning Babylon in the book of Isaiah (Isa 13f) [→**180f**]. It is evident that there are particular traditions which could be picked up in different contexts. The whole thing concludes with the narrative of the sign-act caused by Jeremiah, in which a scroll with threatening words against Babylon is to be sunk in the Euphrates (51.59-64). In retrospect this expresses the fact that Jeremiah had already prophesied disaster for Babylon, when it was still fulfilling the role God had ascribed to it. He was not around to experience the fulfillment of this prediction.

3.11 The prophet in crisis

Jeremiah is in several regards a "prophet in crisis." Like no other prophet before him or after him he is drawn into the greatest crisis in the history of Israel and Judah: the political demise of the remaining kingdom of Judah and the destruction of Jerusalem and the temple. Through his prophetic commission he gets into a dispute with his environment which becomes more and more critical, both with the political and with the religious environment in the confrontation with other prophets. Finally all this leads him in a very dramatic fashion into a personal crisis.

The multifaceted picture of the prophet that the book of Jeremiah presents us with could lead the reader to place Jeremiah's personal fate in the foreground: the trouble and strife with his enemies, the loneliness and suffering. This personal side is not as marked as this in the case of any other prophet, nor does it occupy such a scope. In his suffering for his prophetic commission Jeremiah's life bears exemplary traits. The confessions therefore are rightly seen at the center of any interpretation of Jeremiah. But they must not be separated from the message which Jeremiah has been commissioned by God to proclaim.

At the center of this stands the commission to pass on the word—or words—of God. With no other prophet is this task formulated as expressly or reflected upon so intensively as with Jeremiah, through to the powerful metaphors of the word of God that is fire and like a hammer which smashes rocks. From the call vision through to the end of his lifetime there are constantly words from God which Jeremiah speaks. The conflicts he gets into, as well, are always set in motion by words from God or the sign-acts that underline them, and the loneliness and the suffering that he has to suffer are consequences of the divine sayings and of the reaction of his environment to them.

The themes of his proclamation are determined by the situation into which he has been sent. There are primarily two points of emphasis that constitute what is specific to this proclamation in their mutual connection. They are already clearly formulated in the call vision: Israel has committed the "wickedness" (*rā'āh*) of forsaking God and serving other gods (1.16); God will therefore bring disaster (*rā'āh*) upon Israel (v. 14) [→206]. The worship of foreign gods was not a concern for Isaiah; now it moves more and more into the center of prophetic critique. And the proclamation of the impending judgment gains more and more concrete shape through the political developments, until finally they become terrible reality in the fall of Jerusalem.

But Jeremiah does not simply accept the divine judgment that he has to announce, but tries again and again to turn people away from their misguided and fateful ways and calls upon them to repent. So the word "repent" (*šûb*) becomes a central element in his language [→208]: the call to repent, the note that they are not repenting, the hope of a return in the future, and finally the announcement that God himself will "turn back" their captivity (*šûb šʿbût*).

But when the Babylonians come nearer and nearer [→**222**], the call to repent is replaced by the summons to recognize the inescapably impending disaster as God's judgment and to accept it as a yoke that they must bear. Again and again Jeremiah struggles against the short-sighted and futile resistance against this approaching fate. After it has occurred, he expressly admonishes his hearers to accept the given situation, in which part of the people must live in exile, as one sent and imposed on them by God.

But here we see especially impressively that in Jeremiah's proclamation of judgment the prospect of a prosperous future is never lost from sight. For in the final analysis God does not have plans for the harm (*rā'āh*) of Israel but for its peace and prosperity (*šālôm*) [→**226**]. He will bring the exile to an end and will gather Israel and Judah together and bring them back to their place. And then he will renew the covenant that he made with Israel, by writing the Torah in their hearts, so that they will no longer be able to break it.

Jeremiah himself did not experience the fulfillment of these hopes. He was carried off by his own compatriots from the ruined and occupied Jerusalem away to Egypt, where we lose track of him. But after the turning of the captivity that he predicted had occurred, people remembered his proclamation of the "seventy years" and reminded people of it (2 Chron 36.21; Ezra 1.1) [→**411, 391**].

4. The Book of Ezekiel

4.1 Preliminary considerations

The Hebrew name *yʿhezqē'l* is rendered in the Septuagint by the Greek form Ἰεζεχιήλ. This gave rise to the Latin form *Ezechiel* in the Vulgate, which has evolved into *Ezekiel* in English usage.

The book of Ezekiel [→*In* **219**] as a whole is marked by the person of the prophet. By comparison with the book of Jeremiah his constant presence seems even clearer because the whole book is structured almost like a biography of Ezekiel. The numerous dates given (1.1f; 8.1;

20.1 and so on through to 40.1) show him among the Judeans brought into Babylonian exile with king Jehoiachin in the year 597. In 33.21 we read the report of how news of the fall of Jerusalem reached him in 586. His last vision is dated to the 25th year after the deportation, i.e. 573/2 (40.1). Of Ezekiel himself it is reported that he was the son of a priest. In 1.3 we read that the word of God came "to Ezekiel, the son of Buzi, the priest" or "to Ezekiel the priest, the son of Buzi." Both translations are possible, but since the priesthood was hereditary there is no essential difference between them. It remains open, however, whether Ezekiel had already worked as a priest in Jerusalem before he was taken into exile, where he was unable to exercise priestly office.

The book is formulated as an almost seamless first-person report. The really personal element however remains entirely in the background. The reader learns almost nothing of the prophet's own thoughts and feelings. Only rarely do we hear a lamenting "Oh, LORD YHWH!" (4.14; 9.8; 11.13; 21.5); but even on the death of his wife Ezekiel has to do without the usual mourning rituals and he does it without contradiction (24.15-24). In the frequent vision descriptions (see below) the prophet is constantly physically involved, but there too there are no expressions of any personal emotion.

Instead, the words and actions of God dominate. These are regularly introduced in first-person form, e.g. with the formula "The word of the LORD came to me" (3.16; 6.1; 7.1 etc.); but the person of the prophet then retires entirely behind the divine message. The frequent sign-acts too are introduced as God's instruction to the prophet, e.g. "You, son of man, take ..." (4.1); the prophet's executive action, however, is in general not then reported, though the context presupposes that it has occurred. So in a strange way the prophet is present and yet remains in the background. Only occasionally is he recognizable as a respected person who is asked for information and teaching.

The language of Ezekiel is characteristic and distinct from the other prophetic books. It is a broad, self-confident prose language which shows clear affinities with the "priestly" parts of the Pentateuch. Part of this is the consistent use of formulaic elements, similar to some we have already met in Jeremiah: the word-event formula, "The word of the LORD came to me" (see above), often followed by the messenger formula, "Thus says the LORD YHWH," the latter mainly with the characteristic double designation of God, *'⁴donāy yhwh* "LORD YHWH," as is found also in the divine speech formula *n⁵'um '⁴donāy yhwh* "saying of the LORD YHWH," which frequently concludes units of speech; often the emphatic "For I (the LORD) have spoken" forms the conclusion of a unit. Finally, another of these characteristic elements is the knowledge formula, "They/you will know, that I am YHWH," which appears frequently in an expanded form (cf. Zimmerli 1954).

A particularly prominent element is the visions granted to Ezekiel. Four great visions mark the overall structure of the book: 1.1–3.15; 8–11; 37.1-14; 40–48. They show with particular forcefulness the physical involvement of the prophet: the "hand of YHWH" comes upon him (1.3; 3.14[, 22]; 8.1; 37.1; 40.1), he falls down (1.28; [3.23;] 9.8; 43.4; 44.4) and is set on his feet again by the "spirit" (*rûaḥ*) (2.2; [3.24]) or he is transported to another place (3.12, 14; 8.3; 11.1, 24; 37.1; 40.1f; 43.5); he has to eat a scroll (3.1f), pass through water (47.3f), speak to dry bones (37.4ff) etc. But here too it applies that the person of the prophet is only an instrument for the expression of what is announced in the divine message.

The most important structural element of the book is the taking of Jerusalem, spoken of in ch. 33 (vv. 21f) [→**252**]. Directly before this we find a collection of sayings against foreign nations (chs. 25–32) [→**250**], which have clearly been deliberately set in the middle of the book. A threefold division emerges, in which in chs. 1–24 the words of judgment concerning Judah and Jerusalem dominate, while in chs. 33–48 the proclamations of peace and prosperity dominate. The individual parts are to a large degree linked together. Especially clear are the connections between the first and third parts. Thus right at the beginning we have the announcement, "they will know that a prophet was in their midst" (2.5), repeated at the beginning of the second part (33.33). The discourse about the prophet's role as a watchman also appears at the beginning of both parts (3.16-21; 33.1-9). The dumbness with which the prophet was afflicted after the call vision (3.25-27) is definitively removed with the news of the fall of Jerusalem (33.22; cf. 24.25-27). Further points of contact are evident within various texts.

The unity of the book has been frequently called into question in recent times. There are indeed indications that the book of Ezekiel, like most books of the Hebrew Bible, has been subject to a certain process before arriving at its current final form. How this process is to be assessed and what exegetical conclusions are to be drawn from it find differing responses among interpreters. Zimmerli (1969, 106ff) posits the "continuing writing" of the words of Ezekiel in a "school";

this takes account on the one hand of observations of the multi-layered character of the book, and on the other hand the great affinity of later revisions with the prophet's own words is emphasized. In his "holistic" interpretation Greenberg (1983, 18ff) accepts the given text entirely. (On this cf. Hossfeld 1995, 355f.)

4.2 Son of man, I send you

The heavens open and Ezekiel sees "visions of God" (1.1). Herewith the story of this prophet begins, for whom the visionary experiences and the prophetic commission form an indissoluble unity. He sees something in the wind of the storm and surrounded in flames which he himself can only roughly describe: it "has the form of...," it "looks like ..." (vv. 5, 10, 13, 16): four "living creatures," each with four faces like a human, lion, bull and eagle, and four wings; four wheels, strangely constructed, which go in all directions with the four animals or can rise into the air, "wherever the spirit moves them" (vv. 12, 20). The whole thing forms as it were the undercarriage for the vehicle for a "vault" (*rāqîaʿ*), awesome to behold (v. 22), above which the shape of a throne becomes visible and above that something that looks like the shape of a human being, which however presents itself to the eye only like white gold (? *ḥašmal*) above what looks like its hips and like fire below (vv. 26f). It has the splendor of a rainbow. "This was the appearance of the likeness of the 'glory' (*kābôd*) of the LORD" (v. 28).

This provides a crucial keyword for the whole visionary and prophetic story of Ezekiel: the encounter with the divine *kābôd* [→§15] is given due recognition. In his vision of the enthroned Yhwh Zebaot Isaiah had only heard of Yhwh's *kābôd* in the praise of the Seraphim (Isa 6.2f) [→172], but for Ezekiel it can now itself be "seen" and experienced. Furthermore, the prophet's encounters with the *kābôd* take place at various locations to which the prophet is sometimes "taken" (8.3f; 40.1f with 43.1-5) or to which he goes on divine instruction (3.22f). And these encounters each contain essential elements of the prophetic proclamation with which Ezekiel is charged.

The vision event involves the prophet. He falls down (1.28) and is again raised up (2.1f). And he hears out of this vision "the voice of one speaking" (1.28; 2.2). He addresses him as "son of man" (*ben-'ādām* 2.1), i.e. simply "human," or more precisely individual person, in view of the individualizing *ben* singled out from the collective *'ādām*, which can also mean "humanity." This expression is rather unusual as a form of address, but extremely common in the book of Ezekiel (occurring more than 90 times). In the context of the visions it means that Ezekiel is contrasted with the divine sphere: he is a human, not God (cf. Isa 31.3; Ezek 28.2) [→182, 251].

The divine voice says: "I am sending you" (2.3). Ezekiel is sent (*šālaḥ*) like Moses (Ex 3.12) [→40], Isaiah (Isa 6.8) [→172] and Jeremiah (Jer 1.7) [→204] before him. The difficulty of his task is immediately clear. The Israelites to whom he is sent have been rebellious and sinful since the time of their forefathers, and the sons, the present generation, have obstinate faces and hard hearts. The prophet has only one message for them: "This is what the LORD YHWH says" (v. 4) [→*In* 123]. Actually this is only an introductory formula to a following prophetic speech, but here it stands entirely on its own. It is now for the Israelites to recognize "that a prophet has been among them" (v. 5). And if they refuse to recognize it now (cf. 3.11), then they will recognize it when "it" comes—and it is coming! (33.33) [→253]. So in this commissioning of the prophet the fruitlessness of his preaching is already foreseen. But when the events announced by him occur, then he will be the witness that God has announced all this and brought it about.

Ezekiel is not to be afraid and not to contradict his call, even though he is sent among "thorns" and "scorpions" to a "rebellious house" (2.6-8). Unlike Jeremiah (Jer 1.6) this instruction comes without Ezekiel having already expressed fear or contradiction. Here again we see the withdrawal of the personal element. Ezekiel's equipment in the face of the recipients of his message is also quite different from Jeremiah's. The latter was "reinforced" against attacks (Jer 1.18) [→206], while Ezekiel is as it were equipped against attack with a hard face and a forehead as hard as a diamond (3.8f).

Another parallel to Jeremiah follows: a hand approaches the prophet which physically brings to him the divine word that he is to proclaim (2.9–3.3; cf. Jer 1.9). But in Ezekiel's case this hand-over occurs in a highly concrete and graphic form, which is at once beyond the conceivable: he has to eat a scroll inscribed on both sides with the words "lament, mourning and woe" (2.10). A possible refusal was already rejected beforehand, and so he has to eat it—and it becomes sweet as honey in his mouth (3.3). This is certainly not to say that the eating of the scroll is any easier because of this, but in particular also that he now identifies himself with the task of proclaiming the content of the scroll, however dreadful this may be. Here one can also hear the echo of words in the Psalms, that God's word is as sweet as honey (Pss 19.11; 119.103). And finally Jeremiah too spoke of "eating" the word of God, though in a much more spontaneous way; it delighted his heart too (Jer 15.16) [→**214**].

The scroll on which the divine words are written provides a further connection with Jeremiah. The only place in the Hebrew Bible that speaks about a scroll on which prophetic words are written is the account of the writing down of Jeremiah's words by Baruch (Jer 36) [→**225**]. This too contained "lament, mourning and woe," namely the disaster, *rā'āh*, that God intended to bring upon the house of Judah. Ezekiel may himself have experienced the events of the public reading of this scroll with its consequences through to the burning of the scroll by king Jehoiachim in Jerusalem (Zimmerli 1969, 79). In any case the Bible reader will quickly think of such a scroll.

Finally the commission is once again recapitulated. A remarkable differentiation is evident: Ezekiel is sent to the "house of Israel" (3.4-9) and then once again especially to the community of exiles, the *gôlāh* (vv. 10f). This reveals the double point of view of his mission. It is directed to Israel as a whole, whose center is still Jerusalem; but at the same time the prophet has a very special job to do in relation to those for whom Israel's fate has already progressed a fair way—and who will then be the bearers of the history of God with his people when the catastrophe has occurred [→**§9**]. This is already very clear right at the beginning.

The encounter ends. The *kābôd* rises with loud roaring from its place, while the prophet himself is seized by the "spirit" (*rûᵃḥ*), who brings him back to the residence of the group of exiles, the *gôlāh* (3.12-15). He stays there for seven days under the burden of the "hand of YHWH," overwhelmed and silent.

Once again a word of God comes to the prophet: "Son of man, I have made you a watchman for the house of Israel" (3.17). This brings in a new dimension in the prophetic office. The watchman, the "lookout" (*ṣôfeh*) on the wall, must give a warning when he sees a danger approaching (cf. 33.2ff) [→**252**]. If he performs his duty, it is up to each individual to take the warning seriously, or not; but if the watchman does not give a warning, he makes himself guilty and has ruined his life. With this comparison the task of the prophet is now defined. He receives from the mouth of God the word by which the ungodly, the *rāšā'*, is warned. If he does not pass on the word, he makes himself guilty (3.18); but if he does pass it on, the responsibility resides with the person who hears it (v. 19). The word is directed to the "house of Israel," i.e. to the community as a whole; at the same time, however, it is addressed to each individual, who is thereby called to repent (*šûb*).

The responsibility thereby placed on the prophet makes it impossible for him not to pass on the words he receives from God. This was the case for Jeremiah too. But there it was an essential element of the prophet's suffering for his office. In Ezekiel this too is quite different. The prophet's task is formulated with its alternative aspects in rather legal categories (cf. also ch. 14; 18; 33.1-20) [→**242, 249**]. The special ambivalence in the personality and proclamation of Ezekiel is clearly evident here: he experiences the encounter with God in visions that are dramatic in form—but he speaks like a priest arguing in legal terms.

4.3 Signs and words of judgment

This ambivalence is immediately visible again. Ezekiel experiences once again in a vision an encounter with the divine *kābôd* (3.22f). But instead of a renewed or continuing commission for the public proclamation of the word of God, we now read: "Go, shut yourself up in your house" (v. 24). The isolation from the world around is again reminiscent of Jeremiah (Jer 15.17; 16.5-9 etc.). Here is it described in terms of binding and dumbness (vv. 25f). But the dumbness will always be lifted when God gives the prophet a message for the people.

In 33.22 we read that the dumbness imposed on Ezekiel is lifted on the day news of the fall of Jerusalem reaches him (cf. 24.27). It is disputed whether the meaning is that the dumbness afflicting him had been caused only the previous evening by the "hand of YHWH" or whether we are to understand the dumbness as that imposed on the prophet more than seven years earlier, according to 3.26. But this is not really an alternative, since 3.27 expressly speaks of the lifting (in each case) of the dumbness in order to proclaim the message ordained by God. So the dumbness can be understood as an expression for the complete isolation from the world around, which is lifted only after the fall of Jerusalem.

So Ezekiel's activities begin not with the proclamation of messages from God but with a series of sign-acts. The prophet besieges Jerusalem symbolically (4.1-3), has to lie on his left side and his right side for a long time for the guilt of Israel and Judah (vv. 4-8), has to eat impure "siege food" (vv. 9-17) and conduct symbolic acts with his cutoff hair (5.1-4). All this is interpreted with a long word of judgment introduced by: "This is Jerusalem" (5.5-17). Here it is surprisingly clear that Ezekiel does not speak to hearers in his immediate presence, but that his words are directed against far-off Jerusalem. (This saying may have been spoken—or written—by him also in his house.) As for Jeremiah (Jer 2.4ff) in Ezekiel's sight too the apostasy begins right at the beginning of the story in the land in which God placed Israel— here Jerusalem—"in the midst of the nations." The nations will now be taken as a yardstick: Jerusalem has not only infringed the statutes and commandments that God himself gave it (v. 6), but has not even kept the statutes of the nations (the "heathen") (v. 7). So it is now threatened with a terrible judgment that will be carried out before the eyes of the nations (v. 8). A special reason for this is that Jerusalem has defiled God's sanctuary with its "vile" (*šiqqûṣîm*) and "detestable" (*tôʿᵉbôt*) things (v. 11). The offense against the divine rules and the worship of foreign deities are thus the crucial reproaches against Jerusalem.

In the next chapter too, Ezekiel does not speak to those present but to the "mountains of Israel" (ch. 6), i.e. to the mountainous countryside of the land of Israel. This extends the proclamation of judgment beyond Jerusalem to the whole land. Again the illegitimate cults are in the foreground: the cultic high-places (*bāmôt*), altars and smoking implements (vv. 3-6, 13). There they have brought sacrifices to the "idols" (*gillûlîm*), which are intended to be a "pleasant odor" (*rêᵃḥ nîḥôᵃḥ*) to them, which only Yhwh deserves (Lev 1.9 etc.) [→§11]. The judgment is to bring about acknowledgment: "You will know that I am the LORD" (v. 7). But here the proclamation of judgment is given an important supplement, or even a correction: God will "spare" some (vv. 8-10). Out of their exile among the nations, in view of the judgment that has come upon them they are to come to the insight that they have brought all this on themselves; and "they will know that I am the LORD," and this means, "that I did not threaten in vain to bring this calamity on them" (v. 10). Twice more the "acknowledgment formula" [→§5] occurs in this chapter, each time to emphasize that those addressed will see from the calamity that occurs that the God that brings all this upon them is none other than Yhwh, the "LORD" (vv. 13, 14).

A third great judgment speech (after chs. 5 and 6) is directed to the "land of Israel" (ch. 7). Again it is not specified whether and how the prophet is to carry out the divine word. "The end! The end has come" (v. 2, cf. v. 6); "a disaster is coming" (v. 5), "the time is coming" (vv. 7, 12), "the day is coming" (vv. 10, 12, cf. v. 7), "fear is coming" (v. 25)—dramatic alarm calls and long descriptions of the impending catastrophe resound in quick succession. Again there is talk of "detestable" things; but this time it is said that God will place the people's own detestable things on them in the land of Israel (vv. 3, 4, 8, 9)—very similar to what was frequently said of Jeremiah, that the wickedness (*rā'āh*) of people would come upon them as a disaster (*rā'āh*) (Jer 1.14, 16 etc.) [→206]. The detestable thing consists above all in the fact that people have made images of silver and gold for their "detestable" images (vv. 19f). So all their wealth will be taken away from them. Here too the knowledge formula is again in an emphatic position: at the beginning (v. 4) and at the end (v. 27), and in addition in the expanded form: "You will know that it is I the LORD who strikes the blow" (v. 9).

Call vision, sign-acts and the first great judgment speech form the first clearly marked section of the book of Ezekiel. A new vision forms the next section. Hitherto the view has been directed out from the Babylonian exile towards Jerusalem, into the mountains and the land of Israel; now the prophet is placed directly there.

4.4 Vision about Jerusalem

The following four chapters (8–11) form a self-contained unit. At the beginning Ezekiel is sitting in his house, together with the elders of Judah (8.1); at the end he reports to the *gôlāh*, the committee represented by the elders, about the vision he has experienced (11.25). This framework shows Ezekiel as a recognized personality within the community of exiles. The elders come into his house and "sit before him." This recalls the narratives about Elisha, before whom his disciples regularly sit (2 Kgs 4.38; 6.1) [→143], but on special occasions the elders too (6.32). The conclusion of the framework shows that this vision is not meant only for Ezekiel himself but that he is to pass on the message contained in it to the Judeans living in exile. What is happening in Jerusalem is of great significance to them.

Again "the hand of YHWH" comes upon Ezekiel (8.1). He first sees an individual element of the first great vision: the fiery figure (v. 2; cf.

1.27) [→**234**]. It stretches out "something like a hand," grasps him by the hair and the "spirit" (*rû'ḥ*) transports him to Jerusalem (v. 3); there he then sees the divine *kābôd* as in the earlier visions (v. 4). He is led by this to various parts of the city and the temple, in which all kinds of illegitimate cultic symbols have been set up and cultic practices are being carried out: an "idol of jealousy" with an altar devoted to it (vv. 3b, 5); idolatrous representations of animals on the walls, in front of which a group of the "elders of the house of Israel" are performing burnt-offering ceremonies (vv. 10f); women mourning for Tammuz (v. 14); men worshiping the sun (v. 16). All this is shown to the prophet as a constantly escalating series of "detestable things" (vv. 6, 9, 13, 15, 17). It is all happening because many people think that God does not see it because he has forsaken the land (v. 12).

As if this were not enough: they fill the whole land with violence, to provoke God (v. 17). Together the two things lead to the unmitigated wrath of God, which is now unleashed upon the city (v. 18). Later this is expressly reiterated: the land is full of blood-guiltiness and the city full of transgression. And again we read that they are saying: "The LORD has forsaken the land; the LORD does not see" (9.9).

The judgment on Jerusalem is executed in a manner dictated by divine command (ch. 9). Men with "implements of destruction" appear. The designation of these tools with the word *mašḥēt* (v. 1; cf. also *mašḥît*, vv. 6, 8b) recalls the last of the "plagues" of Egypt, where there is talk of the "stroke of destruction" (*negep l'mašḥît*, Ex 12.13) [→**45**], or, in a personified form, of the "destroyer" (v. 23). This connection is even clearer in that that some are exempted from the destruction and separately marked as such. Six men will carry out the destruction (9.2ff), but the seventh, specially marked out by means of his linen clothing and his equipping with a writing implement, will beforehand mark with a sign on the forehead those who are to be preserved because they sigh and moan over all the detestable things that are happening in Jerusalem (v. 4). In those days in Egypt the Israelites were protected from the destruction by the sign of blood on their door-posts; now it is only a "remnant" (v. 8), and it is only those who have separated themselves from the "detestable" deeds of the great majority by their own behavior.

Surprisingly the prophet sees himself included in what happens in the vision. All around him lies dead, but he himself is "left alone" (v. 8). A sudden cry—not really a petition: "Ah, LORD YHWH! Are you going to destroy the entire remnant of Israel in this outpouring of your wrath on Jerusalem?" But the divine voice replies and repeats that blood-guiltiness and transgression have become so great that there can be no more pity (vv. 9f). And the man dressed in linen announces that the task has been carried out (v. 11). This means the end of the population of Jerusalem. But the man in linen is immediately given another task. For this the vision of the divine *kābôd* is once again unfolded to its full extent, familiar already to the reader from the first chapter of the book (10.1ff). The man's hands are filled with glowing coals from this confusing vehicle, and he is to scatter them around the city (vv. 2, 6f). (The execution of this is not expressly described, but is no doubt to be presupposed.) This seals the fate of the whole city.

The development of the details of the apparition brings the reader an important insight. In the depiction of this vision the prophet has already spoken a number of times of "cherubs" (*kʾrûbîm*) (9.3; 10.1 etc.); finally he "acknowledges" that the "living creatures" of the first vision are cherubs (10.20) [→§11]. The vision thus shows the innermost part of the temple, the holy of holies, as had existed in Jerusalem since the time of Solomon (1 Kgs 8.6) [→119] in accordance with the model of the sanctuary built on Sinai (Ex 25.18-22). And it shows the prophet more than any human has ever seen, when it grants him a sight of the shining figure enthroned above the cherubs. This figure is now itself described as the divine *kābôd*, which can also rise from the place "above the cherub" (9.3; 10.4) and return there (10.18f). From this point of view it now becomes clear once again what an unusual event this was, that this sight had become visible to the prophet outside the temple and outside Jerusalem, indeed in a heathen land.

The whole apparition moves to the eastern gate of the temple (10.19). The prophet is also transported there (11.1). Here he sees a group of 25 men, representatives of the remaining residents of Jerusalem. This is surprising, after the previous mention of the killing of all the inhabitants of Jerusalem. (Some exegetes see a separate vision in this, which was later combined with the first, while others posit a literary expansion.)

The prophet is commissioned to address a divine message to both groups: those who have remained in Jerusalem (vv. 1-13) and those who have been carried away into exile (vv. 14-21). The leaders of the first group are thinking of a reconstruction of the city and see themselves as its valuable contents (v. 4). Concerning the exile they say: "They are far away from the LORD; this land was given to us as our possession" (v. 15) [→**253**]. But those who are speaking are precisely those said earlier to be responsible for blood-guiltiness and transgression of the law in the city (v. 6; cf. 8.17; 9.9). The sword they fear will therefore smite them (vv. 8-11).

A word comes to those living in exile which points far into the future [→**§22**]. God has now scattered them in the lands of the nations; but he has not completely left them alone but has become a "little sanctuary" for them (v. 16). (Targum Jonathan translates: "But I have given them synagogues, second (in rank) to my sanctuary," cf. Greenberg 1983, 190.) He will bring them back together, will give them the land of Israel and above all he will give them a new heart and a new spirit and will restore the covenant relationship: "They will be my people, and I will be their God" (vv. 17-20).

This message to the exiles is the last that Ezekiel hears in his visionary presence in Jerusalem and brings back to them (v. 25). But beforehand he sees how the divine *kābôd* departs from the city and settles on the mountain to the east of the city (vv. 22f). This is an especially enduring sign of the fact that nothing can now stop the destruction of Jerusalem and the temple. God has forsaken his temple. From the ancient Near Eastern point of view, no temple was ever destroyed unless its deity had already abandoned it (cf. Greenberg 1983, 200f). But God will return there when the temple is rebuilt (43.1ff).

4.5 More signs and words of judgment

Sign-acts once again follow the vision (as in chs. 4f following chs. 1–3). Ezekiel gives a dramatic presentation of the impending exile [→**§9**] of the Jerusalemites and their "prince," i.e. of the king, and explains it (12.1-15). The complex text echoes elements of Zedekiah's failed escape attempt (2 Kgs 25.4-7; cf. Lang 1981, 17ff). The prophet then has to eat his bread and drink his water with trembling and shaking (12.17-20) and tackles doubting arguments that seek to dismiss his proclamations as still lying far off (12.21-25, 26-28). In response, his message is: The time is at hand! (v. 23).

Ezekiel has to deal with prophets who proclaim on their own authority and announce "peace" when there is no peace (13.1-16; cf. Jer 6.14; 8.11 etc.) [→**221**] and with women who lead people astray with mantic practices (13.17-23).

Among the exiles too there are still people who hanker after the "idols" (14.1ff). To them the prophet calls: "Repent! Turn (*šûbû*) from your idols and renounce all your detestable practices!" (v. 6). Any who do not repent make themselves culpable; and if even a prophet should be persuaded to support such a course that prophet will be punished in the way laid down by the law (vv. 9f, cf. Deut 13.2-6) [→80]. But all this will happen not just to punish Israel but to open up a new future in which it once again applies that: "They will be my people and I will be their God" (v. 11).

But the question remains: who might be able to avert the divine judgment? The answer is: even the most righteous among the peoples could only save themselves, and not even their sons and daughters, let alone the community as a whole (14.12-20). Those named as examples of the righteous are Noah, Daniel and Job. (Underlying the mention of Daniel and Job there are certainly older traditions, in Daniel's case probably the figure of king Dan'el attested in a Ugaritic text, who is said to have adjudicated the affairs of widows and orphans justly, cf. *ANET* p. 151, V,5-8; *TUAT* III, 1268.) They could no more have averted the judgment than, according to Jeremiah, Moses and Samuel could have done (Jer 15.1). This is at first said in an apparently abstract form about a (any) country and it is repeated like an inalienable rule in strict, as it were legalistic terminology, in four variations, with affliction by hunger, wild animals, the sword and pestilence. But then there is an abrupt change of direction (vv. 21-23). Though all this will come upon Jerusalem, still a host of refugees (*pᵉlêṭāh*) will remain and come to the exiles as a consolation—a consolation not because the escapees were righteous, but on the contrary: despite the fact that their behavior is no better than that of the others in Jerusalem, they will show that God's history with his people is not yet at an end.

Later too sign-acts occur again, sprinkled with words of judgment. "fire" and "sword" are the key terms in ch. 21*. The prophet is to set his face against the south (21.2[20.46]) [→238] and against Jerusalem (21.7[21.2], as in 6.2 against the mountains), is to groan (v. 11[6]), cry out and wail (v. 17[12]) and strike his hands together (v. 19[14]), for the fire and the sword will come upon the land from the south to the north (21.3[20.47]; 21.9[4]). God himself withdraws the sword from the scabbard (21.8-10*), it is sharpened for slaughter (21.14-16*); all have fallen to the sword (21.17f*), which will strike twice, three times (v. 19*), until Yhwh's wrath subsides (v. 22*). The prophet is to represent symbolically the junction of the two roads at which the sword of the king of Babylon stands (vv. 24-26*). It will come upon Jerusalem (vv. 27ff*)—and finally also upon the Ammonites (vv. 33-37*).

4.6 History in pictures

A new feature of Ezekiel's language appears in the metaphorical discourses. They are found in a variety of forms. All of them serve to characterize Israel or Jerusalem, its institutions and its history. Unlike the often extremely lively sequence of images in Jeremiah (esp. chs. 2–6) [→207], in Ezekiel the images are generally painted in broad strokes and carried through consistently (cf. Zimmerli 1969, 45ff).

Many image discourses are short and easy to understand. The wood of the vine is useless, completely so, when it is already half burnt; so are the inhabitants of Jerusalem, who are soon to be consumed by fire (ch. 15). More complex is the image of the cedar, the vine and the two eagles (ch. 17), in which elements of the plant and animal fables of wisdom literature [→§19] are embellished with allegorical features. It is introduced as a "puzzle and parable" (v. 2), and requires detailed interpretation (vv. 11-21). It deals with Zedekiah's misguided political alliances and their failure. But then a conclusion follows: God himself will take a tender seed from the cedar and plant it "on the high mountain of Israel" and it will grow and become a splendid cedar tree (vv. 22-24). Here the hope comes to expression that there will yet be a future for the kingdom of Judah. Later after the fall of Jerusalem Ezekiel will express this hope much more clearly (esp. in ch. 34) [→253]. Chapter 19 too deals with the kings who are here described as "princes of Israel." It is a lament song over the fate of the "princes," in which their mother is represented by the image of a lioness (vv. 2-9) and again under the vine (vv. 10-14); no interpretation is given with the song.

Of quite a different type are the two large picture discourses which present God's relationship to Jerusalem (ch. 16) and to the two states of Israel and Judah (ch. 23) in the metaphorical language of Yhwh's relationships with his unfaithful wives. Chapter 16 tells a far-ranging story of Jerusalem as a foundling child of foreign origins ("your father was an Amorite, your mother a Hittite"), who is abandoned, and then taken up by the first-person narrator, brought up and married (vv. 3-14). In v. 8 the marriage ceremony is designated with the word "covenant" (*bᵉrît*), which is not used elsewhere in this context; here God's relationship to Jerusalem/Israel shines through the metaphor (Greenberg 1983, 278).

Then in the following text a long story of the "prostitution" of this woman unfolds (vv. 15-34). Statements about her lascivious behavior (vv. 15, 25 etc.) at first move into statements about illegitimate cultic practices. She builds high-place sanctuaries (*bāmôt*, v. 16) [→**145**], makes "male (cult) images" (v. 17) and even sacrifices her children ("my children"!) for these gods (vv. 20f). Then the focus of attention shifts and the "prostitution" is seen in political behavior: Israel has "engaged in prostitution" with Egypt (v. 26), Assyria (v. 28) and the "land of merchants," Babylonia (v. 29) [→**§20**]. And that is not the worst of it. Not only has she taken no money for it as a common prostitute would do, but she has even paid her lovers (vv. 33f). And so a great judgment will now come upon her, for the execution of which all her lovers will be called together (vv. 35-43). And all this is because she did not think back to her youth and to what God did for her then (v. 43, cf. v. 22) [→**§16**].

There is another additional aspect to this. Jerusalem has two sisters: Samaria and Sodom (vv. 44-58). But her actions were worse than those of these two. She will thus be ashamed and take their shame upon her (v. 52). But now a turning point is in evidence: God will "turn her fortunes" (*šûb šᵉbût*), first the fate of Samaria and Sodom and then also the fate of Jerusalem "in the midst of them." This removes her special position in respect of her sisters, and she must be ashamed and bear her shame "in giving them comfort" (v. 54); for after all they have proved to be more righteous than she herself (v. 51). But all three will be restored to what they were before (v. 55).

But then follows the decisive final step in the restoration: the shaming of Jerusalem will have a cathartic effect which will prepare Jerusalem to return again to the covenant God made with her (vv. 59-63) [→**§6**]. He will remember his covenant from her youth and will "establish an everlasting covenant" with her (vv. 60, 62). This will show to them "that I am the LORD." So this far-ranging story of Jerusalem's sin and punishment leads into the restoration of the eternal divine covenant with Jerusalem/Israel.

For a second time Ezekiel uses the metaphor of sexual waywardness as the basis for a grand historical review. In ch. 23 the fate of Samaria and Jerusalem, i.e. of the northern and southern kingdoms, is depicted under the names of the two sisters Oholah and Oholibah. The depictions of the unbridled prostitution are no less drastic. The reproaches here, are to start with, focused entirely on the political arena: prostitution with Egypt (vv. 3, 8), Assyria (vv. 5-7, 12f) and Babylonia (vv. 14-17). The elder sister, Oholah, is punished for her prostitution by her lovers, the Assyrians (vv. 9f); this seals the fate of the northern kingdom. The same fate at the hands of the Babylonians is predicted for the younger sister, Oholibah (vv. 22-31). Here the image of the cup of drugged drink crops up again (vv. 32-35) which was found already in Jeremiah as an element of the proclamation of judgment (Jer 25.15-29; 49.12) [→219]. In a second part (vv. 36-49) cultic transgressions of the two sisters are also mentioned. There is talk of "idols" and of child-sacrifices (vv. 37-39, 49), of desecration of the sanctuary and transgression of the sabbath laws (vv. 38f). Once again there is talk of prostitution with men "from far away" (vv. 40ff) and of the resulting punishment, in which there are many echoes of ch. 16. Taken as a whole this chapter is much less developed and in particular it does not contain any prospect of what will come in the future after the punishment has been carried out.

A third great historical review is formulated without metaphors of any kind (ch. 20). Once gain the Elders meet together with Ezekiel. This time we are expressly told that they have come to consult Yhwh (v. 1). But as before in 14.3 God rejects the enquiry (v. 3). Instead, through the prophet he gives them a lecture on their own history. It begins in Egypt. This beginning is described here in very dense theological terms, which echo the reports of the self-annunciation of God in Egypt (vv. 5f). There God "chose" (*bāhar*) the house of Jacob, made himself known to them ceremonially ("I am the LORD, your God," cf. Ex 6.2-8) [→41] and swore to them that he would lead them out of Egypt and give them a land flowing with milk and honey (Ex 3.8). But now something new is added. God said to them: "Get rid of the vile images you have set your eyes on, and do not defile yourselves with the idols of Egypt" (v. 7). This is again underlined by the expression, "I am the LORD, your God." The pentateuchal tradition knows nothing of this. It is not until Josh 24.14 that there is talk of the "gods that your fathers served in Egypt"; but there Joshua himself is the first to raise the requirement before the entry into the promised land that the Israelites should rid themselves of these gods. Ezekiel's view of history is more radical. The idolatry of the Israelites began already in Egypt. (There is also an allusion to this in 23.3.) Already then they refused to stay away from them. And already then God wanted to let his wrath fall on them—but he did not do so (vv. 8f). Here begins a series of God's surges of anger and his decision not to put them into effect "for my name's sake." Three times this is repeated: in Egypt (vv. 8f), in the first generation (vv. 13f) and the second in the wilderness (vv. 21f); for both wilderness generations did not live according to the commandments that God had given them and did not keep his sabbaths. He swore to the first generation that he would not bring them into the promised land (v. 15) and to the second that he would scatter them among the nations (v. 23). Nor is the pentateuchal tradition familiar with the idea that already before the entry into the land God had formed the decision that Israel would end up in exile. But in Ezekiel's view, in what the exiles are already undergoing the plan of God is being carried out, which he was already forming after his unsuccessful attempt to dissuade Israel from the worship of other gods.

And then we read: "I also gave them over to statutes that were not good and laws they could not live by," namely the sacrifice of the firstborn (vv. 25f). This shocking statement goes well beyond what we meet elsewhere in the Hebrew Bible. But it is attached to what precedes it because God had not at all expected Israel to lead a life in the land in accordance with his will. So was it his intention to contribute towards bringing about the predicted catastrophe? Was that why he gave the commandment of the sacrifice of the firstborn: "You must give me the firstborn of your sons" (Ex 22.28b)? Two questions are linked together here: (a) how are we to understand the Old Testament commandments about the sacrifice of the firstborn and what was the cultic practice like; and (b) how are we to take Ezekiel's statement that God himself gave commandments "that were not good"? The first question requires a nuanced answer. But after the difference in historical view that Ezekiel develops here the second question permits of no other answer than that with this commandment God did indeed intend to drive the Israelites—who were sinful in any case—to a point where the boundaries between legitimate Yahweh-worship and the worship of foreign gods were fluid (cf. Levenson 1993, 5ff). For the presentation of the firstborn to Yhwh could easily be confused with the rite of making the children "pass through the fire" (v. 31), which was never Israelite practice. And precisely this is what the Israelites did after God had brought them into the land, together with other cults for foreign gods, to whom they brought sacrifices on the high-places as a "fragrant incense" (vv. 27f; cf. 6.13). So God does not want to be consulted by them (v. 31).

But the Israelites' plan to be "like the nations" (v. 32; cf. 1 Sam 8.5, 20) [→104], will not succeed either. God will not let them go. "With a strong hand and outstretched arm," as he once brought them out of Egypt (Deut 26.8 etc.) [→72], he will lead them out of their dispersion in exile and gather them together again in the wilderness and carry out his judgment on them (vv. 32-38). He will separate off the apostates,

so that they will not come into the land of Israel (v. 38). But after that
all Israel will serve him on his holy mountain. The "fragrant incense"
of the sacrifices will now once again be for Yhwh alone. He will show
himself as the Holy One in the eyes of the nations and the Israelites
will "know that I am the LORD" (vv. 39-42). But for the Israelites this
new beginning will be coupled with a profound shame, as they think
of their deeds up to now (cf. also previously 16.59-63). And they will
recognize that God is acting thus for his name's sake (vv. 43f).

In the last sentences once again the most important elements in this
great sketch of history come together. God acts "for his name's sake"
[→§15]. Right from the beginning this was the determinative element
in his behavior towards Israel, because they already started worshiping
other gods in Egypt, thereby desecrating his name. But he constantly
kept his anger in check so as not himself to desecrate his name in front
of the nations. When he now announces to those in exile that he will
lead them back into the land of Israel again, then he is going to do this
for his name's sake. (This is even more explicitly expressed in 36.16ff;
cf. 1986 [→255].) But for Israel this is at the same time a deeply shaming experience because they will have to become aware that God has
acted towards them graciously for the sake of his name even though
they themselves did not deserve it.

A further chapter of accusations against Jerusalem and its inhabitants
(ch. 22) almost entirely does without images (except for a simile of the
snails that melt in the fire, vv. 17-22) and contains no explicit historical perspective. In the accusations relating to Jerusalem's "despicable
deeds" (*tôʿbot*, v. 2) reproaches concerning misdemeanors in the legal
and social realms as well as the cultic merge together. "Blood(-guilt)"
is one of the dominant words. Jerusalem is a "city of blood" (v. 2)
which sheds blood in its center, making itself guilty (vv. 3f, 13). It is
the "princes" and officials that use their power to shed blood (vv. 6,
25) and to enrich themselves (v. 27); slanderers (v. 9) and the corrupti-
ble (v. 12) work in the same vein. Violence and injustice are added to
the weak, the foreigners, the widows and orphans (vv. 7, 29). This
goes hand in hand with sexual transgressions (vv. 10f) and cultic offenses: the sabbath is desecrated (v. 8), in which the priests also participate as they infringe God's Torah by no longer distinguishing between
sacred and profane and between pure and impure (v. 26). In addition
there is the culticly illegitimate "eating on the mountains" (v. 9; cf.
18.6 etc.), which serves to scorn God's sanctuary (v. 8). Indeed, already in the introduction we read the general judgment that Jerusalem

makes itself "idols" (v. 3). And the prophets whitewash all this (v. 28). Because of all these transgressions God will pour out his wrath on this city (v. 31); he will make it a mockery among the nations (vv. 4f) and it will be considered accursed among them when it is dispersed among them (vv. 15f).

The last metaphorical discourse in this cycle is dated to the beginning of the siege of Jerusalem (24.1-14). In vv. 3-5 it takes up the metaphor that was used before in 11.3, where certain people in Jerusalem say proudly: "The city is a cooking-pot and we are the meat." But then the image shifts. The "city of blood" (v. 6; cf. 22.2) is like a pot that has rust on it. But even if everything is taken out and the pot is made to glow on the fire, the rust does not come off (vv. 9-12). So too Jerusalem's impurity can no longer be removed and its fate is sealed (vv. 13f).

Between all these image discourses and historical surveys there is a text of quite a different kind in ch. 18. Ezekiel tackles arguments circulating in the "land of Israel" in the form of the proverb: "The fathers eat sour grapes, and the children's teeth are set on edge" (v. 2; cf. Jer 31.29). This chapter has perhaps been inserted at this point because the proverb was related to the kings spoken of in chs. 17 and 19 in the form of metaphorical discourses. But the prophet tackles the problem at a much more basic level by generally disputing the truth of the proverb. Each individual person belongs to God and only those that sin themselves will die (vv. 4, 19f). This is developed in a far-ranging argument through three generations (vv. 5-9, 10-13, 14-18). The features of the "righteous person" (*ṣaddîq*, v. 5) [→§10] are listed, as it were a summary of Israelite ethics. It begins with keeping away from illegitimate cults (v. 6): eating on the mountains (cf. 22.9) and worshiping "idols"; also sexual relations with another man's wife and with a woman during her menstrual period belong primarily in the cultic arena here (cf. Lev 18.19f). Then follows a whole series of rules of behavior towards fellow human beings, in particular the needy or oppressed, through to a just judgment in law (vv. 7f). And finally the whole thing is summarized as living and acting in accordance with God's commandments and statutes. Of anyone who does this it may be said that "he is righteous" (*ṣaddîq hû'*) and so he will live (v. 9). Twice more this is all repeated with minor variations: if such a righteous person has a son who does the opposite of all this, then he must die for it (vv. 10-13); but if his son again keeps to the rules of the righteous life, then he will live and not bear the guilt of his father (vv. 14-18).

But it is not just between the generations that there can be a change; the individual "ungodly" person (*rāšāʿ*) can also be converted, and he will then remain alive (vv. 21f). Here in the divine speech the prophet formulates a central sentence of the divine "rules" in dealings with humans: "Do I take any pleasure in the death of the wicked? declares the sovereign LORD. Rather, am I not pleased when they turn from their ways and live?" (v. 23). Be converted, repent (*šûb*), that is what God expects and hopes for from humans. Once again the various possibilities of repentance for good and evil are set out and justified in the face of objections (vv. 24-29), until the whole thing leads into the cry: "Repent! Turn away from your offenses!" (*šûbû*, v. 30). Through the repentance people will as it were create a new heart and a new spirit for themselves (v. 31), as God had previously announced for the time of the return (11.19) [→241]. Then once again: God takes no pleasure in the death of those who die on account of their sins. So: "Repent and live!" (v. 32).

The conclusion to the first part of the book of Ezekiel is formed again by a sign-act (24.15-27). Here the prophet personally is the most immediately involved. His wife, the "delight of my eyes," dies, but he is not permitted to show any expressions of grief and is not to carry out the normal mourning rituals either. It will be so for the house of Israel, when the temple in Jerusalem, the "delight of her eyes," is destroyed and its remaining sons and daughters fall by the sword. Then they will not lament and weep and they will perform no mourning rituals but perish in their guilt (vv. 20-24).

But then there is an earlier announcement of what is reported later (24.25-27; cf. 33.21f). After the fall of Jerusalem an escapee will come to Ezekiel and tell him. And then his dumbness will be taken from him (cf. 3.26f [→237]). So he will become a sign for them, "and they will know that I am the LORD."

4.7 Laments over the fate of the nations

As in the preceding prophetic books (Isa 13–23; Jer 46–51) [→179, 238], in Ezekiel's case too divine words are given against other nations. At first it is a collection of short sayings against the immediate neighbors: the Ammonites (25.2-7), Moab (vv. 8-11), Edom (vv. 12-14) and the

Philistines (vv. 15-17). They have all welcomed the defeat of Judah with glee, and some of them, like Edom and the Philistines, have also engaged in hostile acts against Judah (vv. 12, 15). God will now punish them for this. Tyre, too, was pleased at the fact that its competitor in trade, Judah, had been eliminated (26.2). A similar fate therefore looms for Tyre, though this is depicted in very much more concrete shape: Nebuchadnezzar, king of Babylon, will come, lay siege to the city and take it, destroy it and plunder it (vv. 7-14), so that all neighboring princes will lament it and strike up a song of lament (vv. 15-21). The prophet himself too will be required by God to strike up a lament song (*qînāh*, a dirge [→*In* **127**]) concerning Tyre (27.1f). At first it is a song of praise for the splendor of the Tyrian fleet and its worldwide commercial relations. But then a shipwreck afflicts the fleet (v. 26) and the whole thing turns into a great lament.

Tyre again attracts special attention to itself (ch. 28). Its "prince" (v. 2, in v. 12: king) considered himself equal with God and cleverer and richer than all humans (vv. 2-5). Because of this self-vaunting he will be cut down by his enemies and suffer death (vv. 6-10). The prophet is therefore to strike up a song of lament about him (vv. 11-19). In it again in graphic mythological colors the glory of the king of Tyre is described who was in Eden, God's garden, and whom God himself had set on the "holy mountain" (vv. 12-14). He was blameless until he sinned as a result of his great commercial successes. So God removed him from his mountain, threw him down and annihilated him (vv. 15-19). In this mysterious mythological text there are clearly discernible echoes of the story of the Garden of Eden and of the banishment of the first human couple from it (Gen 2f) [→**15**], though much of the detail remains unclear.

The first collection of sayings against other nations ends with a brief woe against Sidon (28.20-23). The whole thing is related in conclusion to Israel, saying that now its neighbors will no longer present nasty thorns and briars (v. 24). And in a message of salvation appended to it, it is announced that God will gather Israel from its dispersion and that they will then again live securely in their land. As a result God will prove himself to be holy before the eyes of the nations (vv. 25f). So as a whole the sayings against the other nations form an element of the proclamation of salvation for Israel.

The second part of the oracles to the nations deals exclusively with Egypt (chs. 29–32). Its imminent demise is sung about in various ways. Egypt, or rather the Pharaoh, is depicted as a crocodile (29.1-6a; 32.1-

8), as a broken reed (vv. 6b-91) or as a massive cedar in the Garden of
Eden (ch. 31). The powers that will destroy Egypt generally remain
anonymous. But then again and again the Babylonian king appears as
the real destroying enemy. The arm of Pharaoh is broken, but the
arms of the king of Babylon are strengthened when God puts the
sword in his hand (30.20-26; cf. 32.11). Nebuchadnezzar is also mentioned by name (30.10-12); Egypt is given to him as booty in compensation for the poor success of the action against Tyre (29.17-21),
which did not turn out as described in 26.7-14. At the conclusion
there is a great song of lament about Egypt (32.17-32), which has been
kicked into the underworld and is languishing there together with
Assyria (vv. 22f), Elam (vv. 24f), Meshech-Tubal (v. 26), Edom (v. 29)
and the "princes of the north" (v. 30). Here there is no longer a reference to the context of the book as in 28.24-26.

4.8 Behold, it is coming!

The sayings about foreign nations stand at the decisive break within
the book of Ezekiel. After this there has been a fundamental change:
Jerusalem has fallen. The fearful waiting for what was to come, and the
vigorous discussions about how to behave in the face of it, are over.
Attention is now directed to the future. Hitherto it has only been individual sayings in which the prophet has spoken of a blissful future
(6.8-10; 11.16-20; 16.53-63; 20.40-44; 28.25f) [→**238, 241, 245, 248**], but
now this vista opens up to its full extent.

But before the decisive news of the fall of Jerusalem arrives (33.21f),
the prophet is as it were once again placed in his office for this new
chapter in his ministry: he is placed in the office of the watchman,
with which he became acquainted right at the beginning of his prophetic career (33.1-9; cf. 3.16-21) [→**236**]. The talk of the watchman
over the house of Israel, who must warn the ungodly (vv. 7-9), is now
connected with the explanation of the individual responsibility of each
individual, as has already been set out in detail earlier (vv. 12-20; cf.
ch. 18) [→**249**]. But the topic is now developed much more directly *ad
hominem*. The people of the house of Israel lament: "Our offenses and
sins weigh us down, and we are wasting away because of them. How
then can we live?" (v. 10). So now it is not a question of the formal
sacral legal discussion of guilt and punishment in successive generations
as in 18.1-20 but of the lament and the suffering of those directly concerned, who become aware that they share the guilt for the demise of

Jerusalem. So before the discussion of individual responsibility there also stands the call to repentance. With a ceremonial oath formula the assurance is introduced: "I take no pleasure in the death of the wicked, but rather that they turn from their ways and live. Turn! Turn from your evil ways! Why will you die, O house of Israel?" (v. 11). This "Why will you die?" introduces the answer to the desperate question: "How then can we live?" Each one is directed to his own righteousness and each one has the possibility of repentance, of good as well as evil. So also those who lament their sins that weigh heavily upon them can also gain their life back if they repent (vv. 12-20). So no one need stay excluded from the future that is now opening up.

The news arrives: "The city has fallen!" The mouth of the prophet is opened and not closed again (33.21f; cf. 24.26f) [→**237**]. But now the first question to be asked is: whose future is it? Among those remaining in the land there are obviously not only such as suffer for their sins but also others who are trying to realize their claims to possession of the land against those living in exile (v. 24; cf. also previously 11.15) [→**241**]. They appeal to Abraham: "Abraham was only one man, yet he possessed the land. But we are many; surely the land has been given to us as our possession" [→**§8**]. This sounds as if it is aware of tradition, even pious. But it distorts the Abraham tradition into its opposite. For the latter says, after all, that God gave Abraham the land even though he was just one man and could not have taken possession of it in his own strength. But they emphasize that there are "many" of them, thus their own power (cf. Lohfink 1982, 979). But the prophet traces this question back to the decisive point: how can those who insist on their old sins lay claim to the land? These are the same reproaches as before: illegitimate sacrifices, worship of "idols" and violent deeds (v. 25). So God will punish them and lay the land completely waste (vv. 27-29).

But the exiles too have not yet recognized the signs of the times. They are certainly keen to assemble and listen to the prophet. But for them he is like a crooner, singing love songs to anyone who will listen. They have not understood that the historical moment has now come of which Ezekiel has been speaking since the beginning of his ministry: "Behold, it is coming!" Now at last they will "know that a prophet has been among them"—and still is (33.30-33; cf. 2.5; 3.11) [→**235**]. And they will therefore not only listen but they will take what the prophet has to say to them seriously.

For now sayings about the future [→**§22**] awaiting Israel begin. The very first of these messages makes it very clear that the blissful future can arise only against the background of judgment, whether the judgment that is to come or that which has already been suffered, which remains indissolubly linked to the future. In the metaphor of the flock and its shepherds, which we met before in Jeremiah (Jer 2.8; 23.1-4 etc.) [→207], the failure of the monarchy is described (34.1-10). The "shepherds of Israel" were poor shepherds. They thought only of themselves, took the animals' meat and wool but neglected their task as shepherds by not taking care of the weak, the sick, the afflicted, the wayward and the lost; that is why the flock is now scattered (vv. 2-6). But God will put an end to these shepherds (vv. 7-10) and he will himself take care of his flock. He will do everything that the bad shepherds have neglected to do (vv. 11-16). God will also mediate in the conflicts within the flock and provide protection for the weak against the strong (vv. 17-22). So God himself will fulfill the tasks that the kings should in fact have been performing [→§13]. But finally he will raise up a new David (vv. 23f), as Jeremiah also had promised (Jer 23.5f) [→222]. The new David is accorded the honorific title of "Servant" of God. He will be the true shepherd and the "prince" (*nāśî'*), whose position will be marked by his special relationship with God: "I, the LORD, will be your God and my servant David will be prince among you."

This will be the first step towards a fundamental renewal of the relationship between God and Israel. Then God will make a "covenant of peace" (*b'rît šālôm*) [→§6] with them (v. 25). This means in the first instance the establishment of good living conditions: extermination of the wild animals, blessing of the fields and fruit trees (vv. 25-27), but then also protection from the attacks of other peoples (vv. 28f). This will show them that God is with them, that they are his people, his "flock" and that he is their God (vv. 30f). The covenant of peace that is spoken of here is above all a protection agreement, by which God intends to enable and secure the life of his people.

When there is talk of danger from neighboring nations, at this time eyes turn in particular towards Edom (cf. 25.12-14) [→216]. So the prophet is now required to turn his face towards the mountains of Seir, i.e. against Edom (35.1f; cf. v. 15). Once before he had to perform this hostile gesture towards mountains, but that time against the mountains of Israel (6.1f) [→238]; but for these he is now commissioned with a quite different message (36.1ff). Because Edom has interfered with Israel, it will now itself be made a wilderness (ch. 35). The mountains of Israel however will again become fertile and be populated by many people and their cities will be rebuilt (36.1-15).

The view of the desolate mountains of Israel then leads to a surprising retrospect. God had constantly held back from his intention to "pour out his wrath upon them" "for my name's sake," so that his name would not be "desecrated in the eyes of the nations" (20.8f, 13f, 21f) [→247]. But in the end he has done it after all (vv. 20f). So now he will gather Israel again and lead it back into its land "not for your sake but for the sake of my holy name" (vv. 22-24; cf. 1986). Again the view of the nations is a crucial element: "The nations will know that I am the LORD, declares the LORD YHWH, when I show myself holy through you before their eyes" (v. 23). Here there is almost an echo of something like divine self-criticism, or more precisely: his insight that he cannot punish Israel without causing damage to himself and his name by association. If God wants to stay God, then he must remain God for Israel.

So God will now create a new basis for Israel's life before him and with him (36.24-32). He will bring them home and purge them of their impurity, which means in particular: of their earlier idolatry. He will give them a new heart and a new spirit, a heart of flesh instead of a heart of stone and a spirit that dwells inside and enables them to live according to his statutes and commandments (vv. 24-27). These are the same ideas as Jeremiah expressed. God will enable the Israelites themselves to live in his covenant according to his commandments by renewing their inner life, their heart and their spirit (Jer 31.31-34) [→196]. And God will also make their land fertile again and then they will be filled with shame as they recall their evil deeds and in the knowledge that God is not doing all this for their sake (vv. 28-32, 33-38; cf. 16.61-63; 20.43f).

At this point Israel is still far away from all this. They are still without hope, as if dead (37.11). But the prophet experiences a new vision (37.1-14). Again the "hand of YHWH" comes upon him and the "spirit" leads him to a large field of dead people. Here he must himself become active in the vision and "prophesy" over the bones of the dead (vv. 4, 7, 9f). Thereupon they join together again, sinews, flesh and hair grow on them and finally the breath of life comes back into them. The divine word explains to the prophet that these bones are the house of Israel, who are now without hope (v. 11). So he is to "prophesy" again and promise them a future in their land (vv. 12-14). So they are now prepared for what God plans to do with them.

After the vision there follows another sign-act (37.15-28, cf. chs. 4f;
12.1-20). It gives as it were a political concretization of the future
anticipated in the vision. Two wooden staves symbolize the two kingdoms of Judah and Israel. They will in future form a unity under *one*
king: David (vv. 24f). And God will make "a covenant of peace, an
eternal covenant" with them [→§6] (v. 26). His sanctuary (*miqdāš*), his
"dwelling-place" (*miškān*) will be present among them (vv. 26b, 27).
The twice-repeated "covenant formula" (vv. 23, 27) encloses this
paragraph (cf. 1995, 40f). But again the "acknowledgment formula"
follows in a very unusual formulation: "Then the nations will know
that I the LORD make Israel holy, when my sanctuary is among them
for ever" (v. 28). There is anticipation here of the topic of the great
concluding vision in chs. 40-48.

But beforehand the figure of a mysterious and dangerous enemy appears: Gog, from the land of Magog, the great prince of Meshech and
Tubal (chs. 38f). "At the end of years/days" (38.8, 16) he will come
against the people of Israel, which is now living in safety (vv. 8, 11,
14) without walls, bars and gates. But God will prepare a terrible end
for it, the proportions of which will be so massive that the Israelites
will need no firewood for seven years, because instead they will be
able to use the wood of the weapons and shields of the warriors of
Gog (39.9f) and will bury the corpses for seven months (vv. 12-15);
and the birds and the wild animals will satisfy themselves on the flesh
and blood of these warriors and their horses (vv. 17-20). By this
eschatological victory God will prove himself holy in the sight of the
nations (38.16, 23; 39.7, 13, 21).

The concluding section 39.23-29 turns again towards Israel. In a
summary retrospect on the proclamation of Ezekiel we read first that
the nations will know that God has punished Israel for its sins and has
hidden his face from them (vv. 23f). But then follows a word of salvation (vv. 25-29): God will turn the fate of Jacob and have mercy on
the house of Israel. In retrospect they will recognize that it was God
himself who has led them from among the nations [→§9] and then
finally brought them back in their entirety. With this a new period of
relations between God and Israel begins: "I will no longer hide my
face from them, for I have poured out my spirit on the house of Israel,
declares the LORD YHWH."

4.9 I will live here for ever among the Israelites

Once again Ezekiel is seized by the "hand of YHWH" and brought into the land of Israel (40.1). There he is set on a high mountain, on which he sees something like "the building of a city" (v. 2). The further course of the vision makes it clear that this is Jerusalem, more precisely the temple district, which, also according to Isa 2.2 [→**169f**], lies on a mountain overlooking everything. A man whose appearance was "like bronze" (which recalls the "living creatures" of 1.7 [→**201**]) and is equipped with the measuring tools of an architect or master builder, asks Ezekiel to accompany him and to pay careful attention to everything he will show him, so that he can then declare it to the house of Israel (vv. 3f). Here right at the beginning of the vision it is clear that it is not only intended for the prophet himself but that it will be of great significance for all Israel.

On a long tour the prophet is now shown the facilities of the temple with its precise measurements (40.5–42.20). Occasionally the accompanying man gives brief explanations of the designation or function of particular rooms (40.45f; 41.4, 22; 42.13f). But then it is shown that this precise measurement of the temple was the preparation for what now follows: the return of the *kābôd* into the temple (43.1-5). In his earlier vision Ezekiel had seen how the *kābôd* had left the temple [→**241**]. At that time it had left the temple through the east gate in an easterly direction (10.19; 11.23); on the same path it now comes back and fills the temple (v. 5; cf. 44.4). The return is connected with the ceremonial assurance: "This is the place of my throne and the place for the soles of my feet. This is where I will live among the Israelites forever" (43.7; cf. v. 9) [→**§11**]. The "idolatry" of the Israelites will belong to the past. Once again we read that the Israelites will be ashamed of what they have done (vv. 10f; cf. 16.52-54, 61-63; 20.43f; 36.31f) [→**245, 248, 255**]. But this will prepare them for when the prophet informs them of the plan of the temple and writes it down in all its details and announces the instruction (*tôrāh*) of the temple (vv. 10-21).

Quite a variety of individual instructions are added to this great vision with its fundamental consequences for Israel's future, such as concerning the burnt-offering altar and its dedication (43.13-27) and concerning the service of Levites and priests (44.6-31; 46.19-24). The tasks of the "prince" (*nāśî'*) are treated in detail. In the framework of the future prospect of this vision the title "king" is evidently being avoided, so that the "prince" fulfills the functions of the king from the

Davidic house; the new David of the time of salvation was also given this title beforehand (34.23; 37.25) [→**254f**]. However, the task of the prince is described here in a very reticent way; in particular in the temple cult he plays rather a modest role. He does have the privilege that he is the only person to approach the outer east gate from the inside, which has remained locked since God himself entered there in the form of his *kābôd* (44.1-3; 46.1f). In performing his sacrifice the prince has another function, however; he can only watch as the priests perform their duties (46.2). Then he must consume the sacrificial meal at this privileged spot (44.3); but the gate remains locked. In other regards the tasks of the prince's household for the sacrificial service and the prince's participation in communal cultic events are prescribed in detail (45.8-25; 46.4-15).

Finally attention turns beyond the boundaries of the temple and of Jerusalem. For the new beginning after the return from exile the land must be divided up anew. God has sworn to the forefathers to give them the land and now it will come to them again as their inheritance (47.14). So the boundaries are defined (47.15-20) and the land is divided up among the tribes (47.21–48.29; on 48.30-35 see below). Portions of land will also be given in each tribal area to the "foreigners" (*gērîm*) who have been living there on a permanent basis (47.22f). A number of special rulings have to be considered too: for the sanctuary, for priests and Levites, for the city of Jerusalem and for the princes (45.1-8; 46.16-18).

In between, however, quite a different picture opens up: a fountain springs up in the temple (47.1-12). The prophet sees the water bubbling up under the threshold, but the precise location of the source remains hidden. The accompanying man leads the prophet outside and follows the course of the water with him. With his measuring cord he measures the water course and after every thousand ells the prophet has to test the depth of the water himself. At first it comes up to his ankles, then up to his knees, and then to the hips, and finally it is so deep that it is no longer possible to wade through it (vv. 3-5). The man explains that the water flows on down into the Dead Sea (the precise term for this remains unclear in the Hebrew text). Its water will become healthy, many fish will exist in it and on its banks trees will grow with paradisiacal fruitfulness (vv. 9f, 12. A later comment in v. 11 is to provide assurance that the brackish places will serve for the extraction of salt as before.).

With this image of the healing and fruit-giving properties of the temple source the vision's depiction turns away from the area of the rather sober accounts about the future temple and the land around it back into the dimension in which the arrival of the *kābôd* in the temple occurred. For the miraculous spring is certainly a consequence of God's return to the temple and thus into Israel's midst. The source, which grows into a mighty stream, seems quite the opposite of the "gently flowing waters of Shiloah" which the Judeans despised (Isa 8.6) [→**175**]. At the same time this depiction recalls other texts of the Hebrew Bible. The closest to it is the statement in the Psalms: "There is a river whose streams make glad the city of God" (Ps 46.5[4]) [→**334**]. The "paradise" element comes to expression with particular effect in Gen 2.10-14, where the stream that goes out from Eden divides into four arms and therewith waters the whole world. Here in Ezek 47 the crucial emphasis is that God's return and homecoming to Zion not only has significance for Israel but that it heals wounds that were inflicted early on in the history of humanity when God destroyed Sodom and Gomorrah by fire and brimstone, thereby making any life impossible in the water of the Dead Sea. When God returns to his temple [→**§22**], there too life will again be possible, symbolic for the whole of creation.

At the conclusion of the book of Ezekiel, after the dividing up of the land among the tribes (47.21–48.29) there follows another saying about Jerusalem (48.30-35). The city will have twelve gates corresponding to the twelve tribes of Israel. It will thus again become the central point of the whole people of God. Above all, however, it will be given a new name. "From now on the name of the city is: The LORD is there!" The city as a whole is now the place of the presence of God, who on his return to the temple announced: "This is where I will live among the Israelites for ever" (43.7).

4.10 Prophet of radical change

In the case of no other prophet do we see such a clear, even sharp break between two phases in his ministry as with Ezekiel. In the book itself it is brought out very explicitly: "The city has fallen!" (33.21). This profound turning point in the history of Israel and Judah also marks a fundamental change in the proclamation of Ezekiel, in brief terms: the change from the prophecy of doom to the prophecy of salvation. This shorthand comment however requires unpacking in greater detail.

The four great visions present themselves first for this purpose. Two of them are placed before the fall of Jerusalem (1.1-3, 15; 8–11), and two after it (37.1-14; 40–48). In the first, in which Ezekiel is honored for the first time with an encounter with the kābôd ("glory") of God, he is sent to the people, who have been rebellious and sinful since the time of their forefathers (2.3) [→**235**]. The message he has to proclaim is designated by the scroll, which is inscribed with "words of lament and mourning and woe" (2.10). There seems no alternative here. In the second vision Ezekiel becomes a witness as the divine kābôd leaves the sinful temple and thus delivers the city up for destruction (11.22f) [→**241**]. The third vision then occurs after the fall of Jerusalem. Here Ezekiel himself is involved personally in active participation in the resuscitation of the house of Israel, lying there as if dead, which is thereby given new hope (ch. 37) [→**255**]. In the fourth vision the prophet finally becomes a witness of the return of the kābôd into the temple and hears the divine assurance: "This is where I will live among the Israelites for ever" (43.7) [→**259**].

So this marks out the framework within which Ezekiel's proclamation moves. But this certainly does not mean that the proclamations of woe and salvation are to be found exclusively in one or the other section of his ministry, or that they are even mutually exclusive. On the contrary: the proclamation of disaster always contains a basic element directed towards future restoration and future salvation, and the proclamation of salvation is never without a backward look towards earlier accusations and announcements of disaster. This alternating relationship is certainly not always expressed, but it does come to expression in a variety of ways. Thus already the first commission given to Ezekiel to announce the message "Thus says the LORD YHWH" contains the added words: "whether they listen or fail to listen" (2.4f). So they could listen, and the proclamation of the prophet would be pointless if there was not always the possibility that they might listen. In Ezekiel's appointment as "watchman" (3.17-21) [→**236**] it is designated as his task to warn. Herein lies the intent to move those warned to "repentance" (šûb), even if this is not successful (v. 19). In the related text 18.21-32 the word of "repentance" becomes a veritable refrain in the proclamation as a whole (vv. 21, 23, 27f, 30, 32) [→**250**]. The central significance of the call to repentance within the prophetic accusation is reduced here to the formula: "Do I take any pleasure in the death of the wicked? declares the sovereign LORD. Rather, am I not pleased when they turn from their ways and live?" (v. 23). Immediately before the turning point in the proclamation of Ezekiel this is again repeated, expressly reinforced by the direct address: "Why will you die, house of Israel?" (33.11). The solicitation for attention and understanding and the call to repent are among the basic elements of the proclamation, even when that proclamation accuses and predicts disaster and judgment.

This is also clear in the statement, found in many variations: "You/they will know that I am the LORD." One of the most striking observations on the use of this "acknowledgment formula" is that it is used apparently indiscriminately for both positive and negative events. Thus the first time it occurs we read: "Your people will fall slain among you and you will know that I am the LORD" (6.7) [→**238**]; while the last time we read: "Then they will know that I am the LORD their God, for though I sent them into exile among the nations, I will gather them to their own land, not leaving any behind" (39.28) [→**256**]. What will Israel know? What does the apparently formulaic "that I am YHWH" imply? In many cases the context gives some indication. Thus immediately after the passage just cited (6.7), in 6.8-10 a section follows that announces an exception to the judgment. God will leave some remaining, and "they will know that I am the LORD; I did not threaten in vain to bring this calamity upon them" (v. 10). So they will know that God does what he has announced. And they know his announcements through the proclamation of the prophets. A few verses later we read: "You will know that I am the LORD, when your people lie slain among their idols around their altars" (v. 13). Here the connection is even clearer. The slain witness to God's wrath at the Israelites' idolatry. But at the same time this includes the message that all this would not happen, or would not have happened, if the Israelites had desisted from their idolatry. In 7.4, 9 it is the "detestable practices" of the Israelites themselves that God will cause to come upon them, and by this they will "know that I am the LORD" (v. 9: "that it is I, the LORD who strikes the blow"). And in v. 27 we read: "I will deal with them according to their conduct, and by their own standards I will judge them. Then they will know that I am the LORD."

In a grand historical retrospect ch. 20 the acknowledgment formula places positive accents within the thoroughly negative picture of Israel's history. God gave them his sabbaths as a sign "so that you will know that I am the LORD, your God" (v. 20; v.12: "that I, the LORD, make you holy"). Then the formula recurs towards the end of the chapter, when in the gathering of Israel from the dispersion the knowledge will arise that God is separating off the apostate, so that they will not enter the land of Israel (v. 38). The others, however, will "know that I am the LORD" when God brings them back into the land he promised their forefathers (v. 42), and when they realize that God is doing this "for my name's sake" (v. 44). Thus even within the proclamation of judgment and disaster the acknowledgment formula always contains the knowledge that God does not desire the death but the life of his people, and that he is therefore constantly trying to bring them there so that they will obey his will and his commandments.

In a series of cases, however, also in the first part of the book of Ezekiel, the expectation of future salvation is explicitly expressed. Already the announcement that God will leave some "behind" (6.8) [→**238**] contains an element of the prospect of a blissful future. In the context of the second vision it is announced to the exiles in solemn words that they will be brought back and their relationship to God will be restored: "They will be my people and I will be their God" (11.14-21, esp. v. 20). The great parable of faithless Jerusalem also ends with a full proclamation of salvation: the turning of Israel's fate and the restoration of the covenant (16.53-63); also the historical retrospect in ch. 20 (vv. 40-44) [→**248**]. Finally too in the concluding section of the first collection of oracles to the nations the return from dispersion is promised (28.25f), again concluding with the acknowledgment formula.

These future prospects contain a further special element in that the expectation of a turn to salvation is connected with a deep shame, indeed with abhorrence towards their own deeds to date. This is already the case in 6.9, but then especially explicitly in 16.54 and above all in vv. 61 and 63, where the great shaming occurs only after the restoration of the covenant. In 20.43 too we read that after they have been led home and after the restoration of a cult pleasing to God the Israelites will feel abhorrence towards their earlier deeds. Precisely in this motif it is again evident that the proclamation before and after the fall of Jerusalem displays certain common characteristic features; for the moment of abhorrence and shame towards their earlier deeds is also found in 36.31f after the promise of a radical new beginning (vv. 25-27) [→**256**]. And even after the return of the divine *kābôd* to the temple, shame over the earlier deeds is the precondition for the handing over of the plan for the new temple (43.10f). The new beginning will thus certainly not be a triumphal one for Israel, since awareness of their earlier sins and the unmerited nature of the turn in their fortunes will always be with them.

All these texts are determined by a marked way of thinking in historical contexts and historical consequences, unlike anything found in any other of the prophets. Ezekiel develops his historical view in particular detail in the grand overviews in chs. 20 and 23. He reaches back to the beginnings of the history of Israel in Egypt. In 20.5f [→**246**] he speaks entirely in the language of the pentateuchal tradition of the "election" of Israel and of the assurance of the leading out from Egypt into the land of promise. But already there the apostasy to other gods begins (vv. 7f), which is determinative for subsequent history. In the parable of the two sisters Oholah and Oholibah too (ch. 23) the "prostitution" begins already in Egypt (v. 3). Thus here the whole history of Israel from its beginnings onwards appears under a negative light. In the parable about Jerusalem (ch. 16) the "prostitution" begins at the climax of the narrative about the beauty of the young woman (vv. 15ff) [→**245**] and dominates the rest of the account from that point on. Here the question arises of the function of this negative account of history within the proclamation of Ezekiel as a whole. In chs. 16 and 20 the story continues to a proclamation of future restoration. Many exegetes see in this "secondary" additions by another hand. But in the book of Ezekiel as a whole it is beyond question that the prophet does not want to proclaim a history of God with Israel that ends in disaster. The historical surveys are, rather, determined by the question of how things could come to the point that God had to humiliate Israel so profoundly. In addition, the sharpness of the announcements of judgment on Jerusalem is also determined by the fact that up to the fall of the city still far too many believed that the judgment would pass them by. But certainly at no point did the prophet Ezekiel, as the book presents him to us, regard his task of proclaiming this judgment as at an end.

The question of the authorship of chs. 40–48 is related to this. For a long time the dominant view among exegetes was that this "constitutional outline" could not have come from the prophet Ezekiel. Zimmerli then came to the conclusion that the derivation of at least the "basic elements" of these chapters "from the prophet Ezekiel cannot necessarily be excluded" (1969, 994, 1241f). Since then many commentators have followed this example, if they do not assume the unity of the book in an even more resolute way. But right from the beginning of the book there can be no doubt of the fact that the concluding vision of the return of the divine *kābôd* to the temple belongs here. The first great appearance of the *kābôd* (1.1–3.15) summons the prophet to his office, the second (chs. 8–11) reports on the departure of the *kābôd* from the temple. But the book of the prophet Ezekiel or the collection of his sayings can never have concluded with this. Is it really "idle ... to ask about the continuing presence of the divine glory" (Zimmerli 1969, 234)? The book of Ezekiel gives the clear answer: the *kābôd* will return by the same way that it left the city, when the temple is rebuilt (43.1–5). It is only with this that the proclamation of Ezekiel reaches its goal.

5. The Book of the Twelve Prophets

5.1 Preliminary considerations

At the end of that part of the canon called the "Prophets" stands the "Book of the Twelve Prophets." From its earliest citation in Sirach 49.12 the prophetic writings collected here have counted as one book. In Jewish exegetical tradition they are called "The Twelve" (thus in the Babylonian Talmud, *Baba bathra* 14b/15a), in the Septuagint, δωδεκαπρόφητον, while the Vulgate calls them "Prophetae Minores."

At the same time, however, each individual one of the prophetic books collected here is clearly indicated as a separate writing. (In what follows I use the expression "writing" for this in distinction from the "book" of the Twelve Prophets.) This is evident in particular in the introductory superscriptions [→*In* **227**]. For a number of the writings the superscription includes an indication of the period or date of the ministry of the prophet concerned, oriented by the dates of the reign of the king in question in Judah and Israel, or finally the Persian king Darius. This produces a range in date from the middle of the eighth century (Hosea, Amos, Micah) through the late pre-exilic period in the last third of the seventh century (Zephaniah) up to the time of the return and the restoration at the end of the sixth century (Haggai, Zechariah). So this collection essentially spans the same period as the book of Isaiah.

The superscriptions display characteristic differences (tables can be found in Zenger 1995b, 370). They all speak of the receipt of revelation by the prophet concerned, but in differing formulas: as "the word of the LORD" that "came" (Hosea, Joel, Jonah, Micah, Zephaniah, Haggai, Zechariah) or which the prophet "saw" (*ḥāzāh*, Amos) or which came "through" him to Israel (Malachi); as a "vision" (*ḥāzôn*, Obadiah, Nahum) or as a "pronouncement" (*maśśā'*) which the prophet "saw" (Habakkuk). These differences suggest various stages in the compilation of the present collection.

Half of the writings contain the indication of a particular period or time for the ministry of the prophet. As a result the writings of the prophets Hosea, Amos, Micah and Zephaniah stand out as a connected pre-exilic group, divided up again into the three first-mentioned from the time of the existing kingdoms of Israel and Judah plus Zephaniah at the end of the time of the kingdom of Judah; opposite them are the post-exilic prophets Haggai and Zechariah. That no indications of time are made in the other writings can hardly be coincidental, given the carefully considered system of superscriptions. It is entirely conceivable that these writings were added to the first-mentioned in the course of the coming together of the Book of the Twelve Prophets and were connected with them (Nogalski 1993a and b; Schart 1998). As a result, in each case new emphases were given the collection as a whole, while no significance was attached to the temporal classification of the individual writings. Still these new emphases merit attention of their own, for in the understanding of the tradents the whole thing should now be read as a unified prophetic message (cf. Steck 1996).

Nonetheless the contours of the individual prophetic writings have not been smudged, but they have been expressly preserved by means of the superscriptions. However, the prophets that stand behind the individual writings are scarcely visible as persons. This is most clearly the case in the short narrative section in Amos 7.10-17 [→**286**], which shows Amos in a dramatic conflict with the priests of the sanctuary at Beth-El. For the reader this sheds light on the whole of the Amos writing, so that we can visualize this prophet most clearly. At the beginning of the Hosea writing Israel's relationship to Yhwh is presented metaphorically by analogy with the conflict in Hosea's marriage in the very complex section in chs. 1–3 [→**266**]. Here the person of Hosea comes into view from a very "private" angle, while in the often highly charged texts of the following chapters, the situations in which they were spoken are not reported, so that the picture of the person of Hosea in its historical context remains unclear. The words of Micah also frequently reveal tense situations without the person of the prophet ever becoming visible. The same applies to Zephaniah. In Haggai's case the context of his appearance is presented in a narrative way so that here again a prophetic figure is given clear contours; corresponding indications are again missing for Zechariah.

In the undated prophetic writings the prophets remain entirely in the background as persons; the only exception is formed by the Jonah writing, which together presents a prophetic narrative. In Malachi there are again very lively discussions and arguments, but here too the person of the prophet is not discernible.

The exegetical problems of the Book of the Twelve are in many regards comparable with those of the book of Isaiah. Here, as there, very different prophetic voices from very varied times have been combined and now expect to be read in a particular sense as a unity. In the Book of the Twelve, however, the profiles of the individual writings have remained clearly preserved, so that even the individual voices want to be heard, in particular cases evidently also in tension or contrast with others. In our discussion we shall frequently use only the name of the prophet concerned in reference to the voice that calls out in his name.

Exegesis on these questions is still in its infancy, so that much must remain unresolved (cf. 1997c). Of particular interest is the varied position of the writings of Joel, Obadiah and Jonah, which appear in this order after Micah in the Septuagint, while Jonah is found right at the end in an albeit fragmentary manuscript from Qumran (4Q12a) (cf. Jones 1995).

5.2 In the beginning the LORD spoke through Hosea

"When the LORD began to speak through Hosea," we read at the beginning of the Hosea writing (1.2). At the same time the Book of the Twelve is opened.

This beginning marks a topic of far-reaching significance: Israel's apostasy from Yhwh. Israel's failed relationship with God is described with the word "prostitution," and Hosea's marriage becomes a symbolic event. He has to marry a "whore" of a woman and to father "whoring" children. The names of the children mark Yhwh's reaction to Israel's turning away from him: "Jezreel" (v. 4), the name of the royal town as a summarizing critique of the monarchy which has promoted and fostered the cult of Baal since the time of Ahab; *lo' ruḥāmā* "Not loved" (v. 6); *lo' 'ammî* "Not my people" (v. 9). The reader will remember the names given to the children of Isaiah, "A remnant returns" and "Quick to the plunder—Swift to the spoil" (Isa 7.3; 8.3) [→**174**], which also expressed an element of Isaiah's message.

Like at the beginning of the book of Isaiah, which begins with a sharp accusation, which is then developed and given precision in what follows, here too it only becomes gradually clear that Hosea's wife Gomer stands as a representative of Israel and that the lovers she runs after (2.7[5], 9[7]) are the foreign gods [→**§20**], the Baals (2.10, 15, 19★). At the same time this beginning of Hosea surprises us with its sudden change between the sharp critiques and announcements of God's punitive action and the promise of a happy future in which the inglorious names of the children are to be turned into their opposites. Instead of "Not my people" the Israelites will be called "My people" (2.3[1]) and "Sons of the Living God" (2.1[1.10]), and "My loved one" instead of "Not loved" (v. 3[1]), and the "Day of Jezreel" will be a great and wonderful day (2.2[1.11]). This too is again reminiscent of Isaiah, where already at the conclusion of the first unit of prophetic sayings the eschatological pilgrimage of the peoples to Zion is announced (Isa 2.1-5) [→**170**]. Both of these stand right next to each other programmatically right at the beginning: the covering of Israel's guilt with the announcement of punishment—and the promise of a blissful future.

In the following chapters too these two aspects alternate. The husband Yhwh will prevent his unfaithful wife from running after her lovers (2.2-7), will take away the gifts he has given her (vv. 9f, 12), will turn her joy and celebration into shame (vv. 11f), thereby punishing her for her worship of Baal (v. 13). But then he will veritably seduce her and bring her back to the place of her first love: in the wilderness, where everything began after the exodus from Egypt (vv. 14f). And again a further prospect into the future opens up, further than the first time. God will not only "remove the names of the Baals from her lips" (vv. 17f) and build up a new, firmly founded marriage relationship (vv. 19f), but he will also make a covenant with the animal kingdom in her favor (v. 18a), put an end to all military threat (v. 18b) and even reconcile heaven and earth and the whole of nature with Israel (vv. 21f), so that finally, just as the mother learned to say again "my husband" (v. 16), so too the son, who is now called "You are my people," will say: "My God" (v. 23).

Hosea has to enter into marriage anew with his adulterous wife (ch. 3). It is not said whether this is the same one as in ch. 1; this question was evidently unimportant to the tradents, for here the symbolic character of this action is foregrounded from the beginning. For a long time ("many days") the wife will sit in the house without contact with men (v. 3), just as the Israelites will sit for "many days" without their political and cultic institutions (v. 4). Here an exile in a hostile land is announced, something that was always looming as an obvious possibility to people of the time. Israel has now deserved this fate. The reasons for it are not even mentioned in this concise narrative text; the reader knows them from the preceding chapters. But here too there is more than simply an announcement of judgment. "Afterwards," i.e. after these "many days," the Israelites will repent (v. 5). Here the pregnant word *šûb* "repent" occurs. It had already sounded on the wife's lips as an expression of the desire to return to her husband (2.7). Now it is used in a full theological sense: repent, return to God. They will seek him and approach him again, trembling. When will this be? "At the end of days"—a time which plays a role already in Isaiah (Isa 2.2) [→170]. This point in time remains indeterminate, but attention will be focused on this future day, even if in the meantime the sufferings of a long period of exile will be introduced. Here a messianic element flows in too, when we read that they will seek God "and their king David" [→§13].

Thus in the center of the first three chapters of the Hosea writing stands the complaint that Israel has turned away from its God Yhwh in the cultic worship of other gods (so already 1.2), and the announcement of the divine punishment for this apostasy. This remains a dominant theme of Hosea in the following chapters too. From here on it also casts its light on the subsequent prophetic writings in which cultic transgressions are expressly mentioned with much less frequency. There the reproaches and complaints against Israel concern other areas, in particular social matters (Amos and Micah); but they now flow together with the cultic problems into a complex whole. At the same time however the promise of future forgiveness and restoration determines the further writings of the Book of the Twelve, in which again and again we find the often tense juxtaposition and effective clash between proclamations of judgment and promises of salvation.

In Hosea God's argument with Israel now takes on the form of a court case (*rîb*, 4.1). A long series of misdemeanors and crimes is listed (v. 2) [→§16]. They all have their roots in a basic lack (v. 1): there is no "faithfulness," i.e. reliability (*ᵉmet*), no "goodness," i.e. sense of community, mercy (*ḥesed*) and no "acknowledgment of God," i.e. knowledge about God (*daʿat ᵉlohîm*). These are key terms, which are found again and again in Hosea. At this point, however, they are not un-packed, but the prophet concretizes his complaint and sharpens it: not "anyone" (*'îš*) will be accused and called to account but those who are responsible for all this, above all the priests (4.4ff), but then also the royal household (5.1; the prophet mentioned alongside the priest in 4.5 is not otherwise criticized in Hosea, though he appears to be so in other writings of the Book of the Twelve, toward which there is, as it were, an advance reference, thus Mic 3.5f, 11; Zeph 3.4) [→**293, 302**]. In a long speech for the prosecution the priests are charged with being precisely the ones who keep knowledge of God from the people, be-cause they themselves have forgotten God's Torah (4.6). They enrich themselves from the sacrifices (v. 8), and are themselves accomplices in the "prostitution" (vv. 10ff) and the idolatrous worship of the people with "wood" and "stick" (vv. 10ff). Beth-El ("House of God") has thus become Beth-Awen ("House of Wickedness") (v. 15—a clear allusion to Amos 5.5) [→**283**]. The royal house is included in the re-proaches, because it has been entrusted with the law which cannot now be effective (5.1f). Their deeds no longer permit a return to God (v. 4); try as they may, they will not be able to find God (v. 6).

Suddenly the sound of horns rings out (5.8): it is war—and war be-tween brothers! This topic dominates the following chapters. The war between the brothers of the north (Ephraim) and the south (Judah), which also plays a role in Isaiah (cf. Isa 7) [→**175**], has in reality been brought about by God himself; he is the real "enemy" (5.12, 14). So then Assyria cannot help either (v. 13), which is both enemy and ally at the same time. But now God withdraws and waits for the Israelites to acknowledge their guilt and seek him again (v. 15).

And they do indeed come (6.1-3)—but is their repentance genuine (v. 4)? It is still the prophet's task to "cut into pieces" (v. 5) like many others before him, in continuity with whom he sees himself: "Samuel, Ahijah of Shiloh, Elijah, Elisha and finally Moses" (Jeremias 1983, 87). But then the crucial question is not about the sacrifices with which people approach God, but about the inner attitude with which they bring the sacrifices. In an antithesis formulated like a didactic maxim we read: "I desire (*ḥāpaṣtî*) mercy, not sacrifice, and acknowledgment of God rather than burnt offerings" (v. 6). The sentence echoes Sam-uel's words against Saul (1 Sam 15.22f) [→**106**], in which obedience to divine instructions is contrasted with the sacrifices that Saul has brought (*ḥāpaṣ* is an expression from cultic language, cf. 1967, 285f) [→**§11**]. But above all the concern is with those things the lack of which Hosea has mentioned as being the basic evil among the Israelites (4.1): mercy (*ḥesed*) and acknowledgment of God (*daʿat ʾelohîm*). And now too mercy is only like a morning mist that quickly disperses (6.4). What are the sacrifices for? Here it comes very clear that the concern is not with a fundamental rejection of sacrifice but with the right hierarchy, with what God wants above all else, what he "desires" (Luther).

That is why sacrifices are of no use now, because there is no discernible repentance and turning to God. In a long passage the sins of Israel are set out for all to see: violence in the land and in the capital (6.7ff) through to regicide (7.3-7), in which the priests again are particularly prominent (6.9); a foreign policy against the will of God (7.8-12) and finally cultic behavior in which it becomes evident that they are not turning to God but turning away from him (v. 13) and are still following wrong cultic practices (vv. 14f); and when they indeed do "turn," then it is not to God (v. 16).

Again the horn sounds (8.1)! And again a long list of reproaches. Kings and the cult are the themes. Kings are appointed without God's say-so (v. 4a). After Jeroboam II, who still belonged to the dynasty of Jehu inaugurated by Elisha, a fast succession of different kings had come to the throne, always by murdering their predecessor and without any involvement of prophets [→**143f**]. This did not happen on God's orders. In addition they waste costly gold and silver in fashioning images of gods (v. 4b). And finally the "calf of Samaria" (cf. 1 Kgs 12.26-33) [→**129f**], the state sanctuary in Beth-El (vv. 5f, cf. 10.5f)! This is rejected because it was never a legitimate object of the worship of God. Many altars, even if not dedicated to foreign gods, ultimately lead into sin (v. 11) because God does not "desire" the many sacrifices (v. 13, *rāṣāh* in the same sense as *ḥāpaṣ* in 6.6). For Ephraim (i.e. Israel) considers God's instructions, even if so many of them are written down, as something strange (v. 12); in this they are no better than their priests (cf. 4.6). And finally, those misplaced political allegiances once again (vv. 8-10).

So: "They will return to Egypt" (8.13). This is the announcement of exile (9.3) [→**§9**], in which they will lack everything that they are now enjoying (vv. 1-7); at the same time there is an echo here of a "back to the beginnings!" call (vv. 10ff). But the contemporaries can only say: "the prophet is a fool, the inspired man a maniac (*mᵉšuggaʿ*)" (v. 7b). They lie in wait for him, place traps and pursue him into the house of God (v. 8). Their deeds are compared with the "days of

Gibeah," that shameful deed reported in Judg 19. For all this God will exact retribution from them (v. 9).

Suddenly the subject changes. The key words "Egypt" and "Gibeah" have directed attention to the early history of Israel [→§21], of which Hosea now speaks from various angles. It is immediately evident that these are not merely historical observations but that they are there to show the beginnings and causes of Israel's behavior, providing justification for the complaints of the prophet and the announcements of divine acts of punishment. As before in 2.16f (and in Jeremiah, ch. 2) [→207] Hosea's historical retrospective begins with the wilderness period as the time of Israel's first, unclouded relationship with God (9.10). In an impressive metaphor God speaks of the election of Israel as of a "foundling" and indeed of a completely unexpected, because it was totally unrealistic, grape in the wilderness. (The subsequent image of the early figs is also found in Isa 28.4.) But the tone immediately changes: scarcely had Israel's forefathers approached the promised land than they already committed the first great apostasy: that at Baal Peor (Num 25) [→72], when they gave themselves over to "shame" (*bošet*) (Hos 9.10b); here the Baal does not have a concrete name.

The next key term is "Gilgal" (v. 15). This evidently means the beginning of the monarchy, in particular the appointment of Saul as king (1 Sam 11.14f) [→105] and then his sacrifice against the instructions of the prophet Samuel, which led to his rejection (13.8-14). It is certainly no coincidence that Hosea's message concerning what God really "desires" (Hos 6.6) clearly echoes Samuel's words to Saul in 1 Sam 15.22f [→106]. As Saul was then, the Israelites are now "rejected" because they have not "listened" (Hos 9.17; cf. 1 Sam 15.23, 26). Already in Gilgal God began to "hate" them (9.15, the Hebrew word *śānē'* is not as sharp as "hate" in English; cf. *ThWAT* VII, 828ff). Hosea's negative judgment of the monarchy has escalated by comparison with 8.4, and it will escalate still further (cf. 13.11). Here the beginning of the Baal cult and the failed beginning of the monarchy stand immediately next to each other. God will therefore remove all glory (9.11, 13) and fertility from Ephraim (vv. 11-16).

In the following sections too we find historical retrospectives from different points of view. Israel appears as a luxuriant vine (10.1). But again the backward look to the happy beginning merely forms the contrast to what came afterwards. Again it is the all-too abundant altars (vv. 1b, 2, 8), the monarchy (vv. 3f, 7) and the "calf of Beth-Awen" (vv. 4f; cf. 4.15; 8.5), with which Israel has set itself up against God and which God will now remove or destroy. As if in contrast, the next retrospective does not begin with the blissful early days but again with the shameful events of Gibeah (10.9; cf. 9.9). The message speaks of a war (vv. 9f), as does the section that follows later (vv. 13b-15). In between, in a graphic metaphor the early times are conjured up again, when Ephraim was an impressionable young calf that was to be trained up for fruitful work in the fields. "Break up your unplowed ground; for it is time to seek the LORD." But again follows the converse: "But you have planted wickedness, you have reaped evil" (vv. 11-13a).

Once again Hosea starts right at the beginning: with God's love for his young son Israel, when he led him out of Egypt (11.1). But again the reversal immediately follows: they walk away from him, sacrifice to the Baals and present burnt offerings to the idols (v. 2). Nonetheless God has taken loving care of them, but in vain: they must go back to "Egypt" (which is now called "Assyria") (vv. 3-6). This seems to be the end of the salvation history that once began with the leading of Israel out of Egypt. But the text is not yet at an end here. The return to Egypt does not mean the end of the history of God with Israel. For though there is no talk of any repentance on Israel's part, there is talk of a turn-around by God himself! He cannot give up his people, cannot execute his wrath: "My heart is changed within me; all my compassion is aroused" (v. 8). God's regret, his "self-control," which moves him not to execute judgment on his people, has the upper hand. So though Israel still has to go to "Egypt," this does not mean the reversal of salvation history, but they will return from there "trembling" (cf. 3.5) and God will let them come home again (11.11). So salvation history can as it were start from the beginning again.

This is one of the rare texts in the Hebrew Bible that speak of God's "regret" (cf. Jeremias 1975/97, 52ff, 137ff). Here the special feature of Hosea's prophecy, the continual announcement of salvation alongside the proclamation of judgment, finds its clearest expression. It is certainly no coincidence that this breakthrough occurs in connection with the remembrance of the beginning of the history of God's dealings with Israel in the exodus from Egypt; for once before God promised to bring Israel back to the place of its first love, into the wilderness, where everything began after the exodus (2.16f).

The section 11.7-11 forms the conclusion of the large text unit chs. 4–11, just as the joyous prospect in 3.5 concluded the first part (chs. 1–3) [→**268**]. In view of this the new start in ch. 12 is surprising, for here again the history of Israel's guilt is in the foreground. Of particular significance are again the backward references to the early history of Israel, with Jacob now moving into the center of attention. Close connections with the Jacob traditions of Genesis, extending as far as verbatim agreement, are in evidence, even if the intention of some of the allusions remains uncertain for the present-day interpreter.

Many exegetes understand the allusion to the grasping of Esau's heels ('*aqab* v. 4a, cf. Gen 25.26) as "betrayal" in the sense of Gen 27.36 and interpret the following scene of the fight at the Jabbok negatively as "rebellion against God" (Jeremias 1983, 153), although the text uses the same word *śārāh* "fight" as Gen 32.29 [→**30f**], where Jacob's name is changed to "Israel" by use of this word. It seems sensible to understand the text as indicating that here as elsewhere Israel's apostasy constitutes a deviation from the salvation-historical beginnings in the history of God's dealings with the patriarchs (cf. esp. Ackroyd 1963).

Alongside the Jacob tradition there is again talk of Egypt. In a ceremonial self-introductory formula we read: "I am the LORD, your God, from the land of Egypt" (12.10). With this form of words the basic significance of Israel's exodus from Egypt [→**§9**] is brought to expression, not only for God's relationship to Israel, but even for God's own identity. He defines himself as it were as the one who led Israel out of Egypt. That is why Israel "knows" no other God (13.4). The theological significance of the exodus event could scarcely be worded more emphatically (cf. 1997b). The mention of this fundamental divine act for Israel however stands in sharp contrast to Ephraim's "Canaanite" mercenary attitude, which is ruthlessly concerned with the acquisition of wealth (12.8). So God will again lead Israel into the poverty of life under canvas (v. 10b).

Another special feature of the historical understanding of Hosea comes into view here: the great significance of the prophetic precursors. In 6.5 [→**269**] already they appeared as God's tools in his historical dealings with Israel. Now Hosea says in his critical evaluation of the history of Israel, that God always did—and this also means again and again—speak to and through the prophets, so that Israel knew his will and his plans (12.11). But more than this: the exodus from Egypt, which has such a central significance for Hosea, already happened by the hand of a prophet, namely Moses (v. 14). He led and protected Israel along this pathway. Hosea thus "programmatically lays claim to the traditions of Israel's early history as 'prophetic,'" and "sees himself in the *successio mosaica*, the succession of Moses, but also as standing in his authority" (Jeremias 1983, 157). From this position of authority he must now also announce that God is going to punish Israel severely for the bitter offense it has caused him.

Finally ch. 13 stands well isolated from what has gone before. "Baal" [→§20], "idols" and "calves" are again the reproaches against Ephraim (vv. 1f) and the complacency that leads to them forgetting God (v. 6), who is still their "God from the land of Egypt," the only God and savior that they know (vv. 4f). If he now attacks them like wild animals (vv. 7f) then not even their king can help them—the king that God gave them in his wrath and took from them again in his anger (vv. 9-11). The fundamental rejection of the monarchy can hardly be more sharply worded. Death now comes upon Ephraim in various forms (vv. 12-15), and the royal city of Samaria must fall because it has rebelled against God (14.1).

But this cannot be the last word. Once again there is talk of repentance. But this time God himself invites Israel to turn back to him [→§16] (only here in Hosea does the word *šûb* appear in the imperative, 14.2[1]), to confess itself guilty before him and to abandon its failed attempts to find help in false allies or false gods (vv. 2-4*). But before Israel can follow this invitation, God already comes towards it with the assurance that he himself will heal Israel's apostasy (*m'šûbāh*), that his anger has been assuaged and that he will turn his whole love and affection to Israel so that it will have a fruitful and peaceful future (vv. 4-7). The pointlessness of the worship of idols is once again quite evident when God says: "What more has Ephraim to do with idols? I will answer him and care for him" (v. 8). So with its announcement of God's affection for his people in the future, this last chapter once again picks up the message emphasized before in chs. 3 and 11 of the collection of Hosea texts.

Hosea's words have come to an end. Readers will pass on to subsequent generations the question: "Who is wise enough to understand these things?" (v. 9). Within this question lies at the same time the call to be concerned with the wisdom [→§19] necessary to understand all this. The reader will then be led by the insight that God's ways are "straight" and that it is crucial to walk in them as a "righteous person" and not to stumble and fall as a "rebellious person." In all its multilayered variety the Hosea writing aims to lead people to understand and follow this (cf. Sheppard 1980, 129ff).

There are two themes in particular that dominate the Hosea document: the reproach of the Baal cult and the call to repent. The two things stand in a marked contrast to each other: Israel must repent from its false worship—and when it repents, what use will the idols be to it? A further characteristic element in Hosea's proclamation are the backward references to the early history of Israel. Like no other prophet Hosea again and again relates Israel's present situation to the beginnings of its history, and he also sees his own ministry as a prophet in the Mosaic tradition. The Hosea writing thus makes an important contribution to the creation and maintenance of continuity within the canon of the Hebrew Bible. At the same time it presents particular themes for the collection of the Book of the Twelve as a whole, which are picked up again with varying degrees of emphasis in the writings that follow.

5.3 The Day of the LORD is darkness and light (Joel, Amos, Obadiah – and Jonah)

5.3.1 The Day of the LORD is near – salvation is only on Zion (Joel)

While the reader is still pondering the wisdom statement of Hos 14.10[9], again the call to hear resounds (Joel 1.2). It is introduced as the "word of the LORD" to the prophet, of whom we learn only the name: Joel, son of Pethuel (v. 1). The situation has completely changed: a horrendous plague of locusts has come over the land, which forms the occasion for an extended lament (1.2–2.11). Corn, wine and oil, which God had promised Israel for a blissful future (Hos 2.24), have been destroyed (Joel 1.10). So the prophet calls "again" to repentance and penitence (2.12), as Hosea had previously done (Hos 14.2f★), after a first attempt to repent on Israel's part had proved insufficiently serious (6.1-6). The liturgical framework of the penitence (Joel 1.13f; 2.12, 15-17) is reminiscent of the phraseology in Hosea (6.1; 14.3★), as is the talk of the "rending" of the heart (Joel 2.12★; Hos 13.8).

But now this penitential ceremony is held in Jerusalem, in the temple on Mount Zion (Joel 2.15-17). The connection between Hosea and Joel bridges the common history of Israel and Judah. Now in Joel the whole thing is viewed from a new, all-embracing angle. It is the "Day of the LORD" that is coming and is already near (1.15; 2.1f, 11; 3.4[2.31]; 4.14, 18[3.14, 18]). Other prophets too already spoke of this day (Isa 2.12ff; 13.6, 9 etc.), but it is not mentioned in Hosea. It is evident here that Joel is not only connected backwards with Hosea but also forwards with Amos. For in the latter there is talk of the Day of

Yhwh, and it is clear that the prophet is linking up with something that is not only familiar to his audience but which also has a very special, positive significance: "Woe to you who long for the Day of the LORD! Why do you long for the Day of the LORD?" (Amos 5.18) [→**284**]. For the reader of the Book of the Twelve the sudden mention of this day is not surprising, since he has previously read the chapters of Joel in which everything is centered around this day. It is quite conceivable that Joel was placed in this position precisely for that reason, in order to form a bridge between Hosea and Amos.

The Day of Yhwh is a terrible catastrophe which destroys all the basics of life. What is really horrifying about it is that this catastrophe is recognized as "the Day of the LORD": "What a dreadful day!" (1.15). The whole horror of it comes to expression in a play on words: the day comes *kešod miššadday* "like violence from a violent person" (Buber), like devastation at the hands of the Almighty (cf. Isa 13.6). But God himself calls his people to repentance: "Return to me (*šubû 'āday*) with all your heart" (2.12), and the prophet adds: "Perhaps he may think better of it" (lit.: "Who knows, he repents and regrets it," *miyôdēaʻ yāšûb weniḥam* v. 14). The word of God's "regret" sounds again here, which previously played such a central role in Hosea (Hos 11.8) [→**272**]. The prophet has justified his own appeal to repentance (2.13) with a quotation from the great crisis situation in the early history of Israel when God proclaimed his name before Moses on Sinai: "for he is gracious and compassionate, slow to anger and abounding in love" (cf. Ex 34.6) [→**63**]; the prophet has added here: "and he relents from sending calamity" and with this has justified the hope expressed in the "perhaps" with God's fundamental deed of forgiveness which enabled Israel's existence before God in the first place.

The call to repent leads to a great ceremony of penitence and lament on Zion (2.15-17), which climaxes in the urgent prayer: "Spare your people, O LORD. Do not make your inheritance an object of scorn." The shame will also consist in the fact that the nations might say: "Where is their God?" And God is merciful. He is "jealous" for his land, which has suffered so greatly (v. 18) and will not deliver up his people to shame among the nations (v. 19). He gives the land fruitfulness again and as it were replaces the inhabitants' lost years of harvest (v. 25) so that they eat and are satisfied and can praise the name of the Lord (v. 26).

But it is not just a matter of being satisfied. Rather, they will "know that I am in Israel, that I am the LORD your God, and that there is no

other" (v. 27) [→**§15**]. This extended "acknowledgment formula" forms
the conclusion and the climax of this first dramatic chapter of the "Day
of the LORD." Israel has acknowledged that in the threat to which it
was exposed, the Day of Yhwh was being announced. It showed re-
morse, repented, and God heard its prayers. And as a result of this
hearing and saving Israel will now recognize that Yhwh, the only
God, is in their midst. The same acknowledgment formula will form a
concluding emphasis in Joel (4.17★).

But beforehand there is further talk of the "Day of the LORD." Joel
is a sort of collection of texts about the "Day of the LORD" which
view this phenomenon from various angles and are not simply ordered
in a chronological and thematic sequence. Twice a new beginning is
clearly indicated, without these new beginnings however being dis-
cernibly related to each other (3.1[2.28]; 3[4].1).

"It will happen afterwards" (3.1★). This phraseology is quite unusual
in the Hebrew Bible, and it remains open what sort of point in time is
meant by this. An eschatological interpretation suggests itself, as is
expressed in the New Testament adoption of this text: "It will happen
in the last days" (Acts 2.17) [→**§22**]. There is an odd tension here between the introductory "Afterwards" and the "before the Day of the
LORD comes" that follows (3.4★). It is, as it were, an interim time, a
time of eschatological anticipation. What will now happen has reper-
cussions far beyond Israel. God will pour out his spirit on "all flesh,"
i.e. on the whole of humanity (cf. Gen 6.12f, 17 etc.), on old and
young alike, the free and the enslaved (3.1f★). The effect will be that
the recipients of the divine spirit will behave like prophets (*nibb'û*).
Here Moses' desire is effectively fulfilled: "I wish that all the LORD's
people were prophets and that the LORD would put his Spirit on
them!" (Num 11.29) [→**51**]. But much more than that happens, because now the pouring out of the spirit comes upon "all flesh." But
then gigantic changes in nature will announce that the "great and
dreadful Day of the LORD" is about to dawn (3.4★). Unlike the first
description of the Day of Yhwh in chs. 1f, here nothing is said of what
happens on the earth, whether a destructive plague or hostile armies
(as alluded to in 2.4-9). Here the "Day of the LORD" is a veritably
cosmic event which comes upon the whole of humanity.

Who can escape this eschatological judgment? It is this question that
the whole thing is leading up to, and it is answered: "Everyone who
calls on the name of the LORD will be saved" (3.5★). The angle of view
again narrows completely to Zion [→**§14**]: "for on Mount Zion and in

Jerusalem there will be deliverance (*p'lêṭah*, perhaps better: a host of the saved)." This means that those will be saved, and only those, who call upon the name of the Lord. In the context they may come from all the nations, from "all flesh"; and it will be those who have been enabled by the pouring out of the Spirit of God to call on the name of God in this situation of utmost danger. God will answer this call, as it says at the conclusion: "whom the LORD calls." But it will only be a host of the saved, a remnant.

In Joel the Day of Yhwh is again shown from another side: as a day of divine judgment on Israel's/Judah's enemies "on account of my inheritance, my people Israel" (3.1-15). The nations are separately called together into the "Valley of Jehoshaphat" (*y'hôšāpāṭ*, "Yhwh judges," v. 2), in which God will sit in judgment over them (v. 12) and which will become the "valley of decision" (v. 14) when the Day of Yhwh comes. And it is only when the court case has concluded, when Yhwh "roars from Zion" (v. 16a), that Israel comes into view, for which God is a refuge and stronghold. Here again the extended acknowledgment formula appears (v. 17; cf. 2.27), which speaks of God's dwelling on Zion and of the holiness of Jerusalem, and for which a "utopian" prospect is to follow (vv. 18-21).

This is, as it were, the other side of the Day of Yhwh. In chs. 1f this day was described as a day of judgment over Israel, which Israel could avoid by means of fasting and repentance. In ch. 4[3] it is judgment over Israel's enemies, Israel itself not being affected. Between the two, strangely unconnected, is the concise depiction of the eschatological (in the narrower sense) Day of Yhwh in ch. 3 [2.28-32]. All three perspectives were present in Israel and have been brought together here in Joel. This is clearly the real function of this writing: to present the Day of Yhwh from its various sides. At the same time the central role of Zion is significant. In each of the three descriptions of the Day of Yhwh it has a key function. In 2.15 the horn is blown on Zion to launch the fasting assembly, which finally leads to the rescue of Israel; in 4.16* the "roaring" of Yhwh from Zion announces that Israel is exempted from judgment and that God continues to live "on Mount Zion, my holy mountain" (v. 17); and according to 3.5[2.32] the host of the saved, the eschatological remnant, will gather on Zion.

By virtue of the early situation of Joel in the Book of the Twelve, the "Day of the LORD" theme gains great importance for the whole collection. This applies in the first place to the more closely surrounding texts. The only passage in which Amos mentions the Day of Yhwh

(Amos 5.18, 20) [→284] is not now in isolation but is given light from Joel; and Obadiah, the short writing that follows Amos, in which the Day of Yhwh is the only topic, forms together with Joel a sort of framework around Amos (cf. Schart 1998, ch. 8) and is thereby tied into a context of varying viewpoints on the Day of Yhwh. But in the further course of the Book of the Twelve too this topic appears at two more significant points. In Zephaniah it again forms one of the main themes and thereby stands at the end of the partial collection of pre-exilic writings within the book. And finally in Malachi 3 it forms the conclusion to the whole collection and evidently also to the whole prophetic canon in the Hebrew Bible.

With the keyword "Zion," Joel launches a further important topic, which has not been met in Hosea. This at the same time forms a bridge to Amos (cf. Schart 1998, 163ff).

5.3.2 God calls Israel to account (Amos)

The transition from Joel to Amos is not surprising in the context of the Book of the Twelve. The dramatic word "The LORD will roar from Zion and thunder from Jerusalem" from Joel 3.16 is repeated in Amos 1.2. Here it leads on to a cycle of prophetic oracles which are first directed against other nations but then also against Judah and Israel. These oracles continue what was introduced in the last chapter of Joel: the divine judgment against nations [→§20] that have attacked Israel—and now other nations too. The beginning of Amos can be read precisely as the execution of the proclamation that God will sit in judgment "over all the nations on every side" (Joel 3.12); for it is precisely against them that the first words of judgment are directed: against the Arameans of Damascus (Amos 1.3-5), the Philistines of Gaza (vv. 6-8), Tyre (vv. 9f), Edom (vv. 11f), the Ammonites (vv. 13-15) and Moab (2.1-3). They are all accused of having committed "crimes against humanity" with the defenseless and women. And on account of these misdemeanors divine judgment is announced. This time we read "I will not turn (it) back" (1.3, 6, 9 etc.). What does this "it" refer to? In the context of Joel the reader thinks of the announcement of the "Day of YHWH," which will come inescapably upon the nations. Later the reader will again remember the inexorable sound of this statement when the end of God's readiness to forgive is pronounced: "I will spare them no longer" (7.8; 8.2) [→286]. Thus the oracles to the nations in chs. 1f and the visions in chs. 7f form as it were a bracket around the main part of Amos (cf. Jeremias 1995b, 157ff).

The oracles to the nations move resolutely (via the inserted Judah strophe, 2.4f) in the direction of the Israel strophe in 2.6-16. The prophetic speech is thereby given quite a different emphasis than in Joel. There, there was no talk of the sins of Israel, but now they are set out in detail. Unlike the preceding oracles to the nations, here the concern is not with sins against adherents of other nations but against members of their own nations. This shows quite a different point of view than in Hosea. It is not cultic transgressions that are in the foreground but social ones. The complaints are directed above all against the oppression and exploitation of the socially and economically disadvantaged: misuse of the rules of fiefdom, disadvantage in legal cases, sexual exploitation of dependants, squandering of what has been illegally acquired (vv. 6-8). The oppressed are designated by the most varied expressions: they are "in the right" (*ṣaddîq*), poor (*'ebyôn*), insignificant (*dal*), wretched (*'anaw*). Besides their social components these expressions all have religious components, since it is precisely these oppressed groups that God wants to help to gain their rights. The religious element is also evident in this behavior being referred to as desecration of the divine name (v. 7) and in the fact that the orgiastic feasts take place at the sanctuary (v. 8a and b).

This behavior by the Israelites stands in stark contrast to what would have been expected of them. Amos confronts them with some basic elements of the Israelite creed: God first set the preconditions for Israel's life in its land by leading it out of Egypt, guiding it through a long period in the wilderness and finally making it possible for it to take possession of the land (2.9f). He gave them people who should have been the religious leaders and examples, prophets and Nazirites; but the Israelites prevented them from doing what God had commissioned them to do (vv. 11f). As in Hosea, in Amos too the crucial reproaches and complaints are formulated in the opposition with the story of Israel's beginnings. Israel will therefore experience the punishment of God. Unlike in the case of the other nations it will not be a fire that brings about destruction (cf. 1.4, 7, 9 etc.) but God himself will intervene: "I will crush you" (2.13). The depiction of an earthquake moves on into a terrible military catastrophe from which at most only a few naked refugees will be able to escape (vv. 14-16).

Israel's end seems to have arrived. But before the word of the "end" (*qēṣ*) is declared (8.2) [→**286**], a multi-layered and tension-filled collec-

tion of prophetic sayings follows, which were evidently spoken at
various times and for a variety of occasions. Between the sharp critiques and announcements of divine judgment texts and individual
phrases again and again appear in which an albeit generally weak perspective into the future emerges.

At the beginning of this collection stands a brief word of extraordinary importance. The divine speech again recalls the exodus from
Egypt as the beginning of the history of God's dealings with Israel
(3.1) and names the consequence that arises from this for the relationship between God and Israel: "You only have I chosen of all the families of the earth" (v. 2a). The leading out of Egypt justifies the unique
relationship between God and Israel. This came to expression before
in Hosea: "I am the LORD, your God, from Egypt" (Hos 12.10)
[→273]; so Israel "knows" (*yāda'* 13.4) no other God. In Amos we now
read that God "knew," *yāda'*, i.e. "chose," Israel [→§6], the verb selected
here bringing to expression the close, really intimate relationship.

This fundamental statement of faith is followed by a quite unexpected additional clause: "therefore I will punish you for all your sins"
(Amos 3.2b). The election of Israel is not just a privilege; it means at
the same time and to a special degree responsibility towards God, the
duty to live in accordance with the will of God. Israel had not fully
met this responsibility, as Amos has already emphatically pointed out
(2.6-8, 11f). So God now calls Israel to account (*pāqad*). This is not a
retraction of the election; on the contrary, a weighty, far-reaching
consequence of the election is pointed out, though a different consequence than is generally drawn. One might call this the prophetic
consequence. Many interpreters have therefore taken Amos 3.2 as such
a central sentence that it could have served as a motto for the whole of
Amos or even the whole of Israelite prophecy (cf. Jeremias 1995a,
32f). At this point it has the function of introducing what follows.

Before the collection of divine and prophetic sayings to and against
Israel that now follow, which form the center of Amos (chs. 3–6),
there is a fundamental statement about the inescapability of the prophetic commission. With its graphic statements about the cause-effect
relationship (vv. 3-6a) 3.3-8 is resolutely focused on the last sentence:
"The lion roars—who is not afraid? The LORD YHWH speaks, who
will not be a prophet?" Like Jeremiah Amos speaks here of the inescapable necessity of speaking as a prophet. As with Jeremiah, behind
this statement one can discern resistance and hostility to his message

[→**229**], which is only to be expected given the sharpness of his message of judgment and his uncompromising critique of his contemporaries.

Cause and effect are clearly recognizable even amongst all the calamity that is falling on the people. There is no disaster (*rā'āh*) that God has not brought about (v. 6b). An interpretative intermediate sentence extends this insight. God announces his "verdict" (*sôd*) in each case beforehand "to his servants the prophets" (v. 7) so that they will pass it on. But the Israelites stopped the prophets from conveying their message (2.12), so that they have not heard the warning. But Amos is not swayed. He works as a prophet because God has spoken (3.8). And he also announces the disaster that God is going to bring upon Israel.

It is the upper echelons in the capital city of Samaria that will be affected first, whose luxurious lifestyle is depicted dramatically. In their splendid, ivory-bedecked houses ("palaces," 3.10f, 15) they sit and lie on their beds (v. 12). They no longer know (*yāda'*) how to do right; instead they amass violent deeds and oppression (v. 10). The women too, whom Amos calls (fat) "cows of Bashan" (4.1) participate in the oppression of the poor and wretched in the pursuit of their own well-being. The land will therefore be exposed to the destructions of war (3.11, 15), from which no one will escape alive (v. 12). The women will also be led away in the shameful procession of deportees (4.2f).

It is above all the offense against the basic requirements of social justice that Amos is emphasizing (cf. already 2.6-8) and which he names here as the reason for the impending calamity. But in the process the altars of Beth-El will also be destroyed (3.14); for the cult in Beth-El and Gilgal, which Hosea already loudly denounced (Hos 4.15) [→**269**], is in reality a sin, a crime in fact (Amos 4.4; the verb *pāša'* recalls the crime of the nations, *peša'*, in 1.13ff), and does not serve to be "pleasing" to God but only to those presenting the sacrifices (v. 5).

Far too often the Israelites have already given proof of their stubbornness. In a litany-like reiteration, in the following review of the multiple catastrophes that God has brought upon Israel we read: "but you did not turn back to me"—despite hunger (4.6), drought (vv. 7f), catastrophic harvests (v. 9), pestilence (v. 10) and terrible destructions comparable with Sodom and Gomorrah (v. 11).

Only here in Amos does the theme of repentance (*šûb*) resound, and then only in the negative statement: you did not repent—and now it is too late! Israel has to prepare to face its God (v. 12). It remains oddly in the air what is then going to happen. Will it be a meeting with God like that which Israel had to prepare for on Sinai (Ex 19.11, 15) [→**52**]? Or the final judgment?

The text does not leave the reader time to ponder this question for very long, but surprisingly—as it were "on the threshold between life and death" (Jeremias 1995a, 56)—strikes up a hymn, praise to God the creator and Lord of the world and of history (4.13). At first sight this seems to be a μετάβασις εἰς ἄλλο γένος. On closer inspection, however, the hymn shows precisely such sides of God's creative activity that correspond with the ambivalent statement of the preceding verse. God creates the reliable (the mountains) and the ungraspable (the wind); he can turn the light of morning suddenly into darkness and thereby reverse, as it were, the creation process of Gen 1.3f [→**14**]; he strides over the heights of the world showing his superior power (cf. Mic 1.3f) [→**293**]; and he is not only the distant creator, but he informs humans of his plan (cf. 3.7).

At the same time the hymn forms a dramatic conclusion to the collection of prophetic sayings that began with the call to listen in 3.1. It is with the same call that a new collection of prophetic sayings begins (5.1). Now the prophet speaks from his own point of view after the disaster has set in. He sounds a lament for Israel, a dirge (*qînāh*, v. 2) [→*In* **127**], as if Israel has already been decimated by a military catastrophe (v. 3). But then he immediately turns back to those standing in the present with an urgent word from God: "Seek me and live!" (v. 4). There is still a chance—the only one there could possibly be: to live in reference to God. It is extremely impressive how in the midst of the announcements of the ineluctable, indeed already commencing, divine judgment Amos once again calls upon Israel to choose the way of life, "or (*pen*) he will sweep through the house of Joseph like fire." Then in the reiteration of this call in vv. 14f we read: "Perhaps (*'ûlay*) the LORD God Almighty will have mercy."

This "perhaps" is still a possibility. But the possibility is not opened up through people seeking Beth-El and Gilgal (and Beer-Sheba) (5.5). These sanctuaries, after all, Amos had already branded as places where worship did not take place but "crimes" were committed (4.4f). Now he says, in a macabre play on words, that Gilgal must go into exile (*gāloh yigleh*) and that Beth-El, the "House of God" will become a (*bêt-*)*'āwen* "(House of) Disaster" (or of wickedness, cf. Hos 4.15) [→**269**]. "Seeking God" means, rather, seeking "good" and hating evil, concretely:

ensuring the maintenance of justice (5.14f). The "perhaps" applies only in relation to this kind of seeking.

And now it also applies to a "remnant" (5.15). For this dual call, to seek God, stands in the context of thoroughly negative judgments about those addressed. As was the case earlier in Amos, again and again it is reproaches regarding social misdemeanors towards the poor and the helpless (vv. 11f) that are emphatically brought out as offenses against "justice" (*mišpāṭ*) and "righteousness" (*ṣˈdāqāh*) (vv. 7, 10), in sharp contrast with their own luxury (v. 11). But they will no longer be able to enjoy this luxury. The collection of sayings ends where it began: with the lament (vv. 16f). When God strides through Israel's midst (v. 17), as he once strode through Egypt when he struck down the firstborn there (Ex 12.12) [→**45**], then Israel will know what it means to meet God (4.12). But the "perhaps" is not revoked.

The point has now been reached when there must be talk of the "Day of the LORD." The mighty, disaster-bringing intervention of Yhwh reminds the reader of the descriptions of the Day of Yhwh in Joel [→**275**]. The ambivalence of the displays of Yhwh's power has been expressed there many times. One could then hope that on his day Yhwh would destroy the enemies, as is dramatically described at the end of Joel. But Amos opposes such expectations with a clear No. When the Day of Yhwh comes, it can only mean disaster for Israel, only darkness and not light (5.18, 20), unavoidable calamity, from which there can be no escape (v. 19).

Nor is the cult able to save. God takes no "pleasure" in the sacrifices of these Israelites; he "hates" them, he does not like to "smell" them, i.e. acknowledge them as a "pleasing odor" (Lev 1.9 etc; cf. also Gen 8.21), because "justice and righteousness" have disappeared, which should spring forth in Israel like a never-ending stream (5.21-23). Like Hosea (Hos 6.6) [→**269**] and equally Isaiah (Isa 1.10-17) [→**169**] and Jeremiah (Jer 7.21-23) [→**209**], Amos rejects sacrifices which do not correspond to the social and legitimate behavior required of Israel. He does not reject the sacrificial cult *per se* any more than he does these. But he agrees with the whole prophetic tradition that sacrifices alone are of no use and that for God the doing of justice and righteousness— or in Hosea's words: mercy and acknowledgment of God—are more important and are the only life-savers. That is why the critique of the sacrificial cult appears precisely at this point in the face of the impending Day of Yhwh.

A further group of texts follows against the carefree and the self-assured (on Zion and) in Samaria (6.1). Amos again castigates their life of luxury (vv. 4-6) which, however, will soon come to an end when they are taken off into exile (v. 7) and the whole city becomes a morgue (vv. 8-10). Small, local successes like that of Lo-Dabar (v. 13) will not be able to put a stop to the military catastrophe affecting the whole of the land of Israel (v. 14).

Once again something entirely new begins in Amos: "the sovereign LORD showed me" (7.1). Amos reports visions granted him in which he is directly involved [→*In* 121]. In four similarly formed vision reports, presented in pairs, the growing threat to Israel is paraded, which finally leads to the ineluctable end. Twice the catastrophes are natural ones: a plague of locusts (vv. 1f) and an all-destroying drought (v. 4). They are explicitly described as being brought about by God, so that their punitive character is clearly evident. But Amos intervenes. He assumes the intercessory office of the prophet as had been extremely intensively exercised by Moses before him [→62] and as was later forbidden to Jeremiah [→210]. "LORD YHWH, forgive!" it says the first time (v. 2b). But when a catastrophe of veritably cosmic dimensions breaks out—the fire consumes the "great deep"—, he can only call out: "LORD YHWH, I beg you, stop!" (v. 5). The justification for his petition is the same both times: "How will Jacob survive? He is so small!" There is no longer any talk of a hoped-for repentance of Israel. Amos only appeals to God's pity with the helplessness of "little" Jacob—and he is successful. But not because God thinks his punishment inappropriate, but because he "regrets" it (*niham*, vv. 3, 6). As before in Hosea (Hos 11.8) [→272], here too there is talk of the "self-control" of God, with which he himself holds back from carrying out the punishment: "This will not happen." But here too the escalation from the first to the second vision is again discernible. The second time, a "this too" is added, which has at the same time a reinforcing and limiting effect. In the overall thrust it is clear that this means: just this once; God's patience is then definitively exhausted.

Amos has understood. In the two visions that follow (7.7f; 8.1f) he tries not to intervene any more. Here he is drawn into the visionary happenings in a different way, as in response to God's question "What do you see, Amos?" he has to give a name to what he has seen (cf. Jer 1.11, 13) [→205]. The first time it is a metal (*'anāk*), either a plumb-line (the customary interpretation) or tin, as used for weapons (cf.

Jeremias 1995a, 101f). God will "set it among my people Israel," and this means that the sparing has an end: "I can no longer pass over it (to spare it)." In this "no longer pass over" (*'ābar l'*) the reader hears the echo of "I will pass through your midst" (*'ābar b'*, 5.17). This is even clearer in the fourth vision (8.1f). Amos sees a basket with rich summer fruits (*qayiṣ*). Its meaning: "The end (*qēṣ*) has come for my people Israel." Here it is expressed with absolute sharpness and clarity: the end has come.

Between the third and fourth visions, however, there is a section of a special kind (7.10-17), the location of which in this context is significant. It is the only narrative section in Amos. It tells of a dramatic conflict between Amos and the priest Amaziah at the sanctuary in Beth-El, in which the concern is not only with a conflict between the persons involved but with a clash between the prophet speaking at God's behest and the representative of the state cult, who is acting on the authority of the king. Amaziah wants to forbid Amos to appear as a prophet (*hinnābē'*) in Beth-El. He thereby does precisely what Amos reproached the Israelites for in his first accusatory speech: that they say to the prophets: "Do not speak as prophets!" (2.12) [→282]. God has commissioned Amos to speak as a prophet "to my people Israel" (7.15). By trying to prevent him from appearing as a prophet in Israel's state sanctuary, Amaziah is opposing this divine commission. So he is hit by a divine word of judgment, according to which his family and he himself will as it were in advance suffer the impending fate of Israel (v. 17).

So official Israel here rejects the offer of prophetic admonition and direction, thus squandering its last opportunity to stop the "end," of which the fourth vision speaks (8.1f). The texts that follow also merely add detail to the already definitively announced end. Once again offences against the poor and needy are mentioned (8.4-6), new aspects being added, picking up on 2.6f (unfair trade) (v. 5). God will never forget all this (v. 7)—and then a depiction of eschatological cosmic events follows (v. 8). In their introductory formulae, "On that day" (vv. 9f, 13f) and "The days are coming" (vv. 11f), the following sections re-echo the motif of the "Day of YHWH" [→284].

An especially dramatic depiction of the end is again introduced as a vision (9.1-4). The prophet sees Yhwh himself standing at the altar and smashing the capital of the pillars; this produces an earthquake from which no one can escape. Even extreme escape routes into the world of the dead or into heaven, to the summit of Mount Carmel or to the bottom of the sea provide no way out. God's eyes no longer rest on Israel "for good" but "for evil." For Israel has not sought "good" but "evil" (5.14). It must now suffer the consequences.

The depiction of cosmic changes (8.8f) finally takes the shape of a hymn which moves into statements about God's acts as creator (9.5f) and recalls 4.13 (and 5.8). It concludes, like 4.13, with the solemn formula: "YHWH is his name." This points out in an impressive way that the destruction of Israel is not the real aim of God's actions but that the concern in all this—and also in what else happens in the world apart from Israel's "end"—is with God and his name.

This has the effect of a formal conclusion, and perhaps at a particular stage in the development of the Amos writing it was in fact intended as a conclusion. But the message passed on in the name of the prophet Amos does not end here. Readers are bound to ask what happens after this. What does it mean that Israel is at an end? First of all it means that Israel does not enjoy an absolute special place before God (9.7f). Before God Israel is not more than all other nations, e.g. the distant Cushites (Luther: "Moors"); and God has not only brought Israel to its present place of residence but also the hostile neighbors, the Philistines and the Arameans (cf. 1.3-5, 6-8) [→**279**]. If he now destroys the "sinful kingdom" of Israel, then he will certainly not destroy the "house of Jacob." The political entity of "Israel" will come to an end, but not the descendants of the chosen patriarchs. But there will be a sifting: as in a sieve the "sinful" will be retained and delivered up to annihilation, and only what is durable in God's eyes will come through (vv. 9f). Here the idea of "remnant" crops up again, which was expressed earlier in 5.15 [→**284**]. There, there was talk of a "perhaps"; here the hope is more confidently formulated, but again only with reference to that part of the house of Israel that passes the sifting.

And then attention turns on into the future. Once again we read "On that day" (v. 11) and "The days are coming" (v. 13), but this time the phrases introduce hopeful perspectives. The ruined "tent of David" will be erected again "as it used to be." The ideal kingdom of David will give the "house of Jacob" (i.e. Judah) a national shape again, even if only in a modest form, but still enough for it to be able to assert itself against hostile neighbors.

And finally the view passes beyond the real earthly relationships and draws a picture of paradisiacal fertility, where seed and harvest follow each other directly and the mountains and hills drip with wine (v. 13). The peaceful future [→**§22**] of "my people Israel," whose fate God will turn (*šûb š'bût*), is as it were embedded in the picture of a world in which there is no longer any deprivation, poverty or threat (vv. 14f).

This conclusion shows clear connections with Joel. The picture of the mountains dripping with wine is also found in the concluding section there (Joel 4.18★). Close to it in both texts there is a saying about Edom (Joel 4.19★; Amos 9.12), which appears repeatedly in the Hebrew Bible as a particular "close" enemy of Israel's or Judah's. With this key term a bridge is made also to the following writing, Obadiah, in which Edom constitutes the main theme.

5.3.3 Rescue only for the house of Jacob? (Obadiah)

"Vision of Obadiah"—this shortest of all the superscriptions in the Book of the Twelve introduces its shortest writing. It is connected with the preceding writings by two key terms. First, Edom: this neighbor of Israel's and Judah's appears in Amos among the nations reproached for their crimes (Amos 1.1f) [→**279**]. There, there is talk of Edom's transgression against its "brother" (Edom is coterminous with Esau, cf. Gen 25.30; 36.1 etc.), whom it persecuted ruthlessly and mercilessly with the sword. Joel speaks of Edom's violence (*hāmās*) against the "sons of Judah" and of the spilling of innocent blood (Joel 3.19). In Obadiah too Esau is now reproached for his violence (*hāmās*) against his "brother Jacob" (v. 10) and his glee at Israel's calamity (v. 12). (It seems that events in the conquest of Jerusalem by the Babylonians in 586 BCE are in mind here.) The theme of Edom occupies more than half of Obadiah.

It is connected with the second key term, which also links Obadiah with Joel and Amos: the "Day of the LORD." This day is shaped entirely in accordance with the picture developed in Joel 4[3] [→**278**]: as Yhwh's judgment on Israel's enemies. First it is Edom that is "done to, as you have done (to others)" (v. 15b). Then attention turns to "all nations" for which the Day of Yhwh is now close at hand (v. 15a). They must now "drink" (v. 16), the "cup of wrath," that is, of which Jeremiah spoke (Jer 25.15-29) [→**219**], right to the bitter end. "But on Mount Zion will be deliverance" (v. 17). This quotation from Joel 2.32★ is given a fundamentally different meaning here in Obadiah. In Joel, on Mount Zion the host of the saved will assemble, "who call on the name of the LORD." But in Obadiah it is only the house of Jacob, which will again extend its possession from there. In fact, reunited with the house of Joseph (i.e. the northern kingdom), it will become fire and consume the house of Esau like straw, so that no one will escape (v. 18). The returnees from exile will retake possession of everything round about them (vv. 19f) and finally rule the mountainous land of Esau from Zion (v. 21).

For the reader who moves from Joel and Amos to Obadiah, it is irritating how one-sidedly the theme of the Day of Yhwh, which was elucidated from the most varied angles in Joel, is now apparently focused down to a single aspect. In addition, contrary to the warning of Amos (Amos 5.18-20) [→**284**], the "house of Jacob" now stands entirely on the side of the victors. This bias is, however, corrected, or at least mitigated, by the insertion into the present context. The reader still has, after all, the warning of Amos still ringing in his or her ears, and he also understands that in Obad 15f all the nations will be involved in the events of the Day of Yhwh, so that Edom appears as representative of the powers that set themselves up against the people of God (cf. Childs 1979, 414f). In addition, the statements about taking possession (*yāraš*, Obad 17, 19f) clearly echo the conclusion to Amos, where we read: "so that they may possess the remnant of Edom" (Amos 9.12); there too this statement is connected with the proclamation of a permanent residence of the people of Israel in the land that God has given them and in which it has planted them (vv. 14f). And the conclusion of Joel too contrasts the permanent residence of Judah in Jerusalem (Joel 3.20⋆) with the desolation of Edom (v. 19). So it is particularly the one-sided emphasis on this aspect, combined with the haughty vaunting over the neighboring arch-enemy, that produces such an irritating effect in Obadiah.

But now its context is proximity to Amos, so that the reader will not too easily be seduced into a triumphalistic nationalistic understanding of the prophetic message. In addition, the short writing has another concluding sentence: "But the kingdom will be the LORD's." In the final analysis it will only be God himself who rules over Jacob/Israel, over Esau/Edom and, as we read in Ps 22.29⋆ (which Obadiah cites here), "over the nations."

5.3.4 Rescue for the heathen too? (Jonah)

Once again a "word of the LORD" comes, this time to Jonah, son of Amittai. The word contains a commission: "Go!" (1.2), similar to the first word to Hosea, "Go, take…" Hos 1.2 [→**266**]. But then everything is quite different. God orders Jonah to go into the "great city" of Nineveh and "preach against it" (*qārā' 'al*) because its wickedness has come up before God as the wickedness of Sodom and Gomorrah once did (Gen 18.20f) [→**28**]. Jonah, however, does not obey the divine commission, but flees. He presents as it were the counterpart to the prophet as described by Amos: the one that simply *has* to work as a prophet when God speaks (Amos 3.8) [→**281**]. And then to start with there is no longer any talk of divine or prophetic words but the story is told of what happens when Jonah flees. Its narrative character distinguishes Jonah from all other prophetic writings and books. But it is a highly reflective form of story-telling, so that one may describe the writing as "theological prophetic narrative" (Simon 1994, 34).

Why does Jonah flee? The narrative does not give a reason. Is Jonah afraid of the great task, to go to the foreign, hostile metropolis and announce divine judgment to it? Or might Jonah be compared with Jeremiah, who simply falls apart under the burden of his prophetic commission and wishes it would go away? (Jer 20.9) [→**215**]. The narrative does not say. The reader has to leave this question open, as the narrator does. He has to accompany Jonah on his strange trip. First at the harbor and on a ship that leads him "away from YHWH," in the opposite direction, towards Tarshish, the end of the then known world (1.3). But Yhwh does not let Jonah off so easily. He sends a great storm which brings the ship to the brink of destruction.

In their fear the mariners pray "each to his own god"; but Jonah does not pray, he sleeps (v. 5). This contrast gives expression to one of the themes of this complex narrative: the relationship to the "heathen." Here they are depicted as pious and god-fearing. And when Jonah has confessed that he worships the "God of heaven, who made the sea and the dry land," and when the mariners have finally thrown him into the sea on his own advice and the storm has subsided as a result, then they "fear" Yhwh and present him with sacrifices and vows (v. 16).

Jonah's flight is at an end. But this does not mean the end of the divine commission. God sends a great fish which swallows Jonah and finally brings him back to the point at which his flight began (ch. 2). And now Jonah prays, for the first time (v. 3). In the first chapter he did bravely play the role of a witness and accepted his own guilt, but he did not pray. Now he prays a psalm. Surprisingly this is not a psalm of lament or petition but a prayer of thanksgiving [→**§18**]. Jonah is still in the depths of the sea (vv. 3-7) but he is already sure that his prayer is being heard and that he will be saved (vv. 3, 7b). The interpreters disagree as to whether this psalm "originally" belongs with Jonah or was only added later. In the writing as a whole, at any rate, it forms the crucial bridge to the second part. "Salvation comes from the LORD" is the last word of the psalm (v. 10*), before the fish delivers Jonah up again and spews him out on the dry land (v. 11*).

And everything starts all over again. In the same words as at the beginning the word of the Lord comes to Jonah "the second time," as it expressly says (3.1). The commission is the same, too: "Go to the great city of Nineveh and proclaim to it the message I give you" (v. 2). But the reaction is now that of a true prophet: "Jonah obeyed the word of the LORD and went to Nineveh." We are only made party to a single sentence of his preaching: "Forty more days and Nineveh will be destroyed" (v. 4), literally: tipped over, turned upside down, as was the case with Sodom and Gomorrah (Gen 19.25; Amos 4.11). And now something totally unexpected happens: the people of Nineveh believe this message and repent. It is an impressive, even touching depiction of how the whole of Nineveh goes around in garments of repentance and everyone fasts, including the animals. The king calls for repentance (*šûb*), for them to "give up their evil ways and their violence"; for "Who knows? God may yet relent (lit.: "repent," v. 9). The king as it were "quotes" Joel (2.14) [→276]. But this time this expression of hope for a gracious "relenting" of God comes not from a prophet but from the heathen king of the "great city," which is full of wickedness and violence. And it includes the hope that God may perhaps "turn from his fierce anger so that we will not perish." (It was with almost exactly the same words that the ship's captain had called upon Jonah to pray to his God, 1.6). It is a truly exemplary scene of repentance that is played out here. And God does indeed "relent" when he sees all this, and he does not do what he had threatened to do (v. 10).

Here we are at the critical point in Jonah. The heathen repent and God does not carry out the judgment he had announced. This produces as it were a double repentance (Ebach 1987, 113). But it is precisely this unexpected turn of events that Jonah had expected and feared. Now he prays for the second time (cf. 2.2), but this time he is furious: I knew it—and that was precisely why I wanted to flee to Tarshish (4.1f). What he knew he, too, dresses in the words which readers already know from Joel. Unlike the heathen king however he adds, like Joel, the words from the revelation on Sinai: "I knew that you are a gracious and compassionate God, slow to anger and abounding in love, a God who relents from sending calamity" (v. 2; cf. Ex 34.6f) [→62]. But with a remarkable twist he creates not hope from this knowledge but anger. Why? Because God's grace is extended this time to the heathens? But how could Jonah have known this in advance?

The problem lies at a deeper level. God sent Jonah with a message that was *true*. Nineveh will be destroyed because of its wickedness. But the announcement of the divine judgment always also contains the possibility of the repentance of sinners and the resultant repentance of God. This makes the prophetic message (apparently) *untrue*. It is this ambiguity that Jonah cannot stand. It was because he had this possibility in mind that he fled; and so at the end he would rather die than stand there as a "false" prophet. That is how it might appear in the light of the fundamental rule expressed in Deut 18.22 [→83]: "If what a prophet proclaims in the name of the LORD does not take place or come true, that is a message the LORD has not spoken. That prophet has spoken presumptuously." But there are other voices too. Thus we read in Ezek 18.23 in summary form the maxim-like sentiment, elaborated from various new angles throughout that chapter [→250]: "Do I take any pleasure in the death of the wicked? declares the Sovereign LORD. Rather, am I not pleased when they turn from their ways and live?"

It is this message that is developed again in the last scenes of Jonah (in an often apparently satirical way), leading to God's final question: "Should I not be concerned about that great city?" (4.11). Nineveh has repented and so the city is saved. That there is salvation for Nineveh means at the same time: the possibility of salvation for all people if they turn to God and repent.

The reader of this text, living after the end of the Assyrian empire, must, however, wonder how this hopeful expectation of the future fate of the capital, Nineveh, given narrative shape in Jonah, relates to Nineveh's actual fate. Will Nineveh really repent and be saved? This question is picked up again later in Nahum [→298].

But first Jonah concludes the first group of prophetic writings in which there is detailed discussion of the Day of Yhwh. This notion is in the distance in Jonah, it is true; however it picks up a crucial question from the previous writings and adds an extremely important new aspect to it. In this it makes contact with the view of the Day of Yhwh as developed in Joel 2.32: "Everyone who calls on the name of the LORD will be saved." Membership of the people of Israel is immaterial. There remains, however, an essential difference between the two texts, since Joel 2.28-32 is dominated by eschatological ideas that are not to be found in Jonah.

It is difficult to answer the question of how to take the relationship of Jonah ben Amittai of the Jonah text to the prophet of the same name mentioned in 2 Kgs 14.25 [→**135**]. There Jonah is named in a brief note as a contemporary of king Jeroboam II of Israel, to whom he is said to have proclaimed the reconquest of areas that had been lost. Most interpreters date Jonah to a considerably later date, generally to post-exilic times. The narrative itself gives no indications of its chronological situation; "Nineveh" here is the great, sinful city *par excellence.* Finally, the depiction of Jonah as a prophet of judgment is difficult to reconcile with the note in 2 Kgs 14. The question must remain open.

5.4 Judgment and Salvation for Jerusalem (Micah)

Jonah was sent into the world of the nations. In Micah attention turns back inward: to Samaria and Jerusalem (1.1). God calls the nations together to act as witnesses against the two cities and the countries represented by them (v. 2). He descends from his heavenly dwelling and strides over the high-places of the world (v. 3)—like the previous description expressing his superior power in the hymn in Amos 4.13 [→**283**]. The accompanying cosmic phenomena (v. 4) show the significance of what is going to happen: a judgment about the "transgressions of Jacob" and the "sins of Israel." What are the sins of the two separate kingdoms? In a word: Samaria and Jerusalem, their capital cities (v. 5).

Samaria is the first target. The reader needs no further explanation; this is thoroughly familiar from the writings of Hosea and Amos. Samaria will now be smashed together with all its idols, which were only the "wages of prostitutes" and will become such again (1.6f). Here the language of Hosea rings through unmistakably (Hos 1.2; 2.14; 9.1) [→**266f**]. Then the prophet begins a lengthy lament (vv. 8-16), since the calamity turns in the direction of Judah and Jerusalem (v. 9) through the cities of the land. At the end there remains only the shaving of the head as a sign of mourning over the children that have been carried off into exile (v. 16).

Then the real miscreants come into view: those exploiters, who accumulate fields and houses (2.1f), rob people of their possessions (v. 8), drive them out of their houses and exact punitive fines on petty pretexts (vv. 9f). Later those responsible are called the "leaders" and "rulers" (3.1, 9, 11), who do not care for justice but hate and abhor it (vv. 1f, 9), participate themselves in the exploitation (v. 3) or give favorable verdicts for a bribe (v. 11); even the prophets (vv. 5, 11) and priests (v.

11) are corrupt. But those that plan evil (*rā'*, 2.1) now face calamity (*rā'āh*, vv. 3-5); what they have done to others will happen to them (3.2) and it will go dark about the prophets (vv. 5f). So Jerusalem will suffer the same fate as Samaria: it will become a heap of ruins and the temple mount an overgrown hill (v. 12).

These first three chapters bring to the fore the basic elements of Micah's proclamation: his resolute protest against the judicial and social injustices [→§16], the causes of which he denounces as the behavior of the leading classes in Jerusalem. The threat of calamity that will come upon Jerusalem can hardly be exceeded in sharpness. Jerusalem will as it were disappear from the face of the earth as a city and as the location of the temple (3.12). Here Micah shows himself as a Judean who appears against the capital city of his country with the same resoluteness as Amos in the northern kingdom.

Clearly audible though the message of this prophet is, his person remains invisible. There is no scene in which the reader is party to his appearance and its effects. But his proclamation left powerful effects, so that more than a century later it was in the general popular consciousness and could be cited as a weighty argument in a trial against Jeremiah (Jer 26.17-19 quotes Mic 3.12). Only once does the "I" of this prophet come into view, with surprising clarity. He contrasts the divine word about the prophets (3.5-7) with his own prophetic self-consciousness: "But as for me, I am filled with power, with the Spirit of the LORD, and with justice and might, to declare to Jacob his transgression, to Israel his sin" (v. 8). Here Micah presents as it were a counterpart to Jeremiah, who would almost have been in despair at having to declare to Israel its sins.

The interruption of the divine words of judgment by a word of salvation in 2.12f is surprising. This word presupposes that the calamity announced has already occurred and it promises the gathering and return of the exiles. It will only be the "remnant of Israel" that God gathers. But God himself will go before them as king. This alternation between words of judgment and words of salvation is a feature of Micah as a whole. It continues in chs. 4-5.

The change at the transition from ch. 3 to ch. 4 is particularly stark. Zion [→§14], the "mountain of the house" has just lain desolate and waste (3.12), when we suddenly read: "In the last days the mountain of the LORD's temple will be established as chief among the mountains; it will be raised above the hills" (4.1). The contrast is clear: first the announcement of judgment on Jerusalem will be fulfilled; but "at the end of days" Zion will stand at the center of the nations of the world. The reader already knows this text from the beginning of Isaiah (Isa 2.1-5) [→170]. Whoever its author may be, in these two prophetic writings it has a significant function in each case. For Isaiah it forms the crowning of an intense series of words about the fate of Jerusalem which will finally once again be called "City of Righteousness" (Isa 1.26). A straight line leads from this to the central place of Zion, to which the nations make pilgrimages in order to learn Torah there (2.3). In Micah on the other hand the path leads through a morass. The Zion that will be the center of the pilgrimages of the nations at the end of days, will be built on the overgrown ruins of the present Zion.

In Micah this saying contains two elements that it lacks in Isaiah. First, the notion of peace which will extend among the nations is taken further in the picture that "everyone will sit under his own vine and his own fig tree" [→§22]; this is reinforced by the expression "for the mouth of YHWH Zebaot has spoken" (Mic 4.4). This expresses an eschatological repetition of what is reported concerning the time of Solomon as the consequence of comprehensive peace (1 Kgs 5.5) [→118]. Secondly a different concluding sentence is added than in Isa 2.5. A quite particular understanding of the significance of religions for the world of the nations comes to expression here: "All the nations my walk in the name of their gods; we will walk in the name of the LORD our God for ever and ever" (Mic 4.5). Does this mean a self-limitation? Does this supplementary sentence make it clear that the pilgrimage of the nations to Zion does not mean their conversion to the Yahweh religion?

Here again we read (as before in 2.12) that God will assemble people together, and the talk is again of the "remnant" (4.6-8). It is the limping, the lame and the dispersed who will form the "remnant" "on that day." And God will reign as king over them on the restored hill-fortress of his daughter Zion. But for now there are difficult times ahead. Daughter Zion must away from the city, away as far as Babylon. Many nations want to gloat over her fate—until God changes things and Zion overcomes them (vv. 9-13). In a new departure there is again talk of the future ruler, the new David (though the name is not mentioned) from Bethlehem, but who will be more than the first David, since his origins lie way back in primordial times (5.1). Various kinds of ideas are connected with this figure: ideas of the time of those with child (perhaps echoing Isa 7.14) [→174], of the return of the "remnant of his brothers," of his work as a shepherd, his rule until the end of the world and finally his peace-bringing power against the newly threatening Assyria (vv. 2-5).

Once again there is talk of the remnant, this time of the "remnant of Jacob" (5.6f). The concern here is not with the gathering of the remnant (as in 2.12 and 4.7), but with its immediate appearance ("like dew") and its pouncing ("like a lion"). From the viewpoint of the diaspora this means that this "remnant" people is still a force to be reckoned with, that it will again gain its place and assert itself among the nations. Finally God will not only destroy its enemies (v. 8) but also remove all military (vv. 9f) and religious (vv. 11f) self-securities from Israel (Wolff 1982, 130ff). But the nations "who have not heard," despite the call at the beginning (1.2), will experience God's wrath. This ends this complex collection of future-oriented words for Israel in chs. 4–5.

With the call to hear the prophet again turns to the present audience (6.1). God begins a court case (*rîb*) with "his people" Israel (v. 2) [→**§16**]. The trial idea already occurred right at the beginning of the words of Micah, when God himself appeared as a witness against Samaria and Jerusalem (1.2) [→**293**]. There it was the nations that were assembled to "hear." But they did not listen (5.14). Now the mountains and hills are called upon to hear. God's accusation against Israel sounds almost like a self-defense: "My people, what have I done to you?" (6.3). But the following arguments clearly contain the (unspoken) reproach that Israel did not react to God's saving actions in its early history in the way God might have expected of them: the leading out of Egypt, which was a redemption from the house of slavery; the leadership by Moses, Aaron and Miriam; the protection against the plans of Balak by Balaam, acting on God's instructions; and finally the leading into the promised land by way of the Jordan "from Shittim" (Josh 3.1) to Gilgal (4.19)." Like Hosea, Micah mentions the historical saving acts of God in the early days as a contrast to Israel's later behavior (cf. Josh 2.16f; 9.10; 11.1f; 12.10, 14; 13.4f) [→**268, 270f**].

The nation addressed understands the implied reproach. It understands that it has failed decisively, and it asks in return: "With what shall I come before the LORD?" (v. 6). A conversation now begins about the possibility or impossibility of atoning for its failure towards God by means of sacrifices. Burnt offerings are presented in unimaginable quantities, and even the sacrifice of the firstborn son as the last conceivable escalation of the sacrifice (vv. 6f). But the reader expects that it is not sacrifices that are required. The question has already been answered by Hosea (Hos 6.6) [→**269**] and Amos (Amos 5.21-24) [→**284**], and also by Isaiah (Isa 1.10-17) [→**170**] and Jeremiah (Jer 7.21-23) [→**211**]: sacrifices can never be a substitute for right behavior towards God and one's fellows. But the answer is surprising: "He has showed you, O human" (v. 8). There is no need for any new information, for the addressees already know what the issue is, or could at least know it, since it has already been told them long ago. What God demands is "what is good" (*tôb*). Micah himself has already reproached those responsible for hating good and loving evil instead (3.2), and Amos too expressly formulated this alternative (Amos 5.14f) [→**284**]. Micah elaborates in more detail on what is meant by this. "To do justice" (*'aśāh mišpāṭ*), as he already expected of those responsible (3.1, 9); in Amos too the term *mišpāṭ* plays a significant role (Amos 5.7, 15-24; 6.2). "To love a community spirit (*ḥesed*)," i.e. to love and exalt the attitude necessary for the realization of justice in the social life of the community; Hosea too contrasts this term with sacrifices (Hos 6.6) [→**269**]. To "walk humbly (*haṣnē*ᵃ*) with your God" (on the translation cf. Ebach 1995, 21f), attentive in the life of the community before and with God. These requirements seem simple and at the same time difficult and demanding. They show that there is no simple alternative to a sacrifice with which one wants to set everything right again, but that there is a claim upon the whole life of the individual and of the community.

But Jerusalem is now far from the realization of these requirements. Once again the prophet complains at what is now happening there (6.9-12): self-enrichment with false weights and measures (vv. 10f; Amos also raised this reproach in Samaria, Amos 8.5) [→**286**], acts of violence, lies and deception (v. 12). So the city faces calamity, in which all that has been acquired by unjust means will be of no avail (vv. 13-15). This will happen because Jerusalem has acted according to the example of Omri and Ahab, i.e. like Samaria (v. 16); and Micah has already announced the judgment against Samaria right at the beginning (1.6f) [→**293**]. In view of all this only complaint remains (7.1-6).

But then the prophet lifts his eyes and looks out like a watchman on the city wall (7.7). Rescue and help can now come only from God, and he is confident of this. Zion is not yet on its feet and its "enemy" (not further identified) is reveling in its defeat (vv. 8-10)—like Edom in Obadiah (Obad 12f). But the day will come when Jerusalem's walls are rebuilt and those led into exile will return from all points of the compass (vv. 11f). They may gloat as in the days of yore (vv. 14f), but the power of the nations is broken (vv. 16f). Micah ends with a prayer to the God who will turn again to his people, as he swore to the fore-fathers that he would (vv. 18-20).

5.4.1 Has Nineveh not repented? (Nahum)

Once again Nineveh comes on the scene. The name of the city is already given in the superscription to Nahum (1.1) and this indicates that it is the actual theme. For the reader of the Book of the Twelve it is surprising that Nineveh is presented here in a quite negative light and that divine judgment is announced for it. Jonah has reported that the people of Nineveh repented and that their city was therefore spared divine judgment. But now judgment comes home to them. Had Nineveh's inhabitants not repented after all? Or had the city later reverted to its sinful behavior? If the writings of Jonah and Nahum are read in the context of the Book of the Twelve, Nineveh appears in Jonah as an exemplary, sinful heathen city, without any mention of its being a threat to other nations. The message here is that even for such a city and its inhabitants there exists the possibility of repentance and thereby of protection from the wrath and judgment of God. "Nine-veh" too could have repented.

In Nahum it is evident that the real Nineveh did not repent. In Mi-cah already a short passage talks of Assyria, of which Nineveh is the capital and the representative, as being perceived as a threat, from which the future David will rescue his land (Mic 5.4f) [→296]. In Na-hum the end of Nineveh is now described in dramatic scenes. Nine-veh (or Assyria or the Assyrian king) is the *b'liyya'al*, the good-for-nothing, the corrupter (1.11; 2.1); the city is a "city of blood" (3.1) and a "prostitute" (v. 4). Its demise is depicted at several points (1.11-14; 2.2–3.19). For Judah there is reason for joy and celebration (2.1).

The drama of the destruction of Nineveh is placed in Nahum in a world-encompassing context. The psalm-like text at the beginning (1.2-8) depicts God's mighty striding over the earth. God comes full of "jealousy," as a wrathful avenger against his enemies (v. 2). In storm and tempest he strides over the whole earth, so that the mountains shake and the rocks split into pieces, the sea dries up and the rivers dwindle. Then again his fury is like fire and like a raging torrent, which destroys his opponents. Here many kinds of echoes of other hymnic passages in the Book of the Twelve are evident, such as Amos

1.2; 4.13; 5.8f; 8.8; 9.5; Mic 1.3f. Again and again in these texts God's actions towards Israel and the nations in history are seen in the context of his creative power and his rule over the world.

In this description of his powerful appearance God is depicted above all as angry and vengeful. At the same time, however, he is a refuge on the "day of trouble" (1.7). Here there is an echo of the motif of the "day of YHWH," especially since in Obadiah (Obad 12-15) and Zephaniah (Zeph 1.14-16) [→301] the two expressions are used next to each other (cf. also Hab 3.16). God grants refuge to those who seek it of him; for he knows them.

5.4.2 Now come the Chaldeans (Habakkuk)

Nineveh has dropped out of the picture. But a new threat appears: the "Chaldeans" (Hab 1.6), i.e. the Babylonians. Their approach is announced to the prophet Habakkuk as an answer to his complaint (vv. 2-4). He complains passionately about the injustices in his own land: acts of violence and oppression, as Amos (Amos 3.10) [→282] and Micah (Mic 6.12) [→297] had had to complain of, neglect and distortion of the law, so that the unrighteous person (*rāšā'*) triumphs over the righteous (*ṣaddîq*).

The answer seems surprising. It is not help that is announced to the petitioner, but calamity. The answer to the internal troubles will be a threat from the outside. God himself has the Chaldeans raise themselves up and overrun the land in a furious campaign (vv. 5-11). They will bring their own "justice" into effect (v. 7) and practice acts of violence (v. 9); indeed, they make their own power their god (v. 11). The prophet answers with a renewed complaint: will the holy God, with his pure eyes, really permit the unrighteous to swallow up the righteous (vv. 12-17)?

In expectation of an answer to his plea, Habakkuk looks out like a watchman on the tower (2.1; cf. Mic 7.7) [→297]. The answer is announced to him as a "vision" (*ḥāzôn*). He is to write it down, because it will not come into effect until later (cf. Isa 30.8); but the realization will certainly come (vv. 2f). The vision contains a comforting assurance for the righteous: the righteous will live "in perpetuity" (*'emûnāh*; on translation cf. Sweeney 1991a, 76), but his pursuers (i.e. the Chaldeans) will not last (v. 4). A series of five woes are then directed against the Chaldeans (2.6-19). They have plundered many nations and committed violence against lands and cities (vv. 8, 17), and they have relied on their wooden or bronze gods, which are of no use to them (vv. 18f). Standing sovereignly over against them is "the LORD in his holy temple" (v. 20), and he will bring his announcements to fulfillment.

To this God, finally, a great psalm-prayer (*t̲fillāh*, 3.1) [→§18] of the prophet is directed. It contains the description of a mighty theophany, which shakes the earth and recalls the struggle of the creator god against the powers of chaos, intertwined with descriptions of God's struggle against hostile nations (vv. 3-15). Again there are resonances of elements from hymnic passages in other writings of the Book of the Twelve (see above on Nah 1.2-8). The prophet is seized by great fear; but he expects the "day of trouble" that will come upon the enemy nation (v. 16) and ends the prayer with joyful thanks to the "God of my salvation" (vv. 18f).

Nahum began with a psalm (Nah 1.2-8), Habakkuk ends with one. This exalts the statements about Yhwh's struggle against the Assyrians and the Babylonians above purely worldly events. What is happening, or will happen, here, has to do with God's eschatological actions. The fate of Israel is involved in the great context of what happens between creation and the end-times.

5.4.3 The Day of the LORD ... (Zephaniah)

Again we read: "The day of the LORD is at hand!" (Zeph 1.7). It will bring catastrophic events on the whole world and humanity (vv. 2f), but especially on Judah (vv. 4-6). Here, however, the Day of Yhwh is viewed from another perspective than in earlier writings in the Book of the Twelve: for the first time a reason is given why the calamity of this day will come upon Judah. In this Zephaniah is close to the "prophets of judgment" within the book: Hosea, Amos and Micah. The reason for the coming calamity is above all the worship of foreign gods [→§20]: of Baal, the "host of heaven" and of "their king" (*malkām*, i.e. perhaps the Ammonite god Milcom). Their worshipers are turning their back on Yhwh and not seeking him (v. 6).

So the "Day of the LORD" is at hand. It is described as a cultic festival: a sacrifice to which Yhwh has invited guests, "sanctifying" them to participate (v. 7; cf. e.g. 1 Sam 16.5; the addition of "for death" in some translations [e.g. the German *Einheitsübersetzung*] rests on a misunderstanding of the text; the invitees cannot be identical with the sacrifice; rather, the invitees are the nations). On this "feast-day" God will "visit" (*pāqad*, vv. 8, 9, 12) members of the upper classes in Jerusalem for their deeds, not only for their cultic deviations (vv. 8f), but also for their exploitative behavior (vv. 11-13). So once again: "The Day of the LORD is at hand" (v. 14) [→§22]. This "day" is described impressively in all its threatening horror; the word *yôm*, "day," appears no fewer than ten times in vv. 14-18: it is great, bitter, a day of wrath, a day of trouble and oppression, of breaking and bursting, of gloom and darkness, of clouds and black night, and finally of the ram's horn and war-cries. It will come not only upon people in Judah who have sinned against God, but this "day of wrath" will mean an end to all inhabitants of the earth (vv. 14-18).

This dramatic description of a truly eschatological event suddenly changes into an address to the "people," i.e. to those threatened by the approaching day of Yhwh: "Gather together ... seek the LORD" (2.1-3), i.e. do what you have so far refused to do (1.6), before it is too late. Again a repetition to hammer it home: three times "before" (*b'ṭerem*): before the "day of the wrath of the LORD" comes upon you. This "before" has a corresponding "perhaps" (v. 3). Again this reluctant expression of a quiet hope, that perhaps it might not be too late after all, a note heard a number of times before in the Book of the Twelve (Joel 2.14; Amos 5.14; Jonah 3.9). Here as in Amos it is connected with the call to seek the Lord (2.3; cf. Amos 5.4-6, 14f). This also sets up a new theme: "seek the LORD" means acting with justice (*mišpāṭ*) and seeking righteousness (*ṣedeq*). This too has echoes of Amos (Amos 5.15). But a new element is added: "humility" (*'nāwāh*). The call of the prophet is directed towards the "humble (or poor *'nāwîm*) of the land." Does this mean only those oppressed and exploited by the "rich"? The term is used in this sense in Amos (Amos 2.7 [→280]; 8.4 [→286]). In Zephaniah the word later means the whole "remnant of Israel" (3.12f), after "those who rejoice in their pride" have been removed from their midst (3.11). This sense of the word does suggest itself here. The prophet is speaking to those for whom the "perhaps" now applies, because they might in the end belong to the "remnant."

But before this the storm of the Day of Yhwh whips across the nations, over Israel's neighbors, the Philistines (2.4-7), Moabites and Ammonites (vv. 8-11), then the Cushites (i.e. Ethiopians, v. 12) and finally Assyria, the complete destruction of Nineveh being announced once again (vv. 13-15). As in Amos (Amos 1f) this announcement of judgment over other nations leads into a complaint against Israel, i.e. in this case, Jerusalem. In a woe over the city (3.1f) the responsible officials "in their midst" are again (cf. 1.8) accused (v. 3), prophets and

priests included, who "desecrate the holy and do violence to the Torah" (v. 4)—and all even though God himself is present "in their
midst" as the righteous one (*ṣaddîq*) and is exercising justice (*mišpāṭ*, v.
5). Even the fate of other nations and cities did not serve as a warning
to Jerusalem (vv. 6f). So now "the day I will stand up to testify" is at
hand; then God will pour out his "fierce anger" and the "fire of his
jealous anger" will consume the whole world.

But this fire will be like a refining fire. After it God will change
everything: he will change the lips of the nations so that they call on
his name and bring him gifts from afar (3.9f). And Jerusalem no longer
needs to be ashamed, because God is going to remove "those who
rejoice in their pride" "from their midst" (v. 11).

So "in its midst" a new Israel will remain: "the meek and humble
who trust in the name of the LORD" (v. 12). This will be a special
"remnant of Israel." They will not act unjustly and speak no lies and
live in peace, because no one will make them afraid (v. 13).

Thus the dramatic description of the "Day of the LORD" with all its
destructive side-effects ends with a picture of peace—of a life without
ambitions, but in peace with God and protected by him in a peaceful
environment. This picture contains clear reminiscences of the depiction of the eschatological peace in Micah, in which each one will sit
under his own vine and fig-tree (Mic 4.4) [→**295**].

The far-ranging conclusion calls on "Daughter Zion" to rejoice (v.
14) and unfolds the picture of the restored Jerusalem/Israel even further. God has lifted his judgment against her and is now protectively
"in her midst" as king (v. 15) and saving hero (v. 17). She need no
longer fear (v. 16), her enemies have been destroyed (v. 19) and God
will also help the lame and gather the scattered. He will turn Israel's
fate (*šûb šᵉbût*) and lead those who live in the diaspora back home (v.
20).

In the context of the Book of the Twelve this is the conclusion of
the collection of writings from the time of the destruction of Jerusalem
and the deportation of a large part of the population into Babylonian
exile. The reader is very much aware of this, knowing from the introductory dating that Zephaniah's ministry was in the time of Josiah
(1.1) [→**149f**], i.e. shortly before violent end of the kingdom of Judah.
On reading further the first thing the reader will meet is the dating
according to the rule of the Persian king Darius (Hag 1.1).

5.5 Is this the beginning of the messianic age? (Haggai)

With the immediate link between the writing of the prophet Haggai to that of Zephaniah the Book of the Twelve bridges the deep chasm between the violent end of the kingdom of Judah—with the destruction of Jerusalem and the temple as well as the exile of part of the Judean population [→§9]—and the beginning of the return of the exiles. This shows the continuity of prophecy even under the changed circumstances.

But the problems are different ones now. This can already be seen in the fact that the address of the prophet is not directed to the king or any other otherwise known Israelite or Judean representative but to the "governor" appointed by the Persians and to the "high priest" (*hakkohēn haggādôl*), an office that had not previously existed (1.1). Haggai addresses them as those responsible for what he now considers the most important thing: the reconstruction of the temple. He has to counter the notion that the time has not yet come for the building of the temple but that priority should be given to care for one's own place to live (vv. 2-4). Haggai makes this question a *status confessionis*. The temple [→§11] is the place where God is present for Israel. So Israel's attitude towards its God goes together with its attitude to the temple. If they follow the admonition of the prophet, then God's assurance will apply to them: "I am with you" (1.13; 2.4) and "My Spirit remains among you" (2.5). But that their present attitude is wrong is evident to the Israelites themselves. Because God's house lies in ruins (vv. 4, 9), there are failed harvests (vv. 5f, 9) which God himself has brought about (vv. 10f).

Haggai's prophetic warnings are successful, because God "stirs up the spirit" of the governor and the high priest and the rest of the people, so that they take up the work (1.12-15). And when disappointment is about to spread because of the modest new start (2.1-3), the prophet describes the grand context in which this all stands: with the reconstruction of the temple a new period of salvation will begin. God will shake heaven and earth, as Joel had previously announced for the "Day of the LORD" (Joel 2.10; 3.16★) [→275f]. A consequence of this will be that the nations will also tremble and that their riches will pour in and fill the house of God (cf. Isa 60.5-7, 13) [→196]. Thus the "glory" (*kābôd*) of the future house will be greater than that of the first, and it will be a place of peace (or of salvation, *šālôm*) (2.4-9).

Once again the prophet sets about giving a justification of the absolute necessity of the construction of the temple for Israel. In the form
of a prophetic sign-act Haggai holds a *tôrāh* with the priests, instruction
on cultic matters (2.10-14). The question concerns the transferability
of "holy" and "impure." The answers are clear: holy things do not
render other things holy by touching, but impure things render things
impure. Haggai's conclusion: that is how it is with "this people" in
God's eyes (cf. 1.2 etc.; cf. Koch 1967); everything they do, and especially whatever they sacrifice, is impure. Therefore, it will remain impure until the temple has been built and consecrated; for only there
can the rituals of atonement and purification be performed that are
necessary for Israel's life before God (cf. Lev 4f; 16) [→**67**]. And then
God will again give his blessing of fertility (2.15-19).

Finally the eschatological horizon broadens again. The shaking of
heaven and earth will have effects on the nations of the world which
will again recall the descriptions of the "Day of the LORD." Thrones
will be toppled and kingdoms crushed (2.21f). But this will be the
hour of the eschatological ruler [→**§22**], whom God now addresses by
name: Zerubbabel, son of Shealtiel (v. 23). God calls him his "servant"
(*'ebed*), a title often used for David (2 Sam 7.5, 8 etc. [→**113, 254**]); he
describes him as his "signet ring," which is a great distinction; and he
confirms that he has "chosen" him (*bāḥar*), which again awakens consciousness of the David tradition (1 Sam 16.8-10 etc.) [→**107f**]. The
word "king" is not used, nor such a term as "messiah," which might
suggest itself to the interpreter. But this is the only time in the Hebrew
Bible that a potential future ruler is mentioned by name in an eschatological context such as this. But the future will show that this was to
remain an unfulfilled hope.

5.5.1 Zechariah

At almost the same time as Haggai a second prophet appears: Zechariah, son of Berechiah. In his case too the reconstruction of the temple
plays an important role, and with him too the events of those weeks
and months occur in a context of intense eschatological expectation. It
finds its expression in a series of night visions of the prophet, in which
impending events are often represented in picture form, in code.
Unlike the earlier prophetic visions (e.g. Amos 7f [→**285f**]; Jer 1.11-14
[→**205**]) these visions in each case require interpretation by a mediating
angel or interpreting angel ("the angel who spoke with me," 1.9, 13,

14 etc.) [→*In* **122**]. The immediacy of the prophet's access to the vision-ary event clearly no longer exists.

The visions form a cycle. The first three visions announce the resto-ration of Jerusalem. Heavenly riders stand prepared. They have not yet set out, to bring about a fundamental change in political circumstances; but God makes it known through the angel that he is full of great zeal and full of pity for Jerusalem, which will soon be rebuilt (1.7-17). The nations too, which have scattered Israel and Judah, will be flattened (2.1-4). And finally Jerusalem will be measured out; but it will be an open city, for God himself will be a wall of fire around them (2.5-9). The last three visions then describe in coded form the removal of the social miscreants (5.1-4) and of the anti-divine "wickedness" (*riš'ah*, 5.5-11) from the land and finally the sending out of heavenly messen-gers of the Spirit of God (*rū*ᵃ*h*) into the world of the nations (6.1-8).

In the middle of the cycle stand two related texts (taken by some exegetes as two independent visions), in which the concern is with the question who will stand at the head of future Jerusalem. In ch. 3 the highpriest Joshua (Yeshua) stands in the center. In a heavenly scene he is opposed by the *śāṭān* (i.e. the "antagonist" or "accuser"). The reason for this lies in his impure garments. But these very clothes are a sign that Joshua is like "a burning stick snatched from the fire," i.e. one who has escaped a catastrophe (cf. Amos 4.11) [→**282**], a returnee from exile. So the accusation is rejected and Joshua is clothed in new, pure garments, his "guilt" being taken from him at the same time. He is given the solemn divine assurance: "You will govern my house and have charge of my courts" (3.7★).

Chapter 4 presents a different picture: a golden lampstand with seven oil dishes, with an olive tree on each side of it. Who are these two olive trees? After asking a number of times (vv. 4, 11, 12) the prophet is finally given the answer: "These are the two who are anointed (lit.: 'sons of oil'), to serve the LORD of all the earth" (v. 14). Two "anointed" officials, then. Now it is Zerubbabel who receives an added word of confirmation and promise: "The hands of Zerubbabel have laid the foundation of this temple; his hands will also complete it" (v. 9). In the word to Joshua there has already been mention of the second official that God will appoint: "I am going to bring my servant, the Branch" (3.8). There are echoes here of words of Jeremiah (Jer 23.5; 33.15) [→**222f**] and of Ezekiel (Ezek 32.23f) [→**254**] (cf. Hanhart 1990ff, 194-98). Once again there is then mention of a "man whose

name is the Branch" (6.12f). He will build the temple and reign on his
throne [→§13]. At the same time the priest will also be on *his* throne,
and between them there will be harmony (lit.: "counsel of peace, "ṣat
šālôm). So this is the vision of the coming Jerusalem: the harmonious
rule of the king from the line of David, who is at the same time the
rebuilder of the temple, and of the priest who ministers in the temple
and provides atonement for Israel (cf. ch. 3).

Some things remain obscure to the present-day reader. What does the stone
signify which God lays (or sets up) before Joshua, on which there are seven
eyes and on which "his inscription" is engraved (3.9)? And why is Joshua
crowned and why immediately afterwards is there talk of the future ruler called
"Branch," without the relationship between them being explained (6.11-13)?
Is Joshua to pass on the crown to the Davidide who is still preparing to come?
Clearly there are traditions behind this which were intelligible to contemporaries but which we can no longer understand.

The vision cycle is framed by prophetic divine words. At the beginning is a call to repentance, which impressively relates the situation of
the addressees to that of their forefathers [→§7] (1.2-6): "Return to
me—do not be like your forefathers!" The "former prophets" (i.e. the
prophets before the catastrophic end of the kingdom of Judah)
preached again and again to the forefathers: "Return!" But the forefathers did not listen [→§16]. But when the words of the prophets were
fulfilled, then they recognized this and repented (v. 6). An unusual
statement on the lips of a prophet: "they repented." But precisely this
is the precondition for the continuing story of God's dealings with
Israel, or for it to begin again. But the people have not fundamentally
changed, so that even now the prophet must again call out to them:
"Return to me!" But now this call is linked to a further astonishing
statement. The continuation of the sentence reads: "I will return to
you" (v. 3). Never before has a prophet spoken of a "return" of God
to Israel. But how are the two parts of this sentence related? The concise wording of the Hebrew dual sentence (šûbû 'ēlay ... w'ʾāšûb
ʾlēkem) is open to various interpretations. But in the context of Zechariah as in the context of the Hebrew Bible as a whole there is no possibility that the second part of the sentence should be taken in the
sense of "If you turn back to me, *then* I will (also) turn back to you."
Rather, the message of Zechariah is that God has decided to turn again

to Israel and to Jerusalem in particular, in fact concretely: to return to his sanctuary in Jerusalem (1.16; 8.3, 15). This is the precondition for his future dealings with Israel and with Jerusalem. But this certainly does not make the call to Israel to repent superfluous. On the contrary: Israel's repentance is the necessary reaction of Israel, which has to be counseled time and again, to the already decided, anticipated repentance/return of God.

The visions are followed by a series of prophetic divine words, which are connected. The point of departure is a query to the prophet, whether in view of the progressing reconstruction of the temple the ceremony of fasting and lament to mark the anniversary of the destruction of the temple, practiced for the past 70 years, should be maintained (7.1-3). The prophet does not give a direct answer to this question but places it in a wider context. First: basically, fasting is only good for self-satisfaction; the crucial thing, in contrast, is to follow what the "former prophets" already preached and the core of which is the duty of social justice towards the poor and the weak. Because they have not followed this, the Israelites have fallen subject to divine wrath and have been taken into exile (7.4-14).

But a new age has now dawned. God is returning to Jerusalem and taking up residence again in the city, now called the "city of faithfulness" (*'îr hā*ʳ*met*), and on Mount Zion, which is now called the "holy mountain" (*har haqqodeš*). The whole city will be populated by old and young, living peacefully together. This may seem too marvelous to the "remnant of the people," i.e. those who have returned from exile, "but will it seem marvelous to me?" (8.1-6). God will free all Israel from exile [→§9] and bring them home, "and they will be my people, and I will be their God in faithfulness and righteousness" (*be*ʳ*met ûbiṣ*ʿ*dāqāh*, vv. 7f). As before in Haggai, once again the day of the laying of the temple foundations is described as the fundamental turning point. But now the circle is drawn much wider. The "seed of peace" (*zera*ʿ *haššālôm*) that God is now sowing applies not only to the vine, the field and the dew of heaven, but to the whole "remnant of the people." They were a curse to the nations, but they will now become a blessing (vv. 9-13).

So while God has planned calamity up to now, he is now planning something good for Jerusalem and the house of Judah. So "Do not be afraid!" (vv. 9-15). But they will now keep to the message of the prophets and practice real justice, which serves for peace (*šālôm*), and not excessively favor their neighbor, because God hates all that (vv. 16f). And the text then returns to the initial question: what is to happen with the fasting ceremonies? The days of fasting will be turned into festivals of joy. For no longer is there a need to remember past calamities but the salvation that is being experienced (vv. 18f).

Once again the horizon broadens: nations will come to praise the Lord and "seek" him, i.e. to consult him (vv. 20-22), as Micah once predicted for the "end of days" [→**295**] (Mic 4.2 = Isa 2.3; cf. already Zech 2.15). How much Jerusalem has been drawn into the center of things is made clear by the concluding scene: ten men from nations of all languages will grasp a single Judean (or Jew) by the corner of his garment (on which the tassel is discernible, Num 15.38) and ask him if they may join him and the others heading for Jerusalem. "For we have heard that God is with you" (v. 23).

Here something new begins. The superscription *maśśā'* introduces two substantial passages within Zechariah (chs. 9–11; 12–14). The same heading also stands at the beginning of three separate writings within the Book of the Twelve (Nahum, Habakkuk, Malachi), though there it is linked in each case with the name of the eponymous prophet. (It is also found multiple times in the sayings against foreign nations in Isaiah, Isa 13.1; 15.1; 17.1 etc. [→**179**]). So this superscription signals a step beyond the immediate prophecy of Zechariah. A changed self-understanding of these chapters is also evident in the fact that only in one section (11.4-17) does the "I" of the prophet appear; at the same time it is only here that we meet the divine speech formula, "Thus says the LORD" (11.4; in chs. 1–8, by contrast, almost 20 times). Above all a different relationship to "history" underlies these chapters. The "events" described here lie almost entirely in a future that can only be seen in a visionary way, even if sometimes the descriptions are very realistic. Zech 9–14 as a whole can therefore be classed in the realm of "apocalyptic" (cf. Hanson 1975, 280ff) [→**§22**]. But in Zech 1–8 too there are already elements that point in this direction (cf. Gese 1973), so that there is a continuity within Zechariah.

The dominant themes, in these chapters too, are formed by the expectations for the future of Jerusalem and Israel/Judah in the eschaton to come. There is occupation, from various viewpoints, with Yhwh's eschatological battle against the nations on Israel's behalf. The concern is continually with the future fate of Jerusalem. The eschatological king [→**§19**] will enter it amid rejoicing (9.9); he will not himself fight, for God removes the weapons of war, thereby enabling the worldwide reign of peace for the king enthroned in Jerusalem (v. 10). In the midst of changing battles fought "on that day" (12.3, 4, 6 etc.), Jerusalem remains in its place (v. 6). On "that day" a fountain will open up in Jerusalem for the house of David and for Jerusalem's inhabitants for the purging of sin and impurity (13.1).

Finally "a day of YHWH" (*yôm bā'layhwh* 14.1) will come when there will again be an eschatological battle in which Jerusalem and its inhabitants will suffer greatly. But then, accompanied by miraculous phenomena, *one* day will appear, known only to God (v. 7); on this day living water will flow from Jerusalem (v. 8) and the Lord will take up his kingly rule over the whole earth. "On that day there will be one LORD, and his name the only name" (v. 9). Then the whole land will change into a plain and Jerusalem will overlook it; and people will live in security there (vv. 10f). Finally the survivors of the nations that have taken up arms against Jerusalem will come up year by year to worship the Lord and celebrate the Feast of Tabernacles (v. 16). And all Jerusalem will be holy (vv. 20f).

Much in these chapters remains difficult for the present-day reader to understand. This applies for instance to the shepherd allegory in 11.4-17 (cf. Gese 1974) and for the talk of the "pierced" one (12.10-14). The account of the "end of prophecy" in 13.2-6 is also odd.

5.5.2 Malachi
With a surprising about-turn, at its conclusion the Book of the Twelve leaves the apocalyptic mood of the visions of the future and returns to the present. Once again a new section is introduced with *maśśā'* (Mal 1.1). This time the phrase "The word of the LORD" is followed by a name: *mal'ākî*, "my messenger" (usual English spelling: Malachi). The reader is told nothing further about the person that stands behind this unusual name. However the subsequent texts show the picture of lively discussions that Malachi conducts with his contemporaries. At issue, clearly, are problems of the post-exilic community. At the center stands the rebuilt temple (1.6-29; 3.6-12) [→§11]; the relationship to the non-Jewish population is also an important topic (2.10-16), though there is no sign of any armed conflict.

The dominant theme is the question of what life lived appropriately before God should look like. Malachi has to deal with the counter-question whether it is "worthwhile" living according to these rules (2.17; 3.14f etc.). So it is a matter of life in the "here and now"; the eschaton seems for now to have receded into the far distance. Sacrificial practices have become lax (1.6-9). But the question of sacrifice now stands in a quite different context than in the earlier writings of the Book of the Twelve. The temple has become the central symbol for the return of Israel and the restoration of society, and so sacrifices form an important element of the identification of the returning community with this newly granted situation. The sacrifice of less valuable animals is an expression of lack of reverence for God, and so in the divine speech the "holding-to-account formula" customary in the cult is applied negatively to sacrifice: "I take no delight (*ḥepeṣ*) in you, ... and I will accept no (*lo' 'erṣeh*) offering from your hands" (v. 10; cf. 1967, 256). As with the former prophets the attitude of those bringing sacrifices is the decisive reason for their rejection [→170], but this time it is evident in the sacrificial gifts themselves.

Malachi confronts this behavior of the sacrificers with the reverent attitude of other nations [→§20]: "My name will be great among the nations, from the rising to the setting of the sun" (v. 11, cf. v. 14b). An astonishing statement, which is further reinforced in that the reference is even to sacrifices that other nations bring to Yhwh. This contrast of the Judeans with the god-fearing "heathen" recalls Jonah (Jonah 1.14, 16; 3.5ff) [→289f]. In the context of Malachi there is a special sharpening of criticism of the Jerusalemites (cf. v. 14) here.

This criticism is directed above all against the priests (2.1-9). They have deviated from the "covenant" God made with Levi (vv. 4f). Here there is a resonance of the tradition documented in the words to Levi in the Blessing of Moses (Deut 33.8-11; cf. Jer. 33.20f) [→228]. The priests that stand in this tradition have important tasks: they pass on true Torah and knowledge and keep many from guilt (vv. 6f); in fact their ancestor Levi can even be described as a "messenger of the LORD" (*mal'ak yhwh*, v. 7), an expression only seldom applied to humans (cf. Hag 1.13). But the present incumbents have deviated from this path and no longer do justice to the important duties of the priests for the community; God will therefore publicly humiliate them (v. 8).

Another problem concerns not only the priests but the community as a whole: marriages with non-Jewish women (2.10-12). What the concern is here is made clear in the words "daughter (i.e. follower) of a strange god" (*bat-'ēl nēkār*, v. 11). Such marriages hide the danger that the Jewish husband will be seduced into worshiping other gods, as is memorably shown in the tradition of Israel's own history (Num 25 [→72]; 1 Kgs 11.1-13 [→123f]); so they are expressly forbidden in the

Torah (Ex 34.12-16; Deut 7.3f) [→**78**]. The offense against this means
disloyalty, even "profanity" (*tô'ebāh*). Even the argument produced
against this by those concerned is not telling: "Have we not all one
Father? Did not one God create us?" (v. 10). Malachi has refuted this
right at the beginning: in the conflict between Jacob and Esau God has
decided in Jacob's favor and rejected Esau (1.2-5).

The problem is connected with a second problem: separation from those that
have been wives up to now (vv. 13-16). Surprisingly Malachi is fundamentally
in favor of monogamy. There is some dispute, however, about his view of
divorce. It hangs on the understanding of the concise phrase: *kî śāne' śallah* "if
hating, dismiss!" (v. 16). The masoretic text and all ancient translations take
this sentence in the sense of: "If you hate your wife (i.e. no longer love her),
then dismiss her," in accordance with Deut 22.13, 16; 24.3 (cf. *ThWAT* VII,
836). Many recent commentators, however, prefer to take it as the opposite:
"I (i.e. God) hate divorce." (On this whole question cf. Schreiner 1979.)

But then we see that Malachi too stands in the tradition of eschatological expectations. The cynical talk of those who say that the Lord
takes "delight" (*hepeṣ*, cf. v. 10) in those who do evil (*rā'*), or ask
"Where is the God of justice?" (2.17), will be answered in a theophany
(3.1-5). Again the key term "day" crops up: what is about to occur is
"the day of his coming" (v. 2). It will be so terrible that the call of
earlier prophets resounds again: "Who can endure ... and who can
stand?" (cf. Joel 2.11 [→**276**]; Nah 1.6 [→**298**]). God's messenger (*mal'ākî*)
will precede the Lord when he "suddenly" appears in his temple.
  This appearance of God will mean judgment: a purifying judgment
on the priests, the "sons of Levi," so that they will then bring right
sacrifices "as in days gone by, as in former years" (vv. 3f); and a trial of
all those who despise justice in respect of their fellow human beings (v.
5). This last aspect shows that Malachi also stands in continuity with
the ethical demands of the "former prophets."
  "Return to me, and I will return to you"—this sentence from Zech
1.3 [→**306**] appears anew (3.7). It indicates that now already the first
signs of a time of salvation might become visible if the required gifts
are brought to the temple (vv. 8-11). In continuation of the admonitions and promises of Haggai and Zechariah (cf. Hag 2.15-19; Zech
8.9-15), Malachi announces that God will then "throw open the
floodgates of heaven" and pour out blessing, so that there will be rich

harvests. Even the nations will recognize that Israel will be a "land of (God's) delight (ḥepeṣ, v. 12)."

But the people still continue with their cynical talk: "It is futile to serve God," for those who practice wickedness (riš'āh, cf. Zech 5.8) [→305] are blessed (vv. 13-15). But again the eschatological aspect is in evidence. God will write down in a book those who fear him. "In the day I make" they will be his treasured possession and people will again see the difference between the righteous (ṣaddîq) and the wicked (rāšā') (vv. 16-18). For "the day is coming" when the wicked will be burnt like stubble; but for those who fear God's name, the "sun of righteousness" will rise (vv. 19-21).

The concluding paragraph (3.22-24) also speaks again of the "day of the LORD," or more precisely of what is to occur before the day of the Lord comes. Two names are placed in relation to each other: Moses [→§12] and Elijah. Moses gave Israel the Torah. Israel is to live in accordance with it in the time of the coming of the Day of the Lord, i.e. *now*, in the present and the immediate future of the prophet and of his hearers and readers. At the same time attention is expressly drawn to the fact that the message of the prophets is also to be read in the light of the Torah. According to the last words of the Torah Moses himself even was the first and greatest of the prophets (Deut 34.10) [→87].

But then, before the "great and terrible Day of the LORD" appears, Elijah will come—return, one should say, since he did not die, after all, but was taken up to heaven (2 Kgs 2) [→143]. So he still has one task to perform for Israel. (According to Sir 48.10 he is standing prepared for the end-times.) He will come as the "messenger," who precedes the Lord, when he appears in his temple (3.1). His task will be to reconcile fathers and sons. Sirach quotes Mal 3.24 and continues the sentence: "and to restore the tribes of Jacob." This brings the task of the returning Elijah close to what is said of the "servant of God" in Isaiah (Isa 49.5f; cf. Blenkinsopp 1977, 121f). This reconciliation must happen in order for "the land" to be protected from destruction (lit.: banishment) on the day of the Lord. This recalls Zephaniah's admonition: "Seek the LORD" (Zeph 2.1-3) [→301]. The Day of the Lord is the day of judgment; but there will be a difference between the "righteous" (ṣaddîqîm) and those who do "evil" (the rešā'îm), i.e. between those who serve God—in Joel's words, those who "call upon the name of the LORD" (Joel 3.5*) [→277]—and those who do not serve him (cf. Mal 3.18). The task of Elijah the prophet will be to bring fathers and sons together so that they are not subject to judgment.

5.6 The Book of the Twelve in the Canon of the Hebrew Bible

The reader of the Book of the Twelve Prophets has traversed two and a half centuries of prophecy, from "the beginning of the words of the LORD" to Hosea through to the prospect of the impending "Day of the LORD," which contains both threatening and hopeful elements. The collection of the extremely varied prophetic writings in this book gives at the same time a deep insight into the eventful history of prophecy. Some of these prophets have close affinity to the "great" prophetic figures: Amos, Micah and then Zephaniah can be seen in the same tradition as Isaiah as prophets of judgment, for whom the "social" element is very much in the foreground. But as with Isaiah, so too each of these prophets has his own quite personal profile and makes his own individual contribution to the development and theological profile of the religion of Israel. Hosea places special emphasis on reproach of the Baal cult, thereby broaching a topic that comes back into the center under changed conditions in Jeremiah.

But then quite different themes come into play. The most important of them is the "Day of the LORD," which is spoken of in a variety of ways. At the same time the different profiles of the various prophets become clear. What does the Day of the Lord mean? Will it bring Israel salvation or calamity, light or darkness? And what will it mean for the other nations? Is there any chance for them to escape by repenting? And to whom is this chance given—just to Israel, or to the other nations as well? How do the other nations react to the announcement of the Day of the Lord—and how does God react to their behavior? The variety of answers within the collection of the twelve prophetic writings permits the reader an insight into the variety of prophecy, which again forms a mirror image of the Israelite community through the centuries.

At the end of the collection the problems of the reconstruction and consolidation of the community after the exile come to the fore. Will the time of salvation now begin with the restoration of the temple cult in Jerusalem? What shape will it take, and who will be its leaders and representatives? Connected with this, however, is the question of how life in the community is now to be shaped until the "Day of the LORD" arrives. The rules for life together and for cultic behavior still apply as before, "until Elijah comes." The last writings of the Book of the Twelve Prophets thus draw attention once again to the tense relations between the expectation of the eschatological turning point and life in the "here and now."

§ 4

The Writings

1. Introduction to the Writings

The third main part of the canon of the Hebrew Bible is much less uniform than the two preceding parts [→*In* **258**]. The books and writings collected in it belong to quite different areas of life.

At the beginning stands the book of Psalms [→**4**], often called the "Psalter." It brings together a collection of prayers and songs from a whole variety of backgrounds. A proportion of them display evidence of use on religious occasions, which again can differ radically in type. In some of them the liturgical element is dominant, in others the praise of God in hymnic form is in the foreground, while in others again it is the communal lament. In a large number of psalms, however, it is not the community that is speaking but an individual. Here too we find lament as well as praise and thanksgiving; in some of these psalms a connection with the temple and the cult can be recognized, which is, however, lacking in others. Finally we also find texts that have a more reflective character. Here we see elements of "wisdom" thought, which are also found in psalms in the above-mentioned groups.

The wisdom element dominates in several books in the third part of the canon. The most obvious of these is the central significance of wisdom in the book of Proverbs, which can be ascribed as a whole to "wisdom literature." A large number of wisdom sayings are collected in it, especially extensive "didactic speeches" in chs. 1–9, in which "Wisdom" (*hokmāh*) also appears as a person. Notes critical of the notion of wisdom thought and of a kind of behavior determined by it are not found here. Things are quite different in the two other books that stand in the context of the wisdom traditions: the book of Job and Ecclesiastes, the Preacher (Qohelet). These two books are thoroughly marked by wisdom thought, both in language and theme, but both of them, each in their own very different ways, also adopt a critical stance towards fundamental elements of this tradition. The book of the Preacher (Qohelet) is marked by a deep skepticism towards the wisdom traditions, while Job vehemently contests the validity of decisive basic ideas of wisdom doctrine; nonetheless these two writings remain within the common framework of Israelite religion, in which the wisdom traditions also stand.

A number of other writings can be placed with, or close to, these two main groups. Thus the songs of lament belong right next to the Psalms; the Song of Songs can be viewed in proximity to the wisdom writings, which also comes to expression in its ascription to Solomon. Other writings cannot be assigned in this way. Thus we find two narrative books that are quite different in nature. The book of Ruth tells of the fate of an individual, which is played out in the land of Israel and the immediate neighbor, Moab, and which the introduction sets in the time of the judges. The book of Esther, meanwhile, recounts a happily averted persecution of the Jews in the Persian diaspora, thus in a very much later period and outside the land of Israel. The book of Daniel, finally, occupies a special position: it is the only book of the Hebrew Bible that is to be ascribed to "apocalyptic."

At the end of the third part of the canon two books follow which in very different ways take up and continue the historical accounts of the "former prophets." The books of Ezra and Nehemiah (which in fact form one book) start off with their account of the historical events at the point when the restoration of Israel or of Judah begins, after the Babylonian exile, with the decree of the Persian king Cyrus regarding the reconstruction of the temple in Jerusalem; so they continue the historical account of the books of Kings, though in a different form. Quite unlike the books of Chronicles, they begin again right at the beginning with the genealogy of humanity starting with Adam and then repeat with a very distinctive interpretation the history of Israel and Judah under the monarchy of the Davidic dynasty. This book is thus less an account than an interpretation of history from the viewpoint of a later generation.

2. The Book of Psalms

2.1 Introduction

It is "Israel" that speaks in the Psalms (Hebrew *t'hillîm* "songs of praise,"
Greek ψαλμοί or ψαλτήριον) [→*In* 258]. This distinguishes them fundamentally from the preceding parts of the canon. The Psalms can be appropriately described as "Israel's response," in which "Israel before
Yahweh" reacts to the saving acts of its God (von Rad 1962, 366). It is
a multi-vocal and multi-layered response. Often it is the "we" of the
community that sings or speaks; often it is an "I," sometimes a king,
then again a "poor one." Often cultic occasions can be discerned, festive religious assemblies or pilgrimages, then again the lament of an
individual sounds out, who sees himself as persecuted and oppressed or
who suffers in consciousness of his sins, or the communal lament about
the threat to and the devastation of Jerusalem or about life in distant
exile. Praise and thanksgiving are also frequently expressed, together
with theological reflection and wisdom instruction.

This variety does not immediately make orientation easy for the
reader. Each psalm forms a unity in its own right and develops its own
statement, often in a very dense and nuanced form. But it is also evident that the individual psalm does not stand isolated and without
context. Thus we see that particular groups of psalms demonstrate
thematic and linguistic coincidences which permit insights into the
type and place of their original use. The determination of such "genres" [→*In* 104] (German: *Gattungen*) is an important element in the understanding of the significance of the Psalms in Israel's religious life (cf.
esp. Gunkel 1926; Gunkel-Begrich 1933). Thus for example in the
"hymns" which have their *Sitz im Leben* in temple worship, there is
communal praise of God's great deeds in creation (e.g. Ps 104), in the
history of his people (e.g. Ps 105) or in his forgiving acts (e.g. Ps 103)
[→§18]. Some groups of hymns have special themes like praise of Zion
(e.g. Ps 46) or of the kingdom of God (Pss 47; 93; 95–99). The opposite pole to this, so to speak, is formed by the prayers of an individual,
especially the large number of psalms of lament (e.g. Pss 3; 22; 51;
130). There are corresponding psalms in which confidence in divine
aid stands in the foreground (e.g. Pss 4; 16; 23) or thanksgiving for
deliverance experienced (e.g. Pss 30; 32; 34). The psalms of lament in
particular often presuppose a situation of the petitioner far from the

community and the temple, in fact far from the land of Israel (e.g. Pss 42; 120). The people's psalms of lament on the other hand are closely connected with petitionary services and other religious procedures (e.g. Ps 74; 79). In addition there are other smaller genres of various types.

The termination of the genres is not, however, capable of overcoming the isolated consideration of the individual psalms. It was not until recent times that it gradually became recognized that the book of Psalms as we have it today is clearly the result of a very deliberate and nuanced process of compilation. As a result the individual psalm is placed in a broader context which often gives it an additional function and its import is not infrequently given a new accent.

For the reader of the book of Psalms this context is highly significant because it teaches that the individual psalm is to be understood as part of a greater whole into which its message fits and to which it makes its own contribution.

2.2 The Book of Psalms as a whole

Within the book of Psalms it is possible to see a whole series of structural markers. Some of them seem to go back to earlier part-collections of psalms, while others clearly relate to the canonical collection of the 150 Psalms of the Hebrew Bible that we have before us. The latter also doubtless applies to the division of the book of Psalms into five sections or "books." At the conclusion to each of the first four books (Pss 1-41; 42-72; 73-89; 90-106) there is a short doxology, a praise of God, followed by a responding *'āmēn*; the fifth book (Pss 107-150) ends with a whole series of hallelujah-psalms (146-150, introduced by 145.21). The number five is evidently to be understood as a borrowing from the structure of the Torah, the Pentateuch. Closer study of the internal structure of the book of Psalms shows quite clearly that the outline also has significance from the point of view of content (see below). At the same time, however, there are other structural markers which cannot easily be brought into line with the division into books [→*In* **259**]. Some of them point to earlier stages of the present collection (cf. Wilson 1985; Millard 1994).

The clearest indications of psalms belonging together are the superscriptions. A large number of them contain names. One name far exceeds all the others: David. Almost half of all the Psalms (73 of 150) bear his name in the superscription. The majority of them are ordered in groups: Pss 3-41 (i.e. the whole of the first book without the two introductory psalms, 1 and 2); 51–71; 108–110; 138–145. Besides these there are other groups of psalms which are named according to levitical guilds of singers: Korah (42–49; 84–89), Asaph (73–83); as well as many individual psalms with various names, including, alongside David, Moses (90) and Solomon (72; 127). In many of the superscriptions we find other terms which can no longer be precisely clarified; some indicate the type of text, e.g. as "song" (*šîr*, 65–68; 120–134, or *mizmôr* [usually ψαλμός in the Septuagint], very frequent, including 35 times with *l᷎dāwîd*), others perhaps notes on performance, which is suspected to be the case for instance for the also very frequent expression *lam᷎naṣṣēaḥ* (often translated by "for the choirmaster," or similar) (on this topic cf. Kraus 1978/1989, §4). Finally in the fifth book we find the self-contained group of "pilgrimage psalms," or "psalms of ascent" (120–134), each of which contains the superscription *šîr hamma᷎ᵃlôt* (with variants), as well as several groups of psalms that begin or end with *hal᷎lûyāh* (111-118; 135f; 146–150).

These superscriptions and groupings certainly also have significance for the collection of the book of Psalms as a whole; but so far this is only partially discernible to us. The most important signal for the understanding of the book as a whole is given in its introduction. Psalm 1 begins with a blessing for those who live their lives entirely with reference to the Torah. This seems surprising because at first sight the concern is not with the real themes of the Psalms but with the *tôrāh*, the thematic focus of which lies in the Pentateuch [→§10]. If the reference is to intensive study of the Torah (1.2), then this certainly means an available written text, whether the Pentateuch or an earlier stage of it, to which the highest authority is ascribed. This places the book of Psalms in proximity to the book of the Torah; it is classed with it, and at the same time under it (cf. Kratz 1996). The Psalms are God's word, and thus demand intensive study—like the Torah; but the Torah remains superordinate and directive.

This study of the Torah is now viewed from a quite particular angle: the relationship between the "righteous" (*ṣaddîq*) and the "unrighteous" or "wicked" (*rāšāᶜ*). The desired blessing is for those who do not follow the "counsel of the wicked" (1.1) but are intensively occupied with the Torah (v. 2); such persons will blossom and flourish (v. 3). The counterpart are the wicked: they wither (v. 4), they cannot stand in court and have no place in the "community of the righteous" (v. 5). Finally they are placed in opposition to one another: "The LORD knows the way of the righteous, but the way of the wicked will perish" (v. 6). This opposition is one of the basic elements of Israel's "wisdom" tradition [→§19]. In this tradition life experiences and guidelines for living are frequently expressed in antithetical formulations. The basic leading idea here is that there is a connection between what a person does and his or her wellbeing: those who do the right thing do well—and conversely those who do evil do not prosper. This idea, which is frequently expressed and discussed in the wisdom literature, finds its specific form in Ps 1 in the link with the Torah: the righteous who devote themselves entirely to the Torah are on the right, wholesome path; the way of the wicked who despise the Torah leads to perdition.

The theme of Ps 1 is continued in the next psalm. That the two psalms belong closely together is evident already from the fact that Ps 2 is not separated from the previous one by a superscription. To begin with, Ps 2 has a quite different subject: the turmoil of the nations "against the LORD and against his Anointed One" [→§20]. But this theme is closely connected with the previous one. The "nations" who rage against God are the wicked. The kings of the earth are warned not to follow their path, so that their own path will not lead to perdition (*'ābad* 2.11)—like the way of the wicked (1.6). Ps 2 closes with the same blessing formula with which Ps 1 begins (*'aš'rê*, 2.12); this formula encloses the two psalms as an *inclusio*. At the same time, however, in Ps 2 a theme comes to the fore that to some extent dominates the whole book of Psalms. The "Anointed One" of God (2.2), the king [→§13] whom God has appointed on Mount Zion (v. 6) and who himself speaks (v. 7), is none other than David, who from Ps 3 on appears as the "author" of the Psalms. Thus David himself is presented as the righteous man who leads his life in accordance with the Torah (cf. 1 Kgs 2.1-4; 3.14 etc.) [→116]. In the presentation of this "anointed one" appointed by God there is also an echo of the messianic element that is frequently connected with the David tradition (cf. Sheppard 1980, 136ff; Miller 1993).

From here on various lines can be followed through the book of Psalms. The line of Torah piety is resumed in the great Psalm 119. Here the wisdom element is more strongly in evidence and in a variety of forms. The relationship between Pss 1 and 119 has led to the assumption that these two psalms may once have formed the beginning and conclusion of a collection of psalms before the book of Psalms attained its present shape (Westermann 1962). In the present, final form Ps 1 corresponds with Ps 150, a "pure" hymnic song of praise where, unlike the other hymns, no justification is given for the four-part *hal'lûyāh*. The way of obedience to the Torah, to which Ps 1 made the call, has reached its goal. In between, however, there are many stages of doubt and resistance. These come to a climax in Ps 73. Here the petitioner first reflects an experience that is diametrically opposed to the statements of Ps 1: the "wicked" prosper, they are respected, happy and rich (vv. 3-12), so that the petitioner starts to doubt the correctness of his loyalty to the Torah (vv 2, 13). Then ("in the sanctuary") he is granted the certainty that he is on the right path (v. 17), which has him end with a convincing confession of trust in God's guidance and help (vv. 23-28). This psalm can be understood as a turning-point on the pathway from Ps 1 to Ps 150 (cf. Brueggemann 1991, 80ff; Wilson 1992).

Such an understanding of Ps 73 is supported and reinforced by the fact that the psalm stands at a clearly marked break in the book of Psalms. Directly beforehand we read: "The end of the prayers of David, son of Jesse" (72.20). There is no other such note in the book of Psalms. It has certainly not been preserved from an earlier collection but has the function at this point of marking the end of the second book (Pss 42–72) and at the same time of books I (1–41) and II. The other theme of the introductory Psalms 1 and 2 comes into view again: the Davidic monarchy.

The "prayers of David" end with a royal psalm (72), which has the name of Solomon in its superscription. This gives expression on the one hand to the fact that the divine assurances to David apply also to his successors; in addition the psalm contains allusions to the story of Solomon, when there is talk of the "kings of Saba and Sheba" (v. 10) and of the "gold of Saba" (v. 15; cf. 1 Kgs 10) [→123]. At the same time, however, it is pointed out that with the reign of Solomon the great time of the Davidic monarchy already came to an end. This is very clearly evident in the royal Psalm 89 with which the third book (Pss 73–89) ends: the psalm first repeats in detail the divine promises to David and his successors (vv. 2-38), but then suddenly changes into a vigorous lament, that God has rejected his anointed one and given the land up to devastation (vv. 39-52). Now the reader finds himself in the period after the end of the monarchy. This situation is in the center of the lament about the destruction of the temple in Ps 74. In addition in this third book as a whole the lament of the praying community dominates: besides Ps 74 also Pss 79; 80 and 83 are "songs of popular lament" (following Gunkel–Begrich 1933, §4), so that almost all the texts of the book of Psalms that are ascribed to this genre are collected here. So it becomes clear that the time of the monarchy is now coming to an end or has already done so (cf. Wilson 1992; McCann 1993).

There is an impressive counterpart to this in the fourth book (Pss 90–106) in the psalms of the kingship of God (93; 95–99). The perspective has changed: from the kingship of David and his dynasty to the kingship of God [→§13]. Another change is also clearly visible: in the first three books the psalms of lament are dominant, while in the last two books they are very much in the background. Instead, the hymns occupy considerable space, both the hymns that sing of the kingship of God and the large number of hallelujah psalms, which increase steadily towards the end (111–118; 135f; 146–150). So from this point of view it is entirely understandable that the collection as a whole should be called *ṯhillîm* "songs of praise" [→§18]. The book of Psalms, which begins with the call to study the God-given Torah, ends with a song of praise of this God and of his great deeds in creation and in the history of Israel and the nations.

At the turning point from lament to praise stands the only psalm that is ascribed to Moses (Ps 90). Its beginning connects with the Blessing of Moses in Deut 33: "LORD, you have been our dwelling-place throughout all generations. Before the mountains were born or you brought forth the earth and the world, from everlasting to everlasting you are God" (Ps 90.1f; cf. Deut 33.27: "The eternal God is your refuge") [→87]. At the same time there is a resonance of the conclusion of the double psalm at the beginning of the book of Psalms: "Blessed are all who take refuge in him" (Ps 2.12). This completes the arch to the call to a life according to the Torah given by Moses (Pss 1 and 2). Then the psalmist continues and prays as an intercessor, as Moses once did: "Relent, O LORD! How long will it be? Have compassion on your servants" (Ps 90.13). In the psalms that then follow there are constant references to the Moses narratives in the Pentateuch (99.6; 103.7; 106.16, 23, 32; cf. 77.21). This draws attention on various levels to the relationship between the book of Psalms and the book of the Torah (cf. Sheppard 1990, 78f). The canonical context, which has already been clearly indicated by Ps 1, is expressly emphasized again here.

2.3 David prays the Psalms

In the first books of the Psalter the psalms of lament are dominant. (The term psalms of lament is not entirely felicitous, see section 2.4 below.) But who is lamenting? Who is the "I" who dominates these psalms? In the first psalm of lament (Ps 3) the superscription gives an indication: it is David who is lamenting. In a number of passages the superscription sets a psalm in a particular situation in the life of David (cf. Childs 1971) [→§13]. In Ps 3 we read: "When he fled from his son Absalom." So there is a presupposition that the reader knows the David stories. The psalm contains a series of elements that allude to the events described in 2 Sam 15.14ff. [→115]. The "many" enemies of the supplicant (Ps 3.2) correspond to the large number of men that were called out to pursue David (2 Sam 17.1). The "many" who think that God will no longer help the supplicant (Ps 3.3) reflect the large number of those who defect to Absalom's side (2 Sam 5.12). The survival of the night in safety (Ps 3.6) plays a decisive role in 2 Sam 17, because David thereby gains the time he needs. The prayer to God on his "holy mountain" (Ps 3.5) connects with David's flight from Jerusalem, when he had come past the mountain (and perhaps prayed there?) "where people used to worship God" (2 Sam 15.32); he now turns back to that place in prayer. The expression "Arise, O LORD!" (Ps 3.8) corresponds to the call to prepare to move the ark in Num 10.35 [→70]—and David had of course brought the ark to Jerusalem (2 Sam 6) [→112]. So Ps 3 can be read precisely as a "midrash" (a commentary in the rabbinic style of biblical interpretation) on the David story. The superscription to Ps 7, too, which gives as the occasion for the lament the bringing of the news of Absalom's death by a "Cushite" (cf. 2 Sam 18.21ff), belongs in this context, as also the rather obscure superscription to Ps 9, which should be perhaps read as "on account of dying, in reference to the son." Thus a whole group of psalms emerges which relates to the events of Absalom's revolt against David.

Whether some of these psalms were created expressly for the purpose of reflecting and commenting on the David story must remain open. At any rate the reader can and should take and process these psalms on various levels. To begin with these prayers are and remain those of an individual person who turns to God in his distress and prays to him for help. The reader and petitioner who has the texts before him in their current form will place himself and his own problems in them and interpret their words in such a way that they correspond to his needs. But he will also bring in the memory of David, the reports of whose life give such a detailed and graphic account of the great beginnings of the history in which the supplicant himself now stands. Perhaps it will be comforting for him to ponder the fact that David too, this great ideal figure of the early days, had to suffer and was exposed to persecution. The texts that deal with David in the books of Samuel are much more detailed in their account of this side of his life than in the reports of his political and military successes. So David is better suited than any other figure from the "great" history of the people of Israel as a figure for the suffering and lamenting petitioner to identify with.

That the figure of David also constitutes the orientation figure for later kings and for the development of concepts of the kingship, is almost self-evident. Thus the next superscription too, which links a psalm with the biography of David, is placed above a "royal psalm" (Ps 18). It relates the psalm to the time "when the LORD delivered him from the hand of all his enemies and from the hand of Saul." The superscriptions are not in chronological order, then, since these events occurred before those mentioned in Ps 3 [→**108**]. But this is the first royal psalm (after Ps 2), so that the reference to the first victorious phase in David's life is easy to understand. In this psalm a king prays in the first person singular and thanks God for help and victory. No concrete details are mentioned; rather, God's intervention is depicted as a tremendous natural event (vv. 8-16). The king's fate is then raised to the fundamental plane of God's attitude to the righteous: the petitioner has behaved in a righteous manner with respect to God's commandments, and so God has helped him—entirely in keeping with Ps 1. This reminds us that in Ps 2 (in connection with Ps 1) David was seen as the righteous man as depicted previously in 1 Kgs 2.1-4; 3.14 etc. [→**116**]. Finally in Ps 18 the whole people is involved (v. 28), described here as "poor" or "oppressed" (*'ānî*). The link is again made with Ps 2: God protects all who seek refuge in him (*ḥāsāh* 18.31; cf. 2.12). So this psalm already contains several inherent levels: that of the king, who gives thanks for the victory given him by God; that of the petitioner, who is aware of his faithfulness to the Torah and who expects God's help as a result; and that of the poor, oppressed people, which assures itself of God's help. In the context of the book of Psalms David represents all these various aspects.

A quite different side of David the petitioner is displayed in Ps 34. The superscription gives as the occasion the situation in which David feigned madness before the Philistine king in order to escape pursuit (2 Sam 21.11-16) [→**109**]. The psalm itself is an artistic acrostic (alphabetical) poem, which combines elements of the hymn and the song of thanksgiving and bears marked wisdom traits. It speaks of help and rescue from distress and fear, and those who seek refuge in God (*ḥāsāh* vv. 9, 23) are again praised. Here it is not the lamenting person that is represented by David, as in Pss 3 and 7, but the person who gives thanks, as in Ps 18 also.

The lament is again dominant in a whole group of other psalms that have been provided with superscriptions from the life of David. At the beginning of this group stands Ps 51, which is linked to one of the most difficult times in David's life: when the prophet Nathan announced God's punishment on him for his transgression with Bathsheba and his underhand removal of Uriah (2 Sam 11f) [→**115**]. Here the confession of sin and the prayer for forgiveness and restoration are in the foreground. The other psalms relate to earlier events, mainly from the time when David was being pursued by Saul: Pss 52; 54; 56; 57; 59; 60; 63. In all of these the lament dominates. But they are also characteristic of this psalm genre in that alongside the lament there are constant elements of thanksgiving for divine aid experienced on previous occasions.

Once again a psalm with a biographical superscription relating to David stands right at the end of one of the books of psalms: Ps 142. Again it is a lament, and again the petitioner confesses that God alone is his refuge (*maḥseh* v. 6). The reasons why such biographical superscriptions have been added in a series of cases but not in others cannot be determined with precision. But these psalms show in an illustrative way the understanding of the significance of David for the tradition and the prayer of the psalms. For no fewer than 73 of the 150 psalms of the Hebrew Bible bear David's name in the superscription. It is not uncommon for the superscription to consist of only one word: *l*ᵉ*dāwîd*, which is most appropriately translated as "a psalm of David."

It is worth noting the division of the psalms that are ascribed to David within the book of Psalms. The first book (Pss 1–41) is almost dominated by them. In the second (42–72) and third books (73–89) they alternate in groups with the psalms of the levitical choirs of Korah and Asaph. The fourth book (90–106) contains only very isolated psalms of David (101 and 103), and in the fifth book they recede behind other groups—pilgrimage psalms and hallelujah psalms. This observation corresponds with the further observation that in the third book, especially in its two corner pillars, Pss 73 and 89, the end of the monarchy is marked (see above). So David is presented as praying the psalms above all where the kingdom is presupposed as (still) extant. But he does not appear in the first instance as the victorious and triumphant king but as the exemplary supplicant of the song of lament. Towards the end he then joins in with the general praise, as the Davidic psalms 138–145 introduce the great concluding doxology.

2.4 Lament and petition, trust and thanksgiving

The psalms of lament dominate the early parts of the book of Psalms [→*In* 107]. The sufferings of the petitioners that are set out in them appear in a special way as both individual and communal. They are often formulated as the expression of quite personal distress and suffering, but in many cases almost give a stereotypical impression. It is a characteristic feature of most psalms of lament, however, that the distress they speak of does not appear to be limited to a clearly definable area. Very frequently the petitioner sees himself as pursued by enemies, and many times this is the only aspect of suffering that is expressly formulated. Often this includes isolation from the present environment. Alongside this, sickness, even impending death, poverty, and awareness of guilt are given as further reasons for the petitioner's laments. But often several of the reasons are combined and interwoven (cf. Crüsemann 1989).

The "enemies" of the lament-psalm petitioner are also viewed from two angles. On the one hand they are the petitioner's personal enemies, and the way in which they bring their enmity to expression and practice it often delves deeply into the petitioner's personal life. On the other hand they appear very much as representatives of a counterpart world, so that the opposition between the petitioner and his enemies is given the character of a fundamental antithesis that reaches far beyond the individual (cf. Janowski 1995). The petitioner faces the majority, often described as "many," as an individual. But above all the petitioner also understands this conflict as a dispute regarding relationships with God. He does not simply see himself as on God's side; rather he often brings his sinfulness and unworthiness to expression. But he turns to God, reckons on God's help, and he knows that what counts with God is "righteousness," which he makes every effort to achieve. The opponents on the other hand are often represented as mockers, even as those that deny God, so that the petitioner's conflict with his enemies assumes the form of the basic conflict between the righteous and the ungodly.

This is basically the main problem of the psalms of lament. Thus in them the antithesis formulated in Ps 1 between the righteous (*ṣaddîqîm*) and the unrighteous or wicked (*rᵉšā'îm*) is concretized in various ways [→§16]. What is presented in Ps 1 in an instructive form has become an entirely personal problem as far as the petitioner of the psalm of lament is concerned. Reality as experienced by him does not tally with the "theory." The wicked prosper and they oppress the petitioner who is trying hard to be righteous. This leads to the petitioner dealing intensively with the question of how this oppressive reality relates to the conviction set out in Ps 1 and which also determines the tradition within which the petitioner is at home.

The term "psalms of lament" or "songs of lament" is actually rather misleading. The "core" of the genre is the petition (Gunkel–Begrich 1933, 218). In many psalms, right at the beginning stands the request that God will hear this prayer (Pss 4.2; 5.2; 17.1 etc.), or the urgent question why or how long God will remain hidden from the petitioner (10.1; 13.2 etc.), which is then followed by the petition for help (10.12; 13.4) or the call to God to arise and intervene (3.8; 7.7 etc.). The lament is never there for its own sake. As a lament it is also directed to God, from whom the petitioner hopes to receive help. And the prayer for help is also always expressed.

The petitions are often just as lacking in concreteness as the depiction of distress. Thus for instance Ps 6 tells us of a serious illness, but details are not given. The petition "Heal me!" (v. 3) is embedded in the petitions "Be gracious to me!" (v. 3) and "Save me and help me!" (v. 5). This psalm also shows other characteristic elements. The petitioner prays that God will not punish him (v. 2). Behind this evidently stands awareness that his own sin may have contributed to the sickness. Then the petitioner presents a reason that might move God to heal him: "In death no one remembers you" (v. 6). It would as it were be in God's own interest not to lose a faithful worshiper to the underworld (*šᵉ'ôl*, v. 6b). Finally friends turn up, here described as "wicked" (*rᵉšā'îm*, v. 9). They are to move back because God hears—or has already heard—the crying of the petitioner (vv. 9f). Such expressions of confidence that the prayer will be heard or has already been heard, are found time and again in psalms of lament.

The interaction between lament, petition and thanksgiving is evident here. This is especially clear in one of the most deeply moving of the psalms of lament, Ps 22, which begins with the words: "my God, my God, why have you forsaken me?" With his lament the petitioner sounds all the depths of abandonment by God, persecution and personal misery—and then this is suddenly transformed into a public proclamation of assurance that God has heard the prayer, and assurance which adopts hymnic forms (vv. 22ff). Why the petitioner suddenly moves from lament and petition into thanksgiving and praise to God is not made clear. It may perhaps be assumed that on this occasion an assurance of being heard is pronounced by a priest (cf. 1 Sam 1.17) [→103]. But as the psalms were prayed again and again this alternation became an expression of confidence in God's attention and help. Psalm 22 already contains earlier expressions of confidence in God's helping hand. It speaks of God's help and salvation in Israel's history (vv. 4-6) and in the personal life of the petitioner from birth (vv. 10f). In other psalms of lament too there are expressions of confidence which sometimes dominate to such an extent that they might be called psalms of trust (e.g. Pss 4; 16; 23). In general one can say that the petition containing each psalm of lament carries the element of trust in it. Hence no psalm of lament ends in a lament and the lament is certainly not its goal.

A series of psalms speaks out of the situation in which the distress has already been overcome. Here thanksgiving stands in the foreground. While the person praying the psalm of lament generally remains with his lament within the confines of his own house, the person praying the thanksgiving song brings his thanksgiving into the public arena of the religious community: "magnify the LORD with me and let us exalt his name together" (34.4, cf. 30.5; 32.11 etc.) [→§11]. The close connection between lament and thanksgiving is evident in the fact that the person praying the thanksgiving song often reiterates once again his earlier situation, his distress and also his petitions to God.

So in retrospect the petitioner can speak of his distress as if he has already been in death's power: "The cords of the grave (šᵉʾôl) coiled around me; the snares of death confronted me" (Ps 18.4★). This is even clearer in Ps 30: "O LORD, you brought me up from the grave; you spared me from going down into the pit" (v. 3). The petitioner was already in the power of šᵉʾôl. The realm of the dead is an area of power which draws towards itself anyone whose position in the world of the living is in danger. This comes to expression with particular clarity in Ps 88. "For my sword was full of trouble and my life draws near the grave ... I am counted among those who go down to the pit. I am set apart with the dead, like the slain who lie in the grave" (vv. 3-5a). The petitioner is on the brink of the world of the dead and is already "like" the dead. But in this position he is out of God's view and God's thoughts; for God no longer remembers the dead (v. 5b). He performs no miracles for them, nor do they remember his earlier deeds and wonders (vv. 10-12). They are cut off from God and his history with human beings. The worst thing about the suffering, for the petitioner, is that God himself has brought him into this unenviable situation (vv. 6f). So it is only God who can free him from it. (Cf. Barth 1947.)

This psalm makes something else clear as well: the consequence of the suffering is also alienation and isolation from the world around. We read that through his sickness God has alienated the petitioner from his friends and companions (Ps 88.8, 18). In another passage we read that his friends and relatives have become his enemies (41.10; 55.13-15). They have thereby joined the great number of enemies whom many of the petitioners feel themselves surrounded by.

The "enemies" can be spoken of in very different ways. Often they are people from the petitioner's vicinity who turn away from him (31.12; 38.12 etc.), mock him (22.8; 35.15f; 102.9 etc.) or persecute him and attack him (31.14; 35.4; 40.15 etc.). There is also talk of enemy warriors and whole armies (3.7; 27.3; 62.4 etc.), who attack the petitioner with the sword and with other weapons (7.30; 11.2; 37.14 etc.). In this imagery the extent of the true level of opposition has certainly been exaggerated. This is even more clearly the case when the enemy's ambushes are expressed in terms of hunting (7.16; 9.16; 31.5 etc.), or when finally the enemies are described as wild animals (7.3; 10.9; 22.13f etc.). All this makes the extraordinary, terrifying menace and peril of the petitioner clear, from which he can see no escape in his own strength.

But in particular, time and again, it is the words of his enemies that unsettled the petitioner and which he often repeats to God in prayer. "Not a word from their mouth can be trusted ...; their throat is an open grave; with their tongue they speak deceit" (5.10). It is made repeatedly clear that the ultimate concern in these conflicts is the relationship to God. The petitioner is viewed by his enemies as someone who trusts in God, but whose trust is misplaced. "He trusts in the LORD; let the LORD rescue him" (22.8); "God will not deliver him" (3.3); "God has forsaken him" (71.11); "Where is your God?" (42.3,

10). But of themselves they say: "Who will see us?" (64.5); "God has forgotten; he covers his face and never sees" (10.11); "God will not punish. There is no God" (10.4; cf. v. 13). Various expressions are used to describe the enemies' contempt for God (5.11; 10.13). And hence they are constantly described as the *rāš'îm*, the wicked, the unrighteous, the ungodly (7.10; 10.2-4, 13, 15 etc.), as "evildoers" (*po'lê 'āwen*), or troublemakers (6.9; 14.4; 59.3 etc.).

Psalm 1 already spoke of God's attitude towards the *rāš'îm*. But in the psalms of lament, to begin with, the focus is on their own attitude. Above all it is directed against the petitioner in question. The contrast is given expression in the terminology used. The petitioner is often described as the righteous person (*ṣaddîq*), commonly in direct opposition to the *rāš'îm* (Ps 7.10; 11.2f; 31.18f etc.). Or, in similar vein, he is called the "pious one" (*hāsîd*) (12.2; 16.10; 37.28). But then another aspect of the opposition is often evident. The wicked are the rich and the strong, but the petitioner is one of the poor, who are described by the terms *'ebyôn*, *'ānî* and *'ānāw*. These terms are also often used in express contrast to the wicked and the evildoers (9.18f; 10.2ff; 37.10f, 14 etc.). Here again it is very clear that the conflict between the petitioner and his opponents has above all to do with the relationship to God and the Torah. The antithesis of Ps 1 finds its fullest expression in the psalms of lament.

2.5 Hymnic praise

The psalms of lament and thanksgiving do not only dominate the first books of the Psalter. Between them hymnic notes sound time and again, speaking of Israel's experiences with God in a quite different way. Here the hymns do not simply appear without a connection. Thus the lament of Ps 7 ends with a self-challenge to praise God: "I will thank the LORD, for he is just, I will praise the name of the LORD, the Most High" (7.18). This verse leads on to the following hymn (Ps 8), the first psalm of this type in the Psalter. It begins, as announced in 7.18, by praising the name of God (v. 2) and then elaborates on the admiring contemplation of God's creative activity [→§5]. It is contrasted with the work of the enemies, who will have to be silent in the face of this superiority of God (v. 3). It is an individual petitioner who is speaking here (v. 4) and praising God that he has granted the human being, so often persecuted and humiliated, a dominant position in his creation (vv. 5-7), as described already in the account of the creation at the beginning of the Hebrew Bible (Gen 1.26f) [→**14**].

The next hymn, Ps 19, forms the center of a group of psalms, at the beginning and conclusion of which are two texts that speak of the entry into the sanctuary on the "holy mountain" (15.1), the "mountain of the Lord" (24.3)—Zion, as we have been told in 14.7 [→**§18**]. Here we see that the psalms of lament and thanksgiving, in which individual petitioners speak, are not fully separated from the temple service in Jerusalem, even if they are spoken and prayed at other sites, perhaps even outside the land, in exile ("by the rivers of Babylon," 137.1). The special feature of this hymn is that it combines two themes: praise of the creator and of creation with the sun as its central element (19.2-7) and praise of the Torah (vv. 8-15). "The heavens" first praise God's work in the heavenly realm (vv. 2f), which is partly hidden from humans in its grandeur (v. 4). The second part then has to do entirely with the human being, to whom God gives reliable instruction through his Torah [→**§10**]. Here the psalm picks up the theme of Ps 1 again and adds a new element to it in the link with the hymnic praise of creation.

The next hymn (Ps 29) also speaks of creation or, more precisely, of the creator, who expressly displays his creative power. Other notes are audible than those in Ps 19. The powerful demonstration of God's creative power is displayed in thunder-storms, his voice sounding in the thunder. This power, which can also be destructive in its effects, is audible and visible on the earth (vv. 5-9a); but at the same time it is an occasion for praise of the inhabitants of heaven, the "sons of God" (*benê 'ēlîm*, vv. 1f), who worship God in his heavenly palace (v. 9b), in which he is enthroned as king "over the flood," i.e. over the ocean of heaven (cf. Gen 1.7) (v. 10) [→**14**]. But this divine rule is not turned away from the world. So the psalm ends with the petition for strength and peace for God's people (v. 11).

In Ps 8 it was an individual petitioner, and in Pss 19 and 29 it was heaven and its inhabitants that struck up the hymn, but now in Ps 33 it is the "righteous." This hymnic song of praise links up directly with the thanks of those who have learned that their sins are forgiven and "covered," following their confession of them before God (Ps 32). The righteous who have experienced this forgiveness are called to express "joy in the LORD" (32.11). Ps 33 picks this up immediately, by calling on the righteous to sing a "new song" (vv. 1-3). The main theme of this new song is the "word of the LORD." It is as true as his whole activity is reliable (v. 4). This is elaborated upon in various regards: God's word is the guarantee for justice and righteousness, as the righteous have already discovered (v. 5) [→§15]. At the same time it is a powerful word of the creator: "by the word of the LORD were heavens made, their starry host by the breath of his mouth ... for he spoke, and it came to be; he commanded, and it stood firm" (vv. 6, 9). This statement is very close to Gen 1.3ff: "God spoke—and it came to be." But the effects of the word of God are also felt deep in the history of human beings. The words and plans of the nations and peoples must fail if they resist God's plans (vv. 10f). So it is a special distinction for the people that God has chosen for his inheritance (v. 12) [→§6]. The psalm elaborates further on God's superiority over the doings of humans and nations and ends with a confession of the praying community that it hopes and trusts in this God and waits for him (vv. 20-22).

While we encounter each of these hymns in the first book of the Psalter in an environment dominated by the psalms of lament, in the two last books they are primarily in the foreground. In the great hymn Ps 104 the theme is again creation. The psalm sketches a general picture of creation from God's creative activity in his heavenly world (vv. 1-4) by way of the suppression of the waters of chaos (vv. 5-9) step-by-step through to the animal and human domains (vv. 10-23), and finally the greatness and variety of creation and of God's dealings with it (vv. 24-32). This psalm is closely connected with other hymns that precede and follow it. Before it in Ps 103 stands one that elaborates in detail upon God's readiness to forgive. The two psalms are linked by the same blessing formula at the beginning and the end: "Praise the LORD, O my soul!" Ps 103 begins with the petitioner's self-directed call (according to the superscription, to David!), to praise God's "holy name," and then quotes the words with which God declared his name at the reinstitution of his covenant before Moses on Sinai: "the LORD is compassionate and gracious, slow to anger, abounding in love" (vv. 7f; cf. Ex 34.6) [→63]. There on Sinai God declared his readiness to forgive. In its absolutely immeasurable greatness it is a highly significant element of his being (Ps 103.10-13), and in their proneness to fail and their ephemerality humans are totally dependent on it (vv. 14-16). Here the key word "covenant" sounds again (vv. 17f). At the end God appears as the king enthroned in heaven, surrounded by his heavenly court (vv. 19-22), his servants (v. 21), which once again echoes Ps 104.1-4 (esp. v. 4) (cf. Zenger 1991). These two hymns cover the whole area of God's enthronement in heaven and his work in creation through to his grace for his covenant people and for the human being, who is like dust and grass.

The hymn that then follows (Ps 105) tells in great detail the story of Israel's beginnings [→§21] which it presents entirely as the history of God's covenant with his people. The "miracles" that God performs (vv. 2, 5) begin with Abraham, with whom and with whose successors Isaac and Jacob God makes a covenant, which is an eternal covenant for Israel (vv. 8-10). The content of this covenant is: "I will give you the land of Canaan as your inheritance" (v. 11; cf. Gen 15.18) [→27]. The whole story is then told in detail with close reference to the books of the Torah: from Abraham's wanderings through the selling of Joseph to Egypt, Israel's fate in Egypt with the plagues, through to the exodus and finally in brief the way through the wilderness and on to the realization of the promise of the land, with which he "remembered his holy word" which he had given to Abraham (vv. 42-44). The whole thing is told as a pure story of leadership which regards only the miraculous deeds of God. Things come to a neat conclusion at the end, when the aim of the gift of the land is said to be: "that they might keep his precepts and observe his laws" (v. 45). That is the other side of the covenant that God made with the forefathers (vv. 8-10), that Israel should keep the conditions of the covenant.

Psalm 106 is, as it were, "twinned" with Ps 105, since again it speaks of the same history between God and Israel. It too begins with praise of God's great deeds, and it connects with the end of Ps 105 by declaring blessed those who maintain justice and righteousness (v. 3). But before the telling of the story begins we read: "we have sinned, even as our fathers did" (v. 6) [→§7]. And then the story is told again, beginning with the exodus from Egypt, but this time from the opposite point of view: as the history of Israel's sin. Already in Egypt they did not take note of God's miracles (v. 7); and when God had rescued them at the Reed Sea, though they believed his word and sang his praises (v. 12; cf. Ex 14.31; 15.1), they soon forgot about it (v. 13) [→46]. And then follows the history of the time in the wilderness and the stay at Mount Horeb, where God would have destroyed them if Moses had not stepped into the breach (v. 23); the refusal to enter into the land, with its consequence of the long stay in the wilderness (vv. 24-27; cf. Num 13f [→71]); the sin with the Ba'al of Pe'or (vv. 28-31) and—as an afterthought—the waters of Meribah (v. 32f; cf. Ex 17; Num 20); and then their falling in with the inhabitants of the land and their cult, which defiled them and made them fall away from God (vv.

34-39). "Therefore the LORD was angry with his people and abhorred his inheritance" (v. 40). This is the absolute rock bottom. The story would have ended here—if God had not "remembered" his covenant again (v. 45). What was said at the beginning of these two psalms is vindicated: "God remembers his covenant for ever" (105.8). This is one of the most comforting statements in the Hebrew Bible: that in spite of everything God continually remembers his covenant [→§6].

The story of God with Israel also forms the theme of another "pair" of hymns: Pss 135 and 136. There is no tension between them; they both regard the story of Israel's beginnings as the history of the powerful leading of God. They both place this history in the broad framework of God's activity. Ps 136 begins with the creation (vv. 5ff), clearly borrowing from Gen 1, but then goes on in a rather abrupt transition from the creation of the heavenly bodies (vv. 7-9) to the killing of the Egyptian firstborn (v. 10) and from there on describes the pathway along which Israel was led through to its entry into the promised land. So creation and the guidance of Israel are the two great themes that are combined together in this hymn. Psalm 135 places its emphases elsewhere. The same phase of Israel's history from the killing of the Egyptian firstborn through to the giving of the land is summarized succinctly (vv. 8-12). But the dominant message of the psalm is: our God is greater than all other gods (v. 5; the other gods are only images made by human hands (vv. 15-18). God, the only one, also shows his greatness and power in powerful natural events (vv. 6f); but the important thing is that on the basis of his actions with Israel his name will stand for all time and that his name will be "remembered" (v. 13), as God once said to Moses (Ex 3.15) [→40].

The hymns center on the two great themes of creation and history. God is constantly spoken of as the King enthroned on Zion, the mountain to which he led Israel at the beginning (Ex 15.17) and on which he has now set his dwelling in the midst of Israel [→48]. In some hymns Zion itself is the central theme. There it is called "the city of God" (Pss 46.5; 48.2, 9; 87.3), city of the great king" (48.3), "holy mountain" (48.2f), "dwelling-place of the Most High" (46.5; cf. 76.2; 84.2). In Pss 46 and 48 we read of an attack on Zion by nations and kings which God turned away victoriously (cf. also Ps 76). Here historical experiences of the protection of Jerusalem are combined with hymnic praise of the power of God. Jerusalem is both God's dwelling-place and the divinely protected capital city of Israel (esp. of Judah).

Positioned between the two psalms of Zion, 46 and 48, is a third psalm (47) [→§14] in which God himself, enthroned as king on Zion, forms the main theme. Here too nations congregate, but their task is above all to add their confirmation that God is "king of the whole earth" (vv. 2, 8) and "king of the nations" (v. 9). This theme is then taken up again in the fourth book, where a whole group of "Yhwh-as-king hymns" are collected (93; 95–99). In these the call, "Yhwh is king" (93.1; 96.10; 97.1; 99.1; cf. 47.9), resounds again and again. There is much in these psalms to remind us of religious events, which can also be discerned in other psalms: shouts of joy and the sounding of trumpets (47.6; 98.6), falling down in worship (95.6), and the singing and celebration of the assembled community in general. God's "ascent" (*ʿālāh* 47.6) recalls the "bringing up" of the ark to Jerusalem by David (*ʿālāh* hiph.), which was also accompanied by "shouts of joy and the sounding of trumpets" (2 Sam 6.15) [→112]. In other psalms too similar events may be discerned, as for instance in Ps 24.7-10, where the entry of the ark procession into the temple is described with the term "king of glory, Yhwh Zebaot."

God's kingship is described and sung in these psalms from various points of view: God's rule over the world that he has created (Ps 24.1f; 47.3, 8; 93; 95.4f; 96.10, also 29.10); in his leading of his people in history (47.5; 95.7-11; 98.3; 99.6-8); in his establishment and maintenance of justice and righteousness (93.5; 97.2, 6, 8; 98.9; 99.4); in the eyes of the nations (47.2, 4, 9f; 96.3, 7-10; 98.2f; 99.1-3); and above all, his kingship over the gods (95.3; 96.4f; 97.7, 9). Here the confession of God as king becomes an important element of the struggle for the preservation of the purity of Israel's faith in the *one* God from the worship of other gods.

God is king of the world, king above the gods [→§17], king over all the nations, and in all this he is the king of Israel. Thus in the Yhwh-as-king psalms he is called "God ... our king" (Ps 47.7), in the Zion song "my king and my God" (84.4; cf. 68.25). Correspondingly we read in the hymn that the inhabitants of Zion rejoice in "their king," who is also called "their creator" (149.2). God's appellation as "my king and my God" is even found in psalms of lament (5.3; 44.5; cf. 74.12: "God is my king from of old"). So this description of God and the understanding of God that goes with it has become a central element of Israelite piety.

The psalms begin with songs of lament and end with hymns. A series of hallelujah psalms (Pss 146–150) that is reluctant to come to an end forms the conclusion. Israel's singing and praying of the psalms resonates in all the depths of the lament, but it ends with praise of God, who has proven his power not only as creator and king, but again and again also as the helper of the poor and the weak (145.14; 146.7-9; 147.6; 149.4).

3. The Book of Job

3.1 Who is Job?

The book called by the name of Job (in the Latin version, Ijob) [→*In* **263**] begins: "There was a man"—literally: "a man was (there)" (*'îš hāyāh*)—a quite unusual beginning, unique in the Hebrew Bible. It makes it clear that in what follows the concern is only with this one person in his encounter with God. This man lives in the land of Uz (*'ûṣ*). The precise situation of this land remains uncertain and is likely to continue to do so; it lies somewhere in the east, for Job is one of the "inhabitants of the east" (*benê qedem*, 1.3). In the Hebrew Bible the name *'ûṣ* also appears as a personal name in the context of the "Arameans" (Gen 10.23) and as the son of Nahor, brother of Abraham (Gen 22.20f). So in Job we can see a distant relative of Abraham. Is he an Israelite? The question remains open, or rather, it is not asked. But it is clear enough that Job knows God, and that this is the God of whom the whole Hebrew Bible speaks: the God of Israel. He not only knows him, he speaks, prays and cries to him—and also against him, as no other person does in the Hebrew Bible. Whether Israelite or non-Israelite, Job is an exemplary individual, a human being in conversation with God.

It is a feature of Job's special position that we are told scarcely anything about his "world." Apart from his family—and the thieving and murdering "Sabaeans" and "Chaldeans" (Job 1.15, 17)—there is mention of three "friends" who visit him (2.11-13) and who then accompany him as conversation partners throughout the whole book. They too are individuals who come from quite different regions and whose origins remain unclear. (The same applies to Elihu, who first appears in ch. 32.) Right at the end alongside the large family his "earlier acquaintances" turn up (42.11); but even this does not go beyond the inner circle of his world.

Finally, Job is "exemplary" above all in the fact that much of what is said about him moves along the outer extremes of human possibilities and experiences. "Humanness," as it were, comes to its extremest expression in him. Of no other person are such high-sounding statements made in the Hebrew Bible as about Job, and it is even God who makes these statements: he was "blameless and upright, God-fearing and kept from evil" (1.1, 8; 2.3). Of no other person are we told that their behavior and their fate are made the subject of heavenly discussion (1.6-12; 2.1-6). The calamity that overcomes him, and the plagues with which he is afflicted, represent in their seriousness and their accumulation the most extreme affliction that a human being might conceivably experience. In the sharpness of their accusations, his speeches to God exceed anything else found in the Hebrew Bible. And no one else is granted a divine answer comparable with the great divine speeches in chs. 38 to 41.

So Job appears to readers as a human being who comes through all the imaginable heights and depths of human existence, suffering obediently at first, and then questioning wildly, and finally acknowledging God's comprehensive plan.

3.2 "Framework narrative" and "dialogues"

The book of Job begins and ends in prose (1.1-2.13; 42.7-17), while the much more extensive middle section is composed in various poetic stylistic forms. This external difference seems to reflect an inner difference. In the narrative introduction Job appears as the patient sufferer, and in the rest of the book as the presumptuous rebel. Many exegetes therefore regard these two parts as not originally belonging together (so also 1983, 263). The main interest is in the poetic middle section with its often challenging theological problems, while the "framework narrative" is regarded rather as a simple "popular book." However, when exegetical endeavor is applied to the book in its present form, it very quickly becomes clear that this distinction does not do justice to the texts. In recent times more and more exegetes have understood the book in its full complexity as a theological unit (e.g. Greenberg 1980 and 1987; Clines 1989; for interpretation cf. esp. Ebach 1996a and b). This certainly does not exclude the recognition that individual parts of the book have a prehistory of their own; in its present form however the book represents a carefully crafted composition.

The various terms used for God are striking [→§16]. In the narrative parts he is regularly called by the personal name Yahweh, but not in the dialogues between Job and the four friends (with one exception: 12.9); instead, here we have various terms for God: besides the common word *'ēl*, the rarer form *ʾlo'h* and the similarly unusual word *šadday* (cf. Gen 17.1). In the divine speeches on the other hand we find the divine name Yahweh [→27], so that its use or non-use cannot be divided along the lines of framework narrative and speech section.

Many exegetes refer to the introductory narrative as an "idyll": Job is devout, and things are going well for him. But the characterization of his piety goes far beyond what is said about people elsewhere in the Hebrew Bible. That a person is "blameless, perfect" (*tām, tāmîm*) is said only of Noah (Gen 6.9), the one person for whose sake God withdrew his decision to destroy creation [→17]. It is said of Job not only by the narrator (1.1), but by God himself (1.8; 2.3). And God expressly singles Job out from all other people: "there is none like him on the earth." So it is already clear in the first sentence of the book that it is not just a matter of a pious person and not even of an outstandingly pious person, but Job stands as an example for humans, of the person that God wants humans to be.

The apparent idyll, however, is not without its dangers. Job's seven sons appear almost as the ideal embodiment of the divine blessing. What is said of them, however, stands to some degree in contrast with this. They are constantly partying, and they do this in such a way that Job becomes concerned that they might in the process "fall into sin." The example of their sin that is mentioned is that they might have "blessed" God in their hearts, i.e. blasphemed him. And Job takes preventative action against the possible consequences of such behavior and thinking and performs sacrificial rituals in order to "sanctify" his children, i.e. to atone for them (1.4f) [→§11]. In this one can see a rather marked feature of his piety and care. At the same time, however, it is clear that the maintenance of Job's relationship with God is certainly not just a matter of course, and that he believes he must take steps against any possible threat to it.

That it is not a question of a human idyll is made perfectly clear by the abrupt change of scene. Job and the extent to which he pleases God become the object of consideration and discussion in a heavenly assembly (1.6-12). The modern reader has to set aside the many kinds of popular traditions about what goes on "in heaven." What is happening here is once again quite unique in the Hebrew Bible. That the heavenly beings assemble before God may be a common notion, though it is seldom mentioned [→331]. That the topic of discussion is events on the earth is also reported in 1 Kgs 22.19-22 in the context of a prophetic vision [→142]; but there the concern is with fundamental political questions while here it is only Job's behavior that is the subject of discussion. And here the threat to his exemplary behavior is highlighted: the *śāṭān*, i.e. the "adversary" or "accuser," queries the unimpeachability of Job's behavior: "Does Job fear God 'for nothing,'" i.e. without reward? God does after all protect and bless him. But what will happen if God takes all that away from him? Won't Job then "bless" God to his face, i.e. curse him? (vv. 9-11).

This formulates the central theme of the book of Job: how will Job, the exemplary righteous man, behave when things go badly for him? This again is a problem which not only concerns Job as an individual pious man, but in which at the same time the validity of a basic tenet of the wisdom tradition [→§15] that stands behind the book of Job, is opened up to discussion: the relationship between deeds and their consequences, between one's actions and one's prosperity. Are things going well for Job *because* he is pious and God-fearing? Or is Job pious and God-fearing because things are going well for him? Is there a connection between the two things and how can this be determined? It will become evident that this is one of the main points of contention between Job and his friends in the subsequent dialogues.

The problem is considerably sharpened in the fact that it also implies another question. How can God knowingly allow the preconditions for his life of pleasing God to be withdrawn from Job? Does God himself want to "test," as it were, the validity of this basic tenet? Does God himself regard this connection as valid or not? And what consequences are to be drawn for his attitude towards Job? The tension that lies in this double question dominates the whole book. The reader is granted an advantage in information over the persons in the book of Job, since he or she knows the background to Job's suffering—very much as in the narrative of the "binding" of Isaac by Abraham (the Akedah), in which the reader is told at the beginning that God "tested" Abraham (Gen 22.1) [→28].

With God's express permission (v. 12), the adversary robs Job of all his possessions and finally also of his children (vv. 13-19). Job passes this test. He performs the customary mourning ceremonies and prostrates himself on the ground in prayer (v. 20). Then he speaks words of great theological depth and poetic beauty (which are easily prone to become mere formulas through frequent use): "Naked I came from my mother's womb, and naked I shall depart. The LORD gave and the LORD has taken away; may the name of the LORD be praised" (v. 21). This is the very first sentence spoken by Job. It will remain in the reader's consciousness through everything that occurs and everything that is said in what follows.

In the next encounter God settles up, as it were (2.1-3): Job has passed the test. And so God reproaches the adversary for provoking him into afflicting Job "for nothing." This is an extremely sensitive sentence from a theological point of view. The Babylonian Talmud says of this: "If this were not a written verse of Scripture, one would not be permitted to say it: like a human who is led astray and allows himself to be led astray" (*Baba bathra* 16a). God exercises self-criticism, as it were, and acknowledges that he himself must bear responsibility. And what the adversary has done with God's permission proves to be "for nothing." The word "for nothing" has a changed sense by comparison with the provocative question of the adversary whether Job fears God "for nothing" (1.9). While there it said "without reward," now we read "without sense, senseless"; for Job has stuck with his position and has even impressively confirmed it (cf. Ebach 1990).

And nonetheless God once again allows himself to be provoked by the adversary. What will happen when God—through the adversary— stretches out his hand against Job's "flesh and bones"? For this too God gives the adversary a free hand (2.4-6). He afflicts him with bad boils "from the soles of his feet to the top of his head." Job remains alive but his whole energy for living has been taken from him. He sits like an outcast on the rubbish heap outside human society (vv. 7f). But once again he seems to pass the test. At first the text says nothing of his reaction towards God; but when his wife speaks to him, picking up the adversary's words—"bless (i.e. curse) God and die!"—he rejects her words as silly and adds a further significant line himself: "shall we accept good from God, and not trouble?" (vv. 8f).

So has Job passed this test? The text does not answer this question. Nor is there any continuation of the conversation between God and the adversary; the latter does not figure again in the entire book of Job. So the answer must lie in the subsequent text. The section on Job's second affliction ends with the words: "In all this Job did not sin in what he said" (2.10). The Talmud (in the passage cited above) sees a reservation in this: "He did not sin with his lips, but he sinned in his heart." In this would lie an anticipation of Job's subsequent speeches, which at many points move on the boundaries of what might be called "sinning."

The transition to the speeches forms a small, impressive scene. Job's three friends come, perform rituals of mourning and sit down with Job on the ground in silence—for seven days and seven nights (2.11-13). Then Job begins to speak. Against his friends' silence and the fact that they do not give him comforting words the effect of the beginning of this speech is all the more impressive. In the introductory sentence we now find the word for which so far there has been a euphemistic circumlocution: Job curses (3.1). This is the beginning of a long series of alternating speeches. An abundance of themes are addressed which bring a whole variety of aspects of the wisdom tradition to expression, some of them in a rather distinctive form. Some chapters or sections seem to have a prehistory of their own. But now in all their variety of scenes and themes they stand entirely in the context of what is developed in the introductory narrative: the fundamental questions thrown up in the conversations between God and the adversary, as well as Job's fate and his behavior hitherto. Neither the narrative nor the speeches—though a number of individual problems remain—are understandable and meaningful without their interactive relationship.

3.3 Job and his "friends"

Job holds a monologue. He curses "his day," i.e. the day of his birth (3.1). But he does not do what the adversary predicted: he does not curse God, neither at this point nor at any time in the following speeches. The monologue is not addressed to anyone at all; it is nothing but a lament, nothing but a "why?" Job complains that he was born at all (v. 3), or at least that he did not die straight after his birth (vv. 11-13); then at least he would have his peace. But it is precisely the peace that he longs for that he does not now find because of his incessant moaning (vv. 24-26).

It is already evident in this, the first of Job's speeches that the concern is not only with his individual fate, but that he sees his fate and his suffering in a broad context. The day of his birth represents the day *per se*. It would have been better if there had been no day at all (vv. 4-9), if the light had not shone through the darkness, as happened at the beginning of the creation of the world (Gen 1.3f) [→14]. The peace of the grave that Job wishes for himself will ultimately come to all people, the great and the rich (vv. 14f), as well as the wicked, the imprisoned, servants and masters (vv. 17-19). And once more the "why?," "why does he give light to the miserable?" (vv. 20-23). The word "God" is not in the text; the lament almost seems anonymous.

This magnificent monologue is a puzzle to the reader—and also to Job's friends. It complains of suffering—Job's own and that of the world and of humanity—but it gives no indication of how all this relates to what the prologue has described. Nor does it do this in the form of question. Even less does it attempt to give an answer to the question that arises necessarily for the friends of Job, who have been trained in the wisdom tradition, and which they expect Job to pose for himself: namely, what the relationship is between Job's suffering and his deeds.

So then the first of the friends, Eliphaz, begins rather haltingly by calling to mind Job's earlier helpful behavior towards others (4.1-4). But then he formulates one of the foundations of wisdom doctrine: "consider now: who, being innocent, has ever perished?" (v. 7). The key term guilt/innocence is addressed here. This is, after all, the premise which forms the point of departure for the friends—and which Job too, in principle, does not contest—that there is indeed a mutual relationship between one's deeds and one's well-being [→§19], a relationship which however does not work "automatically," but which is put into effect by God (cf. Koch 1955).

A life that is "pleasing" to God is blessed by him; but guilt has suffering as its consequence. Eliphaz does not simply present his arguments in a didactic form, but justifies them from experience: "I have seen" (4.8; 5.3). He even puts forward a weighty sentence as a result of a nocturnal visionary experience: "can a mortal be more righteous than God? Can a man be more pure than his maker?" (vv. 12-17)

As yet Eliphaz does not expressly say that Job must have incurred guilt if things are going so badly for him (which the friends will say very clearly later on). Rather, he gives him the advice: "if it were me, I would appeal to God" (5.8). In Job's suffering he sees "the discipline of the Almighty" and he urges him not to despise it (v. 17). He describes to him how well things will go for him in the end, if he follows this advice. But for all his sympathy for Job's position, Eliphaz's speech admits of no doubt as to the correctness of his arguments and does not show any preparedness to open them up to discussion. Rather, in his view Job's "resentment" is dubious, because this provides the basis for contradiction against God: "resentment kills a fool, and envy slays the simple" (5.2). The friends' dogged maintenance of their positions is also conditioned by the worry that to question them would be to endanger fundamental elements of faith in God (cf. von Rad 1970, 272). Eliphaz then concludes his speech with the definitive declaration and advice: "we have examined this, and it is true. So hear it and apply it to yourself" (v. 27).

This first conversational contribution by one of the friends leaves the reader with an ambiguous impression. On the one hand there is no mistaking the concern to comfort and to pick up. The reader, particularly the modern reader, should not be too quick to take Job's side and to dismiss the concerns of the friends out of hand. On the other hand, however, it is clear that the words of Eliphaz do not really reach Job in his situation. Eliphaz is not actually speaking to Job, but expounding his view of the problem of human suffering. And with all the graphic imagery of his examples they all have in common the basic notion that suffering is a consequence of guilt, but that in the end things will go well for the innocent or the penitent.

This impression is reinforced in the following speeches by the friends. In addition, they now begin to criticize Job expressly and in some cases harshly, as Bildad does in 8.2 and Zophar does in 11.2f. The pastoral tone of Eliphaz's first speech recedes further and further, and the didactic and corrective tone dominates. Bildad supposes that Job's sons are deserving of their death because of their own sins (8.4). As for Job himself, he should "seek" God; God will restore him, "if you are pure and upright" (vv. 5f). Bildad does not know what the reader knows: that God has already expressed precisely this positive verdict about Job. But since the reader has the advantage of knowing this in advance, it is clear also to him or her, to what extent Bildad has missed the mark as far as Job's real situation is concerned. Zophar even speaks expressly of the guilt of Job (11.6), which Eliphaz reinforces and expounds in his second speech (15.5f). On the second occasion Bildad speaks only of the fate of the wicked (ch. 18), which Zophar continues with much verbiage and imagery (ch. 20). Finally, this criticism of Job by his friends reaches its climax in the third speech of Eliphaz (ch. 22), in which he reproaches Job with a long list of sins: "is not your wickedness great? Are not your sins endless?" (vv. 5ff).

3.4 Job's dispute with God

In the meantime it has become very clear that Job responds less and less in his speeches to the words of his friends, but that rather, God himself is his opposite number. At first Job appeared to respond to his friends' arguments, when he challenged them to tell him where he had gone wrong (6.24). But already in the first answer to the friends (chs. 6f) attention moves to the complaint about God's attitude towards him, which quickly develops into an accusation (7.12ff). In the process Job picks up elements from the songs of lament in the Psalms but he turns them into their opposite. The lament singer asks God to pay attention to him; Job says: "let me alone!" (v. 16). And he continues with a veritable parody of a psalm motif: "what is man that you make so much of him" (cf. Ps 8.5) [→**332**]. Job feels pressured by God's constant attention and wishes again that God would turn away from him (vv. 17-19).

Once again he picks up an argument of his friends, and proceeds to take it further in a quite different direction. "Indeed, I know that this is true. But how can a mortal be righteous before God? Though one wished to dispute with him, one could not answer him one time out of a thousand" (9.2f). God and humans are "worlds" apart, in the full sense of the word. For God is the creator of the world, not only of the earth, but of the whole cosmos in its astonishing magnificence (vv. 5-10). Again one finds oneself reminded of the petitioner of the Psalms who contrasts the expanse of the heavens with the insignificance of humans: "when I consider your heavens, the work of your fingers ... what is man that you are mindful of him ...?" (Ps 8.4f). But for Job this contrast has quite different, frightening aspects. In respect of this God humans cannot be in the right, because they cannot gain a hearing. And finally: "it is all the same; that is why I say, 'he destroys both the blameless and the wicked'" (v. 22). God is not only an unjust judge, he is even a wicked person, a guilty person, who has the earth in his hands (v. 24). Job knows that God will view him as guilty in any case (9.28f), even though God knows that he is innocent (10.7). But whether guilty or innocent, he has no chance before God (v. 15). So once again he raises the lament, "why then did you bring me out of the womb?" (v. 18), "turn away from me so I can have a moment's joy before I go to the place of no return" (vv. 20f).

This accusation against God as an unjust judge, who has no concern for justice, is without parallel in the Hebrew Bible. It is all the more surprising to the reader of the book of Job in that it now shows Job from quite a different side than the way in which he was presented in the introductory narrative. So the reader waits in suspense to see how this confrontation will develop. For this can surely not be the last word of Job, of whom God said that he was "blameless" like no other person on earth.

But the picture of Job is complex. After the tremendous accusation against God, quite different tones are sounded in his next speech. The concern is initially with wisdom, the wisdom of Job's friends, which he mocks, the wisdom of God and finally also Job's own wisdom, which is not inferior to that of his friends (12.1-13.2). Then Job accuses his friends of lies and deceit and calls on them to be quiet so that he himself can present his case before God (13.3-13). He begins this with phrases from a court case and emphasizes that he is in the right (v. 18); but finally here too his complaint about heavy-handed oppression by God is again spoken of (vv. 21, 24-27), though this is less massively done than in chs. 9f. And then follows an elegy about human life and its ephemerality (ch. 14). Dominant in the next speech, too, is the tone of Job's lament concerning his situation, as he sees himself once again persecuted by God (16.7-19), but also by people to whom God has delivered him up (vv. 10f), and by his friends (v. 20). The whole thing ends in deep resignation, which sees only the "grave" ahead (ch. 17).

Job now declares quite openly that God has become his enemy. God has caught him in his net, has blocked his path, sullied his honor; he uproots him like a tree and treats him as his opponent (19.6-11). He sets hostile gangs on him, and Job becomes abhorrent even to his nearest and dearest (vv. 12-19). It is God's hand that has struck him (v. 21). But unlike in earlier statements Job does not now want his laments to go down together with him but for them to be written down "with an iron tool on lead, or engraved in rock for ever" (vv. 23f). Why? Because Job knows that his cause will not disappear without trace, but that his "Redeemer" lives (v. 25).

This is one of the most interpreted passages in the book of Job, which nonetheless still leaves open various possible interpretations. "I know that my Redeemer lives," i.e. following linguistic usage in the Hebrew Bible: the *go'ēl*, the closest relative, who is entitled and obliged to redeem an Israelite or his portion of land that has run into slavery (cf. Ruth 4; Lev 25.25ff). In Isaiah (Isa 41.14; 43.14; 44.6 etc.) [→328] and in the Psalms (Pss 19.15; 78.35; 103.4) [→52] God is termed *go'ēl*, and we also read that God has "redeemed" Israel from Egyptian slavery (*gā'al*, Ex 6.6 etc.). So here too only God can be meant. Job knows that the God who can and will finally redeem him "lives" and that he will have the last word (that he will "at last lift himself out of the dust"). It is to this God, the Redeemer from slavery, that Job appeals—as it were against the God that now seems to have become his enemy. And he is certain that he will see this saving God with his own eyes (vv. 26f).

In view of the depths of this lament of Job's the continuation of the "dialogue" seems particularly inappropriate; for once again Zophar now emphasizes the unambiguous and inescapable fate of the ungodly, without responding in any way to Job's lament (ch. 20). Job answers this again, however (21), but only to contrast the didactic speeches of the friends with the horrifying experiences of reality: "why do the wicked live on, growing old and increasing in power?" (v. 7). Reality is quite different than the friends' wisdom doctrine would have it, and all are equal in death (vv. 23-26). So the friends' speeches are emptiness and deception (v. 34).

The third series of speeches (chs. 22) seems to be "disturbed," i.e. more precisely: it does not follow the rhythm of regular speech and counter-speech as shown in the first two series of speeches. The second friend, Bildad, only speaks very briefly now (ch. 25), and the third not at all. On the other hand Job's speeches get longer and longer, and a broad spectrum of themes and forms of speech are collected in them. Whatever the reasons may be for this change in structures (cf. Ebach 1996b, 12f, 26-30), the reader is now introduced once again into the varied and multilayered field of Job's thoughts and experiences.

Job has the pressing desire to make his way through to God's throne and to present his case to him personally (23.3f). We would at least like God to take notice of him (v. 6). But he knows that he cannot find him (vv. 8f), and that God alone will make his sovereign decision as he wills (v. 13). This insight fills Job with horror (vv. 16f). But if God alone is the lord of what happens, how can he permit the world to be as it is? Misery and exploitation prevail in the world. Only the hope remains that God will pay back the exploiters and the violent (ch. 24). Job takes up Bildad's brief interjection, "how then can a man be righteous before God?" (25.4), and develops an image of the size and distance of God, who rules the underworld too (ch. 26). But there is nothing comforting about this insight into God's power, for "who then can understand the thunder of his power?" (v. 14).

As previously in ch. 9, talk of God's rule over creation (ch. 26) is now associated with Job's accusation that God is denying him his rights (27.2-6). On no account does he wish to concede the validity of his friends' reproaches (v. 5). And when in what follows too he uses similar words to those of his friends concerning the fate of the wicked whom God will punish, this time teaching *them* a lesson (vv. 11-23), he makes it clear that he is different from the wicked—and from his friends—in not ceasing to call upon God (vv. 9f).

The conversation with the three friends is at an end (cf. 32.1). They do not turn up again until the concluding narrative chapter (42.7-9) [→**354**], and they have no further chance to say anything. Instead, at this point we have a politically shaped reflection on wisdom (ch. 28) as a device to slow things down. Wisdom is the most valuable thing there is [→**§19**]. Humans may be able by means of great effort and technical aids to gain anything they consider valuable (vv. 1-11)—"but where can wisdom be found?" (v. 12). Humans don't know (*yāda‘*, v. 13), the deep (*t'hôm*) and the sea don't know (v. 14), and even the abyss and death have only heard a rumor of it (v. 22). Wisdom remains hidden from the eyes of all living people (v. 21), and it cannot be bought even in exchange for the most valuable things (vv. 15-19). Only God knows its path and knows (*yāda‘*, v. 23) its place. It was there when God created the cosmos, almost as a category of order (vv. 24-27).

And humans? For humans wisdom has quite a different aspect, which is expressed axiomatically at the end: "the fear of the LORD, that is wisdom—and to shun evil is understanding" (v. 28). The change of perspective is surprising. But as a result the relationship to the context of the book of Job becomes visible. "Wisdom" always also remains the human's relationship with God and his neighbor. In fact it is precisely in that that it is realized, and that *is* wisdom.

This "Song of Wisdom" is within the context of the book part of one of Job's speeches. It stands at the transition between Job's last speech which was still addressed to the three friends (chs. 26f), to a broader more detailed speech by Job which is his last overall (chs. 29–31)—apart from the brief replies to the divine speeches (40.3-5; 42.1-6). This last speech of Job's however leads at the same time to a new (the fourth overall) discourse, in which Job's own speeches are followed first by those of Elihu (chs. 32–37) and then the great divine speeches (chs. 38ff).

The three chapters of this speech by Job once again pick up on three themes of previous discussions in the book. The first concern is with Job's earlier well-being, especially with his respected position in society (ch. 20). This presupposes a city environment, which did not come into view in the introductory narrative. This again shows the complexity of the figure of Job in the book, whose exemplary character is also evident in the fact that it makes human fates visible under quite varied social circumstances. The following chapter then presents Job's present miserable situation contrapuntally, as it were. Now he is even ridiculed by those who live at the lowest level of society (30.1-10), while he is persecuted and attacked by others (vv. 11-14). In the depiction of his misery and his suffering the contours are smudged (vv. 15-19, 24-31), and God does not hear him; in fact he has become his enemy (vv. 20-23).

This sets in motion the third theme which has been alluded to earlier as the most dominant of all: Job's argument with God. In the following chapter, the last one in the cycle of Job speeches (ch. 31), it is specially sharpened once again. Job presents his "case" fully in the form of a court case and declares his innocence in the form of an oath (which might be called a "purification oath") or a sort of self-cursing ("if I have done such and such a thing, then may I suffer the consequences," cf. esp. vv. 7f, 9f; cf. Ex 22.7, 9f; 1 Kgs 8.31f). It is a long list of possible misdemeanors which Job assures us that he has not committed. In many cases these are transgressions that are manifest only in thoughts or intentions, for instance desiring a young woman (v. 1), thinking of divorce (v. 9), feelings of hatred and triumph towards enemies (vv. 29-30), but also false trust in riches (vv. 24f), secret veneration of the heavens (vv. 26-28) and hypocrisy (vv. 33-34); others relate to the social domain such as disregard for the rights of slaves (vv. 13-15), withholding food (vv. 16-18) and clothing (vv. 19-20) for the poor and assistance for orphans (vv. 21-23) as well as infringements of hospitality laws (vv. 31-32); and finally deception (vv. 5f), illegitimate acquisition (vv. 7f) and violence against the cultivated earth (vv. 38-40).

All this comes to a head with the heartfelt wish which begins with the same words as 19.23: "If only there were someone (*mîyittēn*) who would listen to me" (Buber: "Who will give me one to hear me," 31.35). The expression "a hearer" (*šomēᵃ*) sounds very much like an appeal to a court authority. Job would submit his words to him, endorsed with his "mark" (the *taw*, the last letter of the alphabet, taken in the sense of a signature). And he requires, as it were in return, a written indictment. Then he would be able to enter, head held high, as an innocent man (vv. 36f). These words are not only the conclusion to the last chapter but also to the last three, in which once again Job's life-story and fate are presented and then his innocence is emphatically declared. Chapters 29-31 can then be labeled as Job's "challenge speeches." For the reader they end with the question: will God answer?

3.5 Another attempt by a wisdom teacher: Elihu

But first a new conversation partner appears, rather surprisingly: Elihu. He is introduced as someone who has heard the conversations that have been going on between Job and the three friends and now gives his reaction (32.1-5). So he does not belong to that group of the three friends introduced narratively at the beginning of the book (2.11-13). His function in the composition evidently lies in the fact that he has new, "better" arguments to add to those of the three friends. For he is "snorting with anger": at Job, because he "considered himself righteous in relation to God" (possible translation: "considered himself more righteous than God," *mē'elohîm*, v. 2); and at his three friends, because they "had found no way to refute Job and yet had condemned him" (v. 3).

The masoretic tradition indicates here a *tiqqûn sofˁrîm*, an "alteration of the scribes" [→28]. The Hebrew text originally read: "and made God unjust," which was evidently considered inappropriate, so that the name "Job" was inserted instead of "God."

Elihu's speeches are at first more reticent and conciliatory in form than those of the three friends (cf. von Rad 1970, 402n30). He describes himself as the younger one, which is why he has been silent so far (32.6f). Then in courtly detail (vv. 7-22), he gives the justification for why he feels himself led by the "spirit" to speak (v. 18). He picks up Job's complaint that God is not answering him (33.13), and points out that on the other hand God also speaks to people through dreams, especially through frightening dreams, which are intended to bring people away from the false path (vv. 14-18). Even sufferings can be understood as God's warning (vv. 19-22). What is new about Elihu's arguments is in particular that he does not ask about the causes of suffering but about the purpose that God is pursuing by this means. Sufferings can lead to a fundamental change in a person's life. This can occur with a *mal'āk*, a divine messenger (or "angel") appearing as an advocate (vv. 23f). (What is meant by the "ransom money" that the angel has "found" [v. 24] remains unclear.) And finally his physical strength will return (v. 25), and also his relationship with God will be renewed (vv. 26-28); for God wants to bring the sinner back to life (vv. 29f).

Despite Elihu's urgent demand (33.31-33), Job does not answer, neither now nor later. Thus Elihu's speeches within the book remain in the final analysis a monologue, despite his addressing Job repeatedly. And what is there for Job to answer to? Despite new, more sophisticated arguments, Elihu's speeches move entirely in the area of wisdom teaching and are thus unable to reach Job in his real situation. And his tone towards Job now becomes sharper. In a wide-ranging speech before the fictional audience of "wise ones" (34.2) he criticizes Job's attitude as that of a mocker (v. 7) and contrasts it with the greatness and righteousness of God. In Elihu's opinion, all this shows that Job possesses no wisdom and no understanding and that with his speeches against God he only exacerbates his sins (vv. 35-37). This brings him to the same point of general condemnation of Job which his three friends had arrived at previously.

Nonetheless another long cycle of speeches by Elihu follows (chs. 35-37). At the beginning of it we read: "and Elihu answered" (35.1), which after v. 4 is directed at Job and his friends, so that here the Elihu speeches can be related to the preceding dialogue. Elihu extends his argumentation into the domain of creation theology, which was also frequently alluded to in earlier dialogue speeches. He contrasts sin towards one's fellows (v. 8f) with God's remoteness (vv. 5-7, 10-13). But still Job's case is now awaiting God's verdict and is about to be decided (v. 14).

Once again Elihu sets about saying words "for God." This phrase reveals very clearly where Elihu the wisdom teacher is coming from. Despite his constantly expressed humility—he stands on the side of God, about whom he has been instructed through "wisdom" and can now teach others. Cf. 33.33: "listen to me, be silent, and I will teach you wisdom." His teaching is: God is mighty and just (36.5ff); he sends people suffering in order to move them to repentance (vv. 8-10), but then they have to decide whether to hear and be saved (v. 11) or not to hear and to fall into perdition (vv. 12-14). All this applies to Job too (vv. 16ff), but the speech gets lost in reflections on the remoteness and unknowability of God. It takes the shape of a hymn which sings of God as the creator and maintainer of the world and all its creatures (36.27-37.13). At the conclusion Elihu calls on Job to think all this over for himself (37.14-24).

The Elihu speeches have taken us far away from the polemical dispute between Job and his three friends. They have emphasized and developed some of the themes of wisdom teaching more clearly, but have not really advanced the discussion. In the book of Job as a whole, however, they have hinted more clearly at the topic that will dominate the following chapters: the creative power of God. But this also shows the elementary difference between when a wisdom teacher speaks of God's power as creator and when God himself speaks.

3.6 God answers

Will God answer? [→§15] This question has already arisen for the reader a number of times. And Job in particular has raised it for himself. Is God going to answer him? Right from his first complaint, time and again he has addressed God, directly and indirectly; he has complained and accused, begged and provoked him, has appealed to him as his judge and declared him his friend, and finally taken him to court. The friends, Elihu included, have only ever spoken *about* God; they expected no answer, as they already knew everything. But for Job the answer is vital in the truest sense of the word. At this point in the book of Job we see how indissolubly the two parts, the narrative introduction and the long speech duels, belong together. If God will not answer, both would have to remain not only incomplete, but also incomprehensible. But how would he answer?

"Then the Lord answered Job out of the storm" (38.1). God answers, and here, where he himself speaks as in the introductory narrative, he is called by his name: Yahweh, the one and only God. The "storm" (s'*'ārāh*) is a medium for his speaking and acting. It introduces the great vision with which Ezekiel is called to be a prophet, and there we read beforehand that "the word of the Lord" came to Ezekiel (Ezek 1.3f) [→234]; in the great hymnic conclusion of the Psalter it is said, similarly, that the storm announces God's word (Ps 148.8). But it is also this storm that takes Elijah off to heaven, in the opposite direction, as it were (2 Kgs 2.1, 11) [→143].

God answers quite differently from what Job would have expected after all his complaining and accusing. His answer begins with a violent meteorological display, and then words follow which are not answers but questions: "who is it ...?" The first question gets right to the heart of Job's self-understanding: who is this that is speaking "with words without understanding"? (38.2). Knowledge and understanding (*da'at*) —these were precisely the subjects of discussion with the three friends and similarly in Elihu's speeches. In conversation with his friends, Job insisted that his understanding was in no way inferior to theirs (13.2; cf. 12.2), because they wanted to counter him with arguments from the wisdom tradition. He was much better at this than they were. And now we read in the divine speech: "with words without understanding"! This sets a question-mark against the insights of wisdom as fundamental categories of interpretation. When measured against what is really significant, they are bound to fail.

With his "words without understanding" Job has "darkened the plan (*'ēṣāh*)." In his opening lament (ch. 3) he spoke as if his own misfortune demonstrated the senselessness of everything that happens as if there were no meaningful plan in the world at all. He has made his own fate a yardstick and has thereby obscured the plan that guides and sustains the whole thing. God will now set out his plan. He will accept Job's challenge in all regards and enter into a dispute of words with him, as Job has expressly demanded (e.g. 13.22): "I will question you, and you shall answer me."

And he asks him: "where were you when I laid the earth's foundation?" (38.4). In one stroke the situation has changed. This introductory question already makes it quite clear that Job's attempt to interpret the plan of world events from the perspective of his own fate or even to contest the existence of a plan, is misconceived, even nonsensical, "without understanding." And actually Job knows everything that God is now going to explain; didn't he himself say: "how can a mortal be righteous before God? Though one wished to dispute with him, he could not answer him one time out of a thousand ..., he alone stretches out the heavens and treads on the waves of the sea. He is the maker of the Bear and Orion, the Pleiades and the constellations of the South" (9.2f, 8f) [→343]. Job knew that God cannot be called to account, and in particular, that one has to apply the yardsticks of God's actions if one wants to understand the broader context. But already then he set aside this insight and "darkened" it by his exclusive regard for his own misfortune and for the impossibility of demanding "justice" from God (vv. 14ff). The yardsticks are now set straight again (cf. 1987, 46ff [103ff]).

A wide-ranging depiction of creation in all its varied aspects now follows: of heaven and earth, dawn and darkness, snow, hail, wind and rain, constellations and thunderstorms, and then also of animals of all types and of their lives (38.5–39.41). There is so much that humans can understand, but there is much that they cannot. But God's order, his plan, holds sway in all this and far exceeds human insight. This depiction is clothed in the garb of questions to Job, which are repeated many times, often with ironic variations: "Have you ever given orders to the morning?" (38.12), "Have the gates of death been shown to you?" (v. 17), "Can you bind the beautiful Pleiades?" (v. 31), "Do you hunt the prey for the lioness?" (v. 39), "Do you give the horse his strength?" (39.19), and also: "Surely you know, for you were already born! You have lived so many years!" (38.21).

Finally the speech comes back to its beginning, to the challenge to Job to teach God after he has presented him his questions (38.3). Now we read: "Will the one who contends with the Almighty correct him? Let him who accuses God answer him!" (40.2). So God has not simply "steamrollered" Job with the abundance of aspects of his creation, but has granted him a hearing, just as Job had asked; but in so doing he has revealed the inappropriateness of Job's accusations. And this results suitably in Job's answer: "I am unworthy—how can I reply to you?" And with the gesture, "I put my hand over my mouth," he promises to say no more (vv. 3-5). This is a sort of capitulation. Job acknowledges the superiority of his opponent at law. Concerning the content of the subject of discussion here, however, he says nothing.

So a second divine speech follows. While the first tackled the question whether Job might be able to direct the world, the second turns to Job's accusations that God allows the wicked to dominate in the world and that he himself is in the wrong, and might even be unrighteous (esp. in ch. 9). "Would you discredit my justice? Would you condemn me to justify yourself?" (40.8). Job should show that with an "arm like God's" he is able to coerce the wicked in the world, the strong and mighty; then God will praise him, sing a "psalm" to him (vv. 9-14). Here again the ironic element comes to the fore.

But God himself has to deal with quite different strong and mighty ones. While the animals spoken of in the first divine speech belong in the realm of creation, two animals now appear which are not only the most dangerous creatures, and the most difficult to overcome, but which are also considered to be mythical beasts: Behemoth (40.15-24) and Leviathan (40.25-41.26). The mystical significance of Behemoth, the hippopotamus, emerges in particular from Egyptian texts and images (cf. Keel 1978, 127ff); Leviathan, the crocodile, has a similar function in the Hebrew Bible (Ps 74.14 etc.). These are figures that embody the chaos that is the enemy of creation. The divine speech depicts these animals in their strength and dangerousness, as they appear to humans. The message to Job is clear: no human can overcome or master these animals, only God can do that. Even more strongly than in the first divine speech the inappropriateness of Job's complaint against God comes to expression here, which completely misrecognizes and distorts the true state of affairs. So these depictions need no further interpretation.

Job understands the message. His second answer (42.1-6) is no longer in capitulation. Job "acknowledges" (*yāda'*) that God can do anything, but that he himself has spoken of things that were too wonderful for him, without understanding them (*yāda'*). What he has now come up against means a qualitative change: up to now he had only heard of God "by hearsay," but now "my eyes have seen you" (v. 5). What he has heard he has also seen, as it were; the direct encounter with God has opened his eyes. So Job rejects his attitude up to now, because he has learned through this encounter with God that it was wrong, and why. He does this even though his position has not changed; for he is still sitting in the ashes (v. 6; cf. 2.8) [→**340**].

3.7 Job died, old and full of years

Job's last word (42.6) reminds the reader of the situation in which Job finds himself. The reader has perhaps forgotten all about this and concentrated fully on the words that have been exchanged between Job, his friends, and finally God himself. But now the reader is made aware once again what was the cause of these long stretches of discourse and how it came to this. The three friends of course sat there as silent, sympathetic visitors of Job before they began to speak. So their speeches must be seen against the direct background of the situation of the suffering Job. And now God's wrath burns against them because they have "not spoken of me what is right" (42.7). They have spoken as if they knew about God's thought and activity, and have tried to explain Job's situation in the light of their theories. The possibility of the suffering of an innocent person was not foreseen in this, however, and so they had to declare Job guilty, as it were "for God's sake." It is against this that God's anger is directed. (Elihu is not mentioned.)

Job's treatment is quite different. He is expressly contrasted with this (42.7). Despite the free rein given to his outbursts, he never tried to force God's actions into any kind of theory. On the contrary, he sought an answer from God time and again, and called on him to explain his suffering. And finally, when God's answer was granted to him, he saw the error of his attitude and rejected it without reservation. In so doing he has also refuted the prediction of the *śāṭān*, the adversary, that Job would "bless," i.e. curse, God to his face when it came to the "skin" (2.4f). That the adversary does not reappear in the narrative conclusion is thus no coincidence. He has lost his wager.

God calls on the friends to present a burnt offering, at which Job is to assist as petitioner (42.8). The narrative thus harks back to the beginning, where we were told of Job's regular burnt offerings for his children (1.5) [→338]. Job now does not offer the sacrifice himself, but God gives him the role of petitioner at his friends' sacrifice. The precondition for this is Job's "repentance" (v. 6), which—though this is not expressly said—confirms him in the position that God observed at the beginning of the book, that Job was "blameless" and that there "is none like him on the earth" (1.8; 2.3). (The similarly blameless Noah appears alongside Job in 14.14-20 as a potential petitioner.)

God accepts the petition (v. 9) and then he turns the fate of Job the petitioner (v. 10). He turns it literally back to its former state, even doubling it (cf. v. 12). Only the number of children remains the same. But something has changed: Job has no need to worry about them as he did for his first children (1.4f). And his daughters are not only the most beautiful in the land, but Job gives them equal inheritance rights to their brothers (v. 15)—a very unusual act that which is not further justified or commented upon. Did he do this only out of generosity or because he was so rich—or is it an early biblical testimony to the full emancipation of the sexes? Job's relatives and his "acquaintances from before" come, comfort him "over all the trouble the LORD had brought upon him," and bring him gifts (v. 11).

And Job lives on, twice as long as what according to Ps 90.10 is "the length of our days," i.e. 140 years. He sees four generations around him, as is also reported of Joseph (Gen 50.23). Then he dies, "old and full of years" (42.16f). This now proverbial expression is only rarely used in the Hebrew Bible. It again associates Job with Abraham (Gen 25.8) and Isaac (35.29). (Cf. also 1 Chron 29.28; 2 Chron 24.15.) Their lives too were anything but peaceful and conflict-free, but everything turned out well for them in the end.

The comforting nature of this conclusion is simultaneously disturbing for the reader. What is the message of the book of Job? It does not contain any instruction for life and no answer to the question of the applicability of what is said in Job to particular situations and problems. But a number of basic structures are clear.

To begin with: the losers are clearly indicated. First the *śāṭān*, the adversary of God and humanity. His cynicism fails because of Job's piety, which remains the supporting foundation despite all his presumption against God. Then the friends, all four of them. They build entirely on the "teaching" and its infallibility. But the book of Job shows that the teaching of the wisdom tradition, which certainly holds true in many situations in human life, can offer no answers in extreme situations and is bound to fail. The friends are found wanting in particular because they do not consider the possibility that there might be a limit to the interpretative categories of their teaching. With their constantly repeated attempts to reinterpret Job's situation against all appearances in accordance with their teaching, they demonstrate that the attempt to interpret human fate according to fixed rules can become deeply inhuman. And because God forms an essential element in their arguments, they have not spoken of God "rightly" and must therefore seek atonement for this and indeed have to rely on Job's petition on their behalf. Thus one might speak of a "crisis of wisdom" here.

The real significance and greatness of the book of Job lies, however, in the figure of Job himself, his fate and his often desperate attempts to come to terms with it. Here linear and unambiguous models of explanation must fail. The reader who has entered into this book gains the impression that precisely this is the intention of the book: not to put up with simple interpretations. Job is acquainted with all the depths of suffering. In the depictions of his paths one is reminded time and again of the psalms of lament [→**326**]. But he transcends the boundaries of what is conceivable in the Psalms, by calling God to account, indeed even accusing him. But his premises are certainly comparable with those of his conversation partners. But his own experience of suffering leads him into doubt and finally to despair as to the correctness of the traditional teaching, that there is a recognizable link between one's deeds and one's wellbeing, so that a life according to God-given stipulations must have a good fate as its consequence. He knows that he has lived according to these rules yet he still has to endure the experience of succumbing to serious suffering. Being struck personally like this, unlike his friends he does not attempt to adapt reality to the doctrine but rather he questions the doctrine. But because the doctrine says that the rules of the relationship between deeds and wellbeing were set up by God himself and are guaranteed by him, the only person to whom he could direct his questions was God himself.

The pathway there leads Job through heights and depths. Again and again he sinks into deep lament, even to the point where he wishes he had not been born (ch. 3; 10.18ff; 14; 17 etc.) [→**341, 344**]. Often the complaint is directed to God and then develops into the reproach that God himself is persecuting him (7.12ff; 16.7ff; 19.6ff etc.) [→**343f**], indeed that he does not act in accordance with justice and righteousness at all, but is an unjust judge (9f). Repeatedly the wish arises to enter into a judicial dispute with God (13.3ff; 23.3ff), until finally Job challenges God to a real court case (28.31, esp. 31.35-37) [→**348**]. In so doing he has definitively crossed the boundaries of the teaching of the wisdom tradition. The rules no longer apply, and God himself must say what is the true situation.

God's answer is not an answer to the questions that Job has posed. It is more than this: it demonstrates that the questions that Job raises are built on false premises, as if humans could understand God's actions in terms of comprehensible and manageable rules. Job has himself recognized that the rules considered valid cannot fully describe reality and so he has stopped taking these rules as applying to God, as his friends have done. But he has asked for new, better rules with which to interpret the reality of his own life and suffering. God's answer makes him aware that the created order, established and ruled by God, encompasses much more than the fate of the individual human. So God sets the yardsticks straight. Job's question is still open, and must remain so.

4. The Book of Proverbs

4.1 Introduction

"The proverbs of Solomon, son of David, the king of Israel." Thus begins the book of Proverbs [→**In 268**], also called the "Proverbs of Solomon," deriving from its Latin title in the Vulgate: Proverbia. The reader is reminded of the description of the reign of Solomon, in which Solomon's "wisdom" is emphasized as a special characteristic of his, and where it is also reported that Solomon "spoke" a large number of songs and proverbs (1 Kgs 5.9-14) [→**118**]. In Prov 10.1 we again have the superscription "Proverbs of Solomon" and in 25.1 a further collection of sayings is headed: "These are more proverbs of Solomon, copied by the men of Hezekiah, king of Judah." According to this these are not only proverbs by Solomon himself or from his time, but the formation of a continuous collection and tradition at the royal court.

The Proverbs display a great variety of themes and forms. Some reflect conditions in the circle of the royal court and of the city life closely connected with it; others, however, suggest more village and rural conditions and relationships. So wisdom sayings are collected together here from quite different backgrounds and certainly also from various times [→*In* **115**]. The expression "words of the wise" (*dibrê h^ekāmîm*, 1.6; 22.17; cf. 24.23) indicates also, that behind them too stand the "wise" as the bearers of the special intellectual tradition that is designated by the term "wisdom" [→**§18**] (and also by other expressions, see below).

But the book by no means contains only "Proverbs." Other important elements of the wisdom tradition have been transmitted here too. Thus we find extensive didactic speeches, in which the wisdom of themes are dealt with in a more fundamental and more general form (e.g. Prov 1.8ff). In the introductory chapters 1–9, wisdom also appears as a person, first as a woman (1.22-33 etc.), but then also as the first of God's creations, which was with God "at the beginning" of creation (8.22; cf. Gen 1.1) [→**14**]. So a wide-ranging area of the tradition of "wisdom" is visible here, which certainly covers rather lengthy periods in the history of Israel.

The very varied, generally short proverbs are summarized in a number of part-collections: 10.1–22.16 with the superscription "Proverbs of Solomon"; 22.17–24.22 and 24.23-34 in two part-collections which are characterized in each case in the first verse as words of "the wise"; chs. 25–29 "Proverbs of Solomon" from the time of Hezekiah; ch. 30 and 31.1-9 are the only texts in the book to bear the name of an author: Agur (30.1) and Lemuel (31.1), about whom however nothing further is known. These collections of sayings are framed by the more strongly reflective texts: at the beginning by the extensive introduction chs. 1–9 with its didactic discourses and the texts about the female figure of wisdom and at the end by the "praise of the capable woman" (31.10-31) [→**368**], which corresponds to them in a particular way.

4.2 Learn wisdom—and where it starts

In the introduction to the book (1.2-7) it is set out how the texts collected here are to be understood as a whole. They are to be heard and read "in order to learn" (*yāda*ʾ). The collection and transmission of the proverbs has a pedagogical purpose. What the reader or hearer is to learn is in the first instance "wisdom" (*hokhmāh*). This is the key term that stands at the center of the general concerns that have produced this collection. But it is clear that this word cannot be taken in a single, delimited sense. What it in fact comprises is set out in great variety in this book.

The first sentences in the book deal with those areas in which wisdom flourishes and is maintained. Immediately next to wisdom stands the word *mûsār* (1.2f), a didactic term for educational instruction and teaching (1.8; 5.12; 8.33 etc.), extending even to corporal punishment as a necessary means of education (13.24). The primary concern is to understand the reasonable words of explanation and education that lead to insight (*haskēl*, v. 3a). But this insight should not serve personal lifestyle but is directed towards society in which righteousness (*ṣedeq*), justice (*mišpāṭ*) and uprightness (*mēšārîm*) play an important part (v. 3b). This cleverness, insight and circumspection should be passed on to the inexperienced (v. 4); but the wise and understanding too should listen to it and expand their insight, by understanding proverbs, imagery and puzzles of the wise (vv. 5f).

So the wisdom sayings and discourses collected together here are directed to all classes and groups in society, however varied their measure of insight into wisdom may be. The most important thing, however, is that wisdom does not have its basis in itself. It is the "fear of the Lord" that constitutes the beginning of knowledge, wisdom and instruction (1.7). This sentence carries great weight not only in the book of Proverbs, but beyond it too. In the book of Proverbs itself it is found, with certain linguistic variations, once again, first of all, in the conclusion to the first main section of the book (9.10) [→363], so that together with the introductory verse 1.7 it circumscribes this collection and marks it thematically. In 15.33 it introduces a group of texts in which God is spoken of in a particularly concentrated way (15.33-16.9). In the book of Job a corresponding sentence has a crucial function as a concluding sentence in the "song of wisdom" (Job 28.28) [→347], through which wisdom is interpreted for humans as the relationship to God and one's neighbor ("to keep from evil, that is understanding") (cf. von Rad 1970, 91ff).

4.3 My son, hear the instruction

The didactic character of the book appears expressly directly after this introduction. A wisdom teacher begins to speak: "My son ..." (1.8, 10, 15 etc.). This address by the teacher is directed to the young man (cf. v. 4) for whose benefit the wisdom teaching (*mûsār*, cf. vv. 2, 3, 7) is offered. He is to listen to the "teaching of the fathers" and the "instruction (*tôrāh*) of the mothers" (v. 8; cf. 6.20). The word torah has its quite basic sense here, "instruction." It can mean the instruction of the mother (1.8; 6.20) or the instruction of the wisdom teacher ("my *tôrāh*" 3.14.2; 7.2).

The wisdom teacher develops his teaching from one new perspective after another. The instruction consists of very concrete admonitions and warnings to the inexperienced young man (see immediately below). In the center, however, stands wisdom itself and its significance for the life of anyone who opens himself or herself up to it. As before in the introductory verses of the book the term wisdom is developed in many kinds of related expressions which again and again add new aspects of what the concern is with: alongside wisdom and instruction stand insight (*bînāh* 1.2; 2.3 etc. and *t'bûnāh* 2.2, 3, 6 etc.), cleverness (*'ormāh* 1.4; 8.5, 12), knowledge (*da'at* 1.4; 2.6, 10 etc.) and prudence (*m'zimmāh* 1.4; 2.11; 3.21 etc.), and alongside instruction (*tôrāh*) the commandments (*miṣwōt* 2.1; 3.1; 4.4 etc.).

Anyone who opens up to wisdom, who seeks it "like silver" (2.4), will be led to knowledge of God (*da'at 'lohîm*) and to the fear of the Lord (*yir'at yhwh*); "for the LORD gives wisdom, and from his mouth come knowledge and understanding" (2.5f). Here wisdom is again closely linked with the fear of God and especially with the knowledge of God.

Anyone who has accepted wisdom like this can then also be described as "pious" (*hasîd* 2.8), as "straight" (*yāšār* 2.7, 21), i.e. as one who takes the straight path, as perfect, blameless (*tāmîm* 2.21; cf. v. 7b). And he will understand righteousness, justice and uprightness (2.9; cf. 1.3).

Wisdom proves itself above all in that it teaches people to take the right path. Hence the first concrete admonition of the wisdom teacher: "If sinners entice you, do not give in to them" (1.10). Here we meet again this talk of the two ways, which the reader already knows from Psalm 1 [→**319**]. The paths of the "sinners" lead to corruption (1.10-19; cf. 2.12-15); the sinners are blotted out of the land (2.22), but the "upright" and blameless will continue to live in the land (v. 21). This classical wisdom idea is here, as in Ps 1, placed entirely in the theological context in which wisdom is linked closely with the fear and knowledge of God.

Again and again there is talk here of the path and pathways. The paths of wisdom are kind (3.17), sure (3.23) and straight (4.11, 26).

"For these commands are a lamp, this teaching is a light, and the corrections of discipline are the way to life" (6.23). But the path of the wicked and the ways of the evil (4.14) form a temptation for the student of wisdom. The warning against the way to the strange woman is especially sharp (2.16-19; 5.1-14; 6.20-35; 7.1-27). All who go to her do not return and do not make it to the path of life (2.19; 5.6) but to the paths to the underworld and the chambers of death (7.27).

4.4 Wisdom calls

Besides the voice of the wisdom teacher another calls out: that of wisdom herself. She calls on streets and squares, in the midst of the noisy hustle and bustle, to alert and warn those without understanding (1.20-33). Here, right at the beginning of the book, this voice rings out with a striking abruptness and presents an alternative: either those called upon turn to the admonishing instruction of wisdom, in which case she will pour out her spirit on them and announce her words to them (v. 23), or they will refuse to listen and grasp the outstretched hand, "then they will call to me but I will not answer; they will look for me but will not find me" (vv. 24-28). This language is reminiscent of prophetic messages of judgment (cf. Kayatz 1966, 119ff); but then she comes back again to an entirely wisdom-like sentence: "but whoever listens to me will live in safety" (v. 33). What is particularly important here is that wisdom is not simply generally, indiscriminatingly available but that she can withdraw from humans if they lock themselves against her. The loss of this ordering voice can have catastrophic consequences (von Rad 1970, 209f).

But the voice of wisdom can also sound quite different. Again we read that she calls in public in the streets and the city gates (8.1ff). But then the positive side of wisdom instruction in particular is emphasized, which is more valuable than silver and gold and better than pearls (vv. 10f, 19). "By me kings reign," and the rulers and princes (vv. 15f). "I love those who love me, and those who seek me find me" (v. 17). And to whoever loves wisdom she will open up the treasuries (v. 21). Only right at the end of this great poem do warning notes also sound: "But whoever fails to find me harms himself; all who hate me love death" (v. 36).

The real core of this poem, however, is its mid-section (8.22-31). Here wisdom speaks of her own beginning, which precedes everything else in God's creation: "The LORD brought me forth as the first of his works, before his deeds of old; I was appointed from eternity, from the beginning, before the world began" (vv. 22f). An astonishing statement, to which there is nothing comparable in the Hebrew Bible. In a long series of sentences wisdom describes how she was present before the first acts of creation and then at the creation of heaven and earth (vv. 24-29). This recalls the earlier statement: "By wisdom the LORD laid the earth's foundations, by understanding he set the heavens in place; by his knowledge the deeps were divided, and the clouds let drop the dew" (3.19f). But things go an important step further when it is said that wisdom herself in a personal capacity was present already during the events of creation. This expresses the idea that there is nothing in the world that might be ranked above wisdom. Egyptian traditions have a part to play in this, in particular in the notion that wisdom played before God as his favorite (vv. 30f; cf. Kayatz 1966, 93ff; von Rad 1970, 195ff.).

In the context of the book of Proverbs it is significant above all else that wisdom still turns to humans despite this exalted background (8.1-21, 32-36). She is depicted as a hostess who invites all who need instruction, and promises them a long and good life if they accept her teaching (9.1-12). Here once again we glimpse a fundamental contrast that dominates the first part of the book: between wisdom, depicted as a woman, and the "strange woman" (2.16-19; 5.1-14; 6.20-35; 7.1-27), who appears here as the "woman Folly" and sets up a counter-invitation (9.13-18). Behind the seductive attempts of this female figure one may recognize the reflection of foreign cultic practices connected with sexual fertility rites.

The last section on wisdom repeats again, in a slightly varied way, the fundamental sentence from the introduction (1.7): "The fear of the LORD is the beginning of wisdom, and knowledge of the Holy One is understanding" (9.10). This rounds off the first tone-setting part of the book of Proverbs. With this twice repeated sentence the theological reading instructions, as it were, are given for the following collections of proverbs, in which there is much less, and much less explicit, talk of the anchoring of wisdom thoughts and instruction in the fear and knowledge of God.

4.5 The wise man and the fool, the righteous and the wicked

The "proverbs" now begin. The word mashal is found almost exclusively in the superscriptions, and then in the phrase "proverbs of

Solomon" (1.1; 10.1; 25.1). This refers the reader to the description of the wisdom of king Solomon, who expressed himself above all in his "speaking" countless proverbs (3000) and "songs" (*šîr*, 1005) (1 Kgs 5.12) [→**118**]. On closer inspection, however, it is evident that the proverbs and songs of Solomon have other topics in view than in the majority of texts in the book of Proverbs. We read that he spoke about all areas of nature, about plants and animals (v. 13). But such topics are hardly found at all in the book of Proverbs; rather the sayings collected here deal with people, both with people as individuals and above all with people in their social relationships. But the Solomon tradition displays alongside natural wisdom also other features of his wisdom. Right at the beginning of his reign stands the dream vision, in which God promises to give him a "wise and understanding heart" (1 Kgs 3.12). This then proves itself in the unusual judgment that Solomon gives (the "judgment of Solomon," vv. 16-27) and which is understood by "all Israel" as the expression of the "wisdom of God" that was given to Solomon (v. 28). Later the queen of Sheba admires Solomon's wisdom, which comes to expression also in his wealth and the successes of his reign (10.1-10) [→**123**].

The large number of proverbs ascribed to Solomon in 1 Kgs 5.12 bear resemblances to the "list science" of the ancient Near East, in which all the known phenomena of the natural world were collected together in encyclopedic detail. But it is precisely in respect of this type of collective science that the mention of proverbs and songs points to the fact that in the tradition linked with Solomon something new appears: it is not only collecting that has gone on here, but also poetic composition. One might think especially of such texts in which observations of nature, in particular in the animal kingdom, are expressed in the form of artistic proverbs (Prov 30.15f, 18-20, 24-28, 29-31; cf. Alt 1951). But this small group of sayings is situated in relative isolation at the end of the collection.

Thus the book of Proverbs offers a section of what was transmitted in Israel's wisdom tradition and associated with the name of Solomon. The collection and transmission of these texts clearly occurred in court circles and their near environment, as is evident from the superscriptions to the two main parts of the book in 10.1 and 25.1. This was also the place where foreign wisdom traditions were known and could then also be inserted into Israel's own collection (cf. Meinhold 1991, 26-37). So the collection of "words of the wise" in 22.17-24.22 contains texts that often agree verbatim with similar ones in the Egyptian

instruction of Amenemope (cf. Gressmann 1924; text in *AOT* 38-64;
RTAT 75-88; *TUAT* III, 222-250). Otherwise, the themes of the
proverbs cover a broad framework of the various areas of life. They are
in addition largely related to the individual behavior of the individual
person, so that only here and there are particular social structures visible.

Some basic elements of the proverb tradition are immediately evident in the first verses of the collection. "A wise son brings joy to his
father, but a foolish son grief to his mother" (10.1). Here we see
thinking in antitheses, which is characteristic of this tradition. A large
portion of the sayings, especially in chs. 10-15, consists of such short
sentences, formed in antithetical parallelism (cf. the tables in Skladny
1961, 67-71) [→*In* 109]. A typical antithesis sets the one who is "wise"
(*ḥākām*), i.e. one who has already accepted wisdom instruction (cf. 1.2-
6; 2.1-6 etc.) in contrast to the "fool." In the book of Proverbs develops from this perspective a broad field of observations and experiences
concerning the behavior and wellbeing of wise and foolish people (cf.
Westermann 1990a, 64-72). Immediately next to them stands the frequent opposition of the righteous (*ṣaddîq*) and the wicked (*rāšā'*, cf.
Westermann 1990a, 91-101): "The LORD does not let the righteous
go hungry, but he thwarts the craving of the wicked" (10.3). These
two antithetical pairings characterize large parts of the book of Proverbs. In many sayings, however, there is no express designation of
those operating in one sense or another, but various means of behavior
and wellbeing are presented in opposition to each other: "Lazy hands
make a man poor, but diligent hands bring wealth. He who gathers
crops in summer is wise (lit: a wise son), but he who sleeps during
harvest acts disgracefully (lit.: is a disgraceful son)" (10.4, 5).

The first two examples mentioned display quite different angles of
view in these antithetically formulated proverbs. On the one hand
they are concerned with very concrete, practical things in life: hunger
(10.3), industry (10.4f), possessions (10.15f), honesty (11.1) and much
more besides. On the other hand they make more general and more
fundamental statements. Thus between the two above-mentioned
examples there is a sentence about the value and the consequences of
just and unjust behavior: "Ill-gotten treasures (lit.: the gains of wickedness [*reša'*]) are of no value, but righteousness (*ṣᵉdāqāh*) delivers from
death" (10.2). This is one of the numerous sentences in Proverbs in
which the alternative between righteousness and wickedness is presented as decisive for life, i.e. helpful and salvific or as threatening and

deadly. A few verses later we read: "The memory of the righteous will be a blessing, but the name of the wicked will rot" (10.7; cf. also v. 6).

So the frequently expressed view that the book of Proverbs essentially presents a "profane" understanding of wisdom, hardly applies. Certainly there are numerous individual proverbs which express experiences from everyday life, guidelines for prudent behavior and much besides without there being a discernible religious dimension. On the other hand the divine name occurs more than eighty times, distributed throughout the book. But above all the word "righteous" (*ṣaddîq*) appears nowhere else in the Hebrew Bible with such frequency as in Proverbs (66 times), and also in respect of the word "righteousness" (*ṣᵉdāqāh*) the book is in fourth place (cf. the table in *THAT* II, 511). In Proverbs it is not explained or developed what righteousness might be, or who is a righteous person. In this the book stands in a tradition that comprises large parts of the Hebrew Bible and in which these terms, despite all the differences in the detail, are used as it were as ciphers for positively evaluated behavior towards God and one's fellows [→§§10, 15].

4.6 The Lord created them all

The religious evaluation of human actions also comes to expression in the frequent observation that everything is an "abomination (*tô'ēbāh*) to the Lord." in 6.16 a whole range of inter-human modes of behavior is listed, for which this judgment applies. Biased scales, weights and measures are emphasized especially (11.1; 20.10, 23). Also false court verdicts in which justice is turned into its opposite, are an abomination to God (17.15). But above all the attitude and mentality that lies behind the actions is the target of these judgments. So often we find the antithetical formulation: "Lying lips are an abomination to the LORD, but those who act reliably have his goodwill" (12.22). "The way of the wicked is an abomination to the LORD, but he loves one who pursues righteousness" (15.9; cf. also 3.32; 11.20; 15.26; 16.5).

Of particular interest is the opposition in 15.8: "The sacrifice of the wicked is an abomination to the LORD, but the prayer of the upright finds his goodwill" (cf. 21.27). This recalls prophetic criticism of the cult, for instance at such central points as Isa 1.10-17 [→170]; Jer 6.20 etc. Also the proverb "To do justice and righteousness is dearer to the LORD than sacrifices" (21.3) echoes 1 Sam 15.22f; Hos 6.6 and other prophetic texts [→**106, 269f**]. This is all the more remarkable for the fact that the whole realm of the cult is otherwise scarcely mentioned in Proverbs. Decisive here too is again the attitude towards God that lies behind the sacrifice or seeks to hide behind. This is clear in 28.9: "When someone turns his ear away from listening to teaching (*tôrāh*), then even his prayer is an abomination." So it is not just a matter of the sacrifice but of all forms of expression of devotion that are worth nothing when the attitude which gives rise to them does not meet with God's approval. From this point of view the sacrifice is one expression of life among others.

In the last-mentioned quotation the word "abomination" is used without mention of God (cf. also 21.27). This shows that in many cases judgments about human behavior have a religious justification even when these are not expressly mentioned. This leads us once again to the term righteous. In many cases the righteous person is simply a person who does what is right—and this means also: what is right in God's eyes. "The righteous knows the needs (*nefeš*) of his animal, but the inner parts of the wicked are cruel" (12.10). "The just man hates lying words, but the wicked makes himself hated and despised" (13.5). "The heart of the righteous considers what should be answered, but the mouth of the wicked pours forth evil" (15.28). Proverbs is full of similar sayings, whether in antithetical parallelism or without it. In many of them, however, the one presented positively is not expressly termed righteous, but his manner of behavior is shown. According to the overall context of the book, however, one cannot make a fundamental distinction between those who act rightly or in an exemplary way, and those who are explicitly called "righteous." The righteous man in this area of proverbs is the model Israelite, or simply the person who thinks and acts in an exemplary way.

The examples cited so far speak primarily of the thinking and acting of the righteous person; in a number of texts, however, there is talk of their wellbeing. "The righteous will never waver, but the wicked will not remain dwelling in the land" (10.30). "When the storm blows about, the wicked is no more, but the righteous has eternal ground" (10.25). "The name of the LORD is a firm tower, the righteous runs there and is safe" (18.10).

These proverbs, to which we could add many similar ones, regard what marks out the righteous person in much more fundamental respects than the preceding ones. Whoever is righteous will have a share in God's help and protection. This being righteous is certainly not dependent on thinking and acting in the sense of the proverbs cited above. But nor is it something occasional, related to individual acts, but something as it were habitual. Whoever is righteous, that person's life and thought is marked by this mentality, so that the deeds of the righteous person run along particular paths and in accordance with predictable forms of behavior. The person who is righteous in this sense, then, can rely on the fact that God will grant him or her protection and help, which can be expected in accordance with the understanding of life and the world that is the foundation of this belief.

This understanding of the world is frequently called the "deeds—well-being connection" (in German, "Tun–Ergehen–Zusammenhang," Koch 1955). Here it is clear that "deeds" means more than just individual things that one does, and that "well-being" means more than just the immediate consequences of particular deeds. The whole thing is embedded in a broad context, which seeks to embrace human life in its world, a world created by God and maintained by him. This understanding of God is only occasionally expressed. But this shows precisely the almost matter-of-fact obviousness with which this all happens, that this understanding is the basis of everything. "Whoever oppressed the small, despises their creator, but whoever has pity on the needy honors him" (14.31; cf. 17.5). "A listening ear and a seeing eye, the LORD made both of them" (20.12). "Rich and poor have this in common: the LORD is the Maker of them all" (22.2; cf. 29.13). In the introductory chapters of the book the depiction of wisdom as the very first of God's creations places the whole in the context of a developed creation theology (8.22-31) [→362]. Though this means a shift of emphasis by comparison with the collections of proverbs, it certainly does not mean a move to a different basic understanding of the place of humans in God's creation. The thinking and acting of all those spoken of in Proverbs is subject to the same preconditions.

A special place is accorded to some of the proverbs in chs. 28f, in which the word *tôrāh* appears in a sense that goes beyond the realm of wisdom. The clearest case of this is in 29.18, where *tôrāh* appears in parallel to "vision" (*ḥāzôn*), a word used exclusively for the receipt of prophetic revelations (e.g. 1 Sam 3.1; Isa 1.1) [→168]. In 28.4-9 the word *tôrāh* is found multiple times. In v. 4 people who forsake the *tôrāh* are contrasted with those who keep it. Then we read: "Evil men do not understand justice, but those who seek the LORD understand it fully" (v. 5). Here we find a linguistic usage reminiscent of Deuteronomy and texts influenced by it (e.g. Jer 9.12; Ps 89.31; 119.44). Verse 17 again recalls the wisdom use of *tôrāh* (cf. e.g. 3.1). Finally, we read in the above-mentioned v. 9 that the prayer of whose who turn their ear from hearing the torah are an abomination. Here too one thinks of the divine *tôrāh*.

4.7 A capable woman—more valuable than pearls

At the conclusion of Proverbs the reader is introduced to two female figures. One is the mother of king Lemuel, who passes on her cautionary instruction (31.1-9). Alongside warnings about women and alcohol she admonished him in particular to speak up for the case of those who are unable to secure justice for themselves (vv. 8f). He is to judge rightly, as the incumbent functionaries do according to the words of wisdom (cf. 8.16), and he is especially to take the part of the poor and needy, of whom we read just previously that they stand under the special protection of their creator (14.31). So the voice of this woman from the royal household picks up a number of central statements from the preceding collections of sayings.

The concluding poem of the "capable woman" (*'ēšet ḥayil* 31.10-31) then plays a quite special role. This characterization of the woman is also found in 12.4, where we read that such a woman is "her husband's crown." (Cf. also Ruth 3.11 [→**371**].) In this poem, however, the special activities and lifestyle of the woman are focused upon exclusively. At the same time connections with the texts concerning the woman presented as wisdom in chs. 1–9 are found throughout. Wisdom is more valuable than pearls (or corals, 3.15; 8.11) [→**361**]—so too the "competent woman." We read: "Blessed are those who find wisdom" (3.13), and wisdom herself says: "He who finds me finds life and gains the favor of the LORD" (8.35)—so the person who finds such a capable woman is also to be praised (31.1). "Wisdom has built her house" and invites her guests into it (9.1ff)—and so too the woman's care for "her house" is her most important concern (31.15, 21, 27). The woman "opens her mouth in wisdom, and kind instruction (*tôrat-ḥesed*) is on her tongue" (31.26). And finally right at the end we read: "a woman who fears the LORD is to be praised" (31.30), which clearly refers to the statements about the fear of the Lord as the beginning of wisdom that occur at significant points (1.7; 9.10; 15.33). (Cf. Schwienhorst-Schönberger 1995, 258.)

The book of Proverbs is thus rounded of in a surprising and impressive manner. Wisdom, appearing as a woman, who marks the book right from its beginning, has a counterpart in a human woman who manages her household and her business with uncommon independence, being concerned not only with the wellbeing of those in her household (31.21) but also with the poor and needy (v. 20). But she is fully involved in the teachings of wisdom, which she herself passes on (v. 26). And all this is surrounded by the "fear of the LORD" (v. 30). (Cf. Crüsemann 1978b, 34-42.)

5. The Five Megillot

Preliminary remarks

In Jewish tradition, the five shorter books of the "Writings" [→*In* 271] are treated as a group that belong together, under the heading *m'gillôt*, "scrolls." They are performed as ceremonial readings at particular festivals in the liturgical year: the Song of Songs at the Passover festival, the book of Ruth at the Festival of Weeks, Lamentations on the 9th of the month of Av, the memorial day for the destruction of the Temple, Qohelet at the Feast of Tabernacles, Esther at the Purim festival. In many Jewish manuscripts they are also listed in this order, in others in the order that has become common in academic use, as is followed here. The name *m'gillôt* derives from the fact that they were still read, like the Torah, from scrolls, which is still the custom for the book of Esther.

5.1 The Book of Ruth

"In the days when the judges judged"—with this expression, unique in the Hebrew Bible, the book of Ruth transports its readers into the early period of the people of Israel, when there was as yet no king. Readers know that this was a time when the nation was exposed to all sorts of threats as the result of its frequently repeated apostasy from Yhwh [→**100**]. The story told by this little book, however, links up also with the following period of the monarchy, since the child that is born at the end of the narrative is the ancestor of king David (4.17). In the concluding genealogy (vv. 18-22) he is accorded the favored seventh place in the series of ten which begins in the time of the patriarchs with Perez, the son of Tamar fathered by Judah (Gen 38; cf. Ruth 4.12).

But this is not the only intention of the narrative, and not the most important one. In its apparently slick, but extremely artistic account it includes many varied aspects so that it can be read from quite different points of view and be read over and over again. The most striking thing about this narrative is that is essentially a story about women. In no other book of the Hebrew Bible are women depicted in a comparable way as independently active individuals, taking their fate into their own hands (cf. Trible 1993, 190-226). They do not do so on their own initiative, but only after their husbands have died; but the narrative needs only five verses (1.1-5) to reach the point at which the women are on their own and begin to act on their own.

"There was a famine in the land" (1.1). With these words the narrative of Abraham's trek to Egypt begins (Gen 12.10) [→**23**]. The certainly intentional parallel immediately draws attention to the difference, however. Abraham is still the one who acts, while Sarah cannot develop any activities of her own; in the book of Ruth on the other hand Naomi is the one who plans and acts. Her actions stand in a broader context, however. It begins with her hearing in the land of Moab "that the LORD had come to the aid of his people by providing food for them" (1.6). This sets a further basic tone for the narrative: this too is a "guidance story." The actions of people, here those of women in particular, occur independently and to plan; but divine guidance creates the preconditions and circumstances for it, just as God had also previously placed on Naomi her onerous fate through the loss of her husband and of the two growing sons. The people are aware of this connection and frequently express it too.

Naomi decides to go back (šûb, vv. 6f). Her two young widowed Moabite daughters-in-law go with her, but Naomi calls on them to go back (šûb) to their families, where God would show the same goodness (ḥesed) to them that they themselves had shown to their foreign husbands and their mother, letting them find peace (mᵉnûḥāh) in a new marriage (vv. 8f). The topic of "return" becomes the crucial and decisive point: to go with the Israelite mother-in-law to her land (v. 10) or to return to their own home environment (vv. 11f). Naomi pleads with the young women not to tie themselves to her, after the "hand of the LORD" has struck them and presented them with a bitter fate (v. 13). This too comes from God's hand, people can only interpret it (Trible 1993, 195).

Orpah does the most obvious and sensible thing: she goes back "to her people and to her God" (vv. 14f). But Ruth refuses to give in to the insistence of her mother-in-law and return too. "Where you go I will go ... Your people will be my people and your God my God ..." (vv. 16f). The question of return is thus at the same time a question of membership of the people and the religion.

Against all common sense, Ruth decides to follow an old woman to a strange world. In the context of the book she thereby proves her credentials for becoming the matriarch of the dynasty of David. Boaz later expressly emphasizes this: "you left your father and mother and your homeland and came to live with a people you did not know before" (2.11). He adds a detailed blessing for Ruth's further future, mentioning the "God of Israel" as the provider of blessing and protection (v. 12). Thus blessed, Ruth becomes as it were a "matriarch by adoption" (Alter 1981, 59).

The narrative has been moving unswervingly towards this point. On Naomi's and Ruth's arrival in Bethlehem it is initially the women of the town that recognize Naomi, with great surprise. Naomi counters this with the bitter fate that God has laid on her, whom she here calls *Shaddai* (1.20f, alternating with Yhwh v. 21)—like Job (*passim*) [→337]. But then Ruth comes to the fore as she starts actively planning her life. She provides for the sustenance of the two women by gleaning, and in the process meets the man that will turn around their fate. When she tells Naomi about the encounter, she answers with a double "The LORD bless (*bārûk*) him!," first for Boaz's kindness towards the foreigners gleaning the grain (2.19) and then especially because God has shown in this encounter that his goodness has not left the living and the dead (v. 20); for Boaz is one of those who as "redeemers" come into consideration for the family inheritance. He could "redeem" (cf. Lev 25.25ff) [→68] the land that still belongs to the family and—in the view of the book of Ruth—thereby also the childless woman from this family. So Naomi's view of her fate has clearly changed since her arrival in Bethlehem. She no longer speaks any more of the bitterness of her fate (cf. 1.19f) but of the constancy of God's mercy.

Naomi now sees a chance to provide Ruth with a "resting-place" (*mānô°h*, 3.1), just as previously she had hoped her two daughters-in-law would have rest (*m'nûḥāh*) in the house of a new husband (1.9). She thinks up a plan, which Ruth puts into effect. After the celebration of the completion of the harvest, when Boaz has eaten and drunk and has lain down on the threshing-floor to sleep, she is to secretly lie down at the foot-end of his couch, beautifully dressed, having bathed and anointed herself. "He will then tell you what you are to do" (3.2-4). And so it happens—with a small but important difference: he does not tell her what to do, but she tells him what he should do: "Spread the corner of your garment over me, since you are a kinsman-redeemer" (v. 9). And he answers in the same way Ruth answered Naomi's instructions: "I will do for you all you ask" (v. 11). The initiative thus rests entirely with Ruth. A foreigner has called on an Israelite to meet his responsibilities (Trible 1993, 212). Boaz has previously pronounced a blessing, however, and he picks up on his words at their first encounter "The LORD bless you, my daughter ... This kindness (*ḥesed*) is greater than that which you showed earlier: You have not run after the younger men, whether rich or poor" (v. 10). Here two central religious terms of the book connect: blessing and *ḥesed*, which can mean kindness, grace and loyalty (cf. Miller 1994, 290-293).

With this, Boaz has fully accepted and taken on board Naomi's and Ruth's concern. But there is still an obstacle: Boaz is not the first "redeemer," but there is someone else who stands in a closer family relationship to the family into which Naomi married and which she now represents as the only survivor (3.12). This determines the first phase of the narrative. The initiative now rests with Boaz. The women can only wait; but they trust him (v. 18). In a detailed and graphic scene at the gate the case of the "redemption" is dealt with, first concerning the plot of land (4.1-4) and then, with increased suspense, with the "levirate marriage" with Ruth, "in order to maintain the name of the dead with his property" (v. 5).

Boaz acquires the land of Elimelech's family, and he acquires Ruth as his wife and thereby the duty of continuing the family name (vv. 9f). The whole assembly is witness to this, and again the name of God is called upon: "May the LORD make the woman who is coming into your home like Rachel and Leah, who together built up the house of Israel" (v. 11).

This makes the connection with the very beginning of the story of the people of Israel and then again the shorter connection to the beginning of the genealogy of David, to "Perez, whom Tamar bore to Judah" (v. 12). The echo of another story resounds, in which the concern was with a levirate marriage and ultimately about the forced or rather, contrived, preservation of a deceased person's name by a woman (Gen 38).

Finally, once again we see that the story of Ruth is a story of guidance. After the marriage union, God grants Ruth pregnancy, so that she bears a son (4.13). And then the women again dominate the picture and Naomi stands in central position. The women praise God that he has not withheld the "redeemer" from Naomi. And the Israelite aspect also resounds again: "May he become famous throughout Israel!" (v. 14). The daughter-in-law who has given birth to the child, is worth more to Naomi than seven sons (v. 15), but Naomi herself remains in the center. Indeed, finally the woman say: "Naomi has a son" (v. 17). After all, it is her name that has been restored. She is the figure who carries the narrative.

The concluding genealogy (4.18-22) places the whole episode expressly in the context of the dynasty of David. At the same time, by means of the formula "These are the generations" (*'ēlleh tôl'dôt*, v. 18) the story of the patriarchs is once again called to mind, where this formula appears frequently (Gen 11.10, 27; 25.19; 37.2), whereas it is found scarcely anywhere else in the Hebrew Bible.

The book of Ruth is thus a guidance story, a woman's story, and a narrative marked by a quite matter-of-fact piety (cf. also Sasson 1987). People have to act themselves, and they do this with great courage, with consideration and also with cunning. But God sets the terms. He sends famine and he brings it to a close, he sends death and he enables new life. The people know this and they say so. They praise God and bless each other. And in all this a piece of the history of the people of Israel takes place, the early beginnings of which are recounted here in retrospect.

5.2 The Song of Songs

How did the Song of Songs get into the canon of the Hebrew Bible? This frequently asked question arises when one views this book in the context of the other writings. It contains love songs of great beauty and linguistic artistry [→*In* 274]. But it does not speak of God or of the relationship between humans and God, not even indirectly or in code. It speaks of humans, the woman and the man and their relationships with each other.

Tradition has ascribed the book to Solomon (1.1) with the title "Song of Songs" (*šîr haššîrîm*). This certainly has contributed to its canonicization, even if this was constantly in dispute. Later in allegorical interpretation the book was interpreted as relating to the love between God and Israel or between Christ and the Church. In the meantime, however, generally the view has prevailed that the concern here is with real, human love. Can there still be an interpretation of the book in the theological context of the Hebrew Bible?

This occurs most convincingly when the Song of Songs is read as the development of what is said at the beginning of the Bible about the relationship between man and woman: "For this reason a man will leave his father and mother and be united to his wife, and they will become one flesh" (Gen 2.24) [→15]. Sexual love between a man and a woman is expressed very clearly here, but not developed in detail. The Song of Songs can be read as the development of what is only alluded to here. An interpretation like this does not give the texts of the Song of Songs a direct theological meaning. But the free and varied way of experiencing the love between a woman and a man developed in them, it places in the context of the biblical view of creation, in which right from the beginning humans are viewed and presented in their sexual differentiation from each other and their relationship to each other (cf. Trible 1993, 169-190; Crüsemann 1978b, 81-91).

In the immediate canonical context another feature is worthy of note. The book of Ruth shows how in a world whose structures are dominated by men, women take their own initiatives and shape things according their conceptions and wishes. In the Song of Songs too, the loving woman dominates over the man, and here too she is surrounded by other women, the "daughters of Jerusalem," who constantly have a concern for her wellbeing (2.7; 3.5, 10; 5.8-16 etc.). The self-reliance and relative independence of these women is also reminiscent of the "capable woman" at the end of the book of Proverbs (Prov 31.10-31) [→368]. Thus here in the "Writings," on the periphery of the broad stream of biblical traditions, as it were, we meet different texts that show that even in the patriarchal world of Ancient Israel there were successful efforts by women to develop their own identity and to work on their own on the shaping of their fate.

5.3 The Preacher (Qohelet)

5.3.1 Who is Qohelet?

"The words of Qohelet, son of David, King in Israel" [→*In* 278]. The way this book begins is reminiscent of the beginning of the book of Proverbs [→357]. But the difference is immediately clear: the name of the son of David is not given, neither here nor anywhere else in the book. Instead, the word *qohelet* appears, which is found nowhere else in the Hebrew Bible. It is connected with the word *qāhāl* "gathering, community" and is to be understood as a sort of term for an office or function. But what kind of gathering can be meant here? We read a number of times that Qohelet "speaks" (1.2; 7.27; 12.8). Perhaps he is to be thought of as a teacher, as the concluding comment in 12.9 also indicates. Sometimes the word is treated almost like a personal name, for instance "I, Qohelet" (1.12). He says of himself: "I was king over Israel in Jerusalem. I devoted myself to study and to explore by wisdom (*hokhmāh*) all that is done under heaven"(1.12f). It is made clear here that Qohelet styles himself according to the image of Solomon (cf. esp. 1 Kgs 5.9-14) [→118]. This is not applied to the whole book however; thus in 5.7, for instance, it is evident that the person speaking is not one of the "mighty." Here he has taken off the mantle of the king.

In the concluding verses of the book, Qohelet is described as a wise man (*hākām*) who taught the people knowledge (*da'at*, 12.9). But what knowledge that is! "Everything is meaningless ..." (1.2). The word *hebel*, "meaningless," is found more than 30 times in this book, five of them in the opening verse alone. It means "breath of wind" (Isa 57.13), "emptiness, ephemerality, fleetingness" (Pss 144.4; 39.6, 7, 12 etc.). So too in Qohelet: "Everything is emptiness, a chasing after the wind (or: ghost of the air)" (1.14 etc.). What does that mean in the context of wisdom with which Qohelet wants to explore everything? One has to look more closely, to understand what this "Everything is meaningless" brings to expression. (On what follows cf. Lohfink 1993 and Michel 1988 and 1989, *passim*.)

5.3.2 Nothing is gained under the sun

After the aphoristic introductory sentence, which is repeated at the conclusion (12.8), the book begins with the question: "What does man gain from all his labor at which he toils under the sun?" (1.3). The word *yitrôn*, which is found only in Qohelet, means the profit or produce of work. This is described as tedious, often with the almost formulaic expression "the toil (*'āmāl*) with which one toils" (cf. 2.11, 19, 20 etc., cf. Otzen 1989, 217ff). How fundamentally this question is meant, is shown in the addition "under the sun," Qohelet's own, constantly repeated variation on the otherwise customary "under heaven" (which he also uses), in which he includes the whole of the world that is accessible to humans.

In place of an answer, a sort of summarized cosmology follows, or rather a reflection on the human being within the cosmos (1.4-11). "Generations come and go, but the earth remains forever (*lᵉ'ōlām*)" (v. 4). The constant stream of change in human history contrasts it with the immutable identity of the earth, on which this history is played out. The earth does not change, whatever may happen in the changing generations of men. That is how it is with the sun: it runs resolutely from its rising to its setting, but then without a break it returns to its point of departure and rises again (v. 5, cf. Ps. 19.7) [→**331**]. The wind too however. No matter which way it blows, it always returns to the point from which it came (v. 6). Finally the water courses: they flow into the sea, but when they arrive there, their activity is not at an end, for the sea does not fill up, the water turns back to its point of departure, and the streams and rivers constantly stream anew (v. 7). All things are incessantly active; no human can express everything, the eye never has enough of seeing, and the ear never has its fill of hearing (v. 8). So the human being stands in the middle of creation. He can observe and explore it, perhaps admire it too (cf. Ps. 8), but never fully understand it.

As a summary, as it were, we then read: "what has been will be again, and what has been done will be done again; there is nothing new under the sun" (v. 9). Is this already an answer to the opening question? A partial answer in any case: the "gain" cannot consist in humans creating something new. There is nothing "new," because everything has been there before (v. 10). But there is nothing that remains either. Whatever a human may have achieved and created, in subsequent generations there is no memory of the earlier ones, and the subsequent ones too will be forgotten (v. 11). Everything vanishes like a breath of wind.

These general findings are now continued in the scroll of the king (1.12, cf. v. 1) in a quasi-biographical narrative. The word "wisdom" now appears too. It is with this that the king has set about studying and researching everything that is under heaven (v. 13). He has considered everything precisely. Again and again throughout the whole of the book we read: "I saw (*rā'îtî*)." What is meant is not a contemplative gaze but a precise observation, from which conclusions can be drawn. The result of the consideration of "all the deeds that are done under the sun: all is vanity and a chasing after wind" (v. 14). This is an "unhappy business" (*'inyan rā'*) that God has laid upon people (v. 13b), that there is no escaping the effort of considering and studying by wisdom, but that it leads to such a result as this.

The observations are broadened: extension of wisdom [→**§19**] and the attempt to find out what wisdom really is: a chasing after wind (1.16f); to give oneself over to pleasure (2.1f) and wine (v. 3), to build houses and lay out vineyards, gardens and parks (vv. 4-6), buy slaves and livestock, hoard gold and silver, acquire male and female singers and a large harem (vv. 7f), getting bigger and richer with the help of wisdom (v. 9)—yes, all this can be enjoyed. This pleasure is the "reward" that humans can acquire for themselves (v. 10). But then, on further reflection, the verdict is once again: all is vanity and a chasing after wind, because "there was nothing to be gained under the sun" (v.11). The gain towards which the introductory question was addressed (1.3) does not exist. Humans can enjoy their "share" of pleasure if they are given the opportunity. But none of this lasts. There can be no lasting gain "under the sun." Solomon is an example of this: what he acquired and gained, wisdom, wealth and power, has not lasted. In retrospect it is nothing but a breath of wind, a will-o'-the-wisp.

But is not wisdom itself a gain, an advantage? Are not wisdom and stupidity like light and darkness, since the wise have eyes in their heads, but fools grope around in the dark (2.13, 14a)? Experience shows that this too is not a permanent gain, because the same fate awaits both (v. 14b). Both will die, and there will be no memory of them. So everything that happens under the sun is vain and a chasing after wind (vv. 15-17). And all the possessions a person has gained will pass to someone else, and one will not know whether that will be a wise person or a fool (vv. 18-23). So it sounds like a refrain: "all is vanity" (vv. 15, 17, 19, 21, 23).

5.3.3 Everything comes from God's hand
Suddenly the angle of view changes. What is "good" (*tôb*) for people, "happiness" (Lohfink, 1993), does not lie within their own power of disposal but comes from God's hand (2.24). The discourse swings round into the theological. What has been said thus far is not, however, taken back. The good that is spoken of here are the things of the present, earthly life: "to eat and drink and find satisfaction in his work." But God also distributes chances in life: to the one "who pleases him" he gives wisdom, insight and joy, but to another, who "misses the mark," the "sinner," the "business" (*ʿinyān*, cf. 1.13) is given of gathering and storing up wealth to hand it over to "the one

who pleases God" (v. 26). But who is it who is "good in God's eyes"? With this phrase, which is found nowhere else in the Hebrew Bible, Qohelet clearly wishes to bring to expression that this is removed from human view and humans have no influence on it. It is God's own decision, humans can only perceive the consequences. The same applies to one who "misses the mark": the view of the human being sees only the way people prosper and does not know what constitutes the missing of the mark. This inaccessibility of the fates to human view leads Qohelet once again to his refrain, "everything is meaningless, a chasing after the wind."

Again a new tone: a poem on the topic of "a time for everything" (3.1-8). In a strictly worded series of fourteen pairs of opposites Qohelet leads us through a broad spectrum of human life and shows that everything has its appointed time (*'ēt*), its καιρός. The antithetical word-pairs parade the fact that only one of the two things is possible at any one time: to be born or to die (v. 2), but also to plant or harvest, to kill or heal, tear down or build, cry or laugh—through to loving or hating, war or peace (v. 8). This raises the question once again: if this is so, if a person cannot decide at all what he or she should do or not do, "what does the worker gain from his toil?" (v. 9).

Again Qohelet observes this "business" with which God has entrusted humans (v. 10). But this time he does not call it a "heavy burden" (cf. 1.13), since he has recognized that God himself has ordered things this way, that everything is "beautiful," i.e. right (v. 11a) at its proper time. But God has done even more: he has given humans "eternity" (*'ôlām*) in their hearts, i.e. the urge to think beyond "time." But here humans again bump into the boundary that Qohelet complains of so frequently: he cannot "fathom" the work that God does in its entirety (v. 11b). But this time Qohelet does not stay with this negative observation. With a repeated "I have perceived" (*yāda 'tî*) he contrasts two things: for humans it is good (it is "happiness") to enjoy oneself, to find satisfaction, to eat and drink, for this is a gift from God (vv. 12f). But everything that God has made, he has made "for eternity." Nothing can be added to it or taken away from it (v. 14a). And God made it like this, so that people will fear him (v. 14b).

Here Qohelet picks up again what has been said earlier about what is good for people, what is their "portion" (2.10). But he now places it in a broad framework, in which what God does is also in view. The resigned undertone is missing here. Certainly, the distinction and also division between the area accessible to human perception and the area that is reserved for God himself, is clear enough. But we do not find the word "meaningless" in this section, so often repeated elsewhere. Instead, for the first time in Qohelet we find the word "reverence" (3.14b), which is found frequently in the book of Proverbs [→**359, 368**].

Thus, in all his distancing, Qohelet places himself in the context of the wisdom understanding of the relationship between the human and God. In conclusion he again picks up the word that there is nothing new (3.15; cf. 1.9f). But it has a different emphasis here, because it is expressed as it were from God's point of view, who has made everything "for eternity."

5.3.4 Injustice and pointlessness everywhere—but make sure you fear God!

Qohelet now turns his attention to the human society that surrounds him. Again he observes, and he sees injustice (3.16). Here the difference between Qohelet and the wisdom teachers of the book of Proverbs is clearly evident. There the victory of righteousness over unrighteousness was constantly emphasized, in a didactic tone, and therewith also the superiority of the righteous in relation to those who are not righteous, the wicked. Qohelet sees, however, that this does not correspond to reality. The wisdom teacher also knows, of course, that there are unjust verdicts; but his response to this is to say only that they are an abomination to God (Prov 17.15) [→**365**]. Qohelet draws resigned conclusions from this—about the fate of humankind, which is not fundamentally different from that of animals (3.17-21), and that it would be better for humans not to have been born (4.2f). There follow various wisdom sayings, generally longer than in Proverbs, but generally more reflective: about the way humans deal with each other (4.1, 4), about the usefulness of not being alone (4.7-12) and about the fickleness of favor with the people (4.13-16). The whole thing is constantly viewed from a negative point of view, which often opens out into "everything is meaningless" (3.19; 4.4, 7, 8, 16). But in between we read again that there is nothing better (no other "happiness") for humans than to enjoy the pleasure that is their lot (3.22).

Between these reflections comes a surprising passage about religious behavior (4.17–5.6). This also differs from what has gone before in its use of the "you" (second person singular) of wisdom admonitions. "Protect your foot/guard your step when you go to the house of God." The entry into the temple that is in mind here is primarily for the purpose of listening: "Go near to listen rather than to offer the sacrifice of fools" (5.1 [4.17]). Here Qohelet is again fully in line with the wisdom teachers. In Proverbs sacrifices and prayers are contrasted (Prov 15.8) [→**366**] and turning away from hearing doctrine is criticized (28.9). Sacrifices are freewill offerings and are connected with sacrificial meals; the "fools" who form the counterpart to the wise (cf. 2.14) may therefore love this kind of sacrificial occasion. The wisdom disciple who is addressed here, however, is above all to listen, and listen to instruction (*tôrāh*, cf. Prov 28.9) [→**367**]. He should not be too eager or verbose in prayer (5.2). For "God is in heaven and you are on earth, so let your words be few." This is reminiscent of the words of the Psalmist: "Our God is in heaven" … "the highest heavens belong to the LORD, but the earth he has given to man" (Ps 115.3, 16). Thus Qohelet can be described here as the "guardian at the threshold to every righteous prayer" (Zimmerli 1980, 184).

A third aspect of cultic behavior is the vow. The disciple addressed should take care to fulfill any vow made to God, without delay (5.4). Qohelet quotes the corresponding instruction in Deut 23.21a[22a] verbatim. But then the wisdom aspect is evident again when he does not continue with the quotation, which announces a divine "demand" (v. 21b[22b]) but contrasts the "fool" who does not fulfill his vow and thus does not find "favor" (with God, though this is not explicitly said). The sentence that follows in Deuteronomy, that anyone who does not make any vows does not make himself guilty (Deut 23.23[24]), Qohelet changes into a wisdom saying with "better—than" (*tôb—min*, 5.5[4]). After all, one should not let things come to the point where one has to confess (5.6) an unintentional sin (*šᵉgāgāh*) before the "messenger," i.e. the priest (cf. Mal 2.7) [→**310**]. Qohelet is not so concerned with the possibility of obtaining forgiveness for such a sin through the prescribed sin-offering (cf. Num 15.27-29) [→**74**], but with the preceding anger of God and its possible consequences (v. 5b). Instead of relying on cultic restitution, the wisdom disciple should be careful, through prudent and responsible living, not to be reliant on it. And so the concluding, pithy admonition reads: "Fear God!" (v. 7b[6b]).

This theological section (4.17–5.6[5.1–7]) can be viewed as the central section of the book of Qohelet, assuming a planned structure of the whole (Lohfink 1993, 10). Here we see a very detached but certainly not dismissive attitude to some basic questions of the cultic tradition which are regarded in association with a considered, wisdom-oriented life. As before in the book of Proverbs, here one can see clear parallels to the prophetic critique of sacrifice, even if the underlying religious tone is different. In addition, the call to "fear God" echoes Deuteronomy, where this term plays a central role (Deut 4.10; 6.2, 13 etc.) [→**78**].

5.3.5 Live "well"—in the knowledge that we will die

At the beginning of the second half of the book, in the middle of a reflection on the ambivalent aspects of wealth (5.10–6.11[5.9–6.10]), Qohelet once again takes up the topic of what is good, "happiness" (5.18-20[17-19]). Good, which is "beautiful" (*yāfeh*), as God made everything beautiful in its time (3.11), i.e. "complete happiness" (Lohfink 1993), consists in the fact that the human being may enjoy the fruits of the prosperity given him or her by God, without having constantly to think about how short are the days of his or her life.

It is clear here, together with the context in 5.12-16; 6.1f and other texts, that for Qohelet the real threat to human happiness is the knowledge that life is limited in time. This threat can only be escaped temporarily, if God grants this (5.20[19]; but the translation remains uncertain).

Then Qohelet goes on to discuss the "many words which increase the breath of wind" (6.11). These so characteristic words are sentences from the wisdom tradition which Qohelet quotes and criticizes, though it is not always clear where the quotation ends and Qohelet's own words begin. The whole section 6.11–9.6 can be described as ideological critique (Lohfink 1993, 10). Everything is multilayered; beautiful, edifying proverbs are carried on *ad absurdum*. Even the "wise," the educated, are not spared, for their speeches too are breaths of wind (7.5f) and even valuable wisdom is subject to the caveat that no one can straighten what God has bent (vv. 11-13). Even righteousness and wisdom on their own are no guarantee for a good and long life, and it is a matter of finding the right pathway between the extremes; reverence for God helps here (vv. 14-18). But wisdom itself remains far off and deep, very deep (v. 23), and even reverence for God cannot be counted upon to be successful in every case (8.12b-14).

The grandly constructed concluding passage in this section (8.16–9.6) emphasizes once again that even with his most strenuous endeavors the human being cannot "find out" God's deeds in their entirety—even if the wise claim to be able to do so (8.16f). The righteous and the wise are also in God's hands (9.1), they too are included in the fate reserved for all (v. 3). But: life is at any rate better than having died ("a live dog is better off than a dead lion," v. 4), for "the living know that they will die, but the dead know nothing" (v. 5); the memory of them is extinguished, and they no longer have any part in what happens under the sun (v. 6). To know that one is going to die—that is the most that the investigations of human wisdom can attain. But it is more, much more, than a dead person can appreciate. The key thing is to live appropriately with this knowledge.

5.3.6 ... until the dust returns to the earth

The last main section of the book again begins with a second-person address: "Go, eat your food with gladness, and drink your wine with a joyful heart" (9.7). The wisdom disciple addressed (cf. 4.17) is later described as "young man" (11.9). He is expressly called upon to enjoy the pleasures of life. But there is equal emphasis on the two-fold qualification of these pleasures: that they are given by God as one's lot (9.7, 9)—and that this life is a "breath of wind" (v. 9) and leads in the final analysis to the underworld (v. 10). In this framework, sketched again and again by Qohelet, however, an active and responsible enjoyment of life should unfold.

To secure the boundaries, as it were, within which all this has to happen, there follows a reflection in poetic form about time and chance (9.11f; cf. 3.1-8), and then numerous, sometimes very brief texts on various aspects of human behavior: on knowledge and power (9.13-18), stupidity (10.1-3), behavior towards one's ruler (vv. 4-7), wisdom (vv. 8-11) and folly (vv. 12-20); finally, two longer, reflective pieces: on the unpredictability of the future, connected with the call to act vigorously (11.1-8), and a call to enjoy one's youth, before the cares of old age come and finally "the dust returns to the ground it came from, and the breath returns to God who gave it" (11.9–12.7). In this last sentence the echoes of the biblical creation story (Gen 2.7) [→15] are unmistakable. In all his skepticism Qohelet's thinking moves within the framework drawn by the fundamental texts of the Hebrew Bible.

Even the concluding sentence (12.8), which echoes the introductory "everything is emptiness" (1.2) for the last time, does not stand outside this framework. Qohelet has said it time and again: it is emptiness, nothingness, a breath of wind, to search for knowledge that remains hidden from humans, especially knowledge about the profit of life which extends beyond the limits of the lifetime granted to humans. But this limitation has been set by God, and God also grants humans their share in the possessions and joys of this life, until at last the breath that God has given humans returns to God (12.7). Certainly with this viewpoint Qohelet stands on the fringes of the faith traditions of the

Hebrew Bible. But the reader knows of course how multifaceted these traditions are. In many writings the central topics are ones which are not considered at all in others. Even the way in which God is spoken of, varies widely. So the fact that Qohelet does not use the divine name Yhwh and speaks instead of "God" (*'elohîm*, generally with the article), is not so unusual, since for instance in the book of Job the divine name is also entirely absent outside the framework narrative and instead the much rarer word *šadday* (cf. Gen 17.1) is found [→**27**].

The concluding remarks again speak of Qohelet in the third person, like the introductory words. He is described as a wise man who learned knowledge and, like Solomon, composed many proverbs (12.9f). The author of the concluding verses adds some admonitions of his own. He picks up Qohelet's repeated call to fear God and places it in a larger Old Testament context, by adding the keeping of the commands to reverence for God, in deuteronomic terms (cf. e.g. Deut 5.29; 6.2) [→**77**]. The concluding sentence, which speaks of the judgment of God, does not, however, relate to anything in the rest of the book of Qohelet.

5.4 Lamentations

'ēkāh "How...!" is the title of this book in the Jewish tradition [→*In* **280**], in accordance with its first word. The book is often referred to in accordance with the Latin tradition of the Vulgate as Threni or Lamentations (in German: *Klagelieder*, since Luther). Since early times, in the Jewish tradition the prophet Jeremiah has been held to be its author. The book contains laments, lengthy, apparently inconsolable laments, all of which center on one topic: the destruction of Jerusalem and the temple in 586 BCE.

This is a lament of many voices [→**§17**]. The lament about the ruined and abandoned Jerusalem/Zion, sitting like a widow in its misery (1.1ff; 2.1ff etc.), alternates with the lament of the badly afflicted "daughter Zion" herself (1.2ff) and with the we-lament of her bitterly suffering inhabitants (4.17ff; 5.1ff). In between, the voice of an individual is raised (ch. 3) who introduces himself with the words "I am the man who saw misery" (3.1), the identity of whom is not disclosed; his laments are reminiscent of Job and especially the confessions of Jeremiah, which gives some basis for the supposed relationship between the book and Jeremiah.

The laments are accompanied from the beginning with the confession that this catastrophe is the consequence of Jerusalem's own sins (1.5, 8, 14 etc.). "Jerusalem has sinned greatly and so has become unclean." (1.8); the "yoke" of her sins is heavy on her neck (1.14), in fact her guilt is greater than the sins of Sodom (4.6). "We, we have sinned and rebelled and you have not forgiven" (3.42). It is "because of the sins of her prophets and the iniquities of her priests" that enemies have entered through the gates of Jerusalem (4.12f). All this happened on the "day of his wrath," when God mercilessly killed, no longer thinking of his "footstool," i.e. his altar and temple (2.7) (1.12; 2.1, 21).

Nowhere is a voice to be found querying this view of the catastrophe. On the contrary, the heavily beaten Zion confesses: "The LORD is righteous, yet I rebelled against his command" (1.18). The whole book insists almost completely on lament. But from this lament Zion and its inhabitants call constantly on God: "Look, O LORD" (1.9, 11, 20 etc.), "remember, O LORD" (5.1). Only once are comforting and encouraging words uttered (3.21-33): "Because of the LORD's great love we are not consumed, for his compassions never fail. They are new every morning; great is your faithfulness" (vv. 22f); "it is good to wait quietly for the salvation of the LORD" (v. 26). It is not until the very end that we encounter the petition: "Restore us to yourself, O LORD, that we may return; renew our days as of old" (5.21). But this is followed by the doubting question: "unless you have utterly rejected us and are angry with us beyond measure" (v. 22).

The lamentations have much in common with the psalms of lament. But they differ from them in one important respect: that the expressions of confidence and of assurance of being heard, which are found at the conclusion to each psalm of lament [→**327**], are missing. The lamentations are the direct testimony to reaction to the most horrendous catastrophe to have affected Israel in biblical times. And they stand so close to this event that no hope of a new future has found expression in them. (On this in general cf. Westermann 1990b.)

This impression of being directly affected and close to the events does not seem to fit with the fact that the songs are all structured according to an artistic acrostic system. In chs. 1, 2 and 4 each verse begins with the same letter of the alphabet, and in ch. 3 in fact each of the three lines in each verse; ch. 5 contains the same number of 22 verses, or lines corresponding to the number of the letters of the alphabet. Many exegetes thus assume that the songs were given this artistic shape only in the course of the tradition. But one may also surmise that this stylistic form, which is also frequently found of course in the

Psalms, was familiar enough in the authors' circles for them to be able to apply it even for such a purpose as this.

5.5 The Book of Esther

The book of Esther [→*In* 283] tells the dramatic story of the first great persecution of Jews and its happy outcome. It takes place in the time of the Persian Empire under king Ahasuerus (i.e. Xerxes I). The Jews live there as a religious and ethnic minority. From a Jewish point of view this is thus a story from the diaspora. The Jewish motherland is mentioned only once in a comment on the origins of Mordecai, the main male figure in the narrative, among the group of exiles that had been brought from Jerusalem to Babylonia by Nebuchadnezzar (2.6) [→152]; in the narrative itself, however, it plays no part.

A further striking feature is the complete absence of any mention of God, whether with the Old Testament divine name Yhwh or any other term for God. At only one point may there be a reference to a divine power, when Mordecai says in a message to Esther that the Jews might possibly receive help "from another place" (4.14); but the whole sentence remains in the air with a "Who knows?"

The narrative can nonetheless not simply be described as "secular." In the Jewish context of the late OT period it can be taken in advance as a silent assumption that important events do not take place without God. And since the whole narrative has a happy ending for the Jews despite all the dramatic and dangerous twists and turns, it cannot be read in any other way than as a story of divine guidance and leading, even if this remains hidden, and also and especially because the human actors, especially Mordecai and Esther, act in a considered and brave manner. For the narrator of this story, "divine-human cooperation is the most natural thing in the world" (Clines 1984, 157; cf. also Loader, 1992, 220, who speaks of the "relationship between 'God's hidden guidance' and 'human self-assertion'").

Thus, though there are no explicit theological statements in the book of Esther, the book still fits in with OT thinking. This is reinforced by the fact that clear echoes of other OT traditions can be found in the book. Particularly important are the connections with the Joseph story in Gen 37–50 [→31]. In both narratives an Israelite or Jew is promoted to high office in a foreign royal court and saves his or her people from disaster. In the book of Esther the figure of Joseph is as it were duplicated in the person of Mordecai, the rising star among court officials, and that of Esther, who becomes queen of the Persian Empires and in whom the wisdom elements that are clearly in evidence in the book of Esther (cf. Talmon 1963) have gained shape. She represents, as it were, the wise woman who plays such an important role in wisdom literature. (Cf. also Meinhold 1975/1976 and 1983.)

The book of Esther forms the festive legend for the festival of Purim, which is traced back to the events described in it (ch. 9).

Concluding remarks

The texts collected in the Megillot vary widely in type and origin. They do, however, have a certain amount in common, in that in each case they present the voices of "outsiders."

A feature of two of them, the Song of Songs and the book of Esther, is the fact that God is not spoken of in them, at least not explicitly. This certainly does not mean that they are outside the general context of the Hebrew Bible. A comparison of the book of Esther with the book of Ruth shows that the actors in both of them are humans, without there being any question of intervention by God, but that it is the expressed or unexpressed precondition of all human activity that it is in the final analysis directed by God. In the book of Ruth this is expressed again and again, and silently presupposed in the book of Esther. The difference thus lies in particular in the manner in which this form of piety is articulated.

The Song of Songs shows a kind of occupation with human love which stands entirely in agreement with the statements found in the creation account (esp. Gen 2.21-25). Here on the one hand the omission of the divine name is even more clear, but on the other hand nothing is really "missing," since talk of love, when understood in the context of creation concepts, has no need of express naming of God. The special place of the Song of Songs lies in the fact that this topic is developed here in detail; however no religious position at variance with the entirety of the Hebrew Bible comes to expression there.

The book of Qohelet adopts a very emphatic critical stance towards the broad stream of Old Testament wisdom literature. But precisely in this sideline position it develops quite specific conceptions of the relationship between humans and God which in no way depart from the theological framework of the Hebrew Bible. Lamentations also has a special position, since there the lament comes to expression in such elementary depth that there is no room left for words of hope such as are found throughout the songs of lament in the Psalms. But it is clear that this lament, especially in connection with the constantly repeated confession of guilt, has its place in the center of the religion of Israel.

Thus precisely these "minor writings" form an important supplement to the other books of the Hebrew Bible, by showing the breadth of the spectrum of theology and piety that was current at this time.

6. The Book of Daniel

In a number of regards the book of Daniel occupies a special position. [→In 286] In the Hebrew Bible it is situated in the third part of the canon, the "Writings." In the Septuagint and subsequent translations on the other hand Daniel has the position of fourth of the "Major Prophets." The place of the book in the Hebrew canon points, however, to a late, post-prophetic origin. It may be regarded as the only "apocalyptic" book in the Hebrew canon. The late time of composition is also evident in the fact that a large part of the book (2.4b–7.28) is extant in the Aramaic language. In the Septuagint there are in addition extensive supplements, which Luther included among the "Apocrypha" in his translation of the Bible.

The book of Daniel leads the reader to the extreme end of the history of Israel in the biblical period, and at the same time opens up a view of the imminent end of the world age. Its action takes place exclusively in the diaspora. In this regard it is comparable to the book of Esther. But the comparison immediately points up fundamental differences. Unlike the book of Esther, in Daniel the diaspora situation is a constituent element. The acting figures, Daniel and his three companions, are explicitly described as members of the *gālût*, the "deportation" from Judah (2.25; 5.13 etc.). Daniel himself has his windows open towards Jerusalem, in which direction he regularly prays (6.11).

This shows a further fundamental difference: the religious element is constantly and expressly in the foreground. God gives Jehoiachim into the hands of the king of Babylon (1.2); he creates the conditions for the young exiled Judeans to be able to live at the Babylonian court in accordance with the Jewish dietary laws (1.8-16); and he equips them with great insight and understanding (1.17-20). But then the conflicts with the heathen surroundings, in particular, are given religious justification by him: with the rejection of the worship of an idol of the king

[→§20] (ch. 3) and in Daniel's prayer to "his God" (6.11, 13); in the book of Esther on the other hand this aspect appears only indirectly in Haman's claim that the Jews were separating themselves from the other nations and that their laws were different from those of all other nations (Esth 3.8). At the same time this reveals another difference: in the book of Esther the Jews as a "nation" are contrasted with their non-Jewish surroundings, whereas in the book of Daniel the Jews appear as individuals who have to assert themselves. Again the religious element is crucially important, in that the help comes by means of direct intervention by God. Thus Daniel and his companions are saved from mortal danger by miraculous protection: from the furnace (ch. 3) and the lion's den (ch. 6).

These reports of individual rescue miracles express the superiority and uniqueness of the God of Israel [→§15]. In other narratives of the book this is demonstrated even more emphatically in the direct contrast with the heathen kings. Nebuchadnezzar (ch. 4) and Belshazzar (ch. 5) are subject to divine judgment. Nebuchadnezzar has previously ignored the warning given him in a dream which Daniel had to interpret, and has exalted himself proudly (4.26f); with the temple vessels plundered from Jerusalem Belshazzar has set up a hoard that is against God, and the judgment against him is announced through writing on the wall (5.5) which only Daniel is able to interpret (5.25-28). The message of these two chapters is "that the Most High reigns over the kingdom of men and gives it to whoever he wishes" (4.14, 22, 29; cf. 4.32; 5.22f).

This world-historical view of the dominion of God, the "Most High," dominates large parts of the book of Daniel (cf. Koch 1980, 199ff). Daniel confesses: God "changes times and seasons, he sets up kings and deposes them" (2.21). This is developed particularly memorably in the two large chapters that frame the Aramaic part of the book: the dream of Nebuchadnezzar, which Daniel interprets (ch. 2) and the vision which is granted to Daniel himself (ch. 7). Here, with a different image, a sequence of four world empires is presented (from the neo-Babylonian empire to the Hellenistic empire of the Diadochi, cf. Koch 1980, 187), at the end of which God himself will set up an empire that no one will destroy (2.44; cf. 7.27b).

Mysterious figures appear here: an "ancient of days" holds court over the animals which embody the world empires, on a fiery throne (1.9-12); with the clouds of heaven one "like a (son of) man" comes before the ancient of days, and he is granted dominion, honor and kingship

(7.13f); the kingdom is given (also?) to the "holy of holies" (7.18, 22, 27). Much of this remains obscure to today's exegetes (cf. Koch 1980, 214ff). At the same time we see that an eschatological future is envisioned, which lies beyond the time experienced in the present.

Further visions of Daniel point to the "time of the end" (8.17; 11.35 etc.) [→**§22**]. Again much remains mysterious and has to be interpreted to Daniel himself by the angel Gabriel (8.15ff; 9.21ff). Coded numbers play a role in this: "a time, two times and half a time" (7.25; cf. 12.7), half a (year) week (9.27), two thousand three hundred evenings and mornings (8.14), but also the much longer period of seventy (year) weeks (9.24ff). Again much remains entirely or partially obscure to us (cf. Koch 1980, 145ff). In the last two chapters, however, references to the events of the Maccabean period become quite clear. The "abomination" (11.21) is clearly Antiochus Epiphanes, whose wicked acts are depicted in detail in the *vaticinium ex eventu*. The climax of this is the desecration of the sanctuary, the abolition of the daily tamid sacrifice and the erection of the "abomination of desolation" (11.31; 12.11; cf. 8.13; 9.27).

Daniel is initiated into all of this; but he has to keep it secret (8.26; 12.4, 9), because the time of the end has not yet come. But then "many" who have died will "awake, some to everlasting life, others to shame and everlasting contempt" (12.2). Here in the last chapter of the last book of the Hebrew Bible we hear of the expectation of a resurrection of the dead.

7. The Books of Ezra and Nehemiah

Older Jewish tradition knows Ezra and Nehemiah as a single book, the author of which is taken to be Ezra. [→*In* 291] Later a new book was begun with Neh 1.1, probably on the basis of the superscription there relating to the "chronicles of Nehemiah." In Hebrew editions of the Bible the two books are, however, taken as a unity.

The question of the relationship between the books of Ezra–Nehemiah and the books of Chronicles is disputed. That there is a close relationship between them is obvious; but whether they have the same "author" is difficult to determine, not least because in both of them older sources are taken up and quoted on a large scale. In addition, they deal with different time periods: the book of Ezra begins where 2 Chronicles ends. (On this cf. Blenkinsopp 1989, 47-54.) It is surprising in this regard that in the Hebrew biblical manuscripts the books of Ezra–Nehemiah are placed *before* the books of Chronicles. This may have to do with the special understanding of the "canonical" significance of the books of Chronicles. (On this cf. Eskenazi 1988.)

7.1 From the edict of Cyrus to the consecration of the temple

The representation of the history of Israel and Judah ends in the second book of Kings with the catastrophe of the destruction of Jerusalem and the deportation of large parts of the population. The beginning of the book of Ezra now announces the beginning of something new: God wakens the mind of the Persian king Cyrus so that he arranges for the reconstruction of the temple in Jerusalem (Ezra 1.1-4). A new epoch in the history of Israel is thereby introduced, in which both of two things are impressively visible next to each other and in each other: continuity and discontinuity, connection with what has gone before and a new situation with fundamentally changed preconditions.

The new beginning is regarded as by divine decree: God "awakens the spirit" of the Persian king. The new thing that opens up as a result is at the same time the restoration of what was there before: of the temple in Jerusalem as the center of the Jewish religion and as an emblem of the identity of Israel. The turning point however does not come completely out of the blue, since it had been announced in divine messages through the prophets: through Jeremiah, who promised the return (Ezra 1.1; cf. esp. Jer 29–31) [→229], and by the exilic Isaiah, whose words echo very clearly in the statement that God has "awakened" Cyrus (cf. Isa 41.2, 25; 45.13) [→191]. Here we see that the books of Ezra–Nehemiah stand firmly in the earlier traditions, picking them up and carrying them further.

Cyrus issues a decree (in the year 538 BCE). The wording of this has a double tradition: first in the "official" version in Aramaic (Ezra 6.3-5), and secondly in the wording with which the author of the book of Ezra opens this new chapter in the history of Israel (1.2-4). Here it is Cyrus himself who traces this new beginning to a divine decree. In fact, "YHWH the God of heaven" has delivered world dominion to Cyrus, at the same time giving him the task of building a house for this God in Jerusalem. "To build a house" for God was the expression used for the construction of the first temple under Solomon (1 Kgs 5.17, 19; 6.1 etc.) [→119] and so it is now adopted again (Ezra 1.2f, 5; 5.2, 11 etc.): all who belong to the people of this God are to go up (*'ālāh*) to Jerusalem and build "the house of the LORD, the God of

Israel." The reconstruction of the temple in Jerusalem is the critical
goal for the return from Exile.

Another, different context becomes evident: the returning Judeans
are showered with gifts by the inhabitants of the places where they
now live, with silver and gold, with moveable goods and cattle, even
with "freewill offerings" (*n'dābāh*, Ezra 1.4, 6). In the background here
is the memory of the exodus from Egypt, when the Israelites did not
leave "empty" but received valuable "gifts" from their Egyptian
neighbors. There is, however, a notable difference in this reminiscence. In the accounts of the exodus from Egypt these gifts are depicted more as forced gifts, even explicitly "booty" (Ex 3.21f; 12.35f)
[→**46**], but in the foreground now is a willing preparedness to help out.
This also sheds light on the quite different, even opposite characterization of the foreign ruler of that time: Pharaoh is not only presented as
Israel's enemy but explicitly as the opponent of Yhwh (cf. esp. Ex 5.1-
5) [→**44**], while Cyrus praises Yhwh, the God of heaven, who has lent
him world dominion, and thus has a friendly disposition towards
members of the people of Israel.

Cyrus also arranges for the return of the temple objects which Nebuchadnezzar had taken away and brought to Babylon (Ezra 1.7; 6.5;
cf. 2 Kgs 24.13; 25.13-17). Their return had always been a particular
object of hope for a change of fortune (cf. Jer 27.16; 28.3, 6), while
their legendary misuse by the Babylonian king (more accurately,
crown-prince) Belshazzar (Dan 5) is depicted as particularly wicked
[→**217**]. The transportation and return of the objects is described in
detail (Ezra 1.8-11) and appears as an important element in the restoration of the earlier cultic situation.

Thus on the one hand the exodus from exile represents a repetition
of the exodus from Egypt [→**§9**]. On the other hand it is directly oriented towards the critical goal: the restoration of the temple in Jerusalem. God awakens the spirit of the exiles, as he awakened the spirit of
Cyrus, so that they prepare "to go up and build the house of the
LORD" (1.6). This sets out the central theme of the first part of the
book of Ezra. The returnees from exile under the leadership of the
Davidide Zerubbabel and Joshua (Jeshua) the priest (2.2ff) start by re-
erecting the burnt-offering altar of the ruined temple [→**§11**] and rees-
tablish the regular sacrificial cult, including the festival of booths (3.1-
5). The next step is then the laying of the foundations of the temple
(3.6ff). This is carried out with solemn ceremony (vv. 10-13), the tears
of the elderly who had seen the first temple mix with the cries of re-

joicing by others. This one act again expresses both aspects: the link with the former days and the beginning of the new.

But soon the work is frustrated. The precarious position of the returning Judeans in their relationship with other inhabitants of the region becomes evident. The returnees are described as "the *gôlāh*," i.e. as the group of exiles, who now, however, constitute the true, legitimate "Israel" (4.1; 6.19 etc.). Their "enemies" (4.1) are called "the people of the land" (4.4) or "the peoples of the land" (3.3). Their relationship to the construction of the temple that is just beginning is ambivalent. First they declare that they wish to participate, "for we worship your God as you do." They describe themselves as those who were brought here by the Assyrians (cf. 2 Kgs 17.24-41). Here the problem of the purity of the Israelite religion comes into view. Is it enough to worship (*dāraš*) God cultically, or is there more to it than that? The members of the Golah insist that they can only build "for the LORD, the God of Israel," as king Cyrus of Persia ordered them to do (4.3).

In reaction to this rejection the "people of the land" attempt to impede the building of the temple with all means at their disposal (4.4f), and do so right through the whole of Cyrus's reign (i.e. until 530) and through to his second successor Darius (from 522). (The intervening passage 4.6-23 relates to later opposition to the building of the wall in Jerusalem in the time of Xerxes I and Artaxerxes I, the successor of Darius.) Finally the intervention of the prophets Haggai and Zechariah gets the work going again (5.1f), when God again "awakens the spirit of Zerubbabel..., Joshua ... and the whole people" (Hag 1.14) [→303]. A renewed intervention, this time on the part of the Persian satrap (5.3ff), leads to a surprising result: the original copy of king Cyrus's decree ordering the construction of the temple in Jerusalem is found at the Persian court (6.1-5). This clears the way for the building work to be continued and finally the temple is ceremonially consecrated (in 515 BCE) (6.14-18).

The conclusion is formed by a great Passover celebration (6.19-22). This is not the first time that a passover is celebrated at a critical turning point in the history of Israel. Joshua celebrated the first Passover on the soil of the promised land after the whole of Israel had crossed the Jordan (Josh 5.10f); Josiah celebrated the Passover after the execution of his cult reform according to the instructions of the recently discovered "book of the covenant," as it "had not been celebrated since the days of the judges" (2 Kgs 23.21-23) [→151]; and now the members of the Golah celebrate the Passover on the restoration of the temple. The new epoch that is now beginning is thus situated in the broad context of the history of Israel.

The concluding comment in Ezra 6.22b sheds illuminating light on the political situation in which all this took place, and on the clear consciousness of this situation among the Judeans. God had turned the heart of the Persian king (who is here anachronistically referred to as the "king of Assyria") towards the Judeans. His favor had made all this possible, and only his favor and that of his successors can secure the undisturbed continuation of this situation. Thus a bridge is cast to the beginning of the whole account, where we read that God had awakened the spirit of the Persian king Cyrus so that he issued the decree for the reconstruction of the temple in Jerusalem (1.1). Through the spirit and heart of the Persian kings, divine guidance thus surrounds this whole significant episode in the history of the people of Israel.

7.2 Ezra in Jerusalem

The books of Ezra–Nehemiah give an account of the work of Ezra and Nehemiah in Jerusalem. Ezra came first, in the seventh year of the reign of the Persian king Artaxerxes (Ezra 7.8), and then Nehemiah later in the twentieth year of Artaxerxes (Neh 2.1). After that in both cases the king is Artaxerxes I (465-424), so that Ezra's arrival takes place in 458/7 and Nehemiah's in 445/4. These dates are disputed among scholars; the sequence is often reversed and Ezra's arrival dated to the time of Artaxerxes II (404-359), i.e. in the year 398/7. This reversal is not compelling, however, so that the sequence of the canonical text is to be preferred. (On this cf. Blenkinsopp 1988, 139-44.)

No coherent account of the post-exilic period of the history of Israel has come down to us. The books of Ezra–Nehemiah do, however, give us important details about relations between the diaspora and the newly established Jewish community in the land of Israel. Twice it is reported that members of the Jewish diaspora who had attained influential positions at the Persian court come to Jerusalem to set particular things in order: Ezra and Nehemiah. Nehemiah tells us that disconcerting news about the situation in Jerusalem had caused him to ask the Persian king for leave to go and rebuild the city (Neh 1f) [→**397**]. Here the initiative is taken by the diaspora Jew Nehemiah himself and is prompted by a contact between the two, widely separated areas of residence.

In Ezra's case the situation is different. He comes to Jerusalem with the explicit commission of the Persian king Artaxerxes "to enquire about Judah and Jerusalem with regard to the Law of your God, which is in your hand" (Ezra 7.14). We are not told whether there was a particular cause for this commission. It is clear, however, that the concern is primarily with the restoration and securing of law and order in this part of the Persian Empire, i.e. in the areas "beyond the river," where Jews live (vv. 25f). Here "the law of your God" is to be applied as "the law of the king." The Jewish "law" is thus given state sanction and is declared binding on the Persian subjects of the Jewish faith. "Judges and magistrates" are to be appointed to impose this; and it is to be taught to those who are not familiar with it.

Ezra's mission contains another aspect, however: Ezra is to bring to Jerusalem the silver and gold "that the king and his advisers have freely given to the God of Israel, whose dwelling is in Jerusalem" (v. 15). Further donations are to be collected and the whole amount used for sacrifices "on the altar of the house of your God in Jerusalem" (vv. 16f). This reverence towards a foreign cult is in line with Persian policy towards subject peoples. But in particular the religious and cultic side of Ezra's mission comes into view.

Ezra is given various titles in his introduction. First he is depicted as member of a priestly family, whose family tree is traced back to Aaron in the opening verses (1.1-5). Even though he never appears in a priestly function, nonetheless Ezra's origin in a priestly family is clearly important to the author. He repeatedly uses the term "Ezra the priest" (Ezra 7.11, 12, 21; 10.10, 16; Neh 8.2, 9; 12.16). The title *sofēr* (Aramaic *sāfar*), "writer" or "scribe," is also used (Ezra 7.6; Neh 8.1, 4, 13; both titles together in Ezra 7.1.1, 12, 21; Neh 8.9). According to broad opinion the title borne by Ezra was the official title of a Persian civil servant; in Ezra 7.6 the expression is, however, explained as "a scribe, well versed in the Torah of Moses, which the LORD, the God of heaven, had given," which associates him closely with the religious tradition of Israel and points already in the direction of the "scribes" i.e. the expert interpreters and expounders of the Torah (cf. Willi 1995, 106ff).

Ezra's preparation for return looks almost like a repetition of the first return at the time of Cyrus [→**390**]. Again he is joined by numerous Judeans who are keen to return (7.28; 8.1ff), and there is also a detailed description of the carrying and transfer of the gifts for the temple (8.24-30, 33f). It is repeatedly emphasized that the "hand of God" was with Ezra, so that the king granted his every wish and that the dangerous journey took place without incident (7.6, 9; 8.18, 22, 31).

In the first great sacrificial service the returnees are described as "members of the Golah who had returned from captivity (*š᷾bî*)" (8.35). They are thus equated with those who had come already with Zerubbabel and Joshua (2.1), but are also called *b᷾nê haggôlāh* (cf. 4.1; 6.19 etc.) and are thus included in the circle of the restored community.

Accounts of Ezra's activities in Jerusalem are given in two different passages in the books of Ezra–Nehemiah. While in the book of Ezra Ezra's dealings with the problem of mixed marriages are in the foreground (Ezra 9f), Neh 8 tells of a great religious gathering with an extended Torah-reading by Ezra. In the context of the compositional unity of the books of Ezra–Nehemiah this religious service follows immediately the report of the completion of the city wall under Nehemiah's leadership (Neh 6), thus forming a climax in the overall account of the two-volume work. This accepts a chronological discrepancy, in that the appearance of Ezra is inserted into Nehemiah's later time.

Ezra is now presented with a problem: many members of the newly constituted community have married women of the "peoples of the land" and have thus mixed the "holy seed" with these peoples and committed a breach of loyalty (*ma῾al*) towards their God (Ezra 9.1f). This information is placed in a broad, rather dramatic context, in that the foreign nations are described with the "classical," in some cases quite anachronistic series of names familiar to the reader from the Pentateuch (Gen 15.19f; Ex 3.8 etc.) [→48]. In Deuteronomy in particular marriage with members of these nations is expressly forbidden, because this means making a "covenant" (*b᷾rît*) with them (Deut 7.1-5) [→78] and because they could teach the Israelites to copy the "abomination" that they perpetrate with their gods (Deut 20.17f) [→83]. So Israel has done what Moses had prohibited! Herein lies the drama that is expressed in Ezra's reaction. He carries out mourning rites, fasts and pronounces a long prayer (Ezra 9.6-15).

This prayer places the present situation of "Israel" (cf. 9.1) in the broad framework of the history of the nation. From the days of the patriarchs it has been one long history of sinning. That is why the great disaster finally overtook Israel (vv. 6f). God has now granted the surviving remnant (*p᷾lêṭāh*) a moment of peace and restoration (vv. 8f), but they have once again infringed the commandment of the prophets and compromised themselves with the peoples of the land (vv. 10-12). What is now to become of the remnant that God has graciously spared (š˚'ērît ûflêṭāh) (vv. 13f) [→**§22**]? The prayer concludes with the emphatic "LORD, God of Israel, you are righteous!.," which is contrasted with the confession: "We cannot stand in your presence" (v. 15).

Ezra's dramatic behavior leads to a gathering of the "community" (qāhāl, 10.1). The gathered people promise to respond to Ezra's admonitions and to conclude a "covenant" (b˚rît) with God, that they will dissolve their marriages with foreign women (v. 3). The whole thing is reinforced in ceremonial form (vv. 5, 10-12), investigations are carried out (vv. 16f) and lists of those concerned are prepared (vv. 18-43). A brief concluding sentence reports the completion of the exercise (v. 44).

The unreported end of this account about a decision part of Ezra's activity is understandable since Ezra is spoken of again in another important function: in the reading of the Torah in Neh 8 [→**398**], which forms the climax and conclusion of his ministry within the context of the books of Ezra–Nehemiah as a whole.

Nonetheless the reader misses a concluding note here to show how this very invasive action of Ezra's was to be administered and assessed. In particular the question remains open what long-term effect the decisions and measures against marriages with non-Jewish women had. Some time later Nehemiah is confronted with this question again (Neh 13.23-27) [→**399**], which shows that Ezra's actions on this issue did not produce a final solution. (The same problems are also evident in Malachi, Mal 2.10-12 [→**310**]; however, we do not know how this relates in time to the books of Ezra–Nehemiah.)

7.3 The building of the wall, festive Torah-reading and cultic duties

With Nehemiah 1 something new begins: "The words of Nehemiah." The Hebrew expression d˚bārîm can also mean "events" (cf. 1 Chron 29.29; 2 Chron 9.29), so that the superscription can be understood as "Chronicles of Nehemiah." The texts of the book of Nehemiah are largely composed in the first person style, and the whole thing reads like a formal report or a *Denkschrift*. A special feature is the repeated appellation of God: "Remember me with favor, O my God" or similar (Neh 3.36f; 5.19; 6.14; 13.14, 22, 29, 31). It shows that this is not simply a report, but Nehemiah writes all this down to show how he has carried out the task which God "put in his heart" (2.12; cf. 7.5) and what obstacles he met in the process. (Cf. von Rad 1964).

The first main section of this commission is the restoration of the wall in Jerusalem. Nehemiah reports that on the basis of news about the bad situation in Jerusalem and in particular about the condition of the city wall, he applied for and was granted the permission of the Persian king, in whose service he held high office, to journey to Jerusalem and rebuild the wall (Neh 1.1–2.8). This report is accompanied by a long prayer of repentance in which, like Ezra before him (Ezra 9), Nehemiah confesses before God that the situation in which Israel now finds itself has its basis in the sins of the Israelites, in particular in their infringements of the commandments that God gave them through Moses (Neh 1.5-11). He also reminds God that he has promised the people that he will gather them and lead them back if they repent (*šûb*, v. 9), and asks that his prayer be heard and for the success in presenting his concern to the king (v. 11). So he sees what transpires after this as brought about and accompanied by the generous hand of God (2.8, 18).

Nehemiah then gives a comprehensive and detailed account of his journey to Jerusalem (2.9-11), his successful efforts to win over the inhabitants of Jerusalem and the surrounding towns to join in with the work of rebuilding the wall (2.12-18; 3.1-32) and of the building work itself, up to its conclusion (6.15). This description is constantly interrupted by reports of attempts by the governors of the neighboring provinces, Sanballat of Samaria and Tobiah from the transjordanian Ammon to impede the work (2.10, 19f; 3.33-35), including the planning of military attacks (4.1-17) and of assassination attempts on Nehemiah himself (6.1-14; cf. 6.16-19). But when the work has been successfully completed, his enemies have to acknowledge that it was God himself who enabled the completion of this work (6.16).

Before this event can be appropriately carried out, however, Nehemiah is confronted with other problems. "The people," i.e. in context: the poorer groups of the population, raise complaints about their "Jewish brothers," i.e. here: the landowners (according to v. 7 the "nobles" and "officials"). These people exploit the legal options to raise contributions and even the enslavement of the poorer people, who now make use of the claim that they are after all of the same "flesh and blood" (5.1-5). In a great assembly of the people Nehemiah makes a plea for reverence for God and the solidarity of the Jews in response to the enemies surrounding them and he is successful in this. He has the landowners swear solemnly before priests that they will give up their claims against other Jews (vv. 6-13). In so doing he set up new norms of behavior in his official capacity as Persian satrap (cf. Kippenberg 1978, 54-77). He even leads by example in not only giving up his own claims in relation to other Jews (v. 10) but in also not taking the proceeds due to him from his office and contesting the various duties (vv. 14-18).

The work on the city wall has come to an end (6.15f; 7.1-3) and the proper settlement of the restored city is prepared (7.4-72a taking up again a list of returnees from Ezra 2; the execution of this is reported in 11.1f). First, however, the first day of the seventh month (Neh 7.72b) is solemnly celebrated as the beginning of the new year, as had been the case on the first return (Ezra 3.1). But while there the first sacrifices on the re-erected altar stood in the foreground, now interest is focused entirely on the reading of the Torah [→§10]. Ezra thereby comes back into central position. The "whole people" gathers "as one man" on the open square before the water tower, evidently on their own initiative, without there being any mention of a summons to do so. The assembly asks Ezra to bring "the book of the Torah of Moses, which the Lord commanded Israel" (8.2[1]). So this is not a new, unknown book that Ezra now brings at the request of the assembly, but the Torah which had been given so long ago through Moses and which has since formed the constitutional basis of Israel as a religious, social and legal community.

With the public reading of the Torah, however, something new is indeed happening: the Torah is brought to the center of the rebuilt Jerusalem. For this purpose the entire people, men, women and growing children have gathered (8.2), and Ezra is surrounded on his dais by representatives of the people (v. 4). A religious occasion begins: as he opens the scroll of the Torah, all the people rise, Ezra pronounces a blessing, a *b'rākāh*, the people answer with "Amen, amen" and bow in worship (8.5f). There then follows the section-by-section reading of the Torah, with "Ezra the priest" (v. 2) being supported by Levites who explain in detail the passage that has just been read, so that the people understand it (vv. 7f). In this account there are echoes of elements of the later synagogue service.

Nehemiah (who appears here without explanation), Ezra and the Levites encourage the people to rejoice in and celebrate what they have heard and understood (8.9-12), "for the joy of the Lord is your strength" (v. 10). The next day on further study of the Torah they find the long-forgotten requirement of dwelling in "booths" in the festival of booths (Lev 23.39-43); the very varied execution of this requirement is further cause for extended festive celebration, accompanied by daily reading of the Torah (vv. 13-18).

But the reading of the Torah also has quite a different side to it: it is a cause of confession of sins and repentance. So in ch. 9 a great service of atonement takes place. (The succession of festival of booths and atonement service is reminiscent of the festive calendar, where, however, the *yôm hakkipurîm* precedes the festival of booths, Lev 23.26-32, 33-36, 39-43 [→**67**].) Reading of the Torah and confession of sins follow one another (v. 3), and now the Levites lead the service. Finally a long prayer of penitence unfolds (vv. 6-37). It starts by recalling the saving history of God with the world and with Israel (vv. 6-15), but then moves on into the confession of Israel's stubbornness and sinfulness in all its varied repeated instances, to which God responded with his punishments, but time and again also with his mercy, through to the deportation of Israel out of its own land (vv. 16-30); but Israel can still rely on God not to abandon it, "for you are a gracious and merciful God" (v. 31) and the "keeper of the covenant" (v. 32) [→**79**]. This still applies, even though the supplicants have to confess: "But see, we are slaves today ... We are in great distress" (vv. 36f). (Cf. 1997d.)

"In view of all this"—the direct link with the next chapter is made with these words (9.38[10.1]). Because of the serious history of sinning that is elaborated in the prayer, and because of the consequences of this, the gathered community, who now speak as "we," want to commit themselves by means of an oath, "to follow the Law of God given through Moses the servant of God" (v. 29[30]). This self-commitment is to be fixed in writing and sealed (9.38[10.1]). A long list of responsibilities follows (vv. 30ff): rejection of marriages with members of the "peoples of the land," the duty to keep the Sabbath in trade, keeping of the seventh years as a fallow year and for the cancellation of debts, and then in particular responsibilities which have as their center the "house of God," the temple: a temple tax, deliveries of wood, presentations of firstborn and firstfruits of various kinds, and finally the contribution of a tithe for the Levites. In these sentences we find many references to regulations from the Pentateuch, the "book of the Torah of Moses." It can be described as "the oldest preserved document of a detailed Torah-interpretation" (Crüsemann, 1992, 395).

This solemn commitment brings the hearing of the Torah and the confession of sins to an impressive conclusion. Israel has gathered in the restored Jerusalem, with the temple in its center, and has committed itself in its entirety to life in accordance with the Torah. Neh 8–10 thus forms the heart of the books of Ezra–Nehemiah.

The consecration of the city wall, finally, forms the last climax (12.27-43). It is described as a great solemn ceremony, for which the priests and the Levites first purify themselves (cf. Ezra 6.20) and thus also the people, the gates and the walls. The whole people thus becomes "holy." The representatives of the Jewish community, with the levitical singers in front, then march around the wall in two festive choirs under the leadership of Ezra and Nehemiah and finally come together "in the house of God" for a great sacrificial ceremony which develops into a general celebration of the people; "because God had given them great joy" (v. 43). So not only was the wall consecrated but also the temple and the whole city with it, the gates and walls of which had already been "purified." What began with the edict of the Persian king Cyrus (Ezra 1.1-3) has then come to a happy conclusion. The bases for the life of "Israel" (cf. 11.3, 20 etc.) have been re-laid and confirmed.

The following sections, Neh 12.44–13.31, seem to be additions. Some complement the commitment of the community of ch. 10, Nehemiah now appearing again as it were as the executive officer, bringing Nehemiah's first-person account to a conclusion (13.4-31, cf. Eskenazi 1988, 122ff).

7.4 Israel and the Torah

Jerusalem, the "holy city" (Neh 11.1) [→§14], has been rebuilt and encircled by a protective wall. In the middle of it stands the temple, in which the regular cult is carried out in accordance with the rules of the Torah. What was destroyed and ruined has been restored, so that Israel can continue with what earlier generations created and wrote.

But there is much that has changed. The political structures have altered: Israel—or more precisely, Judah—is now part of the Persian Empire without political independence. Political structures of its own, such as the later high priesthood, are not yet in evidence. But above all, Israel no longer lives only in its own land, but also in what can now be called the "diaspora." The exile, understood as temporary, has become an individual, permanent form of life for part of the nation. But this "diaspora Judaism," as it can now be called, is fully aware at least in its best representatives, of its relations to the land of Israel, in fact of its rootedness in it.

This deep-rooted relationship comes to expression with particular clarity in the fact that leading personalities in the diaspora Jewish community, who at the same time also occupy influential positions in the Persian Empire, feel responsible for the fate of the land of Israel and especially of the city of Jerusalem. The books of Ezra–Nehemiah tell of this. They do not give their accounts in isolation, however, and they are not primarily about individuals, but they allow the reader to participate in how the community in and around Jerusalem gains and expresses its self-understanding within the newly consolidated living area. In the central passage Neh 8–10 in particular it is the community itself, the "people" (*hā'ām*) that grasps the initiative for the public reading of the Torah and for the corresponding responsibilities.

The "Torah" and the "law" then appear with two quite different functions in the books of Ezra Nehemiah and also with different terminology. In the Aramaic text of the commission that Ezra receives from the Persian king (Ezra 7.12-26) there is talk of the "law" (*dāt*) which is also described as "the law of your God" (vv. 4, 26, 25 in the plural) or "law of the God of heaven" (vv. 12, 21). "God of heaven" here is the term for the God of Israel from the viewpoint of outsiders. [→§15] This law is at the same time to apply as the "law of the king" and is applied in the whole province in which Jews live and to be supervised in its execution (vv. 25f). The carrying out of this commission is briefly indicated in 8.36.

In Neh 8 we then read of the "Torah." It is introduced as and is simply referred to as "the book of the Torah of Moses, which the Lord commanded Israel" (v. 1) and thereafter simply as "the Torah" (vv. 2, 7, 9 etc.), or "the book of the Torah" (vv. 3, 8, 18). The public reading of it by Ezra is celebrated as a significant event. It has effects on the shaping of the life of the community which thereafter celebrates the feast of booths (8.13-18), publicly confesses its sins (ch. 9) and concludes a solemn commitment to keep the Torah, with special reference to the temple service.

The books of Ezra–Nehemiah thus constitute the witness of the consolidation of Israel in the time of Persian hegemony. Jerusalem with the temple forms the central point, as it had done for centuries before. But now a new element has come in, which from now on becomes the essential basis of Israel's self-understanding: the Torah. Ezra's work thus has fundamental significance. Nonetheless he did not "create" all this and the account shows in a very impressive manner how the newly consolidated community takes its life and its future into its own hands.

8. The Books of Chronicles

The Hebrew name of this book is *dibrê hayyāmîm,* "events of the days," "events of the time." This title does not contain anything specific, since in the books of Kings books with similar titles are often referred to (e.g. 1 Kgs 14.19, 29). The Septuagint divides the book into two parts and describes them as παραλειπομένων "skipped," i.e. things not mentioned in the books of Samuel and Kings. The Vulgate adopted this title as "Paralipomenon." The English title "Chronicles" derives from Jerome's term Χρονικόν.

In the canon of the Hebrew Bible the book belongs in the third section, the "Writings." In some manuscripts it is found at the beginning of the "Writings," but in others and also in all printed editions of the Hebrew Bible it is found at the end. The Septuagint placed it further forward, situating it after the books of Kings; this is followed in the Vulgate and most English translations.

In what follows the books of Chronicles are regarded as a single book and called "Chronicles," and their author—irrespective of the question whether this was a single author or whether there were multiple authors—is referred to as "the Chronicler."

8.1 What is the aim of this book?

In the last book of the canon everything starts up again from the beginning: with Adam, the first human being (1 Chron 1.1). What is the point of this book? How are we to read it after everything that has gone before it? The most striking thing about this book is that it repeats much of what is related before, especially in the books of Samuel and Kings, though fundamental differences are blindingly obvious too. The place of the book in the Hebrew canon shows that it does not aim to be understood as a further historical account to compete, for instance, with the books of Samuel and Kings; rather, its position in the third part of the canon points in a fundamentally different direction. The book does not intend to provide an account, but to explain and interpret.

What is the real subject of this book? The contours of the book give a first answer to this question. After an extensive genealogical introductory part the narrative begins with David's anointing as king over "all Israel" (1 Chron 11.1-3). The Davidic kingship is thus the first and dominant theme of the whole book. This also determines the choice of what is reported. The whole history of the northern kingdom, which had separated itself from the Davidic kingdom after Solomon's death [→**127**] and set up a kingdom of its own, is not mentioned; the northern kingdom crops up only now and again as a counterpart to the Davidic kingdom.

Very soon a second main theme starts up. After David's failed attempt to bring the ark of the covenant to Jerusalem (1 Chron 13) [→**112**], he orders that only the Levites should be permitted to transport the ark, because the Lord has chosen them for this (15.2). From now on the Levites play an important and multifaceted role in the execution of the cult, their use by David always being kept in mind. The true center of the cult however still has to be created. After the averted plague because of the census, David announces that the threshing-floor of Araunah, on which he has built an altar and presented sacrifices [→**115**], is to be the place for the "house of the Lord" (22.1). He then begins right away with preparations for the building of the temple, with the execution of which he entrusts his son and successor Solomon (ch. 22). Here the close connections between the Davidic kingship and the temple and the cult are evident, together with the elevated role of David himself, who has planned and prepared everything.

But the cult is not an end in itself. David links his instructions for the building of the temple to Solomon with the admonition to keep the Torah (1 Chron 22.11-13); the representatives of Israel, who are to support Solomon in this, he requires to seek (*dāraš*) God (v. 19). The two requirements run throughout the whole book. Again and again we hear of infringements (2 Chron 12.14 etc.), but also of the kings and the people humiliating themselves (*kāna'* [niphal], 2 Chron 12.6 etc.). A further distinctive feature of Chronicles becomes clear here: it assumes a reliable connection between the correct relationship with God and the prosperity and fate of the people. Seeking God and humbling oneself results in prosperity and "rest" (e.g. 2 Chron 14.6), and turning away from God results in downfall.

From here on the function of the immaculate depiction of David and Solomon at the beginning of this story becomes understandable. They represent in an ideal form the connection between kingdom, cult and Torah-faithfulness, which is to serve as an example for all subsequent generations—never again attained but always striven for.

This is not historiography but the interpretation of the ground-rules given for the life of the people, which understands itself as the "people of YHWH" (2 Chron 23.16).

The conclusion of the book points into the future. After the land has enjoyed a Sabbath rest, once again a new beginning occurs. God awakens the spirit of the king of Persia, so that he orders that the temple should be rebuilt in Jerusalem and that everyone who belongs to the people of Yhwh may return there (2 Chron 36.22f). Chronicles is written for those who have the history reported here behind them and now belong to those who bear the responsibility for Israel's future [→§9].

8.2 Israel in the world of the nations

The beginning of Chronicles presents the reader with a surprise. For several chapters series and lists of names are enumerated, the connections and structures of which only become clear on close inspection. From the beginnings of the history of mankind starting with Adam (1 Chron 1.1), the list of names first leads straight to Abraham (1.27) and then to the sons of "Israel," i.e. Jacob (2.1f; cf. 1.34). The Israel of the twelve tribes forms the point of departure for everything that follows. First of all the line of Judah is followed on from the sons of Jacob/Israel (2.3ff), in which David also appears (2.15); David's own posterity is then continued in ch. 3 well into the post-exilic period. In the following chapters the genealogies of the other sons of Jacob are dealt with in varying detail. Special attention is paid to the tribe of Levi (5.27–6.66). Here the temple singers are also dealt with (6.39-66). Finally the genealogy of the tribe of Benjamin (ch. 8) is traced through to Saul's family (vv. 29ff). This last section is repeated in 9.35ff, where it forms the transition to the report of Saul's death (ch. 10). (On this cf. Oeming 1990.)

The variety of the material assembled in these chapters shows very clearly that the Chronicler had extensive "biblical" material at his disposal. In many cases passages of text have been taken over verbatim or with minor alterations from sources found in other books of the Bible; thus for instance in 1 Chron 1.1–2.2 we find: Gen 5.1-32; 10.2-4, 6-8, 13-18, 22-29; 11.10-26; 25.13-16, 1-4, 19-26; 36.4-5, 9-14, 20-28, 31-43; 35.22-26; Ex 1.1-5. Chronicles thus reminds its readers of known material, often very familiar material, in order to situate its own account in the broad context of the history of humanity and the people of Israel.

But Chronicles quite obviously does not aim to offer competition or an alternative to the great biblical conceptions it has before it. Adam and Noah (1.1, 4), Abraham (1.27f), Jacob/Israel (1.34; 2.1), Moses (5.29) and Joshua (7.27) are mentioned without the slightest hint of the great events associated with their names. Nor is there any indication that Israel had ever been anywhere else than here in its own land. This aspect is underlined all the more by the fact that the genealogies are frequently linked with geographical data about the residential areas of the tribes. Israel and its land belong indissolubly together (cf. Willi 1995, 124ff) [→§8].

An essential aspect of the Chronicler's message for the readers of his day becomes visible here. Israel's history was from the beginning history in its own land. After the great catastrophe of the division of this land God had granted his people their return. Now everything depends on Israel living in its land in the way that God expects of it and in line with the example given it by the two great kings at the beginning of its history, David and Solomon.

8.3 The ideal age: David and Solomon

What the Chronicler wishes to convey begins with David. A fundamental principle of the whole account that follows is evident here: the Chronicler makes a particular selection from his sources and also alters them again and again, sometimes by slight changes to the wording, sometimes by means of more robust alterations to the text in front of him. So the whole prehistory of David's kingship in Israel goes unmentioned [→107]: his anointing by Samuel, his time in Saul's service, his flight from Saul and his stay with the Philistines, and finally the return and his anointing as king of Judah. The Chronicler's concern is with David's rule over Israel.

Here we see the first changes to the text [→110]. According to 2 Sam 5 "all the tribes of Israel" came to David, i.e. the representatives of the northern tribes, over whom he was not yet king. In 1 Chron 11.1, however, we read: "All Israel came together." The distinction between Judah and the other tribes is not mentioned, and it is "all Israel" that wants to make David king after the death of Saul (ch. 10). The source text is then reproduced largely verbatim, the prehistory also being mentioned, when David was a general under king Saul (v. 2). On David's anointing Samuel too is mentioned in the added comment "according to the word of the LORD through Samuel" (v. 3). Clearly the Chronicler presupposes that his readers know the stories, so that he leaves unmentioned the important tradition of the anointing of David by Samuel on divine instructions.

In 1 Chron 11.4, too, it is again "all Israel," rather than "David's men" (2 Sam 5.6) that sets out to conquer Jerusalem. Before he brings in the ark of the covenant David takes counsel with the "whole community (*qāhāl*) of Israel" (13.1) and when the ark is finally brought in he again calls "all Israel" together (15.3). Here the Levites come into action for the first time. David solemnly declares that no one other than the Levites may bear the ark, "for the Lord has chosen them to bear the ark of the LORD and to serve him forever" (v. 2). Statements from Deut 10.8 and 18.5 resonate here. They again show how deeply rooted the Chronicler's thought is in the traditions of Israel. At the same time an entirely new, broad picture of the activities of the Levites unfolds, who are required in huge numbers not only to carry the ark (v. 15) but also to provide music for worship (vv. 16ff). On his arrival in Jerusalem, David installs Levites to serve with the ark, an important place once again being accorded to music (16.4-6). And then for the first time the strains of the psalm-singing of Asaph and his brothers are heard (vv. 7-36). They sing hymns of praise and thanksgiving of the type familiar from the Psalter. They praise the miraculous deeds (*niplā'ōt*) that God did for the patriarchs, with whom he concluded his covenant (Ps 105.1-15) [→333], and his wonderful rule over all the nations whose gods are "nothing," whereas Yhwh created the world that now sings his praise (Ps 96). The congregation answers with "Amen" and "Hallelujah" (Ps 106.47f) [→335f].

This new picture of David is continued after the decision to erect the "house of God" at the site of Araunah's threshing-floor (1 Chron 22.1). From now on, David's activities are devoted entirely to preparations for the building of the temple and the establishment of the organization of the temple cult. The variety of the dramatic events in David's personal and political life that are spoken of in 2 Samuel, remain unmentioned. The David of Chronicles does not have to confess "I have sinned" [→115], and he does not have to flee from his rebellious son either. David's family does not come into view at all, apart from Solomon. (Only the comment on Michal has remained strangely isolated in 1 Chron 15.29, cf. Japhet 1993, 307f.) In a farewell speech with which he appoints his son Solomon as his successor and the builder of the temple (28.1-10), David publicly repeats his reasons for not being able to build the temple himself, the same reasons he previously gave to Solomon: God has not permitted him to do this because he had blood on his hands from his military campaigns (v. 3, cf. 22.8). He then again passes on to his successor Solomon the quintessence of the Chronicler's theology: "If you seek the LORD, he will be found by you; but if you depart from him, he will reject you forever" (28.9).

David then hands Solomon the blueprint (*tabnît*) of the temple and all the other drawings for the design and furnishing of the temple and the temple cult (vv. 11-21), which he had prepared with God's help (v. 19). He adds rich donations of gold and silver for the temple, which are followed by corresponding gladly given donations from the representatives of the people and the people themselves (29.1-10). David then ends his rule with one last great prayer (vv. 10-19). An important element of the Chronicler's understanding of the kingship is visible in this: God is the true ruler, majesty and power belong to him; he alone can make great and raise up (vv. 11f) [→§13]. David and his people are merely guests and strangers, as the patriarchs were beforehand (vv. 14f). From here on light is shed on the repeated phrase that God plans to appoint David's successor to his own kingly rule (*malkûtî* 17.14) and to the "throne of the dominion of YHWH" (28.5; cf. 29.23). This sounds like an overstatement of human rule; at the same time, however, it is a limitation, since the rule remains God's and the human incumbent on the throne can fall at any time. Thus David's assurance of divine help for Solomon applies "until the whole work for the service of the house of the LORD is completed." This means, first and foremost, the setting of a target: the kingship has the task of completing the temple and the temple service. But at the same time a limitation lies inherent for the time after that (cf. Riley 1993, 74f).

First, however, Solomon sits on his throne and completes the task he had assumed from David. His image as temple-builder was already included of course in his source, in 1 Kings [→119]. The Chronicler concentrates his account once again entirely on his real theme: the Davidic dynasty and the temple and its worship. With this aim in mind he can skip everything in the tradition about the background to Solomon's accession (1 Kgs 1f) [→117], because according to his account the question of the Davidic succession was sorted out without discussion or objection. No shadow is cast on the reign of Solomon either; there is nothing about his being seduced into the worship of other gods by foreign women, nor about external and internal threats to his rule (cf. 1 Kgs 11) [→123]. Together, the reigns of David and Solomon thus form the ideal picture of the divinely appointed dynasty, which devotes itself entirely to the construction of the temple and the maintenance of the cult and is richly rewarded by God for doing so.

At only one point has the Chronicler taken over a text which indicates the possibility that things might possibly have turned out differently. In the second theophany granted to Solomon, there is mention of the fate that would overcome Israel if it were to turn away from God and his commandments (2 Chron 7.19-22; cf. 1 Kgs 9.6-9) [→122]. In 1 Kings the turning point that is in mind is introduced already during Solomon's lifetime. The Chronicler leaves the warning in place, which had also been sounded earlier (1 Chron 28.9), but it is not realized during Solomon's reign. The picture of the David–Solomon era thus remains unclouded.

The most important thing in this ideal first phase of the kingdom is the central role of the temple [→§11]. This is especially clear when one realizes that Chronicles was written for readers in a time in which there was no king, though there was a temple that had been rebuilt in Jerusalem after great efforts. The concentration on the temple is of central importance also for the subsequent history of the divided "Israel."

8.4 Israel between seeking God and abandoning God

The departure of the northern tribes from the dynasty of David is no cause for the Chronicler to go on to give a parallel account of the history of two separate states, as his sources do. The sentence, "So Israel has been in rebellion against the house of David to this day" (2 Chron 10.19; cf. 1 Kgs 12.19) means, rather, that there is now only one legitimate history of "Israel," namely that under the rule of the kings in the dynasty of David, which has its base in Jerusalem, the site of the temple of the Lord. This certainly does not mean, however, that the tribes who joined the northern kingdom are to be simply written off. On the contrary: they are courted again and again. Thus Abijah, the second king of the remaining southern kingdom of Judah in succession to Rehoboam, gives a speech to the army of the northern kingdom, which can be regarded as "a short compendium of the theology of the Chronicler" (von Rad 1962, 365). He begins: "Don't you know that the LORD, the God of Israel, has given the kingship of

Israel to David and his descendants for ever?" He blames them for following after Jeroboam and driving away the priests and Levites, and contrasts this with the regular worship at the temple in Jerusalem. "We are observing the requirements of the LORD our God. But you have forsaken him." So: "Men of Israel, do not fight against the LORD, the God of your fathers, for you will not succeed" (2 Chron 13.4-12).

That there is only *one* real Israel also comes to expression in the fact that alongside the use of the names Israel and Judah for the two part-kingdoms the Chronicler again and again uses the term "Israel" for Judah too, in particular in titles and in connection with the cult. Thus the "leaders of Israel" (*śārê yiśrā'ēl*) in 2 Chron 12.6 and 21.4 are officials in Judah, and the heads of families (*rā'šê hā'ābôt leyiśrā'ēl*) in 19.8 and 23.2 represent Judahite families or clans. With Rehoboam "all Israel" forsakes "the Torah of the LORD," even though Rehoboam is only king of Judah (12.1). Joash had money collected from "all Israel" "in all the cities of Judah" for the repair of the temple (24.5) and was buried in the city of David because of his good deeds "toward Israel, for God and his house." Finally after the victorious war of Jehoshaphat against the Ammonites and the Moabites, which "all Judah" had to fight (20.3f etc.), the other nations acknowledge that "the LORD had fought against the enemies of Israel" (v. 29). With this use of the name of Israel for Judah the Chronicler does not wish to exclude the northern kingdom; rather, he is expressing his conviction that in Judah there is an unbroken continuity with the original *one* Israel (cf. Williamson 1977, 102-110).

The Chronicler tells the lively story of Judah before the separation of the northern kingdom through to the destruction of Jerusalem in his own way. For the overall course of events he allows his source to speak, often in full detail. But he gives the whole thing his own imprint, sometimes by omitting, sometimes by adding events, but in particular through his theological interpretation of them. Thus in the reign of Rehoboam the campaign of Pharaoh Shishak (Shoshenk) is provided with a theological context: Rehoboam "abandoned the law of the LORD" (2 Chron 12.1); when Pharaoh stands before Jerusalem, the prophet Shemaiah mediates a message from God to Rehoboam and the assembled military leaders: "You have abandoned me; therefore I now abandon you"; then they humble themselves and say: "The LORD is just"; then God decides not to ruin Rehoboam entirely (vv. 5-8, 12). Here "humbling oneself" has central position (12.6, 7, 12). It forms the counterpart to the preceding "forsaking" (*'āzab*) of God and his Torah (vv. 1, 5).

At the end of Rehoboam's lifetime another reproach against Rehoboam is raised: he did not "seek" (*dāraš*) God (v. 14). To forsake God and seek God, these two alternating terms run right through Chronicles: David's admonition of Solomon (1 Chron 28.9) is taken up again by the prophet Azariah in relation to Asa (2 Chron 16.2, cf. vv. 12f); at the end of his life, however, Asa no longer seeks God because of his illness (16.12). Jehoshaphat on the other hand does not seek the Baals but the God of his father (17.3f), which is still counted in his favor even despite his relations with the "ungodly" king Ahab (19.2f), especially since he once again seeks the Lord in response to a military threat (20.3).

The turning point in Joash's life, who first takes care of the repair of the temple, but then is threatened by the Arameans and finally falls victim to a conspiracy, is explained on the basis that he forsook God (24.18, 20, 24); the same thing applies to Ahaz (28.6). But it is then Hezekiah that confesses that the fathers forsook God (29.6) and calls for cultic reform. Even members of the northern tribes humble themselves and come to Jerusalem (30.11). At the great Passover festival Hezekiah prays for participants in the festival who have not purified themselves; for to seek "the LORD, the God of their fathers" seems to him to be more important than purification in accordance with the regulations (v. 19). Finally, Hezekiah must humble himself too, because he was too proud in his heart; the Lord's anger was then lifted off him and off Judah and Jerusalem (32.25f).

In the episode of the conversion of Manasseh, freely worded by the Chronicler, the key term is again that he humbled himself (33.12, 19), while it is expressly emphasized that his successor Amon did not follow his father in this (v. 23). But it is then Josiah that seeks "the God of his father David" already in his young years (34.3). In the divine speech through the prophetess Huldin, disaster on the inhabitants of Jerusalem is announced because they have forsaken God (v. 25); Josiah himself however will not have to go through this disaster, because he has humbled himself before God (v. 27). But then the last thing to be said about the last king of Judah is that he did not humble himself (36.12).

Often it is prophets or men inspired by the spirit of God who accompany or interpret events with their words. The concern is frequently with happenings that the Chronicler has not found in his sources but has formulated himself. Thus king Asa is prompted by the prophet Azariah to make a great cult reform (15.1-15, the title *nābî'* in v. 8). Later the "seer" (*ro'eh*) Hanani announces a time of war (16.7-10); Asa's negative reaction to this leads in part to the statement that he did not seek the Lord at the end of his life (v. 12). Joram even receives a letter of the prophet Elijah, who predicts calamity for him because of his idolatry (21.12-15). In the case of a few other prophets too there are reports of conflicts with the kings (24.19-22; 25.15f), while others are listened to (25.7-13; 28.9-15). The reproach against Zedekiah, the last king of Judah is said to be that he did not humble himself before the prophet Jeremiah (36.12). Finally all the officials of Judah, the priests and the whole people ridicule the prophets whom "the God of their fathers" sent as messengers to them (vv. 14-16).

A particularly impressive example of the Chronicler's theology is presented in 2 Chron 20. Jehoshaphat is confronted with a military threat. He then "resolved to inquire of the LORD" and calls a fast (v. 3). In a long prayer he calls upon the "God of our fathers," the "God who is in heaven," who "rules over all the kingdoms of the nations." He reminds him of the saving history in which he gave Israel the land in which they now live and built a sanctuary for his name. But precisely those nations that Israel spared when it occupied the land on God's instructions (cf. Deut 2.4f, 9, 19) are now turning against them in a war of annihilation. The prayer ends with the words: "We do not know what to do but our eyes are upon you" (v. 12). The spirit of the Lord then comes on the Levite Jahaziel of the temple-singer family of the sons of Asaph (v. 14), and he calls to the assembled congregation: "Do not be afraid!" He announces that they will not themselves have to fight, but they should "Stand firm and see the deliverance the LORD will give you" (v. 17). These are the same words that Moses spoke to the Israelites at the Reed Sea (Ex 14.13)! [→46f] The next morning the king gives another war-speech in which he turns the word of Isaiah (Isa 7.9) in a positive direction: "Have faith in the LORD your God and you will be upheld" (v. 20) [→175]. The Levites then line up to head the battle procession in their finery and sing psalms (v. 21). At this point God sends (supernatural?) "ambushes" with the consequence that the enemies kill each other. This narrative depicts a "holy war" as is familiar from earlier texts (e.g. Judg 4.14-16; 1 Sam 7 [→102, 104]). But this time there is no fighting, but everything depends on God's help, and to attain this requires cultic forms. The Levites appointed by David play an important role in this, both in their "prophetic" function and in the liturgical introduction and accompaniment of the "fight." Everything thus becomes "spiritualized" and "leviticized" (cf. von Rad 1951, esp. 80f).

The special evaluation of the prophets by the Chronicler also comes to expression in the fact that he cites them as guarantors in the concluding notes about the individual kings. For David the source has no concluding note. The Chronicler refers to the records of Samuel the seer (*ro'eh*) [→**104**], the prophet (*nābî'*) Nathan [→**113**] and the seer (*hozēh*) Gad (1 Chron 29.29). Here the three terms for prophetic figures are brought together, which are otherwise never found together in the Hebrew Bible. The whole gamut of prophecy is called as witness. Later Gad and Nathan are again found with the same titles in the justification of a regulation given by David in respect of the Levites (2 Chron 29.25). In the concluding note about Solomon the prophet Nathan, the prophecy of Ahijah of Shiloh and the seer Iddo are cited (2 Chron 9.29), for Rehoboam the prophet Shemaiah and the seer Iddo (12.15), for Abijah the prophet Iddo (13.22) and for Uzziah the prophet Isaiah, son of Amoz (26.22), as well as for Hezekiah (32.32).

The last word in the history of Israel–Judah as recorded in the books of Chronicles is from the prophet Jeremiah, or more precisely: "the word of the LORD spoken by Jeremiah" (36.21). In particular the great sermon is recalled which, with the yoke on his shoulders, Jeremiah delivered to Zedekiah and the kings of the neighboring nations, that they should subject themselves to Nebuchadnezzar because they would otherwise be led away from their lands into exile (Jer 27) [→**217**]. This has now occurred, and it will last a long time, as Jeremiah said: seventy years (Jer 29.10) [→**226**]. The Chronicler adduces one more scripture: "Then the land will enjoy its sabbath years all the time that it lies desolate," we read in the great concluding chapter of the giving of the law on Sinai (Lev 26.34f).

But the word of Jeremiah is *fully* fulfilled: "When seventy years are completed for Babylon, I will come to you and fulfill my gracious promise to bring you back to this place." To let this become reality, "the LORD awakens the spirit of Cyrus, the king of Persia," so that he proclaims throughout his empire that "the LORD, the God of heaven" has commanded him "to build a house for him in Jerusalem"; this means nothing other than to rebuild the temple of David and Solomon. And whoever of the people of God is prepared to do so, "may the LORD his God be with him, and let him go up" (2 Chron 36.22f). The story of God's dealings with his people continues. The sabbath years are over, the ruins can be rebuilt. And everything set down in Chronicles concerning the plans and instructions for the temple and its worship will be awakened to new life.

Retrospect and Prospect

The canon of the Hebrew Bible is an entity that has grown by accretion but has at the same time been shaped. Transmitters of tradition, collectors and composers have brought together and combined the texts that were important to them, in order to preserve the traditions of Israel in their entirety and to pass them on to coming generations. Many people shared in the work, and so it has become a multilayered whole. It is very broad in its scope. The history of Israel is placed within the history of the world and humanity created by God. From this it grows through the election of Abraham, to whom God grants a special commission in the context of the world of the nations. The changing story of Abraham's successor and of his grandson Jacob, called "Israel," unfolds in a variety of often changing forms—through to the dramatic events of the destruction of Jerusalem and the temple. The time after that too, the time of the reconstruction and re-orientation in the tense relationships of continuity and discontinuity, is documented in elementary and selective fashion.

Alongside the account and interpretation of this changing story the canon of the Hebrew Bible also contains a variety of texts that are quite different in kind. The words of prophets which accompanied the history of Israel critically through broad tracts of time have been collected in extensive writings of their own. They not only add new emphases to this story and reveal new contours, but they develop themes of their own and aspects of the religious and "theological" traditions of Israel. In the Psalms and related texts the voice of praying Israel is audible, in the wisdom writings the traditions of a reflective dealing with the realities of human life and critical questioning of them.

A Theology of the Old Testament should allow all these voices to be heard. This first part has thus made an effort in running through the canon from its first to its last verse to allow the texts to speak in their present form. In the account itself and in the cross-references attention has been drawn at a number of points to connections between various books and parts of the canon. It will be the task of the Part II to draw out these connections in more detail. This will be done in thematically oriented chapters with constant reference back to Part I, with the aim of creating as comprehensive and nuanced picture as possible of the theological statements of the Old Testament in its entirety.

In a concluding section the basic methodological questions of a canonically oriented Theology of the Old Testament are treated in the context of current scholarly discussion. Attention will then also be paid to the relationship between the Jewish and the Christian understanding of the Old Testament. From a Christian point of view, in particular the question of the relationship between the Old and New Testaments and the possibility and necessity of a "Biblical Theology" will be raised.

Part II

Introduction
Themes of the Old Testament

In its narrative survey of the books of the Hebrew Bible, the first part of this "Theology of the Old Testament" attempted to allow the multitude and multiplicity of voices in these texts to be heard. The cross-references were intended to draw attention to the fact that much of what is talked about in particular texts is also expressed or echoed in other texts, sometimes in the same or similar ways but also in quite different, even contrasting ways. The second part will now attempt to focus more precisely on this variety. We shall proceed by looking into the questions of whether and how the various voices coincide and whether and to what extent they are divergent. In each case the context must be taken into consideration, as far as is possible from our present viewpoint. The radical changes that occurred in the history of Israel in the period covered by the texts of the Hebrew Bible are very clear: from the time of the "Patriarchs" through the exodus from Egypt, the consolidation of Israel in the land given to it, the formation of the state under a monarchy, its end and the stay in Babylonian exile, and finally the return and the renewed consolidation of the life of the community.

Many texts reveal particular situations in this history as their context. Others refer to earlier epochs, often using traditions that have come down to them from these periods. In many cases, however, our chances of greater precision come to an end, both in determining the age of the texts themselves and also with regard to the type and age of the traditions used. In the account presented here however the real concern is not with the clarification of these questions, however interesting and important some of them may be; our interest is focused rather on the statements of the texts themselves in their present form.

An essential element in the variety of the voices lies in the very varied types of text preserved in the Hebrew Bible. It finds its expression already in the threefold division of the canon: Torah, Former and Latter Prophets as well as Writings represent quite varied ways of speaking of God and his relationship with humans and with his people Israel, as well as of human attitudes towards God and to each other. These differences are marked by the various areas of life from which particular texts and groups of texts derive, or for which they were intended. We may distinguish very generally between narrative and legislative texts, prophetic and cultic-liturgical texts, wisdom texts, and texts expressing individual piety. Each of these text groups and types has its own way of speaking; this produces various forms of common themes as well as the articulation of themes peculiar to each.

We have mentioned the rubric of "themes." In its attempt at a synthesis the second part of this book orients itself by particular "themes." It takes these from the account in the first part, retaining the sequence provided by the biblical texts (cf. however also §24.4). The first chapter is thus devoted to the theme of The World as God's Creation (§5). This theme is developed in an impressive manner in the first chapters of the Hebrew Bible; but it is also present in other books of the Hebrew Bible, in all three parts of the canon in fact. This shows that the theme of creation is not only dealt with alone and for its own sake; rather, it stands in a direct relationship with other themes, especially with regard to God's actions in the most varied areas of the world and its history, above all the historical experiences of Israel. In this chapter an attempt is made to relate the manifold statements about creation and the creator to each other and thereby to set out common features and differences as well as different lines of development of the individual conceptions and ideas. No attempt is made, however, to summarize the variety of aspects in a systematic "theology of creation." The latter applies correspondingly to the following chapters: where the totality of the texts adduced in each case produces a relatively self-contained picture, this will be expressed correspondingly; but no attempt is made to produce an overarching system.

The next topic is marked by the key term *covenant* (§6). It first appears in God's covenant with Noah in Gen 9. Here the question arises how far particular terms in the Hebrew text should determine the themes. The Hebrew word *b'rît*, which is generally translated by the English word "covenant," plays a highly significant role in the Hebrew Bible; at the same time, however, it only covers a particular section of the theme to be dealt with here. The similarly significant term *elect* (*bāḥar*) comprises a further section. Other phrases such as for instance the "covenant formula" ("I will be your God and you will be my people") contribute further aspects to this theme. Here it is evident that particular terms, however significant they may be individually, only rarely cover an entire thematic field. In addition, looking backwards it will be clear that for the first chapter there is no corresponding term at all; no noun for "creation" exists in Biblical Hebrew, and various verbs are used for the divine action of creation, and in addition the statements in this area are described and paraphrased in different ways.

In the further course of the biblical narrative the *fathers* of Israel are the key figures. But they are frequently spoken of also in other areas of the Hebrew Bible, and from various points of view. This applies to quite different stages in the history of Israel and often sets weighty theological emphases. It is especially noteworthy how in this theme Israel's self-critical view of its own history comes to expression, in which the fathers are regarded not only as recipients of the promises and of the guidance of God, but also as those with whom Israel's sinful history began (§7). The theme of the *land* has directly to do with this; for it is a central element of the patriarchal history that the fathers were first promised the possession of the land by God. The theme however extends far beyond this, because in many parts of the Hebrew Bible there is talk of the promise of the land, its fulfillment, but also of its being open to question, and again weighty theological statements are associated with this (§8). The theme of *exodus* is linked already with the theme of the "land," in that it was only as a result of Israel's being led out of Egypt that the promise of the land to the fathers could become reality. At the same time this act of leading out from Egyptian slavery is one of the most decisive elements in Israel's self-understanding and of the faith in the God acting in this. At many points the later experiences of the return from Babylonian exile are also understood as a second exodus, in many texts the second exodus echoing already in statements about the first, or one running into the other. This theme is itself a classic example of the way and degree to which themes of the early times are also viewed from the viewpoint of the later phase after the Babylonian exile (§9).

§ 5

The World as God's Creation

1. In the beginning God created

The Hebrew Bible often speaks of the creation, and of God as creator. The basic scheme of Israel's history as found in the Pentateuch begins with the creation, or more precisely with God's act of creation. Some of the great sketches of history that are found later in the Hebrew Bible also begin with this (Ps 136; Neh 9 [→**334, 399**]). But elsewhere too, throughout all parts of the Hebrew Bible in fact, we find an almost innumerable quantity of references and allusions to the creation as the fundamental event that provided the point of departure for the history of the world and humanity.

The first word of the Bible is *b'rēšît*, "in the beginning" (Gen 1.1). Before that there was nothing—other than God himself. Psalm 90 puts it like this: "Before the mountains were born or you brought forth the earth and the world, from everlasting to everlasting you are God" (v. 2). According to Deut 4.32 the ultimate point in time to which one can think back is "the day when God created humans on the earth." And according to Prov 8.22-31 it was the beginning (*rēšît*) of God's activity that he created wisdom before everything else. When the Hebrew Bible considers the question of the beginning of the world and the history of humankind, only one answer is given: God was there before the beginning of everything, and everything had its beginnings in him. To the question how this beginning occurred, the Hebrew Bible gives various answers. In Gen 1.2 we read that before the beginning of the divine act of creation, the earth was in a chaotic state of *tōhû wābōhû* and was covered by the "primeval waters," the *t'hôm* (cf. Ps 104.6) [→**332**]. In ancient thought, "beginning" does not necessarily mean that there was "nothing" beforehand. The notion of a "creatio ex nihilo" was first expressed in the Hellenistic period (2 Macc 7.28). In Gen 1 the concern is not with the contrast between Nothing and the Created but with the Chaos–Cosmos polarity (von Rad 1972, 31). Traditions from Israel's ancient near eastern world resonate here. The *t'hôm* (hereafter "Tehom") has been connected with the Chaos-monster Tiamat, killed in the Babylonian myth by the god Marduk, who then forms the Cosmos out of her body (*Enuma elish*, tablet 4, *AOT* 116ff). Against this background Gen 1.2 was understood as a pale variant of a "Chaos struggle myth," in which the creator-god defeats the personified power of Chaos in battle and then creates the world (Gunkel 1895). The ancient near eastern traditions are however more varied and nuanced (cf. Stolz 1970), and the conflict between God and the chaotic flood is primarily the expression of his superiority over other powers that threaten his creation (Podella 1993). In addition, the overcoming of the powers that are inimical to creation is not a once-and-for-all, self-contained occurrence, but the threat persists permanently, and God has to prove his power time and again (Levenson 1988).

The "weapon" that God uses in Gen 1 is the word. This comes even more clearly to expression in Ps 104, where with his voice of thunder God forces the Tehom, who is here equated with the waters (as in Gen 1.2), to retreat and thus to expose the dry land. Here the element of battle is much more marked than in Gen 1. At the same time it becomes clearer that these anti-creation powers have not disappeared: God sets them a boundary which they may not cross (v. 9, cf. Jer 5.22). In Gen 1 too, God sets limits on the water, in two regards. On the one hand by means of the vault of the "firmament" God "separates" (*hibdîl*) between the water, what is above it, and what remains below it (vv. 6f). On the other hand he assigns particular areas to what is under the water, so that the "dry land" is given its space (vv. 9f). In the "flood" we then see, however, that the destructive power of the waters of chaos is still operative; for with the creator's permission the "great Tehom" bursts up from below, and the water collected above cascades down through the "openings" (Gen 7.11), and thus together they devastate the creation until God grants a respite and the upper and lower openings are closed once again (8.2). In Ps 104.9 we read that they are not allowed to transgress the boundaries set for them; but in the great flood the creator permitted it this one time. The psalm does not speak of God's covenant with Noah; but the psalmist knows that God will not allow the Tehom to flood the earth again. The author of the book of Job is aware of this too. In the great divine speech in Job 38 [→**352**], as in Ps 104 there is talk of the boundary that

God sets for the sea; and here too the decisive instrument is his word: "Thus far and no further!" (vv. 8-11) The sea that is constrained in this way has its fixed place within the great tapestry of creation depicted in this chapter.

The lines of the traditions collected in these texts can be followed further in various directions. The battle motif is found a number of times in even clearer form. Thus in Isa 51.9 God is addressed: "Was it not you who cut Rahab to pieces, who pierced that monster through?" Rahab and the "dragon" (*tannín*) are mythical figures that represent Chaos. God was victorious over them and destroyed them "in the primeval days" (v. 9a), and in the immediate context of this he "dried out the sea, the waters of the great Tehom" (v. 110). Here elements of the tradition of God's battle with the powers of Chaos resonate, and the connection with creation is also clearly expressed. Things are very similar in Ps 74.13-17, where alongside the *tanníním*, whose heads God smashes above the sea, Leviathan appears, whom God also defeats. And again the connection with creation is clear when we read that God created the sun and the moon and set the boundaries of the earth as well as the seasons (vv. 16f; cf. Job 26.12f). There is again talk of Rahab in Ps 89, whom God pierced through and annihilated (vv. 1-11), and this is followed by the statement (vv. 12f) that God had founded the circle of the earth and created (*bārā'* as in Gen 1.1) north and south.

In the last-mentioned texts, however, God's battle against the powers of Chaos is not the actual theme. Rather, the troubles of the prophet's or psalmist's present are in central position. They call on God out of this situation, remind him of his earlier mighty acts and beg him to intervene in their troubles: "Awake, awake! Clothe yourself with strength, O arm of the Lord! Awake as in days gone by, as in generations of old" (Isa 51.9) [→**193**]. "Why do you hold back your hand?" (Ps 74.11). "How long, O Lord? Will you hide yourself for ever?" (Ps 89.46). It is clear that the powers of Chaos are not the real enemies, but the "mortal humans" that Israel fears, thereby forgetting its creator (Isa 51.12f). It is they that have destroyed everything in the sanctuary (Ps 74.3) and who blaspheme God's name (v. 18). In Ps 89.11 "your enemies" are boldly equated (cf. v. 52) with Rahab. The motif of the struggle with the powers of Chaos has attained a high level of current relevance in these texts. God the creator, who proved his unlimited power and superiority in the victory over the powers of

Chaos at the beginning of history, can and will also prove them against the present enemies of his people Israel (cf. Jeremias 1987, 28f).

Another line runs as it were in the opposite direction. The battle motif recedes entirely and the word alone appears as the creative force. "By the word of the Lord were the heavens made, their starry host by the breath of his mouth ... He spoke, and it came to be; he commanded, and it stood firm" (Ps 33.6, 9; cf. Ps 148.5; Isa 48.13) [→**332**]. The sovereignty of the creation by the word as shown in Gen 1 finds its counterpart in these texts. Ps 33 in particular shows that here too the creation is not the only theme, and not even the real theme. Rather, it is the divine word in its various forms that stands in the center here: "For the word of the Lord is right and true; he is faithful in all he does. He loves righteousness and justice" (vv. 4f). The reminder of the creative word at the beginning is a quite essential aspect of this. But God's creative activity cannot be separated from his other activities. In Ps 148 all creatures which God has created by his word, and thus also the mythical traditions, are included in the praise of the creator. The *tannînîm* and the *t'homôt* are to praise him, together with fire and hail, snow and fog and the stormy winds "that do his bidding" (vv. 7f). According to Gen 1.21 God even created the *tannînîm* himself. The verb *bārā'* "create" is used here, which in the first account of creation, apart from the framework passages (1.1; 2.3), is otherwise used only for the creation of humans (v. 27 x3). According to Ps 104.26, God made the leviathan for play. These beings are thus stripped entirely of their mythical character and can no longer endanger the world order (cf. Ebach 1984). At the same time the sovereignty of the creator God Yhwh is convincingly expressed here.

2. When I see the heavens

In the Hebrew Bible the creation and God's creative activity are spoken of in many other forms and aspects. Thus God's creative actions are described with metaphors from the trades: he "stretches the heavens out like a tent" (Ps 104.2; Isa 40.22; 44.24 etc.), "builds his dwelling in the water," which is situated above the "heavens" (Ps 104.3, cf. Ps 24.1f; 29.10; Amos 9.6), and established the earth on stakes, so that it does not waver (Ps 104.5, cf. 93.1, cf. also Amos 4.13). The creation is the "work of his hands" (Pss 19.2; 102.26), indeed the dexterous work of his fingers (Ps 8.4).

Often humans can only observe from afar and say admiringly: "When I see the heavens, the work of your fingers ...!" (Ps 8.4, cf. Isa 40.26) [→**330**]. And they themselves cannot hear the heavens and the changing times of the day proclaiming the praise of the creator among themselves (Ps 19.2-4). But at the same time talk of the creation is always linked with the world of humans. Psalm 104 describes the created world in several stages, the human being becoming involved step by step: God's creation and action in his heavenly world (vv. 1-4), the formation of the Cosmos through the stemming of the waters of Chaos (vv. 5-9); then in a sudden transition the life-giving power of water, even in areas far from the world in which humans live (vv. 10-18, cf. Amos 5.8b; 9.6b: God pours the water of the sea onto the earth); then the alternating relationship between night and day and therewith also between the worlds of animals and humans (vv. 19-23); and finally from there on the view of the breadth and variety of the creation and God's interaction with it (vv. 24-32). In this psalm we see clear connections with Egyptian wisdom texts, especially with Pharaoh Echnaton's great hymn to the sun (*AOT* 15ff; *TUAT* II, 848ff). We see from this that Israel has adopted elements from the most varied areas of the ancient near eastern environment for its view of the world as creation (cf. above on the Babylonian traditions).

But the relationship of creation to the reality of the biblical authors and their audience or readers can also be expressed quite differently. Ps 136 begins with a song of praise to the creator [→**334**]. The account of the first works of creation (v. 49), which closely follows Gen 1, breaks off abruptly after the creation of the stars (which are named here, unlike in Gen 1.16) and moves on to the depiction of the exodus event (vv. 10ff). The might of the creator God has been confirmed in the fact that he led his people Israel "with a strong hand and outstretched arm" (v. 12) out of bondage in Egypt. And thus he also remembers the present situation of the psalmist (vv. 23-25).

The direct connection between God's creative acts and the exodus also comes to expression in Isa 51.10 [→**193**]: God made the Tehom dry out, so that the "redeemed" (*ge'ûlîm*) could march through. The memory of the divine act of creation is here connected backwards from the present of the speaking exilic community with the exodus and forwards with God's hoped-for intervention (see above). The terms used here are reminiscent of the hymn in Ex 15.1-18, where the water of the Reed Sea is termed *t'homot* (vv. 5, 8), through which God led "the people you have redeemed" (*gā'altā*) (v. 13). The great prayer in Neh 9, which follows God's action in creation (v. 6) first with the election of Abraham (vv. 7f) and then the exodus (vv. 9-12), reaches even further back; at the end the hope of a future intervention by God echoes on indirectly in the lament about the desperate present situation (vv. 36f).

The relationship between the creation statements and the problems of the present are especially clear in Isa 40–55 (esp. in chs. 40–45). The word *bārā'* is found more frequently here than in any other part of the Hebrew Bible (cf. Anderson 1967, 124ff). It has almost become an epithet for God, not infrequently in the participial form: "Thus says the Lord, the creator (*bōrē'*), he alone is God" (45.18; cf. 40.28; 42.5; 45.7f. etc.). In these Isaianic texts which date from the time of the Babylonian exile, talk of God as creator has two primary functions: to emphasize his superiority over all other gods (45.18ff etc., see above) and to strengthen Israel's hope in a return home. Over and over again Israel is admonished and encouraged in 40.12-31 to lift its eyes to the works of the creator (v. 26) and to remember: "The Lord is the everlasting God, the Creator of the ends of the earth. He will not grow tired or weary ..." (28ff). Talk of God as creator undergoes surprising turns: God is the "creator of Israel" (43.15, cf. v. 1; with other verbs, 44.2, 21, 24; 45.11; 51.13) or creator of the "servant" (42.6; 49.5) and of Jerusalem (54.5). This can also be extended to individual Israelites: "everyone who is called by my name, whom I created for my glory" (43.7). This statement, which expresses the specially close relationship between God and Israel, always stands in a context proclaiming God's coming saving action on Israel's behalf. It can stand immediately next to the statement that God has "chosen" Israel (44.1f). A further new aspect is the announcement that God "creates" future salvation and new things (41.20; 45.7, 8; 48.7). This has its final climax at the end of the book of Isaiah in the expectation that God will create a new heaven and a new earth (65.17f). The concept of creation is thus on the one hand limited by his relationship with Israel, but on the other hand extended eschatologically. In these changes the action of God, whether in power, care or world-changing, is emphasized by the creation terminology of his sovereignty.

In other parts of the text of the Hebrew Bible, talk of God as creator is less broadly developed, but it still has considerable theological weight. Thus in Deut 10.14f the statement that heaven and earth belong to God is directly connected with the emphasis on the unique election of Israel. In the concluding section of the great discourse of

Moses in Deut 4, the history of God with the world and with Israel, from the creation of humankind onwards (v. 32), is called to mind, to lead on to the recognition that only Yhwh is God (v. 35) "in the heaven above and on the earth beneath" (v. 39). We read something very similar in Solomon's prayer of dedication of the temple in 1 Kgs 8.23: "there is no God like you in heaven above or on earth below." Then later in the same prayer we find the expression "Yhwh, he is God" (*yhwh hû' ha-''lohîm*), i.e. he *alone* is God (v. 60), which is certainly to be understood in the same sense: that the unique deity of Yhwh includes his being creator or that this is on his initiative [→**121**]. The expression is also found in Deut 7.9, 1 Kgs 18.39 and frequently in similar wording (cf. 1994, 19). In Ex 19 also, the promise of Israel's election ends with the words, "for the whole earth is mine."

In some texts the naming of God as creator echoes on without special emphasis. But it is precisely this that shows that this idea is almost regarded as a theological given. Thus Abraham has his slaves swear "by the Lord, the God of heaven and the God of the earth" (Gen 24.3; cf. v. 7). Abraham himself addresses God as the "judge of the whole earth" (18.25), and his authority over the whole world he has created is clear in this. Stronger emphasis is placed on the mention of *'ēl 'elyôn* (the "most high God"), the "Creator of heaven and earth" (Gen 14.19f) [→**589**], who is equated with Yhwh in v. 22. Qohelet too calls on the reader to think of his or her creator (12.1), who has "made everything beautiful" (3.11).

3. To whom will you compare God?

The sovereignty of God the creator must constantly be defended and justified against competing claims and doubts. The question "With whom will you compare me?" (Isa 40.18, 25; 46.5) points in two directions. On the one hand in the elaboration of God's great deeds of creation (40.12-26) it points to the incomparable variety of his actions. The point of this question is to answer the doubting questions of the Israelites living in exile, who feel abandoned by God and unable to believe any longer in his power (vv. 27ff). On the other hand it aims to refute the claim that there are other gods. These are merely dumb idols, made by human hands (46.58). There is only one creator of the world, and this also means: there is only one God. And this is what we find in Ps 96.5: "For all the gods of the nations are nothing, but the

Lord made the heavens" (cf. 95.35). In Jer 10 too we find a broadly developed polemic against the home-made idols with which Yhwh as creator is contrasted (v. 12 as counterpart to v. 11, written in Aramaic) [→**211**].

The question of the existence of other gods plays no role in Job's speeches of accusation against God. The concern is only with why God, who is supposed to be almighty and just, allows Job to suffer. God responds to Job's provocative accusations with the question: "Where were you when I made the earth?" (Job 38.4) [→**352**], followed by a long, long series of rhetorical questions in which God's incomparable work of creation is set out. God thereby more or less quotes Job himself, who had said: "How can a person be righteous before God ..., who alone stretches out the heavens ...?" (19.1ff; 1987, 46ff[103ff]). The question of the justice of God, "theodicy," cannot be taken on its own, separated from consideration of the context of the world as a whole, whose creator is unique: God himself.

This leads to the consequence that this one God alone is responsible for everything that happens in the world. This finds it sharpest expression in Isa 45.6f: "I am the Lord and there is no other: I form the light and create darkness, I bring prosperity and create disaster." This sentence is nothing short of shocking in its abrupt directness. This is reinforced by the fact that the verb *bārā'*, the specific expression for the divine activity of creation [→**14**], is used precisely for the negative sides of God's action: for darkness and disaster. The chaotic darkness (*hošek*), according to this, is not simply integrated into creation (Gen 1.5) but is viewed even as created by God. The parallel clause shows that the issue here is not just a once-and-for-all creative act by God at the beginning of the world; rather, prosperity and disaster are constantly "created" by God. In the immediate context this statement relies on the call of the Persian king Cyrus, whose victory parade will mean salvation for Israel but disaster for the subjects. But it should also be taken on a much more fundamental basis: salvation and disaster as the powers determining the fate of humans and nations are not made by anyone, especially not by other gods. But at the same time the reader of the whole Bible hears and understands that God controls disaster as well as darkness, to which he has assigned a place in the entirety of creation. He can create disaster and he can remove it again or even change it into salvation (cf. Levenson 1988, 124).

4. What is man

The biblical texts were written by human beings and are addressed to human beings. The question of the place of humans in creation is thus far more than just a matter of detail. For even if humans have now learned not to view themselves as the center of creation, it is they who are addressed in the texts in relation to their responsibility within and for creation. Psalm 8 [→330] expresses the tension between the smallness of humans in relation to the creation and the enormity of the honor and responsibility granted them by God: "What is man that you are mindful of him? ... You made him ruler over the works of your hands" (vv. 5, 7).

The two creation accounts at the beginning of the Bible consider the creation from the point of view of the position that the human being has in it. In the first chapter the human being is very emphatically at the conclusion of the whole creation event, in the second he is created first and the creation is built up around him. Thus in both texts he occupies a special place within creation, but his rank in it is given in a variety of ways. His special position is expressed in the first chapter in his relationship to God. God creates him after (or "as," see below) his own image (1.26). This statement has produced an absolutely massive history of interpretation (cf. Westermann 1974, 203ff; Schmidt 1987, 225ff), but some basic questions still remain open and are likely to continue to do so. Here God speaks in the plural: "Let us make man." There is no "royal we" in the Hebrew Bible; so what does the plural mean (cf. also Gen 11.7)? Is God hereby completing his heavenly court (cf. 1 Kgs 22.19; Job 1.6; 2.1, also Isa 6.8)? [→142, 338f] Or does the author of the text want to avoid stating that humans are created according to the image of the creator himself: thus not in the shape of Yhwh, but "only" in the shape of *'lohîm* (von Rad 1962, 158f; 1972, 37ff)? This would also be supported by v. 27: "Then God created man as his image, as the image of *'lohîm* he created him." Ps 8 points in the same direction: "You have made him a little lower than *'lohîm*" (v. 6). Lower than God? Or lower than gods? Or than angels (thus, the Septuagint: ἄγγελοι)? And not equal, but lower? The questions can be multiplied, and no conclusive answer is given. What does "after his image" mean? Is the human being the image of God, i.e. does he resemble him in appearance? Or does the term *selem* point rather to the fact that the human being should be understood as God's representative, so that God created him "for his image" or "as his image"? The context in Gen 1.26 favors this second understanding, where the only thing said in clarification of the "image of God" is that the human is to "rule" over the other creatures. This is again confirmed by Ps 8, where in elaboration of the statement of the creation of humans it is also said that God appointed him as ruler over the other creatures (v. 79). In the historical circumstances of Israel's religious environment, in particular in Egypt, the king is described as the image of God. In Israel this has been "democratized" in its application to humans in general (cf. THAT II.556ff; ThWAT 6.1046ff).

God created humankind as man and woman. The sentence in Gen 1.27 shows the ambivalence of the word *'ādām*: "God created the *'ādām* (singular) ... for the image of *'lohîm* (v. 27a) [→14]—he created them (plural), man and woman" (lit.: "male and female"). The genetic term *'ādām*, "human," is found only in the singular in the Hebrew Bible and can indicate humans as a species, humanity, as an individually differentiable quantity of humans or an individual human being. Usually, the grammatical context is also in the singular. But here in Gen 1.27 the plural is used with emphatic force: the *'ādām* that has now been created is not an individual human being but two, man and woman; together they form *'ādām*. This statement is repeated and strengthened further in 5.1f: "he called their name Adam" (cf. Trible 1993, 36ff). In Gen 2 the creation of humans is presented from a different narrative perspective. The *'ādām* is created from the *'dāmah*, the soil of the field, in order to work it (v. 5b). He is an "earth-creature" (Trible 1993, 99). God makes him a living being by breathing "life-breath" into his nose (v. 7). This earth-creature is not a "man," because as yet there is no sex differentiation. Only when God decides to give him a companion does a sexual distinction and partnership arise between woman (*'iššāh*) and man (*'îš*) (2.18-24) [→15]. The word *ha-'ādām* (with the article) can now indicate the man as distinct from "his wife" (v. 25). But it remains the overall term for humans, as is clear for instance in 3.22-24, where we read that *ha-'ādām* was driven from the garden, which of course affects both man and woman together (Crüsemann 1978, 57).

Despite all the differences, then, the two creation accounts give a "surprisingly sober consensus" (Wolff 1973, 145), that in the beginning God created man and woman. Contrary to the interpretive traditions of post-biblical religions, in neither of the two accounts is there any indication of a subordination of the woman to the man. This is made quite clear in Gen 1.28. After God has created the human pair, he addresses them together. Everything that occurs subsequently happens to both of them without any hierarchical superiority or subordination. "Be fruitful and multiply and fill the earth"—woman and man can only do this together. The following imperatives are also directed to both: "Subdue it (i.e. the earth). Rule over the fish of the sea and the birds of the air and over every living creature that moves on the ground." This instruction should be understood in connection with the statement about humans as the "image of God" (see above). Humans are to represent God by adopting functions of leadership within the world of experience—functions that are inescapably necessary and which no other creature can take on. To judge by ancient near eastern parallels in which the creator God himself and the king appointed by him appear in the function of shepherd in the case of Gen 1.28 one can speak of a veritable "shepherd metaphor" (Zenger 1987, 90). This image should not, however, be romanticized. Leadership also means rule, and this includes the use of violence. All the more so, when one remembers that in antiquity people viewed animals as a threat against which they had to protect themselves and their herd (Ebach 1986, 31ff; Janowski 1993).

One might protest that with the latter consideration an element of disturbance is being brought into the good order of creation as presented by Gen 1. Perhaps the author is thinking rather of a situation as sketched in Isa 11.6-9 in the messianic age of salvation, when complete peace will prevail between animals and between animals and humans. This applies at any rate in the case of the regulation of food that now follows in line with creation (Gen 1.29f). Humans and animals feed only from plants and their fruits. Humans can store food from the seeds and fruits of the plants and produce foodstuffs (v. 29), while the animals feed directly from the plants (v. 30). But the flesh of animals, whether killed by humans or beast of prey, does not belong with foodstuffs in the order of creation. Killing is a feature of the world after the "Fall" and the Flood (Gen 4.1-16; 9.26) [→18f].

In Gen 2 the human task is viewed from another angle: the human is to cultivate the soil of the field (v. 5bβ). God therefore plants a garden and places the human in it "to work it and take care of it" (v. 15). To read the two creation accounts in their present context, this looks like a supplementary view of the call to exercise dominion in 1.28. The relationship here is to the narrower field of human life, and thus it is not on the animals but on the soil of the fields that the work and attention of humans should be focused. So here there is certainly no notion of a situation of "paradise" without work of any kind. The command to take care of the land (*šāmar* also means "guard" and "protect," cf. 3.24; 4.9) also shows that the modern claim that the Bible declares the earth available for exploitation rests on ignorance of the texts (cf. Lohfink 1977, 156ff).

5. Beyond Eden

The account of God forming the human being from the soil of the field and setting him to work in cultivating and maintaining it, has a sequel after the "Fall," but now in an entirely different light. On the expulsion from the Garden of Eden, the narrator repeats the command to humans to cultivate the land (Gen 3.23). But this now has quite a different emphasis. It is the soil "from which he was taken;" and there is an associated echo from the curse in v. 19: "until you return to it." In retrospect the words "for you are dust" sound like an answer to the serpent's words: "You will be like God" (v. 5). Not like God, but dust.

The whole creation event now shifts into a new light. God has made the human from the soil of the field and blown the "breath of life" into him (Gen 2.7). The breath (*nešāmāh*) makes the earth-creature a "living being" (*nefeš ḥayyāh*). The creator of heaven and earth gives breath to all who live on the earth (Isa 42.5), including the animals (Gen 7.22). Breath is part of God's own breath, and so alongside *nešāmāh* the much more common word *rûᵃḥ* ("breath, spirit, wind") can be found (Isa 42.5; Job 27.3 etc.). But at the same time breath is a constant sign of human vulnerability. God gives breath, and he can take it back at any time. "As long as I have life within me, the breath of God in my nostrils"—this is how Job can describe the period of life granted to him (Job 27.3). When God takes his breath back, all living things must die (Ps 104.29; Job 34.14f). But God can also populate the earth anew by sending out his breath (Ps 104.30). God even bridles his anger so that the "breathing beings" that he has created do not perish (Isa 57.16). And finally in the last verse of the Psalter all those who breathe are called to sing praise to God (Ps 150.6).

The creation event moves entirely into the area of the individual human being at this point. Thus in the divine speech to Jeremiah we may read that God formed him in his mother's body (Jer 1.5: *yāṣar* as in Gen 2.7) [→**203**]. The Psalmist too speaks of such forming by God before birth (Ps 139.13-16), and Job depicts this event in astonishing detail (Job 10.8-11). But this amazement stands as it were in sharp contrast to the feeling of being at God's mercy. The Psalmist speaks of the futility of attempts to hide from God (Ps 139.7-12), and Job describes the creation event in almost unbearable contrast to the unjust persecution to which he feels subjected by God (Job 10 *passim*, esp. vv. 8f, 18) [→**344**]. For Jeremiah too, his selection as prophet before he was born is in conflict with his lament about his birth (Jer 15.10; cf. Job 3). So we see again from these texts that the worldview of the Hebrew Bible does not set out from the image of the undisturbed creation described in the first two chapters but from the situation after the "Fall." The life of the human created by God is now limited by death. The human returns to the dust from which he was taken (Gen 3.19). Qohelet adds that the spirit (*rûᵃh*) "returns to God, who gave it" (Qoh 12.7).

Death is the natural end of human life. Thus Joshua can say: "I am about to go the way of all the earth" (Josh 23.14), as can David (1 Kgs 2.2). In these narratives impending death is the occasion to look back on one's own life and to warn those that remain to continue along the pathway that has been laid out for them. Jacob passes on to Joseph and his sons the divine promise: "I am about to die, but God will be with you and take you back to the land of your fathers" (Gen 48.21). So death is at the same time the handover to the following generation.

At the end of a fulfilled life it can be said: "Abraham died at a good old age, an old man and full of years" (Gen 25.8; similarly Isaac, Gen 35.29); the Chronicler reports the same about David (1 Chron 29.28). Astonishingly enough, it is also said of Job that he died "an old man and full of years" (Job 42.17). This shows that the meaning cannot be that the whole of life has passed peacefully and without problems; that was not the case with Abraham and David either. But it is expressed in the fact that a "fulfilled" life comes to its natural end in death.

This "natural" death is generally spoken of in quite undramatic terms in the Hebrew Bible. Often there is just the brief statement: "and he/she died;" a note about the burial frequently follows (e.g. Gen 35.8; 35.19, 29; Judg 8.32; 1 Sam 2.51). This is quite often connected with particular geographical data (Gen 35.8, 19; Num 20.1 etc.), which shows that the graves were known and evidently also venerated; the texts do not, however, give any indication of a regular cult of the dead.

There are, however, a series of texts that show that there was a frequent inclination toward cults of the dead, as are known to us from neighboring religions (Deut 18.11; 26.14; 1 Sam 28; Isa 8.19; 65.4 etc.). Certain cultic texts according to which contact with a corpse renders one "unclean," can be understood as in defense against such tendencies (cf. in particular the stipulations about the "purification water" in Num 19, and also the special provisions for priests [Lev 21.1-4, 11] and Nazirites [Num 6.6-23]; cf. von Rad 1962, 288ff; Levine 1993, 468-479).

But there are also many texts that speak quite differently about death and dying. In the Psalms in particular there is discussion of the necessity of dying and of death, which has its justification on quite different levels. Attention is given to this elsewhere [→**328**]. (Cf. also Crüsemann 1989.)

§ 6

Covenant and Election

1. Preliminary comments

That God is attentive to the world and humanity is expressed in a wide
variety of ways in the Hebrew Bible. Most of these forms of expression
are marked by the language and theology of particular areas of tradition and text within the Hebrew Bible. At the same time however
there are all sorts of connections between them, so that it would vio-
late the theological cohesion of the scriptures as a whole if one were to
try to separate them out fully. From this overall point of view one can
distinguish three main groups of statements:
1. God's covenant with the world and with his people Israel.
2. Israel's election from the nations.
3. The formula "I will be your God and you will be my people" (the
    so-called covenant formula).

These three groups of sayings are on the one hand clearly distinguished
from each other, both in their linguistic forms of expression and in
their theological emphases, and on the other hand they have many
points of contact and overlap. This shows that none of them on their
own can embrace the relationship of God to humans and of humans to
God in all its variety, but that in each case they express certain aspects
of this relationship in different ways. In addition, it is clear again and
again that one can talk about God's relations with Israel and with humanity as a whole even without the characteristic terminology of these
groups. This shows at the same time that basic theological statements
in the Hebrew Bible certainly are not always expressed in specific,
firmly fixed linguistic terms. Terms are important, indeed necessary
orientation aids, but they are never the thing itself.

2. I will remember my covenant

The most comprehensive and the most theologically weighty term for God's attention to humans in the Hebrew Bible is the word *b'rît*, which we usually render in English as "covenant." This translation does have its problems, because the word sometimes has an ambiguity that the Hebrew word does not have in every case. But the word "covenant" has a long history in Christian tradition, so that it is indeed capable of expressing the special relationship between God and humanity.

The most important thing in this respect is that the covenant is always at God's behest and on his initiative. This is very clear in the first passage where we encounter this word in the Hebrew Bible. After the Flood God confirms his promise that the earth will last, despite the unchanged situation of the continuing sinfulness of humans (Gen 8.21f), through the solemn granting of his promised given to Noah (6.18): "But I will establish my covenant with you" (9.9). Here we have a marked terminology: it is God's own covenant ("my covenant"), that he "establishes" (*hēqîm*). He establishes it "with" Noah, his descendants and all living beings that come out of the ark (vv. 9f), or "between me and you" (vv. 12f, 15-17). At the same time God institutes a sign of the covenant (*'ôt habb'rît*, vv. 12f), and he will "remember" this covenant (*zākar*, vv. 15f), for it is an "eternal covenant" (*b'rît 'ôlām*, v. 19). In this covenant God commits himself irrevocably to the continuing existence of the world and of humanity.

The same terminology (which belongs to the priestly layer of composition) is then found in Gen 17 in a covenant agreement between God and Abraham [→**27**]. God establishes his "eternal" covenant between himself and Abraham and his descendants (v. 7, cf. v. 2 as well as the extension of the covenant to Isaac in vv. 19, 21). The subject of the covenant here is first of all the promise that God will endow Abraham (whose name is changed to "Abraham" in v. 5) with numerous progeny (vv. 2, 46) and give him the land of Canaan, in which he is still living as a foreigner, as his permanent possession (v. 8). This promise is, as it were, framed by the "covenant formula" (vv. 7b, 8b, see below), in which God assures Abraham that he will be his and his descendants' God. But the covenant now gains a new aspect in that it also contains a responsibility for Abraham. He is to "keep" (*šāmar*) the covenant by circumcision of all the male members of the family and the household as well as all male descendants (vv. 9-13). This is to be the sign of the covenant (v. 11b). This shows that the covenant is and remains a gift of God, but that there will be a corresponding behavior of observance by the people (and in the person of Abraham this means Israel). The duty to set up the covenant sign is now transferred to the people.

From here various lines can be followed. In Ex 31.12-17 we read that the Israelites are to keep the Sabbath (*šāmar* as in Gen 17) as a covenant sign for the "eternal covenant." The reference back to God's resting on the seventh day of creation (v. 17) creates a connection to the beginning story of creation and thereby also to the first covenant sign that God set (Gen 9). But as in Gen 17 the Israelites themselves are to set up the covenant sign. (According to Lev 24.8 the "eternal covenant" is made concrete on the Sabbath in the "showbread.")

In subsequent history of Abraham's posterity God's "remembering" of his covenant in particular plays an important role. When they are suffering under oppression in Egypt, their groans rise to God, and he remembers his covenant with the fathers (Ex 2.23-25) [→**37**]. Immediately afterwards the history of salvation begins with the birth of Moses. In the central text Ex 6.28 covenant language is then central. God set up the covenant (v. 4) and now he remembers it (v. 5b) and will lead the Israelites out of Egyptian slavery, and fulfill the promise of the land given to the forefathers. The promise that Yhwh will be Israel's God appears again, this time in the dual form: "I will take you as my people and will be your God" (v. 7). This text at the beginning of the exodus story corresponds with the great concluding chapter of the giving of the law on Sinai, Lev 26. At the beginning of it stands the reminder of the covenant (v. 9), again connected with the dual covenant formula (v. 12) [→**68**]. Then after all the suffering that will come as punishment for the failure to keep the divine commandments for Israel, and after the Israelites have acknowledged their guilt (v. 40), God will finally remember his covenant with the forefathers (vv. 42, 45) as he did when he led them out of Egypt, "to be their God." God emphasizes explicitly that he did not wish to break the covenant (*hēpēr* v. 44), the grounds for this being simply: "for I am the Lord, their God." God does not break his covenant. (Cf. also Crüsemann 1990, 125f.)

Outside the Pentateuch, too, this way of speaking of the covenant is found. A similar note to Lev 26 is struck in Jer 14, where the acknowledgement of guilt (v. 20) is followed by the request to God to remember his covenant (v. 21). In Ps 106 too, God finally hears Israel's pleas and remembers his covenant (vv. 44f) [→**245**]. In Ezek 16 the great chapter about the faithlessness of Jerusalem ends with God's remembrance of his covenant, which he concluded with Jerusalem in its youth and which he now wishes to reconfirm (vv. 60, 62, cf. Greenberg 1983, 291f). God's remembering of his covenant has a different emphasis in Ps 105.8, where it comes not at the end of a lament, but at the beginning of a hymn of praise for God's wonderful leading of his people. In Ps 111.5, too, it is a subject of praise. (Cf. in general Schottroff 1967, 202ff.)

In this terminological and theological context God's activity is right in the foreground. God sets up the covenant and remembers it at the appropriate time. The creation stays protected from any new annihilation by a flood, and despite all the dangers, in the end Israel is always rescued. The human side of the covenant is emphasized in the duty of circumcision (Gen 17.9ff) [→**27**] and of Sabbath observance (Ex 31.12ff), but as a whole remains in the background. A special feature of this version of the covenant concept is that God first concludes the covenant with Noah and in it with the whole of humanity, in fact with the whole of creation, and only subsequently with Abraham and in him with Israel. From a terminological point of view both things are on the same plane. So is it one and the same covenant, or are there two "covenants," one with humanity as a whole and one with Abraham/Israel? A number of factors seem to point to the second possibility. But at one point, at least, these two aspects of the covenant are expressly related to each other: in Isa 54.7-10 God assures Jerusalem that after a short period of anger he will turn to it again "as in the days of Noah." As he swore then that he would never again allow a flood, he now swears that he will not scorn Jerusalem again and will not allow the "covenant of peace" (*bᵉrît šālôm*) to waver. Here the Noachic covenant is viewed on the same level as God's covenant with Jerusalem/Israel and in a mutual relationship. (See further below.)

3. You shall keep my covenant

Alongside these linguistically and theologically very uniform statements about God's covenant with the world and with Israel, which in addition have a structuring function for certain parts of the Pentateuch (cf. 1991a), quite different forms of expression are also to be found. Thus God's covenant promise to Abraham appears already in Gen 15.18 [→**27**] in the terms of a covenant agreement, expressed with the verb *kārat*, which is frequently found in biblical Hebrew also as a technical term for the concluding of a *b'rît* between people (e.g. Gen 21.27). (The verb has the basic meaning of "cut" and may be connected with an original covenant agreement ritual, during which an animal was cut up; cf. Jer 34.18 and Gen 15.9f, 17.) The content of the covenant is the promise of the gift of the land to the descendants of Abraham. This is initially surprising, since this promise has accompanied the Abraham story from its beginning (Gen 12.7; 13.15, 17, also 15.7). But here it is confirmed in the solemn form of God's self-commitment in a *b'rît*, after it first seemed endangered by Abraham's own behavior (12.10ff) and then by the conflict with Lot (ch. 13) and finally by the attack of enemy kings (ch. 14). The covenant here contains a self-commitment by God without anything being said of a requirement for Abraham.

In Gen 24.7 Abraham then reminds God of this solemn promise. He does not use the word *b'rît* for this but speaks of God's "swearing." This expression is also used in 26.3f and 50.24. The "swearing" or "oath" is evidently contained in the "covenant" or may indeed constitute it altogether (cf. *ThWAT* VII, 981ff). Thus in the further course of history too the remembrance of the oath by which God promised the land to Abraham and his descendants occurs again and again (Ex 13.5, 11; 32.13; 33.1; Num 11.12; 14.16, 23; 32.11). In Deuteronomy the two lines run together: "The Lord will not forget the covenant with your forefathers, which he swore to them" (Deut 4.31; cf. 7.12; 8.18, also Judg 2.1) [→75].

But a new element comes in at this point. In Gen 17.9ff already there was talk of Abraham's responsibility, and the responsibility of his descendants, to "keep" the covenant by circumcision. On Israel's encounter with God on Sinai we then read in the first divine speech: "Now if you obey me fully and keep my covenant ..." (Ex 19.5) [→53]. This serves to introduce the great giving of the law on Sinai, which from now on is implied whenever there is any mention of God's covenant with Israel. The first group of fundamental divine commandments that opens with the Decalogue (20.1-17), concludes with a solemn covenant agreement ceremony (24.38). Again we meet the phrase *kārat b'rît* (v. 8), this time with the addition that God concludes the covenant "on the basis of all these words." Moses has previously told the people these words (v. 3), written them down (v. 4) and finally read them out from the "book of the covenant" (v. 7). The people answered twice that they intended to do all these words that God had spoken (vv. 3, 7). "Do the words" (*'āśāh*) here is equivalent in meaning to "keep the covenant;" the "doing" grows out of the "hearing" (cf. 19.5. In 24.7, "and we will hear" is added once again; this expresses preparedness to follow all future commandments as well, cf. Jacob 1997, *ad loc.*). What was only starting to become clear in Gen 17 is now discernible in its full significance: God's covenant with Israel proceeds from God himself, but it includes Israel's hearing, keeping and doing in it. It is only the two things together that make the covenant what it is to mean from now on for Israel.

All this also applies after Israel has broken the first Sinai covenant so soon by turning away from the covenant-initiating God and his attention to the self-made "golden calf" (Ex 32) [→**61**]. For God has restored the covenant after Moses' dramatic efforts: "Behold, I make a covenant" (34.10). It is no other covenant than the preceding one. What has changed is the insight that Israel is going to break the covenant time and again ("for they are a stubborn people", Ex 34.9), but that God will nonetheless stand by his covenant. The "keeping" of the covenant remains a constant duty for Israel; but ultimately it is based on the fact that God himself is the "keeper of the covenant" (Deut 7.9 etc.). The two stand in a direct mutual relationship.

After the events on Sinai, alongside the grateful and praising memories of God's "remembrance" of his covenant, the demand comes more and more to the fore that the covenant be kept and that the commandments given with the covenant be observed. And the complaint and accusation is raised time and again that Israel is not meeting this requirement. In Deuteronomy we find all three aspects in a very emphatic form. At the beginning, before the entry into the land of Canaan, Israel is reminded of the "oath" with which God promised the land to the forefathers (Deut 1.8). At the beginning of the great theological chapter, Deuteronomy 4, the two things are linked together: the entry into "the land which the Lord, the God of your fathers, gives you" (v. 1), and the call to "keep the commandments of the Lord, which I command you" without changes (v. 2). In a backward look at the divine revelation on Sinai the word *b'rît* then appears as a term for the commandments given there, and with particular reference to the Ten Commandments that were written on two stone tablets (v. 13, cf. 5.22 and Ex 34.28); but at the same time the other statutes and commandments are added which Moses himself taught the Israelites (v. 14). The exposition of the first commandment (vv. 15ff) then leads on to the admonition not to forget the *b'rît* which God made with the Israelites (*kārat*, v. 23). This admonition moves into an indirect accusation, in that the possibility that Israel might still infringe the first commandment and worship other gods, is described together with its consequences—consequences which at the time this text was composed had already become reality in the deportation of the Israel-ites into exile (vv. 25-28). But then the whole thing takes another turn when those living in exile seek God once more and turn back to him, so that he has pity on them; then "he does not forget the covenant with your fathers, which he swore to them" (v. 31). So here the Sinai covenant and the covenant with the fathers stand in a direct relation-ship to each other. And as the "keeping" of the covenant by Israel and by God himself correspond to each other, so also the opposite, "for-getting," but with the fundamental difference that Israel constantly forgets the covenant, whereas God never does.

Again the question arises: are there two covenants, one with the fa-thers and one on Sinai, or is there just one? A fundamental difference consists in the covenant-mediation of Moses [→**549f**]. It is only through Moses that the covenant with Israel as a nation is concluded. But it is significant that the word *b'rît* in biblical Hebrew never appears in the plural, and that these two main forms of the covenant are never ex-pressly distinguished from each other or separated. On the contrary, they are even closely interwoven, as in Deut 7.12, where we read: "If you obey these commandments, keep them and do them, the Lord your God will keep the covenant and the loyalty he swore to your fathers." Again the reciprocal use of the "keeping" is there, but this time between the commandments of Horeb/Sinai and God's covenant with the fathers. Sometimes the "fathers" can also be those whom God led out of Egypt, as when Solomon is able to say on the occasion of the dedication of the temple in Jerusalem that it provides a place for the ark, "in which is the covenant (*b'rît*) of the Lord that he made with our fathers when he brought them out of Egypt" (1 Kgs 8.21; cf. Deut 29.24; Jer 31.32). Here the fathers, the exodus and Horeb/Sinai come together as part of the same idea of the "covenant."

At the same time the text of Solomon's temple dedication also dis-plays a further development of the concept of *b'rît*. Both stone tablets with the divine commandments from Sinai can be described as the "tables of the covenant" (Deut 9.9, 11, 15, abbreviated in 1 Kgs 8.21 as "the covenant of Yhwh"). According to Deut 10.15 Moses placed them in the ark that he had himself made for this purpose on God's instructions (cf. 1 Kgs 8.9). The ark can thus also be called the "ark of the covenant" (Deut 10.8; cf. Num 10.33). Under this name it ac-companies Israel through many situations along the way (Num 13.33ff;

Josh 3f; 1 Sam 4.3ff), until finally it finds its place in the temple (1 Kgs 8.1). It is again evident here that the same thing can be expressed in different terms in other contexts of tradition within the Hebrew Bible: the ark can also be described as "ark of the testimony" (*"ron hā'ēdut*) because Moses placed the "testimony" in it (Ex 40.20f).

Elsewhere in the Hebrew Bible there are frequent allusions to God's covenant with Israel. It is clear, however, that this term does not occupy a dominant position and that no coherent "covenant theology" can be discerned. The term *b'rît* does not occur in most of the prophetic books (Perlitt 1969, 129ff). In Jeremiah it is more prominent, and from various perspectives: in sermon-like admonitions to hear the "words of this covenant" (Jer 11.1-10), combined with announcement of the consequences of the breaking of the covenant (11.8; 22.19); in the confession of Israel's sins, linked with the prayer to God that he might still remember his covenant (14.21); finally in the promise of a "new covenant" (31.31-34) [→**698**]. The new thing about this covenant promised for the future will not be its content; as before, it is still a question of keeping the *tôrāh*. But God will place it on the Israelites' hearts, so that they will no longer be able to break the covenant (cf. Deut 30.14). Here the term "eternal covenant" (*b'rît 'ôlām*, 32.40) is then once again given a new meaning.

An important element in the keeping of the covenant lies in the setting of limits with respect to the worship of other gods. The breaking of the covenant on Israel's part is often identical to turning to other gods (Deut 29.24f; 31.16, 20; Josh 23.16 etc.). So Israel is forbidden to conclude a covenant with other nations [→**669**], because this has the inherent danger that Israel will be thereby seduced into the worship of their gods (Ex 34.10, 14 etc.). In Ex 23.32 we even read that the Israelites are not to conclude a covenant with the nations they have driven out "and their gods." Here we see very clearly that in many texts the increasingly visible separation from other nations is intended to serve to keep the worship of Yhwh pure and thus to ensure that the covenant is kept.

4. I have chosen you from among the nations

The special history of God with Israel begins in a simple narrative form. God commands Abraham to leave his land and his family for a new land that God will show him (Gen 12.13). In the context of the

Genesis narratives this opens up a new chapter in the history of humanity. The genealogical line of the many forms of humanity focuses down onto this one man (Gen 11.10ff), who is now to be the forefather of the nation with which God wishes in future to shape his special history. In the narrative itself no particular term is used for the separating out of Abraham. In a later comprehensive historical retrospect we read that God "chose" (*bāḥar*) Abraham (Neh 9.7) [→**399**]. This introduces another important term for characterizing God's relationship with Israel.

The term "chosen" is often used in a broader sense without direct connection with a particular term in the Hebrew Bible (e.g. Galling 1928). Rightly so, since terms can only encompass and express a particular aspect of the matter. In this comprehensive sense God's special affection for his people Israel means the choosing of this people. At a crucial point in the story of Abraham the narrative lets us in on God's thinking on Abraham's special position: God has "recognized" him so that he is to become a great nation and lead his descendants on the "way of Yhwh" (Gen 18.18f) [→**28**]. Amos too uses the word "recognize" (*yāda'*) to express Israel's special position (Amos 3.2) [→**281**]. He also adds "from all the nations of the earth." A specific element of the idea of election comes into view here: it means both selection and the giving of prominence over others.

This aspect occurs where the verb *bāḥar* is used. It means the election of Israel "out of all the nations" (Deut 7.6 etc.). This is a very loaded word in Deuteronomic parlance and stands in a broad theological context (cf. 1981). The election of Israel from among the nations of the earth presupposes that God has the whole earth and all the nations that inhabit it at his disposal and thus has the power to choose one of these. The statement about the election of Israel in Deuteronomy is thus indissolubly linked to the confession of God as the creator of the world. This comes formidably to expression in Deut 10.14f. At the beginning stands the statement about God as creator; but although heaven and earth are his, he "only" (cf. Amos 3.2!) cherished Israel's fathers, thereby choosing their descendants. In Deut 4 the detailed discussion of God's covenant with Israel is followed by a further passage in which similarly the election of the descendants of the fathers loved by God and the confession of God as creator are directly linked (vv. 37-39). In addition, the leading out of Egypt is mentioned here as God's act on behalf of the fathers (v. 37), and finally, as in the preceding passage about the covenant, the keeping of the divine laws and commandments is demanded (v. 40). Something very similar is said in 7.6-11, where Israel is described as God's "holy people" [→**543f**], whom God has chosen from among all the nations as the "people of his possession." Here the statement about election is closely connected with the covenant formula (see below). Express reference is made to the "oath" which God swore to the fathers and on account of which he led them out of Egypt (v. 8). Here the statements about election and covenant are again closely interwoven: the choosing God is the faithful "keeper of the covenant" (v. 9).

The connection of the statement of election with God's oath is also found in Ezek 20.5, again in the context of the leading out of Egypt [→**246**]. This word leads into a connection of statement of acknowledgement ("I let myself be known by them") and self-presentation formula: "I am Yhwh, your God." In Ps 105.6-11 statements about election, covenant and oath as well as about God's world rule are linked together. Ps 135.4 sets another tone, where the statements about the election of Jacob/Israel are linked with the description as God's "possession." A notable difference applies in the case of Ps 78.67f: God rejected Joseph and Ephraim and chose Judah and Zion. Reflected here is the historical development in which the northern kingdom which collapsed in 722 was expressly described as rejected and excluded from the election. From here on, everything that can be said of the election of Israel relates only to Judah.

Elsewhere in the prophetic books the statement about election is not very common. In the book of Isaiah, Israel/Jacob is addressed a number of times as the "Servant" whom God has chosen (Isa 41.8f; 43.10; 44.1f) [→**189**]. A remarkable statement is that in Isa 14.1, which says that God will "have mercy on Jacob and choose Israel once again (*'ôd*)." This renewal of the election is linked to the renewed placement in the land. We find something similar in Zechariah, where the renewed election is centered on Zion/Jerusalem (Zech 1.17; 2.16). Here we see that, as in the case of God's covenant with Israel, a renewal of the election can be imagined in a time of bliss that has still to arrive. However, there is no mention anywhere of a withdrawal or lifting of the election.

The statements elaborated by use of the term *bāḥar*, "choose," can however be found as a coherent field of meaning without this expression too. In the opening divine speech of the great Sinai passage in Ex 19.46 we find all the essential elements of this bundling of traditions: the leading out of Egypt, the call to keep the covenant, Israel as the people of God's possession and as a holy nation as well as God's self-description as Creator ("for the whole earth belongs to me," v. 5); but the word *bāḥar* is missing. Here again we see that it does not always do justice to the texts to pay regard only to particular terms.

5. I will be your God and you will be my people

Finally, God's special relationship to Israel also comes to expression in the formulaic-sounding expression "I will be your God and you shall be my people." This is generally referred to as the "covenant formula" (cf. 1995). (The term "belonging-formula" (*Zugehörigkeitsformel*) has also been suggested [Kutsch 1973, 146ff], but this only reflects one particular aspect of what the formula says.) In a series of texts that were dealt with above under the rubrics "covenant" and "election," the covenant formula is an integral component of God's statements about his relationship with Israel. The double formula sometimes occurs with only one of its two statements, in which rather different theological emphases come to expression.

Thus we find the formula with its first part in God's making of a covenant with Abraham in Gen 17.17f [→**27**]. God sets up his "everlasting covenant" with Abraham and all his descendants "to be God for you and your descendants after you." Here the assurance that God will be Abraham's God is practically the explanation of what is meant by *b'rît*. By its repetition of the sentence "and I will be their God" (v. 8b) the covenant formula comprises the promise of the land which forms the other main content of the covenant. The literal translation "to be God for you/them" makes clear the structure of the statement: the concern here is not, as in other passages in the Hebrew Bible, with God's being God as such, but with his being God for Abraham and his descendants.

In the central passage Ex 6.28 [→**41**] the covenant formula then begins in its double-sided form: "I will take you as my people and will be God for you" (v. 7a). Israel has in the meantime become the people (cf. Ex 1.9), and God now includes the entire people in his promise to Abraham. The retrospective view of God's covenant with the fathers therefore stands right at the beginning (v. 4); it is connected with the announcement that God now "remembers" his covenant (v. 5). A whole series of short sentences then follows, leading up to the covenant formula: God leads Israel out of Egypt, frees it from slavery, redeems it with proofs of his power, takes it as his people and becomes

its God (vv. 6, 7a). That God now fully accepts Israel as his people is at
the same time an integral part of his imminent saving action.

Once again the two-sided covenant formula appears in Lev 26
[→68], the great concluding chapter of the giving of the law on Sinai.
Here too it is connected with the leading out of Egypt, and now additionally with God's dwelling in the midst of Israel (vv. 11-13). The
two texts in Ex 6 and Lev 26 correspond to each other and together
embrace the broad context of Exodus and the Sinai events. But the
bridge extends even further. In Deut 29 at the beginning of the first
great speech by Moses after the presentation of the collection of commandments, we read that God solemnly concludes the covenant with
Israel "to confirm you this day as his people, that he may be your
God" (v. 12). Here too the covenant formula specifies the content of
the covenant: Israel's being a people for Yhwh and Yhwh's being God
for Israel. By the addition of the words "as he promised you and as he
swore to your fathers, Abraham, Isaac and Jacob" it is expressly emphasized that this covenant agreement "in the land of Moab" stands in
continuity with the covenant of the fathers. Then finally the "new
covenant" in Jer 31 is also defined by the covenant formula [→698].
The key sentence, which declares what this new covenant consists in,
leads into the covenant formula: "I will be God for them and they will
be a people for me" (v. 33b). Here too the continuity with the covenant concluded earlier with the fathers is preserved, albeit in the form
of a radical critique of the behavior of the "fathers," and for Jeremiah
this means: the behavior of all generations since the exodus from
Egypt. Nonetheless the new covenant will confirm the one in operation hitherto, in that its central content will be and remain the reciprocal relationship between God and Israel.

Thus an essential contribution of the covenant formula to the entirety of Old Testament covenant theology consists in the fact that at
critical points the content of the term b'rît is defined by the covenant
formula: the covenant concluded between God and Israel consists in
his wanting to be Israel's God and Israel being supposed to be his people. This applies both to the early phase in the construction of the
covenant with the fathers (Gen 17) and also the phase of Israel's commitment to the divine commandments given on Sinai/Horeb (Deut
29) and finally also for the "new covenant" expected in the future (Jer
31).

Another important aspect of the covenant formula consists in its
close connection with the notion of the election of Israel by God. At

some central points the two things come to expression in a single sentence: "Yhwh has chosen you to be the people of his possession from among all the nations that are on the earth" (Deut 7.6; 14.2; cf. 4.20). Here the covenant formula appears only with the second part of its statement: that Israel is to be God's people. This shows another theological emphasis than in the texts which use only the first part or the two-part formula. Their shared formula however leaves no doubt as to their theological intention. In addition, at important points in Deuteronomy we also find attestations to the covenant formula in its two-part form (Deut 26.17, 19; 29.12). Thus here the covenant formula contributes to the linking together of various traditions in which the special relationship between God and Israel is expressed.

Finally, the covenant formula also links statements about the already concluded covenant with the "new covenant" expected in the future. The content of the new covenant is no different from the previous one: "I will be God to them and they will be my people" (Jer 31.33). It is placed on a new foundation, whereby the Torah is written on the hearts of the Israelites, as Deuteronomy had also foreseen (Deut 30.14) [→86]. But precisely this, that the covenant is placed on a new footing, was also at the center of the covenant agreement on Sinai, which was reconstituted after Israel's apostasy from God with the "golden calf" (Ex 34.10). To that extent this second Sinai covenant can in a sense be described already as a "new covenant" (Dohmen 1993). Such texts as Lev 25 and Ezek 16 [→244] display the same basic idea: that after a long period of punishment for Israel because of its abandonment of the divine commandments given in the covenant, God nonetheless recalls his covenant, which he never wanted to break, has never broken and never will break. (Cf. also Judg 2.1.)

6. The covenant with Israel and a covenant with David

A number of times in the Hebrew Bible there is talk of a divine "covenant" with David. This expression is not, however, in the foreground of what is said about God's relations with David. The term does not appear in the central passages that speak of God's dynastic promise to Abraham, such as 2 Sam 7 [→113]. It is found primarily in poetic passages. In the "last words of David" in 2 Sam 23 we read that God "gave" David an "eternal covenant" (*bᵉrît ῾ôlām*) (v. 5; the construction with the verb *śîm*, "give," is quite unusual). This text has a special place in that it speaks in a very elevated tone about David as the "anointed one" (*māšîʰh*), through whom the "spirit of the Lord" speaks (vv. 1f). In Ps 89 too, in which a broad, sweeping picture of David is developed, the term "covenant" plays an important role. In the divine speech in v. 4 we read: "I have made a covenant with David, my chosen one (*bāhûr*)." In v. 28[29] the covenant is set in parallel with God's grace (*hesed*) and elaborated in relation to the dynasty promise (v. 29[30]). In vv. 30-34[31-35] God gives the assurance that though he will punish David's descendants if they abandon the Torah, he will not "defile" his covenant. In v. 39[40], however, there is a complaint that this is precisely what God has done: "You have renounced the covenant with your servant and have defiled his crown in the dust." According to this, this covenant with David has thus been ended by God himself.

In 2 Chron 21.7 the Chronicler reinforces his source text: that God wanted to keep a "lamp" for David (2 Kgs 8.19) is justified in the "covenant that he made with David." At another point the Chronicler speaks of God having given David and his sons the kingdom forever as a "covenant of salt" (2 Chron 13.5)—an expression that we can no longer fully understand today (cf. 1985ff, 111). In these texts the concept of the covenant again is found in the context of the dynastic promise. In Jer 33.20f God's covenant with David [→**228**] (and with Levi, see below) is described, in a bold parallelism, as just as indestructible as his covenant with day and night; the statement of 31.35-37, in which the existence of Israel is paralleled with that of the orders of creation, is thereby focused on the Davidic dynasty.

Further texts are sometimes adduced as evidence of a "covenant with David," but incorrectly so. In Isa 55.3 God promises the Israelites in exile that he will make an "eternal covenant" with them, (namely) his "unfailing kindnesses promised to David." Here God's promises to David are interpreted as applying to the people, "democratized," one might say (von Rad 1965, 250). However, there is no mention of a covenant between God and David. Ps 132.11f speaks of an oath that God has made to David, to place his descendants on his throne, "if your sons keep my covenant," and this certainly means the "Sinai covenant."

So we cannot speak of a separate covenant between God and David alongside the covenant with Israel. Some passages use the term covenant for the dynastic promise to David, especially in poetic texts; but it is never found on the same level as the covenant with Israel. In relation to the dynastic promise to David in 2 Sam 7 one may say, especially as regards the prayer of David in vv. 182-9, that the dynastic promise to David has "become a function and an aspect of the 'covenant with Israel.' David has become a pronounced special case of Israel" (Waschke 1987, 167f).

In Jer 33.21 a covenant with Levi is mentioned alongside God's covenant with David. The parallelism is explained in vv. 18 and 22: the concern is with the existence of the priesthood in correspondence with that of the kingship. In Mal 2.4f, 8 this promise is used polemically against the contemporary priests; cf. also Neh 13.29. A similar promise is made to Phinehas in Num 25.12f. It is evident here that in the religious realm as well as the political (cf. e.g. Gen 21.27, 32; Ex 23.32; Josh 9.6, 15; 1 Sam 11.1) the term covenant could be used in a sense that lay on a different level than that of God's covenant with Israel.

§ 7

The Fathers of Israel

1. It all began with the Fathers

The story of God's dealings with Israel begins as a story with Israel's ancestors, with Abraham at the top of the list. In the first chapters of the Bible the story of the beginnings of humanity leads up to this one figure, who is picked out and "chosen" by God, and of whom God intends to make a "great nation" (Gen 12.13) [→21]. Abraham is the father of Israel *par excellence*. He receives from God the promise that is fundamental to Israel's existence as a people: "I will give this land to your descendants" (v. 7). It is with him that God concludes a "covenant" (*b'rît*) which confirms the promise of the land (15.18-21; 17.8) as well as the assurance of a great posterity (17.2, 5f). But above all, this "eternal covenant" contains God's promise "to be God for you and your descendants after you" (17.7f). At the same time it is made clear already that though the covenant is set up by God, it is also two-sided: Abraham and all his descendants are to "keep" it by means of the covenant sign of the circumcision of all male descendants (vv. 9-13).

The story of the "forefathers" or "patriarchs" Abraham, Isaac and Jacob, together with their wives Rebekah, Leah and Rachel, is extensively developed in the book of Genesis (Gen 12–50). It forms a separate, fundamental chapter in the history of Israel. Then in the following books of the Hebrew Bible references and allusions are repeatedly made to the fathers and this story of origins. It begins with Abraham, the one person God had called (Isa 51.2) and chosen (Neh 9.7) [→193]; Abraham was the only one to take possession of the land (Ezek 33.24) [→253]. Israel is the "seed of Abraham" (Ps 105.6), who is also called the "friend" or "beloved" of God (Isa 41.8; 2 Chron 20.7). God remembers Abraham and comes to Israel's aid (Ps 105.42). But it is also said that God concluded his covenant with Abraham, Isaac and Jacob (Ps 105.8-11) and Israel is called the "seed of Abraham, Isaac and Jacob" (Jer 33.26). Here in the same verse there is talk separately of the "seed of Jacob," as, elsewhere too, Jacob is occasionally called alongside Abraham (Isa 29.22; 41.8; Mic 7.20; Ps 105.6; Isa 63.16 Israel). This shows the special position given to Jacob, the youngest of this triumvirate (cf. section 2).

The theological reference back to the patriarchs is connected with the promise of the land especially often. In the patriarchal story in Genesis the divine promise of the possession of the land plays a fundamental role. The wording of the promise changes in this case. On the first occurrence it reads: "I will give this land to your descendants (lit.: your seed)" (Gen 12.7), and then just a little later: "I will give it to you" (13.17) or in a combination of both formulae: "I will give it to you and your descendants forever" (13.15). It becomes clear here that the fathers are the first, key recipients of this divine assurance, but that it will only be their descendants who experience the fulfillment of it. This assurance accompanies Israel on its way and is recalled again and again, often with mention of an "oath" with which God has reinforced his assurance to the fathers (Ex 32.13; 33.1; Deut 1.8; 9.5; 34.4 etc.).

The second important backward reference relates to the covenant that God made with the fathers. At significant points it is said that God remembers this covenant. The rescue of Israel out of Egyptian bondage is introduced by God remembering his covenant with Abraham, Isaac and Jacob (Ex 2.24; 6.5) [→37, 452]. And at the end of the giving of the law on Sinai we read that after Israel has been deservedly led into exile on account of all its sins, God will again remember his covenant with the forefathers (Lev 26.42) [→69]. Here it is very clear that the fathers not only stand at the beginning of the story of Israel, but that this beginning determines the entire subsequent history of the people and its expectations and hopes for the future.

The term "the fathers" refers in the first instance to the three "forefathers." Thus on his self-revelation to Moses God calls himself "God of your/their fathers, the God of Abraham, Isaac and Jacob" (Ex 3.15, 16; 4.5; cf. 3.6). In Deuteronomy too we find the direct connection of the term "your/their fathers" with the name of the three patriarchs (Deut 1.8; 6.10; 9.5 etc., cf. Lohfink 1991, esp. 107; Römer 1990, esp. 266ff). But the notion of the fathers can also be expressed much more broadly. Thus the fathers with whom God made the covenant can also be those whom God led out of Egypt. Solomon says on the dedication of the temple in Jerusalem that the ark also is given its place, "in which is found the *bᵉrît* of Yhwh which he made with our fathers when he led them out of Egypt" (1 Kgs 8.21; cf. 2 Kgs 17.15). Jeremiah too speaks of the "covenant I made with your fathers when I took them by the hand to lead them out of the land of Egypt" (Jer 31.32, also 34.13; cf. also Deut 29.24). According to Deut 5.2f God concluded the covenant on Horeb not (only) with the fathers but (at the same time) with those currently addressed by Moses, who are on the point of crossing the Jordan. Here the "fathers" are the Horeb generation.

The talk of the leading of the "fathers" out of Egypt is found even more frequently elsewhere, e.g. Josh 24.6; Judg 6.13; 1 Sam 12.6; 1 Kgs 8.53 (here next to the statement about the commandments which God commanded to "our fathers," v. 58); 9.9 etc. Where there is mention of the land that God gave to the fathers in connection with captivity and exile, thoughts will go back to the generation that once came into the land (e.g. 1 Kgs 14.15; cf. 2 Kgs 21.8).

2. Jacob, also called Israel

Outside Genesis too, Abraham is occasionally called the one whom God called and blessed (Isa 51.2, together with Sarah) and who was given the land as his possession (Ezek 33.24) [→**253**]. More frequently he appears as the first in a series of the three "fathers" Abraham, Isaac and Jacob (Ex 2.24; 3/6, 15f; Deut 1.8; 2 Kgs 13.23; Jer 33.26 etc.). In the historical retrospect in Ps 105 [→**333**] there is talk of Abraham from various points of view. In the concluding passage we read that in the wanderings in the wilderness God remembered his "holy word" and Abraham his servant (v. 42); here Abraham stands alone as the recipient of the divine promise that has been maintained. In vv. 8-10, however, we read that God remembers the covenant he made with all three patriarchs, with a clear emphasis on Jacob (vv. 10f, see below). And Israel has already been addressed beforehand as "seed of Abraham, his servant, sons of Jacob, his chosen ones" (v. 6). Here, then, Abraham is the ancestor of the people described as the "sons of Jacob," i.e. as the people of the twelve tribes that came from Jacob (cf. 1 Kgs 18.31; Isa 41.8). In the last verse of Micah too (7.20) Abraham and Jacob are mentioned together as the fathers to whom God will maintain loyalty and mercy, from which the present generation will then benefit.

Abraham always remains an individual figure and is never identified with the people. Unlike Jacob. In Genesis already he is accorded the name "Israel" (32.29; 35.10) [→30f], and later "Jacob" is frequently used as a term for the people of Israel, for instance in the form "house of Jacob" (cf. already Ex 19.3, then Isa 2.5f; 8.17; Jer 2.4; Ezek 20.5; Amos 9.8 etc.). In many cases "Jacob" and "Israel" are placed together in *parallelismus membrorum* (Isa 9.7; 10.20; 14.1; Jer 2.4; Ezek 20.5; Mic 1.5; Pss 14.7; 22.24 etc.), especially frequently in the language of Isa 40–55 (40.27; 41.8, 14; 42.24 etc., cf. *ThWAT* III, 771). Ezekiel speaks of God choosing Israel/the house of Jacob in Israel (20.5). According to Ps 114.1 Israel/the house of Jacob fled Egypt. And in Ex 19.3 the community gathered at Sinai is described as the "house of Jacob" and "sons of Israel;" Moses is then to proclaim to them the commandments that follow.

But Jacob can also appear on his own as the bearer of the salvation-historical traditions. Thus Ezekiel expects for his people a future in which they will again live in the land "which I gave to my servant Jacob" (28.25; 37.25). Similarly also in Isa 58.14 it is promised to those who keep the Sabbath that God will feed them with the "inheritance (*naḥ'lāh*) of your father Jacob" [→196]. Psalm 47.5* also praises God for choosing "our inheritance, the pride of Jacob, whom he loves." And in the Song of Moses, Deut 32, Jacob himself is described as God's inheritance, thereby being equated with the people of God.

As in Ezekiel, in Isaiah and Jeremiah too Jacob is repeatedly referred to by the honorific title of "servant." In the divine speech "my servant Jacob" can stand in parallelism with "Israel, whom I have chosen" (Isa 44.1; cf. 45.4; in 44.2 "Jeshurun" instead of "Israel;" cf. also Jer 30.10; 46.27) [→192]. But in Isa 48.20 the term "my servant Jacob" also bears the whole weight of the promise of return.

Jacob is emphasized especially in the divine epithet "God of Jacob" (*'lohê ya'aqob*). It first appears within the series of patriarchs in Ex 3.6, 15; 4.5. But then it often stands alone. In the "last words of David" in 2 Sam 23 the latter is referred to as the "anointed one (*māšîaḥ*) of the God of Jacob" (v. 1). In Isa 2.3 and Mic 4.2 we read that the nations will come up "to the mount of Yhwh, to the house of the God of Jacob." In the Psalms "the God of Jacob" is often found in parallel with "Yhwh Zebaot" in liturgical phrases (Pss 46.8, 12; 84.9). In Ps 81 the festive gathering is called upon to praise the God of Jacob (v. 2), "for this is a decree for Israel, an ordinance of the God of Jacob" (v. 4*); here we see that this divine epithet had its location in the Jerusalem cult. This is also evident in Ps 20, where "the name of the God of Jacob" is called upon for protection (v. 2) and his help is prayed for from Zion (v. 3), on which sacrifices have been brought to him (v. 4). In other Psalms too assistance against enemies (76.7) and the ungodly (75.10) is hoped for, while the latter even wickedly ignore his power (94.7). Also the divine epithet *'ᵃbîr ya'ᵃqob* "the strong one of Jacob" (Gen 49.24) shows a clear relationship with the temple in Jerusalem (Ps 132.2, 5). It is also found in the book of Isaiah in the extended acknowledgement formula, "that I am the Lord, your helper, and your redeemer, the strong one of Jacob" (Isa 49.26; 60.16). Finally, God is also called the "holy one of Jacob" (Isa 29.23) and the "king of Jacob" (41.21).

The personification of Israel as Jacob is found in a very developed form in Amos. In the two first visions in ch. 7 [→**285**] the prophet's petition for his people climaxes in the sentence: "How will Jacob survive? He is so small!" (7.2, 5). Here in the petition for weak, needy Israel, Amos uses the name of Jacob. But in the two following visions, in which no petition is possible for him any more, the name is missing; instead, in the proclamation of judgment of the divine speech we read: "my people Israel" (7.8; 8.2). The name of Jacob thus belongs entirely in the prophetic petition. At other points however the "pride of Jacob" appears, in a strange reversal of Ps 47.4 (see above), as the grounds for a divine proclamation of judgment (Amos 6.8; 8.7; cf. Jeremias 1989). Here there is no longer any question of petition.

In Hosea there is an explicit backward reference to the Jacob traditions of Genesis, together with the Moses tradition of the following books of the Pentateuch (Hos 12). Here there is an emphatic contrast between the saving events of the early times and the later and present actions of Israel: the promise and admonition of God to Jacob at Beth-El (v. 7) is contrasted glaringly with Ephraim's Canaanite attitude towards trade (vv. 8f), and the salvific leading out of Israel from Egypt by the prophet Moses (v. 14) contrasts sharply with the bitter hurt that Ephraim has inflicted on God (v. 15). Between v. 3 and v. 4 a corresponding contrast is also to be seen: the "legal dispute," which God now has with Jacob stands against the background of the early history of salvation.

Many interpreters read v. 47 in the light of v. 3, as if Jacob was already a deceiver in his mother's womb and fought against God on his own [→**273**]. But this relies on an understanding of the text against the wording of the Genesis tradition and in addition isolates this text from the other Jacob traditions of the Hebrew Bible (against this cf. esp. Ackroyd 1963).

So the history of Israel's origins is present in the name of Jacob. At the same time the name contains elements that point to the future [→**170f**]. This applies already to the call to itself in Isa 2.5: "House of Jacob, up, let us walk in the light of the Lord!" Here the hearers and readers are called upon to join the procession of the nations to Zion and to the Torah "at the end of days." Or also concerning the future expectation: "A remnant will return, a remnant of Jacob, to the mighty God" (Isa 10.21). For Jacob a redeemer (*go'ēl* Isa 59.20) and a savior (*môšî*ª') will come, so that Jacob will be able to return and live in peace and security (Jer 30.10), and God will "restore the fortunes of Jacob's tents" (v. 18). Further similar sayings could be added. The special eschatological role of the house of Jacob is finally clear too in Amos 9.8b [→**287**]: God will destroy the "sinful kingdom" from the face of the earth, but he will "not totally destroy the house of Jacob." Here the house of Jacob is the way in which Israel can live on after the inescapable catastrophe.

3. The sequence of the generation of sinners

The "fathers" are not just the "patriarchs" but various generations to which the present generation looks back in various ways (cf. section 1). This is especially clear not only when the earlier generations are mentioned as the recipients of promises and as direct covenant partners with God, but also when they are viewed negatively as the precursors of the present generation. Joshua 24 refers back the furthest [→**679**]: "Long ago your forefathers, including Terah the father of Abraham and Nahor, lived beyond the River and worshiped other gods" (v. 2). No reproach is yet evident in this statement. Rather, the forefathers served the gods of the land or lands in which they lived, as was customary—until God "took Abraham out" of there. The question, however, is how the Israelites plan to behave now that God has led them into the land in which they now live. Obviously among them there is still worship of the gods that the forefathers served "beyond the River" (v. 14). And now there is the added danger that they might serve the new gods of the land, namely the gods of the "Amorites" in whose land they now live (v. 15). Here the Israelites solemnly declare that they will not do this but want to "serve our God Yhwh," who led their fathers (here the "fathers" are the exodus generation) out of Egypt with mighty signs and wonders (vv. 16-18). But the danger persists that the Israelites might again serve "foreign gods" as their forefathers once did.

Ezekiel speaks in detail of the "wickednesses of their fathers" in Egypt which the prophet is to call to mind in the present generation (Ezek 20.4ff). The forefathers worshiped the "idols of Egypt" which the prophet calls "abominations" (*šiqqûṣîm*) (vv. 7f) and refused to give them up. In the wilderness God then called upon their sons to obey his commandments and not to defile themselves with the "gods of their fathers;" but they too refused (vv. 18-21). The next generation of the "fathers" enraged God by sacrificing on the "high places" in the land that God had brought them into (vv. 27-29). In so doing they rendered themselves impure like their own fathers (v. 30) and so God will take them to court as he did their fathers (v. 36). So this is a long story of sinful generations in which each becomes the father genera-tion for the next and each bequeaths its idolatrous tendencies to the next. But then the prophet's speech jumps back to the beginning of the series of fathers when we are told that God will ultimately lead those banished in exile back into the land that he swore to give to their fathers (v. 42; cf. also 47.14). Here the fathers are again in view as the bearers of the promise at the beginning of the story of Israel. Thus in this text two different ways of viewing the "fathers" are contrasted: on the one hand the fathers as bearers of the promise, on the other hand the fathers in the chain of generations, with the negative aspect of the continuation of sinful behavior being dominant.

In the book of Jeremiah there is particularly frequent talk of the "fa-thers." Again the various aspects are evident there. On the one hand numerous passages are to be found which speak of the fathers at the beginning of the story. Repeatedly there is talk of the "day (*b'yôm*) on which I led your fathers out of Egypt" (Jer 7.22; 11.4, 7; 31.32; 34.13) or "on which your fathers left Egypt" (7.25). On this day God con-cluded a covenant with them (31.32; 34.13), commanding them to listen to his voice and follow his commandments (11.4, 7; cf. 7.22f; 17.22; 44.10), and from that day on he sent his prophets to them as warners (7.25). A second group of texts speaks of the "land that I have sworn to give to their/your fathers" (11.5; 32.22) or "have given" (3.18; 7.7; 16.15; 24.10; 25.5; 30.3; 35.15; cf. 7.14; 23.39). In some cases the concern is with the return from exile into this land that was once given to the fathers (3.18; 16.15). Here therefore the fathers are the generation that took possession of the land, who—in line with the account given in Numbers and Deuteronomy—are not identical to the exodus generation. The positive aspect of the promise or giving of the land to the forefathers is foregrounded here.

On the other hand in Jeremiah we also find texts that speak of the fathers as those with whom the history of Israel's sins began. This is evident already in the fact that in the statements about the commandments that God gave to the fathers of the exodus generation, we read the refrain-like comment: "but they did not listen" (7.24, 26; 11.8; 17.23; 34.14; cf. 35.15). Jeremiah expressly brings this topic to the center in his first words after his call. The loyalty and love of Israel in the time of the wandering in the wilderness (2.2f) he contrasts with the reproach against the first generation in the land [→207]: "What fault did your fathers find in me, that they strayed so far from me?" (v. 5). Instead of gratitude for God's having led them out of Egypt, guided them in the wilderness and brought them into the fertile land, "you came and defiled my land and made my inheritance detestable" (vv. 6f). The "nothingness" (*hebel*) is named: Baal (v. 8). What is fundamentally wrong in Israel's relationship with its God, the worship of Baal and other gods "which are worthless," had its beginnings already among the fathers of the first generation after the settlement in the land (cf. 9.13; 23.27; cf. 44.21). It is the "sins of the fathers," from which the Israelites now suffer (14.20), and to which however they constantly return (11.10; 44.9, 17). But if Israel were to turn around, they would also acknowledge that "we and our fathers have sinned" (3.25).

In Hosea we find a message echoing Jer 2.1f concerning the unclouded relationship between God and Israel in the period in the wilderness (Hos 9.10a). Micah too gives the fathers as the recipients of divine favor (Mic 7.20 etc.). However, in Hosea's message the apostasy to Ba'al Pe'or immediately follows (Hos 9.10b). Only the negative aspect is evident in Amos: already the fathers of Judah ran after lies (gods) (Amos 2.4). The book of Zechariah begins with a sermon-like call to penitence, the first words of which read: "The Lord was very angry with your forefathers" (Zech 1.2; cf. also 8.14), and in which the addressees are called upon: "do not be like your forefathers" (v. 4) who did not listen to the preaching of the prophets [→306] and had to suffer the consequences (vv. 5, 6a; whether the concluding sentence in v. 6b, "they returned ..." applies to the forefathers or the hearers of Zechariah's sermon is disputed). Finally, Malachi also speaks positively of the "covenant of our fathers" which his contemporaries are now defiling (2.10), and also of the fact that the Israelites have departed from the commandments of Yhwh "since the days of the forefathers" (3.7).

In the Psalms too the various ways of speaking of the forefathers are found. The fathers told their descendants of God's mighty deeds (Pss 44.2; 78.3): how he gave the Torah in Israel, which the fathers are to pass on to their children (78.5), how he performed miracles in front of them in Egypt and on the path along which he led them (78.12-16). They trusted in him and were saved (22.5). But we also hear other notes that put the image of the forefathers in a dim light. They tested God at Massah and Meribah, even though they had seen his miraculous deeds (Ps 95.8f). And in a strange heightening of the statements we read that God commanded the fathers to teach their children the Torah so that they would not turn out like their fathers (Ps 78.5, 8). Here the duty to pass on the will of God and the insight into their own disobedience run seamlessly into each other. But then the self-accusation in Ps 106 is very clear: "We have sinned, even as our fathers did ... Our fathers gave no thought to your miracles" (vv. 6f) [→333]. Here the sinful chain of generations begins already in Egypt, and this awareness marks the historical picture of this psalm.

Further texts could be added. After the separation of the two part-kingdoms of Israel and Judah we are told that the people of Judah angered God with their sins even more than their fathers (1 Kgs 14.22). The great penitential prayers of the late period also see the history of Israel's sin as beginning already with the fathers. Besides Dan 9.16 and Ezra 9.7 it is Neh 9 in particular [→399] where the story of the leading of the forefathers out of Egypt and their being led in the wilderness is described (vv. 9-15), but where there is then mention of their disobedience which began already in the wilderness, which despite everything met time and again with God's mercy (vv. 16-31), right through to the present situation in which Israel has to confess: "See we are servants in the land that you gave to our fathers..." (v. 36).

Here right at the conclusion the forefathers are again in view as the recipients of the divine gifts that are fundamental for Israel's existence. The chain of generations is thus not only a chain of sinners and sinning, but it is anchored in the figures that stand at the beginning and with which God began his saving history with Israel. The forefathers were not unblemished and sin-free either. But their story was determined by the promises and the leading of God. Israel's history as a whole can thus never be presented and understood without this beginning. The "forefathers" are and remain the "fathers" *tout court*, and Israel's identity is in the first place determined by the fact that this people is the community of the descendants of these fathers.

§ 8

The Promised and Entrusted Land

1. The land that I shall give you

"Go ... to the land that I will show you" reads the divine commission to Abraham, with which the story of Israel begins (Gen 12.1) [→**21**]. The election and call of the "fathers of Israel *tout court*" is indivisibly linked with the land into which the first steps of Israel's historical beginnings lead. It is of fundamental significance for Israel's self-understanding that it does not view this land as a fixed possession right from the beginning, but as the fulfillment of a divine promise. It can be seen precisely as the essential content of God's covenant statement to Israel (Gen 17.7f). And frequently there is almost formulaic talk of the "land that the Lord swore to give to your fathers" (or similar words—Ex 6.8; 13.11; 33.1; Num 14.23; Deut 1.8; 6.10, 18; Josh 21.43; Neh 9.15 etc.).

At the same time however the first phase in Israel's history is marked by the delay in the fulfillment of this promise. Already in the first divine speech to Abraham there is a notable shift of emphasis when we read: "I will give the land to your descendants" (12.7). Abraham himself will thus not experience the fulfillment of the promise of the land and nor will the first generations of his descendants. On the contrary, they will live in a foreign land and have to serve until God leads them out of there—for four generations (15.16) or even four hundred years (v. 13; cf. Talmon 1990). So here right at the beginning of the story of the patriarchs there is anticipation of the sojourn in Egypt and the exodus from there.

The promise of the land and its fulfillment is thus the key element that links together the various stages in the beginnings of Israel's history. Moses will lead the Israelites out of Egypt into the land, which is initially presented as a beautiful and extensive land "flowing with milk and honey" (Ex 3.8) but is then identified as the land promised to the fathers (6.4, 8) [→**41**]. In the decisive crisis on Sinai Moses appeals to God's sworn promise (32.13) and God reissues his command to Moses to lead the people into the land promised to the fathers. The next big crisis has to do with the reconnoitering of the land that "God will give to the Israelites" (Num 13.2). Again it is Moses' petition that enables the continuation of the way into the promised land (14.17-19) [→**71**]; but no one of the generation that has rejected God here (except for Caleb, 14.24) will see the land that God has sworn to give to the fathers (14.23).

When the Israelites finally reach the border of the land, it is established by means of a census that no member of that rebellious generation is still alive (Num 26.64f). Moses will now divide up the land between those that are alive now. The term *naḥ^alāh* "inheritance" (vv. 53ff) appears here, which will play an important part at various times in the future. (Cf. von Rad 1943.)

Excursus: The land as *naḥ^alāh*

In the great speech at the border of the promised land Moses speaks a number of times of the "land which the Lord gives you as a *naḥ^alāh*" (Deut 4.21, 38; 12.9; 25.19; 26.1 etc.; cf. also Ps 105.11). In other texts there is mention of the fulfillment of this promise (Ps 135.12; 136.21; cf. 1 Kgs 8.36; Jer 3.19), but also of its being endangered (Jer 17.4). Alongside the noun *naḥ^alāh* the verb *nḥl* in the hiphil is used in the same sense (Deut 12.10; 19.3; Jer 3.18; 12.14, occasionally also in the qal, Ex 32.13; Deut 19.14).

The word *naḥ^alāh* can be described as a theological legal term. It expresses the fact that the land is given over to Israel for its disposal and use, but that it remains God's possession. The figurative meaning of this term comes to expression in the divine assurance and gift of the whole land to Israel. Everything that goes beyond this is derived from it. Thus Moses is given the task by God of dividing up the land as *naḥ^alāh* among the individual tribes in accordance with their size (Num 26.53-56). Moses delegates the execution of this duty to Joshua (Deut 1.38; 3.28; 31.7). The performance of this commission is noted in summary in Josh 11.23 and then expounded in full detail in chs. 13–21. Thus the whole land that God "swore to give to the fathers" is divided up as *naḥ^alāh*, and Israel has come to the promised "rest"

(21.43-45; cf. Deut 12.9). (In Josh 23.4 instead of the land it is the "remaining" nations that are allocated to the tribes as *naḥᵃlāh*.)

What is presented here as a fundamental theological concept is discernible in other texts in its significance for life in the land and for the questions of the possession of the land. The "wise woman" in Abel Beth Maacah describes the threatened destruction of the city as the destruction of the *naḥᵃlāh* of Yhwh (2 Sam 20.19). Another "wise woman" sees in the killing of her (fictional) son the elimination of her family from the *naḥᵃlāh* of God (14.16). In the same vein, on his flight from Saul David complains that his pursuers are excluding him from participation in the *naḥᵃlāh* of Yhwh and thus want to force him to serve other gods (1 Sam 26.19). So here the land as *naḥᵃlāh* is also the area in which one can worship God who gave the land.

The legal side of the term *naḥᵃlāh* is evident especially where the concern is with the individual's or the individual family's share in the possession of the land. Thus Naboth refuses to hand over his vineyard to king Ahab because it is the "*naḥᵃlāh* of his fathers" (1 Kgs 21.3) [→**140**]. The account of the conflict shows clearly that this is a fundamental tenet of Israelite law to which even the king must submit. This is emphasized sharply when Jezebel, the king's non-Israelite wife, sets herself above this by means of a flagrant distortion of the law. The legal character of the term *naḥᵃlāh* is also evident in Num 27, where there is discussion of the question what will become of the *naḥᵃlāh* of a family when no male heirs are available. Moses produces a divine instruction at this point, which reads: "If a man dies and leaves no son, give his inheritance over to his daughter" (v. 8). So here the *naḥᵃlāh* is the inheritance of the individual family. In Num 36 this question is taken a step further: women who are recipients of a *naḥᵃlāh* should marry within their tribe, so that the *naḥᵃlāh* remains within the tribe.

Finally, the narrative of Naomi and Ruth also belongs in this context. The point at issue is the repurchase of the inheritance of a family which has fallen into other hands as a result of special circumstances. The basis for this is formed by the regulations in Lev 25, where the term *go'ēl*, "redeemer," also appears (vv. 25f) [→**371**], which plays an important role in the book of Ruth (Ruth 2.20; 3.9, 12 etc.). Here the restoration of the family's inheritance is connected also with the problem of "levirate marriage," in which the concern is to "maintain the name of the dead with his *naḥᵃlāh*" (4.5, 10). Here the problem dealt with in Num 27 is seen again from another point of view, because the deceased has not left a daughter either.

In the contexts dealt with last we meet the concept of *naḥ⁽lāh* in connection with the concrete daily affairs of the Israelites. But there is also another side to it. The *naḥ⁽lāh* given by God can also be viewed as God's own *naḥ⁽lāh*. It has been made "detestable" by Israel (Jer 2.7; 16.18) and been plundered by enemies (50.11), but God also gives it life through his rain (Ps 68.10). As a representative of the land the temple mount can also be viewed as God's *naḥ⁽lāh* (Ex 15.17; cf. Ps 79.1). Finally also Israel itself is called God's *naḥ⁽lāh*, often in connection with the term '*am*, "people" (Deut 4.20; 9.26, 29; 1 Kgs 8.51; Isa 47.6; Ps 28.9 etc.) or *šēbeṭ*, "tribe" (Isa 63.17; Jer 10.16; Ps 74.2). According to Ps 33.12 God "chose" Israel as his *naḥ⁽lāh*; and Saul is anointed as *nāgîd* over this *naḥ⁽lāh* of God (1 Sam 10.1; cf. also 2 Sam 21.3).

Thus the term *naḥ⁽lāh* is shown from the most varied perspectives. In the vast majority of cases it is connected with the land. On the one hand it has its concrete legal side in inheritance law as "inheritance" or "share of the inheritance" that is assigned to an individual family; on the other hand it possesses a marked theological aspect as the land given by God, the land promised and given to Israel generally being referred to as a whole as *naḥ⁽lāh*. This theological way of looking at it is as it were transcended when the land or the temple mount and finally even Israel itself can be referred to as God's *naḥ⁽lāh*. In all its various manifestations the *naḥ⁽lāh* is in the final analysis God's possession, which is handed over and left to Israel as a possession given on trust, as it were as a "fief." This is expressed in summary form in the sentence: "The land is mine and you are but aliens and my tenants" (Lev 25.23).

★★★★★

Warning signs are set up before the distribution of the land can take place. The gift of the land does not occur without conditions. In Deuteronomy, Moses' great farewell speech, right at the beginning in a long sermon the interaction between the keeping of the commandments given through Moses and life in the land is emphasized. The introductory sentence reads: "Hear now, Israel, the decrees and laws I am about to teach you. Follow them so that you may live and may go in and take possession of the land that the Lord, the God of your fathers, is giving you" (Deut 4.1; cf. v. 5). The keeping of the commandments is prescribed here at the entry into the promised land (cf. Perlitt 1983). So then the expulsion of Israel from the land and its scattering among the nations is announced as a consequence of the failure to keep the commandments, especially as regards the maintenance of the Yhwh cult (vv. 26f). Here already the exile looms on the horizon as a constantly threatening possibility. This is not, however, the last word; for if Israel turns back, God himself will turn again to Israel. He will not forget the covenant that he swore with Israel's fathers (vv. 30f). At the conclusion the positive link between the keeping of the commandments and Israel's good life in the land given by God is again emphasized (v. 40).

A rather similar admonition and warning is also contained in Lev 26, the great concluding chapter in the giving of the law on Sinai [→**68**]. Here the negative consequences of not keeping the divine commandments are described in various stages. The land is brought into it, in that it no longer produces its fruits (v. 20), wild animals and plagues rage throughout the land (vv. 16, 22, 25) and the land is finally devastated (vv. 31f). Israel itself is scattered among the nations (v. 33). But this is not the last word here either, but at the conclusion we read that God will remember (*zākar*) the covenant with the fathers and also the land (v. 42).

In another direction again Deuteronomy warns Israelites who line up to take possession of the land. When all this has been granted to them they should not think that this is their due. For they are the smallest among the nations and God has done all this "because he loved you and because he kept the oath that he swore to your fathers" (Deut 7.7f). Nor are they to think that it is their own strength with which they have achieved all this; rather it is God himself, "who gives you the ability to produce wealth, and so confirms his covenant, which he swore to your forefathers, as it is today" (8.17f). And finally it is not their own righteousness either, "but on account of the wickedness of these nations, the Lord your God will drive them out before you, to accomplish what he swore to your fathers, to Abraham, Isaac and Jacob" (9.5).

So the reader knows, even before Israel has entered the land, that the gift of the land is on the one hand the fulfillment of the promise that God gave to the fathers and confirmed by his oath, but that on the other hand it is indissolubly connected with the responsibility for Israel to keep the commandments of God given through Moses. And he/she also knows that the infringement of this responsibility can as a final consequence mean the loss of the land. Here we see that the cited texts are not only written with a forward look toward the next stage in the history of Israel, but that they have also taken up and reflected upon the experiences that Israel has itself had in the land, and now look and point forward to these.

2. When you come into the land

The accounts and evaluations of the Israelites' entry into the promised land in the Hebrew Bible are highly complex and sometimes even contradictory. The first part of the book of Joshua (Josh 1–12) describes the completion of the occupation of the land "just as the Lord had said to Moses" (11.23); toward the end of the book this is repeated in detail (21.43-45) [→**100**]. In each case there is talk of the "rest" that God has given the Israelites in the land they have now taken into their possession. The occupation takes place with God's help, accompanied by miraculous events such as the collapse of the walls of Jericho (ch. 6) and the standing-still of the sun at Gibeon (10.12-14). But there are also full reports of violent battles in which the Israelites always prove victorious.

When, toward the end of his life, Joshua is then given the divine task of dividing up the land between the tribes, at the beginning stands the surprising sentence: "Much of the land remains to be possessed" (13.1). There follows a long list of areas that have not been taken (v. 26). In the following it is expressly said a number of times that the Israelites had not taken particular areas (13.13; 15.63; 16.10; 17.11-13). This corresponds with repeated admonitions to take the remaining land (13.1; 18.3; 23.5). At the beginning of the book of Judges too, there is detailed talk of cities and areas of the land that have not yet been taken (1.18f, 21, 27-35; 3.13).

Here it is evident that the Israelites' entry into the land can be viewed from very different points of view. For one thing, the fact that the Israelites lived in the land and that they were granted "rest" there for a time, could be viewed as a whole as the fulfillment of the promises which, according to the tradition, God had given to the fathers. For another, however, the real and certainly not always conflict-free proximity to other neighboring population groups constantly issued a challenge to reflective discussion. The question was bound to arise why the domination of the land was so incomplete and why the proximity to other groups led to conflicts time and again.

In a first farewell speech (Josh 23) Joshua gives an explanation. As previously in Deuteronomy (Deut 4.26f) he renews the commitment to follow all that is written "in the book of the Torah of Moses" (Josh 23.6), and announces expulsion from the land as the consequence for not keeping the law (vv. 13, 15f). The critical point where there is a threat of transgression of the Torah of Moses is the contact with the remaining peoples, which could lead to the worship of their gods (v. 7). Thus these nations are a "snare" and a "trap" for Israel, a whip and a thorn, until Israel will finally "perish from this good land, which the Lord your God has given you" (v. 13). At the beginning of the book of Judges this view is developed again, where we read that God did not drive out these nations in order thereby to "test" Israel (Judg 2.21f; 3.1; cf. 2.3) [→101]. Fraternization with them can only lead to the transgression of the covenant that God made with Israel and its fathers (Josh 23.16; Judg 2.20).

This view is found in the prophets too, that apostasy from the God of Israel began already immediately after the occupation of the land. Thus in Jeremiah we read that during the wanderings in the wilderness Israel's relationship with God was unclouded (2.2f) [→207]; but when they came into the fertile land that God had given them, they no longer asked: "Where is the Lord, who brought us out of Egypt?" but turned to other gods (v. 48), thereby defiling the land, which here in the divine speech is called "my land," and made God's *naḥᵃlāh* "detestable" (v. 7). This reproach is directed to the "fathers," i.e. all the generations that came before those that are now addressed (v. 5), especially the leading *cadres*: in the first place the priests, who are responsible for the maintenance of the Torah, then the "shepherds" of the people and finally even the prophets (v. 8). Similarly, Ezekiel also sees Israel's apostasy on the entry into the land, where the Israelites began bringing their sacrifices "on every high hill and under every green tree" (Ezek 20.27-29) [→247].

In the Psalms we also see the different perspectives from which Israel's entry into the land can be viewed. Thus the two "twin psalms" 105 and 106 [→333] stand in contrast with each other. Psalm 105 is a pure hymn of praise, in which the entry into the land stands at the conclusion as a gift to Israel with no negative undertone. In Psalm 106, however, the history of Israel's sinning begins already in Egypt and carries on through the wilderness wanderings on to the entry into the land. Here we read that they did not wipe out the nations as God had commanded them to do, and had defiled themselves with the "gods of Canaan" (vv. 38f).

This ambivalence in the assessment of the origins of Israel's history is certainly determined in part by the present situation at the time of the composition or redaction of the texts. At the same time, however, it reveals the inner tensions that held sway in Israel and which came to expression time and again especially in the religious realm. In addition, Israel's endangered position is reflected in its political situation between the great power blocks in the south and the north with their own changing fortunes, which often had direct consequences for Israel. In particular the loss of the land, i.e. deportation and captivity in exile, was always there before them as a threatening danger. But again and again this gave rise to the question why this great gift, given to the people by God, could be lost.

3. A Sabbath for the land

"When you enter the land that I am going to give you, the land itself must observe a Sabbath to the Lord" (Lev 25.2). These words introduce a fundamental rule in the administration of the land given by God. It is also found in Ex 23.10f: "For six years you are to sow your fields and harvest the crops, but during the seventh year let the land lie unplowed and unused. Then the poor among your people may get food from it, and the wild animals may eat what they leave." In v. 12 this is paralleled with: "Six days do your work, but on the seventh day you are to rest (*šāmaṭ*)." Here the rhythm of seven years is brought into connection with that of seven days. Just as people and animals are to live in a particular alternation between work and relaxation, so too the land. The determination of the seventh years as a "Sabbath year" is thus not motivated only by the agricultural consideration of giving the land a fallow year to recover, but, just like the Sabbath, contains a fundamental religious element. This might be called a "sacral fallow period." Added to this is the social aspect, as the crops that grow of their own accord during the seventh year are freely available to the needy.

In Lev 25 the regulations about the land are placed under the summary statement: "the land is mine and you are but aliens and my tenants" (v. 23). Here the "Sabbath" of the land (vv. 2-7, 20-22), is linked with other social and legal prescriptions. After seven Sabbath years, i.e. after 49 years, a jubilee year is to be declared in which a general restoration of the earlier owner relationships is carried out (vv. 8-12, with explanations in vv. 13-17). Other regulations are added in which the concern is with the buying-back or ransom of an Israelite who has fallen into poverty, the jubilee year also having a part to play here (vv. 25-55). So here the stress on the economic cultivation of the land has shifted to the social domain. In conclusion we read, in obvious parallel with v. 23: "The Israelites belong to me as servants" (v. 55). The words that follow set this in the broad salvation-historical framework: "They are my servants, whom I brought out of Egypt. I am the Lord your God."

In Deut 15 the Sabbath year is already viewed from the social perspective. It is described as the "(year of) leaving alone" (*šᵉmiṭṭāh*, v. 1) (cf. the verb *šmṭ* in Ex 23.10). It is not said whether the social rules collected here are intended to replace the sacral fallow period or supplement it. But it is clear that Deuteronomy has no independent interest in the agricultural side of the *šᵉmiṭṭāh*.

In Ex 23 the Sabbath commandment is followed by the list of the three annual feasts [→535]: "Three times a year you are to celebrate a festival to me" (v. 14). In the festivals too there is a close connection with the land and the natural cycle of the harvest year. At the beginning stands the "feast of unleavened bread" (*ḥag hammaṣṣôt*, v. 15), during which bread from the new harvest is eaten without the "old yeast." The second is the "feast of harvest" (*ḥag haqqāṣîr*), with "the firstfruits of the crops you sow in your field" (v. 16a); Ex 34.22 speaks of the firstfruits of the wheat harvest, i.e. of the last type of crop to be harvested. The third is the "feast of gathering" (*ḥag hā'āsîp*, v. 16b), i.e. the grape harvest, which is indicated by the addition "at the end of the year." The name that become customary later, "feast of booths" (*ḥag hassukkôt*, cf. Deut 16.13, 16) relates to living in the shelters in the vineyards (cf. Isa 1.8) during harvest time.

In the festivals, then, we see once again the close connection between Israel's life and the land. But the festivals have also undergone a development, in which this original connection became linked with other aspects (cf. 1991e). In particular the festivals were connected with events in Israel's early history. This is already the case for the Massot festival in Ex 23, where the month of Abib is given as the date of the festival: "for in that month you came out of Egypt" (v. 15). Staying in shelters is justified in Lev 23 on the grounds "that I made the Israelites live in booths when I brought them out of Egypt" (vv.

42f). For the second of the three festivals, which is also called the "feast of weeks" (Deut 16.10, 16), there is an indication in the admonition: "Remember that you were slaves in Egypt" (v. 12). The presentation of the firstfruits in Deut 26.1-11 [→**680**], which is linked with a creed-like review of the exodus story, seems also to point to this festival. But this further development will need to be discussed in another context.

4. Promise and fulfillment, loss and recovery

The land as Israel's living space is present in almost all parts of the Hebrew Bible. It bridges the various epochs of the biblical history of Israel from its foundation in the time of the patriarchs to the last stages that have been set down in the canonical texts. At the beginning stands the promise and assurance of God that he will give the land to Abraham and his descendants. This promise is repeated time and again and called to mind in the later phases of the story. In Ex 6.2-8, in the divine speech to Moses [→**41f**], the bridge is cast from the promise to the patriarchs to the situation of the Israelites in Egypt, and the rescue announced here is depicted as the fulfillment of the divine promise. Even after the leading out of Egypt there are constant reminders of the connection between the fathers and the exodus (e.g. Num 20.15f; Deut 26.5-9; Josh 24.4-6).

The assurance that God will give the Israelites the land, however, appears more and more frequently without express reference to the fathers. "The land that I will give you" is, as it were, the leading and accompanying motto in the last phase of the occupation of the land (with variations in the wording: Num 13.2; 15.2; 20.12, 24; 27.12; 33.53; Deut 1.25; 5.31 etc.). The commandments collected in Deuteronomy, which already presuppose life in the land, are also introduced and repeatedly justified like this (Deut 12.1; 16.20; 17.14; 18.9 etc.). And finally this is the light in which the entry into the land under Joshua's leadership is seen (Josh 1.2, 6 [mentioning the fathers], 11 etc.). Then at the conclusion of the reports about the occupation and distribution of the land, once again there is a reminder of God's sworn promise (21.43) [→**100**], which is summarized: "Not one of all the Lord's good promises to the house of Israel failed; every one was fulfilled" (v. 45).

The claim here is that there is a complete correspondence between the promise of the land and its fulfillment. This is echoed again in almost the same words in the blessing with which Solomon concludes the "temple-dedication prayer" (1 Kgs 8.56) [→**121**]. In both texts there is mention of the "rest" that God has granted his people (1 Kgs 8.56 *mᵉnûḥāh*, Josh 21.44 with the verb *nwḥ* hi.). It had also been promised already in Deuteronomy (Deut 12.9f; 25.19; cf. von Rad 1933). It is restated later that the rest was realized during the reigns of David (2 Sam 7.1) [→**112**] and Solomon (1 Kgs 5.18). Here we are even told that everyone could sit in safety "under his own vine and fig tree" (1 Kgs 4.25) [→**118**], an expression found in prophetic texts as an eschatological promise (Mic 4.4; Zech 3.10) [→**295**]. Then in Chronicles the birth of Solomon is announced as "a man of peace and rest" (*'îš mᵉnûḥāh*, 1 Chron 22.9).

In Solomon's temple dedication prayer, however, the possibility is envisaged beforehand that (the) Israelites will sin and therefore be delivered up by God to their enemies and be led captive away from this land into a foreign land, "far or near" (v. 46). This is reminiscent of such texts as Lev 26 and Deut 4, in which deportation from the land is mentioned as the ultimate escalation of the self-induced threat from enemies and other plagues; but like these texts, Solomon's prayer too hopes for a "turn around" and ultimate return of those banished in exile (vv. 47-51). When the northern kingdom comes to an end this expectation then becomes reality, but without the turn for the better that Solomon's prayer hopes and prays for. Israel is carried off to Assyria "to the present day" (2 Kgs 17.6, 23). Later we read: "So Judah went into captivity, away from her land" (25.21). So Israel has walked the path of the promise of the land, through its fulfillment and on to the loss of the land. The land is the constant in Israel's life, in expectation, possession and loss. But loss does not mean the complete end of the story that began with the promise of the land, but exile. Herein lies still the hope of return and the regaining of the land, as the conclusion to the books of Kings cautiously puts it (2 Kgs 25.27-30) [→**152**].

The imminent or already actual loss of the land plays a role also in the prophetic books. In Isaiah's great vision (Isa 6) the prophet's question "How long?" [→**173**] is answered: "Until the cities lie ruined and without inhabitant … and the land is utterly forsaken" (vv. 11f). Later texts in Isaiah speak already from the situation of the ruined and forsaken land that is anticipated here (e.g. 49.17ff; 54.13; cf. 1989, 79 [167f]). Especially in Jeremiah and Ezekiel, contemporaries of the fall of the kingdom of Judah, the end of the undisturbed life in the land is one of the dominant themes. Jeremiah's great temple sermon (Jer 7) ends with the divine announcement: "I will thrust you from my presence, just as I did all your brothers, the people of Ephraim" (v. 15). In ch. 25 we find a long speech in which Jeremiah's proclamations of judgment of twenty-three years of preaching are summarized: the land will soon be visited by Nebuchadnezzar, so that it will lie waste and ruined and not even the basic sounds of human life will be heard (vv. 9–11).

Jeremiah's concern then is primarily with the relationship between those taken into captivity and those who remain in the land (ch. 24) [→225f] and with the question how long the time of exile will last (chs. 28 and 29). The hope of return and restoration then resounds more and more clearly here, as also in the following chapters 30 to 33: "'The days are coming,' declares the Lord, 'when I will bring my people Israel and Judah back (*šûb šbût*) from captivity and restore them to the land I gave to their forefathers to possess'" (30.3). But this is still no more than a hope for the future.

Ezekiel sees the problems as it were from the other side, from the viewpoint of those who have already been afflicted by the loss of the land and are now having to live in exile. His sign-acts and judgment sermons are directed in the first instance against those who have remained in Jerusalem and the land (ch. 47 and *passim*) [→238]. Here we see, even more obviously than in Jeremiah, the shift of theological viewpoint. Those taken into exile have already experienced the judgment of God and are now permitted to hope that they will be brought back some day. Those who have remained in the land, however, are still walking in the old sinful ways, and God's judgment is still ahead of them. But after the fall of Jerusalem (33.21) attention turns toward the future. The desolate mountains will become green again and produce fruit and be inhabited by the numerous returning people of the "house of Israel" (ch. 36) [→254f]. In a vision, Ezekiel himself is allowed to participate in the reviving of the dried-out bones of Israel (ch. 37), which God will then put back into their land (v. 14). And finally in a last vision, Ezekiel sees how Jerusalem and the temple are reconstructed and how at last the land is redistributed among the tribes (chs. 40–48). In this visionary view a new beginning thus comes about as before in the time of Joshua.

And there really was a new beginning! In reality it was, certainly, much more modest than in the prophetic visions. As before in earlier periods of its history, Israel's fate was dependent entirely on developments in the great power centers of the Near East. The conquest of the Babylonian Empire by the Persians and their religious policy, which took quite a different line with respect to the nations they subdued or ruled, opened a new chapter in the history of Israel. God "awakened the spirit" of the Persian king Cyrus, as we read both at the beginning of the book of Ezra (Ezra 1.1) and the end of the books of Chronicles (2 Chron 36.22). This picks up on the hopes and expectations that are found in the prophets. Jeremiah's prediction is expressly mentioned in both texts (cf. Jer 29–31), and talk of the "awakening" of Cyrus sounds just like the texts of the book of Isaiah (Isa 41.2, 25; 45.13).

The return to the land and the readjustment of circumstances are central in the books of Ezra and Nehemiah. But a clear shift of emphasis is discernible by comparison with texts from the time before the exile: interest is primarily focused on Jerusalem. In the first part of the book of Ezra (Ezra 1–6) [**390**], the reconstruction of the temple is in the foreground, while in Nehemiah it is the rebuilding of the city wall (Neh 1–6) [→**396f**]. The "land" is present in its inhabitants, who also help in the building of the wall in Jerusalem (cf. Neh 3 and 11), but it is not a separate object of endeavor or of reflection. (On the extension of Judah in this period cf. Donner 1984/86, 425, ^{2}459.)

But anyhow, Israel has returned to its land. So it can view its history in a continuous context again. The express reference to the origins is made in particular in the great prayers (Ezra 9.7ff; Neh 9.7ff). This shows the consciousness of this continuity, even if the story of Israel's sins is placed in the foreground. Much of what is written in the writings of the Hebrew Bible about the land in Israel's history has to be viewed from the point of view of a retrospective overview like this.

§ 9

The First and the Second Exodus

In the previous chapter we talked about the exodus from the point of view of the land in particular. In the process the dual aspect of the exodus also came into view already: promise and fulfillment, loss and regaining of the land. In what follows the topic of exodus will be considered again in more detail from the point of view of the people of Israel.

1. Israel in Egypt

As the pentateuchal narratives progress an entirely new phase in the history of Israel begins with Israel's stay in Egypt. In place of the figures of the individual "fathers" and their families we now have the "people." It is certainly no coincidence that the expression *'am*, "people," is found first on the lips of the Egyptian Pharaoh, who feels threatened by the growing mass of "children of Israel" (Ex 1.9) [→35]. A conflict is looming.

But first of all this people is silently and helplessly subject to oppression by the Egyptians. And it has no representative who might be in a position to lead it and take its part vis-à-vis the Egyptians. The figure of Moses first appears only on the fringes and without recognizable relation to the desolate situation of the Israelites (Ex 1f). It is not until Ex 3 (prepared for by 2.23-25) that Moses is involved in the action. He is given the commission of leading Israel out of Egyptian slavery. This marks the start of the history of the "exodus." Strictly speaking, however, one should speak not of the "exodus" (ἔξοδος) but of the "leading out," for in the vast majority of passages in the Hebrew Bible that speak of this event, the concern is with God's initiative in "leading out" (*hôṣî*) Israel from Egypt, or having "led" it "up" (*heʿlāh*) or being in the process of doing so (cf. 1997b).

On the level of the present text there are narrative lines of connection with the preceding story. Thus Abraham is granted fulfillment of the promise of the land only for his descendants and only for a time following a lengthy stay in slavery in a foreign land (Gen 16.13-16). Jacob is given the assurance that God will make him a great nation in Egypt and bring him back again (46.3f). Conversely, Moses is promised that God will lead the Israelites out of slavery in Egypt into the land that he promised the fathers on oath (Ex 6.7f) [→**41**]. In some short creed-like formulae such as Deut 26.5 too ("A wandering Aramean was my father") and 1 Sam 12.8 ("When Jacob came to Egypt") a reference back to the time of the patriarchs is discernible. But none of this is to be seen in the first chapters of the book of Exodus. And even in the reminiscence we read only: "We were slaves of Pharaoh in Egypt" (Deut 6.21; cf. also Deut 5.15).

Thus the story of Israel as a people begins in the contour-less shape of the enslaved people in Egypt. A change starts to come about only when Moses has a divine encounter on the "mount of God." At first he can only address the deity he meets here with the quite unspecific expression *hā'ᵉlohîm*, "the deity" (Ex 3.6, 11, 13). But this deity himself then makes the connection with Israel's prehistory, by introducing himself as "the God of your father, God of Abraham, God of Isaac, God of Jacob" (v. 6). Finally God even gives and explains his name: Yhwh (v. 15). The purpose of the events to come is also put into words. God intends to free Israel from its oppressed situation (*hiṣṣîl*, 3.8), in fact he wants to redeem it (*gā'al*, 6.6) and save it (*hôšîᵃ'*, 14.30). In view of the situation in which the Israelites find themselves, this announced divine deed has fundamental significance for Israel's further history: it is only upon its liberation from slavery in Egypt that Israel gains its independent existence as a nation.

2. Exodus as founding experience

The events of the leading out of Israel from Egypt and its prehistory are described in an extremely dramatic manner. They begin with a sharp confrontation between Moses and Pharaoh. But it is immediately evident that the real confrontation is between Pharaoh and the God of Israel. With his abrupt "I do not know Yhwh" (Ex 5.2) [→**44**], Pharaoh presents himself as a resolute opponent of Yhwh. He thereby represents as it were "all the gods of Egypt," over which Yhwh will now execute judgment (12.12).

The ever more acerbic dispute as the plagues escalate has one major aim: to bring about an acknowledgement of Yhwh. Pharaoh himself has already provided the key term in his declaration that he does not "know" (*yāda*') Yhwh and with the inherent refusal to "acknowledge" him. This is now contrasted time and again with the "acknowledgement formula," introduced by the divine message that Moses is to pass on to the Israelites: "You will know that I am Yhwh, your God, who leads you out of Egyptian bondage" (6.7). The Egyptians will then "know that I am Yhwh" (7.5), as will Pharaoh (v. 17). The latter will recognize in particular that "there is no one like Yhwh, our God" (8.10) and "that I, Yhwh, am in this land" (v. 22, cf. 9.14) and indeed that "the earth is the Lord's" (9.29). The Israelites, who are witnesses of all this, will later tell their children of these "signs" that God performed in Egypt, "so that you may know that I am Yhwh" (10.2). (On all this cf. Kegler 1990.)

This is the first important perspective under which the leading out from Egypt has been preserved in the Hebrew Bible tradition: as a result of this fundamental event in its history Israel is to acknowledge and constantly remind itself of the fact that Yhwh alone is God and that he leads his people everywhere and saves them from all calamities. This is very explicitly underlined also by the hymnic confession of the "Reed Sea song" in Ex 15.1-19 [→**48**]. The dramatic depiction of the annihilation of Pharaoh's forces (vv. 4-10) climaxes in the sentence: "Who among the gods is like you, O Lord?" (v. 11). Then attention turns to the following events in which God led "the people you have redeemed" through the encounter with the peoples of Canaan, who were "as still as stone" (vv. 13ff), to the "mountain of your inheritance" (v. 17).

Here we see that the exodus is not just the exit from Egyptian slavery but that it is with this that the history of Israel as a people begins. Again in view here is the land in which the fathers once lived, though this was a land which never became their property. In creed-like formulas it is said that God led Israel out of Egypt "with a strong hand and outstretched arm" and brought them, accompanied by "signs and wonders," into the land "that he had sworn to give to their fathers" (Deut 6.21-23; 26.7-9; cf. Ps 136.10-22). In fact, the leading-out of Israel from Egypt can even become an identity marker of the God of Israel. At the beginning of the proclamation of the fundamental commandments of the Torah on Sinai God introduces himself with the words: "I am Yhwh, your God, who brought you out of the land of Egypt, out of the house of slavery" (Ex 20.2; Deut 5.6) [→53]. Hosea says it in fewer words: "I am Yhwh, your God, from the land of Egypt" (Hos 12.10; 13.4). In Ex 6.7b the leading-out of Egypt has become a component of the acknowledgement formula: "You will know that I am Yhwh, your God, who leads you out from Egyptian bondage."

In some of these fixed formulas exodus and the occupation of the land are directly connected. In others, however, it is clear that between these two events there lies a moment that is of great significance in its own right: Israel's stay in the Sinai desert. In God's first speech to Moses a connection is made between exodus and Sinai immediately after arrival at Mount Sinai: "You yourselves have seen what I did to Egypt, and how I carried you on eagles' wings and brought you to myself" (Ex 19.4) [→52]. Israel, freed from Egyptian slavery, is now "with God." In the course of the giving of the cultic law, this idea is given even sharper expression when we read in connection with the construction of the central sanctuary: "Then I will dwell among the Israelites and be their God. They will know that I am the Lord their God, who brought them out of Egypt so that I might dwell among them. I am the Lord their God" (Ex 29.45f) [→64]. Here it seems almost like the goal of the leading of Israel out of Egypt that God should live among them in his sanctuary on Sinai.

This close connection between God and Israel subsequent to the leading-out of Egypt has a further aspect to it [→542]. In Lev 11.45 the call to Israel to be "holy" is justified as follows: "I am the Lord who brought you up out of Egypt to be your God; therefore be holy, because I am holy." Here the point of the leading-out of Egypt seems to be not only "God's dwelling" among the Israelites, but the closest conceivable relationship: that he wants to be Israel's God. Israel is to have a corresponding "holiness." Thus the leading-out of Egypt forms the basis for Israel's identity. The same idea is found again in Lev 22.32f (cf. also Lev 26.11-13, 45; Num 15.40f). (On this topic cf. Crüsemann 1990.)

There is a shift of emphasis in Deuteronomy. The leading-out of Egypt is placed in immediate connection with the Torah, with the "decrees and ordinances" (*huqqîm ûmišpāṭîm*) that Israel is to keep. So in the instruction for a son we read: "We were slaves of Pharaoh in Egypt, but the Lord brought us out from there … The Lord commanded us to obey all these decrees and to fear the Lord our God, so that we might always prosper and be kept alive, as in the case today" (Deut 6.20-24; cf. 4.32-40; 7.6-11) [→**78**]. Here there is clear emphasis on the fact that the exodus was liberation from slavery and that Israel is to keep alive the memory of this and keep the commandments God has given to the liberated Israel. This is echoed in the laws about slavery (15.15) and about the protection of foreigners and the weak (24.17f, 19-22), where it is said that Israel is to remember its own fate and God's act of liberation. That God has led Israel "out of Egypt, out of the house of slavery" is also cited as an argument for a warning against apostasy from the God of the exodus (13.6-11). Finally, at the feast of Passover, the origin of which is depicted in the direct context of the exodus (Ex 12) [→**45**], this event is called to mind (Deut 16.1, 3, 6), and then also with the feast of weeks, which is also connected with it (16.12). (On this cf. Crüsemann 1992, 256.)

The thankful memory of the leading out of Egypt, as is expressed in the passover, is also echoed in hymnic accounts of the history of Israel. This happens in an especially poignant manner in Ps 136 [→**334**], where the liturgical praise of God's deeds of creation moves directly on to the leading-out from Egypt (vv. 9, 10). In its conclusion the psalm turns to the present and speaks of Israel's oppression as well as its redemption and feeding by God (vv. 23-25). The praise for the leading out from Egypt thus also marks the thanksgiving of the contemporary community. In the parallel psalm, Ps 135, the same sequence of God's action "in heaven and on earth" and the leading-out from Egypt (vv. 5-7, 8f) is embedded in the confession of faith in the God who is greater than all gods (v. 5); his name, which is established forever, is to be remembered from generation to generation (v. 13). In Ps 105 an extensive recapitulation of the history of God's leading of Israel moves from the patriarchs on to the wandering in the wilderness and concludes with thanksgiving for the leading-out of Egypt, which finds expression in the fact that the Israelites keep God's laws and instructions (vv. 43-45).

Quite different notes are sounded in Ps 106: here the history of Israel is primarily a history of its sinning. This began already in Egypt, where the Israelites believed in God's words only for a brief moment following their rescue at the Reed Sea and sang his praise (cf. Ex 14.31; 15.1-21), but then soon forgot his deeds (vv. 12f). Ps 78 too is dominated by the lament that the fathers persisted in sinning, time and again (vv. 17ff, 42f, 51-58) after the divine miracles in Egypt and in the wilderness (vv. 12-16). This view of history is also found in the prophetic books, especially strongly in Jeremiah. For him, the history of God's dealings with Israel begins with the leading-out of Egypt. At that time God gave Israel his commandments. But again and again we read: "but they did not listen" (Jer 7.22-26; 11.7f; 34.13f). For Ezekiel too the disobedience of Israel to the commandments of God begins already in the wilderness, immediately after the leading-out of Egypt (Ezek 20.10-13). A similar picture is given in Hosea: the leading-out of Egypt was the beginning of the history of Israel: it happened under the leadership of the "prophet" Moses (12.14). But Israel responded to this with ingratitude and disobedience (Hos 11.1ff; 12.15; 13.4-6) [→272]. Hosea even carries the idea further, to the point that Israel has to go back to Egypt (8.13; 9.3f, cf. 12.10). But if God has mercy on Israel, they will return alive (11.11). In Amos too the view of the leading-out from Egypt also forms the background to his statement that God will now repay Israel for all its sins (Amos 3.1f). Similarly in Micah, where in God's dispute with Israel the leading-out of Egypt is contrasted with Israel's current sinful behavior (Mic 6.2-8). Thus in all these texts Israel's behavior stands in sharp contrast to God's saving act in leading them out of Egypt.

3. The second exodus: return and a new beginning

In the great divine speech at the end of the giving of the law on Sinai in Lev 26 the leading-out of Egypt appears twice [→68]. In the first place, the phrase "I am the Lord your God, who led you out of Egypt, so that you would no longer be slaves" (v. 13) forms the conclusion of the first part of the speech, which speaks of Israel under the covenant. But then follows the lengthy description of Israel's disobedience and the terrible punishments it has to suffer as a result, including deportation to foreign lands; but God will finally remember his covenant with the forefathers, whom he led out of Egypt "before the eyes of the nations" (v. 45). Here the memory of the leading-out of Egypt is thus closely connected with God's "remembering" of his covenant. This also contains hope for those who still live in the "land of their enemies" (v. 44). There is no mention of a return at this point, but hope in it already resonates unmistakably.

In other texts this connection is expressly made. According to Isa 11.1-16 [→178] God will stretch out his hand a second time to redeem "the remnant of his people" from the lands of captivity and will gather them from the four corners of the earth. He will then make a road for them in the sea of Egypt and in the Euphrates as in the days when they left Egypt (v. 16). The second exodus from the lands of exile will thus be a repetition of the first. In Isa 43.14ff too [→**189f**] the announcement of mighty repatriation of Israel is described with clear echoes of the exodus from Egypt: God will make a way in the sea, will draw out and destroy chariots and horses. In fact, the "new thing" that God will now bring about will even exceed the former thing, so that Israel will not have to remember it any more (v. 18). Jeremiah says it even more clearly: "the days are coming when men will no longer say, 'As surely as the Lord lives, who brought the Israelites up out of Egypt,' but they will say, 'As surely as the Lord lives, who brought the Israelites up out of the land of the north and out of all the countries where he had banished them'" (Jer 16.14f). So the first exodus will become a sort of type of the second, which will exceed it. (Cf. Zimmerli 1963.)

Occasionally the old and the new exodus merge together. In Isa 51.9-11 [→**193**], God's deed of creation through his battle against the powers of chaos is at the beginning. This battle with the waters of the great *t'hôm*, the chaotic primeval torrent (cf. Gen 1.2) merges imperceptibly into the creation of a pathway in the sea for those liberated from Egypt (cf. also the word *t'hômmot* in Ex 15.5, 8); but then these equally imperceptibly become those redeemed from exile, who come to Zion with jubilation, leaving mourning and sighing behind them. The creation, the old and the new exodus are God's great deeds, from which and towards which Israel lives. Finally the exit of the first exiles from exile in Ezra 1 is clearly presented as a repetition of the exodus from Egypt, right through to the detail that as they leave, those that remain in the land give them gold, silver and other gifts (vv. 4, 6). [→**391**]. This exceeds what occurs in the first exodus in that it is even done quite willingly (Ex 12.35f). But then the difference immediately becomes clear: the exodus from Egypt was initially a flight with an uncertain goal, and it was followed by a long period of wandering, until the leavers were finally able to move into the land. Those returning from the exile move resolutely into the land. The first thing they do is to set up the burnt-offering altar again and resume regular sacrifices (Ezra 3.15). Then they get right on with the reconstruction of the temple (vv. 8-13). What now occurs is return, the resumption of life in the land that God had given after the first exodus.

The great significance of the "second exodus" for the thought of post-exilic Israel lies in the fact that new special terminology has been formed for this event. Two conceptions are of special significance and import in this regard: God will turn the fate (or the captivity) of Israel (*šûb šͤbût*) and will "gather" (*qbṣ* pi.) Israel from its scattering among the nations. In the announcement of the turning of Israel's fate in Deut 30 [→**86**] both phrases are found together (v. 3). In the context (v. 2) stands the verb *šûb*, still in the sense of "return, repent:" "when you and your children return to the Lord your God ... then the Lord your God will restore your fortunes and have compassion on you and gather you again from all the nations where he scattered you." The verb "have compassion" (*rḥm* pi.) has been added here, which is also found frequently in this context (Jer 30.18; 33.26; Ezek 39.25 etc.).

In Jeremiah's letter to the exiles in Babylon (Jer 29) [→**226**] the two expressions are also found together. In the context here the concern is not with "turning back" but with "seeking:" "'You will seek me and find me when you seek me with all your heart. I will be found by you,' declares the Lord, 'and will bring you back from captivity. I will gather you from all the nations and places where I have banished you,' declares the Lord, 'and will bring you back to the place from which I carried you into exile'" (vv. 13f).

Elsewhere we see particular emphases in the use of the two formulas: the expression "to turn the fate (or the captivity)" is found with particular frequency in Jeremiah, especially in chs. 29–33 (30.3, 18; 31.23; 33.7, 11 etc.), but also in Ezekiel (16.53; 39.25 etc.) and occasionally in the other prophetic books (e.g. Hos 6.11; Amos 9.14) as well as a few times in the Psalms (Pss 14.7=53.7; 85.2; 126.4). The word about "gathering" has a clear emphasis in Isaiah (11.12; 43.5f; 54.7; 56.8), in 40.11 in the metaphor of the shepherd who gathers the lambs in his arms. The same metaphor is also found in Jeremiah (23.3; 31.10; cf. also 32.37). Ezekiel too uses this term quite frequently (e.g. 11.17; 20.34, 41; 34.13); cf. further Mic 2.12; 4.6 etc., and twice in the Psalms (106.47; 107.3).

Most of these texts speak in a future form of the end of the exile, although some of them were probably not formulated until "post-exilic" times. The turning of Israel's fate and the gathering of the scattered remain a constant subject of hope. In Isa 56.8 the participial form "who gathers the scattered of Israel" (*mͤqabbēṣ*) almost sounds like a divine epithet; it is connected with the assurance that God will gather more people to join those that have already been assembled.

§ 10

The Center of Israel's Life: the Torah

1. The God-given Torah

God gave Israel the Torah. Nothing surpasses this in importance for Israel: the Torah forms the center of Israel's life. In the Hebrew Bible the Torah forms an essential part of the Pentateuch, which taken as a whole might be called Israel's "founding document." Here the gift of the Torah takes place in the middle of Israel's path from liberation from Egyptian slavery into the land promised by God to the forefathers of Israel. In Sinai Israel is "with God" (Ex 19.4) [→**52**] and God sets up his residence in the midst of Israel (Ex 29.46) [→**65**]. Thus finally the first main part of the canon of the Hebrew Bible, the Pentateuch, is given in its totality the label of "Torah."

Sinai (or Horeb), where Israel receives the Torah, is a "utopian place" (Crüsemann 1992, 75), far removed in time and space from the realities of Israel's life. So the Torah is not dependent on a change in circumstances either, but remains valid just as Israel received it there. Israel takes it with it into the land promised by God. After the conquest of the land has been completed Joshua commits the people again to "keeping everything and to doing what is written in the book of the Torah of Moses, not departing from it to the right or the left" (Josh 23.6) [→**100**].

This understanding of the Torah is the result of a long process of tradition. This applies to the fundamental significance of the term *tôrāh* as well as to the variety of texts and collections of texts collected in the books of Exodus through Deuteronomy. To elucidate and describe the history of this process is an interesting and important task, which can open up many kinds of insight into the history of Israel's religion and its social structures. At the end of such research, however, there must be an effort to understand the Torah in its totality, as it stands, as the basis of Israel's life in its various areas and aspects.

In its comprehensive and fundamental meaning the word *tôrāh* signifies the instruction that God gave to Israel through Moses. It can be called "Torah of Yhwh" (e.g. Pss 1.2; 19.8), "Torah of God" (Hos 4.6; Ps 37.31 etc.), "my Torah" (Isa 51.7; Jer 31.33; Hos 8.1, 12 etc.) and also "Torah of Moses" (2 Kgs 23.25; Mal 3.22 etc.). In Deuteronomy it is often called "the Torah" (Deut 4.44) or "this Torah" (1.5; 4.8 etc.) and there is mention of the writing down of the Torah (e.g. Deut 31.9, 24) and of the "book of the Torah" (e.g. Deut 30.10; Josh 1.8). In other writings of the Hebrew Bible too the word *tôrāh* appears in an absolute usage in a comprehensive sense (e.g. Isa 2.3 par. Mic 4.2; Isa 42.4).

This linguistic usage reveals two things: first, the word *tôrāh* is given its terminological impact in Deuteronomy in particular; here it refers in the first instance to the formulations of the divine instruction collected in this "book of the Torah." Second, however, its usage points far beyond the context of Deuteronomy and the other collections of commandments and describes in summary God's instructions as the expression of his will and of his special relationship with his people Israel.

In the Hebrew Bible a more specialized use of the word *tôrāh* is also found. Thus it can describe the instruction of a mother (1.8; 6.20) or that of a wisdom teacher ("my *tôrāh*," 3.1; 4.2; 7.2). A prophet's instruction to his disciples can also be described as "*tôrāh* of Yhwh" (Isa 30.9). The teaching of Torah is especially the task of the priests (cf. Hag 2.11-13); they can be described as those "who administer the *tôrāh*" (Jer 2.8). In the cultic texts of the Hebrew Bible occasionally the expression "this is the *tôrāh* ..." appears as a superscription or subscription for individual regulations (Lev 6.2, 7, 18 etc.; 11.46f; 12.7 and *passim*). This variety of ways in which the word *tôrāh* is used makes it clear that its comprehensive meaning is the result of a quite particular, goal-oriented development.

2. The Decalogue as constitution

Israel received the Torah on Sinai. In a powerful appearance God spoke to Israel and declared to it the Ten Commandments, the Decalogue (Ex 20.1-17) [→**53**]. These commandments are the beginning of the Torah. But they are more than a beginning; for immediately after this first divine speech the people are seized by great terror and they ask Moses, "Speak to us yourself and we will listen. But do not have God speak to us or we will die" (vv. 18f). This marks a break that has great significance: it was only the ten statements of the Decalogue that God spoke directly to Israel. The whole of the rest of the Torah he gave to Moses, who passed it on to Israel. (Cf. Nicholson 1977.)

The fundamental significance of this interruption becomes ever clearer in Deuteronomy. Here the Decalogue appears first only in a detailed narrative context (Deut 5) [→77]. The Israelites are reminded of it, since they had heard it themselves at Horeb. All the other commandments of the Torah God spoke to Moses, who then informs the people gathered in the land of Moab, shortly before the entry into the promised land (chs. 12–26); in between are detailed paraenetic speeches (chs. 6–11). Thus the special position of the Decalogue is emphasized even more strongly than in Ex 20, where in the same chapter already the imparting of further commandments begins (vv. 22ff). (On this, cf. Lohfink 1989.)

The fundamental difference between the Decalogue and the other commandments of the Torah thus lies in the first place in the form in which they are conveyed; it was only the Decalogue that the people heard as a direct divine speech. But this is linked at the same time with a key statement about Moses' position: it is he alone who receives and transmits the entirety of the rest of the Torah, so significant for Israel. He is the sole mediator between God and Israel. And Israel receives the Torah only through him.

A further important aspect of the special place of the Decalogue lies in its dual citation in broadly the same words (Ex 20.1-17; Deut 5.6-21; on the differences see below). In this way the certainly different collections of commandments in the various parts of the Pentateuch are as it were tied together and put on the same plane. Between the announcements of the commandments on Sinai and those in the land of Moab there is no fundamental difference in significance and relevance. They have all come to Israel from God via the mediation of Moses.

The prime place of the Decalogue before all the other commandments is given special significance through its opening statement: "I am the Lord your God, who brought you out of Egypt, out of the land of slavery" (Ex 20.2; Deut 5.6). None of the other larger and smaller collections of commandments that are brought together in the Pentateuch contains such a beginning. Already the phrase "I am Yhwh" (with the full form of the pronoun "I," *'ānokî*), placed in emphatic first position, gives the series of commandments that follows its quite special profile. It is the authoritative statement of the one and only God, who has previously revealed himself as the God of Israel (Ex 3.14f; 6.2f) [→40]. The following reference to the leading-out of Egyptian slavery places the commandments, in addition, in the context of the history of God's dealings with Israel. For Israel after all is on the way from this experience of liberation to the land God has promised them (cf. Ex 6.6-8). At this point God's instruction is now being proclaimed to it.

One might say, then, "that with the proclamation of the Decalogue over Israel, Israel's election is realized" (von Rad 1962, 205). In other words: with the Torah that opens with the Decalogue, God's relationship with Israel is conclusively constituted. The Decalogue has a fundamental opening function. The subsequent commandments develop the content in various ways and add others. A piece of "the theology and social history of the Old Testament law" (Crüsemann 1992 in the title of his work) has been set down here.

The division and enumeration of the commandments is not uniform in the interpretive tradition. In the Jewish tradition the dominant view is that the opening sentence (Ex 20.2; Deut 5.6) on its own is counted as the first commandment, while the prohibition of foreign gods and the prohibition of idols together count as the second commandment (Ex 20.3-6; Deut 5.7-10). The Roman Catholic and Lutheran tradition that goes back to Augustine takes the opening sentence together with the prohibition of foreign gods and the prohibition of idols as the first commandment; the two sentences that begin with "You shall not covet" at the conclusion (Ex 20.17; Deut 5.21) are then counted as the ninth and tenth commandments. A third way of counting, dominant in the Reformed tradition and elsewhere, views the prohibition of idols as a separate second commandment and again counts the last two "You shall" commands as a single (tenth) commandment (cf. Jacob 1997, 606-610).

2.1 No other gods before me

The God who gives Israel the Torah is the one and only God. According to the traditions of the Hebrew Bible there can be no doubt about this. Other gods have come into view only in the form of the powerless gods of Egypt (Ex 12.12; cf. Num 33.4). But the Decalogue looks forward to a time when Israel will come into contact with other gods. So the first instruction, which follows God's initial self-introduction, reads: "You shall have no other gods beside me" (Ex 20.3; Deut 5.7). The formula *'al-pānāy*, which is often translated "besides me," contains an antithetical element which Buber renders appropriately as "into my face" (*mir ins Angesicht*).

Buber's complete sentence reads: "Let another deity not be to you into my face." Buber follows the Hebrew wording closely here. The expression "not be to you" (*lô'* with a following imperfect) represents the most emphatic form of the negative in Hebrew; but it does not contain any verb relating to the addressee as in "you shall." This makes it both more open and sharper. The translation "another deity" expresses the fact that grammatically speaking the Hebrew word *ᵉlohîm* is a plural, but that it can mean both "God" (cf. Gen 1.1) and "gods" or "deities."

This statement points in two directions. First it emphasizes the demand that Israel worship exclusively this one unique God. To worship "other gods" is irreconcilable with Israel's special relationship with this God. Second, it points to the danger that Israel might not meet this demand. Both emphases are found many times in the Hebrew Bible.

Immediately next to the first commandment in the Decalogue is the statement of the prophet Hosea: "I am the Lord, your God, from Egypt. You know no other God than me, and there is no savior (*môšîaʻ*) beside me" (Hos 13.4; cf. 12.10) [→273]. Here, as in the Decalogue, the leading-out of Egypt and the emphasis on the exclusiveness of "knowing" (*yādaʻ*), and this means acknowledging, this God are directly linked together. At the same time we hear the express rejection of the acknowledgment of any other god. In the book of Isaiah there are frequent formulations in which the uniqueness of the God of Israel is emphasized in an extremely trenchant way: "I am the first and I am the last; beside me there is no God (*ᵉlohîm*)" (44.6); "before me no God (*'ēl*) was formed, and there will be none after me" (Isa 43.10). This last sentence continues: "I, I am the Lord and beside me there is no savior (*môšîaʻ*)" (v. 11), with a clear resonance of Hosea.

These words each allow us to see the two viewpoints that also come to expression in the Decalogue's first commandment: the unambiguous emphasis that for Israel there is, and can be, only the *one* God— and the rejection of possible deviations. The exclusive recognition of the *one* God was evidently never entirely taken for granted nor undisputed in Israel. We see this expressed very clearly in other collections of commandments within the Pentateuch. In Ex 34.11-26 the problem is again right at the beginning. Israel is strongly warned against making alliances with the inhabitants of the land because this could lead to Israel "subjecting itself" (*hištaḥ"wāh*) to another god (*'ēl'aḥēr*), being invited to participate in their sacrifices and by marrying their daughters being seduced into "prostituting themselves" after their gods (vv. 12-16). The narrative in Num 25.1-5 [→72] sets out graphically how concrete this danger is. Directly before the entry into the promised land, precisely what is described in Ex 34 happens: Israelites go off with the daughters of the Moabites, follow their invitations to the sacrifices and subject themselves to their gods. "Their gods" are the "other gods," the worship of which is so unambiguously prohibited in the first commandment of the Decalogue.

In the "book of the covenant," in an emphatic concluding function (Ex 23.13, before the subsequent calendar of feasts, vv. 14-19, and the paraenetic conclusion, vv. 20-33) stands the sentence: "Do not invoke (*zkr* hi.) the names of other gods; do not let them be heard on your lips." What is no doubt in mind here is the cultic calling-to-memory of the name of other gods, a further aspect of the cultic worship of other gods alongside the submission to them. The foreign nations play no express role in this. In the concluding paraenesis, however, once again there is a warning of the worship of the gods of the peoples of the land (v. 24). Deuteronomy too focuses on the danger that the Israelites who have come into the land might be seduced into serving "other gods" (Deut 7.1-4) through allying themselves with inhabitants of the land and by intermarriage with them.

At the beginning of the "book of the covenant" stands the prohibition against "making" gods, i.e. manufacturing images (Ex 20.23) [→55]. The second half of the verse relates clearly to images of other gods made of silver and gold. (The first half of the verse is difficult to understand. One might perhaps translate: "You shall not manufacture me," as Crüsemann 1992, 231, says, emending the vocalization of *'ittî* "with me" to *'otî*, "me"). In any case this formula is close to the continuation of the first commandment in Ex 20.4 and Deut 5.8, where there is also mention of idols. This prohibition of images is evidently not a separate "second commandment" (as in the Reformed tradition) but a continuation and explanation of the first commandment (as in the Jewish tradition; in the Lutheran catechism the prohibition of images is not even mentioned; cf. 1999a). The continuation shows that graphic representations are meant which are intended for cultic worship (Ex 20.5a; Deut 5.9a). This applies to images of everything that "is in heaven above and on the earth beneath and in the water under the earth." But it applies equally to graphic representations of Yhwh himself. For the lack of images is one of the fundamental elements of the worship of Yhwh (cf. Mettinger 1995).

The seriousness with which the prohibition of any kind of image-veneration is regarded is unmistakable clear from the continuing words: "for I, the Lord your God, am a jealous God (*'ēl qannā'*)" (Ex 20.5b; Deut 5.9b) [→**629**]. In Ex 34.14 we even read: "the Lord, whose name is Zealous, is a zealous God." It is almost an element of Yhwh's identity that he is called "Zealous."

The word *qannā'* is often translated "jealous." The underlying verbal root *qn'* does indeed contain the element of jealousy between marriage partners (e.g. Num 5.11ff) or family members (e.g. Gen 30.1; 37.11), but also others such as envy (e.g. Gen 26.14), rivalry (e.g. Qoh 4.4) etc. In particular the noun *qin'āh* exhibits a broad spectrum of meaning. The adjective *qannā'* is only used of God, however, and exclusively in the context of the prohibition of worshiping other gods (Ex 20.5; 34.14; Deut 4.24; 5.9; 6.15; cf. *ThWAT* VII, 51-62).

The statement about Yhwh's "jealousy" (or "jealous holiness"—*Eiferheiligkeit*, von Rad 1962, 216ff) has to be understood in the context of the Decalogue. It is Yhwh's reaction to the infringement of the commandment against having other gods besides him, and that means against him. The word may seem emotionally charged, but it is very much tied into the overall context of relations between God and Israel. In the speech that introduces the giving of the law on Sinai Moses speaks of the covenant (*bᵉrît*) which Israel is to keep (Ex 19.5) [→**52**]. This refers back on the one hand to the covenant agreed with Abraham, whose God "remembered" Israel at decisive points along Israel's onward pathway (Ex 2.23-25; 6.4f). On the other hand it contains a forward reference to the solemn covenant agreement which concludes the conveying of the commandments that begins with the Decalogue (Ex 24.3-8) [→**57**]. In Deut 4.13 the keeping of the ten commandments is itself then described as the content of the covenant. So the worship of other gods means at the same time a transgression of the covenant. The zealous anger of God is directed against the destruction of the foundation of the relationship between God and Israel. So this is not a merely emotional anger but a "righteous anger" (Assmann 1991, 99).

This zealous anger of God's has its effects. God's self-predication as "jealous God" has a dual sequel, in each case with an adjectival participle: this God is "visiting the sins of the fathers on the children through to the third and fourth generation on those who hate me; showing goodness to thousands who love me and keep my commandments." The decision to keep the commandments, especially the fundamental commandment to worship exclusively the one and only God, not only decides the fate of each individual, but also affects the fate of the following generations as well.

But what does "visit" mean? It is usually understood in the sense of "punish." This produces a notable problem, however, for the interpretation of Old Testament texts: Biblical Hebrew does not have a word for "punishment" or "punish"! The word *pāqad*, translated here as "visit," can have this meaning; but it also has a much broader range of meaning including quite positive aspects.

The attempt to find a common basic meaning for the varied aspects of the root *pqd* leads to such formulations as "to test," "monitor," "adjudge" (Scharbert 1960, 222), "'observe closely,' the judgement or decision that ensues from the evaluation being included" (André 1989, 709; cf. also Schottroff 1976, 467f). With God as the subject the verb can express God's care and concern for the individual person (e.g. Gen 21.1; 1 Sam 2.21; Ps 8.5 in parallel with *zākar*, "remember") as well as his salvation-historical care for Israel (Gen 50.24; Ex 3.16; 4.31). A large number of passages however speak of critical testing (e.g. Ps 17.3; Job 7.18, in each case alongside *bāḥan*, "test;" Job 31.14). When guilt or sin is involved, to which the divine testing is directed (e.g. Hos 2.15; Amos 3.2), then the consequence that God will draw from this testing is indirectly indicated already. God's "visitation" implies the punishment of the transgression. This punishment is not, however, given concrete form in the Decalogue, as in many other passages.

So one may say: "*pqd* is a function of the *ṣᵉdāqāh*, "righteousness" of God" (Scharbert 1960, 225). It can mean care and salvation but also punishment and calamity. God punishes the transgression of his commandments, especially of the basic commandment; but he plies his kindness on those who keep his commandments. The two ways of behaving toward God that find expression in the following or not following of the commandments are characterized as "love" (*'āhab*) and "hate" (*śānē'*); both verbs can express a broad spectrum of feelings and behaviors and are often used as a pair of opposites (cf. *THAT* II 63).

God's reaction not only affects the individual but involves subsequent generations too, for bad as well as good. The great discrepancy between the three or four generations on the negative side and the thousands on the positive side emphasizes the inequality between God's punishing actions and his kind acts. This aspect is emphasized even more strongly in the partly parallel text in Ex 34.6f [→62]. There the two ways in which God acts appear in the opposite order: first showing kindness to thousands, only then visiting for sin for three or four generations.

But again the question arises what "visiting" means when the reference is to the following generations. Does it mean that three or even four generations will have to suffer as a result of their ancestors' behavior, without consideration for what they themselves have done? In Deuteronomy we find an answer to this question; God "keeps his covenant and his kindness to those who love him and keep his commandments, in a thousand generations; but he pays back those who hate him in their face," i.e. personally to each individual (Deut 7.9f) [→78]. The concluding phrase "to those who hate me" in Ex 20.5 and Deut 5.9 is to be understood in this sense too. This is already the view in the Targumim and the Talmud (*Sanhedrin* 27b), to which Rashi appeals: "if they hold firmly on to the work of their fathers." In the parallel passages in Ex 34.6f and Num 14.18 the terms "love" and "hate" are missing; one can therefore take the formulation in the Decalogue as an express clarification that in the final analysis it always depends on the behavior of the individual (cf. Weinfeld 1991, 299). This view is represented with great emphasis also in Ezekiel (Ezek 18; 33.10-20; cf. also Jer 31.29f; Deut 24.16).

What follows after the first commandment here is thus not a determination of punishment in a legal sense but an elaboration of the consequences that will follow transgression of the fundamental demand for the exclusive worship of the one and only God.

2.2 Do not misuse God's name

With the second commandment (in the Jewish and Lutheran reckoning; third in others) (Ex 20.7; Deut 5.11) the form of the speech changes. God is now spoken of in the third person. This change may have a basis in the early history of the Decalogue. But at the same time it expresses a change in point of view. While so far the concern has been with the direct relationship with God, a new element comes in at this point: the use of the name of God contains an outward orientation; it occurs also in relation to other people (cf. Crüsemann 1983, 50).

There can be no image of God; this is not allowed. The most direct way for a person to express his or her relationship with God is to use God's name. The Hebrew Bible reports that already in the first generations of the history of humanity, people call upon the name of God (*qārā' b'šēm yhwh*, Gen 4.26), and then especially the patriarchs when they built their first altars (12.8; 13.4; 26.25; cf. 21.33). Psalmists call on the name in their distress (116.4, 13, 17; cf. 80.19; Lam 3.55); they praise him (*hll* pi., 69.31 etc.) and "bless" him (*bārûk*, 72.19). People can trust in the name (Isa 50.10) and seek refuge in it (Zeph 3.12). Finally according to eschatological expectations people who call on the name of Yhwh will be saved (Joel 3.5*; Zech 13.9) [→**277**]. (On this cf. van der Woude 1976.)

Calling on the divine name does not only occur, however, in inward-oriented piety. Thus a psalmist calls for a creed-like proclamation of the name of God among the nations (Ps 105.1; cf. Isa 12.4). The creedal element is especially marked in the case of Elijah, who calls upon the name of Yhwh in a dramatic competition with the prophets of Baal, in sharp contrast with the gods of his opponents: "The God who answers with fire, he is the (true) God (*hû' hā'lohîm*)" (1 Kgs 18.24) [→**138**].

Prophecy also occurs in the name of God (Deut 18.9; Jer 11.21). But here we see the danger inherent in the use of the divine name. A prophet can speak "in the name of the Lord" without being authorized by God to do so (Deut 18.20-22) [→**82**]. In Jeremiah especially controversy over this issue plays an important part: the other prophets speak "in my name," but they speak lies (*šeqer*, Jer 14.14f; 23.25; 27.15 etc.; cf. also Ezek 13.6-9). The Decalogue commandment reads: "You shall not lift up the name of the Lord your God to vanity" (Ex 20.7; Deut 5.11).

This phrase is quite unusual and in this form it is found here only. The expression "lift up to vanity" (*nāśā' laššāw'*) is also found in Ps 24.4: "he who does not lift up my (i.e. God's) soul (i.e. me) to vanity and does not swear deceitfully." Here God himself, his *nefeš*, is in place of the name. "To lift up the name" (*nāśā' šēm*) is also found in Ps 16.4, where in reference to foreign gods the psalmist says: "I will not lift their name on my lips," i.e. pronounce their name. The word translated "vanity" *šāw'* can also relate to foreign gods: "They (i.e. the Israelites) sacrifice to vanity" (Jer 18.15). Ezekiel uses the word against the prophets, whom he reproaches for relying falsely on divine messages while their insight is vain (*šāw'*) and a lie (*kāzāb*) (Ezek 13.6-9; cf. 22.28, also Lam 2.14). The word is also found in the legal realm: slander (23.1); false witness (*'ēd šāw'*, Deut 5.20, instead of *'ēd šeqer*, Ex 20.16); false oaths (*'ālāh šāw'*, Hos 10.4); cf. also Ps 24.4.

To lift up God's name "to vanity" thus means to bring it into connection with things that run counter to the nature of God and his commandments. Martin Luther put this aptly in the explanation of the second commandment in the shorter catechism: "We are to fear and love God, not to curse, swear, do magic, lie or deceive with his name but to call on him in all times of distress, pray, praise and thank him." The broad spectrum of possible misuse of the divine name circumscribed here corresponds to the wording of the commandment which can manage without the naming of certain areas or facts.

But this certainly does not mean that the issue remains unclear. Rather, this commandment has a sequel: "for the Lord will not leave him unpunished who lifts up his name to vanity." The misuse of the divine name affects God himself, and so God reacts to it. This sequel, however, like the first commandment, does not contain any indication of the punishment; it speaks of the way God will respond to this disrespect for his name and thus for himself. He will "not leave unpunished" anyone who indulges in such misuse. This is a rather reticent phrase. This is evident in Ex 34.7 [→**62**], where unlike the Decalogue, God's gracious actions are in the foreground, and the opposite statement of "visitation" is introduced afterwards, with a sort of "nonetheless." This is even clearer in Jer 30.11 and 46.28, where we read that he will spare Israel but not leave it unpunished, but punish it "with measure" (*lammišpāṭ*, cf. *ThWAT* V, 106) (cf. 10.24). Misuse of the divine name is not, then, without consequences; but it is not given the same weight as transgression of the first commandment.

2.3 A Sabbath for the Lord

The Sabbath commandment (Ex 20.8-11; Deut 5.12-15) stands "in central position ... right between the first commandments relating to God and those which are concerned only with human actions"

(Crüsemann 1983, 53). It gives the person addressed as "you" (2nd pers. sing.) the obligation of "hallowing" the Sabbath; but this obligation is at the same time a gift to the person which relieves him of the burden of daily work on the seventh day. This dual aspect is expounded explicitly: "Six days you shall labor and do all your work, but the seventh day is a Sabbath to the Lord your God." Then it is explained what a Sabbath is: "On it you shall not do any work, neither you, nor your son or daughter, nor your manservant or maidservant, nor (Deut: your ox, your donkey or) your animals, nor the alien within your gates."

The Sabbath commandment is distinguished from all the other commandments of the Decalogue by its detailed justification. At the same time it is the only commandment in which the two versions of the Decalogue in Ex 20 and Deut 5 vary to any extent. The introductory verbs are already different: "Remember (zākôr) the Sabbath day" (Ex 20.8)—"Keep" (šāmôr) the Sabbath day" (Deut 5.12). Here the different emphases are already evident that are then made explicitly clear in the justifications (cf. Lohfink 1965b).

In Ex 20.11 the justification of the Sabbath commandment is directed entirely towards God's activity: God created the world in six days and rested on the seventh. "And God blessed the seventh day and made it holy" (Gen 2.2f). The Sabbath reflects God's creative act. Israel is to "remember" this and keep the seventh day holy, as God made it holy. On its way to Sinai Israel then experiences the Sabbath even before it knew it or had received a commandment about it. The manna they eat during the time in the wilderness is given them in the rhythm of the Sabbath week: on the sixth day they receive the double amount and nothing on the seventh day (Ex 16.22-30). Moses uses this to explain the nature of the "holy Sabbath to the Lord" (v. 23) and as it were anticipates the words of the Decalogue commandment: "Six days you are to gather it, but on the seventh day, the Sabbath, there will not be any" (v. 26). So already here the prominent role of the Sabbath is clear.

This can also be seen in other texts. In the cultic regulations for the sanctuary on Sinai there is a detailed Sabbath regulation in an emphatic concluding position in Ex 31.12-17. Here the Sabbath is called a "sign" ('ôt v.13), an "eternal sign" ('ôt 'ôlām v. 17) between God and Israel and an "eternal covenant" (b'rît 'ôlām v. 16). The idea of the sanctity of the Sabbath plays an important role here again (vv. 13, 14), as also the danger of desecration (*ḥll* pi.), which carries the threat of death. The report on the erection of the sanctuary begins again with the Sabbath commandment (35.1-3), once again with emphasis on the sanctity of the Sabbath and the threat of death for transgression of the commandment about working. (Here we also have the prohibition of kindling fire on the Sabbath [v. 3], to which there is no parallel elsewhere in the Hebrew Bible; perhaps indirectly in Ex 16.23.) The threat of death for transgression of the prohibition of work on the Sabbath is concretized in Num 15.32-36 in a narrative about the acquisition of a divine instruction through Moses (cf. also Lev 24.10-23).

Deuteronomy 5 draws attention to something else. The introductory sentence in v. 12 is expanded with the addition: "as the Lord your God commanded you;" this corresponds almost word-for-word with the concluding sentence (v. 15b). The listing of those to whom the prohibition of work applies is then expanded with the half-sentence "so that your manservant and maidservant may rest, as you do" (v. 14). Here the manservant and maidservant are mentioned for the second time with the express emphasis that they too are to rest. By means of the connecting "so that" (*l'ma'an*) this social aspect is even declared to be the true purpose of the Sabbath rest. The justification follows immediately afterwards: "Remember that you were slaves in Egypt and that the Lord your God brought you out of there with a mighty hand and an outstretched arm. Therefore the Lord your God has commanded you to observe the Sabbath day" (v. 15). Here the social aspect of the rest from work is anchored in the liberation of Israel from Egyptian slavery. The word "work" (*'ābad*) recalls the situation of the slave (*'ebed*) in Egypt and the liberation from the house of slavery (*bêt 'ᵃbādîm*), spoken of in the opening words of the Decalogue. The Sabbath thus refreshes the memory of the divine act of liberation when Israel was led out of slavery and draws consequences for the common life of those for whom this exodus forms the founding experience in their history.

In the version of the Decalogue in Deuteronomy there is what seems to be a small alteration: before each of the last five commandments, beginning with "You shall not commit adultery," an "and" (*w*) has been inserted, so that this series of commandments is enclosed in a single block. This produces, however, a changed overall structure of the Decalogue, in which five blocks of statements may be discerned: Yhwh-worship (5.6-10), name of Yhwh (v. 11), SABBATH (vv. 12-15), parents (v. 16), moral commandments (vv. 17-21).

The Sabbath commandment has a central position here; it thereby becomes as it were the "main commandment" (Lohfink 1965b, 25f [202f]).

In the prophets, various aspects of the Sabbath are discussed. Amos criticizes merchants who do not regard the Sabbath as a gift but wait impatiently for its end so that they can resume their unsavory business (Amos 8.5) [→286]. He thus presupposes that the Sabbath is generally being kept, but criticizes the way it is regarded by his contemporaries. Things are different in Jeremiah: in a great Sabbath sermon at one of the city gates of Jerusalem (Jer 17.19-27) he castigates the carrying of burdens through the gates of the city on the Sabbath (as well as other types of work, v. 22), and demands instead that the Sabbath be "kept holy" (vv. 22, 24, 27), entirely in keeping with the Decalogue; otherwise the city will be threatened with destruction (which may already have occurred when this text gained its definitive form, v. 27).

In Ezekiel too the aspect of hallowing or desecrating the Sabbath plays an important role. Among the commandments that God has given Israel after the leading-out from Egypt, the Sabbath commandment is the only one to be expressly mentioned (Ezek 20.10-12) [→247]. It is to be a sign between God and Israel (cf. Ex 31.13); it is to show Israel "that I am the Lord, who makes it holy" (v. 12). Israel is also to "keep my Sabbaths holy" (Ezek 20.20); instead they desecrated the Sabbaths (vv. 13, 16, 21, 24), thereby bringing God's wrath upon them. Several times more Ezekiel raises the reproach of the desecration of the Sabbaths (22.8; cf. v. 26; 23.38). Finally in the great concluding part he mentions the keeping of the Sabbaths as a special task of the priests (44.24).

The keeping of the Sabbath has yet another aspect in Isa 56 [→196]. Here it is mentioned as a fundamental criterion for the place of "foreigners" and eunuchs in the Yhwh community (vv. 2, 4, 6), together with the keeping of the "covenant" (i.e. presumably circumcision, vv. 4, 6). The Deut 5.12 terminology of keeping (*šāmar*) the Sabbath (vv. 2, 4, 6) is found immediately next to the statement about desecration (*ḥll* pi. vv. 2, 6), which is in the Ex 20 tradition (esp. v. 11). Here we see that the Sabbath has now gained a central place in Israelite religion, if it can be made a criterion of membership of the community like this. In Isa 58.13f there is a paraenesis relating to the Sabbath commandment which shows that in urban areas in particular business life was certainly being carried on. On the other hand there is praise for anyone who abstains from this and calls the Sabbath instead of the "holy day" "a delight" (*'oneg*). Dominant here again is a viewpoint that is similar to that of Deut 5.14f. Unlike Jer 17 (and Neh 13, see below), however, there is no explicit call to keep the Sabbath commandment. But the significance of the Sabbath is evident in the fact that these two passages on the subject of the Sabbath have been made the framework for Isaiah chs. 56–58 (Westermann 1966, 271).

Finally various aspects of the Sabbath appear in the book of Nehemiah. In the great prayer of repentance in Neh 9 [→**399**] the Sinai commandments are praised as God's good gift to Israel; the Sabbath commandment is the only one to be mentioned separately, in the words: "You made known to them your holy Sabbath" (v. 14). The Sabbath commandment is then described more precisely in the self-commitment of the assembled community "to follow the Law of God given through Moses the servant of God" (10.29): not to buy any goods from the "peoples of the land" who bring these to sell them on the Sabbath (v. 32). In 13.15-22 we see that this was not kept but that vigorous trading went on in Jerusalem on the Sabbath. It is unclear, however, whether the people whom Nehemiah sees at work "in Judah" are Judahites or members of other population groups, as is assumed in 10.32 (cf. Blenkinsopp 1988, 359). At any rate Nehemiah has the city gates closed and guarded for the Sabbath, in order to prevent trading.

Here we see the tendency to a strict interpretation of the Sabbath commandment as developed further in the post-biblical Jewish tradition (cf. Mishnah tractate *Shabbat*). However the dominant aspect in tradition up to the present day is the aspect of enjoyment and gratitude for the gift of rest on this day, on which God himself rested. (Cf. Lau 1988, 112-157.)

2.4 Honor your parents

"Honor your father and mother" (Ex 20.12; Deut 5.16). With this commandment the Decalogue turns from the audience's relationship with God, which characterized the first commandments, to their behavior with regard to other people. In the reports of the reception of the Decalogue by Moses, there is mention of the "two stone tablets" on which the Ten Commandments were written (Ex 31.18; 32.15; 34.1, 4; Deut 4.13; 5.22 etc.); however we are never told how the ten commandments were divided between the two tablets. Many interpreters have the second tablet of the Decalogue begin with the commandment to honor one's parents. The second tablet then becomes the "ethical" counterpart to the "theological" first tablet (cf. Schmidt 1993, 38 and 97). In Jewish tradition, however, the dominant view is that five commandments were written on each of the two tablets. According to this view, as well as the prohibition of images being counted as a separate second commandment, the commandment to honor one's parents is included on the first tablet. This is also how the two tablets are represented in artistic form, as found frequently in synagogues (cf. *EncJud* 5, 1446-1448).

This question cannot be "decided" one way or the other. However, it is clear that the commandment to honor one's parents displays a series of special features that have to do with its position in the Decalogue. Thus only two of the Decalogue's commandments are worded positively: the Sabbath commandment ("remember" or "keep") and the commandment to honor one's parents ("honor," *kabbēd*). They are positioned together in the middle of the Decalogue. In both cases the Deuteronomic version has the addition: "as the Lord your God commanded you" (Deut 5.12, 16). The parent commandment however is "at the top of the list of ethical instructions in the Old Testament as regards the frequency of instances too" (Crüsemann 1983, 59). A number of times it is given as the first commandment in a series (Lev 19.3, before the Sabbath commandment; 20.9) or as the first of the commandments relating to behavior towards other people (Deut 27.16). See also Lev 21.15, 17; and cf. Ezek 22.7; Mic 7.6; Mal 1.6; Prov 1.8; 19.26 etc. After all, this is "the first commandment that has a promise" (Eph 6.2f): "so that your days will be long (Deut: and you will have good success)." The commandment to honor one's parents is accorded very fundamental significance for one's own prosperity. The concern is not primarily with the behavior of children or youths toward their parents but in particular with the care of the parents when they are older (cf. Albertz 1978). This is elaborated in some detail in the earliest exegesis of this commandment in the book of Jesus ben Sirach (Sir 3.1-18). The mention of the "earth" (*ᵃdāmāh*), i.e. the soil of a field, reveals an agricultural background in which the unbroken sequence of the generations is especially important. Thus the promise of prosperity applies not only to the individual but also at the same time to the chain of generations that live on the land God has given them.

2.5 No harming of one's fellow human beings

The commandments that follow at this point all have to do with direct
relationships between people. God is no longer expressly mentioned;
but all these commandments follow the introductory self-presentation
of the God who brought Israel out of Egypt and made them his people
(Ex 20.2; Deut 5.6). This provides incontrovertible justification for
each of the commandments.

These commandments form a series of short sentences which all begin with "not" (*lô'*) in emphatic first position with a following imperfect, as was the case before with the commandments at the beginning
of the Decalogue (Ex 20.3, 4, 7; Deut 5.7, 8, 11). But they are much
briefer; in the first three the "not" is followed only by a single verb, in
the following two (or three) there are also objects or other explanatory
elements. But these commandments—or rather, prohibitions—contain
no justifications of any kind and no indications of punishment or
promises. In the Deuteronomic version these commandments are
joined together by a series of "ands" (*w*). They are reminiscent of
short series of reproaches like those which the prophets throw at their
contemporaries: "cursing, lying, murdering, stealing and committing
adultery" (Hos 4.2) [→**268**]; "stealing, murdering, committing adultery,
swearing falsely and sacrificing to Baal" (Jer 7.9) [→**209**].

Comparison of these texts with each other and with the Decalogue
shows that such series are not exhaustive and that the order of the
reproaches can change. Thus this second part of the Decalogue does
not form a concluding summary of the commandments of the Torah
for human relationships either; others are added in the subsequent
chapters of the report of the giving of the Torah on Sinai as well as in
Deuteronomy. The collection of commandments given here has its
basis in the early history of the Decalogue, about which our information is limited.

The last two (or three) commandments speak of behavior towards
one's "neighbor" (*rē*ᵃ*'*), i.e. one's fellow citizen, who has the same
rights and responsibilities in society, and thus especially in law; these
are matters of juridical relevance. Thee first three commandments do
not have this concept and are thus worded in more generally applica-
ble terms; they relate to all human beings without distinction.

In this last section of the Decalogue the numbering of the verses
varies in the tradition: while the counting customary in English (and

German) translations counts each of the four short "you shall not" sentences as a separate verse (Ex 20.13-16; Deut 5.17-20), other textual traditions and commentaries (e.g. Weinfeld 1991) lump these sentences together as a single verse; this has a knock-on effect on the numbering through to the end of each of the two chapters.

"You shall not kill"

Or: "Do not murder." This brief sentence, which contains no justification and no statements about what happens when the commandment is broken, must arouse associations for each hearer and reader. For this was the first command that God gave to humans: "Whoever sheds the blood of man, by man shall his blood be shed" (Gen 9.6) [→19]. In this first command to humanity there is also mention of the consequences of such an act; it is not said, however, who is to carry them out. But it is especially significant that a justification is given: "for in the image of God has God made man" (cf. Gen 1.27). The killing of a human being is an offense against the divine order of creation.

This command is found in the form of a severe legal statement in Ex 21.12: "Anyone who strikes a man and kills him shall surely die the death (*môt yûmāt*)." The unconditionality of this sentence is then interpretively nuanced: according to whether the deed was an accident, in which "the deity (*hā"lohîm*) let it happen" (v. 13), or whether it was done deliberately by "scheming" (v. 14). In the first case the culprit is to flee to a place that God will determine, in the second case he is to be removed from "my altar," to which he has fled for protective asylum, and killed.

This leads on to the context in which the Decalogue commandment must be understood. The verb used here, *rāṣaḥ*, has a special meaning which may be described as "the violent killing of a person" (Crüsemann 1983, 67; cf. also *ThWAT* VII, 652ff). Outside the Decalogue it occurs in particular in the in some cases very detailed stipulations about the cities of exile (Num 35 *passim*; Deut 4.42; 19.3-6; Josh 20f *passim*). In these texts the killer is described throughout with the participle of this verb as *roṣē"ḥ*. It is also clear that all this is to be viewed in the context of an existing and practiced blood-revenge. The asylum is to protect the unintentional killer from this. The associated legal questions are discussed in detail in the regulations about asylum (cf. Crüsemann 1992, 205-208).

The Decalogue commandment leaves these questions open. The violent killing of a person is in any case an offense against the divine order of creation. In addition, it is an elementary disturbance of the life in society of the community that God led out of Egyptian slavery.

"You shall not commit adultery"

Here too the concern is primarily with life together in community. "Do not commit adultery" means not breaking into the existing marriage of someone else. This succinctly worded prohibition has to be viewed in its social-historical and legal context (cf. esp. Crüsemann 1978b). In Old Testament times the family is the basic foundation of life in society. "Family" in this context means the extended family in which all the essential processes of life are played out, in particular the production of the necessities of life. Breaking into someone else's marriage means endangering this community and thus the foundation of existence for those concerned and their whole families. (Cf. also the last verse of the Decalogue in Ex 20.17b; Deut 5.21a.)

It is clear in various penal regulations how seriously this problem is taken: the death penalty is threatened in the case of adultery (Lev 20.10; Deut 22.22). The elaboration of this in Deut 22.23ff shows that the critical point is whether the woman was married or at least engaged, i.e. whether the legal prerequisites for marriage were in place (e.g. by payment of a dowry). In such cases "in-breaking" is a fact; the death penalty automatically threatens for the man. The same applies to the woman if she was married or if the act of sleeping together took place within the locality where the fiancée could have called for help. But if it took place in the open air the fiancée is not to be punished; she is given the benefit of the doubt and it is assumed that her cries for help could not be heard. If the girl was not engaged, however, the legal situation is quite different: the adulterer must marry the girl, paying the dowry, and the latter must not dismiss his wife. (In Ex 22.15f there is a slightly different ruling.) It is clear from this last stipulation that the primary concern is not with sexual morality but with a socio-legal problem. (Cf. also Otto 1994, 39-47.)

The problems of sexual relations are also viewed from another perspective, however. In Lev 18 the concern is with relationships within the extended family. They are not to be disturbed and endangered by legal claims and family relationships getting confused; forbidden sexual relationships are thus set out in great detail (cf. Elliger 1955). Penal rules are not given here. But once again it is clear that the primary concern is not with questions of sexual morality but with the prevention of disturbances of community life. But the whole thing is then placed in a different light: setting boundaries with regard to the practices of other peoples, in particular those "of the land of Egypt, where you lived" and "of the land of Canaan, where I lead you" (v. 3, cf. v. 24). By indulging in such practices Israel would defile itself (*ṭm'* hithp., vv. 24f).

From here on the line leads to language in which adultery becomes a metaphor for Israel's apostasy from Yhwh through the worship of other gods. In Hosea God's relationship with Israel is viewed from this point of view right from the outset [→**266**]. Several times use is made of the verb *nā'ap*, "commit adultery," which is used in the Decalogue (Hos 3.1; 4.13f), as well as the word *zānāh*, "prostitute oneself" (1.2; 4.12 etc.), occasionally both in *parallelismus membrorum* (4.14f). In Jeremiah and Ezekiel this metaphorical depiction of Israel's adulterous relationships with other gods is painted in great detail: Israel indulges in prostitution "on every high hill and under every green tree" (Jer 2.20) [→**207**], as well as her sister Judah (3.2f); once again the words "commit adultery" and "prostitute oneself" occur in parallel (3.8f etc.). In Ezekiel too in the two great chapters 16 and 23 [→**245**] the verb "prostitute oneself" is dominant (16.15, 26, 28; 23.3, 5 etc.). In the word "commit adultery" we hear the echo of the legal background that it has in such texts as Deut 22: "I will sentence you to the punishment of women who commit adultery and who shed blood" (Ezek 16.38; cf. 23.45).

Alongside this metaphorical use, however, in the prophets too the original use of the word *nā'ap* continues, as e.g. in the above-mentioned series of reproaches in Hos 4.2 and Jer 7.9. In Jer 9.1-5 the word is found at the beginning of a long accusation about the destruction of the community, which again is reminiscent of the context of the Decalogue commandment (cf. also 23.10, 14). In Malachi the religious and legal aspects are linked together under the heading "acting unfaithfully" (*bāgad*): "Judah has broken faith ... by marrying the daughter of a foreign god" (Mal 2.11); and individual Israelites are also unfaithful toward the "wife of your youth" (2.14-16).

"You shall not steal"

While the concern in the previous commandment was for the marriage of one's neighbor and thus with the protection of the family, the following commandments are primarily directed to the protection of property. In a society whose members do not live in luxury, a loss of property can make a considerable dent in the circumstances in which one lives. At the same time theft also means a disturbance of life together in community. Stealing (*gānab*) is thus mentioned time and again in the list of offenses against life together in society. In addition to Hos 4.2 and Jer 7.9, Lev 19.11 should be mentioned. Here the sentence "You shall not steal" stands at the head of a long, well-constructed series leading up to the commandment "You shall love your neighbor as yourself" (v. 18). The series is given special weight by the fourfold "I am the Lord" (vv. 12, 14, 16, 18).

The terse commandment "You shall not steal" leaves various elaborations open. In other collections of laws there is express mention of: theft of cattle (Ex 21.37), including the theft of cattle given to someone for safe keeping (22.9-13) or lent to them (e.g. for plowing) (vv. 13f); of money or valuables given to another person for safe keeping, e.g. while one is away on a journey (22.6f); and finally in the extreme case the theft of a person (for enslavement) (Ex 21.16; Deut 24.7) [→56]. The Decalogue leaves this whole spectrum open. Legal rulings are not its topic either. Certainly they will have been in existence at the time the Decalogue was fixed in one form or another, so that hearers or readers will have been familiar with them.

"You shall not bear false witness against your neighbor"

This commandment, or prohibition, ties up directly with the previous one. Theft is an offense against the rule of law. In order to clear up and punish such offenses there is a need for legal processes. Reliable and responsible witnesses are of great importance for such processes, while false witnesses mean the endangerment of life together in a law-abiding community. The word '*ēd*, generally translated as "witness," also means the person who reports an offense or crime and therefore also appears as complainant in the court case (cf. Seeligmann 1967, 262ff; *THAT* II, 212f).

In the Decalogue commandment the protection of the rights of the individual member of the law-abiding community is in the foreground. For the Israelite addressed, the other person is the "neighbor" (*rē*ᵃ'), to whom he should be useful, not harmful. But a "false witness" ('*ēd šeqer*, Ex 20.16; Deut 5.20, '*ēd šāw*'), who can also be a person who brings a false accusation, can be very dangerous to someone accused of a crime. The awareness of this danger has left clear traces in the texts of the Hebrew Bible. So a single witness is never enough in matters of life and death (Num 35.30); there must be "two or three witnesses" (Deut 17.6) [→82], and in addition they must reinforce their statements by being the first to raise their hand at a stoning (v. 7). In Deuteronomy the requirement for two or three witnesses is even set generally for any form of misdemeanor (19.15).

This shows too what interests may drive a false statement. An essential point is that no partiality should be shown on account of someone's social standing (Deut 16.19; cf. 1.17). The concern here is with the fundamental matter of equal treatment for all members of society, both "small" and "great" (Deut 1.17; cf. Lev 19.15). But the danger of false testimony pertains in both directions. Going along with the crowd can lead to a statement in court which leads to the "insignificant" (*dal*) being advantaged (Ex 23.2f). But in the same context there is a warning against twisting the rights of the "poor" (*'ebyôn* v. 6). In what follows the greatest danger is mentioned: bribery. "A bribe blinds the eyes of the wise and twists the words of the righteous" (v. 8, cf. Deut 16.19). Prophetic texts reveal that this is a significant problem in life together in society (Isa 1.23; 5.23; Mic 3.11 etc.) [→293]. In contrast to this, in Deuteronomy's list of God's qualities there is special emphasis on the fact that he "shows no partiality and accepts no bribes" (Deut 10.17); God is therefore the true guarantor of justice for all.

"You shall not covet"

The concluding two sentences are concerned with the property of one's neighbor. In the context of the Decalogue, "You shall not covet" means you are not to take steps to acquire something that belongs to your neighbor. The word "covet" or "desire" (*ḥāmad*) does not inherently mean something negative; but it is often found in a context where the desiring contains an intent to possess, which ultimately leads to "taking:" thus Eve sees that the tree is desirable (*neḥmād*), and she helps herself to its fruit (Gen 3.6; cf. also Josh 7.21). Mic 2.2 speaks of the snatching of fields and houses by force as the consequence of desiring, and also makes it clear that this implies a deep incursion into the social situation of the person concerned (cf. Kessler 1999, 111ff). Thus this concluding commandment forbids any desiring that can result in appropriation.

The two sentences of the commandment which are introduced by "You shall not covet" clearly have the function of describing the area of what is to be protected by them in sufficient breadth and nuance. In the version of the Decalogue in Ex 20, the neighbor's household is at the beginning (v. 17a). This again reminds us of the passage just quoted from Mic 2.2, which reads: "They defraud a man of his home." Here the term "home/household" means more than just the building; it means the whole area of life for which the man is responsible in the social order of the day. This also comes to expression in a greeting such as in 1 Sam 25.6: "Good health to you and your household! And good health to all that is yours!" The concluding expression corresponds to the one at the end of the Decalogue: "everything that belongs to your neighbor" (Ex 20.17b; Deut 5.21b).

In the Ex 20 version (v. 17) the "household" is fleshed out further as the area of responsibility: the neighbor's wife is the first in this category, which again clearly emphasizes the social and legal significance of the prohibition of adultery. Then slaves (manservant and maidservant) are mentioned, who belong to the "household" in another legal capacity; further the domesticated animals with the most important representatives, cattle and donkeys. Finally the whole thing is expanded again and summarized: "and everything that belongs to your neighbor."

In the Deuteronomic version a certain shift in emphasis is evident. At the head in this case stands the prohibition against coveting one's neighbor's wife (Deut 5.21a); this emphasizes the fundamental socio-legal significance of the prohibition of adultery even more strongly. In the further elaboration another verb of "desire" is then used (*'wh* hithp.), though this does not seem to make much difference in content. Here, however, the term "household" is taken more concretely and supplemented by "field." These divergences between the two formulations of the Decalogue show again, as in the case of the Sabbath commandment, that the text of this fundamental collection of divine commandments and prohibitions was open to alterations as a result of further consideration and changes in circumstances, up to the time each collection was committed to writing.

3. Multi-layered and tension-filled elaboration

With its commandments the Decalogue has described a broad area: from the exclusive worship of the one and only God through the concretization of the worship of God on the Sabbath through to the problems of life together in human society. In the previous sections we have often talked about how these commandments are reflected in other texts of the Torah (Pentateuch) and in the Hebrew Bible as a whole, but how they were also developed further and given precise shape. (In the history of the beginnings in the Pentateuch some texts are probably older than the Decalogue and will have been used as a source or working document when it was put together.) We shall now investigate this more closely.

3.1 The purity of the cult—outwardly and inwardly

The commandments that Moses receives from God and passes on to the Israelites immediately following the divine imparting of the Decalogue begin like the Decalogue itself with instructions as to the correct form in which God is to be worshiped. This displays a fundamental element of the Torah: as far as Israel is concerned, the most important thing is the duty of exclusive acknowledgement and worship of the one and only God, who has revealed himself to Israel and led it out of Egyptian slavery. Thus at the beginning of the commandments that follow the Decalogue (in the "book of the covenant") we find the demand that Israel should make no images of gods, neither of God himself (Ex 20.23a) nor of other gods (v. 23b) [→**56**]. Another collection of commandments that appears in a later passage in the Sinai account (Ex 34.11-26) is dominated entirely by questions of the worship of God. There the demand "You shall not bow down to any other god" (v. 14) is embedded in the prohibition of making alliances with the inhabitants of the land, because this could lead to the worship of other gods (vv. 11f, 15f, cf. also 23.32).

In both texts the altar plays an important role. In Ex 20.24f the prohibition of the manufacture of images is immediately followed by an altar law. In a prominent position a fundamental element of the cultic worship of God is given. The call to destroy altars that serve for the worship of other gods corresponds to this. This call appears in Ex 34.13 in the context of the prohibition of alliances with the older inhabitants of the land and of participation in their cultic acts. It is then repeated with forceful emphasis in Deuteronomy (Deut 7.1-5; 12.2f; cf. Crüsemann 1992, 153-156) [→**78**].

Next to the altar, in Ex 34 (and Deut 4 and 12) two further cultic elements are mentioned which the Israelites are to destroy: massebah and Asherah, i.e. cultic symbols made of stone and wood (cf. also Deut 16.21f; in Ex 23.24 only massebah). The massebah (*maṣṣēbā*) is an erected stone, generally a religious symbol. It appears in the story of the patriarchs as a legitimate Israelite cultic symbol representing the presence of God: Jacob designates the massebah he erects at Beth-El at the site of the nocturnal appearance of God [→**31**], as the "House of God" (*bêt ᵉlohîm*, Gen 28.12, 22; cf. 31.13; 35.14f); a massebah serves as a "witness" before God for the agreement between Jacob and Laban (31.45, 51-53); and Jacob erects a massebah over Rachel's grave (35.20). On Sinai Moses erects twelve massebahs for the twelve tribes of Israel with whom God concludes the covenant (Ex 24.4; despite the number twelve the word *maṣṣēbā* is in the singular here!) [→**57**]. The twelve stones spoken of in Josh 4 (vv. 3ff) also belong in this context, as well as the stone as witness before God in Josh 24.26f. Finally for Hosea too the massebah (singular) is one of the legitimate elements of the cult for which Israel has long been reproached (Hos 3.4) [→**268**]. Massebahs can also serve for the worship of other gods. Israel should thus remove "their massebahs" (plural) as well as "their altars" (Ex 23.24; 34.13; Deut 7.5; 12.3). In Deut 16.22 the erection of massebahs is prohibited altogether, "for the Lord hates it." Here a general negative verdict on the massebahs has won the day.

Alongside the massebahs, Asherahs are often mentioned. *'Aśērāh* is the name of a female deity who plays an important role especially in neighboring Ugarit (the form of the name there being *'Aṯirat*) as the escort of *'El*, the most high God (cf. *ThWAT* I, 473-481). This deity is represented by a wooden cultic symbol, a tree or a post (cf. Deut 16.21) [→**81**]. Thus we read of the "tearing down" of the altars and the "smashing" of the massebahs and of the "breaking down" (Ex 34.13), "knocking down" (Deut 7.5) or "burning with fire" (Deut 12.3) of the Asherahs.

Unlike the massebah the Asherah is never found as a legitimate cultic object in the Hebrew Bible. It is mentioned first in narrative contexts in the book of Judges. In the introduction to the first of the Judges narratives we read in Judg 3.7: "The Israelites did evil in the eyes of the Lord; they forgot the Lord their God and served the Baals and the Asherahs" [→**101**]. Here the Asherah (generalized in the plural) as the female escort of Baal is a central element in the apostasy of the Israelites from the worship of Yhwh. This is made concrete in the story of Gideon in Judg 6.25-32: Gideon is given the divine commission to tear down the altar of Baal and to knock down the Asherah standing next to it (vv. 25, 26, 28, 30). Here Asherah means a wooden cult image that stands next to the altar. (Deut 16.21 forbids such an arrangement of the altar of Yhwh, so that at times there was evidently a tendency to do this.) In the account of the history of the period of the monarchy the setting up of Asherahs is mentioned time and again as an especially serious reproach (1 Kgs 14.15; 15.13; 16.32f; 13.6; 2 Kgs 17.16; 21.3, 7; together with massebahs in 1 Kgs 14.23; 2 Kgs 10.26f; 17.10). In 1 Kgs 18.19 Elijah's opponents include the prophets of Asherah alongside the prophets of Baal. Finally, Josiah's Reform is directed in particular against the Asherahs and the Asherah cult in Jerusalem and on the cultic high-places as well as the temple of Beth-El (2 Kgs 23.4, 6, 7, 14, 15).

The lines that are becoming visible here are also evident in the prophetic criticism of Israel's cult. Hosea complains of the multiplicity of altars and massebahs (in the plural here, unlike 3.4), which Israel has set up in consequence of its prosperity, and announces their destruction because Israel's heart is "false" (Hos 10.1f) [→271]; however legitimate these cultic objects may be *per se*, Israel has gone and misused them. In Micah, in the concluding paragraph of the part collection Mic 4–5, alongside the destruction of weapons in order to bring about peace (5.9f; cf. Kessler 1999, 174f) there is also the removal of religious means of self-security: sorcery, diviners, then idols (*pesîlîm*) and massebahs, and finally also Asherahs (vv. 11-13). Here the massebahs are classed as the "work of your hands" in between idols and Asherahs. This shows a generally low view of massebahs, as in Deut 16.22. Jeremiah mentions altars and Asherahs in his polemic against the high-place sanctuaries (Jer 17.2). In Isa 17.8 it is said in relation to a future that has yet to occur that "the human" will then look only to his or her creator and no longer to the self-made altars and Asherahs. And according to Isa 27.9 the destruction of the altars and Asherahs will constitute a contribution toward the atonement of Israel's sins. Despite all the various differences between these texts, it is common to all that in the view of the prophets consorting with cultic symbols has led Israel onto a wayward path and that—for Israel's own good—they must therefore be removed.

But this is only one side. The other is seen in that in the Torah itself detailed stipulations for the establishment of the cult are given. There has already been mention of the altar law at the beginning of the "book of the covenant" (Ex 20.24f) [→55]. Later the Sabbath commandment is taken up again (Ex 23.12; cf. 34.21), though there is talk there only of the "seventh day," on which there is to be rest from work, while the name "Sabbath" is not (yet?) mentioned. Here the

Sabbath is linked with the immediately following stipulations about the three annual festivals (23.14-17; cf. 34.18, 22-24) as well as the instruction about the submission of firstfruits (23.19a; cf. 34.26a). In addition, before the Sabbath commandment stands the requirement of the keeping of the Sabbath year, i.e. the seventh year, in which the fruits of the land are not to be harvested (23.10f). They are to be for the benefit of the "poor of your people." Thus the rules of the Sabbath year on the one hand express the religious aspect that the land belongs to God, and on the other hand they contain a social element. The latter is then developed further in different ways in Deut 15 and Lev 25. The connection between these two elements is fundamental for the Torah as a whole. In the Torah the concern is always with the relationship to God and to one's fellow human being, one's neighbor, which has already found its striking expression in the Decalogue.

From Ex 25 on there then follow detailed instructions for the whole area of the cult in the narrower sense. They comprise a large part of the texts through to the point when Israel leaves Sinai (Num 10.11). Attention thereby turns now inward, as the rules for matters in the inner area of the cult are developed. (For details see §11.) For the reader who comes from the Decalogue and the collections of commandments emanating from it, the breadth and variety of what is collected in the Torah becomes clear in these quite varied texts. But nowhere is there any indication of a difference in religious or theological evaluations of the various aspects of the Torah (as e.g. in the sense of a low view of the "ritual laws" as is common in the Christian tradition).

Here there are dangers of quite a different sort. The cultic prescriptions need to be kept precisely; infringements of these could have fatal consequences. This is emphasized especially in the rules for the behavior of priests: the wearing of leg apparel during the worship service (Ex 28.42f); the washing of hands and feet before entry into the sanctuary (30.18-21); abstinence from alcohol during the priestly service (Lev 10.9); the relinquishing of particular mourning rites (Lev 10.6; cf. 21.10) etc. A particular dramatic description is given to the danger of infringing cultic regulations in the forbidden smoke offerings of two sons of Aaron, Nadab and Abihu, who were struck by divine punishment on account of this "foreign fire" ('ēš zārāh, 10.1-5) [→67]. In the introduction to the law about the "day of atonement" there is express reference to the prohibition that Aaron (i.e. the high priest) is not "at any time" to enter the holy of holies (16.1f). (Whether there were other occasions beside the day of atonement for entering the holy of holies, is left open at this point; for discussion on the Jewish history of interpretation see Milgrom 1991, 1021f, 1061f; cf. also Heb 9.7).

The various purity regulations (Lev 11–15; 20; Deut 14 etc.) also belong in this area of "purity and endangerment" (Douglas 1966/1985). At the same time they are tied into the broad context of what is included under the term "holy" (*qādoš*) [→**542**]. This comes forcibly to expression in the fact that the formula "You shall be holy, as I am holy" concludes the chapter on "clean" and "unclean" animals (Lev 11.44, 45), while it also opens the chapter Lev 19 in which at great length ethical commandments are presented (v. 2). Both aspects, however fundamentally different they may seem from modern thinking, belong inseparably together in the Torah.

3.2 The rights of slaves, foreigners, widows and orphans

The cult-related introduction in Ex 20.22-26 is followed immediately by the first of the legal ordinances (*mišpāṭîm* 21.1), regulations of slave law (21.2-11). Slaves were mentioned before in the Decalogue in the context of the Sabbath commandment (20.10), and the social aspect of rest from work has been extensively elaborated in the Deuteronomic version of the Decalogue (Deut 5.14f). Now as the commandments given to Israel are further expounded the stipulations regarding the rights of slaves are in prime position. Precisely because slaves are the weakest members in the social order, their rights need to be made especially secure. Some stipulations relate only to slaves as such, such as the rules about being set free after seven years (Ex 21.2-6) and about giving female slaves in marriage (vv. 7-11). Frequently in the following regulations too special rules are established that take account of their special place in society. Thus abduction, the intent of which is to enslave the abducted person, carries the threat of death (v. 16); in regulations about assault there are special rules for slaves (vv. 20f, 26f), and also for cases in which a slave is gored and killed by a bull (v. 32).

The slave laws reflect certain social changes. Ex 21.2 speaks of a "Hebrew" slave (*'ebed 'ibrî*). The derivation and precise meaning of the word *'ibrî* are disputed; it can contain ethnic as well as social elements (cf. *EKL*[3], 393f). In Deut 15.12 the "Hebrew" slave (the male and the female slave) is termed "brother," i.e. Israelite. In the foreground here is the release in the seventh year (vv. 12-18). In Lev 25.39-43 there is mention only of the impoverished "brother," and it is stated expressly that he is to be treated not as a slave but as a paid worker. "Because the Israelites are my servants, whom I brought out of Egypt, they must not be sold as slaves" (v. 42, cf. v. 55).

What applies to slaves applies by the same token also to "foreigners" and equally to widows and orphans: they have no voice of their own in legal matters. Thus at the end of the "book of the covenant," corresponding to the regulations about slave law at the beginning (Ex 21.2-11), we find the prohibition of oppressing foreigners, widows and orphans (22.20-23; 23.9). This prohibition has a notable addition: "Do not take advantage of a widow or an orphan. If you do and they cry out to me, I will certainly hear their cry" (22.22). The cry of distress (*ṣāʿaq*), the cry for justice, will be addressed to God himself, and God will hear it. Israel is to remember that its people were themselves "foreigners" in Egypt (22.20; 23.9) and that God heard and answered their "cries" at that time (Ex 2.23; 3.7, 9). In the context of God's commandments to Israel, however, this means that Israel itself is to deal appropriately with the legal rights of these groups, so that God will not have to intervene and punish them (22.23).

Finally the "poor" (*ʿānî*) and "needy" (*ʾebyôn*) are mentioned separately; these are Israelites who are not outside the community as far as the law is concerned, but who have become dependent as a result of economic need. No interest is to be exacted from them (Ex 22.24) and if one takes a poor person's only garment as deposit for a loan, one is to give it back to him before sunset (vv. 24f; cf. also Deut 24.10-13). Similarly the poor and needy casual laborer is to be paid his wage before sunset (Deut 24.14f). The needy are also to eat of what grows on the uncultivated fields in the seventh year (Ex 23.10f). The same ruling is given in relation to the poor and foreigners in Lev 23.22. In Deut 15.7-11 there is an even more basic demand that one should be open-handed towards one's poor and needy brethren; for there will always be such in Israel (despite the utopian wish expressed in v. 4). Finally, the rights of the needy should not be abused in legal cases either (v. 6), but nor should partiality be shown to the disadvantaged (*dal*) (v. 3; cf. Lev 19.15). (The terms *ʿānî*, *ʾebyôn*, and *dal* are not clearly distinguished.)

3.3 The rights of the individual (a man and his neighbor)

One of the most common words in the regulations that immediately follow the Decalogue is the word "man" (*'îš*, often translated by "anyone" or "whoever"). Rather than slaves and foreigners this means the Israelite citizen who bears full responsibility in relation to the law. If two men get into conflict, the other is referred to as the "neighbor" (*rēaʿ*) (Ex 21.14, 18, 35 etc.). A large number of stipulations give rules for social life with all its conflicts large and small. Two topics are in the foreground here: life—with the whole area of endangering and damaging of physical inviolability (21.12-36)—and property (21.37–22.16). Both topics also play an important role in the Decalogue (20.13, 17; Deut 5.17, 21).

Unlike the Decalogue, which does not have rules about punishments or restitution, here the consequences of infringements of the commandments are dealt with in detail. In a series of cases restitution is required (21.19, 22, 30 etc.), and for serious misdemeanors the death penalty is threatened (21.12, 14-17). It is clearly evident here that these commandments have legal force and that the availability of legal enforcement is presupposed. One will think in the first place of the local magistracy "in the gate" (cf. Ruth 4.1-12; cf. Köhler 1931) [→372]. But there were also frequently cases where the local magistracy was not able to make a decision on its own, so that a higher authority was necessary. The establishment of such a supreme court was prescribed in Deut 17.8-13. In 2 Chron 19.5-11 it is reported that the Judean king Jehoshaphat established such a court, and Ex 18.13-27 may also be read as an (etiological) reference to such an authority (cf. Macholz 1972b; Knierim 1961). Regardless of the historical problems of these very different texts, the legal background for the stipulations of the "book of the covenant" may be seen here (Crüsemann 1992, 113ff).

The collection of commandments in Lev 19 has different emphases. Here the commandments about human relationships (vv. 11-18) lead to the sentence "You shall love your neighbor as yourself" (v. 18). The legal aspects take second place here. Instead, this passage is emphasized by means of the fourfold "I am the Lord" (vv. 12, 14, 16, 18). In addition, it comes under the overall topic expressed at the beginning of the chapter: "Be holy because I, the Lord your God, am holy" (v. 2 [→543]. Cf. Ruwe 1999, 218ff).

3.4 Israel's justice

Many of the Old Testament commandments are directed to a singular "you" (2nd pers. sing.), while others are addressed in the 2nd person plural. Both forms of address can mean the legally responsible individual Israelite; in many commandments however the community as a whole is being addressed. (Occasionally the number in the verb form changes within a sentence or passage, cf. e.g. Ex 22.20-23; the variation is particularly frequent in Deuteronomy, cf. Weinfeld 1991, 14f; *ABD* 2, 173f). The instructions of the Torah apply to Israel as a whole.

The legal aspect that was discernible already in the commandments of the "book of the covenant" is viewed here from the other point of view. Israel is addressed as an entity: "Appoint judges and officials for each of your tribes in every town the Lord your God is giving you, and they shall judge the people fairly (*mišpaṭ ṣedeq*)" (Deut 16.18). The great significance of this ruling comes to expression in the immediately following sentence: "Justice, justice (*ṣedeq ṣedeq*)—you are to follow, so that you may live and possess the land the Lord your God is giving you" (v. 20). Israel's justice has its essential foundation in the institutions responsible for the maintenance, interpretation and further developments and in particular the application of the law, i.e. the Torah. But the people appoint the judges, and the responsibility remains with the people; this is clear from the fact that in Deuteronomy alongside the judges there is frequent mention of the elders with juridical functions (21.2; see also 19.12; 21.18-21; 22.13-21; 25.5-10; 27.1 etc.; cf. Crüsemann 1992, 278ff).

From this point, threads can be followed through the various areas of the Hebrew Bible. The maintenance of the law is constantly a critical matter, and correspondingly the neglect or abuse of the maintenance of the law is an essential cause for prophetic criticism (cf. §16.2). Finally the establishment of law and justice is also one of the most important hopes for the future (cf. §22.3).

§ 11

The Location of Life before God: the Cult

1. The Place where I make my Name known

1.1 You shall make me an altar

In all parts of the Hebrew Bible it is one of the fundamental elements
of the relationship between humans and God that they accord him
cultic worship. The first reported human act "beyond Eden" is the
bringing of sacrifices to God (Gen 4.3f). It appears as something that is
taken entirely for granted, needing no special justification or explanation, that each of the two brothers Cain and Abel present God with a
"gift" of the produce of their labor: of the yield of the field and of the
animals of the flock. Here the word *minḥāh* is a collective term for
sacrifices of vegetable material and sacrifices of animals, which where
otherwise generally separated. This word is also the only biblical term
for sacrifice that is used also outside the cultic area; in the political area
it can mean a tribute (e.g. Judg 3.15, 17f), in other cases a present as an
expression of submission (Gen 32.14, 19, 21f; cf. 1967, 192-195;
1985ff, 87f). So what we have here is not a more precise statement
about the type of sacrifice brought by the two brothers, but the simple
fact that in the rhythm of their life in agriculture and animal husbandry
they bring appropriate gifts to God.

It is more difficult to answer the question why God reacts so differently to the
two sacrifices and wherein this comes to expression. The verb *ša'ah*, "look,"
occurs only here in a cultic context (cf. *ThWAT* VIII, 349f). The following
divine speech to Cain largely escapes our understanding. (Gen 4.7 has been
called the "most obscure verse in Genesis.")

The first thing reported of Noah doing after his rescue from the flood
catastrophe is also that he brings sacrifices to God (Gen 8.20). Here
they are a very marked expression of thanksgiving for the rescue. In

the first place Noah builds an altar for this purpose. This brings us face to face with a quite crucial point in cultic life: the altar is an essential precondition for the cultic worship of God. The narratives about the patriarchs also regularly report the erection of altars. Another important feature becomes evident here: the place where an altar is erected is not chosen by human whim. It is reported of Abraham that the first thing he does on his journey to the land of Canaan is to go to a particular place (*māqôm*) where God appears to him; there he erects an altar (Gen 12.6f). Jacob erects an altar in Beth-El after his return from Haran, at the place where God had appeared to him when he was fleeing from his brother Esau (35.1-7; cf. 28.10-22). The precondition for the establishment of the altar is thus that God himself has "appeared" at this place, that at a certain moment in time he was present there.

What is given narrative expression here is expressly formulated at the beginning of the "book of the covenant:" "'Make an altar of earth for me and sacrifice on it your burnt offerings and fellowship offerings, your sheep and goats and your cattle. Wherever I cause my name to be honored, I will come to you and bless you'" (Ex 20.24; cf. Crüsemann 1992, 201ff) [→56]. The narratives of Abraham and Jacob read almost like explanations of this cult law. Here God has made himself known, by appearing to the fathers.

On other reported occasions of the establishment of altars, corresponding experiences of God are certainly to be presupposed. When Abraham calls upon (or exclaims) the name of "Yhwh, the Eternal God" (*Yhwh 'ēl 'ōlām*, Gen 21.33), or when Jacob calls the places where he founds altars "El, God of Israel" (33.20) or "El of Beth-El" (35.7), there are echoes of encounters with God. The naming of prominent local landmarks such as the "Terebinths of Mamre" (Gen 13.18) may indicate the special features of a sacred place. The context in the Exodus narrative is clearer: Moses sets up an altar after the victory over the Amalekites, achieved with God's help, and calls it "Yhwh is my Banner" (Ex 17.15). In Gideon's case too the connection between a divine appearance and the construction of an altar is quite marked (Judg 6.24). (On Judg 6.25-32 see below.) Finally, we should also mention the story of David's census of the people and its consequences in 2 Sam 24 [→116]: at the express request of the prophet Gad, David erects an altar at the place where he saw the "destroying angel" (*hammal'ak hammašḥît*) when the plague that came over Israel came to a halt (vv. 18-25). We can probably see an etiology here for the place where the temple of Solomon was later built.

These texts, in all their variety, show the fundamental significance of the altar for the cultic exercise of relations with God. Its name *misbe'h* (place of slaughter) expresses the fact that sacrifices generally occupy central place in this cult. The expression "call upon (or exclaim—Buber) the name of the Lord," which we meet many times in the stories of the patriarchs (*qārā' bešēm yhwh*, Gen 12.8; 13.4; 21.33; 26.25), puts an even more comprehensive aspect into words. One can almost see in this a "fixed term to give expression to the establishment of relations with Yhwh" (cf. *ThWAT* VII, 122). Sacrifices, as a more or less taken-for-granted form of worship, are no doubt included in this.

In texts that speak of the establishment of the cult in the sanctuary on Sinai—and thus in anticipation in the temple in Jerusalem—(Ex 25-31; 35-40; Lev 1-7; 16), the altar occupies a central position. Lev 1-7 [→530] in particular shows that the altar is the place where the community's and the individual's turning to God takes place most directly. The Israelite can approach God as far as this point, and he brings everything here that he wants to, or must, present to God. Thus the Psalmist, who is far from the temple, can pray to God to bring him to his holy mountain, Zion, and to his dwelling-place, the temple so that "Then will I go to the altar of God" (Ps 43.4). Another compares the sense of security in the nearness of God at the altar with that of a bird that has found its nest (84.4).

The central significance of the altar comes especially clearly to expression in the new start of cultic life after the Babylonian exile. At the beginning of the seventh month, i.e. at the beginning of the new year according to the Jewish calendar, the returnees first rebuild the altar so as to bring sacrifices on it, "as it is written in the Torah of Moses, the man of God" (Ezra 3.1-6) [→391]. They begin with the daily sacrifices and then continue two weeks later with the feast of tabernacles with the festive offerings "according to the law" (v. 4, cf. Num 28f). The cult is thus back in force in its basic structure. After this the returnees then begin preparations for the reconstruction of the temple (vv. 7-13).

1.2 The Sanctuary

1.2.1 They shall make me a sanctuary

On Sinai God showed Moses the model of the sanctuary (*miqdāš*) that
he was to build him, saying: "I will live among them." The sanctuary
is thus also called "dwelling-place" (*miškān*, Ex 25.8f). But the "dwelling" is obviously not meant in the static sense. At the conclusion of
the regulations about the daily offerings that are to be brought to the
altar (*tāmîd* offerings) we read: "There I will meet you (i.e. Moses) and
speak with you; there also I will meet with the Israelites, and it (i.e.
the sanctuary) will be consecrated by my glory (*kābôd*)" (29.42f). So
the altar remains the place of God's encounter with the Israelites even
after it has found a home within the sanctuary. There is another specific way in which God is encountered in the sanctuary, through the
ark (Ex 25.22; cf. 30.6, 36; Num 17.19; see also 1.2.2 below [→**514**]).
After all, the sanctuary that is to be set up in Sinai is called generally
"tent of meeting" (*'ohel mô'ēd*, Ex 27.21 etc.).

That God does not constantly "dwell" in the sanctuary in a static
sense, also comes to expression in the fact that God constantly comes
down to the sanctuary in the cloud, so that his *kābôd* fills the "dwelling-place" (Ex 40.34). Here the descent in the cloud is expressed by
the word "dwell" (*šakan*), which can be taken concretely in the sense
that it was not possible for Moses to enter into the sanctuary, which
was filled with the cloud (v. 35). It may also mean that God "appears"
in the cloud (*rā'āh* niph., Lev 16.2).

Through the presence of God the sanctuary (*miqdāš*) is "sanctified"
(Ex 29.43). The Hebrew root *qdš* and its derivatives plays a crucial part
in this context. Thus God himself says that he will sanctify the tent of
meeting, the altar, as well as Aaron and his sons as priests (v. 44). This
is the full framework of the cult, which thereby as an entirety stands
under the concept of the holy. Within this framework there are then
various differentiations, some of which have their own systems. A
basic boundary marker is worded as a task of the priests: "to distinguish between the holy and the profane, between the pure and the
impure" (Lev 10.10). This distinction marks the external boundary for
the cultic area.

Within this area there are various stages of holiness, each of which
has its own system of reference. The most basic is the boundary of the
"holy of holies" (*qodeš haqqadāšîm*) in the innermost part of the sanctu-

ary; it is separated from the "holy" (*qodeš*) by a curtain (Ex 26.33;
40.3), which itself is separated off by an additional curtain from the
"outer court" (26.36; 40.5). This holy of holies, which is called *dᵉbîr* in
the temple built by Solomon (1 Kgs 8.6) [→**119**], forms the center of
the Israelite cult in a very special way. In it is found the central element, the ark (*'ᵃrôn*). Its prominent position is already clear from the
fact that it is mentioned first in the detailed description of all that is
necessary for the creation of the divine "dwelling" (Ex 25.10-22). The
ark is described as a box-shaped container, in which Moses later places
the "testimony" (*'ēdût*, 25.16; 40.20), i.e. the "tablets of the testimony" which he receives from God (31.18; 32.15; 34.29); that is why
it is also called the "ark of the testimony" (*'arôn hā'ēdût*, 25.22; 26.33
etc.), which is occasionally expanded into a description of the entire
sanctuary as "dwelling-place of the testimony" (*miškān hā'ēdût*, Ex
38.21 etc.).

But above all the ark serves as the place where God "meets" Israel
(Ex 25.22; 30.6, 36), by "appearing" (Lev 16.2; cf. Num 7.89). For
this Moses makes an artistically formed golden pedestal (*kapporet*),
flanked by two winged "cherubs" (*kᵉrûbîm*).

The exact meaning of the word *kapporet* is as disputed as its function. The
Septuagint translates it with ἱλαστήριον, thus relating the word to *kipper*,
"atone." The translation "throne of grace" (cf. Luther's *Gnadenstuhl*) takes on
also the aspect of the divine throne. More recent translators often prefer the
translation "covering," taking *kapporet* as the lid on the ark. The derivation of
kipper seems more obvious, however, leading to the suggestion that the translation should be "marker of atonement" or "place of atonement" (cf. Janowski
1982, 271-354, esp. 271f, n. 457; cf. *ThWAT* IV, 312).

The direct encounter with the God who appears in the holy of holies
on the *kapporet* is reserved to Aaron and thereby in turn to his successors. But even he is not allowed to enter the holy of holies "at any
time" (Lev 16.2), but only once a year on the "day of atonement," the
yôm hakkippurîm (Lev 16; 23.26-32). On that day he performs the basic
acts of atonement; for the holy of holies, the "tent of meeting," the
altar, the priests and the whole assembled people (16.33).

In the gradated system of holiness, the altar too is described as "a
holy of holies" (*qodeš qadāšîm*, without the article, Ex 29.37). This
means that no unauthorized person may touch the altar, i.e. no one
apart from the priests, who are themselves "sanctified." The same ap-

plies to the smoke-offering altar (30.10; again summarized in vv. 26-29). Finally the smoking facility is also described as a "holy of holies," so as to preclude its use for profane purposes (vv. 34-39). Thus the whole sanctuary and its facilities are included in this area of holiness.

1.2.2 Make an ark out of acacia wood

The ark is spoken of from very different points of view in the Hebrew Bible. If the texts are read in context, the impression may be gained that the ark was first constructed for the sanctuary on Sinai but then became as it were self-perpetuating. Thus the way God guided the Israelites as they departed from Sinai is expressed in two different ways. On the one hand we read that the "cloud" covers the dwelling-place; when it lifts, the Israelites move on, and where it comes down, that is where they set up camp (Num 9.15-17) [→**70**]. On the other hand it is also said of the ark that it moves ahead of the Israelites and points the way to the next camp-site (Num 10.33). Thus Moses accompanies their departure and their settlement in each case with a statement introduced by "Arise, O Lord," or "Turn back, Lord" (vv. 35f). Here the ark appears to be entirely on its own, separated from the sanctuary. Here it is referred to for the first time as "ark of the covenant" (*ʾᵃrôn bᵉrît yhwh*)—an expression that reappears frequently later (see below). Afterwards the ark is mentioned just once more during the wilderness wanderings: it remains with Moses in the camp while the Israelites conduct their self-initiated military campaign against the Amalekites and Canaanites (Num 14.44). On the other hand there is frequent mention of the sanctuary being carried with them, under a variety of names: dwelling (*miškān* 9.15ff; 10.11 [*miškān haʿēdût*]; 16.9 etc.), sanctuary (*miqdāš* 10.21; 18.1 etc.) and especially frequently tent of meeting (*ʾohel môʿēd* 11.16; 12.4), above which the "glory (*kābôd*) of Yhwh" appears (14.10; 16.18f; 17.7f).

In the further course of the account, the relationship between the ark and sanctuary shifts. In the book of Joshua the ark is right in the foreground as the symbol of guidance for the Israelites on their way to the promised land [→**99**]. Here it is now frequently called "ark of the covenant" (*ʾᵃrôn habbᵉrît* Josh 3.6, 8, 11; 4.9 etc.) or "ark of the covenant of Yhwh" (3.3, 17; 4.7 etc.) or even simply "ark of Yhwh" (3.13; 4.5), and occasionally again with the addition "of the Lord of the whole earth" (*ʾᵃdôn kal-hāʾāreṣ* 3.11, 13); the latter shows particularly clearly the great significance that is attached to it here. At the beginning stands the procession through the Jordan (Josh 3). It has almost the character of a cultic march; Joshua charges the Israelites to "sanctify" themselves (*qdš* hithp., v. 5) before the priests carry the ark of the covenant ahead of the people; the water of the Jordan (at high-water level at this point) stands in front of them like a wall (*nēd* vv. 13, 15; cf. Ex 15.8), so that the entire people can cross the Jordan without getting their feet wet—as Israel once did through the Reed Sea (Ex 14). In the narrative of the conquest of Jericho the miraculous element is even more marked (Josh 6). The ark is carried around the city while the priests blow on the horns. However, the ark retires into the background as soon as the battle proper begins (vv. 15ff).

The presence of the ark is presupposed also in the following accounts. This is evident in Josh 7.6, where it is reported that after the ill-fated attempt to conquer the city of Ai Joshua throws himself down before the ark. It has a special role to play when Joshua, carrying out Moses' instruction (cf. Deut 27.1-8), sets up an altar on Mount Ebal and writes down a copy of the "Torah of Moses" on stones (Josh 8.30-35). Here the whole community stands on both sides of the ark, facing the levitical priests (v. 33). Thus the ark forms the central point, in religious terms, for the assembled people.

The tent of meeting then turns up again. The whole "community" (*'ēdah*) gathers together in Shiloh and sets up the tent of meeting there (Josh 18.1). This is clearly meant as the conclusion of the settlement of the land, as is evident from the supplementary clause "the land lay subject to them." A division of the rest of the land by means of lottery now takes place "before the Lord at the entrance to the tent of meeting" (19.51). In the continuation of the tradition the tent of meeting and the ark are presupposed as being together in the same location, namely in Shiloh. The sanctuary there is referred to by the term "temple" (*hêkāl*), which occurs here for the first time (1 Sam 1.9; 3.3), also as "tent of meeting" (2.22) [→103]. Here we also find the ark (3.3). (According to an isolated comment in Judg 20.27f the ark was previously in Beth-El.)

A new chapter in the history of the ark now begins, as it goes beyond its guidance function and becomes a helper in military need. After a defeat at the hands of the Philistines the Israelites decide to bring the ark of the covenant of Yhwh from Shiloh to the military camp, "so that he will save us from the hand of our enemies" (1 Sam 4.3). When the ark then comes and the Philistines learn the reason for the loud cries of jubilation, they cry out in horror: "God has come to

them, into their camp!" (v. 5). By this means the author indicates that
he means that God himself is present with the ark. This recalls the
statements about the ark made by Moses in Num 10.35f (see above).
Another aspect of the presence of God is expressed by the epithet "the
throne of the cherubim" (v. 4), used here for the first time, for the
God of the ark. It is linked to his name Yhwh Zebaot, and this powerful connection is called in 2 Sam 6.2 the "name that is named above
the ark" [→587].

The ark is lost, however, in battle with the Philistines (1 Sam 4.11).
But it then proves its mysterious powers as the Philistine god Dagon,
in whose temple the ark has been set up, lies smashed on the ground
and the inhabitants of the Philistine cities into which the ark had been
successively brought are afflicted by a plague of boils (1 Sam 5). Finally
the Philistines send the ark back, and it finds a place for the time being
in Kiryat-Jearim (1 Sam 6.1–7.2). There is no longer any mention of a
connection between the ark and the tent of meeting. (On 1 Kgs 8.4
see below.)

The ark thus has its own history. Especially for the phase of the entry into the land up to the beginning of the monarchy it plays an important role. It generally appears as the only sanctuary for Israel as a
whole. Only in the scene on Mount Ebal is it mentioned alongside an
altar (Josh 8.30-35). Otherwise, in this period no altar is mentioned
with a function for Israel as a whole.

Through David the ark finally attains a pan-Israelite function in the
true sense. After he has become king of Judah and Israel and has made
Jerusalem his royal city, David brings the ark, which by now has become all but forgotten, in a festive procession to Jerusalem (2 Sam 6)
[→112]. There he has it placed in a tent erected specially for it (v. 17).
Clearly this tent was set up as a sanctuary. This is already evident in
the fact that after the ark is set up in the tent David presents burnt
offerings and communal offerings "before the Lord," a formula regularly used in the sacrificial rituals at the altar (Lev 1.5, 11; 3.1, 7 etc.).
This is expressed more clearly in 1 Kgs 2.28, where Joab flees to the
"tent of the Lord" and grasps the horns of the altar, in order to claim
asylum. A similar scene at the altar is reported also of Adonijah,
though there the tent is not expressly mentioned (1.51). In 1.39 we
read, in addition, that Zadok the priest takes the horn of oil from the
tent to anoint Solomon with as king; evidently this was housed there
in a cultically privileged place. It is reported of Solomon that he brings
sacrifices "before the ark" (3.15), which presupposes a corresponding

cultic facility. (The Septuagint supplements the text with express mention of the altar.)

Later "all the sacred objects that were in the tent" are brought into the temple
together with the ark (1 Kgs 8.4). In addition to the "tent," there is mention
of the "tent of meeting." This is clearly an addition intended to establish again
the connection between the ark and the tent of meeting. A similar concern is
served also by the statement in 2 Chron 1.3f, according to which the tent of
meeting was situated on the "cultic high-place" (*bāmāh*) in Gibeon and David
had only transferred the ark to Jerusalem.

Finally Solomon transfers the ark into the temple he has built. It is
carried in there with due ceremony (1 Kgs 8.1-9) and set up in the
dᵉbîr, the holy of holies (v. 6) [→**119**]. A fundamental difference from
the Sinai sanctuary is visible here. Solomon had had two cherubim set
up already before the ark was brought into the *dᵉbîr* (6.23-28). So here
they are not connected to the ark. In addition, they have quite different measurements: each of them is 10 ells high, i.e. approx. 5 meters,
while the ark was only about 75 cm high according to Ex 25.10 (cf.
37.1). It seems that two quite different traditions have come together
here. And the more precise details of the placing of the ark "under the
wings of the cherubim" (1 Kgs 8.6-8) remain unclear (cf. Janowski
1991, 250f[266f]).

Surprising at this point is the information that there was nothing in
the ark apart from the two stone tablets which Moses had put in them
on Horeb (v. 9; in the Septuagint they are called "tablets of the covenant," cf. Deut 9.9, 11, 15). This reflects the corresponding report in
Deut 10.1-5 (cf. also Ex 40.20f). In comparison with the priestly version of the setting up of the ark with the *kapporet* (Ex 25.17-22; 37.6-
9) and the cultic functions resulting from it this appears to be more an
indication of a non-cultic significance of the ark. This accords with the
fact that the ark is only mentioned one more time in the introduction
to Solomon's "temple dedication prayer" (v. 21), again with reference
to the tablets (which here are called "the covenant of Yhwh" [*bᵉrît
yhwh*]). After that there is no further mention of it in the entire books
of Kings. Apart from Chronicles it only occurs twice more in the Hebrew Bible: in Jer 3.16 and in Psalm 132. (On Jer 3.16 see below, p.
521.)

Psalm 132 is of great significance in this regard [→**567**]. In cultic-
poetic language it reflects the bringing of the ark to Jerusalem by
David. David's decision to bring in the ark is accentuated strongly by

the fact that it is described as a vow that God is requested to remember (vv. 1-5). David is said to have wanted to find a place (*māqôm*) for Yhwh, and a dwelling-place (*miškān* plur.) for the "strong ones of Jacob" (v. 5). The "dwelling-place" is spoken of again in v. 7, in connection with the expression "his footstool" (see below). A call is then directed to God (thought of as enthroned on the ark?): "Arise O Lord!" (v. 8), which picks up the ark saying of Num 10.35. But here God is not to arise for battle but for his "rest," which David wants now to prepare for him and "the ark of your might." The cultic character of the whole thing is again made clear in the fact that the priests are mentioned, who are to be "clothed with righteousness (*ṣedeq*)" (v. 9); according to v. 16 God himself will clothe them with "salvation" (*yešaʿ*). The psalm then climaxes with God's assurance to David for the permanency of his dynasty (vv. 11f), as well as in the statement that God has chosen Zion and has decided to dwell there (vv. 13f).

Here quite disparate ark traditions have merged together. The connection is certainly not purely literary, but rather shows the vivacity of these traditions. Especially significant is the fact that here the ark and Zion are mentioned in direct relation to each other. (In 1 Kgs 8.1 we again find the older terminology in which Zion was the name of the southerly situated city of David, the "stronghold of Zion" [2 Sam 5.7].) The ark tradition thus appears here as an element of the religious tradition of Zion (cf. Jeremias 1971). (See 1.3 below.)

1.2.3 And Solomon built the house and completed it

The representation of the sanctuary on Sinai is certainly to be taken as a backward projection of the temple in Jerusalem. The abundance of details points to the fact that what we have here comes from extensive priestly knowledge. It is very clear that it is a matter of an inside view of the temple and the temple cult. The texts contain many details, e.g. with regard to the performance of sacrifices or purification rituals which could not have been accessible to lay persons and could have had no relevance to them either.

The Jerusalem temple is viewed from quite a different angle in the report of its construction and dedication by Solomon in 1 Kgs 6 and 8. The altar, which was originally the central feature of any sanctuary, withdraws into the background here; its construction is mentioned in a rather offhand way alongside other things (6.20, 22; 7.48). The altar is then mentioned as the place from which Solomon speaks his prayer before the dedication of the temple (8.22, 54) [→121]. The altar does not appear until the end in its function as place of sacrifice; but there we read that it was too small for the large number of sacrifices that were being presented, so that Solomon "consecrates" (*qdš* pi.) the whole outer court for this purpose (v. 64). So here the significance of the altar is comparatively moderated.

Center stage is occupied all the more by the ark itself. This has to do above all with its prehistory in the preceding narratives (see the previous section), which came to a head with David bringing the ark to Jerusalem and placing it in a tent there (2 Sam 6.1-19) [→**112**]. When he then made plans to build a house for the ark, he was prevented from doing so by the prophet Nathan (2 Sam 7.1-19). But in the prophetic divine speech it was said about the promised descendant of David: "He will build a house for my Name" (v. 13). What Solomon now builds is thus the house for the ark which his father David had planned. The dedication of the completed temple thus begins with the ceremonial bringing-in and setting-up of the ark (1 Kgs 8.1-11). This produces a clear connection with the establishment of the sanctuary on Sinai: after the ark has been set up in the holy of holies, the "cloud" and in it the "glory (*kābôd*) of Yhwh" fills the "house of Yhwh," so that the priests are unable to enter (vv. 10f), which is precisely what happened long ago on Sinai (cf. Ex 40.34f) [→**66**]. This lends express emphasis to the continuity between these two traditions.

Nonetheless the differences remain striking. In particular in the tradition of Solomon's building of the temple there is (almost) no mention of "holiness." Besides the "consecration" of the outer court as a place of sacrifice in 8.64 it is not until the following chapter, in a divine speech to Solomon, that it is said that God has himself "consecrated" (*qdš* hithp.) this house, in order to place his name there forever (9.3, cf. v. 7: "this house I have consecrated for my Name"). Here the "Name" of God appears again, which was already associated with the ark in 2 Sam 7.13. But there is nothing here of the great significance attached to the whole area of holiness in the tradition of the Sinai sanctuary. Nor is there any mention of "atonement" and all that goes with it. So here there is no mention either of the *kapporet* and no mention of a corresponding atoning function of the ark.

Particularly striking, finally, is the distribution of roles in the construction and dedication of the temple. Everything lies in the hands of the king. The priests only bring the ark into the temple and place it in the *d'bîr*, the holy of holies (1 Kgs 8.3-6). Then they are only mentioned again in the scene with the cloud that fills the sanctuary (vv.

10f). According to this account they have no cultic functions, not even for sacrifices. And it is Solomon himself who performs the "consecration" of the outer court as a place of sacrifice (v. 64). The reader gains the impression that the report only depicts the outside view of the temple in its "public" function in direct relation to the royal rule, as it were *ad maiorem gloriam* of king Solomon. Thus everything that has to do with the inner area of the cult in the temple remains unexpressed.

Later it is mentioned once again that three times a year (cf. Ex 23.14-17) Solomon presented sacrifices on the altar he had set up (1 Kgs 9.25). Here it is again Solomon himself who presents the sacrifices (*'lh* hi.) and even lets them "go up in smoke" (*qtr* hi.), which had always been the task of the priest (cf. Lev 1.9, 13 etc.). It is, however, said here that Solomon brought the sacrifices "before Yhwh," which may be meant as an emphatic counter-statement to the earlier information that Solomon used to bring sacrifices on the high-places (1 Kgs 3.3).

Quite different again is the viewpoint from which the restoration of the temple is spoken of in Ezek 40–48 [→257]. This is a visionary account, which on the one hand contains very precise details with exact measurements (40.5–42.20), but on the other hand is evidently not concerned with a full overall description. Here the reader finds him- or herself again in the area of the inside view of the "priestly" conception of the Sinai sanctuary. Thus the concept of holiness dominates this whole section: the innermost part of the temple is again called "the holy of holies" (*qodeš haqqadāšîm*, 41.4, 21 etc.), as are the special sacrifices which only the priests are allowed to eat (42.13); also the priests' rooms are "holy," as well as the clothes in which they perform the sacrifices (v. 14). The entire grounds of the temple are enclosed by a wall "to separate the holy from the common" (v. 20, cf. Lev 10.10), and it is the "torah of the house (i.e. of the temple)" that its whole area is "holy" (43.12).

The altar again plays an important part here (43.13-27). The tasks and functions of the priests, too, are described in detail (42.13f; 43.19, 24, 27 etc.), as well as the details of the performance of the sacrifice (43.18-27; 46.4-7 etc.). There is a broad level of agreement with the data given for the sanctuary in Sinai (cf. 1967, 26-30). In comparison with the report of Solomon's temple the quite different distribution of roles in particular is striking. All the activity here lies with the priest. There is no talk of the king, but instead the "prince" (*nāśî'*) (apparently in view of the uncertain political future for the time after the exile). There is detailed discussion of his dues and his responsibilities for the sacrificial service (45.8-25; 46.4-15), but he is expressly prohibited from active participation in the sacrificial cult (46.2).

Of crucial importance, finally, is the return of the "glory (kābôd) of Yhwh" to the re-erected temple (43.1-5). The kābôd fills the house (v. 5), as was reported before of the sanctuary in Sinai (Ex 40.34) and of the temple of Solomon (1 Kgs 8.10f). And the voice of God proclaims to the prophet: "Son of man, this is the place of my throne and the place for the soles of my feet. This is where I will live among the Israelites forever" (43.7). Here again the saying about God's "dwelling" appears, as expressed right at the beginning in relation to the Sinai sanctuary (Ex 25.8f; 29.45f).

The temple design in the book of Ezekiel differs in one essential regard from the two others, however: there is nothing about the ark. Nowhere in the Hebrew Bible are we told what happened to it [→518]. In the report of the conquest and destruction of Jerusalem and the temple and about the removal of the objects from the temple (2 Kgs 25.13-17) the ark is not mentioned, nor when the objects that Cyrus gives back to the Judean exiles in the context of his decree about the reconstruction of the temple (Ezra 1.7-11). Similarly, there is no mention of the ark during the reconstruction and the dedication of the temple. Does Ezekiel say nothing about it because it has been lost and because he does not know whether it can ever be restored?

The only text in which this problem is discussed is a saying in Jeremiah (Jer 3.16f): if Israel will repent and new life will develop under the shepherds appointed by God, "men will no longer say, 'The ark of the covenant of the Lord.' It will never enter their minds or be remembered; it will not be missed, nor will another one be made." The ark has been lost, and there seems to be some discussion as to whether a new one should be made (von Rad 1965, 280). Jeremiah counters this with the view that in the future time of salvation there will no longer be any talk of the ark, but of Jerusalem, the "throne of the Lord;" the ark will therefore no longer be needed. This does not imply any devaluation of the significance of the ark up to now; there would then be no call for this discussion. But here a new view of the presence of God is evident here, which will no longer be tied to individual cultic objects or buildings but will comprise Jerusalem as a whole, i.e. Zion (cf. v. 14). (For discussion of the fate of the ark cf. Schäfer-Lichtenberger 2000.)

1.3 Where is God present?

Worship takes place only where the deity is believed to be present. But how and in what the divine presence manifests itself can find expression in very different ways. The preceding paragraphs have shown that a variety of concepts have been maintained in the Hebrew Bible.

At the beginning of the history of the Israelite cult stands the altar, as the site of encounter with God (see 1.1 above). He is not tied to a sanctuary (temple, tent etc.), but evidently to a sacred place that is legitimated by a manifestation of the presence of God. The report of a theophany by which the holiness is justified—or perhaps the preserved and transmitted memory of it—is one of the preconditions of the cult in a particular place. But this cannot be just a memory of something in the past. According to the central formula in Ex 20.24 it is a matter of God himself "making known" or "calling to remembrance" (*zkr* hi.) his name. Other texts view this as it were in the opposite direction: that people call upon or exclaim the name of God (cf. e.g. Gen 12.8). What is decisive in each case is the presence of God which finds expression in the solemn naming of his name.

The freestanding altar, however, is not the place of a constant presence of the deity. Things are different with the sanctuary. There is often talk of God's "dwelling" here. Thus the Sinai sanctuary itself is described as God's "dwelling-place" (*miškān*) (Ex 24–40 *passim*). God told Moses that the Israelites should build him a sanctuary, "so that I may dwell with you" (25.8; cf. also 1 Kgs 6.13) [→**64**]. The dwelling-place is then sanctified by the presence of God (29.43-46). The notion of God's dwelling however can be articulated quite differently. Thus in Deuteronomy there is talk of the place which God will choose "to let his name dwell there" (Deut 12.11; 14.23; 16.2 etc. [→**80**]; cf. "in order to place his name there," 12.5, 21; 14.24). Here the notion of God's dwelling is connected with the idea of the presence of the name. This resonates also in Nathan's promise to David, which says that his successor will "build a house to my name" (2 Sam 7.13); Solomon appeals to this on the dedication of the temple (1 Kgs 8.17-21). Then later in the divine speech about the temple we read that God himself has sanctified this house in order to set his name there forever (9.3; cf. v. 7); here the name of God is connected with the idea of holiness. Different again is the way the concept of dwelling appears in the great vision of Ezekiel, where the return of God's "glory" (*kābôd*) is commented upon with the words: "This is the place of my throne and the place of the soles of my feet, where I will dwell for ever among the Israelites" (Ezek 43.7). Here the *kābôd* represents the presence of God; at the same time the notion of the "enthronement" of God appears in the temple.

But the ark too can be the place of God's presence. The sayings about the ark in Num 10.35f, with their "Arise, O Lord" presuppose the presence of Yhwh on the ark. In the narrative of the struggle against the Philistines too, we read that with the entry of the ark God has come into the camp (1 Sam 4.5). Here it is then primarily the expression "the throne of the cherubim" (*yošēb hakkerûbîm*, 1 Sam 4.4; 2 Sam 6.2) which very emphatically presupposes a presence of Yhwh Zebaot—indicated specifically by the manner of the enthronement. Perhaps the notion of the ark as "his footstool" (Ps 132.7) is relevant here. When it is brought into the temple clearly essential elements of the ark tradition accompany it into the temple.

With regard to the expression "throne of the cherubim" and the associated conceptions the prevalent view is that they were originally connected with the ark and were taken over from there into the temple. However, in the report about the construction of the temple there is detailed discussion of the cherub figures which Solomon had set up there (1 Kgs 6.23-28), while there is no indication of an actual connection between the ark and cherubim. Thus the dominant view has become dubious. One might think rather of a retrojection of the temple onto the ark. This might have had political grounds, in order to tie the ark, linked with the northern Israelite Shiloh, more closely to Jerusalem. Whether the talk of "his footstool" can be related to a throne footstool has also become doubtful. Thus the question of what traditions were in fact connected with the ark remains open. (On this cf. Janowski 1991.)

The temple in Jerusalem is the place where the various ideas of the presence of God in the sanctuary in Jerusalem have come together. They have certainly not become harmonized in this process, but express very different aspects of the presence of God. There is, however, a fundamental degree of commonality between all the conceptions: the God who is experienced as present is never presented in visible form. Even where the notion of the presence of God seems concentrated on a particular point—especially there in fact—the thought is always of an invisible God. This applies especially to the notion of God's sitting on a "throne." Both on the ark and also on the "throne of the cherubim" in the temple, God is presented as invisibly enthroned. Yhwh's throne is always an "empty divine throne." (See further §14.2 [→**578**].)

But the notion of God's sitting on a throne is not static, any more than the concept of God's dwelling in the Sinai sanctuary. Thus the same expressions can refer to God's enthronement in heaven: he is "the One enthroned in heaven" (*yôšēb baššāmayim*, Ps 2.4; cf. 123.1); he has set up his throne in heaven (103.19; cf. 11.4); the place of his enthronement (*mᵉkôn šibtô*) can also be in heaven (33.14), and he can also be called upon as the one "enthroned between the cherubim" (80.2; cf. v. 15). But the talk of God's enthronement in heaven generally doest not express his distance, but precisely his saving concern for humans on earth: "The Lord looked down from his sanctuary on high; from heaven he viewed the earth, to hear the groans of the prisoners and release those condemned to death" (102.20f; cf. 11.4; 33.13-15; 113.5f; cf. Metzger 1970). The connection between God's heavenly throne and the earthly temple comes especially strongly to expression in the vision of Isaiah (Isa 6): "King Yhwh Zebaot" (v. 5) is surrounded on his throne by heavenly beings; but the train of his robe fills the earthly temple. And the prophet is involved in the heavenly events.

Where is God present? It is the Psalms in particular that give a multi-vocal response to this question. We see once again another side of the cultic events and the experience of the cultic: here it is not the inside view of priestly cult practice, even less the royal court-representing outer view of the temple and the cult. Rather, here above all expression is given to the viewpoint of the participant in the cult, the "layperson." This applies in particular to the many psalms in which the "we" of the cult community or the "I" of an individual supplicant speaks. But also hymns, liturgical texts etc. ring out in the context of public worship in the presence of the community. The fact that they are collected in the book of Psalms certainly points to their having belonged also to the stock of religious material that was familiar to the laity.

In the Psalms the presence of God is closely connected with the temple. This is the place where the individual and the community participate directly in the cultic event. So there is a series of psalms that focus completely on the temple. This begins with the question, "Lord, who may live on your holy hill?" (Ps 15.1); the answer is given, as it were, as rules of admission: "He whose walk is blameless and who does what is righteous and speaks the truth from his heart" (vv. 2ff; cf.

Koch 1961). An unjustly persecuted person gives an assurance that he keeps away from the congregation of the evildoers and the ungodly and devotes himself to God's altar; for "I love the house where you live, O Lord, the place where your glory dwells" (*miškān k'bôdêkā*, Ps 26.5-8). Another person in a similar position prays to God: "Send forth your light and your truth, let them guide me; let them bring me to your holy mountain, to the place where you dwell. Then will I go to the altar of God" (43.3f; cf. 5.8). An entire psalm praises the "loveliness" of the dwelling-place of the Lord Almighty, for "Better is one day in your courts than a thousand elsewhere" (Ps 8; cf. 27.4). In the group of "pilgrimage psalms" (120–134) the orientation to Jerusalem and the temple find expression especially in Ps 122. These psalms, like many others, are marked by a personal piety in the center of which stands the temple in Jerusalem.

In many psalms, however, the connection and interrelationship between God's presence in the temple and in heaven also comes to expression. The two cannot be separated (cf. Metzger 1970). Thus Ps 20 first prays for divine aid "from the sanctuary (*qodeš*), from Zion" (v. 4) and gratefully acknowledges the help experienced "from his holy heaven" (*š'mê qadšô*, v. 7). Similarly, Ps 76 speaks of God's dwelling-place on Zion (v. 3), but then of the fact that God makes his judgement known from heaven (v. 9). Of the God who "dwells" on Zion, in Jerusalem (135.21), it is also said: "The Lord does whatever pleases him, in the heavens and on the earth" (v. 6).

In the liturgical context too there is mention of the presence of God in the temple. Thus the "king of glory" (*melek hakkābôd*), Yhwh Zebaot, passes in solemn procession (on the ark?) through the gates and "ancient doors" into the temple (Ps 24.7-10). In the background to Ps 132 too there seems to be an ark procession on Zion, God's "resting-place" (vv. 8, 14). In the Zion-psalm Ps 46, it is said of the "city of God:" "God is within her, she will not fall" (v. 5[6]). But here too it is the case that God is often addressed as the one who lives and is enthroned in heaven.

The majority of the psalms, however, stand outside what can be counted as the area of the cult. The question of where God was believed to be present and was experienced as such is thus by no means limited to this area. (On this see also §§14, 15, and 18.)

2. Sacrifices

2.1 The variety of sacrifices

Our account needs first to turn back to what happens in the cult, in the narrower sense. We have seen that the presentation of sacrifices is one of the rudimentary expressions of life among people "beyond Eden." When it is first mentioned in Gen 4.3f the summarizing term *minḥāh* is used for the sacrifice of fruits of the field as well as produce from animals of the herd. A rather distinct differentiation then becomes apparent. Noah presents sacrifices from those saved in the ark, sacrifices of "clean" animals, i.e. animals that may be sacrificed. This sacrifice is called a "burnt offering" (*'ōlāh*, in the plural in Gen 8.20). This introduces the most common of the terms for sacrifice in the Hebrew Bible. The characteristic element of this sacrifice is that the sacrificial animal is burned in its entirety, so that no part of the animal can be used for any other purpose. This is a "whole offering," a *holocaustum*. The meaning of the burning lies in the fact that the whole sacrificial animal "goes up in smoke" and that the smoke rises to God. The aroma of the sacrifice is called a "soothing aroma" (*rê'ḥ nîḥo'ḥ*), an expression found frequently as a technical term in sacrifice rituals (cf. e.g. Lev 1.9, 13, 17).

In Noah's sacrifice we read the graphic description of God "smelling" the aroma of the sacrifice (v. 21) and of the resulting retraction of his decision to annihilate the whole of creation. This anthropomorphic concept of "smelling" also appears a number of times elsewhere. Thus when David is on the run, in one of the dramatic situations when he spares Saul, he says: "If the LORD has incited you against me, then may he accept (smell) an offering (*minḥāh*)" (1 Sam 26.19). Here the idea is expressed that God's anger might be tempered by means of the "soothing aroma." This contrasts with the abrupt words in Amos: "I will no longer smell your festive gatherings" (Amos 5.21) [→284]; this means that the time of hope in God's intervention is now over. Cf. also Lev 26.31. It is evident in these texts that the "soothing aroma" is an essential element of the sacrificial cult. This helps the understanding when we read that gods "made with hands" cannot smell (Deut 4.28; Ps 115.6; cf. *ThWAT* VII, 384).

Besides the burnt offerings, in the altar law of the "book of the covenant" (Ex 20.24) [→522] a second type of sacrifice is mentioned, the *š'lāmîm*. These two sacrifices are evidently regarded as the most important sacrifices that are to be brought regularly to the altar; they are often mentioned together elsewhere too, especially in the context of official or public occasions as e.g. the re-establishment and dedication of altars (Ex 20.24; Deut 27.5-7; Josh 8.31; 1 Kgs 9.25; 2 Kgs 16.13; Ezek 43.27; cf. 2 Sam 24.25). In the case of the *šᵉlāmîm* too, the sacrifice is of animals; the verb used for the presentation of the sacrifice is often *zābaḥ*, "slaughter" (Ex 20.24; Deut 27.7; Josh 8.31 etc.). The texts do not give us details of the rite. However, an important indicator is provided by the connection made between this type of sacrifice and another, the "slaughter victim" (*zebaḥ*). This is always associated with a meal (Gen 31.54; Ex 34.15; Deut 12.27 etc.). In many cases (e.g. Lev 3.1, 3, 6, 9; 7.11, 18) the double expression *zebaḥ-šᵉlāmîm* is used as a fixed sacrificial term. This reveals a particular development, since in the double expression the concern is predominantly with sacrifices by an individual rather than public sacrifices (see below).

The translation of the term *šᵉlāmîm* is disputed. The generally customary translation with "thank-offering," "atonement offering" etc. rests on the echo of the word *šalôm* and corresponding translations in the Septuagint with forms of the adjectives σωτήριος or εἰρηνικός etc. Other suggestions relate more closely to the function of the sacrifice, thus "concluding sacrifice" (Köhler 178) and "communal sacrifice" (Noth 21). The latter goes on to render *zebaḥ-šᵉlāmîm* as "communal slaughter victim" (cf. 1967, 132; 1985ff, 125-127; *ThWAT* VIII, 110f).

These two forms of animal sacrifice represent two fundamentally different but connected aspects of sacrifice. The burnt offering means the complete transfer of the sacrifice to God's ownership. The person or community bringing the sacrifice thereby gives part of what they have received from God back to him. The occasions for this can be quite varied. In Gen 4 no occasion is mentioned; rather, the sacrifice appears as an element in the rhythm of life in agriculture and stock-farming, which needs no further justification. One can draw a line from this to the sacrificial calendars (esp. Num 28f), in which the burnt offering appears as a daily sacrifice (see 2.1.2). But in addition there are also quite spontaneous occasions for a burnt offering, e.g. joy at the return of the ark that had been plundered from the Philistines (1 Sam 6.14; on v. 15 see below). Other texts show the burnt offering as the central demonstration of the deity of Yhwh in contrast to the worship of Baal, as in the case of Gideon (Judg 6.25-32) and especially Elijah (1 Kgs

18.30-39) [→**138**]. The burnt offering can also be taken as atonement: just in case, when transgressions may have occurred (Job 1.5) and in atonement for misdemeanors committed, supported by intercession (Job 42.7-9). Finally the burnt offering forms the central main sacrifice in the regular temple cult (Num 28f etc.; see 2.1.2).

The slaughter sacrifice displays a quite different side of the sacrificial cult. It is a meal offering, in which the major part of the animal is consumed by those gathered for the meal (cf. Gen 31.54; 1 Sam 9.13; 16.3, 5 etc.). It is often the family that gathers around the sacrificial victim, so that one might almost speak of a "family sacrificial victim" (*zebah mišpāhāh*, 1 Sam 20.29; cf. v. 6; cf. also the annual family slaughter-sacrifice in 1 Sam 1f). But the eating of an animal from the herd, possession of which people owe to God, cannot occur without God first being given part of it back. The account in 1 Sam 2.12-17 shows in a graphic way that the fat must first "go up in smoke" before anything else can be done with the meat of the animal (vv. 15f). This is then described in detail in the sacrifice ritual in Lev 3 (see 2.1.2).

It is not uncommon for burnt offerings and slaughter-offerings to be mentioned together. Contrary to the mention of burnt offerings and *š'lamîm* together (see above), however, in this case the sacrifices are not generally public events. Thus the presentation of burnt and slaughter offerings by Jethro, Moses' father-in-law, is described more in terms of a slaughter offering meal (Ex 18.12). In other cases the mention of the two together seems like a summary of the sacrificial cult, as when in 1 Sam 15.22 [→**106**] the question is asked in an apparently formulaic sentence whether God views burnt offerings and slaughter offerings with the same favor as he does obedience towards him; similarly in Ps 51.18 and (with the sacrificial terms in the opposite order) 50.8. In Isa 56.7 we read that God will accept with favor the burnt offerings and slaughter offerings of "strangers" that want to turn to God.

It is not only animals that are sacrificed, however. This becomes clear already in Gen 4.3: Cain brings an offering from the fruits of the field. Here the term *minhāh* in v. 4 is also used of Abel's animal sacrifice; elsewhere too this expression is frequently found as a sacrificial term with a rather unspecific meaning. As late as the latter prophet Malachi this is the generally used term for sacrifices (1.10, 11, 13; 2.12, 13; 3.3, 4) [→**310**], and it is clear here that the concern is (also) with animal sacrifices (cf. 1.7f, 13f). In the area of "priestly" texts the term *minhāh* is, however, used exclusively for the sacrifices of plant matter ("vegetable" or "grain offerings"). (Luther's term, still favored in German, is *Speisopfer*, "food offering.")

A special feature of the term *minḥāh* lies in the fact that it can be used to indicate the time of day. In 1 Kgs 18 we read that the prophets of Baal get into a frenzy from midday "until the time for the *minḥāh*" (v. 29) and that Elijah then ended the preparations for his sacrifice "at the time of the *minḥāh*" (v. 36). In contrast, in 2 Kgs 3.20 we read: "the next morning, about the time for offering the *minḥāh*." The evening *minḥāh* is also mentioned in Ezra 9.4f; Dan 9.21 as a time of prayer; cf. Ps 141.2. While these texts do not expressly say what kind of sacrifice they are talking about, in 2 Kgs 16.15 there is talk of a morning *'ōlāh* and an evening *minḥāh*. (Cf. 1967, 195f.)

2.2 The sacrificial system
The variety of statements about sacrifice and the lack of uniformity in the terminology shows that the bringing of sacrifices on the one hand is one of the things that were taken for granted in Israel's common life—as elsewhere in the ancient Near East—but on the other hand that different conceptions and practices were operative from place to place and from time to time. In the Hebrew Bible we find an area in which all this is more or less consistently systematized: the "priestly" account of the erection of the sanctuary on Sinai and a number of other groups of related texts. There can be no doubt that these texts reflect conditions in the temple in Jerusalem. At the same time, however, this means that the variety of cultic places and occasions is no longer apparent in this systematization. What was required in the book of Deuteronomy has in fact come into being: Israel's sacrificial cult is to be practiced at only one single place (cf. esp. Deut 12). And this place can be nowhere but Jerusalem.

In the much-discussed question of the age of these texts we may assume that the systematization with reference to cultic practice in the Jerusalem temple represents a relatively late stage. The term "late," however, should in fact be used only relatively. We have no way of determining what stage in the Jerusalem cult the system presupposed here relates to, or whether these texts even brought the system about. Frequently the language of the priestly texts as a whole is said to be "late." However, we possess no texts at all on the details of the cult in the Jerusalem temple in any other linguistic form, so that no conclusions can be drawn as to their age. Nor do we know to what extent these cultic rules and rituals were subject to change. We may assume there was a great capacity for adhering to them. At the same time we may, in my view, assume that the practice systematized in these texts corresponds to the real circumstances at the time of the final formulation of the canonical text of the Pentateuch. Such central texts for the religious life of the Jewish community would certainly never have attained canonical status if they did not correspond to cultic realities at the time of the canonization. Exegesis thus has the task of tracing this picture of the cult in the temple in Jerusalem.

Leviticus 1–7 lists the most important types of sacrifice and describes the details of their performance. Chapters 1–5 contain ordinances for their performance, which are also of significance for laity that brought sacrifices, while chs. 6f present regulations more specially for the priests. In chs. 1–3 first the three types of sacrifice are mentioned that we also find in other texts: burnt offering and fellowship offering, and then the grain offering. The burnt offering has first place (ch. 1). Sacrifices of cattle (1.3-9), domesticated animals (vv. 10-13, the Hebrew word *ṣo'n* includes sheep and goats) or poultry, i.e. the two types of dove (vv. 14-17), may be brought. Its character as a whole offering is described in detail: the sacrificial animal is separated into parts which are then placed in layers and burnt as a whole. Directly after the slaughtering and before the sacrificial process per se, the blood of the sacrificial animal is sprinkled around on the bottom part of the altar (v. 5b, 11b; the rite is correspondingly different in the case of birds, v. 15). In the case of the burnt offering and the fellowship offering (cf. 3.2, 8, 13) this act is not part of the sacrificial process per se, unlike the "sin offering" (see below and cf. 1985ff, 52-54).

The presentation of the rite ends in each case with the formulaic sentence: "It is a burnt offering, an offering made by fire, an aroma pleasing to the LORD" (*'iššēh rê'ḥ nîḥoaḥ lyhwh*, 1.9, 13, 17). Here the expression "pleasing aroma" familiar already from the Noah story (Gen 8.21) is combined with a specific sacrificial term found almost exclusively in the priestly cultic texts. (The frequent translation of *'iššēh* as "fire offering" comes from a medieval exegetical tradition; cf. 1985ff, 63-65). The same formulaic expression is then also found in relation to the two following types of sacrifice, the grain offering and the fellowship offering (2.2, 9, 16; 3.5, 11, 16 with individual variations). These three sacrificial types thus belong closely together as the "gifts of the aroma pleasing to YHWH."

Here the grain offering has got between the two animal sacrifices, the burnt offering and the fellowship offering (Lev 2). In priestly parlance the term *minḥāh* is unambiguously tied to the sacrifice of vegetable material. The grain offering is generally found as a sacrifice additional to the animal sacrifices. This is most clear in the sacrificial calendar given in Num 28f (cf. also Num 15.1-16). This evidently also has to do with the special character of this sacrifice: only a small portion of the sacrificial material, a "handful," goes up in smoke as a "memorial portion" (*'azkārāh*, cf. 1985ff, 100f); the remainder belongs to the priests (2.2f, 9f). Here we gain an insight into the internal organization of the cult. In Lev 7.6-10 the priestly portions are listed in summary. At the conclusion of the sacrificial laws they are expressly described as the divine instruction on the appointment of the priests (cf. Lev 8). (On the grain offering in general see Marx 1994.)

In the priestly texts the slaughter offering is found largely in the form of the "fellowship offering" (*zebaḥ-šelāmîm*, Lev 3). The actual sacrifice, the "gift for YHWH" (vv. 3, 9, 14), consists in the fact that the priest causes the internal fatty parts of the sacrificial animal (which are listed in great detail in vv. 3f, 9f, 14f) to "go up in smoke" (cf. also 1 Sam 2.16). What happens to the rest of the animal's meat is not said. However, this is evident from the character of the *zebaḥ* or *zebaḥ-šelāmîm* as a meal offering: it is eaten by the participants at the sacrifice. In the last verse of the chapter it is expressly emphasized that the fat of animals (in the sense of the definition in the sacrificial ritual) is not allowed to be eaten (v. 17). The fundamental character of this regulation is then emphasized by means of the formula "a lasting ordinance for the generations to come, wherever you live." The prohibition of eating blood is included. This is traced back to a fundamental divine decree in the early days of human history (Gen 9.4). In addition, the ritual removal of the blood before the sacrificial procedure itself (see above) shows that it must remain excluded from human consumption.

Finally one further element of the ritual with the sacrificial animals should be mentioned: the sacrificing layperson brings his sacrificial animal "to the entrance of the tent of meeting," i.e. to the place prescribed for this purpose in the outer court of the temple, and "lays his hand on the head of the sacrificial animal" (1.4; 3.2, 8, 13, also 4.4ff). This is one of the elements of Old Testament cultic tradition that is nowhere explained and which can only be explained from the context. The particular difficulty lies in the fact that any attempt to explain it presupposes a particular understanding of the sacrifice. But the sacrifices are nowhere explained, either.

The procedure of the laying-on of hands is not limited to sacrifices. Moses confers his authority to Joshua by this means (Num 27.18, 23; Deut 34.9). The blessing of the sons of Joseph by Jacob may also be compared (Gen 48.13, 16). Aaron also carries out a rite of transference with the goat that is sent to Azazel in the wilderness (Lev 16.21). For the laying-on of hands in relation to sacrifice the most varied theories have been considered. The notion that an identification takes place by this means between the sacrificer and the sacrificial animal, so that the latter as it were vicariously suffers the death of the sinful person (thus Janowski 1982, 220f following Gese 1977, 97) could only apply to the sin offering, but not to the burnt offering and even less to the slaughter (fellowship) offering, in which the sacrificer of course eats the meat himself. It seems more logical to think that by the laying-on of hands the sacrificer expresses the fact that this is *his* animal, which is to be presented in *his* name by the priest (cf. 1985ff, 32-48, esp. 43f; see further *ThWAT* V, 886).

In the systematic arrangement a sacrifice now appears which is mentioned outside the priestly texts: the "sin offering" (Lev 4). The name itself is already remarkable: the word *ḥaṭṭaṭ* means both "sin" and "sin offering." (It is, however, clear from the context what is meant in each case.) A special feature in relation to the three sacrifices discussed above lies in the introduction in each case. So far we have read: "if his presentation is a burnt offering" (1.3, similarly 3.1) or simply "if someone brings a grain offering" (2.1); in the foreground in each case is thus the type of sacrifice. Now we read: "if someone sins" (4.2 etc.). The occasion for the sacrifice is central here: the sin offering has to be brought where there is sin. (In view of its function and significance it might be better to call it "atonement offering," but I shall stay with the customary term.)

This also marks the structure of this sacrificial regulation, since the crucial matter is *who* sins. This produces a fourfold structure: if the "anointed priest" sins (4.3-12), the "whole community of Israel" (vv. 13-21), the "prince" (vv. 22-26) or an "individual person" (vv. 27-35). Of fundamental significance here is the more precise definition of the sin for which the sin offering can and must be brought: only if it is a matter of an unintentionally committed sin (*biš'gāgāh*, v. 2). This term is explained later in Num 15.27ff: the atonement obtained by the sin offering is valid for the person who sins unintentionally; but for anyone who has sinned "with raised hand," i.e. deliberately and in full awareness of what he was doing, there can be no atonement.

The sin offering thus has quite a different function from the three earlier sacrifices. The key term is not the "pleasing aroma" of the sacrificial offering; this term does not occur in the sin offering. Instead, the dominant terms are "atonement" and "forgiveness." At the conclusion of the individual rituals we read in each case: "the priest carries out the atonement act (*kipper*) for them (i.e. the community) or him; it is forgiven them/him (*nislah*)" (vv. 20, 26, 31, 35). The collaboration of these two elements is the crucial thing: the act of atonement carried out by the priest is the precondition for God's forgiveness. The passive formulation "it is forgiven them/him" describes the divine action. (On the lack of this concluding sentence after v. 11, see on Lev 16 below.)

Viewed from this perspective the meaning of the blood rite in the sin offering also becomes clear. It has quite a different shape and function here compared with the other sacrifices. In the sin offering of the "anointed priest" and in that of the community as a whole the blood is first sprinkled seven times "before YHWH," i.e. before the curtain that separates the holy of holies from the rest of the temple (4.6, 17). The blood is brought as close as possible to the place where God himself appears from time to time (cf. 16.2). This is a provisional anticipation of what the high priest himself will do once a year in the holy of holies (cf. Lev 16.11-19): a removal of sin from the holy of holies. Then something of the blood is painted on the horns of the smoke altar (vv. 7, 18); this altar stands directly in front of the curtain, closest to the holy of holies (cf. Ex 30.6; on the horns cf. v. 2, cf. *BRL*², 8f; Keel 1972, 127f). Here the atoning or purifying action is repeated at the altar.

After these two rites the entire remainder of the blood is "poured away," at the base of the burnt offering altar (4.7b, 18b), i.e. where the blood of the burnt offering and the fellowship offering was sprinkled (1.5 etc.; 3.2 etc.). In the sin offering it is now quite clear that the concern is not with a sacrificial act in the true sense, but that the blood is removed and thus withdrawn from human use.

In the sin offering of the "prince" (4.22-26) and of the individual (vv. 27-35) only the second part of the blood rite takes place, the painting of the horns of the altar. However, there is an essential difference: these are now the horns of the burnt offering altar (vv. 25, 30, 34). Here once again the difference between the "great" and the "small" blood rite is made clear. The former is carried out in the area of the "holies," where the smoke altar also stands, the latter on the other hand in the "court" accessible to laity, the center of which is formed by the burnt offering altar.

The further procedure with the sacrificial animal of the sin offering, the burning of the internal fatty parts, corresponds to that in the fellowship offering, which is also expressly emphasized (4.10, 26, 31, 35). But the flesh of the sin offering has quite a different quality, so that it cannot be eaten by the person or persons bringing the sacrifice. Rather, here again a distinction emerges between the first two occasions for a sin offering and those that follow. In the first two no one may eat of the meat because of their greater "holiness"; it is burned "outside the camp" at a "pure place" (vv. 11f, 21). What happens with the meat in the case of the other sin offerings, we learn of in Lev 6: the priest who has carried out the atonement rite is to eat the meat (v. 19). The difference from the sin offerings is emphasized with the "great" blood rite: their meat is not to be eaten but has to be burned (v. 23).

Unintentionally committed sins are now distinguished from those that were committed unknowingly and whose sinful character only becomes apparent to the person concerned at a later date (5.1-13). The cases dealt with here are generally less serious ones. Thus in the case of poverty they can be atoned for also with doves (vv. 7-10) or even with flour (vv. 11f). Finally another type of sacrifice is added: the "guilt offering" ('*āšām* 5.14-26). The concern here is with disloyalty and other misdemeanors which damage either temple property (vv. 15f) or other persons (vv. 21-26) and whereby material compensation has to be made in addition to the guilt offering (on the rite, see 7.1-7). Finally, the special case is dealt with too, when someone thinks he may have committed a sin but is not entirely sure (vv. 17-19). The person therefore brings a guilt offering instead of a sin offering.

These regulations in Lev 5 show the intensive concern to deal as well as possible with the many circumstances in which sins may be committed and viewed. The lists of possible transgressions show that these are examples that may serve as a precedent for similar or comparable cases. In the final analysis all this comes together in the totality of "impurities and sinnings" of the Israelites which have to be and can be atoned for and removed once a year, on the "day of atonement" (Lev 16.16, 21).

3. Festivals

3.1 Three times a year you are to celebrate a festival to me

"Three times a year you are to celebrate a festival to me" (Ex 23.14). Thus reads Israel's oldest calendar. "All the men" are to assemble three times a year for a communal festival (Ex 23.17; 34.23; Deut 16.16): for the "feast of unleavened bread" (*ḥag hammaṣṣôt*), for the "feast of (cutting) the harvest" (*ḥag haqqāṣîr*, Ex 23.16), also called "festival of weeks" (*ḥag [haš]šābu'ôt*, Ex 34.22; Deut 16.10, 16), and to the "feast of ingathering" (*ḥag hā'āsîp*), i.e. the wine harvest (Ex 23.16; 34.22), which is also called the "feast of tabernacles (or booths)" (*ḥag hassukkôt*, Deut 16.13, 16). These festivals were no doubt originally harvest festivals, so that their dates depended on the circumstances of the harvest year. Later they were then given a more precise date (see below on the festival calendars and cf. 1991e) [→**537**].

That the festival gatherings took place at sanctuaries is in the nature of the case. The texts speak of all males having to "appear" before Yhwh's face. (Perhaps the Hebrew text originally meant "see Yhwh's face" [→**604**], borrowing an expression from the religious environment for visits to the sanctuary.) This presupposes that the festivals were celebrated at various sanctuaries in the land, which were within traveling distance for festival participants. The festivals are those also referred to as "pilgrimage festivals." We also read that the pilgrims were not to come before God's face "empty," i.e. empty-handed (Ex 23.15b; 34.20bβ; Deut 16.16b). Deut 16.17 adds that everyone should "bring a gift in proportion to the way the LORD your God has blessed you." Gifts to the sanctuary are thus part and parcel of festival attendance.

One festival that was later to gain great significance is not mentioned in these early lists of three: the Passover (*pesaḥ*). This is quite a different type of festival. Its origins are set narratively in connection with the "plagues" in Egypt and the exodus from there (Ex 12) [→**45**]. The ritual is also explained in this context: the lamb of a sheep or goat is slaughtered, roasted and eaten within the family or neighborhood circle in a single night, as an expression of the exodus situation. The Passover is thus not a sacrifice; rather, the whole animal is eaten by the participants in the festival. The blood, however, does have a special function: some of it is brushed onto the entrances to the homes (vv. 7, 22) in order to protect them from the great "plague" that will come upon the Egyptians, the killing of the firstborn (vv. 13, 23). So the

Passover is primarily a memorial festival, in the center of it the liberation from Egyptian slavery.

The Passover is mentioned more frequently in narrative texts, in each case at particular turning points in the narrated history of Israel. Thus in the first year after they break camp from Sinai Moses receives the divine instruction to celebrate the Passover (Num 9.1-14) on the date given in the festival calendar (see on Lev 23 below). Exceptions to the Passover regulations of Ex 12f are added (highly anachronistically, travel abroad is given as a valid impediment, v. 10). Then on the settlement of the land it is one of Joshua's first deeds after the circumcision of the generation born during the wilderness period (Josh 5.2-9) to celebrate the Passover (vv. 10-12). With the eating of unleavened bread from the harvest of the land, the manna now comes to an end. A further emphatically presented Passover feast is organized by Josiah "as it is written in this (i.e. the now 'discovered') book of the covenant" as no Passover had been observed "since the days of the judges who led Israel" (2 Kgs 23.21-23) [→**151**]. And finally the celebration of the Passover is the first thing that the returnees from exile do after the reconstruction of the temple (Ezra 6.19-22) [→**393**].

In the Passover celebrations in Josh 5 and Ezra 6 the eating of unleavened loaves is also mentioned. The two things are already closely associated in Ex 12f. In Deut 16 it is then clear that the Passover festival was connected with the Massot festival: while in v. 16 the familiar series of the three festivals is mentioned, in vv. 1-8 there is instead a detailed set of regulations about the Passover, followed by the festival of weeks (vv. 9-12) and the festival of booths (vv. 13-15). The Passover (vv. 1ff) and Massot festivals (v. 16) are evidently identical here. This is also the case in the calendars of festivals and sacrifices in Lev 23 and Num 28f. In Lev 23 the series of festivals in the narrow sense begins with this dual festival, the beginning of which is spread over two days: Passover on the fourteenth day of the first month (v. 5), the Massot festival on the fifteenth day, which is then celebrated for seven days (vv. 6-8). The same thing is found in Num 28 (vv. 16 and 17-25).

This is therefore associated with a historicization of the originally agrarian Massot festival: it is now celebrated, together with the Passover, in memory of the exodus. In Ex 12.34 the missing yeast dough is already explained in the context of the hasty departure situation. In the calendar of festivals in Lev 23 a historicization is also found for the festival of booths, which also refers to the exodus or the subsequent wandering in the wilderness: the Israelites are to live in booths for seven days in memory of the fact that "I made the Israelites live in booths when I brought them out of Egypt" (vv. 42f). The inherent anachronism is self-evident, especially when one considers the immediately preceding description of the fruits of the trees, palm fronds and branches with plenty of leaves which are to be used for building the booths (v. 40). But the salvation-historical historicization evidently does not find this a problem. No express historicization is given us for the festival of weeks. However, in Deut 16.22 we read at the conclusion of the section of the festival of weeks: "Remember that you were a slave in Egypt." This recalls such texts as Deut 6.20ff, where the early salvation history of Israel is recapitulated for the benefit of later generations, beginning with the words: "We were slaves of Pharaoh in Egypt." So all three (or four) festivals were in course of time more or less explicitly placed in the salvation-historical context of exodus, wilderness-wandering and settlement of the land.

3.2 You are to proclaim sacred assemblies

A more advanced stage in the festivals is summarized in two annual calendars: the calendar of festivals in Lev 23 and the calendar of sacrifices in Num 28f. In Lev 23 the festivals are together referred to as "sacred proclamations" (*miqrā'ê qodeš*, v. 2). This extends the circle of holy days. At the beginning stands the Sabbath (v. 3). It is also referred to as a "sacred proclamation," though the observance of it consists only in resting from work. But it is a particularly strict form of rest, which is already announced in the double expression, *šabbat šabbātôn* ("a strict Sabbath"). We read further that "no kind of work" (*kol-m'lā'kāh*) may be done. This comprehensive phrase is otherwise found only in relation to the day of atonement (Lev 23.28, 30, 31). On the other holy days the double expression, *kol-mele'ket 'abodāh* expresses a restriction relating to hard work or work in one's occupation (cf. *ThWAT* IV, 908). The Sabbath is thus a special holy day, even though nothing is said here about sacrifices or other cultic procedures.

The Sabbath is followed by the double festival of Passover and Massot (vv. 4-8). Here the dating of the festival year now begins: Passover takes place on the eve of the fourteenth day of the first month (v. 5), the Massot festival on the fifteenth day, which consists of the eating of unleavened loaves for seven days (v. 6). The first and the seventh days are festival days with the "sacred proclamation" and the limited prohibition of work (vv. 7f). In addition, a sacrifice (*'iššeh*) is to be brought on all seven days (v. 8), but no further detail is given about this sacrifice.

The festival of weeks that now follows is placed in a broader framework. To begin with, the presentation of a first sheaf from the new harvest is ordered (vv. 9-14), linked with a burnt offering in addition to supplementary sacrifices: grain offerings and "drink offerings" (*nesek*; the latter is regularly found in the priestly texts as supplementary sacrifice, but is nowhere described as a separate sacrifice; cf. 1967, 169-72). These sacrifices are to be "a gift of pleasing aroma for YHWH" (v. 13) [→**45**], borrowing the familiar expression from the sacrificial laws in Lev 1–3. From here on "seven Sabbaths" are counted, i.e. seven weeks or 49 days, until the festival of weeks begins on the fiftieth day. The enumeration of these days and weeks later became a fixed custom in Judaism, the word *'omer*, which actually means sheaf, becoming an object of counting (cf. *EncJud* 12, 1382-89). At the festival of weeks (vv. 15-21; the name "festival of weeks" is not expressly mentioned but is expressed by the seven weeks that are to be counted) a "new grain offering" (*minḥāh ḥᵃdašāh*) is presented (the ritual for which may perhaps be found in Lev 2.14; cf. 1985ff, 112f), and again burnt offerings, this time in larger numbers, with the supplementary sacrifices we have met before (v. 18; cf. v. 13).

Surprisingly enough another sin offering now follows, additional to the other sacrifices and in the form of a scapegoat (v. 19a). Here we see a development that comes fully into its own in Num 28f: each sacrificial act on festival days concludes with a sin offering (see below). In Lev 23 there is just this one reference; this festival calendar is clearly less interested in the detail of cultic performance. (The mention of the fellowship slaughter sacrifice in v. 19b is quite unusual. The explanation may lie in the fact that a reviser concerned with completeness wished to list the whole range of sacrifices, in the order given in Lev 6f; cf. 1967, 25).

A whole series of festivals now follows. To begin with, the first day of the seventh month is a festival (23.24). This is the start of the new year. (The expression that later became customary, *ro'š haššānāh*, "beginning of the year," is found only in Ezek 40.1.) Originally the seventh month was the first, because it was then that the harvest year began; the counting of the months was later adapted in accordance with Mesopotamian practice—perhaps under political pressure—to begin in the spring, but the religious calendar remained unaffected by this (cf. *BRL* 167f). New year's day is a "sacred proclamation" with a limited prohibition of work, together with a ceremonial "noisy trumpeting" (*t̄rû'āh*). This is only mentioned at new year in the festival and sacrifice calendars (also Num 29.1), and further at the proclamation of the jubilee year (Lev 25.9), where it is expressly stated that it is performed with a ram's horn (*šôfār*). In Lev 23.24 this trumpeting is called "commemorative trumpeting" (*zikrôn t̄rû'āh*), as it is intended to call God's remembrance to the festival and the year that is now beginning (cf. Num 10.9f).

New year's day is as it were the preparation for the festival that now follows: the day of atonement (*yôm hakkippurîm*) [→**67**], which takes place on the tenth day of the seventh month (vv. 26-32). The further development of the festival year beyond the three originally agrarian festivals is especially clear here, as the day of atonement is quite different in character from the other festivals. However, this is no more than hinted at in the festival calendar. Thus on the day of atonement, as on the Sabbath, the complete prohibition of work applies (v. 28), underlined once again by the double expression *šabbat šabbātôn* (v. 32). Here it is even reinforced by the "elimination formula" (v. 30). Additionally we read: "you are to humble your souls (i.e. yourselves)" (vv. 27, 32), which is generally taken to be a fasting regulation; according to v. 29 "elimination" is also threatened in the case of transgression of this rule. The work prohibition is finally underlined by the sentence: "because it is the Day of Atonement, when atonement is made (*l'kapper*) for you before the LORD your God" (v. 28) [→**534**]. Thus the cultic performance of atonement determines the entire day of atonement. (See on Lev 16 below.)

Finally there follows on the fifteenth day of the seventh month the festival of booths (vv. 33-36, 39-42). This takes seven days (v. 34); an eighth day is added (v. 36) which like the first "sacred proclamations" is with a limited prohibition of work. (It is also referred to by the term *'ʷṣeret*, the interpretation of which is uncertain, cf. *ThWAT* VI, 336f.) In a supplementary note this festival is singled out from the circle of the other festivals as "the festival of the Lord" (vv. 39-42). Details of the performance of the festival are given: the bringing-in of fruits of the trees, together with palm-fronds and other branches, the precise use of which is not further explained and is therefore evidently presupposed as familiar (v. 40). Finally the seven-day stay in booths is prescribed in memory of the exodus from Egypt (vv. 42f). This completes the annual cycle. The older list of three or four festivals and holy days is now extended by the Sabbath, the new year festival and the day of atonement.

In the calendar in Num 28f the cycle of culticly significant days is extended even further. This calendar as a whole has a different emphasis: it is a calendar of sacrifices, as 28.2 explicitly states. It therefore begins with the daily sacrifice (*'iššeh*): two one-year-old lambs are to be brought as burnt offerings, one in the morning and one in the evening (vv. 3-8), and the supplementary sacrifices familiar from Lev 23: grain offerings and drink offerings (vv. 5, 7f; cf. 23.13, 18). This daily sacrifice is named *'olat tāmîd*, "regular burnt offering" (vv. 3, 6) and is often referred to as Tamid sacrifice. On the Sabbath comes further burnt offering with supplementary sacrifices (vv. 9f).

The beginning of the month (*ro'š hodeš*), i.e. the day of the new moon, now appears as a feast-day (vv. 11-15). The sacrificial animals get bigger and more numerous here: two young animals, a ram and seven lambs, and in addition the precisely prescribed supplementary sacrifices. In particular, however, a sin offering is now added (v. 15a), as was previously the case in Lev 23.19 on the occasion of the festival of weeks. This then continues regularly in the whole calendar of sacrifices, always only in the shape of a scapegoat, regardless of the steadily increasing amount of other sacrificial animals (28.22, 30; 29.5, 11, 16 etc.). So the crucial thing is simply the atoning function of this sacrifice, which is emphasized repeatedly by the expression "to bring about atonement for you" (*l*'*kapper* '*lêkem*, 28.22, 30; 29.5).

The festival that now follows is still called Passover here (vv. 16-25), but the duality remains: Passover is on the fourteenth day of the first month and on the fifteenth day begins the seven-day eating of unleavened bread. The festival of weeks then follows, here called also the "day of firstfruits" (*yôm habbikkûrîm*, vv. 26-31), which is followed by the new year festival (29.1-6). The day of atonement that comes after this (29.7-11) is here distinguished only by the complete prohibition of work (cf. Lev 23.28). Otherwise the same number of sacrificial animals as in the two previous festivals applies. But we are then told that these sacrifices are to be presented "except for the atonement-sin offering" (*ḥaṭṭāṭ hakkippûrîm*, v. 11b). In the context of this calendar, the real subject is thus not the day of atonement as such but the sacrifices that mark this day, in which the entire community participates.

The concluding regulations for the festival of booths (29.12-38) are quite sweeping. This recalls the special term "festival of the LORD" in

Lev 23.39. Here for each of the days separately the number of sacrifices and accompanying sacrifices is stipulated, the number of the largest sacrificial animals, the young bulls, decreases from day to day: from thirteen on the first day to seven on the seventh day, and on the eighth day it is only one, as on new year's day (29.2) and the day of atonement (v. 8). Particular historical developments appear to stand in the background here, which we are no longer able to determine. Finally, here too, the sin offering has its place at the conclusion (v. 39).

3.3 Once a year atonement for the sanctuary and for the whole community of Israel

"Once a year"—in the Hebrew Bible this phrase is found only in association with the "day of atonement" (*yôm hakkippûrîm*) in Lev 16.34 and Ex 30.10. This is the only divine instruction (*ḥuqqat 'ôlām*, "lasting ordinance") that is to be performed once a year. At the center of this stands the term *kipper*, "perform the act of atonement." Lev 16.33 lists the individual steps that are taken within the chapter of acts of atonement: for the holy of holies (with the double term *miqdaš haqqodeš*, which appears only here, cf. v. 16a), for the sanctuary as a whole (here termed the "tent of meeting," cf. v. 16b), for the altar (v. 18), for the priests (i.e. Aaron and his "house," cf. vv. 6, 11f) and for all Israel (with the double expression *'am haqqāhāl*, cf. vv. 17, 24b, which also appears here only). Verse 34 views the whole thing in relation to the Israelites, for whom the act of atonement is performed, to purify them from all their sins (*ḥaṭṭā'ôt*).

Both aspects together form the central significance of this day. (In the Hebrew Bible the day is called *yôm hakkippurîm* [Lev 23.27, 28; 25.9] and in the post-biblical tradition *yôm kippur*.) It is concerned, for one thing, with the "atonement" or "expiation" of the sanctuary. This shows quite a special aspect of the term *kipper*: here it means the removal of the consequences of "impurities" or "defilements" of the Israelites; for the tent of meeting "dwells with them in the midst of their impurities" (16.16). In the preceding chapters there has been detailed discussion of the most varied types of impurity and defilement (Lev 11–15). These impurities also defile the sanctuary, so that there is a regular need of cleansing in order to maintain its full efficacy. For this purpose the high priest may, and must, enter the holy of holies just this one time in the year, and under the strictest of safety measures (16.12f).

Atonement means above all cleansing. At the same time, however, it is also the day when the acts of atonement that are generally carried out in the context of the sacrificial cult reach their climax. This is clear particularly in the case of the sin offering of the "anointed priest" (i.e. in later terminology the "high priest"). At the end of the section on his sin offerings in Lev 4.3-12 the concluding statement about the act of atonement and the following divine absolution (see above) are missing; for no one can perform the act of atonement for the high priest. But once a year he can and must do this himself, by bringing about atonement "for himself and his house" (16.6, 11). And "for the whole community of Israel" too he carries out the atonement (v. 17b). This then relates not only to the defilements but also the sins that are mentioned previously in v. 16. Thus this day of atonement forms the climax to and the turning point of the year. Israel's life depends on this day being celebrated regularly.

It is of significance that unlike Lev 4f *kipper* here means an act of the high priest, who functions on his own account, and thus no statement about divine forgiveness follows. (This is also evident in the fact that the word *kipper*, when it relates to humans, is not linked with *'al-*, "about," but with *b'ad*, "for," 16.6, 11, 17, 24.) This may mean that the sins are thereby transferred to the high priest himself and that he therefore has to confess them over the scapegoat, thus unloading them onto it, and send it into the wilderness (vv. 21f; so Kiuchi 1987, cf. Crüsemann 1992, 364). However, the meaning of this ritual remains uncertain.

The expression "for Azazel" (vv. 8, 10, 26) is generally taken to refer to a demon of the wilderness by this name, to which the goat is sent. Perhaps, however, it originally indicated the purpose of an archaic elimination ritual, which lies in the background here (cf. Janowski 1993b). But this too remains disputed.

4. You shall be holy, as I am holy

In view of the central significance of the "day of atonement" it is certainly no coincidence that ch. 16 of Leviticus is found in the middle of the book and thus at the same time at the center of the Pentateuch, the Torah. It is framed by texts which deal in the most varied ways with the topic of "purity" and the corresponding topic of "holiness" (Lev 11–15 and 17–26). How closely these two things are related is evident, in an almost programmatic way, in the fact that the first chapter that deals with purity and impurity concludes with the repeated sentence: "you shall be holy as I am holy" (11.44f) [→**505**]. This statement is then repeated in 19.2 at the beginning of a chapter that develops various aspects of life in accordance with the will of God, and again in 20.26.

The correspondence between holy and pure is also evident in the way the priests' task is described, "to distinguish (*l^ehabdîl*) between the holy and the profane, between the unclean and the clean" (Lev 10.10) [→**513**]. So the concern is with distinction and the setting of limits. The demand addressed to Israel that it should distinguish finds its justification and premise in the distinction that God himself has already made. This context is expressed in a particularly marked way in the conclusion of Lev 20: "I am the LORD, your God, who have set you apart (*hibdaltî*) from the nations; you must therefore make a distinction (*w^ehibdaltem*) between clean and unclean animals ..., which I have set apart as unclean for you. You are to be holy to me because I, the LORD, am holy, and I have set you apart (*wā'abdîl*) from the nations to be my own" (vv. 24b-26). The separation from the nations is given more precision elsewhere with the sentence: "for I am the LORD, who led you out of the land of Egypt, to be your God. You shall be holy, for I am holy" (11.45). The leading-out of Egypt is thus the essential precondition for the demand that Israel should correspond to this action on God's part and be "holy." At the same time, however, being holy means active sanctification. Here too the actions demanded of Israel are preceded by the actions of God: Israel is to sanctify itself (*hitqaddēš*) because God sanctifies (*qdš* pi.) Israel (20.7f; cf. 22.32f; cf. Zimmerli 1980b, 503).

In Deuteronomy too, we find the connection between holiness and purity. Deut 14 contains a list of clean and unclean animals, largely identical to those given in Lev 11. Here too, both the beginning and the end speak of holiness: "for you are a people holy to the LORD, your God. Out of all the peoples on the face of the earth, the LORD has chosen you to be his treasured possession" (v. 2); and once again at the conclusion: "for you are a people holy to the LORD your God" (v. 21). Here the same basic idea is expressed in Deuteronomistic language: with the election of Israel God has created the preconditions for Israel to be able to be a "holy people."

In Deuteronomy it now becomes clear again that the holiness of Israel is not limited to the area of purity. In Lev 19 already the whole chapter, which is introduced by the sentence about Israel's holiness (v. 2), is concerned with the maintenance of Israel's special God-given position in the varied areas of everyday life. In Lev 20, which concludes with the detailed statements about Israel's being separated out and its holiness (see above), the concern is with particularly serious infringements in some of these areas. In Deuteronomy the statement about Israel as "holy people" is now right at the beginning in the context of the prohibition of participating in a foreign cult (7.6). Towards the end it then crowns the festive ceremony of commitment, in which the God-given commandments are confirmed as the basis of the covenant relationship between God and Israel (Deut 26.16-19).

Thus the term holiness extends over a broad framework: from the varied aspects and gradations of holiness in the cultic area through the rules about keeping purity and on to the demands of ethics and the shaping of everyday life. To put it another way: holiness extends from the "holy of holies" in the temple, via abstinence from unclean animals through to the commandment that "You shall love your neighbor as yourself" (Lev 19.18).

§ 12

Moses

The greater part of the Pentateuch, from Ex 2 to its last section in Deut 34, is concerned with Moses. All the events reported in the four books of Exodus through Deuteronomy, and all the commandments and instructions imparted in these books, are more or less directly connected with his person. Who is this Moses, the figure of whom marks the fundamental beginnings of the history of Israel in such an all-pervasive manner?

If anywhere, then it is clear at this point that this can be no "historical" question. The texts assembled in the Pentateuch are so multilayered and clearly reflect such a range of different epochs of Israel's history and literature, that the question can only be: what do these texts convey by the picture they sketch of Moses? In correspondence with the complexity of these texts and the differences between the traditions taken up and reworked in them, this picture is in no way uniform or consistent. On the other hand, the various elements come together into an overall picture. This will be the focus of our attention in the following pages.

1. The called savior

At the beginning of the story of Moses, and thus at the beginning of the history of Israel as a nation, stands the account of the saved savior. The history of Israel as a people begins with its oppression by the Egyptian king, the Pharaoh (Ex 1.8ff). A child, hidden in an imaginative way from persecution by the Pharaoh and thereby saved, arrives at the court of this very same Pharaoh and grows up there (1.15–2.10) [→36]. After a further digression (2.11-22) this Israelite with the Egyptian-sounding name *Mošeh* is called by means of a divine encounter to be the savior of his people from oppression (3.1-20). This beginning emphatically sets out the special position that Moses has. He is picked out of the fate of the oppressed Israelites in a quite extraordinary way, to be then acquainted with the crucial task given him for the further history of the people.

The account of Moses' call at the same time forms the bridge to the previous section on the early history of Israel. God reveals himself to Moses from the burning thorn-bush, as the God of Abraham, Isaac and Jacob (3.6). This sets in motion a long conversation between God and Moses (3.7–4.17), which is followed by many further encounters between God and Moses. In their directness ("face to face," Deut 34.10) they are comparable only with the confrontation between God and Abraham (Gen 15; 17; 18.16-33; cf. 1997f) [→**26**]. Neither before nor after is anyone else granted such a direct encounter with God.

The comparison with Abraham makes another fundamental difference clear, however. Abraham stood alone facing God; but in Moses' case already in the first sentence of the divine speech it is "my people" (3.7). Moses is called as the leader and savior of the people of the "children of Israel," whom he is to lead out of Egypt (3.10 etc.). Thus he stands in-between God and the people right from the beginning. At the same time the connection is again made backwards: Moses is to lead the Israelites into the land which God swore he would give to Abraham, Isaac and Jacob and which he now wishes to give to the present generation as their inheritance (6.8).

This fundamental element runs right through the whole story related, with many variations, in the Pentateuch: Moses is called by God to be the savior of his people. He carries out this task through reverses of many kinds but also through the greatest climaxes in the history of the people of Israel, until finally he is permitted to see with his own eyes the land God promised the forefathers (Deut 34.1-4) [→**87**]. In the greatest crisis in relations between God and his people occasioned by the construction of the "Golden Calf" on Sinai, Moses is able to assuage God's anger by taking him at his word, by which he promised the land to the forefathers (Ex 32.11-14) [→**61**].

The call of Moses contains another central element too: God declares his name to Moses. The reader knows the name from the narratives about the beginning of human history (Gen 2.4); occasionally it is also reported that God addresses one of the patriarchs with the solemn expression "I am YHWH" (Gen 15.7; 28.13). But now, at the beginning of a new, fundamental section of the history of God's dealings with Israel, God expressly introduces his name: first in the veiled form

"I will be what I will be," and then in the unveiled word (of which, however, only the consonants have come down to us): *Yhwh*. This again makes the connection with the patriarchs, as in this first express naming of his name God reveals himself at the same time as the "God of your fathers, the God of Abraham, the God of Isaac and the God of Jacob" (Ex 3.14f). This express naming of the divine name is repeated once again in another context, where there is a reminder of the earlier self-presentation of God to the patriarchs as *'ēl šadday* (6.2f) [→**27**].

In the call narrative it starts to become evident that Moses will not only be the bearer of an individual "office." He is called as the savior of his people from Egyptian slavery. At the same time, however, he is the first to whom the name of the God of Israel is fully announced. This means that from now on he will also be the religious leader and guide of his people. The call story also already contains an indication of the events in which this side of his commission will come to its full development: "this will be a sign for you that I have sent you: when you lead the people out of Egypt, you will serve God on this mountain" (3.12). For the reader the meaning of this reference becomes clear later, when the Israelites arrive at Mount Sinai and Moses purposefully climbs up the mountain "to God" (19.3) [→**52**].

As the called savior, Moses represents his people to the outside world. Right at the beginning of the first speech to Moses, God announces to him that he will send him to Pharaoh to demand Israel's release (3.10) [→**44**]. This means confrontation with Pharaoh as the representative of the power that is oppressing Israel. At the same time this commission reveals another "office" for which Moses is prepared: he is to oppose Pharaoh with the prophetic formula: "Thus says the LORD" (4.22; 5.1). Previously too the prophetic element resounded when God announced to Moses that he would "send" him (*šālaḥ*, 3.10, 12), as is later said repeatedly of the prophets (e.g. Isa 6.8; Jer 1.7; 7.25; Ezek 2.3).

Finally the narrative certainly does not describe this relationship in the first detailed encounter between God and Moses as at all lacking in suspense. To start with, Moses is not prepared to accept the call to be his people's savior. First he doubts that the Israelites will believe him (Ex 4.1), then he points to his lack of gifts as a speaker (v. 10), and finally he turns the commission down altogether (v. 13). But God sticks to his commission and assigns his brother Aaron, who is more of a speaker, as his co-worker (4.14-16, 27-31). The moment of quarrelling with God however remains preserved in the picture of Moses. It stands in the context of the conflicts between the people and Moses, which arise in connection with the preparation of the "Golden Calf" (Ex 32.7-14, 31f) [→60]. In what the transgression of Moses and Aaron consists in the account of the "water of quarreling" (Num 20.1-13) remains unclear (cf. Milgrom 1989, 448ff); but it is mentioned expressly as grounds for the fact that neither of them will be permitted to enter the land to which they have led the people (20.12; 27.12-14).

2. The recipient of the Torah

The pathway of the people liberated from Egyptian oppression leads first to Mount Sinai (Ex 19.1f; cf. 1991d). There begins the second stage in Moses' ministry. It shows him once again in the role of mediator between God and the people of Israel, but this time in the area of religion. As the history of Israel as a nation only starts to unfold under the leadership of Moses, the called savior, so too it is under the mediation of Moses at Sinai that it gains its crucial features. Neither here nor anywhere else in the Hebrew Bible is Moses described as or termed the "founder" of Israelite religion (cf. 1975). His call is quite expressly anchored in the previous history of God with the patriarchs; in addition, the notion of an individual founding personality would be incompatible with the thought of the Hebrew Bible. A fundamental and unmistakable element of the religion of Israel is, however, linked with the name of Moses: the Torah.

Once again Moses stands between God and Israel, this time in a particularly marked way. The Ten Commandments with which God's instructions for his people begin, are announced by God to the entire nation (Ex 20.1-17) [→53]. But the people are seized by great fear and beg Moses: "Speak to us yourself and we will listen. But do not have God speak to us or we will die" (vv. 18f). In Deuteronomy this is depicted in even more detail, where Moses expressly says: "At that time I stood between the LORD and you" (Deut 5.5). From this point on the whole of the rest of the Torah is received by Moses and passed on to the people. Moses is the sole mediator between God and Israel, and Israel receives the Torah only through Moses. So the Torah can be called the whole Torah of God (Pss 1.2; 19.8 etc.), but also the Torah of Moses (Josh 8.31f; Mal 3.22).

Even more than through his leading role in the freeing of Israel from Egyptian slavery, through his mediation in the receipt of the Torah Moses becomes the great, dominant figure in the fundamental

beginning chapter in the story of Israel. For the Torah, i.e. the Pentateuch, which is marked throughout by the figure of Moses, is not
merely an account of past events; it prescribes Israel's life to the tiniest
detail [→**500**]. This not only applies to legal or juridical questions in the
narrower sense, but for many fundamental questions in Israel's religious life. The texts of the Pentateuch authorized by the name of
Moses contain extensive cultic regulations that concern not only temple service, but also the personal life of individual Israelites, male and
female, as in the purity regulations, the ordering of festivals and holy
days, regulations for agriculture (Ex 23.10f etc.) and much more besides.

3. The Covenant mediator

The receipt and transmission of the Torah by Moses is closely connected with the solemn covenant agreement on Sinai. Already at the
beginning of the great encounter with God that is granted to Israel on
Sinai, there is talk of the covenant (*bᵉrît*), which Israel is to "keep," or
better: "maintain" (Ex 19.5) [→**53**]. This points forward to the solemn
ceremony with which after the conclusion of the proclamation Moses
then conducts the covenant agreement (24.1-8) [→**57**]. The commandments that Moses has received and passed on form the central
content of the covenant agreement. Moses first presents "all the Lord's
words and laws (*mišpāṭîm*)," and the people respond with "Everything
the Lord has said we will do" (v. 3). Moses then writes these words
down and later reads them out once again from the "book of the
covenant" (*sēfer habbᵉrît*, v. 7), again followed by the answer of the
people. Covenant and Torah are indissolubly linked here.

Moses acts, as on the receipt of the Torah itself, in the role of mediator between God and the people [→**436**]. Herein lies the crucial
difference between God's covenant agreement with the patriarchs and
the covenant agreement on Sinai. In the case of the patriarchs there
was no need for a mediator; Abraham stood and faced God alone. But
Moses now stands "between" God and the people. We can again see
the unique nature of Moses' position here (cf. 1999b). Torah and
covenant, these two great themes that are so central for Israel are indissolubly linked to its whole being.

Moses' position as mediator is evident in a particularly impressive
way in the dramatic situation of the transgression of the covenant by

the Israelites with the fashioning of the "Golden Calf" (Ex 32). Moses demonstratively smashes the "tablets of the testimony" (v. 19, cf. v. 15): the covenant is broken—or rather, Israel has broken the covenant. But already before this Moses prayed earnestly to God not to destroy Israel but to remember his covenant promise to Abraham, Isaac and Jacob/Israel, to make their descendants numerous and to give them the promised land—and God relented (vv. 11-13). So the way is clear for the eventual renewal of the covenant agreement (34.10). God has not broken the covenant. And Moses is once again the mediator for this restoration of the covenant.

In the great sermon at the beginning of Deuteronomy (Deut 4) [→52] the connection between the two aspects is once again developed extensively. Torah and covenant are identified: the covenant that Israel is to "do" is equated with the Ten Words that God wrote on the stone tablets (v. 13). Moses is given the task by God of teaching Israel further commandments and sentences of law (*ḥuqqîm ûmišpāṭîm*), after he has already spoken of the Torah which—in renewed and expanded form—he is now in process of presenting to Israel. And Israel is warned not to forget the covenant which God has concluded with it (v. 23); at the same time, however, Israel is assured that God will not forget the covenant that he made with Israel's forefathers and which he sealed with his oath (v. 31).

4. The paradigmatic prophet

God "sends" Moses (*šālaḥ*, 3.10, 12), just as later he will repeatedly send prophets (cf. Isa 6.8; Jer 1.7; 7.25; Ezek 2.3 etc.). He gives him the task of confronting Pharaoh with the prophetic formula: "Thus says the Lord" (4.22; 5.1), as Moses then does a number of times (7.17, 26; 8.16 etc.). In the further course of the Pentateuch too, the prophetic character of Moses' ministry is brought out. At the same time, however, Moses' special position is emphasized: as a rule, God makes himself known to prophets by means of visions and dreams. "Not so, my servant Moses;" with him God speaks "mouth to mouth" and not through riddles or parables (Num 12.6-8) [→51]. Moses is more than a prophet.

The towering stature of Moses' prophetic charisma comes to narrative expression in the same context: God takes "(some) of the spirit (*rûaḥ*) that rests on him (Moses)" and distributes it among seventy elders, who then fall into prophetic ecstasy (*hitnabbē'*). Two of those chosen for this who remained in the camp are also affected. Moses answers the disquiet that arises from this with the words: "I wish that all the LORD's people were prophets and that the LORD would put his Spirit on them!" (Num 11.16f, 24-30). This account raises a number of questions (cf. Gunneweg 1990; Sommer 1999); but it is quite clear that the intent is to show that a thoroughly superhuman measure of prophetic spirit has been granted to Moses.

That Moses is the yardstick against which all prophecy is measured, is expressed in a pointed way by Deuteronomy, when it characterizes the prophets that God will raise in Israel as prophets "like Moses" (Deut 18.15: "like me," v. 18 "like you") [→82]. In contrast to the diviners and soothsayers of other nations (vv. 9-13) the prophets will stand in the tradition of Moses, who heard the voice of God on Horeb at the request of the people and passed on what he heard to the people. So God will also give future prophets his word on their lips, which they are then to pass on to Israel; Israel will listen. Here prophecy is defined by reference to Moses. To that extent the sentence "Moses was a prophet" would be a tautology (Watts 1998, 419); rather, the reverse is the case—prophecy is defined as Mosaic (Blenkinsopp 1992, 235; cf. also Perlitt 1971, 597).

At the end of Deuteronomy, however, it is again specified that Moses is more and remains more than all the prophets after him: "Since then no prophet has risen in Israel like Moses" (Deut 34.10) [→87]. Moses' special position, which was previously put into words in Num 12.8, is emphasized once again: "God knew him face to face" (*yāda'*). The other prophets are "like Moses" in that they receive and pass on the word of God. But in the immediacy of his relationship with God he remains unique and alone.

The characterization of Moses as a prophet is not limited to the Pentateuch. In Hosea we read: "The LORD used a prophet to bring Israel up from Egypt, by a prophet he cared for him" (Hos 12.14[13]) [→273]. This leads us back again to the narrative of Moses' call, where he is given the commission of leading Israel out of Egypt in the language of a prophetic call: "I send you ... and you will lead my people out" (Ex 3.10) [→40]. Here Hosea is evidently picking up on a tradition he can assume to be familiar to his hearers or readers (cf. Perlitt 1971, 606f).

The image of the "prophet Moses" is not a uniform one, like the picture of prophecy itself. But this aspect is an essential part of the picture of the biblical Moses.

5. The leading advocate

Already in the call account we see a characteristic feature in the picture of Moses: his suffering in his office: "Who am I, that I should go to Pharaoh and bring the Israelites out of Egypt?" (Ex 3.12[11]); and then: "What if they do not believe me or listen to me?" (4.1); and again: "I have never been eloquent ...; I am slow of speech and tongue" (v. 10); and finally: "O LORD, please send someone else to do it" (v. 13). This sounds very much like a refusal to accept the task prepare for him. Though God does get angry (4.14), he sets Moses' brother Aaron at his side, who is to be his "mouth" (v. 16). God has previously equipped Moses already with a miracle-working staff (vv. 3-9).

Moses' suffering in his office continues when the Pharaoh reacts to the desire to leave by intensifying the conditions of forced labor. It is initially the suffering of the people that brings Moses to his complaint to God: "LORD, why have you brought trouble upon this people?" But then he adds: "Is this why you sent me?" (5.22). Here Moses' position between God and the people comes clearly into view for the first time: in view of the suffering of his people Moses complains about the futility, indeed the detrimental effect, of his mission (v. 23). He does not explicitly ask God for help, but God grants it (6.1). The short account in Ex 5.22–6.1, especially in comparison with others (see below), can be taken as a scene of intercession, more precisely as "intercessory complaint" (Aurelius 1988, 160f).

In the traditions about the Israelites' wanderings in the wilderness the element of Moses' suffering in his office is found in various constellations. In the account of the "brackish water" (Mara, Ex 15.22-25) [→50] we first meet the word "grumble" (*lwn* niph., v. 24), which then repeatedly characterizes the behavior of the people [→638]. Here it is expressly stated that the people grumbled against Moses (v. 24). Moses feels attacked by this and "cries" to God, who helps him by miraculous means to make the water potable (v. 25). Moses' "crying" (*ṣāʿaq*) is the cry for help of one oppressed by the people and does not contain the element of intercession. The situation in Ex 17.1-7 is similar. Here the "grumbling" (v. 3) is exacerbated by the "accusing" (*rîb* v. 2, cf. v. 7); this also expresses a fundamental criticism of the leading-out of

Egypt: "to make us and our children and livestock die of thirst" (v. 3). Moses even fears for his life and "cries" to God (v. 4), who enables him to perform the miracle of getting water to spring out of the rock (vv. 5f). Here too Moses' cry is one of distress, not intercession. Moses' suffering in his office is presented as his personal suffering, caused by the obstinacy of the people. (In the parallel narrative in Num 20.1-13 Moses does not pray at all, but only throws himself, together with Aaron "on his face," whereupon the "glory of YHWH" appears to them and speaks with Moses [vv. 6f].)

In other narratives the people complain "before the ears of the LORD" (Num 11.1) or speak "against God and Moses" (21.5), which immediately gives rise to punitive reactions on God's part: by a fire that threatens the camp (11.1) and by (fiery?) snakes (21.6). It is only when the people "cry" to Moses (11.2) or confess their sinful behavior to him (21.7) that Moses takes a hand and makes intercession (*yitpallēl*) for the people. The fire is extinguished, and Moses receives the task of setting up a "brazen serpent," the sight of which keeps those bitten by snakes alive. Here we have a picture of Moses in which he appears in an intercessory role between God and the people God punishes.

This aspect is evident in an especially striking way in the account of Israel's sin with the "Golden Calf" (Ex 32–34) [→**60**]. There is scarcely any other occasion when Moses' position between God and the people is more clearly marked, and scarcely anywhere else is Moses' intercession of such fundamental significance. God introduces his decision to annihilate Israel by saying to Moses: "Now leave me alone so that my anger may burn against them" (32.10). Moses stands between God and the people; he should as it were stand to one side to allow free rein to God's anger. Instead, Moses attempts to "soothe the face of the LORD his God." He reminds him that he himself has led Israel out of Egypt "with great power and a mighty hand;" that the Egyptians would say that he has led them into misfortune, to wipe them out; and that he swore to the forefathers that he would make their descendants numerous and give them the promised land (vv. 11-13). "Then the LORD relented and did not bring on his people the disaster he had threatened" (v. 14). Moses brought about this "relenting" of God's by reminding God of his oath towards the patriarchs (cf. Jeremias 1975, 59ff).

Several times more in the multi-layered chapters of Ex 32–34 Moses raises his voice as petitioner on Israel's behalf. While the first conversation (32.11-14) took place between God and Moses only, the people are then brought in. Moses points out to the Israelites their great sin and then once more ascends Mount Sinai in order to ask God for forgiveness for the sin of the people. Once again he emphasizes his solidarity with the people: if God will not forgive the people, then he should obliterate Moses "from the book that you have written" (32.30-32). Moses thereby reinforces once more his earlier rejection of God's declaration that he would make him alone a great nation (v. 10). He does not want his fate to be better than that of the rest of the people (Cassuto 1967, 423). God's answer is multi-layered: Moses cannot be wiped out of God's book, for only "whoever has sinned against me I will blot out of my book" (v. 33). God does not express an explicit promise of forgiveness for the people's sins; however, he gives Moses the task of leading the people now to the goal promised by God (v. 34a). The danger that the exodus from Egypt might fail is thereby obviated for the time being. (There follows a strange warning: "When the time comes for me to punish, I will punish them for their sin" [v. 34b]. It remains unspecified when this is to take place. Some interpreters see in this a threat to the northern kingdom because of the bull-images that Jeroboam I had erected in Beth-El and Dan; cf. 1 Kgs 12.25-30.)

The restoration of the covenant, too, is represented as God's direct answer to Moses' renewed petition for forgiveness (34.8-10). Here Moses' tension-filled relationship with the people is again evident. On the one hand he says that they are a "stiff-necked people;" on the other hand he associates himself with them when he prays that God should forgive "*our* guilt and sin" (v. 9). God replies: "I am making a covenant with you" (v. 10).

Finally a similar situation is repeated to that at Sinai after the sending-out of spies into the land that Israel is to settle (Num 13f) [→**70**]. After the report of the spies on the strength of the inhabitants the people refuse to carry on. They grumble against Moses and Aaron and want to appoint a new leadership and return to Egypt (14.1-4). God reacts as he did on Sinai: he purposes to destroy the people and make Moses a greater and mightier people (vv. 11f). Moses' answer contains the same arguments as in his first petition on Sinai (Ex 32.11f), this time in even greater breadth: the Egyptians and the other nations will doubt God's power to bring his people into the land that he has sworn to give them (Num 14.13-16). And Moses repeats the words that God himself said to him in the theophany: that he is merciful and gracious and forgives misdeeds and transgressions (vv. 17-19; cf. Ex 34.6f). And

Moses then prays God: "forgive the sin of these people, just as you have pardoned them from the time they left Egypt until now" (Num 14.19). And God replies: "I have forgiven them, as you asked" (v. 20). But at the same time he determines that the present generation of rebels will not reach the land (vv. 21-23).

Here once again the ambivalence of Moses' situation between the grumbling and stubborn people and God appears explicitly. It is evident that Moses' petition has its focus after the granting of the Torah and the covenant agreement on Sinai. It is an answer to God's wrath and threatened punishment towards the people, since the people are in a new legal relationship with the Sinai covenant and have thus entered into a new set of responsibilities towards God (cf. Schart 1990, 50f).

The image of Moses the intercessor is supplemented by a number of narratives about his intercession on behalf of individuals. The narratives about the Egyptian plagues repeatedly contain the feature that Pharaoh asks Moses to pray for him, to end the current plague, and that Moses grants this request (Ex 8.4-9, 24-27; 9.27-33; 10.16-19) [→**456**]. Here the petition is an element in the conflict with Pharaoh, through which Moses' legitimation is displayed as the divinely appointed savior of Israel. Moses' petition on Miriam's behalf, too, who contested his claim to the leadership and was struck by God with a rash as a result (Num 12.13), stands in the context of the presentation of the legitimation of Moses. Finally Moses (this time together with Aaron) asks God not to destroy the entire community together with the rebels supporting Korah (16.20-24). Here the divine punishment is not averted, but limited to the immediate group of the culprits.

Common to all the accounts of Moses' intercession is the fact that they expressly demonstrate and legitimate Moses' special position. No one besides him has the ability to protect the people—and occasionally individuals too—from the wrath and punishment of God through his intercession on their behalf. At the same time, these accounts show in various ways that Moses' intercession emerges out of conflict situations in which rejection and contradiction constantly arise against his office. The intercession is thus often also an expression of Moses' suffering in his office, which accompanies his pathway right from the beginning.

Finally, the capacity for effective intercession is also a special feature of the prophet. The Amos tradition tells us that his petition was heard by God (Amos 7.2, 5) [→**284**], but that he was then unable to continue it further (7.7-9; 8.1-3); Jeremiah is given by God the express prohibition of continuing the intercession that he had previously been engaged in (Jer 7.16; 11.14; 14.11; cf. 18.20) [→**210**]. Intercession is also required of Isaiah (Isa 37.4). But also before the writing prophets, intercession plays a part as a feature of the prophet. Samuel, the prophet (1 Sam 3.20) is also depicted as the disciple of Moses in that he makes petition on Israel's behalf. Like Moses he prays and thereby achieves victory over the Philistines for Israel (1 Sam 7.7-12; cf. Ex 17.8-13). And he grants Israel that even after the appointment of a king against his will he will not stop praying for Israel (1 Sam 12.19, 23). Thus in Jer 15.1 Moses and Samuel are mentioned together as the paradigmatic intercessors. Finally, Abraham is granted the title of prophet because a disaster God had decreed was averted through his effective petitioning (Gen 20.7, 17).

6. The Servant of God

"And Moses the servant of the LORD died" (Deut 34.5). This sentence marks the end of an epoch, as is clearly shown by its repetition in Josh 1.1f: "Moses my servant is dead." Moses is here given the honorific title of "Servant of the LORD" (*'ebed yhwh*). This title expresses an especially trusted position in relation to a higher-placed person, linked with a corresponding authorization (cf. the "servant of the king," 2 Kgs 22.12). Thus God can say of "my servant" Moses that he "is faithful in all my house" (Num 12.7); opposition to him is at the same time against God (v. 8b). This title also expresses the close religious connection between God and Moses; thus we read after the miraculous rescue of the Israelites at the Reed Sea: "the people feared the Lord and put their trust in him and in Moses his servant" (Ex 14.31) [→**46, 98**].

Above all, this title is frequently found in association with the Torah of Sinai. Thus before the entry into the land of Canaan Joshua is expressly warned by God to "be careful to obey all the law my servant Moses gave you" (Josh 1.7) [→**98**]. On Mount Ebal Joshua erects an altar "as Moses the servant of the LORD had commanded the Israelites. He built it according to what is written in the Book of the Law of Moses" (8.31), and carries out the ritual of the public proclamation of the Torah according to the instructions of Moses, the servant of the Lord (v. 33). After the completion of the conquest of the land, the transjordanian tribes of Joshua are warned to continue to keep to the Torah of Moses, the servant of the Lord (22.2, 5). The end of the northern kingdom is justified on the grounds that the Israelites had not listened to the voice of God and had transgressed against the covenant, i.e. they had not done all "that Moses the servant of the LORD had commanded" (2 Kgs 18.12). In respect of the cultic deviations of Manasseh, too, the requirement is called to remembrance, to observe "the whole Torah that my servant Moses commanded them" (21.8); and the person who prays the prayer of repentance in Daniel confesses disobedience to the Torah, which has brought about the implementation of the curse "which is written in the Torah of Moses, the servant of God" (Dan 9.11). In this regard, the community of returnees from exile commit themselves to "follow the Law of God given through Moses the servant of God" (Neh 10.30) [→**399**], and concretize this with detailed self-commitments. Finally, the prophet Malachi gives an admonition, in view of the day of the Lord that is to come, to remember "the Torah of my servant Moses" (Mal 3.22) [→**313**].

A second thematic field in which Moses is termed "servant of the Lord" is the promise of the land, as well as its distribution among the tribes. The title frequently appears in this connection in the book of Joshua, especially in relation to the land that Moses assigned to the transjordanian tribes (Josh 1.13, 15; 12.6; 13.8; 18.7; 22.4; cf. also 9.24; 11.12, 15; 14.7). At the end of the prayer of dedication of the temple, Solomon prays to God again for the people that he has singled out as his inheritance from among all the nations "just as you declared through your servant Moses when you, O Sovereign LORD, brought our fathers out of Egypt" (1 Kgs 8.53). And in the subsequent blessing, Solomon gives thanks that God has given his people rest and that "not one word has failed of all the good promises he gave through his servant Moses" (v. 56). In the books of Chronicles the title appears a few more times in connection with cultic affairs: 1 Chron 6.34; 2 Chron 24.6, 9.

The term "my servant" in the divine speech is not limited to Moses. It can also be used in reference to Jacob/Israel (Isa 41.8f; 44.1f etc.), the "servant of God" (Isa 42.1, 19; 52.13; 53.11), the "messianic" figure of Zerubbabel (Hag 2.23), but also Isaiah (Isa 20.3) and Job (Job 1.8; 2.3; 42.7f). However, it appears with particular frequency, again in a titular sense, for David (Isa 37.35; Ezek 34.23; 37.42f), who is expressly called the "servant of the Lord" (Pss 18.1; 36.1). Here we see the drawing of a conscious parallel with Moses.

7. Moses, Israel's paradigmatic leader figure

With the death of Moses, the first, fundamental epoch in the history of Israel comes to a close. In a sense it is prehistory: it does not yet take place in the land in which Israel then lives, and it contains only a provisional draft of the structures and institutions that will later determine Israel's life. Everything is, as it were, summarized in the person of Moses. As yet there are none of the offices that will then develop in Israel. It is only Moses who fulfills all the functions that are necessary for Israel's life.

One can go further than this: through his leading of the people out of Egyptian slavery Moses first created the conditions for Israel's life as a nation. Without Moses Israel would not be what it is. He as it were gave the nation its identity. Here we also see already a crucial element of Moses' special position: he receives the instructions for everything he does directly from God. In all the "offices" that Moses fulfills, this is the fundamental difference in comparison with all later incumbents. Here lies the key to Moses' uniqueness as it is presented to us in the texts.

In the "office" of the prophet the outstanding special position of Moses is expressly emphasized many times: his dealings with God are fundamentally different from those of all the prophets that follow him (Num 12.7f) and no one comes close to him (Deut 34.10-12) [→**51, 88**]. The most striking thing about this, however, is that his comprehensive leadership function resists comparison with later offices. This function too is marked by his direct relationship with God. This applies to the role of the called savior, and it finds tension-filled and often dramatic expression in particular in the role of the suffering intercessor. The task of leading and guiding the people then shifts in a limited sense to Joshua; but this ends with Joshua's death. The charismatic figures of the time of the judges only very partially bridge the vacuum that is produced. But it is only after that that the uniqueness of Moses' position becomes entirely clear: the king, who now assumes the leadership of the people, requires appointment and legitimation by a prophet; he himself has no "spiritual" authority of any kind. From here on it becomes clear in retrospect what the figure of Moses expresses: Israel needs a leadership that stands in a direct relationship with God. The "prophet" Moses has fulfilled this task in a paradigmatic way. But after him there is no leader figure who can do justice to these demands. The prophet Samuel has to transfer the "worldly" leadership to someone else.

At one more point a comparison between the role of Moses and that of the king suggests itself. In Israel's ancient Near Eastern environment the king is the legislative authority. There is no trace of this in Israel. "Where elsewhere the king stands, in Israel Moses stands." There is therefore a great deal to suggest that the extended and differentiated shaping of the legal texts in the Pentateuch should be interpreted with reference to the necessities and the development of the Israelite legal system (cf. Crüsemann 1992, 76-131 [quotation p. 113]).

Finally it is significant that there is one important office that Moses does not fulfill: that of the priest. It is one of the most important elements in the establishment of the cult that Moses appoints Aaron and his sons as priests (Lev 8) [→67]. It is only on this occasion that Moses himself performs the sacrifices. Afterwards he never has a priestly function. But at the same time this means that the appointment of Aaron and his sons as priests is irrevocable and can never be changed by anyone else. Moses has no successor who could perform this function.

Thus it is evident from various points of view that Moses is a model figure. In many areas he has a paradigmatic function, which however is so elevated, from a religious point of view, that it can never be equaled by a later incumbent of one of his offices. In the figure of Moses ideal forms of particular offices and institutions have been designed and imported into the early history of Israel, against which later incumbents and administrators will be measured, though they will not be able to match them.

From this point of view, it is remarkable that the figure of Moses is absolutely not drawn two-dimensionally and free of contradiction. Quite the contrary: often enough there is mention not only of the wrath of God but of the wrath of Moses (Ex 32.19 etc.). And often enough his anger is not only directed against his people, but also against God (Num 11.10-15). But then we also find the surprising sentence: "Now Moses was a very humble man, more humble than anyone else on the face of the earth" (Num 12.3). In the immediate context this is probably intended to explain the fact that Moses does not presume to defend himself against the querying of his elevated position (v. 2). But it is significant that the image of Moses is thereby given a broad spectrum. Moses is as little an ideal figure as the patriarchs are, or any other figure in the Hebrew Bible.

§ 13

The Kingship of David

1. The disputed beginnings

"In those days Israel had no king; everyone did as he saw fit" (Judg 21.25) [→**102**]. This concluding sentence of the book of Judges characterizes Israel as without leader and without orientation. The reader of the Hebrew Bible knows, however, that there was once a time when Israel possessed an ideal leadership in Moses and when it used to take its orientation entirely from the Torah of Moses. In addition the reader also knows the experiences of a time when the lamentable circumstances of the period of the judges had been overcome because Israel had a king.

The institution of the kingship, however, was certainly not uncontested in Israel. The associated problems are reflected in the texts in various ways. First, already for the time of the judges there are reports of attempts to appoint a king, and in a wide variety of ways. For one thing, we read that the Israelites ask the successful, charismatic Gideon, whom God had called, to rule over them, in the form indeed of a hereditary dynasty. But Gideon rejects this with the words: "I will not rule over you, nor will my son rule over you. The LORD will rule over you" (Judg 8.22f). This gives emphatic expression to the irreconcilability of a kingship over Israel with the sole reign of God. However, neither the word "king" (*melek*) nor "reign as king" (*mālak*) is used.

An entirely different perspective comes in the narrative of the kingship of the usurper Abimelech (Judg 9). In his case there is no religious agenda of any sort; it is a kingship set up by force, which comes to an ignominious end. The element of arbitrariness in this reign is exposed in all its absurdity in Jotham's fable of the rule of the thorn-bush over the trees (vv. 7-15). Here we can discern a critique of the kingship which regards this institution as inherently dangerous.

Finally the problems of the kingship are discussed at a fundamental level when the elders of Israel ask Samuel to appoint a king over Israel "like all the nations" have (1 Sam 8.5) [→**104**]. Chapters 8–12 of 1 Samuel contain an extremely tense collection of texts in which this question is viewed from a wide variety of angles. On the one hand there are reports, in several different narrative variants, of a divine legitimation of Saul, his appointment as king and his first victory (9.1-10; 10.16; 11). On the other hand in chs. 8 and 12, which frame the whole body of material, the kingship is evaluated as a rebellion against God (8.7) and also as an intervention in the property circumstances of the free Israelite peasants (8.11-17) (cf. also 10.17-27). An anti-royal attitude is reflected here, which presupposes experiences with the kingship. The result shown in 1 Sam 8–12, however, is that despite some fundamental misgivings the kingship is recognized as an institution legitimated by God and instituted by the "prophet" Samuel. (On this whole issue cf. Crüsemann 1978a.)

Nonetheless the kingship of Saul ends with his rejection by God. "Because you have rejected the word of the LORD, he has rejected you as king" (15.23) [→**106**]. In this extremely ambivalent narrative (cf. Brueggemann 1997, 367ff) the selection and anointing of David as his secret successor (16.1-3) already plays a crucial role.

2. David as model king

David's kingship is presented right from the beginning in contrast to the kingship of Saul: David's anointing by Samuel occurs explicitly as an alternative to Saul, whom God has rejected (1 Sam 16.1). In all the vicissitudes of their relationship, the disputes between David and Saul which then follow have a clear tendency in presenting David's steady rise to prominence despite all difficulties and dangers (cf. 1971). But special attention is paid to the fact that David himself does not attack Saul, despite having the opportunity to do so on several occasions; for he sees in him the "anointed (*māšîaḥ*) of YHWH" (24.7, 11; 26.9, 11, 16, 23), against whom no one has the right to raise his hand (cf. 2 Sam 1.14, 16). David is no usurper but Saul's legitimate successor, appointed by God, who awaits his appointed hour. The reader will later remember these statements of David's, when David himself is described as *māšîaḥ* (2 Sam 22.51; 23.1) [→**109**].

At the beginning of his reign, David takes two steps that will have far-reaching significance for the further development of Israel and in particular for the elaboration of Israelite religion. The first is the capture of the city of Jerusalem (2 Sam 5.6-9). The significance of this step lies, first of all, in the fact that David creates a city of residence that is independent of the interests and rivalries of the tribes. Its fundamental religious significance Jerusalem gains through the second step: the bringing in all the "Ark of God" (2 Sam 6.2-4 etc.) or "Ark of the Lord" (vv. 9, 11 etc.) to Jerusalem. This provides the precondition for Jerusalem's role as the central and ultimately the only sanctuary site for Israel. How strong the memory of this step of David's persisted in the religious tradition is strikingly evident in Psalm 132, which tells the story of this event in a poetic and liturgical form. Here we also meet the term "Zion" for the place that God has "chosen, to live there" (v. 13) [→575].

The question of the suitable "dwelling-place" for God is explicitly linked with the future of the kingship of David in David's conversation with the prophet Nathan (2 Sam 7.1-17) [→113]. The premise is David's wish to set up a house for the Ark of God, which at the time is still "living" in a tent (v. 2). The divine answer provided through Nathan shifts the theme of a house for God to a house for David: God is going to build David a house (v. 11), and he intends to establish his kingship beyond his immediate heirs for all time (*'ad 'ôlām*, v. 16). So David's immediate heir is to build a house to God's name (v. 13).

In 2 Sam 7 the approach taken towards an overall picture of David as the chosen king of Israel becomes evident. At the beginning is the call from the humblest of circumstances: God has taken David from "behind the flock" and made him "*nāgîd* over my people Israel" (v. 8, cf. 1 Sam 16.1-13). God has then been with him on his paths and in his deeds and will make his "name great as the name of the great on the earth" (v. 9). All this, however, will take place not for David's sake but for Israel's. Here the horizon extends to a view of the history of God's dealings with Israel: God will give his people a place to live and "plant" it there (v. 10). This is reminiscent of the thanksgiving song after the Israelites pass through the Reed Sea, where we read: "You brought them in and planted them on the mountain of your inheritance—the place, O LORD, you made for your dwelling, the sanctuary, O LORD, your hands established" (Ex 15.17). The planting on the mountain of God's residence corresponds to the anticipatory view of the construction of the house for God's name in 2 Sam 7. The metaphor of the "planting" of the people then also appears in prophetic promises of salvation for the restoration of Israel (Jer 32.41; Amos 9.15).

In David's prayer which follows the "wise saying of Nathan" (2 Sam 7.18-29) [→114] it is again pointed out what significance the divine promises to David have for Israel. With clear echoes of the language of Deuteronomy the greatness of God and the uniqueness of his actions towards Israel are praised, whom he has redeemed by means of mighty deeds and made his people (vv. 23f; cf. Deut 4.7, 34). The two things now belong indissolubly together. "Then men will say, The LORD Almighty is God over Israel! And the house of your servant David will be established before you" (v. 26).

This sounds a signal for everything that will follow. David's story itself begins in a way that is anything but straightforward: David's adultery with Bathsheba and the treacherous removal of her husband Uriah (2 Sam 11), David's confession of his sin (ch. 12), the intrigues surrounding the Davidic succession, his flight, Sheba's rebellion (chs. 12–20)—in all this hardly anything is evident of the divine blessing that was spoken of in the prophecy of Nathan and the prayer of David that follows it. It is not until the two psalm-like texts at the end of the story of David, both of which are introduced as the words of David, that different notes are again sounded: 2 Sam 22 (largely identical to the "royal psalm" Ps 18) calls David the "anointed of YHWH" (v. 51) and speaks in detail of the divine rescue from his enemies which the praying king has experienced (esp. vv. 1, 18, 38-49).

In this "thanksgiving song of David" a further key term is evident, which adds a new feature to the picture of David: the praying David speaks of his righteousness (*ṣ'dāqāh*) in an exemplary character (2 Sam 22.21-25; previously we have had only a very brief note that as king over Israel David had done "justice and righteousness," 2 Sam 8.15), and he describes himself as "blameless" (*tāmîm*, v. 24). Here we can see yardsticks against which David's successors would later be judged. In the "last words of David" in 2 Sam 23.1-7 this picture is further reinforced when David calls himself the "anointed of the God of Jacob" (v. 1) through whom the "spirit of the LORD" has spoken (v. 2). Here we also read that God had "given" (*śām*, v. 5) David an "eternal covenant" (*b'rît 'ôlām*).

Thus at the end of David's reign an ideal picture of this God-chosen king is sketched, which lifts him way above the narrated reality and makes him a model and yardstick for all subsequent kings. On Solomon's accession this picture is given a further accent. David admonishes his son Solomon to walk in God's ways and to keep the commandments and statues "as written in the Torah of Moses" (1 Kgs 2.1-4) [→116]. The whole following story of the kingship is then tied into the bases of Israel's life at the time of the inauguration of the kingship when under Joshua the Torah of Moses was the guideline for the leadership of the people.

In this farewell speech of David's the measuring of his successor by his figure is prepared for with the insertion of a conditional element in the recapitulation of the Nathan prophecy which is not found in 2 Sam 7: "If your descendants watch how they live ... you will never fail to have a man on the throne of Israel" (1 Kgs 2.4). In his prayer of dedication of the temple Solomon himself repeats this conditional limitation (8.25), and in the second dream vision of Solomon's it is further developed and sharpened in the divine speech (9.3-9). Finally at the end of Solomon's reign the "functioning" of the promises to David are again emphasized, but once again restricted: in a divine speech it is announced to Solomon that God will "snatch" the kingdom from him (11.11). This is then doubly qualified, however: this will not happen during Solomon's life-time (v. 12), and it will not be the entire kingdom that is snatched away from Solomon's son, but one tribe will be left to him (v. 12). The two things are justified "for David, your father's sake," or "for my servant's sake." Verse 12 adds: "and for the sake of Jerusalem, which I have chosen." Here in retrospect the situation is described as it then transpired: the kingdom of David is limited to the southern kingdom of Judah, where, however, it lasts for a long time.

At this point a strange *ritardando* occurs: the prophet Ahijah announces to Jeroboam that he will transfer the kingdom to him in Solomon's succession (1 Kgs 11.29-39) [→127]. Here he repeats, as it were, in mirror form the announcement that was made to Solomon in the divine speech: that he will leave one tribe to Solomon's son "for the sake of my servant David" (vv. 32, 34). But above all he makes the same promises to Jeroboam that Nathan the prophet had once made to David: God will be with him and make him a lasting house, as he did for David (vv. 37f). In this announcement Jeroboam appears as the true successor of David or at least as a rival king with comparable legitimacy and with a "house," i.e. a dynasty. In fact, we can even read that God has "snatched away" the kingdom from the house of David and given it to Jeroboam (14.8). So then Rehoboam's behavior, which finally leads to the fall of the northern tribes from the Davidic dynasty, is interpreted by the narrator as the fulfillment of this prophetic promise to Jeroboam (12.15).

This promise does, however, again contain the proviso, as we find previously in Solomon's case: "If you listen to all that I command you ..., as my servant David did" (11.38). The further history of the kingdom of Jeroboam then shows that he did not do justice to the expectations placed on him. On the contrary: his cultic measures amount to sin as far as the house of Jeroboam is concerned (13.34), so that the prophet Ahijah has to observe that "you were not like my servant David" (14.8) and therefore announce to the "house of Jeroboam" that it will be wiped out (vv. 10, 14). Henceforth the "sins of Jeroboam" will lie like a dark shadow over the history of the northern kingdom (14.16; 15.30; 16.31 etc.). Here no long-term dynasty will be formed.

In Judah on the other hand, the dynasty promise to David is realized, albeit in an extremely vicissitudinous history. An important key term in the interpretation of this history appears in the speech of the prophet Ahijah to Jeroboam: God will leave a tribe to the son of Solomon, "so that my servant David may always have a lamp (*nîr*) before me in Jerusalem, the city where I chose to put my Name" (1 Kgs 11.36). A "lamp" for David in Jerusalem—this is one of the leitmotifs by which the subsequent history of the kingdom in Judah is to be seen. It appears in quite special times of crisis: the first son of Rehoboam walks "in all the sins of his father," so that the continuation of the dynasty seems endangered; but nonetheless God does not allow the "lamp" to be put out for David (15.3-5) [→**145**], so that a connection is laid to Asah, of whom we read that he "did right in the eyes of the LORD," "like his father David" (v. 11). And when later the danger becomes apparent that Judah will under king Joram and his northern Israelite wife Athaliah go the same way as the northern kingdom, in anticipation of the usurpation by Athaliah, the only interruption in the reign of the dynasty of David, we read that God did not want to destroy Judah but to keep his promise to give his servant David a "lamp" (2 Kgs 8.19).

The comparison with David remains the dominant criterion for the judgment of the Judahite kings in the following centuries. Asah is the first of whom it is said that "his heart was devoted (*šālēm*) to the LORD" (1 Kgs 15.14), as was previously said of David: "He did right in the eyes of the LORD, just as his father David did" (2 Kgs 18.3). Hezekiah is also given the promise that God will protect Jerusalem against the attacks of the Assyrians "for my sake and for the sake of my servant David" (19.34; 20.6). And finally it is said of Josiah, with special emphasis and detail: "He did right in the eyes of the LORD and walked in the ways of his father David and turned neither to the right nor to the left of it" (22.2).

In Josiah's case the second element in the picture of David appears again: the close association with the Torah. In the concluding note about Josiah's reign we read that there was never a king before or after him who turned to the Lord with his whole heart "according to the whole Torah of Moses" (2 Kgs 23.25; cf. 1 Kgs 2.1-4). One can see here the "confluence of two streams of tradition:" the David tradition and the Moses tradition (von Rad 1962, 350). The Moses tradition of course also lies in the background, when in the divine speech Solomon is accused of not having kept "my covenant and my commandments that I commanded you" (1 Kgs 11.11). Of Hezekiah, on the other hand, we read that he kept the commandments "which the LORD commanded Moses" (2 Kgs 18.6). And when we read that the heart of a king was turned "undividedly" to God (1 Kgs 15.14), or that a king "did right in the eyes of the LORD" (1 Kgs 15.5, 11; 22.43; 2 Kgs 10.30; 12.3; 14.3; 15.3, 34; 18.3; 22.2), then this must be taken in the sense of the keeping of the commandments. The exemplary function of David is thus in the final analysis oriented to his relationship to the Torah of Moses.

Already in the books of Kings it is evident that the judgments of the kings according to the example of David are at least partially formulated with a backward look to the end of the kingdom in Jerusalem. In the books of Chronicles this is perfectly plain. Here the Davidic kingdom is the first and dominant theme, even though it ceased to exist long ago. This shows the close interconnection between the kingdom and the temple and the cult as well as in particular the special place of David himself, who planned and prepared everything. He gave a plan (*tabnît*) to Solomon (1 Chron 28.11) [→**407**], in which the construction of the temple and its erection are described in the fullest detail. This is a "writing by the hand of the LORD" (v. 19). David is thus set in parallel to Moses, to whom God showed the blueprint (*tabnît*) for the construction of the sanctuary (Ex 25.9, 40) [→**65**]. Here a new view of David comes into view: he is the founder of the temple cult in Jerusalem that exists at the time of the narrator and his readers, the Levites

playing a significant role in this (cf. 1 Chron 15.2; 2 Chron 35.3 etc.).
Thus the temple and the cult are legitimated by the authority of "an
idealized and divinely inspired king David" (De Vries 1988, 639).

3. The Davidic king in the Psalms

The books of Samuel and Kings accord us an insight into the origins
and development of the figure of David as an example and model for
the kings of Israel and Judah. According to this, a legitimate kingship is
only possible in the Davidic succession and in orientation to his figure,
which has become paradigmatic. This picture of David has frequent
echoes in other areas of the Hebrew Bible.

In the Psalms further features are added to the biographic and exemplary aspect of the figure of David, which have their locus in one
way or another in the cult. At the beginning of his reign David laid
the foundation stone for the cultic and religious center of Israel by
bringing the Ark to Jerusalem. In the account of this it is expressly
emphasized that "the name of YHWH Zebaot, enthroned above the
cherubim" was mentioned (2 Sam 6.2) [→112]. It is therefore notable
that this solemn divine name plays an important role in the "prophecy
of Nathan" (2 Sam 7.8, 26f). The house for God is not built until
later, it is true, but David prays "before the LORD" (v. 18), "and this
certainly means in the sanctuary of the Ark" (Noth 1957, 127f=341f).
This gives expression to a real connection between David and the
sanctuary in Jerusalem and its cult.

This connection is spoken of quite directly in Ps 132 [→**517**]. Here
the story of the installation of the Ark by David is retold in a liturgical
framework: David wanted to find a "place (*māqôm*) for the Lord, a
dwelling-place (*miškān* plur.) for the strong one of Jacob" (v. 5); God
is asked to remember David for this (v. 1). But then the psalm turns to
the present: God is called upon "For the sake of David your servant,
do not reject your anointed one" (v. 10). Here the "anointed one"
(*māšîaḥ*) is clearly the presently incumbent king, who reminds God of
his oath to let the line of David sit for ever on his throne—though
with the limitation "if your sons keep my covenant and the statues I
teach them" (vv. 11f). Finally the psalm speaks of Yhwh's election of
Zion as his resting-place and dwelling-place (vv. 13-16) and then turns
back once more to David, to whom God promised that he would

prepare him a "horn" and a "lamp" here and let his crown shine (vv. 17f).

Here the figure of David has a firm place in cultic affairs in the sanctuary and on Zion. We hear on the one hand that David establishes the sanctuary on Zion as God's dwelling-place (v. 5), but on the other hand that God himself has chosen Zion as his residence (v. 13; cf. 78.68; 9.12; 74.2; 76.3 etc.). The cultic aspect joins the biographic aspect and changes the perspective. In Ps 78 the two things stand immediately next to each other when there is mention of the divine election (*bāḥar*) of Zion (v. 68) and of David (v. 70) [→**576**]. In Ps 89 the biographic element of the election (vv. 4, 20) and anointing of David (v. 21) and of the divine covenant oath (vv. 4, 29, 35f, 50) is set in a worldwide context: God is praised as the Creator and Lord of the world (vv. 6-15), and David is depicted as a world ruler, who is not only victorious over his enemies (vv. 23f) but whose ruling hand God also places on the sea and the rivers (v. 26). Finally we read that God has appointed him as the firstborn, who will call God his father (vv. 27f).

Quite a different dimension in conceptions of the kingship comes into focus here. We find it already at the beginning of the book of Psalms in Ps 2 [→**320**]: God has appointed his king on Zion, his holy mountain (v. 6) [→**576**]; this king is described as the "anointed one" (*māšîaḥ*) of God (v. 2); he can call himself the son of God (v. 7) and God will subject his enemies to him (vv. 8f). The same conceptual world is evident in Ps 110: God has the king take his place at his right hand and places his enemies at his feet (vv. 1f). In Ps 72 the notion of the world rule (vv. 8-11) is extended into cosmic dimensions: the king will live as long as the sun and moon continue to shine (v. 5); he will fall down like rain (v. 6) and under his rule nature will produce rich fruit (v. 16).

Here statements are made about the Davidic king enthroned on Zion which go far beyond all human measure. These are texts that have their *Sitz im Leben* in cultic-ritual processes centered on the enthronement of a new king. We are given an insight into such processes in such texts as 1 Kgs 1.32-40 and 2 Kgs 11.4-12 (cf. von Rad 1947). Elements from other Near Eastern religions, Egyptian in particular, have been borrowed in this area. This includes especially the designation of the king as "son of God." In the context of Israelite religion this cannot be understood in a mythological sense as the physical divine sonship of the king. Rather, we do better to think of an adoptionistic understanding or perhaps of an *interpretatio israelitica* in which a mythological understanding was reshaped (cf. Mettinger 1976, 259ff). The wording in Ps 2.7, "My son are you, today I have begotten you" expresses the fact that this sonship begins at a particular point in time, i.e. at the enthronement. We read something similar in Ps 89.28: "I will make him the firstborn." (On this in general see Noth 1950; Krause 1979, §4.)

These concepts however certainly do not determine the picture of the Davidic king in the Psalms. In the group of "royal psalms," alongside God's help against the king's and the people's enemies (Pss 18; 20; 21; 89.23f), the king's justice and his contribution to legal judgments are an especially prominent element. Some psalms are entirely or predominantly devoted to this subject. In Ps 101 the king proclaims in a sort of "pledge of loyalty" (Kraus 1978, 858) his full commitment to the maintenance of the law in his realm. In Ps 72 God is called upon to lend the king "your justice (*mišpāṭ*) and your righteousness (*ṣᵉdāqāh*)" so that he can judge his people in righteousness (*ṣedeq*) and lawfulness (*mišpāṭ*)" and the land can bear "wellbeing (*šālôm*) and righteousness (*ṣᵉdāqāh*)" (vv. 1-3). Later on in the psalm this is developed further (vv. 12-14) and extended to nature, which for its part is to bring forth righteousness and salvation in consequence of the king's actions (vv. 6f). Here it is evident what high expectations are placed in the king's actions for the implementation and maintenance of the law (cf. also Ps 122.5; see further Macholz 1972a).

The picture of David in the Psalms has quite another side to it, however. A number of psalms are related to events in David's life by means of superscriptions. In the main these are songs of lament which are related in their superscriptions to situations in which David had cause for complaint: in Ps 3.1 we read: "when he fled from his son Absalom," which reminds us of Absalom's revolt, which was such a danger to David, forcing him to flee from Jerusalem (2 Sam 15-19). This was one of the low points in David's reign; the mourning for his son Absalom—beloved in spite of everything (18.19–19.9), spoken of in the superscription to Ps 7. David had fallen even deeper through his affair with Bathsheba and the treacherous removal of Uriah (2 Sam 11f) [→**115**], which is referred to in the superscription to Ps 51. David's confession "I have sinned against the LORD" (2 Sam 12.13) echoes a number of times in this psalm. Immediately following it a whole group of psalms are related in the superscriptions to events in the early days of the story of David, when he was being pursued by Saul (Pss 52; 54; 56; 57; 59; 63). The lament dominates in these too. (The lament-psalm Ps 142 also belongs with these.) Another event in this period, in which David escapes danger by means of a ruse, is referred to in the superscription to Ps 34, in which the supplicant expresses gratitude for his rescue. Only once is it a royal psalm that is provided with such a superscription (Ps 18), speaking of rescue and victory. (Psalm 60 is also related to a victorious event in the superscription.)

These psalms show quite a different picture of David than the texts that are connected with coronation and court-cultic ceremony. These are oriented entirely to the person of David, as presented in the texts of the books of Samuel and Kings. Above all it is the suffering and complaining David, but also the sinful David that is the focus of interest. He is an example for the psalmist in quite a different way than the highly tuned psalms can be that sing of the Davidic kingship. This impression is reinforced by the fact that almost half the psalms (73 out of 150) are labeled by their superscriptions as "psalms of David," and that these psalms are found mainly in the front part of the Psalter, in which the psalms of lament dominate.

4. David as anticipatory ideal figure

In the prophetic books the figure of David and the Davidic king is viewed from yet another side. Here we see the tension between the elevated expectations of the actions of the kings and disappointment at the actual situation. It finds expression in texts that look forward to a future king.

Isaiah addresses the "house of David" and promises it as a divine sign the birth of a child by the name of "Immanuel" ("God with us," Isa 7.13f) [→174]. In his day there will be great changes—for salvation and for disaster (vv. 15-26). It remains unexpressed who is meant by this child. But then clear words announce that a child is to be born that will sit on the "throne of David" (9.5f; as in Ps 2.7 and 89.28 we may think of the institution of divine sonship at the enthronement). This announcement stands in the context of high expectations: "the people that walks in darkness" will see a "great light" and be freed from all the threats of their enemies (vv. 1-4). The child on whose shoulders the rule will rest is named with great, ceremonial throne-names: "Wonderful Counselor, God-Hero, Eternal Father, Prince of

Peace" (v. 5). In his rule there will be peace (*šālôm*) without end, and "justice and righteousness" will reign. This kingdom will exceed all that has gone before, and it will last "from now on forever." But it will not be set up by human strength but "the zeal of YHWH Zebaot will perform it" (v. 6). God will do it not just for Israel's sake but for his own sake. This characterization of the future king is reminiscent of statements in the Psalms (cf. Pss 2; 89; 110) [→**320, 445**]. But here this is all projected much more strongly into the future. It opens up the expectation of a blissful, just world, in which everything that now influences and endangers life in this world will be overcome.

This picture of the rule of a king of the future is exceeded again in Isa 11.1-10 [→**178**]: the story of the house of David will begin again from the beginning with a new shoot of the house of Jesse, David's father (1 Sam 16), as it were with a new David. The "spirit of the LORD" will rest on him as it once came upon David (16.13). But this spirit will be much more comprehensive than could ever have been said of David: a "spirit of wisdom and insight, spirit of counsel and strength, spirit of knowledge and the fear of the LORD." Here the framework of what could be expected of a rule and also what was said in an idealized picture of David is far exceeded. This future king is not just a political ruler but equally a spiritual and religious one. Nonetheless it is his actions as a ruler, or to be more precise as a judge, that are first placed in the foreground (vv. 3-5). Again it is righteousness that is above everything else, here with the special emphasis that the actions of this regal judge will above all benefit the poor and oppressed in the land.

But then the text leaves consideration of the area of what a human ruler can achieve entirely behind it. Not only will relations between people be set straight but disturbances in creation will be removed, between animals among themselves and between animals and humans (vv. 6-8). The picture drawn here is nothing short of paradise: predatory animals settle down next to peaceful domesticated animals, the offspring of both graze together and even little children need have no fear of adders and snakes. All the disturbances in the coexistence of created beings have been removed. Surprisingly the text then returns to the human world, or rather: back to the world of Israel: no one will sin any more "on my holy mountain," and the land will be filled with the knowledge of the Lord (v. 9). Both things belong together in this picture of the future: the hope of a world without injustice and sin and of an unendangered life within creation.

This word of the book of Isaiah reaches out furthest in the anticipation of what is expected of the coming of an eschatological king of the line of David. Other prophetic texts remain in the inner-world area. Thus in the book of Micah the thought that the Davidic kingship will begin all over again, at the place where it had its beginning: in Bethlehem (Mic 5.1). The origin of the new ruler of Israel will lie long before the beginnings of the present kingdom, however, in the primeval times (*qedem*), in the remote days of the earlier times (*'ōlām*). Thus his rule will not simply be a continuation of what there has been so far. Even the title "king" is avoided and instead there is talk of the "ruler" (*mōšēl*). His actions are described as "grazing" (v. 3), a picture that is also found in the David tradition (2 Sam 5.2). His rule will even extend over the whole world, so that people will live in safety "to the ends of the earth." And peace will reign (v. 4).

In the book of Jeremiah the metaphor of the shepherd who leads the people to pasture, is used of the political class. In Jer 23 a woe against the shepherds who have forgotten their responsibilities (vv. 1f) is contrasted with the proclamation that God will gather the rest of the flock and give them new shepherds (v. 4). This is, as it were, crowned by the promise that God will awaken a "righteous shoot" (*semah saddîq*, v. 5), a "true shoot that truly gives honor to his ancestors" (Rudolph 1968 *ad loc.*). Again it is in particular "justice and righteousness" that mark the actions of this king, and under him Judah and Israel will live in security (v. 6). Here from the critique of the present king the expectation arises of a new Davidide, whose name is clearly alluded to: in the name of the future ruler *yhwh sidqēnû*, "YHWH is our righteousness" we hear the name Zedekiah (*sidqîyāhû*, "my righteousness is YHWH." This expectation of a new Davidide thereby remains entirely in the area of present political hopes. (Cf. also 33.14-16.)

Ezekiel extends the shepherd metaphor: God himself will lead the flock to pasture instead of the irresponsible shepherds (Ezek 34.1-16). But then he will appoint a single shepherd over his people who will lead them to pasture, namely "my servant David" (v. 23). Thus God will delegate the office of shepherd he has assumed, to a new David. The latter does not thereby stand in God's place, but carries out his duties on God's instructions and with a clear subordination: "I, the LORD, will be their God, and my servant David will be prince (*nāśî'*) in the midst of them" (v. 24). Lying here in the echo of the "covenant formula" is also a legitimation for the promised ruler (cf. 1995a, 41).

In 37.23 the announcement of a new David appears in a new context again: the promise of the reunification of the two separated kingdoms of Judah and Israel (vv. 15-28). This time "my servant David" is described as king, who will at the same time be *one* shepherd for all (v. 24; in v. 25 the title *nāśî'* is taken up again). The reunited people will return to its land and God will make an eternal covenant of peace with them (v. 26). Here the promise of a new David extends forward into an area of history that lies entirely outside the present realities. Nonetheless it remains still in the realm of what is historically conceivable.

In the case of the post-exilic prophets too the expectation of a new ruler constitutes an important part of their future expectation. The name David is not mentioned in this connection, but there can be no doubt that the picture of the king in these prophets is marked by the tradition of the Davidic kingship. In Haggai the expectation of a new ruler is given a surprising concrete form when it is linked with the name of a particular person: Zerubbabel, the descendant of David, is called "my servant" in the divine speech and said to be chosen by God (Hag 2.23) [→**304**]. He thus stands squarely in the Davidic tradition. God will appoint him "on that day" when the dramatic eschatological changes occur of which the preceding verses speak (vv. 20-22). God will then make him "like a seal," like a confirmation of the divine action. Perhaps a part is played here also by the memory of the saying in Jeremiah that God will "tear off" king Jehoiachin, who is like a seal-ring on his right hand (Jer 22.24). Now with Zerubbabel the opposite is to occur. Here the expectation of eschatological changes is connected with a high-tension, imminent expectation that is directed towards a concrete person.

In Zechariah too, an eschatological king is expected. He will come into Jerusalem to the accompaniment of the jubilation of the "daughter of Zion;" but he will not himself create the conditions for the change of circumstances, but God will remove the weapons of war (Zech 9.9f) [→**308**]. The first sign of this ruler will be that he is righteous—a central element of the David tradition (cf. Pss 72; 101 etc.). Features sketching a decidedly unwarlike picture then follow: he will be one that is or was helped (*nôšā'*—not "a helper;" Buber: a "liberated one"); he will take up his royal office after God has created the circumstances for this. He will be "poor" (or perhaps better: humble), as was once said of Moses (Num 12.3). He will ride on a donkey, i.e. not in a warlike procession but on a suitable, noble steed (cf. Gen

49.11; Judg 5.10; 10.4 etc.). And then he will announce peace to the world and begin his worldwide rule.

Despite all the differences the prophetic expectations of a new king from the dynasty of David have basic things in common. When the king starts his reign, basic disturbances in the present situation of Israel, in fact of the whole world, will be removed. But the eschatological king will not himself create the conditions for his rule, but God will do this, so as to prepare the way for his rule of peace (Isa 9.2-4; Ezek 34.11-16, 20-22; Hag 2.21f; Zech 9.1-8, 10). The scope of his rule is described variously. In some prophetic passages expectations relate entirely to the extent of Israel (Isa 9; Jer 23; 33; Ezek 34; 37). In others there is talk of world-affecting changes and of a worldwide rule of the eschatological king (Mic 5.3; Hag 2.22; Zech 9.10). In Isa 11 the effective scope of the eschatological turmoil is extended to the whole of creation, in which all enmity will be removed (vv. 6-8).

One of the essential qualities of the expected king will be his righteousness and his just juridical actions (Isa 9.6; 11.3-5; Jer 23.5f; Ezek 37.24; Zech 9.9). In particular his juridical championing of the disadvantaged, the "poor and wretched," is emphasized (Isa 11.4). But the word that towers above all else is "peace" (*šālôm*, Isa 9.5f; Mic 5.4; Jer 23.6; Ezek 34.25; 37.26; Zech 9.10). This will be the crucial sign of the forthcoming end-time, in which the expected Davidic king will exercise his office as the one commissioned and appointed by God to do so.

The figure of an end-time king is often referred to as "Messiah." This does not, however, correspond to Old Testament linguistic usage. The underlying word *māšîaḥ*, "the anointed one," often means the reigning king in Israel—even Saul, whom God rejected (1 Sam 24.7; 26.9 etc.)—but also the Persian king Cyrus (Isa 45.1) as well as the "anointed" priest (Lev 4.3, 5 etc.), once in the language of the Psalms also the forefathers of Israel (Ps 105.15); on the other hand the word is not used of a future king. This changes, however, in the early post-biblical period, when with the arising of a "messianic" expectation the word *māšîaḥ* or its Greek equivalent χριστός becomes the title of an expected king (cf. e.g. *Pss Sol* 17.21ff; 18.5-9). The word ὁ χριστός (with the article) is also found in this sense in the New Testament (e.g. Matt 16.16; 24.23). Twice the Graecized Hebrew word Μεσσίας (John 1.41; 4.25) also appears here. Thus in the interpretation of Old Testament texts the term "messianic" can be used in a broader sense, but not the expression "the Messiah."

§ 14

Zion

"Zion" is one of the names most heavily filled with content in the Hebrew Bible. There is a wide variety of different concepts associated with this name. The critical and original point is the erection of the temple in Jerusalem on the ridge that has since borne the name Zion. Through its recognition as the only legitimate sanctuary Zion became the central point for Israel's cult and religion.

A central element is the presence of God on Zion. God has chosen Zion and has decided to live there (Ps. 132.13f etc.). A second important element thus comes in here: God not only dwells on Zion but is enthroned there as king: Mount Zion is the "city of the great king" (Ps 48.3) [→334f]. Finally the name of Zion also becomes a term for the city of Jerusalem and its inhabitants and beyond this also for Judah as a whole: "Zion will be redeemed with justice, her penitent ones (or: returnees) with righteousness" (Isa 1.27).

The central and comprehensive significance that the name of Zion has taken on makes it seem justified to view the traditions circulating Jerusalem as Israel's central cultic site together under the term "Zion," even if the name itself certainly does not appear everywhere. So it is striking, for instance, that in the psalms that deal with the topic of the kingdom of God (see section 2) the name of Zion appears only once in reference to this kingdom (Ps 99.2; further 97.8 as a term for the city and its inhabitants, cf. section 3). And in a book like Ezekiel, which centers so markedly on Jerusalem and the temple, the name Zion is entirely absent (cf. Zimmerli 1969, 63; evidently Ezekiel represents an understanding of the cult which is oriented entirely towards the establishment of the cult on Sinai; thus in chs. 40–48 the name Jerusalem is also absent, the talk being instead of the "city" [40.2; 45.6 etc.]).

1. Zion, the site of the temple

Zion was initially the term for a particular part of the city of Jerusalem. When the city is taken, it is reported that David took the "mountain strongholds of Zion," which was evidently an especially important part of Jerusalem, probably the acropolis (2 Sam 5.7; cf. *ThWAT* VI, 1008f) [→**111**]. David made it his royal seat and called it the "city of David" (v. 9, cf. v. 7). In 1 Kgs 8.1 we then read that Solomon brought the Ark of the Covenant up "out of the city of David, that is Zion" to the new palace and temple precincts (adjoining to the north, in a more elevated situation). With this transposition of the political and religious center of the city the name Zion also moves to the temple precincts. In the historical traditions about pre-exilic times the name is no longer found. (In 2 Kgs 19.21, 31 it is found in a prophecy.) It appears all the more frequently in the Psalms and prophetic literature.

Mount Zion is the place where the temple stands. This aspect is central in the Psalms, though there is scarcely any talk of the temple cult in the narrower sense. Only occasionally are sacrifices mentioned: grain offerings and burnt offerings (Ps 20.4), burnt offerings as votive offerings (66.13, 15), "just" fellowship offerings (*zibḥê ṣedeq*, 4.6) and thank-offerings (*zebaḥ tôdāh*), as brought by the individual on experiencing divine help (107.22; 116.17; cf. 27.6; 50.14, 23; 56.13); in addition however we find critical comments toward the sacrifices as are familiar to us from the prophetic critique of sacrifice (40.7; 51.18, but cf. v. 21). From some texts indications can be deduced about processions with the Ark (132.7f; 24.7ff); Ps 26.6 speaks of walking around the altar, 118.27 of a round dance during which perhaps ropes or garlands were wrapped around the "horns" of the altar; 68.25f describes God's solemn procession into the sanctuary.

Because of the temple Zion itself becomes the place of the presence of God: "The Lord has chosen Zion, elected it as his residence" (Ps 132.13) because he loved it (78.68). He "dwells" on Mount Zion (74.2; cf. 9.12; 76.3; 135.21), which is thus also called the "holy mountain" (2.6; 3.5; 48.2 etc.; in the "Song of the Reed Sea" it is called the "mountain of your inheritance [*naḥ⁽ᵃ⁾lāh*]," Ex 15.17). The designation of the mountain as the "extreme north" (48.3) is apparently a borrowing from Ugaritic mythology, where *ṣāphôn* (Hebrew "north") is the name of a widely visible mountain that was venerated as the residence of the god Ba‘al (cf. Isa 14.13; *ThWAT* VI, 1093ff).

From Zion, the "crown of beauty," God appears radiantly (50.2). From there God's help (14.7; 20.3) and blessing (128.5; 134.3) are hoped and prayed for, and there praise and vows are brought to him (65.2). The pilgrims who come to Zion "see" God there (84.8).

In the psalms of individual petitioners a strong emotional tie to the temple is expressed. Thus in Ps 84 the psalmist speaks of his love for the "dwelling-places" of Yhwh Zebaot (v. 1), of his longing for the "courts of the LORD" (v. 2, cf. v. 11), of living in God's house (v. 5), where he finds security at the altars of Yhwh Zebaot, like the bird in its nest (v. 4); and those who go through the "valley of distress" will ultimately see God there on Zion (vv. 7f). Other psalms too speak of love for the temple (26.8), of "dwelling" in the temple, in "God's house" (27.4) and in its forecourts (65.5), in God's "tent" on his "holy mountain" (15.1); the psalmists hope to flourish in God's house and its courts like an olive tree (52.10), or like a palm and a cedar of Lebanon (92.14). It is due to God's kindness that the psalmist can go into God's house and pray (5.8) and that he can keep coming back there his whole life long (23.6). The pilgrims rejoice as they go into the house of the Lord (122.1) and then stand in the temple and its forecourts (134.1; 135.2). The petitioner remembers this in times of oppression (42.5) and abandonment (55.14f). And those sitting in exile in Babylon can only weep when they think of Zion (137.1).

The significance of Zion as the place of God's presence extends beyond the temple area to the city of Jerusalem. Thus in "Zion psalms" there is repeated mention of the "city of God" or "city of the LORD" (Pss 46.5; 48.2, 3, 9; 87.3; cf. 101.8). In other psalms the name of Jerusalem appears in association with the temple (68.30; 79.1; 116.19) or Zion and Jerusalem stand in a relationship of *parallelismus membrorum* (51.20; 102.22; 128.5; 135.21; 147.12). Jerusalem is also the goal of pilgrims (122.2, 3, 6), and memory of Zion in exile is directed to Jerusalem as a whole (137.5-7). (On the further use of the name Zion for Jerusalem see section 3.)

Of the prophetic books it is the book of Isaiah especially, in which the name Zion plays an important role, and in all its parts; in no other book of the Hebrew Bible do we find the name Zion as frequently as in Isaiah (cf. 1984, 305-309 [149-52]). In some texts elements of the religious Zion tradition are addressed with this name. Thus as the conclusion of the first unit of prophetic sayings there stands the vision of the pilgrimage of the nations "to the mount of the LORD, to the house of the God of Jacob," where the latter say: "For the Torah goes

out from Zion, the word of the LORD from Jerusalem" (2.1-5; cf. Mic
4.1-5) [→**170**]. Here a significant connection between the Zion tradition and the Torah tradition comes into view. In a moment that is
crucial for him personally, Isaiah speaks of "YHWH Zebaot, who
dwells on Mount Zion" (Isa 8.18), echoing central elements of the
Psalms tradition. In 18.7 too there is talk of the "place of the name of
YHWH Zebaot, Mount Zion," in 24.23 and 52.7 of the kingdom of
God on Zion, and in 28.16 of a mysterious foundation stone that God
lays on Zion. Finally the "liberated of the Lord" will return with jubilation to Zion as the pilgrims once did (51.11 = 35.10).

In the majority of instances in Isaiah the name Zion indicates the
city of Jerusalem. This also applies to the larger part of the references
in the other prophetic books. Only occasionally do we find elements
of the Zion tradition. Thus in Jer 31.6 in an eschatological text a call
summoning the pilgrims to Zion echoes on. In 50.4f there is talk of an
eschatological return to Zion; similarly also in Mic 4.7, where God
will reign as king over the returnees on Zion. (On Mic 4.1-5 see
above on Isa 2.1-5.) In Zech 8.3 the tradition of Zion as the "holy
mountain" is connected with the other one of Jerusalem as the "city of
loyalty," and in 9.9 Zion is called upon to celebrate the festive procession of the eschatological king.

Zion has a special role in the book of Joel. Here everything is over-
shadowed by expectation of the "day of YHWH." In 2.15-17 there is a
summons to a great celebration of repentance and lament on Zion. In
4.16 the "roaring" of Yhwh from Zion announces the fact that Israel
is exempted from the eschatological court and that God continues to
dwell "on Zion, my holy mountain" (v. 17, cf. 21b). In between there
is the other statement: only those will be saved "who call upon the
name of the LORD;" and this salvation will be on Mount Zion (3.5).
Here Zion is ascribed a central role in the eschatological events; and
according to the context the eschatological rescue applies not only to
Israel but to "all flesh" (3.1), as long as it calls upon the name of the
Lord. (Cf. also 2.1, 23; 4.21.)

2. Zion, the seat of God's throne

Zion is called the "city of the great king" (48.3). Here there is a combination of the concept of Zion as God's dwelling-place with the notion that God is "king." In the "temple dedication prayer" of Solomon
(1 Kgs 8.12f) [→**120**] the two things are side by side: God wants to live

in the dark of the clouds—and Solomon has built him a "house of dominion," a "place of enthronement (mākôn l'šibtekā) for all time." The same expression is found in the "Song of the Reed Sea" in Ex 15: "You brought them in and planted them on the mountain of your inheritance, the place, O LORD, you made for your dwelling, the sanctuary, O LORD, your hands established" (v. 17). This is followed by the solemn formula, "The LORD will reign for ever and ever" (v. 18). Here we see an important shift in the concept of God's enthronement: it has been extended from the temple building to the "mountain of your inheritance (nah⁴lāh)," i.e. Zion. This name does not occur at this point; but in Ps 132 we read that God has chosen Zion for his resting-place, where he will be enthroned forever (v. 13). Thus God can be praised precisely as the "One enthroned on Zion" (yošēb ṣiyyôn, Ps 9.12). (On this topic cf. Mettinger 1982.)

This conception was given cultic shape in the temple in Jerusalem. It gained expression in particular in a group of psalms that are known as "Psalms of Ascent" or "Yhwh-King Psalms" (47; 93; 95–99) [→335]. They are characterized by the formula "YHWH reigns as king" (yhwh mālak, 93.1; 96.10; 97.1; 99.1; in 47.9 mālak ⁴lohîm). The real theme in each of them is the kingdom of God. But this is developed in quite different directions. Thus in Ps 93 God's reign as king is celebrated as the dominion over the world he has himself created. In the language of the "raging waters" (vv. 3f) there are echoes of the mythological tradition of the battle of the creator god against the sea of chaos (cf. also Pss 74.13-17; 89.10-12). But there is no longer any mention of a battle. God has established the earth firmly (v. 1b) and his throne was established long ago (v. 2). He sits enthroned above the pounding waters "on high" (v. 4, cf. 29.10: "The Lord sits enthroned over the flood [heavenly ocean]"). In v. 5, however, "your house" evidently means the temple, in which the worshiping community is gathered. In these psalms it is clear throughout that the heavenly and the earthly residence of God cannot be separated (cf. also Isa 6; Metzger 1970).

In Ps 47 God's dominion over the world is described as dominion over the nations. The subjection of the nations means at the same time the prime position of Israel, whose inheritance (nah⁴lāh) God has chosen (vv. 4f). Israel can therefore call God "our king" (v. 7). God "has ascended amid shouts of joy, the LORD amid the sounding of trumpets," i.e. in a cultic ceremony; the expression recalls the procession of the Ark in Jerusalem (2 Sam 6.15) [→112]. The climb leads to the ascent of the "holy throne" (v. 9) in the temple on Zion. Here God is enthroned, but not only as king of Israel, but over the nations. Their representatives are gathered before the throne "as the people of the God of Abraham" (v. 10)—a quite singular statement which recalls Gen 12.3, according to which "all the nations of the earth" will have a share in the blessing promised to Abraham.

In other psalms of this group a new aspect comes in: Yhwh is king over the gods (Pss 95.3; 96.4; 97.9). The gods of the other nations are "nothings" (96.5; 97.7), but Yhwh is the creator of the world (95.4f; 96.5b, 10). Here this theme is connected with the first-mentioned one, that God has established the earth and his throne has thus been there from ancient times (93.1f). Israel will now tell of the glory and wonders of its God among the nations (96.3), and the nations will come and worship God in the temple courts (vv. 7-9).

A further important aspect of the divine kingdom is the establishment and exercise of justice and righteousness. Thus we read that righteousness and justice (*ṣedeq ûmišpāṭ*) are the supports of God's heavenly throne (97.2) and that the heavens proclaim his righteousness (v. 6). God himself will judge the world and the nations with righteousness (98.9). With this theme the cultic community's attention is then turned inward: in Ps 97 we read that Zion also rejoices over the divine judgments (*mišpāṭîm*, v. 8) and there is talk of the righteous (*ṣaddîqîm*) that live by them. According to 99.4 the divine king has established equity and created justice and righteousness (*mišpāṭ ûṣ'dāqāh*) in Jacob (i.e. Israel). So for Israel, God's reign as king is played out in that the God-given gifts of justice and righteousness determine the life of Israel and of each individual.

The inward view is at the same time a view of their own history. In Ps 99.6-8, continuing on directly from the talk of justice and righteousness, three great figures of Israel's early days are mentioned: Moses, Aaron and Samuel. "They called upon the LORD, and he heard them." They are thus said to be intercessors. (For Moses cf. Ex 32.11-14, 31-34; Num 14.13-20 etc.; for Samuel 1 Sam 7.5-10; 12.16-25; for both together Jer 15.1.) This presupposes that Israel will constantly have need of intercession on its behalf. And God will grant this, just as he was a forgiving God (*'ēl nōśē'*) to the great intercessors. (On this cf. Jeremias 1987, 118-22.)

In Ps 95 the inward view has a dual aspect. First God's nearness to his people and his care for them are described with the imagery of the shepherd and his sheep (v. 7a, cf. 79.13; 100.3). But then the text moves into an admonition: Israel is to listen to God's voice and not harden its heart (vv. 7b, 8). As a salutary example they are reminded of Israel's wandering in the wilderness, where "your fathers" "tempted" God, first at Massah and Meribah (Ex 17.2, 7) and then later shortly before reaching the promised land (Num 14.22) [→**71**]. At that time God swore in his anger that this generation would not come into the land (14.23, 30), which is here termed "my rest." Thus the psalm ends with the warning not to gamble away again the gift of the land that was granted to the subsequent generation. The knowledge of God's dominion is no guarantee for a permanent life in God's rest. This note is only sounded in this one psalm; however, it shows that even the hymnic praise of God in the temple does not remove the responsibility to listen to the admonishing and warning voice of God. (On the Yhwh-King psalms cf. also Janowski 1989.)

God's reign on Zion comes, finally, to expression also in the fact that he appoints his "anointed one" (*māšîaḥ*) as it were as his representative as king "on Zion, my holy mountain" (Ps 2.6, cf. v. 2). In a slightly different perspective we read that God sends his king the "mighty scepter from Zion" (Ps 110.2). Combined here in the Zion tradition are the two weighty concepts of the kingdom of God and the kingdom of David, and thus the Davidic dynasty.

It is very likely that particular psalms reflect religious activities such as processions, in which the Ark would presumably have played a role (cf. 132.7f; 24.7ff). However it is no longer possible to determine more detail about these. There have also been assumed to be special Zion festivals, especially in connection with the "psalms of ascent" (cf. esp. Mowinckel 1922), but discussion on this remains open.

3. Zion, that is Jerusalem

The name Zion means more than this, however. Already in the texts so far mentioned we find repeatedly the concept of the city. Thus the city of Jerusalem can also be termed Zion. Frequently the two names are given in parallel (Pss 102.22; 128.5; 135.21 etc.). In some texts both aspects can be discerned, that of the temple and that of the city with its inhabitants. Thus God is asked: "In your good pleasure make Zion prosper; build up the walls of Jerusalem" (51.20[18]). Here the aspect of the temple is still dominant, as the context speaks of sacrifices

(vv. 18f⋆, 21⋆). The city aspect however recedes into the background when we read: "The LORD loves the gates of Zion more than all the dwellings of Jacob" (87.2) or: "God will save Zion and rebuild the cities of Judah" (69.36[35]; cf. 48.12; 97.8, which speaks in the same vein of the "daughters of Judah"). The city of Zion is also personified when the text speaks of the "gates of the daughter of Zion" (9.15) or when Zion is called upon to sing to its God (147.12; cf. 146.10). When, finally the turning of Zion's fate is spoken of (126.1), it is not just the city that is meant but the fate of Israel as a whole (cf. 137.1).

In the book of Isaiah, where the name Zion plays a significant role (see above), in the majority of texts it is a term for the city of Jerusalem. At the beginning, almost programmatically, we read that the "daughter of Zion" is threatened and abandoned "like a shelter in a vineyard" (1.8). This threat to Zion is one of the dominant themes in the whole book of Isaiah. It presents itself from various aspects, partly as a threat from enemies but partly also through the behavior of its own inhabitants. Here the theme of "Zion" is linked with that of "justice and righteousness" (Isa 1.21-27) [→169]. This shows that the city of Jerusalem/Zion is measured especially against the standards set by God's Torah (2.3). The future expectation of the book of Isaiah is thus oriented entirely to the restoration of justice and righteousness in Jerusalem. Already in 1.27 we read that Zion will be redeemed through justice and righteousness; in 11.9 the future vision reaches its conclusion in the expectation that no one will sin any more on the "holy mountain;" and in chs. 60–62 [→196] the description of the shining eschatological future of Zion amounts to the fact that righteousness radiates over it so that all the nations can see it (62.1f).

In other passages in Isaiah, in the most varied contexts, there is talk of God's helping Zion against the threats of its enemies (10.12; 29.8; 31.4, 9; 33.20; 34.8; 37.22), especially when "the people of Zion, who live in Jerusalem" call upon him for help (30.19). Finally, Zion will be the place where the "remnant" of those who "are left" will gather under the shelter that God will set up over Zion (4.2-6; cf. 14.32; 37.32) and "everlasting joy will crown their heads" (35.10 = 51.11).

The middle part of Isaiah (chs. 40–55) [→184], too, is dominated entirely by the hope and expectation that God will redeem and restore Zion/Jerusalem. Here again there are grounds for viewing the texts concerning Jerusalem and Israel together under the heading "Zion." In what follows we shall restrict ourselves to mentioning only a few of those that expressly mention the name of Zion. At the beginning of this block of chapters stands the call of the "joyful messenger (female) of Zion," who announces God's coming (40.9). When the "redeemed of the Lord" have returned home to Zion with jubilation (51.11) there will again be messengers of joy who proclaim to Zion that her God is king and has returned to Zion (52.7f). Because Zion complains that God has abandoned and forgotten her, she is told that her walls are always before God's eyes, because he has drawn them on his hands (49.14-16), and that God will comfort her (51.3). As if in a new act of creation God will "extend the heavens and found the earth and say to Zion, 'You are my people'" (51.16). So Zion will get up, adorn herself and shake off the dust, because her captivity has come to an end (52.1f). (Cf. also 41.27; 46.13.)

Similar language also dominates the third part of Isaiah [→**195**]: Zion, that is Jerusalem. The redeemer (*gōʾēl*) will come for Zion (59.20) and her enemies will fall down before her and call her "The City of the LORD, Zion of the Holy One of Israel" (60.14). Even when Zion lies in ruins (64.9), still comfort and restoration are promised to those who mourn in Zion (61.3). For "for Zion's sake" God cannot be silent, but will cause her righteousness (*ṣedeq*), her salvation (*yešûʿā*) and her glory (*kābôd*) to shine over her (62.1f). It will be heard to the ends of the earth when people say to Zion: "See, your salvation (*yēšaʿ*) comes!" (v. 11). (Cf. also 66.8.)

In Jeremiah the name of Zion appears in quite varied contexts. In the series of calls to repentance in ch. 3 we read in v. 14 that God will bring the returnees to Zion, and that Zion/Jerusalem will be called "throne of the Lord" (v. 17). In the following chapters Zion is then often named in connection with military events that break upon Judah. Here Zion stands as the main target of hostile attacks and as the exemplary suffering one (4.6, 31; 6.2, 23; 8.19; 9.18; 14.19). In a later section of the book (the "book of comfort," chs. 30f) [→**226**] the restoration of Zion is announced (30.17) and the joyous return of the exiles to Zion (31.6, 12; cf. also 50.4f, 28; 51.10). Also retribution for what Babylon has done to Zion is expected (51.24, 35). As a whole the statements about Zion have an eschatological tone, as was discernible at a number of points already in the book of Isaiah.

In Micah a number of texts speak of the impending reign of God (as king) on Zion in a tradition that is related to the book of Isaiah (4.2, 7, see section 1). Other texts expect the restoration of the "kingship of the daughter of Jerusalem," i.e. the Davidic kingship, to come to the "daughter of Zion" (4.8, cf. vv. 10, 11, 13). But this expectation will only apply at a time when judgment has come upon the sins of the daughter of Zion (1.13) and its chiefs (3.9f), ending with a complete destruction of Jerusalem and the temple mount (*har habbayit*, 3.12). According to the context this destruction also means the end of the rule of the previously mentioned responsible persons who built "Zion with blood and Jerusalem with wickedness" (v. 9[10]). So here the wonderful prospect of the next chapter is not yet addressed, but the door is opened to it (cf. Kessler 1999, 166ff).

In Zechariah too, the name of Zion occurs several times in specially emphasized passages. Thus we read twice, at the beginning and end of the first main part of the book, that God is "very jealous for Jerusalem and Zion" (1.14p 8.2). At the beginning it is announced that the city will be rebuilt and that God will comfort Zion and choose Jerusalem again (1.17). At the end we hear the promise that God himself will return to Zion/Jerusalem and dwell there and that Jerusalem will be called "city of faithfulness" and the mountain of Yhwh Zebaot will be called "holy mountain" (8.3). In 2.14 also God proclaims to the daughter of Zion the joyful message that he will come and live in the midst of Zion, after the exiles living in Babylon have previously been called upon to escape to Zion (2.11). In the second main part of Zechariah Zion is then called upon to celebrate the solemn entry of the eschatological king (9.9) [→**308**].

The statements about Zion have their own weight in the concluding part of the book of Zephaniah which speaks of the "remnant of Israel" that will be left after the storm of the day of Yhwh (3.12). The daughter of Zion is now called upon to rejoice (v. 14) and she is told "Do not fear, O Zion" (v. 16).

On Joel, see above pp. 578f. Cf. further Amos 1.2 with Joel 4.16, also Amos 6.1. Obad 17 quotes Joel 3.5, cf. also v. 21.

The book of Lamentations is entirely dominated by the lament over Zion's fate [→**383**]. Nowhere else does this lament reach such depths and especially such exclusiveness. More evident here even than in the prophetic books is the awareness that the cause of the catastrophe that has come upon Zion/Jerusalem and thus Judah/Israel is its own sin: "Jerusalem has sinned greatly and so has become unclean" (1.8); in fact her guilt is greater than the sin of Sodom (4.6). In the lament a good deal is embraced by the term "Zion": feast-day and Sabbath, king and priest, altar and sanctuary, the walls of the palaces and of the city (2.6-

8), and especially in many variations the suffering of the personified "daughter of Zion" (1.6, 8f; 2.1 etc.) and her inhabitants, male and female (1.11; 2.11, 20f etc.).

Despite all the differences in the detail, it is clear that the term "Zion" is used above all for the city and its inhabitants where the concern is with its threatenedness and vulnerability through to its destruction, but then also with its comfort and restoration. The threat to Zion by no means emanates only from external enemies but is also viewed by the prophets as the consequence of the sinful behavior of its inhabitants and especially of its leading classes; the laments too are dominated entirely by this point of view. Correspondingly the reestablishment of justice and righteousness is an essential element of the restoration of Zion (Isa 1.27; 62.1f). The expectation and promise of its ultimate restoration frequently bears eschatological features.

Thus the name of Zion, with its various meanings as temple site, God's throne and a second name for the city of Jerusalem, has a high emotional value which comes to expression in a variety of ways in the different parts of the text. The frequently used term "theology of Zion" thus needs nuancing to the extent that in parts of the prophetic books and especially in Lamentations Zion/Jerusalem are spoken of in a highly human way, of the military attacks on her and of her sufferings, but also of her transgressions and sins. Her personification also as "daughter of Zion" (or: "daughter Zion") expressly emphasizes the human side. (This expression appears only once in the psalms, in Ps 9.15.) In its very complexity Zion frequently represents Judah/Israel as a whole.

§ 15

Speaking of God

Preliminary remarks

The Bible speaks of God, literally, from the first to the last verse. (This applies to the Hebrew canon as well as the Christian Bible.) But God is not a "topic" of the Bible. God is constantly present in the Bible; he is the ground that enables the Bible to be written in the first place. But only rarely is he himself the subject. In particular the Bible does not speak of God "per se" but of what God says, how he acts and how he is experienced. The concern is thus always with God in his relationship to the world and to humans and quite especially to Israel. Thus the first sentence of the Bible speaks of God; but it does not speak of whether God *is*, or who he is, but expresses the fact that God *acts*. The verb that describes his action appears even before the mention of God himself: "In the beginning *created* God."

God's action is experienced by people in a wide range of ways. The texts of the Bible speak of this. They bring these experiences to expression in their variety and also in their contradictoriness. So talk of God in the biblical texts is anything but uniform. Often the texts reflect disputes over experiences of God and thereby show quite different aspects and opinions. But in all the variety of the experiences and conceptions, for the authors of the texts and writings of the Hebrew Bible it is beyond any doubt that God is *one*. This also includes the fact that he is God of the whole world, and this also means of all the nations. This only becomes a separate topic where another understanding of God contradicts it, whether in contrast to other nations and religions or within the history of their own people. From this there constantly emanate disputes, apparent crises, within Israel which have found their way into the texts. We shall need to discuss these in a separate chapter (§16).

"Speaking of God" in this context comprises the various ways in which the authors or the persons in their texts speak. Often they speak of God in the third person; the psalmists and many other texts speak to God in the second person; and even the divine speech, in which God speaks in the first person, is discourse spoken by prophets and/or written down by the authors of the texts, so that it too is "speaking of God."

1. The Name of God

1.1 The divine name and terms for God
The God of the Hebrew Bible, the one God, has a name—like most gods in the ancient Near East. This name has come down to us only by way of the writing of the consonants: YHWH. Already at the end of the Old Testament period the name was no longer pronounced and when the text was read aloud it was replaced by the word *ᵃdonay*, "my Lord" (in a plural form used only as divine address); this can be inferred e.g. by the usage of κύριος, "Lord," in the Greek translations of late antiquity. In the vocalization of the text in the middle ages the consonants Yhwh were given the vowels for *ᵃdonay*, which later led Christian readers to the erroneous pronunciation *Jehovah*. In addition we find a punctuation (attested in the Biblia Hebraica) that points to the pronunciation *šemā'* = Aramaic "the Name" (Hebrew *haššēm*). In more recent times, from late antique transcriptions the pronunciation *Yahweh* was reconstructed, but this, though it is taken for granted by many, remains only a conjecture. Whether an original meaning can be derived from the etymology of this name is doubtful (cf. *ThWAT* III, 533ff); nowhere can it be discerned that such a meaning found expression in particular aspects of the concept of God.

The name Yhwh is by far the most common term for God in almost all the books of the Hebrew Bible. It unambiguously means the *one* God, the God of Israel, who is both the creator and Lord of the earth. In one part of the Old Testament literature we find the combined form *yhwh ṣᵉbā'ôt* ("Yhwh Zebaot"). Its original meaning is disputed. (The most likely meaning lies in a connection with the word *ṣābā'* "hosts," cf. Josh 5.13-15; 1 Kgs 22.19; cf. Mettinger 1982b; *idem*, 1988, 123-57; *ThWAT* VI, 876ff.) It is found in a cultic context associated with the Ark (2 Sam 6.2 etc.) [→112], and also as an especially elevated divine title in the prophetic literature (e.g. Isa 6.3, 5) [→**172**]; in the Pentateuch it is not found at all.

Alongside the divine name, the Hebrew Bible frequently uses the term *ʾlohîm* (henceforward "Elohim"), "God." It is less unambiguous since it can also be used of other gods; since grammatically speaking the word represents a plural, it can also mean "gods," often in the expression "other gods" (cf. the beginning of the Decalogue, Ex 20.3). But when this term for God is used without further additions it expresses just as clearly as the divine name that the concern is with the one and only God. That the term does not express any other evaluation, or even a lesser evaluation, is quite clear in the fact that God is introduced by the term Elohim in the very first verse of the Bible. The equation of the terms comes with particular clarity also in the creed-like phrase "YHWH is God" (*yhwh hûʾ hāʾlohîm*, Deut 4.35 etc.; cf. 1 Kgs 18.39; see 1994, 19) [→**76, 138**].

A special feature of the word Elohim compared with the divine name Yhwh consists in the fact that it can be supplemented with additions providing greater precision: "my God," "our God" etc., but also in genitival constructions, e.g. with personal names: "the God of Abraham" etc., or "the God of your father/fathers," or even "the God of heaven." In this expanded and specified form Elohim is often found in direct connection with Yhwh: "Yhwh, the God of your fathers," "Yhwh, the God of Israel" etc. Thus the divine term Elohim can express special aspects of relationships with Yhwh and of experience with him.

A further term for God that is frequently encountered in the Hebrew Bible is the word *ʾēl* ("El"). It is also found in other semitic languages and religions, which is why particular questions regarding a possible early stage in Israelite religion are related to this (cf. 1994, 4f). Regardless of the possible borrowing of older traditions, in the present context of the Hebrew Bible there can be no doubt that the God referred to by this term was never any other God than the *one* God of Israel. In a series of cases El is a closer determination or more exact characterization of God. Thus for Jacob he is "the God who has appeared to you" (Gen 35.1, cf. v. 3). Other emphases are made by statements such as the statement that Yhwh is a "jealous God" (Ex 20.5 etc.) or "a merciful and gracious God" (Ex 34.6 etc.). The name *yiśrāʾēl*, "Israel," is also formed with the divine name *ʾēl*.

Some combinations with El raise special questions: in Gen 14.18-20 *'ēl 'elyôn*
"the Most High God" is named as the God of pre-Israelite Jerusalem; he is
called the "creator of heaven and earth." Underlying this is an older non-
Israelite tradition of El as the creator of the earth; the description as creator of
heaven is, however, part of the Israelite adoption of this tradition (cf. 1966,
284ff [179ff]; Niehr 1990, 124). The word *'elyôn* on its own is frequently
found, in addition, as a term for God as the "Most High" (e.g. 2 Sam 22.14;
Ps 7.18).

The divine term *'ēl šadday* is unclear as regards its origins and precise
meaning (cf. *ThWAT* VII, 10078-1104). In "priestly" texts this marks
a primitive stage in the self-presentation of God before the final declaration of the name to Moses (cf. Gen 17.1 and Ex 6.3) [→**27**]. There is
a different emphasis in the term *šadday* on its own, which is found in
particular in the book of Job (Job 5.17; 6.4 etc., 31 times in total). The
Septuagint usually translates this by παντοκράτωρ, the Vulgate with
omnipotens, the "Almighty." In no case is the word ever used to indicate anyone other than the *one* God of Israel.

Whether the texts use the divine name, or whether with or without
particular additions or whether they use various terms for God, depends largely in each case on the traditions that are given expression in
them. In some cases this is clearly discernible to the present-day reader,
as for instance the fact that in Job the divine name is used in the
framework narratives and the divine speeches, but not in the dialogues
between Job and his friends, or the "elohistic" revision of Psalms 42–
83, just to mention two examples. In each case, however, careful interpretation is called for, in which the name given to God can only be
one factor alongside others. (This applies in particular to the alternation between Yhwh and Elohim as a tradition criterion for separating
out the sources of the Pentateuch, cf. Blum 1984, 471-75.)

1.2 The varied aspects of the divine name
The fundamental significance of God's name for his relationship to
Israel, and especially for Israel's relationship to God, finds striking expression in the narrative of the call of Moses in Ex 3 [→**38**]. In order to
legitimate his task to the Israelites, Moses needs to know the name of
the God who has sent him, whom to begin with he can only identify
as "the deity" (*hā'lohîm*, v. 13). Via the description "I will be who I
will be" (v. 14) the divine speech leads on to the full proclamation of
the name Yhwh: "This is my name for ever" (v. 15). The supplemen-

tary clause states a fundamental function of the name: it is the form of "remembrance" (*zēker*) by which Israel is to remember God "from generation to generation." This comes to expression especially in hymnic texts in which the divine name and the "remembering" stand in parallelism (Pss 30.5; 97.12; 102.13; 135.13, cf. Isa 26.8: "your name and 'remembrance'"). In Hos 12.6 we read simply: "YHWH is his 'remembrance.'" And the psalmist laments: "No one remembers you when he is dead" (Ps 6.6[5]). Without the remembering of God the connection with God is torn apart.

For the reader the name is not introduced anew with its express proclamation to Moses. Rather, in the Hebrew Bible it is the way in which God is "called upon" right from the beginning of the history of humankind: "At that time men began [lit.: it was begun] to call on the name of YHWH" (Gen 4.26). This sentence speaks of Yhwh as the one and only God, who from the beginning is the God of humanity. Thus the name is introduced already with the beginning of the second creation account, first in the quite unusual double expression *yhwh ʾᵉlohîm* (from 2.4), and then on its own (from 4.1). The sons of the first human couple, Cain and Abel, present their sacrifices to Yhwh as a matter of course (4.3f). Of the patriarchs it is reported that each time they built an altar they called upon "the name of the LORD" there (*qārā' bešēm yhwh*, Gen 12.8; 13.4p 26.25; cf. 21.33). It is said of Abraham that he erected an altar at the place where God had appeared to him (12.7). This corresponds to the altar law in Ex 20.24, according to which an altar should be erected "wherever I cause my name to be remembered (*'azkîr*)." Here it is God himself who brings about the remembering of his name; and he will then come to those offering sacrifices at this altar and bless them. The remembering and reminding can thus occur in both directions. It can also correspond to the calling-upon (or calling-out) of the name on the part of humans: "Call upon (or: out) his name ..., call to remembrance (*hazkîrû*), that his name is exalted" (Isa 12.4). Here the translation "call out" seems appropriate, as the intervening clause "proclaim his deeds among the nations" shows (cf. Ps 105.1).

Calling upon the name has quite a different emphasis in the dispute between Elijah and the prophets of Baal. Each of the two sides is to call upon the name of its God, and the God that answers with fire is the (true) God (*hû' hā'ʾᵉlohîm*)" (1 Kgs 18.24) [→**138**]. Elijah sets up an altar "to the name of the LORD" (*bešēm yhwh*, v. 32), and Yhwh sends fire from heaven, thereby proving himself over Baal as the one of whom the people then proclaim, in an act of confession: "The LORD is the true God" (v. 39). An element of the hymnic language points in the same direction: statements about the world-embracing and world-moving power of God conclude with an emphatic "YHWH (Zebaot) is his name" (Amos 9.5f; 4.13; 5.8; Isa 51.15; Jer 10.12-16=51.15-19 etc.). Here statements about God's action in creation, which in other religions is ascribed to other gods, are claimed in an emphatic declaration of the name for the God of Israel as the only true God (cf. Crüsemann 1969, 95ff). In the polemic against the worship of foreign gods the statement that Yhwh is a "zealous God" (*'ēl qannā'*) can even be amplified in the words: "Zealous YHWH is his name" (Ex 34.14).

In immediate proximity to the last-mentioned passage, however, there is quite a different development of the content of the name Yhwh. God himself calls out his name in the hearing of Moses: "YHWH, YHWH, the compassionate and gracious God, slow to anger, abounding in love and faithfulness, maintaining love to thousands, and forgiving wickedness, rebellion and sin. Yet he does not leave the guilty unpunished; he punishes the children and their children for the sin of the fathers to the third and fourth generation" (Ex 34.6f; cf. 33.19) [→623]. This is, so to speak, the external side of the name Yhwh. In the foreground here is not his defensive "jealousy" but his longsuffering and gracious attitude towards Israel, which always has the upper hand over punitive actions towards sinners. In the Decalogue the two aspects are found connected together. The expression *'ēl qannā'* is turned inward here; but here too the divine mercy dominates by a long way over his punitive action (Ex 20.5f; Deut 5.9f).

Frequently the word "name" (*šēm*) stands for God himself. In the characteristic stylistic form of *parallelismus membrorum* (cf. 1983, 109) the two things can stand opposite each other without any discernible difference in content or shift of emphasis: "Therefore I will praise you among the nations, O LORD; I will sing praises to your name" (Ps 18.50[49]=2 Sam 22.50); "Glorify the LORD with me; let us exalt his name together" (Ps 34.4[3]) etc. (cf. the list in Grether 1934, 36f). But there is a special emphasis in statements that speak of "knowing" or "acknowledging" (*yāda'*) God's name. Thus in some psalms there is talk of the pious "who know your name" (Ps 9.11; cf. 91.14). For the happy future the prophet expects that "on that day" "my people will know (or: acknowledge?) my name;" this means in particular that they will acknowledge that it is God himself that says "Here I am" (Isa 52.6; cf. 65.1). For God will himself "make my holy name known (*hôdîᵃ*) among my people Israel" (Ezek 39.7). And finally "all the peoples of the earth will know your name" (1 Kgs 8.43; cf. Isa 64.1; Jer 16.21). To know the name of God means to acknowledge God himself. (On this cf. 2.4.)

The word *yādāh* (usually in the hiphil form, *hôdāh*), often translated by "give thanks" (e.g. "Give thanks to the Lord, for he is good," Ps 136.1), "praise" (cf. Westermann 1953 *passim*), can also have the meaning "confess" (esp. in the hithpael). In this sense it is related to God's name: in Solomon's temple dedication prayer, the confessing of God's name in situations of distress is connected with the "turning" (*šûb*) from sinful behavior that has brought about the calamity (1 Kgs 8.33, 35; cf. without mention of the name Ps 32.5) [→**121**]. At the conclusion of the extensive and detailed confession of Israel's transgressions through the generations the psalmist responds to God's concern, which ensues despite everything, and expresses the hope of return from the diaspora with the confession of "your holy name" (Ps 106.47). In other texts too the psalmist confesses the name of God not from the situation of hymnic praise but from a situation of distress in which he hopes for, or has already received, help and rescue by God (Pss 7.18; 18.50[=2 Sam 22.50]; 44.9; 52.11; 54.8 etc.; also Isa 25.1). Here too the confessing of God's name means confessing God himself.

Swearing by the name of Yhwh is also an act of confession: "Fear the LORD your God, serve him only and take your oaths in his name" (Deut 6.13; 10.20). The Israelites can even be characterized as those "who swear by my name" (Isa 48.1), and foreigners can learn from them and "swear by my name, saying, 'As surely as the LORD lives'" (Jer 12.16). But "swearing falsely by my name" means "profaning the name of your God" (Lev 19.12; cf. Zech 5.4). So we read in the Decalogue: "You shall not misuse the name of the LORD your God" (Ex 20.7; Deut 5.11) [→**486**]. And whoever curses God's name deserves to die (Lev 24.10-16).

In Ps 106 there is talk of confessing the "holy name" (v. 47, see above). In the hymnic Psalm 33, too, which speaks of God's actions in creation and in the steering of human fates, we read in the closing confession: "We trust in your holy name" (v. 21); at the conclusion of the hymn Ps 145, "all flesh" is called upon to praise God's holy name (v. 21, cf. v. 1). In other psalms God's holy name is already mentioned in the hymnic introduction (103.1; 105.3). Ps 99.3 calls for confession of the great and terrible name of God with the pointed concluding clause: "Holy is he." In the prophetic message of salvation we read of the high and exalted God that his name is holy (Isa 57.15). There is also talk of the "hallowing" of God's name. Thus in a prophetic announcement of salvation the expectation is expressed that the saved will hallow God's name when they see the work of his hands (Isa 29.23).

But above all it is God himself who hallows his name. In the great historical retrospect in Ezek 20 [→**246**] we read that God constantly held back his wrath "for my name's sake," to "keep it from being profaned in the eyes of the nations" (vv. 8f, 13f, 21f, cf. v. 44). But this has now occurred, as the Israelites scattered among the nations "profaned my holy name, for it was said of them, 'These are the LORD's people and yet they had to leave his land'" (36.20f). So "for the sake of my holy name, which you have profaned among the nations" God will now sanctify his name again, i.e. restore the holiness of his name (vv. 22f). Later we read that God "will make known (*hôdî‛*) my holy name among my people Israel," so that the nations too will acknowledge (*yāda‛*) "that I am the LORD, the Holy One in Israel" (39.7). And finally God will "turn (*šûb šᵉbût*) the fate of Jacob" and "be zealous for my holy name" (v. 25).

In Isaiah, like in Ezekiel, we also read that God holds back his anger "for my name's sake" (Isa 48.9). In the great historical retrospect in Ps 106 there is talk of God's help at the Reed Sea "for his name's sake" (v. 8). This expression also appears as part of the language of the prayer: God is asked to help in this distress, despite Israel's sins, "for your name's sake" (Jer 14.7, 21); in the Psalms too we find this expression time and again in the request for God's forgiveness (Pss 25.11; 79.9) and help (31.4; 109.21; 143.11), but also in thanks for God's guidance (23.3; cf. 33.21). Another aspect is evident in the last chapter of Isaiah, where we read that certain people "hate" and "exclude" their brothers "because of my name" (Isa 66.5), i.e. on account of their express confession to God, which was evidently a cause of contention in the situation presupposed here. Finally in Solomon's temple-dedication prayer, God is asked to hear the prayer of a foreigner "who has come from a distant land because of your name" (1 Kgs 8.41) [→**121**]. Here the talk of God's name is developed still further in the two following verses: the foreigners hear of God's great name and his mighty deeds and therefore come to the temple in Jerusalem to worship him (v. 42); and may God hear their prayer, so that "all the peoples of the earth may know your name" and also acknowledge "that this house I have built bears your Name" (v. 43).

In the last phrase the concept of God's name is closely connected with God's "house," the temple. This recalls the promise of the prophet Nathan to David, that his son will "build a house to my name" (2 Sam 7.13), to which Solomon later appeals (1 Kgs 8.17-20). The connection of God's name with the sanctuary is especially marked in Deuteronomy, where there is repeated discussion of the "place which the LORD will choose to let his name dwell (šākan, qal) there" (Deut 12.11; 14.23; 16.2, 6, 11; 26.2) [→80] and God's dwelling-place (miškān), which is found in the most varied contexts in the Hebrew Bible (e.g. Ex 25.8f; Lev 8.10; 2 Sam 7.6; 1 Kgs 6.13; Ezek 37.27; Ps 26.8; 1 Chron 6.17), is interpreted in a quite particular way. Unlike the altar law in Ex 20.24 [→56], according to which an altar is to be set up "wherever I cause my name to be honored/remembered," here it is expressly a single, particular place where the legitimate cult can and may exclusively take place. Here God will be present in his name. Some exegetes see in this a deliberate distinction between the God who lives in heaven and his name, which lives in the earthly sanctuary (cf. Grether 1934, 34). But the formula that is used as an alternative, "the place the Lord will choose to place his name there (śûm)" (Deut 12.5, 21; 14.24) makes it clear that the prime concern is not with where God "lives," but with the presence of the divine name at this single legitimate cultic site. God "places" his name on the temple in Jerusalem, but he does not thereby separate himself from his name, but is himself present in it. According to 1 Kgs 9.3 not only is God's name present in the temple, but also his eyes and his heart. And the "placing" of God's name is not a once-and-for-all act, but God commissions Aaron and his sons to "put my name on the Israelites, and I will bless them" (Num 6.27). (Cf. van der Woude 1976b, 953ff; Mettinger 1982, 38-79.)

Blessing in God's name is also described as a task of the members of the tribe of Levi (Deut 10.8), or in Deuteronomic terms the "levitical priests" (21.5), together with "serving in the name of the LORD" (cf. 18.5, 7; 1 Chron 23.13). Only once is it said of David that after bringing the Ark into Jerusalem he blessed the people "in the name of YHWH Zebaot" (2 Sam 6.18; 1 Chron 16.2). Reflected here are clearly different traditions about particular cultic functions.

A special feature of the prophets is their speaking in God's name. In Deuteronomy the expression "in the name of YHWH" or "in my name" appears in the same chapter for the "levitical priests" (Deut 18.5, 7) [→**82**] and for the "prophet like me (i.e. Moses)," or "like you" (vv. 15, 18) whom God will raise up. While the priest serves and blesses "in the name of the LORD," it is the task of the prophet to speak "in my name" (vv. 18f). In Deuteronomy the concern in this context is primarily with the distinction between true and false prophets and with the recognition of the latter (vv. 20-22). This question is constantly present in Jeremiah too. Jeremiah's opponents want to stop him prophesying in the name of Yhwh (Jer 11.21), or accuse him on account of the message of judgment on Jerusalem which he has proclaimed in the name of God (26.9) [→**220**]. But the argument that he has "spoken to us in the name of the LORD, our God" is then validated in his favor (v. 16; in vv. 20-23 the counter-example of another prophet is reported, who also prophesied in the name of Yhwh and was executed for doing so). But there are also prophets who presume to speak in God's name without being authorized by God to do so: "The prophets are prophesying lies in my name. I have not sent them" (14.14, 15; 23.25; 27.15; 29.9, 21, 23). The dispute over the distinction between true and false prophecy "in God's name" had a huge impact on Jeremiah's life. In his deepest crisis he wanted "no longer to speak in your name;" but he could not refrain from doing so, because it would have burned inside him (20.9).

1.3 I am Yhwh

The central significance of the divine name finds its especially marked expression in the highly charged phrase "I am YHWH" (*ˀnî yhwh* or *ˀānōkî yhwh*). In this concise for as a separate sentence it is first found in Ex 6.2 [→**41**] in connection with the fundamental announcement of the divine name to Moses. Here at the same time it becomes clear that this succinct, formulaic statement is more than the imparting of the name; it appears three times in vv. 2-8: as the beginning of the divine speech to Moses (v. 2), as an introduction to what Moses is to pass on to the Israelites (v. 6), and as a conclusion to the divine speech (v. 8). Here it proves to be a very emphatic rhetorical form of God's self-presentation. (Zimmerli 1953 calls it "self-presentation formula" [*Selbstvorstellungsformel*]; thereafter "I-am formula." Cf. also 1961, 32ff [=50ff].) Besides this, it appears one further time in this text in an expanded form as part of the "acknowledgment statement:" "You will know that I am YHWH, your God" (v. 7; see 2.4).

In an elevated position this formulaic expression then appears as the introduction to the Decalogue: "I am the LORD, your God, who brought you out of the land of Egypt, out of the house of slavery" (Ex 20.2; Deut 5.6 [→**54**]; the divine "I" appears here in the fuller form *'ānokî*). Here God's self-presentation is expanded by a relative clause in which God's fundamental saving act towards Israel in leading them out of Egypt is effectively a further definition of the name. This recalls God's fundamental self-presentation in Ex 6.7, where in different terminology we read: "who led you out of the oppression of Egypt."

In Ezek 20.5, as in Ex 6.2 [→**246**], the I-am formula stands as a separate sentence, in fact as the only content of the divine speech that the prophet is to pass on: "On the day I chose Israel, I swore with uplifted hand to the descendants of the house of Jacob and revealed myself to them in Egypt. With uplifted hand I said to them, 'I am the Lord your God.'" Zimmerli: "Everything that Yahweh has to say and announce to his people appears as a development of the basic statement: I am Yahweh" (1953, 188 [=20]).

This fundamental reverberant statement appears in the most varied parts of the text of the Hebrew Bible, with quite differing meanings and functions. In the strict form, "I am Yhwh" (sometimes with the additional words "your/their God") is found frequently in particular "priestly" collections of commandments, especially in the "holiness code" (cf. Ruwe 1999, 71ff). It stands as the conclusion to commandment texts of varying length and expressly emphasizes their binding nature as divine commandments (Lev 18.2, 4, 5, 6 etc.). Occasionally it is supplemented by the addition "who sanctifies you/them/him" (Hebrew participle, 20.8; 21.8, 15, 23 etc.) [→**543**]. Because God himself is holy, Israel is to make and keep itself holy by keeping the appropriate commandments. In Lev 26.44f [→**69**] the formula is found twice in connection with God's assurance that despite Israel's sins and the resulting sufferings they must undergo he will not break his covenant. The God who presents himself so often with the simple sentence "I am Yhwh" does not break his word.

This precision of the divine "I" by means of the memory of the leading-out of Egypt, as found in Ex 6.7 and 20.2, is found elsewhere in the most varied contexts. Thus in Num 15.41 a collection of commandments concludes with a broadly extended sentence: "I am the LORD your God, who brought you out of Egypt to be your God. I am the LORD your God." Here, then, the "covenant formula" is brought in (cf. also Lev 25.38). The almost identical words in Lev

11.45 add the charge to be holy (cf. v. 44). In Hosea the reference to the leading-out of Egypt is shortened to the phrase: "I am YHWH, your God, from the land of Egypt" (Hos 12.10; 13.4), using a short form of the leading-out formula, so to speak (cf. 1997b, 502). In a series of passages in the priestly texts of the Pentateuch, the I-am formula is adapted in being extended into an "acknowledgement statement" as previously in Ex 6.7: "You (sing. or plur.)/they will know that I am YHWH." (See 2.4 below.)

In the prophetic books the I-am formula is found only in certain contexts. It plays a highly prominent role in the second half of the book of Isaiah, especially in chs. 40–49. There we find the programmatic statement, as it were: "I am YHWH; that is my name! I will not give my glory (*kābôd*) to another or my praise to idols" (42.8). That is the concern here: with the unambiguous delimitation in respect of other gods, which are only "idols" (*p'sîlîm*). And then in the addressing of the Persian king Cyrus, commissioned by God, we read: "I am YHWH and no other; besides me there is no God" (45.5; cf. v. 21). According to this, the name Yhwh simply means "God." Besides this name there is no God. The prophet sharpens the statement even further by repeatedly replacing God's name with God's "I": "I am he (*"nî hû'*); I am the first and I am the last" (48.12; cf. 41.4; 43.10, 13 etc., *'ānôkî hû'* 43.25; 51.12). As the name did before, here the simple "I" of Yhwh stands for "God."

The I-am formula is found even more frequently in Ezekiel. Sometimes it functions as an emphatic introduction (Ezek 20.19) or as a conclusion (20.7) to a unit of discourse. But primarily it is found in two expressions which signify a continuation and in a sense a resolution of the real formula. One is found frequently as the conclusion to a discourse unit: "I, YHWH, have spoken" (5.15, 17; 21.22, 37; 26.14; 30.12; 34.14, 24); or as an introduction (12.25; 24.14). In an elaborated version we find, further: "I, Yhwh, have spoken and I will do it" (17.24; 22.14; 36.36; cf. 24.14; 37.14). So the concern here is not with a self-presentation by God but with an express underlining of what has just been said or of what is about to be said on Yhwh's authority. The other elaboration is found in the "acknowledgement statement" (see 2.4).

Thus the "I am Yhwh" formula represents an especially potent and impressive way in which God speaks, as has been formulated by prophets or by authorized authors. It represents God's sovereignty which proclaims itself to people in various ways and wants to be recognized and acknowledged by them.

2. How God appears and makes himself known

2.1 The varied ways in which God appears

God appears to humans in various ways. In the patriarchal narratives we read on a number of occasions: "The LORD appeared to him and said ..." Sometimes this looks like no more than a speech introduction, without further description of the appearance. But as the text continues it becomes clear that this is no everyday event. In Abraham's case this expression introduces the first divine speech in which the promise is made to him that God will give "this land" to his descendants; afterwards Abraham builds the first altar in this land "to the Lord, who appeared to him" (Gen 12.7). The next time, God announces to Abraham the covenant he wants to make with him, and Abraham prostrates himself in worship (17.1-3). In the narrative of the binding of Isaac Abraham calls the place where it occurs "the Lord sees" (*yir'eh*, v. 14a), thereby pointing back to the expectation of divine intervention that he himself had expressed at the beginning: "God will provide the lamb for the sacrifice" (v. 8). A later commentator sees here a reference to the "appearance" of God (*yêrā'eh*, v. 14b; cf. Jacob 1934, 501).

In one divine speech Isaac is given the instruction to remain in the land and not (as Abraham had done) to move to Egypt (26.2), and he obeys (v. 6). Later God appears to him again and assures him of his help; Isaac then builds an altar and calls upon "the name of the LORD" (vv. 24f). Jacob experiences a theophany at Beth-El, containing a twice introduced divine speech: first the blessing and the name-change to "Israel" (vv. 9f), then the assurance of posterity and the promise of the land (vv. 11f). Thereupon Jacob too erects a sanctuary, this time not an altar (as in v. 7) but as in the earlier nocturnal theophany at Beth-El, a massebah, over which he pours oil (v. 14; cf. 28.18). Jacob later appeals to this theophany in the blessing of Joseph's sons (48.3).

In these texts, the "appearing" of God means that God comes into direct contact with the persons addressed; the type of appearance is not made concrete. But twice after the conclusion of the divine speech or the conversation between God and Abraham we read: "God went up from him (or: from Abraham)" (17.22; 35.13). So here there is the notion of the presence of the deity in the appearance, though this is given no more detailed description. Another form of God's appearance is the nocturnal dream, as Jacob had at Beth-El (28.11-19) [→**30**]. There he is granted a glimpse of God's world, the important aspect for humans being the connection of God's heavenly world and the "angels" surrounding him (plural, *mal'akê 'elohîm*, v. 12) with the earthly world of human beings. This leads Jacob to the insight: "Surely the LORD is in this place, and I was not aware of it" (v. 16). In a striking way this graphic nocturnal dream experience brings to expression an experience that runs through the whole of the Hebrew Bible: God is present both in heaven *and* on the earth.

The patriarchal tradition, however, shows another quite different picture. With the same expression, "The LORD appeared to him," a very real encounter between Abraham and God begins (18.1) [→**28**]. In the veiled form of one of three "men" (v. 2), he gradually becomes more and more distinct from them: in v. 9 the speech is introduced: "They spoke," in v. 10, "He spoke," in v. 13 finally, "The LORD spoke." And then follows the walk together to Sodom and finally a direct face-to-face conversation between Yhwh and Abraham (vv. 22-23).

How unusual this face-to-face situation is, in the biblical context, is evident from the fact that the "scribes" altered the text, which originally read, "and YHWH remained standing before Abraham" (v. 22b), to "and Abraham remained standing before YHWH." They noted the emendation in the margin.

Abraham is the only one of the patriarchs—and besides Moses the only person at all—to have been granted such a direct encounter with God. This narrative shows, however, how broadly stretched is the framework within which God's appearance can be imagined and depicted in the Hebrew Bible. Thus in the Abraham story already quite a different view is evident in the story of the binding of Isaac. Here God is first introduced in a veiled form as *hā'"lohîm* (Gen 22.1). Then in the crucial scene the "angel of YHWH" (*mal'ak yhwh*) intervenes by calling "from heaven" (v. 11). In what he calls, however, it is quite clear that it is none other than God himself who is speaking: "Now I know ..." (v. 12; in v. 15 he uses the formula "utterance of YHWH," *n'"um yhwh*). The "angel" here is a form in which God himself appears. But this is quite different from the immediate, quite physical encounter that is described in the visit at Mamre (Gen 18). The different forms of appearance are clearly deliberately used by the authors of the texts as a means of presentation in order to bring different experiences of God to expression.

Jacob's nocturnal encounter with God at the Jabbok (Gen 32.23-32) [→30] remains mysterious. Jacob has to survive a fight with a "man" whom he cannot see in the dark of the night and who does not give his name. But in the explanation of the new name, Israel, which the unknown person gives Jacob, the incognito is removed: "You have wrestled with God and man ..." (v. 29). And Jacob afterwards expresses it thus: "I have seen God face to face" (v. 31). So it was God himself that Jacob was fighting with here, this time in a quite unusual disguise for which there are no parallels in the Hebrew Bible. This narrative however again broadens the spectrum of the forms of God's appearances that we find in various contexts in the tradition.

The "angel of YHWH" that is spoken of in the Abraham tradition (Gen 22.11) appears elsewhere in the most varied contexts. In the narrative of the banishing of Hagar it is clear that the "angel of YHWH" in Gen 16.7-13 represents God himself, since he grants Hagar promises in the first person in the divine speech (v. 10); it is the same with the "angel of God" who appears to Jacob in the dream (31.11-13). In the second Hagar narrative God (Elohim) hears the child's crying but then the "angel of God" speaks to him (21.17-20); here the "angel" appears as the side of God that is turned towards humans. In Jacob's blessing for Ephraim and Manasseh it seems almost like an intensification when Jacob first speaks of "God" who has led his fathers and himself, and then of the "angel who has delivered me from all harm" (48.15f; cf. von Rad 1972, 343). In the narrative of the call of Moses it is again the "angel of YHWH" who "appears" to Moses, veiled in the flame of fire in the thorn-bush (Ex 3.2). But then God himself (Elohim) calls out of the thorn-bush (v. 4b) and finally reveals himself as "YHWH" (v. 15). Here the identity of the "angel" with Yhwh himself unfolds step by step.

In a series of texts we read that God sends his "angel" ahead as a helping guide. In the story of the forefathers this occurs in the narrative of the seeking of a bride for Isaac (Gen 24.7, 40). Then it is a topic above all in the reports of the leading-out from Egypt. In Ex 14.19 there is rather abrupt mention of the "angel of God who had been traveling in front of Israel's army." In 23.20, however, we read: "See, I am sending an angel ahead of you to guard you along the way and to bring you to the place I have prepared." A distinction is made here between the sending God and the "angel" that is sent by him (in

v. 23 the term is "my angel"). But then God admonishes Israel to obey the "angel," "since my Name is in him" (v. 21). This expresses in quite an unusual way that the "angel" represents God himself, and even that disobedience to him will not be forgiven.

Another aspect becomes clear after the conflict with the "Golden Calf" and the restoration of the covenant. Here God gives the commission once more to break camp and move on into the land that has been promised by oath (32.34; 33.1f) [→**62**]. He repeats his assurance that he will send an "angel" (32.34 "my angel") ahead of Israel; but then he limits this assurance: "I will not go with you, because you are a stiff-necked people" (33.1-3). God stands by his promise to lead the people by means of the "angel" he commissions, but he himself will not be present in the angel as he had announced in 23.21. The figure of the "angel" thus does not necessarily mean the same thing as the presence of God, but can also fulfill separate tasks assigned to him. Thus the "angel of YHWH" "appears" in other contexts too, to pass on a message from God to particular persons (Judg 6.12ff; 13.3ff etc.; cf. also 1 Kgs 19.7 [→**139**]; 2 Kgs 1.3, 15; in a punitive function, 2 Sam 24.16f; as an interpreting angel, Zech 1.9, 13, 14 etc.).

The limitation that God will not himself go up with Israel causes Moses once again to ask "whom you will send with me" (Ex 33.12). God's answer is: "My Countenance (*pānîm*) will go with you" (v. 14). Is *pānîm* here a further representative of God like the "angel"? The subsequent conversation shows that this is a term for God himself: Moses asks God to "go with us" (v. 16), and God grants this request (v. 17, cf. also Deut 4.37). In Isa 63.9 it is explicitly emphasized that "not a messenger (?) or angel, but his presence (i.e. he himself) helped them." (Cf. van der Woude 1976, 446-48.)

The talk of God's "appearing" shifts subsequent to the erection of the sanctuary on Sinai to the appearance of the divine *kābôd* ("glory," henceforward "Kabod"). To begin with this is described as a cultic phenomenon. Before the presentation of Aaron's and his sons' first sacrifice Moses announces: "Today the LORD will appear to you" (Lev 9.4). After the completion of the sacrifices and after Moses and Aaron have blessed the people, this appearance then occurs before the whole nation in the shape of the divine Kabod (v. 23, cf. v. 6). No description is given. But previously there has been mention of the Kabod a number of times: before Moses ascends Mount Sinai to receive the instructions and specifications for the construction of the sanctuary, the Kabod covers the mountain. Here it is equated with the "cloud," and we read further that his appearance is like "consuming fire" (Ex 24.15-17) [→**64**]. After the completion of the sanctuary and its facilities the Kabod-cloud then fills the sanctuary, so that Moses cannot enter (40.35f). This is repeated on the dedication of the temple built by Solomon in Jerusalem (1 Kgs 9.10f) [→**120**].

The Kabod also appears as a demonstration of the power of God in protecting Moses and Aaron against the rebellious Israelites (Num 14.10; 16.19; 17.7; 20.6; cf. also Ex 16.10). This function too can only be performed by the "cloud." It demonstrates the presence of God and lends authority to the stance taken by Moses and Aaron (Ex 19.9, 16; 33.9f; 34.5; Num 11.25; 12.5, 10; 17.7). After the departure of the Israelites from Egypt the "cloud" also appears regularly as a visible sign of God's guidance and protection of Israel. It leads Israel in the day-time in the form of the "pillar of cloud" and is relieved at night-time by the "pillar of fire" (Ex 13.21f) [→**49**]. In this function it protects Israel at the Reed Sea from the pursuing Egyptians (14.19f, 24; in v. 19 together with the "angel of God"). On moving on from Sinai and afterwards it also gives the sign to break camp and to strike camp (Ex 40.36-38; Num 9.15-23; 10.11f, 34; cf. 14.14).

In some psalms there is talk of God's Kabod as of a heavenly phenomenon (Pss 19.2; 29.1f, 9) [→**331**], which however is visible to all the nations (97.6). This is so also in Isaiah's great vision: "Holy, holy, holy is the LORD of Hosts; the whole earth is full of his Kabod" (Isa 6.3; cf. also Num 14.21; Ps 72.19). The visibility of God's Kabod for "all flesh" will mean a proof of the triumph of his power (Isa 40.5). But it still remains the subject of hope in the future restoration of Zion (Isa 60.2; Ps 102.17; see in general 1961, 23-34 [=41-50]).

A quite different picture of God's Kabod is drawn by the book of Ezekiel. The prophet's great visions are determined by the appearance of the Kabod, the highly peculiar features of which he describes in detail (Ezek 1.4-28) [→**234**]. Here the Kabod is closely connected with the temple in Jerusalem (8.2ff; 11.22f; 43.2ff); Ezekiel thus stands in the sanctuary tradition of Ex 40.35f and Lev 9.4, 23 etc. But the special thing with Ezekiel is not that the Kabod leaves the temple, thereby giving up the sinful city for destruction (11.22f), but that later it returns there to live there forever (43.2-9). The cultic side of the Kabod tradition is extended here to open up the prospect of a still outstanding blessed future.

2.2 Can a person "see" God?

When we are told that God "appears," this is often expressed by a particular form of the verb *rā'āh*, "see" (niphal). This could also be rendered "God lets himself be seen" or "God becomes visible"—like the rainbow in the sky (Gen 9.14). But can one "see" God?

The Hebrew Bible frequently says that a person has seen God, but this is always associated with an additional sentence expressing the unusual and unexpected nature of this encounter and its consequences (actual or missing). Thus Jacob calls the place where he fought with God "P^eni'el, for I have seen God face to face and my life was spared" (Gen 32.31) [→30]. There is an underlying awareness of what God said to Moses: "No one can see me and remain alive" (Ex 33.20). So it is something quite unexpected that has overtaken Jacob. In an impressive way it underlines the special place that Jacob has been granted by being renamed "Israel." In Ex 24.9-11 [→58] we are told that Moses ascends Mount Sinai with the Elders of Israel, and then we read: "They saw the God of Israel." Here too, a sentence is appended: "But he did not stretch out his hand against the Elders; they saw God and ate and drank" (v. 11). This can be seen against the background of God's instruction to Moses to warn the people not to come to close on the mountain, "to see YHWH, and many of them fall" (19.21). God now makes an exception; but it remains a unique event, such as could only take place at this central place of God's direct encounter with his people. (The eating and drinking can perhaps be understood in connection with the preceding report of the covenant conclusion as a sort of covenant meal.)

In an impressive vision Isaiah sees "the Lord (*'^adonay*) sitting on a high and elevated throne" and hears the praises of the Seraphim. He is terrified because as a human being with unclean lips he has "seen the king YHWH of Hosts" (Isa 6.1-5) [→172]. Here the threat associated with seeing God is reinforced further by the knowledge of his own unworthiness. In answer to this Isaiah's lips are purified by one of the Seraphim with a glowing coal; this prepares for the reception of the proclamation commission that follows. One has to take this to mean that the danger of death is also lifted: for Isaiah had been called to "see" God and to accept his commission. This shows once again that it is possible only in quite special, exceptional situations and with express divine confirmation, that a person can see God and live to tell the tale.

Two narratives in the book of Judges tell of the same problem on the appearance of the "angel" of God. Gideon calls out, "Woe to me,

LORD YHWH! For I have seen the angel of the LORD face to face."
But he is given the comforting answer by God himself: "Peace be with
you! Do not be afraid, for you will not die" (Judg 6.22f). It remains
open whether the seeing of the "angel" here is taken to be less dangerous than the seeing of God himself, or whether as in Isaiah the
intention is to express the fact that in quite special situations there can
be a "seeing" of God in connection with a divine commission. One
can see the Judg 13 narrative of the announcement of the birth of
Samson in the same way (esp. vv. 22f).

The cultic usage of the notion of "seeing Yhwh's face" creates a special problem. Several times we read: "Three times a year all males are to appear under
you before the face of YHWH" (Ex 23.17; 34.23; Deut 16.16). Many exegetes
think that the consonantal text should be read: "see the face of YHWH" (*yir'eh*)
and that the Masoretic punctuation as a niphal (*yērā'eh*) is intended to prevent
God being viewed visibly as in the sanctuary (cf. Nötscher 1924, 88ff; cf. also
Ex 23.15b; 34.24; Deut 31.11; 1 Sam 1.22; Isa 1.12; Ps 42.3). This may indeed be the case; but one can certainly not conclude from this that the "seeing" of a cultic image is meant, which was never present at an Israelite sanctuary; rather, it is a matter of the adoption of a familiar expression from the
religious environment for visiting the sanctuary.

A quite different form of "seeing" God is demonstrated in the prophetic view, the vision granted to Isaiah (Isa 6.1-5). However, seldom
is there mention of such an immediate visionary encounter with God
as in Isaiah. Micaiah ben Imlah describes a vision (1 Kgs 22.19ff)
[→142], the beginning of which is comparable with that of Isaiah: he
sees Yhwh on his throne, surrounded by his heavenly court. But Micaiah remains an independent observer of the heavenly scene and is
not drawn into it himself. Amos too sees the Lord (*"donay*) standing
"on the altar" (Amos 9.1) [→286]. No detailed description of a vision
event follows this, but a divine word, so that Amos—unlike in the
visions in 7.1-3, 4-6, in which there is no mention of seeing God—is
not himself drawn into the vision event. Ezekiel sees in his visions the
Kabod of God, i.e. a form in which God appears, which veils God
more than it makes him visible (see above 2.1). On one occasion we
read that he saw a figure "with the appearance of fire" (Ezek 8.2)
[→239]: perhaps this should be read with the Septuagint "like a man"
(*'îš* instead of *'ēš*), but to judge from the context the "man" is not God
himself, who again appears in the form of the Kabod (v. 4).

2.3 God makes himself known

In Ex 6.3 [→**41**] we read: "I appeared (*wā'ērā'*) to Abraham, Isaac and Jacob as El Shadday, but my name YHWH I did not announce to them (*lo' nôda'tî lāhem*)." According to this, "announcing" is a new step in God's self-proclamation, "revelation" (for which there is no term in Hebrew, cf. 1961); for this sentence is a development of the formula "I am YHWH" (v. 2), which appears here for the first time. It almost sounds like a repeat of Ex 6 when in Ezek 20.5 we read: God chose Israel in Egypt, proclaimed to them (*wā'iwwāda'*) and spoke with a raised hand: "I am YHWH, your God." (Cf. v. 9, *nôda'tî.*)

In the Psalms too the connection of God's self-proclamation with his name is evident: "God is made known in Judah, his name is great in Israel" (Ps 76.2); this is followed by a depiction of preservation against oppressive enemies (vv. 4, 6f). In Ps 48.4[3] a similar description is introduced about the preservation of Zion, the city of God: "God is in her citadels; he has shown himself to be her fortress." In the double psalm Pss 9/10 the psalmist thanks God as the helping judge: "The LORD has made himself known, has exercised justice; the wicked are ensnared by the work of his hands" (9.17[16]). We are also told that God's hand will show itself (Isa 66.14). In another form of the verb (*hôdî'* hiphil) we are told that it is God himself who will show his hand and his power (Jer 16.21) or his help (Ps 98.2), just as he previously "made known his ways to Moses, his deeds to the people of Israel" (Ps 103.7). (In Ps 98.2 this is paralleled by the verb *gālāh* in the piel: God "reveals" his righteousness.)

In Jer 16.21 the verse, and thereby the whole chapter, ends with: "so that they may know that my name is YHWH." This is a changed form of the "acknowledgment statement" into which the I-am formula has been expanded (see 1.3 above) [→**595**]. Here we see that the self-proclamation and acknowledgment of God are directly connected and related to each other. Here also the sequence of God's deed and the acknowledgment of humans is clearly in evidence. If one looks for an equivalent for the term "revelation" (a term from post-biblical Christian theology) in the Hebrew Bible, the closest thing to it is talk of God's self-proclamation, though this does not correspond to it entirely (cf. 1961).

2.4 Knowing God

There has been frequent talk in this chapter of "acknowledging" or "knowing" God. The large number of perspectives from which these statements can be viewed has become apparent. No attempt will be made at this point to systematize these perspectives. However we shall isolate some of the characteristic elements and inquire into their interrelationships.

The large majority of the statements point to an acknowledgment of God that has still to take place. This applies in particular to the "acknowledgment statement" (or "acknowledgment formula"): "You (sg. or pl.) will / they will know that I am YHWH." This statement generally follows the announcement of some action by God. It seems then that acknowledgment of God is human reaction to God's action. This observation applies in a very basic way: "The sequence: deed of Yahweh—acknowledgment by a person, which cannot be reversed, is constitutive of the description" (Zimmerli 1954, 40[80]).

The content of what is to be acknowledged is generally indicated by the concise, formulaic expression, "that I am YHWH." So it is not just that they should acknowledge *me*; rather the loaded I-am formula [→595] with the large number of aspects that go with it expresses the comprehensive meaning of what it is to acknowledge the fact that Yhwh is God, and indeed uniquely and exclusively God. But the acknowledgment is not an acknowledgment of who Yhwh is, or what he is like, but the acknowledgment that it is *he* who acts and proves himself in what is announced.

Occasionally this expression is expanded: "You were shown these things so that you might know that the LORD is God; besides him there is no other" (Deut 4.35, cf. v. 39). Here once again it is explained unambiguously what it means that Yhwh is he himself: he is *the* God (*hāʾlohîm*), the only one. The expansion can, however, also contain statements about the content in which Yhwh proves himself to be he himself. Thus in Ex 6.7 we read: "You will know that I am YHWH, your God, who brought you out from under the yoke of the Egyptians." Here it is by the basic experience of the exodus that Israel will know that Yhwh is *he himself.* Then in a later historical phase we read: "Then they will know that I am the LORD their God, for though I sent them into exile among the nations, I will gather them to their own land, not leaving any behind" (Ezek 39.28). Here it is the whole history of exile and return in which God wants to be known as himself.

The goal of the exodus is articulated in a quite particular sense when we read that "They will know that I am YHWH, their God, who brought them out of Egypt so that I might dwell among them" (Ex 29.46) [→**65**]. It is in the presence of God among his people, first on Sinai, but then in an exemplary way for the temple in Jerusalem, that God proves himself as himself. Ezekiel promises for the time after the exile: "My dwelling-place will be with them; I will be their God, and they will be my people. Then the nations will know that I YHWH make Israel holy, when my sanctuary is among them for ever" (Ezek 37.27f) [→**256**]. The Sabbath too will "be a sign between me and you for the generations to come, so that you may know that I am YHWH, who makes you holy" (Ex 31.13).

Often it is experiences of God's actions in history that will lead to Israel acknowledging who God is. This becomes very graphic in the collection of prophetic narratives in 1 Kgs 20. In the face of the threatening enemy army an anonymous prophet announces in a divine message to king Ahab: "I will give it into your hand today, and then you will know that I am YHWH" (v. 13) [→**141**]. In a later situation this procedure is repeated. The justification in this case is particularly interesting: "Because the Arameans think YHWH is a god of the hills and not a god of the valleys, I will deliver this vast army into your hands, and you will know that I am YHWH" (v. 28). Here the promise of God's help for his people is given a particular emphasis through the demonstrative rejection and refutation of the apostate statements of the Arameans about the God of Israel.

In the book of Ezekiel, in which we meet the "acknowledgment statement" with particular frequency, above all it is experiences of imminent judgment that can bring about acknowledgment of God: "And when I have spent my wrath upon them, they will know that I, YHWH, have spoken in my zeal" (Ezek 5.13; cf. 6.7, 10, 13, 14; 7.4, 9, 27 etc.). But finally Israel will then experience God in his saving acts in gathering and returning his people (39.28). A similar note is sounded in Isaiah: "You will know that I am YHWH, your savior and your redeemer, the mighty one of Jacob" (Isa 60.16).

In the almost verbatim equivalent text in Isa 49.26 we read that "all flesh" will recognize this. Not only will Israel acknowledge God in his actions, therefore, but "all flesh" or "the nations," as the text often says. This idea plays a part already in the exodus tradition. Here it is the Egyptians (Ex 7.5; 14.4, 18) and Pharaoh (7.17; 8.18) that will come to recognize through his actions that Yhwh is God. The idea is then found in a very emphatic form in Solomon's temple dedication prayer, "so that all the nations of the earth will know your Name" (1 Kgs 8.43, cf. v. 60). The stories about Jethro, Moses' father-in-law, and the Aramean Naaman read almost like graphic illustrations of this; Jethro has recognized "that YHWH is greater than all gods" (Ex 18.11), and Naaman "that there is no God in all the world except in Israel" (2 Kgs 5.15). In Ezekiel too this expectation is frequently expressed (21.10; 25.17; 26.6 etc.). It is again generally found in connection with a divine judgment on the nations. But when at the end God will fulfill his promises concerning Israel, then in view of this event the nations too will acknowledge him (36.23; 37.28).

At this point we might also recall the statements that speak of the "knowing" or "acknowledging" (*yāda‘*) of the *name* of God: the righteous know the name of God (Ps 9.11), and in a prosperous future Israel will know him (Isa 52.6), for God will make himself known (Ezek 39.7), and finally all the nations of the earth will acknowledge him (1 Kgs 8.43).

Only seldom do we come across talk of acknowledgment of God in an imperatival form. Thus in the hymnic call to praise of God we read: "Know that YHWH himself is God" (Ps 100.3). Here the "knowing" is to be taken more as an acknowledgment in hymnic praise. In Ps 46.11 the call is issued to representatives of enemy powers (v. 10), to desist from their military plans: "Desist and know that I am God." (In the "elohistic" revision of the psalm *’lohîm* replaces *yhwh* here.) The acknowledgment of Yhwh's world dominion will be an essential precondition for the world peace that he is working towards. In Ps 4.4 it is an individual pious person (*ḥāsîd*) who calls on the mighty to acknowledge how God leads and hears those that are his.

Another aspect of the acknowledging of God, finally, is evident in Hosea. Here we meet the substantival formula "knowledge of God" (*da‘at ’lohîm*, Hos 4.1; 6.6, in 4.6 twice *hadda‘at*) [→269]. The context points in another direction. Knowledge of God is found here in a series with goodness (*ḥesed*) and faithfulness (*’met*); all three of these are now lacking in Israel (4.1). Knowledge of God is thus not just to be brought about through God's actions, but should be simply present in Israel. The priests are held responsible for the lack of knowledge of God; they have themselves rejected the knowledge of God and have forgotten the Torah (4.6). So here knowledge of God is something that must be taught and learned, in a similarly fundamental way as the Torah. Its content can be deduced from passages which talk verbally of "knowing" God: the leading-out of Egypt (13.4), guidance in the wilderness (v. 5), gift of the fertile land (2.10), in short: the "classic" contents of the basic themes of the tradition as they have come down to us in the Pentateuch. This knowledge of God might be called "knowledge about God" (Wolff 1953).

3. Conceptions and depictions of God

3.1 The varied aspects of the image of God

No one can know what God is really like. People can experience God in different ways: his creative and formative power, but also his judging and destructive power, his affection and his nearness, his security and his absence. And they can bring these experiences to expression. They can say how they imagine God and his actions and can depict him in language and also in visible images. Visible divine images do, however, have the inherent danger that they can be worshiped; so their manufacture is permanently prohibited in Israel (Ex 20.4f; Deut 5.8f; cf. 1999a).

The linguistic conceptions and images by which Israel expresses its experiences with God are extraordinarily varied. It is not possible to do more than make a rough summary of these. In particular they resist attempts at systematization. The best thing is probably to take an approach on the basis of form. So with Brueggemann (1997, 117) I would tend to assume that the concern is always with *speech about God*. The various manifestations of speaking are included here: the speech of the biblical authors or the persons in their texts, when they speak of God in the 3rd person, the speaking of worshipers addressing God in the 2nd person, and equally divine speech in the 1st person, which is speech spoken and/or written down by prophets or the authors of the texts.

In the Hebrew Bible God is spoken of primarily in the form of verbs—God creates, liberates, rules, judges—, less frequently in the form of adjectives—God is just, gracious—, and finally, as it were in generalization, in the form of nouns—God as king, as judge, as shepherd (cf. Brueggemann 145ff). But it is in keeping with the character of the Hebrew Bible that such nouns are rare, and that in particular fundamental statements about the actions of God are made almost exclusively in verbal form. Thus there is talk of God's activity as creator with the most varied verbs: God creates (*bārā'*), makes (*'āśāh*), forms (*yāṣar*), founds (*qānāh*) and has things come into being through his word. But there is no word for the "creator;" and the participles of these verbs are used only seldom too: *bôrē'* is found almost exclusively in Isa 40–66, where the participles of other verbs are also found in abundance (cf. the table in Anderson 1967, 124ff; *qonēh* is another name for El elyon of Jerusalem, Gen 14.19, 22).

But this certainly does not mean that God's activity is not spoken of in non-graphic terms. On the contrary, a large proportion of the statements about God are highly graphic, "anthropomorphic," one might say. This applies, though certainly in very different ways, to all areas of Old Testament literature. (Criticism of the anthropomorphism of biblical language is an element of the criticism of biblical religion as a whole; so in the context of the representation of biblical statements it has no meaningful function, cf. *EKL³*, 1559.) Thus God's creator activity is made concretely conceivable by means of verbs taken from the realm of handiwork: from the "forming" of humans and animals (Gen 2.7, 8, 19) to the "stretching" of the heavens (Ps 104.2). The adoption of battle motifs from neighboring religions (Isa 51.9 etc.) [→420] is also highly graphic. But it is also clear that the verbs utilized in relation to Yhwh's fighting and gaining victory are meant metaphorically, to describe the power and strength of the creator God. To that extent they do not express anything fundamentally different from other verbs that instead of God's fighting describe his creative speaking (Ps 33.6, 9 etc.). There are various ways of expressing something that can only be described in vague terms. And there are no other means of expression available for use than concrete graphic depiction using terms from the human realm.

The same thing can be shown in relation to other themes. The "covenant" (*bᵉrît*) that God makes with humanity and then with Israel in particular, has its models in agreements between human beings (e.g. Gen 31.44) and nations (e.g. 1 Kgs 15.19). The word "choose" (*bāḥar*) too has its meaning in the secular realm in the sense of "select" (e.g. Gen 13.11). When God reinforces his promises to Israel's forefathers by means of an oath, he is doing something that is common in everyday relationships between humans (e.g. Gen 26.31).

The verbs used for the leading-out of Israel from Egypt are more varied. In Ex 6.6 three verbs follow each other in close succession:

God will "lead out" Israel (*yāṣā'* hiphil), a word with a large number of secular meanings; he will "save" (*nṣl* hiphil) Israel, a word that can also be used in a non-religious sense (e.g. Deut 25.11; 1 Sam 17.35) and in the vast majority of cases means rescue from danger; he will "redeem" (*gā'al*) Israel, a word from legal language (e.g. 25.25ff; 35.19), which however becomes a central theological term (e.g. Isa 43.1, often also in the participle *go'ēl*, e.g. 41.14). In other texts, alongside "lead out" the verb "lead up" (*'ālāh* hiphil) is also used (e.g. Ex 3.8), which also appears frequently in secular usage; in Deuteronomy in *pādāh* "redeem" a further legal term is found, related to *gā'al* (e.g. Deut 7.8; cf. Stamm 1940).

All this has been extensively discussed in the previous chapters of this book and will not be repeated here in any detail.

3.2.1 God as king

In the majority of cases mentioned so far, the verbs are concerned with the description, or more precisely, the attempted description, of a purposeful action on the part of God. Other verbs on the other hand express a continuous divine activity. Thus the verb "rule" (*mālak*) presupposes a more or less closely delimited realm of dominion, unlike for instance terms used in connection with the leading-out of Egypt which express precisely movement and inconclusiveness. So it is no coincidence that in the word *melek*, "king," we meet one of the few nouns that are used in describing God. It designates the continuity and the, as it were, institutional stability of the rule of God. Here too it is clear that the concept has been borrowed from the realm of human life in society. The king is a well-known and generally a key figure throughout the whole of the ancient Near East. In addition, in the religious environment of Israel the notion of the kingdom of a god was widespread, so that Israel has certainly borrowed some ideas from there (cf. Schmidt 1966 and 1996, 204-12).

In application to God, the title "king" is a metaphor that expresses God's superior power: God rules *like* a king. The concept of Yhwh's kingdom can then relate to quite a variety of realms of dominion: "The LORD has established his throne in heaven, and his kingdom rules over all" (Ps 103.19); as "king forever" (*l'ʿōlām*) he is enthroned above the heavenly ocean (*mabbûl*) and the "sons of God" will honor him (29.10, 1f); he is "a great king above all gods" (95.3), who are to

bow down and worship him (97.7). Here God's dominion encompasses the whole of creation that he himself has made (95.4f). So all
gods are subject to him too, since none of them can claim to have
made the world.

God is also "king of the whole earth" (Ps 47.3, 8) and reigns as king
over the nations (v. 9), who are called upon to praise him (96.7-10).
Here the notion of God's heavenly dominion is combined with that of
the earthly. It is evident that the notion of God's kingdom also relates
to Israel—and perhaps primarily so; for the statement that God is king
of the whole earth and over the nations (Ps 47.3, 8f) corresponds to
the other statement that he has chosen Israel as his inheritance (*naḥᵃlāh*)
and subjected the nations to Israel "under our feet" (vv. 4f). Here the
rule of God is not grounded in his creative acts, but in his dealings
with Israel in history.

An important aspect of the notion of God as king is the talk of his
"throne." In the statements about the place where he has set up his
throne we see the same alternation between the heavenly and the
earthly dominion: his throne is in heaven (Ps 103.19); he is enthroned
above the heavenly ocean (29.10); he is surrounded on his throne by a
"great heavenly host" (1 Kgs 22.19) [→**142**]. But when the nobility
among the nations gather around the throne of the "king above all
nations," then the latter is imagined as being located on the earth (Ps
47.9f). This can only mean Jerusalem or Zion. Thus in the "Song of
the Reed Sea" in Ex 15 Zion becomes the "mountain of his inheritance" and "place of his enthronement," where God will rule as king
forever (vv. 17f); and God is described as "the one enthroned on
Zion" (Ps 9.12).

But the notions of the levels of dominion do not stay unseparated.
This comes to particularly graphic expression in Isaiah's vision (Isa 6):
the prophet experiences the vision of the enthroned "king YHWH
Zebaot" (v. 5) in the temple in Jerusalem. But the temple (*hêkāl*) can
only contain the hem of the robe of the enthroned God (v. 1) because
his figure towers up into heaven. There God is surrounded by heavenly figures singing his praises. The prophet is brought into this scene;
but the scene still features the earthly temple as one of the Seraphim
takes a glowing coal from the altar (v. 6; cf. Metzger 1970, 144f). Finally, in Isa 66.1 we are told that "heaven is my throne and the earth is
my footstool." Here God's enthronement stretches over both levels of
his dominion. There is an echo here of what is said in Solomon's

"temple-dedication prayer: "The heavens, even the highest heaven, cannot contain you. How much less this temple I have built!" (1 Kgs 8.27; cf. Westermann 1966, 327f).

The notion of God as king is associated particularly strongly with Zion. This has found expression in certain religious procedures which are reflected especially in the "psalms of ascent." (See §14.2 above.) From here the idea then gained entry into the extra-cultic language of piety. In the Psalms God is constantly addressed and praised as king. Thus the psalmist calls him "my king" (Pss 5.3; 44.5; 68.25; 74.12; 84.4), "YHWH, you king" (20.10) or "my God, you king" (145.1). In other psalms he is praised as "eternal king" (10.16; 146.10; cf. 29.10). All Israel is called upon to rejoice in its creator and king (149.2; cf. Isa 43.15 and also the rare description of God as "king of Israel," Isa 44.6; Zeph 3.15). Here the notion of God as king has left the cultic context and has become an expression of personal piety. The greatness and power of the king is not reduced as a result; on the contrary, as the expression of the individual supplicant's confidence it gains added significance for the religious life of the community.

3.2.2 God as judge

Abraham calls God "judge of the whole earth" (Gen 18.25; cf. Ps 94.2) [→28]. With the term "judge" (*šofēṭ*) a title is again conferred on God which functions as a term for human officials in Israel. In this case the title is not an independent noun but a participle, alongside which a verb used frequently to describe the activity of a judge is used, namely the verb *šāfaṭ*, which means "to judge, pass judgment," but also "to rule." The participle still has its own function as a term for an office, however; in application to God it expresses not only the actions of a judge in each case but also a permanent state: it is God who creates justice. In Gen 18 the area in which God's activity as judge takes place is clearly defined: his concern is to maintain the distinction between the righteous (*ṣaddîq*) and the wicked (*rāšā'*) because otherwise "the righteous would be like the wicked." Because God does this, he is called the "righteous judge" (*šofēṭ ṣedeq*, Jer 11.20; Ps 9.5 or *šofēṭ ṣaddîq*, Ps 7.12), who sits on his throne and dispenses justice (Ps 9.5). Here the proximity between the titles "judge" and "king" becomes clear: in Ps 97.2 we read that righteousness and justice are the supports of the throne of the divine king. In Isa 33.22 the two titles are juxtaposed: "The LORD is our judge, the LORD is our lawgiver, the LORD is our king—he will help us." Here we see, as previously with the title of king, the transference of the title into the realm of personal piety.

Thus the relatively few texts in which God is expressly referred to as "judge" cover a broad area: the heavens declare the righteousness (*sedeq*) of God the judge (Ps 50.6); he is the judge of the whole earth (Gen 18.25; Ps 94.2) and judge over the nations (Ps 7.12, cf. v. 9); he will decide between Israel and its opponents (Judg 11.27), he will save Zion (Isa 33.22, cf. v. 20). For the psalmist, who sees God as the righteous judge on his throne (Ps 9.5), from where he judges the whole earth (vv. 8f), this is at the same time cause for thanksgiving for the judging and saving action of God towards him personally (vv. 1-5) and hope for the poor and needy (vv. 10, 19). The psalmist in Ps 94 calls upon the judge of the world to pay pack the arrogant for their deeds (v. 2). Just as God as judge decides between the righteous and the wicked (Gen 18.25), so too in this capacity he will humiliate one and raise up the other (Ps 75.8). And finally Yhwh Zebaot, the righteous judge, who tests the reins and hearts, grants justice to Jeremiah against his enemies from Anathoth (Jer 11.20).

These texts display a range of perspectives from which God's activity as judge is viewed. This variety is even more marked if we take a closer look at the verb *šāfaṭ*. Here an important difference from the conception of God as king is also evident: the latter means primarily the continuous, powerful presence of God as king, while the activity of the "judge" is effective or hoped for in his active work and intervention in concrete situations. "Try me (*šāfṭēnî*)" (Pss 7.9; 26.1; 35.24; 43.1; cf. 82.8); a corresponding call to the king to fulfill his office would be inconceivable. (The imperative of the verb *mālak* is found only in satire, Judg 9.8-14.) It can, however, be said of king Yhwh, "He comes, he comes to judge the earth. He will judge the world in righteousness (*sedeq*) and the peoples in his truth (*ʾmûnāh*)" (Ps 96.13). Where the king performs juridical functions, the active character of his actions come to the fore.

Talk of God's actions as judge often relates to the inter-human realm. The Psalms which refer to God as judge in heaven (Ps 50.6) and on earth (94.2) and over the nations (7.9) are concerned with problems of the psalmist, whether as a community (Pss 50; 94) or as individuals (Ps 7). An important function of the judge lies in deciding questions of competing claims to justice by individual people or groups. Thus God is to "judge" between Abraham and Sarah (Gen

16.5), between Laban and Jacob (31.53), between David and Saul (1 Sam 24.13, 16), but also between Israel and the Ammonites (Judg 11.27). In the metaphor of God as shepherd we are told that he will "judge" between the fat and unscrupulous animals and the thin, oppressed animals of the flock (Ezek 34.20, 22, cf. v. 17). Finally in the eschatological view of the future there is the hope that God will "judge" between the nations, so that they will no longer wage war with each other (Isa 2.4 = Mic 4.3). (Cf. Liedke 1971, 62ff.) It is especially clear here that *šāfaṭ* means the restoration of a situation that has been disturbed by enmity between the nations.

Psalm 82 shows God in a juridical function within the gathering of the gods. It reproaches the gods for fundamental shortcomings in their function as the guarantors of "just" conditions: they have judged unjustly and favored the wicked, but they have omitted to help the poor, the orphans and the needy to gain justice and to deliver them from the hands of the wicked (vv. 2-4). God therefore denies that they are gods at all (vv. 5-7) and he himself will "judge the earth," i.e. do everything that the "gods" have failed to do (v. 8). Here in a world-spanning context we learn what God's concern is in his capacity as judge: on the one hand to deal with the wicked (*rešāʿîm*) as is their due (cf. Gen 18.25); on the other hand to show special favor towards those who are oppressed or who are unable to achieve justice for themselves. These are mentioned together here in an unusual conglomeration: the insignificant (*dal*, twice), the orphaned (*yātôm*), the wretched (*ʿānî*), the poor (*rāš*), the needy (*ʾebyôn*). (On the parallel terms cf. *THAT* II, 347f.) The problem of their social situation is made clear in the fact that achieving justice for them (*hiṣdîq*) means at the same time rescuing them from the hands of the wicked (vv. 3f). Once again God shows himself in the role of the just judge who takes care of a clear distinction between justice and injustice, but who also in a special way accepts the weak and those in need of protection in society.

There is quite a different picture of the judging God in the book of Ezekiel. Here it is the punishing judgment of God that comes upon Israel: "I will judge each one according to his way" (Ezek 18.30; 33.20). This sentence can also contain the call to repent (18.30), or it can direct attention to a subsequent turn in fortunes (36.19, 21ff). But it can also be part of the announcement of imminent judgment when God says of the land of Israel: "The end is now upon you and I will unleash my anger against you. I will judge you according to your conduct and repay you for all your detestable practices" (7.3, 8; cf. 16.38). But all this is not simply a judgment of annihilation. Rather, the people concerned will, as a result of God acting "according to their conduct" and judging them "according to their own ways (*mišpāṭ*, cf. v. 23)," "know that I am YHWH" (v. 27, cf. also 11.10). This acknowledgment embraces far more than the immediate occasion of judgment and what precedes it.

3.2.3 God as Shepherd

"Hear us, O Shepherd of Israel, you who lead Joseph like a flock" (Ps 80.2[1]). The metaphor of God as shepherd sets another tone. God is the "shepherd of Israel," and Israel is "his people, the sheep of his pasture" (100.3; 79.13; cf. 95.7). In this idea Israel's dependence on God's guidance and care comes to expression in a special way. The picture of the flock can also stand alone, without the shepherd being expressly present. The majority of texts in which this metaphor appears presuppose a situation of distress in which the help of God the shepherd is prayed and hoped for. Thus the call in Ps 80.2[1] forms the introduction to a psalm that laments the destruction of the vineyard that was planted by God and prays for its restoration. Ps 74.1 introduces a lament about the desecrated sanctuary.

Other texts already announce the end of the time of distress: "He who scattered Israel will gather them and will watch over his flock like a shepherd" (Jer 31.10). This expectation also runs through the book of Micah: God will gather the "remnant" of Israel [→705] like a flock (Mic 2.12) and in particular take up the lame among the exiles (4.6f); at the end of the book God is called upon in prayer to give pasture to "the flock of his inheritance" (7.14; cf. Kessler 1999, 305). Isa 40.10f describes God's expected return to Zion: first with the concept of the powerful ruler, then with that of the caring shepherd; this picture is quite lovingly painted, as God takes up the lambs in his arms, hides them protectively in his robes and leads the ewes. The picture of the shepherd here is very close to that of the king in his protective and guiding function. In Mic 4.7 it is the other way round: the picture of the caring shepherd escalates into that of the king on Mount Zion.

The metaphor is elaborated in greatest detail in Ezek 34 [→254]. Here we see a remarkable interaction in the use of the term "shepherd(s)" for human "officials" and as God's own term for himself. Because the shepherds, i.e. the responsible leaders of the people, have not done justice to their tasks of care and protection for their flocks, so that the animals of the flock are scattered and at the mercy of the wild animals (vv. 1-6), God will call them to account (vv. 7-10) and will take his flock to himself (vv. 11-16). Here the activity of the good shepherd is elaborated in detail: he will gather the flock and bring it out of dispersal into its land and give it good pasture, and he will do all that the bad shepherds have failed to do: he will seek the lost, bring back the scattered, bandage the wounded and strengthen the weak (v. 16, cf. the contrast in Greenberg 1997, 706). In the graphic imagery the historical situation of Israel addressed here rings through: God will lead the "flock" out of dispersal, i.e. exile, back into "their" land and they will graze on the "mountains of Israel." In addition, in the dispute within the flock he will "judge" between the strong and the weak (vv. 17-22); the metaphor of the judge comes in here too. Finally, however, God will transfer the office of shepherd back to a human being: "I will place over them one shepherd, my servant David, and he will tend them" (v. 23). God himself will, as it were, assume the office of the shepherd in the interim, until he can transfer it to the new David in the expected time of salvation. But the order of things is clear: "I the LORD will be their God, and my servant David will be prince among them" (v. 24). And the relationship between God and Israel remains constant too, even when God will have transferred the title of shepherd to the eschatological David: "You my sheep, the sheep of my pasture, are my people, and I am your God" (v. 31).

The same expectation is expressed in a much more concise form in Jer 23.1-4: the bad shepherds are held responsible for the dispersal of the flock, but God will gather the "remnant" of his flock (cf. Mic 2.12) "out of all the countries" and will lead them back to their pasture; then he will appoint shepherds over them again. The "messianic" element of the new David that we find in Ezek 34.23ff is missing (as yet) here. In Mic 2.13 it is God himself who will lead the flock as "one who breaks open the way" (i.e. as lead animal) out of exile and then go before them as king. The metaphor of God as shepherd is thus developed differently in detail in the various contexts.

Finally, like the metaphor of God as king, this metaphor has become an expression of personal piety. In Ps 23.1-4 God's care as shepherd is developed in detail: God gives green grass for pasture, fresh water, secure guidance on the path, protection and comfort at night. The relationship of these concepts and images to Ezek 34.11-16 is obvious; but here everything remains in the personal realm. Jacob too speaks in retrospect of the guiding of his life by God, who has led him as a shepherd, going on to an "angel" (*mal'āk*) who has redeemed him (Gen 48.15f). Here Jacob's personal fate stands for the leading of Israel by God in the early days of its history.

In all the various nuances it is very clear that the metaphor of God as shepherd brings to expression a quite different area of the understanding of God and of the relationship with God than that of king and judge. The concern in this case is not with power or with justice but with the experience of guidance and protection in the life of the nation and of the individual and above all with hope of this in the future.

3.2.4 God as Father and Mother

"As a father has compassion on his children, so the LORD has compassion on those who fear him" (Ps 103.13). "As a mother comforts her child, so will I comfort you" (Isa 66.13). The comforting care of parents is an essential element of the biblical image of God. It is not surprising that in the patriarchally biased world of the Hebrew Bible and its environment we find the metaphor of the father more frequently than that of the mother. It evokes a broad spectrum of associations.

Israel is God's firstborn son. This idea is found expressed from various aspects in texts on the beginnings of God's history with Israel. God has called his son, whom he loves, out of Egypt (Hos 11.1), he has demanded the release of his firstborn from Pharaoh (Ex 4.22); he has carried him all the way on the path of wandering, "as a man carries his son" (Deut 1.31; cf. Hos 11.3). But Israel has proved ungrateful and has not understood God's fatherly care (Hos 11.3; cf. Deut 32.6). God has waited in vain for Israel to call him "my father" (Jer 3.19f) and to give him the honor due to him (Mal 1.6). Here we see that the picture of God as father also contains an element of demand; and time and again God has to note that Israel has not fulfilled the demands that arise from the parent-child relationship. (Cf. also Isa 1.2, 4.) So the wrath of God can enter the picture again (Hos 11.9). But at the same time there is talk of the overcoming of this anger. In Hos 11.8f the internal tension in God is striking: "How might I give you up, Ephraim, deliver you up, Israel? ... My heart has turned around in me, my regret has burned up with power. I cannot execute my burning anger, cannot ruin Ephraim again: for I am God, not man, the holy one in your midst: I do not allow the embers of wrath to arise" (translation with reference to Jeremias 1983, 139). Similar notes are to be heard in Jer 31.20: God must have mercy on his "dear son" Ephraim because otherwise his heart will break. (Cf. also v. 9.) In Ps 103 too, the pathway extends from God's anger (v. 9) through to the loving mercy of the father (v. 13). (Cf. also in wisdom language Prov 3.12.)

In the exilic situation the prophet announces that God will require the return of his sons and daughters from the north and the south as he once did of Pharaoh (Isa 43.6f; cf. Ex 4.22). The picture of the creator is added to that of the father when God speaks of having created (*bārā'*), formed (*yāṣar*) and made (*'āśāh*) these children that are named by his name (cf. v. 1; also Deut 32.6; Mal 2.10). The accent here lies on the expression "for my honor"; for this is the special thing about *these* creatures of God's, that they are at the same time in a very special sense his sons and daughters. So he has every right to restore them to their earlier state. In 45.9-13 too God rejects all criticism of his support for Israel: as little as the clay can criticize the potter, so little can anyone say to the father: "Why do you beget?" and to the mother: "Why do you give birth?" No one can dictate to God, the creator of the world, how he should act in relation to his children, the "work of his hands."

In a great prayer of those returning from exile (Isa 63.14–64.11 — "evidently the most impressive psalm of popular lament in the Bible," Westermann 1966, 311), it is now humans who speak of the fatherhood of God. It sounds like an echo of the text just cited: "Yet, O LORD, you are our Father. We are the clay, you are the potter; we are all the work of your hand" (64.7[8]). The petitioners cling in real desperation to their exclusive dependency on God: "You are our Father, though Abraham does not know us or Israel (Jacob) acknowledge us" (63.16). All bridges to the past seem to be in ruins; so the petitioners now expect a completely new start: "You, O LORD, are our Father, our Redeemer from of old is your name." God as creator, as father and redeemer—this encompasses the whole horizon of what Israel has experienced of God, what it knows and what it hopes for.

Only rarely is God's fatherhood described in biological terms. This occurs in a particularly marked fashion in Deut 32.18: after in v. 6 the terminology of God as creator has been used, in v. 18 (according to the customary translation): "the Rock, who fathered (*yālad*) you, you deserted, and you have forgotten the God who gave you birth (*ḥyl*, pol.)" The second half of the verse is clearly talking about God as the one giving birth; the verb *yālad* in the first half of the verse can mean both "to father" and "to give birth to," so that the whole verse could also speak of God as mother (so the translation in von Rad 1964, 137; cf. Rupprecht 1988; Trible 1993, 79ff). (For God this verb is otherwise used only in Ps 2.7 for the fatherhood of God in relation to the king on Zion.)

So Deut 32.18 carries us into talk of God as mother. She appears in this text as the one who gives birth; the verb used for this also means "to be in labor" and can thus connote the associated pains. This comparison is also found in Isa 42.14: God has been silent for a long time, but "now, like a woman in childbirth, I cry out, I gasp and pant." With this issue begins a phase of new creation of nature and a turnaround in the fate of the captives (vv. 15f).

Another aspect of this metaphor is evident in Num 11.11f: Moses complains to God that he has laid on him "the burden of this whole nation." In a rhetorical question he gives the responsibility for this back to God: "Did I conceive all these people? Did I give them birth? Why do you tell me to carry them in my arms, as a nurse carries an infant?" The implied answer is: no, it was not me, it was you yourself, and so you must now bear the responsibility yourself. In the image of God as mother the boot, as it were, is on the other foot compared with Deut 32.18. There the concern was with the people's responsibility not to forget God, here it is with God's responsibility to take the part of his people (cf. Brueggemann 1997, 258).

In Isa 49.15 it is God himself who expresses this concern for his people: "Can a mother forget the baby at her breast and have no compassion on the child she has borne? Though she may forget, I will not forget you!" God's attitude to Zion is as elementary as the attitude of a mother to her child—more so, indeed: even in the unlikely case that a mother should forget this fundamental relationship, this cannot occur in God's case. The same idea is expressed in Ps 27.10, this time in relation to father and mother: "Though my father and mother forsake me, the Lord will receive me." God is not only like father and mother, he is more than them. In Isa 66.10-13 the picture of Jerusalem as the suckling mother changes to God himself: "As a mother comforts her child, so will I comfort you." Again the close similarity of God's actions to those of a mother are emphasized.

So the psalmist can say: "From the womb (*rehem*) I was cast upon you; from my mother's body (*beten*) you have been my God" (Ps 22.11). God sees himself even more closely connected with the mother's body in the prophetic speech: "Listen to me, O house of Jacob, all you who remain of the house of Israel, you whom I have upheld since you were conceived, and have carried since your birth. Even to your old age and gray hairs I am he, I am he who will sustain you" (Isa 46.3f). "The imagery of this poem stops just short of saying that God possesses a womb" (Trible 1978, 38).

It is especially noteworthy that the noun "womb" (*reḥem* or *raḥam*) comes from the same root as the verb "have mercy" (*rḥm*, pi.), the noun "mercy" (*raḥᵃmîm*) and the adjective "merciful" (*raḥûm*), which is used almost exclusively of God. This corresponds with the fact that the image of God as mother contains only this concerned, caring aspect and not the demanding, even angry element like the image of the father. Thus the metaphor of the maternal God, even though it is not attested very frequently, is fundamental material in the biblical image of God.

A new perspective on the image of God emerges as a result of this, which comes to expression in the report of the creation of humans at the beginning of the Bible. "So God created man in his own image, in the image of God he created him; male and female he created them" (Gen 1.27). On the one hand this makes a statement about humans: humans are male and female; the two together form "man" in his unity and difference. But at the same time it contains a statement about God, since this male-female human being is created "in the image of God." This "image of God" thus embraces both the male and the female. But the difference between "God" and the "image of God" remains intact. The image opens up to us a new perspective on God; but it remains a statement about his image. More than this is not revealed; the transcendence of God remains preserved. (Cf. Trible 1993, 30ff, esp. 42f.)

3.3 God's "qualities"

Further metaphors for God's work and actions might be added. Thus there is talk of God as warrior and fighter. But there is no title for this. God's designation as "man of war" (*'îš milḥāmāh*) in Ex 15.3 is linked with other predicates, part of a hymnic praise of the strong and helpful God, ending with the emphatic "YHWH is his name." The hymn sings of the wonderful rescue of Israel at the Reed Sea, which God brings about by his "right hand" (vv. 6, 12), with which he directs the forces of nature by which the Egyptians are destroyed; then he has his "arm" transfix the enemy peoples to enable Israel's passage (v. 16). In Isa 42.13f the designation of God as "man of war" is followed by the metaphor of moaning like one giving birth. In Isa 40.10f the image of the "ruling arm" of God changes into the arm of the shepherd, with which he gathers the lambs, and in 52.10 we read that God bares his arm before the eyes of the nations, so that "the ends of the earth will see the salvation of our God." In other texts the metaphor of the fighting God appears in the battle of the creator with the forces of chaos (Isa 51.9f; Ps 74.13ff).

The metaphors by which God is portrayed have very graphic features. Each of the shapes that God assumes in the metaphors displays quite particular characteristic traits. In biblical discourse these become God's qualities: for instance, when we read that God is angry, this means that humans experience God as angry, or more precisely, they experience something that they understand, or try to understand, as God's anger. Thus particular adjectives, "qualifiers" in English, become statements about the behavior and the nature of God. But it is evident that none of the designations of the qualities can quite comprehend and embrace God's "nature." In the case of metaphors in nominal expressions it has emerged clearly that they can only ever comprehend and represent a partial aspect of the nature of God. The same applies to the adjectives too; unlike the nouns, however, they can occur in association with other terms and so contemplate and illuminate God's nature from various angles. So in what follows we shall need to pay attention to both: to the specific statements that the individual adjectives make as well as what they indicate in combination.

An especially illuminating example of this is the almost formulaic statement: "The LORD is merciful and compassionate, patient and full of goodness." If we compare two of the particularly striking passages where this is found, a fundamental difference is plain: in Ps 103.8 this sentence stands at the beginning of an almost overflowing series of statements about the goodness and mercy of God (vv. 8-13); in Ex 34.6f the text continues, however, with the statement that God "certainly does not leave sins unpunished;" here God's mercifulness appears in a tension-filled interactive relationship with his punitive anger. The two aspects appear in other passages in the Hebrew Bible in different expressions, sometimes on their own, sometimes together. If we first look at them individually we must constantly keep this in mind. Later we shall return to the connections between the different aspects.

3.3.1 God is compassionate and gracious
a. The "grace formula"

The Lord is compassionate and gracious, slow to anger, abounding in love" (Ps 103.8; Ex 34.6). This "grace formula" (*Gnadenformel*, Spieckermann 1990) is probably the most impressive and effective statement about God's qualities. It is found in quite a variety of contexts in the Hebrew Bible, sometimes in similarly worded terms, sometimes in adapted phraseology (Ps 86.14; 145.8; Neh 9.17; Joel 2.13; Jonah 4.2 etc.). It begins with two adjectives that are used almost exclusively for God and which can thus be seen as especially characteristic divine qualities: "compassionate" (*raḥûm*) and "gracious" (*ḥannûn*). This word-pair, the sequence of which can also vary (e.g. Ps 111.4; 145.8), brings quite different areas together: "compassionate" is, as said above, derived from the verb "to have mercy" (*rḥm* pi.). This word group also contains the noun "compassion" (*raḥᵃmîm*) and then especially the word for the "mother's womb" (*reḥem* or *raḥam*). This adjective is thus an expression for the "maternal" side of the image of God; that it is also found in the image of God as father (cf. Ps 103.13: twice the verb), shows the close interweaving of these two aspects (see 3.2.4 above) [→**618**].

But this is only part of the picture. The verbal statement that God has mercy is found frequently in texts in which this compassion stands in opposition to a previous or still continuing negative situation or action by God. For instance, "For a brief moment I abandoned you, but with deep compassion (*raḥᵃmîm*) I will bring you back. In a surge of anger I hid my face from you for a moment, but with everlasting kindness I will have compassion on you (*riḥamtik*)" (Isa 54.7f). Or, "I will restore the fortunes of Jacob's tents and have compassion on his dwellings (*ᵃraḥēm*)" (Jer 30.18). So the talk of the mercy and compassion of God also always contains the element of God's relenting from his anger and the overcoming of the disaster or rescue from distress and danger (cf. also Ps 78.38).

The word "gracious" (*ḥannûn*) takes us into quite different contexts. The noun *ḥēn* covers a broad area: from the aesthetic beauty of a piece of jewelry (Prov 1.9; 4.9) and the gracefulness of an animal (5.19) or a woman (11.16; 31.30), through the mellifluence of language (Ps 45.3; Prov 22.11) and on to goodwill and favor among people. The latter finds expression in the common phrase "find grace/favor in someone's eyes." When this term is used between people it can be a courtesy formula, for instance as the introduction to a request (Gen 18.3; 30.27;

47.29 etc.) or as an expression of gratitude (1 Sam 1.18; Ruth 2.13), but it can also express personal esteem (Gen 39.4, 21; 1 Sam 16.22) or friendship (20.3). "Find grace in God's eyes" on the other hand has quite different weight. In Noah's case it means the critical turning-point in the fundamental crisis at the beginning of history of human-kind (Gen 6.8). In the dramatic conversations between God and Moses after Israel's sinning with the "Golden Calf" Moses takes God at his word, as he said to Moses, "You have found grace in my eyes" (Ex 33.12) and introduces his urgent requests that God accompany Israel on its further pathway repeatedly with the expression "If I have found grace in your eyes" (33.13; 34.9; cf. 33.16); here this expression is anything but a courtesy formula, and it is answered by God with the repetition of his assurance: "You have found favor in my eyes" (v. 17). In Moses' complaints about the burden God has laid on him with the leadership of the people, this expression also plays a part (Num 11.11, 15). And in the great chapter of the proclamations of salvation in Jer 31 we read at the beginning: "The people that escaped the sword have found grace in the wilderness" (v. 2).

Confidence in this human-oriented side of God finds quite specific expression in the fact that the psalmist constantly calls upon God with the imperative form of the verb *ḥānan*, "Be gracious to me" (Pss 4.2; 6.3; 9.14 etc., altogether more than twenty times). Here again the different accent is clear by comparison with the root *rḥm*, since an appeal in prayer like this is not found anywhere else. So this word-pair forms a tension-filled unity of God's ways of behaving towards humans, which the latter experience as positive. Two further examples of this: "Yet the Lord longs to be gracious to you; he rises to show you compassion" (Isa 30.18). And: "The Lord is gracious and righteous; our God is full of compassion (*m'raḥēm*)" (Ps 116.5). Here the word "righteous" (*ṣaddîq*) is added, a word which will concern us later (see 3.3.3).

This word-pair has a special emphasis in a text that precedes the "grace formula" in the multi-layered pericope Ex 32–34 at 34.6. God answers Moses' request, "Show me your glory (*kābôd*)" with the words: "I will cause all my goodness to pass in front of you, and I will proclaim my name, the LORD, in your presence. I will have mercy on whom I will have mercy, and I will have compassion on whom I will have compassion" (33.18f). The highly charged linguistic form of the second sentence recalls the introduction of the divine name to Moses:

"I will be who I will be" (Ex 3.14, cf. Vriezen 1950). The emphasis lies on the fact that God will be gracious and merciful; but the decision as to who will benefit from his grace and compassion rests with him. The sounds rather like an anticipatory interpretation of the "grace formula" (cf. Aurelius 1988, 125). Rashi (Commentary, *ad loc.*) sees in the subsequent covenant agreement (34.10) a confirmation that the assurance of grace and compassion will never return "empty."

In the grace formula the statements of the word-pair "compassionate and gracious" are continued by the words "patient and of great goodness." The word "patient" renders two Hebrew words: *'erek 'appayim*, literally "long with regard to anger." The expression is often translated by "longsuffering;" the translation "slow to anger" (cf. Trible 1993, 17ff) is a better rendering of the sense, since again the concern is with the wrath of God, and the positively experienced attitude of God is understood as the opposite pole to this. This shows once again that God's behavior described here can certainly not be taken for granted.

"Rich in goodness" (*rab-ḥesed*) is then again a thoroughly positive-sounding statement. In some uses of the "grace formula" it is linked with the additional word "faithfulness" (*'emet*), a favorite term in the Psalms in particular (more than 120 times); here it has also found full use in a liturgical context (e.g. Pss 136; cf. 118.1-4, 29). In the "grace formula" it finds its fullest expression (cf. *THAT* I, 600-621; *ThWAT* III, 48-71). The same applies to the word *'emet*, the meaning of which covers the range of "faithfulness, reliability, truth" (cf. *THAT* I, 177-209; *ThWAT* I, 333-341). The combination of the two expressions is characteristic of religious usage in the Psalms (e.g. Pss 25.10; 89.15; 117.2).

On its "wanderings" through the scriptures (cf. Trible 1993, 17ff; also Jeremias 1975/97, 94ff) the "grace formula" is rarely found in a context that does not clearly indicate what the assurance of the compassion and grace of God is responding to; thus in Ps 145.8, a psalm that gives unlimited praise to the kingship of God, and in a shortened form in the wisdom psalm, Ps 111.4. Jonah quotes a version which adds at the end, "and relents concerning the calamity" (Jonah 4.2); this fits the context of Jonah and also draws attention to the fact that God's compassion means an express aversion from a planned calamity. This version is also found in Joel, but in a quite different, veritably dramatic context: "Return! Rend your hearts and not your clothes! Return to the LORD, your God, for he is gracious and compassionate, slow to

anger but rich in goodness and relents from the calamity" (Joel 2.12f).
Joel continues: "Perhaps he may relent" (v. 14), the immediate situa-
tion-relatedness of this addition being clear. In Jonah the same form of
words is found in the proclamation of the king of Nineveh (Jonah
3.9); but while Jonah looks back in indignation and anger at God's
relenting, which has now taken effect, Joel hopes it will come in the
future as God's response to the people's repentance.

Psalm 103 explains in a highly impressive manner that the compassion of God finds expression in the forgiveness of sins. Even before the
"grace formula" is quoted (v. 8[9]) we read at the beginning of the
psalm: "He forgives all your sins" (v. 2[3]). The impact of the formula
itself is then reinforced by the assurance that God will not remain angry "forever" (v. 9) and not deal with us in accordance with our sins
and transgressions (v. 10) but remove our transgressions from us "as
the heavens are far from the earth" (vv. 11f). The subsequent image of
the father who takes pity on his children (*rhm* pi., v. 13), shows, like
the comparisons of humans with the "dust" from which they are
formed (v. 14; cf. Gen 2.7; 3.19) and with the grass and the quickly
fading flower of the field (vv. 15f, cf. Isa 40.6f), that what moves God
to act graciously and with forgiveness is certainly not due to human
merit. But the psalmist also says that this is no *carte blanche*, but that
God's goodness (*hesed*) is for those who fear him (v. 11) and that these
are precisely those on whom God has pity like a father (v. 13). In the
concluding assurance that the goodness of God and his righteousness
(*s'dāqāh*) are immutable ("from everlasting to everlasting"), we are
further told that to fear God means "to keep his covenant and remember and obey his precepts" (vv. 17f).

A quite different note is struck by Psalm 86. The psalmist describes
himself as "poor and needy" (*'anî w''ebyôn*, v. 1), and he calls to God
in his distress (v. 7). In his laments and petitions we frequently hear the
motif of the "grace formula:" God is of "great goodness" (*rab-hesed*)
towards all who call upon him (v. 5); the psalmist himself has experienced God's great goodness, when God saved him from the "underworld" (*še'ôl*, v. 13). And finally when threatened by violent men who
seek his life (v. 14), he exclaims the "grace formula" (v. 15). Here
there is no help and rescue in sight; the psalmist hopes only for a sign
that God will stand by him and comfort him (v. 17). That God is
compassionate and gracious, he knows from the religious tradition in
which he himself stands, and from his own previous experience.

An impressive example of the elaboration of religious traditions is provided by the great prayer of repentance in Neh 9.6-37 (cf. 1997d). The person declaiming this public prayer tells the story of God's dealings with Israel, reminding God of all that he has done for Israel. The first great break comes with Israel's refusal to continue on the path prescribed by God to the promised land (vv. 16, 17a). At this point attention turns with an emphatic "but you" from Israel's behavior do the deeds and behavior of God (v. 17b). Here, as it were programmatically for all subsequent stages, the "grace formula" is introduced. God is addressed with the quite unusual words "God of forgiveness" (*ʾᵉlôᵃh sᵉlîḥôt*); this expresses the function of the formula as a reminder and as a guarantee of God's readiness to forgive. Added at the end of the formula is "and you did not abandon them." In this form the "grace formula" is the interpretive framework for everything that follows: in the wilderness God did not abandon them "in your great compassion" (v. 19); he delivered them into the hands of their enemies, but when they cried to him he gave them saviors "in your great compassion" (vv. 27, 28); and also after God had delivered them into the hands of the nations, he did not make an end of them "according to your great compassion" and did not abandon them, "for you are a compassionate and gracious God" (v. 31).

b. God does not leave unpunished

The first and fundamental formulation of the "grace formula" as "called out" by God before Moses on Sinai, differs in one important regard from all previously discussed versions: it continues immediately with the addition, "who shows goodness to thousands, forgives transgressions and sins, but certainly does not leave unpunished but visits the guilt of the fathers on the children and children's children, to the third and fourth generation" (Ex 34.7). Much of what in other texts was already evident from the context is put expressly into words here: the compassion and grace of God can only be understood in their tension with God's punitive anger.

How the two things relate together is stated in this divine word at the first critical turning-point in Israel's history. The premise is the compassion and grace of God. It finds expression in the forgiveness of sins for the "thousands," that is for an almost unimaginable number. (Deut 7.9f speaks of "a thousand generations".) But a limitation follows: "He certainly does not leave unpunished" (*naqqēh lōʾ yᵉnaqqeh*). This deals emphatically with the misunderstanding that transgressions against God's commandments might not be taken into account because God is compassionate. Rather, he will "visit" them [→**485**], and indeed on into subsequent generations.

The same problem can also be viewed from another angle, however. In the Decalogue the sequence is reversed: first the "visiting" of guilt through to the third and fourth generation is spoken of, then of the goodness that God will show to "thousands" (Ex 20.5f; Deut 5.9f). The immediate grounds for this lies in the fact that this opposition here follows the prohibition of idol worship, to which special importance is attached as the elaboration of the first commandment. At the same time the whole thing is given a different accent, however. The point of departure is the self-presentation of God as "zealous God" (*'ēl qannā'*) [→**629**]; that is why the first concern is with the "visitation." Then the two groups of people are separated into those who "hate" God, i.e. those who act in contravention of his commandments, and the others "who love me and keep my commandments."

The Ex 34.6f version finds an echo a number of times in texts in which the "grace formula" is only partially cited, or not at all. In the crisis after the visit of the reconnaissance spies to the promised land Moses reminds God of his earlier words and quotes in abbreviated form what God had said to him on Sinai (Num 14.18). Briefer still are the formulae that Jeremiah uses in a prayer (Jer 32.18). Deuteronomy sets another tone, describing God as "the faithful God (*ne'mān*), keeping his covenant of love to a thousand generations of those who love him and keep his commands. But those who hate him he will repay to their face by destruction" (Deut 7.9f). Here God's faithfulness to his covenant is given as the crucial grounds for his showing love (*hesed*). In these texts God's forgiveness comes before his retribution.

That God's compassion has the last word is also attested to in other texts. Thus in Isa 54.8 we read that "In a surge of anger I hid my face from you for a moment, but with everlasting kindness I will have compassion on you." Similarly in Ps 30.6: "For his anger lasts only a moment, but his favor lasts a lifetime." And the petitioner in Hab 3.2 can ask God: "In wrath remember mercy." The beginning of Hosea presents a very explicit development of this tension-filled relationship: Hosea is to call his "child of prostitution" *lô ruhāmāh*, "Without-Mercy," "for I will no longer show mercy to the house of Israel" (Hos 1.6). But we then read, "Yet I will show love ..." (2.1[1.7]), and in the envisioned future the name will be changed to *ruhāmāh*, "Mercy" (2.3[1]).

Irrespective of the question whether this indicates different stages in the development of the text, the message of the text of Hosea to the reader is: ultimately God will have mercy.

3.3.2 God is jealous and angry

God is a "zealous God" (*'ēl qannā'*, Ex 20.5b; Deut 5.9b; Josh 24.19 etc.). This means God is zealous for his cause. In the Decalogue the concern is with the fundamental commandment not to worship other gods; any contravention of this arouses God's "jealousy" (*qin'āh*, cf. Num 25.11; Deut 29.19) and his anger (Deut 9.19; 29.26f). Here the divine jealousy is directed "inwards," i.e. against those to whom this commandment has been given and who still act against it.

But God's "jealousy" can also be focused on something quite different. Thus in Isaiah the proclamation of a new ruler concludes with the solemn sentence: "The jealousy [NIV: zeal] of YHWH Zebaot will accomplish this" (Isa 9.7). Here the thing that God is jealous (or zealous) about is the future restoration of a kingdom in Jerusalem in accordance with his will. The same formulaic sentence underlines the promise that a "remnant" will remain in Jerusalem (Isa 37.31f; 2 Kgs 19.31). We are not told here what form this zeal of God's will take. In other texts, however, this zeal assumes military features. Thus in the metaphor of God as a warrior, we are told that he "awakens" his zeal (Isa 42.13), or that in addition to putting on righteousness like a breastplate and salvation like a helmet, he puts on zeal like a cloak (59.17); in another passage the petitioner asks what has become of God's zeal and his heroic strength (*gebûrāh*, 63.17). In a further metaphor there is talk of the "fire of my/your zeal" (Ezek 36.5; Zeph 1.18; 3.8; Ps 79.5).

This warlike and fiery jealousy (expressed also by the verb *qn'* pi.), can be directed "inwards" against Israel and "outwards" against Israel's enemies. God certainly does not act arbitrarily in this, but it is also evident from the texts what it is that God is zealous about. When this zeal is directed against Israel then this is generally justified by its transgression of the Decalogue commandment not to worship other gods; the anger of the "zealous God" (Ex 20.5; Deut 5.9) is constantly directed against his people Israel or against particular groups in this people when they transgress this commandment. This is expressed particularly pointedly in Ezekiel: because Jerusalem has defiled God's sanctuary with its idols he will vent his anger on it "so that they will know that I, the Lord, have spoken in my zeal" (Ezek 5.13). In the great similes of Jerusalem as unfaithful wife the talk of God's jealousy takes on another special slant: God himself as the jilted husband will judge Jerusalem (16.38, 42) and punish her (23.25). But in this same book of Ezekiel we see the other side too: God directs his zeal against Edom because it has attacked Israel (35.11; 36.5f); and when God finally turns the fate of Jacob and has pity on him, he will do this because he is zealous for his "holy name" (39.25). It is made clear here that God's zeal is closely connected with his holiness, so that one might even speak of his "zealous holiness" (*Eiferheiligkeit,* von Rad 1962, 216ff).

In Zephaniah talk of God's zeal is linked to the anticipation of the "day of the Lord." This will be the "day of the wrath of the LORD, when the 'fire of his zeal' will consume everything" (Zeph 1.18; 3.8). But this will at the same time be the turning-point. This fire will be like a purifying fire and God will afterwards leave a purged "remnant of Israel" behind, "a humble and poor people that seeks its refuge in the name of the LORD" (3.12f). In Joel the description of the "day of the Lord" tells us that God will "be zealous for his land" (Joel 2.18) and in Zechariah, "I am zealous for Jerusalem and Zion with great zeal" (Zech 1.14) "and with great anger" (8.2). As before in Ezekiel, after it has brought judgment on Israel, God's jealousy will be directed entirely to a prosperous future.

So this is the common point of departure for all the various, often apparently mutually contradictory expressions of the "jealousy" and anger of God: that God is zealous for his cause, for his "holy name," that he should be acknowledged and worshiped as the only God, and thus also for Israel, but for an Israel that remains faithful to its calling, its being chosen by God out of all the nations as *his* people. Here lies the reason why God's zeal is constantly directed against Israel: because Israel keeps forgetting its calling and is unfaithful to it and thereby threatens to remove the foundation for God's relationship with his people. So God's zeal is directed towards restoring this foundation and to letting Israel become fully his people again, albeit in the form of a "remnant" (cf. 2000a).

3.3.3 God is righteous

The tension between the compassion and the anger of God constantly leads to the complaining and accusing question: Why? Many psalmists ask this (Pss 10.1; 22.2; 74.1, 11 etc.). Most have no answer to offer; all that remains to them is the request that God should intervene: "Arise, O Lord" (10.12); "Awake, O Lord! Why do you sleep?" (44.24); or even "Rescue me and deliver me in your righteousness"

(71.2). The word "righteousness" (*ṣᵉdāqāh*) here means the divine rescue of the petitioner out of his distress; the petitioner will later tell of this, and he also calls this righteousness "help" (*tešû'āh*, v. 15). Here God's "righteousness" is thus his helping, saving action. In this sense the word can also be supplemented and extended with other words. Alongside the "help" there is talk of his "truth" (*'emûnāh*), "goodness" (*ḥesed*) and "faithfulness" (*'emet*) (Ps 40.1; cf. Crüsemann 1976). There is a veritable stacking-up of terms here in the description of God's action, and each of them adds another aspect within the framework of the psalmist's view of God.

The hope of a helpful, saving righteousness of God is oriented to the future. But even when the help seems delayed or absent, the certainty that God is just proves stronger. This appears with particular impressiveness in several prayers of repentance out of the oppressed, hopeless situation after the Babylonian exile. Ezra's great prayer of repentance in Ezra 9 ends with the confession: "O Lord God of Israel, you are righteous (*ṣaddîq 'attāh*)! We are left (*niš'arnû*) this day as a remnant (*pᵉlêṭāh*)" (v. 15, cf. also vv. 8, 13, 14). That God is righteous is, as it were, the key to the understanding of the history of Israel who in the form of the company of survivors, the "remnant," are now faced with a new probationary test (v. 14). The confession-like character of the statement "you are righteous" comes even more strongly to expression in the second great prayer of repentance in Neh 9. Here the first, foundational stage in the history of God's dealings with Israel is first sealed, as it were, in the election of Abraham, the covenant agreement and the promise of the land with the sentence: "For you are righteous" (v. 8). There then follows an account of the history of God's leading of Israel which is constantly frustrated by Israel's disobedience and contrariness (vv. 16, 26, 28, 29), until finally God delivers them into the hands of the "peoples of the lands" (v. 30). In this situation the prayer again confesses "You are righteous" (v. 33). That God is righteous forms the continuum of the history of God and his people from its happy beginnings through to the desperate present of the praying community (cf. 1997d). In the third related prayer of repentance in Dan 9, too, we read: "For the LORD, our God, is righteous" (v. 14; cf. also v. 7: "With you, O LORD, is righteousness," cf. v. 16).

The confession that God is righteous stands in a dual context here: First, the praying community's confession of its own guilt forms the dominant theme of these prayers and in each case is expressed in the immediate context of confession of God's righteousness (Ezra 9.15; Neh 9.33; Dan 9.14). Reflected here is a particular tradition of services of repentance and fasting in which the praying community confesses its own guilt and declares God to be righteous (cf. 1 Kgs 8.33ff; 2 Chron 12.6; also Lam 1.18); perhaps the origins lie in cultic "court doxologies" (cf. von Rad 1971; also 1962, 369f; von Rad refers in this context also to Josh 7.19).

At the same time the prayers of repentance speak repeatedly of grateful awareness of God's compassion. In Neh 9.17 the "grace formula" is found, which echoes again in v. 31; in addition there is frequent mention of God's "great compassion" (vv. 27, 28, 31). The prayer in Dan 9 opens with a variant of the "grace formula:" "the great and awesome God, who keeps his covenant of love with all who love him and obey his commands" (v. 4; for the expression "keeper of the covenant and goodness/love," *šomēr habb'rît u'hahesed*, cf. also Deut 7.9; 1 Kgs 8.23; Neh 1.5; 9.32). Trust in God's keeping of his covenant enables the petitioner to call upon him. Then he addresses him as "God of compassion and forgiveness" (v. 9) and at the end we read: "We do not make requests of you because we are righteous, but because of your great mercy" (v. 18).

In the Psalms too God's righteousness or justice is viewed together with his compassion and grace: "The Lord is gracious and righteous; our God is full of compassion (*m'rahēm*)" (Ps 116.5, similarly 112.4). God's righteousness and goodness belong together too: "The LORD is righteous in all his ways and loving (*hasîd*) towards all he has made" (145.17). And finally in Isaiah, Yhwh, the God besides whom there is no god, is called "a righteous and saving God" (*'ēl ṣaddîq ûmôšîaʿ*, Isa 45.21).

Thus the statement that God is righteous adds a further feature to the multifaceted picture of God's qualities. This is also a combining element which together with others makes it evident that none of the "qualities" that can be experienced of God can on its own express who he is. It is only the combined force of this whole complex of experiences that produces a fuller picture; but even this can only provide an incomplete understanding and depiction of God's reality.

3.3.4 God is holy

The "qualities" of God mentioned thus far all relate to God's behavior towards people, especially towards Israel. When God is called (or calls himself) the "Holy One," a broad field opens up, only part of which is directly concerned with God's relations with humans. The closest thing to the aspects treated thus far comes when God sets his holiness in opposition to his wrath: "I will not carry out my fierce anger, nor devastate Ephraim again. For I am God, and not man—the Holy One among you" (Hos 11.9). Here the term holiness justifies "precisely not God's will for justice but his will for salvation" (Wolff 1965, 262). God's zeal for his "holy name" can also find expression in the fact that he turns Jacob's fate and thus proves himself holy "in the eyes of the nations" (Ezek 39.25, 27).

In Isaiah the expression "the Holy One of Israel" (*q'doš yiśrā'ēl*), which is characteristic of the book, appears a number of times in connection with the reproach that Israel has abandoned the Holy One of Israel and rejected his Torah (1.4; 5.24; cf. 5.19; 30.11; 31.1). This contrasts with "the holy God will show himself holy by his righteousness" (5.16). Here God's holiness corresponds to his punitive righteousness. But this is not the last word, but we also find quite different notes: "This is what the Sovereign LORD, the Holy One of Israel, says: 'In repentance and rest is your salvation, in quietness and trust is your strength'" (30.15). In another passage the expectation is expressed that "on that day" the "remnant" of Israel will rely on the Holy One of Israel (10.20; cf. 17.7; 29.19, 23). And in the psalm at the end of the first main section of the book of Isaiah we read: "Shout aloud and sing for joy, people of Zion, for great is the Holy One of Israel among you" (12.6). Here it is clear that God's holiness like his other "qualities" can on the one hand be an occasion for God's wrath and for announcements of judgment, while on the other hand it can appear also in connection with announcements and anticipations of salvation.

The holiness of God appears in quite a different fashion in the great vision granted to Isaiah: God is surrounded by heavenly beings singing his praises: "Holy, holy, holy is the LORD Zebaot. The whole earth is full of his glory (*kābôd*)" (Isa 6.3). This scene recalls Psalm 19, where we read: "The heavens declare the glory of God, the skies proclaim the work of his hands" (v. 2). But the context is quite different here: the psalm responds to the heavenly song of praise with praise of the divine Torah, which has been given to humankind (vv. 8ff); in Isaiah's vision on the other hand the commissioning of the prophet is followed by the terrible message of Israel's stubbornness and the divine judgment that will follow (Isa 6.9ff). Here the holiness of God is directly connected with his wrath. It is only at the end that a view opens up of a possible prosperous future, and the "seed" that is announced here is called "holy" (v. 13).

Then in the second part of Isaiah the title "the Holy One of Israel" turns positive: "Do not be afraid ... I myself will help you ... Your Redeemer (*gō'ēl*) is the Holy One of Israel" (41.14; cf. 43.14; 47.4; 48.17; 49.7; 54.5). Other positive attributes are also connected with this title: "Savior" (*môšîa'*, 43.3), "Creator" (43.15; 45.11; 54.5; cf. 41.20), "the One who chose you" (49.7) and who "endows you with splendor" (55.5). God's holiness has become a marker of his saving action, in the history of Israel thus far, and above all in the future that is to come.

The formulaic statement "be holy, for I am holy" (Lev 11.44, 45; 19.2; 20.26; 21.8) [→**542**] leads into quite a different area. The holiness of God has its counterpart in the holiness of Israel: "You are to be holy to me" (20.26). God has "separated" Israel (*hibdîl*) from the nations "to be your God" (11.45); Israel is therefore to complete the "separation" by distinguishing (*hibdîl*) between pure and impure (20.25). In the first instance this has to do with the narrower area of cultic purity; but it extends beyond this into the broad field of the interhuman behavior which God orders (ch. 19). Israel is to keep God's commandments, for "Do not profane my holy name. I must be acknowledged as holy by the Israelites. I am the LORD, who makes you holy" (22.32). So Ezekiel, finally, can speak of Israel having defiled God's holy name among the nations, so that he himself must restore their holiness (Ezek 36.22f). Here too the concern is with pure and impure; for God will once again purify Israel of its impurities caused by idolatry (v. 25). And God will then "make known (*hôdîa'*) my holy name among my people Israel," so that the nations too will know (*yāda'*) that I the LORD am the Holy One in Israel" (39.7).

In these conceptions, which are ultimately rooted in the cult, the holiness of God is not related to Israel; rather, for its part Israel must behave in such a way that the holiness of God is not compromised but preserved. Only when this does not happen does God himself act against Israel to restore his holiness. The concept of God's holiness thus cannot be fixed to any particular area. Rather, it serves to lend expression to the uniqueness of God by comparison with the heathen world.

4. God is *one*

That God is one, and that he alone is the true God, is beyond any doubt as far as all the authors of the texts and writings of the Hebrew

Bible are concerned. The texts however also reveal that this was disputed among the Israelites at a whole range of different times. This will need to be dealt with in a separate chapter.

At this point one of the fundamental differences between a "Theology of the Old Testament" and a "History of Israelite Religion" emerges. An account of the theology of the Hebrew Bible can and must sketch the disputes about the question of appropriate worship of the one God that have found their way into the texts of the Hebrew Bible. But it will do this from the point of view of the authors of the texts themselves, for whom there is no doubt that Israel, *as Israel*, never worshiped any other gods than this *one* God. "Polytheism," "Polyyahwism" etc. are terms in a history of religions that tries to reconstruct the positions rejected and fought against in the texts of the Hebrew Bible. The religion-historical viewpoint of the modern author is bound to play a part in the reconstruction or even determine it completely. This is where the attraction of such attempts may lie; but at the same time it indicates its limits and justifies the uncertainties and constant fluctuations of such attempts at reconstruction.

There is no indication that more than one God was ever worshiped as "Israel's God" at some (early) time. Even primitive forms of Yhwh religion can only be discerned "against the sense of the present text" (Schmidt 1996, 31). But the texts do clearly reveal that the image of God changed in the course of time, or that different aspects came to the fore. In Genesis we see two quite different points of view. In the first chapters God is depicted as creator of the world and as the God of all humanity: from the quite intimate relations with the first human couple (Gen 1–3), through to the world-embracing catastrophe of the flood (chs. 6–8) and the renewal of God's relationship with humanity in the covenant concluded with Noah (ch. 9), through to the worldwide development of humanity, which is presented in a "table of nations." A brief note indicates that beginnings were made already in this early period at "calling on the name of Yhwh" (4.26); but who is meant by the passive phrase "at that time it was begun" (*'āz hûḥal*), remains open. This line is then continued via the differentiation between the three sons of Noah, where Yhwh is described as the "God of Shem" (9.26), to the call of Abraham, the descendant of Shem, which begins with the words: "Then YHWH spoke to Abram" (12.1). From here on in Genesis God speaks and acts only with Abraham and his direct descendants. The reader now has two quite different viewpoints in front of him or her: Yhwh as the God of all humankind—

and Yhwh as the God of an individual family. But there is no doubt, not for a moment, that this is one and the same God.

In Exodus a new point of view is added. For the first time the term "people of Israel" now appears (first in the expression "people of the Israelites," *'am benê yiśrā'ēl*, Ex 1.9). Moses is to tell the Israelites: "YHWH, the God of your fathers, the God of Abraham, the God of Isaac and the God of Jacob has sent me to you" (3.15). This introduces the subsequently dominant view of Yhwh as the God of Israel; at the same time it is connected backwards and identified with the previous view as the God of the family of Abraham. This connection is presupposed and constantly reformulated in what follows in the entire Hebrew Bible. The first view of God as the Creator and the God of all humankind remains intact and comes expressly to discussion in the most varied contexts.

That God is one is put into words in a highly emphatic manner in the "Hear O Israel" (*Šema' yiśrā'ēl*) of Deuteronomy: "Hear O Israel! YHWH is our God. Yhwh is *one*" (Deut 6.4). How this sentence is to be understood is clearly evident from the wording of the great introductory discourse of Deuteronomy: "YHWH, he is *the* God" (*hā'lohîm*); there is none beside him" (4.35). And once again: "YHWH is *the* God in heaven above and on the earth beneath, none other" (v. 39). In comparatively unambiguous terms this is then expressed again and again in Isa 40ff in particular—right through to the extremely emphatic statement: "I am the LORD, and there is no other. I form the light and create darkness, I bring prosperity and create disaster; I, the LORD, do all these things" (45.6f). Here one must clearly speak of "monotheism," if the term is to be used at all. In a canonical reading these formulations can rightly be understood as the key to the understanding of God in the Hebrew Bible as a whole. Certainly few texts put this so unambiguously into words, but equally certainly there are no texts in the Hebrew Bible which run counter to such an interpretation.

That God is *one* is also stated at the beginning of the Decalogue, Israel's "constitution." Here God's self-presentation is immediately supplemented by the sentence: "You shall have no other gods before me" (Ex 20.3; Deut 5.7). Here it is clear that the unambiguous requirement of exclusive worship of the one and only God has to be reinforced time and again and that deviations and counter-movements have to be rejected and resisted. In quite different ways this problem occupies large parts of the Hebrew Bible. (For detail see further §16.)

§ 16

Israel in Conflict

"Talk of God" has many voices in the Hebrew Bible and it is not infrequently controversial. The tensions and contradictions however lie on quite different planes. The reader of the biblical texts experiences them essentially from the point of view of the author in question. In many cases the authors display a clearly discernible religious and theological profile, from which certain conclusions can be drawn as to the theological interests of the group or institution to which they belong. But there is another plane which is discussed only indirectly in the biblical texts. Through the entire Bible runs the dispute between the authors of the texts or the figures represented by them and the "others" against whom the texts are directed, often argumentatively, often also polemically. They too belong to "Israel," and in many cases they clearly represent the majority. The disputes that become visible in the texts thus bring to expression tensions and contrasts within Israel. This is the intended thrust of the title of this chapter, "Israel in Conflict."

With regard to the Hebrew Bible as a whole we should broaden the question a little further: it is not only a matter of Israel in conflict, but also of people in conflict. This is of course the remarkable thing about the opening chapters of the Bible, that on the one hand people are presented as God's creatures, with all the beautiful and positive things that go with this, but that on the other hand it is reported right from the start that people do not behave in the way intended in God's plan of creation. This produces a change in human living conditions, which already provides the justification for the tension that makes the human an inherently contradictory being. Thus the history of people before God is from the start the history of humans in conflict, and not infrequently in conflict with themselves. We touched on this above in §5.

Here, however, our special concern will now be with Israel in conflict, and this means Israel in conflict with itself and with God. This tension is evident right at the beginning of the history of Israel as a people. First we read twice that the Israelites believe: when Moses tells them that God will lead them out of Egyptian slavery (Ex 4.31), and after the rescue at the Reed Sea (14.31). But immediately after this the narratives about the Israelites' "grumblings" begin (15.24; 16.2; 17.2f) [→50]. This grumbling is directed against Moses, but Moses is quick to see it as resistance against God (17.2). This resistance reaches its climax against God on Sinai, when the Israelites coerce Aaron into making them "another God" (32.1) [→60], as it were "in God's face," in blatant contravention of the commandment that God has given them on Sinai (20.3).

But this is only one side of the story. In the Pentateuch there are only certain parts of the narrative tradition that show Israel in conflict or even in resistance against God's envoys or against God himself. In other regards the bases of the religious tradition of Israel are developed in great breadth, without there being any talk of contradiction or resistance. On the contrary: at key points it is expressly emphasized that the Israelites were united in their assurance that they intended to hear (Ex 19.3; 24.7) and/or obey (19.8; 24.3, 7) the commandments that Moses would proclaim or which were already written down. And the law collections that then follow show at many points that long experience in living with these divine commandments is reflected in them. So when we speak of "Israel" we must first and foremost think of the religious foundations on which this community was established and grew.

The conflict into which Israel gets and which the biblical texts tell us of, is to an essential degree justified in the tension that emerges in any society, especially in any religion, between its premises and foundations on the one hand and their practical application in the everyday life of the community and the individual on the other. One can thus view any community from various sides. (One might think of the extreme contrasts between particular tradition-conscious approaches to Christian dogmatic theology and the polemical representations of the history of the sins of Christianity that are now common.) An attempt will be made in this chapter to focus more closely on some of the contrasts and disputes that come to discussion in the texts.

1. Only *one* God?

One of the key issues in relation to conflict in Israel is the exclusive worship of the *one* God, Yhwh. This question has an elevated position already in the structure of the Hebrew Bible. In the Decalogue the first sentence worded as a commandment, or prohibition, is: "You shall have no other gods beside me" (Ex 20.3; Deut 5.7). Israel's first great crisis comes about through its manufacture and cultic worship of another "god" (Ex 32). On the Israelites' first contact with the land they are to enter on God's instructions and under Moses' leadership, things go so far that there is participation in the cult of the Moabite god Ba'al Pe'or, followed by a divine court case (Num 25). The first phase after the settlement of the Israelites then begins with a turning away to the Canaanite gods, referred to collectively as "Baals" (Judg 2.11 etc.); the goddesses Astarte (2.13) and Asherah (3.7) are also mentioned, both of them similarly in the plural.

In the further course of Israelite history too, this question continues to play a crucial role. The end of the Davidic-Solomonic empire is essentially justified on the basis of Solomon's turning away to "other gods" (1 Kgs 11.4, 10). The phraseology is the same as in the Decalogue (Ex 20.3; Deut 5.7), which is also found repeatedly in Deuteronomy (Deut 6.14; 7.4; 8.19; 13.3, 7f; 18.20 etc.). In Solomon's case the names of other gods are also mentioned, and they are connected with particular foreign nations: Astarte with Sidon, Milcom with the Ammonites (1 Kgs 11.5), Kamosh with the Moabites (v. 7; Molek is insecure in the text, but cf. Lev 18.21; 2 Kgs 23.10 etc.). Here it is clear that the concern is with the gods of other nations; they are also referred to as "foreign gods" (Deut 31.16; 1 Sam 7.3; Jer 5.19 etc.).

A climax is reached in the account of the monarchy with the great dispute between the prophet Elijah and the Baal cult of his time (esp. 1 Kgs 18) [→**137**]. Here too it is in the first place the king, Ahab in this case, who is accused of the cult of Baal, to whom he even had a temple built in the capital Samaria (16.31f). It is expressly emphasized that the Baal cult was introduced by the king's consort, the Phoenician princess Jezebel. But then we see that Elijah has to argue with the "whole people" (18.21ff). He presents the Israelites with an alternative: "If YHWH is God, then serve him; but if Baal, then serve him." The alternative presented here makes it quite clear that the issue is a straight either-or choice. There is no discussion either here or anywhere else in the Hebrew Bible of a mixing of Yhwh with other deities. "Yahweh was never a part-element in stories of gods or constellations of gods" (Lohfink 1985, 25).

The dispute with the Baal cult also marks Israel's and Judah's further history in the bloody removal of Ahab's descendants and the worshipers of Baal by Jehu (2 Kgs 10) [→**135**] as well as the ending of the rule of the usurper Athaliah (ch. 11). And finally the end of Israel (and of Judah) is justified, in summary, by its worship of other gods, its construction of sanctuaries, bringing of sacrifices etc. (2 Kgs 17.7ff) [→**149**]. In these reflections the theological context is also recalled in which this "apostasy" from pure Yahweh worship is to be seen: the leading-out of Egypt, which Israel has forgotten (v. 7), and the covenant that God made with their forefathers and which they have despised (v. 15).

The character of the texts provides its own justification for depicting the history of the monarchy largely in reference to the behavior of the various kings. In the Elijah tradition we see, however, that the worship of Baal that Ahab introduced met with a positive response from the population, which is evident in Elijah's reproach that the Israelites "hop on two crutches" (waver between two opinions) (1 Kgs 18.21). But then the people acknowledge the outcome of the competition between God and the gods (cf. Thiel 1990, 221) with the confession: "YHWH is *the* (i.e. the only) God" (v. 39). The fact that extermination of the dynasty of Omri by Jehu (2 Kgs 9f), undertaken in the name of "zeal for YHWH" (2 Kgs 10.16) also apparently met with "relatively broad acceptance among the population" (Albertz 1992, 243), allows one to conclude that at this time Yhwh worship was undisputed in Israel as a whole.

The frequent indication that the people presented sacrifices on the "high-places" does not necessarily contradict this. The local high-place (*bāmāh*) was in each case the site where Yhwh worship took place until the temple was built in Jerusalem. The narrative of Saul's visit to Samuel is told in quite relaxed terms (1 Sam 9.12-14). Before the erection of the temple, Solomon too sacrifices on the "great high-place" in Gibeon (1 Kgs 3.4ff), and God appears to him and speaks to him there; the "high-place" is therefore valid here as a legitimate site of the Yhwh cult, as is emphasized in the introduction (v. 2; by use of a limiting "only," v. 3 however sets the high-place cult in contrast to Solomon's otherwise exemplary behavior; see below on 1 Kgs 22.44; 2 Kgs 12.4 etc.). But the "high-place" then appears once more when Solomon sets it up for the Moabite god Kamosh (11.7). By this point the term has lost its positive or at least neutral religious connotation.

When David's empire falls apart, following the end of Solomon's reign, in the northern kingdom a cult develops which, in the author's view, lies outside the boundaries of legitimate Yhwh religion. Jeroboam sets up two "Golden Calves," one in Beth-El and one in Dan, with the same words with which Aaron once presented the "Golden Calf" on Sinai: "Here are your gods, O Israel, who brought you up out of Egypt!" (1 Kgs 12.28; cf. Ex 32.4) [→**130**]. He thereby picks up on the darkest hour of Israel's early religion, when in the Sinai everything stood on a knife-edge and only the intervention of Moses was able to save Israel from perishing. From this point of view Israel (in the narrower sense) has taken a wrong path. This is further reinforced by the fact that Jeroboam sets up "high-place houses" for a cult which is clearly presented as an alternative to Jerusalem (vv. 31f). Here the term "high-places" has an unambiguously negative content.

In the course of the history of Judah, in the evaluations of the individual kings we read the almost stereotypical comment that the "high-places" were not removed. This observation often contrasts explicitly with an otherwise positive evaluation of the king concerned (1 Kgs 15.14; 22.43f; 2 Kgs 12.3f; 14.3f; 15.3f, 34f). It is also said in each case (except in 1 Kgs 15.14) that "the people continued to offer sacrifices and burn incense" on the "high-places." Behind these very general comments there may well be memories of local Yhwh cults that were viewed as legitimate and continued to be used before the temple in Jerusalem established itself as the only legitimate cultic site. But there is already another factor at play here: the term generally translated "burn incense" (*qtr* pi.) is always used for illegitimate sacrifices. So these retrospectively formulated comments point to a tendency which was already beginning to develop despite the positive evaluation of the kings concerned.

The cultic high-places then also become the key points in cultic disputes. This begins with Ahaz, of whom we read the introductory comment that he did not "do right in the eyes of the LORD like his father David," but went "on the path of the kings of Israel" (2 Kgs 16.2f) [→**147**]. He adopted foreign cultic customs, the "detestable things of the people which the LORD had driven away before the Israelites," by letting his son "pass through the fire" (on this cf. Albertz 1992, 300), and he "made sacrifices and burned incense on the high-places and on the hills and under every green tree" (v. 4; on this phrase see below). Here the "high-places" are clearly signs of deviation from legitimate Yhwh worship. (We do not, however, learn anything here either about the nature of the cult conducted there; still it is striking that the cult on the "high-places" is never expressly connected with the worship of other gods. Nor do we learn anything about the cult at the altar set up by Ahaz on an Assyrian model [16.10-16].)

So it seems only consistent that in his grandly conceived cult reform the first thing Hezekiah does is to dismantle the "high-places" (18.4). Manasseh, for his part, begins his counter-reform by rebuilding the "high-places which his father Hezekiah had destroyed" (21.3). He is said, further, to have built altars for Baal. This places Manasseh in a series with Athaliah and thereby also with the northern Israelite dynasty of Omri (see above on 2 Kgs 9–11). Alongside Baal and Asherah, however, the "hosts of heaven" also appear, pointing to Assyrian influence. Evidently one or several altars in the Jerusalem temple are in mind here (vv. 3-5); in the account of Josiah's reform there is mention in very general terms of the removal of "all the articles made for Baal, the Asherah and the hosts of heaven" (23.4).

In this reform of Josiah's (2 Kgs 23) [→**150f**] the high-places are also removed once again. But the talk here is of quite different "high-places," the cult staff also being mentioned. In v. 8a the "priests of the cities of Judah" are mentioned who had carried out sacrifices on the "high-places" and whose "high-places" Josiah now "desecrates." That these are Yhwh priests is evident from the fact that Josiah has them come to Jerusalem, where, though they are not permitted to perform any cultic functions, they are fed "with their brothers" (v. 9). So here the existence of local cultic sites of the Yhwh cult is presupposed, which are not removed until Josiah does so. (In relation to the admission of these "country priests" to cultic service in Jerusalem there is, however, a difference from Deut 18.6-8, according to which they are to be admitted without restriction.) In v. 5, however, there is mention of "pagan priests" ($k^e m \bar{a} rim$) who had once been appointed by the kings of Judah and whose "high-places'" are now destroyed. In addition, various more special high-places are listed as being removed: the "high-places at the gates" (v. 8b, frequently emended to "high-places of the spirits of rams"); the "high-places" built by Solomon for foreign deities (v. 13; cf. 1 Kgs 11.7); the "high-places" built by Jeroboam in Beth-El (v. 15; cf. 1 Kgs 12.32); and finally "all the houses of the high-places in the cities of Samaria," there even being mention of the killing of all the priests of the "high-places" (vv. 19f). Here the distinction between the cultic deviations in Judah and those in Israel is drawn out very clearly.

The account in the books of Kings essentially shows the picture of "official" Israel. In the prophetic books, on the other hand, the religious behavior of people in Israel is a much more prominent topic, both as a community and as individuals. In the majority of the prophets the criticism of Israel's behavior stands in the foreground, as it was this that led to a spoiling of relations with God. The reasons for this disturbance are presented quite differently by the various prophets. For some of them the problem is primarily the exclusive worship of the *one* God, while in other books it is other themes that dominate. Thus Isaiah speaks right from the beginning in very sharp tones of the Israelites having "abandoned the LORD, and rejected the Holy One of Israel" (Isa 1.4 etc.). However, the problem of the worship of other gods is not a topic in Isaiah.

Things are quite different in Hosea. The "prostitution" of Israel, depicted as an unfaithful wife, consists in the fact that she does not acknowledge that it is Yhwh who has given her her corn, wine and oil (Hos 2.10), but forgets him and turns to the "Baals" (v. 15). Israel's turning to "other gods" (3.1) is the central theme of Hosea, which he varies a number of times. He speaks of Baal (13.1), the Canaanite god, with whom the prophet Elijah (1 Kgs 18) and later king Jehu (2 Kgs 10) were in conflict; but he also uses the plural "Baals" (2.16; 11.2), which appears to be used to summarize foreign gods (cf. 3.1; cf. Albertz 1992, 271 n.115). Hosea characterizes them as "idols" made by hands (8.4; 13.2), as "images" (11.2; cf. 13.2) and speaks disparagingly of "wood" and "sticks" which Israel consults (4.12). Also the "calf" of Beth-El (10.5f, corrupted as Beth-Awen, "house of distress" or "of wickedness," cf. Amos 5.5), the state sanctuary of Samaria (8.5), is subjected to the criticism of the prophet; after all it too has only been made by a craftsman, so it is no God. And if the Israelites also sacrifice on the mountains and hills (4.13) and build many altars and Massebahs (8.11; 10.1), these will be destroyed (10.2). Hosea words his criticism in very radical terms: Israel can sacrifice as much meat as it wants, God takes no "pleasure" in it (8.13); what "pleases him," rather, are love (*ḥesed*) and "knowledge of God" (*da'at ʾlohîm*, 6.6). Here Hosea turns cultic terms ("to be pleasing," *rāṣāh* and *ḥāpaṣ*) into their opposites.

In Jeremiah too, the Israelites' occupation with other gods is one of the central themes. Thus right at the beginning we read of "their wickedness in forsaking me, in burning incense to other gods and in worshiping what their hands have made" (Jer 1.16). From Jeremiah's point of view this began right at the start of the history of Israel, when the "fathers" did not ask "Where is the LORD, who brought us up out of Egypt?" but instead turned to other gods (2.5f) [→**207**]. Jeremiah frequently speaks in the plural of the "other gods" (1.16; 7.6, 9, 18 etc.) and of "foreign gods" (5.19); he describes them as "worthless" (*hebel*,

2.5; 8.19; 10.3, 15 etc., in 8.19 "worthless foreign idols") of wood and stone (2.27; 3.9); they are useless (2.8, 11), like a scarecrow in a field of cucumbers (10.5). Above all, these are gods that Israel does not know (7.9), i.e. which do not belong to the faith tradition that Israel has learned from preceding generations. But it is not just anonymous "gods;" Jeremiah also names names: above all Baal (2.8; 7.9; 11.13, 17; 19.5 etc.); it is evident here that the Baal cult also plays a role in the southern kingdom of Judah. In addition Jeremiah also speaks of domestic worship of the "queen of heaven" (the Babylonian Ishtar, 7.17f; cf. 44.17-19, 25) and of the cultic worship of the sun, moon and the hosts of heaven (8.2; cf. 19.13). The "high-places" again play a part (17.3; 19.5; cf. 7.31); there are altars and Asherahs there (17.2). The "high-places" appear especially in the metaphor of the "prostitution" that Israel commits "on every high hill and under every green tree" (2.20; 3.6-8, 13; 17.2).

As in Hosea, Jeremiah's critique leads to severe censure of the current cultic practice in the temple: the temple service is useless when the "living and doing" contradicts the divine commandments (7.2ff). Social demands also come into view here (vv. 5f). Jeremiah announces even that God will deal with the temple in Jerusalem as he once did with the temple in Shiloh (vv. 12-15). And he heightens the alternative so that he can say that it was not sacrifices that God ordered when he led the forefathers out of Egypt, but obedience to his word (vv. 21-23).

In Ezekiel too the cultic worship of other gods is in the foreground. He speaks first of the situation that has become the occasion for the destruction of Jerusalem and the leading of its inhabitants into exile: Jerusalem has desecrated God's sanctuary with "abominations" (*šiqqûṣîm*) and "detestable things" (*tô''bôt*, Ezek 5.11) [→**238**]; on the cultic high-places are altars and facilities for burnt offerings (6.3-6) which Israel has set up for its "idols" (*gillûlîm*). In these drastic expressions Ezekiel speaks of the foreign gods but mentions no names. In the great historical sketches in chs. 16, 20 and 23 the concern is essentially with Israel's or Jerusalem's and Judah's relationship to other gods; cf. also 14.1-11; 18.6, 12, 15. Ezekiel announces that God will ultimately bring the "abomination" that Israel has committed upon the people themselves (7.3, 4, 8, 9). In the vision Ezekiel is transported into the ruined Jerusalem, where he is shown what "abominations" are currently occurring there: he sees an "idol of provocation" with an altar (8.3b, 5), women mourning for Tammuz, and men worshiping the sun (v. 16). But Ezekiel promises that God himself will finally purify Israel of all the impurities (36.25; 37.23) and restore the pure sanctuary (chs. 40ff).

The critical view of Israel's cultic behavior in the historical accounts and the prophetic books shows only one side of the picture, however. The Psalms present quite a different view. This applies both to the public realm and to the personal life of individuals. One could generalize and say that the Psalms represent the public cult and private piety from which those who are the focus of critical accounts and prophetic critique deviate. Thus in the contrast between these different bodies of literature the conflict *within* Israel comes to expression.

The Psalms reveal nothing of a critical attitude towards the kings. Rather, these are involved entirely in the Israelite cult. This is very impressively evident in Ps 132, for instance, where the king participates as God's "anointed one" (*māšî'ḥ*, v. 10) in a cultic ritual with the Ark; cf. also Ps 2; 110 etc. The praying community requests that God will hear his anointed one and remember his sacrifices (20.7, 4). Where the voice of the king himself is heard, it is a matter of thanksgiving for rescue from oppression by enemies (Ps 18 etc.), but also for equipping him with the capacity to act justly (Pss 72; 101 etc.). Nowhere is there any talk of cultic aberrations by the kings; indeed, even the marriage of a king with a foreign princess is celebrated (Ps 45, esp. vv. 11-13).

The psalmists themselves are clearly not among those who are criticized by the prophets either; in fact, they are vigorously opposed to these people. These are the "fools" (14.1), even the "ungodly" (*r°šā'îm*, 10.4) who say, "There is no God." The psalmists themselves often display a deep piety and firm confidence in God. They count themselves among the "righteous" (*ṣaddîqîm*, 5.13; 7.10; 14.5 etc.; cf. 1.5f) or the "pious" (*ḥasîdîm*, 4.4; 12.2; 16.10 etc.). The conflict lies in particular in the fact that the "pious" feel persecuted by the ungodly, the wicked. They are thus also referred to as the "poor," using various terms (*'ebyôn, 'ānî, 'ānāw*, 9.13, 19; 10.2; 12.6 etc.). Where more detail is given, it is largely a question of disputes in the social arena (on this see §16.2). So these psalmists present a side of the picture of "Israel" that is not the target of prophetic critique.

2. Justice and righteousness

The picture is similar with regard to the second important area of the conflict within Israel, which might be described by the double term "justice and righteousness." In the summary characterization of David's reign (2 Sam 8.15; cf. 1 Kgs 3.6) and Solomon's reign (1 Kgs 10.9 on the lips of the Queen of Sheba), the ideal image of the Israelite ruler is marked by these terms. This ideal doubtless underlies the evaluations of the kings of Israel and Judah, who are compared with David (1 Kgs 15.11; 2 Kgs 14.3; 16.2; 18.3; 22.2) [→145]. In Isaiah the image of a future ideal king is described in these terms (Isa 9.6; 11.3-5; cf. 32.1) [→175f].

In Isaiah, however, we also see that this theme is by no means limited to the area of the king's reign. Zion was once full of justice and righteousness (Isa 1.21), and it is to be redeemed by means of justice and righteousness and then be called once again "city of righteousness" (Isa 1.26). But justice and righteousness are now absent, as is graphically lamented in the parable of the vineyard (5.7). It is evident here that Isaiah sees one of the main problems in current Israelite society in the fact that justice and righteousness do not reign. The next verse makes an especially important point: "Woe to you who add house to house and join field to field till no space is left and you live alone in the land" (5.8). Obviously individuals succeed in acquiring other people's land, thereby fundamentally changing the given equality-based property relationships. The same reproach is raised by Micah: "They covet fields and seize them, and houses, and take them. They defraud a man of his home, a fellow-man of his inheritance" (Mic 2.2).

Amos too makes accusations that point in the same direction: the economically advantaged oppress others and exploit them (Amos 2.6; 5.11; 8.6) [→280]. Characteristic terminology is used here: the oppressed are described as "poor" (*'ebyôn*, 2.6; 4.1; 5.12; 8.4, 6; *'ānî*, 8.4; *'ānaw*, 2.7; 8.4) and "insignificant, weak" (*dal*, 2.7; 4.1; 5.11; 8.6), but also as "righteous" (*ṣaddîq*, 2.6; 5.12). Group conflicts within Israelite society find expression here which represent a clear infringement of the premises for inter-personal relationships set out in the Torah.

Once again in the Psalms we see the picture from the other side. In many cases the psalmists themselves or those in whose name they speak are described as the poor and insignificant; these are the same adjectives that Amos uses for the oppressed and persecuted. It is said of them that they suffer violence (paradigmatically Pss 70; 12.6; 35.10;

37.14; 82.4 etc.). They are also called the righteous, and the oppressors the "ungodly," i.e. evildoers, the wicked (*rʾšāʿîm*); the two are often directly juxtaposed (7.10; 11.2f, 5; 31.18f; 37.12, 32 etc.). Once again, the psalmists are not among those criticized by the prophets; they are precisely those to whom injustice is done by others.

Finally the opposition between the "righteous" and the "ungodly" in the wisdom literature again appears from another perspective. The alternative is not viewed from a situation of persecution and suffering here, but from the point of view of those who as "righteous" are certain of God's help. The contrast with the wicked plays a fundamental role here too. This alternative is already expounded in Psalm 1. In Proverbs [→**365**] it occurs in multiple variations: "The righteousness of the upright delivers them, but the unfaithful are trapped by evil desires" (Prov 11.5); "the house of the righteous contains great treasure, but the income of the wicked brings them trouble" (15.6; cf. von Rad 1970, 172; Westermann 1990a, 91-101). Here this certainty is developed in a rather didactic way, and no audible doubts are raised about it within the book of Proverbs. But doubts were not always absent, as the books of Job and Qohelet impressively show, in their different ways.

3. Israel must turn around

Thus the conflict within Israel proves to be a theme that appears in many different contexts and from a wide variety of perspectives. But it is not enough that this conflict is complained about or opposed. Again and again the question is raised, how it might be overcome. The central term for what must happen is "turning" or "repentance" (especially with use of the Hebrew verb *šûb*).

Israel must repent—this is the heart of the prophetic message. In retrospect on the history of Israel and Judah during the monarchy we are given the summary: "The LORD warned Israel and Judah through all his prophets and seers: 'Turn from your evil ways. Observe my commands and decrees, in accordance with the entire Law that I commanded your fathers to obey and that I delivered to you through my servants the prophets'" (2 Kgs 17.13). This is how things look in the retrospective account of Israel's history: the prophets constantly warned Israel to keep the Torah given by Moses and called the Israelites to repentance when they turned away from it.

When it comes to detail, however, the picture varies greatly between the prophets. It is only rarely that we find the explicit call "Repent!" (Hos 14.2; Jer 3.14; Zech 1.2 etc.). But the theme is present in various ways, both in terms of content and in terms of the language used. The breadth of meaning of the verb *šûb* comes into play here. Thus the name of Isaiah's son Shear-Yashub (*še'ar yāšûb*, "a remnant will repent") is interpreted with reference to the fate of the "remnant of Israel" and the "host of exiles of the house of Jacob" (Isa 10.20): "A remnant will return, a remnant of Jacob will return to the Mighty God" (*'ēl gibbôr*, v. 21). Repentance and return are very close here, in fact they merge into one another. In Isa 1.27 [→169] too, the two connotations are present: "Zion will be redeemed with justice, her penitent ones (or: returnees) with righteousness." Using the example of a wife's return to her first husband (impossible with humans), Jeremiah shows that repentance also means return (Jer 3.1; cf. Hos 2.9). But repentance is also a turning away: "So turn from your evil ways, each one of you, and reform your ways and your actions" (Jer 18.11; 25.5); at the same time it is active turning away (of one's face, *šûb* hiphil) from sins (Ezek 14.6) or from idols (18.30), which finds appropriate expression here in the word-play *šûbû wᵉhāšîbû* ("turn around and turn away").

But repentance is above all turning towards God and turning back to God himself. "If you repent, Israel, you turn back to me" (or: "If you want to repent, you may turn back to me," Jer 4.1); "turn to me, for I have redeemed you" (Isa 44.22). In Jeremiah, in the parable of the two baskets of figs we read: "They will return to me with all their heart" (Jer 24.7). Finally the acceptance of this return by God can be expressed as a mutual relationship: "Turn back to me, and I will turn to you" (Zech 1.3; Mal 3.7).

But to begin with, the dominant experience of the prophets is that Israel does not repent. Thus Amos says in the stereotypical repetition of the response poem: "but you have not turned to me" (Amos 4.6, 8, 9, 10, 11) [→282]. In Isaiah we read: "In repentance and rest is your salvation, in quietness and trust is your strength, but you would have none of it" (Isa 30.15). Hosea sounds a note of readiness to repent: "Come, let us return to the LORD. He has torn us to pieces but he will heal us; he has injured us but he will bind up our wounds" (Hos 6.1); but this readiness is like mere morning mist and like the early dew that disappears (v. 4).

Thus a full repentance remains the object of promise and hope. The ideas of repentance and return link together, as for example in Deut 30.1-5, where the great historical sketch of ch. 28 is brought to its conclusion. (In Lev 26.40-45, where there is also talk of the critical turning-point, the terminology of repentance and return is not to be found.) But nowhere is there any talk of a definitively completed repentance on Israel's part. Rather, in post-exilic prophecy too the call to repentance is raised; here it is combined with the remembrance of the forefathers who did not repent: "Repent ... Do not be like your forefathers" (Zech 1.3f; cf. Mal 3.7). Finally the promise of return is once again given a new emphasis when we read that God himself will return to Zion (Zech 1.16; 8.3).

Preliminary remarks to §§ 17-19

Three settings in life in Old Testament literature

One of the reasons for the often confusing variety of texts in the Hebrew Bible lies in its varied *Sitz im Leben*. What we mean by this is the various life-situations in which the texts came into being and for which they were intended. The first two main parts of the Bible, the Pentateuch and the "Former Prophets," essentially contain narrative and legislative texts. Generally speaking, the modern reader does not find these difficult to access, the detailed problems of understanding and interpretation aside. Things change fundamentally when the reader leaves this area. The conclusion of the books of Kings in the Bible is followed by the book of Isaiah: after information on the situation of the Judahite king Jehoiachin, in captivity in Babylon (2 Kgs 25.27-30), comes the cry: "Hear, O heavens. Listen O earth!" The reader is entering another world, that of *prophetic* literature.

The reader of an English translation of the Bible meets the change in a different way: from the book of Esther (in the Protestant tradition) or from 2 Maccabees (in the Catholic tradition) to the book of Job. Here the reader enters the world of *wisdom* literature. While prophetic literature contains many echoes of ideas and themes in the first two sections of the Hebrew Bible, these are almost entirely absent in wisdom literature. A further change occurs when the reader comes to the book of Psalms. (The reader of the Hebrew and Jewish Bible comes directly from the prophets to the Psalms.) Here the reader enters the world of prayer and liturgy. The themes are different again, especially in the prayers of individual pious persons in which their own situations of distress and problems with faith take center stage.

The next three chapters intend to draw attention to these varied realms of life that find their voice in the Hebrew Bible and which contribute in a fundamental way to the breadth and depth of biblical statements. There will be many references to matters already discussed in detail at different points above, so that these chapters can be kept concise.

§ 17

Prophecy

This chapter begins with an excursus which brings together some comments on terminology in relation to prophets, prophetic speech and behavior, which may additionally shed light on some of the things discussed above in this book. See in particular the "Interlude: Continuity and Discontinuity in Old Testament Prophecy" (pp. 157ff).

Excursus: Terminology of prophets and prophetic speech

The word "prophet" is derived from the Greek προφήτης. This word is used throughout the Septuagint to translate the Hebrew *nābî'* (and correspondingly the feminine προφῆτις to translate *n'bî'āh*) and also for the terms *ro'eh* "seer" and *ḥozeh* "visionary." In application to prophetic figures the term *'îš 'elohîm* ("man of God") is also found in the Hebrew. These terms are often used alongside one another, not infrequently in relation to the same person. This overlap has occasionally led to interpretive notes. Thus in 1 Sam 9 for instance Samuel is first referred to by the epithet "man of God" (vv. 6-8, 10) and later as "seer" (vv. 11, 18); he also applies the latter term to himself (v. 19). In between there is the explanatory comment: "Formerly in Israel, if a man went to enquire of God, he would say, 'Come, let us go to the seer,' because the prophet of today used to be called a seer" (v. 9). So here the terms "man of God," *nābî'* and "seer" are interpreted in terms of each other.

In other circumstances the expressions *ḥozeh* and *nābî'* are equated. The priest Amaziah in Beth-El addresses Amos as *ḥozeh*: "Get out, you seer! Go back to the land of Judah." Amos retorts: "I was neither a prophet nor a *ben-nābî'* (prophet's disciple)" (Amos 7.12-14). Here the terms *ḥozeh* and *nābî'* are tacitly equated. Amaziah defines the term *ḥozeh* also by using the verbal forms of the root *nb'*, which indicates various ways in which the *nābî'* appears (see below). So a *hozeh* can also act like a *nābî'*.

That there was no uniform terminology for the "prophets" is also clear in a number of narratives in which various terms are used for the same person. Thus in 1 Kgs 20 there is first talk of a *nābî'* but he remains anonymous (v. 13); on his next appearance he is described as "the *nābî'*" (v. 22). As the narrative progresses we see that this is the same prophet who in v. 28 is called "the man of God." Later "one of the *bᵉnê hann'bî'îm*, the "disciples of the prophets" appears (v. 35), who is called "the *nābî'*" in the subsequent text (v. 38). Finally the king acknowledges that he was "of the *n'bî'îm*" (v. 41). In this chapter, then, on the one hand the terms *nābî'* and "man of God" are used as synonyms but on the other hand a member of the *bᵉnê hann'bî'îm* group (see below) can also be called simply *nābî'*. (On the odd contrast between "prophet" and "man of God" in 1 Kgs 13 cf. Blum 2000b.)

This leads us to the question of the relationship between prophetic groups and individual prophets. The texts do not provide a uniform and unambiguous answer to this either. The whole history of prophecy is dominated by the prophetic personalities that appear individually. But a number of times some of them have a rather close relationship with prophetic groups. Samuel, who always works on his own, appears as the "president" of a "conventicle" of prophets (1 Sam 19.20) and he has previously prepared Saul for his encounter with a similarly ecstatic "host of prophets" (10.5f). Elijah appears as the great loner; but in the last act of his ministry we suddenly meet groups of *bᵉnê hann'bî'îm* who are well informed as to his imminent ascension (2 Kgs 2.3, 5). Elijah had himself already complained that he alone remained of the "prophets of Yhwh" (1 Kgs 18.22; 19.2); to judge by this his isolation was not of his own volition. Elisha has a closer, regular connection with the *bᵉnê hann'bî'îm*. They form an order-like community with a communal assembly room in which they "sit before Elijah" (2 Kgs 6.1f), and with communal meals (4.38-41). Their description as *bᵉnê*, literally "sons of," here indicates adherence to a group of *n'bî'îm*, so that it is possible to speak of "members of a group of prophets;" the term "disciples of the prophets" is frequently used too. Elisha often appears on his own, however (e.g. 2 Kgs 5), and he can be described as "the *nābî'* who is in Samaria" (2 Kgs 5.3) and even as "the *nābî'* in Israel" (5.8; cf. 6.12).

So we cannot assume there was a fundamental distinction or even division between individual prophets and groups of prophets; they may indeed belong closely together. One may thus suspect that in many cases the individual prophetic figures were special personalities who stood out from the group of *nᵉbî'îm* and also appeared on their own, without giving up their connection to the group entirely. Occasionally however an individual *nābî'* is confronted by a group of *nᵉbî'îm*, as in 1 Kgs 22. The *nᵉbî'îm*, a four-hundred-strong group, are assembled to "seek the counsel of YHWH" (vv. 5f). Under the leadership of a president, singled out by the mention of his name (v. 11), they all "prophesy" (v. 11) (see below) as the king requires (vv. 10, 12, cf. v. 6). Their close connection with the king or even dependence on him is clear from the narrative and is also expressed by reference to "his" or "your prophets" (vv. 22f). Micaiah ben Imlah confronts them alone. He is expressly described as "still a prophet of YHWH" through whom one can "inquire" of Yhwh (vv. 7f). So the difference lies neither in the title nor in the fundamental qualification for declaring the will of God, but in the content of what the prophet in question announces. This also raises the question of "true" and "false" prophets.

The activity of prophets is occasionally described by the use of the verb that derives from the noun *nābî'*, the root of which, *nb'*, is found only in the niphal and the hithpael (cf. 1960, 797). It has a broad range of meaning: in 1 Sam 10.5f, 10f, 13 the hithpael designates the ecstatic behavior of the *nᵉbî'îm*, which also affects Saul as the "spirit of Yhwh/God" comes upon him (*rûᵃḥ yhwh/'elohîm*, vv. 6, 10). The same thing is repeated later on, when Saul's envoys are also affected (19.20f, 23f). The niphal is used twice in these texts, when people who are not (yet) affected observe the ecstatic things that are going on (10.11; 19.20). In 1 Kgs 18.29 the niphal indicates the continuing efforts of the prophets of Baal to get their god to hear them. Finally Saul's attempt to murder David in 1 Sam 18.9f is viewed as the consequence of a *hitnabbē'* caused by the "evil spirit from God;" so here the verb has come into its own as a term for "madness" in contrast to the prophetic phenomenon. (Cf. also Num 11.25-27.)

Only once in the books of the "former prophets" does the verb also indicate prophetic speech: in 1 Kgs 22 the hithpael (v. 8) and the niphal (v. 12) are used for the words of the various prophets. In the same context, in v. 10 the action of the *nᵉbî'îm* "before" the kings is described as *hitnabbē'*, which finds visible expression in Zedekiah's sign-act (v. 11). So here the various aspects of prophetic activity are expressed by the verb. It clearly means "to act or speak as (or like) a prophet."

In the prophetic books (cf. 1960, 804-807) the terms *ro'eh* "seer" and *'îš 'elōhîm* "man of God" are not found for the various "writing prophets," and *ḥozeh* "visionary" is only once used on the lips of the priest Amaziah (Amos 7.12, see above). The relationship of the prophets or the authors to the title *nābî'* remains ambiguous. One should bear in mind that the title is used overwhelmingly in a narrative context, so that one would in any case expect it to appear less frequently in collections of prophetic sayings. Hosea is described as a *nābî'* by his opponents, though the title *per se* does not seem to be used pejoratively (Hos 9.7f). Amos rejects the title in application to himself, as well as the term *ben-nābî'* (Amos 7.14); but it is not made clear whether this implies that he wishes to distance himself from bearers of this title, especially since Amos himself takes up the verb *nb'* (in the niphal) as a term for his prophetic activity (vv. 15f, see below). Isaiah is described as a *nābî'* only in chs. 37–39 (Isa 37.2; 38.1; 39.3); the term *nᵉbî'ah* in 8.3 clearly refers to Isaiah's wife, but no conclusions can be drawn from this as to Isaiah's own relationship with this title (and none as to any prophetic function on the part of Isaiah's wife). In Jeremiah the positive use of the title is quite unambiguous. He is called by God as *nābî'* for the people (Jer 1.5), and elsewhere too Jeremiah is often referred to by this title, especially in narrative contexts (e.g. 28.5f, 10f; 29.1). In Ezekiel too the title *nābî'* appears with very positive emphasis in the call vision (Ezek 2.5; cf. 33.33). Finally it is used in the Book of the Twelve in Habakkuk, Haggai and Zechariah, right from the introduction, as well as elsewhere in the same work (Hab 1.1; 3.1; Hag 1.1, 3, 12; 2.1, 10; Zech 1.1, 7). So overall one may say that the title *nābî'* does not appear with any frequency in reference to the writing prophets, but that with the exception of Amos 7.14 there are no indications of a rejection or conscious avoidance of the title.

The prophetic books also use the title *nābî'* in a positive sense for other prophets. This happens twice in the singular. Hos 12.14[13] reads: "The Lord used a prophet to bring Israel up from Egypt, by a prophet he cared for him;" the reference is of course to Moses. In Mal 3.23, right at the end of the canon of the prophets, there is talk of the return of the *nābî'* Elijah. Moses and Elijah are thus the two great prophetic figures that the writing prophets look back to.

Frequently there is talk of the *n'bî'îm*, in the plural, in a positive sense. God had to "cut you in pieces with my prophets" as a punitive measure in Israel's upbringing (Hos 6.5) and spoke through the prophets time and again (12.11). He called the *n'bî'îm* and Nazirites, but they were impeded in their work by the Israelites (Amos 2.11f). We also find the formula familiar from the historical books that God acts and speaks through "his servants, the prophets" (Amos 3.7; Jer 7.25; 25.4 etc.; Ezek 38.17: "prophets of Israel"). Jeremiah sees himself in a long series of prophets of disaster and it is thus that he demonstrates his legitimacy (Jer 28.8). Zechariah, finally, speaks of the "former prophets" (*n'bî'îm rišonîm*) who called the forefathers to repentance, and calls them God's servants (Zech 1.4-6; 7.7, 12).

Besides the above there are a number of texts in which the *n'bî'îm* are spoken of critically or negatively. In Hos 4.5 the *nābî'* is mentioned alongside the priest in a message of disaster, though without further justification. Similarly, in Isaiah the *nābî'* appears alongside other functionaries and dignitaries (Isa 3.1-3; 9.13f; 28.7ff; 29.10); in 9.14 it is said that the *nābî'* "teaches lies." 28.7ff evidently presents a polemic by priests and prophets against Isaiah. Micah accuses the *n'bî'îm* of being open to bribery (Mic 3.5-7, 11). The argument going on in these texts has scarcely any institutional traits, as is often assumed. The named *n'bî'îm* cannot be taken to be incumbents of an office that differs fundamentally from that of the writing prophet who is speaking.

In Jeremiah the argument with the *n'bî'îm* is broad in scope (cf. Auld 1984). Two things are clear here. For one thing, Jeremiah constantly sees himself as an individual in opposition to a large number or group of other people who claim to have the same task or the same office as he does; occasionally this argument leads to a direct confrontation with a single representative of this other group (Jer 28). Second, despite all the oppositions it is not clear that Jeremiah himself sees his own task and the office of these *n'bî'îm* as something fundamentally different. The problem is really the legitimacy of the mission. The most common reproach is that the *n'bî'îm*'s prophecy lies (*šeqer*, 5.31; 6.12; 14.13f etc.). They speak in the name of Yhwh, even though he has not sent them (14.14f; 23.21, 32 etc.). Their words are dreams (23.25-32). They preach *šālôm*, peace (6.14; 14.13; 29.8-10), whereas Jeremiah has to announce the opposite. So the concern here is not with two different forms of prophecy but with whether the prophecy in each case is "true" or "false." The confrontation between Jeremiah and Hananiah in Jer 28 is very similar to that between Micaiah ben Imlah and Zedekiah in 1 Kgs 22. Then in Ezekiel there are quite similar accusations against the *n'bî'îm* (13; 14.1-11).

The verb *nb'*, derived from the noun *nābî'*, in the niphal or the hithpael, is found with particular frequency in Jeremiah (cf. 1960, 796-799). Before Jeremiah it is found only in Amos. In a key statement about his calling as a prophet Amos says: "The Lord YHWH has spoken—who can but be a prophet (or prophesy)?" (Amos 3.8). In the dispute with the priest Amaziah the verb is first found on his lips in his banishment of Amos to Judah (7.12) and in his prohibition against his "prophesying" in Beth-El (v. 13). Amos retorts that this is precisely the task Yhwh has given him to do (v. 15) and announces to Amaziah that God will judge him because of this prohibition (v. 16). In both passages the verb (in the niphal) is a key term for Amos's own prophetic activity. In addition, he reproaches the Israelites for having prevented the prophets God has appointed from "prophesying" (Amos 2.12).

In Jeremiah the verb, like the word *nābî'*, is used both for Jeremiah himself (e.g. 19.14; 20.1; 26.12) and for his opponents. For the latter it is often found in close connection with the noun *n'bî'îm*: "the prophets that prophesy"; as for instance in the reproach that they proclaim "lies" (5.31; 14.14; 23.25 etc.) or that they claim to speak in the name of Yhwh (14.15; 27.15 etc.). In the majority of cases it is clear from the context that the verb indicates prophetic speech, whether legitimate or illegitimate. Thus, the verb is frequently directly linked to the term *dābār* "word"—"speak a prophetic word (or words)" (20.1; 23.16; 26.12; 27.16 etc.)—, or the text says "speak prophetically in the name of Yhwh" (11.21; 14.14f; 23.25; 26.9, 20 etc.). So this verb also shows that the concern is not with an institutional difference between the "writing prophets" and their opponents, but with the question of whom Yhwh has really sent to speak in his name. The considerable potential difficulty in answering this question is again particularly evident in the confrontation between Jeremiah and Hananiah, in which it is divine word against divine word (Jer 28).

In the book of Ezekiel the verb has become a frequently used formulaic element: "Son of man, turn your face against … and prophesy" (6.2; 13.17; 21.2, 7 etc.) or, "Son of man, prophesy … and say" (13.2; 21.14, 33; 30.2 etc.). Here the development of the verbal concept has come to an end and the latter has become a fixed expression for prophetic speech (13.2, 16). The effect of the prophetic word introduced by the verb in Ezek 37 is quite special: on the field of dry bones the prophet must first speak prophetically to the bones (vv. 4, 7), then call the spirit (*rû'ḥ*) of life upon them (vv. 9f), and finally speak over the graves of Israel (v. 12).

The conclusion of the history of the meaning of the verb is strangely ambivalent. On the one hand Joel expects a pouring-out of the divine spirit (*rû'ḥ*) in the time of salvation, which will produce a general prophetic effect (Joel 3.1). On the other hand in Zech 13.2-6 a complete end to prophecy is prophesied for the end-times, and where it persists it will be deemed a shameful crime, worthy of death. Is this passage perhaps a conscious counterpart to Joel 3, according to which prophecy must end when all Israel is filled by the prophetic spirit (Müller 1986, 162f)?

In conclusion the verb *ḥāzāh* "envision" should be mentioned. Apart from Num 24.4-16 this is found only in the prophetic books, independently of the noun *ḥozeh* "visionary," sometimes together with the noun *ḥāzôn* "vision," sometimes without. As a rule it means the reception of divine words, i.e. "hear prophetically." In a series of prophetic books the verb appears in the book's superscription: Isa 1.1; Amos 1.1; Mic 1.1; Hab 1.1. Isaiah "envisions" a "vision," Amos envisions "words," Micah a "word of Yhwh," Habakkuk an "utterance" (*maśśā'*). The noun *ḥāzôn* also appears, without the verb, in the superscriptions Obad 1 and Nah 1.1. In Isaiah the verb *ḥāzāh* is found twice more at significant points in the superscription or introduction: Isa 2.1 and 13.1. It is also used, differently, a few more times in Isaiah, and also in Ezekiel, Micah and Zechariah.

1. The LORD speaks

The first sentence of prophetic speech that has come down to us in the books of the "latter prophets" (the so-called "writing prophets") formulates the crucial and fundamental element of this domain of Old Testament literature: "The Lord speaks" (Isa 1.2). The prophetic books contain almost exclusively speeches, only sporadically supplemented by narrative texts. The large majority of these speeches are formulated as divine speech; it may be God himself speaking, or the prophet may pass on what God says, on his instructions.

This expresses the basic precondition for prophetic self-understanding: the prophet is "called" by God and "sent" to pass on God's word. In the account of the call of Jeremiah we read: "Now, I have put my words in your mouth" (Jer 1.9). This sets the prophets in the succession of Moses, as is expressly stated in Deuteronomy: "I will (time and again) raise up for them a prophet like you from among their brothers; I will put my words in his mouth, and he will tell them everything I command him" (Deut 18.18).

But at the same time the comparison with Moses demonstrates the fundamental difference. The divine words which Moses receives can be divided (broadly) into two clearly distinct categories. First, Moses speaks on God's instructions to particular people directly: to the Israelites during his call phase (Ex 3f), to Pharaoh in the conflict that leads to the exodus from Egypt (Ex 5–11) and once again to the Israelites in the dispute about the Golden Calf (Ex 32–34) and in various situations during the wandering in the wilderness (Ex 16f; Num 11–14 etc.). But the great majority of the divine words that Moses passes on are permanently valid; they become the "Torah of Moses."

The prophets differ fundamentally from Moses at this point. They have no permanently valid commandments or statutes to proclaim. Rather, they stand together with the Israelites to whom their words are directed, within the space delimited by the Torah given through Moses. Here they have the special divine commission constantly to remind Israel of, and call them back to, what is the foundation of its life as the people of God. It is this that all the prophets have in common.

When it comes to the detail, the way in which the prophets perceive this task varies considerably. Each one of them is a personality in his own right, with his own background and biography and with his own experiences. In addition the contemporary political and religious circumstances in which each of the prophets works has a considerable influence on the manner of their appearance and the content of their message. Nonetheless, what unites them is that they know themselves to be those commissioned with conveying the word of God that has been entrusted to them.

2. The prophet passes on the message

How the prophets received the word of God, or how they were sure of receiving it, lies outside our purview. Just occasionally individual prophets give a glimpse of their experiences and emotions on receiving the word. Jeremiah speaks of having "swallowed" God's words (Jer

15.14) but also of God wanting to make his words burn in Jeremiah's mouth (5.14); Ezekiel tells us that God gave him a scroll to eat, and that this was as sweet as honey in his mouth (Ezek 2.8–3.3). These texts add color to the events, but no not make them more "understandable" as far as the present-day reader is concerned. When finally we read "Is not my word like fire, and like a hammer that breaks a rock in pieces?" (Jer 23.29) it is clear that the reception and transmission of the divine words is anything but a purely intellectual affair as far as the prophet is concerned.

But it is important to the prophets to mark the words they pass on to their hearers as a previously divine message (on the following discussion cf. 1983, 123ff). This occurs for instance with the "messenger formula" "Thus says the Lord," which is found already in the words of Moses (Ex 4.22; 5.1; 7.17 etc.), but then especially in Jeremiah (Jer 2.5; 4.3, 27; 5.14 etc.) and in Ezekiel, where the formula has established itself as a term for prophetic divine speech (Ezek 2.4f; 3.11, 27); or with the "word event formula" "Then the word of the LORD came to ..." (1 Sam 15.10; Jer 1.4, 11, 13 etc.; Ezek 6.1; 7.1; 11.14 etc.); or with the (often concluding) formula, "saying of the LORD" (n^e'um $yhwh$, Isa 1.24; 3.15; Jer 1.19; 2.3 etc.; cf. 1954b). The frequency of such formulas in the various prophetic books varies greatly; in some, like Hosea for instance, they are entirely lacking, while in others, such as Jeremiah, they are found in abundance. The reason for this lies primarily in the nature of the collection and redaction of the words of these prophets and does not express some fundamental difference in the understanding of the prophetic message.

The words of the prophets are received and passed on as the word of God. But this certainly does not mean that the prophets confront their audience directly in their own areas of life. Thus Isaiah's rhetorical question "The multitude of your sacrifices—what are they to me?" (Isa 1.11) [→170] addresses the regular cultic practice of his hearers; but then the prophet turns his attention in an unexpected direction: "When you spread out your hands in prayer ... your hands are full of blood" (v. 15). So "wash and make yourselves clean ... Stop doing wrong, learn to do right! ... Defend the cause of the fatherless, plead the case of the widow" (vv. 15-17). The new, unexpected thing here is the contrast between two apparently independent areas of the hearers' (or readers') lives: that of the cult and that of social life, in particular with respect to the law.

This example from the first chapter of the "writing prophets" collection is representative from various points of view. The hearers are addressed about what they do (or do not do) in their own lives. The precondition for this prophetic critique is that the addressees know—or at least could or should know—what is expected of them as members of Israelite society. The prophets do not dream up some new yardstick for the behavior of the Israelites but measure them against the yardsticks that apply, or at least should apply, to this society. So the prophets' premise is "emphatically from the old Yahweh traditions." They "certainly do not see themselves as the revolutionary speakers of a social group. Step by step one can see how they practice statutes of the ancient divine law" (von Rad 1965, 185).

But this does not apply to the cultic or the social arena. Rather, it is evident that the prophets are broadly familiar with the historical and religious traditions of Israel and can assume that their hearers also know them. An example of this is found, again in the first chapter of Isaiah, in the mention of Sodom and Gomorrah (Isa 1.9, 10); it presupposes that its hearers are familiar with the traditions referred to. In many of the prophets the traditions of Israel's early days are picked up in the most varied ways: forefathers, exodus, wilderness period, settlement of the land etc. These themes are often interpreted in a very subjective way and brought into the context of the argument in question. But it is also the case here that the prophets stand squarely within the traditions of Israelite society.

The special position of the prophets does not therefore consist in the fact that they introduce other, new themes, but that in an extremely consistent way they are convinced of the validity of the fundamental traditions of Israel and measure the social reality of their present against them, confronting it with them. This radicalism makes them largely individualists. Still, these are not "outsiders," since they criticize their fellow Israelites not "from the outside" but rather "from within," from the center of Israelite religion. However, they give many of the fundamental traditions a new emphasis or a new interpretation. To that extent the words of the prophets form a quite special component of the religious traditions of Israel. In relation to the entirety of the tradition as we have it, the voice of the prophets is no longer the voice of individuals either, but a very formidable and significant part of this whole.

3. The words of the prophets are collected and explained

The words of the prophets are in essence *spoken words*. But they have come down to us as *written* words. This shows us, first, that it was important to the prophets, or those that wrote down their words, to preserve and transmit the words beyond the present moment and beyond the current situation of the prophetic proclamation. This is already evident in such passages as Isa 8.16-18 and 30.8 as well as the narrative in Jer 36, according to which the prophets themselves took the first step towards the preservation and transmission of the prophetic messages in writing. It is also clear from this that there is a concern for the applicability and efficacy of the prophetic words beyond the present situation. Thus begins a long path of recording, collection and continuing interpretation of the prophetic words, which eventually emanates in extensive prophetic books (Isaiah, Jeremiah, Ezekiel) as well as a consciously shaped collection of prophetic writings in the Book of the Twelve Prophets. (Cf. §3.1 and 3.5.1.)

The significance of this procedure for the understanding of prophecy has only recently become fully evident (cf. esp. Steck 1996). It is particularly important not to stay with the (only hypothetically possible) distinction between the "original" words of the individual prophets and the later supplements, revisions etc., but to view the whole trajectory from the spoken prophetic word to the final form of the texts as we have them as part of the *one* prophetic tradition. This trajectory can be considered under the heading of "prophetic interpretation of the prophets (*prophetische Prophetenauslegung*)" (Steck 127ff). If we view things this way, it becomes clearer what was meant above when we touched upon the independent adoption and continuation of the traditions by the prophets. In the course of the interpretive transmission of the prophetic words, the traditions transmitted, which the prophets themselves often adopted in ways quite their own, were thought through further and constantly reinterpreted. The changing circumstances, with their often dramatic interruptions and alterations, played a basic role in this, especially in relation to the question whether and how the prophets' words were confirmed in these events. A crucial point here is the experience that the prophetic announcements of divine judgment on Israel were confirmed; this is connected, however, with the conviction that the history of God's dealings with his people is still not at an end.

Judgment and salvation are the two great poles between which the prophetic proclamation moves. Often they are presented as alternatives. But in the prophetic books as they have come down to us there are no pure "prophets of doom." No doubt for some prophets, such as Amos, the proclamation of judgment is very much in the foreground, and there are good grounds for the assumption that the concluding proclamation of salvation (esp. Amos 9.11-15) [→**701**] has been formulated in the course of the "reception history" sketched above (cf. Koch 1991, 223f), as a continuing interpretation of the message of the prophet Amos in the general context of prophecy. For other prophets the relationship between these two basic elements of prophetic speech is less clear. For some of them one might assume that their view of the history of God's dealings with his people changed as a result of the experiences of rejection of their message by their contemporaries and as a result of the new political circumstances. But the proclamation of judgment *and* salvation, in all their contrasting difference and yet in their mutual relationship is one of the essential features of Old Testament prophecy.

Prophecy thus has its own very distinctive profile. But we should recall again that the tradition context in which prophetic speech and the ensuing reception history moved is to be found, or has its roots, to a large extent also in other areas of Old Testament literature. This applies in particular to the Pentateuch. Thus one might in a sense speak of a separate "prophetic theology." This is, however, a partial aspect of "biblical theology" as a whole, which must always be thought of in terms of its harmony with other aspects.

§ 18

Israel at Worship and Prayer

The Psalms take the reader into quite a different area of life. While the prophetic books are dominated by God's speech to humans (mediated by the prophets), the direction in which the Psalms work is the reverse: people speak to God, or they speak about God in song, prayer or contemplation. The Psalms represent "Israel's answer" (von Rad 1962, 366). The themes of the Psalms are thus often different from those we find in the prophetic literature. In particular there is not the critical argument with the divine demands that plays such an important role in the prophetic books. On the contrary, in the case of various themes it is evident that the psalmists are not among those against whom the prophets' criticism is directed; this applies to cultic behavior as well as to the realm of social justice (cf. §16.1 and 2).

Part of the Psalter reflects cultic procedures in the Jerusalem temple. It is here that the celebrating and praying community assembles, and their speaking and singing is entirely focused on God. "Enter his courts with thanksgiving and his courts with praise" (Ps 100.4). Praise and thanksgiving are the prime concern in many of the psalms. Attention turns in various directions and to quite different realms. God is praised as the Creator of the world, "who made heaven and earth" (Pss 115.15; 121.2 etc.), who is enthroned in heaven (2.4; 11.4 etc.), above the floods (29.10), among the "sons of the gods" (29.1), where his praise is sung far away from human beings (19.2-4). But he not only reigns as king over the gods (95.3) but also over the whole earth (47.3) and over the nations (v. 9); and above all he is "our king" (v. 7) who sits enthroned on Zion, in the "city of the great king" (48.2f). So the service in the Jerusalem temple is the place where the reign of God, which encompasses heaven and earth, is celebrated.

In a series of psalms attention is turned to God's actions in history. A whole range of emphases can be seen: Israel's history can appear as a pure history of the "miracles" that God performed for Israel (Ps 105)

[→**333**], as the history of God's leadership (136), as the proof that God is greater than all gods (135)—or as a history of sinning, which began so long ago with Israel's forefathers (106). Reflected here are the tension-filled traditions of the historical accounts in the Pentateuch.

But the Psalms do not only express the voice of the worshiping and praying community; more frequently still it is the voices of individual supplicants. This shows a strong emotional tie to the temple on Zion, which God "chose" as his dwelling-place (Ps 132.13) because he loved it (78.68). Thus the psalmist speaks of his love for the "dwellings" of Yhwh Zebaot (84.2), of his longing for the "courts of the Lord" (v. 3, cf. v. 11); it is from there that God's help (14.7; 20.3) and blessing (128.5; 234.3) are hoped and prayed for, and it is there that praise and vows are presented to him (65.2). The pilgrims who come to Zion "see" God there (84.8), while the exiles sitting "by the waters of Babylon" can only weep when they think of Zion (137.1).

Many psalms permit an insight into the spiritual situation of the individual supplicant. The lament is dominant. There are two areas in particular in which the psalmists express their distress in psalms. First there are the religious straits, brought about by their own awareness of sin and the feeling of distance from God or abandonment by God; here we find moving expressions of a deep individual piety (e.g. Pss 22; 51) [→**328**]. Then the psalmists complain about "enemies" who make life difficult for them. This shows a deep split in Israelite society, in which much is reminiscent of the social critique of the prophets; but here the psalmists are the persecuted and oppressed who are often described as the "righteous" (*ṣaddîqîm*), while their enemies are the "evildoers" (*rešā'îm*) (e.g. 7.10; 31.18f). In these psalms much tends to be expressed in stereotypes, so that such psalms may conceivably have been used as set prayers. (The counterpart to the psalms of lament are thanksgiving psalms, in which the psalmist's distress comes back into view—but now as overcome.)

These excerpts and examples from Psalms literature show that the reader is again entering quite a special realm of life here. But it is much less alien to the present-day reader than the prophetic realm. As in the case of prophetic literature, here too we can see a clear connection with other realms, especially with the Pentateuch; and despite all the contrasting differences there are also clear connections with prophecy.

§ 19

Israel's Wisdom

The wisdom-influenced literature leads us, finally, into quite a different area of life once again. It is not easy for the reader to make a connection with the other areas of life. A basic difference lies in the very fact that the word "Israel" is found only once in the book of Proverbs, in fact in the superscription in which this book is attributed to king Solomon (Prov 1.1). The same applies in Qohelet (Qoh 1.12) and similarly in the Song of Songs (Song 3.7); the name Israel is missing altogether in the book of Job. Israel is not a theme in the literature of this area of life.

The wisdom literature is neither speech from God like prophecy nor speech to God as in the Psalms. Its topic is the life and behavior of the individual person in his or her social circumstances. The OT wisdom literature has a range of connections with comparable traditions in the ancient Near Eastern environment, and sometimes direct borrowings (e.g. Prov 22.17–24.22). The *Sitz im Leben* of the wisdom traditions is on the one hand the realm of the court, which also reflects city influences, but on the other hand we see elements of rural/peasant society, where one might speak of "tribal wisdom." The didactic character of the speeches is evident at various points (cf. Prov 1.8ff); in the expression "words of the wise" (1.6) the figure of a wisdom teacher is visible; the mention of the "wise" alongside the priest and the prophet also points to this (Jer 18.18).

But the wisdom traditions are certainly not purely "secular." Proverbs often speaks of God, generally using the divine name Yhwh. A key sentence reads: "The fear of the LORD is the beginning of wisdom" (in different wording in Prov 1.7; 9.10; 15.33) [→359]. Here we see that speech about God is entirely related to wisdom in the sense of the experiences and instructions developed here. The concern is with a life that is pleasing to God; anything at odds with this is "a detestable thing" to the Lord (*tô'ēbāh*, 3.32; 6.16; 11.1 etc.).

A person who lives according to the teachings of wisdom is called a "righteous" person (*ṣaddîq*). Wisdom literature shows a distinctive profile in this regard too: this understanding of what constitutes a "righteous" person can hardly be reconciled with the picture that the prophets show us, on the one hand, and the Psalms on the other. In the wisdom literature this term lacks the religious dimension in the true sense. And above all, this literature is marked by a clear thinking in alternatives: whoever follows the teachings of wisdom is righteous, while others are "evildoers" or "ungodly" (*rešāʿîm*). The contrast between these two dominates the book of Proverbs as a whole. Behind all this stands the view that people's behavior and their resulting prosperity or otherwise have a necessary causal relationship. This is called the "deeds-and-wellbeing relationship" (*Tun-Ergehen-Zusammenhang*, cf. Koch 1955). Certainly this connection is viewed as a divine given. But it is still regarded as something that operates, as it were, in accordance with fixed laws.

This is the point at which criticism arose: the almost unquestionable, regulated nature of this connection, which is presupposed in many of the statements made in this literature. It is one of the most interesting phenomena of Old Testament literature that prominent critical voices are heard in it and have been preserved and transmitted in it: in the books of Job and Qohelet. In Job in particular the discussion of the validity of these apparent rules takes on quite dramatic forms. It comes to a head above all in the fact that Job's "friends" view the deeds-and-wellbeing relationship as it were from the other end in their arguments, when they deduce a person's deeds, i.e. their behavior in relation to the rules of "wisdom," from their state of wellbeing, in this case Job's suffering. Job simply *must* be guilty, otherwise he would not be suffering. This provides the reader of the Hebrew Bible with the possibility of tackling these questions him/herself.

§ 20

Israel, the Nations, and the Gods

1. Israel a nation among nations

Israel has always been aware of being a nation among other nations. This awareness, however, has found highly divergent expression at various times and in changing political circumstances. If we consider the overall account of the Hebrew Bible, some striking features are evident.

The Hebrew Bible initially draws a picture of the world of the nations which spreads worldwide after the Flood and God's covenant with Noah. As yet there is no mention of Israel. It is only with Abraham's call that the history of Israel begins, as it were, to grow out of the general history of humanity. Abraham's departure from his family home is a detail in the great history of humanity. There is no concern as yet with the nations. It is only later in Egypt that Jacob's descendants living there as dependent slaves form into a nation. At this same time this provides justification for a distinction from the surrounding world. At first this is just the Egyptians; in the narrative context, however, the talk is impersonally of "Egypt" (*miṣrayim*), while Israel's real opponent is Pharaoh.

With Israel's encounter with the promised land, other nations come into view. The reports of relations with these peoples reflect a wide range of traditions and memories from various phases in Israel's history. In summary one can initially distinguish between two groups of peoples: on the one hand Israel's neighbors in the time of its settlement in the land, in particular the eastern neighbors, Edom, Moab and Ammon. Genesis contains traditions of related contacts with all three: Moab and Ammon are taken as sons of Lot's daughters, fathered after the destruction of Sodom (Gen 19.30-38); Edom is equated with Esau, Jacob's brother (Gen 25.30; 36.1 etc.). Reflected in these traditions are neighborly proximity as well as tensions and conflicts which in part date back to before the conquest of the land by the Israelites (Num 20.14-21; 22–24; 25.1-5; Deut 2.19, 37). The western neighbors, the Philistines (1 Sam 4–6 etc.), have a different ethnic origin.

The second group is the pre-Israelite inhabitants of the land itself. The land is called "the land of Canaan" (Gen 11.31; 12.5 etc.) and on Abraham's arrival we read: "at that time the Canaanites lived in the land" (12.5). "Canaanites" is probably a collective term for various pre-Israelite population groups in this stretch of land. (In addition we find changing lists of inhabitants of the land, in which the Canaanites are mentioned alongside other peoples; Gen 15.21; Ex 3.8; Deut 7.1 etc.). Israel's position in relation to the Canaanites is clearly negative; this is traced back as far as the primordial history, where there is mention of Noah cursing Canaan (Gen 9.25).

Later further nations come into view. Following Israel's political consolidation foreign-policy relations and conflicts arise. Alongside the immediate neighbors an important role is played by the greater political powers of the immediate and wider surroundings: first the Aramean states (2 Sam 8.3-8; 2 Kgs 16.5 etc.), then the empires of the Assyrians (2 Kgs 16.19f, 29 etc.) and, after a brief Egyptian interlude (23.29, 33-35; 24.7), the Babylonians (24.10-17; 25). Finally the power relationships in the Near East change again and Israel (or Judah) comes under the rule of the Persian Empire (2 Chron 36.22f; Ezra 1ff).

This brief run-through of Israel's history shows that Israel's relationship to the various nations had to be highly varied. The greater nations, especially the Assyrians and the Babylonians, were initially seen as a threat; later the small remnant of the Judean empire managed to come to an accommodation with Persian rule. The relationship with the immediate neighbors and with the Canaanites was ambivalent. On the one hand there were constant armed disputes of various kinds with them too. On the other hand, however, the greater proximity brought about mutual cultural and especially religious influences which have left their mark in various ways on the traditions of the Hebrew Bible.

In particular the relationship with the inhabitants of the land is viewed as a danger because overly close relationships could lead to intermarriage and thereby also to participation in the cults of other nations. Hence the repeated prohibitions in the Torah of making a "covenant" with the inhabitants of the land (Ex 23.32; 34.12-16; Deut 7.2-5). The social boundaries required clearly have religious motivations.

2. Israel and the gods of the nations

In the Decalogue we read: "You shall have no other gods beside me" (Ex 20.3; Deut 5.7). "Other gods" are in particular the "gods of the nations around you" (Deut 6.14; 13.7f; Judg 2.12). They are regarded as the first and immediate danger as regards Israel's turning away from the exclusive worship of the only God. In Num 25.1-5 [→**72**] there is a graphic description of how this danger might become reality: the first encounter with the Moabites leads to sexual contact and then also to participation by Israelites in cultic events held by the Moabites, with communal meals and worship of the Moabite gods. "So Israel joined in worshiping the Baal of Peor" (v. 3).

This is the first mention of the Canaanite god Baal. In the book of Judges we then read the initially very general comment: "Then the Israelites did evil in the eyes of the LORD and served the Baals. They forsook the LORD, the God of their fathers, who had brought them out of Egypt. They followed and worshiped various gods of the peoples around them" (Judg 2.11f). The name Baal appears here in a generalizing plural, in which the "gods of the peoples" are also included. Judg 6.25-32 [→**102**] speaks more concretely of a dispute in which Gideon destroys his father's Baal altar. Here a picture is sketched in which a proportion of the Israelite population are Baal-worshipers. The narrative does not tell us whether and how a distinction can be made between Israelites and Canaanites in this period. But it makes it very clear that the fight against Baal is fought on behalf of and in the name of the God of Israel and that it is a crucial matter of Israel's identity. Baal worship is incompatible with Israel.

Even clearer is the polemical stand taken against the Baal cult in Elijah's dispute with the prophets of Baal (1 Kgs 18) [→**138**] and in the subsequent removal of the dynasty of Omri, which Elisha brings about at Jehu's behest (2 Kgs 9f) [→**143**]. Here too the question must remain open whether Israelites and Canaanites can be ethnically distinguished ("if it was ever possible at all," Donner 1984/86, ²1995, 293). What is clear, however, is that the dispute with the cult of Baal is a matter of crucial importance for Israelite religion and society. Baal is the god of the "other" peoples *par excellence*, to which Israel sees itself opposed and with which it must deal. In Judah there is then mention of Baal worship especially in connection with the rule of the usurper Athaliah (2 Kgs 11). Here too the Baal cult appears as an import from Canaanite tradition which Athaliah has brought with him from his family back-

ground (8.26f). Whether and to what extent this was well received in
the Judahite population cannot be determined from the texts; at any
rate the opposition against Athaliah's rule proceeded from the Yhwh
priest Jehoiada and reached its conclusion in the destruction of the
elements of the Baal cult (11.18). After this, Baal worship is mentioned
once more in the context of Manasseh's cultic "counter-reform"
(21.3) and its reversal by Josiah (23.4f).

But "other gods" are not always understood as gods of the other nations. As we have already mentioned, it is very much open to question
whether and for how long a distinction can be made between Israelites
and Canaanites. Of the prophets, it is Jeremiah in particular who complains in detail, and constantly, that Israel turns to other gods (Jer 1.16;
7.6, 9, 18 etc.). He also speaks of the continued worship of Baal (2.8;
7.9; 11.13 etc.). According to his picture of history, this all began right
back at Israel's entry into the land promised by God (2.5-8) [→**207**].
But it is not the other nations that are held responsible for this. The
"Canaanite" traditions have long since become an element of their
own religious ideas, which stand in conflict with the worship of
Yhwh.

This fits with certain statements that not only see the religions of
other peoples as a danger but which also respect them as separate traditions. A particularly striking statement is found in Mic 4.5 [→**295**]: "All
the nations may walk in the name of their gods; we will walk in the
name of the LORD our God for ever and ever." This sentence can be
read with different emphases (cf. Wolff 1982, 94; Kessler 1999, 187f);
in any case it concedes that the other peoples worship other gods,
without criticizing this fact. We might compare what is said of the
sailors in the book of Jonah, where we read that "each cried out to his
own god" in his distress (Jon 1.5). Even broader and more fundamental is the statement in Deuteronomy that Israel is not to worship the
sun, the moon, the stars and the whole host of heaven, because these
God has "apportioned to all the nations under heaven" (Deut 4.19)
[→**75**]. These statements show that Israel's religious conflicts have become internal conflicts, providing for the possibility of respecting the
religions of the other nations.

In the situation of the post-exilic community of returnees, however,
the problem faced by Israel on its first encounter with the peoples of
the land, is viewed once again in a new light: the close contacts with
non-Israelite population groups leads to numerous mixed marriages.
On Ezra's visit to Jerusalem this is publicly acknowledged and pre-

sented as a transgression of the Torah's commandment not to enter into marriage with the "peoples of the land" (Ezra 9; cf. Ex 34.16; Deut 7.3). But the emphasis has shifted here: this is not about the worship of other gods—at least not expressly so. Rather, the concern is with mixing the "heavenly seed" (Ezra 9.2; the expression is singular) with the "peoples of the land," i.e. with the maintenance of the purity of the returning community, the "Golah." Thus the prohibition of the worship of other gods is reinforced here to include the social element of the protection of the now small nation from dissipating into the non-Israelite environment. The problem also surfaces in Malachi. Here, however, the religious concern is given much greater emphasis, when Malachi reproaches his contemporaries for marrying "the daughter of a strange god" (Mal 2.11) [→**310**]. Here too, however, the accusation regarding the worship of this "strange (foreign) god" is not expressly raised.

3. Do the gods exist?

What does the Hebrew Bible mean when it speaks of "other gods"? Are there other gods? The answer to this question is clearest in the second part of Isaiah, Isa 40–55. Here in multiple variations this one truth is formulated: "I am the first, and I am the last, and beside me is no God" (44.6). This may also be rendered: "no other God exists apart from me."

We encounter this position in the time of the Babylonian exile in a very vigorous and developed form (cf. Hermisson 2000). But there are numerous texts in the Hebrew Bible which put the same viewpoint into words much earlier. We can go back as early as the Gideon narrative in Judg 6.25-32 [→**102**]. This account shows clearly that Joash, Gideon's father, expresses the viewpoint of the narrator: "if he (i.e. Baal) really is a god, he can defend himself when someone breaks down his altar" (v. 31). But Baal does not budge—precisely because he is not a god.

In the great dispute in the time of the prophet Elijah the concern is not just with the question of which God Israel is to worship, but of who God *is*, Yhwh or Baal: "If YHWH is God, then follow him; but if Baal is God, follow him" (1 Kgs 18.21). And then once again: "the god who answers by fire—he is God" (v. 24) [→**138**]. The account demonstrates very impressively that Baal is not a god, since he cannot show proof. The alternative is already clear in the form of the word itself: only one can be "*the* God" (*hā'elōhîm*). There can be no "gods" in the plural.[1]

Hosea speaks in detail of the Israelites worshiping "other gods" (Hos 3.1); he also calls them "Baals" [→**267**] (2.15; 11.2; in the singular in 13.1). But he describes them as "idols" made with hands (8.4; 13.2), as "images" (11.2; cf. 13.2), and he ridicules Israel for consulting "wood" and a "stick" (4.12). He confronts this with the statement: "I am the Lord your God, from Egypt. You shall acknowledge no God but me, no Savior except me" (13.4). So it is quite obvious that in Hosea's opinion the other gods do not "exist"—there is only the one God, Yhwh. In Jeremiah, the "other gods" are described as the "work of their hands" the first time they are mentioned (Jer 1.16). They are wood and stone (2.27; 3.9), like a scarecrow in a field of cucumbers (10.5); in fact they are even "nothing" (*hebel*, 2.5; 8.19; 10.3, 15 etc.), they are no gods at all (2.11; 5.7; 16.20). Ezekiel does not even grace the foreign gods with the term "gods," but speaks of "idols" (*gillûlîm*, Ezek 6.4-6, 9, 13; 8.10 etc.), of "vile images" (*šiqqûṣîm*) and "detestable idols" (*tô'ēbôt*, Ezek 5.11; 7.20; 11.18, 21 etc.).

In Isa 40–55 this is developed in very broad and graphic terms. Isa 44.6 has already been quoted: "I am the first, and I am the last, and beside me is no God." Again and again we read: "no one beside me": "I am the LORD and no other, beside me there is no God" (45.5); "Before me no god was formed, nor will there be one after me" (43.10; cf. 45.14, 21, 22; 46.9). The statement is made concrete: "a righteous God and a Savior; there is none but me" (45.21); "Turn to me and be saved, all you ends of the earth; for I am God, and there is no other" (45.22): Yhwh proves himself to be God, since he is the only one who can save and help. And finally: "I am YHWH, and there is no other. I form the light and create darkness, I bring prosperity and create disaster; I, YHWH, do all these things" (45.6b, 7) [→**191**]. There is no other who can be held responsible for anything at all, not even darkness and evil. So this unique God cannot be compared with others: "'To whom will you compare me? Or who is my equal?' says the Holy One" (40.25). The reason: "Lift your eyes and look to the heavens: Who created all these? He who brings out the starry host one by

---

[1] In line with English-language convention, the "true" God (only) is capitalized here. This is a formal distinction that cannot be made in Hebrew (or German).

one, and calls them each by name" (v. 26). Even the stars, the highest conceivable "gods," are his creations. In a fictive court case (41.21-29) it is shown that the other "gods" can do nothing at all, not even answer. They are "nothing" (vv. 24, 29).

So what "Deutero-Isaiah" is expounding here is certainly nothing new. Rather, in earlier texts too there is no indication that the authors of these texts themselves had assumed that such other gods might "exist." The controversy is not about the question whether Israel should worship this God rather than another, but only about whether Israel is faithful to the worship of the one God, besides whom there are and can be no gods. This is the only thing at issue in the conflict in which Israel constantly finds itself embroiled.

One can certainly assume that the Israelites who turned in worship to other gods took these to be in some sense gods deserving of the name. And it can be of interest from the point of view of the history of religions to investigate these ideas further. But there is no indication that at any time any "other god" was regarded in Israel as the God of Israel. Rather, it is crystal clear from the texts that from early times the sentence "Israel is defined by Yahweh" (Hermisson 2000, 111) was considered valid.

4. The God of Israel and the nations

We are back at the beginning: right from the earliest times Israel is a people among peoples. The call of Abraham means on the one hand a separation from among the peoples, but on the other hand the peoples are also in view: "in you shall all the nations of the earth be blessed" (*w^enibr^ekû*, Gen 12.3; on the translation cf. Westermann 1981, 175f). This promise is passed on to Isaac (in slightly different wording) in Gen 26.4 and to Jacob in 28.14.

The idea that the nations will have a share in Israel's special relationship with God is not frequently but nonetheless clearly expressed in the Hebrew Bible. Thus we are told initially in various contexts that individual members of other nations recognize the God of Israel and confess him. In this connection we may mention the Midianite priest Jethro, Moses' father-in-law, who confesses: "Now I know that YHWH is greater than all other gods" (Ex 18.11). Another example is the Aramean Naaman, who acknowledged that "there is no God in all the world except in Israel" (2 Kgs 5.15). In Solomon's temple dedication prayer the idea that foreigners will also come to worship Israel's God in the temple is given a section to itself (1 Kgs 8.41-43); here God is asked to hear their prayer "so that all the peoples of the earth may know your name" (v. 43). At the end of the temple dedication prayer we read once again: "so that all the peoples of the earth may know that YHWH is *the* God (*hāʾlohîm*) and that there is no other" (v. 60). A text at the beginning of the third section of Isaiah also speaks of foreigners as participants in the Israelite cult. Here the foreigner who has decided to follow Yhwh is promised full fellowship in the cult (56.3, 6f). In mind here are individual non-Israelites who live in community with Israel and wish to participate in the cult. The section concludes, however, with a sentence that takes things much further: "For my house will be called a house of prayer for all peoples" (v. 7).

The prophetic books mention the turning of the peoples to the God of Israel in the twice transmitted promise that the nations will stream to Zion "at the end of days" in order to learn the "ways" of the God of Israel: the Torah (Isa 2.2-5; Mic 4.1-5) [→**170, 295**]. This expectation is echoed in Ps 102.22f: "So the name of the LORD will be declared in Zion and his praise in Jerusalem when the peoples and the kingdoms assemble to worship the LORD." Similarly, Ps 22.28. Zephaniah expects that God will "purify the lips of the peoples, that all of them may call on the name of the LORD and serve him shoulder to shoulder" (Zeph 3.9). Similarly Zechariah: "Many nations will be joined with the LORD in that day and will become my people" (Zech 2.15[11]; cf. 8.20-22; 14.16). This expectation is also expressed in the statement that "My name will be great among the nations, from the rising to the setting of the sun" (Mal 1.11; cf. Isa 45.6; Ps 113.3).

A very unusual future expectation is found in Isa 19.16-25: Egypt will enter into a relationship with Yhwh on its own account, and then Assyria will also join them and there will be a divinely blessed community between Egypt, Assyria and Israel. When it is said that the "language of Canaan" is spoken in Egypt (v. 18) and that there is an altar to Yhwh there (v. 19), evidently underlying this are experiences and hopes of Jews living in Egypt in post-exilic times. But the expectations expressed here remain quite isolated within the Hebrew Bible.

The texts collected here indicate a line that runs from the beginnings of the history of God's dealings with Israel through to its late phases within the Hebrew Bible. But they do not paint the whole picture. There are many texts which speak of a very critical relationship between God and the peoples, whether with particular individuals or with the peoples as a whole; sometimes this relationship can even be characterized as aggressive. This applies in particular to a series of "oracles to the nations" in the prophetic books. I must repeat what was said in our discussion of the prophetic books: the first main section of the oracles to the nations in the book of Isaiah (chs. 13f) shows the key interest of these texts—God turns against the hubris of any people and any nation that rejects him, as he does against the hubris of Israel (Isa 2.12ff). So it would be to misunderstand these texts to suggest the meaning is that God's judgment on other nations means salvation for Israel. Israel is often completely in the background in these texts. (Cf. esp. Hamborg 1981.)

So the picture that the authors of the Hebrew Bible sketch of the relationship between God and the nations is certainly not a uniform one. The principal reason for this lies no doubt in the changing political circumstances in which the texts were written and in which they were transmitted. The texts reflect the ever-changing situation of Israel as a "people among peoples."

§ 21

How does Israel view its Past?

1. Sketches of history

"The Old Testament is a history book." The oft-quoted sentence of Gerhard von Rad's (1952/53, 23 = 278) must be taken together with its continuation: "It represents a history of God's word from the creation of the world to the coming of the Son of Man." In the Old Testament history is never related for its own sake. And as a rule it is not reported with the presuppositions and intentions of modern thinking about history. So the reconstruction of the history of Israel in OT times is only possible with reservations, as is very clear in the current controversy in scholarly discussion.

In the context of a Theology of the Old Testament, however, the concern is not with such attempted reconstructions but with the representation and interpretation of what the biblical texts say about history, how their authors or those whose voices we hear experienced and interpreted it. So the concern in these texts is with the experience of history and with thinking this history through. To put it another way: the concern is always with narrated history, in which the narrating of the experience gives expression to the experience and processing of history.

In English-speaking scholarship there are interesting attempts to distinguish between *history* (what really happened) and *story* (history as experienced and narrated). This distinction is more difficult to make in German (the word *Geschichte* means both history and story). (Cf. Barr 1967; *idem* 1999, 345-361; Ritschl & Jones 1976.)

The Pentateuch tells the story of the beginnings of the world and of humanity through the first catastrophe in human history, the election of Abraham, the migration of his descendants to Egypt, their miraculous leading-out from there, the fundamental encounter with the God of Israel on Sinai and the further wanderings through to the borders of the promised land. This broad context is the result of the growing together and thinking-through of various traditions and different experiences with the people's own history and the overarching history of God's activity in the world. Two things in particular are evident here. First, Israel does not view its own history as the beginning of history as such. On the contrary: Israel's history grows as it were out of the general history of humankind. Abraham's departure from his ancestral home is a detail in the great history of humanity. But from this point on attention in the account is focused on the section that begins here. Second, the great theological sketch provided by the Pentateuch deals only with the history of the period when Israel was not yet settled in its land. The real history of the people of Israel as a tangible political entity begins only after this.

In the books of the "former prophets" which follow, the history of Israel is presented from the occupation of the land through to the end of the monarchy and the deportation of part of the nation into Babylonian captivity. But the manner in which the story is told is very different from that of the Pentateuch. Despite the various differences, the latter always deals with the history brought about by God or about history that is viewed and presented directly in its relationship to God. In the following books on the other hand history is presented largely in a "secular" manner, so that for stretches at a time it is quite possible to reconstruct a "history of Israel" in the modern sense. But this history is frequently accompanied by prophets, sometimes in the form of active cooperation (in particular through Samuel [1 Sam 8–16] and in a different way by Elisha [2 Kgs 9]) and sometimes through anticipatory or accompanying interpretations of the divine will. In addition the history of the individual kings in its present context is continually subjected to theological evaluation. So here too the account can hardly be called "secular."

In the books of the "latter prophets" too there is constant talk of history from a wide variety of viewpoints: of history hitherto in the tension between the election and failure of Israel, of the current history as a continuation of apostasy and the experience of divine punishment, and of the history that is still to be played out in the hope and expectation of a new future. Finally in many psalms history is also a dominant theme. Even more clearly than in the prophets quite different conceptions and emphases in relation to accounts of history are evident, both with regard to their beginnings and to their further course and to the role played by Israel itself in this history. There are few books in the Hebrew Bible in which history does not play a part.

However, in the prophetic books, and even more so in the Psalms, we see very different approaches to the consideration and representation of Israel's history. An important point here is the question where the account of history starts. But the course of the history too is presented in very varied ways. Particular epochs or events are given special attention or treated and interpreted in greater detail than others; the question of how far the account of history is taken also plays a part in this. And finally there are fundamental differences in the interpretation and evaluation of the story as a whole. These questions will be examined in the following paragraphs.

2. Where does Israel's history begin?

The Pentateuch's great historical account begins with the creation. This point of departure is rarely found in other texts. Thus Ps 136 [→**334**] begins with a hymnic praise of God "who alone does marvelous deeds" (vv. 1-4) and then mentions creation as the first of these deeds, borrowing phraseology from Gen 1 (vv. 5-9). Then in a rather abrupt-sounding transition we read: "to him who struck down the firstborn of Egypt and brought Israel out from among them with a mighty hand and outstretched arm" (vv. 10-12). Again the issue is a mighty divine deed, as also in the following events: the dividing of the Reed Sea (vv. 13-15), the leading of Israel into the wilderness (v. 16), the defeat of enemy kings (vv. 17-20), and finally the gift of the land to Israel (vv. 21f). The concluding sentences generalize praise of God for the help and care of those that are his ("we," vv. 23f) and of the whole of creation ("all flesh," v. 25). Here the history of Israel is an important part of the wonderful and powerful action of the creator God.

The view of history in the great prayer of repentance in Neh 9.6-37 [→**399**] is quite different. In two introductory sentences, constructed in parallel ("You yourself, Lord," *'attāh-hû' yhwh*), God is addressed as the creator of the world (v. 6) and as the one who chose Abraham (v. 7). The point of departure for everything that follows is the covenant that God made with Abraham, to give the land to his descendants (v. 8). This first section concludes with the confession: "You are just" (*'attāh ṣaddîq*). A detailed account follows of the "signs and wonders"

(v. 10) which God performed on Israel's behalf in the leading-out from Egypt, the rescue at the Reed Sea, the leading in the wilderness, the gift of the good commandments, instructions and statutes on Sinai and of the manna and the water in the wilderness (vv. 9-15). But then the account turns into a depiction of the stubbornness and disobedience of the forefathers throughout the whole of the wilderness period (vv. 16-21) and then again to the gift of the land (vv. 22-25), so that God finally delivered them into the hands of their enemies (vv. 26-30); but he still did not put an end to them, for he is a "gracious and compassionate God" (v. 31). In the current, desperate situation of his people the supplicant confesses that God "keeps his covenant of love" (v. 32) and then again: "You are just" (v. 33).

The special significance of the creation event is emphasized by the fact that the historical account begins with this, and this first great divine deed is followed by the election of Abraham as the second great deed. This is in line with the intention of the pentateuchal sketch in which the call and election of Abraham is the crucial event after creation, which determines and influences the following history. At the same time it is clear here that Abraham is an extraordinary individual figure, while the term "(fore)fathers" designates the generation of the exodus (v. 9) and the wilderness wanderings (v. 16), the latter giving rise to the "sequence of the generations of sinners." Finally in this prayer of repentance the point of departure in the current desperate situation is quite different from that in the general mood of thanksgiving in Ps 136.

Abraham also has a prominent role in the overview of history, which reaches back furthest to the beginnings of the history of the people: in Josh 24.2-13 we read: "your forefathers lived beyond the River (i.e. the Euphrates) ... and served other gods" (v. 2). Here the term "forefathers" even includes the generation before Abraham. Then with Abraham something new begins, when God leads him out from there and brings him to Canaan (v. 3). However, in what follows there is no special emphasis on the person of Abraham; Isaac, Jacob and also Esau are mentioned after him, and Jacob travels with his sons to Egypt (v. 4). It is then the "fathers" that God leads out of Egypt soon afterwards (v. 6). And finally once again the farthest-reaching concept of "(fore)fathers" is taken up when the generation of Joshua is called upon to remove the gods "which your fathers worshiped beyond the River and in Egypt" (v. 14). The term "fathers" is thus lacking in precision and serves primarily as a polar opposite to the generation addressed in the narrative. The intention is that this generation will be primed against repeating the mistakes of the forefathers.

In Gen 15.13-16 [→**27**] Abram is the recipient of a preview of the story of his descendants, who will live for a long time in adverse circumstances in a foreign land, but will finally leave. In this brief outline of history the history of the forefathers and the exodus are linked together and related to each other. In the context of the chapter the promise to the descendants of possession of the land is the subject of the covenant that God concludes with Abram (vv. 18-21). The same point of departure is also found in Neh 9.8. Psalm 105 also begins its detailed historical retrospect after the hymnic introduction (vv. 1-6) with the reminder of the covenant with Abraham, the key content of which was the promise of the land of Canaan (vv. 8-12). The psalm is quite different from the prayer of repentance in Neh 9, however, attuned entirely to the note of thanksgiving for God's miraculous leading.

In some cases a historical overview begins with a brief reminder that the forefathers first came to Egypt. This applies to some of the texts which von Rad called "the short historical creed" (von Rad 1938, 2ff [11ff]): "My father was a wandering Aramean, and he went down into Egypt" (Deut 26.5); with the express mention of Jacob in 1 Sam 12.8: "When Jacob came to Egypt ..."; similarly Josh 24.4 (see above). But in Deut 6.20f the "creed" that is to be passed on to one's son begins directly with: "We were slaves of Pharaoh in Egypt ..."

So the majority of historical retrospects also begin with the leading-out from Egypt, without mention of the prehistory of the Israelites' stay in Egypt. The "forefathers" are now quite clearly the exodus generation. Repeatedly we find the statement that God concluded a (or: the) covenant with the forefathers at the time of their departure. Thus on the dedication of the temple we read that in the Ark lies "the covenant" (i.e. the tablets of the covenant) "which he made with our forefathers when he led them out of the land of Egypt" (1 Kgs 8.21). Jeremiah speaks very similarly of the "covenant which I made with your forefathers when I took them by the hand to lead them out of the land of Egypt" (Jer 31.32; similarly 34.13; cf. 11.3f; further Deut 29.24; 2 Kgs 17.15); according to Ex 20.5 God "chose" Israel in Egypt and raised his hand to swear an oath, which in v. 6 is explained to be the announcement of the leading-out from Egypt and the gift of the land. Elsewhere too we find even more frequent mention of the leading-out of the "forefathers" from Egypt (e.g. Judg 6.13; 1 Sam 12.6; 1 Kgs 8.53; 9.9; Jer 2.5f etc.).

Occasionally a retrospect on the history of God's dealings with Israel begins only with the wilderness, when God "found" Israel (Hos 9.10; cf. Deut 32.10). "Find" in this context is a metaphor for "choose." In Jer 2.2f [→207] it is clear that this early time in relations between God and Israel in the wilderness was the "time of first love," which is now looked back upon with mourning. At the same time it is evident that the fact that the author starts his historical retrospect at this point does not mean that he did not "know" the traditions going back further than this. Both Hosea and Jeremiah after all speak frequently of the earlier stages in the history of Israel (Hos 11.1; 12.3-5, 13f; Jer 2.6f; 7.22, 25; 11.4, 7 etc.). Rather, this shows that often an episode in Israel's history (or better: in the history of God's dealings with Israel) comes into view from a special angle, without other stages in this history being expressly mentioned.

What has just been said applies also to all the brief mentions of this history that are found at many points in the Hebrew Bible. It is often only a sentence or a short phrase that expresses or emphasizes something particular in the context. An example of this would be the many instances of the "leading-out formula" found scattered throughout the Hebrew Bible, which are often not followed by any further details of this history. A classic version of this is the brief wording in Hosea: "I am the LORD, your God, from the land of Egypt," in which the "self-presentation formula" and the "leading-out formula" are linked together (Hos 12.10; 13.4; cf. 1997b).

3. Why is Israel's story told?

Historiography is always the *telling* of a story. In the Hebrew Bible history is never narrated for its own sake. However, the reason for and intent of the narrating of history can vary widely, and this has a powerful influence on the character and features of the account.

History can be narrated in order to instruct: "When your son asks you ..." (Deut 6.20). But it is immediately clear here that instruction does not occur in order to provide information or further education. The question itself does not relate to events but to the "stipulations, decrees, and laws" whose meaning is to be conveyed to the next generation. This is why history is narrated: beginning with the slave-existence in Egypt through the leading-out from there and God's mighty deeds through to the leading into the land promised to the forefathers (vv. 21-23). This history justifies the divine call to keep his commandments and the preparedness of those that have experienced this history to respond appropriately to this call (vv. 24f).

The almost bleak sobriety of this recapitulation of the fundamental historical event is clear if one compares it with the superficially parallel text of Deut 26.5-9. The historical "facts" are essentially the same, but the tone of the account is quite different: the nameless Aramean father became a *stranger* in Egypt, i.e. one without rights; then we (!) were *oppressed* by the Egyptians and *cried* to the Lord, and the Lord heard our cry and saw our *misery*, our *fear and distress*; the leading-out from Egypt was accompanied by *horrors from God*—and then God gave us the land flowing with *milk* and *honey*. All this is now a cause for gratitude, which finds expression in the presentation of the firstfruits, and for joy, and last but not least for attention to "the stranger in your midst" (vv. 10f).

Gratitude and praise for God's great deeds are expressed with different emphases in several psalms. Ps 105 begins with Abraham (vv. 8f) [→333] and then leads the story in great detail through the stay in Egypt to the gift of the "lands of the peoples" (v. 44); unlike Deut 26 there is no more than an allusion to Israel's suffering in Egypt (v. 25). In Ps 136.10-22 (see above) this aspect is entirely absent, as also in Ps 135.8-12. In this psalm a quite different reason emerges for the retrospect on Israel's history, namely the message that our God is greater than all gods (v. 5), who are merely the work of human hands (vv. 15-18).

Psalm 106 stands in abrupt contrast to the tone of these psalms. Even before the historical account begins, we read: "We have sinned along with our fathers" (v. 6). The whole story is then retold in detail from this perspective, as a history of God's great deeds and of the constantly repeated sinful reactions of the Israelites, from the leading-out from Egypt to the fraternization with the inhabitants of the land and the worship of their gods (vv. 34-39); this was the last straw, which moved God to deliver them into the "hands of the peoples" (v. 41). The reason why this is not the end of the story lies exclusively in the fact that God recalled his covenant (v. 45). So the confident closing prayer can also be spoken: "Save us, O LORD our God, and gather us from the nations, that we may give thanks to your holy name and glory in your praise" (v. 47). The history of sinning is not recounted for its own sake here but as a justification for a remorseful and hopeful prayer by those who are still captives of the peoples (v. 46).

We also meet the history of Israel as a history of sinning in other, quite varied, contexts. In Ezekiel this topic is common: twice in the form of metaphors in the narratives of unfaithful wives (Ezek 16 and 23), and once without metaphor in ch. 20 [→**246**]. In this case the history of sinning begins already in Egypt, where the Israelites defiled themselves with idols (vv. 7f). After a long, vicissitudinous history the prophet prophesies an end when all Israel will serve God on his "holy mountain" (v. 40). The same motif of shaming as a result of the ultimate saving act of God is found at the end of the metaphorical account of Jerusalem as an unfaithful wife, this time linked to the restoration of the covenant that God made with Jerusalem in its youth (vv. 59-63).

The great prayer of repentance in Neh 9.6-37 [→**399**] too tells the story as a history of sinning. There too we are told that God is "a gracious and compassionate God" and that he "keeps his covenant of love" (vv. 31f). But here at the end there is no hopeful view of the future opening up. The supplicant confesses: "You have been just in all that has happened to us" (v. 33); but the last words read: "we are slaves today ... we are in great distress" (vv. 36f). In the prayer in Daniel 9, which is related in a number of respects, a brief retrospect on the leading-out from Egypt also ends with the confession: "We have sinned" (v. 15). But then follows a long, pleading prayer that God will turn his anger and let his face shine upon his ruined sanctuary (vv. 16-19). In this respect this text is close in intent to Ps 106.

But there are also historical accounts that are quite different in nature, as when in the divine speech or as a speech of Moses the consequences of keeping or not keeping the divine commandments are expounded, as for instance in the great overviews in Lev 26 or Deut 28 and 30 [→**68**]. They begin in the present, and it is clear that not the narrated situation in the Sinai desert or on the borders of the land is in view but a present time which has already experienced a long history in the land and also has the exilic situation behind it. They set out the positive and—in much more detail—the negative consequences of Israel's behavior in respect of God's commandments, and they end with a view of the future when Israel will again stand in the place it should stand in accordance with God's will. The intent of this account of history at this point is quite clear: Israel can only continue to live if it keeps the divine Torah. In Deut 30.11-14 [→**86**] there is the encouraging additional assurance that the Torah can indeed be kept.

Finally the recalling of history represents an important argument in support of the keeping of particular commandments. In the Deuteronomic version of the Decalogue the Sabbath commandment is expanded with the clause "so that your manservant and maidservant may rest, as you do" (Deut 5.14). And then we read: "Remember that you were slaves in Egypt and that the LORD your God brought you out of there with a mighty hand and an outstretched arm. Therefore the LORD your God has commanded you to observe the Sabbath day" (v. 15). The reminder of their own liberation from a state of slavery is a critical argument for the requirement that slaves be properly treated. This is given expression in the law about the freeing of a Hebrew slave (Deut 15.15). In Deut 24.17-22 it is extended to other groups of people: foreigners, widows and orphans; here too slavery in Egypt is expressly recalled (vv. 18, 22). In Ex 22.20; 23.9 the commandment not to oppress strangers is justified in that "you were strangers in the land of Egypt." So in these brief mentions of the sojourn in Egypt, and thus the leading-out from there, the exodus, their specific significance is evident.

4. Where does Israel's story end? —Does Israel's story end?

This question has various aspects to it. First: where do the accounts or sketches of Israel's history end? A broad spectrum is again in evidence here; much of this was already indicated in the preceding section. In a series of texts the point of departure of the story that is recalled is at the same time its goal. This applies in particular to the many mentions of the fact that God led Israel out of Egypt. This can serve as instruction (e.g. Deut 6.20-25), justification for particular regulations (*ibid.*) or behavior (e.g. Deut 5.14f; 24.17-22) or as praise for the mighty acts of God in history (e.g. Ex 13.9; Deut 7.19; cf. 1997b, 515-517). In other cases the emphasis shifts to the leading of Israel into the promised land. Here too the concern is above all with thankful praise for God's mighty action, which has proved itself in particular in victory over enemy kings (e.g. Pss 136.10-12; 136.17-22).

In texts of this sort Israel's current situation does not have a role of its own (or only by implication as in Ps 136.23f), and they do not explicitly contain any view of the future. Israel looks back on God's actions which brought it to where it can now live and present itself in the psalm-singing during the liturgy. But this is quite different in the case of texts in which the story is told primarily as a story of Israel's sinning. They all speak from a situation in which Israel must bear in the present the consequences of Israel's long history of sinning since the time of its forefathers. Some of these texts do not end with the confession of Israel's own sinfulness but with hope in a future in which despite everything that has happened God will accept his people once again (e.g. Ps 106.44-47; Ezek 20.40-44; Lev 26.40-45). In some texts, however, we still have the desperate cry of distress from the current situation (Neh 9.36f; Ezra 9.13-15). In the context of these prayers, however, we are permitted to hear hope (albeit a desperate hope) of a change in fortunes.

The question is represented from a quite different point of view when we direct it to the great coherent accounts of Israel's history or of particular parts of it. The Pentateuch opens up Israel's history and points expressly and constantly to the coming times. They are to orient themselves by what is set out in the Pentateuch and measure themselves by the yardsticks provided there. There is an explicit emphasis that none of the later religious and political leader figures will or can match these standards that were set up in the figure of Moses. But still this account is quite open to a future which will run the course set out here. And in the Pentateuch there are also attempts at a continuation and further development of what is set down there "on through the generations" (Num 15.23; cf. Crüsemann 1992, 419-423).

The next great narrative context that covers the period from Israel's settlement in the promised land to the end of the monarchy is not clear as far as the question of the "end" of the history of the people of Israel is concerned. Some interpreters have interpreted the "Deuteronomic History" in such a way that its authors "(have) seen in the history of the people of Israel a self-contained event which began with certain proofs of divine power and found its definitive conclusion in the destruction of Jerusalem" (Noth 1943, 103). However, in the estimation of those who transmitted and developed this work after the return from exile and the resumption of the reconstruction in Jerusalem, this was clearly no way to conclude things. Rather, the time of the kings in Israel and Judah, about four centuries after all, became an epoch which remained in the consciousness of the following generations in its whole ambivalence. The more so for the fact that the prophetic writings from these centuries were similarly transmitted and in many cases shed additional and new light on this period. In these writings the warnings and admonitions which are also clearly to be heard in the historical books, were extraordinarily sharpened and deepened. Israel now lived very consciously in the succession of this great and highly ambivalent time. In the prophetic books we constantly see indications of a time still to come in which the negative elements of this history will be overcome.

The books of Chronicles sketch another picture of these centuries: they depict them as an ideal time under the rule of the Davidic monarchy. The intention here, however, is basically the same: after God has given through the Persian king Cyrus the task of reconstructing Jerusalem and the temple (2 Chron 36.22f), Israel is to tackle this task and orient itself by this ideal period. So for the books of Chronicles too, Israel's history is far from concluded; rather the shaping of the present and the immediate future is the task now laid upon Israel.

In a sense, one can view the great prophetic books or collections as general sketches. The book of Isaiah leads the reader from the political circumstances in the second half of the eighth century through the time of Babylonian exile through to the restitution and reshaping of the social and religious conditions in Jerusalem in the post-exilic period. Towards the end, from the discussions of current problems prospects of a future in which the current adversities will be overcome arise time and again. For Zion a splendid future is expected (Isa 60–62), and finally God will create "a new heaven and a new earth" (65.17; 66.22). But this will not be a world "beyond" but a world in which people will live, freed of the problems that hold sway in the present world. In this view, then, the history of Israel is far from at an end but will be carried over in an entirely new way into the future.

The new Jerusalem too, which is outlined in the last part of Ezekiel (Ezek 40–48), is not an "otherworldly" or even "heavenly" Jerusalem; despite all the wondrous changes it will come about at the place where the temple stood right from its foundations, and the history of Israel will find its continuation there. Finally the Book of the Twelve Prophets, comparable in this respect to the book of Isaiah, leads from the conflicts of the eighth century into the post-exilic period. Here too it is evident that towards the end expectations and hopes of a new future are expressed. But the construction of this collection of prophetic traditions makes it clear that such expectations certainly do not exempt the people from responsibility for the future course of history, "until Elijah comes" (Mal 3.23).

Israel's history is not yet at an end. Nor will it simply end, according to the expectations of the biblical texts, even if radical changes and new developments will occur. For even as it awaits the return of the prophet Elijah Israel remains duty-bound to remember the law of Moses (Mal 3.22). Israel will then have to perform the duties assigned to it by God.

§ 22

What does Israel expect in the Future?

1. Implicit and explicit answers

Israel's history is not at an end. But what does Israel expect of its future? There are a wide variety of answers to this question, explicit and implicit. The reader of the Hebrew Bible can gain implicit answers from the structure of the individual greater and smaller components of the canon. Thus the Pentateuch as a whole looks to a future in which Israel will live in the promised land and take its orientation from what is set out in the Pentateuch.

This future expectation is also expressed in detail. In the Decalogue the commandment to honor one's parents is "the first commandment that has a promise" (Eph 6.2): "so that your days will be long (and it will go well with you) in the land that the LORD, your God, gives to you" (Ex 20.12; fuller version in Deut 5.16). Deuteronomy repeats this promise again and again: at the end of the great sermon in ch. 4 (v. 40); in the admonition that follows the Decalogue (5.33); at the beginning of the paraenetic sermon in ch. 6 (v. 2); further in 11.9; 22.7; 25.15 and finally once again very emphatically in Moses' last admonition before his death in 32.47. Israel's good and long life in the land given it by God is, right from the start, a task in which Israel must cooperate and the fulfillment of which is still in the future; and this duty remains in force as long as Israel lives in the land, but also in times of exile and fully after the return to the land. For readers of these texts have the changing history of Israel in mind and are themselves involved in it.

In the following books certain quiet points are depicted. At the end of the book of Joshua we read that after the occupation of the land God gave Israel rest; "Not one of all the Lord's good promises to them house of Israel failed; every one was fulfilled" (Josh 21.43-45; cf. 23.14). A very similar form of words is used by Solomon at the conclusion of the temple dedication prayer (1 Kgs 8.56). Solomon's time is marked by the fact that in Judah and Israel everyone could "sit under his own vine and fig-tree" (5.5[4.25]). The occupation of the promised land and the establishment of the monarchy appear as points of rest at which what was promised by God and hoped for by Israel became reality. But in the case of both Joshua and Solomon, the admonition and warning is raised that this rest is always going to be endangered whenever Israel turns away from the pathway indicated by the Torah and the covenant of God (Josh 23.12f, 16; 1 Kgs 9.6-9). And the reader knows how true this has proved to be. So there is renewed confirmation here that the complete fulfillment of what Israel hopes for is still to come.

In the account of the centuries after Solomon there are no longer any times of rest. Generally speaking the basic tendency of the account is thoroughly negative. Internally the empire created by David splits into two component parts, between which there is a constant series of disputes. Religious conflicts play a large part in this. In this respect Elijah's struggle against the Baal cult, the end of the dynasty of Omri inaugurated by Elijah and then also the fall of Athaliah are climaxes, because to a large degree the central demand of exclusive worship of Yhwh is achieved at these points. And this applies especially to the great cult reforms of Hezekiah and Josiah. But the downward slide in the history of Israel and Judah is not arrested by this. Israel's expectations and hopes have not been realized.

So the account of the history from the beginning of the monarchy to the destruction of Jerusalem and the deportation of a significant part of the population to Babylon ends with an open question: what can Israel expect of the future? The books of Kings left this question open; they did not even explicitly pose it. Centuries later the books of Chronicles offer an answer: with the commission to reconstruct the temple in Jerusalem a new section in Israel's history begins. This is at any rate one of the possible answers that were given to this question in Israel itself: much more than before, the Torah can now become the basis and the center of Israel's life (cf. Crüsemann 1992, 381-423).

But these implicit answers are only a partial aspect of what the Hebrew Bible tells us of Israel's expectations of the future. In the prophetic books especially there are numerous explicit statements about what will occur in the future. If one takes the term "future" in a broader sense, one may say that the large part of the prophetic sayings deal with future matters. The concern can be with an imminent future, but also with a future that lies far ahead, which perhaps lies beyond what is currently conceivable. To put it simplistically: the expectations and announcements of the prophets pick up the implicit future expectations and lead them on: what will happen "afterwards"?

This "afterwards" describes the non-fulfillment or the failure of the expectations and hopes in the context of the history of a politically independent Israel. The end of this Israel meant at the same time the end or at least the questioning of the notions and expectations that went with Israel's central institutions and symbols, prime among them the monarchy and Zion, and last but not least, the land. The weightier part of the prophetic statements about the future deals with this "afterwards." It is not essential to know—and in many cases it can no longer be determined—whether the individual prophetic words saw the political catastrophe coming or whether they were spoken or written after it had occurred. (This applies also to the question of the "authenticity" of the individual prophetic sayings, which from a canonical point of view is of limited significance; this does not exclude the possibility that in certain cases a temporal succession of individual prophetic sayings is discernible and can be shown.)

Can these expectations be described as "eschatological"? In the narrower sense, as a designation of talk about the ἔσχατα, the "last things," certainly not. But many expectations and hopes are focused on an "afterwards," on a time that will differ in one way or another from the present time. In many prophetic sayings it is initially a question of negative events that will come upon Israel and which will be sent or directly effected by God. But in all the prophetic books the hopeful expectations come into their own. There are also announcements of a fundamental change of things that one could describe as eschatological in the narrower sense.

However, the future notions and expectations are not oriented to the world "beyond." Even when there is talk of a "new heaven" and a "new earth" (Isa 65.17; 66.22), expectations remain within the realm of the conceivable, even if sometimes they brush against the borders of this. But in particular there is as yet no idea of a world "beyond" and of an "eternity" that is fundamentally different from "time." The word *'ôlām*, which is often translated as "eternal" or "eternity," can mean the most distant imaginable time, the earliest as well as the last times. The expression "from eternity to eternity/for ever and ever" (*mê 'ôlām w' 'ad-ôlām*) encompasses this entire time-span (Jer 7.7; Ps 90.2 etc.). It is only in the book of Daniel that the word *'ôlām* (or its Aramaic equivalent *'ālam*) seems to "tend toward the meaning 'world age' (Gk αἰών)" (Dan 7.13f, 18, 27; 9.24; 12.1-3; cf. Koch 1980, 214f). In post-biblical times it is possible to speak of "this world" (*ha'ôlām hazzeh*) and of the "world to come" (*ha'ôlām habbā'*) (e.g. *Pirqe Avoth* 4.1). (On this whole topic cf. Jenni 1952/53.)

2. The future of the monarchy

The non-fulfillment of the expectations and hopes is first and most clearly evident in the reality of the kingship. Prophetic voices are raised against its failures. (For detail see §13.4 [→**570**].)

Even while a legitimate representative of the Davidic dynasty is on the throne, Isaiah announces the arising of a new king. These texts contain a quite open critique of the current kingship. In Isa 7.10-17 already the announcement of the birth of "Immanuel" occurs against the express refusal of the receipt of a sign by the reigning king; the future of this figure remains unexpressed, however. Then in 9.5f the birth of a future king is announced, whose rule will be characterized in particular by justice and righteousness, the current lack of which Isaiah has just criticized (e.g. 1.21; 5.7). In 11.1-5 the criticism is then taken a whole lot further: the present Davidic kingship will be cut back to the root, and then a new king will emerge from this, on whom the spirit of God will rest—which certainly no one would say of the currently reigning king—, and whose rule once again will be marked in particular by righteousness.

In the book of Micah criticism of the kingship and the proclamation of a new beginning are even more radical (Mic 5.1-4). After Zion has become a heap of rubble everything will start again in Bethlehem (cf. 1 Sam 16). But the origin of the new ruler (*môšēl*; the expression "king" is evidently consciously avoided here) will not, as in Isa 11.1, be the family of Jesse, from which David came, but will lie far back in primordial times (*'ôlām*). His rule is characterized by the term "pasture" (v. 3), a metaphor that Jeremiah also picks up (Jer 3.16; 10.21 etc.): God will replace the shepherds who neglect their duties with new ones (Jer 23.1-4), and finally "days will come" when God will also appoint a new king (vv. 5f). Jeremiah has no qualms about describing him as the "shoot of David." Again righteousness stands at the heart of what is expected of this king; in fact he is even given the name "YHWH is our righteousness" (cf. also 33.15f) [→**222**].

Ezekiel too uses the metaphor of the shepherd. He first applies it to God, who himself will lead his flock to pasture as a shepherd (Ezek 34.1-16) but will then appoint *one* shepherd: "my servant David" (v. 23). Ezekiel thereby replaces the Davidic dynasty, which no longer exists, with a new, eschatological David. But this new David exercises his office on God's instructions and with a clear subordination: "I, the LORD, will be their God and my servant David will be prince (*nāśî'*) in their midst" (v. 24). In 37.24f we then read that "my servant David" is to be king and shepherd of the reunited kingdoms of Judah and Israel.

In post-exilic prophecy, for a short time a concrete hope centers on the Davidide Zerubbabel. Together with Haggai he participates in the reconstruction of the temple (Hag 1.12, 14), and the prophet expects that Zerubbabel will have a leading role after the imminent eschatological turmoil, because God has "chosen" him (2.20-23) [→**304**]. In Zechariah his name crops up once again. He is described as the builder of the temple (Zech 4.9) and in the prophet's vision he and Joshua the priest stand together as the two "sons of anointing" before the "Lord of the whole earth" (v. 14). Similarly in 6.12f there is talk of a joint eschatological rule by a man called "shoot" (cf. 3.8; Jer 23.5f; 33.15f) and Joshua the priest. But it is really just this short-term prophetic hope.

Finally in Zech 9.9f [→**308**] the "daughter of Zion" hears the announcement of the coming of its king, who will enter Jerusalem after God has removed all the weapons of war and thus created the preconditions for a worldwide reign of peace. One of his characteristic features is that he is "righteous;" this takes up and continues the long tradition of the prophetic expectations of an eschatological king.

The prophetic expectations of a new king from the line of David thus show fundamental similarities despite the various differences. When the king assumes his rule, basic disturbances in Israel's present situation, and in fact in the whole world, will be removed. But the eschatological king will not create the preconditions for this rule himself with military means, but God will do this so as to prepare the way for his reign of peace (Isa 9.2-4; Ezek 34.11-16, 20-22; Hag 2.21f; Zech 9.1-8, 10). The extent of his kingdom is described in various ways. In some of the prophetic statements, expectations relate entirely to the realm of Israel (Isa 6; Jer 23; 33; Ezek 34; 37). In others there is

mention of global changes and of a worldwide reign of the eschatological king (Mic 5.3; Hag 2.22; Zech 9.10) [→**177**]. In Isa 11 the area
affected by the eschatological turmoil is extended to the whole of creation, where all enmity will be removed (vv. 6-8).

One of the essential qualities of the expected king will be his righteousness and his just actions as a judge (Isa 9.6; 11.3-5; 32.1; Jer 23.5f;
33.5; Ezek 37.24; Zech 9.9). His championing of the disadvantaged,
the "poor and needy" is emphasized here (Isa 11.4). But above all
stands the word "peace" (*šālôm*, Isa 9.5f; Mic 5.4; Jer 23.6; Ezek 34.25;
37.26; Zech 9.10). This will be the decisive feature of the end-time to
come, in which the expected Davidic king will exercise his office as
the one commissioned and appointed by God.

Nonetheless, this is not exactly a uniform expectation of a future
king or a successor figure. In particular, these expectations remain
limited to specific areas of the prophetic literature. In the second part
of Isaiah the title "king" is used only of God (Isa 41.21; 43.15; 44.6).
The name David appears only once (55.3) and signals a complete break
with the David tradition: the "unfailing kindnesses" (*ḥasdê dāwîd*) that
God has promised and shown to David are now transferred to Israel.
God will make an "everlasting covenant" with Israel, as he did before
with David; but God himself has ended the covenant with David (Ps
89.40, 50).

In other literature from the time after the catastrophe there is no
sign of beginnings of an expectation of a new king. In the books of
Ezra and Nehemiah David only appears as the founder of cultic regulations (Ezra 8.20; Neh 12.24, 36, 45f).

On the term "Messiah" see above, p. 574.

3. Righteousness and peace

One of the key points of prophetic criticism is the lack of "justice and
righteousness." This criticism is by no means directed solely at the
kings. Rather, the prophets recognize this lack also in the relationships
between Israelites themselves. Justice and righteousness have disappeared from Zion (Isa 1.21) and from the "vineyard" of Israel as a
whole (5.7; cf. 58.2; 59.14; 64.5). It is largely the way the legal system
works that is subjected to sharp prophetic criticism. Isaiah mentions
especially the civil servants (*śārîm*) who accept bribes and do not grant
justice to orphans and widows (1.23; cf. v. 17); they acquit (*ṣdq* hiphil)

the guilty in return for gifts and deny justice to those who are in the right (5.23); in fact they even legislate written law which deprives the insignificant (*dallîm*) of legal recourse and rob the needy (*ˁaniyyîm*) of their rights, so that they can exploit widows and orphans (10.1f; cf. Crüsemann 1992, 31ff). Similar reproaches are found in Amos (5.10-12; cf. 2.7), Micah (2.9-11; 7.3), Jeremiah (5.28; 7.6; 22.3) and elsewhere. The behavior that is criticized here is in clear opposition to the protective rules set out in the Torah for behavior towards the social groups that have no voice of their own in the legal process (Ex 22.20-23; 23.9).

The prophets balance their criticism with the expectation that an eschatological king will stand out by virtue of his righteousness and his fair administration of justice (Isa 9.6; 11.3-5; 32.1; Jer 23.5f; 33.15; Ezek 37.24; Zech 9.9). His support as a judge for the disadvantaged, the "poor and needy," is especially emphasized (Isa 11.4). But just like the prophetic criticism, the future hope extends to Israel as a whole. In Isaiah the complaint that justice and righteousness have departed from Jerusalem is followed by the assurance that God will give Zion just judges "as at the beginning," so that it will be called "The City of Righteousness, The Faithful City" (Isa 1.26f; cf. 33.5); then Torah will go out from Zion for all peoples (2.3) and no one will sin any longer on the "holy mountain" (11.9). When "the Spirit from on high" is poured out upon Israel, then "justice will dwell in the desert and righteousness live in the fertile field" and righteousness will bear its fruits (32.15-18); and finally righteousness will radiate over Zion, so that all the peoples will see it (62.1; cf. Zech 8.3).

In the second part of Isaiah, among the duties given to the "Servant of the Lord" is to ensure justice (*mišpāṭ*) and to establish it in the earth (Isa 42.1-4). So here too the restoration of justice is an essential element of the expected eschatological changes. Ezekiel promises the Judeans living in exile that God will lead them back to their land and then give them a new heart and a new spirit, so that they will keep God's commandments and statutes; and they will then be his people once again, and he will be their God (Ezek 11.17-20; cf. 36.26f).

All these prophetic expectations and hopes direct attention back to the basis for all just behavior: the Torah. A just king could create the conditions for the reestablishment of justice and righteousness, but their realization will also lie in the co-existence of people in Israel itself. This is what people hope for.

In various texts it is said that justice and righteousness stand in a broader context of eschatological changes. The second basic aspect comes into view here: the hope of peace. Here too the concern is with hope of the restoration of what has been lost. Looking back on the completed occupation of the land, at the end of the book of Joshua we read that God had fulfilled his promises to Israel and "given rest" to them (Josh 21.43-45). What had been announced (Deut 12.9f; 25.19) had thus come to fruition. In respect of the reign of David and Solomon it is again stated that God gave Israel rest (2 Sam 7.1; 1 Kgs 5.4f, 18). In this context we also find the key term "peace" (*šālôm*, 1 Kgs 5.4). The gift of peace is expressed by means of an expression found elsewhere in prophetic hopes for the future: "Everyone sat under his vine and his fig-tree" (v. 5; cf. Mic 4.4; Zech 3.10). Here we see the interactive relationship between the retrospect on the lost ideal time and the prospect of the future hope. In Lev 26.3-6 the assurance of peace in the future if the divine commandments are kept is connected with a fertility of the land which goes beyond anything anyone has previously experienced. Peace and fertility together form the lost conditions that people hope will be restored.

The hope of peace then finds expression in different ways in the prophetic future expectations. The savior-king expected in Isaiah is not only called "Prince of Peace" (*śar-šālôm*), but "everlasting peace" will be in his domain, and justice and righteousness will reign (Isa 9.5f). Here the two great lines are connected. In Jeremiah too the expected "just shoot" will reign in justice and righteousness, and Israel will live in safety (Jer 23.5f). Ezekiel promises that in the time of the eschatological David that God will appoint, he will make a "covenant of peace" (*bᵉrît šālôm*) with Israel and cause them to live in security (Ezek 34.25; cf. 37.26. In Mic 5.3 the statement "they will live" should probably be taken in this sense; whether the word "peace" in v. 4a relates to the ruler is disputed.). Finally also the just king expected in Zechariah will create peace (Zech 9.19).

But the expectation of peace is not tied to the figure of a future king. Jeremiah writes to those deported to Babylon that God has thoughts of peace (or: of salvation) for them, to give them a "future and hope" (Jer 29.11). In the hoped-for end-times "the fruit of righteousness will be peace; the effect of righteousness will be quietness and confidence forever" (Isa 32.17). In Isa 52.7 the title of king is transferred to God when the "joyful message" announces peace, goodness and salvation and calls to Zion: "Your God is king!" God's sovereignty

696 The Canonical Hebrew Bible

is expressed in the fact that he creates salvation/peace (*šālôm*) and disaster (*rā'āh*), and that he lets righteousness reign from heaven, so that righteousness and salvation spring up from the earth (45.7f). According to Isa 54.10 God will not let his "covenant of peace" (cf. Ezek 34.25; 37.26) fall. In future days God will appoint peace and righteousness as the authorities (60.17); and finally he will spread peace over Jerusalem "like a river" (66.12). Haggai connects the rebuilt temple with the hope that the glory (*kābôd*) of this new house will be greater than that of the first, and that God will give peace "to this place" (Hag 2.9).

So from quite different sides and various perspectives a relatively uniform picture emerges: righteousness and peace are the two great hopes for the time of the future. Only God can give peace. But for the restoration and continuing existence of righteousness Israel itself can and must make its own contribution since it must be perfected and lived. The basis for this is and remains the Torah.

4. Repentance and return. God turns

In the future expectations in the Hebrew Bible the experiences of return from exile have a fundamental part to play. In pre-exilic times there were certainly all sorts of future expectations and hopes. But most of the books of the Bible reached their final form only in post-exilic times, so that the experiences of the exile and the return have found their way in too. Experiences of earlier historical periods have also been seen in a new light and set in new contexts. A representative example of this is the way the first exodus is seen in the light of the second (see §9.3) [→475].

In this whole context the Hebrew word *šûb* plays a crucial role. It is precisely the ambiguity of this verb that gives it its key position. It can mean "turn around," both in the sense of turning away (e.g. from sin or from the worship of foreign gods), and in the sense of turning towards, i.e. to God; in addition it can mean "return" in the spatial sense. In Hosea we find all these meanings: the Israelites "turn away," i.e. away from God (Hos 7.16); they must "return," to Egypt (8.13; 9.3; 11.5); the hope is that in the future they will "turn back" to God (2.9; 3.5); they will "return" as they once did from Egypt (14.8). "This means, consequently: Israel's guilt, its punishment, its hoped-for change and its ultimate salvation are expressed in one term!" So *šûb* "has become really the central, indeed constitutive key term in the eschatology of the book of Hosea" (Jeremias 1995b, 68f).

The subject of the verb can also be God, however. This is especially prevalent again in Hosea. God will heal Israel's "apostasy" (*m'šûbāh*) by "turning away" his anger from Israel, i.e. by refraining from punishment (14.5). So it is "impossible to speak of Israel's turning away/return without speaking of Yahweh's turning away/return" (Jeremias, *loc. cit.*). God can also be the direct subject of the verb (in this case transitively used): "Restore us again (*šûbēnû*), O God our Savior, and put away your displeasure towards us" (Ps 85.5; cf. Zenger & Horsfeld 2000, 524). So God is asked to take the initiative himself for the return of Israel to its earlier status.

Finally, God is always the subject of the expression *šûb-š'bût*, which is common in Jeremiah, especially in chs. 29–33 (30.3, 18; 31.23; 33.7, 11 etc.). Its literal translation is disputed: "turn the captivity," "turn the fate," or with a more eschatological tinge: "restoration of the former things" in the sense of a *restitutio in integrum* (cf. *THAT* II, 886f). At any rate the term designates an active move on God's part, by means of which Israel's present situation is turned fundamentally to the better; God turns Israel's fate around. The interrelationship between Israel's turning and the turn in God's action is impressively evident in texts in which this change is found in the immediate context of another use of the verb *šûb*: "If you return (*šûb*) to the LORD, your God … then the LORD, your God, will restore your fortunes (*šûb-š'bût*) and have compassion on you and gather you again from all the nations where he scattered you" (Deut 30.2f). Israel's return and the turning of its fate by God are directly connected here.

And God himself turns around: "Return to me, and I will return to you" (*šûbû 'ēlay … we'āšûb 'ʰlēkem*, Zech 1.3; cf. Mal 3.7). The reciprocity comes even more directly to expression here. God's relationship with Israel will be placed on a new footing if Israel should really turn around. God, in fact, has already turned around: "I have returned (NIV: I will return) to Jerusalem" (*šabtî lirûšalayim*, Zech 1.16); "I have returned (NIV: I will return) to Zion" (8.3; on the translation cf. Hanhart 1990ff, 56f, 513). What Ezekiel has experienced in the view of the future, that God has returned to his house (Ezek 43) has in Zechariah's view become reality with the beginning of the restoration of the temple on Zion.

This view of Zechariah's makes it clear that in the context of eschatological expectations, what is expected, what is happening now and what has already happened can flow into each other. Life in eschatological expectations moves on the boundaries of present reality. But it is only in apocalyptic writing that this is fully developed.

5. The renewed covenant

"The time is coming when I will make a new covenant with the house of Israel and with the house of Judah" (Jer 31.31). With these words begins one of the most frequently quoted and interpreted texts of the Hebrew Bible. It is also a text which confronts exegesis with particularly difficult questions. The more so in that this text has gained a very far-reaching meaning all its own in the Christian tradition, which is consciously or unconsciously present for the interpreter, but which should not in principle influence his or her interpretation. (Cf., however, 1991f; Crüsemann 2000.)

The special status of this text is already expressed in the fact that the term "new covenant" (*b'rît hadāšāh*) occurs only here in the Hebrew Bible. But what does "new" mean here? The Hebrew root *ḥdš*, which derives from the adjective "new," is most frequently found in the word *ḥodeš*, "new moon," which also means simply "month;" the moon becomes "new" over and over again. The same occurs in the rhythm of the year, so that there is talk of new corn (Lev 26.10) and new fruits (Song 7.14). But also new beginnings of some significance in human life are also thus called: a new coat (1 Kgs 11.29f), a new house (Deut 20.5; 22.8), a new, i.e. recently married, wife (Deut 24.5) etc. And God himself constantly "renews the face of the earth" (Ps 104.30) and the youthful vigor of a person (103.5); there is the prayer: "renew our days as of old" (Lam 5.21) and he is thanked for the fact that his compassion is new every morning (3.23). So the concern is always with renewal, but which is often experienced as a new beginning.

In the prophetic literature it is only from the time of the Babylonian exile onwards that the word "new" is found: in the second part of Isaiah, in Jeremiah and Ezekiel. In Isa 42.9 the "new thing" is contrasted with the "former thing," which has occurred and which one should thus no longer think about (43.18); God will "from now on tell you of new things, of hidden things unknown to you" (48.6). Jeremiah places the emphasis differently: Israel will not experience something new from God; the basis of the covenant is, and will remain, the Torah. The new thing will be the way in which the Israelites respond to the Torah. Time and again, Jeremiah has sharply criticized their attitude to the Torah: they have rejected the Torah (6.19) and abandoned it (9.12); their forefathers already forsook God themselves by not keeping the Torah (16.11). The reproaches apply especially to those in positions of responsibility: kings, princes, priests and prophets (32.32f; 2.8; 8.8). And in Jeremiah's temple speech the call to keep the Torah is connected with the announcement of the destruction of the temple (26.4-6). But then the days will come when God will "turn the fortunes of my people Israel and Judah" and will bring them back into the land "which I gave to your fathers" (30.3). Then a great deal will happen, which chs. 30–33 tell us about.

A climax comes in the prophecy about the "new covenant." Again we read: "the days will come" (31.31). God will then perform a fundamental renewal by concluding a new, i.e. a renewed, covenant with Israel and Judah. What is new about this covenant is initially put negatively: "it will not be like the covenant I made with their forefathers when I took them by the hand to lead them out of Egypt" (v. 32). Hearers and readers are familiar with the juxtaposition of the leading-out from Egypt and the events on Sinai from Jeremiah's "covenant sermon" (11.3f); but now Jeremiah represents the breaking of the covenant, which began with the sin with the "Golden Calf" (Ex 32) as it were as a feature of this covenant: "(*'ašer*, it is true of this that) they broke my covenant" (v. 32b).

The precise meaning of the following clause, "though I showed myself a master to them," remains uncertain. Is the verb *bā'al* "to be lord or master" (which can also mean "marry") meant rather in a neutral sense here—"though I was their Lord" (cf. NIV: "though I was a husband to them")—or in a punitive sense, "so that I had to show myself as Lord to them" (cf. Luther 1545; von Rad 1965, 222; Ruldoph 1968 *ad loc.*)?

The positive exposition of what is new about this covenant is linked with a renewed time indication that points beyond everything that has gone before: "after those days" (v. 33). This expression, unique in this form in the Hebrew Bible, expresses the fact that this announcement will not be realized until all has transpired that has been previously announced as happening "in those days." The "new covenant" will thus really be an "eschatological" episode, a final event. God will conclude this covenant with the "house of Israel," i.e. with the entire covenant people. What is new about it will not, however, be its content. As before, it is about keeping the Torah; covenant and Torah remain inseparable. At the same time this tells us that the covenant there has been up to now will not be revoked. But God will create the conditions to make it impossible for this covenant ever to be broken again. For then the Torah will no longer be a written one, heard "from outside," to which each individual must respond with a personal act of compliance, but God will "put my law in their minds and write it on their hearts," so that it will become a "natural" thing to live in accordance with this Torah, which means keeping the covenant.

A new way of knowing God will be associated with this. They will not have to teach each other, but each person will acknowledge the Lord individually (v. 34). This recalls an earlier prophecy in Jeremiah. In the parable of the two baskets of figs we read: "I will give them a heart to know me, that I am the LORD" (24.7). So knowledge of God will be a product of the renewal of the heart. These two aspects, the Torah in the heart and the new knowledge of God, are connected in the covenant formula (v. 33b). This too points back again to 24.7 (cf. 1995a, 39). The announcement that God will give the Israelites a new heart is also found in Ezekiel. It is expressed in very graphic terms here: God will take the "heart of stone" out of their bodies and give them a "heart of flesh." Here too the concern is to "walk in my commandments" and to "keep my statutes," and here too the covenant formula follows (Ezek 11.19f; 36.26-28). (The terms "covenant" and "Torah" are, however, absent in this context in Ezekiel.)

From this point of view it is surprising that Deuteronomy seems to take as a given what Jeremiah announces in an eschatological promise: "The word (i.e. "this commandment," *miṣwāh*, v. 11) is very near you; it is in your mouth and in your heart so that you may obey it" (Deut 30.14). This quite uneschatological view of things is "somewhat odd" (von Rad 1964, 131), especially as Deuteronomy is also well aware that the fulfilling of the Torah can certainly not be taken for granted; the consequences of the non-observance of the Torah are set out in an impressive way in ch. 28. But ch. 30 then speaks of a turning and a new beginning; in v. 6 there is mention of the circumcision of the hearts. Should v. 14 be read from this perspective?

The use of the covenant formula in connection with the "new covenant" again shows that this will not be *another* covenant. In this the "new covenant" promised by Jeremiah stands in continuity with the Sinai covenant, which was renewed and confirmed after the apostasy of the Israelites; this too was in a way a "new" covenant (Dohmen 1993). And in other texts too we read that God will ultimately remember his covenant and enforce it anew (e.g. Lev 26; Ezek 16). Here in Jeremiah the emphasis lies entirely on what is to happen "after these days."

The term "everlasting covenant" also gains new meaning in the context of the proclamation of salvation in Jer 29 and 33. When all the predicted calamity has fallen upon Jerusalem, God will at last gather his people together and take them back there, and he will put the fear of God into the hearts of those returning home (32.39f). The observance of the Torah and the knowledge of God spoken of in the promise of the "new covenant" (31.33f), are now joined by the fear of God. Together with the others, this will be the sign of the "everlasting covenant" (*b'rît 'ôlām*, 32.40), i.e. of the covenant that God will renew and confirm in "those days."

6. The day of Yhwh

Many prophetic passages speak of the day or the days when what they have announced will occur. The variety of terms used in this shows that the contours of this complex of ideas are not firmly fixed. On the other hand there are clear characteristics in the language used and in the intent of the various means of expression, and awareness of this can make a contribution to our understanding of the future expectations of the prophets. As a cautionary note we should mention that these terms certainly do not occur in all the prophecies of the future, so that we are dealing only with a selection from them.

Excursus: The day and the days

The word "day" (*yôm*) is one of the commonest words in the language of the Hebrew Bible. The term used for a particular day when something happened, or is going to happen, is "that day" (*hayyôm hahû'*) or "on that day" (*bayyôm hahû'*). This phrase is found frequently in prophetic language. In the book of Isaiah in particular we find an extended usage, though with a very striking distribution: more than 40 times in chs. 1–39, but only once in chs. 40–66 (in 52.6). This tallies with the fact that in the main the expression "on that day" points to, or announces, events to come. These are in particular menacing events which are sent or brought about by God, or their accompanying circumstances (Isa 3.18; 4.1; 5.30; 7.18 etc.). In the other prophetic books the situation is similar, though the expression "on that day" is also less common. Some examples: Jer 4.9; 25.33; Ezek 30.9; Hos 1.5; Amos 2.16; 8.3; Mic 2.4.

In a number of texts, however, the expression "on that day" speaks of what will happen afterwards, after the catastrophe. Thus there is talk of the survivors, the "remnant" (Isa 10.20; 11.11), or of God's wrath being averted (12.1, 4; 25.9; 26.1 etc., also 52.6). Similarly, Jer 30.8; Ezek 24.26f; 29.21; Mic 4.6; Zeph 3.11 etc. Elements that might be called eschatological are part of this picture: that a shoot will sprout forth from the stem of Jesse, cut off at the root (11.10), or that in an eschatological reiteration of the battle with chaos in creation God will kill the leviathan with his sword (27.1). Similarly, Hos 2.20, 23; Amos 9.11; Hag 2.23 etc.

In addition we also find the plural expression "in those days" (*bayyāmîm hahēm*). While talk of the day emphasizes more strongly the coming of an event, with the plural a longer period of time is in view. The concern is always with the time "afterwards." This expression is particularly common in Jeremiah, while it is absent from Isaiah. Far-reaching changes can be indicated by this: people will no longer think of the Ark (Jer 3.16); Judah and Israel will come home together (3.18); God will renew his covenant with Israel (31.33, here with the words "after those days"); he will make a righteous shoot sprout from David's line (33.15); Israel's sin will no longer be found, because God will forgive it in the case of those who remain, the "remnant" (50.20). The related plural phrase "days will come," often introduced by "behold" (*hinnēh yāmîm bā'îm*), is found especially in Jeremiah (7.32; 9.24; 16.14 etc.).

All three expressions can introduce a prophecy; the singular form is often expanded by the prefaced phrase "it will come to pass" (*wᵉhāyah*). Occasionally we find whole series of prophecies with an introduction like this, which thus looks formulaic: e.g. Isa 7.18, 20, 21, 23; 17.4, 7, 9; 19.16, 18, 19, 21, 23, 24; Zech 12–13 (9 times). In the commentaries there is a common tendency to regard these introductory formulae as exchangeable elements of "secondary" additions (cf. Wolff 1969, 373). But as a result the clearly intentional difference between "day" and the "days" is lost. This is particularly clear in Amos 9: in v. 11 the singular phrase expresses God's action in restoring the "tabernacle of David" with its immediate effects is announced, while the plural phrase in v. 13 looks forward to a time of prosperity which will be characterized by fundamental changes in nature and in the fortunes of the people of Israel.

Finally there is also talk of the "end of days." The expression *b''aḥarît hayyāmîm* can point forward to a close or a distant future in which something will happen. Thus in the "blessing of Jacob" Jacob tells his sons what they will face in the period after his death (Gen 49.1); the announcements cover the prospect of longer periods in the history of the individual tribes. Jeremiah announces in the divine speech that Israel will at last acknowledge God's action (Jer 23.20 = 30.24). Hosea expects that after a lengthy period of suffering the Israelites will repent and seek God (Hos 3.5). Balaam's announcement to Barak of what Israel will do to his people in the future (Num 24.14) includes the prediction that a "star will come out of Jacob" and a "scepter will rise out of Israel" (v. 17); here one can discern a certain "eschatological" element. This emerges more clearly in Isa 2.2 = Mic 4.1, where the prophecy announces the end-time journeying of the peoples to Zion. Ezekiel announces an eschatological disaster when Gog of Magog will descend upon Israel (Ezek 38.16). Finally in the book of Daniel the expression relates to the last epoch in history, to which the apocalyptic writer looks forward (Dan 2.28 [Aramaic]; 10.14). This is the first time that this expression speaks of the last phase of history, of the ἔσχατα, the term generally used in the Greek translation.

★ ★ ★ ★ ★

In a series of texts there is a greater density of statements about the future day using the expression "day of Yhwh" (*yôm yhwh*, henceforward "Day of the Lord"). This is clearly a fixed term which stands out clearly from the other statements about "the day" or "the days." A wide variety of ideas can be associated with this. In each case the concern is with an event that is directly instigated by God; and these events are in the main menacing ones that spread horror and fear. But the question is, against whom are they directed, against Israel, or against its enemies? And this means: will the Day of the Lord bring Israel salvation or disaster?

It with this question that Amos confronts his contemporaries: "Woe to you who long for the Day of the LORD!" (Amos 5.18). So among his hearers there are those who view the Day of the Lord as a positive, desirable event. Amos points out that "the Day of the Lord is darkness and not light" (vv. 18, 20). This need not mean that Amos is the first to oppose a generally dominant view that the Day of the Lord means salvation for Israel (cf. Hoffmann 1981, 42f). Isaiah already tells us in a context directed against the "house of Jacob" (Isa 2.6) that the "Day of the LORD Zebaot" will come upon "the proud and lofty" (vv. 12-21). In Isa 13, however, there is also a text in which the Day of the Lord (vv. 6, 9) is a judgment of annihilation on Babel. So there are two quite different aspects to the expectation of what the Day of the Lord will mean for Israel. Then the book of Zephaniah is entirely dominated by the depiction of mighty events in which the Day of the Lord (Zeph 1.7) will punish the sins of the ruling classes in Jerusalem but will then extend also to all the inhabitants of the earth (1.14-18). The day is impressively depicted in graphic terms: it is great and bitter, "a day of wrath, a day of distress and anguish, a day of trouble and ruin, a day of darkness and gloom, a day of clouds and blackness, a day of trumpet and battle cry" (vv. 15f). This "day of wrath" will put an end to all the inhabitants of the earth (v. 18). Similar descriptions are also found in other texts (e.g. Isa 13.6ff; Joel 2.1ff).

But in Zephaniah this is not all. The cry out of this dramatic scenario is: "Gather together ... seek the LORD!" (2.1, 3). This means, "See righteousness—and humility." This call is associated with a hesitant hope of preservation on the "day of the wrath of the LORD:" "perhaps" (v. 3). And then the Zephaniah document ends with a saving conclusion: God will leave a "remnant of Israel" (3.13), "a meek and humble people who trust in the name of the LORD" (v. 12); and God will gather them and bring them home and turn their fortunes (*šûb šᵉbût*, v. 20). So the Day of the Lord stands in the general context of an end-time which will ultimately be a time of prosperity for the "remnant" of Israel.

All the complexity of the tradition of the Day of Lord is evident in the Joel document. In chs. 1f [1.1–2.27] this day is described as the day of judgment on Israel and in ch. 4 [ch. 3] as judgment on Israel's enemies. Between them in ch. 3 [2.28-32] stands the description of an eschatological event in the narrower sense: God will pour out his spirit on all flesh, and in heaven and on earth devastating events will occur in nature, "before the coming of the great and dreadful Day of the LORD" (3.1-3[2.29-31]). But then there will be salvation for "all who call on the name of the LORD," on Mount Zion (v. 4[2.32]). The distinction between Israel and its enemies seems to have been removed here, in that of "all flesh" all those are saved who call upon the name of the Lord on Zion.

The great significance of the expected Day of the Lord, finally, is also evident in the fact that this theme has become an important element in the collection and composition of the Book of the Twelve Prophets. The Joel document is placed before the Amos document, so that the reader has the complexity of notions of the Day of the Lord in mind when in the central passage in Amos he or she reads the question: "What will the Day of the LORD be to you?" (Amos 5.18). Amos is followed by the little document of Obadiah, which is entirely dominated by this theme but deals with it in a very biased way from the point of view treated in Joel 4 of judgment on Israel's enemies, in this case Edom. We may suppose that this bias was to be relieved by the connection with Joel and Amos. In Zephaniah, the last of the pre-exilic prophets, this theme is again a focus. And in the last chapter of the book Malachi speaks of the expectation that God will send the prophet Elijah "before the great and dreadful Day of the LORD comes" (Mal 3.23[4.6]). (On this topic cf. 1997c [=2000c] and 1998.)

7. Israel's remnant

The Hebrew Bible often talks in a variety of contexts of a "remnant" being "left" in Israel. Unlike other common ideas, e.g. covenant, election, grace, Torah etc., there is no comprehensive terminology for the notion of the remnant. This is not a "theological" concept in the narrower sense, either. To put it more precisely: its theological significance is not discernible at first sight.

The Hebrew terms to be considered here express in different ways that something or someone remains from a larger crowd or community. This can be said with a negative or positive evaluation, or neutrally. A few examples: Samuel presents Saul with the remaining meat (*hanniš'ār*) that has been kept for him (1 Sam 9.24); after the plague of frogs, frogs are to remain only in the Nile (Ex 8.5, 7); when sacrificing a dove, after the sprinkling rite the priest is to squeeze out the remaining blood at the foot of the altar (Lev 5.9).

In relation to humans, the character of the "remnant" is more clearly evident: before the encounter with Esau, Jacob divides his family and all his possession into two parts, so that at least the remaining half can form a "band of survivors" (*p'lêṭāh*, Gen 32.9[8]). Naomi remains with her two sons, when her husband dies (Ruth 1.3), so that the continued existence of the family is imperiled; but for this "remnant" of the family there is still a future. In Jehu's revolution the entire royal house of Ahab is wiped out, so that no one remains (2 Kgs 10.11, 17); there is no future for this dynasty. "Remain" or "survive" can thus mean a future; but where there is no "remnant" there is no longer a future.

In the biblical primordial history there is already talk of the "remnant." In the Flood everything "that was on the earth" is obliterated; "only Noah remained and what was with him in the ark" (Gen 7.23). This is a very significant text: the entirety of humankind after the Flood is a "remnant." And with Noah, as the representative of this remnant, God concluded an "everlasting covenant," that he would never again destroy "all flesh" (9.11; this connection was already pointed out by Jesus ben Sirach: Sir 44.17-19; cf. Clements 1993, 938). A very positive view of the remnant is evident here: this is *only* a remnant, but God's promise for the future rests on it. The interpretation that Joseph gives his brothers concerning his own fate is very similar: "God sent me ahead of you to preserve for you a remnant (*š'ērît*) on earth and to save your lives as a great band of survivors (*p'lêṭāh gedolāh*)" (Gen 45.7). It is out of this saved and surviving remnant that the people of Israel then grows.

In the further course of the story there are repeatedly points where the remnant idea is discussed. Before the separation of Israel and Judah we read in the prophecy of Ahijah that God will leave only one tribe to the Davidide Rehoboam "for the sake of David and Jerusalem" (1 Kgs 11.32) and in order to give David a "lamp" (v. 36). Judah is what is left of the twelve-tribe people that once developed in Egypt out of the saved and surviving remnant of Jacob's descendants (Ex 1.9). But still it is in Judah, and not least also Jerusalem, that the history of God's dealings with Israel and Israel's history with God continues.

The remnant idea has a special part to play in the Elijah story. In the divine message to Elijah we read: "I reserve seven thousand in Israel— all those whose knees have not bowed down to Baal and all whose mouths have not kissed him" (1 Kgs 19.18). This prophecy is set in a broader context: Elijah complains that he alone remains of all the prophets of Yhwh, because queen Jezebel has eliminated them all (18.22; 19.10, 14). The divine word sounds like an answer: Elijah will not remain on its own, but a remnant will remain in Israel. More precisely: God will leave a remnant. It remains open who the seven thousand are or will be; but there is no conditional element here in the sense that this might depend on whether such are to be found. "God determines the remnant. He already knows of those whose existence has so far remained hidden to Elijah" (von Rad 1965, 30). And the remnant will not simply "remain," but it will be "left" by God.

In the books of Kings the theme of the remnant appears in two more very different contexts. First, Hezekiah receives from the mouth of Isaiah the assurance that the group of survivors that remains of the house of Judah will again set down roots and bear fruit, and that "out of Jerusalem will come a remnant, and out of Mount Zion a band of survivors" (2 Kgs 19.30f = Isa 37.31f). Here the saving tradition of the remnant idea finds its sequel. Things are quite different in the prophecies against Manasseh: God will wipe out Jerusalem and deliver "the remnant of my inheritance (*š^e'ērît naḥ^alātî*)" into the hands of its enemies (2 Kgs 21.13f). The picture of the threatening catastrophe that will come upon Judah and Jerusalem is already painted here.

But this is not the last word to be found about the expectation of a remnant of Israel in the Hebrew Bible. In the prophetic books quite new dimensions open up. In the first chapter of Isaiah already we read in respect of the "remaining daughter (of) Zion:" "Unless the Lord Almighty had left us some survivors, we would have become like Sodom and Gomorrah" (Isa 1.9; on the following, cf. 2000a). Here the remnant idea is closely associated with Zion/Jerusalem, and the "leaving" of the remnant (*śārîd*) is understood as a deliberate action by God. The context makes it clear that those remaining might be included among those in the prophet's address to "you rulers of Sodom, you people of Gomorrah" (v. 10). But in Jerusalem God has left a remnant, without posing the question of a minimum number of "righteous" as before in Sodom (Gen 18.23-32).

Talk of the remnant carries on through the whole of Isaiah. The expectations and hopes associated with this are shown from various perspectives. In Isa 4.2-6 an announcement of salvation is made to the "band of survivors of Israel" in Zion/Jerusalem, specified as "all who are recorded among the living in Jerusalem;" those included are called "holy" (v. 3). Membership of the remnant is presented almost as an honorific title here. But this does not exclude the possibility that this may be a small remnant, a remnant that is scarcely perceptible as such, even if the stump of the tree is cut down; but this remnant too is "holy seed," because new life will grow from it (6.13). In the context of Isaiah's vision (ch. 6) one might almost say that into this seed, "this tiny point at the end of the vision, the entire holiness is compressed which the Seraphim sang about" and that it is at the same time the opening up of a significant future (Landy 1999, 80).

In Isa 7 the name of Isaiah's son, Shear-Yashub (*š᷾'ār yāšûb*, "a remnant will return"), contains a specific message, since Isaiah is expressly required in the prophecy to take his son with him. This message, however, is not immediately deciphered; the reader can however understand it in the broader context in which it is found in Isaiah. To begin with, this name points to the other name mentioned in this narrative: Immanuel (*'immānû'ēl*, "God with us"). The "we" that speaks in this name is the remnant that God is with, even if he has abandoned Israel as a whole. (This is the only name in the Hebrew Bible formed with the 1st person plural pronoun; cf. Rice 1978, 223.) In 8.8 the land is called "your land, Immanuel." So in the context it seems reasonable to take the "disciples" and "children" of Isaiah (8.16, 18) as the collective Immanuel, which means: as the remnant. So the "we" in Immanuel could also include 1.9 (cf. 2000a, 272).

The name Shear-Yashub also reappears: "A remnant will return (*š᷾'ār yāšûb*), a remnant of Jacob will return to the Mighty God" (10.21). This remnant that is prepared to return is equated with the "remnant of Israel" and the "band of survivors of the house of Jacob" who will now rely only on the Lord, the Holy One of Israel (v. 20). But even if the people of Israel have been as numerous as the sand on the seashore, only a remnant will return (once again: Shear Yashub, v. 22). Finally following the promise of an eschatological king and a kingdom of peace (11.1-9), we read that God will "reclaim the remnant of his people (*š᷾'ār 'ammô*)" that is left among all the surrounding peoples (v. 11). And then God will deal with the "sea of Egypt" and the Euphrates as before with the Reed Sea, so that the remnant of his people can pass through on dry land (vv. 15f). The return of the remnant from exile will be a second exodus.

So the talk of the remnant in the first great collection of Isaianic prophecies (chs. 1–12) has clear features. On this basis one can also understand the concluding psalm (ch. 12) as the hymn of praise which the remnant community will sing together "on that day" in Zion/Jerusalem (Webb 1990, 73). The close link between the remnant idea and Zion has already been clear in other passages, as we have seen (cf. on 1.8f and 4.3). It is here that further texts in Isaiah belong, in which the notion of the remnant comes clearly to expression, even if the characteristic terms (which are by no means uniform) are not used. Thus we hear of the re-established rule of Yhwh Zebaot on Zion with a (remnant) community represented by the "elders" (24.23) and of the great homecoming of the lost and outcast from all the ends of the earth to Zion, the "holy hill in Jerusalem," where they will worship the Lord (27.12f). "On that day" God will be a crown and a wreath for the remnant of his people (28.5; cf. 11.11); those that are left, i.e. the remnant, will be like a signpost on a mountaintop and like a field sign on a hill (30.17). Finally the community of the "redeemed of the Lord" will gather on Zion in jubilant praise (35.10), as the first main section of Isaiah ends in a similar way to the first great collection in ch. 12. (On Isa 37.31f see the discussion of 2 Kgs 19.30f. above.)

In Isa 40–55 two important emphases are made by means of talk of the remnant. In 51.11 the message of 35.10 is repeated verbatim: the "redeemed of the Lord" will return to Zion with jubilation. The conclusion in 55.12f is very similar: the returnees will leave in joy, and mountains, hill and trees will rejoice and clap their hands. None of the customary terms is used here again, but it is clear that the subject is the returning remnant. This time it is the returnees who are the remnant. This also became clear back in 46.3, where the prophet addresses the exiles as "the whole remnant (*š'erit*) of the house of Israel."

In Isa 56–66 the situation has changed fundamentally. The returnees are the remnant, though this is not expressly stated. Within this remnant new criteria of identity are developed. They are already evident in the introductory key position of "justice and righteousness" (56.1). From this point of view foreigners, i.e. non-Israelites, can also be God's "servants" and be among those who worship him cultically in his house on the "holy mountain" (v. 6). Thus the idea of the remnant is on the one hand extended:" "all flesh," i.e. also all the members of the peoples who have demonstrated that they are among the servants of God, will participate in the great eschatological worship service (66.23); on the other hand however, those who have turned away from God (*poš'îm*) are delivered up to destruction (v. 24). "While the remnant may be inclusive it is not universal. The remnant is a remnant still" (Webb 1990, 80).

In the other prophetic book the remnant theme appears only sporadically; but it is clear that it is an element of the tradition that does not have to be reintroduced. Thus we read in Amos: "Perhaps the LORD, the God Zebaot, will be gracious to the remnant of Joseph" (Amos 5.15). The "perhaps" is again restricted to the remnant here. (Cf. also Zeph 3.12f.) In the concluding section of Amos the idea then crops up in another graphic form when we read that God will shake the house of Israel "as in a sieve" (9.9f). Read together with v. 8, this means that only those members of the "house of Jacob" will be saved who remain after this sieving process (cf. Jeremias 1995a, 133).

In Micah talk of the remnant appears at three important points. The divine speech in Mic 2.12f provides "the first hope for the banished and scattered" (Kessler 1999, 136ff). God wants to gather "Jacob as a whole" and bring the remnant of Israel together; he will bring them to safety like a shepherd his flock, and he will himself go before them like a king. According to the context this assurance of salvation is directed in particular to those who have previously been exploited and driven into misery (1.16; 2.2, 9). In 4.6f there is again talk of gathering and bringing together. The image of the shepherd also crops up again, this time especially with reference to the animals of the flock, which are only rescued as "lame," as injured (cf. on 3.1-4). But the present fate of the flock is at the same time also the consequence of God's action in bringing calamity (v. 6b), which will now be at an end. And the lame are now "made a remnant" (*w'samtî ... liš'ērît*, v. 7). A quite positive aspect of the remnant idea is evident here; it is tantamount to an award, a title of honor. This is expressed with even more force in the special position accorded in 5.6f to the remnant of Jacob "among many generations:" it will be like dew, which falls to the ground without human collaboration and becomes a blessing, or on the other hand like a lion that no one can stand up to. This double aspect stands still in its ambivalence. But the crucial thing is that this remnant will not be some pathetic left-over but something new, something special, which will play its own part among the peoples.

A striking lack of uniformity in the idea of the remnant arises in the book of Jeremiah. First Jeremiah explains explicitly, a number of times, that there will be no remnant for Israel when the announced judgment of God comes in (6.9; 8.3; 15.9). But then a positive aspect turns up when Jeremiah announces in the dispute with the bad "shepherds" that God himself will gather the "remnant of my flocks" from all the countries to which he has banished them, and will give them new shepherds (23.1-4), in fact even a new "righteous shoot" from the house of David (vv. 5f). But then we see that the term "remnant" is not fixed when in the vision of the two baskets of figs the bad figs are described as "the remnant (*š*e*'ērît*) of Jerusalem, those who remained (*hanniš'ārîm*) in the land" (v. 8), while the whole promise for the future applies to those in exile in Babylon (vv. 5-7). In the assurances of salvation to the exiles in Jeremiah's letter in ch. 29 the remnant terminology is not to be found. In ch. 31 however there is a call to rejoice because God has helped his people, the "remnant of Israel" (v. 7). Here we see the same positive understanding of the remnant as in the other prophets. —But a new term occurs here: those living in exile are termed the *gālût* (24.5) or *gôlāh* (29.4), a term which has a clearly positive sound to it. We shall return to this later.

First we must consider two more extremely different ideas of the eschatological remnant in prophetic texts. Zechariah continues the line discernible so far, but he also takes it a step further. He speaks of the remnant as an already existing entity: "'It may seem marvelous to the remnant of this people at that time, but will it seem marvelous to me?' declares the LORD Zebaot" (Zech 8.6). The "remnant in those days" are the present inhabitants of Jerusalem (vv. 1ff). But the eschatological restoration of life in Jerusalem is not yet complete, so that the announcement can still seem "too marvelous." The "remnant of this people" is thus expressly promised, once again, the change and renewal of their living circumstances (vv. 11f).

A quite different notion of the remnant is to be seen in Joel 3[2.28ff]. When God pours out his spirit on "all flesh" at the end of days, then "all those who call on the name of the LORD" will be saved; "for on Mount Zion there will be a band of survivors (*p*e*lêṭāh*), as the LORD has said, among the survivors (*še*rîdîm*) whom the LORD calls" (v. 5[2.32]). So here it is not a remnant of Israel or Judah, but of all those who call upon the name of the Lord. In the context they may come from all the peoples, from "all flesh;" and they will be those who have been equipped by the pouring-out of the spirit of God to call on God's name in this situation of extreme danger. God will answer this cry, as we read at the end: "whom the Lord calls." But it will only be a band of the saved, a remnant. —Here there is a remarkable parallel to the expectation at the end of the book of Isaiah, that "all flesh," i.e. including all members of the peoples that have shown they are among the servants of God, will take part in the great eschatological worship service (66.23). But the difference is also obvious in the type of end-time expectation.

The book of Ezra presents as it were the counterpart to this: here the concern is with the remnant of Israel. The term *gôlāh* plays a crucial role in this. This word is found already in Jeremiah (see above). It first means the process of leading into captivity (2 Kgs 24.25f etc.) but then becomes a term for the group of exiles in Babylonia, as in Jer 29.1, 4, 20, 31 etc. Dominant here are the tones of salvation: the Golah is the remnant on whom the promise for Israel's future rests. Then in Ezra the term begins to be connected closely with the remnant idea. In Ezra 1.4 we read in the continuation of the decree of Cyrus after the departure to "go up" (*'ālāh*) to Jerusalem: "the people of any place where survivors remain (*niš'ār*)" and a few verses later there is then mention of the departure of the Golah from Babylon to Jerusalem (v. 11). In the arguments that now follow, the returnees who begin with the temple construction are designated as "all members of the Golah" (4.1). In 6.19 the entire community that gathers to celebrate the Passover is so described. Then v. 21 is especially important: the Passover is eaten by the "Israelites who had returned from the exile ... together with all who had separated themselves from the unclean practices of their Gentile neighbors." So here the returned members of the Golah form the real worshiping community, whose numbers are however swelled by the Judeans who remained in the land, who are prepared to "seek the Lord, the God of Israel," i.e. to submit themselves to the cultic regulations of the Golah.

In Ezra's day the situation seems to have change. Now it is the "people of Israel" and its representatives (9.1) who have been guilty of mixed marriages, so it is a misdemeanor of the Golah itself (v. 4), which is here equated expressly with "Israel." And this happens at a moment when God has after a long history of sinning and persecution left his people a band of survivors and thus granted them a "firm place in his sanctuary" (v. 8). Should this remnant, this band of survivors, now be endangered anew (vv. 13-15)? Here the key terms *š'ērît* and *p'lêṭāh* appear together again and also in close association with the term Golah.

For the time being this is the end-point. In the multifarious versions of the remnant idea it has become clear time and again that it is the "remnant" that the promises apply to, and that has a future. The remnant *is* Israel. In Ezra's time this certainty is transferred to the Golah: the Golah *is* Israel—just as the host of the children of Jacob were saved from famine with their families and the new generation remaining after the wilderness period and similarly Judah which remained after the "division of the kingdoms" and finally also the Golah in Babylonia, as addressed and comforted by the prophet in Isa 40–55 and Jeremiah. This self-understanding of the returning community as the remnant and as Israel that comes to expression in Ezra has already been outlined clearly in Isa 35.10 and 51.11.

8. What does Israel expect in the future?

What has been brought together in the preceding paragraphs resists systematic summary. But a number of common basic features may be discerned.

The first and most important is that the expectations for the future are not "utopian" but that they are oriented to the experiences that Israel and the individual Israelites have had to date. Israel expects and hopes that fundamental elements of life and coexistence that have been disturbed or destroyed in one way or another will be restored. The most important of these foundational elements are righteousness and peace. The two are found in comprehensive contexts. Righteousness is a crucial element of the structure of society. It can be disturbed or prevented by the misuse of hierarchical structures just as much as by economic inequality. This can have a variety of causes and be affected by different developments. So the future expectations are directed towards a society in which such differences will be overcome.

The question of an appropriate leadership for the society is of great significance here. The hope of a restoration of a kingship that will do justice to these tasks is extremely important. The associated expectations for life together in society are given graphic expression in the metaphor of the shepherd. Another fundamental aspect associated with hope in the restoration of the monarchy is the hope of peace. A just king can create internal peace, and a successful king can also secure peace with external enemies. But it is crucially important that the king has God's help. A further fundamental aspect comes into the frame here: only a king who keeps the Torah can be a ruler in accordance with God's will. And the Torah is also the plumb-line against which internal peace founded on righteousness must be shaped and secured.

A further important element is the fact that Israel never dreamed of external greatness. There is no mention of this in the future expectations either, however much these occasionally provide the external affairs with features removed from the realities of life. On the contrary, the concept of the "remnant" that is left comes frequently to expression in the future expectations too. Thus many of these expectations look to God's fulfilling of the expressed hopes for the "remnant." The frequent concentration of expectations on Zion also stands in this context.

Many of the future expectations contain features that may be termed "eschatological." This term is used in a wide variety of ways today; here it is meant in the sense sketched above as talk of that which will come "afterwards." The expected time is often depicted with features that go beyond present reality. But generally speaking they still remain within the realm of the conceivable. Things are different in the realm of "apocalyptic," which is represented in the Hebrew Bible by certain parts of the book of Daniel. The basic difference lies in the fact that in apocalyptic material attention is focused on an end of the world order in which the structures of present reality lose their significance. Thus the fundamental elements of Israel's history, the restoration of which is hoped for and described in the eschatological future expectations, would also be inconsequential. To that extent apocalyptic is not representative or characteristic of the future expectation of the Hebrew Bible. Rather, it points ahead to developments that occurred in a period after the conclusion of the Hebrew Bible.

Is the Hebrew Bible as a whole oriented towards the future? This question requires a dual answer. First, the large part of the texts and writings are dominated by the consciousness that the present situation does not or does not yet correspond to what Israel hopes for and what it has been promised. So Israel must itself work towards the realization of that hope. Above all, this realization requires constantly hoping and praying for the help of God.

Second, the Hebrew Bible texts look forward constantly to an anticipated "afterwards," i.e. to a time after the things that now stand in the way of the realization of the hopes and promises have been over-come. But this hope is not directed towards something that lies "be-yond" present reality, but to a reformation or reshaping of this reality in line with the hopes and promises. Part of this reality is the firm certainty that, in the future too, God will never dissolve or break the covenant he has made with Israel.

Part III

The Hermeneutics of an Old Testament Theology

§ 23

Methodological Considerations

The Old Testament is a theological book. This sentence, with which this book began, will now be picked up and developed further, as we look back on the two preceding main sections. The statement made in this sentence implies a series of premises.

1. What does "final canonical form" mean?

The history of the discipline of "Old Testament Theology" has been set out in detail many times. (In orientation we may mention: Reventlow 1982; Hayes & Prussner 1985; Hasel 1991; Preuß 1991, 1-22; Brueggemann 1997, 1-114, and especially Barr 1999.) This history demonstrates that the question of how a Theology of the Old Testament is conceived is determined by many kinds of advance decisions, the justification for which is to be found only partially within Old Testament studies itself; they also reflect general theological developments which are themselves influenced by social and political developments.

Most accounts see in the appearance of Gerhard von Rad's *Theology of the Old Testament* the start of a new era (cf. also Schmidt 1972; 1991a). The new thing about it is determined also by the emergence of the theology of Karl Barth and by the end of the Second World War, but equally by developments within Old Testament Studies, associated in particular with the names of Albrecht Alt and Martin Noth. All these set the preconditions for a new theological beginning, which was then marked by the theological personality of Gerhard von Rad.

In the Introduction to the first part of this book, I sketched briefly what my own account owes to von Rad's approach. I would like to repeat the critical aspect of this: von Rad sees the course of his account as essentially provided already by the biblical texts in their contexts. There is a fundamental difference here in relation to most other approaches, whose accounts are determined either by a systematic concept—either borrowed from the dogmatic tradition or otherwise justified—or by a historical or religion-historical set of questions (cf. 1991a).

In this regard the ambitious approach of Walter Brueggemann (1997) has a special position: here the author raises quite specific questions, from a varying range of perspectives and adducing an abundance of generally very brief text citations. This gives rise to an extremely lively and stimulating picture; but the biblical texts do not come into view in their contexts. (Cf. 1999c, 21.)

I call this approach "canonical." I have taken this term from the debate that was first carried out in the English-speaking world in the 1970s (cf. 1983; Sheppard 1992; Barr 1999, 378ff). In the meantime the term has been much discussed, and it has been shown that it can be used in very different ways and with a very wide variety of intentions. So what we mean by this needs to be set out and delimited more precisely. I follow the line first discussed in 1983, which I have since taken up again and continued further in various contexts (cf. 1995c).

The crucial stimulus for me was the book by Brevard Childs, *Introduction to the Old Testament as Scripture* (1979). I took two essential points from this. First, in a theological interpretation of the Hebrew Bible the issue is the exposition of the texts in the form in which we now have them. This approach is significant from various angles. To begin with, it contains a critical element towards the broadly accepted and practiced type of historical-critical treatment of the biblical texts. In this regard I had already expressed my misgivings and attempted to try out new paths. In regard to the Pentateuch the results of source division had become questionable, which led to a critical querying of the method as such (1977). Then some years later with regard to the book of Isaiah I presented an attempt to draw attention to some elements that run through the whole of the book which point to the conclusion that the book as a whole has been deliberately shaped (1984). In the meantime comparable approaches have appeared in the most varied of places (cf. 1996 and 1997c), so that in Old Testament Studies today the exposition of biblical texts in commonly practiced in the overall context of the books that have come down to us.

The form in which the books of the Bible have come down to us are often referred to in this context as the "final form." This phrase is frequently criticized, from various points of view. First, the argument is that no concluding final form exists, since the transmission of the oldest manuscripts and the ancient translations shows that many texts were not finally fixed at all, but that there were different versions in circulation. Associated with this is the other argument that one cannot speak of a "canonical" final form because it is not possible to show historically the mandatory fixing of a particular text form.

On the first argument we may say that certainly there is a certain open-endedness to the final form of the texts, especially since under ancient conditions deviations between different manuscripts were unavoidable. In the context of hermeneutical debate, however, these deviations are not particularly significant; for the concept of the final form is in this case primarily an alternative to the form of the text obtained by critical "reconstruction," which is often taken as a basis for exegesis. This means "that the issue is *the* theology *of the* biblical texts, and not especially the theology of our literary and historical reconstructions" (Crüsemann 1995, 71).

In my view of things, however, this cannot mean we should ignore or even reject the results of historical-critical exegesis. Rather, it is a matter of changing the set of questions to be asked and the exegetical interest. Historical-critical exegesis, especially in the German-speaking world, generally proceeds with the questions posed by "literary criticism" (*Literarkritik*). Its first concern is with the question of the "literary unity or lack of unity" of the text, and to start with in regard to the "individual text." In the case of "revelation of breaks, unevenness or tensions" an attempt is then made to ascribe the "text parts obtained" to "meaningful sequences in narrative and action" and then to set them "in broader—again meaningful—contexts" (quotations from Schmidt 1991, 120). With this procedure, in each case a new text is "reconstructed," which implies that the present final text at least is not meaningful. But the primary exegetical interest has turned from the present text and towards a new, "reconstructed" text. An interpretation of the present text can then—if it can be undertaken at all—only address itself in a second step to a collated text that is viewed as secondary.

My argument is that the question should be turned around: the first and primary task of a theologically motivated exegesis is the exposition of the existing text. This change of question implies a fundamental change in the exegetical interest. The dominant literary-critical way of looking at things is by definition interested in the earlier stages of the present text and thus also in the history of its coming into being. It is "historical-critical" in the fact that it asks about the history that led to the emergence of the present text and is reflected in the different stages behind the text. So it turns its exegetical interest especially towards the individual text elements that have been deduced; as a result, the text at hand in its present form disappears from consideration.

This exegetical interest is associated with a quite particular evaluation of the various stages in the text. The present form of the text is generally accorded the least intrinsic value; rather, it is viewed as the result of "secondary" and often not "meaningful" (see above) revision and reshaping. The previous, earlier, "more original" stages of the text which are discerned in the analysis of the text, are given a higher rating; in consequence, it attracts the greater weight of exegetical interest. This interest can shift when greater attention is paid to the redactional processes, so that the pathway that led to the present form of the text and thus this form itself come once again into view. Of course it is not the present text as such to which interest is directed, but a historically attuned process by means of which the text has ultimately reached its present form.

The reversal of the question which seems necessary to me proceeds from the fact that each biblical text in the form in which we now have it has its own statement to make. The authors of the biblical texts—I expressly include those to whom we owe the shaping of the "final form"—have passed these texts down to us in precisely this form and not in some other previous form. Here the other aspect of the term "canonical" comes into play: the biblical text, in the form we now have, forms the basis for the faith and life of the two great communities of faith, the Jewish and the Christian. Theology is done in this context, and it is only meaningful in this context. (This applies especially in the Christian context; on the question of a Jewish "Theology of the Tanakh" see §24.3.) So a theologically grounded access to these texts must take the current form of the texts as its starting-point.

This does not mean, as I have said, that we should reject the results of historical-critical exegesis. Rather, what matters is its place and its position in the framework of a Theology of the Old Testament. The question of the dating of the texts and the resulting consequences play an important role here. So it is not unimportant in this connection to bear in mind the hypothetical nature and the associated uncertainty and changeability of many results of historical-critical exegesis.

The "classical" example of this is again the Pentateuch. The picture that the critical analysis of it produces has changed dramatically in recent decades. While previously, at least in German-speaking circles, it was possible to speak, almost without fear of challenge, of a "Yahwist" situated in the early period of the monarchy, who formed the basis for the theological interpretation of the Pentateuch, today it is frequently disputed that it is possible to establish substantial continuous "sources" in the Pentateuch; and where a "Yahwist" is still taken into account, he is dated to the exilic or post-exilic period (cf. Zenger, in Zenger *et al.* 1998, 113-118). The implications of this for a theological exegesis of the pentateuchal texts and for their place within a Theology of the Old Testament are far-reaching, because essential elements of what used to be assumed to be pre-exilic theology have fallen by the wayside. One needs only to think of the picture that von Rad sketched of the "Yahwist" as a theologian from the "free-thinking era of Solomon" (1938, 63[76]) and certainly of the "new spirit" of the time of "Solomonic humanism" (1962, 62-70) (cf. also 1953)!

In other areas of the Old Testament literature too, the question of the dating of the texts or of the traditions adopted in them is the subject of lively debate and in the process of change; this has in some cases fundamental consequences for the reconstruction of the history of Israel, especially in post-exilic times, and thus also for the theological classification and interpretation of many texts. But at the same time the question arises, what significance the resulting (or currently dominant) datings of texts should have for the presentation of the theology of the Old Testament.

2. An example: Creation

The various ways of presenting the biblical statements need to be briefly sketched, taking as an example the way the creation and God the creator are spoken of in some more recent Theologies of the Old Testament.

In an introductory paragraph on "methodological problems" Brevard Childs (1992) sets as the "aims of the analysis" of the biblical material the need first to determine "the original place of a witness within the history of Israel," and then "to follow a line of development in its use and its application in Israel's history," and finally "to recognize the unity and difference of the faith of Israel within the Old Testament" (97). Here then, the dependence of the account of the Old Testament material on the historical classification of the texts is explicitly emphasized.

In his execution of this, Childs then begins with a chapter on the creation; for according to Genesis the story does not begin with Israel but "with the preparation of the stage for world history." But then follows a detailed discussion of the literary-critical problems of the first two chapters of Genesis, which ends finally in a separate treatment of the Priestly document (P) and the Yahwist version (J). Only right at the end is there a short passage on "the unification of the sources into a continuous narrative" (113). The function of this—"canonical," as I would call it—reading of the text is not further elaborated. At the conclusion, however, we read the sentence: "the remarkable success of the redactional unification is confirmed by the history of interpretation, which had little difficulty up to the Enlightenment in reading the chapters as a unity." But no conclusions are drawn from this insight.

Walter Brueggemann's approach (1997) is quite different. In the first main chapter on the "Testimony of Israel" the discussion begins with statements about God's activity and within this again with a section on God's activity as creator ("Yahweh, the God who Creates," 145ff). The texts cited here do not, however, come from the first chapters of Genesis, but in particular from Isa 40ff and the Psalms. In justification of this, a section follows on the "Context of the Exile," beginning with the observation: "In the Old Testament, belief in creation is given its fullest elaboration in the Isaiah of the exile" (this is Brueggemann's term for Isa 40–55) (149). It is only later that a brief section follows on Gen 1.1-2, 4a as a "liturgical narrative," in which, however, the statements of this chapter are not discussed in detail. The general view then is not oriented to the concept of the Hebrew Bible itself, but to the assumed late stage of the development of the theme of creation.

Different again is Werner H. Schmidt's treatment of the theme of creation in the 8th edition of his book, *Alttestamentlicher Glaube* (1996).

Here the creation appears as a separate topic in the chapter about the monarchy in a paragraph about "The New Statements about God" (233ff). This paragraph is preceded by another about "The Significance of Canaanite Gods in the Old Testament" (195ff), and immediately before the section on "The Creation" there is one with the title "The Battle with the Chaos Dragon" (229ff). The religious-historical classification of the Old Testament creation ideas thereby expressed is explicitly emphasized when in the first sentence of the section on creation we read that Israel seems "originally to have had no creation story of its own." A little later: "Yahweh seems, however, originally not to have been worshiped as creator" (234). In what follows the disparate nature, the "colorful juxtaposition" (240) of the Old Testament creation ideas is then discussed in particular. Only from the exilic period onwards does "a certain change" come about, for "it is only the newly addressed assurance of salvation following the completed sentence in the exile that for the first time does not base itself any longer on a historical event, such as leading or election, but on the creation" (240). Here, then, the diachronic account of the assumed religious-historical development dominates, while the "canonical" view of the Hebrew Bible is not discussed.

These examples show on the one hand the dependence of theological statements about biblical texts on literary, historical or religious-historical premises, and on the other hand the varied interest of individual theologians in an overview of the statements of the biblical texts. In Childs's sketch dependence on the dominant literary-critical classification of the texts stands in the way of the express interest in a "canonical" overview. But his remark that before the emergence of modern biblical criticism the opening chapters of Genesis were certainly read as a unity is significant. For Brueggemann too the statements about God's actions as creator stand expressly at the beginning of the biblical statements about the actions of God. His view of the full elaboration of the creation belief in the time of the Babylonian exile leads him, however, not to adduce the creation statements of Genesis as primary witnesses. His clearly marked interest in an overview of the Old Testament "testimony" is itself not oriented to the texts in their given contexts. For Schmidt the questions that arise on the basis of his history-of-religions-oriented overall concept are different from the start. The late development of a separate belief in creation in the Old Testament is not situated in a theological overview. In the concluding chapters on "The Old Testament Inheritance" (§19) and "Elements of

Biblical Theology" (§20), too, we find only very brief mentions of Old Testament ideas of creation (p. 438).

In my own account I have taken my lead from the general outline of the Hebrew Bible, in which the creation stands very emphatically at the beginning. In the discussion I have then attempted to set the various aspects of the creation statements in thematic relationship to each other. Diachronic aspects have hardly been discussed. At certain points, however, reference has been made to exilic or post-exilic perspectives. Such texts as Isa 51.9f, for example, in which there is talk of Yhwh's battle with the chaos monster Rahab, make clear the limitations to what diachronic observations can say; for here an archaic element in the tradition appears here in a relatively late (probably exilic) text. Of greater significance, however, is the insight that in this and other texts the creation ideas are set in new theological contexts, in this case the "second exodus." This is certainly not an argument in favor of a general ascription of creation belief to a "late" phase in the history of Old Testament belief; rather, it shows that such diachronic classifications do not do justice to the overall theological vision of the Hebrew Bible, in which the creation stands at the beginning.

3. Diachronic and synchronic exegesis

"The 'Old Testament as a whole' is a composite of texts. As such it is a composite of meanings. Knowledge of its prehistory and background is important for the interpretive evaluation of this composite of meanings. But such knowledge does not itself constitute the meanings, let alone provide the all-important key to exegesis" (Lohfink 1989, 86[234]). These sentences, which could be matched by others, can be used to characterize the concept that can be termed "canonical exegesis." The tension between a "synchronic" and a "diachronic" consideration of the texts comes in here. In order to discern and appreciate the composite of texts of the Old Testament as a composite of meanings, a synopsis or overview is necessary that can be called synchronic. This applies to smaller or larger units of text as well as to overarching thematic contexts. Insights into the prehistory of the texts and the ideas they contain, which have been obtained by means of historical or religious-historical considerations, i.e. with a diachronic set of questions, can indeed be important. But they cannot determine the overall view as such but must be placed in the service of such an overview.

The relationship between diachronic and synchronic exegesis has been discussed in present-day Biblical Studies especially since the emergence of canonical interpretation (on the history of this cf. Barr 1999, 378ff; Lohfink 1992, 31-34[92-95]). Although discussion to date has not been carried out systematically, it is evident that there is a degree of agreement that these approaches are not mutually exclusive but that these are different sets of questions and viewpoints which can complement each other (cf. 1995c; Crüsemann 1995, 72). Still, they need to be clearly distinguished, especially with regard to the difference in exegetical interest.

Once again the opening chapters of Genesis provide a suitable example. The division of Gen 1 and 2 into different sources or layers is one of the oldest results of literary-critical analysis and doubtless has good grounds to support it. In a theological survey of the Hebrew Bible however the question necessarily arises how the authors of the present final form wished this text to be read in its context. On the presupposition of this exegetical interest, both chapters are open to illuminating interpretation in their interaction with each other. But for larger contexts too a synchronic view opens up new insights, as for instance is shown in recent work on the book of Isaiah (cf. 1984 and 1996). It proves time and again to be the case that in many cases a synchronic treatment does not contest the diachronic insights but even presupposes them. But it then takes the next step by investigating the intention of the author(s) of the extant final text. That a satisfactory answer to this question is not always to be found can hardly be used as a counter-argument, for diachronic exegesis also faces comparable difficulties often enough.

The crucial thing, as we have said, is the exegetical interest, i.e. the intention with which the text is read. Once again the aspect of "canonical" exegesis comes into view here, which reads the biblical texts as the holy scriptures of the Jewish and Christian community of faith. We recall Childs's reference to the history of the interpretation of Gen 1 and 2, which "had little difficulty up to the Enlightenment in reading the chapters as a unity" (Childs 1992, 113). It seems doubtful whether it is a gain for the theological exegesis of this and other texts if the historical-critical interpretation produces difficulties that did not previously exist. I regard synchronic interpretation etc. as an attempt to overcome such difficulties through an approach in which the texts are read and interpreted in their given contexts. This cannot simply happen by undoing or ignoring the results of historical-critical text analysis, however; rather, what is needed is a deliberate, methodologically self-aware step towards a new understanding of the final text. The intention of this attempt is not anti-critical but theological. That in some cases the interpretation can thereby pick up insights of "pre-critical" scripture exegesis is certainly not an argument against it.

Excursus: Formulaic speech

The language of the Hebrew Bible is extraordinarily varied and multi-faceted. The reasons for this lie in the quite varied *Sitz im Leben* of the individual texts (cf. 1983, 80ff), and also in the individual style of the various authors. It is all the more remarkable that particular linguistic elements are frequently found in quite different contexts, the linguistic character of which can be otherwise very different. This applies in particular to expressions that can be called formulaic, in the narrower or broader sense. Many of them also have a particular *Sitz im Leben* which is also reflected in their use in Old Testament texts. In the detailed study of such expressions the question of their provenance and origins and precisely of this *Sitz im Leben* is in the foreground. In our context, however, interest is addressed to the question how "formulaic" texts can fulfill particular theological tasks in different contexts.

A first example is provided by the formulaic introduction to prophetic speech as divine speech: "Thus says the LORD" (often called the "messenger formula," cf. 1962b). It is found in the prophetic books in varying frequency (most frequently in Jeremiah) as well as in narrative texts which report the ministry of prophets (e.g. Judg 6.8; 1 Sam 2.27; 2 Sam 7.5). In Ezekiel's pregnant language the formula can even stand alone as an unambiguous sign of the authenticity of the prophet (Ezek 2.4f; 3.11, 27). It is striking in this regard that the formula first appears in the Hebrew Bible in the context of Moses. He is regularly told by God to confront Pharaoh and to introduce his speech with this formula (Ex 4.22; 7.16f, 26 etc.). One may certainly assume that the formula has its "original" setting in connection with the ministry of the prophet. But it is just as certain that one cannot describe its usage in the sending and ministry of Moses as simply "secondary" borrowing of the formula. Rather, the formula here is a separate element with which the special sending of Moses is brought to expression. In Deuteronomy Moses is then expressly described as the paradigmatic prophet (Deut 18.15, 18; 34.10), so that one can almost say that here prophecy is defined by reference to Moses (cf. §12.4). The messenger formula has gained a separate function in the characterization of Moses as the model against which all prophecy must be measured.

A further important example is formed by formulaic expressions which contain the divine name. The basic forms are "I am YHWH" and "you/they will know that I am YHWH." They are found in a range of forms and variations, which were discussed in detail in the sections on the name of God (§15.1.3) and acknowledgment of God (§15.1.4). Walther Zimmerli devoted extensive research on these formulae (Zimmerli 1953 and 1954). They will now be examined once again from the point of view of their functions in a synchronic reading of the texts.

The I-Am formula (Zimmerli: self-presentation formula) is found in an especially emphasized version in the divine speech in Ex 6.2-8. This text occupies a key position from various points of view. Zimmerli made an important synchronic observation about this: the self-presentation formula "cannot in essence appear earlier, and in essence it cannot go quiet afterwards" (1953, 186[=18]). The formula therefore has a crucial function within the composition (see §15.1.3 above). Zimmerli's assertion relates in the first place to the "priestly" narrative; but it applies to the character of the pentateuchal narrative as a whole (cf. Blum 1990a, 232ff). Here the section of the story that is beginning, so fundamental for Israel's identity, is linked backwards with the story of the forefathers and forwards with the gift of the promised land. This is expressed in a unique linking and interweaving of different characteristic form elements (for detail cf. 1995a, 20ff). The I-Am formula opens the section (after an introductory formula as divine speech) in a very emphatic sole position: "I am YHWH" (v. 2). It then follows twice more: as the introduction to the message that Moses is to pass on to the Israelites (v. 6) and in an emphasized concluding position (v. 8) which forms together with v. 2 the frame around the whole tapestry of formulae.

Then the arch reaches backwards: the newly introduced self-presentation "I am YHWH" is related to the self-presentation "I am *'ēl šaddāy*" (v. 3, cf. Gen 17.1; 35.11): what began then now enters a new, decisive stage in the history of God's dealings with Israel. Towards the end of this divine speech there then appears the other shape of the "I am YHWH" in the "acknowledgment formula," also for the first time: "You will know that I am YHWH, your God" (v. 7). The interaction between these two formulae is emphasized in the concluding repetition of the I-Am formula at the end of this discourse section (v. 8).

At the same time the divine self-presentation is connected with two other themes which have also found expression in characteristic forms. First, the "covenant formula." The new self-presentation by God is followed by a retrospect on God's conclusion of a covenant with the forefathers (v. 4), linked with the announcement that God will now "remember" his covenant (v. 5); this remembrance will be realized in God's imminent intervention on Israel's behalf. God will lead Israel out of Egypt, free them from slavery and redeem them with proofs of his mighty power—and all this leads to the covenant formula: "I will take you as my people and will be God to you" (vv. 6, 7a). In this complex of sentences the "leading-out formula" is also included: "I will bring you out from under the yoke of the Egyptians" (v. 6) and once again as an extension of the acknowledgment formula: "who brought you out from under the yoke of the Egyptians" (v. 7); here the formula is continued on through the assurance of leading into the land that God swore to give to the forefathers (v. 8).

This central section in Ex 6 shows how the various fixed formulae can take on an important synchronic function in a particular context. As a further example we might mention the beginning of the great historical retrospect in Ezek 20. Here the I-Am formula stands again as a separate sentence, in fact as the real content of the divine speech that the prophet is to pass on: "On the day I chose Israel, I swore with uplifted hand to the descendants of the house of Jacob and revealed myself to them in Egypt. With uplifted hand I said to them, 'I am the LORD your God'" (Ezek 20.5). God's self-presentation, reinforced by an oath, is here linked with the election of Israel. With a repetition of the oath formula the leading-out of Egypt and the gift of the promised land are then included (v. 6). After a call to dispose of the "gods of Egypt," finally the introductory divine speech is concluded with the repeated, asyndetically placed I-Am formula at the end (v. 7). So here we find both things: the emphasized singling-out of the I-Am formula as the quintessence of what Israel is to know of God and to acknowledge, and the connection with other elements of the theological tradition.

A third example: in Lev 18 the I-Am formula appears for the first time in the so-called "holiness code," with various functions. First in vv. 1f in an individual position (comparable with Ezek 20) as the actual content of the introductory divine speech. But this is the only time that the formula stands as an introduction within the "holiness code." Otherwise in ch. 18 and the following chapters it always forms the conclusion of individual speech units, where it clearly has a structuring function (cf. Zimmerli 1953, 181 [=12f]; Ruwe 1999, 72ff). The group of texts that begins in ch. 18 is thereby marked as belonging together. (In ch. 17 the formula is absent; its regular appearance as a concluding formula extends as far as ch. 22. The conclusions to be drawn for the question of the "holiness code" need to be examined more closely; cf. the provisional comments of Blum 1990a, 318ff.)

Finally it should be pointed out that in its central position as the introduction to the Decalogue, the I-Am formula is linked with the leading-out formula: "I am the Lord, your God, who brought you out of the land of Egypt, out of the house of slavery" (Ex 20.22; Deut 5.6). Here these two formulaic elements have come into a quite close, indissoluble connection with each other. (Cf. further §15.1.3 above.)

Other observations may be made for the second version of the formulae formed with the divine name, the "acknowledgment formula." To begin with, here too a basic form is discernible: "You (sing./plur.) will/they will know that I am YHWH." But it can be seen that this formula is much more variable than the simple I-Am formula. This also depends on a very much stronger context-relatedness of the formula. It always relates to the immediately preceding text, in which as a rule a divine action is announced; the knowledge of God is expected as the reaction of the addressed person(s) to this divine action. The various linguistic versions of the formula are all worded accordingly: "And you will know (*wîda'tem*) (i.e. you will recognize by this) that I am YHWH" (Ex 6.7); "then you will (or: should) know (*b'zo't tēda'*) that I am YHWH" (7.17); "so that you will know (*l'ma'an tēda'*) that I am YHWH" (8.18); "in order to know (*lāda'at*, i.e. so that you will know) that I am YHWH" (Ezek 20.20).

The question of the original *Sitz im Leben* for the acknowledgment formula proves to be unanswerable. Rather, we see that it "neither belongs exclusively to the prophetic, nor exclusively to the priestly word, but is found in both and beyond both in third-party passages too" (Zimmerli 1954, 43[=95]). The context-relatedness of the formula is especially marked in the frequent expansions of the statement about the object of knowledge. The wording "know that I am YHWH" already has an inherent weighty theological statement in it; but it can be explained in quite different ways according to the context. Frequently we read: "that I am YHWH, your God" (Ex 6.7); then there are participial expansions: "that I am YHWH, who sanctifies you" (*m'qaddiškem*, 31.13); or verbal ones: "that I, YHWH, have spoken" (*dibbartî*, Ezek 5.13); or we read: "that I, YHWH, their God, am with them" (34.30). Watered-down versions of the formula are also to be found: "that I did not do all this in vain..., utterance of YHWH" (14.23). (On this whole topic cf. Zimmerli 1954, 6ff [=42ff].)

The acknowledgment formula thus forms a quite separate element of formulaic speech. On the one hand its formulaic character is very marked, while on the other hand it is a very adaptable element which can appear in a wide variety of contexts and be used with quite different intent as to meaning. So the understanding of this is largely a matter for exegesis of the context. (For further detail see §15.2.4 above.)

In the tapestry of formulae in Ex 6.2-8 an important role is played also by the "covenant formula" (cf. Smend 1953; 1995a). It represents a very pregnant statement about God's relationship with Israel. In Ex 6.7 it is found in a form in which the two-sidedness of this relationship comes to expression: "I will take you as a people and will be God to you" (vv. 6, 7a). An important synchronic observation can be attached to this: the two-sidedness of the connection between God and Israel as people could not be expressed earlier because it is only now in the departure from Egypt that Israel becomes a people. This recalls Zimmerli's comment on the self-presentation formula in the same text (see above). The covenant formula is found already in the statement made in the first part of the divine speech to Abraham: "I will be God to them" (Gen 17.8; cf. v. 7); in Ex 6 the second aspect is now added.

The covenant formula in Ex 6 is also connected with the acknowledgment formula. Israel will know from the fact that God takes Israel as his people and will himself be Israel's God "that I am YHWH, their God" (v. 7). The identity of this God is then specified by means of a brief overview of the history of God's dealings with Israel in the past and the future: the leading-out of Egypt and the leading-into the land that God swore to the forefathers he would give them and which he now intends to pass into Israel's possession. A similar connection between covenant formula and acknowledgment formula is evident in Ex 29.45f. Here the leading out of Egypt proceeds to the proclamation of God's dwelling in the midst of Israel. In Deut 7.6-11 too there is a comparable connection between the two formulae (esp. v. 6 and v. 9). In Jer 24.7 the two formulae are linked together very succinctly and tellingly; they are associated with the expectation that Israel will turn back to God "with their whole heart." In Jer 31.31-34 the covenant formula (v. 33b) is followed by a watering-down of the acknowledgment formula. No one will teach another person: "Know Yhwh!" Instead, they will all know him (v. 34). We see in these texts that the various formulae certainly are not used "formulaically" in a schematic sense, but that they are used as set forms of speech, which readers or hearers recognize, to express certain theological matters.

A detailed treatment of the covenant formula was given above in §6.5. Here we shall draw attention once again to the predominant synchronic function of the formula. In the structure of the Pentateuch as a whole the covenant formula has an important function. It stands at the beginning in connection with Abraham in Gen 17.7 and at the end in Deut 29.12. In both texts the covenant formula appears as the direct explanation of the "covenant" (*bᵉrît*); this close connection is found only in these two passages in the Hebrew Bible, which can scarcely be regarded as a coincidence. Furthermore, it is striking that the two-part covenant formula stands only at this point in Deuteronomy, while otherwise (with the exception of 26.17) it is always only the second part of the formula that appears, in which Israel is addressed as the people of God. (The special position of Deut 29 is also clear from the fact that outside the Decalogue the expression "I am YHWH" is found only here in Deuteronomy, within the acknowledgment formula in v. 5.) To some extent Ex 6.2-8, where the two-part formula is found for the first time (and thus also for the first time in the Pentateuch), forms the bridge between Gen 17.7 and Deut 29.12 (cf. 1995a, 29f; 70f). Thus the covenant formula encompasses "priestly" as well as Deuteronomic texts in the present final form of the Pentateuch.

A number of times we have already spoken of the "leading-out formula" (cf. 1997b). In its striking formulation as the introduction to the Decalogue it is linked with the self-presentation formula: "I am the Lord, your God, who brought you out of the land of Egypt, out of the house of slavery" (Ex 20.2; Deut 5.6). This formula is always context-related, since it begins with a backward reference to the previously mentioned divine name, whether as here in the form of a relative clause (with *ᵃšer*), or by means of a participial verb form with an article (e.g. *hammôṣî*, Ex 6.7). In many cases it is followed by a more detailed specification of what is regarded in that context as the goal or point of the leading-out from Egypt: life in the God-given land with its produce (Deut 26.8f) or "to live among you" (Ex 29.46) or "to be God for you" (Lev 22.33), to mention but a few characteristic examples. On the other hand, in the Decalogue for instance there is no discernible connection between the introductory leading-out formula and the commandments that follow.

In Ex 6.2-8 the leading-out formula is also connected with the covenant formula (see above). A similarly dense composition of formulae is found in Ex 29.45f. God will live among the Israelites, "and I will be God for them." Then the acknowledgment formula is added, which is explained by the leading-out formula: "They will know that I am the LORD their God, who brought them out of Egypt;" then again, "so that I might dwell among them;" and finally inclusion the self-presentation formula: "I am the LORD their God."

The leading-out formula can bear different emphases in its context. It can make statements about God himself: *I* am the one who led you out of Egypt. This is especially marked in the concise statement in Hosea: "I am YHWH, your God, from the land of Egypt" (Hos 12.10; 13.4), as also in the introduction to the Decalogue (Ex 20.2; Deut 5.6). On the other hand the formula can make statements about God's actions, as e.g. in Deut 26.5ff: God brought us out of Egypt and gave us this land (vv. 8f). Certainly these two aspects cannot be completely separated from each other; but they indicate the broad radius in which the statements about the fundamental exodus event can appear in its dominant form.

Frequently the leading-out formula appears with expansions in which the mighty act of God in the leading-out is described in more detail, especially so in Deut 26.8: "with a mighty hand and outstretched arm, with great terror and with miraculous signs and wonders." Other expansions characterize Egypt as the "house of slavery" (Ex 20.2; Deut 5.6) or as the "iron-smelting furnace" (Deut 4.20). The leading-out formula is given quite a different emphasis when the behavior of the Israelites is held up in contrast to it. This starts at the beginning of the book of Judges: "I brought you up out of Egypt ... yet you have disobeyed me" (Judg 2.1f). Then again: "They forsook the LORD, the God of their fathers, who had brought them out of Egypt" (v. 12). This contrast between God's act in the leading-out of Egypt and the negative reaction of Israel is then found repeatedly in the historical books and in the prophets, e.g. Jeremiah: "They did not ask: Where is the LORD who led us out of the land of Egypt?" (Jer 2.6); instead they ran after other gods. Here the function of the formula is reversed: it no longer serves to emphasize God's might or the greatness of his actions, but has the effect of contrasting this with the present behavior of the Israelites, which deviates from the pathway God has traveled with his people since he led them out of Egypt.

Thus in the variety of its formulations and its application in different contexts, the leading-out formula too shows what the linguistic options are for expressing primarily theological matters and connections in the flexible use of formulaic elements; and it shows how these are perceived by the authors of the Hebrew Bible texts. Many kinds of connections and links are also clear particularly between the formulae dealt with so far: self-presentation formula, acknowledgment formula, covenant formula and leading-out formula.

We are taken into quite a different area, finally, by the "grace formula." A striking difference is evident already in the fact that the formulae dealt with so far do not appear in the Psalms, while the grace formula is concentrated precisely there. Here we find the "classical" formula: "The Lord is compassionate and gracious, slow to anger, abounding in love" (Ps 103.8; in identical or similar wording in Pss 78.38; 86.5, 15; 99.8; 111.4; 112.4; 116.5; 145.8). The grace formula also differs fundamentally in content from those discussed so far: it makes statements about God's qualities. The two adjectives "compassionate" (*raḥûm*) and "gracious" (*ḥannûn*) are used almost exclusively of God and can thus be considered especially characteristic statements about God's qualities. (For detail see above §15.3.3.1a.)

At the same time, however, the observation is significant that the formula is usually found in a context in which the other side of the qualities and behavior of God is discussed. Thus in one of the basic formulations we read in connection with the restoration of the covenant on Sinai: "maintaining love to thousands, and forgiving wickedness, rebellion and sin. Yet he does not leave the guilty unpunished; he punishes the children and their children for the sin of the fathers to the third and fourth generation" (Ex 34.7). A similar opposition, this time with the sequence reversed, is found in the Decalogue, where there is mention first of the "visiting" (punishing) of guilt to the third and fourth generation and then of the goodness that God will show to "thousands" (Ex 20.5f; Deut 5.9f). Finally, we find statements which speak of God's own repentance: "For a brief moment I abandoned you, but with deep compassion (*raḥ°mîm*) I will bring you back. In a surge of anger I hid my face from you for a moment, but with everlasting kindness I will have compassion on you (*riḥamtîk*)" (Isa 54.7f).

In its various forms, the grace formula thus puts God's qualities into words in an exemplary manner and shows itself thus to be an important element of the linguistic shaping of the theological insights and experiences of the biblical authors.

In the language of the Hebrew Bible we find plenty of other formulaic expressions, but as a rule these remain limited to their immediate area of validity. Alongside introductory formulae of various kinds we might mention for instance the conventional oath formula: "as the LORD lives" (Judg 8.19; 1 Sam 14.39, 45 etc.). Then it is in particular in the cultic domain that formulaic expressions are used. This applies for instance to sacrificial rites, in which such formulae have the function of marking the cultic correctness and the effect of particular sacrifices. For instance: "It is a burnt offering, an offering made by fire, an aroma pleasing to the LORD" (Lev 1.9, 13, 17; cf. 2.2; 3.5 etc.); or "the priest will make atonement for them, and they will be forgiven" (Lev 4.20, 26, 31, 35). In the liturgy too we find formulaic expressions, as when God is proclaimed king in festive singing: "YHWH is king" (Pss 93.1; 96.10; 97.1; 99.1; cf. 47.9). These are just a few examples of the formulaic expressions that are not used outside their own area of application and thus are not the subject of this excursus.

★ ★ ★ ★ ★

4. The significance of the canon-formation period

In Old Testament Studies today there is no consensus regarding the question of the time when the texts of the Hebrew Bible were set down. It is, however, clear that the parameters have changed. Half a century ago there was a majority opinion according to which many of the traditions that have found their way into the texts date from a relatively early phase in Israel's history and were given their first and crucial literary shape in the early monarchic period. This consensus no longer exists today. It has not been replaced by another generally recognized concept (cf. 1993). However, the time of the Babylonian exile and the period that followed it are thought to have played a very important role in the shaping of the Old Testament traditions. In our account up to this point this has frequently been spoken of. It now needs to be reflected upon once more with respect to its hermeneutical significance.

For this purpose I shall make use of the term "canon-formative period" (*kanonbildende Periode*, Crüsemann 1995, 71). It is becoming clearer and clearer that the period that begins with the Babylonian exile has become of great significance for the shaping of the canon. The expression "shaping of the canon" implies that much of the text and tradition material that is shaped into the canon at this time was already in existence and available to the process of canon-formation. A nuanced view must come into play here, in which the relationship between diachronic and synchronic consideration is also taken carefully into account. Great importance is attached here once again to the question of the exegetical interest. In the context of a Theology of the Old Testament interest will turn increasingly to the synchronic consideration of the canonical shape of the texts.

A basic consideration in this is "that the early period becomes more and more important in the late period, the account of it broader and broader" (Crüsemann, *ibid.*). This applies in particular to the Pentateuch, in which the story of Israel's foundation is reported, including its prehistory. This whole early epoch in history is presented, without problems, as in a time before the settlement of Israel in the land of Canaan. But it is clear that the account we have is presented from the point of view of an Israel that is settled in the land. There are good grounds for the assumption that the overall composition of the Pentateuch, however we are to imagine its shaping in matters of detail, is not to be set before the time of the Babylonian exile (cf. esp. Blum 1990a). But this means that the "canonical" overall sketch of Israel from the beginnings of its own history has been shaped retrospectively from the time of consolidation after the catastrophe of the destruction of Jerusalem and the temple. (Cf. §1.4.)

In particular the detailed system of the cult at the "utopian" site of Sinai (Crüsemann 1992, 75; cf. §10.1) doubtless reflects the situation in the temple in Jerusalem. The synchronic meaning of this sketch is clear: the cult in Jerusalem is performed as was ordered in the divine commission given through Moses on Sinai. The diachronic questions that arise here are more difficult to answer. We have no way of determining at what stage in the Jerusalem cult these texts correspond to the deduced systems, since we possess no comparable texts outside the priestly Pentateuch. Nor do we know to what extent these cultic rules and rituals were subject to change. We may assume there was a strong capacity for persistence. At the same time, in my view we must assume that the practice systematized in these texts corresponds essentially with the real circumstances at the time of the concluding formulation of the canonical text. Texts that were of such central importance for the religious life of the Jewish community would scarcely have been accorded canonical status if they did not correspond with the cultic realities of the time of canonization. Exegesis at any rate has the primary task of drawing this picture of the cult in the temple in Jerusalem with its theological implications (cf. §11.2.2).

For other thematic areas of the canonical texts of the Pentateuch too, important observations can be made with regard to the significance of the early period in the late. The story of Israel begins with the call of Abraham. In the opening text of this story two characteristic elements immediately stand out: God calls Abraham as an individual from the great world of the nations and promises to make him a "great people" (Gen 12.1f)—and at the same time God promises to give the land into which he has led him, to his descendants (v. 7). It is immediately clear that these two aspects have fundamental significance for Israel's self-understanding.

The theme of the land promise is marked from the beginning by delay and danger (cf. §8.1). In God's first speech to Abraham we read: "To your offspring I will give this land" (Gen 12.7). So Abraham himself will not experience the fulfillment of the promise of the land. The patriarchal stories then make it quite clear that the land in which the forefathers live is not their own. In Gen 15.12-21 it is also expressed that the first generations of Abraham's descendants will not experience the fulfillment either, but that for a long time they will have to live in a foreign land, until God finally leads them out of there and gives them the land. So here right at the beginning of the story of the forefathers there is an anticipation of the stay in Egypt and the departure from there, the "exodus." But the pathway from Egypt to the promised land is then fraught with many problems and difficulties, as the narratives of Exodus and Numbers and finally also the book of Joshua show. It is only at the conclusion of the reports about the conquest and distribution of the land that the topic comes to a provisional point of rest, when the fulfillment of the land promise is declared (Josh 21.43-45). But already before this the possibility had been countenanced that Israel might itself throw away the gift of the land. In Deut 4.25-28 and much more extensively in Lev 26 (esp. vv. 32f) and Deut 28 (esp. vv. 63f) the deportation from the land and the scattering among the nations is depicted as the climax of the punishments that God will cause to come upon Israel if it does not keep his commandments. Here the exilic fate is presented in dramatic form (cf. §8.4).

From this first basic theme of the early period, then, we see how strongly marked its presentation and interpretive emphasis is by the experiences, but also by the hopes and fears, of the later period. Exegesis will have to give due weight to this aspect of the time of narration. With regard to diachronic questions, different answers will necessarily be given in respect of the individual texts of the patriarchal traditions, which will then have to be meaningfully arranged in the synchronic overview.

With regard to the other theme of the first divine speech, the call of Abraham, things are a little different. Here it is Deuteronomy in which the theme of "election" is conceived theologically in the term *bāḥar* (cf. §6.4 and 1981). This does not contradict the statement that the early period becomes increasingly important in the late period. But it extends the horizon of what is meant by "late period." Clearly it was not just the catastrophe of the years 597 onwards that led Israel to rethink their own early history and confront the present situation with it. Rather, one may say that precisely the availability of a theologically considered view of their own history, as is provided in Deuteronomy, was an important precondition for the success of the new start. The various "deuteronomistic" elements in the canonical shape of a wide range of books speak eloquently in this regard. So the election of Abraham and his offspring (*zera'*, Deut 10.15; cf. Gen 17.19; Lohfink 1991, 71) is a further theme of the early period that gained new and fundamental significance in the late period.

An important aspect of the "late period" as the epoch of the formation of the canon is also evident in the composition of the prophetic books. Here the concern is not with the "early period" of Israel's history, which is seen and presented in a new light, but still with a significant epoch in pre-exilic history. It is perfectly clear that the book of Isaiah contains elements from pre-exilic, exilic and post-exilic times. But while scholarly research used to be occupied essentially with the distinction and separation of the various elements, in recent times increased interest has been focused also on the shaping of the canonical final form (cf. 1996). In Isaiah's case this is particularly desirable, necessary in fact, because the text of the book itself gives no indications that the various parts come from different periods and must accordingly also have different authors. Evidently the composers of the final canonical version were not interested in making the reader aware of this. In addition, in the first, pre-exilic part (Isa 1–39) we find numerous elements that present-day insights tell us have affinities with the later parts, which suggests that what we are seeing here is the canon-forming activity of the composers of the final form. So the book of Isaiah as a whole is marked by the canon-formative late period but also contains highly important traditions from the mid-monarchic period.

In the Book of the Twelve Prophets things are different again. Here there is a quite obvious tension between the writings of the individual prophets, which are marked as separate writings, and its transmission as one book (cf. §7.5). As in Isaiah, writings from pre-exilic times have been combined with post-exilic ones. Here too in the older ones of these writings we find elements that have been formulated from a post-exilic point of view. This produces hermeneutical problems of interpretation which resist a simple choice between diachronic and synchronic consideration; a particularly well-known example of this is the positive conclusion of Amos (cf. Crüsemann 1995, 72). So the Book of the Twelve is also an example of theological work from the post-exilic canon-formative period. (On this cf. 1997c [=2001a]; further Nogalski & Sweeney 2000.)

Finally to the Psalms. Here the questions of date are particularly difficult and in many cases they are unanswerable. This applies especially to the large number of psalms in which an individual psalmist is speaking. These are so concentrated on the individual problems of the psalmist that it is impossible to order them chronologically. But also in the case of community psalms there is often nothing to go by as regards date. This applies to many psalms of thanksgiving and lament, in which the content of the prayer offers no indications of particular temporal circumstances; but it also applies to psalms in which a cultic situation can be discerned, since we know too little about the development of the cult, and especially about the question of what the interruption in the destruction of the temple and its later reconstruction meant for it.

In some psalms, however, the exilic or post-exilic situation is quite clearly discernible, for instance when Psalms 74, 79 and others speak of the destruction of the sanctuary or when the psalmists say of themselves that they sat "by the rivers of Babylon" (137.1); Ps 126 speaks of the (already arrived or still expected) restoration of Zion and the return of the captives. In other psalms much speaks for a pre-exilic date. This applies in particular to a series of royal psalms, as for instance to Ps 132, in which the bringing of the Ark into the temple is carried out liturgically by David in the presence of the king, or to Ps 110, in which the divine election of the enthroned king is celebrated.

But precisely in the area of the royal psalms we also see deep-seated changes as a result of the canon-forming composition. In the third book of the Psalms collection (Pss 73–89) the demise of the monarchy is marked (cf. esp. Ps 89.39-52). But also the composition of the Psalter as a whole reveals a shift: in Ps 2 the king, whom God has appointed on Mount Zion, is described as the "anointed one" (*māšî*ᵃ*ḥ*). In the context of Ps 1 he is the exemplary righteous one (*ṣaddîq*) and from 3.1 onwards he frequently appears as the author of the psalms, but now not as the victorious ruler, but as the suffering righteous one. So here the kingship is interpreted anew from the post-exilic perspective in a "messianic" sense. This then also has great significance for the liturgical use of the psalms that speak of the king.

(On the question of the canon cf. also §6.4.)

§ 24

Jewish and Christian Theology of the Hebrew Bible/Old Testament

Preliminary remarks

In the past two decades I have repeatedly, and in a wide range of contexts, expressed my views on matters of Christian-Jewish relations. This topic has since become central to my own theological thinking. In what follows I shall pick up on some of the material I have published in other places already. I mention some of the studies in which the questions to be dealt with here have been discussed in one way or another: the essay "Zur Bedeutung des Kanons für eine Theologie des Alten Testaments," in the Festschrift for Hans-Joachim Kraus (1983); the conversation with Jon Levenson in response to his essay, "Why Jews are not interested in Biblical Theology" (1991g); the contribution to the discussion in the *Jahrbuch für Biblische Theologie*, "Die Hermeneutik einer kanonischen Theologie des Alten Testaments" (1995c); the essay in the volume of essays *Eine Bibel—zwei Testamente*, entitled "Die Bibel Israels als Buch der Christen" (1995d); the lecture at the Tübingen seminary, "Theologische Vorarbeiten zu einem christlich-jüdischen Dialog," of 1996 (1998a); the essay "A Christian Approach to the Theology of Hebrew Scriptures" in the collection *Jews, Christians, and the Theology of the Hebrew Scriptures* (2000e); and some material from the booklet *Christen und Juden heute* (1998c).

1. Israel's Bible

"The most important theological event in the second half of this century is Christian theology's discovery of Judaism." It is appropriate that this sentence, written in 1995 (1995d, 97 [=2001a, 30]), should preface the following considerations. From the point of view of the theology of the Old Testament it means above all: the rediscovery of the Old Testament as Israel's Bible. The term "Israel's Bible" deliberately has a different emphasis than the term used so far in this book, "Hebrew Bible." The latter was chosen with regard to the linguistic character and the canonical shape of the collection of scriptures which generally forms the basis of exegesis and theological interpretation in scholarly usage beyond the boundaries of religions and denominations. It is also increasingly being used in international discussion, frequently in the variant Hebrew Scriptures (cf. Bellis & Kaminsky 2000). By contrast, the term "Israel's Bible" places emphasis on the fact that this collection of scriptures was Israel's Holy Scripture during the process of its composition through to its concluding canonical composition (cf. Dohmen in Dohmen & Stemberger 1996, 14ff).

Within this Israel, which in this period can also be termed the Jewish people, there emerged in the first century of the common era the messianic movement from which Christianity grew. In its beginnings this movement was fully part of the community of the Jewish nation and the Jewish faith. Accordingly, Israel's Bible was also their Bible. This applies to Jesus as well as the authors of the New Testament writings. For them Israel's Bible was the "Scripture" by which they lived, which they often quoted, and which they interpreted.

This generally known historical fact (cf. von Campenhausen 1968) is today being gradually recognized for its theological significance. The consequence of this recognition must, even when the questions come from Christian theology, be to understand and interpret in the first place the first part of the two-part Christian Bible, the "Old Testament," for what it itself has to say. In the practice of exegetical work, in commentaries and scholarly publications as well as in the field of the "theology of the Old Testament," this is indeed what the great majority of Christian Old Testament scholars do (cf. 1995d, 100f [=33f]). The theological discussion of the consequences of this insight has, however, barely begun.

For this, a fundamental change of theological approach is required. As a rule the question of the Christian meaning of the Old Testament is viewed from the perspective of an established Christianity with a fully formed theology, i.e. from a point of view situated far beyond the experiences and contacts of Jesus and the authors of the New Testament writings with their "Scriptures." This narrows down the questions that can be asked from the beginning, because the Old Testament is confronted with Christian theology, which did not develop until much later, so that the questions about what distinguishes them shift to the foreground. The problem is thus viewed back-to-front, as it were; but this distorts the order given in the Christian Bible to its opposite, because there the Old Testament comes *before* the New. One might speak of a "pre-position of Israel's Bible" (Dohmen in Dohmen & Stemberger 1996, 154ff). The question of "what justifies the use of the Hebrew Bible in the church and thus its place in the Christian canon of Scripture" (Dohmen & Oeming 1992) must therefore be regarded as inappropriate. This question is not posed to us as Christians. Since the church's decision against Marcion there can be no Christianity without the *whole* of Scripture. So today we do not have to "justify" all over again a decision that was taken in the early period of church history.

If the question of what is distinctive or "specifically Christian" is foregrounded, then a narrow self-understanding of Christian faith is evident; for this is to lose sight of the sequence of the articles of the Christian confession: the first article of the Apostles' Creed is "pure Old Testament." And the abundance of Christian experiences that are justified by faith in God the creator and by trust in him, needs no supplementary questioning as to its "correctness" from a Christian point of view. We might add something else: Luther placed the Decalogue at the beginning of the catechism without offering a special "Christian" justification for doing so; rather, in the Greater Catechism he said that one should keep the Ten Commandments "dear and valued above all other teachings as the highest treasure given by God." Or: no Christian pastor or priest will ever see the need to provide the use of psalms in the liturgy he leads with a special "Christian" justification. These examples show very clearly that the whole Bible belongs to the foundation of the faith of Christians.

This applies particularly markedly to Jesus and the first generations of Christians, especially also for the New Testament writers. For them the "Scripture" is their Bible, the use of which they take for granted, requiring no justification. On the contrary, they justify what they have to say often enough with the authority of "Scripture." And central statements on the significance of the life and fate of Jesus are interpreted precisely as having occurred "according to the Scriptures" (e.g. Luke 24.44f; 1 Cor 15.3f). "There is no Christology, there is not even a material foothold for one, outside the Scripture and its validity" (Crüsemann 1997, 16).

Right through to the time of Christian origins, including the period of the emerging New Testament, there is thus only *one* Bible: Israel's Bible. Its authority as Holy Scripture is undisputed among all Jews, including those that formed a group of their own as disciples of Jesus. So any occupation with the theology of the Bible must start here and interpret Israel's Bible as Holy Scripture from itself.

2. The dual sequel

Toward the end of the first century two developments occur independently of each other which lead to a dual sequel in the history of Israel's Bible. After the destruction of Jerusalem and the temple in 70 CE, in the small coastal town of Yavne (Gk *Jamnia*) a new center of Jewish scholarship forms under the leadership of Yohanan ben Zakkai. What takes place here in the following years is "a fundamental re-ordering and re-constitution of Judaism, which enabled the survival of the Jewish religion and the Jewish people" (Schäfer 1975, 54[=45]). "Judaism" in the narrower sense thereby comes into being, also called "rabbinic Judaism" or "classical Judaism" (Stemberger 1979).

In the course of this reconstitution the canon of the writings of the Hebrew Bible is finally fixed. This does not appear to have happened by means of a formal decision; it is often assumed that the scope of the collection was in essence firmly established earlier. The important thing, however, is that an independent form of scripture exegesis now develops for which the precise extent of the canon and precise wording of the text form a crucial precondition. This canon is termed the "written Torah." Rabbinic exegesis is added as a supplement and continuation as the "oral Torah." (This term remains in use even though these texts were then set down and passed on in writing.) In the course of the centuries rabbinic exegesis grows enormously and exceeds the biblical canon in extent many times over. Nonetheless the distinction between written and oral Torah is maintained. The Bible, the "Holy Scriptures" (*kitbê haqqodeš*), remains the foundation.

This high view of the Hebrew Bible finds expression in the further history of the transmission of the text. Here we can observe the efforts made to fix definitively a uniform wording of the consonantal text (cf. Fabry in Zenger *et al.*, 1998, 58ff), ultimately leading also to the addition of vowel pointing by the "Masoretes" (probably around 700 CE, cf. Fabry 43ff) in order to ensure uniform pronunciation of the biblical text.

In the same period in which rabbinic Judaism was constituted, but independently of this, the messianic Jesus movement begins to develop into a community separate from Judaism. But there is no change in the fact that Israel's Bible remains valid as Holy Scripture. Nor do things change when in the further course of this development this community collects scriptures of its own and finally canonizes them as the "New Testament." (For detail cf. Trobisch 1996.) The name of this collection corresponds to the term "Old Testament," now coming into use for Israel's Bible.

This development hits a serious crisis around the middle of the second century as a result of Marcion's call for the fixing of a Christian canon with a "purged" selection of New Testament writings and in particular without the Old Testament. Marcion's exclusion as a heretic (c. 144) and the associated decision to keep the Old Testament as part of the Christian Bible brought this dispute to a conclusion (cf. von Campenhausen 1968, 173ff). "Old" and "New Testament" have since together formed the Holy Scriptures, the Bible of the Christian community.

Here we see a fundamental difference in relation to rabbinic Judaism: while there the difference between the "written" and the "oral Torah" remains strictly observed and only the former is valid as Holy Scripture, in Christianity a new biblical canon emerges, which comprises both the "Old Testament" and the "New Testament." As a result, entirely new questions arise in relation to the "Old Testament" (cf. also Koch 1991).

3. Jewish theology of the Hebrew Bible

"Biblical theology" or "theology of the Old Testament" is a Christian interest in terms of its approach and its history. (The history of scholarship has been presented many times; see above p. 717.) Above all the term "theology" designates a set of questions that is alien to the Jewish tradition. In the famous words of Gabler (see 1991a, 2), fundamental for the Christian tradition, the issue is the distinction of "biblical" from "dogmatic" theology. Here the term theology is presupposed as a given, and at the same time it becomes clear that this term belongs originally in the field of dogmatics. Dogmatics in the sense meant here is, however, something that is specifically Christian, unknown in the Jewish tradition.

Thus until quite recently it was considered settled that there could be no Jewish "theology of the Hebrew Bible" or "theology of the Tanakh." In the meantime, however, a lively discussion has arisen (cf. Barr 1999, 286-311). First there appeared in 1987 (exactly 200 years after Gabler!) two essays by well-known Jewish biblical scholars, in which at first sight opposing viewpoints are expressed. Jon Levenson wrote "Why Jews are not interested in Biblical Theology." This sounds like a fundamental dismissal of occupation with biblical theology. But on closer examination it is mainly a critique of the dominant Christian theology of the Old Testament with its efforts to systematize and unify the polyphonic voices of the Hebrew Bible and of its interpretation of Old Testament statements in the context of Christian theological schemes. As a special example Levenson criticizes von Rad's exegesis of Gen 15.6 under the title "The Reckoning of Faith as Righteousness" (German 1951). His conclusion: "It is precisely the failure of the biblical theologians to recognize the limitation of the context of their enterprise which makes some of them surprised that Jews are not interested in it." Levenson does not raise the question of a separate Jewish biblical theology here. But only a year later he publishes a book which can scarcely be termed anything other than a piece of biblical theology, *Jewish* biblical theology of course: *Creation and the Persistence of Evil. The Jewish Drama of Divine Omnipotence* (1988). In the Preface Levenson expressly refers to this book as "a theological study," which he has written because of the perceived "lack of sophisticated theological reflection upon even such central and overworked aspects of the religion of Israel as creation and covenant." Levenson can thus now be counted as one of those who concern themselves with a suitably Jewish "biblical theology."

Also in 1987 an essay appeared by Moshe Goshen-Gottstein, in which this intention was unmistakably expressed already in the title: "Tanakh Theology: The Religion of the Old Testament and the Place of Jewish Biblical Theology." Goshen-Gottstein analyses the history of Old Testament theology and comes to the conclusion that the more recent development in which Christian theologians have begun to explain the Old Testament "from the inside," "in its own terms," makes it essential to think carefully about a theology of the Tanakh (624f). This "is not only possible, but necessary as a new central area of biblical studies" (633).

In the meantime discussion has progressed. Thus in Chicago in 1996, under the leadership of Michael Fishbane and Tikva Frymer-

Kensky a conference was held on "Jewish Biblical Theology" (cf. Brettler 1997). In the same year at the Annual Meeting of the Society of Biblical Literature there was a session on this topic with four papers, by two Jewish and two Christian speakers. This produced a collection of essays, published in 2000, with the title *Jews, Christians, and the Theology of the Hebrew Scriptures* (Bellis & Kaminsky 2000). Here Jewish and Christian biblical scholars endeavor to come together to a new understanding of what they agree to call "theology of the Hebrew Bible." This shows at the same time a fruit of international and inter-religious cooperation between biblical scholars, as now takes place worldwide, with a clear center of gravity in North America. The editors of this volume chose as a motto Joseph's word to his brothers: "You will not see my face unless my brother is with you" (Gen 43.3). They explained the figurative sense of this motto by a word from Paul: "Now we see but a poor reflection; then we shall see face to face" (1 Cor 13.12).

As yet no contours of a program for a theology of the Hebrew Bible have emerged. But it is significant that Jewish biblical scholars are now speaking unselfconsciously of "theology" and of the need to be occupied with it. The term "theology of the Hebrew Bible" can also be taken on board by Christian biblical scholars (cf. 2000e). For them the "theology of the Old Testament" then has a further dimension which has no immediate relevance for their Jewish colleagues. Conversely for Christians, the same is true of rabbinic exegesis, which, though of great interest—and it ought to be studied much more than it is—, cannot have a direct influence on their exegesis of the Hebrew Bible.

Excursus: The term "Old Testament"

On the following discussion cf. especially Zenger 1991, 144-154; also 1998c, 73-77.

The term "Old Testament" is a purely Christian term. It only makes sense if there is also a "New Testament" that is to be distinguished from the "Old." This terminology is documented from the late second century (cf. Trobisch 1996, 68f). It was only at that time, when the Christian scriptures were collated into a canon, that the "Scriptures" which Jews and Christians together venerated as Holy Scripture were expressly singled out as a separate entity. Since then, for the Christian community the canon of Holy Scripture consists of two parts, the second of which contains only the specifically Christian text tradition. To that extent the naming of the first part as "Old Testament" marks the meanwhile completed distinction between and separation of the two communities of faith. That the Old and New Testaments together now form a single canon of scripture, however, is also an expression of the fact that they belong closely together. The inherent tension in this has since variously characterized the relationship between the two religions and their understanding of scripture.

The two parts of the Christian Bible also form a unity as a result of their common language. The Bible of the worldwide Jewish community was in those days the Greek translation, the "Septuagint." The New Testament writings were also written in Greek and furthermore influenced in their language by the Greek Bible. After the Septuagint had been canonized in the two-part Christian Bible, however, its use in the Jewish world was discontinued. The Greek version differs in many respects from the Hebrew original: for one thing the sequence of the books is different, and for another there are additional writings that were not included in the Hebrew canon. To that extent the Old Testament is not identical to the Hebrew Bible. Hence the discussion here as to the appropriate term for the first part of the Christian Bible.

In conversation between Jewish and Christian biblical scholars it is relatively easy to agree on particular terminology. The basis for collaborative work is without doubt the Hebrew Bible. So the use of this term, or the alternative English term "Hebrew Scriptures," is an immediate option. Even if Jewish conversation-partners use the term *Tanakh*, this is no problem for Christians. For their part they can continue to use the term "Old Testament" for the first part of the Christian Bible. (On this see also §6.4.) This term is used without problem in the international and inter-religious arena, e.g. in the context of the "International Organization for the Study of the Old Testament," in whose congresses many Jewish scholars participate; when the 1986 congress was held in Jerusalem, no one thought of changing its name.

The term "Old Testament" however has become the subject of discussion for reasons of quite a different nature. The word "old" has often been, and continues to be, used in the sense of "outdated, discarded." Correspondingly the New Testament has been seen (and still is) as the message of the New by which the Old has been superseded; the new covenant was seen (and for many is still seen) as the superseding and replacement of the old covenant, which has lost its validity. Such views also gave new impetus to Christian anti-Judaism, which was acknowledged to be one of the roots of anti-Semitism. Committed

Christian circles (cf. 1998a) opposed this, and in this connection the term "Old Testament" was also queried.

Here the term "Hebrew Bible" is not equally suitable as an alternative. Firstly because the original linguistic form plays no separate role in general Christian understanding. Thus "Hebrew Bible" can seem strange and alienating outside the context of specialized theological language. In addition, in its Bible translations the Catholic tradition takes its premise not from the Hebrew but from the Latin text of the Vulgate, which corresponds in its structure to the Greek text of the Septuagint. This means that scriptures that have not been passed down in Hebrew are also part of the biblical canon. Luther on the other hand took the Hebrew text as the basis for his translation and added the other writings as "Apocrypha." But all modern Christian translations follow the structure of the Septuagint and thus do not correspond to the three-part structure of the Hebrew canon.

The expression "Israel's Bible" (see above §24.1) avoids the potentially alienating term "Hebrew," instead indicating clearly that this Bible is meant before and outside its unification with the New Testament. To that extent it can also serve to make people aware that the first part of the Christian canon is and remains also the Bible of Israel, i.e. the Jewish Bible. The term "Jewish Bible" for the first part of the Christian canon would be misleading, because the term "Judaism" is appropriate only for a phase after the fixing of the Hebrew canon (see above, §24.2).

For a number of years now, the term "The First Testament" has been frequently used (cf. Zenger 1991). Certainly "the first" does not evoke the same negative associations as "the old." Instead, the prior position of the first in relation to the second is in the foreground. On the other hand the term "the first," like "the old" assumes that something is to follow it, at least a second. So it expresses an incompleteness. This term would not therefore be acceptable to Jews, because their Bible would thereby be marked as incomplete and as in need of continuation and revision.

We return, finally, to the expression "Scripture" or "the Scriptures," which is used to designate the Jewish holy scriptures (see above §24.1). No doubt the use of this term would be very sensible. It could, however, be objected that in Christian usage (though certainly this is somewhat outdated) the Bible as a whole is called "Scripture." Crüsemann (1997, 16) is certainly right to say: "If we follow the evangelical scriptural principle, then the Old Testament is the *scripture of scripture.*" How this can translate into linguistic usage remains to be seen.

To conclude these observations, it is evident that though the problems associated with the term "Old Testament" have often been recognized, so far no generally accepted alternative suggestion has emerged. So in my view it is advisable to use other terms alongside the term "Old Testament" and to indicate the pros and cons in each case.

★ ★ ★ ★ ★

4. Christian theology of the Old Testament

It is of crucial significance that the church has maintained Israel's Bible unchanged, in the contemporary Greek version (see below). One cannot say it has "taken it over," because this Bible of course was the Holy Scripture to the Christian community right from the beginning. So it is one of the necessary changes of theological approach to set this question on its head: the church did not "take over" the Old Testament at some point but from the beginning it lived with its Bible and it had its own self-understanding and, last but not least, developed its interpretation of the life and fate of Jesus from this Bible. There is no Christian history and no Christian theology without this Bible (cf. also Koch 1991; Crüsemann 1997).

The corollary of this is that Christian theology does not begin with the message of the New Testament. We have already looked at the fundamental significance of particular Old Testament themes for Christian faith and thinking: belief in creation, the Ten Commandments, many Psalms, etc. (see above §24.1). Examples could be multiplied. So the unpacking of the theological statements of the Old Testament is an integral part of Christian theology. It cannot be a matter of selecting those texts and themes that seem to the interpreter from the point of view of his or her own presuppositions to be "Christian." Nor can the selection criterion consist in what texts and themes are discussed, by extension, in the New Testament (see §24.5). Rather, the task of theological interpretation of the Old Testament lies in unpacking the entirety of the message of the first part of the Bible.

At this point we must return to what was said above in the context of the term "biblical theology" or "theology of the Old Testament" and its presuppositions. The term "theology" in these phrases is a Christian term, both in approach and in its history (see above §24.3).

The distinction between "dogmatic" and "biblical" theology, which goes back to Gabler, remains within the context of the Christian understanding of theology. (There is a difference in approach here from a "history of Israel's religion," which does not presuppose any allegiance of the author to a particular religion. If on the other hand the term "theology" is now used also for the Jewish theology of the Hebrew Bible, then a theological exegesis in the context of the Jewish religion is meant.)

The connection with Christian theology has consequences already for the type of questions asked. The procedure we have followed with the thematic discussion in this book is no doubt led by a "systematic" interest, the origins of which lie in theology. This is already true of the choice and formulation of the "themes." They do not emerge on their own but are chosen and named on the basis of the theological insights and certainly also of the theological interest of the author.

Here again we see the significance of the "canonical" approach to the theology of the Old Testament. In my selection of themes I have taken my lead from the structure of the canon of the Hebrew Bible. But here there is a tension between the terms "Hebrew Bible" and "Old Testament," since Israel's Bible, in the Greek version, the Septuagint, was joined together with the New Testament that had come into being in the meantime, to make the Christian Bible. The number and especially the sequence of the writings in the Greek version do not, however, correspond to those of the three-part canon of the Hebrew Bible. The basic difference lies in the fact that in the Hebrew Bible the Prophets follow the Torah, while in the Septuagint the Prophets are found at the end of the collection.

Now, in the New Testament, we see that at first "Torah and Prophets" were established as binding, i.e. canonical, since "Scripture" is frequently cited as "the Law (νόμος = *tôrāh*) and the Prophets" (Matt 5.17; 7.12; John 1.45; Rom 3.21 etc.) or as "Moses and the Prophets" (Luke 16.29, 31; 24.27; Acts 28.23). This implies that the other writings did not yet have canonical status. One can interpret the difference between the Hebrew Bible and the Septuagint as lying in the fact that in the Hebrew Bible the other writings were added as a third part of the canon, while these were inserted in the Septuagint between the fixed parameters of the Torah and the Prophets. In both versions, then, the canonical superiority of the Torah and the Prophets is maintained. In the Hebrew Bible the Torah perspective dominates so that both the Prophets and the Writings are read and understood from the perspective of the Torah (cf. Mal 3.22; Pss 1.1f; 119), while in the Septuagint the Prophets perspective is determinative, so that everything is oriented towards the future prophesied by the Prophets (Dohmen in Dohmen & Stemberger 1996, 150-154; cf. the table on p. 151; for a suggested interpretation that goes a step further, cf. Zenger in Zenger *et al.* 1998, 34f).

The difference between the Hebrew Bible and the Christian Old Testament thus does not affect the fundamental theological agreement between the two versions and thus also between the theologians interpreting them. For the Christian theologian, though, the tension between the two versions of the text continues to quite an extent, because from the time of the Reformation onwards the original Hebrew text has formed the basis for Bible translations, while at the same time the sequence of scriptures provided by the Septuagint has been kept. But the scriptures that are not available in Hebrew have not been adopted in the churches of the Reformation; Luther added them as a supplement to his translation as "Apocrypha." On the other hand the Catholic Church has kept these writings in its translations of the Bible. Despite these differences for all Christian theologians the Hebrew text of the Bible forms the generally accepted common basis for scholarly theological biblical interpretation.

How the theology of the Old Testament relates to Christian theology as a whole must be thought through in further theological steps.

5. Biblical theology

The term "biblical theology" can be used in a wide variety of ways (cf. Barr in *EKL*[3] I, 488-494; Janowski 1998/99). Gabler brought this term into play with his distinction between biblical and dogmatic theology (cf. 1991a, 2). In the same sense Barr distinguishes between biblical theology and other theologies, such as "doctrinal" or "philosophical theology" (Barr 1999, 1). Accordingly, "Old Testament theology" and "New Testament theology" are two forms of biblical theology; but if a theology is meant that comprises both the Old and New Testaments, Barr likes to speak of "pan-biblical theology," with which he picks up on the title of Oeming's book (1985). In German discussion, however, the term *Biblische Theologie* is used primarily in precisely this sense as theology of the whole Bible, as represented by Reventlow's book (1983). And this is how the term is being used here.

First the basic question arises: what should be the criteria for pursuing a theology that views the Old and New Testaments together as the Bible, Holy Scripture? In light of all that has been presented so far the basic premise for a "biblical theology" is the insight that Israel's Bible was from the beginning the Holy Scriptures of the Christian community. This means that Christian theology does not begin only with the message of the New Testament. Nor can one judge the significance of the Old Testament for the Christian church from the New Testament or from a theology derived from it. This would radically contradict the history of the origins of the Christian Bible and the theological decisions made in this history.

How little correspondence there is between such an approach and the self-understanding of the two-part Christian Bible is shown very impressively if one reads on from the end of the Old Testament in the canonical sequence of the Christian Bible (see above §24.4). The call by the prophet Malachi to bear in mind that God will send the prophet Elijah (Mal 3.22f) is followed immediately by the family tree of Jesus Christ, the son of David, son of Abraham (Matt 1.1). As so often in the Hebrew Bible, the text starts off with the genealogy beginning with Abraham. (It can hardly be a coincidence, either, that the superscription to the first Gospel, Βίβλος γενέσεως, is a quotation from Gen 2.4.) So this provides an unbroken transition for the reader.

But this certainly cannot mean that the Old Testament as it were is absorbed into the New Testament, losing its own dignity. On the contrary: the many cases where the New Testament appeals to the Old show very clearly how very much alive the latter continued to be in the consciousness of early Christianity. If one wanted to take stock of the theological thinking (in the broader sense) of the early Christian community, one would first have to give an extensive account of Old Testament faith traditions (cf. 1998c, 61-69). One might appropriately cite the beginning of Hebrews: "In the past God spoke to our forefathers through the prophets at many times and in various ways" (Heb 1.1). Especially illuminating are those texts in which there is explicit mention of the Old Testament as authority. This applies, for instance, to the commandment to love one's neighbor (often labeled as specifically Christian), which Jesus expressly quotes from the "Scripture" (Matt 19.18f; Mark 12.29-31). In Luke's version Jesus even has the scribe who has asked him "What must I do to inherit eternal life?" himself give the answer from Scripture (Luke 10.25-28). For both

conversation partners the Scripture is the common source and acknowledged authority for matters of life and faith.

So "biblical theology" cannot avoid the question of what is "different" in the New Testament in comparison with the Old, or in what
sense the Old Testament is "fulfilled" in the New. Certainly such
questions arise, and they must be asked, but they cannot be the first
consideration. In particular they are not appropriate to the message of
Jesus, because this stands squarely in the context of the Judaism of his
day. Biblical theology must first sort out the still valid significance of
the Old Testament in the Christian community and in its own writings, i.e. in the New Testament.

To that extent there is continuity between the Old and New Testaments. This continuity needs greater precision. First it must be
considered how much discontinuity there is within the Old
Testament. The canon of the Hebrew Bible or the Old Testament
comprises a very wide variety of texts from many different periods,
both in the narrative sections and in the history reflected there. There
are also quite profound disjunctions in it, above all the demise of Judah
and the Babylonian exile, but also the demise of the northern kingdom
and the dramatic reduction of "Israel" that went with it. For the
reader of the Hebrew Bible it is very clear that the entire history of
Israel—and this also means the history of God's dealings with Israel
and of Israel's with God—has entered the tradition from the point of
view of the post-exilic community represented by Ezra (see above
§24.4). Finally, there is quite some discontinuity also in the quite
different areas of life in the Old Testament literature (cf. §§17–19).

All this is not disguised in the canon of the Old Testament, but
openly recorded. So despite all the tensions and contrasts, the overview displays a "composite of meanings" (see above §23.3). One
might therefore view the transition from the Old Testament to the
New in the same light: here a new chapter begins in the story of God's
dealings with Israel and with humanity as a whole. This means continuity between the Old and New Testaments; together they form a
"contrasting unity" (Janowski 1998, 16f [=264f]). But this new beginning is emphasized as something that is fundamentally new. The quotation from the beginning of Hebrews continues: "but in these last
days he has spoken to us by his Son" (Heb 1.2). This means discontinuity: God's varied and multiform speaking is continued, but at the
same time it comes to an end because of the unique character of this

last communication from God. However, this discontinuity "only really becomes understandable against the background of the continuity" (Janowski, *ibid.*).

The element of discontinuity is articulated in a particularly emphatic way through the concentration on *one* point: Christology. The comments of Westermann are particularly noteworthy in this regard: "The OT represents a long epoch, more precisely a series of epochs, and the NT only a brief period of time in the middle of which stands one event, the ministry, suffering and death of Jesus. While the OT is conceived from the start on a grand scale ..., the NT has the character of an excerpt, or section, of a concluding section in fact." Differences emerge from this: "The NT, because it is concentrated on one thing, must also be biased; the OT, oriented towards the entirety of what is happening, must be multifaceted, manifold and in various forms" (Westermann 1986, 19). This means that though the life and faith of Christians is decisively determined and stimulated by the events reported in the New Testament, in order to develop, it still requires the variety of the Old Testament witness. Once again we can draw on what Hebrews says: God's last communication does not make his various previous communications superfluous or meaningless. On the contrary, it is only in this context that the New Testament message can be understood and lived out.

It is worth bearing in mind in particular that even fundamental matters of Christian faith are not developed in the New Testament. Thus "the New Testament authors saw no need ... to develop a doctrine of God" (Dunn 1995, 186, with reference to Childs 1992, 367 [= vol. 2, 32f]). The same also applies to the understanding of God as creator: "the Old Testament's understanding of God as creator was simply assumed and largely taken for granted as true" (Childs 391). Thus "biblical theology" protects us from "supporting New Testament theology only on what is directly explicit" (Dunn *ibid.*). Finally one must not lose sight of the fact that within the New Testament itself there are also considerable discontinuities: "fundamental here is the question of what the relationship is between the—plurifom, though not amorphous—theology of the Old Testament and the—similarly plurifom and similarly not amorphous—theology of the New Testament" (Söding 1995, 173).

These are just some of the questions that need examination and clarification in a "biblical theology." This can certainly only be achieved in close collaboration between representatives of the two disciplines who agree on particular common premises. As far as I can see, we are currently a long way from this. "Biblical theology" is therefore a topic that is much discussed and written about, but which has so far been only rarely presented in a coherent study. As recently as 1983 Reventlow could say in the introduction to his survey on this topic: "No 'Biblical Theology' has yet been written" (Reventlow 1983, vii).

This sentence is now out of date following the appearance of B. Childs's *Biblical Theology of the Old and New Testaments* (1992). However, Childs's book sets out quite a different basic concept than the one discussed up to this point. A glance at the table of contents already makes this clear: to start with there are two long chapters on particular themes in the (separately treated) Old and New Testaments ("The discrete witness of the Old/New Testament"), but then an extensive chapter (which occupies almost the whole of the second volume in the German translation) with the title "Theological reflection on the Christian Bible." In this chapter everything is geared to Christian doctrine, as Childs takes the path in each individual sub-section from the Old Testament—sometimes via (early) Judaism—to the New, reaching the end of the path in dogmatics. Biblical theology is understood here as a partial aspect of Christian theology as a whole. Childs assumes that the Old and New Testaments bear the same core message: "the Old Testament also served as Christian 'Scripture' because it witnessed to Jesus Christ" (64). This was possible because "the Evangelists read the Old Testament retrospectively from the point of view of the New," thereby "transforming" it. This notion of a transformation of the Old Testament by the reading and adoption of the New Testament authors is diametrically opposed to our discussion above. For the maintenance of the "Scriptures" in the form in which it was transmitted in the Jewish faith community is precisely an essential element of continuity between the Old and the New Testaments (see above §24.4).

So this first attempt at a detailed "biblical theology" shows the range of possibilities that arise, and reveals at the same time the theological controversies that unavoidably arise in the process (cf. 1994b). In addition it opens a perspective on a further chapter: the question of the relationship between biblical theology and dogmatics. This too is something that has not yet been studied very much, and the positions of those who raise this question lie far apart. Barr has made some important contributions to the formulation of the problems (Barr 1999, 62ff, 240ff, 513ff etc.).

I have seen it as my task in this book first to set out the statements made by the Old Testament texts in their various contexts: in their context in the various biblical documents or books and in a thematic survey within the Old Testament as a whole. This is no doubt a theological task, if one does not want to tie oneself to a particular understanding of theology as is prevalent for instance in systematic theology, especially in dogmatics. One can be much more open in saying that "by the term 'theological' we mean quite simply that effort to order the phenomena in broader contexts." This endeavor is discernible at many points in the Old Testament, as the texts themselves "interpret the events and ... seek to open them up to understanding faith" (von Rad 1965, 382f). The theology of the Old Testament, and biblical theology too, can take this interpretation a good step further by picking up these interpretive premises and developing them further. This too is a theological task, not least because interpreters approach it as theologians, bringing their own theological tradition and their own understanding of this tradition with them. The understanding of theological tradition that informs this book is also significantly influenced by a lifetime's occupation with the Old Testament.

Works Cited

Abbreviations used in the Bibliography

ÄAT	Ägypten und Altes Testament
AB	Anchor Bible
ABD	*Anchor Bible Dictionary*
AKuG	Archiv für Kulturgeschichte
AOAT	Alter Orient und Altes Testament
ATD	Das Alte Testament Deutsch
ATANT	Abhandlungen zur Theologie des Alten und Neuen Testaments
BEATAJ	Beiträge zur Erforschung des Alten Testaments und des Antiken Judentums
BETL	*Bibliotheca ephemeridum theologicarum Lovaniensium*
Bib	*Biblica*
BibInt	*Biblical Interpretation*
BibSem	Biblical Seminar
BJS	Brown Judaic Studies
BK	Biblischer Kommentar
BN	*Biblische Notizen*
BRL²	*Biblisches Reallexikon*, 2nd ed.
BSt	Biblische Studien
BTS	Biblisch-theologische Studien
BZ	*Biblische Zeitschrift*
BZAW	Beihefte zur Zeitschrift für die alttestamentliche Wissenschaft
ConBOT	Coniectanea Biblica, Old Testament Series
CBQMS	Catholic Biblical Quarterly Monograph Series
EdF	Erträge der Forschung
EKL³	*Evangelisches Kirchenlexikon*, 3rd ed.
EncJud	*Encyclopedia Judaica*
EvT	*Evangelische Theologie*
FAT	Forschungen zum Alten Testament
FOTL	Forms of the Old Testament Literature
FRLANT	Forschungen zur Religion und Literatur des Alten und Neuen Testaments

FS	Festschrift
GAT	Grundrisse zum Alten Testament (= ATD supplementary series)
HAR	*Hebrew Annual Review*
HAT	Handbuch zum Alten Testament
HBT	Horizons in Biblical Theology
HK	Göttinger Handkommentar zum Alten Testament
HTKAT	Herders Theologischer Kommentar zum Alten Testament
IBC	Interpretation: A Bible Commentary for Teaching and Preaching
Int	*Interpretation*
JBT	*Jahrbuch für Biblische Theologie*
JR	*Journal of Religion*
JSOT	*Journal for the Study of the Old Testament*
JSOTS	Journal for the Study of the Old Testament, Supplement series
JSS	*Journal of Semitic Studies*
KAT	Kommentar zum Alten Testament
KT	Kaiser Traktate
KuDB	Kerygma und Dogma, Beihefte
NEchtB	Neue Echter Bibel
NTOA	Novum Testamentum et Orbis Antiquus
OBO	Orbis Biblicus et Orientalis
OTL	Old Testament Library
QD	Quaestiones disputatae
RBL	*Review of Biblical Literature*
RTAT	Religionsgeschichtliches Textbuch zum Alten Testament
SBA	Stuttgarter Biblische Aufsatzbände
SBL	Society of Biblical Literature
SBLDS	Society of Biblical Literature, Dissertation Series
SBLSP	Society of Biblical Literature, Seminar Papers
SBLSymS	Society of Biblical Literature Symposium Series
SBS	Stuttgarter Bibelstudien
SKGG	Schriften der Königsberger Gelehrten Gesellschaft. Geisteswissenschaftliche Klasse
SUNT	Studien zur Umwelt des Neuen Testaments
stw	suhrkamp taschenbuch wissenschaft
SVSKHF	Skrifter udgifna af Videnskabsselkabet i Kristiania – Historisk-Filosofisk Klasse
TB	Theologische Bücherei
THE	Theologische Existenz heute
THAT	*Theologisches Handwörterbuch zum Alten Testament*
TLZ	*Theologische Literaturzeitung*

TS	Theologische Studien
TViat	*Theologia Viatorum*
ThWAT	*Theologisches Wörterbuch zum Alten Testament*
TW	*Theologische Wissenschaft*
TTZ	*Trierer Theologische Zeitschrift*
TZ	*Theologische Zeitschrift*
TUAT	*Texte aus der Umwelt des Alten Testaments*
UF	*Ugarit-Forschungen*
UT	Urban Taschenbücher
VF	*Verkündigung und Forschung*
VT	*Vetus Testamentum*
VTS	Vetus Testamentum Supplements
WMANT	Wisschenschaftliche Monographien zum Alten und Neuen Testament
ZAW	*Zeitschrift für die alttestamentliche Wissenschaft*
ZBK	Zürcher Bibelkommentare
ZDMG	*Zeitschrift der deutschen morgenländischen Gesellschaft*
ZTK	*Zeitschrift für Theologie und Kirche* (new series)

Bibliography

Note:
The publications are in each case cited by name and date, but some only by date. "Luther" and "Buber" without further qualification refer to the respective Bible translations. Generally speaking, dictionary articles are not separately listed in this bibliography.

Ackroyd, P.R., 1963. "Hosea and Jacob," *VT* 13, 245-59
——1978. "Isaiah I–XII: Presentation of a Prophet," in: VTS 29, 16-48 (= *Studies in the Religious Traditions of the Old Testament*, 1987, 79-104)
——1982. "Isaiah 36–39: Structure and Function," in: *Von Kanaan bis Kerala*, FS J.P.M. van der Ploeg, AOAT 211, 3-21 (= Studies [cf. 1987], 103-20)
Albertz, R., 1978. "Hintergrund und Bedeutung des Elterngebots im Dekalog," *ZAW* 90, 348-374
——1989. "Die Intentionen und die Träger des Deuteronomistischen Geschichtswerkes," in: R. Albertz *et al.* (eds.), *Schöpfung und Befreiung*, FS C. Westermann, Stuttgart, 37-53
——1992. *Religionsgeschichte Israels in alttestamentlicher Zeit*, 2 vols., GAT 8/1 and 2
Alt, A., 1925. "Jerusalems Aufstieg," *ZDMG* 79, 1-19 (= Kleine Schriften zur Geschichte des Volkes Israel, vol. 3, 1959, 243-57)
——1951. "Die Weisheit Salomos," *TLZ* 76, 139-44 (= Kleine Schriften, vol. 2, 1953, 90-99)

Alter, R., 1981. *The Art of Biblical Narrative*, New York

Alter, R. and F. Kermode, 1987. *The Literary Guide to the Bible*, Cambridge, MA

Anderson, B.W., 1967. *Creation versus Chaos: The Reinterpretation of Mythical Symbolism in the Bible*, New York (repr. Philadelphia 1987)

——1984. *Creation in the Old Testament*, Philadelphia/London

André, G., 1989. "פָּקַד, *paqad*," *ThWAT* VI, 708-723

Assmann, J., 1991. *Politische Theologie zwischen Ägypten und Israel*, Carl Friedrich von Siemens Stiftung, Themen 52

Auld, A.G., 1983. "Prophets through the Looking Glass. Between Writings and Moses," *JSOT* 27, 3-23

——1984. "Prophets and Prophecy in Jeremiah and Kings," *ZAW* 96, 66-82

Aurelius, E., 1988. *Der Fürbitter Israels. Eine Studie zum Mosebild im Alten Testament*, Lund

Barr, J., 1961. *The Semantics of Biblical Language*, Oxford

——1966. *Old and New in Interpretation*, London

——1999. *The Concept of Biblical Theology. An Old Testament Perspective*, London

Barth, C., 1947. *Die Errettung vom Tode in den individuellen Klage- und Dankliedern des Alten Testaments*, Zürich (ed. B. Janowski, 1997)

Barton, J., 1986. *Oracles of God. Perpceptions of Ancient Prophecy in Israel after the Exile*, London

Baumgartner, W., 1917. *Die Klagegedichte des Jeremia*, BZAW 32. ET: *Jeremiah's Poems of Lament*, trans. D.E. Orton, Sheffield, 1987

Begg, C., 1986. "The Non-mention of Amos, Hosea and Micah in the Deuteronomistic History," in: *BN* 32, 41-53

Bellis, A.O. & J.S. Kaminsky, 2000. *Jews, Christians, and the Theology of the Hebrew Scriptures*, SBLSymS 8

Blenkinsopp, J., 1977. *Prophecy and Canon. A Contribution to the Study of Jewish Origins*, Notre Dame

——1983a. *A History of Prophecy in Israel. From the Settlement in the Land to the Hellenistic Period*, Philadelphia

——1983b. *Wisdom and Law in the Old Testament. The Ordering of Life in Israel and Early Judaism*, Oxford

——1988. *Ezra-Nehemiah. A Commentary*, OTL

——1992. *The Pentateuch. An Introduction to the First Five Books of the Bible*, New York

——1995. *Sage, Priest, Prophet. Religious and Intellectual Leadership in Ancient Israel*, Louisville, KY

——1998. *A History of Prophecy in Israel. From the Beginnings to the Hellenistic Period*

Blum, E., 1984. *Die Komposition der Vätergeschichte*, WMANT 57

——1990a. *Studien zur Komposition des Pentateuch*, BZAW 189

——1990b. E. Blum *et al.* (eds.), *Die hebräische Bibel und ihre zweifache Nachgeschichte* (FS R. Rendtorff), Neukirchen-Vluyn

——1996/97. "Jesajas prophetisches Testament. Beobachtungen zu Jes 1–11,"

ZAW 108, 547-68; 109, 12-29

——2000a. "Noch einmal: Jakobs Traum in Bethel – Genesis 28,10-22," in: S.L. McKenzie & T. Römer (eds.), *Rethinking the Foundations. Historiography in the Ancient World and in the Bible, Essays in Honor of John Van Seters*, BZAW 294, 33-54

——2000b. "Die Lüge des Propheten. Ein Lesevorschlag zu einer befremdlichen Geschichte (I Reg 13)," in: E. Blum (ed.), *Mincha. Festgabe für Rolf Rendtorff zum 75. Geburtstag*, Neukirchen-Vluyn, 27-46

Blum, R. and E., 1990c. "Zippora und ihr חתן דמים," in: E. Blum 1990b, 41-54

Brettler, M.Z., 1997. "Biblical History and Jewish Biblical Theology," *JR* 77, 563-583

Brueggemann, W., 1991. "Bounded by Obedience and Praise: The Psalms as Canon," *JSOT* 50, 63-92

——1997. *Theology of the Old Testament. Testimony, Dispute, Advocacy*, Minneapolis

——1999. "Walter Brueggemann, *Theology of the Old Testament: Testimony, Dispute, Advocacy*. Review Essay," *RBL* 1, 1-21; including review by Rolf Rendtorff (11-17) and a response by Walter Brueggemann (17-21, esp. 20f) (May also be consulted at http://www.bookreviews.org)

Buber, M., n.d. *Die Schrift. Verdeutscht von Martin Buber, gemeinsam mit Franz Rosenzweig*

——1942/1984. *Der Glaube der Propheten* (Heb. 1942; Germ. 1950, 2nd ed., Darmstadt 1984)

Campbell, A.F., 1986. *Of Prophets and Kings. A Late Ninth-Century Document (1 Samuel 1–2 Kings 10)*, CBQMS 17

Campenhausen, H. von, 1968. *Die Entstehung der christlichen Bibel*, BHTh 39

Carlson, R.A., 1964. *David, the Chosen King. A Tradito-Historical Approach to the Second Book of Samuel*, Stockholm

Carroll, R.P., 1969. "The Elijah-Elisha Sagas: Some Remarks on Prophetic Succession in Ancient Israel," *VT* 19, 400-15

——1979. *When Prophecy Failed. Reactions and Responses to Failure in the Old Testament Prophetic Traditions*, London

——1981. *From Chaos to Covenant. Uses of Prophecy in the Book of Jeremiah*, London

Cassuto, U., 1961/1964. *A Commentary on the Book of Genesis*, Part I: *From Adam to Noah, Genesis I–VI 8* (Heb. 1944); Part II: *From Noah to Abraham, Genesis VI 9–XI 32* (Heb. 1949), Jerusalem

——1967. *A Commentary on the Book of Exodus* (Heb. 1951), Jerusalem

Childs, B.S., 1971. "Psalm Titles and Midrashic Exegesis," *JSS* 16, 137-50

——1974. *Exodus. A Commentary*, OTL

——1979. *Introduction to the Old Testament as Scripture*, London

——1986. *Old Testament Theology in a Canonical Context*, Philadelphia

——1992. *Biblical Theology of the Old and New Testaments. Theological Reflection on the Christian Bible*, Minneapolis

Clements, R.E., 1977. "Patterns in the Prophetic Canon," in: G.W. Coats & B.O.

Long (eds.), *Canon and Authority. Essays in Old Testament Religion and Theology*, Philadelphia

——1993. "שַׁעַר, ša'ar," *ThWAT* VII, 933-950

Clines, D.J.A., 1978. *The Theme of the Pentateuch*, JSOTS 10

——1984. *The Esther Scroll. The Story of the Story*, JSOTS 30

——1989. *Job 1–20*, Word Biblical Commentary 17, Dallas

Coats, G.W., 1988. *Moses. Heroic Man, Man of God*, JSOTS 57

Collins, T., 1993. *The Mantle of Elijah. The Redaction Criticism of the Prophetical Books*, BibSem 20

Conrad, E.W., 1988. "The Royal Narratives and the Structure of the Book of Isaiah," *JSOT* 41, 67-81

——1991. *Reading Isaiah*, Minneapolis

——1997. "The End of Prophecy and the Appearance of Angels/Messengers in the Book of the Twelve," *JSOT* 73, 65-79

Cross, F.M., 1973. *Canaanite Myth and Hebrew Epic*, Cambridge, MA

Crüsemann, F., 1969. *Zur Formgeschichte von Hymnus und Danklied in Israel*, WMANT 32

——1971. "Kritik an Amos im deuteronomistischen Geschichtswerk. Erwägungen zu 2 Könige 14,27," in: H.W. Wolff (ed.), *Probleme biblischer Theologie*, FS G. von Rad, Munich, 57-63

——1976. "Jahwes Gerechtigkeit (ṣedāqā / ṣädāq) im Alten Testament," *EvT* 36, 427-450

——1978a. *Der Widerstand gegen das Königtum. Die antiköniglichen Texte des Alten Testaments und der Kampf um den frühen israelitischen Staat*, WMANT 49

——1978b. "'… er aber soll dein Herr sein' (Genesis 3,16). Die Frau in der patriarchalischen Welt des Alten Testaments," in: F. Crüsemann & H. Thyen, *Als Mann und Frau geschaffen. Exegetische Studien zur Rolle der Frau*, Gelnhausen, 13-106

——1981. "Die Eigenständigkeit der Urgeschichte," in: J. Jeremias & L. Perlitt (eds.), *Die Botschaft und die Boten*, FS H.W. Wolff, Neukirchen-Vluyn, 11-29

——1983. *Bewahrung der Freiheit. Das Thema des Dekalogs in sozialgeschichtlicher Perspektive*, KT 78 (= Gütersloh 1993)

——1985. "Israel in der Perserzeit. Eine Skizze in Auseinandersetzung mit Max Weber," in: W. Schluchter (ed.), *Max Webers Sicht des antiken Christentums*, stw 548, 205-32

——1989. "Im Netz. Zur Frage nach der 'eigentlichen' Not in den Klagen der Einzelnen," in: FS Westermann (cf. Albertz 1989), 139-48

——1990. "Der Exodus als Heiligung. Zur rechtsgeschichtlichen Bedeutung des Heiligkeitsgesetzes," in: FS. R. Rendtorff (cf. Blum 1990b), 117-129

——1992. *Die Tora. Theologie und Sozialgeschichte des alttestamentlichen Gesetzes*, Munich

——1995. "Religionsgeschichte oder Theologie? Elementare Überlegungen zu einer falschen Alternative," *JBTh* 10, 69-77

——1997. "Wie alttestamentlich muß evangelische Theologie sein?" *EvT* 57, 10-18

——2000. "Der neue Bund im Neuen Testament. Erwägungen zum Verständnis des Christusbundes in der Abendmahlstradition und im Hebräerbrief,"in: *Mincha* (see Blum 2000b), 47-60

De Vries, S.J., 1988. "Moses and David as Cult Founders in Chronicles," *JBL* 107, 619-639

Dietrich, W. & C. Link, 1995. *Die dunklen Seiten Gottes. Willkür und Gewalt*, Neukirchen-Vluyn

Dohmen, C., 1987. *Das Bilderverbot. Seine Entstehung und seine Entwicklung im Alten Testament*, 2nd ed., BBB 62

——1993. "Der Sinaibund als Neuer Bund nach Ex 19–34," in: E. Zenger (ed.), *Der Neue Bund im Alten. Zur Bundestheologie der beiden Testamente*, QD 146, 51-83

Dohmen, C. & M. Oeming, 1992. *Biblischer Kanon, warum und wozu?* QD 137

Dohmen, C. & T. Söding (eds.), 1995. *Eine Bibel – zwei Testamente. Positionen Biblischer Theologie*, UTB 1893

Dohmen, C. & G. Stemberger, 1996. *Hermeneutik der Jüdischen Bibel und des Alten Testaments*, Stuttgart

Donner, H., 1959. "Art und Herkunft des Amtes der Königinmutter im Alten Testament," in: FS J. Friedrich, 105-45 (= Aufsätze zum Alten Testament, BZAW 224, 1994, 1-24)

——1984/1986. *Geschichte des Volkes Israel und seiner Nachbarn in Grundzügen*, 2 vols., GAT 4/1 and 2 (2nd ed. 1995)

Douglas, M., 1966. *Purity and Danger. An Analysis of the Concepts of Pollution and Taboo*, London

——1993. *In the Wilderness. The Doctrine of Defilement in the Book of Numbers*, JSOTS 158

Dozeman, T.B., 1989. *God on the Mountain*, SBLMS 37

Dunn, J.D.G., 1995. "Das Problem 'Biblische Theologie'," in: C. Dohmen & T. Söding (eds.), 179-193

Ebach, J., 1984. *Leviathan und Behemoth*, Paderborn

——1986. "Bild Gottes und Schrecken der Tiere. Zur Anthropologie der priesterlichen Urgeschichte," in: *Ursprung und Ziel. Erinnerte Zukunft und erhoffte Vergangenheit*, 16-47

——1987. *Kassandra und Jona. Gegen die Macht des Schicksals*, Frankfurt am Main

——1990. "'Ist es "umsonst", daß Hiob gottesfürchtig ist?'," in: FS R. Rendtorff (cf. Blum 1990b), 319-35

——1995a. *Hiobs Post*, Neukirchen-Vluyn

——1995b. "'… und behutsam mitgehen mit deinem Gott'". *Theologische Reden* 3, Bochum

——1996a. *Streiten mit Gott. Hiob*, Part I, *Hiob 1–20*, Neukirchen-Vluyn

——1996b. *Streiten mit Gott. Hiob*, Part II, *Hiob 21–42*, Neukirchen-Vluyn

Edelman, D.V., 1991. *King Saul in the Historiography of Judah*, JSOTS 121

Elliger, K., 1951. "Der Jakobuskampf am Jabbok. Gen 32,23ff als hermeneutisches Problem, *ZTK* 48, 1-31 (=Kleine Schriften zum Alten Testament, 1966, 141-173)

——1955. "Das Gesetz Leviticus 18,"*ZAW* 67, 1-25 (= *Kleine Schriften*, ThB 32, 1966, 232-269)

Eskenazi, T.C., 1988. *In an Age of Prose: A Literary Approach to Ezra-Nehemiah*, SBLMS 36

Eslinger, L., 1989. *Into the Hands of the Living God*, JSOTS 84

Even-Shoshan. *A New Concordance of the Old Testament*, ²1989

Exum, J.C., 1983. "'You Shall Let Every Daughter Live': A Study of Exodus 1:8–2:10," in: *Semeia* 28, 63-82

——1992. *Tragedy and Biblical Narrative. Arrows of the Almighty*, Cambridge

Fishbane, M., 1979. *Text and Texture. Close Readings of Selected Biblical Texts*, New York

——1985. *Biblical Interpretation in Ancient Israel*, Oxford

Galling, K., 1928. *Die Erwählungstraditionen Israels*, BZAW 48

——1977. *Biblisches Reallexikon*, 2nd ed., ed. K. Galling, HAT 1st series, 1 (= *BRL*²)

Gaston, L., 1980. "Abraham and the Righteousness of God," *HBT* 2, 1980, 39-68 (=*Paul and the Tora*, Vancouver 1987, 45-63)

Gerstenberger,E.S., 1988. *Psalms. Part I with an Introduction to Cultic Poetry*. FOTL 14, Grand Rapids

Gese, H., 1973. "Anfang und Ende der Apokalyptik, dargestellt am Sacharjabuch," in: *ZTK* 70, 20-49 (= *Vom Sinai zum Zion. Alttestamentliche Beiträge zur biblischen Theologie*, BEvTh 64, 1974, 202-230)

——1974. Nachtrag: Die Deutung der Hirtenallegorie Sach 11,4ff, in: *Vom Sinai zum Zion*, 231-238

Goshen-Gottstein, M.H., 1987. "Tanakh Theology: The Religion of the Old Testament and the Place of Jewish Biblical Theology," in: P.D. Miller *et al.* (eds.), *Ancient Israelite Religion*, FS F.M. Cross, Philadelphia, 617-644

Greenberg, M., 1973. "Mankind, Israel and the Nations in the Hebraic Heritage," in: J.R. Nelson (ed.), *No Man is Alien. Essays on the Unity of Mankind*, Leiden, 15-40 (= *Studies in the Bible and Jewish Thought*, Philadelphia 1995)

——1980. "Reflections on Job's Theology," in: *The Book of Job. A New Translation according to the Traditional Hebrew Text*, Philadelphia, xvii-xxiii (= *Studies*, 327-333)

——1983. *Ezekiel 1–20*. The Anchor Bible, vol. 22, Garden City

——1987. "Job," in: R. Alter & F. Kermode (eds.), *The Literary Guide to the Bible*, Cambridge MA, 283-304 (= *Studies*, 335-357)

——1997. *Ezekiel 21–37*, AB 22A, New York

Greßmann, H., 1913. *Mose und seine Zeit. Ein Kommentar zu den Mose-Sagen*, Göttingen

——1924. "Die neugefundene Lehre des Amen-em-ope und die vorexilische Spruchdichtung Israels," in: *ZAW* 42, 272-296

Grether, O., 1934. *Name und Wort Gottes im Alten Testament*, BZAW 64

Gunkel, H., 1895. *Schöpfung und Chaos in Urzeit und Endzeit*, Göttingen

——1910. *Genesis*, HK I/1 (3rd ed.) (⁶1977)

——1926. *Psalmen*, HK II/2 (⁶1986)

Gunkel-Begrich, 1933. H. Gunkel, *Einleitung in die Psalmen. Die Gattungen der religiösen Literatur Israels, zu Ende geführt von J. Begrich*, Göttingen 1933 (⁴1985)

Gunneweg, A.H.J., 1985. *Esra*, KAT XIX/1

——1987. *Nehemia*, KAT XIX/2

——1990. "Das Gesetz und die Propheten. Eine Auslegung von Ex 33,7-11; Num 11,4–12,8; Dtn 31, 14f.; 34,10," in: *ZAW* 102, 169-180.

Hamborg, G.R., 1981. "Reasons for Judgement in the Oracles against the Nations of the Prophet Isaiah," *VT* 31, 145-159

Hanhart, R., 1990ff. *Sacharja*, BK XIV/7

Hanson, P.D., 1975. *The Dawn of Apocalyptic. The Historical and Sociological Roots of Jewish Apocalyptic Eschatology*, Philadelphia (rev. ed. 1979)

Hasel, G., 1991. *Old Testament Theology. Basic Issues in the Current Debate*, 4th ed., Grand Rapids

Hayes, J.G. & F.C. Prussner, 1985. *Old Testament Theology. Its History and Development*, Atlanta & London

Hermann, S., 1971. "Die konstruktive Restauration. Das Deuteronomium als Mitte biblischer Theologie," in: FS G. von Rad, Munich, 155-170 (= Gesammelte Studien zur Geschichte und Theologie des Alten Testaments, Munich 1986, 163-178)

——1986ff. *Jeremia*, BK XII

——1990. *Jeremia. Der Prophet und das Buch*, EdF 271

Hermisson, H.-J., 2000. "Gibt es die Götter bei Deuterojesaja?" in: FS. W.H. Schmidt (cf. Rendtorff 2000a), 109-123

Hoffmann, H.-D., 1980. *Reform und Reformen. Untersuchungen zu einem Grundthema der deuteronomistischen Geschichtsschreibung*, ATANT 66

Hoffmann, Y., 1981. "The Day of the Lord as a Concept and a Term in the Prophetic Literature," *ZAW* 93, 1981, 37-50

Horst, F., 1956. "Recht und Religion im Bereich des Alten Testaments," *EvT* 16, 49-75 (= *Gottes Recht. Studien zum Recht im Alten Testament*, TB 12, 1961, 260-291)

Hossfeld, F.-L., 1995. "Das Buch Ezechiel," in: E. Zenger *et al.*, 1995, 345-359

Hossfeld, F.-L. & E. Zenger, 1993. *Die Psalmen. Psalm 1–50*, NEB

Jacob, B., 1934. *Das erste Buch der Tora. Genesis, übersetzt und erklärt*, Berlin (repr. New York, n.d.)

——1992. *The Second Book of the Bible: Exodus*. Trans. with an introduction by Walter Jacob in association with Yaakov Elman, Hoboken, New Jersey

Janowski, B., 1982. *Sühne als Heilsgeschehen. Studien zur Sühnetheologie der Priester-*

schrift und zur Wurzel KPR im Alten Orient und im Alten Testament, WMANT 55

——1987. "'Ich will in eurer Mitte wohnen'". Struktur und Genese der exilischen Schekina-Theologie," *JBTh* 2, 165-193

——1989. "Das Königtum Gottes in den Psalmen. Bemerkungen zu einem neuen Gesamtentwurf," *ZTK* 86, 389-454 (= *Gottes Gegenwart in Israel. Beiträge zu Theologie des Alten Testaments*, Neukirchen-Vluyn 1993, 148-213)

——1990. "Tempel und Schöpfung. Schöpfungstheologische Aspekte der priester-schriftlichen Heiligtumskonzeption," *JBTh* 5, 37-69

——1991. "Keruben und Zion. Thesen zur Entstehung der Zionstradition," in: D.R. Daniels *et al.*, *Ernten, was man sät*. FS Klaus Koch, Neukirchen-Vluyn, 231-264 (= *Gottes Gegenwart in Israel*, see 1989, 247-280)

——(ed.), 1993a. *Gefährten und Feinde des Menschen. Das Tier in der Lebenswelt des alten Israel* (with U. Neumann-Gorsolke & Uwe Gleßmer), Neukirchen-Vluyn

——1993b. "Azazel und der Sündenbock. Zur Religionsgeschichte von Leviticus 16,10.21f," in: *Gottes Gegenwart in Israel* (cf. 1989), 283-302

——1995. "Dem Löwen gleich, gierig nach Raub. Zum Feindbild in den Psalmen," *EvTh* 55, 155-173

——1998. "Der eine Gott der beiden Testamente. Grundfragen einer Biblischen Theologie," *ZTK* 95, 1-36 (= *Die rettende Gerechtigkeit. Beiträge zur Theologie des Alten Testaments*, 2, Neukirchen-Vluyn 1999, 249-284)

——1998/99. "Biblische Theologie I," *RGG*⁴ 1, 1544-1549; expanded in: *Die rettende Gerechtigkeit*, 285-298 (ET forthcoming in *RPP*. Leiden)

Japhet, S., *The Ideology of the Book of Chronicles and its Place in Biblical Thought* (Hebr. 1977, Engl. 1989, quotations from 1989)

——1993. *I & II Chronicles*, OTL

Jaspers, K., 1949. *Vom Ursprung und Ziel der Geschichte*, Munich. (Unabridged edition Fischer Bücherei, Frankfurt 1955.)

Jenni, E., 1952/53. "Das Wort ʿōlām im Alten Testament," *ZAW* 64, 197-248; 65, 1-35)

——1971. "יוֹם, jôm, Tag," *THAT* I, 707-726

Jeremias, J., 1971. "Lade und Zion. Zur Entstehung der Ziontradition," in: FS von Rad (cf. Crüsemann 1971), 183-198 (= 1987, 167-182)

——1975/97. *Die Reue Gottes. Aspekte alttestamentlicher Gottesvorstellung*, BSt 65 (2nd ed. BTS 31, 1997)

——1983. *Der Prophet Hosea*, ATD 24/1

——1987. *Das Königtum Gottes in den Psalmen. Israels Begegnung mit dem kanaanäischen Mythos in den Jahwe-Königs-Psalmen*, FRLANT 141

——1989. "Jakob im Amosbuch," in: M. Görg (ed.), *Die Väter Israels*. FS J. Scharbert, Stuttgart, 139-154 (= 1995b, 257-271)

——1990. "Schöpfung in Poesie und Prosa des Alten Testaments. Gen 1-3 im Vergleich mit anderen Schöpfungstexten des Alten Testaments," *JBTh* 4, 11-36, esp. 35f.

——1995a. *Der Prophet Amos*, ATD 24/2

———1995b. Hosea und Amos. Studien zu den Anfängen des Dodekapropheton, FAT 13

Jones, B.A., 1995. "The Formation of the Book of the Twelve. A Study in Text and Canon," SBLDS 149

Jüngling, H.-W., 1985. "Der Heilige Israels. Der erste Jesaja zum Thema 'Gott'," in: E. Haag (ed.), *Gott, der einzige. Zur Entstehung des Monotheismus in Israel*, QD 104, 91-114

———1995. "Das Buch Jesaja," in E. Zenger, *et al.*, 1995, 303-318

Kayatz, C., 1966. *Studien zu Proverbien 1-9. Eine form- und motivgeschichtliche Untersuchung unter Einbeziehung ägyptischen Vergleichsmaterials*, WMANT 22

Keel, O., 1972. *Die Welt der altorientalischen Bildsymbolik und das Alte Testament. Am Beispiel der Psalmen*, Zürich & Neukirchen-Vluyn (⁵1996)

———1978. *Jahwes Entgegnung an Ijob. Eine Deutung von Ijob 38-41 vor dem Hintergrund der zeitgenössischen Bildkunst*, FRLANT 121

Kegler, J., 1983. "Arbeitsorganisation und Arbeitskampfformen im Alten Testament," in: L. Schottroff & W. Schottroff (eds.), *Mitarbeiter der Schöpfung. Bibel und Arbeitswelt*, Munich, 51-71

———1990. "Zur Komposition und Theologie der Plagenerzählungen," in: FS R. Rendtorff (see Blum 1990b), 55-74

Kessler, R., 1999. *Micha*, HTKAT

Kippenberg, H.G., 1978. *Religion und Klassenbildung im antiken Judäa. Eine religionssoziologische Studie zum Verhältnis von Tradition und gesellschaftlicher Entwicklung*, SUNT 14

Kiuchi, N., 1987. *The Purification Offering in the Priestly Literature. Its Meaning and Function*, JSOTS 56

Knierim, R., 1961. "Exodus 18 und die Neuordnung der mosaischen Gerichtsbarkeit," *ZAW* 73, 146-171

Köckert, M., 1989. "Leben in Gottes Gegenwart. Zum Verständnis des Gesetzes in der priesterschriftlichen Literatur," *JBTh* 4 (1989), 29-61

Koch, K., 1955. "Gibt es ein Vergeltungsdogma im Alten Testament?," *ZTK* 52, 1-42 (= *Spuren des hebräischen Denkens. Beiträge zur alttestamentlichen Theologie, Gesammelte Aufsätze*, vol. I, Neukirchen-Vluyn 1991, 65-103)

———1961. "Tempeleinlaßliturgien und Dekaloge," in: R. Rendtorff *et al.* (eds.), *Studien zur Theologie der alttestamentlichen Überlieferungen.* FS G. von Rad, Neukirchen, 45-60 (= *Gesammelte Aufsätze*, I, see Koch 1955, 169-183)

———1967. "Haggais unreines Volk," *ZAW* 79, 52-66 (= *Gesammelte Aufsätze* I, 206-219)

———1978/80. *Die Profeten I. Assyrische Zeit* (³1995), II. *Babylonisch-persische Zeit*, UT 280/281

———1980. *Das Buch Daniel* (with T. Niewisch & J. Tubach), EdF 144

———1981. Das Profetenschweigen des deuteronomischen Geschichtswerks, in: J. Jeremias & L. Perlitt (eds.), *Die Botschaft und die Boten*, FS H.W. Wolff, Neukirchen-Vluyn, 115-128

——1987. "P – kein Redaktor! Erinnerungen an zwei Eckdaten der Quellenscheidung," *VT* 37, 1987, 446-467

——1991. "Der doppelte Ausgang des Alten Testaments in Judentum und Christentum," *JBT* 6, 215-242

Köhler, L., 1931. *Die Hebräische Rechtsgemeinde* (= *Der Hebräische Mensch*, Tübingen 1953, 143-171)

——1966. *Theologie des Alten Testaments*, 4th ed., Tübingen

Kratz, R.G., 1996. "Die Tora Davids. Psalm 1 und die doxologische Fünfteilung des Psalters," *ZTK* 93, 1-34

Kraus, H.-J., 1978. *Psalmen*, BK XV/1 and 2, 5th ed. (^{6}1989)

——1979. *Theologie der Psalmen*, BK XV/3 (^{2}1989)

Kreuzer, S., 1988. *Die Frühgeschichte Israels in Bekenntnis und Verkündigung des Alten Testaments*, BZAW 178

Kutsch, E., 1973. *Verheißung und Gesetz. Untersuchungen zum sogenannten 'Bund' im Alten Testament*, BZAW 131

Landy, F., 1999. "Strategies of Concentration and Diffusion in Isaiah 6," *BibInt* 7, 58-86

Lang, B., 1981. *Kein Aufstand in Jerusalem. Die Politik des Propheten Ezechiel*, 2nd ed., Stuttgart

Lau, I.M., 1988. *Wie Juden leben. Glaube – Alltag – Feste*, Gütersloh (^{4}1997)

Levenson, J.D., 1982. "The Paronomasia of Solomon's Seventh Petition," *HAR* 6, 135-138

——1985. *Sinai and Zion. An Entry into the Jewish Bible*, New York

——1987. "Why Jews are Not Interested in Biblical Theology," in: J. Neusner *et al.* (eds.), *Judaic Perspectives on Ancient Israel*, Philadelphia, 281-307 (= *The Hebrew Bible, the Old Testament and Historical Criticism. Jews and Christians in Biblical Studies*, Louisville 1993, 33-61)

——1988. *Creation and the Persistence of Evil. The Jewish Drama of Omnipotence*, San Francisco

——1993. *The Death and Resurrection of the Beloved Son. The Transformation of Child Sacrifice in Judaism and Christianity*, New Haven

Levine, B.A., 1993. *Numbers 1–20*, AB 4A

Liedke, G., 1971. *Gestalt und Bezeichnung alttestamentlicher Rechtssätze*, WMANT 39

Loader, J.A., 1992. *Das Buch Ester*, ATD 16/2, 199-280

Lohfink, N., 1965a. "Verkündigung des Hauptgebots in der jüngsten Schicht des Deuteronomiums (Dt 4,1-40)," in: *Höre Israel! Auslegung von Texten aus dem Buch Deuteronomium* (Die Welt der Bibel 18), Düsseldorf, 87-120 (= *Studien zum Deuteronomium und zur deuteronomistischen Literatur* I, SBA 8, Stuttgart, 167-191)

——1965b. "Zur Dekalogfassung von Dt 5," *BZ* n.s. 9, 17-32 (= *Studien* [see 1965a] I, 193-209)

——1967. *Die Landverheißung als Eid*, SBS 28

——1972. "'Israel' in Jes 49,3," in: J. Schreiner (ed.), *Wort, Lied und Gottesspruch*,

FS J. Ziegler, Würzburg, vol. II, 217-229

——1977. *Unsere großen Wörter. Das Alte Testament zu Themen dieser Jahre*, Freiburg

——1982. שׁרֹ,, *jāraš*, Th*WAT* III, 953-985

——1985. "Zur Geschichte der Diskussion über den Monotheismus im Alten Israel," in: E. Haag (ed.), *Gott, der einzige. Zur Entstehung des Monotheismus in Israel*, QD 104, 9-25

——1987. "Die Kultreform Joschijas von Juda. 2 Kön 22-23 als religionsgeschichtliche Quelle." ET in P.D. Miller *et al.* (eds.), *Ancient Israelite Religion*, FS F.M. Cross, Philadelphia 459-475

——1987b. "'Diese Worte sollst du summen'. Dtn 6,7 *w'dibbartā bām* – ein verlorene Schlüssel zur meditativen Kultur in Israel," *Theologie und Philosophie* 62, 59-72 (= *Studien* [see 1965a] III, 181-203)

——1989. "Kennt das Alte Testament einen Unterschied von 'Gebot' und 'Gesetz'? Zur bibeltheologischen Einstufung des Dekalogs," *JBT* 4, 63-89 (= *Studien zur biblischen Theologie*, SBA 16, 1993, 206-238)

——1991. *Die Väter Israels im Deuteronomium. Mit einer Stellungnahme von Thomas Römer*, OBO 111

——1992. "Der weiße Fleckt in Dei Verbum Artikel 12," *TTZ* 101, 20-35 (= SBA 16, 78-96)

——1993. *Kohelet*, NEB, 4th ed.

Long, B.O., 1984. *1 Kings, with an Introduction to Historical Literature*, FOTL 9

McCann, J.C., 1992. "The Psalms as Instruction," *Int* 46, 117-128

——1993. "Books I-III and the Editorial Purpose of the Hebrew Psalter," in: J.C. McCann (ed.), *The Sahpe and Shaping of the Psalter*, JSOTS 159, 72-92

Macholz, G.C., 1972a. "Die Stellung des Königs in der israelitischen Gerichtsverfassung," *ZAW* 84, 157-182

——1972b. "Zur Geschichte der Justizorganisation in Juda," *ZAW* 84, 314-340

——1980. "Psalm 29 und 1. Könige 19. Jahwes und Baals Theophanie," in: R. Albert *et al.* (eds.), *Werden und Wirken des Alten Testaments*, FS C. Westermann, Göttingen/Neukirchen-Vluyn, 325-333

Marx, A., 1994. *Les offrandes végétales dans l'Ancien Testament. Du tribut d'hommage au repas eschatologique*, VTS 57

Matheus, F., 1990. *Singt dem Herrn ein neues Lied. Die Hymnen Deuterojesajas*, SBS 141

Meinhold, A., 1978/76. "Die Gattung der Josephsgeschichte und des Estherbuches: Diasporanovelle I und II," *ZAW* 87, 306-324; 88, 72-93

——1983. *Das Buch Esther*, ZBK 13

——1991. *Die Sprüche, Teil 1: Sprüche 1-15, Teil 2: Sprüche 16-31*, ZBK 16/1 & 2

Melugin, R., 1976. *The Formation of Isaiah 40–55*, BZAW 141

Mettinger, T.N.D., 1976. *King and Messiah. The Civil and Sacral Legitimation of the Israelite King*, ConBOT 8

——1982a. *The Dethronement of Sabaoth. Studies in the Shem and Kabod Theologies*, ConBOT 18

———1982b. "YHWH SABAOTH – The Heavenly King on the Cherubim Throne," in: T. Ishida (ed.), *Studies in the Period of David and Solomon and Other Essays*, Tokyo, 109-138

———1983. *A Farewell to the Servant Songs. A Critical Examination of an Exegetical Axiom*, Lund

———1988. *In Search of God. The Meaning and Message of the Everlasting Names*, Philadelphia

———1990. "The Elusive Presence. YHWH, El and Baal and the Distinctiveness of Israelite Faith," in: FS R. Rendtorff (see Blum 1990b), 393-417

———1995. *No Graven Image? Israelite Aniconism in its Ancient Near Eastern Context*, ConBOT 42

Metzger, M., 1970. "Himmlische und irdische Wohnstatt Jahwes," *UF* 2, 139-158

———1985. *Königsthron und Gottesthron. Thronformen und Throndarstellungen in Ägypten und im Vorderen Orient im dritten und zweiten Jahrtausend vor Christus und deren Bedeutung für das Verständnis von Aussagen über den Thron im Alten Testament*, 2 vols., AOAT 15

Michel, D., 1988. *Qohelet*, EdF 258

———1989. *Untersuchungen zur Eigenart des Buches Qohelet*, BZAW 183

Milgrom, J., 1989. *Numbers*, The JPS Torah Commentary

———1991. *Leviticus 1–16*, AB 3

Millard, M., 1994. *Die Komposition des Psalters. Ein formgeschichtlicher Ansatz*, FAT 9

Miller, P.D., 1993. "The Beginning of the Psalter," in: J.C. McCann (ed.), 1993, 83-92

———1994. *They Cried to the Lord. The Form and Theology of Biblical Prayer*, Minneapolis

Mitchell, G., 1993. *Together in the Land. A Reading of the Book of Joshua*. JSOTS 134

Moberly, R.W.L., 1983. *At the Mountain of God. Story and Theology in Exodus 32–34*, JSOTS 22

———1992. *The Old Testament of the Old Testament. Patriarchal Narratives and Mosaic Yahwism*, Minneapolis

Mosis, R., 1989. "'Glauben' und 'Gerechtigkeit'—zu Gen 15,6," in: M. Görg (ed.), *Die Väter Israels*, FS J. Scharbert, Stuttgart, 225-257

Mowinckel, S., 1914. *Zur Komposition des Buches Jeremia*, Kristiania

———1922. *Psalmenstudien II. Das Thronbesteigungsfest Jahwäs und der Ursprung der Eschatologie*, SVSKHF 4

Müller, E.L., 1939/1973. *Die Vorstellung vom Rest im Alten Testament*, Leipzig (expanded, revised edition by H.D. Preuß, Neukirchen-Vluyn, 1973)

Müller, H.-P., 1968. "Wie sprach Qohälät von Gott?" *VT* 18, 507-521

———1986. נָבִיא, *nabî'*, *ThWAT* V, 140-163

Naumann, T., 1999. *Ismael*. OBO

Nelson, R., 1987. *First and Second Kings*, IBC

Nicholson, E.W., 1977. "The Decalogue as the Direct Address of God," *VT* 27, 422-433

——1986. *God and His People. Covenant and Theology in the Old Testament*, Oxford

Niehr, N., 1990. *Der höchste Gott. Alttestamentlicher JHWH-Glaube im Kontext syrisch-kananäischer Religion des 1. Jahrtausends v.Chr.*, BZAW 190

Nogalski, J. 1993a. *Literary Precursors to the Book of the Twelve*, BZAW 217

——1993b. *Redactional Processes in the Book of the Twelve*, BZAW 218

Nogalski, J.D. & M.A. Sweeney, 2000. *Reading and Hearing the Book of the Twelve*. SBLSymS 15, Atlanta (= 2001a, 139-151)

Noth, M., 1943. *Überlieferungsgeschichtliche Studien I. Die sammelden und bearbeitenden Geschichtswerke im Alten Testament*, SKGG. 18/2, Halle (³1967 Tübingen)

——1948. *Überlieferungsgeschichte des Pentateuch*, Stuttgart (=³1966)

——1950. "Gott, König, Volk im Alten Testament," *ZTK* 47, 157-191 (= *Gesammelte Studien* 1957, 188-229)

——1957. "David und Israel in 2. Samuel 7," in: *Mélanges Bibliques rédigés en l'honneur d' André Robert*. Travaux de l'Institut Catholique de Paris, 4, 122-130 (= *Gesammelte Studien* ²1960, 334-345)

——1962. *Das dritte Buch Mose. Leviticus*, ATD 6 (¹1982)

——1966. *Das vierte Buch Mose. Numeri*, ATD 7 (⁴1982)

——1968. *Könige (1 Kön 1–16)*, BK IX/1 (21983)

Oeming, M., 1983. "Ist Genesis 15,6 ein Beleg für die Anrechnung des Glaubens zur Gerechtigkeit?" *ZAW* 95, 182-197

——1985. *Gesamtbiblische Theologien der Gegenwart. Das Verhältnis von AT und NT in der hermeneutischen Diskussion seit Gerhard von Rad*, Stuttgart

——1990. *Das wahre Israel. Die "genealogische Vorhalle"1 Chronik 1–9*, BWANT 128

Ollenburger, B.C., 1987. *Zion, The City of the Great King: A Theological Symbol of the Jerusalem Cult*, JSOTS 41

Olson, D.T. 1985. *The Death of the Old and the Birth of the New: The Framework of the Book of Numbers and the Pentateuch*, Chico, BJSt 71

Otto, E., 1994. *Theologische Ethik des Alten Testaments*, TW 3,2

Otzen, B., 1989. עָמָל, *'amal*, *ThWAT* VI, 213-220

Patrick, D., 1995. "The First Commandment in the Structure of the Pentateuch," *VT* 45, 107-118

Perlitt, L., 1969. *Bundestheologie im Alten Testament*, WMANT 36

——1971. "Mose als Prophet," *EvTh* 31, 588-608

——1977. "Sinai und Horeb," in: H. Donner *et al.* (eds.), *Beiträge zur Alttestamentlichen Theologie*, FS W. Zimmerli, Göttingen, 302-322

——1983, "Motive und Schichten der Landtheologie im Deuteronomium," in: G. Strecker (ed.), *Das Land Israel in biblischer Zeit. Jerusalem-Symposium 1981*, Göttingen, 46-58

Podella, T., 1993. "Der 'Chaoskampfmythos' im Alten Testament. EIne Problemanzeige," in M. Dietrich & O. Loretz (eds.), *Mesopotamica—Ugaritica—Biblica*, FS K. Bergerhof, AOAT 232, 283-329

Preuß, H.D., 1982. *Deuteronomium*, EdF 164, Darmstadt

——1991. *Theologie des Alten Testaments*, vol. I: *JHWHs erwählendes und verpflichtendes Handeln*, Stuttgart etc.

——1992. *Theologie des Alten Testaments*, vol. II: *Israels Weg mit JHWH*, Stuttgart etc.

de Pury, A. (ed.), 1989. *Le Pentateuque en question. Les origines et la composition des cinq premiers livres de la Bible à la lumière des recherches récentes*, Le Monde de la Bible, 19, Geneva (²1991)

von Rad, G., 1930. *Das Geschichtsbild des chronistischen Werkes*, BWANT 54

——1933. "Es ist noch eine Ruhe vorhanden dem Volke Gottes. Eine biblische Begriffsuntersuchung," *ZZ* 11, 1933, 104-111 (= *Gesammelte Studien* I, 101-108)

——1938. *Das formgeschichtliche Problem des Hexateuchs*, BWANT 78 (=*Gesammelte Studien* I, TB 8, 1958, 9-86)

——1943, "Verheißenes Land und Jahwes Land im Hexateuch," *ZDPV* 66, 191-204 (= *Gesammelte Studien* I, 87-100)

——1944. "Der Anfang der Geschichtsschreibung im alten Israel," in: *AKuG* 32, 1-42 (=*Gesammelte Studien* I, 148-188)

——1947a. *Deuteronomium-Studien*, FRLANT 58 (²1948)

——1947b. "Das judäische Königsritual," *TLZ* 72, 211-216 (= *Gesammelte Studien* I, 205-213)

——1951a. *Der Heilige Krieg im alten Israel*, ATANT 20

——1951b. "Die Anrechnung des Glaubens zur Gerechtigkeit," *TLZ* 76, 129-132

——1952/53. "Typologische Auslegung des Alten Testaments," *EvT* 12, 17-34 (= *Gesammelte Studien* II, 1973, 272-288)

——1953. "Josephsgeschichte und ältere Chokma," in: *Congress Volume Copenhagen 1953*, VTS 1, 120-127 (= *Gesammelte Studien* I, 272-280)

——1962/1965. *Theologie des Alten Testaments*, 2 vols., 4th ed., Munich (following editions unchanged)

——1964a. "Die Nehemia-Denkschrift," *ZAW* 76, 176-187

——1964b. *Das fünfte Buch Mose. Deuteronomium*, ATD 8 (subsequent editions unchanged)

——1970. *Weisheit in Israel*, Neukirchen-Vluyn (=Gütersloh 1990)

——1971. "Gerichtsdoxologie," in: *Schalom. Studien zu Glaube und Geschichte Israels*, FS A. Jepsen, Berlin & Stuttgart, 28-37 (= *Gesammelte Studien* II, 1973, 245-254)

——1972. *Das erste Buch Mose. Genesis*, ATD 2-4, 9th ed. (following editions unchanged)

Rendtorff, R., 1954a. "Die theologische Stellung des Schöpfungsglaubens bei Deuterojesaja," *ZTK* 51, 3-13 (=*Gesammelte Studien zum Alten Testament*, Munch 1975, 209-219)

——1954b. "Zum Gebrauch der Formel *n'um jahwe* im Jeremiabuch," *ZAW* 66, 27-37 (= *Gesammelte Studien* 256-266)

——1960. "Προφήτης κτλ. B. נָבִיא im Alten Testament," *ThWNT* 6, 796-813

——1961. "Die Offenbarungsvorstellungen im Alten Israel," in W. Pannenberg *et al., Offenbarung als Geschichte* (KuD.B 1, ⁵1982), 21-41 (=*Gesammelte Studien* [see 1954] 39-59)

——1962. "Erwägungen zur Frühgeschichte des Prophetentums in Israel," *ZTK* 59, 145-167 (=*Gesammelte Studien* [see 1954a] 220-242)

——1962b. "Botenformel und Botenspruch," *ZAW* 74, 165-177 (= *Gesammelte Studien* [cf. 1954a], 243-255)

——1966. "El, Ba'al und Jahwe. Erwägungen zum Verhältnis von kanaanäischer und israelitischer Religion," *ZAW*, 78, 276-291 (= *Gesammelte Studien* [cf. 1954a], 172-187)

——1967. *Studien zur Geschichte des Opfers im Alten Israel*, WMANT 24

——1971. "Beobachtungen zur altisraelitischen Geschichtsschreibung anhand der Geschichte vom Aufstieg Davids," in: FS von Rad (cf. Crüsemann 1971), 428-439

——1975. "Mose als Religionsstifter? Ein Beitrag zur Diskussion über die Anfänge der israelitischen Religion," in: *Gesammelte Studien* (cf. 1954a), 154-171

——1977. *Das überlieferungsgeschichtliche Problem des Pentateuch*, BZAW 147

——1981. "Die Erwählung Israels als Thema der deuteronomischen Theologie," in FS H.W. Wolff (cf. Crüsemann 1981), 75-86

——1983. *Das Alte Testament. Eine Einführung*, Neukirchen-Vluyn (⁵1995)

——1983b. "Zur Bedeutung des Kanons für eine Theologie des Alten Testaments," in: H.-G. Geyer *et al.* (eds.), *"Wenn nicht jetzt, wann dann?" Aufsätze für Hans-Joachim Kraus zum 65. Geburtstag*, Neukirchen-Vluyn, 3-11 (= *Kanon und Theologie* [see 1991a], 54-63)

——1984. "Zur Komposition des Buches Jesaja," *VT* 34, 295-320 (= *Kanon und Theologie* [see 1991a], 141-161)

——1985ff. *Leviticus*, BK III/1ff

——1986. "Ez 20 und 36,16ff im Rahmen der Komposition des Buches Ezechiel," in: J. Lust (ed.), *Ezekiel and His Book. Textual and Literary Criticism and their Interrelation*, BETL 74, 260-265 (= *Kanon und Theologie* [see 1991], 180-184)

——1987. "'Wo warst du, als ich die Erde gründete?' Schöpfung und Heilsgeschichte," in: G. Rau *et al., Frieden in der Schöpfung*, Gütersloh, 35-57 (= *Kanon und Theologie* [see 1991], 94-112)

——1989. "Jesaja 6 im Rahmen der Kompostion des Jesajabuches," in: J. Vermeylen (ed.), *The Book of Isaiah. Le livre d'Isaïe: Les oracles et leurs relectures. Unité et complexité de l'ouvrage*, BETL 81, 73-82 (= *Kanon und Theologie* [see 1991a], 162-171)

——1991a. "Theologie des Alten Testaments. Überlegungen zu einem Neuansatz," in: *Kanon und Theologie. Vorarbeiten zu einer Theologie des Alten Testaments*, Neukirchen-Vluyn, 1-14

——1991b. "'Bund' als Strukturkonzept in Genesis und Exodus," in: *Kanon und Theologie* (see 1991a), 122-131

——1991c. "Die Geburt des Retters. Beobachtungen zur Jugendgeschichte Samuels im Rahmen der literarischen Komposition," in: *Storia e tradizioni di Israele. Scritti in onore di J. Alberto Soggin*, Brescia, 205-216; also in: *Kanon und Theologie* (see 1991a), 132-140

——1991d. "Der Text in seiner Endgestalt. Überlegungen zu Exodus 19," in: D.R. Daniels *et al.* (eds.), *Ernten was man sät*, FS Klaus Koch, Neukirchen-Vluyn, 459-470

——1991e. "Die Entwicklung des altisraelitischen Festkalenders,"in: J. Assmann (ed.), *Das Fest und das Heilige. Religiöse Kontrapunkte zur Alltagswelt*. Studien zum Verstehen fremder Religionen, 1, Gütersloh, 185-205

——1991f. "Was ist neu am 'Neuen Bund'?", in: *Kanon und Theologie* (see 1991a), 185-195; also in: M. Stöhr (ed.), *Lernen in Jerusalem – Lernen mit Israel. Anstöße zur Erneuerung in Theologie und Kirche*, Berlin 1993, 26-37

——1991g. "Wege zu einem gemeinsamen jüdisch-christlichen Umgang mit dem Alten Testament," *EvT* 51, 431-444 (= *Kanon und Theologie* [see 1991a], 40-53

——1992. "Some Reflections on Creation as a Topic of Old Testament Theology," in: E. Ulrich *et al.* (eds.), *Priests, Prophets and Scribes*, FS J. Blenkinsopp, JSOTS 149, 204-212

——1993. "The Paradigm is Changing: Hopes – and Fears," *BibInt* 1, 34-53 (= 2001a, 83-102)

——1994. " 'El als israelitische Gottesbezeichung. Mit einem Appendix: Beobachtungen zum Gebrauch von הָאֱלֹהִים," *ZAW* 106, 4-21

——1994b. Review of Brevard S. Childs, *Biblical Theology of the Old and New Testaments. Theological Reflection on the Christian Bible*, *JBT* 9, 359-369

——1995a. *Die "Bundesformel". Eine exegetisch-theologische Untersuchung*, SBS 160

——1995b. "Sihon, Og und das israelitische 'Credo'," in: S. Timm *et al.* (eds.), *Meilenstein*, FS H. Donner, ÄAT 30, 198-203

——1995c. "Die Hermeneutik einer kanonischen Theologie des Alten Testaments," *JBT* 9, 359-369

——1995d. "Die Bibel Israels als Buch der Christen," in: C. Dohmen & T. Söding (eds.), *Eine Bibel – zwei Testamente. Positionen Biblischer Theologie*, UTB 1893, 97-113 (= 2001a, 30-46)

——1996. "The Book of Isaiah: A Complex Unity. Synchronic and Diachronic Reading," in: R.F. Melugin & M.A. Sweeney (eds.), *New Visions of Isaiah*, JSOTS 214, 32-49 (lightly revised version in: Y. Gitay (ed.), *Prophecy and Prophets. The Diversity of Contemporary Issues in Scholarship*, Atlanta 1997, 107-128)

——1997a. "Kontinuität und Diskontinuität in der alttestamentlichen Prophetie," *ZAW* 109, 169-187

——1997b. "Die Herausführungsformel in ihrem literarischen und theologischen Kontext," in: M. Vervenne & J. Lust (eds.), *Deuteronomy and Deuteronomic Literature*, FS C.H.W. Brekelmans, BETL 133, 501-527

——1997c. "How to Read the Book of the Twelve as a Theological Unity," in *SBLSP* 420-432

——1997d. "Nehemiah 9: An Important Witness of Theological Reflection," in: M. Cogan *et al.* (eds.), *Tehillah le-Moshe: Biblical and Judaic Studies in Honor of Moshe Greenberg*, Winona Lake, IN, 111-117

——1997e. "Samuel the Prophet: A Link between Moses and the Kings," in: C.A. Evans & S. Talmon (eds.), *The Quest for Context and Meaning*, FS J.A. Sanders, BibInt Series 28, 27-36

——1997f. "Some Reflections on the Canonical Moses: Moses and Abraham," in: E.E. Carpenter (ed.), *A Biblical Itinerary. In Search of Method, Form and Content. Essays in Honour of George W. Coats*, JSOTS 240, 11-19

——1998a. "Theologische Vorarbeiten zu einem christlich-jüdischen Dialog," in: 2001a, 3-19

——1998b. "Alas for the Day! The 'Day of the LORD' in the Book of the Twelve," in: T. Linafeldt & T.K. Beal (eds.), *God in the Fray. A Tribute to Walter Brueggemann*, Minneapolis: Fortress, 186-197 (= 2001a, 253-264)

——1998c. *Christen und Juden heute. Neue Einsichten und neue Aufgaben*, Neukirchen-Vluyn; including "Als Christ das 'Alte' Testament lesen," 42-87

——1999a. "Was verbietet das alttestamentliche Bilderverbot?" in: R. Bernhardt & U. Link-Wieczorek (eds.), *Metapher und Wirklichkeit. Die Logik der Bildhaftigkeit im Reden von Gott, Mensch und Natur*, FS D. Ritschl, Göttingen, 54-65 (= 2001a, 201-212)

——1999b. "Noah, Abraham and Moses: God's Covenant Partners," in: E. Ball (ed.), *In Search of True Wisdom. Essays in Old Testament Interpretation in Honour of Ronald E. Clements*, JSOTS 300, 127-136 (2001a, 155-163)

——1999c. Review of Brueggemann, W., 1999 (see there), 11-17

——2000a. "Israel's 'Rest'. Unabgeschlossene Überlegungen zu einen schwierigen Thema der alttestamentlichen Theologie," in: A. Graupner *et al.* (eds.), *Verbindungslinien. Festschrift für Werner H. Schmidt zum 65. Geburtstag*, Neukirchen-Vluyn, 265-279 (= 2001a, 272-286)

——2000b. "Wie sieht Israel seine Geschichte?" in: S.L. McKenzie & T. Römer (eds.), *Rethinking the Foundations. Historiography in the Ancient World and in the Bible. Essays in Honour of John Van Seters*, BZAW 294, 197-206

——2000c. (= 1997c). "How to Read the Book of the Twelve as a Theological Unity," in: J.D. Nogalski & M.A. Sweeney, *Reading and Hearing the Book of the Twelve*. SBLSymS 15, Atlanta, 75-78 (=2001a, 139-151)

——2000d. "Er handelt nicht mit uns nach unsern Sünden. Das Evangelium von der Barmherzigkeit Gottes im Ersten Testament," in: R. Scoralick (ed.), *Das Drama der Barmherzigkeit Gottes. Studien zur biblischen Gottesrede und ihrer Wirkungsgeschichte in Judentum und Christentum*, SBS 183, 145-156

——2000e. "A Christian Approach to the Theology of the Hebrew Scriptures," in: A.O. Bellis & J.S. Kaminsky (eds.), *Jews, Christians, and the Theology of the Hebrew Scriptures*. SBLSymS 8, Atlanta, 137-151

——2001a. *Der Text in seiner Endgestalt. Schritte auf dem Weg zu einer Theologie des Alten Testaments*, Neukirchen-Vluyn (contains 1991d, 1993, 1994, 1995b,

1995c, 1996, 1997b, 1997c, 1997e, 1998a, 1999a, 1999b, 2000a, 2000c)

Reventlow, H. Graf, 1982. *Hauptprobleme der alttestamentlichen Theologie im 20. Jahrhundert*, EdF 173

——1983. *Hauptprobleme der Biblischen Theologie im 20. Jahrhundert*, EdF 203

Rice, G., 1978. "A Neglected Interpretation of the Immanuel Prophecy," *ZAW* 90, 200–227

Riley, W., 1993. *King and Cultus in Chronicles. Worship and the Reinterpretation of History*, JSOTS 160

Ritschl, D. & H.O. Jones, 1976. *'Story' als Rohmaterial der Theologie*, TEH 192

Römer, T., 1990. *Israels Väter. Untersuchungen zur Väterthematik im Deuteronomium und in der deuteronomistischen Tradition*, OBO 99

——1991. Response to Lohfink 1991, 111–123

Rost, L., 1926. *Die Überlieferung der Thronnachfolge Davids*, BWANT 42

Rudolph, W., 1968. *Jeremia*, HAT I,12, 3rd ed.

Rupprecht, K., 1977. *Der Tempel von Jerusalem. Gründung Salomos oder jebusitisches Erbe?*, BZAW 144

——1988. "'Den Felsen, der dich gebar, täuschtest du …' Gott als gebärende Frau in Dtn 32,18 und anderen Texten der Hebräischen Bibel," in: *KuI* 3, 53–61

Rupprecht, E., 1980. "Exodus 24,9–11 also Beispiel lebendiger Erzähltradition aus der Zeit des babylonischen Exils," in: FS. C. Westermann (cf. Macholz 1980), 138–173

Ruwe, A., 1999. *"Heiligkeitsgesetz" und "Priesterschrift". Literaturgeschichtliche und rechtssystematische Untersuchungen zu Leviticus 17,1–26,2*, FAT 26

Sæbø, M., 1982. םוֹי, *jôm*, *ThWAT* III, 559–586

Sasson, J.M., 1987. "Ruth," in: Alter & Kermode, 320–328

Schäfer-Lichtenberger, 1989. "'Josua' und 'Elischa' – eine biblische Argumentation zur Begründung der Autorität und Legitimität des Nachfolgers," *ZAW* 101, 198–222

——1995. *Josua und Salomo. Eine Studie zur Autorität und Legitimität des Nachfolgers im Alten Testament*, VTS 57

——2000. "'Sie wird nicht wieder hergestellt werden'. Anmerkungen zum Verlust der Lade," in: E. Blum (ed.; cf. E. Blum 2000b), 229–241

Scharbert, J., 1960. "Das Verbum PQD in der Theologie des Alten Testaments," *BZ* n.s. 4, 209–226

Schart, A., 1990. *Mose und Israel im Konflikt*, OBO 98

——1998. *Die Entstehung des Zwölfprophetenbuchs. Neubearbeitungen von Amos im Rahmen schriftenübergreifender Redaktionsprozess*, BZAW 260

Schmid, H., 1966. *Wesen und Geschichte der Weisheit. Eine Untersuchung zur altorientalischen und israelitischen Weisheitsliteratur*, BZAW 101

Schmidt, W.H., 1966. *Königtum Gottes in Ugarit und Israel. Zur Herkunft der Königsprädikation Jahwes*, 2nd ed. (1st ed. 1961), BZAW 80

——1972. "'Theologie des Alten Testaments' vor und nach Gerhard von Rad," *VF* 17, 1–25 (= *Vielfalt und Einheit des alttestamentlichen Glaubens*, I, 1995, 113–

138; references are to this)

——1983. *Exodus, Sinai und Mose*, EdF 191, Darmstadt (²1990)

——1988. *Exodus*, BK II/1, Neukirchen-Vluyn

——1993. *Die Zehn Gebote im Rahmen alttestamentlicher Ethik, in Zusammenarbeit mit Holger Delkurt und Axel Graupner*, EdF 281

——1996. *Alttestamentlicher Glaube*, 8th ed., Neukirchen-Vluyn (earlier editions have the title *Alttestamentlicher Glaube in seiner Geschichte*)

Schottroff, W., 1967. *"Gedenken" im Alten Orient und im Alten Testament. Die Wurzel zākar im semitischen Sprachkreis*, WMANT 15 (2nd ed.)

——1976. "פקד *pqd* heimsuchen," in: *THAT* II, 466-486

Schreiner, S., 1979. "Mischehen – Ehebruch – Ehescheidung. Betrachtungen zu Mal 2,10-16," *ZAW* 91, 207-228

Schwienhorst-Schönberger, L., 1995. "Das Buch der Sprichwörter," in: E. Zenger *et al.*, 1995, 255-262

Seeligmann, I.L., 1967. "Zur Terminologie für das Gerichtsverfahren im Wortschatz des biblischen Hebräisch," in: *Hebräische Wortforschung*, FS W. Baumgartner, VTS 16, 251-278

Seitz, C.R., 1988. "Introduction: The One Isaiah // The Three Isaiahs, and: Isaiah 1–66: Making Sense of the Whole," in: *idem* (ed.), *Reading and Preaching the Book of Isaiah*, Philadelphia, 13–22 and 105-126

——1989. "The Prophet Moses and the Canonical Shape of Jeremiah," *ZAW* 101, 3-27

——1993. *Isaiah 1–39*, IBC

Seybold, K., 1973. "Elia am Gottesberg. Vorstellungen prophetischen Wirkens nach 1.Könige 19," *EvTh* 33, 3-18

——1986. *Die Psalmen. Eine Einführung*, UT 382

——1993. *Der Prophet Jeremia. Leben und Werk*, UT 416

Sheppard, G.T., 1980. *Wisdom as a Hermeneutical Construct. A Study in the Sapientialization of the Old Testament*, BZAW 151

——1990. *The Future of the Bible: Beyond Liberalism and Literalism*, The United Church of Canada

——1992. "Canonical Criticism," in: *ABD* I, 861-866

Simon, U., 1994. *Jona. Ein jüdischer Kommentar*, SBS 157

Ska, J.-L., 1982. "La place d'Ex 6,2-8 dans la narration de l'exode," *ZAW* 94, 530-548

——1989. "Quelques remarques sur Pᵍ et la dernière redaction du Pentateuque," in: de Pury, *Pentateuque*, 95-125

Skladny, U., 1961. *Die ältesten Spruchsammlungen in Israel*, Berlin

Smend, R., 1963. *Die Bundesformel*, ThS 68 (= *Die Mitte des Alten Testaments, Gesammelte Studien*, I, BevTh 99, 1986, 11-39)

——1982. "Theologie im Alten Testament," in: E. Jüngel *et al.* (eds.), *Verifikationen*, FS G. Ebeling, Tübingen, 11-26 (= *Die Mitte des Alten Testaments. Gesammelte Studien* 1, 1986, 104-117)

Smith, M., 1971. *Palestinian Parties and Politics that Shaped the Old Testament*, London (²1987)

Söding, T., 1995. "Probleme und Chancen Biblischer Theologie aus neutestamentlicher Sicht," in: C. Dohmen & T. Söding (eds.), 159-177

Sommer, B., 1999. "Reflecting on Moses: The Redaction of Numbers 11," *JBL* 118, 601-624

Speckermann, H., 1990. "'Barmherzig und gnädig ist der Herr ...'," *ZAW* 102, 1-18

Stamm, J.J., 1940. *Erlösen und Vergeben im Alten Testament*, Bern

Steck, O.H., 1975. *Der Schöpfungsbericht der Priesterschrift*, FRLANT 115 (²1981)

——1985. *Bereitete Heimkehr. Jesaja 35 als redaktionelle Brücke zwischem dem Ersten und dem Zweiten Jesaja*, SBS 121

——1991a. *Der Abschluß der Prophetie im Alten Testament. Ein Versuch zur Frage der Vorgeschichte des Kanons*, BTS 17

——1991b. *Studien zu Tritojesaja*, BZAW 203

——1993. "Prophetische Prophetenauslegung," in: H. Geißer *et al.* (eds.), *Wahrheit der Schrift – Wahrheit der Auslegung. Eine Zürcher Vorlesungsreihe zu Gerhard Ebelings 80. Geburtstag*, Zürich, 198-244 (an expanded version is also published in Steck 1966, 127-204)

——1996. *Die Prophetenbücher und ihr theologisches Zeugnis. Wege der Nachfrage und Fährten zur Antwort*, Tübingen

Stemberger, G., 1979. *Das klassische Judentum. Kultur und Geschichte der rabbinischen Zeit (70 n.Chr. bis 1040 n.Chr.)*, Munich

Stolz, F., 1970. *Strukturen und Figuren im Kult von Jerusalem. Studien zur altorientalischen, vor- und frühisraelitischen Religion*, BZAW 118

Strauß, H., 1985. "Das Meerlied des Mose – ein 'Siegeslied' Israels? Bemerkungen zur theologischen Exegese von Ex 15,1-19.20f," *ZAW* 97, 103-109

Sweeney, M.A., 1991a. "Structure, Genre, and Intent in the Book of Habakkuk," *VT* 41, 63-83

——1991b. "A Form-Critical Reassessment of the Book of Zephaniah," *CBQ* 53, 388-408

Talmon, S., 1963. "'Wisdom' in the Book of Esther," *VT* 13, 419-455

——1990. "'400 Jahre' oder 'vier Generationen' (Gen 15,13-15): Geschichtliche Zeitangaben oder literarische Motive?" in: FS R. Rendtorff (cf. Blum 1990b), 13-25

Terrien, S., 1978. *The Elusive Presence. The Heart of Biblical Theology*, San Francisco

Thiel, W., 1973. *Die deuteronomistische Redaktion von Jeremia 1–15*, WMANT 41

——1981. *Die deuteronomistische Redaktion von Jeremiah 26–45*, WMANT 52

——1990. "Zur Komposition von 1 Könige 18. Versuch einer kontextuellen Auslegung," in: FS R. Rendtorff (see Blum 1990b), 215-223

Trible, P., 1978. *God and the Rhetoric of Sexuality*, Overtures to Biblical Theology, (6th printing 1989), Philadelphia

Trobisch, D., 1996. *Die Endredaktion des Neuen Testaments*, NTOA 31

Tucker, G.M., 1977. "Prophetic Superscriptions and the Growth of a Canon," in: G.W. Coats & B.O. Long (eds.), *Canon and Authority*, Philadelphia, 56-70

Uehlinger, C., 1990. *Weltreich und "eine Rede"*. *Eine neue Deutung der sogenannten Turmbauerzählung (Gen 11,1-9)*, OBO 101

Utzschneider, H., 1988. *Das Heiligtum und das Gesetz. Studien zur Bedeutung der sinaitischen Heligtumstexte (Ex 25–40; Lev 8–9)*, OBO 77

Van Winkle, D.W., 1996. "1 Kings xii 25–xiii 34: Jeroboam's Cultic Innovations and the Man of God from Judah," *VT* 46, 101-114

Vriezen, T.C., 1950. "'*Ehjeh 'ašer 'ehjeh*," in: W. Baumgartner *et al.* (eds.), FS A. Bertholet, Tübingen, 498-512

Waschke, E.-J., 1987. "Das Verhältnis alttestamentlicher Überlieferungen im Schnittpunkt der Dynastiezusage und die Dynastiezusage im Spiegel alttestamentlicher Überlieferungen," *ZAW* 99, 157-179

Watts, J.W., 1998. "The Legal Characterization of Moses in the Rhetoric of the Pentateuch," *JBL* 117, 415-426

Webb, B.G., 1990. "Zion in Transformation. A Literary Approach to Isaiah," in: D.J.A. Clines *et al.* (eds.), *The Bible in Three Dimensions*, JSOTS 87, 65-84

Weinfeld, M., 1991. *Deuteronomy 1–11*, AB 5

Weippert, H., 1972. "Die 'deuteronomistischen' Beurteilungen der Könige von Israel und Juda und das Problem der Redaktion der Königsbücher," *Bib* 53, 301-339

——1983. "Die Ätiologie des Nordreiches und seines Königshauses (I Reg 11,29-40)," *ZAW* 95, 344-375

Wellhausen, J., 1899. *Die Composition des Hexateuchs und der historischen Bücher des Alten Testaments*, 3rd ed., Berlin (⁴1963)

——1905. *Prolegomena zur Geschichte Israels*, 6th ed., Berlin (= 1927)

Westermann, C., 1953. *Das Loben Gottes in den Psalmen*, Berlin

——1962. "Zur Sammlung des Psalters," in: *TViat* VIII, 1961/62, 278-284 (= *Forschung am Alten Testament*, Munich 1964, 336-343)

——1966. *Das Buch Jesaja, Kapitel 40–66*, ATD 19 (⁵1986)

——1971. "חָדָשׁ *ḥādāš* neu," in: *THAT* I, 524-530

——1974. *Genesis 1–11*, BK I/1

——1975. *Genesis 12–50*, EdF 48, Darmstadt (²1987)

——1981. *Genesis 12–36*, BK I/2 (²1989)

——1986. "Zur Frage einer Biblischen Theologie," *JBT* 1, 13-30

——1990a. *Wurzeln der Weisheit. Die ältesten Sprüche Israels und anderer Völker*, Göttingen

——1990b. *Die Klagelieder. Forschungsgeschichte und Auslegung*, Neukirchen-Vluyn

Wildberger, H., 1960. "Die Thronnamen des Messias," *ThZ* 16, 314-332

——1971. *Jesaja 1–2*, BK X/1 (²1980)

Willi, T., 1972. *Die Chronik als Auslegung*, FRLANT 106

——1991. *Chronik*, BK I/1

——1995. *Juda – Jehud – Israel. Studien zum Selbstverständnis des Judentums in per-*

sischer Zeit, FAT 12

Williamson, H.G.M., 1977. *Israel in the Books of Chronicles*, Cambridge

——1994. *The Book Called Isaiah. Deutero-Isaiah's Role in Composition and Redaction*, Oxford

Wilson, G.H., 1985. *The Editing of the Hebrew Psalter*, SBLDS 76

——1992. "The Shape of the Book of Psalms," *Int* 46, 127-142

——1993. "Shaping the Psalter: A Consideration of Editorial Linkage in the Book of Psalms," in: J.C. McCann 1993, 72-92

Wolff, H.W., 1951. "Das Thema 'Umkehr' in der alttestamentlichen Prophetie," *ZTK* 48, 129-148 (= *Gesammelte Studien zum Alten Testament*, 1964 [²1973], 130-150)

——1953. "'Wissen um Gott' bei Hosea als Urform von Theologie," *EvT* 12, 533-554 (= *Gesammelte Studien* [cf. 1951], 182-205)

——1965. *Dodekapropheton 1. Hosea*, BK XIV/1, 2nd ed. (⁴1990)

——1969. *Dodekapropheton 2. Joël und Amos*, BK XIV/2 (³1985)

——1973. *Anthropologie des Alten Testaments*, Munich (³1977)

——1982. *Dodekapropheton 4. Micha*, BK XIV/4

van der Woude, A.S., 1976a. "פָּנִים *pānîm* Angesicht," in: *THAT* II, 432-460

——1976b. "שֵׁם *šēm* Name," in: *THAT* II, 935-963

Zakovitch, Y., 1991. *"And you shall tell your son". The Concept of the Exodus in the Bible*, Jerusalem

Zenger, E., 1983. *Gottes Bogen in den Wolken. Untersuchungen zur Komposition und Theologie der priesterschriftlichen Urgeschichte*, SBS 112 (²1987)

——1986. *Das Buch Ruth*, ZBK 8

——1991. "Israel und Kirche im gemeinsamen Gottesbund. Beobachtungen zum theologischen Programm des 4. Psalmbuches (Ps 90-106)," in: M. Marcus *et al.* (eds.), *Israel und Kirche heute*, FS E.L. Ehrlich, Freiburg etc., 236-254

——1991b. *Das Erste Testament*, Düsseldorf

——1995a. "Heilige Schrift der Juden und der Christen," in: E. Zenger *et al.*, 1995, 12-33

——1995b. "Das Zwölfprophetenbuch," in: E. Zenger *et al.*, 1995, 369-436

——1995c. "Das Buch Ester," in: E. Zenger *et al.*, 1995, 201-210

Zenger, E. *et al.*, 1995/1998. *Einleitung in das Alte Testament*, Stuttgart (³1998)

Zenger, E. & F.-L. Hossfeld, 2000. *Psalmen 51–100*, HTKAT

Zimmerli, W., 1953. "Ich bin Jahwe," in: W.F. Albright *et al.*, *Geschichte und Altes Testament*. FS A. Alt, BHT 16, 179-209 (= *Gottes Offenbarung* [cf. 1954], 11-40)

——1954. *Erkenntnis Gottes nach dem Buche Ezechiel. Eine theologische Studie*, ATANT 27 (= *Gottes Offenbarung. Gesammelte Aufsätze zum Alten Testament*, Munich 1963, 41-119)

——1963. "Der 'neue Exodus' in der Verkündigung der beiden grossen Exilspropheten," in: *Gottes Offenbarung* (cf. 1954), 192-204 (French 1960)

——1969. *Ezechiel*, BK XIII (²1979)

——1980. *Das Buch des Predigers Salomo*, ATD 16/1, 121-249

——1980b. "'Heiligkeit' nach dem sogenannten Heiligkeitsgesetz," *VT* 30, 493-512

——1983. "'Unveränderbare Welt' oder 'Gott ist Gott'? Ein Plädoyer für die Unaufgebbarkeit des Predigerbuches in der Bibel," in: H.-G. Geyer *et al.* (eds.), *"Wenn nicht jetzt, wann dann ...?"*, FS H.-J. Kraus, Neukirchen-Vluyn, 103-114

Zobel, H.-J., 1982. "יֵעָקֹ(וֹ)ב *ja'ᵃqo(ô)b*," *ThWAT* III, 752-777

Indexes

All the indexes are selective. Please use also the cross-references in the text and the detailed table of contents at the front of the book.

The assistance of Nelleke Yakubu, Rahman Yakubu and Judith Kronenberg in the preparation of the indexes is gratefully acknowledged.

Index of Names and Subjects

Index of Hebrew Words

Index of Biblical References

This index is selective. For additional orientation see the table of contents, the index of names and subjects, and the cross-references provided in the text. The discussion referenced in each case may extend beyond the given page.

556, 637
15.1ff 46
15.1-21 475f
15.1-19 471
15.1-18 422
15.1-17 45
15.1-9 47
15.3,12,16 621
15.6 515
15.11 45
15.14-16 47
15.17 47, 121, 334, 460,
    563, 577f, 612
15.22-26 50
15.22-25 552
15.24;16.2 638
15.24 50
16 50, 657
16.1 52
16.3 50
16.8 50
16.10 602
16.13 50
16.16 20,
16.22-30 489f
16.32,34 120
17.1-7 50, 552
17.8-13 555
17.8 65
17.15 511
18.8-16 50
18.11 608, 673
18.12 59, 528
18.13-17 507
18.13ff 37
19–24 55
19ff 38
19 55, 57
19.1 51, 52, 548
19.2 52
19.3 39, 52, 450, 546, 639
19.4-6 52, 57, 441
19.4 55, 65
19.5f 60
19.5 52, 56, 57, 59, 61,
    423, 436, 442, 484,
    549
19.6 57, 58
19.7 58
19.8 57, 59, 137
19.9 602
19.11,15 696

19.16ff 53
19.16,21 602f
20.1-17 436, 479f, 548
20.2-17 53, 55
20.2 47, 53, 472, 480f,
    494, 595f, 728, 741f
20.3-5 60
20.3 54, 481, 494, 588f,
    669
20.4f 56
20.4 54, 483, 494, 609
20.5f 63
20.5 483, 485, 588, 591,
    628f, 733
20.5a 54
20.5b 54
20.6 54
20.7 486, 494, 592
20.8-11 488
20.10 505
20.11 489, 491
20.12 492, 688
20.13-16 495
20.13 16, 507
20.16 488, 499
20.17 481, 496, 499f, 507
20.18 55, 479, 548
20.19 54
20.21 120
20.22-23.33 55, 79
20.22 55, 480
20.23 55, 483, 501
20.24ff 56
20.24 501, 503, 510, 523,
    527, 590, 594
21.1-22.16 56
21.1-11 505f
21.2,12-36 507f
21.16 498, 506
22.20* 24, 34, 56, 684
22.21* 56
22.24-26* 56
22.24f 506
22.26 491
22.28 247
23.1-8 56
23.1 56, 488
23.2,6,8 499
23.2 56
23.3 56
23.4f 56
23.6 56

23.7b 56
23.8 56
23.9 24, 56, 684, 694
23.20-33 482
23.20-24 49
23.20ff 56, 62, 601
23.24 56, 483, 496f
23.32f 72
23.32 56, 73, 100, 438,
    447, 501, 669
24 53, 55, 57
24.1-8 549
24.1 58, 63
24.3 57, 59
24.3-8 57, 436, 484
24.3-5 60
24.3,7 137, 436, 638
24.4 57, 501
24.4b 60
24.5 57, 61
24.7 55, 57, 59
24.8f 64
24.9-11 58, 60, 602f
24.10 58
24.11 58
24.12ff 59
24.13 98
24.15-17 602f
24.16b 66
24.16f 66
24.18 65f
24.28 64
25–31 59, 60, 64, 65, 512
25 504
25.5-10 508
25.8f 65
25.8 512, 522f, 594
28f 67
28 61, 67
28.42 505
29.20f 58
29.34-39 514
29.36f 67
29.38-42 67
29.42 66, 512
29.43-46 523
29.43f 513
29.43 66
29.45 120, 472, 522, 731f
29.45f 65
29.45b 66
29.46 66, 91, 478, 607,

8.46-51 460, 467
8.53 449, 558, 680
8.54 519
8.56 466, 558, 688
8.58 449
8.60 423, 608, 674
8.64 519, 520
9.3-7 519, 523, 594
9.3-9 564
9.6-9 408, 689
9.6 155
9.9 449, 680
9.25 521, 527
10 320
10.1-10 363
10.9 646
11 408
11.1-13 310
11.4,10 565, 638
11.5,7 229, 639, 643
11.11-13,29-39 564, 566
11.14-22 26
11.29 699
11.32,36 565, 706
11.38 565, 566
12.15 565
12.19 409
12.25-30 554
12.26-33 269
12.28,31 60, 640
12.32 643
13 652
13.6 502
13.34 565
14.8,10,16 564, 565, 566
14.15,23 449, 502
14.19 402
14.22 457
14.29 402
15.3-5,30 565
15.5,11,14 565, 566, 640, 646
15.13 502
15.19 610
16.31 565, 639
16.32 502
17.1 28
18 643, 669
18.19 502
18.21 639, 671
18.22 652
18.24 486, 590, 672

18.29 529, 653
18.30-39 528
18.31 449
18.32 590
18.36 529
18.39 423, 588, 590, 639
19.2 652
19.7 601
19.8ff 38
20.13,22,28 607, 650
20.35,38,41 651
21.3 459
22 655
22.5-12,22 652
22.19 427, 588, 604, 612
22.20-22 215
22.27 217
22.28 39
22.43f 568, 640

2 Kings
1.3,15 601
2 313
2.1,31 351
2.3,5 652
3.4-27 229
3.20 529
4.38-41 652
4.38 239
5.3,8 652
5.15 608, 673
6.1f,12 652
8.19 128, 445, 565
8.20-22 26
8.26 670
9–11 641
9 640, 669, 677
10 639, 643
10.11,17 706
10.26 502
10.30 566
11 639, 670
11.4-12 568
11.7 640
11.18 670
12.3f 566, 640
13.23 449
14.3 566, 640, 646
14.7 26
14.25 707
15.3,34 566, 640
15.19,29 668

16.2,10-16 566, 641, 646
16.5 529, 668
16.13 527
17.6 467
17.7 639
17.10,16 502
17.13-23 220
17.13 648
17.15 449, 639, 680
17.23 467
17.24-41 392
18–20 183
18.3,6 565, 566, 646
18.4 641
18.12 556
18.13–20.19 159
19.21 576
19.30 707, 709
19.31 576, 629
19.34; 20.6 565
21.3-5,7 502, 641, 670
21.8 449, 556
21.13 707
21.24 82
22.2 566, 646
22.12 556
23.4 502, 641, 670
23.6f,14f 502
23.8,13 229
23.9 641
23.10 639
23.21-23 393, 537
23.25 479, 566
23.29,33-35 668
23.30 82
24.7,10-17 668
24.13 392
24.25 712
25 668
25.4-7 242
25.13-17 392, 522
25.21,27-30 467, 649
25.27 16

Isaiah
1.2,4 619, 633, 643
1.2 13
1.8 465, 582, 709
1.9 29, 659, 707f
1.10f,15-17 659
1.17,21 646, 691, 693
1.21-27 582

Tools for Biblical Study series

ISSN 1566-2101

1. J.P. Fokkelman, *Reading Biblical Narrative. A Practical Guide*. ISBN 90 5854 001 4.
2. G.W. Dawes (ed.), *The Historical Jesus Quest. A Foundational Anthology*. ISBN 90 5854 007 3.
3. A. Piñero & J. Peláez, *The Study of the New Testament. A Comprehensive Introduction*. ISBN 90 5854 006 5.
4. J.P. Fokkelman, *The Psalms in Form. The Hebrew Psalter in its Poetic Shape*. ISBN 90 5854 017 0.
5. M.J. Boda, *Haggai and Zechariah Research. A Bibliographic Survey*. ISBN 90 5854 023 5.
6. J. Bekkenkamp & F. Dröes (eds.), *The Double Voice of Her Desire. Texts by Fokkelien van Dijk-Hemmes*. ISBN 90 5854 003 0.
7. R. Rendtorff, *The Canonical Hebrew Bible. A Theology of the Old Testament*. ISBN 90 5854 020 0.
8. D.F. Watson, *The Rhetoric of the New Testament. A Bibliographic Survey*. ISBN 90 5854 028 6.